# British History

**(⊕) SEE WEB LINKS**

This is a web-linked dictionary. There is a list of recommended web links in the appendix, on page 705. To access the websites, go to the dictionary's web page at http://www.oup.com/uk/reference/resources/britishhistory], click on Web links in the Resources section and click straight through to the relevant websites.

**Professor John Cannon** held the chair of Modern History at the University of Newcastle upon Tyne until 1992. He has edited several titles, including *The Letters of Junius* (1978), *The Blackwell Dictionary of Historians* (1988), which was awarded a Library Association prize for reference works, and *The Oxford Companion to British History* (1997). His other publications include *The Fox–North Coalition* (1969), *Parliamentary Reform* (1973), *Aristocratic Century* (1984), *The Oxford Illustrated History of the British Monarchy* (1986, 1998), *Samuel Johnson and the Politics of Hanoverian England* (1994), and with Anne Hargreaves *The Kings and Queens of Britain* (2001).

## Oxford Paperback Reference

The most authoritative and up-to-date reference books for both students and the general reader.

A Dictionary of
# British
# History

REVISED EDITION

*Edited by* JOHN CANNON

OXFORD
UNIVERSITY PRESS

# OXFORD
UNIVERSITY PRESS

Great Clarendon Street, Oxford OX2 6DP

Oxford University Press is a department of the University of Oxford.
It furthers the University's objective of excellence in research, scholarship,
and education by publishing worldwide in

Oxford New York

Auckland Cape Town Dar es Salaam Hong Kong Karachi
Kuala Lumpur Madrid Melbourne Mexico City Nairobi
New Delhi Shanghai Taipei Toronto

With offices in
Argentina Austria Brazil Chile Czech Republic France Greece
Guatemala Hungary Italy Japan Poland Portugal Singapore
South Korea Switzerland Thailand Turkey Ukraine Vietnam

Oxford is a registered trade mark of Oxford University Press
in the UK and in certain other countries

Published in the United States
by Oxford University Press Inc., New York

© Oxford University Press 2001, 2009

The moral rights of the author have been asserted
Database right Oxford University Press (maker)

First published 2001
Reissued with new cover and corrections 2004, revised 2009

All rights reserved. No part of this publication may be reproduced,
stored in a retrieval system, or transmitted, in any form or by any means,
without the prior permission in writing of Oxford University Press,
or as expressly permitted by law, or under terms agreed with the appropriate
reprographics rights organization. Enquiries concerning reproduction
outside the scope of the above should be sent to the Rights Department,
Oxford University Press, at the address above

You must not circulate this book in any other binding or cover
and you must impose this same condition on any acquirer

British Library Cataloguing in Publication Data

Data available

Library of Congress Cataloging in Publication Data

Data available

Typeset by SPI Publisher Services, Pondicherry, India
Printed in Great Britain
on acid-free paper by
Clays Ltd., St Ives plc

ISBN 978-0-19-955037-1

1 3 5 7 9 10 8 6 4 2

R0430192302

# Contents

# Preface to the First Edition

Who forgot Goschen? Why was the Amritsar massacre so significant? What was a nabob? When was trial by battle abolished? Why did the band play 'Nearer my God to thee'? Which queen was 'nothing so fair as reported'? Which Viking king of York was known as 'Squinty'? Where would you find the Honours of Scotland? What was Peter's Pence? Who said 'they make a desert and call it peace'? How did the British acquire Hong Kong? Which MP said, 'the great speakers fill me with despair, the bad with terror'?

No one—not even the most learned historian—is born knowing who won the battle of Flodden or when *The Wealth of Nations* was published. Students of history need lots of information and need it quickly. We spend our time checking, comparing, and trying to understand the past. First, the facts—then the significance of the facts. This volume is intended to help at all levels.

We have done our best to see that the information is correct and that the interpretations are not tired or outdated. Our formula has been to bring together a large number of good scholars, at home in their chosen fields. Consequently the *Dictionary* is based upon the *Oxford Companion to British History*, to which more than 100 authors contributed. Their names are printed on p. viii and it is a pleasure for me to acknowledge their help. We have updated the entries where necessary and corrected them in the light of comments sent in by readers. Since history is a collective endeavour (all sensible historians being well aware of their own limitations), we would be glad to receive further suggestions or advice. We have added a brief chronological survey, not only to help place events or books in a context, but to stimulate thought about the relationship between political events and scientific, religious, and cultural change. Perhaps this is most easily seen in literature which can breathe life into dry bones. *The Ruin (of Bath?)*, written by an eighth-century Saxon, conveys a sense of wonder at the departed grandeur of Roman Britain: more than 1,000 years later, Trollope's *The Way We Live Now* (1874) expressed doubts about the march of international finance, which have yet to vanish. Asterisks guide readers to related entries, so that they can follow up themes.

Answers to the twelve questions may be found on p. 711.

John Cannon
*January 2001*

# Note to the Reader

Entries are arranged in letter-by-letter alphabetical order up to the first punctuation in the headword. For example, the entry on **Quebec, capture of** precedes **Quebec Act**. We have tried in all cases to use the most appropriate headword, particularly the name by which people were best known. It would be unhelpful to have entered **Disraeli** under 'Beaconsfield', a name by which he was known for only the last five years of his life, and it would be unreasonable to expect all readers to remember that Lord **Melbourne** was William Lamb. Where there have been second or third creations for a title, all the holders of that title are arranged together in straightforward alphabetical order for simplicity of reference. Holders of titles created in the Scottish peerage are distinguished by [S] after the headword, for example **Melville, George Melville, 1st earl of [S]**, and similarly [I] denotes titles created in the Irish peerage.

An asterisk within the text indicates a cross-reference to another relevant headword. An item is normally marked with an asterisk only at its first appearance in any entry, and if the reference is merely incidental it has not been marked. We have not asterisked sovereigns after 1066 for England or after Malcolm II (d. 1034) for Scotland, since they all have entries. 'See also' at the end of an entry indicates that there is another substantial entry with a bearing on the subject.

In addition to entries there is a chronology at the back of the book. The chronology, spanning over 2,000 years from 55 BC to the present day, places events in government and politics alongside other events.

# List of Contributors

Geoffrey Alderman
David Aldridge
Stephen Alford
Douglas Allen
Stephen Badsey
Richard Bailey
C. J. Bartlett
David Bates
John Beckett
Hugh Berrington
Clyde Binfield
Jeremy Boulton
Keith Branigan
Roy Bridges
Dauvit Broun
Nicholas Bryars
Angus Buchanan
John Butt
Kenneth Button
Euan Cameron
James Campbell
John Cannon
Sue Cannon
Harold Carter
Stuart Carter
Muriel Chamberlain
Judith Champ
J. A. Chartres
Thomas Clancy
A. S. E. Cleary
Colin Coates
June Cochrane
Bruce Coleman
John Collis
Eric Cross
Anne Curry
John Derry
Ian Donnachie
J. A. Downie
Sean Duffy

Sandra Dunkin
David Dutton
T. E. Faulkner
David French
Ian Gentles
John Gillingham
Brian Golding
Peter Gordon
Tim Gray
Ralph Griffiths
John R. Guy
Andrew Hanham
A. S. Hargreaves
John Harrison
Robert Holland
Michael Hopkinson
Kenneth Ingham
Alvin Jackson
Andrew Jennings
Clyve Jones
J. R. Jones
Ian Keil
David Knight
Christopher Lanigan
Clive Lee
Bruce Lenman
Andrew Lewer
Simon Lloyd
Roger Lockyer
Henry Loyn
Charlotte Lythe
Norman McCord
Audrey MacDonald
Norman Macdougall
Gordon Macmullan
William Marshall
Ged Martin
Roger Mason
Lewis Mates
H. C. G. Matthew

R. J. Morris
Maureen Mulholland
David Palliser
R. A. C. Parker
Nicholas Phillipson
John Pimlott
Anthony Pollard
Bernard Porter
John Presley
Michael Prestwich
Martin Pugh
A. E. Redgate
Glynis Ridley
Pamela Ritchie
Lynda Rollason
Edward Royle
Andrew Sanders
John Saunders
Eleanor Scott
J. A. Sharpe
Gary Sheffield
Richard Simmons
Alan Sked
E. A. Smith
Richard Smith
R. L. Storey
Keith Stringer
Roland Tanner
J. B. Trapp
John Walton
David Washbrook
Martyn Webb
Bruce Webster
D. C. Whaley
David Wilkinson
Margaret Wilkinson
Peter Willis
Austin Woolrych
Barbara Yorke

**abbeys and priories** Abbots were the spiritual heads of the larger monasteries (abbesses for nuns), with priors in charge of smaller or daughter houses. Until the Reformation some 27 mainly 'mitred abbots' attended the House of Lords. Great abbeys like Evesham, Pershore, Buckfast, Selby, or Sherborne had vast estates. The *Valor Ecclesiasticus* of 1535, which preceded the dissolution of the monasteries, identified some 563 religious houses. The largest group, with more than 170 houses and 22 nunneries, belonged to the Augustinian canons, whose first house at Colchester was founded *c.*1100. Next came the Benedictines, or black monks, with some 130 houses and over 60 nunneries. The Cistercians, or white monks, had some 76 houses in England and Wales, often built in remote areas, and the remains of Tintern, Rievaulx, and Fountains are among the most beautiful in the country. The proliferation after the Reformation of private estates such as Woburn abbey, Hitchin priory, or Grantham grange demonstrates that most of the monastic estates finished up with the gentry or aristocracy.

**Abbey theatre** First permanent home of the Irish National Theatre, founded in 1904 by Lady Gregory, Edward Martyn, and W. B. *Yeats to foster native drama. Dramatic scenes came four years later with riots at the first night of J. M. *Synge's *The Playboy of the Western World*. The original building was destroyed by fire in 1951.

**Abbot, George** (1562–1633). Bishop of Lichfield (1609), London (1610), and archbishop of Canterbury (1611–33). As a fellow of Balliol (1583) and master of University College (1597) he established a reputation as a preacher. In 1604 he was among those appointed to prepare a new translation of the Bible. His defence of hereditary monarchy and work in Scotland promoting episcopacy (1608) won him the favour of James I and the primacy. From 1621 his ministry was overshadowed by his accidental killing of a gamekeeper, and under Charles I his influence was eclipsed by that of *Laud.

**abdication crisis,** 1936. A constitutional *scandale* stemming from the determination of Edward VIII to marry Mrs Wallis *Simpson, an American lady who had divorced her first husband and was about to divorce her second. At first Edward hoped that he might enter into morganatic marriage. *Baldwin, prime minister, issued an ultimatum: the king must choose between the throne and Mrs Simpson. Edward chose the latter, and abdicated on 11 December.

**Aberconwy, peace of,** 1277. This treaty, which brought to a conclusion the war between Llewelyn ap Gruffydd and Edward I, marked the beginning of the end of Llewelyn's ambitions. His rule was confined to 'Lesser' Gwynedd, west of the Conwy, and five years later he was killed near Builth.

**Aberdeen,** a royal burgh (1178) with two universities by 1600, became a significant port and developed a range of industries after 1750, including linen, cotton and woollens, shipbuilding and engineering, distilling, paper, white fish, and granite. In 1970 oil was first tapped in the North Sea, and Aberdeen became the capital of the British offshore oil industry.

**Aberdeen, battle of,** 1644. After his victory at *Tippermuir on 1 September 1644, *Montrose advanced upon Aberdeen against a superior covenanting force. After heavy fighting on the 13th, Montrose's troops entered the city. Incensed by the murder of a drummer-boy, Montrose gave Aberdeen over to pillage.

**Aberdeen, cathedrals** St Machar's cathedral, built on the site of a church founded by one of St *Columba's disciples (*c.*580), was rebuilt in granite after destruction by Edward III in 1336. Alternately under presbyterian and episcopal rule 1560–1690, then wholly presbyterian, the glory of its surviving interior is the nave's oak ceiling (1520). The central tower fell after a storm (1688). The episcopal cathedral, erected 1816–17 as St Andrew's chapel, is regarded by American episcopalians as their mother church.

**Aberdeen, George Hamilton-Gordon, 4th earl of** (1784–1860). As prime minister during the *Crimean War Aberdeen paid a high price for underestimating public anxiety about the conduct of the war. Yet he had a long career of public service behind him. Educated at Harrow and Cambridge he first made his mark as a diplomat. In 1828 he became foreign secretary in *Wellington's administration and in 1841 was again foreign secretary under *Peel. He achieved some improvement in Anglo-French relations, and settled the long-standing border dispute between Canada and the USA. He ended the war with China by the treaty of *Nanking in 1842, which leased Hong Kong to Britain. Aberdeen loyally supported Peel, resigning with him after the repeal of the Corn Laws in 1846.

When Russell's government fell in 1852 Aberdeen headed a ministry which held out every prospect of stability. But Aberdeen was unlucky in that he was drawn into war with Russia. British suspicions of Russia were well founded, but although the political nation was convinced of the wisdom of containing Russian designs, public opinion was soon appalled by the incompetence exposed by the war and demanded scapegoats. He had little choice but to resign when *Roebuck's motion calling for an inquiry into the condition of the army was carried in the Commons by 305 votes to 148 on 29 January 1855.

**Aberfan disaster** On 21 October 1966 an avalanche of sludge from a coal tip buried the primary school of this south Wales village, causing the loss of 144 lives, mostly young children. The subsequent inquiry blamed the tragedy on the lack of any National Coal Board tipping policy.

**Abernethy, submission of,** 1072. After the *Norman Conquest, the boundary between England and Scotland remained in doubt and Malcolm Canmore, king of Scotland, gave refuge to *Edgar the Atheling, whose sister he married. In 1072 William led an expedition to Scotland and at Abernethy, near Perth, forced Malcolm to submit and expel Edgar.

**Abyssinian War,** 1935–6. Conflict between Abyssinia and Italy. Mussolini used a border incident in December 1934 at Walwal as a pretext for pursuing his aim of imperial expansion in north Africa. The Italians invaded Abyssinia on 3 October 1935 and captured the capital Addis Ababa on 5 May 1936. The League of Nations branded Italy the aggressor and imposed limited sanctions to no avail.

**Aclea, battle of,** 851. A major victory for King Æthelwulf of Wessex over Danish raiders. In 850, for the first time, the Danes wintered on Thanet in Kent. Men from 350 ships stormed Canterbury and London, driving the Mercians to flight, before facing the West Saxon king south of the Thames. The Wessex men made 'the greatest slaughter of a heathen host' heard of to that day.

**Acre, defence of,** 1799. Bonaparte, in Egypt, advanced into Syria to menace the Turks, then in alliance with Britain. Sir Sidney *Smith flung troops and guns into the fort of Acre, which resisted the French for two months. Three months later Bonaparte abandoned his men and sailed back to France.

**Acre, siege of,** 1189–91. The siege and capture of Acre during the Third Crusade was a great event. Acre was the chief town of the kingdom of Jerusalem and the siege commenced in 1189. Richard I joined the besiegers in June 1191. Despite efforts by Saladin to relieve the city, it surrendered in July. But the crusaders' advance south on Jerusalem stalled and in October 1192 Richard left Acre on his ill-fated journey home.

**Acton, Sir John, 1st Baron Acton** (1834–1902). Historian and liberal Roman catholic. From an old Shropshire family on his father's side, Acton had a German mother and was brought up mainly on the continent. He first came to public attention writing articles for liberal catholic periodicals. He reported the 1870–1 Vatican Council, opposing papal infallibility. Acton was an MP 1858–65 and was created a peer by *Gladstone in 1869. In 1895 he became regius professor at Cambridge, and delivered a famous inaugural lecture (11 June 1895). He edited, but did not contribute to, the *Cambridge Modern History*. Acton never finished any of his own grand projects, but his published output was larger than is often allowed. Though not an easy author to read, Acton was a sharp epigrammist; his most famous epigram—'Power tends to corrupt and absolute power corrupts absolutely'—was written to Mandell Creighton on 3 April 1887.

**Acts of Parliament** *See* PARLIAMENT.

**Adam, Robert** (1728–92). Scottish architect who, with his brothers John (1721–92) and James (1730–94), trained in the office of their father William Adam (1689–1748). After a spell at Edinburgh University, and a grand tour, Robert Adam started his architectural practice in London in 1758 and soon developed a light and decorative style inspired by his travels in Greece and Italy. His interiors combine domes, columned screens, and apses with classically derived surface patterns in delicate colours. The 'Adam style' can be seen in Kedleston (1760–1), Syon (1760–9), Osterley (1761–80), or Kenwood (1767–9), with elegant plasterwork, furnishings, and fabrics. Robert Adam's finest civic work was in Edinburgh, notably Charlotte Square (1791–1807), the *Register House (1774–92), and the first stage of the university (1789–93).

**Adams, Gerry** (b. 1948). Politician. Born in West Belfast and attending St Mary's Christian Brothers grammar school, Adams was interned in the early 1970s and in 1983 became President of *Sinn Fein and was elected to the Westminster Parliament for Belfast West. He did not take the seat and lost it in to *SDLP in 1992, recovering it in 1997. He also served in the Northern Ireland Assembly and supported the power-sharing pact with *DUP in 2007, whereby his ally Martin McGuinness became Deputy First Minister. Adams has always denied being a member of the Provisional *IRA.

**Addington, Henry, 1st Viscount Sidmouth** (1757–1844). Prime minister. During a long political career Addington suffered from the denigration of foes and the condescension of friends. The son of a country doctor, he was educated at Winchester and

Oxford. Entering the Commons in 1784 he made little impact until *Pitt pushed him as Speaker in 1789. He proved to be capable and fair-minded, and because of his opposition to *catholic emancipation was George III's choice to succeed Pitt as prime minister in 1801. Despite its defects the peace of *Amiens was initially popular and Addington's policies of fiscal economy were generally approved. The breakdown of the peace settlement exposed his limitations and in 1804 he was replaced by Pitt. Raised to the peerage in 1805 he served in Pitt's second ministry, in the Ministry of All the *Talents, and in *Perceval's administration. When *Liverpool formed his ministry in 1812 Sidmouth became home secretary, holding the office until 1821, when he remained in the government as minister without portfolio. At the Home Office Sidmouth was responsible for the surveillance of radical activity. He was convinced that concessions made to popular pressure would be dangerous. Yet during several industrial disputes in the troubled post-Waterloo years he sympathized with the strikers. If his advice had been followed in 1819 there would have been no '*Peterloo massacre': he had cautioned the magistrates at Manchester against any confrontation. Nevertheless, he thought it necessary to support the magistrates in the face of criticism. After he left office in 1824 he remained a staunch opponent of catholic relief and parliamentary reform, voting against both measures in 1829 and 1832.

**Addison, Joseph** (1672–1719). English writer and politician. Educated at Charterhouse, Queen's College, and Magdalen College, Oxford, where he became a fellow, Addison found favour with the Whigs on account of *The Campaign* (1705), a poem celebrating *Marlborough's victory at *Blenheim. Appointed under-secretary of state in 1706, he was elected MP for Lostwithiel in 1708, accompanying the lord-lieutenant, Lord Wharton, to Ireland in 1709. Addison's close friendship with Richard *Steele and Jonathan *Swift led to his involvement in the *Tatler* (1709–10), but he is best known for his contributions to the *Spectator*, which included most of the 'Sir Roger de Coverley' papers. Returning to office on the accession of George I in 1714, Addison became secretary of state, marrying the countess of Warwick in 1716.

**'Addled Parliament'** (5 April–7 June 1614). The second Parliament of James I was bedevilled by controversy over the king's levying of *impositions, which members feared would leave him rich enough to rule without Parliament. Deadlock ensued and James dissolved Parliament before any bills had been passed.

**Adela of Louvain** (c.1100–51), queen of Henry I. Henry's second wife, Adela, married him after the death of his only legitimate son in the *White Ship disaster. The marriage's chief—and unfulfilled—purpose was to provide Henry with a male heir. When it had manifestly failed to do so, Henry persuaded his chief subjects to agree to the succession of his daughter, the Empress *Matilda.

**Adelaide** (1792–1849), queen of William IV. Adelaide of Saxe-Meiningen was suggested by Queen *Charlotte as a suitable wife for her son William Henry, then duke of Clarence, hoping that he would end his relationship with Mrs Jordan. Marrying in July 1818, Adelaide's reserved personality complemented William's exuberant nature. The death of two infant daughters clouded Adelaide's life. But following William's accession in 1830, she performed her royal duties with dedication. Initial unpopularity sparked by a belief that she meddled in politics gave way to respect for her charitable works.

**Aden** A port in the Middle East, commanding the entrance to the Red Sea. In 1839 Aden was ceded to the British by the Turkish sultan. It became a free port in 1850 and was developed as a coaling station on the steamship route from Suez to Bombay. After the civil war (1965–7) the British withdrew from Aden and it became the capital of the People's Republic of South Yemen.

**Admiralty** Until a permanent royal navy came into being, organization did not need to be elaborate. A commander was appointed for the campaign, after which most of the vessels, being converted merchantmen, returned to their home ports. The first admirals were appointed in the late 13th cent. Henry VIII made a considerable effort to strengthen naval power. In 1540 Lord *Bedford was named lord admiral and in 1545 a Council for Marine Causes was established—the genesis of the Navy Board. *Buckingham, Charles I's favourite, was made lord high admiral and after his murder in 1628 the office was put into commission. This arrangement, with a 1st lord of the Admiralty, became permanent after 1708. The growing importance of the navy in the 17th cent. was underlined by the fact that the lord high admiralship was taken at the highest level—by James, duke of York, 1660–73, and by Charles II himself 1673–84.

The Navy Board took responsibility for administration and implementation, the Admiralty Board for appointments and strategy. The fleet to which Charles I had devoted considerable care deserted him at the Civil War. The Commonwealth regime abolished both boards, but found it necessary to replace them with commissioners of the Admiralty and naval commissioners, under whom the navy, particularly with *Blake's leadership, acquitted itself well. Charles II in 1660 restored the old order and was fortunate enough to find in Samuel *Pepys a remarkably capable civil servant. The same efficiency was scarcely maintained in the 18th cent. and the great victories were won more by tactics, morale, and personnel than by administration. Since the 1st lord was always a politician, often with no experience of the sea, professional naval advice came from a 1st sea lord.

The dual system came to an end in 1832, partly as a measure of economy, when Sir James *Graham brought the Navy Board into the Admiralty structure and redefined channels of responsibility.

In the 20th cent. the degree of autonomy built up by the Admiralty was weakened by a number of factors—spiralling cost, an acceleration of technological change, and, not least, after 1945, by the remarkable shrinking of the navy itself. In 1931, for the first time since 1709, the 1st lord was briefly not a member of the cabinet, and in 1964, after a great run-down of the navy in the wake of the Second World War, the post of 1st lord was discontinued. In a unified Ministry of *Defence the spokesman for the navy was the chief of naval staff and 1st sea lord.

### Admonition to the Parliament, 1572.
A puritan manifesto, composed by John Field and others, arguing against the author-

ity of bishops and urging a presbyterian church government. It was not presented to Parliament but was published in June 1572 after a puritan bill had been abandoned, when the House was informed that the queen 'utterly misliketh it'.

**Adomnán, St** (*c*.628–704). Irish scholar, diplomat, and ninth abbot of Iona. Born into the royal Uí Néill dynasty and educated at Durrow, probably where he taught the future King Aldfrith of Northumbria, he moved in the 670s to Iona, where he wrote his *Holy Places*. He visited Aldfrith twice, in 686 as emissary of the king of Brega, and in 688 when he accepted the Roman Easter. Failure to convert his monks perhaps influenced his writing (688–92) a life of his kinsman *Columba, the monastery's founder, and his return to Ireland in 692. Adomnán's cult flourished in Ireland and Scotland.

**Adrian IV** (*c*.1100–59). Name taken by Nicholas Breakspear, still the only Englishman to be pope. Elected in 1154, he soon found himself at odds with the Emperor Frederick I (Barbarossa). In 1155–6 he granted lordship over Ireland to Henry II. According to a papal bull (known from its opening word as *Laudabiliter*), Adrian made the grant so that Henry could reform 'a rough and ignorant people'— and scholars still debate whether the bull was a forgery.

**Adrian, Edgar Douglas, 1st Baron Adrian** (1889–1977). Scientist. Born in London, Adrian went to Westminster School and Trinity College, Cambridge. Specializing in physiology, he became a fellow of his college in 1913 and then spent the First World War treating cases of shell-shock. Adrian returned to Cambridge in 1919 and published extensively on the nervous system. He shared the Nobel prize in 1932, held the chair of physiology from 1937 to 1951, and was master of Trinity from 1951 to 1965.

**Adullamites** was the name derisively given to Robert *Lowe and nearly 40 Liberal MPs who opposed Lord *Russell's programme of parliamentary reform in 1866. They were dubbed by John *Bright on 13 March in allusion to the cave of Adullam (1 Sam. 22), where David was joined by the discontented. Their opposition brought about the fall of the government but a further measure of reform was introduced by the Conservative government of *Derby and *Disraeli.

**advowsons** are the right of appointing a parson in the Church of England to a parish or other benefice. The system survived from pre-Reformation power struggles between church and state until the right became protected in English civil law. The Benefice Measure of 1978 provided for involvement of the parish in appointments but not for abolition of this form of patronage.

**Adwalton Moor, battle of,** 1643. *Newcastle and the *Fairfaxes were manœuvring in the spring of 1643 for control of Yorkshire. In the battle on Adwalton Moor, 30 June, east of Bradford, the royalists achieved an important victory. Bradford and Leeds fell immediately.

**Æd** (d. 878), 'king of the Picts' (876–8), anachronistically regarded as 4th king of Scotland. Son of *Kenneth I, he succeeded his brother *Constantine I. This was the worst period of Scandinavian devastation. Two rivals on record are the obscure *Giric and Æd's nephew *Eochaid, son of Rhun of Strathclyde. Either of these may have been Æd's final opponent in battle at Strathallan, which left Æd fatally wounded.

**Ædan mac Gabhrain** (d. *c*.608), king of Dalriada. He was crowned on Iona in 574 by St *Columba, his spiritual adviser. Ædan established a powerful kingdom, first gaining authority over the Irish Dalriada at the convention of Druim Cett in 575. Successful campaigns included expeditions to the Orkneys and the Isle of Man. But in 603 he led a great army against the powerful Northumbrian king *Æthelfryth at *Degsastan. Soundly defeated, he fled, which may be why, in Welsh tradition, he is known as 'Ædan the traitor of the North'.

**Ælfheah** (954–1012), archbishop of Canterbury, was a monk at Deerhurst and at Bath before being appointed bishop of Winchester in 984. In 1006 he succeeded Ælfric as archbishop of Canterbury. A Danish host burned Canterbury in 1011 and took the archbishop prisoner: on 19 April 1012 at Greenwich he was battered to death. He was buried in St Paul's and then at Canterbury.

He is recognized as a saint, usually as St Alphege.

**Ælle** (d. *c*.514), founder of the South Saxon kingdom, is said to have landed near Selsey Bill in 477, traditionally with three sons and three ships, driving the Britons back into Andredesweald. His next recorded battle, in 485, took place near an unknown stream, Mearcredes burna, and in 491, Ælle and his son Cissa successfully stormed the fort of Anderida, near Pevensey. Named by *Bede as first of the *bretwaldas, a powerful overlord, he was probably leader of a general Anglo-Saxon push against Britons in the south.

**Ælle** (d. 867), king of Northumbria (*c*.863–7 or, possibly, his reign was confined to 867). He was the last independent English king of Northumbria. Though probably not of royal birth, he sought to usurp power from his predecessor Osberht. Danish armies took York in November 866. Ælle and Osberht united in an effort to regain the city on 21 March 867. They penetrated the walls, but both were then killed.

**Æthelbald** (d. 757), king of Mercia (716–57). The young Æthelbald was driven into exile in the reign of his second cousin Ceolred, but succeeded Ceolred as king. Writing in 731 *Bede says that all the kingdoms of the English, south of the Humber, are under the authority of Æthelbald. A charter of 736 describes Æthelbald in language supporting this claim. His relations with the church were forceful. He seems to have established a firm exploitation of monasteries and he misconducted himself with nuns. He died at the hands of his own military household.

**Æthelbert** (d. 616), king of Kent (560–616), was the king who welcomed the Christian missionaries led by St *Augustine to England in 597. He exercised overlordship over all the English peoples south of the Humber, and as a direct result of his support the Christian mission was firmly established in the south-east, with bishoprics set up at his principal centre, *Canterbury, *Rochester, and *London. Sources suggest that he began his reign as early as 560 or 565, but it is more likely that his reign commenced in the late 570s or early 580s. Sometime before 589 Æthelbert married Bertha, daughter of Charibert, a Frankish king of Paris. She was a Christian, and brought a Christian priest, the bishop Liudhard, with her. They practised their faith in a church on the site of St Martin's. Æthelbert allowed Augustine to preach, allotting him the church at St Martin's and a site in the city which became the cathedral church. The king was quickly converted and many of his people with him. The new faith drew him into yet closer contact with Francia and ultimately with Rome. Æthelbert continued to exercise effective authority in the south-east but Kentish pre-eminence weakened after his death in 616.

**Æthelburg** (b. *c*.605) was the Christian daughter of Æthelbert of Kent. Her marriage to the Northumbrian king Edwin (625) brought about his baptism and the initial conversion of his kingdom by Bishop *Paulinus, who had accompanied her north. Edwin's defeat and death in 633 forced queen and bishop to flee back to Kent.

**Æthelfleda, lady of the Mercians** (d. 918), was the last independent ruler of Mercia. The daughter of Alfred of Wessex and his Mercian wife Ealhswith, she was married to Æthelred of Mercia, probably in the second half of the 880s. Even before his death in 911, Æthelfleda is recorded as exercising regalian power in the province. In particular she provided a ring of burhs (fortified centres) around western Mercia and conducted successful military campaigns against the Welsh, the Hiberno-Norse Vikings, and the Danes of York. After Æthelfleda's death in 918, Edward the Elder deposed her daughter Ælfwynn and took over control of the province.

**Æthelfryth** (d. *c*.616), king of Northumbria (*c*.593–*c*.616), was said by *Bede to be the cruellest enemy of the Britons. It was probably Æthelfryth who defeated the British at Catterick (north Yorks.). His defeat of King *Ædan at *Degsastan in 603 subdued the Irish in Scotland. His victory over the men of Powys at *Chester *c*.616 separated Britons in Wales from their northern compatriots. But Æthelfryth's demise was at the hands of Anglo-Saxons. Threatened by Æthelfryth if he did not hand over Edwin, claimant to the Northumbrian kingdom of *Deira, who had taken refuge at his East Anglian court, *Rædwald attacked, killing Æthelfryth near the *river Idle (Lincs.) c.616.

**Æthelheard,** king of the West Saxons (726–40). Æthelheard succeeded to the throne of Wessex when *Ine abdicated to go to Rome. His succession was challenged by Atheling Oswald, who claimed descent from King *Ceawlin. Æthelheard suffered from the expansion of Mercian power.

**Æthelnoth** (d. 1038). Archbishop of Canterbury from 1020. Often referred to as 'the Good', and thought to have influenced *Cnut. Æthelnoth restored the church at Canterbury, damaged during Danish raids, and in 1023 had the remains of his martyred predecessor *Ælfheah translated there with great ceremony.

**Æthelred** (d. c.716), king of Mercia (675–704). All we know of Æthelred, son of *Penda, suggests a world no less pious than brutal. Its realities can be glimpsed, not recaptured. In 676 he ravaged Kent, and not least its churches. In 679 he won an important victory over the Northumbrians on the *Trent. In 697 his nobles murdered his royal Northumbrian wife Osthryth. In 704 he abdicated to become a monk.

**Æthelred** (d. 796), king of Northumbria (774–8/9, 790–6). Knowledge of Northumbrian history at this time is 'nasty, brutish, and short'. Æthelred was displaced after five years' rule by a member of another line, Ælfwald. Regaining power upon Ælfwald's murder in 790, Æthelred butchered Ælfwald's sons and sought to secure himself by marrying the daughter of *Offa of Mercia. In 796 he was murdered.

**Æthelred I** (d. 871), king of Wessex (865–71). The third son of *Æthelwulf to succeed to the kingship of the West Saxons, Æthelred had to endure the first major onslaught of the Danes. From bases set up in *East Anglia in 866 they first turned their attention to *Northumbria and *Mercia, delaying moves against *Wessex until the autumn of 870. After a series of skirmishes, Æthelred died on campaign in April 871, to be succeeded by his younger brother *Alfred.

**Æthelred, lord of the Mercians** (d. 911). Of unknown origins, by 883 Æthelred was in control of western Mercia, left under

Anglo-Saxon control when Vikings conquered the rest. Æthelred found it expedient to accept the overlordship of *Alfred of Wessex and married his eldest daughter *Æthelfleda. The two provinces co-ordinated activities against the Vikings, but Æthelred became increasingly plagued by ill-health so that well before his death in 911 Æthelfleda had become the effective leader of the Mercians.

**Æthelred II** (d. 1016), king of England (978–1016). Æthelred *Unræd*, the 'Unready', or more accurately the 'ill-advised', lost his kingship 1013–14, when the Danish king, *Sweyn Forkbeard, forced him into exile in Normandy, the home of his second wife *Emma, whom Æthelred had married in 1002. The Anglo-Saxon Chronicler who composed a full account was heavily biased against the king, painting a grim picture of impotence, vacillation, and treachery. Modern approaches have been kinder, noting solid evidence for effective government in the legal and financial spheres and pointing to the cultural and religious elements of strength in the period. No one denies the incompetence, notably later in the reign after 1006, when Æthelred relied too much on the treacherous ealdorman Eadric Streona. It was the king's misfortune that, no military leader himself, he had to face renewed Viking onslaught which reached a peak after the defeat and death of the ealdorman Byrhtnoth at the battle of *Maldon in 991. This was followed by attempts to buy off the Danes by the payment of immense sums. Sporadic violent reaction also occurred as when on the morrow of *St Brice's day, 13 November 1002, Æthelred ordered 'all the Danish men in England' to be slain. In the later stages of the reign things got completely out of hand. *Ælfheah, archbishop of Canterbury, was martyred by the Danes in 1012, and Sweyn's success the following year may be attributed in part to English war-weariness. After Sweyn's death, Æthelred was recalled but died on 23 April 1016 in London, itself under threat from *Cnut's invading and ultimately victorious army.

**Æthelthryth (Ætheldreda, Audrey), St** (c.630–79). Daughter of King Anna of East Anglia, and virgin wife of Tondbert, of the south Gyrwe, and secondly of Ecgfrith of

Northumbria, who eventually released her to monastic life at Coldingham, north of Berwick. Æthelthryth founded a double monastery at Ely, perhaps the first south-eastern house for women. The promotion of her cult by *Wilfrid showed Gallic influence and, after *Æthelwold refounded Ely (c.970), gave title to church and to lands, to her community, and respectability as rulers of East Anglia to her royal West Saxon devotees.

**Æthelwold, St** (c.908–84). Winchester-born leader of the 10th-cent. reformation, and major influence on King *Edgar. Probably a noble, Æthelwold served King *Æthelstan, became a monk under *Dunstan at Glastonbury, and was made, by King Edred, abbot of Abingdon (c.955) and, by Edgar, bishop of Winchester (963). He replaced the clerks of the Old and New Minsters with monks (964), and developed Winchester as a centre of art and learning. Æthelwold's *Benedictional* (collection of blessings), which combined two liturgical traditions, proved very influential. Heavily involved in politics, he worked closely with Edgar and Queen Ælfthryth. Æthelwold elevated royal authority, implying parallels between king and Christ.

**Æthelwulf** (d. 858), king of Wessex (839–58). The son of *Egbert (802–39) and father of four kings, the youngest of whom was *Alfred the Great (871–99), Æthelwulf is a far from negligible figure. He was a competent military leader, conducting substantial campaigns against the Danes at *Aclea in Kent in 851 and against the Welsh of Powys in 853. Much of his personal interest seemed, however, to lie in ecclesiastical directions. He made generous provision for the financing of churches (his Decimations). In 855 he yielded his authority to his eldest son Æthelbald, and went on pilgrimage to Rome. Æthelwulf was away for a twelvemonth, and on his return with a Frankish princess as a bride (a young girl, Judith) he was forced to agree to a division of the kingdom with his own authority confined to the south-east.

**Aetius, Flavius** (d. 454). Roman general. Gildas's work *On the Ruin of Britain* contains the passage known as The Groans of the Britons: 'To Agitius thrice consul, the groans of the Britons....the barbarians push us back to the sea, the sea pushes us back to

the barbarians.' The Agitius of the text is usually identified as Flavius Aetius, consul for the third time in 446 and last effective Roman commander in Gaul.

**Afghan wars** From 1807, when the armies of Tsar Alexander I reached its northern borders, Afghanistan became an uneasy neutral zone between the Russian and the British Indian empires around which 'the Great Game' was played. The British launched three military interventions—in 1838–42, 1878–81, and 1919–21. None was successful. The first Afghan War against Dost Mohammed saw a British expeditionary force capture the capital, Kabul. However, surrounding tribes forced a desperate retreat through mountainous country and only one member of the original army of 16,000 lived to cross the Khyber pass back into India. The second war was precipitated by Lord *Lytton's forward policies, which subsequently were repudiated by *Gladstone's incoming 1880 government. The third war arose when Habibullah Khan demanded recognition by the British of the absolute independence of his kingdom. British arms, once more, found the Afghan terrain and peoples intractable. Afghanistan's sovereignty at international law was formally recognized on 21 November 1921. A fourth and unexpected intervention in Afghanistan began in 2001 when the Americans, with British assistance, drove out the Taliban as part of their campaign against international terrorism. But the struggle proved protracted and difficult.

**Africa, partition of** Africa is the nearest continent to western Europe, yet its colonization lagged far behind more distant regions, partly because of the health risks it presented to Europeans, and partly because there seemed little to take them there. The main exception was trade, in slaves and other goods, which could be carried on perfectly well through African and Arab middlemen at the coasts. A number of maritime nations had posts in Africa from the 16th cent. onwards, including the Portuguese, Spaniards, and—a little later—the Dutch and British. As late as the 1860s, however, their presence in tropical Africa was marginal. Britain seemed content. In 1865 a parliamentary select committee recommended withdrawing from three of her four west coast settlements altogether. Shortly after that, however, interest in Africa revived.

The reasons for this were the use of quinine as a prophylaxis against malaria; missionary activities; a new demand for Africa's natural products; booming trade to the East, and native rebellions. Other European countries also became involved, especially France. In 1882 Britain took control of Egypt after a rebellion there against the local khedive threatened her own interests, particularly in Suez. That sparked off the main stage of the 'scramble for Africa', in which several European nations vied for control.

To prevent conflict, the German chancellor Bismarck called a conference in Berlin in 1884, which parcelled west and central Africa. That was done with relatively little fuss, mainly because none of the claimants felt desperately strongly about it. The only new colony to feel the effects of this immediately was the Congo 'Free State', chiefly because of its bloody exploitation by its new owner, the Belgian King Leopold II.

In the 1890s action shifted to the east and south. Here the lion's share went to Britain, including the *Sudan, most of east-central Africa, and the *Rhodesias. This time the competition was keener, threatening conflicts with France over *Fashoda in 1898, and Germany on the eve of the second *Boer War. By 1900 the process was completed, leaving virtually the whole of Africa—barring only Ethiopia and Liberia—in European hands.

**Africa Company** *See* ROYAL AFRICA COMPANY.

**Agadir crisis,** 1911. A Franco-German colonial crisis triggered by a German gunboat in a Moroccan port (July 1911) led ministers to resolve an inter-service dispute over the role of the army in any future war with Germany by agreeing 'in principle' that it should be sent to the continent.

**Agincourt, battle of,** 1415. Henry V landed in France on 13 August 1415, laying siege to Harfleur. As the town held out until 23 September, and his army was much depleted, he decided to return forthwith to England via Calais. The French army, perhaps over 20,000 strong, attempted to block his approach to Calais. Henry had little choice but to give battle on 25 October though he now had only about 900 men-at-arms and 5,000 archers. He drew up his troops, all on foot, within 300 yards of the

enemy, across a narrow front bordered by trees, with archers on the flanks. The French cavalry charged into this funnel, hampered by volleys of arrows and by the wet ground. Many were killed or captured, amongst them the duke of Orléans.

**Agreement of the People,** 1647. A set of counter-proposals from the radical members of the army, who were concerned at the concessions which the army council had offered the king in the *Heads of the Proposals. The Agreement, formulated in October 1647, became the basis for the discussions at the army debates in *Putney. It urged a substantial widening of the parliamentary franchise. *Cromwell and *Ireton retorted that the security of property would be undermined. When the Agreement was submitted to Parliament, it was rejected.

**Agricola, Gnaeus Iulius** Governor of Britain 77–83. Agricola came of a senatorial family in southern Gaul. He was exceptional in spending all three of his periods of provincial service in Britain, culminating in an unusually long governorship. He first served in Britain as a military tribune at the time of the *Boudiccan revolt (60/1). He returned as legate (commander) of *legio XX Valeria Victrix* 69–73, during which time his legion took part in the advance north of the Humber–Mersey line. He served as a consul in the year 77 and probably arrived in Britain as governor late that year. Tacitus' account of Agricola's governorship is dominated by narratives of the seven seasons of campaigning, advancing Roman power far into Scotland and culminating in the defeat of the Caledonian tribes under *Calgacus at the battle of Mons Graupius (83/4).

**agricultural revolution** This was traditionally regarded as taking place simultaneously with the *industrial revolution, and involving the introduction of new crop rotations in which roots and artificial crops were cultivated, improvements in livestock breeding, and the reorganization of land as a result of parliamentary enclosure. These changes were held to have raised the productivity of land in such a way that the population was fed (with some help from imports) without resort to massive labour inputs which would have slowed down the industrial revolution by restricting the flow of labour from the countryside to the town. Without doubt the end results deduced by this argument are correct. Food supply did more or less keep pace with population and urbanization. By 1850 an estimated 6.5 million extra mouths were being fed from home production compared with 1750. However, questions have been raised about the nature, and particularly the timing, of the agricultural revolution.

Modern understanding of the agricultural revolution sees it loosely as a three-stage, overlapping, process. The first phase, completed by c.1750–70, saw two developments: first, the introduction of new crops, particularly root crops such as turnips and swedes, which could be grown between grain crops; and second, a considerable rise in the productivity of labour. As a result of these changes less land needed to be left fallow, additional animal feedstuffs were grown, and greater quantities (and quality) of manure became available.

During the second phase, lasting from around 1750 to 1830, demand increased rapidly. In this period the slack in the agricultural economy which had been partly taken up by grain exports disappeared and by the early 19th cent. an import balance existed. The reorganization of the land through enclosure and the gradual growth of larger farms, brought a slow rise in productivity, and a growing trend towards regional specialization. Norfolk farmers had pioneered the cultivation of clover in England, but it was only after 1740 that the principal benefits of the new crop were felt.

The third phase, beginning in about 1830, and sometimes called the second agricultural revolution, saw for the first time farmers using substantial inputs purchased off their farms, in the form of fertilizers for their land and artificial feedstuffs for their animals. Together with the introduction of improved methods of drainage, the results were seen in the era of high farming between the 1840s and 1870s, which soon gave way to a severe and prolonged agricultural depression.

In Scotland the agricultural revolution took a rather different form. Although, as in England, there has been a tendency to view it as a long-term change, it is now thought that, at least in the Lowlands, this underplays the transformation which occurred in the second half of the 18th cent. A rapid move towards single tenancies and production for the market was partly stimulated by the pace of population growth, and particularly of urbanization (notably Glasgow and Edinburgh) in the second half of the 18th cent.

The result, in the second half of the 18th cent., was seen in the adoption of new technologies and crops, a shift to long leases with improving clauses written in, and higher productivity. Many of the existing farmers adapted to the new demands upon them, so that there was no Lowland equivalent of the Highland clearances. Overall the result was a radical departure from the patterns of the past in the last quarter of the 18th cent., not simply measured in terms of physical enclosure, but also in the more effective use of land involving liming, sown grasses, and the organization of labour. It was a structural change, and not simply an intensification of existing trends, since it produced a dramatic increase in crop yields, allowing Scottish cultivators to catch up on English levels of output within a few decades.

**Aidan, St** (d. 651). First abbot of *Lindisfarne, site of his see (634–51). Sent from *Iona, replacing a severer colleague, to work closely with King *Oswald in restoring Christianity in Northumbria, Aidan's legacy was profound: Lindisfarne, and his royal pupil *Hilda, were stars in the later 7th-cent. firmament. Aidan's rejection of worldly behaviour and elevated associations partly explains the eclipse of his cult by *Cuthbert's and his relative obscurity. Some of Aidan's relics were taken from Lindisfarne to Ireland by Colman, and his cult was revived at *Glastonbury in the 10th cent.

**aids, feudal** *See* FEUDAL AIDS.

**Ailred of Rievaulx** (1110–67), known as the 'St Bernard of the North', was the leading figure in the *Cistercian order in England in the mid-12th cent. The son of a priest of Hexham (Northd.), he entered the abbey of *Rievaulx, where he remained for nine years before being chosen as first abbot of Revesby (Lincs.), daughter house of Rievaulx. Four years later he was recalled to be abbot of Rievaulx itself. The monastery prospered and expanded, its numbers increasing to 150 choir monks and 500 lay brothers and servants. Ailred himself became a figure of national importance, beyond Cistercian circles, through his many friends, contacts, and writings.

**Aix-la-Chapelle, treaty of,** 1748. Between March and November 1748 all the belligerents in the War of the *Austrian Succession met to negotiate a settlement. The British and French put together an agreement that they persuaded their respective allies to sign. There had been no clear victor in the war and the peace merely acknowledged the status quo. Prussia had made a separate peace with Austria in 1745, but her conquest of Austrian Silesia was recognized at Aix-la-Chapelle. Don Philip of Spain was granted the dukedom of Parma, and Anglo-Spanish trade disputes were adjudicated.

**Akeman Street** This Roman road linked *Cirencester and *Verulamium, running across the south midlands via Alchester (Oxon.). The modern name derives from the Anglo-Saxon words meaning 'oak-man'.

**Alabama case** The *Alabama* was the largest of several commerce raiders built in Britain for the Confederate South in the American Civil War. The *Alabama* collected her armament outside Britain, and in two years of high seas raiding seized 62 merchantmen. She was finally sunk in June 1864 by the Union warship *Kearsage*. Arbitration in Switzerland in 1871 awarded higher damages against Britain than the sums claimed by the US government.

**Alanbrooke, Alan Brooke, 1st Viscount** (1883–1963). Soldier. Chief of the imperial general staff for much of the Second World War, Brooke was the son of an Irish baronet and a member of the protestant ascendancy. After the Royal Military Academy at Woolwich from 1902 he spent the Great War on the western front as an artillery officer. At the outbreak of the Second World War he was a lieutenant-general in charge of anti-aircraft defence. After commanding in France, he was appointed commander-in-chief home forces in 1940 after Dunkirk and the following year became chief of the imperial general staff. He was capable of standing up to and working with *Churchill, whose boldness and imagination he complemented with sober planning.

**Alba, kingdom of** The name 'Alba' was Irish and originally applied to Britain ('Albion'). It was then adopted by the kingdom created by *Kenneth MacAlpin of *Dalriada when he took over the kingdom of the Picts in the 840s. By the 11th cent. it was more commonly known as Scotia or Scotland, but it remains the Gaelic name for Scotland today.

**Alban, St** Protomartyr of Britain, known from early medieval hagiographies. These portray him as a Roman officer who sheltered a priest and was martyred at *Verulamium. Dates in the early and late 3rd cent. have been put forward. The description of the trial and passion of Alban reflects the actual topography of Verulamium and St Albans abbey may perpetuate the site of his death or burial.

**Albany, Alexander Stewart, 1st duke of** [S] (c.1454–85). Second son of James II of Scotland, created earl of March [S] (1455), lord of Annandale, and duke of Albany (1458). As admiral of Scotland and march warden in the 1470s, Albany was an obvious focus for Scottish opposition to his brother James III's English alliance (October 1474). Indicted for treason in October 1479, Albany fled to France, where he married and fathered the son who, as John, duke of *Albany, acted as governor (1515–24) for James V. He was killed in 1485 by a lance splinter at a tournament in Paris.

**Albany, John Stewart, 2nd duke of** [S] (1484–1536). When James IV of Scotland was killed at *Flodden in 1513, his son was 17 months old. Albany, a grandson of James II, was heir presumptive. He was summoned to become regent to his young cousin and held office from 1515 until 1524. Bred in France, Albany strove to restore the *Franco-Scottish alliance and by the treaty of *Rouen (1517) negotiated marriage for James V to a French princess.

**Albany, Murdac Stewart, 2nd duke of** [S] (c.1362–1425). Son and heir of Robert, 1st duke of Albany (d. 1420), Murdac served as royal justiciar north of Forth. Captured by the English at *Homildon Hill (1402), he spent more than thirteen years in captivity. Murdac returned to Scotland in 1416 and succeeded his father as governor in 1420. He officiated at James's coronation at Scone (21 May 1424), but was arrested in Parliament the following March, and beheaded at Stirling on 25 May 1425.

**Albany, Robert Stewart, 1st duke of** [S] (1339–1420). Third son of Robert II and uncrowned ruler of Scotland for 32 years (1388–1420). While still a young man, Robert acquired the earldoms of Menteith [S] (1361) and Fife [S] (1371); he became royal chamberlain in 1382; and in December 1388 was made guardian for his infirm elder brother John, earl of Carrick [S] (later Robert III, 1390–1406). In 1398 Robert was created duke of Albany, a title which reflected his ambitions.

Albany's guardianship was characterized by intermittent hostility towards England, consistent support (until 1418) of the antipope Benedict XIII, a growing commitment to the French alliance, and a ruthless elimination of political opponents.

**Albert, prince consort** (1819–61). Albert was the second son of Ernest, duke of Saxe-Coburg, and Louise, daughter of Duke Augustus of Saxe-Coburg-Altenburg. His parents were divorced in 1826. He was a shy and delicate child but exceptionally diligent and serious-minded. The possibility of a match with his cousin Queen Victoria was fostered by their uncle Leopold, king of the Belgians, but they did not meet until 1836 when they were both 17 years old. Victoria then found him 'extremely handsome'. When they met again at Windsor three years later Victoria fell instantly in love and Albert soon responded. Five days after their meeting she proposed to him and they were married on 10 February 1840.

If Albert was unexpectedly swept off his feet by Victoria's ardour, he was less enthusiastic about her country, nor did her subjects take to him. He was not thought important enough to marry the queen of England, and the facts that he was German, Victoria's first cousin, lacked wealth and position, and was hardly known in England all counted against him. He was variously (and wrongly) supposed to be a 'Coburg adventurer on the make', a political radical, a papist, and (even worse because accurately) an intellectual. Parliament reduced the allowance that was proposed for him, and refused to grant him precedence next to the queen. Precedence was nevertheless conferred on him by letters patent, but he received no title and was not officially designated prince consort until 1857.

Victoria adored her husband but was reluctant to admit him to share in her political duties. He did however guide his wife towards political neutrality, weaning her from her previous Whig partisanship and reconciling her after 1841 to *Peel. After 1842 he acted as Victoria's informal counsellor, private secretary, and sole confidant. In many ways he was a natural bureaucrat—efficient, painstaking, and absorbed by detail. He was happy to become, on Peel's suggestion, chairman of the Fine Arts Royal Commission and he threw himself energetically into his favourite project to make South Kensington a centre for the arts and for education. His attempt to promote the causes of social improvement, science and technology, and the public patronage of the arts and sciences culminated in the organization of the *Great Exhibition of 1851. Nor was he inactive in other public fields. He attempted to guide British foreign policy in peaceful directions and tried to insist that *Palmerston should submit his policies and dispatches to the queen. Palmerston's refusal led to his dismissal from the Foreign Office in 1851. Nevertheless, Albert was unable to avert the outbreak of the *Crimean War in 1854 and Palmerston's return as prime minister in 1855. Almost his last act on his deathbed in 1861 was to tone down an aggressive dispatch to Washington on the *Trent affair which probably averted war with the USA.

Perhaps Albert's most lasting contribution to his adopted country was the example he set, with Victoria, of a respectable and devout private life. They produced nine children, to whom Albert was a loving and devoted though heavy-handed father. His relations with his eldest son, the future King Edward VII, suffered from 'Bertie's' resistance to the ambitious system of education which his father devised and supervised. The pressure placed on the prince of Wales resulted in his alienation from his parents and increased the anxieties from which Albert increasingly suffered. His habits of overwork and his weakened physical constitution resulted in an inability, and perhaps a lack of will, to resist attacks of ill-health and he died of typhoid fever on 14 December 1861 at the age of 42.

**Albert Memorial** When Prince *Albert died in 1861 a competition was held for a national monument, which Sir G. G. *Scott, inevitably, won. It stands in Hyde Park, just across Kensington Gore from the Albert Hall.

The latter is cheap and rather boring, designed by an army engineer. The memorial makes up for that—tall, Gothic, spiky, colourful, and crammed with decorations and sculptures celebrating the achievements of the high Victorian age.

**Albion** is a poetical personification for Britain. It was first used in classical literature in the 6th cent. BC and referred either to the Celtic name or to the white cliffs of Dover.

**Albuera, battle of,** 1811. On 16 May 1811 an Anglo-Spanish-Portuguese force of 35,000 men under Marshal Beresford blocked Marshal Soult's French army of 24,000 moving to lift the siege of Badajoz in Spain. Both sides lost heavily. But the allied army succeeded in repulsing the French in a confused battle which featured the epic action of the 'astonishing infantry' of the Fusilier Brigade.

**alchemy,** an art of ancient origins, can be interpreted as an enquiry into man's relationship with the cosmos and the will of the Creator, manifested as either a devotional philosophy transforming sinful man into perfect being ('esoteric'), or attempted transmutation of base metals into gold or silver ('exoteric'). The catalyst required was the elixir of life, tincture, or philosophers' stone, the search for which long obsessed men of all ranks.

Probably arising in Hellenistic Alexandria, alchemy (*al-kimia*) was transmitted to Europe through Islamic culture. Whilst earlier Taoist alchemists had aimed principally for longevity, medieval western alchemists' objectives were gold-making or creating superior medicines. Since the gold-makers' skills rendered them vulnerable to avaricious magnates, circumspection was advisable, but public credulity encouraged conjuring and dishonesty. Practical alchemy, nevertheless, had much to offer medicine, giving rise to metallic rather than herbal remedies, much favoured by Paracelsus, and eventually to iatrochemistry.

Despite interest from John Dee, Kenelm Digby, the 'Wizard' 9th earl of *Northumberland, Walter *Ralegh, and even Charles II, alchemy received its death-warrant in the mid-17th cent. when Robert *Boyle demolished the theory of the four 'elements'.

**Alcock, John** (1430–1500). Ecclesiastical statesman. Born in Beverley, Alcock attended the University of Cambridge. From 1472 to 1476 he was bishop of Rochester, transferring to Worcester in 1476, and to Ely in 1486. He was in high favour with Edward IV, holding office as master of the rolls, lord chancellor (joint), president of the Council of Wales, and as tutor to Edward, prince of Wales. Henry VII brought him back into service, appointing him again as lord chancellor. Alcock was the founder of Jesus College, Cambridge.

**Alcuin** (*c.*735–804) was a Northumbrian, probably noble, deacon, adviser to Charlemagne, and architect of the Carolingian Renaissance. He was born between 735 and 745, and succeeded his teacher Ælbert as master of the school at York in 767. He travelled on the continent, and after meeting Charlemagne at Parma in 781 was invited to his court.

Alcuin became involved in political life and influenced Charlemagne's thinking. Authorship of some of Charlemagne's texts is still credited to Alcuin. He wrote against the heresy of adoptionism. He probably composed the letter to Pope Leo III wherein pope's and king's functions are defined, and he may have been partly responsible for Charlemagne's taking the Roman imperial title in the west (in 800). His writings include one of the earliest, medieval, political essays. An ideal of warrior kingship is presented in Alcuin's poem on *The Bishops, Kings and Saints of York*, the first major extant Latin verse history in the medieval West, it offers *Edwin as supreme kingly example and Ælbert as ideal prelate.

Alcuin's writings include textbooks, saints' lives, compilations of commentaries, missals, and Charlemagne's epitaph for Pope Hadrian I. His epitaph for himself became a literary model. His revisions of the lectionary (lessons to be read at mass) and of the (Latin) Vulgate text of the Bible became standard. His letters offer evidence of low standards in the late 8th-cent. English church and amongst the Northumbrian elite, and his York poem for 8th-cent. Northumbrian history, the development of the York school, and York's wealth and commercial activity.

**Aldhelm** (*c*.639–709) was one of the most learned men of his time. Thought to be related to West Saxon kings and educated at Malmesbury under the Irish scholar Maildubh, he also studied briefly at the Canterbury school flourishing under Archbishop *Theodore and Abbot Hadrian after 669. A distinguished scholar and teacher, ecclesiastically energetic, appointed abbot of Malmesbury *c*.675, and first bishop of *Sherborne *c*.705, Aldhelm founded monasteries, built churches, and a surviving letter shows him writing to Geraint, king of *Dumnonia, urging conformity with the Roman observance of Easter. His largest work, *De virginitate*, dedicated to the nuns at Barking (Essex), is a twofold treatise in prose and verse, which became a stylistic model for subsequent Anglo-Latin works.

**Alexander I** (*c*.1077–1124), king of Scots (1107–24). The second of the three sons of *Malcolm Canmore to become king, he succeeded his elder brother Edgar. He ruled north of the Forth–Clyde line while his younger brother David (later David I) governed Strathclyde and much of Lothian in his name. He maintained friendly relations with England by marrying Sybil, one of Henry I's illegitimate daughters, and by campaigning with Henry in Wales in 1114.

**Alexander II** (1198–1249), king of Scots (1214–49). Son and successor of William the Lion. He swiftly asserted himself against King John by allying with the barons of *Magna Carta, who formally recognized Scottish claims to Northumberland, Cumberland, and Westmorland. In 1216 the Yorkshire rebels paid homage to him, and he marched as far south as Dover to meet Prince Louis of France, claimant to the English throne, who acknowledged his right to the border counties. Following John's death and the royalist victory at *Lincoln, the ground was cut from beneath the Scots, and in December 1217 Alexander made peace with Henry III, relinquishing his war gains. These events introduced a new realism into Anglo-Scottish relations, and both kingdoms adopted more conciliatory policies. His marriage to Henry III's sister *Joan reinforced the new understanding between the crowns, and by the treaty of *York (1237) he renounced all claims to the border shires. Scottish re-

sources were now concentrated on the vigorous assertion of authority in the north and west of Scotland. Alexander died of a fever on the island of Kerrera in Oban Bay while leading a major expedition against the Western Isles.

**Alexander III** (1241–86), king of Scots (1249–86). Only son of Alexander II and his second wife, Marie de Coucy. The view that his reign was a 'golden age' for Scotland was first fully articulated by 14th- and 15th-cent. Scottish chroniclers, who boosted his reputation in order to stress Scottish national identity. Nevertheless, there is much to be said for their assessments. The reign began badly with the factional squabbles of Alexander's minority (1249–60). Thereafter Alexander dealt with the great lords firmly but sensitively. Continuing earlier processes, he campaigned extensively in the west, and brought matters to a successful conclusion in 1266, when sovereignty over Man and the Western Isles was relinquished by Norway. Their annexation to Scotland, one of the greatest triumphs of Scottish state-building, was facilitated by amicable relations with England. Alexander had married Henry III's daughter *Margaret in 1251, and although Henry intervened in the minority power struggles, he repeatedly reassured the Scots of his respect for their liberties. Cruel circumstances jeopardized this 'golden age'—the deaths of Alexander's three children between 1281 and 1284, and his own untimely death at the age of 44, when he was thrown from his horse. Even so, by 1286 Scotland had emerged as a unified and sturdily autonomous state.

**Alexander, Harold Rupert Leofric George, 1st Earl Alexander** (1891–1969). From an Anglo-Irish aristocratic family, Alexander fought throughout the First World War, commanding a brigade at the age of 27. In 1939–40 he served in France, and, until 1942, in Britain. Then he took charge of the British retreat from Burma. In August 1942, he became commander-in-chief, Middle East, but left *Montgomery a free hand with the 8th Army.

Polite, elegant, and tactful, Alexander's 'easy smiling grace won all hearts' (*Churchill). In ground command of Anglo-American forces in Tunisia he 'won the adulation of his

American subordinates' (Bradley). Soon, however, the Anglo-American campaign in Sicily exposed Alexander's inability to impose his orders on self-willed subordinates when Montgomery seized priority for his army over Patton's. On 12 December 1944 he became allied C.-in-C., Mediterranean, and field marshal, backdated to restore his seniority over Montgomery. In 1946–52 he was the last non-Canadian governor-general of Canada, was given an earldom, and became minister of defence in Churchill's government until 1954.

**Alexander, Sir William, 1st earl of Stirling** [S] (c.1576–1640). Alexander was born at Menstrie in Clackmannanshire. He established an early reputation as poet and dramatist, served at the court of Prince *Henry, and was knighted. In 1614 James VI and I made him master of requests [S], a post he held until his death. From 1626 until his death he served as secretary of state [S], was granted a viscountcy in 1630, and raised to the earldom of Stirling [S] in 1633. But his record was not distinguished. 'Unactable plays and unreadable poems' is a verdict on his literary output.

**Alexandra** (1844–1925), queen of Edward VII. Born in Copenhagen, eldest daughter of the future Christian IX of Denmark, Alexandra retained warm Danish sympathies all her life. Her marriage to Edward, then prince of Wales, took place in 1863. The couple, popular with the public, took much of the attention shunned by the widowed Victoria, and became society figures. The marriage was affectionate, though Edward was far from faithful. Family life was the focus of her existence, partly because of her initial difficulty with English, and then her growing deafness. She devoted much of her time to nursing and hospitals: Alexandra Day was instituted in 1913 to sell paper roses for hospital funds. Following Edward's death in 1910 she led a quiet, private life, mainly at Sandringham.

**Alexandria, battle of,** 1801. Napoleon's expedition to Egypt was cut off in August 1798 by *Nelson's victory of the *Nile, and a year later Napoleon abandoned his men and returned to France. In March 1801 a British force of 14,000 men under Sir Ralph Abercromby fought its way towards Alexandria. On the 21st, after heavy fighting in which

Abercromby was killed, the French capitulated.

**Alford, battle of,** 1645. Alford was one of *Montrose's brilliant victories. Pursued by Baillie's troops, Montrose took his men over the hills until Baillie retired on Inverness. On 2 July he found Montrose at Alford, west of Aberdeen. Baillie's forces could not withstand the ferocity of Montrose's charge and were badly beaten.

**Alfred** (849–99), king of Wessex (871–99). A popular image of Alfred is of national superman; destined by his father's (*Æthelwulf) will to be king, despite having three surviving older brothers (Æthelbald, Æthelbert, and *Æthelred I); saviour of the English from the Vikings; architect of a united England; founder of the navy, reformer of the army, townplanner; patron of the church; promoter of universal education and father of English prose; saintly, and easy to know. Revisionists emphasize his skill as propagandist, downgrading his achievements.

Perception of Alfred's personality, policies, and methods depends largely upon his seemingly intimate hagiographical biography by *Asser. But there was probably a different side to Alfred's character. And if the denial of the text's authenticity, powerfully reasserted in 1995, should carry the day, significant elements of the traditional account of Alfred's career will disappear.

Asser says Alfred was born in 849 in Wantage and married a Mercian lady in 868. The quality of his own writings suggests that he had a sound education in Latin. He assisted Æthelred against the 'great army' which invaded in 865, and his accession in 871 was most likely not a certainty. The 870s saw continuing war against the Danes, who were numerous, skilled, treacherous, well led, wanting conquest and settlement. In 878, surprised by *Guthrum at *Chippenham, Alfred fled to Athelney (Somerset), but defeated the Danes in a desperate laststand battle at *Edington. The results were the treaty of *Wedmore, Guthrum's baptism and retirement to be king of East Anglia.

The West Saxon dynasty was the only one to survive the Viking threat and Alfred gained authority over all the English outside Danish control. Mercia (under Burgred) had been an ally, and was handled tactfully. Alfred

a

married his daughter *Æthelfleda to Ealdorman *Æthelred, probably of Mercian royal stock, allowed him to operate as subking, and ceded London after its recapture from the Danes (886).

Alfred's success depended on his own abilities and on the excellence of his administration. Earlier dynastic stability contributed to royal control over local government, though Alfred's rota for *thegns' attendance at court and the system of division of his revenues are recorded by Asser alone. His new 60-oared design for 'long ships' was not immediately successful, his division of the *fyrd into two (home and away) was perhaps to safeguard agriculture. His most effective reform was the development of burhs. Various sites, chosen so that nowhere in Wessex was further than 20 miles from one, were fortified and their defence and maintenance imposed on the people. Some 27,000 men were required in all.

Alfred's government was expensive. It is probable that he bought peace with heavy payments to the Danes, for example in 896. Wealth was necessary to ensure aristocratic support, for building, against Vikings, and also against dynastic rivals. Alfred's nephews Æthelhelm and Æthelwold challenged his disposition of Æthelred's property before the witan and could be expected to challenge his son *Edward for the kingship. Asser asserts that Alfred spent lavishly on art, architecture, alms, and gifts to the church. His coinage shows he was not short of silver, and his will that he was hugely wealthy in 899.

Alfred's relationship with the church seems superficially harmonious. Ninth-cent. West Saxon kings seem not to have pressured the church economically: the *Anglo-Saxon Chronicle records Alfred sending alms to Rome, and receiving gifts from Pope Marinus, and Asser recounts his foundation of monasteries at Athelney and Shaftesbury (for women). Yet evidence from Abingdon suggests Alfred was resented there as a despoiler, other evidence that he appropriated monastic properties right across Wessex, and it is as a threat to the church that he appears in a papal letter in 878.

The support Alfred needed was not automatic, so he attempted to teach his subjects about their duties, his authority, and their collective destiny. The authorship and dates of texts produced in his reign have been much discussed, and depend in part on the degree of credence given to Asser's account of Alfred's intellectual development. Alfred's law code referred to the laws of *Æthelbert of Kent and *Offa of Mercia, and included *Ine's, perhaps to appeal to Kentish and Mercian sentiment. The code's purpose was to promote the king as lawgiver, rather than to serve as a handbook, and Alfred's preface offers a history of law beginning with the Ten Commandments, suggesting that his people were a new people of God. The *Chronicle* was perhaps composed in 896–7 under Alfred's direction, its content and structure suggesting that it was commissioned to tie Alfred into West Saxon history and Wessex into world history, to emphasize Alfred's fitness to rule, to represent the West Saxon kings as struggling for Christianity against paganism, to set Alfred's cause and people in a context of contemporary world powers and events, and to celebrate his achievement.

Alfred proposed, in his prose preface to his translation of Pope Gregory I's *Pastoral Rule*, a programme of translation of books 'most necessary for all men to know'. He complained that clerical knowledge of Latin and educational standards generally had greatly declined. But his own and his team's activities betray this to be an exaggeration. Alfred himself refers to Asser, Plegmund, Wærferth, Grimbald, and John. For their attendance on and education of Alfred, the plans for mass education, and for reading tests for ealdormen and reeves, we depend on Asser. Alfred's *Pastoral Rule* was sent to his bishops, to educate them and to urge them to teach. Alfred also translated two contemplative works, Boethius' *Consolation of Philosophy* and Augustine's *Soliloquies*, and a number of psalms.

The West Saxon take-over of England, 10th-cent. economic development, the burhs as sites of mints and centres of administration, can all be traced back to Alfred. Though vernacular literature failed to take off, the education of bishops may have contributed to the 10th-cent. reform movement since its leaders were bishops. Alfred's legal innovations may have laid a foundation for the English common law of Henry II's time.

Asser exaggerated Alfred's contemplative quality. The reality was a ruthless, shrewd ruler with a keen historical sense, a sensitivity to public opinion, and a genuine sense of duty.

**Alfred the Atheling** (*c.*1008–*c.*1037) was a younger son of *\*Æthelred by \*Emma of Normandy. Her second marriage, to \*Cnut, dispossessed the sons by her first marriage and they were brought up in Normandy. In 1035, on the death of Cnut, Alfred made an ill-judged visit to England. He was captured by Earl \*Godwine, blinded, and died in Ely.

**Algeciras** A great-power conference (January–April 1906), which resolved the first Moroccan crisis of 1905–6, during which Germany had vainly tried to weaken or destroy the Anglo-French \*Entente.

**Algiers, bombardment of,** 1816. On 27 August 1816, Lord Exmouth, in command of nineteen British warships, bombarded Algiers for eight hours, destroying much of the town. The Dey then agreed to abolish Christian slavery in his dominions.

**Allen, William** (1532–94). Founding principal of Douai College (1568–85) and cardinal (1587). A Lancashireman, educated at Oriel College, Oxford, he became principal of St Mary's Hall (1556–60), then joined catholic exiles at Louvain (1561). Briefly in England (1562–5), he was ordained at Mechlin, visited Rome, and founded the college at Douai (1568) to give English catholics university education and train missionary priests for reconverting England. He retired to Rome (1585) in poor health, became cardinal-priest, and died there.

**Allenby, Edmund, 1st Viscount Allenby** (1861–1936). Soldier and administrator. After extensive service in Africa before 1914, Allenby fought in France before being posted to Palestine in June 1917. In the Middle East he proved himself a master of mobile warfare. In October 1917 his troops defeated the Turks at Gaza and by Christmas he had occupied Jerusalem. Further rapid progress was halted when his army was milked of reinforcements to be sent to France. But when he resumed his offensive in September 1918, operating in co-operation with the Arab forces organized by Colonel T. E. \*Lawrence (of Arabia), he destroyed the Turkish armies in Palestine and Syria at the battle of Megiddo.

**Alliance Party** Formed in April 1970 to bridge the gap between unionists and nationalists in Northern Ireland. The party was represented at the Sunningdale conference (December 1973) and in the power-sharing executive (January–May 1974). Its share of the vote peaked in 1977, when its candidates secured 14.4 per cent in the district council elections: recent electoral performance has been weaker. Though the Alliance party has never won a seat in the Westminster Parliament, it has seven seats in the Northern Ireland Assembly elected in March 2007, together with a number of local councillors.

**Alma, battle of,** 1854. On 20 September, a week after disembarking in the \*Crimea, British, French, and Turkish troops under \*Raglan and St Arnaud launched an attack on Menshikov's forces blocking their advance on Sebastopol at the Alma river. After heavy fighting at bayonet point, the Russians were forced to retreat.

**Almanza, battle of,** 1707. On 25 April an allied force under the command of Lord Galway, comprising about 15,000 English, Dutch, and Portuguese troops, attacked a larger Franco-Spanish army under Marshal Berwick near Valencia. Despite initial allied success, a Portuguese defeat on the right flank exposed the English and Dutch, over 3,000 of whom were forced to surrender.

**Almenara, battle of,** 1710. On the river Noguera in Aragon, on 27 July, an allied army of 24,000, commanded by the Austrian Count Stahremberg, and including an English contingent under \*Stanhope, attacked a Spanish army of roughly equal size, commanded by General Villadarias with Philip V in attendance. Caught by surprise, the Spanish were defeated, chiefly by Stanhope's men.

**almshouses,** also known as bede-houses, are buildings to provide accommodation for aged or frail people. They were established at a time when there was no alternative welfare provision. Usually they were paid for by a benefactor, whose intentions were set out in a deed stipulating who might be given help.

The origin of almshouses lay in medieval monasteries, which built houses from which alms and hospitality were dispensed. The religious links remained: often almshouses were intended to contain small communities

**a**

who had to attend regular services to pray for the souls of the benefactor. The houses frequently included a chapel and generally the priest who took the services supervised the residents. Generous benefactors established funds to pay for fuel, clothing (sometimes a uniform), and even some food and drink.

By the early 14th cent. the endowment of almshouses had become a favoured form of charitable bequest. After the Reformation, almshouses continued to be established in many towns and villages, and are often architecturally agreeable. Benefactors often specified that only members of the Church of England were eligible.

**Alnwick, battle of,** 1093. During the reign of Malcolm III of Scotland there were repeated clashes over the border with England. After William Rufus had taken possession of Cumberland and Westmorland, negotiations broke down. Malcolm invaded Northumberland and besieged Alnwick castle. A relief force on 13 November 1093 killed both Malcolm and his eldest son Edward.

**Alnwick, battle of,** 1174. In pursuit of his claims to the northern shires, William I 'the Lion', king of Scotland, invaded England in 1173 and 1174. In 1174, having failed to take Carlisle, Wark, and Prudhoe castles, William decided to ravage the coastal plain of Northumberland. On the morning of 13 July, William and the few knights he had with him were caught completely by surprise outside Alnwick castle by a force loyal to Henry II led by Ranulf *Glanvill. A sharp fight followed before William was led away in captivity to Henry II who imposed severe terms.

**Alnwick castle** is a major medieval fortress in Northumberland and a principal residence of the Percy family since the early 14th cent. It stands above the river Aln amongst parkland created by Capability *Brown around 1765. In its present form the castle is mostly mid-19th cent., the creation of Algernon, 4th duke of Northumberland.

**Alresford, battle of** See CHERITON.

**Althorp, John Charles Spencer, Viscount, 3rd Earl Spencer** (1782–1845). Althorp preferred the pleasures of private life to the tribulations of politics. Not an eloquent speaker, he won the confidence of the Commons by his honesty. In both the *Grey and *Melbourne administrations he was important as chancellor of the Exchequer. He welcomed the 1832 Reform Bill, was involved in drafting it, and prominent in securing its passage through Parliament, but in 1834 he could not support an Irish Coercion Bill and this contributed to Grey's decision to resign. Melbourne believed Althorp's presence in the Commons was essential and it was a great blow when Althorp succeeded his father as Earl Spencer in November 1834. The result was Melbourne's resignation. Althorp was happy to leave politics and immersed himself in farming and country sports.

**Amboyna massacre,** 1623. The island of Amboyna in the Moluccas became the focus of Anglo-Dutch rivalry in the spice trade. In 1623, the English settlement was wiped out by the Dutch. The massacre soured relations between Dutch and English for many years.

**Ambrosius Aurelianus,** 'the last of the Romans', was a British leader who emerged during the twilight years of Roman Britain to resist the onslaught of invading Saxons. This resistance culminated in the battle of *Mount Badon at which the Saxons were defeated.

**America** The thirteen colonies later formed the United States of America. All except Georgia, founded in 1732, resulted from 17th-cent. crown grants, mainly to companies or proprietors. Most were eventually taken under crown control, so that by 1750 they had similar institutional and political systems. The original Indian inhabitants were gradually dispossessed and marginalized by aggressive settlers.

In the south, Virginia (1607) became a royal province in 1624. Its neighbour, Maryland (*see* BALTIMORE), was taken under royal control, but reverted to proprietary rule in 1715. Tobacco, a major export crop, shaped the development of both colonies. The demand for labour was met by indentured servants from the British Isles, who worked for a term of years in return for a free passage. After about 1680 African slaves gradually displaced them. In South Carolina (1663) rice became the great export crop; here slavery was more concentrated and harsher. South Carolina and North Carolina became royal colonies. In Georgia, founded by humanitarians as a refuge for poor persons, attempts to ban slavery and strong drink failed; it developed as a plantation-based society.

In the north, no staples dominated. Families rather than indentured servants went to Massachusetts (*see* MASSACHUSETTS BAY COMPANY), and to Connecticut, which received a royal charter in 1662. In both, the religious convictions of the early settlers helped shape social and political institutions. Hostilities between congregationalists, baptists, and quakers played a major role in the development of religious toleration in Rhode Island, settled from 1636. New Hampshire, first settled by New England congregationalists, was chartered in 1679.

The middle colonies, founded after 1660, became the great receptacles of continuing white migration. New York was granted to James, duke of York (later James II), in 1664. From it he granted New Jersey to a number of proprietors. Both territories later came under direct royal control. Pennsylvania's (*see* PENN, WILLIAM) early life was dominated by members of the Society of Friends. Its southern neighbour, Delaware, was formed from Pennsylvania's three lower counties. New York City and, especially, Philadelphia became substantial urban centres.

In the 17th cent. the colonies were seen in Britain as receptacles for a surplus population, but by the end of the century, the need for a large labour force at home was stressed. Although immigration continued from mainland Britain, its major sources became northern Ireland and protestant Germany. This led to increasing religious diversity as Ulster presbyterians ('Scotch-Irish') and a variety of German baptists, Lutherans, and Moravians arrived. Even so, natural increase more than migration fed population growth. This was formidable, a distinguishing feature in the development of the colonies, underpinning a burgeoning self-confidence.

British opinion was that the colonies were primarily of value to the development of a profitable maritime commercial empire. Regulatory measures included various acts of trade ('*Navigation Acts') from 1651 onwards in the face of Dutch competition. Foreign-built and/or -crewed ships were excluded from colonial trade and most exports and imports were to be carried via English and (after 1707) Scottish ports. In 1696 the foundation of the Board of *Trade provided a focus for colonial administration and attempts were made to tighten British control, especially during times of war.

These were not continued with any force under Sir Robert *Walpole and the duke of *Newcastle, a period characterized as one of 'salutary neglect'. Only renewed struggles with Spain and France, and the rise of a group of imperially minded politicians and colonial governors, created demands for stronger executive control. By this time colonial political identities were almost fully formed. The original crown charters had conferred large powers of self-government on the colonies, allowing them representative assemblies with substantial legislative powers, chosen by wide electorates. These assemblies assumed fiscal authority and control of local government, a process shaped by the emergence of élite groups of successful families.

Warfare between France and England in North America in 1754 necessitated co-operation between a mother country and colonies whose differences were masked by shared ambitions for victory over a catholic power. British plans for colonial union in 1754 failed in the colonial assemblies. The course of the *Seven Years War revealed the jealous self-interest of the colonial assemblies towards each other and towards London. Overwhelming advantages in terms of wealth and population enjoyed, for example, by New York and New England over French Canada, together with the deployment of British regular troops, failed to bring victory until 1759–60.

Success brought rejoicing for a God-ordained triumph of protestantism and liberty. The reality was a huge increase in the British national debt, provoking fears that colonial expansion, no longer checked by the French and their Indian allies, would precipate expensive new conflicts with the frontier tribes, concerns fed by the Cherokee War (1759–61) and by a major middle-colony Indian war in 1763. When British ministers introduced new measures to raise larger revenues from America, colonial political awareness was stimulated and intercolonial co-operation increased. Resistance and revolution followed.

**American War** *See* WAR OF 1812.

**American War of Independence,** 1775–83. The roots of American independence go as deep as the original settlements—colonists of a dissenting disposition, the development of a more egalitarian society without bishops or noblemen, colonial assemblies gaining political experience, and a population increasing in size, prosperity, and confidence. In 1715 the colonists numbered fewer than half a million, of whom 70,000 were negro slaves. By 1770 there were more than 2 million.

The crisis was triggered by the *Seven Years War, during which the British drove the French out of Canada. Only the threat of falling prey to Spain or France had kept the colonists in check. That check was removed at exactly the moment that the British became alarmed at the rising cost of the plantations: they were determined that the Americans should bear more of the imperial burden. *Grenville's *Stamp Act of 1764 led to a storm of protest. Though the Stamp Act was repealed in 1766, the *Declaratory Act which reaffirmed British sovereignty deprived the gesture of much of its appeal. The imposition of the *Townshend duties provoked violence. The *Boston massacre of 1770 was followed by the seizure of the Gaspée in 1772 and the *Boston Tea Party in 1773. By 1774 the Americans had summoned a congress to concert resistance.

Once fighting began at *Lexington in 1775, Britain faced a difficult military task. To occupy and garrison so vast a country was out of the question. But many Americans remained loyal to the crown and British armed intervention could give them the upper hand. The first phase finished when *Burgoyne's grandiose plan to cut off *New England ended in capitulation at *Saratoga in October 1777. Though the disaster could have been retrieved, it brought France and Spain into the conflict. Nevertheless the issue remained in doubt and *Washington experienced great difficulty in holding his troops together. In 1780 *Cornwallis led a major expedition to the southern colonies. He was cut off and his surrender at *Yorktown in October 1781 brought the conflict to an end. American independence was recognized by the treaty of *Versailles in 1783.

The short-term consequences were less dramatic than many expected. Though Britain's eclipse as a world power was confidently predicted, her economic recovery was swift. But in the long run there was a great shift of power across the Atlantic and

the population of the USA passed that of the mother country soon after the American Civil War, in the 1860s. In the long perspective of world events, the colonization and the loss of America, together with the spread of the English language and English parliamentary institutions, seems the single most important development in British history.

**Amherst, Jeffrey Amherst, 1st Baron** (1717–97). Amherst, a career soldier, entered the army at an early age and was lieutenant-colonel by 28. After serving with distinction in the War of the *Austrian Succession at *Dettingen and *Fontenoy, he was made commander-in-chief in America in 1758, and acquired a great reputation by the conquest of Canada. At the outbreak of hostilities with the American colonies, Amherst was brought into the cabinet, raised to the peerage in 1776, and made formally C.-in-C. 1778–82. He was dismissed at the fall of North's ministry, but brought back as C.-in-C. from 1793 to 1795. George III remarked sardonically in 1772 that Amherst's services, undoubtedly great, 'would not be lessened if he left the appreciating them to others'.

**Amiens, mise of,** 1264. After the struggle between Henry III and the baronial party had gone on for several years, it was agreed to put the validity of the provisions of *Oxford (1258) to Louis IX of France for arbitration. Louis decided emphatically in favour of his fellow king. The result was not to settle the dispute but to force de *Montfort and his supporters into open rebellion.

**Amiens, treaty of,** 1802. The treaty provided the only break in the long war between Britain and revolutionary and Napoleonic France from 1793 to 1814. By 1801 the conflict was near to stalemate. The resignation of *Pitt in 1801 made it easier for his successor *Addington to seek peace. Britain retained Ceylon and Trinidad but restored the Cape of Good Hope to the Dutch. Malta was to be given back to the Knights of St John and guaranteed. The French were to withdraw from Naples and central Italy, and Egypt was to return to Turkish rule. Each side dragged its feet on fulfilling the terms and the peace, little more than an armed truce, lasted only until May 1803, when Britain declared war. Napoleon then began planning an invasion of England.

**Amritsar massacre,** 1919. On 13 April 1919 at Jallianwalla Bagh in Amritsar, General R. E. H. Dyer ordered his soldiers to fire on a protesting though unarmed crowd, killing 400 people. The massacre became a symbol of British oppression. Mahatma *Gandhi led nation-wide demonstrations, which brought him to leadership of the Indian national movement.

**anabaptists** held that baptism should be postponed until people were capable of understanding the promises made. But the hatred they encountered stemmed from the widespread belief that they intended to overthrow the whole social order. There were different groups within the movement but those anabaptists who held power in Münster 1533–5 were radical, advocating common property and practising polygamy. This served to smear the whole movement and 'anabaptist' became a term of abuse. Henry VIII thought them 'a detestable sect' and burned a number: James I in the preface to *Basilikon doron* denounced them as 'a vile sect' and burned more.

**anarchism** Though mistrust of the state is a commonplace in the British political tradition, formal anarchism has received little support. Anarchist elements have been traced in the Commonwealth period, though they were more probably collective agrarianists, and the theory developed only after the French Revolution. *Paine declared that government was, at best, a necessary evil: 'a great part of what is called government is mere imposition.' *Spence went further. His vision of the future was of parish communities, with minimal powers reserved for the state. The *Cato Street conspiracy to murder the cabinet in 1820, the work of some of Spence's supporters, gave anarchism a lurid image. The First International split in 1871 between the supporters of Marx, who wanted a proletarian state, and those of Bakunin who argued, with some prescience, that it might itself become an engine of despotism. The small British groups made little impact. A sensational episode was the siege of 100 Sidney Street, Stepney, in 1911, with two foreign anarchists holed up. There was some interest in anarchist theory among left-wing circles involved in the Spanish Civil War in the 1930s. But fear of anarchy, an important ingredient of the conservative tradition, was always in Britain more influential than anarchism itself.

**Ancrum Moor, battle of,** 1545. The death of James V after the disaster at *Solway Moss in 1542 encouraged Henry VIII to propose a marriage between his son Edward and the infant queen of Scotland, Mary. When the negotiations faltered, Henry resolved on a strong-arm policy, the famous '*rough wooing'. In 1544 Hertford (*Somerset) sacked Edinburgh. The following year another expedition, led by Sir Ralph Evers and Sir Brian Latoun, gutted Melrose. But the regent, *Arran, and the earl of *Angus gathered a Scottish army and on 17 February inflicted a heavy defeat on the invaders, killing both the leaders.

**Anderson, Elizabeth Garrett** (1836–1917). First Englishwoman to qualify in medicine. Elizabeth Garrett was born in Aldeburgh (Suffolk), where she is buried. Her tenacious efforts led to her becoming a licentiate of the Society of Apothecaries (1865) and the first female MD in France (1870). Concentrating on treating women and children, she founded the first hospital wholly staffed by women, eventually becoming dean of the London School of Medicine for Women.

**Andrew, St** (d. *c.* AD 60). Fisherman of Galilee, among the first of Jesus' disciples, and first missionary. Little is known of his life after the Crucifixion, though it is generally thought he was crucified at Patras in Achaia. Patron saint of Scotland, the saltire cross associated with his death represents Scotland on the Union Jack. St Andrew's day is 30 November.

**Andrewes, Lancelot** (1555–1626). Bishop of Chichester (1605), Ely (1609), and Winchester (1619–26). Educated at Pembroke Hall, Cambridge, Andrewes was a scholar of great erudition, conversant with fifteen languages. One of those appointed to prepare a new translation of the Bible (1604), he was largely responsible for the Pentateuch and historical books of the Old Testament.

**Aneurin** (late 6th cent.). Bard. Almost everything known about Aneurin has to be conjectured from the epic poem he composed, *Y Gododdin*, recounting a disastrous raid on the Anglo-Saxons of *Bernicia and *Deira by the Britons of *Gododdin in Lothian (*c.*600). *Nennius, *Historia Brittonum* (*c.*796), named him along with *Taliesin as one of the five Welsh bards during the struggle against the Northumbrians.

**Angevin empire** The term commonly used to describe the collection of lands held, or claimed, by Henry II and his immediate successors. Henry II first brought the constituent parts of the empire together by combining under his rulership three distinct inheritances. These were, first, the former Anglo-Norman realm, comprising the duchy of Normandy and the kingdom of England, brought into being in 1066. Henry also claimed suzerainty over the duchy of Brittany, and over Wales and Scotland, claims inherited from previous kings of England. This was Henry's inheritance from his mother, the Empress *Matilda, daughter of Henry I. From his father Henry inherited the county of Anjou (hence *Angevin* empire), and the counties of Maine and Touraine. Thirdly, there was *Aquitaine, the inheritance of *Eleanor of Aquitaine, which came to Henry following their marriage in 1152. Ireland also came into the Angevin orbit following Henry's invasion of 1171–2. Henry, accordingly, was lord of a vast territory stretching from the Pyrenees to Scotland, making him the most powerful ruler in western Europe.

The evidence suggests that it was Henry II himself who created the Angevin empire. He brought together the three different inheritances between 1150 and 1156, when Geoffrey the Younger rebelled but was forced to submit. The implications of this are important. If the empire was essentially the product of Henry's opportunism, then its decline and collapse in 1204, within fifteen years of its creator's own demise in 1189, is more explicable.

Those who maintain that the empire's collapse was inevitable stress the fact that neither Henry II, Richard I, nor John sought to centralize. Rather, each lordship remained in its institutions, laws, and customs, with a bare minimum of 'imperial legislation', no common currency, and no single political centre. On the contrary, changing circumstances forced the Angevin lords to accept ever greater implications in their feudal relationship to the Capetian kings of France, so

far as their French fiefs were concerned, culminating in the terms of the treaty of *Le Goulet (1200). Only in England were they juridically equal to their French overlords. Nor was there any intention that the different dominions should pass as one inheritance. As early as 1169, at Montmirail, Henry II made plain his wish that each of his sons should receive a part. In addition, the sheer extent of the Angevin lands made effective government difficult, a problem exacerbated by the extraordinary rivalries and tensions within the ruling family itself.

Powerful though these arguments are, the fact remains that until 1202–3 the Angevin empire remained essentially intact. Allowance must be made for the comparative abilities of John and Philip II, the Capetian king at the time. Philip was much more of a match than his father Louis VII had been, partly because of his own abilities, but also because he commanded far greater resources. He had a more compact principality to defend than the sprawling mass of the Angevin empire in France. In addition, John played into Philip's hands. Between 1200 and 1204 he managed to fritter away the advantages he had enjoyed.

The combination of these factors meant that by the end of 1204 only the *Channel Islands and a much reduced Gascony remained in John's hands. In 1259 Henry III bowed to the inevitable and renounced his claims to Henry II's French inheritance. In return, Louis IX acknowledged him as rightful duke of Gascony. An era had come to an end.

**Angles** *See* ANGLO-SAXONS.

**Anglesey** Island county of north-west Wales, separated from the mainland by the Menai Straits. In 1974 it became the district of Ynys Môn in the county of Gwynedd, but was reconstituted as a county in 1996. Its location, together with the protective barrier of the Snowdonian mountains, made it a traditional centre of resistance to invaders, Roman and Norman. But after conquest by Edward I it was created a county of the principality of Wales in 1284, a status confirmed at the Act of Union of 1536.

**Anglesey, Henry William Paget, 1st marquis of** (1768–1854). Soldier and administrator. In 1794 Anglesey served in

Flanders under the duke of York. In 1808 he commanded the cavalry with distinction during the *Corunna campaign. At *Waterloo he showed undaunted bravery, leading the heavy brigade in the terrible charge which overwhelmed the comte d'Erlon's division. He lost a leg in the battle and was created marquis for his services. In 1828 Anglesey became lord-lieutenant of Ireland, favouring catholic emancipation, an opinion which led to his recall in 1829 by *Wellington. Anglesey was reappointed by *Grey and faced opposition from *O'Connell.

**Anglicanism** See CHURCH OF ENGLAND.

**angling** is the art of catching fish with rod, line, and hook, with live or artificial bait. The name derives from the Old English *angle*, a hook. The success of Izaak Walton's *The Compleat Angler* (1653) testifies to the popularity of the pastime in the 17th cent. A National Federation of Anglers was formed in 1903.

**Anglo-catholicism** Developing rapidly from *tractarianism in the 19th cent., it reached its peak in the 1920s and 1930s. Charles Gore transformed old tractarianism from a marginal phenomenon into the central force in the church; he achieved what *Newman could not. Whereas tractarianism had stressed Anglican continuity from ancient times, extreme Anglo-catholicism became a copy of ultramontane Roman catholicism, but at its best it was socialist in ethos, vigorous in socially deprived areas. After establishing more frequent communion, they added the trappings of candles, vestments, incense, reservation of the sacrament, and confession. In the 1920s, with *evangelicalism weakened, Anglo-catholicism was the moving force. But the second Vatican Council (1962-5) by 'protestantizing' catholic liturgy left the old-style Anglo-catholics an isolated group, for whom the ordination of women (1990s) became a major stumbling-block.

**Anglo-Dutch wars** Three wars, 1652-4, 1665-7, 1672-4, provide a unique element of continuity between the Commonwealth and the restored monarchy. All were intended to redress the commercial imbalance between England and the Dutch Republic. In the first war security was also an objective. The Dutch rejected a union which the Common-

wealth demanded (1651), and sent a fleet into English waters to prevent Dutch ships being searched. An accidental clash precipitated war. The lighter-armed Dutch navy suffered heavy defeats, one in 1652, three in 1653, and their trade was paralysed. Cromwell conceded lenient terms (April 1654). He did this because, by a separate agreement, the leading province of Holland excluded the house of Orange from all offices.

James, duke of York (later James II), brought about the second war, assuming that victory was assured. He defeated a rebuilt Dutch fleet off *Lowestoft (June 1665) but failed to exploit the success. Each side won an expensive victory in 1666 but this campaign exhausted English finances. Shore defences failed to prevent the Dutch destroying English ships in the river *Medway and seizing the *Royal Charles*. The third war aimed to annihilate the Dutch Republic. The French overran its eastern provinces, but the English fleet could only fight drawn battles, one in 1672, three in 1673. This war, launched by the pro-catholic *cabal, with France as an ally, became unpopular. Opposition, stimulated by William of Orange's propaganda, made Parliament refuse further money, forcing Charles to make peace.

**Anglo-Irish agreement,** 1985, signed at Hillsborough, Co. Down, on 15 November 1985, by Margaret *Thatcher and the taoiseach (prime minister) of Ireland, Dr Garret FitzGerald. The agreement was intended to promote reconciliation within Northern Ireland, and co-operation between the British and Irish governments. Ulster Unionists saw it as establishing a form of joint authority, and mounted a ferocious campaign of opposition in 1985-6.

**Anglo-Irish ascendancy (protestant ascendancy).** The term 'protestant ascendancy' appears to have been coined in 1782. However, the origins of this interest lay with the land confiscations of the 17th cent. The Ulster plantation (1608-9) brought a substantial transfer of property from the Gaelic lords to English investors and settlers; the Cromwellian confiscations (1652-3) brought the expropriation of the great majority of catholic landowners throughout the rest of Ireland. The victory of the Williamite cause in the war of 1689-91 paved the way for further confiscations, and for a series of measures designed to bolster the new protestant landed interest.

The 18th cent. was, therefore, the golden age of the ascendancy. The height of ascendancy political power came after 1782–3, with the grant of legislative independence to the gentry-dominated Irish Parliament. But increasingly powerful catholic and dissenter interests challenged this dominance in the 1790s, and the apparent helplessness of the ascendancy during the 1798 rising made it vulnerable to English intervention. The Act of *Union (1800) abolished the Dublin Parliament, and represented a severe blow to the political authority of the Irish landed interest. Further political set-backs came with *catholic emancipation (1829) and with the rise of a radical peasant nationalism. Land purchase legislation, especially the *Land Act of 1903, facilitated the transfer of land to the former tenant farmers, and brought a swift end to the economic predominance of the Anglo-Irish ascendancy.

**Anglo-Irish treaty,** 1921. A truce on 11 July ended the war between the *Irish Republican Army and the British army which had been raging since 1919. Negotiations began in earnest in October with Arthur Griffith and Michael *Collins representing Ireland. A treaty was signed on 6 December whereby Ireland became a free state, with the six counties of Ulster remaining as part of the UK, but with full dominion status. The Dáil eventually accepted the treaty on 7 January 1922 by 64 votes to 57 and it came into effect on 6 December.

**Anglo-Japanese treaty,** 1902. Concluded to improve British security against France and Russia in the Far East, each party agreed to fight only if the other became involved in war with at least two other powers. The treaty promised to localize any war, and facilitated Japan's decision to attack Russia in 1904. It was renewed in 1905, each party agreeing to assist the other in a war with only one opponent. American objections brought about its demise in 1921–2.

**Anglo-Russian entente,** 1907. The convention was concluded on 31 August 1907 to try to resolve long-running Anglo-Russian rivalries in Persia, Tibet, and Afghanistan. The Foreign Office also hoped to improve the balance of power in Europe and the Near East against Germany. Only Russian weaknesses after defeat by Japan and revolution at home made agreement possible.

**Anglo-Saxon Chronicle** *Alfred in the early 890s was responsible for putting into shape the *Anglo-Saxon Chronicle*, providing a record of events on an annalar basis in Old English. The *Chronicle* was kept up to date at great ecclesiastical centres where literate clerks could be found. Surviving manuscripts associated with Canterbury, Worcester, York, and Abingdon provide very full accounts for some periods (the reign of Alfred and the reign of *Æthelred conspicuously, and then the reign of *Edward the Confessor and the Norman kings), but give only distressingly jejune entries at others.

**Anglo-Saxons** is the name collectively applied to the descendants of the Germanic people who settled in Britain between the late 4th and early 7th cents. Their backgrounds varied. Some came as mercenaries, others as invaders. They included, besides Angles and Saxons, Jutes and other groups. The eventual use of the name 'English' and 'England' for people and territory probably owes something to *Bede, whose *History of the English People* dealt with the whole. He followed Pope Gregory I, who knew the people as Angles.

Much about the invasion and settlement is obscure, but for most of its history Anglo-Saxon England is one of the best-documented early medieval European societies. Besides Bede's *History*, historical sources include a number of saints' lives, and the *Anglo-Saxon Chronicle*. Many letters survive, those of the Anglo-Saxon missionary to the continent, *Boniface, of particular importance. A great body of evidence relates to royal ideology, government, and administration: vernacular law codes (beginning with that of *Æthelbert of Kent), charters, writs, and wills. Historians also benefit from the study of the language of vernacular texts, from that of place-names, of art (including sculpture), and of architecture. Archaeology, of burials, settlements, towns, kings' halls (*Yeavering, Cheddar), monasteries, and churches, is critically important. Yet there are still uncertainties. Gaps in the evidence, problems of its interpretation and of reconciling different types, generate lively debate. Some may never be solved: it is salutary to realize that important subjects depend on chance survivals or discoveries—the ship-burial at *Sutton Hoo and the poem *Beowulf* for example.

From obscure beginnings the Anglo-Saxons formed a number of kingdoms. The 7th-cent. trend was a shift in the balance of power from south and east (*Kent and *East Anglia) to north and west (*Northumbria, *Mercia, *Wessex), and the take-over of smaller kingdoms by larger ones, the so-called *heptarchy. The 8th cent. was a period of Mercian dominance and Northumbrian independence, the 9th of the rise of Wessex, and of the threat of the Vikings. They established their own kingdoms of East Anglia and Northumbria. In the 10th cent. Wessex united England.

To the forging of one people *Alfred, *Athelstan, and *Edgar made significant contributions. Encouragement was to be found in the pages of Bede and in the needs of the church. But the England of 1066 was not inevitable. Quite different borders could have been established. In the late 7th cent. one kingdom south of the Humber and another north, including southern Scotland, was a possibility; in the 10th a kingdom pushing into Wales rather than the Scandinavian-held north.

Society and culture changed over time. Anglo-Saxon paganism is not fully known. The great period of conversion was the 7th cent., an age of saints, especially in Northumbria (the missionary *Aidan, the home-grown *Wilfrid, *Cuthbert, and others) and monastic foundations (including *Lindisfarne, *Whitby, *Ripon, *Hexham, and Monk-wearmouth-Jarrow). A stratified society, in which *ceorls and gesiths (royal companions) had different *wergelds, its political life was dominated by the aristocracy. Historical development brought a growth in royal power and authority in a society wherein the participation in government of free men had a long history. On some issues—marriage and war, for example—the new religion might conflict with traditional values. Some features of Anglo-Saxon society seem alien, even incomprehensible, to modern eyes at first sight: the practice of blood-feud, the institution of the retinue (war-band), both of which contributed to a high level of violence in elite society, the combination of genuine piety with ferocity in warfare, and its

condoning by clerics. Yet others seem modern: the status of women has been seen as comparatively high, some queens and royal ladies, particularly *Æthelfleda, lady of the Mercians, and abbesses, notably *Hilda and Ælfflæd of Whitby, playing an important part in political and religious life.

The Anglo-Saxon arrival had ended Britain's involvement with Roman culture and institutions, but this was recreated in the late 6th cent. Christianity, purveyed to the Anglo-Saxons almost entirely by non-British teachers, from the Irish, from Frankish Gaul, and from Rome (beginning with the mission of *Augustine), brought England into the Mediterranean, Christian, Roman world. Missionaries worked amongst the Anglo-Saxons' still pagan continental kin. *Boniface was prominent in Frankish church reform and functioned as representative of the pope to the Franks. Anglo-Saxon veneration of the papacy was strong and contributed to the growth of papal authority. *Alcuin of York was adviser to Charlemagne and a leading figure in the Carolingian Renaissance.

But England owed much to Europe. The books collected on the continent by *Benedict Biscop, and the school of Canterbury, established by Archbishop *Theodore, himself from Tarsus, brought Christian culture and scholarship. From an early period Frankish support and influence were factors in English dynastic politics, most clearly visible in Charlemagne's support for some of *Offa of Mercia's enemies. Carolingian ideas concerning church reform and kingship, Carolingian administrative and governmental institutions and practices, Carolingian coinage, and Carolingian art all had an impact in the 8th cent. Alfred learned much from Carolingian example. Government in the 10th and 11th cents. has much about it that seems Carolingian. Involvement with Normandy came in the late 10th cent. Trade, especially in slaves in the early period and wool in the later, brought great wealth, probably the main attraction for Cnut and William the Conqueror.

The Anglo-Saxon achievement was cultural, religious, economic, and political. Art, architecture, vernacular and Anglo-Latin writing, and scholarship are all remarkable. Not, originally, an urban people, Scandinavian activity and the development of Alfred's burhs lay behind their 10th- and 11th-cent.

towns. Coinage was firmly under royal control. Prosperity sustained the frequent collection of large *Danegelds. By the 11th cent., with its hundreds, shires, ealdormen and reeves, law courts, and tax-collecting, Anglo-Saxon England was, by European standards, remarkably sophisticated and advanced. There was no capital, but *Winchester was almost a capital city. The country was united, though it was not uniform in every particular. The compilation of William I's *Domesday Book would not have been possible without Anglo-Saxon administrative genius. This genius, largely West Saxon, is visible elsewhere, in the rational distribution of mints in the 10th cent., and in the shire system, almost unchanged until 1974.

**Anglo-Scottish border** *See* MARCHES OF SCOTLAND.

**Anglo-Scottish wars** *See* SCOTTISH WARS OF INDEPENDENCE.

**Angus, Archibald Douglas, 5th earl of** [S] (*c.*1449–1513). Son and heir of George, 4th earl of Angus [S] (d. 1463), and the great political maverick of late 15th- and early 16th-cent. Scotland. Angus was involved in the seizure of James III at Lauder bridge (July 1482)—hence the much later nickname 'Bell-the-Cat'—and he rebelled against James III in 1488. Yet Angus was a friend of James IV, providing the king with his first mistress, Marion Boyd, the earl's niece, in 1492; and he was chancellor from 1492 to 1497. Losing royal trust, Angus was warded (imprisoned) from 1501 to 1509. He opposed war with England in 1513, and missed *Flodden, dying at Whithorn late in 1513.

**Angus, Archibald Douglas, 6th earl of** [S] (*c.*1490–1557). Douglas inherited the earldom from his grandfather in 1513. Later that year he married *Margaret, queen dowager of Scotland. The daughter of the marriage became countess of *Lennox and was mother of Lord *Darnley. Angus was a member of the Council of Regency for James V 1517–21 and 1523–6 and chancellor in 1527. On bad terms with the young king and divorced by his wife, he was in exile in England from 1528 to 1542. He returned to Scotland in 1542 after the death of James, abandoned the English connection, and fought with distinction at *Ancrum and *Pinkie.

**Angus (Oengus) MacFergus** (*c.*690–761), king of the Picts. Under Angus Pictish power was at its height. Succeeding in 729, Angus established himself as over-king. The king of Atholl was defeated *c.*734 and his son drowned (a formal ritual killing): the king himself was drowned *c.*739. In 736 Angus attacked *Dalriada and captured Dunedd. But when he turned his attention to the Britons of *Strathclyde he was not so successful. With the aid of Eadberht of Northumbria, he captured their stronghold of Dumbarton in 756, but his army was wiped out ten days later.

**Anjou** District around the city of Angers in France. The counts of Anjou played a crucial role in the politics of northern France. This led, in 1127, to Henry I marrying his daughter *Matilda to the young count, Geoffrey 'le Bel'—otherwise known as *Geoffrey Plantagenet. In 1154 Henry of Anjou became King Henry II of England and for the next fifty years Anjou remained the homeland of three successive kings of England: Henry II, Richard I, and John. In 1203–5 John's incompetence allowed Philip Augustus of France to wrest Anjou as well as Normandy from the family's grasp.

**Annates, Acts in Restraint of,** 1532, 1534. These formed part of the campaign by Henry VIII to cajole the papacy into granting an annulment of the king's first marriage, or to give statutory authority for the English church to act independently. 'Annates' were taxes levied by the papacy on recently appointed clergy. The Act in Conditional Restraint of Annates (23 Hen. VIII c. 20), passed in spring 1532, required that these payments be suspended. In the November–December 1534 session, after the pope had excommunicated Henry, the Act in Absolute Restraint of Annates (25 Hen. VIII c. 20) abolished annates entirely.

**Anne** (1665–1714), queen of England, Scotland (Great Britain from 1707), and Ireland (1702–14). The conventional picture of Queen Anne as a weak-willed and ineffectual monarch has been subjected to substantial revision. Re-examination has revealed a much less insipid personality. She was the younger daughter of James, duke of York, and his first wife Anne *Hyde. The doctrines of the Church of England in which she was educated provided an important political and emotional prop for the rest of her life. In 1683, aged 18, she married Prince *George of Denmark, a distant cousin, and their relationship quickly blossomed into one of lasting devotion. Anne deserted her father at the revolution in 1688 and joined William of Orange and his wife, her elder sister Mary. Before long, however, relations with them became strained with bitterness, especially after Anne succeeded where they had failed and produced a healthy son, the duke of Gloucester, in 1689. Anne's hatred of the king deepened as William persistently excluded Prince George from any share in government. Her particular intimates were the *Marlboroughs and Lord *Godolphin. In Sarah Marlborough, especially, she found the feminine support she needed as she endured one failed pregnancy after another. By 1700, when her seventeenth and last pregnancy ended in miscarriage, she was, at 35, practically an invalid. That same year her one surviving child, William of Gloucester, succumbed to illness and died.

Anne became queen on William III's death in March 1702. She had patiently waited for what she had said would be her 'sunshine day'. In the early years of her reign she gave fresh impetus to court life and ceremonial in a conscious effort to elevate her regal image. Wherever she travelled she was received with acclamation. Away from royal panoply, Anne industriously fulfilled the position she occupied at the centre of government. She presided once or twice weekly at cabinet meetings, conferred with individual ministers, regularly attended debates in the Lords, and gave active encouragement to major national ventures, such as the war with France, the union with Scotland (1707), and after 1710 the drive for peace.

Until 1710 her administrations were headed by the 'duumvirs', her old friends Godolphin, at the treasury, and Marlborough, in command of the army. Neither of them were party men in the conventional sense, but acted primarily as 'political managers'. Like her predecessor, Anne was anxious to avoid becoming the captive of 'party'. In 1702 the high Tory grandees, mindful of Anne's affinity with Toryism, expected the lion's share of governmental appointments, but she resisted their demands for a purge of Whigs. After 1705 Godolphin's efforts to persuade

her to placate the powerful and well-organized *Junto Whig faction placed a growing strain on their association, but she reluctantly yielded to a series of Whig appointments. Sarah Marlborough's less tactful bullying on behalf of the Junto was a major source of irritation, but Anne could ill afford to dismiss her, fearing that she would use her influence with Marlborough and Godolphin to induce them to resign.

The queen's third 'manager', Robert *Harley, gradually gained her confidence with his notion of a 'moderate' ministry of both parties, a venture in which he was assisted by his cousin Abigail Masham, who had replaced Sarah as Anne's closest friend and confidante. However, in 1708 Harley's attempt to implement this plan with the queen's co-operation backfired when the 'duumvirs' forced Anne to dismiss him from his post of secretary of state.

By 1710 Anne was willing to sacrifice Godolphin for Harley (later Lord Oxford), though the Tories' huge electoral success in the summer ruled out her favoured objective of 'moderation' and forced her to accept an exclusively Tory government under Harley's lead. As her health became more precarious in 1714, Lord *Bolingbroke seemed increasingly likely to succeed Oxford, although the queen remained non-committal. Two days after dismissing Oxford on 27 July, Anne fell mortally ill, but her acceptance of the politically neutral duke of *Shrewsbury as next lord treasurer on the 30th was crucial in ensuring that after her death on 1 August the transition to the Hanoverian dynasty occurred without the political turmoil which many had feared.

**Anne of Bohemia** (1366–94), queen of Richard II. Born in Prague, the eldest daughter of Emperor Charles IV, Anne was the first wife of Richard II, king of England, chosen for her nobility and gentleness. The marriage took place on 14 January 1382 at St Stephen's chapel, Westminster, followed by her coronation on the 22nd. Plain and unassuming, Anne was devoted to Richard, helping him through severe depression.

**Anne Boleyn** (c.1507–36), 2nd queen of Henry VIII. Sir Thomas Boleyn, Anne's father, descended from London merchants, was a courtier and became gentleman of the bedchamber to Henry VIII. Anne spent several years at the court of France. Returning in 1522 she was given a post in the household of *Catherine of Aragon. The king's interest at this time was in her sister Mary, who became his mistress. Anne was dark-haired, with large eyes, composed, and cultivated. By 1527 Henry was initiating annulment proceedings against Catherine, but not until 1532, it seems, did he and Anne become lovers. Anne was made marchioness of Pembroke in September 1532. Early in January 1533 Anne knew she was pregnant and was married privately to Henry on the 24th. The birth of a princess, Elizabeth, on 7 September 1533 was a disappointment, but more ominous was a miscarriage in September 1534. The king was already beginning to look elsewhere. Publicly, Anne's position was strong—the Princess Mary had been declared illegitimate, and Anne's marriage was protected by a new Treason Law. But in January 1536 Catherine of Aragon died, opening up the possibility of another marriage free from any dubiety. Anne was once more pregnant but at the end of the month, she gave premature birth to a dead son. Henry was now paying marked attention to *Jane Seymour, one of Anne's ladies-in-waiting. At the end of April 1536, Anne was accused of adultery with several men and incest with her brother George. On 2 May she was taken to the Tower, and after a trial presided over by her uncle *Norfolk, she was executed. Her daughter Elizabeth was deprived of her rank, but succeeded to the throne 22 years later.

**Anne of Cleves** (1515–57), 4th queen of Henry VIII. The daughter of John, 3rd duke of Cleves, Anne was suggested by Thomas *Cromwell as a wife for Henry VIII to strengthen the protestant alliance. On first meeting, in December 1539, Henry was dismayed to find her 'well and seemly...but nothing so fair as reported', alluding to *Holbein's flattering portrait. He was persuaded to go through with the marriage in January 1540. After Cromwell's fall and the swing back towards catholicism, Henry sought swiftly to extricate himself, citing grounds of non-consummation. The annulment was declared in July 1540, according Anne a handsome settlement and residences, on condition that she remain in England and accept the status of royal sister. Not surprisingly, Anne felt that she had fared rather well. She lived at Chelsea until her death in July 1557 and was buried in Westminster abbey.

**Anne of Denmark** (1574–1619), queen of James VI and I. Anne was daughter of Frederick II of Denmark and Norway. The marriage to James VI on 23 November 1589 was followed by her coronation in May 1590. Anne was interested in the arts, patronizing both Ben *Jonson and Inigo *Jones. An amiable woman, who enjoyed masques and dancing, her husband James, with a taste for theological disputation, found her frivolous.

**Anne Neville** (1456–85), queen of Richard III. Anne was a pawn in the ferocious political game of the later 15th cent. She was the second daughter of Richard Neville, earl of *Warwick ('the Kingmaker'). In 1470 Anne was married to *Edward, prince of Wales, heir to Henry VI. But her father was killed at *Barnet in 1471 and her new husband at *Tewkesbury, three weeks later. With the *Yorkists temporarily on top, Anne was transferred to the other side and in 1472 became wife of Richard, duke of Gloucester, one of Edward IV's brothers. On Edward IV's death in 1483, Richard usurped the throne and Anne was crowned on 6 July. Her only son *Edward died in April 1484 aged 8, leaving the royal couple childless. Her life as queen lasted less than two years and her husband's as king did not last much longer.

**Anselm, St** (1033–1109). Archbishop of Canterbury (1093–1109). Anselm was born at Aosta in northern Italy. He travelled to northern France in the late 1050s, where he became a monk at Le Bec and a pupil of *Lanfranc. Thereafter he rose to be both prior and abbot of the monastery. A great philosopher whose works include the *Monologion*, the *Proslogion*, and *Cur Deus homo*, he was promoted to Canterbury in March 1093. Anselm subsequently quarrelled bitterly with both William II and Henry I. His disputes ultimately focused on his belief that obedience was owed first and foremost to the papacy. By 1097 the breach between Rufus and Anselm was irreparable and the archbishop went into voluntary exile. Recalled in 1100 by Henry I, Anselm was for a time able to hold ecclesiastical councils and rule the church as he wished. Fresh quarrels developed about lay investiture of bishops, still practised in England, although prohibited by the papacy since the 1070s, and in 1103 Anselm again went into exile. A settlement was not finally reached until 1106–7. Anselm was in some respects representative of a changing intellectual and political climate, in which notions of authority were being redefined. His preference for the quiet world of the monk masked a robust personality who saw it as his duty to engage with the world.

### Anson, George, 1st Baron Anson
(1697–1762). A circumnavigator of the world, Anson shared some attributes with plundering Elizabethan 'sea-dogs' but his work also pointed Britain towards a modern commercial imperialism. Anson rose to command a Pacific expedition in 1739. He captured a Spanish treasure ship and sailed westwards to reach home in 1744 a rich man. Further active service and politics qualified him for a peerage and spells as 1st lord of the Admiralty from 1751 to 1762.

### Anti-Corn Law League
Agitation against the *Corn Laws, which imposed duties on imported foodstuffs to protect British producers, increased after the Corn Law of 1815, and peaked in 1838–46. The creation of a Manchester Anti-Corn Law Association in 1838 led in 1839 to the establishment of a national league. Its leader, Richard *Cobden, advocated direct political involvement, and the league contested a by-election at Walsall early in 1841. Its candidate was beaten, but his intervention showed that the league had some muscle. In the general election of 1841, a few free traders were returned. The league's organization, increasingly sophisticated, became a model for later political agitations. It fought elections, and sought to multiply supporters on the electoral registers and expel opponents. Considerable sums of money were raised, much of it from industrial interests who resented the dominance of the landed aristocracy. In 1843 Cobden was joined in Parliament by John *Bright, and their rhetorical partnership proved effective in and out of Parliament. In 1845 and again in 1846, the potato crop, on which many Irish had become dependent, suffered a catastrophic failure, threatening widespread starvation. Peel decided that all obstructions to the import of food must go, including the Corn Laws. This split the governing Conservative Party, but with the aid of opposition forces, including Whigs and the league, Peel was able to repeal the Corn Laws in 1846.

**Antigua** is one of the Leeward Islands in the eastern Caribbean. With Barbuda it forms an independent state within the Commonwealth. It was visited and named by Columbus but colonized in the 17th cent. by English settlers.

*Anti-Jacobin* A weekly journal which ran from November 1797 until July 1798. Its prospectus declared its prejudices in favour of the established institutions of church and state, and its satire was directed against British radicals—*Paine, *Godwin, Holcroft, Thelwall—and their Whig allies, with sideswipes at the Noble Savage, sensibility, and Gothick. Among its more memorable items is the denunciation of the Whig as 'the friend of every country but his own', and Canning's celebrated 'The Friend of Humanity and the Knife-Grinder'.

### Antiquaries, Society of
Founded in 1707 by a group of like-minded men meeting weekly at the Bear tavern in the Strand (London), it has had continuous existence since 1717. Gaining a royal charter (1751), then launching *Archaeologia* (1779), it moved to its present home, Burlington House, in 1875.

**antislavery** Slavery was regarded in later 18th-cent. Britain as essential to the exploitation of the West Indian colonies and there was strong opposition to any interference with the institution, particularly from centres like Bristol and Liverpool. The moral objections to slavery arose mainly from the *evangelical movement of the second half of the century, reflecting concern for the spiritual and physical welfare of all mankind. A national committee of nine quakers and three Anglicans was set up in London in 1787, headed by Granville *Sharp with Thomas *Clarkson as secretary. It was decided to aim first at the suppression of the slave trade. In 1788 William *Wilberforce, the son of a Hull merchant, joined the cause after his evangelical conversion, and supplied parliamentary leadership. He persuaded his friend William *Pitt to give it unofficial backing and committees were set up in provincial towns, the most active being in Manchester. However, the abolitionist cause suffered from the reaction against the French Revolution. The agitation was revived by Clarkson's speaking tours in 1804, by which time the economic importance of the West Indies had lessened, and in 1807 Lord *Grenville, an early convert, gave his government's backing to an abolition bill, forcing it through the Lords.

The campaign to abolish slavery itself throughout the British empire began in earnest in 1823, when the Anti-Slavery Society was formed in London by evangelicals, quakers, and methodists. A campaign during the 1830 general election encouraged *Grey's government to put through a bill abolishing slavery in the British empire in 1833, substituting apprenticeship for seven years.

**Antonine Wall** The second and more northerly of the two walls constructed across northern Britain by the Romans in the 2nd cent. On the death of *Hadrian in AD 138 his successor Antoninus Pius reoccupied Scotland up to the Forth–Clyde line. Following the example of his predecessor he had a linear barrier constructed, running from the Forth, west of modern Edinburgh, to the Clyde, west of modern Glasgow. Only half the length (37 miles) of Hadrian's Wall, the Antonine Wall was constructed of turf on a stone base.

**Antrim** was until 1973 one of the six counties of Northern Ireland, with close links with Scotland, 13 miles distant from Torr Head: there is a major ferry route from Larne to Stranraer and Cairnryan. The Giant's Causeway is off the north coast and Belfast Lough indents the south-east coastline. Antrim, Lisburne, Larne, Ballymena, and Coleraine developed as market towns before the spectacular growth of Belfast in the 18th and early 19th cents. The county has the smallest Roman catholic population in Northern Ireland.

**Anzacs** The Australian and New Zealand Army Corps was raised at the beginning of the First World War. Australia, with a population of 5 million, raised 322,000 volunteers, of whom 60,000 lost their lives—one of the highest casualty rates. New Zealand, with 1.1 million people, raised 124,000 troops, of whom 17,000 died. They took a major part in the 1915 landings at *Gallipoli, a plan imaginative in concept, disastrous in execution.

**Apology of the Commons,** 1604. Less an apology than a vigorous assertion of parliamentary rights, it arose out of a dispute over the electoral return for Buckinghamshire, the Commons insisting that they were the sole judge of their own elections. Though the matter was compromised, they resolved to address the king. The apology was couched in respectful terms, but the House maintained that its privileges were of right, not of grace. 'The prerogatives of princes may easily and do daily grow,' James was advised.

**Appeals, Act in Restraint of** (1533). The Act (24 Hen. VIII c. 12), largely the work of Thomas *Cromwell, was a crucial step in Henry VIII's assertion of royal supremacy. He had already moved against the clergy with accusations of *praemunire and in 1532 forbade the payment of *annates or first fruits to Rome. The Act, passed in the first week of April, forbade appeals to Rome and had two objectives—to allow *Cranmer to give a ruling on Henry's marriage to *Catherine of Aragon which could not be appealed, and to intimidate the pope generally.

**appeasement** is generally used to describe the policy towards Nazi Germany pursued by Prime Minister Neville *Chamberlain between 1937 and 1939, and has negative connotations. In fact, appeasement had a more respectable history. British unhappiness with the reparations required to be paid by Germany after the First World War led to a policy of economic appeasement. During the early years of Nazi rule in Germany (1933–6) a similar policy operated in relation to trade; in April 1933 an Anglo-German Trade Pact was concluded by Ramsay *MacDonald's National Government, in the belief that although the Nazis were not likeable, one ought to do business with them.

Anglo-French acquiescence in Hitler's remilitarization of the Rhineland (March 1936), in violation of the treaties of *Versailles and *Locarno, marked a new phase of appeasement. In March 1938 Hitler ordered the anschluss, the union with Austria forbidden at Versailles, and indicated his determination also to meet the demands (real or imaginary) of Germans living in the Sudetenland, in Czechoslovakia, for union with Germany. At Munich, on 29 September 1938, the Sudetenland was transferred to Germany. Chamberlain, who visited Hitler twice during this crisis, was a national hero. Only after the German occupation of Prague (March 1939) was appeasement abandoned.

**appellants** Richard II's political opponents of 1387-8 are known as the appellants, for it was by means of the legal process of appeal that they proceeded in Parliament against the king's ministers. The king had been humiliated in Parliament in 1386, when his chancellor Michael de la *Pole, earl of Suffolk, was impeached. In the *'Merciless Parliament' of February 1388, Richard's five chief opponents, the earls of *Gloucester, Arundel, Warwick, Derby, and Nottingham, appealed Suffolk, de Vere, the archbishop of York, Robert Tresilian (the chief justice), and Nicholas Brembre of London, accusing them of treason. Tresilian and Brembre were executed; the archbishop of York was translated to St Andrews, while Suffolk and de Vere both died in exile. In 1397 Richard II revenged himself on the appellants, engineering an appeal against Gloucester, Warwick, and Arundel.

**Apprentice Boys** The Apprentice Boys are an Ulster loyalist organization whose title celebrates the thirteen apprentices who shut the city gates of Derry before the Jacobite siege (April–July 1689). The Apprentice Boys remain in existence, with a membership of around 10,000.

**apprenticeship** refers to the period of service as a learner of a trade or handicraft. The apprentice, usually a boy at the beginning of his working life, was bound by a legal agreement to serve an employer for a fixed number of years during which the employer promised to instruct him. The system developed during the Middle Ages when guilds of craftsmen in particular trades established control of their trades by regulating the number of recruits and their training. The statute of *Artificers of 1563 gave magistrates power to compel compliance with apprenticeships. At the end of their apprenticeships trainees became journeymen, fully skilled tradesmen. If they could afford to set up in business they became masters in their own right.

Apprenticeship in a wide variety of traditional skilled work continued in the second half of the 20th cent. However, challenges to such 'training on the job' combined with expanding provision of formal technical education led to a decline in traditional apprenticeship.

**Aquitaine** Rich wine-producing region in the south-west of France. Originally a province in Roman Gaul, after the 9th cent. Aquitaine became a more or less independent duchy in the kingdom of France. In 1154 when *Eleanor of Aquitaine's husband became King Henry II, the duchy became one of the king of England's dominions and remained so, though within fluctuating borders, until 1453.

**Arbroath, declaration of** The name usually given to the letter of the Scottish barons to Pope John XXII, dated at Arbroath on 6 April 1320, which proclaimed the ancient independence of Scotland and denounced English efforts at conquest. It was part of Robert I of Scotland's response to his threatened excommunication for failing to observe papal demands for a truce. The letter attracted little attention till the late 17th cent., since when it has often been described as a Scottish 'Declaration of Independence'.

**Arch, Joseph** (1826-1919). Trade unionist and politician. Arch was the son of a Warwickshire farm labourer and began work at the age of 9 scaring birds. He gained experience in public speaking as a primitive methodist lay preacher and in 1872 launched a National Agricultural Labourers' Union. Arch entered Parliament as a Liberal in 1885 but was defeated the following year: he served again from 1892 until 1900—the first farm labourer in the House of Commons.

**archaeology** is a branch of historical study which has developed its own specialized and highly sophisticated techniques for recovering, dating, and identifying material found largely in the ground, such as skeletons, grave-goods, and the foundation of buildings. For societies which have left little or no literary evidence, it is essential; but it may also be used to correct or modify literary sources. The slightly misleading term 'industrial archaeology' has been popularized to describe the recovery and preservation of modern industrial remains, such as mills, railways, mines, pumping-engines, and canals. Marine archaeology is another specialized branch dealing with the recovery of wrecks.

**archbishops** are, literally, chief bishops. By the 5th cent. AD the title was applied to the occupants of sees of major ecclesiastical importance, particularly those of metropolitan bishops. This designation originated in the bishop of the principal city of a district or division of a country, the *metropolis*, being the usual president of any assembly of bishops of that area. Ecclesiastically, such a district or division formed a province. Thus Milan, residence of the emperors during the 4th cent., became the metropolitan see for much of northern Italy. There is little evidence to suggest that, prior to the withdrawal of the Roman legions, the church in Britain was organized along provincial or metropolitical lines. Not until the arrival of *Augustine (597) was *Canterbury established as an archbishopric, and *York did not become a separate province until the 8th cent.

However, attempts by Canterbury to assert its precedence over York were fiercely resisted, particularly in the 11th and 12th cents. The argument was not resolved until the 14th cent.—in Canterbury's favour. The independence of the Scottish bishops from the province of York was recognized by Pope Celestine III in 1192, though the primatial see (*St Andrews) was not raised to archiepiscopal status until 1472. *Glasgow became an archbishopric in 1492. In Ireland *Armagh, *Cashel, *Dublin, and *Tuam all achieved archiepiscopal status during the 12th cent., the primatial see being at Armagh. The number of Anglican archbishoprics was reduced to two (Armagh and Dublin) by the Ecclesiastical Commission in the 1830s.

**archdeacons** Literally chiefs of the deacons. The office traces its origins to the New Testament church, where the ministry of Stephen and others is described in the Acts of the Apostles as their *diaconia*. As dioceses were established and grew in size, their bishops delegated administrative authority in a specified area to an archdeacon, thus giving him a territorial title, a practice discernible in England by the late 12th cent. From the mid-12th cent. archdeacons held regular visitations, and following the third

Lateran Council they became responsible for ensuring that church buildings in their jurisdiction were kept in repair.

**archery** developed as a sport from the use of the bow and arrow in hunting and warfare. The English and Welsh longbow dominated the battlefield from the 11th to the 15th cent., and governments frequently forbade other sports, particularly football, in order to encourage archery practice. When guns developed and the bow became redundant as a weapon, the sport was maintained. The Company of Archers, founded in Edinburgh in 1676, eventually became a royal bodyguard. The Royal Toxophilite Society was established in 1781.

**Arcot, siege of,** 1751. Robert *Clive, a young captain in the army of the *East India Company, while attempting to relieve Mahomet Ali in Trichinopoly, was besieged in Arcot by a vastly superior French and Indian force. He defended it for 50 days until help came. It was Clive's first major victory and a check to French progress in the Carnatic.

*Areopagitica,* an impassioned plea by John *Milton (1644) for liberty of the press, was written in response to the Licensing Ordinance of 1643 that no book should be printed unless previously approved by an authorized officer. Although aware that liberty was double-edged, Milton abhorred such control before rather than after publication.

**Argyll, Archibald Campbell, 5th earl of** [S] (1532–73). A committed protestant whose political allegiances frequently changed. Signing the first 'Common Band' of the protestant nobles as Lord Lorne (1557), Argyll succeeded his father in 1558. However, he did not formally join the lords of the *Congregation until May 1559. During the personal reign of Mary, queen of Scots, Argyll was a favoured privy counsellor until charged with treason in 1565, for his part in *Moray's rebellion against *Darnley. Having been reconciled with Mary in the spring of 1566, Argyll was appointed lieutenant of her forces, losing at *Langside in 1568. Abandoning the Marian cause to support James VI, he was made a privy counsellor by *Mar in September 1571. In January 1573, Argyll was appointed chancellor by *Morton, until his death nine months later.

**Argyll, Archibald Campbell, 1st marquis of** [S] (*c.*1607–61). Campbell's father, the 7th earl, became a catholic, and was declared a traitor in 1619. Campbell, as a protestant, took over the enormous estates at the age of 12, and succeeded to the earldom in 1638. His subsequent conduct was erratic. A violent *covenanter in 1639–40, he made terms with Charles I in 1641 and was advanced to the marquisate. He then rejoined the covenanting party but was routed by *Montrose at *Inverlochy and *Kilsyth in 1645. Next he joined in welcoming Cromwell but in 1651 took part in *Charles II's coronation at Scone, having been promised a dukedom. He made his peace with the Cromwellian regime and served in the Parliament of 1659 as MP for Aberdeenshire. In 1660, at the Restoration, he was arrested, and executed at Edinburgh. A small, red-headed, squinting man, Clarendon described him as of 'extraordinary cunning', though in the end his contorted tergiversations overwhelmed him.

**Argyll, Archibald Campbell, 9th earl of** [S] (1629–85). Campbell's father, the 1st marquis, was executed for treason in 1661. Campbell, who had fought on the royal side at *Dunbar and *Worcester, was restored to the earldom in 1663. His presbyterian sympathies placed him in jeopardy during James, duke of York's government of Scotland, and in 1681 he was lodged in Edinburgh castle. He escaped in disguise and joined *Monmouth in Holland. Involved in the *Rye House plot, he led an expedition to raise the west of Scotland in May 1685 to coincide with Monmouth's rising. There was little support, divided counsels, and he was captured. Executed at Edinburgh, where his father had suffered before him, Argyll died with composure and bravery.

**Argyll, Archibald Campbell, 10th earl of** (d. 1703). Scottish politician. Following the execution in 1685 of his father, the 9th earl, Argyll's chief objective was to assume his patrimony as head of the Campbell clan. Failing to obtain recognition from James II, he joined William of Orange in 1688. Accordingly, he was admitted as earl of Argyll to the convention of Scottish estates in April 1689 which declared in favour of William and Mary, and in June his father's attainder was rescinded. By the mid-1690s he and the mar-

quis of Queensberry effectively led the court interest in Scotland. He was created a duke in 1701.

**Argyll, Archibald Campbell, 3rd duke of** [S] (1682–1761). Campbell succeeded his brother John in 1743, having been created earl of Islay [S] in 1706. He was a keen supporter of the Union and fought on the government side at *Sheriffmuir in 1715. He held the privy seal [S] 1721–33 and the great seal [S] from 1733 until his death. For many years he was the Whig government's adviser on Scottish affairs. While his brother was high-spirited, imperious, and a celebrated orator, Islay was a man of business.

**Argyll, Colin Campbell, Lord Lorne, 1st earl of** [S] (d. December 1492/January 1493). Colin Campbell was the grandson of the 1st Lord Campbell [S] (1445). Colin's elevation to earl (1458) was followed by a steady acquisition of lands and offices. Argyll combined the attributes of a shrewd royal councillor and the ambitions of an immensely powerful Highland clan chief. He supported the English alliance of 1474, yet opposed James III at Lauder (July 1482). In 1483 he became chancellor, but was suddenly sacked by James III in February 1488. Joining the formidable magnate coalition against the king, Argyll recovered the chancellorship on James's death at *Sauchie Burn.

**Argyll, Colin Campbell, 6th earl of** [S] (*c.*1542–84). Campbell succeeded his half-brother in the earldom in 1573. After a quarrel with Regent *Morton over certain crown jewels, brought to Argyll by his second wife, he seized the young king James at Stirling in 1578 and forced him to dismiss Morton. Argyll was appointed lord chancellor [S] and held the post until his death.

**Argyll, John Campbell, 2nd duke of** (1678–1743). Soldier and politician. While still in his twenties, Argyll emerged pre-eminent among the Scottish magnates, and as lord high commissioner (1705) played a key role in opening negotiations for the Anglo-Scottish union. He afterwards commanded with distinction in the War of the *Spanish Succession, though he conceived a lasting hatred of the duke of *Marlborough. But his association with *Harley's Tory administration turned sour during a spell as commander-in-chief in Spain (1711–12). In 1712 he became commander of the army in Scotland, and in 1715 suppressed the Jacobite uprising. He lost office during the Whig divisions of 1716–19 but was reinstated, and by 1725 was in control of Scottish affairs. His relations with *Walpole deteriorated after the *Porteous episode (1736–7), and in 1742 his contingent in the Commons contributed appreciably to the minister's downfall.

**aristocracy** A vague term, derived from the Greek *aristokratia*, meaning the rule of the best. It is broader than peerage or even nobility. In common parlance it was usually taken to mean the upper classes or 'betters', but was confined largely to landowners. The 'golden age' of aristocracy was between 1688 and 1832, with the monarchy safely limited yet the threat of democracy still distant. Its legacy was the parks and country houses, such as Belton (1685), Petworth (1690), Chatsworth (1696), Castle Howard (1700), Woburn (1747), Harewood (1759), and Heveningham (1778).

**Arkinholm, battle of,** 1455. In the spring of 1455 James II of Scotland moved to rid himself of the powerful 'Black Douglases'—James, earl of Douglas, and his three brothers, Ormond, Moray, and Balvenie. Douglas fled to England but the three brothers gave battle at Arkinholm near Langholm on 1 May. They were utterly defeated. Moray was killed in the battle, Ormond captured and executed, and Balvenie fled.

**Arklow, battle of,** 1798. Despite the repulse at *New Ross on 5 June 1798 the Wexford rebels remained dangerous. They had captured Gorey, and threatened Arklow. But the government reinforced the small garrison at Arklow and when the rebels attacked on 9 June, they were driven back, largely by artillery.

*Ark Royal* The name given to a series of warships in the Royal Navy. The first *Ark Royal*, originally called *Ark Raleigh*, was purchased by the crown in 1588. It was used as the flagship of Lord *Howard of Effingham against the *Armada.

**Arkwright, Sir Richard** (1732–92). Born in Preston, Arkwright was apprenticed to a barber, and established a business in Bolton. Travelling around northern textile districts to buy hair for wig-making, Arkwright met craftsmen attempting to improve cotton production and lured John *Kay away in the 1760s; together they produced the water frame, a roller-spinning machine which Arkwright patented (1769). His first horse-driven factory was established at Nottingham (1769); in 1771 he moved to Cromford (Derbys.). Lancashire cottonmasters successfully attacked his patent (1781 and 1785), but Arkwright deserves the title of 'father of the factory system'.

**Arlington, Henry Bennet, 1st earl of** (1618–85). Having fought for the crown in the Civil War, the future foreign minister of Charles II represented him at Madrid during Cromwell's alliance with France against Spain. Financially dependent on office, he did little to improve Anglo-Dutch relations, though in 1666 he married a Dutch wife. Distrustful of France, as secretary of state Bennet was similarly flaccid in falling in with Charles II's French policies. He contrived Charles's first secret treaty of *Dover with Louis XIV in May 1670, was granted a barony in 1665 and promoted to an earldom in 1672. Disgraced as secretary in 1673, Arlington became an Admiralty commissioner, and assisted in withdrawing the garrison at Tangier.

**Armada, Spanish** The invasion fleet sent against England by Philip II of Spain in July 1588 comprised some 138 vessels, perhaps 7,000 seamen, and 17,000 soldiers. The number of soldiers would be doubled once the forces of the duke of Parma in Flanders were embarked. English naval forces comprised 34 royal warships and some 170 privately owned ships under the command of Lord *Howard of Effingham. The quality of English guns and their handling were of an order with which the Spaniards could not compete, yet the English, in turn, could not compete with Spanish soldiery if it came to hand-to-hand fighting at sea, or on land. Philip II's purposes behind the Armada were to end English attacks on Spain's commerce with her American dominions, to assert his sovereignty in Flanders, and, above all, to bring heretic England back into the fold of Rome.

Under the command of the duke of Medina-Sidonia, the Armada took three weeks to make Corunna from Lisbon. From the Lizard Point in Cornwall on 29 July its disciplined crescent formation was only twice broken by English forces before it reached Calais on 6 August. Here Parma had failed to prepare his troops. The Armada's congestion made it vulnerable to Howard's fireship attack on the night of 7 August, and the following day there was heavy Spanish loss of life in a sustained battle off Gravelines. Deteriorating weather drove a dispersed Armada up the North Sea, pursued by Howard. Driven round Scotland and Ireland, in unseasonably severe weather, two-thirds of the Armada were brilliantly navigated back home, but upwards of 30 ships were lost in the Hebrides and western Ireland. Some 11,000 Spaniards may have died. Although the elements had principally saved England, the campaign brought her high international repute, while Spain had proved she could place a huge naval force in northern latitudes.

**Armagh** was the smallest of the six counties of Northern Ireland. The chief town is Armagh which has been an archbishopric since the 12th cent.: there is also a Roman catholic archbishopric. The catholic population is strong in the south and in 1921 Armagh council protested against the creation of Northern Ireland and was dissolved.

**Armagh (Ard Machae), archiepiscopal diocese of** Its strong associations with St *Patrick made Armagh inevitably the seat of both the Catholic and Anglican primates of all Ireland. By the Council of Raithbressail (1111) Armagh became the metropolitan see of Leth Cuinn (northern half of Ireland) with twelve dioceses. Later, by the Council of Kells-Mellifont (1152) when Ireland was divided further into four provinces, the province of *Tuam for western Ireland was carved out of Armagh, while Armagh, with its eleven dioceses, still retained overall primacy. Armagh has two cathedrals, both dedicated to St Patrick.

**Arminianism** Under Elizabeth I, though against her will, the Church of England eschewed ritual and adopted the grim Calvinist belief that God, when creating human beings, had predestined them to either salvation or damnation. The 1590s saw a reaction set in, similar to that which was taking place in Holland under the impetus of Jacob Arminius, and English anti-predestinarians came to be called Arminians. The Arminians were given only limited advancement by

James I, but with the accession of the high-church Charles I in 1625 they came to dominate the episcopal bench. Charles's identification with them was one of the principal causes of the lack of trust between him and his subjects.

**armour** There are relatively few surviving pieces of medieval date, so the study of armour is largely dependent on the evidence of monumental effigies, manuscript illuminations, and documentary sources. Three periods of development have been identified. The first period, *c.*11th–13th cent., saw the predominance of mail. A knee-length mail hauberk, sometimes hooded, was worn over a padded garment (aketon). By the mid- to late 12th cent., a surcoat of linen was commonly worn over the hauberk. Helmets were at first conical with a descending plate to protect the nose, but developed into rounder, cylindrical forms with visors (the great helm). In the third period, from the late 14th to early 16th cent., full plate armour was worn, covering the trunk as well as the legs and arms. A padded coat (or arming doublet) would be worn under a solid breast- and backplate. Helmets came in many shapes, often protecting the whole head by means of a visor. Even in this third period mail might still be worn to protect the groin and armpits. The second period links the first and the third but overlapped with both. It saw the development of the coat of plates, a cloth-covered body armour which was essentially a fabric garment reinforced internally with metal plates (subsequently called the brigandine). This might be worn with mail, and also with solid, and later articulated, plate protection on the arms, hands, legs, and feet. The great helm persisted but was giving way to the head-hugging bascinet, which sometimes had a visor. Our picture of armour is too often derived from the top of the range—the most expensive apparel of the aristocratic and knightly classes. The rank and file continued to rely on mail shirts, reinforced cloth armours (brigandine and jak), and simpler headgear (sallets, kettle hats, etc.). Tournament armour can be misleading. Because of the desire to protect life in what was, after all, a sport, it tended to be heavier and more defensive than armour for war: visors, for instance, were *de rigueur*, whereas in battle faces might be left uncovered. The most expensive and most fashionable armours in the later Middle Ages came from northern Italy and southern Germany. Generally speaking, however, the rank and file had to make do with locally produced, and probably often recycled, armour.

**Arms, Assize of** Henry II made an Assize of Arms in 1181. It bound all freemen of England to swear on oath that they would possess and bear arms in the service of king and realm. The assize stipulated precisely the military equipment that each man should have according to his rank and wealth. The assize, frequently renewed, effectively revived the old Anglo-Saxon *fyrd duty.

**Arms, College of** *See* COLLEGE OF ARMS.

**Armstrong, William Armstrong, 1st Baron** (1810–1900). Armstrong was the son of a Newcastle merchant. Trained as a solicitor, he was interested in technical experiments from boyhood. In 1847 he established the Elswick engine works near Newcastle to manufacture hydraulic machinery. During the *Crimean War he became involved in gunmaking and this led in 1859 to the Elswick Ordnance Company. During the later 19th cent. it became one of the world's leading engineering, shipbuilding, and armaments firms, taking over the Whitworth company in 1897. Armstrong acquired a Northumberland estate at Cragside in 1863 and commissioned Norman Shaw to build a mansion for him. He received a peerage in 1887.

**army** Long before the Norman Conquest, military obligation seems to have divided into two basic forms. One was an obligation for service by all adult males, established in English law as the *militia by the Assize of *Arms of 1181. The other was a small permanent standing army, usually represented in the medieval period by the warriors of the royal household.

By early modern times, English armies consisted almost entirely of troops paid in some fashion. However, any form of standing army was considered a potential instrument of royal despotism. The *Yeomen of the Guard, founded by Henry VII in 1485 as a small royal bodyguard, is the earliest unit of the British army that has survived. The granting of money by Parliament to finance armies

on a temporary basis became one of the most important issues between crown and Parliament. It reached a crisis in 1639–41 when Parliament refused Charles I money to repel a Scots invasion, and would not trust him with control of an army to suppress the Irish rebellion.

The direct ancestor of the modern British army is usually considered to be the parliamentary *New Model Army of 1645. However, its part in enforcing Cromwell's rule in England and in subjugating Scotland and Ireland helped to establish a prejudice against soldiers which lasted well into modern times. The first properly constituted standing army, of tiny proportions, was created in 1661 by Charles II, and entitled 'His Majesty's Guards and Garrisons'. The existence and function of the army was based on royal prerogative rather than statute, an issue which came to a head in the reign of James II and played a part in his overthrow. Thereafter the 1689 *Declaration of Rights established that a standing army was illegal without Parliament's approval, granted every year in the *Mutiny Act until 1953, when this was replaced by a five-yearly Armed Forces Act.

Particularly after the Act of *Union with Scotland of 1707, and the subsequent defeat of *Jacobite uprisings, a large army at home was not required. Instead, the British needed a minimum force to keep order, garrisons for their overseas possessions, and small forces to contribute to coalitions for European wars. The British army developed in a manner regarded by European standards as both eccentric and old-fashioned, with a central core of units providing the basis for a much larger army that could be expanded and disbanded according to need.

Whereas in some countries the army became the focus of political and social reform, in Britain it was always seen as a bastion of reaction. Particularly after the French Revolution, the army was deliberately kept apart from British society (through the building of barracks), and practices regarded as obsolete in continental warfare, such as officers purchasing their commissions, regiments having considerable autonomy from central authority, and the flogging of soldiers, persisted well into the 19th cent. Parliamentary fears of militarism meant rigid control of the army's budget, a deliberately divided command system, and a toleration of inefficiency in order to keep the army politically weak. Officers were drawn largely from the lesser gentry, with an admixture of the aristocracy, and recruits from the poorest classes.

After the loss of the American colonies in 1783, the largest single focus for the British army was India, following the crown's absorption of the East India Company army as the Indian army in 1858. Garrisoning British India with both British and Indian troops became the major army role of the late 19th cent. A series of reforms following the *Crimean War (1853–6), associated in particular with the abolition of purchase by Edward *Cardwell in 1871 and with the creation of the 'county regiments' structure ten years later, produced a largely infantry army to serve overseas. The revelation of serious military deficiencies in the Second *Boer War (1899–1902) produced reforms to prepare the army for warfare in Europe, particularly associated with Richard *Haldane.

The British tradition of a small long-service army for use overseas meant that at the start of the *First World War (1914–18) Britain was the only belligerent country without conscription, introduced with reluctance in January 1916. The creation of a mass citizen army for the war was of great social as well as political significance for Britain, marking the first real contact between the army and British society since the Civil War. Ultimately the British army was the most successful of the war, inflicting a crushing defeat upon Germany. However, with no shared military tradition to draw upon, the social and cultural impact of the war upon Britain was devastating, and persisted to the end of the 20th cent.

The experience of the First World War enabled Britain to cope rather better with the *Second World War (1939–45). For the first time in British history peacetime conscription was introduced in 1939, shortly before the outbreak of war. Although Britain once more emerged victorious, it faced in 1945 a changed military situation. In particular the traditional roles of the British army of garrisoning the empire and fighting in Europe were ceasing to be relevant. After 1945 Britain maintained, again for the first time in its history, peacetime conscription (known as National Service) until 1963, after which the army reverted once more to an all-volunteer force. Its two major roles

were from 1949 membership of *NATO (the North Atlantic Treaty Organization) as part of the collective defence of western Europe against the Soviet Union until 1991, covering the 'Retreat from Empire', a succession of wars as Britain dismantled its empire. The 21st-cent. army has been obliged to adjust to the pace of technological change and has been stretched by a number of campaigns, including Northern Ireland (1969–2005), the Falkland Islands (1982), two Iraq wars (1990, 2003) and a long-running conflict against the Taliban in Afghanistan (2001 onwards).

**Arnhem, battle of,** 1944. British and Polish parachute troops attempted to secure bridges at Arnhem over the Rhine in September 1944, while US forces seized crossings further south. The Americans succeeded; the British drop met overwhelming counter-attack from SS Panzer divisions resting nearby. Montgomery's decision to attack in spite of warnings from ULTRA intelligence was a gamble in an attempt to finish the European war in 1944.

**Arnold, Matthew** (1822–88). Poet and critic. Son of Thomas *Arnold, headmaster of Rugby School, Matthew was educated also at Winchester and Oxford, before election to an Oriel fellowship (1845). From 1851 to 1883 he was an inspector of schools. Emerging as a mature poet by 1853, he was professor of poetry at Oxford 1857–67. He broadened the accepted form of the critical essay, and in *Culture and Anarchy* (1869) famously classified English society into 'Barbarians, Philistines and Populace'.

**Arnold, Thomas** (1795–1842). Headmaster of Rugby School. Arnold was educated at Winchester and Corpus Christi College, Oxford. In 1818 he became vicar of Laleham (Middx.). Appointed to the mastership of Rugby, a prosperous public school, in 1828, he built a chapel at the school, then an unusual feature. Dr Arnold brought with him what has been termed 'muscular Christianity', a good picture of which can be found in Tom Hughes's *Tom Brown's Schooldays* (1857).

**Arran, James Hamilton, 2nd earl of** [S] (*c.*1517–75). Arran was a great-grandson of James II of Scotland. On the death of James V in 1542 he was heir presumptive to the Scottish throne, Mary being a tiny infant.

From 1543 he was regent on her behalf. At first pro-English and anxious for a marriage between Mary and Edward VI, when this fell through and war followed, he abjured protestantism and moved towards the French interest. In 1554 he gave up the regency to *Mary of Guise, though he retained hopes of a marriage between Queen Mary and his own son. He opposed the *Darnley marriage and was obliged to leave the kingdom between 1565 and 1569. On his return, he supported the queen's party.

**Arran, James Hamilton, 3rd earl of** [S](c.1538–1609). Arran himself was one of the many contenders for the hand of Elizabeth, and, failing that, of Mary, queen of Scots. He was abroad from 1550 to 1559 and on his return to Scotland became a leader of the protestant party. But in 1562 he was declared insane and in 1581 was persuaded to resign his earldom in favour of his relative James Stewart.

**Arran, James Stewart, 4th earl of** [S] (c.1550–95). James Stewart was a second son of Lord Ochiltree [S]. After service with the Dutch he returned to Scotland in 1579 and was soon in favour with James VI. He took an active part in the prosecution of *Morton. His relative the 3rd earl of Arran, who was insane, was placed in his charge and in 1581 consented to renounce the earldom in Stewart's favour. In 1583 he was temporarily ousted by the protestant lords in the *Ruthven raid, but recovered his position in 1584 and had *Gowrie executed. He became chancellor [S] and for a time wielded great power. But he was overthrown in the coup of November 1585, attainted, and exiled. Though he returned, he was murdered by Sir James Douglas in revenge for his part in Morton's downfall.

**Arras, Congress of,** 1435. Marked an attempt by the papacy and the Council of Basle to bring about peace between England and France. It was presided over by two cardinals and attended by embassies representing Henry VI, Charles VII of France, and Philip, duke of Burgundy, still technically in alliance with the English. It came to naught because the English refused to abandon Henry VI's rights to the French throne. They withdrew their delegation on 6 September, leaving the way clear for a Franco-Burgundian alliance, finalized on 21 September.

**array, commissions of** This was a means of raising local troops. The commissions instructed individuals to raise troops in their area and were first issued by Edward I. Parliament succeeded in obtaining a number of concessions. Edward III promised in 1327 not to employ the men outside their county, save in case of invasion; in 1344 that the crown would pay wages if they were asked to serve outside the kingdom; in 1350 that commissions would only be issued with the consent of Parliament. After mid-16th cent. it was more convenient to ask the *lords-lieutenant to raise levies and commissions fell into disuse.

**Arrow War,** 1856–60. The war occurred when the ship *Arrow* was boarded at Canton, in October 1856, by the Chinese on suspicion of piracy. Although the crew and owner were Chinese, the ship was registered in Hong Kong and flew the Union Jack. The incident was used by western powers as an opportunity to extract concessions. On 29 December 1857 an Anglo-French force occupied Canton and then proceeded to *Tien-Tsin, where a treaty was signed in June 1858. China agreed to open ports and receive legations at Peking. However, in 1859 British and French ministers were refused permission to enter Peking. A second Anglo-French force landed at Pei-Tang on 1 August 1860 and took Peking in October. On 18 October the Chinese agreed to honour the Tien-Tsin treaty and ceded Kowloon, the mainland opposite Hong Kong, to Britain. *See also* CHINA WARS.

**Arsuf, battle of,** 1191. On 22 August 1191 Richard I led the armies of the Third Crusade out of Acre towards Jaffa, whence they would strike inland to Jerusalem. The army marched close to the sea-shore, its right flank protected by Richard's fleet. Saladin's forces harassed the crusaders, but could not break their close formation and Saladin realized that he would have to risk open battle. On 7 September, on the plain to the north of Arsuf, the two armies met. The day was won when the massed crusader cavalry charged and forced Saladin to withdraw.

**Arthur** King Arthur and his circle are creations of medieval writers drawing on history, folklore, mythology, and imagination. Arthurian material has been continually reshaped and developed, reflecting aspects of contemporary life, morality, and aspirations. The 'real' Arthur is a hero referred to in the British poem the *Gododdin* (*c.*600), in the 9th-cent. *Nennius' Historia Brittonum*, and in two entries in the 10th-cent. *Annales Cambriae*. The original warlord, who defies identification, was developed by the 9th- and 10th-cent. Welsh into a great Welsh victor. Welsh tradition in turn contributed to oral traditions in Cornwall, and in Brittany, where it came to be believed that he still lived. It was probably Breton bards who were responsible for the Round Table motif. But Arthur and his world were definitively formed in the 1130s by *Geoffrey of Monmouth in his fictional *History of the Kings of Britain*. In this, Arthur is the ideal king, conqueror of much of Europe, attacking even Rome. Finally defeated and mortally wounded, he is borne to Avalon.

Arthur's court proved a magnet for heroes and their deeds, and in much Arthurian material Arthur's own profile is low. The legend of Tristan and Isolde, one of the most popular, was tacked on to Arthur's. Other tales, however, developed out of it. The Grail element, combining Celtic traditions of magical testing-vessels and blessed food-producing horns with Christian sentiment, first crystallized in French. Chrétien of Troyes in the 1170s and 1180s also introduced courtly love, made the Round Table a centre of chivalry, and identified Arthur's capital as Camelot. The first treatment in (Middle) English was Layamon's *Brut* (late 12th cent.), which introduced the element of faerie. The greatest English production was the late 14th-cent. *Sir Gawain and the Green Knight*.

The cult of chivalry was a European phenomenon. Arthurian romances portrayed its ideals, and its organization and trappings. Arthurian characters and deeds were emulated in tournaments, sometimes in Arthurian dress, and in ceremonial, as in Edward III's foundation of the Order of the *Garter. Arthurian matters could be politically useful. Honour paid by Edward I to what were apparently bones of Arthur and Guinevere, at Glastonbury in 1278, was flattering to the Welsh, while emphasizing that hope for a Messianic delivery from him was pointless.

In the early modern period the popularity of Arthurian material declined. It survived in the English-speaking world because of Sir Thomas *Malory, whose work, completed about 1469, retailed the story as a tragedy. It was printed in 1485 by *Caxton as the *Morte Darthur*. Henry VII exploited Welsh interest, for example naming his elder son *Arthur, and making him prince of Wales in 1489, but Arthur's significance under the Tudors was chiefly in pageantry and literature. There was some drama and poetry, and Arthur was taken up by Edmund *Spenser in his *Faerie Queene*. *Shakespeare, however, gave him no attention.

Arthurian romance was next popular in the 19th cent., though *Dryden wrote a play which was set to music by *Purcell. Sir Walter *Scott and William *Wordsworth wrote some Arthurian material, but the boom began with *Tennyson's poems, from 1832, based on Malory. Tennyson's characters often symbolize particular qualities, and his works are moralizing. Other Arthurian writers include Algernon Swinburne, William *Morris, Matthew *Arnold, and (satirically) the American Mark Twain.

In the 20th cent. Arthurian settings and circles were an enduring theme for novelists and poets of very different kinds. British musical treatments include works by Boughton, Bax, *Parry, and *Elgar. There have been a number of films.

Many attempts have been made to identify Arthurian sites. Through the ages Camelot has been located at Cadbury (where an Iron Age hill-fort was a centre of British power in the late 5th cent.), Caerleon, Colchester, Winchester, Tintagel, and, recently and controversially, near Stirling. The origin of Arthur's association with Cornwall is not clear. Castle Dore and Tintagel (with their late 5th- and early 6th-cent. secular aristocratic dwellings) are 'identified' as settings for Tristan and Isolde. Glastonbury was associated in the mid-12th cent. with an abduction of Guinevere, and became identified with Avalon. In 1190 or 1191 the monks 'discovered' the burial of Arthur and Guinevere, and in the mid-13th cent. they added Joseph of Arimathea, with whom the Holy Grail was associated, to their history.

**Arthur, Prince** (1187–c.1203). As the post-humous only son of Geoffrey and Constance of Brittany, Arthur was duke of Brittany from the moment of his birth. Greater prospects opened up in 1190 when his uncle, Richard I, nominated him as heir presumptive to the throne, but by 1199, when Richard died, John had taken over as the acknowledged successor. Arthur's moment came in 1202 when King Philip Augustus, at war against John, decided to recognize him as rightful ruler of Normandy and Anjou. But he was captured by John in August 1202, imprisoned at Rouen, and never seen again.

**Arthur, prince of Wales** (1486–1502), was the eldest son of Henry VII and *Elizabeth of York and the elder brother of Henry VIII. At the age of 15 he was married to *Catherine of Aragon and set up court at Ludlow. Five months later he was dead of consumption and buried in Worcester cathedral.

**Artificers, statute of,** 1563. Growing concern at the number of masterless men, increasing vagabondage, and escalating crime underlay the promulgation of conditions of service between masters and servants. All unmarried persons below 30 who had received craft training could not refuse to serve if requested, those between 12 and 60 obliged to serve in husbandry were defined, and unmarried women between 12 and 40 could also be made to serve. Wage rates were to be set yearly at the Court of Chancery, and then proclaimed in every county. Anyone failing to carry letters testimonial was punishable for vagrancy.

**Arundel, Henry Fitz Alan, 12th earl of** (1512–80). Arundel steered a dextrous course through the rapids of mid-Tudor politics. He was in favour with Henry VIII, served with distinction against the French, and was awarded the Garter. During the reign of Edward VI Arundel was at odds with the duke of *Northumberland and spent a year in the Tower. In 1553 he ostensibly supported Lady Jane *Grey, but took out an insurance by reporting everything to Mary. Under Mary he was Lord Steward and, as a fellow-catholic, once more in favour. In Elizabeth's reign, he was mentioned as a possible husband. But he was implicated in the *Ridolfi plot in 1571, and in the later 1570s lived in quiet retirement.

**Arundel, Philip Howard, 13th earl of** (1557–95). Philip Howard's father was the 4th duke of *Norfolk, executed in 1572: his mother, daughter of Henry, earl of *Arundel, died soon after his birth. The dukedom was under attainder from 1572 but in 1580 Howard succeeded his grandfather as earl of Arundel. In 1584, he converted to catholicism, and the following year was arrested and imprisoned in the Tower. In 1588 he was tried for treason as having prayed for the success of the *Armada, was condemned to death, and died after seven more years in prison.

**Arundel, Thomas Howard, 14th earl of** (1585–1646). Howard's father spent the last eleven years of his life in the Tower. Howard was restored to the title by James I in 1604, received the Garter in 1611, and converted back to protestantism in 1615. In 1621 he was made earl marshal for life. In 1639 he was put in charge of the army to restore order among the Scots, but since the campaign ended without fighting, his military qualities were not tested. He was lord steward 1640–1 and presided over the trial of *Strafford.

**Arundel, Thomas** (1352–1414). Archbishop of Canterbury. The third son of Richard Fitz Alan, 8th earl of Arundel, Thomas was an Oxford undergraduate when he became bishop of Ely in 1374. When the baronial critics of Richard II took control in 1386, Arundel was appointed chancellor and promoted to the archbishopric of York in 1388. He was replaced as chancellor after Richard's resumption of authority in 1389, but again held the office from 1391 until he was translated to Canterbury in 1396. Next year, Richard destroyed the leadership of the former opposition and Arundel was deprived of his archbishopric by fictitious translation to St Andrews. He regained Canterbury in 1399 by supporting Henry IV's usurpation. In the new reign, Arundel was again chancellor from 1407 to 1410, when his resignation marked the rise of a faction headed by Prince Henry (later Henry V). On its fall, Henry IV reappointed Arundel as chancellor, in 1412. The accession of Henry V in 1413 ended Arundel's role as a power behind the throne.

**Arundel castle** in Sussex was started by Roger, earl of Shrewsbury, soon after the *Norman Conquest. It was later in the possession of the Aubigny family until 1243, passed by marriage to the Fitz Alans until 1580, and subsequently to the Howards, dukes of Norfolk.

**Ascham, Roger** (1515/16–68). Protestant classical scholar, born in Yorkshire. He went up about 1530 to St John's College, Cambridge, and was there influenced by Sir John *Cheke, whom he supported on Greek pronunciation. Ascham himself taught Latin, Greek, and logic, being also university public orator. His *Toxophilus, the School of Shooting* (1545), a beautifully written account of the merits of archery, secured him patronage. After tutoring both Princess Elizabeth and the future Edward VI, Ascham went on embassy to Germany in 1550. A sympathizer with Lady Jane *Grey, he suffered little under Mary, for whom he acted as Latin secretary; and was in favour with Elizabeth. Ascham's best-known work, *The Schoolmaster, or Plain and Perfect Way of Teaching Children the Latin Tongue* (1570), advocated an education based ultimately on Quintilian.

**Ashanti (Asante) wars** The Ashanti empire, in the hinterland of the Gold Coast, reached its peak in the late 18th cent. An attempt by the Ashanti to establish their dominion over the territory adjacent to British trading posts in 1807 threatened British trade, but did not lead to armed conflict until 1824 when the Ashanti were victorious. The British government's ambivalence emboldened the Ashanti to seize the coastal territory again in 1863. After another reversal of policy, Britain sent a military force under Sir Garnet *Wolseley to challenge Ashanti claims in 1873. Wolseley destroyed the Ashanti capital, Kumasi. The rapid expansion of French and German colonization in the region induced Britain to demand Ashanti submission in 1896. When the Ashanti resisted, another British expedition (1900–1) destroyed the empire, which became a British crown colony in 1902.

**Ashburton treaty,** 1842. After the *War of 1812, relations between Britain and the USA remained difficult, with border disputes in Maine. In 1841 when *Peel took office, the situation was bad enough to call for naval deployments in case of war. Peel dispatched Lord Ashburton, who had an American wife, as a special envoy. By the treaty, signed in April, Britain dropped the right of maritime search, the Maine border was adjusted, and the boundary with Canada agreed as the 49th parallel.

**Ashdown, battle of,** 871. In 870 a Danish army camped at Reading and began raiding the surrounding countryside. *Æthelred, king of Wessex, and his brother *Alfred gave battle at Ashdown on the Berkshire downs about 8 January 871. The struggle raged round a stunted thorn-bush and, according to the *Anglo-Saxon Chronicle*, 'went on till nightfall'. The Danes were driven back—the first major check to their advance—but a follow-up against their camp failed. Æthelred died within weeks and, his sons being too young to lead in battle, Alfred became king.

**Ashdown, Jeremy, 1st Baron Ashdown** ('Paddy') (b. 1941). Politician. After serving in the Royal Marines from 1959–72, Ashdown worked in the Foreign and Commonwealth Office. In 1983 he was returned to Parliament for Yeovil as a Liberal Democrat and became leader of the party, succeeding David *Steel, in 1988. He presided over a significant increase in the parliamentary strength from 20 seats in 1992 to 46 in 1997. Friendly towards the Blair government, he failed to persuade it to introduce electoral reform. After giving way to Charles *Kennedy in 1999, he was appointed a life peer in 2001. From 2002–6 he served as High Representative in Bosnia, but a move in 2007 to appoint him UN envoy to Afghanistan was frustrated.

**Ashingdon, battle of,** 1016. This was the final battle in the struggle between *Edmund Ironside and *Cnut and took place near the river Crouch in Essex. The defection of Eadric, ealdorman of Mercia, who led the Magonsaete of Herefordshire from the field, contributed to a crushing Danish victory, with 'all the flower of the English nation' cut down. The two leaders met subsequently at Deerhurst in Gloucestershire to divide the kingdom but Edmund's death weeks afterwards gave the whole realm into Cnut's hands.

**asiento** (Spanish: contract) was the concession made by Spain to Britain at *Utrecht in 1713 of the right to supply negro slaves to the

Spanish empire. Intended to last for 30 years, the trade was never as profitable as the British hoped and disputes about its implementation were among the causes of the War of *Jenkins's Ear in 1739. The British relinquished the concession in 1750 for £100,000 compensation.

**Aske, Robert** (d. 1537). A Lincolnshire attorney, Aske led the *Pilgrimage of Grace in 1536–7, a rising against the *dissolution of the monasteries and in favour of the old religion. An outbreak in Lincolnshire was followed by Aske's Yorkshire rising, strong enough to persuade Henry VIII to offer pardons and agree in November 1536 to grant Aske an audience. But after renewed activity in January 1537, Aske was seized, and in July executed in York. A moderate who had tried to restrain his followers and urged them to trust Henry's good faith, Aske paid with his life for such naivety.

**Asquith, Herbert Henry, 1st earl of Oxford and Asquith** (1852–1928). Prime minister. Between 1908 and 1914 Asquith enjoyed an outstanding record, pushing through a series of major constitutional and social reforms. But he had less success as a wartime premier from 1914 to 1916, and his reputation declined during the undignified period of infighting within the Liberal Party from 1918 to 1926.

Asquith's early life was spent in Morley and Huddersfield where his relatives were minor employers in the woollen trade. He soon left these modest origins behind and advanced by means of a scholarship to Balliol College (1870), to the bar, and to a safe seat in Parliament—East Fife—which he held from 1885 to 1918. His first wife Helen, by whom he had five children, died in 1891, and when he re-married in 1894 it was to a very different character, Margot Tennant, the daughter of a wealthy Scots chemicals magnate. Margot was a terrible snob who insisted on calling her husband Henry not Herbert, and described him as 'incorrigibly middle-class'.

Though his attendance at Westminster was restricted by the need to maintain his legal income, Asquith's abilities were quickly recognized. His systematic working habits and skill in mastering a brief made him a formidable parliamentarian. In 1892 *Gladstone gave him the vital experience as home secretary

which placed him in line for the premiership. Subsequently, however, Asquith's career entered the doldrums for a time. In 1898 he declined the chance to lead the Liberals in the Commons, largely for financial reasons. Worse, Asquith became associated with the *Liberal Imperialist cause during the South African War which detached him from the mainstream of the party. However, between 1903 and 1905 he worked his passage back into favour by championing *free trade against the protectionism propagated by Joseph *Chamberlain. When offered the Exchequer in December 1905 he quickly accepted.

Asquith proved to be one of the most important, innovative chancellors of modern times. He made it compulsory to provide an annual return of income to the Inland Revenue; he drew up the scheme for non-contributory old-age pensions; and he prepared the ground for the 'People's Budget' of 1909 by forcing the Treasury to abandon its opposition to a supertax on incomes above £5,000.

When Campbell-Bannerman retired in 1908 Asquith seemed to be the natural successor as prime minister. He presided over a highly talented cabinet, and was never afraid to promote able and ambitious men like *Lloyd George and Winston *Churchill. As premier Asquith played a key role in supporting Lloyd George's 1909 budget against criticism in the cabinet. As a result of the ensuing controversy he led the Liberals through two general elections in 1910 and ultimately resolved the problem that had hampered them since Gladstone's days; the 1911 *Parliament Act curtailed the powers of the House of Lords and excluded it altogether from financial legislation.

The outbreak of war brought further proof of Asquith's skills. Against expectations he succeeded in taking his cabinet to war with only two resignations. But his cold, legalistic temperament was not well suited to the emotional atmosphere of wartime. Asquithian cabinets—during which the prime minister often wrote long letters to Venetia Stanley, a young woman with whom he was infatuated—were protracted and inconclusive. But he was unlucky that neither the generals nor the admirals proved capable of scoring a military victory. His decision to form a coalition government with the Conservative and Labour parties in May 1915 was the beginning of the end for Asquith. Increasingly the Liberals began to blame him for right-wing policies like conscription. When presented with an ultimatum by Bonar *Law and Lloyd George in December 1916, he misjudged his strength by resigning. The result was a new coalition under Lloyd George and a split in the Liberal party. This led to the disastrous 'coupon' election in 1918 in which Asquith lost his seat and the Liberals were displaced by Labour on the opposition front bench. Though he achieved a comeback by winning a by-election at Paisley in 1920, he was by then a negative force, intent upon keeping the party out of the hands of Lloyd George. He finally surrendered the leadership in 1926.

**Asser** (d. 909). Bishop of Sherborne. Author of the *Life of King Alfred*, Asser was a Welshman who was a monk and priest at St David's in Dyfed until recruited by Alfred in 885 to become one of a group of scholars at his court. His famous biography of Alfred was written by 893 and makes use of the recently completed *Anglo-Saxon Chronicle*. He succeeded Wulfsige c.900 as bishop of Sherborne.

**assizes** The word has a number of different meanings in legal history. It was used to describe (*a*) a session of an official body, especially the king's council (e.g. the Assize of *Clarendon 1166); (*b*) the edicts or enactments made at such sessions; (*c*) the forms of action or procedures instituted by such edicts; (*d*) the system of travelling courts which became part of English life from the reign of Henry II until 1971. In the 13th cent. the term 'assize' came to be the general term applied to the visits of the judges on circuit. After 1340 the justices of assize were required to justices of the Court of *Common Pleas or *King's Bench or serjeants at law. The assizes continued until 1971 on the circuits ordained by Henry II, the assize towns being visited periodically by assize judges, who would hear serious criminal and important civil cases. Although the Courts Act 1971 abolished the assizes, senior judges still go 'on circuit' to hear cases in important modern centres of population.

**Astley, Sir Jacob** (1579–1652). A professional soldier who fought for the king and was given a barony in 1644. He was present at the beginning and end of the conflict. At Edgehill on 23 October 1642 he led his troops into battle with a soldier's prayer: 'O Lord,

thou knowest how busy I must be this day. If I forget thee, do not thou forget me.' At the end, in the market-place of Stow-on-the-Wold, on 21 March 1646, he surrendered the king's last sizeable force. Sitting on a drum, he told his captors, 'you may now go to play, boys, unless you fall out among yourselves.'

**Astor, Nancy W.** (1879–1964). Politician, and daughter of an American railway developer in Virginia. Nancy Astor had an unhappy first marriage, which ended in divorce in 1903. The following year she travelled to England, marrying Waldorf Astor three years later; when Waldorf, Conservative MP for Plymouth, Sutton, succeeded to the peerage in 1919, Nancy was returned in his stead at the subsequent by-election, becoming the second woman to be elected to Parliament. As a parliamentarian (1919–45) Nancy was outspoken —perhaps too much so—in favour of those causes she held dear: opposition to divorce (despite her own experience); raising to 18 the age at which it was legal to purchase alcohol; lowering to 21 the voting age for women; above all, appeasement of Nazi Germany.

**asylum** was the right Britons afforded generations of foreign refugees fleeing from religious or political tyrannies. Early beneficiaries were the French Huguenots who came there after 1685. Like most best British liberties it rested on the absence of any laws to exclude them, rather than one to protect them specifically. During the French wars this was modified, by an Alien Act passed in 1793; but still thousands of royalists sought shelter in Britain, and the Act was repealed in 1826.

Throughout Victoria's reign, therefore, refugees poured in, mostly left-wingers. They included Mazzini, Marx, Victor Hugo, Herzen, Kropotkin, and Louis Napoleon (from the other side). In 1858 a great row blew up with France after the ex-refugee Orsini's attempt on the life of Napoleon III with a bomb. That led to *Palmerston's fall when he tried to appease the tyrant emperor.

When Britain's free-entry policy was eventually dropped, it was for social rather than political reasons. None the less the 1905 Alien Act, directed against Jews, did specifically exempt refugees. The first real inroad into this traditional British freedom came during the *First World War. Refugees still entered Britain after that, but on sufferance, rather than as a right. In the 1980s and 1990s, when economic advancement became a more powerful motive than political safety, the issue came to the fore in politics.

**asylums** for the insane had medieval origins in Britain, with London's Bethlem Hospital (*Bedlam) the most famous. Its shortened name passed into the language as befitted a frame of mind in which madness was equated with brutishness and kept in check with chains and whips. The patients in Bedlam were a spectacle for curious visitors. At the turn of the 18th and 19th cents. reformers began to claim that asylums could be turned into therapeutic environments, in which insanity could be cured by seclusion from external stresses. This line was taken by the Tuke family at their York Retreat. An Act in 1808 empowered counties to set up asylums for pauper lunatics with a view to possible cure as well as custody. In 1845 legislation required the general establishment of pauper asylums, and commissioners in lunacy were established to inspect, remedy abuses, prescribe best practice, and deal with alleged cases of wrongful confinement. Charles Reade's mid-Victorian novel *Hard Cash* dealt forcefully with this issue; but the promise of cure made asylums seem less frightening. But as asylums filled up with incurable patients and were unable to attract staff with suitable attitudes, patient–staff ratios increased, and they reverted to custodial control rather than cure. The abuses of the system came to seem to outweigh its therapeutic pretensions, and physical as well as moral restraints were reintroduced. The emergent psychiatric profession had used 'moral treatment' to enhance its credibility, but failed to deliver cures in significant numbers. The sheer scale of Victorian investment in the system, and the administrative power of the psychiatrists, kept it in being until the last quarter of the 20th cent., when a fashion for the liberation of inmates led to replacement with so-called care in the community, whose limitations were quickly apparent.

**Athelstan** (d. 939), king of England (924–39). One of the greatest of Anglo-Saxon kings, Athelstan, son of *Edward the Elder, succeeded in uniting all England under his rule. Brought up in the household of his father and of his aunt, *Æthelfleda, ruler of the Mercians, he was well received by the Mercian as well as by the West Saxon nobility. At a meeting held at Hereford he brought the Welsh to submission, and their princes, notably *Hywel Dda, regularly attended his courts. His military successes were great. From 927 he established direct control of York. He led expeditions against the Scots, culminating in a battle at *Brunanburh in 937 when he and his brother and successor, *Edmund, led a joint force of West Saxons and Mercians to victory against a force of Scandinavians, Irish, and Scots. Athelstan established a firm internal peace, issuing important codes of law, to apply to all his subjects. His central courts developed into virtual national assemblies, attended by magnates drawn from all England, as well as Welsh princes. On the international scale he extended the range of the monarchy, arranging marriages for his sisters with Hugh, duke of the Franks, and with the future Otto the Great of Germany. His charters, written in an elaborate Latin style, betray an advanced secretariat for the age, and accord the king formal titles that indicate effort to express his special dignity. His coinage was placed under strong royal control, and after 927 his style on coins was normally given as *rex totius Britanniae*, king of all Britain. Athelstan's reign was a vital stage in the move towards the unification of England under the West Saxon dynasty.

**Athenry, battle of,** 1316. The battle, near Galway, on 10 August 1316, was a heavy defeat for the O'Connors, who were in alliance with Edward *Bruce. They were opposed by an Anglo-Irish force led by Richard de Bermingham and William de Burgh. Their chief Felim O'Connor was slain, and their power broken. But Edward Bruce continued his struggle to create an Irish kingdom for himself.

**Atholl, James Murray, 2nd duke of** [S] (*c.*1690–1764). Atholl was one of the greatest men in the Highlands because of his vast estates and because of his possession of two-thirds of the county of Perthshire. His elder brother William, marquis of Tullibardine, was attainted after the '15. His father had not countenanced the rising, so it proved possible to obtain an Act of Parliament in 1715 transferring the succession to James. He succeeded in 1724. His rights were confirmed by an Act in 1733, when he also succeeded Islay (*Argyll) as lord privy seal. In 1738, through Stanley ancestry, he inherited the sovereignty of the *Isle of Man.

In 1745 James fled south, leaving Tullibardine, the Jacobite duke, to take control of Perthshire. By joining *Cumberland's army on its march north, Duke James secured his return. Among the beneficiaries was John, son of Lord George *Murray, who despite his father's attainder was allowed to succeed as 3rd duke, after selling to the crown the lordship of Man.

**Atholl, John Murray, 1st marquis of**
[S] (1631–1703). Murray's grandfather was earl of Tullibardine but resigned the title in 1626 on promise of the earldom of Atholl, given to his son in 1629. Murray joined Lord *Middleton in 1653 in the Highland rising on behalf of Charles II. At the Restoration he was in favour. From 1663 to 1676 he served as justice-general [S] and in 1670 succeeded a cousin as earl of Tullibardine. From 1672 to 1689 he was keeper of the privy seal and in 1676 was raised to the rank of marquis. In 1679 he fought with *Monmouth against the covenanters at *Bothwell Bridge, and took an active part against *Argyll's invasion of 1685. In 1687 James II gave him the Thistle. His vacillation at the *Glorious Revolution earned him widespread mistrust and, in the end, he took refuge in visiting Bath to take the waters.

**Atholl, John Murray, 1st duke of** [S]
(1660–1724). Murray was a strong supporter of the *Glorious Revolution, was created earl of Tullibardine in 1696, and succeeded his father as marquis of Atholl in May 1703. A month later he was raised to the dukedom. From 1696 to 1698 he served as secretary of state [S], resigning on losing ground to the *Queensberry interest, and lord privy seal from 1703. But in 1705 he resigned and offered vigorous opposition to the *Union, arguing that Scottish opinion had not been properly consulted. Henceforth he acted with the Tories.

**Atholl, John Stewart, 4th earl of** [S]
(c.1528–79). Atholl succeeded his father as a boy. He was a Roman catholic and supported the cause of Mary, queen of Scots.

He opposed the religious reforms of 1560 and was appointed to the council in 1561 on Mary's return from France. At *Corrichie in 1562 he helped to put down a rising by his father-in-law, Lord *Huntly. He gave support to the *Darnley marriage but opposed *Bothwell and was against Mary in the confrontation at *Carberry Hill. He was in the Council of Regency until *Moray's return in 1567. In 1578 Atholl joined forces with *Argyll to challenge the regent *Morton and was appointed chancellor [S]. A reconciliation restored Morton to the council but in April 1579, immediately after banqueting with Morton, Atholl fell ill and died. Rumours of poison circulated, but Morton denied it at his own execution in 1581.

**Atholl, Walter Stewart, earl of** [S]
(c.1360–1437). Second son of Robert II's marriage to Euphemia Ross. Lord of Brechin until 1402, Walter Stewart acquired the earldom of Caithness [S] in that year, and that of Atholl [S] and the lordship of Methven in 1404. His main territorial ambitions centred on the earldom of Strathearn [S], which he received in life-rent from his nephew James I in 1427. Atholl was an old man when his sons David and Alan predeceased him. Fears that James I was seeking to undermine his position in Perthshire led Atholl and his grandson Robert to organize a successful assassination plot. The king was murdered at the Perth Blackfriars (20 February 1437), but Atholl was beheaded for regicide on 26 March 1437.

**Atholl, John of Strathbogie, earl of**
(d. 1306). Scottish earl who played a leading if inconsistent role in the Wars of Independence. He was captured at *Dunbar (1296) and imprisoned in the Tower of London. Reconciled with Edward I, he became warden of northern Scotland in 1304. He reverted to the Scottish allegiance, attended the coronation of Robert Bruce, his brother-in-law, in 1306, and was retaken by the English three months later. Hanged in London, then decapitated and burned, he was the first earl to be executed in England since 1076.

**Atlantic, battle of the,** 1939–45. A decisive Second World War battle. Before the war British naval experts thought 'Asdic' countered submarines and, like the highest German authorities, considered surface warships the best means of interrupting transport to Britain. Hitler allotted priority to submarines only after the fall of France, which gave German submarines greater range from Bay of Biscay harbours. In the first half of 1941 the Germans began to win, using 'wolf-packs' of submarines to overwhelm convoys. In June, however, the British started to decode orders, generated by German 'Enigma' machines, giving U-boat assembly areas in the Atlantic. In July 1941, shipping losses from submarine attack fell to less than one-third of those in June. Early in 1942, the Germans recovered; they began to read allied convoy orders and again made their own orders indecipherable. Losses to allied ships exceeded combined British and American building. In 1943, however, at twelve times the volume of 1941, US construction far exceeded losses. 'Very long-range' aircraft and small escort aircraft carriers improved allied reconnaissance and attack, together with high-frequency direction finding, which enabled warships to locate U-boats as soon as they made radio signals. The allies won the battle of the Atlantic for good in summer 1943.

**Atlantic charter** This was drawn up at the first of the *Churchill–Roosevelt wartime meetings (9–12 August 1941) during one of the darkest periods of the war. The two powers renounced territorial aggrandizement; condemned territorial changes contrary to the wishes of the people concerned; pledged that peoples should be free to choose their own form of government, and to live in freedom from want and fear. A British bid for Soviet endorsement elicited only a vague statement of approval.

**Atrebates** A British tribe and *civitas*. The tribe seems to have had origins in Gaul (France) where a tribe of the same name is recorded by *Caesar. Indeed, the king of the Gallic Atrebates, *Commius, fled to Britain and appears to have established a dynasty ruling over the British tribe. From about 15 BC, the Atrebates seem to have re-established friendly relations with Rome, and it was an appeal for help from the last Atrebatic king, Verica, which provided *Claudius with the pretext for the invasion of Britain in 43. The tribal territory lay south of the Thames in Berkshire.

**Attacotti** A British tribe or people. They seem to have inhabited a corner of north-western Britain, most probably the Outer Hebrides. They are mentioned only in late Roman sources such as Ammianus Marcellinus and St Jerome, amongst whom they had a reputation for savagery.

**attainder, Acts of** These were unpleasant political weapons whereby the accused was denied a proper trial and the normal laws of evidence could be set aside. In form they were bills of Parliament, passed by both Houses and receiving the royal assent: life, property, and titles were all forfeit. Parliamentary indictment was used against the *Despensers, favourites of Edward II, and during the Wars of the *Roses, Lancastrians and Yorkists in turn used attainders against their opponents. Thomas *Cromwell was attainted in 1540 without being heard in his own defence. The attainder of *Strafford, after his impeachment had broken down, was a crucial episode in the power struggle before the Civil War. In 1689 the Jacobite Parliament at Dublin used attainder wholesale against the supporters of William III.

**Atterbury, Francis** (1663–1732). Anglican priest and high-church Tory. A King's Scholar at Westminster School, Atterbury was then educated at the high Anglican Christ Church, Oxford, where he became a don. By 1710 Atterbury was the leading Tory spokesman for the high-church vision of a revitalized Anglican church–state and a strong defender of the rights of *convocation. By the time he became bishop of Rochester and dean of Westminster in 1713, he was of the radical Tory school epitomized by Henry St John (*Bolingbroke). The destruction of the Tory Party after 1715 appalled him. No Jacobite before 1716, he was driven to Jacobite intrigue by one-party tyranny and Whig Erastianism. Detected and exiled by *Walpole in 1723, he was a minister of the Jacobite court until 1728, but long before his death had become totally disillusioned by its incompetence.

**Attlee, Clement, 1st Earl Attlee** (1883–1967). Prime minister. The son of a solicitor, Attlee grew up in a comfortably middle-class environment. He was educated at Haileybury and University College, Oxford. Called to the bar in 1905, he forsook the law for a career in social work after viewing poverty at first hand in London's East End. Meanwhile Attlee became committed to socialism, joining the *Fabians in 1907 and the *Independent Labour Party in 1908. He volunteered for military service in the *First World War, fighting with distinction in Gallipoli, Mesopotamia, and France. In later years he retained the title of 'Major', setting himself apart from the strong anti-militarist strain within the Labour movement.

With the war over Attlee became mayor of Stepney and was elected to Parliament as member for Limehouse in 1922. He immediately became parliamentary private secretary to Ramsay *MacDonald and was appointed under-secretary at the War Office in the short-lived Labour government of 1924. He became chancellor of the duchy of Lancaster in November 1930, but was soon promoted to be postmaster-general. When this second Labour government collapsed in the summer of 1931, Attlee refused to follow MacDonald when the latter re-emerged as prime minister of an all-party *National Government.

Ironically, Labour's catastrophic performance in the general election of that year worked to Attlee's advantage. So depleted was the party's front bench that Attlee faced no opposition when the pacifist George *Lansbury was forced out of the leadership in 1935. Even so, it was widely expected that Attlee would be only a stop-gap leader. After the general election of 1935, however, he retained his position in a contest with Herbert *Morrison and Arthur Greenwood.

It was always easy to underestimate his qualities. He was no orator. Even his private conversation was clipped and uninformative. But Attlee emerged as a consummate politician, capable of controlling difficult and wilful colleagues. During the 1930s he played his part in curbing the excesses of Labour's left and re-establishing Labour as a viable party of government. In May 1940, following the debate on the ill-fated Norwegian campaign, he made it clear that Labour would not serve in a government headed by Neville *Chamberlain.

Under *Churchill Attlee served successively as lord privy seal, dominions secretary, and lord president. From 1942 he was also designated deputy prime minister and was the most powerful figure on the home front. With the resumption of party politics in the

general election of 1945 Attlee was the beneficiary of the mood of popular radicalism. He emerged as the head of the first majority Labour government in British history.

As prime minister 1945–51 Attlee helped shape the development of British politics for the next quarter-century. The administration presided over a substantial extension of the public ownership of British industry, the development of the welfare state including the creation of the National Health Service, and the establishment of Britain's position within the western alliance. Attlee headed a talented, if not always harmonious, group of senior ministers, which included Ernest *Bevin, Hugh Dalton, and Herbert *Morrison. Despite considerable difficulties, Labour sustained its public support.

Though Labour was again victorious in the general election of 1950, its massive majority of 1945 was all but wiped out. Party unity came under severe strain, while the outbreak of the *Korean War imposed new difficulties. Conservative tactics in the House of Commons made the business of government difficult and Attlee went to the country again in October 1951. Labour was narrowly defeated and the moment was perhaps opportune for Attlee to resign the leadership. As leader of the opposition Attlee engaged in little more than an exercise in damage limitation, failing to define a new role for the Labour movement. After a further electoral defeat in 1955, Attlee resigned and went to the House of Lords with an earldom.

A modest man by nature, Attlee came to enjoy great respect from the majority of those who worked under him and the electorate at large. Though the ideas of central planning, state intervention, and welfarism have been less in vogue over the last two decades, his historical reputation remains high.

**attorney-general** The chief law officer of the crown who acts as the crown's representative in legal proceedings. The title attorney-general of England was first used in 1461. During the 17th cent. the attorney-general was often accused of subservience to the monarch and of being over-zealous in prosecuting in state trials, as in the notorious prosecution of Sir Walter *Ralegh by *Coke in 1603. The modern attorney-general is a hybrid member of the government in that he is the government's legal adviser and representative, but also has historic functions relating to the administration of the law. In these cases he is required to be non-political.

**Attwood, Thomas** (1783–1856). Banker, currency reformer, and founder of the *Birmingham Political Union, Attwood argued that the economic ills of the nation were caused by hard money, and that the cure lay in an abundant supply of paper currency. Although now remembered chiefly for his support of parliamentary reform, he saw this as secondary to the need for a change in monetary policy. Attwood regarded himself as representing the Birmingham 'industrious' classes, meaning businessmen, masters, and skilled workers. He was returned for Birmingham in the reformed Parliament of 1832 and wrote continuously on monetary reform until 1847.

**Aubrey, John** (1626–97). A Wiltshire country gentleman of antiquarian interests, reduced to penury by litigation and imprudence. The only work he published himself was *Miscellanies* (1696), dealing with astrology, but his copious notes on antiquity and topography were used by others. In 1680 he sent to Anthony à Wood at Oxford his *Minutes of Lives*, sketches mainly of contemporaries. They were not published until 1813. A classic of quizzical humour. the best known is his description of Thomas *Hobbes, also from north Wiltshire. To Aubrey, we owe Hobbes at 40 taking up Euclid's theorems and declaring, '"By God, this is impossible" . . . This made him in love with Geometry.'

**Auchinleck, Claude** (1884–1981). British field marshal. Auchinleck succeeded Wavell as commander-in-chief, Middle East, in July 1941. On 17 November the 8th Army, under Alan Cunningham, attacked westward into Cyrenaica. Rommel counter-attacked on 22 November and Cunningham retreated, but Auchinleck took direct command and replaced Cunningham by Neil Ritchie on 26 November. The 'Crusader' offensive continued, clearing Cyrenaica by 6 January. Rommel counter-attacked again on 21 January and drove the 8th Army back by 4 February. Churchill felt Auchinleck to be dilatory in offensive action and Rommel struck first in May 1942. By mid-June the 8th Army's retreat, with the fall of Tobruk, became near rout. On 25 June Auchinleck took over command, organized a defence at El Alamein, and finally stopped Rommel. However, in August, Churchill flew to Cairo, and substituted *Alexander and *Montgomery respectively as C.-in-C. and army commander. Auchinleck ended his career as C.-in-C. of the Indian army. He refused a peerage, distressed by the partition of India.

**Auckland, George Eden, 1st earl** (1784–1849). Auckland was a Whig who served as president of the Board of Trade under *Grey and as 1st lord of the Admiralty under *Melbourne. In 1835, he was appointed governor-general of India. Auckland pursued commercial expansion from India into Afghanistan and central Asia and was responsible for undertaking the first *Afghan War, which initially was prosecuted with success and gained him an earldom. However, incautious policies towards 'the tribes' soon stirred revolt. In the winter of 1841–2, British forces were obliged to retreat and were shot down or frozen to death. Of 16,000 men who set out from Kabul only one, Dr Brydon, survived to proclaim himself, famously, 'the army of the Indus'. Lord Auckland was recalled in disgrace in February 1842.

**Auckland, William Eden, 1st Baron** (1744–1814). Politician and diplomat. Eden trained as a lawyer after leaving Oxford. He entered Parliament in 1774 for Woodstock and quickly established himself as a useful man, with a particular interest in economic matters and in penal reform. He was employed by Lord *North in the abortive negotiations in 1778 with the American rebels, served as chief secretary in Ireland from 1780 until 1782, and stayed with North during the coalition. But soon afterwards, he accepted an invitation from *Pitt to negotiate a commercial treaty with France and was pilloried in the *Rolliad* as chief rat. He was raised to the Irish peerage in 1789 and to the British in 1793. From 1798 until 1804 he served as joint postmaster-general, and during the Ministry of All the Talents was president of the Board of Trade.

**Auden, W. H.** (1907–73). Poet, whose name is often given to the literary generation of the 1930s when, it has been said, 'the red flag was intertwined with the old school tie'. Marx, Freud, and *Eliot all influenced *Poems*

(1930). Yet he was as ready to write 'in praise of limestone', the Icelandic sagas, or simple human love. Intellectually restless, a brilliant chronicler of the times, in 'Spain' (1937) he wrote one of the definitive poems of a 'low, dishonest decade'. On the eve of war he emigrated. He returned to Oxford in 1955 as professor of poetry.

**Audley, Thomas, 1st Baron Audley of Walden** (1488–1544). Audley was a lawyer from Essex, who became town clerk of Colchester in 1514 and was elected to Parliament for the borough in 1523. He was a member of *Wolsey's household but avoided going down with his master. He succeeded *More as Speaker. On More's resignation as chancellor in 1532, Audley was appointed keeper of the great seal and in 1533 lord chancellor. In this capacity he presided over the trials of More, *Fisher, and the accomplices of *Anne Boleyn. In 1538 he was given a barony and he acquired the estates of the abbey of Walden at the *dissolution of the monasteries.

**Aughrim, battle of,** 1691. The battle of the *Boyne in July 1690 did not end the conflict in Ireland. The Jacobites held Limerick and Galway. The task of subduing them was left to William's Dutch commander, Ginkel, who took Athlone on 30 June 1691. The Jacobites, under the command of Saint-Ruth, a French nobleman, dug in near Aughrim, defended by bogs, streams, and stone walls. On 12 July Ginkel, with just over 20,000 men, launched his attack against the same number. Heavy fighting continued all day but after Saint-Ruth had been killed the Jacobites broke. Galway surrendered later in July, Limerick in October.

**Augustine, St** (d. *c*.604). Augustine was chosen by Gregory the Great to lead an evangelistic mission to the Anglo-Saxons. In 597 they landed on Thanet in Kent, where *Æthelbert was the most powerful king south of the Humber, and his Frankish wife *Bertha was a Christian. Impressed by their sincerity, Æthelbert supplied them with food, a house in Canterbury, use of an old Roman church, and permission to preach. *Bede records that Æthelbert himself was ultimately baptized. Augustine returned to Arles, in Gaul, for episcopal consecration, after which he is said to have converted

thousands. He established his see in *Canterbury, where he built his church, and outside the walls founded the monastery of SS Peter and Paul (St Augustine's).

Augustine is perhaps overshadowed by Gregory, who conceived and directed the mission. Yet Gregory's letters reveal a diligent servant who faced enormous difficulties in securing a new church based on orthodox Roman lines. Augustine established Christianity, and introduced to an illiterate Germanic society the influence of Mediterranean civilization, through Latin learning and classical architecture. With Æthelbert's support, he consecrated two bishops, establishing sees at *Rochester in Kent and in East Saxon *London. To secure continuity, he consecrated his successor, *Laurentius, before he died.

**Augustinian canons** ('Regular' or 'Black' canons) had their origin in the mid-11th-cent. ecclesiastical reform movement. Earlier communities of clerics (or 'canons') staffing cathedrals and large churches and organized in a quasi-monastic rule had long existed. Reformed canons, particularly in southern France, Italy, and Germany, increasingly adopted a rule based on that drawn up by St Augustine of Hippo (354–430). Many Augustinian priories were sited in towns, where their canons fulfilled a wide range of roles, serving in parish churches and cathedrals, running hospitals (such as St Bartholomew's, London), and functioning as teachers. In England, where the first truly Augustinian priory was founded at Colchester *c*.1100, they tended to be more contemplative, often emerging from communities of hermits.

**Augustinian (Austin) friars** were founded by Pope Alexander IV in 1256 from a number of small hermit communities in Italy. They were given the rule of St Augustine of Hippo (*see* AUGUSTINIAN CANONS) which the *Dominicans, whose constitution they largely followed, also observed. In England, where their first community was founded at Clare, by the *dissolution they were found in nearly 40 places, usually substantial towns or ports, such as Grimsby, Hull, and King's Lynn, as well as Oxford and Cambridge.

**Auld Alliance** *See* FRANCO-SCOTTISH ALLIANCE.

**Auldearn, battle of,** 1645. *Montrose was unable to follow up his great victory at *Inverlochy in February 1645 when many of his followers returned home. This time a covenanting army under Sir John Hurry tried to surprise Montrose on 9 May at Auldearn, east of Nairn. The issue was decided by a spirited cavalry counter-attack by the Gordons and Hurry fled to Inverness.

**Aulus Plautius** commanded the Roman invasion of Britain in AD 43. Consul in 29, he had probably governed Pannonia on the middle Danube; experience together with political and family influence made him a suitable choice for *Claudius' British expedition. The invasion was successfully mounted with four legions and an equivalent number (*c.*20,000) of auxiliary troops. The major settlement at Camulodunum (*Colchester) surrendered in the presence of the emperor. By the time Plautius left Britain in 47, the greater part of the island south-east of the Humber–Severn line was under Roman control.

**Auray, battle of,** 1364. Sir John Chandos, who had fought at *Crécy and *Poitiers, was engaged in 1364 in supporting the claims of John de Montfort to the duchy of Brittany against those of Charles de Blois. On 27 September, while besieging Auray, he was attacked by Bertrand du Guesclin. The French were defeated, Blois killed, and du Guesclin captured.

**Austen, Jane** (1775–1817). Country parson's daughter who became one of England's best-loved novelists. As she says in *Emma* (1816), 'one half of the world cannot understand the pleasures of the other', and for some, minute attention to nuances of bygone manners makes her simple romances parochial. For others, her awareness of the realities of money and class and their bearing on human happiness is compelling. Though she rejected suggestions to try her hand at historical subjects, confident that '3 or 4 families in a Country Village is the very thing to work on', it is misleading to think of her as a miniaturist. The Napoleonic wars occupy her only in letters from her sailor brothers, but her penetration and seriousness reflect an admiration for Dr *Johnson. He could not have matched the sprightly ironic comedy of *Pride and Prejudice* (1813) but would have appreciated the moral dilemmas of *Mansfield Park* (1814). Three years later, still unmarried, she was dead, leaving her sister Cassandra to supervise publication of *Northanger Abbey* and *Persuasion* (1818).

**Austin, Herbert** (1866–1941). Motor car manufacturer. Austin served his engineering apprenticeship at Langlands Foundry, Melbourne. He became manager of the Wolseley Sheep Shearing Company and in 1893 returned to England to work for the company in Birmingham. He was one of the first British engineers to envisage the possibilities of the petrol-driven car and built his first three-wheeled Wolseley car in 1895. In 1905 he went into business for himself as the Austin Motor Company Ltd. at Longbridge, Birmingham. The following year he produced 120 cars with a work-force of 270. The Austin Seven (Baby Austin), launched in 1922, brought motoring within the means of the masses.

**Australia, Commonwealth of** A federation of six states, *New South Wales (founded 1788), Western Australia (1829), Tasmania (formerly Van Diemen's Land, 1825), South Australia (1834), Victoria (1851), and Queensland (1859), and the self-governing Northern Territory (1863), together with Australian Capital Territory (1911), Norfolk (1856), Heard and McDonald (1947), Cocos (1955), Christmas (1958), and Coral Sea (1969) Islands, and the Australian Antarctic Territory (1933).

Australia is the smallest, most arid, and least populated of the world's continents. Its mainland, together with Tasmania, is 35 times the size of Great Britain and had an estimated population of 21 million in 2001. Australia took its name from the mythical Southern Continent first postulated by classical geographers, *Terra Australis Incognita*. First sighted by Portuguese and Spanish navigators during the late 15th cent., it became known through 17th- and 18th-cent. Dutch, British, and later French voyages.

Australia's Aboriginal people entered the country more than 40,000 years ago across a land-bridge created during a low sea-level period. They greatly modified the Australian environment by the extensive use of fire and hunting to extinction of its mega-fauna, and developed a distinctive way of life. Completely isolated from the rest of the world, Aborigines developed a strong attachment to and intimate knowledge of the land. Estimates put their population at the time of the coming of the British at 500,000.

The modern era began with the arrival on 26 January 1788 of the 1st Fleet of eleven vessels under the command of Captain Arthur Phillip RN, who took formal possession of land already named New South Wales and claimed on Britain's behalf in 1770 by Captain James *Cook. The British began to occupy New Holland in 1827, and, with the formal possession and change of name to Western Australia and the founding of the Swan River Colony under Captain Stirling RN in 1829, laid claim to the whole continent.

On arrival at *Botany Bay on 18 January 1788, Captain Phillip, finding it less fertile than he had anticipated, sailed a few miles into Port Jackson (now Sydney Harbour), where, on 26 January, he commenced landing 736 convicts (including 188 women). He was followed by the commercially organized 2nd and 3rd Fleets, which embarked a further 3,100 convicts. The transportation of convicts to New South Wales ceased in 1840, to Van Diemen's Land in 1853, and to Norfolk Island in 1855. Between 1850 and 1868, 10,000 convicts were shipped as a subsidy to poverty-stricken Western Australia, making a grand total of 160,000 convicts transported before 1868. The Aborigines offered no effective resistance to the British.

The early days of New South Wales were under near famine conditions and the colony was not self-sufficient in wheat until 1797. However, the crossing of the Blue Mountains behind Sydney in 1813 revealed a belt of millions of acres of rich savannah grasslands. Here, flocks of fine wool-bearing merino sheep (first imported from the Cape Colony in 1797) spread out and by 1880 it supported over 60 million sheep. The export of wool provided the staple upon which to found a viable economy, helped end convict transportation, and created a new class of politically powerful and capitalist large-landholding squatters (graziers).

The discovery of gold in 1851 caused a dramatic leap in immigration and the combined population of New South Wales and Victoria rose from 267,000 in 1850 to 886,000 in 1860; 538,000 were located in the newly proclaimed colony of Victoria. Melbourne, its capital, rapidly became Australia's financial and industrial centre. A miners' revolt at Eureka Stockade near Ballarat in 1854 eventually forced the introduction of democratic reforms far in advance of those in England. These included the adoption of secret ballot (1856), adult male franchise (1857), paid parliamentarians (1870), and eventually votes for women (1908).

The gold rushes and the rise of agriculture encouraged commerce, finance, trade, and industry in Sydney and Melbourne, the latter growing to more than half a million by 1900. The spread of wage labour in mines, factories, ports, and shearing sheds saw the rise of trade unionism during the 1870s. The defeat of the great strikes of 1888–95 led to the setting-up of union-backed Labour parties. The first, but short-lived, minority Labour governments took office in Queensland in 1899, and federally in 1904.

Following a series of meetings during the 1890s, six colonies agreed by referendum to become a federation. This was inaugurated on 1 January 1901 as the Commonwealth of Australia. One of the Commonwealth government's first acts was to introduce the so-called 'White Australia policy' to protect the Australian working man's standard of living. The outbreak of the First World War in 1914 severely tested the new federation. An Australian Imperial Force (AIF) comprising 322,000 troops was sent overseas to fight alongside the allies. The period between the First and Second World Wars was at first prosperous with assisted British immigration until development was stopped by the Great Depression of the 1930s. At times, unemployment exceeded 25 per cent of the workforce. Australia's support for British empire preference helped maintain her exports to Britain. With the fall of Singapore in 1942, the withdrawal of the British to India, and the Japanese invasion of Papua New Guinea, the Second World War came to the shores of Australia with the bombing of Darwin. Wartime Labour Prime Minister John Curtin turned to America for military help. Australian forces played an important part in the Pacific War and were the first to defeat the Japanese on land in the battle for New Guinea (Kokoda).

Post-war mass European immigration, assisted by the Labour government, was made possible by an assured British market, a high Australian tariff wall, a 1960s boom in mining, especially for bauxite and iron ore, and the discovery of new reserves of petroleum, natural gas, and coal; 500,000 European immigrants, one-third from the British Isles, came to Australia 1945–9. Immigration peaked at 170,000 in 1952. The balance shifted toward Asian migration after the war in Vietnam in 1972, whence Australia had accepted more than 100,000 refugees. Australia's population, which had passed the million mark by 1860 and the 5 million mark by 1920, was by 1998 approximately 19 million.

Australia looks west to Europe, east to the USA, and north to her burgeoning Asian neighbours. Although now officially multicultural, Australia has still not resolved her relation with her own indigenous people, the Aborigines. The granting of native title by federal law in 1993 will in the long run markedly change the position of Aborigines, but unlike Australia's European and Asian immigrants, a high proportion of the nearly 300,000 Aboriginal people are still both culturally and geographically 'fringe dwellers'.

With the rise of the new industrializing countries of east Asia, Australia's relative industrial and economic strength has declined. Furthermore, since Australia no longer has preferential access to European markets, she is now in direct competition with other primary raw material producers. Though retaining all the political, organizational, and governmental structures inherited from Britain, Australia is no longer the Anglo-Celtic culture that she was before 1945 and republican sentiments have grown as the composition of the population has changed.

**Austrian Succession, War of the** Most of western Europe was plunged into war through Frederick the Great's invasion of Austrian Silesia in December 1740, though Britain was already fighting the War of *Jenkins's Ear with Spain. The eight years of continental and colonial warfare that followed killed half a million people. Spain and France were closely allied, with periodic links to Prussia. Britain, Piedmont-Sardinia, the United Provinces, and Austria were ranged against them. British, Austrian, and Dutch troops fought against the French in the Low Countries. George II himself fought at *Dettingen (1743), but before the peace of *Aix-la-Chapelle in 1748, the French army had thrust deep into Dutch territory. In central Europe, British money helped Maria Theresa in her fight against the onslaughts of France and Prussia. At sea Britain was triumphant, the French navy having been destroyed by late 1747, largely due to the skill of *Anson and *Hawke. In India the French had considerable success, but in America the British predominated, capturing Louisbourg in June 1745.

At home, the war helped to end the career of *Walpole and assisted the rise of *Carteret. Apart from the Jacobite rising of 1745–6, the conflict seemed remote to the British people and was not popular in the manner of the *Seven Years War.

**Authorized Version** *See* BIBLE.

**Avon** was a county formed under the Local Government Act of 1972. It was based upon Bristol, Bath, and Weston-super-Mare, but incorporated a slice of Gloucestershire, and a part of north Somerset. The name was taken from the river Avon, which runs through Bath and Bristol. The county town was Bristol. Avon was abolished in 1996.

**Avranches, compromise of** On 21 May 1172, at Avranches cathedral (Normandy), Henry II was publicly absolved from complicity in the murder of Archbishop Thomas *Becket on condition that he provide 200 knights to serve in the Holy Land for one year, take the cross himself and fight either in the Holy Land or against the Moors in Spain, restore all properties seized from the church of Canterbury, and allow appeals from the English church to Rome.

**Babbage, Charles** (1792–1871). Babbage made the first (clockwork) computers. He studied mathematics at Peterhouse, Cambridge, and in 1828 was elected to the Lucasian chair of mathematics. He hoped to eliminate errors in mathematical tables by calculating them mechanically, and in 1834 oversaw the construction of his difference engine. Before it was finished, he saw how much more powerful it would be as an analytical engine, but the government cut off finance: the principles were later realized electronically.

**Babington plot,** 1586. Anthony Babington (1561–86), a Derbyshire gentleman and a catholic page in Mary Stuart's service in England, was contacted by John Ballard, a catholic priest. The plan was to kill Elizabeth and secure the freedom of Mary. Babington's failure was engineered by Sir Francis *Walsingham, who recruited a catholic, Gilbert Gifford, as an agent. Babington was executed in September 1586 and the plot sealed the fate of Mary by convincing Elizabeth that she was incorrigible.

**Bacon, Francis, 1st Baron Verulam, 1st Viscount St Albans** (1561–1626). Lawyer, philosopher, and essayist. The son of a prominent lawyer, Bacon went to Trinity College, Cambridge, and then to the Inns of Court. In 1584 he became an MP. On the accession of James I, Bacon achieved rapid promotion, prosecuting *Ralegh, raised to the peerage, and ending up as lord chancellor. But in 1621 he was convicted of taking bribes, and though soon pardoned, he had to give up public life.

His witty and pithy *Essays* were first published in 1597, and are splendid examples of English prose; in 1605 he brought out his *Advancement of Learning*. In this first exercise in writing about science, he was highly critical of the humanistic education he had

received at Cambridge. In 1620 he published his *Novum organum*, presenting his philosophy of science in the form of aphorisms. In retirement, he collected and published information of a miscellaneous kind, in what was to be the *Great Instauration*. He died a martyr to science, from a chill caught trying to preserve a chicken by stuffing it with snow. After his death, the fragmentary *New Atlantis* was published in 1627: with its vision of an island governed by an Academy of Sciences. This is the most accessible and exciting of his writings on science. Bacon's science was organized common sense; and his vision of utility was gripping.

**Bacon, Sir Nicholas** (1510–79). Statesman. Nicholas Bacon, a great work-horse of Elizabeth's government, owed his rise in part to college friendship. He was at Corpus Christi College, Cambridge, with Matthew *Parker, afterwards archbishop of Canterbury. Later, he formed a friendship with William Cecil (*Burghley), whose wife's sister he married in 1553. He read law at Gray's Inn and was employed on the *dissolution of the monasteries, managing to acquire estates for himself. He served as MP for Westmorland (1542) and for Dartmouth (1545). Though a protestant, he survived Mary's reign without disaster. Bacon's boat came in, with that of his two friends, at Elizabeth's accession. Cecil was reappointed secretary of state in November 1558, Bacon became keeper of the great seal in December 1558, and Parker archbishop of Canterbury in 1559. Fat and cheerful, he was also efficient and honest. His son Francis *Bacon was created Viscount St Albans in 1621.

**Bacon, Roger** (c.1214–92). Philosopher. A Franciscan friar, Bacon was born in Somerset and probably studied at Oxford before teaching in Paris. From c.1250 to 1257 he was again in Oxford but his Franciscan superiors returned him to Paris, where he was under a cloud. In 1265 Pope Clement IV asked him to prepare a treatise on the knowledge of the day. This high patronage did not last, for Clement died in 1268, and Bacon was soon in trouble again. His *Opus majus*, dating from the 1260s, has been hailed as a foundation work in modern science. Bacon laid stress on useful knowledge, on ascertaining facts, and on the need for experimentation. His work in alchemy gained him a popular reputation as a magician.

**Baden-Powell, Robert** (1857–1941). Founder of the *Boy Scouts. Baden-Powell joined the army in 1876 and specialized in reconnaissance. In 1897 he was appointed to command the 5th Dragoon Guards stationed in India. He explained his methods in *Aids to Scouting* (1899). During the Boer War he took part in the defence of *Mafeking, which held out for 217 days against overwhelming forces. He was made inspector-general of the cavalry in 1903. He retired from the army in 1910 to devote his energies to the Boy Scout movement he had founded several years earlier.

**badminton** took its name from the Gloucestershire seat of the dukes of Beaufort, where it is believed to have evolved in the 1870s from the older game of shuttlecock. It was much played in the Indian army and rules were drawn up in Poona. The convenience of a vigorous and sociable undercover game led to its rapid spread, particularly in Scandinavia and the Far East.

**Baffin, William** (d. 1622). Explorer. Baffin made a number of voyages in the 1610s looking for the North-West Passage. He was killed in India in a skirmish with the Portuguese. In 1821 the large island he had discovered to the north of Hudson Bay was named after him.

**Bagehot, Walter** (1826–77). Journalist. From a banking family in Langport (Som.), his father a unitarian, Bagehot attended University College London and began to study law. But he moved into banking, wrote copiously, and from 1860 edited his father-in-law James Wilson's paper *The Economist*. Though capable of brilliant writing and subtle insights, much of Bagehot's work is marred by a habitual superciliousness towards the 'stupid' masses and his inability

to resist a *bon mot*. His best-known work, *The English Constitution*, which came out in the 1860s, was enormously successful and seriously misleading. Written at the time of Victoria's seclusion after Albert's death, it is understandable that Bagehot should have exaggerated the weakness of the monarchy: 'the queen must sign her own death warrant if the two Houses unanimously send it up to her' is more piquant than profound.

**Baginbun, battle of,** 1170. In 1169 Richard de Clare, earl of *Pembroke, known as Strongbow, decided to seek territory in Ireland. A small advance party commanded by Raymond le Gros dug in at Baginbun Head and was attacked by a vastly superior force of Norsemen and Irish. The invaders were successful. Strongbow then joined them, took Waterford and Dublin, and declared himself king of Leinster. The first English foothold in Ireland had been obtained.

**Bahamas** These islands lie off the coast of Florida and form an independent state within the Commonwealth. The larger islands include Grand Bahama and Andros: the capital, Nassau, is situated on New Providence Island. The economy depends greatly on tourism and on the large mercantile fleet flying the Bahamian flag.

**Baird, John Logie** (1888–1946). Television inventor. Baird came from Helensburgh (Dumbartonshire) and studied electrical engineering at Glasgow University. In poor health, he moved to Hastings in 1922, where he experimented with a crude home-made transmitting apparatus. By 1925 he was able to demonstrate shadowy television in Selfridge's store and followed with a public demonstration to members of the Royal Institution. An experimental BBC television service was started in 1929 and regular broadcasts from Alexandra palace in 1936.

**Bakewell, Robert** (1725–95). Bakewell was one of the pioneers of the agricultural revolution as a result of his animal breeding activities at Dishley, near Loughborough, particularly the 'New Leicester' breed of sheep. He selected more rigorously than other landlords and was more sophisticated in the choice of animals he selected from.

**Balaclava, battle of,** 1854. On 25 October 1854 the Russian commander in the Crimea, Menshikov, attempted to lift the siege of Sebastopol by attacking with 25,000 troops at Balaclava. The 'thin red line' of 93rd Highlanders repulsed a charge by Russian cavalry. This was followed by a successful attack on the main body of the Russian horse by the numerically inferior British heavy [cavalry] brigade and by the notorious *Charge of the Light Brigade.

**Baldwin** (d. 1190). Archbishop of Canterbury. A native of Exeter, Baldwin entered the Cistercian monastery at Ford, Devon (c.1170), becoming abbot and then bishop of Worcester (1180). He was Henry II's own choice as archbishop in 1184. He took the cross (1188), preaching the crusade in Wales with 'the energy and style of Bernard of Clairvaux'. After attending Henry on his death-bed and crowning Richard I, he set out for the East. Heading the English advance guard, he arrived at the siege of *Acre (October 1190), but died soon after.

**Baldwin, Stanley** (1867–1947). Prime minister. Educated at Harrow and Cambridge, Baldwin entered the family ironmaster's business but on his father's death in 1908 succeeded him as Conservative MP for Bewdley (Worcs.). He served in the Lloyd George coalition governments from 1917 to 1922, but became increasingly alarmed at the adventurism associated with the later years of Lloyd George's premiership. Baldwin made the key speech at the Carlton Club meeting of Conservative backbenchers in 1922 that brought down Lloyd George, after which he served as chancellor of the Exchequer in the short-lived Conservative administration of the dying Andrew Bonar *Law, succeeding to the premiership in May 1923. Baldwin's industrial experience told him that free trade had had its day, and he determined on its abolition. He called a general election on the issue of protection but the Conservatives lost their overall majority, thus permitting the formation of the first Labour government.

But while Baldwin lacked Lloyd George's political cunning, he preserved in public life values of probity, charity, and conciliation. He was known to be a man of simple country pleasures who had, during the Great War,

donated one-fifth of his private fortune. Baldwin's conciliatory spirit seemed preferable to a Labour Party tinged with extremism and a Liberal Party in a state of civil war. Following the general election of 1924, which saw the Liberal Party reduced to 40 seats, the Conservatives emerged with a majority of over 200 in the Commons. Baldwin was once more prime minister.

The composition of the cabinet was not, however, conducive to the pursuit of the policy of national unity which Baldwin had preached. In order to make peace with the Conservative free traders, Baldwin gave the Exchequer to Winston *Churchill. His one inspired appointment was to put Neville *Chamberlain in charge of the Ministry of Health. Churchill's return to the gold standard (1925) had a predictable effect on employment, and the cabinet took an equally predictable line on the *General Strike the following year. Baldwin brushed aside George V's advice to pursue a military solution and appealed instead to the quietist instincts of the British public and to the moderate elements within the Labour movement. This policy paid handsome dividends, since the Trades Union Congress abandoned the miners and called off the industrial action. However, in 1927, and against his own better judgement, the cabinet pushed through the vindictive Trade Disputes Act, by which the principle of 'contracting out' of the political levy collected by trade unions was replaced by 'contracting in'. It was hoped that this provision would reduce Labour Party membership and income, which it did.

Between 1929 and 1931 Baldwin fought a bitter duel with the empire free traders, led by the press barons Lords *Beaverbrook and *Rothermere. The age of free trade was clearly drawing to a close, but Baldwin understood better than most the sensitivities this issue aroused within his party. On 17 March 1931 he made a dramatic appeal to the Conservative public to choose between him and 'the engines of propaganda for the constantly changing policies, desires, personal wishes, personal likes and personal dislikes of two men . . . What the proprietorship of these papers is aiming at is power, but power without responsibility—the prerogative of the harlot throughout the ages.'

Baldwin survived, and his leadership of the Conservative Party was never again seriously challenged. In 1931 he agreed to serve under Ramsay *MacDonald as lord president of the council, succeeding MacDonald as prime minister in 1935. Baldwin was not slow in perceiving the vital necessity of a programme of rearmament in the face of international aggression. In November 1935 he called a general election, during the course of which he protested his support for the *League of Nations. The election resulted in a resounding Conservative victory, but Baldwin's advocacy of the League was in fact a sham. Baldwin knew that the League's sanctions against Italy (which had invaded Abyssinia) would not be effective if they excluded oil; it was precisely for this reason that he supported them. When his foreign secretary, Sir Samuel *Hoare, signed an agreement with Pierre Laval, the French prime minister, proposing the cession of Abyssinian territory to Italy, Baldwin forced him to resign.

Baldwin's handling of the abdication crisis, the following year, cannot be faulted. In advising Edward VIII against a morganatic marriage to Mrs *Simpson he acted with constitutional propriety, and with the backing of the Labour leader Clement *Attlee, and of the dominion prime ministers. The smoothness of George VI's succession was due primarily to Baldwin's calm assuredness. He stayed in office long enough to attend the new king's coronation; two weeks later, aged almost 70, he resigned, accepting the customary earldom.

**Balfour, Arthur James, 1st earl of** (1848–1930). Prime minister. Essentially a mid-Victorian, Arthur Balfour seems miscast as a 20th-cent. prime minister. Naturally fitted for life in a rural vicarage or an Oxford college, Balfour did in fact produce an original work, *A Defence of Philosophic Doubt* (1879), which critics thought summed up his approach to politics admirably.

Balfour grew up on the family estate at Whittingehame in the Scottish borders; his father had been a Tory MP and his mother was a sister of Robert Cecil, the future Lord Salisbury. The young Balfour remained a solitary, intellectual figure, especially after the death in 1875 of his intended wife, May Lyttelton. He never married. Having no particular purpose in life, he decided to enter politics, and from 1874 to 1885 represented Hertford, the Cecil family's pocket borough. A poor speaker, Balfour underlined his rather detached position by involvement with Lord Randolph *Churchill's '*Fourth Party'.

However, around 1885-6 Balfour's career took off. He left the security of Hertford and contested a new, popular constituency, East Manchester, which he held until 1906. He served briefly as president of the Local Government Board (1885) and as secretary of state for Scotland (1886), but made his reputation as chief secretary for Ireland (1887-91). First he ruthlessly suppressed rural violence, earning thereby the epithet 'Bloody Balfour'. Second, he attempted to conciliate nationalist opinion by social intervention, including the sale of land to tenant farmers on easy terms, and investment in light railways and seed potatoes.

By promoting his nephew as leader of the House in 1891-2 and 1895-1902, Salisbury placed him in line for succession as prime minister in the latter year. Unhappily, Salisbury also bequeathed to Balfour accumulated problems. In particular, the financial cost of the South African War led Joseph *Chamberlain to take up the cause of tariff reform. Though Balfour cleverly manoeuvred Chamberlain into resigning from the cabinet, this only led him to launch a campaign from 1903 onwards which largely captured the party for protectionism. Balfour struggled to maintain party unity by offering a compromise. This meant adopting 'retaliation', in effect to use the threat of tariffs to force other states to reduce their barriers against British goods. However, Balfour's clever dialectics merely convinced colleagues that he did not care much about the issue. Free traders felt he had failed to support them in their constituencies, while the protectionists blamed his approach for losing the 1906 election. None the less, Balfour's government did take several important initiatives including the passage of the 1902 *Education Act, the Anglo-French *Entente of 1904, and the establishment of the Committee of Imperial Defence and the Royal Commission on the Poor Laws.

After 1906 the parliamentary party became predominantly protectionist and Balfour exercised little effective leadership. In 1909 he made no attempt to stop the Tory majority in the Lords from rejecting *Lloyd George's budget. It resulted in Balfour having to lead his party through two unsuccessful elections in 1910, and as a result 1911 saw the development of a 'Balfour Must Go' campaign. He resigned—the first in a long line of modern Tory leaders to fall victim to their own backbenchers.

Yet a remarkably long career as a respected elder statesman still awaited Balfour. From the outbreak of war in 1914 he became an unofficial adviser to the Liberal government, and, not surprisingly, *Asquith appointed him 1st lord of the Admiralty in the coalition of May 1915. Subsequently he served Lloyd George as foreign secretary (1916–19), in which capacity he produced the famous *Balfour declaration committing the government to the establishment of a national homeland in Palestine for the Jews. His last role was as lord president of the council under Lloyd George (1919–22) and under *Baldwin (1925–9).

**Balfour declaration** Partly with a view to securing the support of world Jewry for the allied war effort, *Lloyd George's government authorized Foreign Secretary A. J. *Balfour to send a letter (2 November 1917) to Lord Rothschild (lay leader of Anglo-Jewry) pledging the support of the British government for the establishment in Palestine of a 'National Home' for the Jewish people, but safeguarding the rights of Palestine's non-Jewish inhabitants. Growing Arab resentment and violence led to the abrogation of the declaration by Neville *Chamberlain's government in 1939.

**Ball, John** (d. 1381). Contemporary chroniclers saw John Ball as the evil genius behind the *Peasants' Revolt of 1381. Little is known about this man, who described himself as formerly a priest of St Mary's, York, and then of Colchester. Early in 1381 his attacks on the established church order led to his excommunication and imprisonment at Maidstone in Kent, from where the rebels released him. He was soon linked by chroniclers with *lollardy, but his preaching during the revolt, with its egalitarian message, was in a well-established tradition. After the rising, Ball was sentenced to be hanged, drawn, and quartered.

**Balliol, Edward** (c.1280–1364). Son of John *Balliol, king of Scots, and himself titular king of Scots (1332–56). He had good prospects in youth, being betrothed in 1295 to the niece of the French king, and recognized as heir to the Scottish throne as late as 1301. But the Wars of Independence marginalized the Balliols, and after his father's death in 1313 Edward lived in obscurity in Picardy.

Edward III's coup in England (1330) opened up new possibilities. There were others who had lost Scottish estates, and in 1331, Balliol returned to England and put himself at the head of a group of 'disinherited'. Landing at Kinghorn they were at first dramatically successful: after a victory at *Dupplin Moor (11 August 1332), Balliol was made king at Scone. By the end of the year, however, he had been forced to flee ignominiously to England. This provoked Edward III to intervene in person, defeating the Scots at *Halidon Hill (19 July 1333), and reimposing Balliol as king. In 1334 Balliol had to pay the price, performing homage to Edward for his kingdom, and ceding much of southern Scotland to Edward III's direct rule.

There followed five years of devastating guerrilla warfare. Though he himself took part in several expeditions, he was evidently only the agent of Edward III. In 1356, disgusted with his prospects and burdened by age, he resigned his title to Edward III in return for a pension.

**Balliol, John** (c.1250–1313), king of Scots (1292–6). The son of John Balliol of Barnard Castle, he was descended through his mother from David, earl of Huntingdon, the brother of William the Lion, king of Scots (1165–1214). The Balliol family held lands in France, in northern England, and in Galloway. These last gave John a stake in Scotland and a number of strong supporters when the crown became vacant on the death of *Margaret, the 'Maid of Norway', in 1290.

The verdict of Edward I's Parliament at Norham went to Balliol and he was duly enthroned as king of Scots on 30 November 1292. There is every reason to think that this judgment was acceptable to the majority of Scots. Edward I, however, had insisted that all the claimants acknowledged his right to be lord superior of Scotland. Balliol therefore had to perform homage to Edward before his enthronement. Edward's claims were to plague John's entire reign. He faced nine appeals to Edward from disgruntled litigants. Far more serious was Edward's demand in 1294 for military service in his French wars by John himself and all the most prominent nobles of Scotland. Edward was for the moment distracted by a serious Welsh revolt, and the Scots were able to get away with excuses. But it was clear that Edward would not let this go on indefinitely, and the Scottish nobles, distrusting King John, set up in July 1295 a council of twelve which took power out of his hands. The council allied formally with Philip IV of France in October 1295, and prepared to resist Edward by force. From this point, John lost control. In 1296 Edward I took Berwick. Scottish resistance was destroyed by Earl *Warenne at *Dunbar, and John was forced to resign his kingdom into Edward's hands in July. Balliol was brought a prisoner to London; and the rest of his career had little impact. Balliol himself in 1298 declared formally that he never wanted to have anything to do with Scotland again. In 1299 he was transferred to papal custody and in 1301 was released to his ancestral lands in Picardy.

**Ballymore Hill, battle of,** 1798. Father Murphy, leading the Wexford rebels, ambushed a small detachment of British troops on 4 June near Enniscorthy, killing their commander, Colonel Lambert Walpole. Though no more than a skirmish, it gave great encouragement to the rebels.

**Balmoral (Aberdeenshire).** The Scottish holiday home of the royal family. The present house was built in 1853–6 for Queen Victoria by the architect William Smith of Aberdeen (1817–91) as a replacement for an earlier house in Jacobethan style erected in 1834–9. 'This dear paradise', as she called it, is a white granite mansion in Scots baronial style, and embodies modifications suggested by Prince *Albert. Queen Victoria spent part of every spring and autumn at Balmoral, her love of Scotland finding public expression in her books *Leaves from the Journal of our Life in the Highlands* published in 1869, with a second part, *More Leaves*, appearing in 1883.

**Baltimore, George Calvert, 1st Lord** (c.1580–1632). Royal servant, MP, and secretary of state from 1619 to 1625, Calvert relinquished office when he openly declared his conversion to catholicism. After visiting the Chesapeake, he obtained from Charles I in 1632 proprietary rights to land carved out of Virginia. The Maryland (named after Charles I's catholic wife) charter gave the Baltimore family palatinate powers of government.

**Bamburgh castle** in Northumberland is sited on an outcrop of basalt rock, overlooking the North Sea. A citadel of the Anglo-Saxon kings of *Bernicia, it was close to their palace at *Yeavering and the royal monastery of *Lindisfarne. Later the site became a centre of power of the earls of Northumbria. It was allowed to fall into decay after being severely damaged in the siege of 1464, when held by the Lancastrians against Edward IV. *Warwick the Kingmaker pounded it with heavy guns, despite the king's wish that it be taken whole. Its present condition is due to modern restorations, especially by Lord *Armstrong.

**Bamford, Samuel** (1788–1872). Lancashire radical and poet. Brought up a Wesleyan in Middleton near Manchester, he worked as a warehouse boy, farm labourer, on coal ships plying between Tyneside and London, and as a bookseller before setting up as a hand-loom weaver. Under the influence of William *Cobbett he became a radical, founding the Middleton Hampden Club in 1816 and being arrested for treason for advocating parliamentary reform in 1817. Acquitted, he was present at '*Peterloo' on 16 August 1819 and was sentenced to a year in Lincoln gaol for treason. His autobiography was written in 1841–3 to justify his turbulent past and warn *chartists against the use of violence.

**Banbury, battle of** See EDGECOTE.

**Bancroft, Richard** (1544–1610). Archbishop of Canterbury. Born in Lancashire and educated at Christ's College, Cambridge, Bancroft was successively canon of Westminster (1587), chaplain to Archbishop *Whitgift (1592), bishop of London (1597), and archbishop (1604). From 1597 he was virtually acting primate during Whitgift's illness and attended Elizabeth at her death. A powerful advocate of episcopacy, his profound animosity towards presbyterianism was evident at the *Hampton Court conference (1604).

**Banda, Hastings Kamuzo** (*c.*1902–97). Malawian nationalist statesman. Banda trained as a doctor in the USA and in Scotland and practised medicine in England (1945–53) and in Ghana (1953–8). He protested against the creation of the Central African Federation in 1953, but returned home to lead the campaign against federation as president of the Nyasaland African Congress in 1958. In 1959 the colonial government declared a state of emergency and Banda was imprisoned. Released a year later, he became successively minister of natural resources and local government in 1961 and prime minister in 1963. In the latter year, the Federation was dissolved, Banda retaining his office when Nyasaland became independent and was renamed *Malawi in 1964. Malawi became a republic in 1966 with Banda as president, an office he assumed for life in 1971.

**Bangladesh** proclaimed itself a sovereign state on 25 March 1971 although it was not until 15 December that *Pakistan conceded this status. Previously, the country had been known as East Pakistan, united with West Pakistan in the state created at the time of India's partition in 1947. East Bengal's place in the new Pakistan was never comfortable. Power was narrowly concentrated in the landed-military élites of the West. In the 1960s, a movement developed around the Awami League demanding, at least, provincial autonomy. It was repressed but reasserted itself strongly in 1970 when President Yahya was obliged by US pressure to hold Pakistan's first general elections. The Awami League won 160 of the 162 East Pakistan constituencies. West Pakistan's military and political leaders struck back, arresting the president of the Awami League and unleashing tanks on Dakha. Brutalizing violence drove 10 million refugees into neighbouring India, whose army then intervened. On 15 December 1971, West Pakistan forces surrendered and the 'liberation' of Bangladesh was confirmed.

**Bangor, diocese of** The foundation of the church at Bangor is ascribed to Deiniol in the 6th cent., his sphere of influence as a bishop extending throughout the principality of *Gwynedd in north-west Wales. Work on the cathedral began in the 12th cent. under Bishop David (1120–39). The diocese includes the island of Anglesey, the holy island of Bardsey, burial place of many of the Welsh saints, and the mountainous countryside of Snowdonia. Worship in many of the churches is conducted in the Welsh language.

**Bangorian controversy** Loosed by Benjamin *Hoadly, appointed to the bishopric of Bangor in 1715. The following year he launched an attack on the *non-jurors. In 1717 he preached a sermon, in which he adopted an extreme position—that Christ had not vested authority in any secular persons, that private judgement was sacrosanct, and that sincerity of belief was the ultimate test. Hoadly appeared to his opponents to open the floodgates to religious anarchy. The revival of religious controversy was extremely unwelcome to Whig ministers and when the matter was raised in the lower house of *convocation, that body was hastily prorogued, not to meet again until 1852.

**Bank Charter Act,** 1844. The culmination of government efforts to create an effective legal framework to achieve a stable currency, the Act defined the roles of the Bank of England. One department had the exclusive duty of issuing notes having a minimum value of £5 as legal tender in England and Wales. The other department undertook banking business, with powers which included fixing the minimum cost (interest) of borrowing money.

**Bank Holiday Act,** 1871. Introduced by Sir John Lubbock, this Act compelled the clearing banks to close on certain days, thus making them public holidays. In England and Wales Easter Monday, Whit Monday, the first Monday in August, and Boxing Day became public holidays. In Scotland New Year's Day, the first Monday in May and August, and Christmas Day were declared holidays.

**banking** A system of trading in money which involved safeguarding deposits and making funds available for borrowers, banking developed in the Middle Ages in response to the growing need for credit in commerce. The lending functions of banks were undertaken in England by money-lenders. Until their expulsion by Edward I in

1291, the most important money-lenders were Jews. They were replaced by Italian merchants who had papal dispensations to lend money at interest. In the 13th cent. credit was essential to finance commerce and major projects. The most important was the wool trade but other examples included large buildings such as Edward's castles in north Wales. When Italians had their activities in England curtailed in the early 14th cent., they were replaced by English merchants and goldsmiths, whose rates of interest were sufficiently low to avoid the usury laws.

Monarchs had borrowed from merchants and landowners for centuries. By the late 17th cent., the growth of parliamentary power over government expenditures required more regulation. The *Bank of England, founded in 1694, gave the government and other users of credit access to English funds. Similar developments occurred in Scotland and Ireland. These banks remained without serious competition until the later 18th cent., when expanding commercial activities gave scope to merchants, brewers, and landowners to establish banks based on their own cash reserves. Errors of judgement sometimes occurred and 'runs on the bank' took place when depositors, fearing for the security of their money, demanded its return.

Fluctuations in the value of money because of the return to a gold-based currency after the end of the Napoleonic wars (1815) precipitated a series of crises. To stabilize the currency the government eventually introduced the 1844 *Bank Charter Act, which gave the Bank of England the functions of supervising the note issue and of monitoring the activities of the banking system. Regulatory powers were put in place in 1845 to control banking in Scotland and Ireland.

In the 19th cent., overseas trade and the expanding British empire reinforced the place of London as a centre of merchant banking. The skills of these specialist bankers attracted business from foreign firms and governments seeking loans. These arrangements made possible the rapid development of railways, heavy engineering, mines, and large commercial developments. Many of these merchant banks survive, including Rothschilds, Lazard Brothers, Kleinwort Benson, and Schroders. Internal trade was funded mainly by a larger number of

local banks which, after the middle of the 19th cent., became consolidated into a much smaller number of banks. Numbers continued to diminish so that by 1980 banking was dominated by four companies: Barclays, Lloyds, Midland, and National Westminster.

Banking has been characterized, largely because of technological innovation, by an increasingly sophisticated provision of banking services and an expansion of consumer credit. The business of safeguarding and lending money is often arranged through machine-readable cards and continuous access by telephone.

One of the most severe crises in banking took place in 2007 when, after a number of bad mortgage debts in America, Northern Rock, based in Newcastle, ran into severe difficulties. Though given respite by a large government-backed loan, Northern Rock's predicament led to accusations that many bankers had pursued irresponsible and damaging lending policies.

**Banks, Sir Joseph** (1743–1820). Explorer, and for over 40 years president of the *Royal Society. Educated at Harrow, Eton, and Christ Church, Oxford, Banks developed an extra-curricular interest in botany. Graduating in 1763, instead of going on a grand tour, he sailed to Newfoundland and Labrador on HMS *Niger*. Inheriting great wealth in land in 1764, he resolved to join Captain *Cook's voyage to observe Venus from Tahiti and then to search for the unknown southern continent (1768–71). Returning a hero, he was elected president of the Royal Society in 1778, holding the office to his death. Putting down what he saw as rival institutions, but promoting the *Royal Institution, *Kew Gardens, and the colonization of Australia, he became the formidable autocrat of science in Regency Britain.

**Banks of England, Ireland, and Scotland** Founded in 1694, the Bank of England was a private company, the first to offer services in England. By the 19th cent. it had become the central bank and currency manager for the state. In 1946 it was taken into public ownership.

The Bank of Ireland was created by legislative charter of the Irish Parliament in 1783. Although it dominated banking in Ireland during its first half-century, its position was never that of a central bank. It continues to function as a commercial bank.

The Scottish Parliament in 1695 licensed a partnership to establish the Bank of Scotland with the intention of providing coherence for the finances in Scotland. After the Act of *Union in 1707 the Scottish financial system was linked to that of England although the Bank of Scotland together with other Scottish banks retains the right to issue its own bank-notes.

**Bannockburn, battle of,** 1314. Early in 1314 Edward II assembled a large army to restore his crumbling authority in Scotland and to relieve Stirling castle, besieged by supporters of Robert I Bruce. The English thought it unlikely that the Scots would offer a pitched battle. But Bruce massed his spearmen, and dug pits to protect them from the cavalry. On 24 June, the Scots gained the upper hand in heavy fighting. The Scottish victory was decisive and reaffirmed the independence of the country.

**Banqueting House** (Whitehall). The Banqueting House is one of the finest rooms in the country. Built by Inigo *Jones for James I, between 1619 and 1622, it was one of the few buildings to survive the fire at Whitehall palace in 1698. The ceiling was finished in 1634 by Rubens and is largely devoted to themes illustrating the wisdom and virtue of James I: its baroque exuberance is in strange contrast with the restraint of the hall. From this building Charles I stepped through a window to the scaffold in 1649. Cromwell declined the crown there in 1657 and William and Mary accepted it there in 1689.

**baptists** formed one of the main protestant dissenting groups, holding that baptism should be undertaken by adults who could understand the ceremony, and that it should involve total immersion in water. These views may have been inherited from the 16th-cent. *anabaptists, but baptists managed to shed the odium which had attached to the earlier group. The first baptist community was established in London in 1612 and the movement spread rapidly. The writings of John *Bunyan in the Restoration period gained for baptists widespread respect. Baptists did little more than maintain their num-

bers in early Hanoverian England but in the 19th cent. expanded greatly and by 1851 had more than 2,700 congregations in England and Wales.

**Barbados** An island in the eastern Caribbean some 200 miles north-east of Trinidad. Extending 21 miles by 14, it is a little larger than the Isle of Wight. It was uninhabited in 1627 when settled by the English, who began growing sugar cane in the 1630s. The capital is Bridgetown and tourism is augmented by light industry.

**Barebone's Parliament** When Cromwell expelled the *Rump on 20 April 1653, he had no plans for an alternative government. After deliberation, he decided to vest the supreme authority in a nominated assembly. He and his officers chose 144 members to represent all the English counties, and also Ireland, Scotland, and Wales. The assembly met on 4 July and soon voted to call itself a Parliament; it gets its familiar sobriquet from Praise-God Barebone, leather-seller, lay preacher, and MP for London. Barebone was not a typical member, however, for most of the House were gentlemen, and moderate men outnumbered religious and political radicals. But the latter strove for extreme changes in religion and the law, until the moderate majority, to Cromwell's relief, staged a walk-out on 12 December and resigned their authority back into his hands.

**Barham, Charles Middleton, 1st Lord** (1726–1813). Middleton was a cousin of Henry *Dundas, the intimate of Pitt the Younger, treasurer of the navy and secretary at war. Hence Middleton had access to the centre of government almost from the time he became comptroller of the navy in 1778. His active naval career had been more profitable than distinguished, but he found his métier in the comptrollership. Appointed to the Admiralty Board in 1794 Middleton resigned in 1795; but ten years later his enduring reputation brought him to the 1st lordship in succession to Dundas. Middleton was created Lord Barham. His outstanding administrative record was crowned by a foresight which ensured the ship-strength available to *Nelson at *Trafalgar.

**Baring, Evelyn, 1st earl of Cromer** (1841–1917). Proconsul. Baring spent the years 1858–72 in the Royal Artillery and then went to India as private secretary to his cousin, Lord *Northbrook, the viceroy. In 1877 he began his life's work when he was sent as commissioner to Egypt to attempt the enormous task of placing its finances on a firm footing. For 30 years he was the effective power in the land, comptroller-general from 1879 to 1880, consul-general 1883–1907. Restoration of Egyptian solvency meant withdrawal from the Sudan and Baring acquiesced, with misgivings, in the choice of *Gordon to carry out the task, watching helplessly when Gordon was trapped at Khartoum. Not until the 1890s was *Kitchener able to restore Egyptian control over the Sudan. Baring, meanwhile, accumulated honours—a barony in 1892, viscountcy in 1899, and earldom in 1901.

**Barnardo, Thomas John** (1845–1905). Philanthropist. In 1866 he entered the London Hospital as a missionary medical student and visited slums where he was saddened by the number of homeless children. He abandoned his plans to go to China as a missionary in order to help them. On 15 July 1867 he founded the East End Juvenile Mission for the care of sick and destitute children. Under the patronage of Lord *Shaftesbury he opened a boy's home, later followed by a series of similar houses known as 'Dr Barnardo's Homes'. His work expanded both in Britain and in Canada and before his death he had rescued 59,384 children and assisted as many as 500,000.

**Barnet, battle of,** 1471. *Warwick, Edward IV's great ally at *Towton, turned against him in 1470 and drove him out of the kingdom. Returning in March 1471, Edward landed near Hull. Warwick, in possession of London, marched out to confront him. They met at Barnet, 14 miles north, on 14 April. Warwick's men won initial success, but confusion and mistaken identity led to cries of treason and a fatal collapse of morale. Warwick himself was cut down trying to reach his horse. Three weeks later, Edward secured his position beyond doubt with his crushing victory over Queen *Margaret at *Tewkesbury.

**baronets** are hereditary knights. The order was instituted by James I in 1611 as a means of raising money for the army in Ulster. Baronets remained commoners and were therefore eligible for membership of the House of Commons. Pledges to limit the number granted were soon broken.

**barons** The name was first used loosely to mean any great landowners or lords and then acquired a precise meaning as the lowest of the five ranks in the peerage. The word came into use after the Conquest to describe the more important tenants-in-chief. In time a class of greater barons emerged who were summoned specifically to the host or the king's council. The emergence of Parliament in the 13th cent. meant that barons were summoned by writ to the House of Lords and then sought to make the privilege hereditary. But from 1385, the establishment of superior titles of duke, marquis, and viscount pushed barons into the lowest rank of the nobility.

**Barrosa, battle of,** 1811. Since 1810 Cadiz had been besieged by the French under General Victor. In January 1811 an Anglo-Spanish force attempted to lift the blockade by landing 50 miles to the south at Tafira. On 5 March Victor, hiding in Chiclana Forest, attacked the allied flank and captured Barrosa ridge. General Graham, commanding the British troops, in a bold but bloody counter-attack managed to repulse the French.

**Barrow, Henry** (c.1550–93). An early puritan separatist, Barrow was born in Norfolk, educated at Clare Hall, Cambridge, and became a member of Gray's Inn. While living a dissolute life, he had a conversion experience (c.1580) and dedicated himself to theology, especially *Brownist ideas. Arrested in 1586, he was examined personally by *Whitgift and *Burghley. From prison he smuggled his illicit writings to the Netherlands. Eventually he and John Greenwood were tried for writing 'with malicious intent' and hanged.

**Barry, Sir Charles** (1795–1860). Victorian architect. After travel in 1817–20 through France, Italy, Greece, Turkey, Egypt, and Syria, he returned to London and built several churches in a Gothic idiom. Turning to the Greek revival, he designed first the Royal Institution of Fine Arts (1824–35) and then the Athenaeum (1837–9), both in Manchester. By this time he was using Italian *palazzi* as models for the Travellers' (1830–2) and Reform Clubs (1838–41) in Pall Mall. His *magnum opus*, the \*Houses of Parliament, won in competition in 1836, was in the required 'Gothic or Elizabethan' style, but its construction took its toll on Barry's health and hastened his death in 1860.

**Barton, Elizabeth** (*c.*1506–34). Prophetess. Known as the Maid of Kent, Elizabeth Barton, a domestic servant, developed religious mania, with trances and visions. But when she took up the cause of \*Catherine of Aragon and declared that Henry VIII would die if he divorced her, the Maid moved into deep waters. For a time she was protected by \*Warham, \*More, and \*Fisher, but when \*Cranmer succeeded Warham as archbishop he interrogated Barton and obtained a confession that her revelations were feigned. She was executed at Tyburn in April 1534.

**Basilikon doron** (1598), a manual on the practice of kingship, was written by James I and VI for his eldest son, Prince \*Henry. Though less polemical in tone than *The Trew Law of Free Monarchies*, composed about the same time, it made apparent James's exalted view of kingly power.

**bastard feudalism** The term bastard feudalism, seemingly invented in 1885, has been adopted as a label to distinguish a social structure different from its predecessor in the post-Conquest period. The essence of the feudal system introduced by William I was that tenants of manors had obligations to their lords. With bastard feudalism the bond between a man and his lord was not tenurial but financial, not hereditary but personal; it was often made by a written contract, by which a retainer undertook to attend his lord whenever required, suitably armed and equipped. The proliferation of this pattern of relationships coincided with the \*Hundred Years War. Edward III and his successors raised their armies by indentures with lords and other captains who undertook to provide certain numbers of mounted men and archers. All were to be paid wages of war.

The political hazards of this dependency could be reduced by good kingship. Public order was assisted if lords kept their retainers in order. It was otherwise when lords competed for regional dominance, as did the dukes of Norfolk and Suffolk, and the Ne-

villes and Percies, in a period of weak monarchy. In 1384 the parliamentary Commons complained that wrongdoers expected to escape retribution through the patronage of the lords whose liveries of cloth or badges they wore. Eventually bastard feudalism was curbed, though not abolished, by Henry VII's conciliar jurisdiction and his statute of 1504, which prohibited retaining without royal licence.

**Bastwick, John** (1593–1654). Bastwick was an indefatigable opponent of \*Laud and the bishops. Born in Essex, he went to Emmanuel College, Cambridge, and then practised as a physician. In the 1630s he published several pamphlets urging presbyterianism and denouncing the church which was 'as full of ceremonies as a dog is of fleas'. In 1637, with \*Prynne and Burton, he was sentenced to the pillory, to a fine, life imprisonment, and to have his ears cropped. Bastwick was exiled to the Scillies but brought back in triumph by the \*Long Parliament in 1640.

**Basutoland** *See* LESOTHO.

**Bath** The Roman settlement of Aquae Sulis developed where a number of thermal springs erupt from the floor of the Avon valley. Chief of these is the King's Bath Spring which delivers nearly 250,000 gallons of water a day and was the focus of Roman activity. Late Iron Age coins recovered from the spring and the presence of a presiding Celtic goddess, Sulis (assimilated to Minerva), suggest pre-Roman veneration. The religious and thermal precinct at Bath is the earliest and grandest Roman civil building complex in Britain. Round about 200, major refurbishment of the buildings included modifications to the temple, the replacing of the timber roofs of the baths with a tile barrel-vault, and the enclosing of the reservoir within a barrel-vaulted containing building. In the later 4th cent. maintenance of the complex started to lapse, with silt accumulating. After the end of Roman rule, the complex fell into ruin, though the town is mentioned in the *Anglo-Saxon Chronicle* for 577. Bath did not slide into total insignificance. \*Edgar was crowned there in 973 and in 1090 the diocese was transferred from Wells to Bath. The *Gesta Stephani* of 1138 referred to visitors from all over England making their way to the baths. *Leland, in the 1530s, commented that Bath was much frequented by people 'diseased with lepre, pokkes, scabbes and great aches'. Queen Elizabeth paid a brief visit in 1591 but found the smell disagreeable.

The transformation of Bath into the fashionable spa of Georgian England was the work of two men—Richard 'Beau' *Nash and John Wood. Nash was master of ceremonies from 1705 to 1761 and imposed order and decency, insisting that rank be put aside—the 'happy secret of uniting the vulgar and the great'. To the baths were added concerts, receptions, balls, fireworks, the theatre, milliners, booksellers, coffee-houses, card parties, and pleasure walks in Spring Gardens (1735) and Sydney Gardens (1795). Wood began the massive reconstruction of Bath from medieval huddle to Georgian spaciousness, under the patronage of Ralph Allen, whose estate at Prior Park above the city provided the stone. The glory of Bath lasted until the early 19th cent., by which time success had bred disaster and Nash's vulgarians had taken over. Catherine Morland in Jane Austen's *Northanger Abbey* (1818) found that in the Pump Room on Sundays there was 'not a genteel face to be seen'.

**Bath, Order of the** Bathing as a symbol of purification was an element in the creation of spotless knights and the practice grew up of dubbing numbers of knights on grand occasions like coronations. By the time of Henry V they were known as knights of the Bath. In 1725 John Anstis, Garter King of Arms, suggested the 'revival' of the order. *Walpole and George I agreed, partly to add lustre to the new regime, partly to fend off aspirants. The red ribbon became coveted. The Order was extended in 1815 and 1847.

**Bath and Wells, diocese of** The present see, created in 909, is roughly conterminous with the old county of Somerset. Though Wells itself was founded in c.704 as a religious centre by *Ine, king of Wessex, it was not until 909 that *Edward the Elder split the bishopric of Sherborne into four, Wells being the new see for Somerset. In 973 *Dunstan crowned *Edgar as king of all England at Bath abbey. The first Norman bishop, John de Villula (1088–1122), became abbot of

Bath, to which he transferred his see (1090). This led to friction between the monks of Bath and the canons of Wells over episcopal elections. In 1176 Pope Alexander III resolved the dispute by declaring the cities to be joint-sees. The magnificent 13th-cent. cathedral stands within a complex of buildings, including the moated bishop's palace, started by Burnell, and the 14th-cent. Vicars' Close.

**Bathurst, Henry, 3rd Earl Bathurst** (1762–1834). Bathurst's grandfather was one of the twelve Tory peers created in 1712 to carry the treaty of *Utrecht and in 1772, aged 88, had been promoted earl; his father was lord chancellor 1771–8 and lord president of the council 1779–82. As Lord Apsley, Bathurst entered Parliament for Cirencester as soon as he was of age and was appointed a lord of the Admiralty by *Pitt, a personal friend. He held the post until 1789 when he became a lord of the Treasury, and from 1793 to 1802 was a commissioner of the Board of Control. He had a long career in the Tory ministries of the early 19th cent.—president of the Board of Trade 1807–12, secretary for war 1812–27, and lord president of the council 1828–30. According to *Greville, once his secretary, he made moderate talents go a long way.

**'Bats, Parliament of',** 1426. Competition between Humphrey, duke of *Gloucester, and Henry *Beaufort, bishop of Winchester, to dominate government in the minority of Henry VI assumed dangerous proportions with a riot on London bridge, 30 October 1425. A Parliament was called to Leicester for 18 February 1426, then adjourned to Northampton. Members and their attendants had orders not to come armed, but many carried clubs or 'bats'. The quarrel was submitted to arbitration and peace was made, for the time being.

**Baugé, battle of,** 1421. On 22 March 1421 Thomas, duke of Clarence, while campaigning in Anjou, was killed in a rash sortie. No more than a nasty reverse, Baugé heralded the French recovery after *Agincourt. Henry V left for France to restore the situation but died on the campaign in 1422.

**Baxter, Richard** (1615–91). Puritan divine. A Shropshireman, Baxter was educated locally and became master of Bridgnorth Grammar School (1638). Contact with nonconformists, however, sowed doubts about Anglicanism and episcopacy. After a spell as vicar of Kidderminster (1642) and parliamentary army chaplain, he became disillusioned by both sides in the Civil War. In 1660 he welcomed Charles II back, but his inflexibility at the *Savoy conference helped its breakdown. After refusing the see of Hereford, he preached in London until ejected after the *Act of Uniformity (1662). Having helped overthrow James II, he welcomed William and Mary.

**Bayeux Tapestry** An extraordinary work: it is a major work of art, unique for its time, a stunning piece of political propaganda in support of the Norman claim to the English throne in 1066, and a record of immense importance for the study of subjects ranging from contemporary ship construction and navigation, military tactics, and equipment, to the more homely—clothes and fashions, furniture and fittings.

Strictly speaking, the tapestry is an embroidery, some 230 feet long and around 20 inches high. It is worked in eight coloured wools on a plain linen ground, its masses of colour, in couched and laid work, defined by stem or outline stitch. It was produced in six separate pieces, the consistent quality indicating very close monitoring by the overall designer. It consists of one single horizontal line of action set within two borders (above and below), and takes the form of a sequence of vignettes.

Politically, the tapestry records some of the events of 1064-5/6 which culminated in the death of Harold II at *Hastings. But it is not objective. It seeks to impart a political message which splices with its overarching moral—the inevitable fate that awaits any man who breaks a solemn oath. Since Harold is shown swearing such an oath to Duke William of Normandy in full public view, the tapestry's essential story is that of Harold's downfall after he committed perjury by taking the English throne on Edward the Confessor's death.

Internal evidence indicates that the tapestry was produced for Bishop *Odo of Bayeux, William's half-brother. It is now generally accepted that it was made in England, prob-

ably in Kent, of which Odo was earl (1067-82).

**Beachy Head, battle of,** 1690. Command of the Channel was of critical importance in 1690, when William III and James II struggled for control of Ireland and the French threatened to invade England as a diversion. In June, de Tourville put to sea with a French fleet of 78 vessels. *Torrington, commanding the joint Anglo-Dutch fleet, was apprehensive. On 29 June the brunt of the action fell upon the Dutch, who lost six ships. Torrington withdrew to the safety of the Thames estuary. He was court-martialled, but acquitted.

**beagling** is the hunting of hares on foot with the aid of beagle hounds, specially bred for the purpose. It was practised in the classical world and held its popularity in England until gradually replaced in the 18th cent. by fox-hunting.

**Beale, Dorothea** (1831–1906). Headmistress. Born into a pious family, Dorothea Beale's religious convictions led her into teaching. She entered Queen's College, London, in 1848 where she was offered the post of mathematics tutor, followed by the headship of the college's preparatory school. But it is as principal of Cheltenham Ladies' College that she is remembered. In 1858 the college was in danger of closure. Beale improved the calibre of the teaching staff and broadened the syllabus, with dramatic results. She was instrumental in establishing St Hilda's Hall, Oxford, as a teachers' training institution.

**bear-baiting** Reputedly introduced from Italy in the 12th cent., the spectator sport of setting dogs onto a bear chained to a stake occurred usually in an arena known as a bear garden, such as that at Bankside, south of the Thames, attended by Henry VIII and Elizabeth. Many Tudor nobles kept bear 'sleuths' (packs), and baits were held at markets and fairs. Despite Macaulay's remark that the puritans hated bear-baiting for the pleasure afforded the spectators rather than concern for the bear, there were stirrings of disapproval, but the sport declined only slowly, not legally banned until 1835.

**Beatles** The Beatles, a 1960s Liverpool pop group, were the decade's most commercially successful rock-pop musicians and a social phenomenon ('Beatlemania') epitomizing youth culture. The later musical experimentalism of John Lennon (murdered, 1980) and Paul McCartney, the songwriters of the 'Fab Four', subverted, revolutionized, and continues to influence popular culture.

**Beaton, David** (c.1494–1546). Cardinal. Beaton was the nephew of Archbishop Beaton of Glasgow and St Andrews, whom he succeeded as archbishop in 1539. He already held a French bishopric, was a cardinal, and had been much employed in James V's French matrimonial negotiations. After James's death in 1542 *Mary of Guise relied upon him greatly and he was chancellor [S] 1543–6. His life-style was magnificent and his behaviour profligate. In March 1546 Beaton was instrumental in the burning of George *Wishart, a reformer. Two months later, friends of Wishart burst into the castle of St Andrews and murdered him.

**Beatty, Sir David, later 1st Earl Beatty** (1871–1936). Admiral. In 1914 Beatty was one of the youngest admirals in the Royal Navy, and, as commander of the battle-cruiser squadron of the Grand Fleet, held one of the navy's most prestigious appointments. He led the battle-cruisers at the *Dogger Bank and *Jutland, where he lost three of his ships. Beatty was a demonstrative, flamboyant, and aggressive commander. In December 1916 he succeeded *Jellicoe as commander of the Grand Fleet. But despite his own criticisms of Jellicoe's lack of aggression at Jutland, he pursued the same strategy designed to keep the German surface fleet bottled up. At the end of the war he was appointed 1st sea lord, a post he held until 1927.

**Beauchamp, Richard, 13th earl of Warwick** (1382–1439). Warwick's early years were spent fighting Welsh rebels with Prince Henry (later Henry V) and winning an international reputation as a paragon of chivalry. His pilgrimage to Jerusalem in 1408–10 was punctuated with 'feats of arms' in France, Italy, and Prussia. He served Henry in major embassies and the conquest of Normandy. Although a regular member of Henry VI's council, he still periodically campaigned in France. He was appointed lieutenant-general there in 1437 and died in Rouen.

**Beaufort, Edmund, duke of Somerset** See SOMERSET, EDMUND BEAUFORT, DUKE OF.

**Beaufort, Henry** (c.1375–1447), cardinal bishop of Winchester. The second son of *John of Gaunt, Beaufort rose rapidly in the church, becoming bishop of Lincoln in his early twenties, translating to Winchester in 1404. As half-brother of Henry IV, he was rarely far from the heart of Lancastrian government, being chancellor of England under three kings in 1403–5, 1413–17, and 1424–6. Yet his relationship with the royal family was ambivalent. He quarrelled both with Henry V, over his acceptance of a cardinal's red hat, and with Humphrey of *Gloucester for pre-eminence in England during the minority of Henry VI. Proud, ambitious, and avaricious, delegating his spiritual responsibility in his diocese to subordinates, he stands as the exemplar of a worldly political prelate in late medieval England, outshining even Thomas *Wolsey.

**Beaufort, Joan** See JOAN BEAUFORT.

**Beaufort, Lady Margaret** (1443–1509). The mother of Henry VII, Margaret Beaufort was one of the most remarkable women of the 15th cent. She was married to Edmund Tudor, earl of Richmond, as a child and conceived Henry when she was only 12. Tudor died when she was six months pregnant; she outlived two further husbands, but had no more children. She was separated from her son in 1461, when he was 4, and apart from a one-week reunion in 1470, did not see him again until he was king. Nevertheless, she devoted herself to his cause, throwing herself into the conspiracy which triumphed on the field of Bosworth. As mother of the king, for 24 years Margaret wielded immense political influence. She was the founder of two colleges at Cambridge, Christ's and St John's. At Oxford, she founded the first chair of divinity, and the first women's college, Lady Margaret Hall (1879), was named after her.

**Beaumaris castle,** on the south coast of Anglesey, was started for Edward I after the Welsh revolt of September 1294. The castle was built over the site of Llanfaes, a Welsh royal manor and principal port of the island.

The houses of the town were dismantled and re-erected in the new English borough of Beaumaris, close by, the inhabitants being transported to Newborough or re-established in the English town.

**Beaverbrook, Lord** (1879–1964). Newspaper proprietor. Born to a Scots-Canadian family in Ontario, William Aitken worked as a company negotiator, and became a millionaire. In 1910 he journeyed to England, where his fellow Scots-Canadian, *Andrew Bonar Law, found him a seat as a Conservative MP. He cultivated the acquaintance of *Lloyd George, played a murky part in Lloyd George's overthrow of *Asquith, and was rewarded with a peerage (1916).

Beaverbrook had, meanwhile, bought the *Daily Express*: by 1936 it had achieved a world-record circulation of 2.25 million copies per day. In 1923 he acquired control of the *Evening Standard*. In 1940 Churchill made him minister of aircraft production. The choice was inspired. Beaverbrook's ruthless methods helped ensure the victory of the Royal Air Force in the Battle of Britain.

**Bechuanaland** *See* BOTSWANA.

**Becket, Thomas** (*c.*1120–70). Archbishop of Canterbury who was murdered in his own cathedral and became a saint. Son of a Norman merchant settled in London, Becket entered the service of Archbishop Theobald of Canterbury in 1145. Soon after being crowned by Theobald, Henry II appointed Thomas chancellor. In this office he displayed a wide range of talents, administrative, diplomatic, and military. His zeal in the king's interests, even when they appeared to conflict with the church's, gave Theobald cause for concern and led Henry to believe that Thomas was his loyal friend. When Theobald died, Henry decided that Thomas should succeed him. In June 1162 Becket was consecrated archbishop.

At once Becket began to oppose the king. He campaigned for the canonization of *Anselm, a monk-archbishop who had defied kings. Whatever Becket's motives, Henry felt betrayed. King and archbishop were soon at odds over a wide range of issues, among them the question of 'criminous clerks', i.e. *benefit of clergy. At the Council of Northampton (October 1164) Henry brought charges against Becket arising out of his conduct while chancellor. Becket, see-

ing that the king was determined to break him, fled to France, where he remained in exile until 1170. After years of fruitless negotiations, the coronation of *Henry the Young King in June 1170 by the archbishop of York brought matters to a head. In Becket's eyes crowning the king was a Canterbury privilege. He agreed terms with Henry and returned to England with the intention of punishing those who had infringed that privilege. In November he excommunicated the archbishop of York and two other bishops. They complained to the king, then in Normandy. Henry's angry words prompted four knights to cross the Channel and kill Becket in his own cathedral on 29 December 1170, a murder that shocked Christendom. Little more than two years later, in February 1173, he was canonized by Alexander III.

Becket's murder changed everything. It put Henry in the wrong and forced him to do penance. The church of Canterbury clearly gained. *The *Canterbury Tales* bear witness to the fact that for centuries Becket's tomb in the cathedral was the greatest pilgrimage shrine in England.

**Bedchamber crisis,** 1839. After the resignation of Lord *Melbourne in 1839 Robert *Peel was summoned to form a ministry. Peel wanted the queen to dismiss those ladies of the bedchamber whose husbands were Whigs. The queen refused and appealed to Melbourne; the Whig statesmen reluctantly returned to their posts. With the fall of the Whig administration in 1841 the question rose again. This time the Prince *Albert arranged for the ladies to resign voluntarily and settled the difficulty.

**Bede, St** (672/3–735/6). First English historian, author of the *Ecclesiastical History of the English People* (*c.*731). Deacon, priest, and monk, Bede is generally associated with Jarrow, but probably lived mostly in the monastery of Monkwearmouth, which he entered in 679/80. He travelled a little to Lindisfarne and York.

Bede was particularly interested in miracles and in the calculation of dates and time. Some of his scientific scholarship was advanced and his historical influence profound. He was the first systematically to use the *anno domini* dating system and his idealized portrait of the 7th-cent. church inspired King *Alfred and Bishop *Æthelwold, who attempted its re-creation. Modern scholars depend heavily upon him.

In historical writing Bede was influenced by the 4th-cent. Eusebius of Caesarea, but the greatest non-biblical influence upon him was probably Pope Gregory I. His purposes were varied. The prime one was to facilitate the salvation of his people. The *Ecclesiastical History*'s parade of exemplars, like *Aidan, *Cuthbert, and *Oswald, entailed much selection. Bede's attempt to impose order on a complex past produced his so-called list of *bretwaldas. He may have felt that a 'national' history would encourage 'national' unity. He may have been offering a Christian alternative to secular sagas.

Bede was in touch with highly placed people (including King *Ceolwulf, Acca, bishop of Hexham, and Egbert, archbishop of York). Yet lack of experience outside his monastery may have made him so idealistic as to be considered isolated. But the quarrels generated by *Wilfrid may have inspired his presentation of an alternative version of 7th-cent. ecclesiastical history to that offered in Wilfrid's biography.

Well written and researched, Bede's works are subtle and complex. Some attempt was made to promote his cult, but Viking raids caused Monkwearmouth and Jarrow to be abandoned c.800. Remains claimed to be Bede's were moved in the 11th cent. to Durham cathedral.

**Bedford, John of Lancaster, duke of**
(1389–1435). The third son of King Henry IV, John was created duke of Bedford by his brother Henry V in 1414. Throughout his life he identified himself with his brother's policies. He was lieutenant of the kingdom during Henry's absences in France. He also proved himself an able soldier, commanding the ships which defeated the French fleet before relieving Harfleur in August 1416. After Henry's death in August 1422 Bedford was appointed regent of France. In alliance with John, duke of Brittany, and Philip, duke of Burgundy, whose sister Anne he married in June 1423, he prosecuted the war, at first with considerable success. But his position in France was made difficult by both lack of funds and the uneasy state of England induced partly by the actions of his brother Humphrey, duke of *Gloucester, lord protector to the in-

fant Henry VI. After the failure of the siege of Orléans in 1429 Bedford resigned the regency in favour of Philip of Burgundy but retained the government of Normandy, where he secured the coronation of the young Henry VI in Paris in December 1431. The death of Duchess Anne and Bedford's marriage to Jacqueline, daughter of the comte de Saint-Pol, in 1433 destroyed friendly relations between England and Burgundy. Bedford died at Rouen in September 1435, his policies in ruins, after the failure of peace negotiations at the Congress of *Arras, which had seen Duke Philip finally desert the English cause.

**Bedford, Francis Russell, 4th earl of**
(1593–1641). Bedford hoped to resolve the political crisis of early 1641, since he was acceptable to Charles I as well as the parliamentary leaders. In concert with his client John *Pym, a key figure in the Commons, he planned to accept office in the king's government, take control of the Treasury, and restore the royal finances. Bedford was prepared to save Strafford's life, but could not carry his parliamentary associates with him. At this critical moment, he was struck down by smallpox and died on 9 May.

**Bedford, John Russell, 1st earl of**
(c.1485–1555). The founder of the fortunes of the house of Russell was born in Dorset of gentry stock and became a gentleman of the bedchamber to Henry VII and Henry VIII. In 1537 he became comptroller of the household, and in 1539 was created baron and given the Garter. From 1540 to 1543 he served as lord high admiral and from 1542 to his death as lord privy seal. His gains from the *dissolution of the monasteries were gigantic, and included Tavistock in Devon, Woburn in Bedfordshire, and Covent Garden in London. Though he endorsed the proclamation of Lady Jane *Grey in 1553, he succeeded in retaining the favour of Mary.

**Bedford, John Russell, 4th duke of**
(1710–71). Succeeding to one of the wealthiest dukedoms in Britain in 1732, Bedford served as 1st lord of the Admiralty (1744–8) and as southern secretary (1748–51). He returned to office in 1757 and was lord-lieutenant of Ireland until 1761. In September 1762 he went to Paris to negotiate peace and signed the resultant treaty in February 1763. Thereafter his followers often acted

with those of *Grenville, fully supporting a hard-line attitude towards the American colonies.

**Bedford level** was by far the most ambitious drainage scheme attempted in the Fens. A group of 'adventurers', under Francis, 4th earl of *Bedford, was granted authority in 1630 to proceed and Vermuyden, the Dutch engineer, put in charge. There was strong opposition from local people, acute financial and technological difficulties, and an interruption caused by the civil wars. The work was officially declared complete in 1652, though much of the reclaimed land was of dubious value and maintenance proved expensive.

**Bedfordshire** is a small, low-lying, and predominantly agricultural county, drained largely by the river Ouse. In pre-Roman times it formed part of the kingdom of the Catuvellauni. In 571 a victory of the English over the Britons seems to have secured the northern parts of the area for the kingdom of the *Middle Angles, and later for *Mercia. In the 9th cent., Alfred, king of *Wessex, divided the region with Guthrum, the Danish leader, who took the eastern lands. Forty years later, it was recovered by *Edward the Elder, king of Wessex, who fortified the town of Bedford in 919. It succumbed once more to the Danes in the early 11th cent. By that time Bedfordshire was taking shape as a county and was mentioned in the *Anglo-Saxon Chronicle* for 1011. Bedford itself commanded an important river crossing over the Ouse, and was the point from which the river was navigable by barges.

Despite its nearness to London, Bedfordshire remained something of a backwater. The cottage industry of straw-plaiting brought a modest prosperity, but in 1793 John Byng described Bedford as a 'vile, unimproved place'. The 19th cent. saw dramatic changes. By 1851 Luton had overtaken Bedford as the largest town. A boost to the local economy was the coming of the railways: the line from Bedford to St Pancras opened in 1868. Brick-making developed as an alternative to the declining hat trade and Luton turned to engineering. The Vauxhall car company established its headquarters in the town in 1907. By 1961 Bedford's population had risen to 63,000, Luton's to 131,000.

**Bedlam,** more properly **Bethlem hospital,** was originally attached to the priory of St Mary Bethlehem outside Bishopsgate, founded in 1247 and used for the 'distracted' from 1377. After the priory's dissolution (1546), it was granted to the city, and from 1557 jointly managed with *Bridewell. The only public madhouse and a popular resort for sightseers from the early 17th cent., it became infamous for the cruelty meted out to the insane—'bedlam' is still used figuratively for any place of uproar.

**Beecham, Sir Thomas** (1879–1961). Self-taught English conductor. Financed by the family business, Beecham founded many leading orchestras, including the Beecham Symphony Orchestra (1909), London Philharmonic Orchestra (1932), and Royal Philharmonic Orchestra (1946). His vast repertoire included many small-scale 'lollipops', although he was an early champion of the operas of Richard Strauss and the music of *Delius.

**Beeton, Mrs** (1836–65). Isabella Mary Beeton, Mayson, was born in 1836 in London. Although her father died when she was 4, she received a rounded education, attending finishing school in Heidelburg and becoming an accomplished pianist. However, it is for her cookery and household management books that she is remembered. In 1856 she married Samuel Orchard Beeton, a publisher. Mrs Beeton became a regular contributor to his monthly household publication. Her practical style coupled with attractive illustrations ensured enduring success for her book, *Household Management*, published between 1859 and 1860.

***Beggar's Opera, The*** John Gay's ballad opera began its record-breaking run at the theatre in Lincoln's Inn Fields on 29 January 1728. A satire on Italian opera set in Newgate prison and making use of folk-tunes and popular songs, the ubiquitous references to statesmen, politicians, and 'great men' were interpreted as reflections on Sir Robert *Walpole, the prime minister.

**Behn, Aphra** (1640–89). Dramatist and novelist, Aphra Behn was born on 10 July 1640 at Wye, Kent. Her early childhood, spent in the West Indies, later provided inspiration for her novel *Oroonoko*, a forerunner to Rousseau's 'natural man'. Her marriage to a wealthy merchant in 1663 gave her entrance to the court. In 1666, Charles II chose Behn, then widowed, to carry out spying missions in Holland. She returned to England to concentrate on writing. Although much of her work was published anonymously, fellow Restoration writers, including *Dryden, held her in esteem.

**Bek, Anthony** (c.1240–1311). Bishop of Durham. Bek came from Lincolnshire, went to Oxford University, and in 1270 entered the household of Prince Edward. He accompanied Edward on crusade and returned with him when he succeeded as Edward I in 1274. Henceforth he was one of the king's closest advisers, accompanying him on campaigns in Wales and Scotland, fighting at *Falkirk, and given the lordship of the Isle of Man. In 1283 he was elected bishop of Durham, where he possessed palatine powers.

**Belfast** is the second largest city in Ireland, and the economic and political capital of Northern Ireland. Although the Normans established a fort at Belfast in the 12th cent., a substantial town only developed at the beginning of the 17th cent., and was incorporated by royal charter in 1613. The most remarkable years of expansion were from 1860 to the First World War, coinciding with the development of the shipbuilding and engineering industries, and the consolidation of linen manufacturing: the population of Belfast grew from 87,000 in 1851 to 349,000 by 1901. With the Government of *Ireland Act (1920), and the partition of the island, Belfast became the administrative capital of the newly created Northern Ireland.

The swift expansion of Belfast partly determined its politics. The proportion of catholic citizens grew from virtually nothing at the beginning of the 18th cent. to one-third by the late 19th and 20th cents. The industrial growth of the city brought closer links with the British economy: this, in combination with a protestant domination of capital, helped to determine the predominantly unionist character of the city's politics. The city suffered greatly in the 1980s and 1990s from the *IRA bombing campaign but the cease-fire of 2002 gave an opportunity for it to recover some of its former prosperity.

**Belgae** A British *civitas*. The Romans applied the name Belgae to a whole group of tribes in north-west Gaul, but the appearance of a *civitas* of this name in Britain is a mystery. The *civitas* of the Belgae was most probably an artificial creation of the Roman administration, and was established in c. AD 80 following the death of King *Cogidubnus. Its administrative capital at Winchester was known as Venta Belgarum.

**Belize** in central America is a little larger than Wales and was originally part of the Maya empire. English colonists were repeatedly driven out by the Spaniards. In 1862 it was formed into a colony as British Honduras and was renamed Belize in 1973. Though it became independent in 1981, British troops remained as protection against Guatemalan claims.

**Bell, Alexander Graham** (1847–1922). Inventor of the telephone. Bell followed his father in teaching his system of 'visible speech' to the deaf. In 1870 he emigrated to Canada and in 1873 was appointed professor of vocal physiology at Boston University. During his research Bell conceived the idea of the electrical transmission of speech. In March 1876 the first intelligible sentence was transmitted. He won a 50,000-franc prize for his invention, which he used to establish the Volta laboratory for research into deafness.

**Bell, Andrew** (1753–1852). Founder of the Madras system of education. Bell was educated at St Andrews University, Scotland. In 1789 he became superintendent of the Madras Male Orphan Asylum, founded by the East India Company. The teachers were few and inefficient, so Bell experimented with a system of delegated instruction whereby clever boys were placed in charge of others. This system was described in a pamphlet written in 1797. There was open rivalry with Joseph *Lancaster, who claimed to have originated the system. The Church of England in 1811 formed the *National Schools Society for Promoting the Education of the Poor with Bell as its first superintendent.

**Bell, Gertrude** (1868–1926). Traveller, archaeologist, and diplomatist in the Middle East. Bell took a first in modern history at Oxford at the age of 18 and then made herself expert in Persian before turning to Arabic in 1899 when she first visited the Middle East. Four major caravan journeys through the Syrian and Arabian region and some archaeological digs between 1905 and 1913 led to an RGS medal and several books, the best known being *The Desert and the Sown*.

**Bell, Henry** (1767–1830). Bell became a millwright, but spent part of his career as the proprietor of a hotel in Helensburgh, where he conceived the idea of a steamboat to bring his customers from Glasgow. Another Scotsman, William Symington, had already demonstrated the effectiveness of a steam-engine in a canal boat in 1789. Bell, however, converted the idea into an economically viable proposition, commissioning the first commercially successful steam vessel, *Comet*, launched in 1812. *Comet* plied regularly between Glasgow and Greenock until it was wrecked in 1820.

**Benburb, battle of,** 1646. After the Irish rebellion of 1641, the situation was extremely confused. The Irish catholic confederacy fought against royalists, parliamentarians, and with a Scottish army sent over under Monro to protect the Ulstermen. In 1643 a truce or 'cessation' enabled *Ormond to begin sending troops back to England to fight for the king. After Charles surrendered in May 1646 hostilities in Ireland continued. In June, Monro's troops were badly beaten at Benburb on the Blackwater by Owen Roe *O'Neill and the confederates. Parliament's response was to send first Michael Jones, then Oliver *Cromwell, to restore English rule.

**Benedict Biscop** (628–c.690) at 25 left his position at *Oswiu's Northumbrian court to undertake the first of several pilgrimages to Rome. Twenty years later, after becoming a monk at Lerins (near Cannes), he returned to Northumbria, founding the twin monasteries of Monkwearmouth (674) and Jarrow (681/2). Concerned to establish a stable, obedient order, his rule combined the best of seventeen monasteries observed on his travels.

**Benedictines** The monastic order of St Benedict of Nursia (c.480–c.550) had its origins at Monte Cassino, south of Rome, where c.540 Benedict drew up a rule. This codification became dominant, until challenged by the rule of St Augustine in the 11th cent. One of its chief strengths was its adaptability, and

many interpretations were introduced. The first Benedictine abbeys were probably those founded by *Wilfrid of York at Ripon and Hexham at the end of the 7th cent. Thereafter the order spread rapidly. The Viking raids of the 9th cent. severely affected most Benedictine houses, some of which were destroyed; others were refounded, and some new ones established in the mid-10th cent. under the influence of *Æthelwold, bishop of Winchester, Archbishop *Dunstan of Canterbury, and *Wulfstan, bishop of Worcester, all themselves monks. Following the Norman Conquest some abbeys lost land, but most soon recovered under new, Norman abbots, and new abbeys were founded. There was also an increase in the number of Benedictine nunneries, though the most prestigious were Anglo-Saxon foundations like Shaftesbury or Wilton.

The Benedictines were challenged by the rising appeal to lay society of new orders, like the *Cistercians and the *Augustinians, and the *friars who presented a new spirituality. By the 16th cent. the number of Benedictine monks had declined and their dynamic had largely been lost.

**benefit of clergy** was fought for by Archbishop Thomas *Becket and conceded by Henry II in 1176 in the aftermath of Becket's murder. It exempted clergy from trial or sentence in a secular court on charges arising from a range of felonies and offences. This exemption was allowed to all who could prove themselves literate by reading a verse of Scripture. It was abolished by Parliament in 1827.

**benevolences** These so-called free gifts, offered out of the goodwill or *benevolentia* of the subjects, were outlawed by statute in 1484, but monarchs continued to solicit them. They eventually fell into disuse because of their low yield. *Forced loans were more effective.

**Bengal, acquisition of** On 12 August 1765 the Mughal emperor Shah Alam proclaimed the English *East India Company his *diwan* (administrator) for the revenues of the provinces of Bengal, Bihar, and Orissa. This confirmed the company's transformation from a trading to a political power in India and made Bengal the 'bridgehead' of its new empire. The process was brought to completion in 1773 by Warren *Hastings, who removed the residual powers of the nawab of Bengal.

**Bennett, Arnold** (1867–1931). Like George *Eliot, Bennett was a fine novelist of provincial middle-class society—in his case that of the Potteries, a landscape of canals and kilns and trams and chimneys and dust. *The Old Wives' Tale* (1908) tells of two sisters, daughters of a draper in Bursley (Burslem). *Clayhanger* (1910) recalls the introduction of steam-printing into the Potteries. Bennett, born in Hanley, was a solicitor but went to London in 1888 where he made a living editing and writing short stories.

**Benson, battle of,** c.777. This was an important victory in Oxfordshire in the struggle between *Mercia and *Wessex. *Offa of Mercia defeated *Cynewulf of Wessex and took possession of territories south of the Thames.

**Benson, Edward** (1829–96). Archbishop of Canterbury. Born in Birmingham and educated at Trinity College, Cambridge, he taught at *Rugby and was successively first master of Wellington College (1859–72), first bishop of Truro (1877), and archbishop (1883). A lover of pageantry, he dealt with the ritualist case against the saintly Bishop Edward King of Lincoln in a revived archiepiscopal court, thus reclaiming for Canterbury oversight of common worship.

**Bentham, Jeremy** (1748–1832). English utilitarian and philosophical radical. Educated at Oxford University, Bentham qualified as a barrister before he was 20, though he never practised. He was highly critical of English law for its obscurantism, and devoted his life to systematizing it on the basis of utility. In his first substantial publication, *A Fragment on Government* (1776), Bentham launched a broadside against *Blackstone's defence of England's constitution. His most important contribution to moral philosophy was contained in his *Introduction to the Principles of Morals and Legislation* (1789), where he elaborated his theory of utility in terms of the greatest happiness of the greatest number. In his 'felicific calculus', he demonstrated how alternative courses of action could be evaluated by estimating the total quantity of plea-

sure they would generate. His intellectual leadership of the philosophical radicals was a critical factor in achieving many of the legal, social, industrial, economic, and political reforms that took place in England during the 19th cent.

**Bentinck, Lord George** (1802–48). Bentinck personified integrity in politics and sport. A son of the duke of Portland, Bentinck was private secretary to *Canning, his uncle by marriage, and an MP from 1828. With other Canningites he abandoned *Wellington in the late 1820s, though supporting *catholic emancipation, and backed *Grey's ministry and, with reservations, the Reform Bill. With the *Derby Dilly, he moved back towards the Tories. Declining office from *Peel in 1841, Bentinck remained silent in the House, devoting his time to sport. In 1845-6 he emerged as an enraged opponent of Peel's policy of *Corn Law repeal: 'What I cannot bear is being sold!' His personal standing helped to give him the leadership of the protectionist revolt in the Commons and he succeeded in bringing down Peel's government. Bentinck continued to champion protectionism but he alienated his party by voting for the admission of *Jews to Parliament in 1847 and resigned the leadership. Returning briefly, he died suddenly of a heart attack.

**Bentinck, Lord William** (1774–1839). Soldier and administrator. In 1803 he became governor of Madras but was recalled after being held responsible for the sepoy mutiny at Velore in July 1806. He subsequently saw action in the Mediterranean, commanding the British forces in Sicily (1811) and conducting a successful expedition against Genoa (1814). From 1827 to 1835 Bentinck acted as governor-general of Bengal. He instituted reforms to eradicate debts, reorganized the legal system, abolishing such practices as suttee (widowburning), improved communications, introduced education programmes, and opened up official posts to natives. In 1833 he became the first governor-general of India.

**Bentley, Richard** (1662–1742). Scholar and polemicist. After attending Wakefield Grammar School and St John's College, Cambridge, Bentley was appointed royal librarian in 1694. His reputation as an outstanding classicist was established by the controversy over the *Letters of Phalaris*, which Bentley showed to be forgeries. In 1700, he was elected master of Trinity, Cambridge. His relations with the fellows were acrimonious and there were repeated attempts to deprive him of his mastership, all of which Bentley defeated.

**Beowulf** Anglo-Saxon poem. This anonymous epic was written *c*.1000. Provenance, date, and genesis are uncertain: Northumbria or Mercia in the 8th cent. have long been favoured. The principal setting is southern Scandinavia *c*.500, but there is also reference to *Hengist, King *Offa, and other figures from English history. It surveys Danish legend before depicting three great monster fights. In the first two, the young Geat hero Beowulf frees King Hrothgar and the Danes from the predations of the evil fen-dwellers Grendel and his mother; in the last, Beowulf, now an aged king, loses his life while slaying a treasure-guarding dragon.

**Berengaria** (*c*.1164/5–*c*.1230), queen of Richard I. The daughter of Sancho VI of Navarre, Berengaria was married to Richard while he was on the Third Crusade. On her journey to the Holy Land, Berengaria was shipwrecked off Cyprus and threatened by the ruler, Isaac Comnenus. Richard captured the island and married Berengaria, who was also crowned queen, in Limassol in May 1191. Thereafter, she saw her husband only rarely and England never.

**Berkeley, George** (1685–1753). Philosopher and bishop. One of the most renowned philosophers of his day, Berkeley was born in Kilkenny of English descent. He became a fellow of Trinity College, Dublin, but spent 1713–20 in London or on continental travel. In 1724 he was appointed dean of Derry but his main interest was in raising support for a college in Bermuda to preach the gospel and he was in America 1728–32. From 1734 he was bishop of Cloyne and spent almost all his later years in the diocese. His idealist philosophy, attacking the materialism of *Locke and *Newton, is to be found largely in *Treatise Concerning the Principles of Human Knowledge* (1710) and *Three Dialogues* (1713).

**Berkshire** is an area south of the upper Thames, which separated the county from Oxfordshire and Buckinghamshire. Through the centre of the county run the chalk hills, from Uffington to Streatley—the line of the *Icknield Way and the Berkshire Ridgeway. There were therefore two east–west corridors—one north of the downs, one south.

In Roman times, the area was the territory of the *Atrebates. From the early days of the Saxon occupation, it was disputed between *Mercia and *Wessex. Mercia gained the upper hand in the mid-7th cent. and the region was still held by *Offa of Mercia in the 770s. It was recaptured by King *Egbert for Wessex in the early 9th cent. Wantage was a royal estate and *Alfred the Great was born there. It was probably one of the earliest shires to be organized and placed under an *ealdorman. Berkshire was first in the diocese of *Dorchester, just across the river in Oxfordshire, then in *Winchester, and from 909 in *Ramsbury in Wiltshire, whence it was finally transferred to the new diocese of *Salisbury. This suggests that it was border country, lacking a powerful capital. In 1066 William crossed the Thames at Wallingford and began building the castle at *Windsor, soon established as a major royal residence. Its position astride one of the main routes to London gave Berkshire strategic importance. In the civil war between King Stephen and *Matilda in the 12th cent., Wallingford castle was held for the latter. During the 17th-cent. civil wars, the county was on the border between royalist and parliamentarian: Wallingford was held throughout the war for the king, Windsor for his opponents.

Berkshire remained a quiet rural area, the downs feeding the sheep, and Newbury and Abingdon gaining reputations for cloth. Reading's place on the river gave it steady prosperity: in the 1720s, Defoe found it 'large and wealthy, the inhabitants rich and driving a very great trade'. But the extensive areas of downland and the barren, sandy heathland in the east kept the population down. The Kennet and Avon canal in the south, opened in 1810, gave a modest boost to trade, but the Wiltshire and Berkshire, a canal completed in 1809, had desultory traffic from the beginning. The market towns of the shire remained small, until the great expansion of Reading itself—9,000 in 1801, 60,000 by 1901, 134,000 by 1991: Huntley and Palmer's biscuit partnership dates from 1841. Didcot grew considerably in the 20th cent. as a rail junction, but Wantage, Wallingford, and Faringdon, bypassed by the main lines, stayed small. Berkshire remained essentially a shire to be passed through, from east to west. Brunel's Great Western railway cut a large swathe through the north of the county in the 1830s, and the Taunton to Reading line, through Hungerford and Newbury, opened in 1847. The M4 motorway, completed in 1971, bisected the county from Bray in the east to Membury in the west. By the local government reorganization of 1972, the county gained Slough and Eton from Buckinghamshire, but lost Abingdon, Faringdon, Wantage, and Wallingford to Oxfordshire—Mercia's belated triumph.

**Berlin, Congress of,** 1878. A summit conference under the presidency of Bismarck, in June 1878. Lord *Salisbury and Lord Beaconsfield (Benjamin *Disraeli) represented Britain. European opinion was uneasy at the gains Russia had made by the treaty of San Stefano at the end of the Russo-Turkish War. San Stefano had provided for a 'Big Bulgaria', an autonomous principality including half the Balkan peninsula, which seemed likely to be under Russian influence. This was divided and part returned to Turkish jurisdiction. Austria was to 'occupy and administer' Bosnia and Herzegovina. Britain was to lease Cyprus from Turkey. Disraeli returned to London boasting that he had secured 'peace with honour' but Salisbury later concluded that they had 'backed the wrong horse' in trying to prop up the Turkish empire.

**Bermuda** is a group of islands in the western Atlantic, 600 miles from the east coast of the United States. It has the status of a dependent territory with internal self-government. It was named after the Spanish explorer Juan Bermudez, though it remained in British hands from 1612 onwards.

**Bernicia, kingdom of** This kingdom may have had its origins in Anglo-Saxon settlements around the rivers Tyne and Wear, but it expanded rapidly in the late 6th and 7th cents. to control all the land between the Tees and the Forth. The first recorded king was *Ida (c.547–59). His grandson *Æthelfryth (592–616) and great-grandsons *Oswald (634–42) and *Oswiu (642–70) were responsible for the military expansion

which enabled Oswald and Oswiu to establish a wide-ranging overlordship over other Anglo-Saxon and Celtic kingdoms. The supremacy of the Bernician dynasty in northern England was only seriously challenged by *Edwin of Deira (617–33) who ruled in both Bernicia and Deira, but by the end of the reign of *Ecgfrith (670–85) Deira had been integrated with Bernicia to form the province of *Northumbria. The disastrous defeat of Ecgfrith by the Picts at *Nechtansmere put an end to further overlordship of the northern Celtic peoples. When much of Deira was overrun by Scandinavians after 867, Bernicia (or a substantial part of it) re-emerged in effect as a separate province under a dynasty known as 'ealdormen of Bamburgh'.

**Bertha,** daughter of the Frankish king Charibert, married King *Æthelbert of Kent sometime before 597, on condition that she could continue to practise her Christian faith. She did not convert her pagan husband. Pope Gregory the Great, writing to her in 601, rebuked her for this, but it seems likely that the relationship with the greater Merovingian rulers influenced Æthelbert's acceptance of *Augustine's Christian mission in 597. She died before 616.

**Berwick, treaty of,** 1357. David II, king of Scotland, was captured at *Neville's Cross in 1346. Eleven years later, by the treaty of Berwick, he was ransomed for 100,000 marks.

**Berwick, treaty of,** 1560. The years 1558–60 were critical in Anglo-Scottish relations. The death of Mary Tudor in 1558 placed a protestant on the English throne. Mary, queen of Scots, became queen of France in 1559, with her mother *Mary of Guise as regent for her in Scotland. Her catholicizing policy was opposed by the lords of the *Congregation, a group of noblemen, supported by the zeal of John *Knox. By the treaty of Berwick of February 1560, Elizabeth I undertook to support the rebellious lords.

**Berwick-on-Tweed** Northumbrian coastal town at the mouth of the river Tweed. Berwick was a disputed Anglo-Scottish border town and changed hands thirteen times before finally being recognized as English in 1482. The Elizabethan fortifications, built in

1558, followed the latest Italian system, and are the only surviving walls of their kind. Berwick has three very different bridges. The 17th-cent. Old Bridge is an elegant structure which took a quarter of a century to build. The Royal Border Bridge, an impressive railway viaduct, was designed by Robert *Stephenson and built 1847–50. The Royal Tweed Bridge, of concrete construction, was built in 1928 to carry the main road north.

**Bessemer, Sir Henry** (1813–98). Bessemer distinguished himself as a professional inventor. His most successful invention was the process which bears his name for making steel—previously an expensive material in short supply—available in bulk. Invented in 1856, it involved blowing air through molten cast iron so that it combined with excess carbon in the melt to produce mild steel in substantial quantities. Steel from 'Bessemer converters' came to be used extensively on railway lines, ship plate, and forgings for large guns.

**Betjeman, Sir John** (1906–84). Poet laureate and essayist, whose eccentricity has encouraged an undervaluation of his literary gifts. His *Collected Poems* (1958) sold over a million copies and as a broadcaster he became a national institution, championing Victoriana and the disappearing 'Metroland' of his youth. Unhappy at Marlborough, he blossomed at Oxford, where he moved in literary circles. He documented the doings of middle-class suburbia with a mixture of nostalgia and irony. Betjeman had something of Thomas *Hardy's sadness and simplicity, but a greater capacity for enjoyment.

**Bevan, Aneurin** (1897–1960). One of the most controversial of Labour Party politicians, Bevan was born in Tredegar, a miner's son in a dissenting family. His creation of the National Health Service in 1948 remains Labour's most enduring legacy. During the war years he was virtually a one-man opposition to *Churchill and had no ministerial experience when *Attlee appointed him minister of health in 1945. He resigned when his cabinet colleagues in 1951 imposed charges on dental and ophthalmic treatment. His followers, known as Bevanites, were accused of forming a party within a party around *Tribune*. But they also found Bevan difficult, especially after he denounced unilateral nuclear dis-

armament at the 1957 party conference, declaring that no Labour foreign secretary should be sent 'naked into the conference chamber'. His jeer in 1948 (much interpreted) that the Tories were 'lower than vermin' gave his adversaries a propaganda feast.

**Beveridge, William H.** (1879–1963). Social reformer. Educated at Oxford, Beveridge joined Toynbee Hall, in London's East End, where he met Sidney and Beatrice *Webb. In 1908 he joined the Board of Trade and played a major part in drafting the Labour Exchanges Act of 1909 and the National Insurance Act of 1911. In 1919 he became director of the London School of Economics (LSE). While firmly establishing LSE's reputation in the social sciences, his inclination to autocracy caused inevitable clashes; in 1937 he resigned to become master of University College, Oxford. At the outbreak of war in 1939 Beveridge was asked to chair an inquiry into post-war social services. His two reports on social insurance (1942) and full employment (1944) formed the basis of the Labour government's welfare legislation in the later 1940s.

**Beverley** Yorkshire town, in the Hull valley. John, bishop of York, founded or restored a monastery there; he was later canonized as St John of Beverley (1037). The archbishops of York were lords of the town, and in the 1120s *Thurstan granted its burgesses the same liberties as York. The minster, rebuilt *c.*1220–1400, surpasses in both size and beauty some English cathedrals. Beverley flourished, and by 1377 was one of the twelve largest English towns. Its trade and industry decayed in the 15th and 16th cents.

**Bevin, Ernest** (1881–1951). Trade unionist and Labour politician. The illegitimate son of a village midwife, Bevin left school at 11. He became a full-time official of the Dockers' Union in 1911, and by 1920 was assistant general secretary. Bevin gained national attention in the immediate post-war years through his evidence to the Shaw Inquiry in 1920 on dock labour. He master-minded the amalgamation of eighteen unions into the Transport and General Workers' Union, of which he became the first general secretary in 1922. The failure of the *General Strike of

1926 underlined his belief that unions should negotiate from strength.

The collapse of the Labour government of 1929-31 compelled Bevin further into the political arena and he played a major role during the 1930s in committing Labour to realistic policies on the economy and rearmament. A devastating speech at the 1935 party conference helped remove the pacifist George *Lansbury from the leadership. By 1937 Bevin was chairman of the TUC and one of the most influential figures in the Labour movement.

When Labour joined *Churchill's wartime coalition in May 1940, the prime minister made the surprise but inspired appointment of Bevin to the Ministry of Labour. At the age of 59 he entered Parliament. Probably no other figure could have secured the same level of co-operation from the work-force.

With the election of a majority Labour government in 1945 Bevin went to the Foreign Office. Here he laid the foundation stones of British foreign policy for the next 40 years. To the approval of the Conservative opposition, Bevin took a consistently strong line towards the Soviet Union. Under Bevin's influence the government went ahead with the construction of a British atomic bomb, and played a leading role in the creation of *NATO in 1949.

Bevin had been in poor health since the 1930s. After the 1950 general election he was no longer capable of fulfilling his duties, and he died within a month of leaving office. He was a man of great intelligence, despite his lack of formal education.

**Bible** The Bible is a library of different literary types rather than a single book (Greek *biblia*—books (plural)). The larger part, the Old Testament (OT), is a collection of Jewish sacred writings, originally in Hebrew and consisting of teaching (or Law—*Torah*), history, prophecy, and poetry. The New Testament (NT), originally in Greek, also includes diverse literary forms—letters of Paul and other apostles, historical narrative (Acts), apocalyptic writing (Revelation), and four Gospels which are not history but arrangements of remembered acts and sayings of Jesus.

The first English translations were spasmodic—paraphrases attributed to *Cædmon (*c.*680), *Bede's translation of part of John's Gospel (673–735), and Middle English metrical versions. The first full versions were 14thcent. NT translations from the Vulgate, made under *lollard influence. Illicit MS translations continued to appear, until a powerful impetus was provided by the printing of the Vulgate (1456), the Hebrew text (1488), and Erasmus' Greek NT (1516), which inspired *Tyndale to make the first English NT translation from the original Greek (1526) and of the Pentateuch from the original Hebrew (1529–30). *Coverdale, whose first complete English Bible (1535) was partly based on Tyndale, superintended publication of the Great Bible (1539–40). A new version (1557), issued in Geneva—the first with verse-divisions—formed the basis of the so-called Geneva Bible, dedicated to Elizabeth (1560). *Parker, however, authorized yet another, this time more Latinate, revision of the Great Bible, the Bishops' Bible (1568). Meanwhile exiled English catholics in Rheims translated their own NT from the Vulgate (1582), followed by the OT at Douai (1609–10). At the *Hampton Court conference (1604) James I commissioned a panel to produce the King James (or so-called Authorized) Version of 1611, a comprehensive revision of previous translations. Its superb quality enabled it to supplant all previous versions, and for 250 years it was the only one used. Though new scholarship led to a conservative Revised Version (1881-5), translations proliferated in the 20th cent.: James Moffatt (1922, 1924), Ronald Knox (1945, 1949), followed by the Revised Standard Version (1952), the New English Bible (1961, 1970), Jerusalem Bible (1966), and others.

**Bible Christians** were a methodist connexion founded in 1815 in north Devon by William O'Bryan (1778–1868), a Wesleyan farmer of Anglican and quaker descent, an attractive but refractory personality. The Bible Christians joined with the New Connexion and United Free Churches in 1907 to form part of the United Methodist Church which, in turn, entered the methodist church in 1932.

**Bible Society** The evangelical revival's largest pan-denominational organization was formed in 1804 to promote the international distribution of the Scriptures. Based in London, with a committee of fifteen Anglicans, fifteen dissenters, and six foreigners, its fundamental principle was that only bibles authorized by public authority should be circulated, without note or comment. By the 1970s it issued 1,000,000 bibles annually, in over 1,000 languages.

**Biedcanford, battle of,** *c.*571. Though Biedcanford was clearly an important battle, it is difficult to identify. The *Anglo-Saxon Chronicle* seems precise, attributing a victory over the Britons to Cutha, brother of *Ceawlin of Wessex, who went on to take the towns of Lygeabyrig, Aeglesbyrig, Benesingtun, and Egonsham. These have with some confidence been identified as Limbury (now part of north Luton), Aylesbury, Benson, and Eynsham. But Stenton denied that the name referred to Bedford and historians have puzzled whether Britons could have been holding the vale of Aylesbury as late as 571.

**Big Ben,** the name given to the clock in the eastern tower of the Houses of Parliament, Westminster, was originally applied only to its 13-ton bell, supposedly named after Sir Benjamin Hall, commissioner of works (1859).

**Bigod, Roger, 5th earl of Norfolk** (1245–1306). One of the most powerful barons in Edward I's reign, Bigod succeeded his father Hugh Bigod, justiciar, in 1266 and his uncle as earl and hereditary marshal of England in 1270. His life was spent in the service of Edward I and he saw much campaigning in Wales and Scotland. But relations with the king were by no means easy. In 1297 Bigod refused to lead a campaign in Gascony. 'You will either go or hang', Edward is reported to have said, to be met with the retort, 'I will neither go nor hang.' Edward was forced to give way and confirm charters. Bigod's political position was weakened by debt and in his last years he was obliged to come to terms with Edward.

**billeting** The right of the crown to demand accommodation for its troops was always part of the royal prerogative. Though it was never popular, since remuneration was often inadequate, it did not become a major constitutional issue until the 17th cent. The *petition of right (1628) complained that 'great companies of soldiers and mariners have been dispersed into divers counties and the inhabitants against their will have been com-

pelled to receive them into their houses'. After the *Glorious Revolution, the law was modified: ordinary citizens were not required to find billets, but innkeepers were obliged to accept troops and a scale of charges laid down.

**billiards and snooker** Billiards is a game which evolved as a popular pursuit in the 19th cent. A modern billiards room was opened in Covent Garden and then in many London clubs. Snooker developed from it in the Indian army and is believed to have taken its name from the slang term for a new cadet. Billiards has never achieved wide popularity but snooker has acquired a considerable TV following and its simpler variant, pool, is played in many pubs, on smaller tables.

**Bill of Rights** Passed by Parliament in December 1689 this gave statutory force to the *Declaration of Rights presented to William and Mary on 13 February 1689. The bill closely followed the declaration in its recital of ancient rights, and the recent abuses of the royal prerogative by the catholic James II, deemed to have abdicated and hence vacated the throne. The succession was stated to lie in the heirs of the protestant Mary, and then her younger sister Anne. None could succeed who were of the catholic faith, or had married catholics. In the early 21st cent. there have been proposals that the Bill of Rights should be replaced, or substantially modified, and calls for the restrictions on catholics to be removed.

**Birgham, treaty of,** 1290. Anglo-Scottish treaty, initially drawn up at Birgham (Berwickshire) on 18 July and ratified at Northampton on 28 August 1290. It provided for the marriage of *Margaret 'the Maid of Norway', granddaughter and successor of Alexander III, to Edward of Caernarfon (later Edward II). It became redundant on Margaret's death in September 1290.

**Birkenhead, HMS,** 1852. On 25 February 1852 at night the paddle-steamer *Birkenhead* taking 480 soldiers and 13 women and children for the Kaffir War sank off Cape Town. The troops were ordered to stand fast on deck to avoid swamping the women's boat and almost all perished in shark-infested waters. Hailed by the Victorians as a matchless example of courage, it has also been condemned as a needless sacrifice.

**Birmingham** The rise of Birmingham from local to national importance was largely an 18th-cent. development, when improvements in roads and canals enabled it to turn to advantage its central situation. The name indicates the ham or settlement of the people of Beorma, presumably a Saxon leader, and at the time of Domesday Book (1086) it was no more than a tiny hamlet. It grew during the Middle Ages, but was overshadowed politically by Warwick and Coventry. By 1700 it had well over 10,000 inhabitants. It still had no parliamentary representation and no corporation. But by 1830 the *Birmingham Political Union had taken the lead in pressing for reform and the town acquired two MPs in 1832 and a council in 1838. Under the mayoralty of Joseph *Chamberlain in the 1870s Birmingham became celebrated for municipal enterprise, and Mason's College, founded in 1870, received a charter as a university in 1900. Birmingham's economy diversified, with Cadbury's established at Bournville in 1879, General Electric in 1896, the Dunlop Rubber Company at Castle Bromwich in the 1890s, and the Austin Motor Company in 1905.

**Birmingham, diocese of** Largely conterminous with north Warwickshire and including the city of Birmingham, the see was created mainly out of the diocese of Worcester in 1905. The cathedral is the former parish church of St Philip, built by Thomas Archer (1711-19) with 19th-cent. windows by Burne-Jones and William *Morris.

**Birmingham Political Union** Formed in 1830 by Thomas *Attwood to press for parliamentary reform as a remedy for economic distress. Led by local businessmen and manufacturers, the BPU aimed to unite middle- and working-class reformers in a programme based on currency reform and household suffrage. After the passing of the 1832 Reform Bill, the BPU fell apart and was virtually dissolved in 1834.

**Birmingham riots,** 1791. A foretaste of the great conservative revulsion against the French Revolution, directed against its sympathizers. Joseph *Priestley, a unitarian scientist, had foolishly written of placing gunpowder beneath superstition and error, and was henceforth known as 'Gunpowder Priestley'. On 14 July 1791, after a dinner to celebrate the storming of the Bastille, his house, library, and scientific apparatus were destroyed by the mob. Four rioters were executed.

**birth control** techniques appear to have been widely available long before the 19th cent. Herbal mixtures were advocated to reduce the sex drive or induce abortion. Contemporaries also seem to have been aware of the withdrawal technique since at least the early 18th cent., when the practice of coitus interruptus was linked by quack literature to an awesome list of debilitating medical complaints. Male contraceptives were advertised by the early 18th cent., when such 'armour', made of animal gut, was used to avoid contracting venereal infections. The 1820s and 1830s saw the first open discussion of birth control techniques. More public debate followed the creation of the so-called Malthusian League (1877-1927), which distributed some 3 million pamphlets advocating birth control.

Before the third quarter of the 19th cent., however, there is little statistical evidence that English couples were practising much family limitation. Birth control before 1870 was restricted to higher social classes and some groups of industrial workers. All this changed after 1870 when, within a few generations, Britain underwent the so-called fertility transition. Between 1880 and 1930 the fertility of women of child-bearing age declined by over 60 per cent and the average size of British families fell by almost two-thirds. This declining birth rate was due largely to the adoption of birth control within marriage. It is also clear that the contraceptive techniques used in the early stages of this decline were largely traditional methods such as abstinence, coitus interruptus, and 'safe periods' rather than mechanical aids such as condoms, caps, or sponges. The adoption of birth control within marriage may have been due to a new decision by women to limit the size of their families, prompted by the impact of feminist arguments, growing information regarding the dangers of repeated childbirth, and the impact of universal compulsory schooling in 1880, which reduced the contribution children might make to the household economy.

The development of the female contraceptive pill in the 1960s had wide moral and social implications. Its use was advocated by people concerned at the increase in teenage pregnancies.

**bishops** The office and work of a bishop has evolved from that of the apostles in the New Testament church. That church recognized two differing forms of ministry, that which was local and settled (pastors and teachers) and the itinerant ministry of apostles, prophets, and evangelists. The word *episcopus* (bishop), literally 'overseer', well defines this apostolic ministry.

The jurisdiction of a bishop is a diocese, a word taken from a territorial administrative unit of the Roman empire. There were certainly Christians in the British Isles by the beginning of the 3rd cent. AD and several bishops in the country by 314, when three of them attended the Council of Arles. The churches in Wales, Ireland, and Scotland remained episcopal during the period Christianity was forced underground in England after the withdrawal of the Romans.

The gradual re-establishment of the Christian church in England and revival of episcopal government followed the mission of *Augustine (597), but early Anglo-Saxon dioceses could be vast in extent. After the Norman conquest, the sees of a number of bishops were transferred to larger towns (e.g. *Sherborne to *Salisbury, *Selsey to *Chichester). The reformed Church of England retained bishops and Henry VIII established five new dioceses (*Bristol, *Chester, *Gloucester, *Oxford, and, briefly, Westminster). With the development of major conurbations in the 19th cent. further dioceses were founded (*Ripon 1836, *Manchester 1848, *St Albans and *Truro 1877, *Liverpool 1880, *Newcastle 1882, *Southwell 1884, and *Wakefield 1888), a process which continued into the 20th.

**Bishops' wars,** 1639–40. Charles I assumed that religious diversity was a source of weakness in a state. In 1637, therefore, he ordered the Scottish presbyterian church to use a new prayer book on the English model. This provoked a protest, culminating in the drawing up of a national *covenant to defend 'the true religion'. Charles raised an army but his troops were an undisciplined rabble and he accepted the pacification of Berwick in June 1639. In 1640 Charles again took up arms. The outcome was worse. The Scots promptly invaded England, brushed aside Charles's army at *Newburn on 28 August, and occupied the north-east of the country. They refused to contemplate withdrawing unless and until he summoned Parliament. Charles's policy had collapsed.

**Black and Tans** was the nickname, derived from a Limerick hound pack, or the colour of the uniform, for an auxiliary police force recruited in Britain 1920–1 from ex-servicemen to reinforce the hard-pressed *Royal Irish Constabulary (RIC). The ill-disciplined force was associated with drunken brutality and reprisals following *Irish Republican Army (IRA) atrocities.

**Blackburn, diocese of** The see, created in 1927 mostly out of the *Manchester diocese, comprises much of Lancashire except for Liverpool and Manchester, a mixture of countryside and cotton-mill towns. The cathedral is the former parish church of St Mary's, built in 1818, early Gothic Revival in style.

**Black Death** An epidemic of catastrophic proportions, the Black Death first struck England in the summer of 1348. This first outbreak probably killed between a third and a half of the population, as is shown by figures showing death rates for the clergy, and for peasant landholders. It is usually considered to have been bubonic plague, spread by fleas and rats. The Black Death had major economic effects, although these did not become fully apparent until the 1370s. The area under arable cultivation was sharply reduced and some lands were turned over to pasture. Labour became more expensive, and attempts to revive peasant labour services were unsuccessful.

**Blackheath, battle of,** 1497. A formidable rising of Cornishmen in the summer of 1497 protested against taxation to support Henry VII's campaign against James IV of Scotland, arguing that this was a purely northern responsibility. Under the leadership of Thomas Flammock and James, Lord Audley, the rebels marched through Wells, Salisbury, and Winchester towards London. But Lord Daubeney and the earl of Oxford led the army prepared for Scotland against the insurgents at Blackheath and dispersed them. Flammock and Audley were executed.

**Black Hole of Calcutta** By legend, on 20 June 1756 Nawab Siraj-ud-Daula, Robert *Clive's great enemy, packed 146 Englishmen captured at Calcutta into a small guardroom. The next day only 21 were left alive. There is today dispute about Siraj-ud-Daula's culpability and the actual number of victims, which may have been 43.

**Black Parliament,** 1320. A parliament held at Scone on 4 August 1320 to try conspirators who had intended to kill Robert I and place Sir William Soulis, the son of a competitor in the *Great Cause, on the throne. Soulis was sentenced to life imprisonment. Some were not so fortunate. Sir Roger Mowbray, dead before the trial, was none the less sentenced to be drawn, hanged, and beheaded.

**'Black Prince'** *See* EDWARD THE BLACK PRINCE.

**Blackstone, Sir William** (1723–80). Blackstone is acknowledged as one of the greatest writers on the common law. He was both a practising barrister and an academic, and in 1758 was appointed as the first Vinerian professor of law at Oxford. His *Commentaries* have been one of the most authoritative and revered sources of English law.

**Blackwater, battle of** *See* YELLOW FORD.

**Bladensburg, battle of,** 1814. The defeat of Napoleon in 1814 allowed Britain to take the offensive in the *War of 1812 against the USA. A force of 4,000 men, under General Robert Ross, was landed at Chesapeake Bay. A militia force at Bladensburg on 24 August was brushed aside and the British entered Washington, burning the White House in retaliation for the American sack of Toronto in 1813.

**Blair, Anthony ('Tony')** (b. 1953). Prime minister. Educated at Fettes College, Edinburgh, and St John's College, Oxford, Tony Blair followed his elder brother William to Lincoln's Inn and qualified as a lawyer. He entered Parliament in 1983 as Labour MP for Sedgefield, Durham, and soon made his mark as an articulate and forceful speaker and an adroit TV performer. He was elected to the shadow cabinet in 1988 and was spokesman on Home Affairs when John *Smith died in 1994. Blair won the leadership contest with ease, defeating John Prescott and Margaret Beckett. He pursued Neil *Kinnock's policy of working to shed Labour's 'loony left' image: 'New Labour's' reward was a massive majority at the general election of May 1997. Insisting that his administration would be a radical reforming ministry, he undertook a series of initiatives, not all of which seemed thought out. The consequences of devolution in Scotland, Wales, and London appeared to surprise the government when local people claimed influence and the nationalists did well. Abolition of the hereditary element in the Lords was carried without, it seemed, much idea of what was to follow. Blair's sympathy for the EEC was inhibited by the poor performance of the Euro, and he found some difficulty in wooing the business community without alienating traditional Labour support. Knitting together Old and New Labour proved, at times, difficult. Blair's personal popularity remained high but the Conservative opposition under William *Hague managed a considerable comeback. Nevertheless, at the general election of 2001 Blair's government was retained for a second term with its majority intact and faced the challenge from the spread of international *terrorism. His third election victory in 2005 made him the most successful leader his party had ever had.

Whereas the threat of terrorism helped to unite the country, and perhaps gained support for the government of the day, Blair's intervention in Iraq, in conjunction with the Americans, proved deeply divisive. His government was accused of doctoring evidence to gain support for the war. An engaging television style and a mastery of the House of Commons helped Blair to retain much personal popularity. His most remarkable political success was probably helping to bring peace to the shattered province of Northern Ireland, though this owed much to the attack upon the Twin Towers in New York in 2001 which persuaded a number of Americans who had given support to the *IRA that terrorism was a doubtful policy. But Blair's third term proved difficult as power drained away. Like many prime ministers, he outstayed his welcome. In contrast to the speed with which Saddam Hussein in Iraq had been overthrown, pacification of the country proved protracted and bloody, and was not helped by a resurgence of fighting in Afghanistan after the Taliban had regrouped. At home there were damaging accusations of corruption and croneyism and the prime minister was singed when he was interviewd by the police in the 'sale of peerages' case. In 2007 he made way for his long-serving chancellor, Gordon *Brown and accepted the post of UN envoy to the Middle East. In retrospect Blair's ten years in office seem curiously ephemeral, beset by initiatives which were ill-thought out and reforms uncompleted. 'A short attention span' was one laconic valediction.

**Blake, Robert** (1599–1657). Admiral. Educated at Oxford, Blake volunteered for the parliamentary army in 1642, and distinguished himself at the sieges of Lyme and Taunton. In February 1649 he was one of three colonels appointed admiral by the Commonwealth. His first assignment was to neutralize the royalist navy under Prince Rupert besieging Kinsale. Having done this, he chased Rupert to Lisbon. Defeated by the Dutch commander Tromp at *Dungeness (30 November 1652), he avenged his humiliation at *Portland and Beachy Head (18–20 February 1653). In 1654 he was given command of the Mediterranean fleet, where he campaigned against Turkey and Spain. His victory over the Spanish West Indies fleet in April 1657 was the occasion of a public thanksgiving in London.

**Blake, William** (1757–1827). Artist, engraver, philosopher, visionary, and poet. His first major work was *Songs of Innocence* in 1789, and *Songs of Experience* was published in 1794. Blake longed for fame and an enthusiastic audience, to build a New Jerusalem, but spent many years in poverty. He spent his later years drawing rather than writing, surrounded by admirers. Individual, nonconformist, experimental, Blake's work still challenges and mystifies, yet it includes two of the best-known poems in the English language, 'Tyger, tyger' and 'Jerusalem'.

**Blanketeers, March of the,** 1817. After the *Spa Fields riots of November 1816, the government suspended habeas corpus and banned meetings of more than 50 people. A large gathering of some 5,000 weavers met in St Peter's Fields (Manchester), on 10 March 1817, intending to march to London to petition the prince regent. They carried blankets and rugs with them. After the Riot Act had been read, most were dispersed by the cavalry, but 300 reached the bridge at Stockport, where almost all were turned back.

**Blatchford, Robert** (1851–1943). English socialist and nationalist. Author and journalist, Blatchford wrote for the British newspaper the *Sunday Chronicle* 1885–91, before cofounding the *Clarion* in 1891, a popular socialist weekly, which he edited for 20 years. Blatchford's socialism was the homely message of William *Morris, not the revolutionary doctrine of Karl *Marx, and it spawned a host of organizations—such as the Clarion Scouts, the Clarion Field Clubs, and the National Clarion Cycling Club. His most important book, *Merrie England* (1894), sold over 2 million copies, and has been described as the best recruiting document ever produced by socialists in Britain.

**Blenheim, battle of,** 1704. In early 1704 the French and Bavarians in the War of the Spanish Succession were threatening the imperial capital of Vienna. The duke of *Marlborough marched from the Low Countries to the Danube to link up with his allies under Eugene of Savoy. On 13 August 1704 Marlborough attacked the 60,000-strong Franco-Bavarian forces under Marshal Tallard at the village of Blindheim (or Blenheim) in Bavaria. The battle was decided by a major blow against Tallard's centre, which gave way as Eugene pushed forward on the right flank. The Franco-Bavarian force lost 38,000 men while the victors lost 12,000.

**Blenheim palace** (Oxon.). Home of the dukes of Marlborough and birthplace of Sir Winston *Churchill. Situated in Woodstock, Blenheim palace was given to John Churchill, 1st duke of *Marlborough, in gratitude for his victory in 1704 over the French at *Blenheim. The architect was Sir John *Vanbrugh, soldier and dramatist. Henry Wise (1653–1738) was largely responsible for the formal gardens, and a plan of 1709 signed by *Bridgeman shows the main avenue stretching across Vanbrugh's bridge into the park. From about 1764 this area was planted and flooded by Capability *Brown. The palace itself consists of a pedimented centre block, with flanking courts on each side. Inside the heroic scale is sustained in the great hall, saloon, library, and other rooms, with their paintings, furniture, bronzes, and tapestries. Sir Winston Churchill is buried in the churchyard at Bladon, on the edge of Blenheim Park.

**Bligh, William** (1754–1817). Sailor. Born in Plymouth, Bligh joined the navy at 16. In 1787 he commanded an expedition to the Pacific to procure bread-fruits, taking HMS *Bethia*, renamed *Bounty*. Fletcher Christian, his mate and the leader of the mutiny, was a friend. Bligh was an excellent navigator, but irritable and prone to coarse language. After the mutiny on 28 April 1789, he and eighteen men were placed in an open boat. They reached Timor after 41 days and well over 3,500 miles, with the loss of only one man, killed by natives. On his return to Britain, Bligh was court-martialled and exonerated. He resumed his career, served as governor of New South Wales, and died a vice-admiral.

**Blitz** British colloquialism for air attacks on UK towns, particularly at night in 1940–1, derived from *Blitzkrieg*, lightning war. Towns important for war, like Belfast, Manchester, Sheffield, Glasgow, Hull, Plymouth, Coventry, suffered but the main 'Blitz' descended on London, which was bombed every night but one for over two months. Human casualties were less than feared; damage to buildings greater. In 1940–1, before the attack on the USSR diverted the German air force, about 42,000 were killed in the UK.

**Bloemfontein, convention of,** 1854. The British government was puzzled by the Great Trek of 1836–7 when thousands of Boer farmers moved out of the Cape, leaving British jurisdiction. In 1845 it annexed *Natal and in 1848 followed up by annexing the *Orange River Territory, pursuing the Boers. But it was difficult to establish control and in 1852 the British signed the *Sand River convention acknowledging the independence of the Boers in the Transvaal in the hope that they would not assist the Boers in the Orange River Territory. But the Orange River Territory remained unstable and, in a startling switch of policy in 1854, by the Bloemfontein convention, power was handed back to the

Boers. This arrangement did not prove satisfactory and two Boer wars resulted.

**Blois, treaty of,** 1572. Elizabeth I, excommunicated in 1570, was in a vulnerable position and in 1571 the *Ridolfi plot against her life was exposed. To protect herself, she sought reconciliation with the French, who had supported Mary, queen of Scots, but were in rivalry with Spain. *Walsingham conducted negotiations and on 21 April 1572 Charles IX of France agreed at Blois to a treaty of mutual defence.

**Bloody Assizes** was the name given to the mass trials of *Monmouth's rebels in 1685, presided over by *Jeffreys and four other judges. The judges indicated that pleas of not guilty would invariably mean death sentences and ordered execution on the day of conviction. These examples produced pleas of guilty which enabled courts to sentence 500 in two days at Taunton, 540 at Wells in one. The executions of some 250 were dispersed in towns over the area of the rebellion, and pickled heads and quartered bodies were publicly displayed throughout the western region.

**Blore Heath, battle of,** 1459. *Warwick's father, the earl of *Salisbury, supported the duke of *York in 1459 when he rebelled against Henry VI. He marched from Yorkshire to join York, who was in Wales, near Ludlow. Royalist forces mustered under Lord Audley at Market Drayton to prevent the junction and attacked Salisbury's men on Blore Heath on 23 September. Audley was defeated and slain, and Salisbury joined York.

**Blyton, Enid Mary** (1897–1968). Children's author. Born in East Dulwich (London), Blyton trained as a kindergarten teacher. Her first books, poems in *Child Whispers* and stories in *The Enid Blyton Book of Fairies*, were published in 1922 and 1924. Her wide range of books included a series of school stories beginning with *The Naughtiest Girl in the School* (1940) and the well-known 'Famous Five' and 'Secret Seven' adventures. Noddy and his Toyland friends became television personalities. Her work has been severely criticized for its limited style, moral attitudes, and for perceived racist, sexist, and snobbish elements in her stories, but nevertheless have been popular with children.

**Boat Race** The Oxford and Cambridge universities' challenge race for eights was first rowed at Henley in 1829, with Oxford winning. It moved to London in 1836 and became an annual event in 1839. The race is over 4¼ miles from Putney to Mortlake.

**Boer wars** The first Boer War (1880–1), hardly more than a skirmish, was won by the Boers (Dutch-origin South African farmers) after victory over a British force at *Majuba. That gave the Boer republics of the *Transvaal and *Orange Free State the independence they craved except in foreign policy. Britain accepted this while they were poor and backward. That changed, however, when the vast Witwatersrand goldfield was discovered in the Transvaal in 1886. In 1899 Britain went to war again against the Boers, and got it back.

Britain had other reasons for noticing the Boers' new wealth. If it made them too powerful, they could threaten her supremacy in the rest of South Africa, possibly in league with Germany. The aftermath of the *Jameson Raid fuelled that fear. The kaiser sent a telegram congratulating the Boer president on repelling the raid. There were also complaints of mistreatment of immigrant diggers ('uitlanders') in the goldfields, though these were mostly exaggerated. Britain negotiated to ease these grievances, but possibly not genuinely, since her main agent in South Africa, *Milner, seems to have wanted war. In the end, on 10 October 1899, it was the Boers who issued the ultimatum. Most foreign opinion saw Britain as the aggressor, Goliath against David.

David did well initially. The first months of the war went disastrously against Britain, with the Boers advancing deep into Natal. Only in May 1900 did the tide begin to turn, mainly through the numbers Britain could deploy. By October the Transvaal had been largely reconquered, Kruger, its president, had fled, and both republics were annexed to the British flag. But the war was not over. The Boers continued a 'guerrilla' warfare, which was only crushed in the end by methodical land-razing, farm-burning, and by herding non-combatant Boers—mainly women—into unhealthy 'concentration camps'. In June 1901 *Campbell-Bannerman, the Liberal leader,

publicly attacked this as 'methods of barbarism'.

When the last Boers eventually surrendered, in May 1902, most Britons were heartily sick of the war: 5,774 Britons had been killed (more than on the other side). The Boers had been beaten, but not bowed. In the treaty of *Vereeniging (31 May) they stuck out in defence of their racial policies. In Britain, the army's poor showing proved salutary, leading to a cessation of aggressive *imperialism for a while, and a great national self-examination. The fact that many volunteers were found to be unfit for army service contributed to a revival of the 'condition of England' question and assisted the introduction of improvements in welfare and health.

**Bohun, Humphry de, 4th earl of Hereford** (c.1276–1322). Bohun succeeded his father as earl of Hereford and constable of England in 1298 when there was still considerable tension between Edward I and his leading barons. But in 1302 he married a daughter of Edward I, widow of John, earl of Holland. In the reign of Edward II, Bohun was a leading *Ordainer and took part in the murder of *Gaveston. He was taken prisoner by the Scots after the defeat at *Bannockburn, but exchanged. His opposition to the *Despensers in 1321 led him to take up arms with Thomas of Lancaster, and he was killed at *Boroughbridge.

**Bolingbroke, Henry St John, 1st Viscount** (1678–1751). St John was Tory MP for Wootton Bassett (1701–8) and Berkshire (1710–12), secretary at war (1704–8), secretary of state for the northern department (1710–13) and for the southern department (1713–14). He was in charge of the negotiations for the peace of Utrecht (1713) ending the War of the Spanish Succession. The growing rift between him and Robert *Harley paralysed the Tory ministry. Dismissed office by George I, he was attainted and fled to France into the service of the pretender. He was pardoned and returned to England in 1723, and was restored to his estates in 1725, though barred from the House of Lords. Moving into opposition to *Walpole, he provided much of the intellectual backbone to the 'patriot' and Tory parties with his writings, particularly in the *Craftsman*.

**Bombay (Mumbai)** An island off the west coast of India originally in Portuguese possession. It was given to Charles II in 1661 as part of the dowry of *Catherine of Braganza. In 1673, the English *East India Company moved its west-coast station there from Surat. Following the defeat of the Maratha Peshwa in 1818, Bombay city became the capital of a large presidency. By 1901 its population had reached 850,000, making it the third largest city in the British empire after London and *Calcutta.

**Bondfield, Margaret** (1873–1953). Trade union leader and first woman cabinet minister. Bondfield left school at 13 and became a shop assistant. She immersed herself in socialist politics, joining the Fabian Society. Her first-hand knowledge of the plight of shop-workers assisted her promotion within the National Union of Shop Assistants, of which she became assistant secretary (1898). Elected to Parliament in 1923, she served in the Labour government of 1924 as parliamentary secretary to the Ministry of Labour, and in the second Labour government (1929–31) as minister of labour. She identified herself with the fiscal conservatism of Philip *Snowden, and in August 1931 supported the cabinet's decision to cut unemployment benefit. At the general election, she lost her seat.

**Boniface, St** (c.675–754). St Boniface was perhaps the greatest of early Anglo-Saxon missionaries. Named Wynfrith, he left England in 718, working first with *Willibrord in Frisia before beginning his own work in Hesse and Thuringia as regional bishop. Appointed archbishop in 731 and ultimately papal legate, supported by Frankish rulers, he became a leading ecclesiastical figure in Europe. In 754 he returned to evangelize in Frisia, where he and his followers were killed by heathen robbers.

**Book of Common Prayer** By a proclamation of 23 September 1548, Edward VI set up a commission to oversee the preparation of 'one uniform order [of service] throughout the kingdom'. The Act of *Uniformity (March 1549) ordered the exclusive use of the new Book of Common Prayer. The Prayer Book contained morning and evening offices, and forms for the administration of the sacraments (e.g. baptism and the eucharist) as well as the psalter.

After 1549, reformed ideas, particularly from Germany and Switzerland, rapidly gained ground among English scholars, and were reflected in the Second Prayer Book, issued in 1552. This book was little used, as the accession of Mary I saw a temporary return to the older Latin services. In 1559 a modified 1552 Prayer Book came into use under Elizabeth I, and this formed the basis of the 1662 book, which remained the norm of Anglican worship until the 20th cent.

**book of sports** Sunday, the one non-working day in the week, was traditionally a time for recreation, but *puritan clergy, equating it with the sabbath, kept it 'holy' by banning customary pastimes. This threatened to alienate public sentiment from the established church. In 1618, therefore, James I issued a declaration asserting the right of all persons to engage in 'lawful recreation' on Sundays after divine service. Charles I reissued this 'book of sports' in 1633.

***Books of Discipline,*** 1560, 1578. Both works expounded an ideal never fully realized. The *First Book of Discipline* (1560) was largely the work of the uncompromising Calvinist John *Knox. It was heavily dependent upon the *Ordinances* of Calvin's church in Geneva. Knox died in 1572 and three years later Andrew Melville began drawing up a *Second Book of Discipline*, intended to purge the Scottish church of the last vestiges of episcopal government.

**Boot, Jesse** (1850–1931). Boot was born in Nottingham, where his father, a Wesleyan lay preacher, ran a herbal medicines shop. Boot saw the advantages of meeting demands for mainstream medicine and employed a licensed pharmacist to dispense drugs in every shop. The business became nationwide by establishing branches and by purchasing chains of other retailers.

**Booth, Charles** (1840–1916). Booth, a wealthy Liverpool shipowner and social investigator, refused to accept the findings of the *Social Democratic Federation that about 25 per cent of the working population were living in poverty. He began his own investigation and published seventeen volumes on the life and labour of London's poor between

1889 and 1903. His main finding was that the SDF estimate was too low: 30.7 per cent were living in poverty. Booth greatly influenced the practice of later social investigators and the Liberal government (1906–14).

**Booth, William** (1829–1912). Revivalist and founder of the *Salvation Army. Booth joined the methodists in Nottingham and in 1844 was converted. He set up a mission in London's East End in 1865, from which developed the Salvation Army. For some time Booth waged his holy war solely on the spiritual front; but experience showed that poverty was a great impediment to salvation, and in his book *In Darkest England* (1890) he outlined plans for social reform.

**Booth's rising,** 1659, was one of many attempts by royalists to overthrow the Commonwealth regime. *Penruddock's rising in Wiltshire in 1655 had failed completely but in 1659 Sir George Booth succeeded in rousing a substantial number of supporters in Cheshire to exploit the uncertainty following the death of Oliver *Cromwell. John *Lambert crushed the rebels without difficulty at Winnington bridge on 19 August. Booth was imprisoned in the Tower but released in 1660. He was created a peer in Charles II's coronation honours.

**Borders** From 1973, an administrative region of Scotland, comprising the counties of Berwick, Peebles, Roxburgh, and Selkirk. A hilly area, its economy has continued to be dominated by sheep-farming and textile-manufacturing, with a growing presence of tourism attracted by its castles and abbeys, its peaceful countryside, and its small towns.

**Borneo, North** Although the Spanish touched the region in the 16th cent., it was not until Alexander Dalrymple's expedition of 1759 that it was connected to the outside world. The *East India Company opened several settlements and, in 1846, Labuan was occupied as a crown colony. In 1877 the British North Borneo Company began to establish a government. The Japanese invasion of 1941–2 eventually led to crown colony status in 1946. Representative government and membership of the Malaysian Federation followed in 1963.

**Boroughbridge, battle of,** 1322. Thomas of Lancaster, in rebellion against Edward II and the *Despensers, retreated into Yorkshire to join the Scots. At Boroughbridge, on 16 March 1322, he found the crossing of the Ure blocked by a strong force of archers commanded by Sir Andrew Harcla, sheriff of Cumberland. Lancaster, who surrendered, was executed for treason.

**boroughs** The word 'borough' ('burgh' in Scotland) has caused endless confusion. The Old English (Anglo-Saxon) terms *burg, burh*, and *byrig* were used originally for fortified places. By 1086, however, *Domesday Book was using the word, in its Latin form *burgus*, to mean 'town', and was referring to its inhabitants as *burgenses* (burgesses). In the 12th cent. burgage tenure came to be seen as the normal characteristic of an English borough: each burgess held a burgage, usually a house, for a money rent. In the 13th cent. the larger towns developed rules to define who were 'free burgesses', and to ensure that burgesses, the only townspeople with political rights, were defined as those who were sons (or sometimes widows or daughters) of burgesses, who had served an apprenticeship, or had paid a fee.

Between the 13th and 17th cents., as many towns acquired privileges, 'borough' developed multiple meanings. From the late 13th cent. royal officials tended to confine the word 'borough' to the more privileged urban places, and to distinguish certain boroughs as having separate juries for the administration of justice; they have been called 'juridical boroughs'. Others, not always the same, have been termed 'taxation boroughs' because they paid royal taxes at different rates from other towns, especially after 1334. Finally, sheriffs in the 13th and 14th cents. had to choose which places in their counties were to be represented in parliaments: these are often called 'parliamentary boroughs'. By the 16th and 17th cents. 'borough' was being used chiefly in two senses: as a legally corporate town, usually with privileges granted by royal charters, and as a town which sent members ('burgesses') to Parliament. Most important towns were both, but a few places without chartered privileges were parliamentary boroughs (e.g. Gatton), while some important and growing towns were not represented in Parliament (e.g. Birmingham and Manchester).

Modern boroughs begin with the 1830s. The 1832 *Reform Act revised the parliamentary franchise, both in terms of which boroughs were represented and of who was entitled to vote. In 1835 the *Municipal Corporations Act dissolved the corporations of nearly 200 boroughs, and replaced them by councils elected by ratepayers. New places, such as Birmingham and Manchester, were incorporated as boroughs in 1838.

**Boston,** on the river Witham in Lincolnshire, was once one of the greatest English ports. It became a town only after 1066, but rapidly flourished by exporting wool. In the 13th cent. it paid more tax than any port except London. It is still dominated by the medieval church of St Botolph ('Boston stump') with its 272-foot tower.

**Boston 'massacre',** 1770. The 'massacre' resulted from the clash between British troops, who fired without orders, and an urban crowd, on 5 March 1770 in Boston (Mass.). Three persons were killed. Its propaganda value was quickly utilized, notably by Paul Revere, the engraver. In an ensuing trial, the soldiers were acquitted of manslaughter.

**Boston Tea Party,** 1773. This marked a stage on the road from resistance to insurrection in North America. The unpopular tea duty was continued after the repeal of the other *Townshend duties. In 1773 the East India Company was allowed to export dutied tea directly to America. A group of men disguised as 'Mohawks or Indians' 'emptied every chest of tea' on board three ships into Boston harbour on 16 December 1773. This attack on British property provoked the *'Intolerable Acts' of 1774.

**Boswell, James** (1740–95). Writer. Educated at Edinburgh High School and Edinburgh University, the son of Lord Auchinleck, Boswell owes his significance to Samuel Johnson. Their friendship enabled him to write *Life of Johnson* (1791) as well as *Journal of a Tour to the Hebrides* (1785). Boswell's non-Johnsonian literary achievement was his *Account of Corsica* (1768). Boswell lacked sufficient dedication to be a successful lawyer and his hopes of entering Parliament were never realized.

**Bosworth, battle of,** 1485. Richard III's usurpation of the throne of Edward V was challenged by Henry Tudor, the future Henry VII. Henry landed at Milford Haven. Richard concentrated his forces at Leicester where he could watch events. The armies met on 22 August near Market Bosworth. Richard chose a strong position on Ambien hill, but his considerable superiority in numbers was offset by the defection of Lord *Stanley. Richard was cut down fighting on foot and his body slung on horseback for burial at Grey Friars, in Leicester.

**Botany Bay,** discovered on 29 April 1770 by Captain *Cook, who named it, probably to honour the botanists aboard HMS *Endeavour* led by Sir Joseph *Banks. Banks later (1786) advocated Botany Bay as an ideal place for a penal colony. The 1st Fleet landed there on 20 January 1788 and, finding Banks's account much exaggerated, moved on to Port Jackson, landing there at Sydney Cove. Nevertheless, the name Botany Bay became synonymous with Australia, first as a convict settlement,

**Bothwell, James Hepburn, 4th earl of** (*c.*1535–78). The family influence was in the south of Scotland. Though a protestant, Bothwell was at first a supporter of *Mary of Guise and strongly anti-English. He had no part in the murder of *Rizzio, and as relations between Mary, queen of Scots, and *Darnley deteriorated, he became close to the queen. In 1567 events moved to a melodramatic climax. In February, Bothwell was the chief instigator of the murder of Darnley. On 7 May he was divorced, on 12 May created duke of Orkney, and on 15 May married Mary at Holyrood palace. Outraged at his elevation, his enemies confronted him. Mary and Bothwell fled to Borthwick castle, from which Bothwell escaped, but after the encounter at *Carberry Hill on 15 June, they parted for ever—Mary to captivity in Lochleven castle, Bothwell to Orkney and Shetland. Thence he fled to Norway, under Danish rule. The king of Denmark kept him in prison as a useful pawn, first in Malmö, then in Dragsholm on Zealand, where he died insane. His embalmed body is preserved in a crypt in the church at Faarvejle nearby.

**Bothwell Bridge, battle of,** 1679. After the murder in May 1679 of Archbishop

James *Sharp of St Andrews, a zealous episcopalian, the *covenanters rose in the south-west. They defeated John Graham of Claverhouse (Viscount *Dundee) at *Drumclog on 1 June and occupied Glasgow, but were routed by James, duke of *Monmouth, at Bothwell Bridge on 22 June.

**Botswana** Former British protectorate of Bechuanaland. British influence in the region was established by the *London Missionary Society and traders operating northward from Cape Colony in the early 19th cent. It was not until pressure from the Boers of the South African Republic (*Transvaal) to the east and the establishment of a German colony to the west threatened the region that the British government declared a protectorate in 1885. It became independent in 1966.

**Boudicca** British queen of the *Iceni tribe. Boudicca led the British rebellion against the Romans in AD 60/1. Her husband Prasutagus had become a client king of the Romans at the time of the invasion. However, when Prasutagus died in AD 60 the Romans decided to incorporate his kingdom into the province of Britain. The take-over seems to have been badly handled and, according to the Roman historian Tacitus, ended up with Boudicca being flogged and her two young daughters raped. The rebellion which she instigated was joined by the Iceni's neighbours, the *Trinovantes. They captured and destroyed the new Roman colony at *Colchester, repeated their success at *London, and then destroyed *Verulamium, the capital of their traditional foes the *Catuvellauni. The Roman governor *Suetonius Paullinus eventually managed to assemble a large enough force to take on the rebels in a pitched battle. The British were defeated and the rebellion collapsed. Boudicca died shortly afterwards, by her own hand.

**Boulton, Matthew** (1728–1809). Birmingham entrepreneur and engineer. Boulton developed his father's button business from 1759, establishing his new Soho Works (1760–2). Like his associate *Wedgwood, he integrated manufacturing with mercantile functions. Already chronically short of water power by 1771, he acquired a two-thirds share of *Watt's 1769 patent (1773), and entered partnership (1775).

**Bourchier, Thomas** (c.1410–86). Archbishop of Canterbury. A great-grandson of Edward III, Bourchier became chancellor of the university and bishop of Worcester while studying at Oxford. Because of his 'great blood', he was chosen as archbishop in 1454 by the baronial council ruling during Henry VI's insanity. He welcomed the Yorkist descent on London in 1460, agreed to Edward IV's assumption of the crown, and seemed ready to accept *force majeure*, crowning both Richard III and Henry VII.

**Bourges, treaty of,** 1412. This agreement between *Henry IV, king of England, and the duke of Orléans arose out of the French civil war. In return for Henry's aid against the Burgundians, Orléans accepted English claims to sovereignty over the duchy of Aquitaine. Henry dispatched an army in July 1412, but as the Orléanists had reached a temporary peace with Burgundy, the treaty was never fulfilled.

**Bouvines, battle of,** 1214. On 27 July 1214 was fought one of the decisive battles in European history. Near Bouvines (Flanders), the army of Philip II 'Augustus', king of France (1179–1223), crushed the forces of the coalition against him: an expeditionary corps from England, dispatched by King John; the detachments of Rhineland princes; and Otto of Brunswick, John's nephew and Holy Roman emperor. Philip's victory set John upon the road to Runnymede and *Magna Carta.

**bowls** is one of the oldest and most popular of all sports and like many others blossomed in late Victorian Britain: London, which had only one municipal green in 1895, had 76 by 1907. The modern game developed when biased bowls were brought into use, permitting tactical play. The Scottish Bowling Association was formed in 1892, the English in 1903, and the International Board in 1905. Crown green bowls, played on a convex green, is popular in the midlands and north.

**Bow Street runners** were constables attached to the Bow Street Police Office, established by the magistrate Sir John Fielding in the mid-18th cent. Seven police offices were established in London in 1792 on the Bow Street pattern. Valuable public servants but poorly paid, they were superseded by the Metropolitan Police Act (1829).

**Boxer Rising,** 1900. The spread of European influence led to strong anti-foreign feelings in northern China. Encouraged by Dowager Empress Tzu Hsi, young Chinese formed an organization called the Society of Harmonious Fists or 'Boxers'. They attacked converts to Christianity, missionaries, and workers on foreign-controlled railways. On 20 June a Boxer uprising occurred in Peking. A six-nation force landed at Tien-Tsin on 14 July and marched 80 miles to relieve Peking on 14 August.

**boxing** developed from uncontrolled encounters, in which wrestling, kicking, gouging, biting, hair-pulling, and kicking opponents when down were practised. Early prize fights went on until one of the combatants could not continue. By 1838 London Prize Ring rules were in use, with a roped-off ring. The Queensberry rules from 1867 onwards took some time to establish themselves: they included padded gloves, 3-minute rounds, and a 10-second knockout. The Amateur Boxing Association was set up in 1880 and boxing was brought into the Olympic Games in 1904. In professional boxing, the British Board of Control has supervised since 1919, though international authorities have proliferated.

**Boyle, Robert** (1627–91). Famous for his work on air pressure, Boyle was the youngest son of the 1st earl of Cork. During the 1650s he belonged to the 'invisible college', so called because they never all met together, associated with John *Wilkins at Wadham College, Oxford. Crucial in the *scientific revolution in England, this was a nucleus for the *Royal Society.

**Boyne, battle of the,** 1690. James II's attempt in the summer of 1689 to reassert his rule over all Ireland faltered on the resistance of *Derry and Enniskillen. The Williamite victory at *Newtown Butler in July 1689 was the start of the counter-attack. Derry was relieved the following day. In June 1690 William III arrived to take personal command and began his advance south. The Jacobites decided to give battle on the line of the Boyne, north of Dublin. When they met on 1 July, James's army was some 25,000

strong, William's a little more. In the end, the day was decided largely by a frontal assault across the Boyne. Though casualties were not heavy, the outcome was decisive.

**Boys' Brigade** Founded by William Alexander Smith in Glasgow in 1883. Smith started the brigade as a means of controlling the boys who attended his Scottish free church Sunday school. He sought to use military drill and discipline for the religious and moral improvement of the boys. The crest of the brigade was an anchor and its motto 'Sure and Stedfast'. The uniform consisted of a 'pill-box' cap, belt, and haversack.

**Boy Scouts** Youth movement founded by *Baden-Powell in 1908. Baden-Powell was inspired to establish the Boy Scouts by the interest shown in his army training manual, *Aids to Scouting*, and by the example of the *Boys' Brigade. He held a trial camp on Brownsea Island in Poole Harbour from 29 July to 9 August 1907. The following year Baden-Powell established the Boy Scouts and wrote *Scouting for Boys*. Within two years there were 100,000 members. Unlike the Boys' Brigade, he believed that drilling boys destroyed individuality. Other branches were added to the organization; the Wolf Cubs in 1914, the Rover Scouts in 1919, and the Beavers in 1982. Today the movement has spread to 150 countries and has around 16 million members.

**Bracton, Sir Henry** (c.1210–68). Bracton, one of the greatest writers on the common law, was born in Devon and became the dean of Exeter cathedral. He served Henry III as a justice in Eyre and a justice of King's Bench, but his fame rests on his great work *De legibus et consuetudinibus Angliae* ('On the Laws and Customs of England'). But it has been suggested that most of the book was written by others.

**Braddock Down, battle of,** 1643. Parliament and the king were still contending for supremacy in the south-west early in 1643. At Braddock Down, near Liskeard, on 19 January 1643, Sir Ralph *Hopton defeated a parliamentary force.

**Bradford** Though Bradford received a charter as early as 1251, it remained a cloth town of local importance. During the 17th cent. it lost ground. Celia Fiennes in the 1690s did not mention it and *Defoe in the 1720s ignored it, though he devoted a long description to Leeds. Its revival was due to the development of the worsted trade and the growth of the canal network. Bradford canal, completed in 1774, and the link to the Leeds and Liverpool canal (1777), gave access to the east and west coasts. By the early decades of the 19th cent., Bradford had begun its prodigious growth. By 1851 it was the seventh largest town in the country, with a population of well over 100,000. From 1846 onwards it was also joined to the rapidly growing railway system. In the 20th cent. Bradford was less well served. It suffered comparatively little from the attentions of the Luftwaffe but severely at the hands of post-war town planners. Many evocations of Edwardian Bradford, when wool was still king, are to be found in the works of J. B. Priestley, particularly *Bright Day*, a threnody for 'Bruddersford' trams.

**Bradford, diocese of** The see was created in 1919 out of sections of the *Wakefield and *Ripon dioceses, to accommodate the increasing population in this heartland of the woollen industry. The cathedral is the former 15th-cent. parish church with 18th-cent. fittings and notable modern extensions (1953–65).

**Bradlaugh, Charles** (1833–91). Radical, atheist, and republican journalist. Born in London, he rose from solicitor's clerk and part-time *secularist lecturer to become one of the most formidable public speakers in Victorian Britain. He owned the *National Reformer* from 1862, formed the National Secular Society in 1866, and launched the National Republican League in 1873. Notoriety was achieved with the republication of the 'Knowlton Pamphlet' on birth control with Annie Besant in 1877. In 1880 he was elected to Parliament for Northampton, but as an avowed atheist was not allowed to take the oath. His attempt to secure entry to the Commons, not successful until 1886, made him the leader of democratic opinion in Britain.

**Bradshaw, John** (1602–59). President of the High Court of Justice which tried and condemned Charles I to death. At the trial he was out of his depth. Discomfited by the king's challenge to the court's legality, Bradshaw twice ordered him removed. At the end of the trial, after sentencing Charles as a 'tyrant, traitor and murderer', he denied the king's request to be heard. Elected president of the *Council of State, Bradshaw nevertheless challenged *Cromwell's right to dismiss the *Rump Parliament in 1653. When the Rump was recalled in 1659, Bradshaw resumed his presidency of the Council of State, but died a few months before the Restoration.

**Bramham Moor, battle of,** 1408. Henry Percy, earl of *Northumberland, who had escaped disaster in 1403 when his son Hotspur was killed at *Shrewsbury, raised rebellion against Henry IV again in 1408. He marched south to Thirsk but found little support. He was defeated and killed at Bramham Moor, on 20 February 1408.

**Brandywine, battle of,** 1777. John Burgoyne set out from Canada on his march south against the American rebels in June 1777. The following month, *Howe took a force from New York by sea, landed in Maryland, and moved north. *Washington moved south to protect Philadelphia and took up position on the Brandywine Creek. On 11 September Howe outflanked him and went on to occupy Philadelphia. British elation was short-lived when news came through in October that Burgoyne had surrendered at *Saratoga.

**Braose, William de** (d. 1211). King John's treatment of William is the most notorious example of his capricious approach towards his subjects. William, a major Welsh marcher lord, supported John's claim to the throne in 1199. But his capture of John's nephew and dynastic rival *Arthur of Brittany, at Mirebeau in 1201, proved his downfall, for he was one of the few who knew that Arthur had been murdered. John became increasingly concerned about his loyalty. From 1205, he determined to destroy him after Matilda, William's wife, blabbed something about Arthur's fate. John ruthlessly hounded the family. Matilda and her sons disappeared, and William died in exile in France in 1211.

**'Bread or blood' riots,** 1816. The years after *Waterloo saw high prices, unemployment, and a trade recession. The agricultural labourers of the fenland were a depressed group, badly paid and housed. They complained of tithes, enclosures, threshing-machines, and the hiring of Irish labour, and arson, tree-cutting, and cattle-maiming were not infrequent. The worst disturbance was at Littleport in May 1816 when a large crowd was dispersed by the yeomanry, with two killed. In the event, five were hanged and nine transported. The protesters were said to have carried placards threatening 'Bread or blood'.

**Brecon cathedral** *See* SWANSEA.

**Breconshire** Border county of south Wales taking its name from the Welsh kingdom of *Brycheiniog. Its Norman successor was the lordship of Brecon. At the Act of *Union with England in 1536 the lordships of Brecon and of Builth to the north were merged to form the county. In 1974 it became a district of the new county of Powys and remained part of that county after the revision of 1996.

Breconshire is dominated by hills, including the Brecon Beacons (Pen-y-Fan 2,906 feet), one of the country's national parks, the Black Mountains, and Fforest Fawr. Only some 6 per cent of the county is below 500 feet, the lower land being formed by the valleys of the rivers Wye and Usk.

**Breda, declaration of,** 1660. In April 1660, while he was still in exile in Holland, Charles II issued the Breda declaration. It was a skilful political document, conciliatory but vague. It promised a general amnesty, payment of arrears to *Monck's troops, and an assurance that 'tender consciences' in religion would be respected. Most contentious issues were left to a free Parliament.

**Breda, treaty of,** 1667. Signed on 31 July, the treaty ended the second *Anglo-Dutch War. The most important clause left England in possession of New Netherlands, including New Amsterdam, renamed New York. The *Navigation Act of 1651 was modified to allow the Dutch to bring to England exports from the southern Netherlands.

**Brémule, battle of,** 1119. Fought on 20 August between Henry I and Louis VI of France. Louis invaded Normandy and was keen to bring Henry to battle. He launched poorly controlled cavalry attacks against the English and Norman household troops. Henry himself received some blows on his helmet, but the French were beaten off and fled in disorder.

**Brétigny, treaty of,** 1360. After the Black Prince's great victory at *Poitiers in 1356, Edward III resumed campaigning in 1359. But he was unable to land a knock-out blow and negotiations commenced in May 1360 at Brétigny, near Chartres. King John's ransom was to be cut and, in exchange for abandoning his claim to the throne of France, Edward was to have Guînes and Aquitaine in full sovereignty.

**bretwalda** The term first appears in the *Anglo-Saxon Chronicle*'s annal for 829. The A version says *Egbert of Wessex was the eighth king who was bretwalda (ruler of Britain). The other versions use 'brytenwalda' (wide ruler). There is dispute as to which term is 'right'. More significant is the relationship of the term to *Bede's statement that there were seven rulers who had *imperium* over much or all of our island: the earliest *Ælle of Sussex (late 5th cent.), the latest *Oswiu of Northumbria (d. 670).

If, as is likely, 'bretwalda' is an early term, it is of a poetically glorifying kind. Bede's observation on *imperium,* and who held it, derives from some topos of grouping rulers in sevens (to be found later in *Nennius' idea of seven Roman emperors who ruled in Britain). Two questions arise. First, whence did Bede get his information? Why, for example, dig up the exceedingly obscure Ælle? Second, granted the almost infinite obscurity of early political arrangements, may not Bede be transmitting traditions which derive from something which lay between the poetically rhetorical and the institutionally defined?

**Brian Boru** (d. 1014), the greatest of Ireland's *high kings, belonged to what had been a minor *Munster dynasty, Dál Cais, which rose to prominence in the mid-10th cent. Brian's father, Cennétig mac Lorcáin, began the family's rise to power and died in 951 as king of north Munster (Thomond). Brian succeeded his brother Mathgamain in 976 and rose swiftly, dominating the Viking towns of Limerick and Waterford. At this point he challenged the reigning high king, the midlands ruler Mael Sechnaill mac Domnaill of the southern Uí Néill, who finally submitted to Brian as high king in 1002. Brian adopted the title 'Emperor of the Irish' in 1005. A revolt by the Leinstermen and the Hiberno-Norse of Dublin led to Brian's great victory over them in the battle of *Clontarf in 1014, at which, however, he himself was slain.

**Bridewell** The London Bridewell, set up in 1555, was the first 'House of Correction' and the term was often used henceforth to describe such institutions. The 16th cent. saw a massive increase in the numbers of poor and indigent, and houses of correction were used for the punishment and reformation of petty offenders. In 1610 houses of correction were set up generally throughout England.

**bridge** developed in the 19th cent. from whist and is believed to have originated in the Near East. The word itself is doubtful, but may derive from the Russian *biritch* meaning no trumps. The essential difference from whist is the bidding process to establish the trump suit and the forecast. The large number of local bridge clubs are affiliated to the English Bridge Union, which issues points, enabling players to qualify as club masters, district masters, and the like.

**Bridgeman, Charles** (d. 1738). Royal Gardener to George II 1728–38, Bridgeman played a major role in the evolution of the English landscape garden. Stylistically his work lay between the geometric layouts of the late 1600s and the freer designs of William *Kent and Lancelot 'Capability' *Brown. For the crown he was active at *Hampton Court, *Kensington, *Richmond, *St James's Park, and *Windsor, whilst his private commissions included Claremont, Eastbury, and Wimpole.

**Bridgwater, Francis Egerton, 3rd duke of** (1736–1803). Bridgwater succeeded his brother as duke in 1748 at the age of 11. After the collapse of his proposed marriage to the widowed duchess of Hamilton (one of the Gunning sisters) in 1758, he devoted his time to exploiting the coal resources on his Lancashire estates. To this end he employed *Brindley in 1761 to construct a canal from Worsley to Salford, with a famous aqueduct at Barton over the river Irwell, and followed it with the Manchester to Liverpool canal, of 28 miles. He died un-

married and was buried at Little Gaddesden (Herts.), near his Ashridge estate.

**Brigantes** A British tribal federation and *civitas*. The name means 'upland people' or 'hill-dwellers', which is appropriate to the Pennine heartland. Not surprisingly, such a vast area was not the fiefdom of a single tribe but rather a loose confederation. There may have been a central place for the whole federation, possibly at Almondsbury near Huddersfield or at Stanwick near Scotch Corner. Certainly by the time the Romans reached their southern borders, the Brigantes were led by a single ruler, Queen *Cartimandua.

**Briggitines** Established *c.*1346 as a double order of men and women by St Bridget of Sweden (*c.*1303–73). They followed the *Augustinian rule and constitutions drawn up by Bridget, including the 'Rule of the Saviour'. There was only one English house, Twickenham, founded by Henry V in 1415 and transferred to Syon in 1431.

**Bright, John** (1811–89). Radical politician and son of a Rochdale textile manufacturer, his first public speech (on temperance, 1830) marks the strong quaker influence on him. A leading public speaker for the *Anti-Corn Law League (1839–46), Bright was elected MP for Durham (1843), Manchester (1847–57), and thereafter Birmingham. He supported *free trade, opposed legislation limiting the hours of adult workers in textile factories, and, in the 1850s, called for peace, retrenchment, and reform, gaining unpopularity for his opposition to the *Crimean War. He entered Liberal cabinets as president of the Board of Trade (1868–70) and chancellor of the duchy of Lancaster (1873–4, 1880–2), resigning on the latter occasion in protest at the naval bombardment of Alexandria. Said to be the most belligerent of pacifists, Bright was one of the greatest orators of the 19th cent.

**Brighton** Originally Brithelmston, a Sussex fishing village, Brighton developed rapidly from the mid-18th cent., when Dr Richard Russell recommended its health-giving air. It was patronized by Fanny *Burney, Samuel *Johnson (1770), and from 1784 by George, prince of Wales. Brighton's original classical Royal Pavilion, built by Henry Holland

(1784), was redeveloped by *Nash in oriental style with an Indian exterior and Chinese interior (1817).

**Brigit, St** (c.450–c.525). Patron saint of Ireland, with *Columba and *Patrick. Born in Faughart (Co. Louth), she took the veil in her youth, having evaded marriage by disfiguring her face. Her monastery of Cill-Dara (Kildare), founded c.470, developed as a centre of learning and spirituality.

**Brihuega, battle of,** 1710. Under pressure from a revitalized Franco-Spanish army of 12,000 troops under the duc de Vendôme, an English force of 4,000 men commanded by Lord *Stanhope was forced to retreat from Madrid into Catalonia. Caught at Brihuega on 9 December, Stanhope's troops stood firm until their powder ran out. Reduced to less than 500 men, Stanhope had no choice but to surrender.

**Brindley, James** (1716–72). Brindley, an engineer, was born in Derbyshire and set up as millwright at Leek in Staffordshire. In 1759 he was put in charge of the duke of *Bridgwater's canal between Worsley and Manchester. Brindley subsequently supervised the building of a number of canals, including the Liverpool to Manchester, opened in 1767; the Trent and Mersey, 140 miles long and involving a 2,880-yard tunnel at Harecastle; and the Staffordshire and Worcester.

**Bristol** A city at the junction of the rivers Avon and Frome. It is not recorded before c.1020, but by 1066 was a flourishing port. The Normans built there one of the key strategic castles of England. By 1216 Bristol was influential enough to have an elected mayor. In 1377 it ranked in the poll tax as the largest provincial town after York; its importance was recognized in 1373 when the king made it a county corporate; later its status was further enhanced when it became a cathedral city (1542). Bristol enjoyed a golden age in the late 17th and 18th cents. Its wealth came chiefly from transatlantic trade (especially in slaves) and its associated new industries (sugar and tobacco). By 1800, however, it was overtaken in importance by Liverpool, Manchester, and Birmingham. In the 1830s and 1840s I. K. *Brunel helped to make Bristol an important terminus for railways and for Atlantic steamships, and from 1868 new docks at Avonmouth helped the city recover prosperity.

**Bristol, diocese of** The see, founded in 1542 by Henry VIII, is now roughly conterminous with the city of Bristol. Its poverty, and the need to create the Ripon and Manchester dioceses without increasing the total bench of bishops, led to its brief union with the *Gloucester diocese in 1836. Rising population made this merger clearly undesirable, and the bishopric had its independence restored by an Act of 1884. The cathedral is the former St Augustine's abbey.

**Bristol riots,** 1831. The rejection of *Grey's second Reform Bill by the House of Lords was greeted by widespread demonstrations and rioting. Bristol had a reputation for disorder and the riots there were as much against an oligarchical corporation as against the Lords' action. The flash-point was a visit on 29 October by the recorder, Sir Charles Wetherell, an outspoken opponent of the bill, to open the assizes. The Mansion House, Customs House, Bishop's palace, and half of Queen Square were then attacked and looted. After two days, troops cleared the streets, with twelve killed and 100 arrested. Thirty-one persons were condemned to death and five eventually executed.

**Britain, Battle of,** 1940. On 18 June 1940, Churchill declared 'the Battle of France is over; I expect that the Battle of Britain is about to begin'. On 2 July Hitler reluctantly ordered planning for the invasion of England. The Churchill government, supported by most public opinion, chose to fight on. The invasion was impossible without German air superiority. The battle was a German attempt to destroy RAF Fighter Command and so win control of the air. The single-seat aircraft in the decisive encounters were evenly matched. The Messerschmidt 109E was as fast as the British Spitfire and faster than the Hurricane; the British types were more manœuvrable. German bombers began by attacking shipping from mid-July to mid-August. The plan was to force the RAF to attack German fighter escorts. On 13 August, the Germans began the main battle, attacking airfields and aircraft factories. British losses in aircraft and pilots began to exceed replacements. On 7 and 9 September heavy attacks hit London; the Germans lost

84 aircraft. Evidently the RAF was not defeated and Hitler postponed the decision to invade. On 15 September a renewed attack on London gave the RAF another success: 60 German aircraft and only 26 British were lost. On 17 September Hitler again postponed the invasion and on 12 October it was abandoned. The British lost fewer than 800 aircraft; the Germans nearly 1,400. Fewer than 3,000 British aircrew took part, of whom 507 were killed. Churchill was correct: 'Never in the field of human conflict was so much owed by so many to so few'.

**Britannia,** the Roman name for the British Isles revived by *Camden (1586), has become the poetic name for Britain. Personified as a seated female figure, she appeared emblematically (modelled by Frances Stewart) on Charles II's 1667 peace of *Breda medal and copper coinage (1672); the 'union' shield resting alongside bore the crosses of St George and St Andrew.

**British Academy** In response to a resolve for a world-wide Association of Scientific and Literary Academies (Wiesbaden, 1899), the British Academy was established in 1901. It soon received a royal charter, but many years passed before it affected the humanities' world as the *Royal Society did science. By the mid-1940s it was moribund, but under Sir Charles Webster (president, 1950–4) and Mortimer Wheeler (secretary), efficiency and scope slowly broadened: by 1970 it had active research committees, funds to support younger scholars, an improved government grant, new premises in Burlington House, and foreign exchanges. Its headquarters are at 10, Carlton House Terrace, London.

**British and Foreign School Society** The society stemmed from the work of Joseph *Lancaster, who established a school and training institution in Southwark in 1798. With the promise of £100 p.a. from George III, Lancaster formed 'The Society for Promoting the Royal British or Lancasterian System for the Education of the Poor' in 1808, later changed to the British and Foreign School Society. Lancaster's proposal for a system of teaching through monitors enabled mass education at an elementary level to be provided on a scale never previously

attempted and almost 4,000 British schools were established by the Society.

**British Association for the Advancement of Science** This peripatetic body, founded in 1831, has been important in promoting public awareness of science. The *Royal Society was London-based and like a gentleman's club; the *Royal Institution fashionable and expensive. Provincial pride and fear of scientific decline were important factors in the British Association's establishment; the first meeting was in York, then came Oxford and Cambridge, and then commercial and industrial cities.

**British Broadcasting Corporation (BBC).** Britain's key media organization, which oversaw the introduction of radio (1922) and television (1936). Founded in 1922 as the British Broadcasting Company, it became a corporation five years later. From the start it was a monopoly organization to avoid what was seen as the 'chaos' of free enterprise broadcasting in the USA.

The tone for the BBC was set by its founder, John *Reith, managing director of the company 1922–6, and director-general of the corporation 1927–38. His Scottish presbyterian values ensured that the BBC fulfilled its remit to inform, educate, and entertain, and observe due impartiality. To ensure its impartiality, the early BBC was banned from dealing with controversial issues, and even when the ban was removed by the government in 1928, the BBC trod carefully. It introduced more varied fare to supplement its Home Service during the war, with a forces programme of light music (to become the Light Programme in 1945) and a Third Programme of high art and classical music. This pattern remained until the 1960s saw it reshaped into Radios 1, 2, 3, and 4 (with the addition of Radio 5 in the 1990s) and the start of BBC Local Radio in 1967. In television, BBC broadcasting became popular with its postwar relaunch, and a second channel, BBC2, from 1962. In an era of cable, satellite, and interactive media, the BBC's privileged status as a publicly funded body is increasingly questioned and it has frequently been accused of an institutional 'liberal' bias.

**British empire** At its apogee, around 1920, the British empire was the largest ever known, reputed to cover a quarter of the world's land area, and a fifth of its population. Like all mighty oaks, this one had a tiny origin. It grew out of the seafaring voyages of the Tudor age. The first British colony was Virginia, settled in 1585, but not for long. A ship returning four years later found that the colonists had disappeared. In 1607 the colony was re-established, and survived. Other places were also colonized, especially some Caribbean islands. Trading posts were established in India.

It was mainly a commercial empire, run by chartered monopoly *companies, and defended by the Royal *Navy. Britain made sure its benefits accrued to her exclusively, by a series of *Navigation Acts passed in the mid-17th cent. to prevent the colonies dealing with anyone else. The *Seven Years War saw Britain take control of much of India (1756–7). That marked the peak of what later came to be called the 'first' British empire, which came to an end with the rebellion of the thirteen American colonies in 1776.

The loss of America (except Canada) threatened the British empire as a whole. In fact, however, it continued to expand. Even while America was being lost, Captain *Cook was sniffing out new possibilities in the antipodes. The first colony there, *New South Wales, was established in 1788. *Sierra Leone in west Africa was established as a home for freed slaves at the same time. Other gains—*Trinidad, *Malta, *Gibraltar, the *Cape of Good Hope—were made as a result of the French Revolutionary wars.

In the 1880s Britons became infused with a conscious mood of *imperialism. They sought empire deliberately, instead of merely accepting its growth in what the imperialist J. R. Seeley called 'a fit of absence of mind'. It sparked off the Scramble for *Africa, which added much of the eastern and southern part of the continent to Britain's collection. The culmination of this phase was the second *Boer War (1899–1902). The only substantial additions to the British empire after this were the '*mandated' territories—ex-German and Ottoman possessions—which were allocated to it in the wake of the *First World War.

This was the empire's zenith. Most Britons felt it was beneficial: 'the greatest secular agency for good that the world has seen', according to Lord *Rosebery, though there were other opinions, voiced by J. A. *Hobson. The wonder was that so small a country as

Britain was able to exercise so wide a sway. How was it done?

The simple answer to that is: 'with difficulty'. Britain's empire would have been too much for her, if she really had tried to dominate it. She succeeded in holding it mainly by persuading others to take the strain. In the 'white' dominions these were the European settlers, who were given effective self-government from early on in the 19th cent. Elsewhere local governors utilized divisions amongst natives, or adopted a policy of preserving native social and power structures, so as to keep disruption to a minimum. Every colony had its class of collaborators. Later they proved less willing, especially as Britain's strength came to look more vulnerable. That, in the end, was what brought the empire down, in the aftermath of the *Second World War, when *decolonization began.

The empire left legacies on both sides. For the ex-colonies it brought stability for a while. It helped the spread of capitalism, Christianity, parliamentary institutions, English as a lingua franca, and (most beneficially) cricket. Afterwards it conferred membership of a new club, the *Commonwealth of Nations. So far as Britain is concerned, the balance sheet is controversial. She may not have profited as much as she thought from the empire. Its collapse was felt as a loss, however, economically and emotionally. Some of the country's problems in the second half of the 20th cent. were undoubtedly aggravated by her difficulty in coming to terms with its disappearance.

**British Empire, Order of the** This was the first democratic or meritocratic order and was established in June 1917 in the darkest days of the First World War. Though far less aristocratic than previous orders, it was nevertheless divided into five sections—the Knights Grand Cross, the Knights Commander, Commanders, Officers, and Members. Of equal significance was that a large number of women were, for the first time, admitted to honours.

**British Guiana** See GUYANA.

**British Honduras** See BELIZE.

**British Museum and Library** Founded in 1753 to house three historic collections (Cotton, Harley, Sloane) acquired by the nation, the museum was funded by public lottery and established in Montagu House, Bloomsbury. The British Library was established by statute (1973) as the national centre for reference, and is a copyright deposit library. The museum has outgrown its original home since opening in 1759, but removal of the library to the new building at St Pancras has enabled the great court to be opened up to improve facilities. The existing building in Neo-Greek style was by Sir Robert Smirke and opened in the 1850s.

**British National Party** Founded in 1982 as an off-shoot of the *National Front, the BNP has no seats at Westminster, Cardiff or Edinburgh, but claims some 48 seats on local councils. Its constitution commits it to seek to restore 'the white make-up' of Britain by encouraging voluntary repatriation. Its stance has moved from anti-semitism to denunciation of fanatical Islamism. Other policies include the return of capital punishment, strong disapproval of homosexuality, and withdrawal from the European Union.

**British Somaliland** Former British protectorate near the mouth of the Red Sea. In 1884, during the 19th-cent. partition of Africa by European powers, Britain declared a protectorate over part of Somali territory. In the Second World War British troops occupied the neighbouring Somali territory, previously controlled by Italy, and in 1960 the two former dependencies were united to create the independent state of Somalia.

**British Union of Fascists** The BUF was founded in 1932 by Sir Oswald *Mosley's New Party and various small British fascist groups. The Blackshirts, a paramilitary organization, were formed in self-defence against attacks from militant Jewish youths and communists. However, the crisis in British society which Mosley expected did not materialize. The BUF failed to create a nationwide, mass movement. It suffered a set-back after the Olympia meeting in June 1934 when unnecessarily strong action was taken by the Blackshirts to silence hecklers. When on 4 October 1936 1,900 fascist marchers were turned back by 100,000 opponents at the 'Battle of Cable Street' in the East End of London, the government decided to take action. The Public Order Act (1936) prohibited political uniforms and gave the police powers to ban marches. Many BUF members

were interned in 1940 but the movement was never a threat to the stability of government.

**Britons** The peoples living in Britain during the Roman occupation. The name, which the people of Britain seem to have given themselves, first appears in the account of the voyages of the Greek explorer Pytheas in the late 4th cent. BC. The Greek form of the name is Prettani (or Pritani): Latin authors such as Catullus and Caesar wrote of the Brittani, whence came the name of the Roman province, Britannia. The meaning is uncertain, but is thought to be something like 'the tattooed people'.

In general, Roman authors presented a dismal picture of the Britons, as barbarians who wore skins or went naked, and practised a form of polygamy. Strabo, who claimed he had seen British youths in Rome, described them as relatively tall, but bow-legged and graceless. But Caesar recognized that not all Britons were the same, identifying those around the south-east coast as more civilized and of different stock from the people of the interior. Even before the invasion, the Britons in the south-east were becoming socially and politically sophisticated and acquiring a taste for things Roman. They were using gold and bronze coins, and exporting raw materials (gold, silver, and iron) along with grain and hides. In exchange, they received manufactured goods such as bronze- and silverware and fine pottery, together with wine. These products are found mainly at a limited number of major tribal centres like Camulodunum (*Colchester) and *Verulamium (St Albans).

To some extent, therefore, political and social developments in the century before the Claudian invasion of AD 43 paved the way for the political system that conquest by Rome brought with it. Nucleated settlements which acted as centres of administration for large tribal territories were known to both the invaders and the natives. Equally, both Romans and Britons were used to a society in which power was in the hands of a single individual, supported by an élite class.

The Romans developed a system of provincial administration which perpetuated, at least initially, the existing tribal framework. Thus in Britain they created, between AD 70 and AD 120, about fifteen self-governing tribal authorities (*civitates*), each with elected magistrates and council and each based on a major town. The first such grants of local self-government were in the areas which had shown political sophistication before the invasion—Kent, Essex, Hertfordshire, and Buckinghamshire, where the *Cantiaci, the *Trinovantes, and the *Catuvellauni were established. Other *civitates* were added later, and there is little doubt that the first magistrates and councillors were drawn from the old tribal élites. By AD 80, according to Tacitus, the Britons were widely adopting Roman fashion in housing, clothing, language, and diet. Houses with mosaics, plastered walls and ceilings, under-floor heating, and their own bath-suites were built in town and country alike. Roman shoes and sandals were made. Along with wine, a variety of amphorae demonstrate that olive oil, fish-sauce, and other exotic foodstuffs were imported from the Mediterranean.

Just how widespread the adoption of a Romanized life-style was is debated. There were probably fewer than a hundred towns in Roman Britain, mostly very small, and with a total population unlikely to have exceeded 200,000 people. The villas, even if we assume 3,000 of them, would add little to this total, since the greatest part of a villa's population would be the agricultural labour force and servants. If we compare this to recent estimates of the total population of Roman Britain, at around 2–3 million, we can see that the Romanized element of the population was in the minority. Yet even in rural settlements which show few signs of Romanized architecture, imported pottery and glass, coins, Roman-style jewellery, and occasional Latin graffiti are found. There were some changes in agricultural practice too, with new agricultural implements and crops, new methods of land management, and an increasing emphasis on cash-crops and farming for profit. These changes, not surprisingly, are best attested in those areas where villas were most prolific. Outside this area, the clearest signs of Romanization are often found in the civilian settlements that grew up to serve the soldiers in the garrison forts of the north and west. For a minority, changes in life-style were dramatic, but for the vast majority of the population, the impression is that much of life went on as before.

**Britten, Benjamin** (1913–76). The most distinguished English composer of his generation, Britten showed talent from an early age. Educated at the *Royal College of Music (London), his roots were firmly in East Anglia, where he had his home for 30 years. In 1945 Britten's opera *Peter Grimes* was premièred in London. Its impact was remarkable: Britten had written an opera which quickly established itself in the international repertoire and which combined a distinctively modern style with the ability to appeal to the general musical public. Thereafter Britten's prolific output demonstrated his fluency in writing for the human voice. A brilliant pianist, Britten's commitment to musical performance was reflected in the foundation of the Aldeburgh Festival in 1948.

**Brontë family** In 1820, the Irish-born Patrick Brontë brought his Cornish wife and six young children to Haworth parsonage, near Bradford. After the deaths of Mrs Brontë and the two eldest girls the children were cared for by an aunt but thrown very much on their own resources. After erratic schooling, then short teaching posts, Charlotte, Emily, and Anne returned to Haworth to care for their father; anxiety over their irresponsible debt-laden brother Branwell deepened as he became addicted to alcohol and opium. Charlotte's discovery of some of Emily's poems led to publication of *Poems by Currer, Ellis, and Acton Bell* (pseudonyms corresponding to their initials), which, though selling poorly, encouraged them towards novels. Charlotte (*Jane Eyre*, 1847; *Shirley*, 1849; *Villette*, 1853) became a literary celebrity, but Emily's *Wuthering Heights* (1848) was too innovative and passionate for many tastes; Anne (*Agnes Grey*, 1847; *Tenant of Wildfell Hall*, 1848) might have been overpowered by her more brilliant sisters, but continues to be quietly appreciated. Although Branwell's debts were discharged, he died in 1848, to be followed shortly by Emily, then Anne the following summer. Charlotte eventually married her father's curate (1854), but died soon after.

**Brooke, Sir Basil, 1st Lord Brookeborough** (1880–1974). Prime minister of Northern Ireland 1943–63. Descended from Ulster plantation landowners, Brooke came to politics after a military career. He was behind the establishment of the Ulster Special Constabulary, minister of agriculture 1933–40, and the most active of Sir James *Craig's administration. Minister of commerce 1940–3, his criticism of the ineffective response to wartime led to his premiership. He was an intransigent opponent of concessions to the catholic minority and conservative in economic affairs.

**Brooke, Sir James** (1803–68). Brooke, 'the White Raja of Sarawak', was born at Benares, educated in England, and joined the Madras army in 1819. Wounded in the first *Burmese War (1824–6), he resigned his commission in 1830. Inheriting a fortune five years later, he became an explorer in southeast Asia. In 1841, he heard that his friend, the raja of Sarawak, was facing a major rebellion. He rushed to the raja's aid and helped to crush the rising. As a reward, and after the death of the raja, he was offered the rajadom by its overlord, the sultan of *Brunei. He accepted and established a dynasty.

**Brougham, Henry Peter, 1st Baron Brougham and Vaux** (1778–1868). From a minor gentry family in Westmorland, educated at Edinburgh University, Brougham was one of the most eminent lawyers of his time. He helped to found the *Edinburgh Review* and his contributions made it the leading political journal of the day. He qualified for the English bar in 1802 and entered the House of Commons in 1810. He was a brilliant speaker, supporting the liberal wing of the Whig Party and espousing the causes of anti-slavery, popular education, and legal reform.

Brougham was mistrusted by his party leaders who considered his support of Queen *Caroline to be motivated by desire for personal advancement. His support of popular causes, particularly anti-slavery, gained him election as MP for Yorkshire in 1830, and when the Whigs came to power he expected high office. He reluctantly accepted the post of lord chancellor with a peerage because it meant giving up the House of Commons and a lucrative income at the bar. He carried through a series of important legal reforms but disagreements with his colleagues led *Melbourne not to reappoint him in 1834. Brougham never returned to office and became markedly eccentric in later life.

**Brown, James Gordon** (b. 1951). Prime minister. Born in Glasgow, son of a Church of Scotland minister, Brown was educated in Kirkaldy and took a First in History at the University of Edinburgh. After working in television, he was returned to Parliament in 1983 as the Labour member for Dunfermline East. With Tony *Blair he set out to remodel the party as 'New Labour' and in 1997 became Chancellor of the Exchequer in the first Blair government, holding the post for a record ten years.

One of his first actions was to give greater independence to the Bank of England in monetary policy and he was credited with a long period of financial stability and economic growth. Long regarded as Blair's destined successor, rumour suggested that Brown found the period of waiting increasingly trying. He took over as prime minister in September 2007 and was accorded a respectful welcome. There were strong indications that he might launch an early general election to confirm his own authority, and when he decided not to do so he was accused of dithering—a slightly odd charge against one who had previously been seen as dictatorial and heavy-handed—a 'clunking fist'. Of far greater consequence was the financial crisis which followed the collapse of Northern Rock in late 2007 and which many attributed to the extravagant borrowing which had characterized Brown's later years as Chancellor. Towards the European Union he is reputed to be less enthusiastic than his predecessor. Another decision which has returned to plague him was to support *devolution to undermine Scottish nationalism. Instead the *SNP made gains, taking control of the Scottish Parliament in a minority administration, and leaving Brown to argue the case for retention of the Union. He is married with two sons.

**Brown, Lancelot** (1715/16–83). English landscape designer, generally known as 'Capability' because of his references to the 'capabilities' of the places about which he was consulted. Born in Northumberland, he worked first for Sir William Loraine at Kirkharle but by 1741 had moved south to Stowe. Brown took a prominent part in the evolution of the Stowe landscape for which *Gibbs and *Kent were providing buildings. Soon Brown established his own distinctive landscape style with its clumps, belts, bridges, irregular lakes, and encircling woodland and lawns. Major commissions began to come his way, among them Croome (from 1750), Longleat, Burton Constable, *Chatsworth (from 1761), and *Blenheim (from about 1764). In 1764 Brown was appointed master gardener at Hampton Court. *Walpole wrote of him: 'So closely did he copy nature that his work will be mistaken for it.'

**Browne, Robert** (c.1550–1633). An early puritan separatist, Browne was born in Rutland of a wealthy family. After graduating from Corpus Christi College, Cambridge (1572), he had a spell in London as a schoolmaster and open-air preacher (1572–8) and then in Cambridgeshire. Hostile to any form of church government, he established independent congregations, later known as Brownists, in East Anglia. Accepting episcopal ordination (1591), he was rector of Achurch (Northants) until his death.

**Browne, Sir Thomas** (1605–82). Physician and author. London-born, educated at Oxford, Montpellier, and Padua, Browne received a Leiden MD (1633) before returning to practise near Halifax. He settled in Norwich (1637) and in 1643 published the authorized version of his most famous work *Religio medici*. Its reflections on the mysteries of God, creation, and man were an immediate success. *Urn Burial* and *The Garden of Cyrus* (1658) reflected antiquarian interests.

**Browning, Robert** (1812–89). Born in Camberwell, son of a clerk in the Bank of England, Browning read widely as a boy in his father's library. Much of his early work was historically based. *Paracelsus* (1835) was a verse drama about the 16th-cent. physician. *Strafford* (1837) was a lifeless poetic drama; *King Victor and King Charles* was on the unpromising subject of a dynastic dispute in 18th-cent. Piedmont and was never performed; *A Blot on the 'Scutcheon* (1843) ran for three nights and convinced Browning to abandon the theatre. *Dramatic Lyrics* (1842) included 'My Last Duchess', 'Soliloquy in a Spanish Cloister', and 'The Pied Piper'; *Dramatic Romances and Lyrics* (1845) added 'Home Thoughts from Abroad', 'The Lost Leader', and 'How they Brought the Good News from Ghent to Aix'.

In 1846 Browning married Elizabeth Barrett, already an established poet, and they lived mainly in Italy until her death in 1861. His greatest success, *The Ring and the Book* (1868–9), took a melodramatic murder story from late 17th-cent. Italy and presented it from different viewpoints.

**Bruce, Edward** (d. 1318). Brother of Robert I king of Scots, earl of Carrick from 1313, titular king of Ireland (1315–18). Edward Bruce was an outstanding if savage soldier, but an over-ambitious man. As soon as Robert I took the throne in 1306, Edward became one of his foremost commanders. In 1308 he ravaged Galloway, confining English authority in the area to a few castles; further campaigns followed, culminating in the siege of Stirling castle which began in 1313. At *Bannockburn (24 June 1314), Edward was in command of the leading brigade.

Next, with Robert's full backing, he embarked on an expedition to Ireland. He seems to have landed in Ulster at the end of May 1315, with the support of Ulster nobles, but then forced them to acknowledge him as king of Ireland. He proceeded to the south, but did not find the support he expected. Edward's position as king was impossible to sustain; and in October 1318 he was killed in battle at Faughart, near Dundalk.

**Bruce, James** (1730–94). British explorer. Bruce established his claim to fame by revealing to the western world that the Blue Nile had its source in Lake Tana, in Abyssinia (Ethiopia). From Cairo in 1768 he travelled upstream as far as Aswan continuing his journey to Lake Tana, which he reached in November 1770. After a perilous homeward journey he reached England in 1774, only to encounter serious doubts about the truth of his discoveries. His claims were vindicated by later travellers.

**Bruce, Robert** (1210–95). Known as the 'Competitor'. Leading member of the 13th-cent. Scottish nobility and grandfather of King Robert I. His extensive lands stretched from Middlesex to Aberdeenshire, the most important concentrations lying in Essex, Co. Durham, and south-west Scotland. His transnational interests are reflected in his marriage to Isabel de Clare, daughter of the earl of Gloucester. He also served as sheriff of Cumberland and supported Henry III against Simon de *Montfort at *Lewes. A truly cosmopolitan figure, he went on crusade to the Holy Land (1271–2). Descended through his mother from David I, he was one of the chief claimants or 'competitors' for the vacant Scottish throne in 1291–2, and was bitterly disappointed when Edward I declared in favour of John *Balliol.

**Bruce, Robert** (d. 1304). Eldest son of Robert *Bruce (d. 1295) and father of Robert I. His marriage to Marjorie, widow of Adam of Kilconquhar, brought him the earldom of Carrick—a promotion which involved the Bruces in rivalry with their neighbour John *Balliol, lord of Galloway. Bruce–Balliol rivalry intensified when Robert's father and John Balliol were the main challengers for the Scottish throne in 1291–2. When Balliol was enthroned, Robert refused to recognize him. After the English victory at *Dunbar (27 April 1296), he asked for the Scottish throne—a request to which Edward famously responded: 'Have we nothing else to do but win kingdoms for you?' Despite this rebuff, Robert remained in the English allegiance until his death.

**Bruce, Robert I of Scotland** *See* ROBERT I.

**Brudenell, James Thomas** *See* CARDIGAN, 7TH EARL OF.

**Brummell, George** (1778–1840), known as 'Beau' Brummell. English dandy. Son of Lord North's private secretary, with a reputation for fastidiousness and repartee, he utilized a generous inheritance to become an arbiter of fashion. Supremely self-centred, he was an intimate friend of George, prince of Wales until royal favour was withdrawn in 1811. Accumulating debt eventually forced retirement to Calais (1816).

**Brunanburh, battle of,** 937. Brunanburh was the crowning military achievement of Athelstan's reign, which saw *Wessex advances into Devon, south Wales, and the north. In 937 a formidable coalition attempted to hold him at bay. Constantine II of Scotland was joined by Owain of Strathclyde and Olaf Guthfrithsson from Dublin. In savage fighting, probably near the Humber, Athelstan and his brother Edmund prevailed.

**Brunei** rose as a powerful Islamic sultanate in the 15th cent. In 1888, surrounded by the Brookes' Sarawak and the domains of the British North Borneo Company, it was taken under a British protectorate. The sultan was restored to his government and, in 1963, declined to join the *Malaysian Federation.

**Brunel, Isambard Kingdom** (1806–59). Engineer. Son of the distinguished émigré Sir Marc, Brunel was scientifically educated in Paris. Sickness incurred at his father's Thames Tunnel (1826–8) led Brunel to convalesce at Bristol, where he gained appointments as engineer of the Clifton bridge (1829–31), the floating harbour (1830–1), and the Great Western railway (from 1833). Brunel's engineering of the GWR demonstrated his vision and his failings: the commitment to the broad (7-feet) gauge promised quality and speed, but delivered inflexibility; his vision of the Atlantic crossing from Bristol encapsulated by his first two major ships, *Great Western* (1837) and *Great Britain* (1843), exceeded the bounds of commercial technology proven in the outstandingly advanced *Great Eastern* (1858). A driven man, chronic overwork contributed to early death as his two greatest achievements, the Albert bridge at Saltash and the *Great Eastern*, neared commissioning.

**Brussels, treaty of** Signed on 17 March 1948 between the United Kingdom, France, Belgium, the Netherlands, and Luxembourg, it set up the Brussels Treaty Organization, also known as *Western European Union. The Brussels treaty was therefore a vital step on the road to the formation of *NATO.

**'Brutus'** The extraordinary legend that Britain had been 'founded' by Brutus, great-grandson of Aeneas of Troy, haunted men's imagination for centuries. *Geoffrey of Monmouth, in the 12th cent., related how Brutus, after many adventures, visited England (landing at Totnes), subdued the race of giants who inhabited it, gave his name to it, and founded London as New Troy.

***Brut y tywysogyon*** ('Chronicle of the Princes') is the most valuable narrative source for the history of medieval Wales. Translated from a lost Latin original, three independent versions in Welsh survive from the 14th cent. as continuations of *Geoffrey of Monmouth's *Historia regum Britanniae*. They begin with Cadwaladr Fendigaid, whose death (682) was regarded as a key event in the history of Britons and Saxons. They end with the equally crucial death of Llywelyn ap Gruffydd (1282).

**Brycheiniog** was a medieval Welsh kingdom whose dynasty is said to have begun with Brychan, the son of a 5th-cent. Irish chieftain and the daughter of the king of Garthmadrun in the Vale of Usk. His line ended *c*.940, when Brycheiniog fell under *Deheubarth's influence. It was conquered by Bernard of Neufmarché (1093), whose marcher lordship was known as Brecon (a corruption of Brychan).

**Buchan, John Comyn, earl of** [S] (d. 1308). Buchan's career shows the difficulties faced by prominent Scots who wished to maintain the integrity of their country. He was a supporter of John *Balliol, and hostile to the claims of Edward I. Yet he had at times to compromise, submitting to Edward in 1296 and being sent by him to suppress the rising of Andrew Murray in 1297. Instead, he joined the rebels, fought at *Falkirk against Edward, and was a leading figure on the Scottish side till what seemed to be Edward's final victory in 1304. Bruce's murder of his cousin John *Comyn of Badenoch forced him finally onto the English side. He was routed by Bruce at *Inverurie in 1308.

**Buchan, Alexander Stewart, 1st earl of** [S] (d. *c*.1406). Lord of Badenoch. The fourth son of Robert II, he was made a justiciar in northern Scotland (1372), in which post he earned his nickname of 'Wolf of Badenoch'. He became earl of Buchan in 1382 as a result of his marriage to Euphemia, countess of Ross. He was associated with bands of caterans, and was sacked from his justiciarship in 1388.

**Buchanan, George** (1506–82). The most distinguished Scottish humanist of his era, Buchanan was educated at Paris, where he gained a reputation as a neo-Latin poet and dramatist. Deeply influenced by Erasmus, his anticlerical views led to frequent brushes with authority culminating in imprisonment by the Portuguese Inquisition. On his return to Scotland in 1561 he was associated both with the court of Mary Stuart and with the new protes-

tant kirk. Following the queen's deposition in 1567, he emerged as the most influential of Mary's detractors, justifying resistance to tyranny in his elegant dialogue *De jure regni apud Scotos* (1579) and his monumental *Rerum Scoticarum historia* (1582).

**Buckingham, Edward Stafford, 3rd duke of** (1478–1521). Stafford's father, a prominent supporter of Richard III, was seized and executed at Salisbury in 1483. Stafford was restored to the title by Henry VII. He had royal blood, through Thomas, duke of *Gloucester, younger son of Edward III, and his mother, Catherine Woodville, sister to Edward IV's queen. Under a suspicious king, this was a dangerous heritage. In 1520, an anonymous letter accused the duke of treasonable words. He was summoned from Thornbury and executed on 17 May 1521.

**Buckingham, Henry Stafford, 2nd duke of** (1455–83). Buckingham came from a staunchly Lancastrian family. He could expect little favour from the Yorkist establishment, but Edward IV's death opened the door. Allying himself with Richard of Gloucester, the two dukes swept to power in the summer of 1483. With Gloucester crowned as Richard III, Buckingham looked well set. Yet within four months he joined southern gentry in rebellion. Betrayed to the king, he was summarily executed at Salisbury on 2 November. He may have been converted to Henry Tudor's cause; he might have judged that he was again joining the winning side; or he might even have had fantasies about the crown.

**Buckingham, George Villiers, 1st duke of** (1592–1628). Buckingham attracted James I's attention by his good looks, and by 1616 had replaced Robert *Carr as favourite. Unlike Carr, however, he displayed considerable administrative ability. The king's repeated affirmations of his dependence upon Buckingham meant that he was blamed for unpopular policies such as the 'Spanish match' (for Prince Charles). Only in 1623, during his enforced stay in Spain, did he emancipate himself from James's tutelage. He planned to build up an anti-Spanish alliance, of which France was to be the linchpin, but religion complicated the situation, for the French protestants of La

Rochelle were under attack from their own king and appealed to Charles to save them. Buckingham sent out expeditions against Cadiz in 1625 and in support of La Rochelle in 1627, but both ended in humiliating defeat. The Commons attempted to impeach him in 1626, and two years later denounced him as the cause of all England's evils. This inspired John Felton to assassinate him at Portsmouth in August 1628. Subsequent events showed that he was a symptom rather than the cause of malfunctioning in the English polity.

**Buckingham, George Villiers, 2nd duke of** (1628–87). Heir to his father the 1st duke, he was brought up with the royal children. He fought in the Civil War, but recovered his estates in 1647. Personally involved in the Scottish invasion on Charles II's behalf in 1651, Buckingham was able to return to England from exile in 1657. Enjoying preferment at the Restoration, lack of managerial capacity combined with pathological irresponsibility rendered Buckingham the least weighty of 'the *cabal's' members.

**Buckingham palace** (London). The official London residence of Her Majesty the Queen. Buckingham House (as it then was) was built in 1702–5 for John Sheffield, 1st duke of Buckingham, by the architect William Winde (d. 1722). It was bought in 1762 by George III, who had it enlarged by Sir William Chambers in 1762–9. In 1825 George IV approached his friend John *Nash for designs, who incorporated Buckingham House in Buckingham palace. Some of the rooms were opened to the public in 1993 to help pay for the rebuilding of parts of *Windsor castle after the fire in 1992.

**Buckinghamshire** has little geographical unity. The chalk hills of the Chilterns run across the middle of the county from southwest to north-east. Communications between north and south have always been poor, and Olney in the north, where William Cowper lived, was in a different world from Stoke Poges in the south, where *Gray wrote 'Elegy in a Country Churchyard'. The diffuseness of the shire was increased by the fact that the county town was not Aylesbury, near the middle, but the smaller town of Buckingham in the extreme north-west corner.

Pre-Roman Buckinghamshire was in *Catuvellauni territory, and *Cunobelinus, grandson of *Cassivellaunus, is believed to be commemorated in Great and Little Kimble, near *Chequers. In the 6th cent. the area was disputed between the Britons and the English, the latter reported by the *Anglo-Saxon Chronicle* to have captured Aylesbury in 571. The region became part of the kingdom of *Mercia. As a county Buckinghamshire probably developed after *Edward the Elder, king of Wessex, launched his great advance against the Danes and fortified Buckingham as a frontier outpost in 918. It was first mentioned as a county in 1010 when most of it was overrun by a second Danish advance. In *Domesday Book, Buckingham appears to have been substantial, but did not maintain its pre-eminence and was overtaken by Aylesbury, Wycombe, Marlow, and Chesham. Industrial development came late to Buckinghamshire. Slough did not even merit a separate entry in the 1801 census but was included in the parish of Upton. The 19th cent. gave the county a network of railways, which stimulated the growth of Wolverton, Slough, and Wycombe. Proximity to London led to great changes in the 20th cent., the balance of population moving south. The development of Milton Keynes in the north-east as a new town promises to restore the balance.

**budget** The practice of devising an annual programme for financial legislation has been attributed to William Lowndes, an official in the Treasury throughout the half-century after 1675. The term dates from the 1730s and is derived from the wallet or 'bougette' in which the chancellor of the Exchequer carried his proposals. In the 19th cent. the practice developed by which the annual budget comprised an assessment of Exchequer income and expenditures for the past financial year, together with estimates of expected spending needs in the forthcoming year and the fiscal steps required to provide for them. As the range of economic instruments at the disposal of the state has increased, the budget has lost some of its importance.

**'Bulge, battle of the'**, 1944. In September 1944 Hitler decided to counter Anglo-American success in France and Belgium by secretly preparing powerful forces, including twelve Panzer divisions, to break through in the Ardennes and retake Antwerp. Selecting a period of bad weather to palliate allied air superiority, the Germans attacked on 16 December 1944. The British and Americans contained the initial success gained by the Germans. Moreover, the American defenders held road junctions, notably at Bastogne where 101 Airborne, hurriedly moved there, withstood a six-day siege.

**Bunker Hill, battle of,** 1775. After the encounter at *Lexington in April 1775, General Gage found himself trapped in Boston by the American rebels. The town was dominated by the Charlestown peninsula to the north. On 16 June the Americans dug in on, near Charlestown, and the following day Gage sent 2,000 troops to dislodge them. This they accomplished but at the cost of more than 1,000 killed and wounded.

**Bunyan, John** (1628–88). Puritan author. Son of a brazier near Bedford, Bunyan suffered a severe religious crisis initiated by his wife's piety. Subsequently joining a nonconformist group in Bedford, he began to preach (1657). The Restoration revived hostilities against conventicles, so his refusal to abandon preaching led to imprisonment for most of the next twelve years, until the *Declaration of Indulgence (1672). The enforced leisure produced a stream of theological and devotional works. The vitality of *Pilgrim's Progress*, written in gaol, made him a household name.

**Burford, battle of,** c.752. *Æthelbald of Mercia was defeated by *Cuthred of Wessex, enabling Wessex to extend its territories north of the Thames. Wessex's gains were wiped out by *Offa's victory at *Benson c.777.

**burgages** were forms of tenure. In the royal burghs of Scotland, they were properties held from the crown for rent and with the obligation of performing *watch and ward. In England, they were properties in certain boroughs held freehold: in parliamentary boroughs they could carry the right to vote, which gave them a value far in excess of their economic worth.

**Burgh, Hubert de** (c.1175–1243). A younger son of Norfolk gentry, he rose to govern Plantagenet England and marry a sister of a king of Scotland. Hubert entered John's service in the 1190s. His reputation was made by his defence of the castle of Chinon in Anjou against Philip Augustus in 1205. Recalled to England he was appointed *justiciar at the height of the *Magna Carta crisis and remained in that office until 1232. He played a decisive part in the war of 1215–17, successfully resisting Prince Louis of France's siege of Dover castle (1216–17), and commanding the victorious English fleet at the August 1217 battle of *Sandwich (or Dover). From 1219 onwards Hubert was the most influential figure in Henry III's minority government. In 1221 he married, as his third wife, Margaret, sister of Alexander II of Scotland, and four years later was created earl of Kent. In 1232 Peter des Roches persuaded Henry to dismiss and imprison him. He made a dramatic escape in 1233, but never recovered his former influence.

**Burghley, William Cecil, 1st Lord** (1520–98). Cecil, created Lord Burghley in 1571, was the son of Lincolnshire gentleman Richard Cecil. After education at Grantham and Stamford grammar schools, he matriculated at St John's College, Cambridge, in 1535. He became part of the important humanist circle of Roger *Ascham, Thomas *Smith, John *Cheke, and Walter Haddon. Cecil married Cheke's daughter Mary in 1541 and entered Gray's Inn the same year. Mary died a year after the birth of their first son Thomas, but Cecil remarried in December 1545. His new wife was Mildred, daughter of the protestant humanist Sir Anthony Cooke.

His political career gathered pace after the early 1540s. According to Cecil's own chronology of his life, he sat in Parliament in 1543. He was knighted in 1551, and became a member of the Privy Council (and the principal secretary) from 1550 until 1553. He spent the last three years of Mary's reign privately in Wimbledon. Cecil's public life began again in November 1558, when he started working on the day of Mary Tudor's death to secure a comfortable accession for Elizabeth. Until he was appointed lord treasurer in 1572, Cecil was principal secretary and the queen's private secretary. He was at the centre of the campaign in 1559–60 to support the protestant lords of the

\*Congregation in Scotland. Like his Privy Council colleagues, Cecil wanted Elizabeth to marry; this was the central political issue of the decade because it involved Mary Stuart, her French connections, Scotland, and the competing ideologies of protestantism and catholicism.

Cecil collaborated with Sir Francis \*Walsingham in 1584 to involve Englishmen in a 'bond of association' to take action in the event of Elizabeth's assassination by catholic foreigners. Although the second part of his Elizabethan career—between 1585 and his death in 1598—is generally viewed as more 'conservative', Cecil was still active as a parliamentary patron, co-ordinator of the Privy Council, master of the court of wards, and lord treasurer.

Cecil's reputation is mixed. Some of his earliest biographers and contemporaries emphasized his anxiety over England's Roman catholic enemies, his political success, and his patronage of learning. \*Macaulay argued that Cecil was purely an administrator. But Cecil had a keen sense of providence and a strongly apocalyptic view of the struggle between the protestant and catholic European kingdoms.

**burghs,** a variant spelling of boroughs, is the Scottish term for privileged towns. David I is traditionally credited with the first foundations of royal burghs; after 1450, burghs founded by subjects became more numerous. Scottish burghs differed in many respects from English boroughs: they were more uniform in their laws and customs; they had a more unified voice in national politics until 1707; and indeed the royal burghs had their own \*Convention from the 16th cent.

**Burke, Edmund** (1729–97). Whig politician and conservative political philosopher. Burke was born in Ireland to a catholic mother and protestant father. Brought up as a protestant, he was sent to Trinity College, Dublin. He studied law in London, but quickly turned his attention to writing. He became a member of Parliament in 1766 and remained an MP for virtually the rest of his life. Burke had an unrivalled gift for portraying the issues of the day in terms of general principles, and as a result many of his speeches contain disquisitions on political philosophy.

Burke has often been accused of inconsistency. His stance on the plight of catholics in Ireland—he deplored their savage treatment by the protestant ascendancy—and of Indians in Bengal is contrasted with his rejection of the idea of natural rights advanced by the French revolutionaries. Similarly, Burke's sympathy for the American colonists appears to contradict his insistence on the sovereign authority of Parliament. However, if we bear in mind the organizing ideas of his political philosophy, we can see that there is an underlying coherence in his writing. In his defence of the Irish catholics, the Bengali Indians, and the American colonists, Burke was not arguing that they had natural rights to determine their own destiny, but that there had been abuse of legitimate (i.e. traditional) authority. Similarly, we can see consistency in Burke's apparently contradictory endorsement of the 1688/9 Whig revolution in England, yet denunciation of the 1789 revolution in France. In both cases he sought to defend traditional modes of political authority. The Whig revolution in England was a revolution averted, in that it preserved the established Anglican state from an unconstitutional conversion by James II into a Roman catholic polity. By contrast the French Revolution was a real revolution, perpetrated against the wholesome foundations of a 'noble and venerable castle', the traditional and settled French state. His \*Reflections on the Revolution in France (1790) is generally regarded as the epitome of conservatism, defending traditional political cultures. However, he recognized that some change was inevitable—indeed he held that a state without the means of change was without the means of its own conservation.

As a practising politician and statesman, Burke also left his mark. His impassioned defence of the formation of political parties as a means of resisting the unconstitutional influence of the crown was an important step in legitimizing party politics in Britain. Moreover, although he only held minor office (that of paymaster-general) for two short spells, Burke exerted considerable influence on the government. His vehement condemnation of the revolution in France helped to stiffen anti-French policy in Britain. Similarly the sympathetic tone he adopted toward the American colonists contributed towards the *rapprochement* which was eventually reached by the British government. Finally Burke's obsessive pursuit of the impeachment of Warren *Hastings in the House of Lords for his rule as governor-general of Bengal succeeded in creating an irresistible momentum for the reform of the East India Company.

**Burma (Myanmor)** was ruled by the Alaungpaya dynasty from 1752 to 1885. Initially, the dynasty was expansionary, conquering (although failing to hold) Thailand. However, it was severely checked and ultimately defeated by a counter-expansionary drive coming from the British in India. The British conquest of Burma was piecemeal, beginning in 1826 and not reaching completion until 1885. Originally ruled as a province of British India, the country was given its own administration in 1937. Between 1942 and 1945, Burma was overrun by the Japanese. After the war, hopes continued in the Colonial Office for a restoration of British dominance. However, an Anti-Fascist People's Freedom League had arisen to organize large-scale popular resistance to the Japanese. Now it was turned against the British. On 4 January 1948, the Independent Republic of Burma came into existence.

**Burma campaigns** (1941–5). These involved three objectives. One commanded American support, the attempt to reopen the land route to nationalist-held China. The second involved guarding British-controlled India; the third the reconquest of lost British territories, particularly Malaya, rich in rubber and tin. In 1944 General *Slim defeated a Japanese offensive and in 1945 *Mountbatten's South-East Asia Command organized the reconquest of Burma.

**Burmese wars** The British in India fought three wars against the Alaungpaya dynasty (1752–1885), kings of Burma. The first, between 1824 and 1826, was a reaction to Burmese expansion which was considered to threaten *Calcutta. Following a victory notable for its heavy casualties, the East India Company annexed Assam, Arakan, and Tenasserim and established a resident at the royal court. The second war in 1852 was provoked by a revolt against interference in

Burmese affairs by the resident and led to the annexation of Pegu. The third war, in 1885–6, was a response to the throne's attempts to promote anti-British sentiments. In its wake, the dynasty was displaced, upper Burma annexed, and the whole of the country ruled directly as a province of British India.

**Burney, Frances (Fanny)** (1752–1840). Novelist and dramatist. Frances was a daughter of music historian Charles Burney, in whose circle she met Samuel *Johnson and Edmund *Burke. A quiet observer of mankind, her first novel, *Evelina*, was published anonymously in 1778 and well received. The second, *Cecilia*, in 1782, brought her society introductions, which led to a minor appointment at the court of Queen *Charlotte in 1786. Five years later, to the surprise of her friends and family, she married General d'Arblay, an impoverished French refugee. Between 1802 and 1812 they lived in France, and at the time of Waterloo she was in Brussels. Her diary contains many descriptions of court and literary life.

**Burns, John E.** (1858–1943). Trade union organizer and exponent of 'Lib-Labism'. Burns was born in London. Despite little education he became an engineer, and involved himself in the Amalgamated Society of Engineers. An accomplished orator, he was one of the organizers of the London dock strike of 1889. In 1884 Burns had joined the *Social Democratic Federation, and acquired a reputation as a socialist militant. But by the 1890s he had broken both with Marxism and with trade unionism, supporting instead the furtherance of working-class interests within the Liberal Party. Elected as an independent Labour MP for Battersea in 1892, in 1905 he accepted office as president of the Local Government Board in the Liberal administration. Burns resigned from the government in 1914, apparently in protest against war with Germany.

**Burns, Robert** (1759–96). Poet, son of an Ayrshire tenant farmer. Well educated by an enlightened parish schoolmaster, Burns grew up with an appetite for literature. His first creative period coincided with his father's death in 1784, his own unsuccessful attempts at farming, and a passionate affair with Jean Armour. It culminated in the publication of his *Poems Chiefly in the Scottish*

*Dialect* (1786). This carefully crafted selection of poems was a literary sensation and marks the beginning of a Burns cult that has prospered. Being lionized in Edinburgh proved an unnerving experience for Burns, who was on the point of emigrating to Jamaica when marriage, the offer of a farm, and an appointment in the excise in 1789 made him decide to stay in Scotland. The second creative period of his career was marked by his contributions to James Johnson's *The Scots Musical Museum* (1789–1803). These took the form of more than 100 brilliant vernacular songs and lyrics. He died in poverty in Dumfries in 1796 at the age of 37.

**Burton, Sir Richard** (1821–90). Traveller, Arabist, and great Victorian outsider, Burton joined the Indian army in 1842. In India he learned numerous languages and much obscure lore, not least about Islam. Hence he was credible when he travelled to Mecca disguised as an Arab in 1853. Now famous, he led an expedition to Harar in north-east Africa before being chosen by the Royal Geographical Society to lead their great east African expedition of 1856. Burton discovered Lake Tanganyika in 1858. Later travels took him to the Gold Coast, Mount Cameroon, Dahomey, Brazil, and the American West. He published translations of the *Arabian Nights* and the *Kama Sutra*. This and other exploits shocked many Victorians, including his wife, who destroyed most of his papers.

**Bury St Edmunds and Ipswich, diocese of** The see, roughly conterminous with Suffolk, was created in 1914 out of the *Norwich diocese. Suffolk then had its own see for the first time since the *Dunwich bishopric collapsed under the weight of the Danish invasions. The cathedral at Bury St Edmunds is the former 15th-cent. Perpendicular parish church adjoining the tower of the ruined former Norman abbey.

**Busaco, battle of,** 1810. After making peace with Austria, Napoleon resolved to drive the English out of Spain and Portugal. Masséna was dispatched with a large force while *Wellington prepared his defensive line at *Torres Vedras. On 27 September 1810 Masséna launched an attack at Busaco, north-east of Lisbon, but failed to make progress. Wellington retired to Torres Ve-

dras, from which he counter-attacked the following year.

**Buss, Frances Mary** (1827–94). A pioneer of higher education for women, Frances Buss started teaching at 14. She entered Queen's College, London, in 1849 and went on to found the North London Collegiate School for Girls the following year. Starting with 35 pupils, a year later it had 135. Buss was a fervent supporter of women's suffrage and campaigned to have university examinations opened to girls, giving much help to Emily *Davies in founding Girton College, Cambridge.

**Bute, John Crichton-Stuart, 3rd marquis of** (1847–1900). Philanthropist and scholar. Bute inherited the title at the age of 6 months. After education at Harrow and Christ Church, Oxford, he converted to the catholic church. Much of his time was devoted to the development of Cardiff docks and to the family estates in Glamorgan. In Scotland, he was a benefactor of Glasgow and St Andrews universities, and took a keen interest in Scottish history. From 1892 to 1898 he was rector of St Andrews.

**Bute, John Stuart, 3rd earl of** ([S] 1713–92). Prime minister. Bute served as tutor to the prince of Wales from 1755, thereby acquiring an influence which gave rise to political controversy after the latter's succession as George III in 1760. Initially holding only a court appointment, Bute rose to become secretary of state in 1761 and 1st lord of the Treasury in May 1762 until his resignation the following April. Disheartened by the difficulties in implementing the theoretical reign of virtue which had so impressed his royal pupil, Bute gave up the struggle. Exaggerated fears about his continuing influence (as a 'minister behind the curtain') destabilized the administrations of both *Grenville and *Rockingham. Beyond the sphere of politics, he was not only a patron of education, literature, and the fine arts, but also a keen student of science, with a particular interest in botany.

**Butler, Josephine** (1828–1906). Campaigner for women. Born in Northumberland, daughter of John Grey, she married George Butler, an academic and later dean of Winchester, in 1852. She first took up philanthropic work amongst poor women in Oxford and continued it after moving to Liverpool in 1864. She became president of the North of England Council for the Higher Education of Women (1869-70) and secretary (1869-85) of the Ladies' National Association for the Repeal of the Contagious Diseases Acts, passed in 1866-9 to regulate prostitution in garrison towns and ports. She withdrew from public life after the death of her husband in 1890.

**Butler, Richard Austen** (1902-82). Born in India and educated at Cambridge, 'Rab' Butler entered Parliament in 1929 as MP for Saffron Walden. As president of the Board of Education he was responsible for the Education Act (1944), which introduced a tripartite secondary system and the '11-plus' examination. He served in all three of the great offices of state, as chancellor (1951-5), home secretary (1957-62), and foreign secretary (1963-5). He was twice passed over for leadership of the party in favour of *Macmillan in 1957 and Douglas-*Home in 1963. Butler retired from politics in 1965 and accepted the mastership of Trinity College, Cambridge.

**Butt, Dame Clara** (1872-1936). English contralto, who studied at the Royal College of Music. Her first major success was as Orpheus in Gluck's opera at the Royal College in 1892. Her career, however, centred on the concert platform, where her tall, imposing figure was matched by a powerful voice. She was particularly associated with the music of Elgar, singing the première of his *Sea Pictures* (Norwich, 1899).

**Butt, Isaac** (1813-79). Founder of the *Home Rule movement. At the outset, Butt was a vigorous defender of Orange Toryism. Increasingly, however, his unionism and his commitment to property right were tinctured with a strong national feeling. Defending the *Young Irelanders in May 1848, he urged that the detrimental economic consequences of the British connection might be offset through a subordinate parliament in Dublin. Although he sat for Youghal (1852-65), he languished for a time on the margins of national politics. His defence of the *Fenian conspirators in 1868 restored his patriotic reputation. He was returned to Parliament in 1871 as a Home Ruler, representing Limerick. Butt helped to create a national organi-

zation through the Home Rule League (1873), but by the time of his death he had been superseded by more militant lieutenants.

**Butterworth, George** (1885-1916). English composer and one of countless examples of the pity and waste of war. Educated at Eton and Trinity College, Oxford, Butterworth was a leading member of a group of musicians, including Cecil Sharp and Ralph *Vaughan Williams, interested in English folk-song. His compositions were few and small scale, but Butterworth developed a distinctive voice, with a full and at times lush orchestration in his idylls *A Shropshire Lad* (1912) and *The Banks of Green Willow* (1913). He died in action on the Somme on 5 August 1916.

**Bye plot,** 1603. James VI and I, plagued by plots in Scotland, was confronted by fresh ones as soon as he arrived in his new kingdom. The Bye plot was a hare-brained scheme, hatched by William Watson, a catholic priest, to seize the king at Greenwich and force him to grant a general toleration. It fizzled out, but the subsequent investigations led to the *Main plot, which brought down *Ralegh.

**Byland, battle of,** 1322. The victory of his supporters at *Boroughbridge in March 1322 encouraged Edward II to undertake another campaign against the Scots in the summer. After besieging Berwick without success, he retired, pursued by Robert I Bruce. While the king was at Rievaulx abbey, Bruce's men attacked over the hills from Northallerton. They dispersed the royal rearguard at Old Byland on 14 October, but Edward escaped to York. A king of England in flight in his own country was mortifying.

**Byng, John** (1704-57). Byng's naval career got off to a flying start. He was a younger son of Viscount Torrington, the hero of *Cape Passaro and 1st lord of the Admiralty 1727-33. He entered the navy at 14, was present at Cape Passaro, and reached rear admiral in 1745. On the outbreak of war in 1756 he was dispatched with a squadron to protect *Minorca. He found an enemy force landed on the island and a French fleet cruising outside. Byng's ships engaged the enemy but came off worse and Byng retired to Gibraltar, leaving Minorca to its fate. When it surrendered, the outcry was thunderous. Byng was recalled at once, court-martialled, and sentenced to death. The recommendation for mercy was ignored and he was shot on the quarter-deck of the *Monarque* in Portsmouth harbour. Byng died with courage and composure. Voltaire's *Candide*, published in 1759, contained the famous observation that the English liked to shoot an admiral from time to time, *pour encourager les autres*.

**Byrd, William** (*c.*1543–1623). Britain's leading composer during the Elizabethan and Jacobean periods, Byrd's large output included English anthems and consort songs, Latin motets and masses, and keyboard and instrumental consort music. A pupil of Thomas *Tallis, he was appointed organist and choirmaster at Lincoln cathedral in 1563. In 1570 he became a gentleman of the Chapel Royal, where he was joint organist with Tallis, with whom he was granted a royal monopoly of music printing.

**Byron, George Gordon, 6th Baron Byron** (1788–1824). Poet. He succeeded to the barony and Newstead abbey in 1798. After Harrow and Cambridge he embarked on the grand tour which provided material for his verses, in 1812 waking to find himself famous with the publication of the first two cantos of *Childe Harold*. In politics associated with the Holland House set, his maiden speech was on the Nottinghamshire framebreakers' bill, but he left England in 1816 after separating from his wife, heiress Annabella Milbanke. Saluted in Italy as 'il poeta della rivoluzione', in 1824 his love of liberty took him to fight in the Greek War for Independence. He died of fever, his masterpiece *Don Juan* unfinished.

b

**cabal** Word meaning secret clique or conspiracy, given to Charles II's administration of 1671–3. The ministers, whose initials formed the word cabal, each had different objectives. Lord *Clifford, who climbed from being a Devon squire to become lord treasurer, became a catholic and advocated war to seize Dutch commercial wealth. *Arlington, a courtier and careerist, tried to implement what he interpreted as Charles's wishes. *Buckingham wanted to become chief minister: he affected popularity and favoured religious toleration. Lord Ashley, advanced to be earl of *Shaftesbury, also advocated toleration. The cynical *Lauderdale governed Scotland. The cabal disintegrated 1673: Clifford died, Buckingham and Shaftesbury went into opposition.

**cabinet** The executive committee of the government, appointed by the *prime minister. It evolved in the later 17th cent. out of the *Privy Council, which had become too large. Two developments of crucial importance were the withdrawal of the monarch from attendance during George I's reign, allowing the first minister to take the chair and impose his views on his colleagues, and the growth of the principle of cabinet solidarity.

In the 18th cent., the cabinet was overwhelmingly aristocratic. George *Grenville in the 1760s had a cabinet of nine, in which he was the only commoner—yet he was the younger brother of an earl. Not until the later 19th cent. did commoners predominate. Like most committees, the cabinet has tended to grow. The Fox–North coalition in 1783 had seven cabinet members; *Peel in 1841 had fourteen; *Salisbury in 1895 had nineteen; John *Major in July 1995 had 23.

In *Bagehot's words, the cabinet links the legislative part of the state to the executive. Its members are normally drawn from the majority party in the House of Commons, together with some peers: at the same time, they head the executive departments. The government as a whole consists of about 100 ministers, ministers of state, junior ministers, and whips: as a body, it never meets.

The extension of the state's functions imposed a burden on an institution better suited to the minimal state of the 19th cent. Committees had long been a feature of the cabinet but they were *ad hoc* and temporary. The modern system of permanent standing committees of the cabinet dates effectively from the Second World War. Small committees of ministers deal with matters too important, too sensitive, or too broad to be determined within a single department. By 1995 there were nineteen cabinet committees or subcommittees.

Recent discussion has emphasized the increasing power of the prime minister and the declining status of the cabinet. There is little doubt that during the 20th cent. the office of prime minister expanded in power. However, the cabinet remains the ultimate court of appeal within the government.

**Cabot, John** (d. 1498) and **Sebastian** (1474–1557). Much obscurity surrounds the lives of the Cabots, father and son. But they discovered and defined the north-east American coast as part of a continent and Sebastian set the British on the fruitless search for polar passages to the Orient. Genoese-born, but working for Venice and Spain, John came to Bristol in 1493 and was inspired by Columbus to try to cross the Atlantic. After one failure, he reached Cape Breton and Newfoundland in the *Matthew* in 1497, thinking initially that he had reached Cathay. He died on an attempted repeat voyage. Sebastian certainly attempted the North-West Passage to the Orient in 1508. Possibly he reached the entrance to Hudson's Bay before navigating southwards along the North American coast.

**Cade, Jack** (d. 1450). Leader of Kentish rebellion. Cade's identity remains a mystery. Military experience is suggested by his capacity to organize, lead, and attempt to discipline thousands of men from Kent who began to rise late in May 1450. Cade harnessed a spontaneous movement of protest against the incompetence of Henry VI's government which could not prevent the rebels entering London on 3 July. Here Cade's control of his followers crumbled, and the rebels were persuaded to disperse. Although himself pardoned, Cade remained belligerent and was fatally wounded resisting arrest on 12 July.

**Cadoc, St** A leading 6th-cent. Welsh scholar. Trained by an Irish monk in Wales, he sought further instruction in Ireland, allegedly under Mochuta, abbot of Lismore, returning to study rhetoric at Llanspyddyd. His principal foundation at Llancarfan became a centre of religious and literary learning.

**Cadwaladr** (d. 664), Welsh king. Son of *Cadwallon who devastated Northumbria before being killed by King *Oswald in 634. Cadwaladr himself suffered a serious defeat by the West Saxons at Pinhoe near Exeter in 658. His death in 664–5 seems to have marked the end of British hopes of recovery from the Saxon invasion. Though his deeds are not recorded, he is a significant figure in later prophetic poems, becoming, like *Arthur, a semi-mythical hero, who would rise again and lead his people to victory.

**Cadwallon** (d. 634), king of Gwynedd. With his ally *Penda of Mercia, Cadwallon was responsible for the death of *Edwin of Northumbria at the battle of *Heathfield in 633 and for those of his successors Osric of Deira and Eanfrith of Bernicia the following year. In 634 he was himself defeated by Eanfrith's brother *Oswald at the battle of *Heavenfield, near Hexham.

**Cadwgan (Cadogan)** (d. 1111), Welsh prince. Cadwgan was one of the sons of Bleddyn ap Cynfyn who ruled Gwynedd and Powys from 1063 to 1075. He began in the 1080s by waging war against *Rhys ap Tewdwr of Deheubarth, who was killed in 1093 by the Normans. The following year Cadwgan led a great counter-attack against the Norman advance in Wales, in league with *Gruffydd ap Cynan, king of Gwynedd. William Rufus himself led two expeditions to restore control. In 1102 Cadwgan joined with Robert of Bellême, earl of Shrewsbury, in revolt against Henry I but was defeated. He was murdered while trying to re-establish himself in Powys.

**Cædmon** (d. 680). An elderly uneducated herdsman at the monastery of Whitby who, in a dream, miraculously received the gift of composing vernacular religious poetry. When he awoke, he remembered his song in praise of God and added more verses. Learning of his new-found ability, the abbess *Hilda took him into the monastic community to receive instruction. Only a few lines survive, recorded by Bede.

**Cædwalla** (c.659–89), king of Wessex (685–7). A member of the royal kin of Wessex, Cædwalla is first met as an exile in the wild lands (*deserti*) of the Chilterns and the Weald. He made himself king of Wessex and extended his power widely. In particular he conquered the Isle of Wight, exterminating its royal dynasty. Not long after, he abdicated and went to Rome. There he was baptized, died, and was buried in St Peter's.

**Caen, treaty of,** 1091. On his death-bed in 1087 William the Conqueror gave England to his second son William Rufus, and the duchy of *Normandy to his first son, *Robert. In 1091 Rufus led an expedition to Normandy, forcing Robert to a treaty at Caen or Rouen. They joined forces to dispossess their younger brother Henry (later Henry I) in Cotentin but by 1094 were at war with each other again.

**Caerleon** in Gwent was the legionary base of the *legio* (Roman legion) *II Augusta*. It became its permanent headquarters in the mid/late 70s AD, probably under the governor Frontinus. Excavations at Caerleon have revealed impressive structures such as the military bath-house.

**Caernarfon castle** (Gwynedd) was begun in June 1283 during the second Welsh War. It incorporates the ancient motte of the castle of Hugh, earl of Chester, built at the end of the 11th cent., and thus resumes a lordship symbolized by the earlier fortification. Caernarfon's Christian Roman associations were consciously fostered. In 1283, during building work, a body, thought to be that of Magnus Maximus (383–8), alleged father of the Emperor *Constantine, was discovered. The castle was built with polygonal towers and banded masonry, imitating the land walls at Constantinople. The king's tower, seat of government in the principality, was decorated with imperial eagles. Finally, Edward chose the castle to be the birthplace of his son, the future Edward II, the first English prince of Wales.

**Caernarfonshire** County of north Wales. It was part of the tribal territory of the Celtic Venedotae, later the Welsh kingdom of *Gwynedd. 'Arfon' is the land over against Môn (*Anglesey) and the county's name is derived from the Roman fortress Castrum (or Caer) of Segontium—Caer yn Arfon. Arfon, together with the Lln peninsula, Eifionydd to the south, and Arllechwedd, the land west of the Conwy river, were joined together by the statute of *Rhuddlan in 1284 as Caernarfonshire. At the Act of *Union with England in 1536 the county remained, but in 1974 became part of the county of Gwynedd. In 1996 Môn was detached and Caernarfonshire, Eifionydd, and Aberconwy remain as the new county of Gwynedd.

The county was dominated by the Snowdon massif (Eryri) with the highest peaks in Wales (yr Wyddfa, 3,560 feet). It is predominantly agricultural with sheep-farming as the main enterprise but extensive slate-quarrying and mining in the 18th and 19th cents. have scarred the landscape. In 1901, 89.6 per cent spoke Welsh with 47.7 being monoglot Welsh. By 1991 the percentage speaking Welsh had fallen to 61.5.

**Caerwent** Roman town in Gwent and tribal capital of the *Silures (Venta Silurum). Roman occupation in south Wales pivoted around the legionary fortress at Caerleon until the Hadrianic stimulation of AD 121–2. Hadrian clearly considered the area ready for local self-government and the Roman town of Caerwent was developed. The administration of the tribe by the town council is specifically attested in an inscription.

**Caesar, Julius** Roman politician and general. Born in 100 BC of a leading patrician family, Caesar rose to be consul in 59 BC. His command included the Roman province of southern Gaul. In a series of brilliant campaigns from 58 to 54 BC he conquered Gaul as far as the Rhine. Late in the campaigning

season of 55 BC he invaded Britain, but retreated when his fleet was wrecked by storms. The following year he returned and defeated the tribes of south-eastern Britain under *Cassivellaunus. For these incursions into a semi-mythical island the Senate voted a longer thanksgiving than for the conquest of Gaul.

**Calais, possession of** Calais was in English hands from its capture by Edward III in 1347 to its loss in 1558. It was essentially a 'little bit of England overseas', being represented in the English Parliament from 1536. Soon after its capture, English settlement was encouraged. Thenceforward, the town's officials, garrison, and merchants were almost exclusively drawn from the homeland.

**Calais, treaty of,** 1360. By this treaty, based on terms agreed at *Brétigny in May, Edward III gained Aquitaine, Poitou, Ponthieu, Guînes, and Calais in full sovereignty, giving up in return his claim to the French throne and to Normandy, Anjou, and Maine, and agreeing to ransom the French king, John II.

**Calcutta (Kolkata)** was founded on 24 August 1690 by Job Charnock of the English *East India Company at Kalikata on the banks of the Hooghly river in *Bengal. It grew quickly as Bengal displaced *Madras as the company's leading commercial region. The town attracted a large British community and in 1834 became recognized as the official capital of British India. In 1901 the city was the second largest in the British empire after London. However, in 1912 the capital was removed to *New Delhi and Calcutta began a long decline.

**Caledonii** The people of the Scottish Highlands. For a people on the fringes of the known world, the Caledonians make an appearance in the works of a surprising number of Roman writers. Xiphilinus tells us that they were actually a confederation of tribes rather than a single entity. Confederation is confirmed by Tacitus, who records that *Calgacus, who addressed the Caledonians before the battle of Mons Graupius, was 'one of many leaders'. Tacitus described them as red-haired and large-limbed.

**calendar reform,** 1751. To remedy the imperfections introduced by Julius Caesar, most of Europe adopted after 1582 the reform proposed by Pope Gregory XIII. Some protestant countries stayed with the old calendar, which became increasingly out of line. The Act 24 Geo. II c. 23 remedied this by eliminating eleven days in September 1752. At the same time, England fell into line with Scotland by starting the year on 1 January instead of 25 March. The protests were less concerned with 'give us back our eleven days' than with the genuine difficulties when contracts or birthdays fell between 2 and 14 September 1752, which disappeared.

**Calgacus** is the name given by *Tacitus to the leader of the Caledonian confederacy at the battle against the Romans under *Agricola at Mons Graupius in 83/4. Calgacus appears only to give a speech exhorting his followers to resist as free Britons. It contains the famous epigram 'ubi solitudinem faciunt pacem appellant', 'they create a desert and call it peace'. However, such speeches are a convention of Graeco-Roman histories.

**Callaghan, James** (1912–2005). Prime minister. Callaghan had the unique record of having held all the highest offices of state: chancellor of the Exchequer (1964–7), home secretary (1967–70), foreign secretary (1974–6), and finally prime minister (1976–9). He left school at 16 to obtain a job in the civil service. He joined the union, becoming assistant general secretary of the Inland Revenue Staff Federation in 1936.

In 1945 Callaghan was elected to Parliament as Labour MP for Cardiff South. He quickly established his reputation and in the 1950s became recognized as a Gaitskellite. In 1960 he was defeated in the deputy leadership election by George Brown. After Gaitskell's death in 1963 Callaghan stood for leader but came third behind Harold *Wilson and Brown. When Labour assumed power in 1964 Callaghan became chancellor of the Exchequer. However, his authority was challenged by the creation of a new Department of Economic Affairs under Brown. Callaghan's term was dogged by speculation against sterling which resulted in the devaluation of the pound in 1967.

Callaghan moved to the Home Office, where he attempted to deal with the problem of immigration from Commonwealth countries and was responsible for sending British troops into Northern Ireland in August 1969. As the only senior minister with trade union connections, he thwarted measures put forward by Barbara Castle and Wilson, in 1969, to reform trade union law.

Callaghan's term as foreign secretary coincided with the controversy surrounding Britain's entry into the EEC. The issue had split the Labour Party, Callaghan having criticized the idea of entry without fully opposing it. He set out to renegotiate the terms of entry agreed by the Heath government. Between June 1974 and March 1975 he visited foreign capitals to settle details concerning the EEC budget, Common Agricultural Policy, and arrangements for Commonwealth countries. But the changes were largely cosmetic.

In 1976 Wilson announced his resignation and Callaghan beat Michael *Foot to assume the party leadership and prime ministership. The outlook for Callaghan's term was gloomy. Inflation was rampant and in September 1976 the government was forced to apply to the International Monetary Fund for stand-by credit of £2.3 billion. The government had no effective majority and in 1977 Callaghan had to strike a deal with the Liberals to survive, the price being devolution bills for Scotland and Wales.

During the 'winter of discontent' (1978–9) Britain was crippled by strikes as protests against wage restraint. In March 1979 the devolution referenda failed. The Labour government lost a vote of no confidence by one vote and the subsequent general election. In October 1980 Callaghan resigned as leader and in 1987 became a life peer. The succession to Wilson had proved something of a poisoned chalice.

**Calvert, George** See BALTIMORE, 1ST LORD.

**Calvinism,** the creed of Jean Calvin (1509–64), was largely as formulated in his *Institutes*, published 1536. Calvin was greatly influenced by St Augustine in inferring predestination from divine foreknowledge, and he therefore presumed that the elect, chosen for salvation, were known to God from before the creation. Free will was an illusion. Church organization followed from that basic premiss, that the chosen of God—the elect—should share government with the ministers.

Taken into Scotland from Calvin's Geneva in 1559 by John *Knox, Calvinism became the national creed and was recognized as the established church in 1690. In England it struggled first to influence Anglicanism, then to overthrow it. After 1660 it was at first the most powerful of the dissenting sects but lost ground rapidly to the *baptists and *congregationalists and in the early 18th cent. was infiltrated by *socinianism and *unitarianism.

**Cambridge, Great St Mary's** Commonly called the university church, this is a fine late Perpendicular parish church on a splendid site between King's Parade and the Market Square. The west tower, started in 1491, was only half-finished in 1550, completed in 1608, and the proposed spire was never added.

**Cambridge, Richard of Conisborough, 1st earl of** (1385–1415). Richard was the younger son of Edmund, duke of York, and a grandson of Edward III. With no lands, he depended on Exchequer annuities which were irregularly paid until after his clandestine marriage to Anne Mortimer, sister of Edmund Mortimer, earl of March, in 1408. Apparently unhinged by resentment, Richard devised hare-brained seditious schemes and persuaded himself that Edmund Mortimer shared his motives for rebellion. It remains a mystery how Henry, Lord Scrope, became entangled in this half-baked conspiracy. Convicted for plotting the deaths of Henry V and his brothers, Cambridge and Scrope were beheaded at Southampton.

**Cambridgeshire** was a quiet, thinly populated, agricultural county, pleasantly hilly in the chalk south, flat in the north where it joins the Fens. The river Cam bisects the southern part of the county, flowing north to join the Ouse near Ely. It was a county of small landowners, puritan and nonconformist in sympathy, and politically independent. By the Local Government Act of 1972, Cambridgeshire took over Huntingdonshire and the soke of Peterborough, adding more than 50 per cent to its area. Modern Cambridge-

shire has seen the development of science and technological parks and the A14 from Huntingdon has become one of the busiest and most congested roads.

Cambridge was a Roman settlement, the centre of a network of roads, joining to cross the Cam. Its importance was enhanced by the fact that it became the southern point of a complex pattern of inland navigation, centred on the Ouse. It was early colonized by the Angles and in the 7th cent. was much disputed between the East Angles and the Mercians. A development in 673 was the foundation of a monastery at Ely. It rapidly prospered and survived sacking by the Danes in 870. Work on the Norman cathedral began in 1083 and it was given cathedral status in 1109. Ely's unique position was responsible for the bishop being granted quasi-*palatine status. The Isle of Ely was given its own county council in 1888, March becoming the county town, but was once more merged with Cambridgeshire in 1958.

Cambridge town went down before the first Danish onslaught in 870, was liberated by *Edward the Elder in the early 10th cent., but fell to the Danes once more in 1011. After the Norman Conquest, William I built the castle in 1068 and the town received a charter in 1201. Stourbridge fair on Midsummer common was one of the largest in Europe. The growth of the university in the 13th cent. produced prolonged antagonism between town and gown, and is responsible for that mixture of seat of learning and East Anglian market town which characterizes Cambridge today.

The northern parts of the county remained for centuries almost completely cut off by fen and water. Their inaccessibility made them a natural shelter for refugees, of whom *Hereward, leader of resistance to the Normans, was the most famous. Proposals for draining the fens were put forward repeatedly. In the 17th cent. a start was made, and the earl of *Bedford, through the work of Vermuyden, the Dutch engineer, succeeded in reclaiming vast areas.

The fen part of the county has always been an acquired taste. Camden wrote of the 'Fenmen, a sort of people (much like the place) of brutish, uncivilized tempers, envious of all others ... and usually walking aloft on a sort of stilts'. Admiration for Ely cathedral was usually tempered by disgust at the town itself. Celia Fiennes in 1698 found Ely 'the dirtiest place I ever saw...a perfect quagmire, the whole city...I had frogs and slow-worms and snails in my room.' Wisbech was a flourishing port and displayed some elegant buildings, but Pevsner wrote laconically in 1954 that the Fens 'grow much potato, sugar-beet and other root crops, and wheat, but they have never grown much architecture'.

**Cambridge University** dates back to 1209, when, after a clash with the townspeople, some of the clerks at Oxford migrated to Cambridge. The first college was Peterhouse, established in 1284 by Hugh de Balsham, bishop of Ely. Royal patronage led to expansion: Henry VI founded King's College in 1441 and Henry VIII established Trinity College in 1546. After the Reformation, the poor students largely disappeared, to be replaced by the sons of wealthy families. Many of the leading figures of the Renaissance of learning were associated with Cambridge, including Erasmus, *Ascham, and *Fisher. As puritanism flourished in East Anglia, Cambridge supported the parliamentary cause in the Civil War. Academically, Cambridge was characterized by the growth of science, with *Newton at Trinity its best-known exponent. Cambridge's scientific reputation was further enhanced with the opening of the Cavendish Laboratory in 1873. Two women's colleges were established at this time, Girton in 1869, Newnham in 1871.

For the first six centuries of its existence, Cambridge, like Oxford, was a seminary, and until 1871 fellows were required to be celibates in holy orders. The older foundations date from the Middle Ages, like Corpus Christi College (1352), Pembroke (1357), and Trinity Hall (1390). Several are Tudor, such as Christ's (1505), Trinity, and Emmanuel (1584). Downing was founded in 1800 after a protracted and troublesome legal action over the original bequest by Sir George Downing in 1717. Selwyn and St Edmunds came in the late 19th cent. (1882, 1896). During the 1960s, no fewer than six new colleges came into existence, Churchill (1960), Darwin (1964), Lucy Cavendish (1965), Clare Hall (1966), Fitzwilliam (1966), and Wolfson (1969). Robinson College opened in 1977. One of the greatest 20th-cent. developments was the move of the University Library to West Road, opened in 1934

and designed by Sir Giles Gilbert Scott: the late 20th cent. saw a notable growth of scientific facilities clustered round the University.

**Cambuskenneth abbey** (Stirling) was one of several *Augustinian priories founded by David I of Scotland in the 1140s. James III was buried here in 1488 and a lavish rebuilding occurred early in the 16th cent. Little now remains but a 14th-cent. detached bell-tower.

**Camden, battle of,** 1780. In December 1779 Sir Henry Clinton took an expedition to South Carolina in the hope of drawing on loyalist support. In May 1780 Charleston was captured with 6,000 rebel prisoners. Clinton then handed over to *Cornwallis. A counter-thrust by De Kalb from North Carolina was met at Camden on 16 August. Though Cornwallis was heavily outnumbered, the Americans were routed and De Kalb killed.

**Camden, Charles Pratt, 1st Earl** (1714–94). Camden was called to the bar in 1738. In 1757 he became attorney-general under *Pitt and MP for Downton. In 1761 he was promoted to chief justice of Common Pleas. His most famous case in 1763 involved *Wilkes and the libellous *North Briton. Camden ruled that *general warrants were illegal and gained great popularity. He became lord chancellor in Chatham's second administration and retained the great seal until 1770. He remained in opposition until the death of Chatham, but became president of the council in the *Rockingham administration, retaining the post until his death.

**Camden, William** (1551–1623). Camden was one of the finest of schoolmaster-historians. Born in London, he was educated at St Paul's and then at Oxford. From 1575 until 1597 he taught at Westminster School, where he became headmaster. He produced two major works—*Britannia* (1586), a survey of the antiquities of Britain, and *Annals of Queen Elizabeth* (1615), which established the view of her reign as a *via media.*

**Cameron, David** (b. 1966). Politician. Educated at Eton and Brasenose, Oxford, Cameron was returned to Parliament for Witney in 2001 and became leader of the Conservative Party in 2005. He has endeavoured to reposition the party and rebrand its image, paying particular attention to environmental and green issues. His performances in the House of Commons have been spirited but critics have accused him of trendiness and vagueness.

**Cameronians** Known as the 'Society people' until 1690, these covenanters of south-west Scotland followed the extensive field preaching of Richard Cameron (1648–80) and Donald Cargill (c.1627–81). After Cameron was killed in battle and Cargill hanged, the various dissident societies combined against the *Test Act. After 1690 they raised the prestigious Cameronian regiment against James. The Cameronians refused to join the restored presbyterian Church of Scotland which they saw as Erastian, and finally became the free church (1876)

**Campaign for Nuclear Disarmament (CND).** The largest organization associated with the two waves of agitation against the British nuclear deterrent and US nuclear bases in Britain. It was formed in 1958 by establishment intellectuals such as Bertrand *Russell and urged unilateral British nuclear disarmament. It soon became involved in demonstrations organized by the smaller anarchist-orientated Direct Action Committee. The Easter 1958 march to the Aldermaston nuclear base in Berkshire attracted up to 10,000 supporters and 1959 and 1960 saw numbers approaching 100,000. The success of a unilateralist motion at the 1960 Labour Party Conference was a high point, but *Gaitskell managed to reverse the decision in 1961 and the signing of the 1963 Test Ban treaty caused CND to lose momentum.

It re-emerged as a mass movement in the 1980s as a result of a new iciness in American–Soviet relations. By 1982 it had about 100,000 members and drew an estimated 400,000 people to its Hyde Park rally. Further multilateral agreements to control nuclear weapons were both welcome to CND and blunted its cutting edge.

**Campbell, Sir Colin, 1st Baron Clyde** (1792–1863). Campbell was born in Glasgow and entered the army in 1807. He fought in the Peninsular War (1808–14); the Demerara insurrection (1823); the Opium War (1839–42); the second *Sikh War (1848–9); and the *Crimean War (1854). On the outbreak of the mutiny

in 1857, he was appointed commander-in-chief of the Indian army and was principally responsible for relieving the sieges of *Lucknow and *Cawnpore.

**Campbell-Bannerman, Sir Henry** (1836–1908). Prime minister. A genial and popular politician, Campbell-Bannerman acquired a reputation as uninspired. In fact he proved to be more shrewd and determined than his rivals. He held the Liberal Party together during a difficult, post-Gladstonian period, leading it to its greatest electoral victory in 1906.

'C-B' was educated in Glasgow and at Cambridge, and became a partner in the family firm. As MP for Stirling Burghs from 1868 C-B showed himself a radical Gladstonian, supporting Scottish disestablishment and *Irish Home Rule.

However, C-B made little impact as a junior minister in *Gladstone's 1868 and 1880 governments. In 1884–5 he served briefly as chief secretary for Ireland and reached the cabinet as secretary of state for war in 1886. He retained this post in Gladstone's last administration in 1892 and under *Rosebery in 1894–5, though by that time he harboured ambitions to become Speaker. Instead he was destined to fill the vacuum left by Gladstone's retirement. Rosebery quit in 1896, and Sir William *Harcourt resigned as leader in 1898. When both John *Morley and H. H. *Asquith declined the poisoned chalice, C-B became leader almost by default.

He was promptly faced with the task of guiding the divided Liberal Party through a period dominated by the *Boer War. The use of concentration camps by *Kitchener to quell the Boers provoked C-B's memorable words: 'When is a war not a war? When it is carried on by methods of barbarism in South Africa.' His prospects were rapidly transformed during 1902–4 as the *Balfour government split over tariff reform. As prime minister 1905–8 he successfully bridged the gap between New Liberal policies and Gladstonian traditions. Adopting the role of a firm chairman, he gave free rein to his exceptionally able ministers. Important reforms were enacted in connection with trade unions and school meals; old-age pensions were devised by Asquith and the British army reorganized by *Haldane. By the time of his retirement through ill-health in 1908, C-B had pointed the Liberals towards their next great goal—the reduction of the powers of the Lords.

**Camperdown, battle of,** 1797. Camperdown is a coastal village in Holland. Offshore the Dutch fleet was defeated by a British fleet under the command of Admiral *Duncan on 11 October 1797. By then the Dutch were effectively under the rule of revolutionary France, and their navy had been designated to assist in an invasion of Ireland. Both Dutch flagships and nine other ships were taken.

**Campion, Edmund** (1540–81). Jesuit martyr. Son of a London bookseller, Campion studied at Oxford, where he was ordained deacon (1568) despite catholic inclinations. Conscience prevailing, he was received at Douai (1573). Part of the Jesuits' 1580 mission to English catholics and carefully non-political, Campion's 'sweetness of disposition' and eloquent preaching alerted the authorities, especially after *Decem rationes*, denouncing Anglicanism, appeared at St Mary's, Oxford. Captured and taken to the Tower, his refusal to recant led to torture. Trumped-up charges of conspiracy to overthrow the queen brought hanging at Tyburn.

**Canada** A self-governing dominion since 1867, much of Canada was colonized by the British and the French. Ships from the west country probably located the Grand Banks fisheries even before John *Cabot's explorations of 1497. Despite official discouragement, *Newfoundland became the first overseas British colony.

In 17th- and 18th-cent. usage, the name Canada referred primarily to the St Lawrence lowlands. Here the British involvement is usually dated from *Wolfe's victory on the Plains of Abraham (1759), but this was not the first British attempt to capture the colony. In 1629 the Kirke brothers seized the fort at Quebec. It was returned to the French three years later. More unsuccessful attacks took place in 1690 and 1711.

From 1670, through the *Hudson's Bay Company, England claimed sovereignty over Rupert's Land. The expanding fur trade led the company to set up posts in the far north and on the west coast, establishing British claims to this region. In the long-running 18th-cent. conflict with France, the British acquired Acadia, renamed *Nova Scotia,

in 1713. Unable to secure allegiance from the Acadian population, British authorities deported them.

With the 1763 treaty of *Paris, British control over North America was unrivalled. The attempt to integrate the French catholic population formed a major objective during the next century. The *Quebec Act (1774) guaranteed religious freedoms and legal customs, but in doing so, it heightened tensions between Britain and its colonies to the south.

When conflict between Britain and its other North American colonies broke out, Nova Scotia obeyed the military garrison at Halifax. Quebec maintained its allegiance for fear of the more radical protestants of the rebel colonies. In the aftermath of the American Revolution, loyalist refugees streamed north. The arrival of the Anglo-American refugees created new exigencies. Nova Scotia was divided into two colonies, *New Brunswick and peninsular Nova Scotia. *Prince Edward Island had already acquired a separate administration in 1769, and *Cape Breton Island enjoyed a separate status as a refuge for loyalists for 40 years. In 1791, Quebec was divided along the Ottawa river to create Upper and Lower Canada. Henceforth, Upper Canada contained primarily an English-speaking population.

The North American colonies were more of strategic than economic importance to the British. With the fisheries secured, the colonies served two other purposes. They provided primary resources, such as wheat, timber, and minerals: they also offered a place for British emigrants. After 1815, Highland Scots and northern Irish flocked to Canada. These huge influxes exacerbated tensions between colonial politicians and the mother country and were important factors in the rebellions of 1837–8 in Lower Canada. A third constitution, the Union Act, tried to address the problem, uniting the two Canadas, in the hope of swamping the French-speaking population. However, French-Canadian politicians made alliances with reformist English-speaking colleagues to defeat the attempts. The fourth constitution, the British North America Act of 1867, rejected the assimilationist policy, by separating again Upper and Lower Canada, and joining them with Nova Scotia and New Brunswick. The four provinces received important degrees of autonomy, within a federal system. This constitution has proved the most successful. But Quebec separatism, as demonstrated by the referendum of 1995, remains strong.

With the BNA Act, the name Canada extended to take in the provinces involved. Other territories were either annexed or joined the federation subsequently: the Northwest Territories through purchase from the Hudson's Bay Company in 1870; Manitoba (1870); British Columbia (1871); Prince Edward Island (1873); the Arctic Islands (1880), Yukon (1898); Alberta and Saskatchewan (1905); Newfoundland (1949). Constitutionally equal in status to Britain according to the statute of *Westminster (1931), until 1949 the final court of appeal for Canada remained the Judicial Committee of the Privy Council in London.

Between 1902 and 1912 alone, over 1.5 million British emigrants left for Canada. More immigrants arrived following the Second World War. Cultural and emotional links to Britain in English-speaking Canada remained strong and Canada contributed greatly to the allied war effort in both world wars. However, following the Second World War, Canadian politicians and diplomats have attempted to carve out a separate space in world affairs.

By 2007 the population had reached 33 million. Since the Second World War trade between Canada and Britain has levelled out at a lower, but not inconsequential, level. As the economic clout of the USA has expanded, so has its influence over Canada. The passage of the Free Trade Agreement in 1989 (and later the North American Free Trade Agreement) recognized and indeed enhanced Canada's continental orientation.

**canal system** Britain was late to develop its canal network, being well endowed with improvable rivers and ready access to coastal shipping. *Exeter was linked to Topsham by a new cut in 1564–6, the first recorded use of the pound lock, the critical technology for inland navigation. By the 1630s, it had been applied on the Lea, the Thames, and Warwickshire Avon.

The first modern development was the Newry canal (opened 1745), which linked the Tyrone coalfield with sea-borne access to the Dublin market. The first English canal, the Sankey Brook navigation, linked St Helens coal to the river Mersey and *Liverpool (1757). While the Sankey was an extensive

parallel cut, the duke of *Bridgwater's canal (1761) was the first to take a route independent of any river. When completed in 1767, it linked the duke's pits north-west of Manchester to Runcorn in the south-west, a broad 30-mile contour route without locks.

Trunk route development followed from the boom of 1766–72, when most schemes involved James *Brindley. The key links were those of the Grand Trunk canal (1777), which connected the Trent and Mersey, and through the Birmingham canal (1772) connected the midland manufacturing regions with the ports of *Hull and Liverpool; the Staffordshire and Worcestershire (1772), tying both to the river Severn; the Thames and Severn (1789), Coventry (1790), and Oxford (1790) canals which completed links from the north-west to London. *Birmingham became the hub of the English canal system. Lateral trunk routes linked Bristol and London through the Kennet and Avon Canal (1810), and Leeds and Liverpool (1815); the first trans-Pennine crossing was the Rochdale canal (1804); in Scotland, the Forth and Clyde canal (1790) linked Edinburgh and Glasgow, and the Caledonian canal through the Great Glen (1822) cut out the hazardous journey by way of the Pentland Firth.

The canals had creative effects: new towns were established, notably Stourport, Runcorn, Ellesmere Port, and Goole. They created employment: around 37,000 men and 2,500 women were recorded as canal employees in 1851. Canal-building engaged many of the greatest engineers of the era—Brindley, *Smeaton, *Rennie, and *Telford for example.

The system was completed only in the 1820s, but immediately proved inflexible in the face of growing traffic. Mixed gauge development reduced real integration, with the bulk of the system being Brindley model narrow (7-foot) canals. Water shortages limited carriage, and stemmed from the problems of maintaining reservoirs. By the mid-1840s, carriers such as Pickfords were rapidly abandoning canals in favour of railways.

Canal usage continued to fall in the First World War, and declined further in the interwar years, reviving little between 1939 and 1945. Nationalization in 1948 left trends unchanged: although the volume of goods carried grew until 1953, 36 per cent of the remaining 2,100 miles were seen as redundant in 1955. By the 1968 Transport Act, around 1,000 miles were identified as 'cruising waterways' and leisure usage has predominated subsequently, with some restoration by preservation groups, notably of the Kennet and Avon and Rochdale canals.

**Canning, Charles John, 1st Earl** (1812–62). Canning served as under-secretary to Robert *Peel and as postmaster-general to Lord *Aberdeen before being appointed governor-general of India in 1856. His years in office were dominated by the *Indian mutiny of 1857. He recalled an army from China and insisted on military reconquest. Afterwards he resisted demands for widespread vengeance, earning the nickname 'Clemency Canning'. His post-mutiny policies centred on reorganizing the army and promoting the loyalty of Indians to Britain. He founded the first Indian universities, passed tenancy legislation, guaranteed the continuity of princely states, and banned interference in Indian religion and custom.

**Canning, George** (1770–1827). Prime minister. The most brilliant disciple of the younger *Pitt, Canning was distrusted as an intriguer. He also suffered from the fact that his father had died in penury and that his mother had been an actress. Rescued by a wealthy uncle, Canning was educated at Eton and Oxford. Entering the Commons in 1794 he shone as an orator and writer of witty polemical verses, denouncing the French Revolution and supporting the war against France. When *Portland became prime minister in 1807 Canning was made foreign secretary. He prevented the Danish fleet from falling into French hands and supported the Spaniards and Portuguese in their struggle against Napoleon. But the failure of the *Walcheren expedition heightened distrust of Canning and he sought to make *Castlereagh the scapegoat. The outcome was the famous duel which consigned both men to the back benches. Only in 1818 did Canning return to office as president of the Board of Control and in 1822 he was about to sail for India as governor-general when Castlereagh's suicide led to his appointment as foreign secretary. His success was as dazzling as it was controversial. Always opposed to the *Congress system, he disengaged from Europe with enthusiasm. By recognizing the independence of the Spanish American co-

lonies, he opened up Latin America for British commerce. When he was asked to form a government in 1827 *Wellington and *Peel refused to serve under him. Canning's ministry was a coalition of liberal Tories and conservative Whigs. His unexpected death in August 1827 after only three months meant that his premiership did not fulfil its promise.

**canon law** was the law of the universal church and from the 4th cent. became a complete legal system, taking much inspiration from the civil (Roman) law. All European countries accepted the authority of canon law and the conflict between church and state in many countries, and in England notably between Henry II and Thomas *Becket, arose from disputes over the boundaries between canon law and domestic law in matters such as *advowsons (the right to present to a clergy living), criminous clerks, or other jurisdictional disputes.

**Canterbury** Succeeding an important late Iron Age settlement, the *civitas*-capital of Durovernum was laid out on either side of the Great Stour in the later 1st cent. By the later 4th cent. the town was in decay. It re-emerged as the capital of a pagan English kingdom of *Kent, to which St *Augustine was sent by Pope Gregory the Great in 597. Gregory intended the new English church to have archbishops at London and York, but a series of historical accidents led to Augustine and his successors remaining at Canterbury. Canterbury became one of the larger English walled towns, with a self-governing corporation, but it was dominated until the 1530s by its two great abbeys of Christ Church (the cathedral) and St Augustine's. The city suffered economically from the dissolutions at the Reformation, but revived modestly through silk-weaving introduced by Walloon refugees, and later as a social centre for gentry and clergy.

**Canterbury, metropolitan diocese of** The diocese, comprising east Kent, was founded in 601 at the instigation of Pope Gregory the Great, four years after *Augustine's arrival in Kent. The boundaries of the diocese itself have changed little. The number of sees in the Canterbury province, however, has varied from 12 in 735 to 29 today. Disestablishment removed the Welsh bishoprics in 1920. In the late 8th cent. the short-lived metropolitan status of *Lichfield almost eclipsed Canterbury. Pope Leo's decision to restore the primacy to Canterbury was confirmed by a synod at Clofesho in 803. Since Gregory's blueprint for two provinces of Canterbury and York left their relationship unclear, York claimed independence from Canterbury. The dispute reached a peak in 1070 when *Lanfranc demanded obedience from Thomas of York, but following a council at Winchester in 1072, Canterbury's precedence was confirmed. It arose again in 1118 and continued until Innocent VI (1352–62) resolved the question. York was to have metropolitan authority over the north as 'primate of England', Canterbury to have national precedence as 'primate of all England'. Though still retaining his diocesan seat at Canterbury, the archbishop's official residence as primate since *c.*1185 has been at *Lambeth palace.

**Canterbury Tales** Late 14th-cent. unfinished masterpiece by *Chaucer. The General Prologue presents portraits of diverse pilgrims congregated at the Tabard inn (Southwark), including a battle-worn Knight, sweetly pretentious Prioress, and emaciated scholar-Clerk. They lighten the journey to Thomas *Becket's shrine at Canterbury by exchanging twenty-four tales, which range from high romance set in ancient Greece (Knight) to low comedy in contemporary England (Miller, Reeve).

**Cantiaci** A British tribal grouping and *civitas*. The Cantiaci seem to be a creation of the Roman government, for there is no record of either a tribe or federation of this name before the Roman conquest. The capital of the new *civitas* was established at *Canterbury, and was given the name of Durovernum Cantiacorum.

**Cape Breton Island** has formed part of *Nova Scotia since 1820. Named Île Royale by the French, who built *Louisbourg, it was ceded to Britain in 1763.

**Cape Finisterre, battles of,** 1747. The two encounters, in May and October 1747, were similar in character, since they arose from the Royal Navy's attempt to cut French communication with its American possessions. In the first, *Anson annihilated a smaller squadron protecting a convoy. In the second, *Hawke sank six warships, though most of the merchantmen managed to escape.

**Cape of Good Hope** Cape Town was captured by the British from the Dutch in 1795 and formally ceded in 1814. Strained relations between British immigrants and the Dutch settlers (Boers) over slavery and religion led to the Boers' Great Trek in 1835 to re-establish their own territories. The Cape became a crown colony in 1853. In 1910 the Cape became a province of the Union of South Africa along with the Boer republics of Natal, Transvaal, and the Orange Free State.

**Cape Passaro, battle of,** 1718. Cape Passaro is the southerly cape of Sicily. On 31 July 1718 a British fleet under Sir George *Byng defeated a Spanish fleet, destroying or capturing seventeen Spanish warships. Britain was not yet at war with Spain but was already committed to supporting the ambitions in southern Italy of the Emperor Charles VI.

**Cape St Vincent, battle of,** 1797. On 14 February 1797, four months after the start of hostilities with Spain, 15 ships under Sir John *Jervis met the Spanish fleet of 27 ships off the south-western cape of Portugal. *Nelson in *Captain* broke out of the line to prevent the westerly Spaniards rounding the British rear to reunite with their easterly ships. *Captain* was fought to a standstill; Nelson then vaulted with boarding parties first into the *San Nicolas* and then into *San Josef*: his 'patent bridge'. In all, four Spaniards were taken.

**capitalism** Capitalism is the name given to the market economy system, which did not come to full fruition until the restrictive practices of the medieval and mercantilist eras had been eroded. During the past two centuries world economic growth has been achieved very largely through the free market system and mainstream economic theory has provided theoretical justification for it. But it has also been subject to sustained criticism, both in the mild form that its inherent limitations required that it should be modified by government intervention and, at the extreme, that its inherent flaws would ensure its eventual collapse.

The positive case for free market capitalism is based on the liberty of individuals to pursue their objectives subject only to the constraint of law. The competitive environment, idealized in perfect competition, represents the most efficient structure. Such a structure implies that all participants benefit: competition weeds out inefficient producers and ensures that consumers pay the lowest possible price.

It is, of course, generally recognized that this is not an entirely accurate description of either the modern economy or its precursors. A range of obstacles inhibits the free working of markets. Monopoly power constitutes such an obstacle. Another type of perceived imperfection has been the interference of government policy. Monetarist theorists like Friedman have explained inflation as the result of weak control of the monetary system by the state. According to this perspective, the market system is totally satisfactory provided various imperfections can be eliminated. But one area of difficulty lies in the provision of public goods by the state because market failure means they are not adequately supplied by private producers. Examples include transport networks, law and order, welfare benefits, defence, health, and education. The difficulty lies in the fact that payment is indirect, through taxation.

More familiar criticisms have come from those whose vision of capitalism is not of an ideal state marred temporarily by imperfections. The Keynesian tradition, following the work of John Maynard *Keynes, made the basic assumption that the market system needs to be managed by the state because it will seldom produce outcomes optimal for society as a whole. Adherents to this tradition believe, for example, that state intervention can reduce unemployment and generate economic growth. A far more radical view of capitalism is taken by Marxists. Marx argued that capitalism was based not on complementarity of interest but upon conflict between the classes. Further, he argued, capitalism contained the seeds of its own destruction through that conflict. The acquisition of colonies was one means of postponing eventual collapse by securing new and additional markets. Others have explained the continued failure of the capitalist world to collapse, as predicted by Marx, as a result of artificial demand created by governments in the form of military expenditure.

**capital punishment** was formerly of central importance in all European criminal justice systems. Although the history of capital punishment in Scotland has been little studied, it is clear that hanging was the standard method of executing on both sides of the border. Under English law, decapitation, hanging, drawing, and quartering, or (in the case of women) burning at the stake were reserved for traitors.

Evidence from burial sites suggests that capital punishment was known in Anglo-Saxon England. Calculating levels of capital punishment for this and the medieval period is impossible, although it seems they were low. This changed drastically in the Tudor period. By Elizabeth's reign many convicted criminals were executed, a trend which continued after 1603.

The 18th cent. provides better documentation on ceremonies and crowd reactions at executions. It also experienced a lower level of executions than the early 17th, with many convicted persons being reprieved, notably before being transported to the American colonies. The early 19th cent. experienced a rapid transition in thinking on punishment. Transportation to Australia or incarceration in one of the new prisons became the standard punishment for serious, non-homicidal offenders. By the mid-19th cent. capital punishment was restricted to murderers and, after 1868, was carried out inside prisons rather than in public. By that date the abolition of the death penalty was already being mooted. Debate on this issue surfaced intermittently in the 20th cent., leading to its abolition for all practical purposes in 1965.

**Caracalla** Roman emperor. The eldest son of the Emperor *Septimius Severus, his real name was Marcus Aurelius Antoninus, Caracalla being a nickname from his habit of wearing the military cloak. He came to Britain with his father in 208 to take part in the campaign into Scotland. After his father's death at York in 211 he withdrew the troops to *Hadrian's Wall before returning to Rome to substantiate his claim to the throne by murdering his brother. He was assassinated in 218.

**Caratacus,** British king. Caratacus was one of several sons of the great British king *Cunobelinus and on his father's death around AD 40 he and his brother Togodumnus appear to have divided the *Catuvellaunian kingdom. Their forces opposed the Roman invasion in AD 43 but Togodumnus died shortly after the battle at the Thames and Caratacus fled west. He re-emerged five years later leading the *Silures of south-east Wales. When the Romans planted fortresses at Kingsholm (*Gloucester) and Wroxeter, Caratacus withdrew into central Wales and began to organize the *Ordovices. In a pitched battle, perhaps near Caersws, his forces fought well but lost. He himself escaped and fled to *Brigantia, but was handed over to the Romans by Queen *Cartimandua. Taken in chains to Rome, he made a bold speech before *Claudius (imaginatively recorded by Tacitus) which won him and his family a pardon. He spent the rest of his life in exile in Rome.

**Carausius** Roman imperial usurper, AD 286–93. In 286 Carausius revolted in advance of disciplinary action by the western *Augustus* (emperor) Maximian. Appointed to command patrols of the English Channel, Carausius had acquired too much booty for Maximian's liking. Carausius declared himself emperor and controlled Britain and north-western Gaul 286–93. In 293 Constantius Chlorus (Maximian's *Caesar* or deputy) made military gains against Carausius in Gaul: Carausius was assassinated by his finance minister Allectus.

**Carberry Hill, encounter at,** 1567. Mary, queen of Scots' marriage to *Bothwell in May 1567 provoked widespread protest. On 15 June at Carberry Hill, east of the city of Edinburgh, they were confronted by a superior force. While negotiations continued, Mary's troops began to desert. Bothwell fled north and finished up in lifelong captivity in Denmark. Mary abdicated in favour of her infant son James.

**Carbisdale, battle of,** 1650. Early in 1650 *Montrose sailed from Bergen to Orkney with a small force. He moved to the mainland and on 27 April was surprised at Carbisdale, near Dornoch. His supporters were routed, Montrose captured and hanged in Edinburgh the following month.

**Cardiff** The capital of Wales located at the mouth of the river Taff. Cardiff was the site of a Roman fort constructed in AD 76. During the Dark Ages the Celtic St *Teilo founded his church at Llandaff to the north. But it was with the coming of the Normans that the site was revitalized, Robert *Fitzhamon setting up his castle within the Roman fort. A charter was granted sometime after 1147. Although large by Welsh standards, later evidence suggests a town of no great significance. At the first census of 1801, with a population of 1,870, it ranked only 21st amongst Welsh towns.

With the beginning of the iron industry, Cardiff began its rapid growth as the main port, linked to the interior by the Glamorgan canal (1798) and then the Taff Vale railway (1840–1). But from the middle of the century, coal export rose to dominance, reaching 13.5 million tons by 1913. In 1881, when its population was 82,761, it became, and has remained ever since, the largest Welsh town. The rise of Cardiff is intimately associated with the marquises of Bute, who owned great swathes of urban estate. The series of docks, constructed by the estate, was unique in Britain, since the development was provided by a single private estate.

Cardiff became a county borough in 1889, was designated a city in 1905, and slowly acquired a new role as the Welsh metropolis. The most significant modern development is that of Cardiff Bay, where the old docklands are being transformed in a characteristic 'inner harbour' development. The population of Cardiff in 2001 was 305,000. The city is home to the Welsh Assembly.

**Cardigan, James Brudenell, 7th earl of** (1797–1868). As Lord Brudenell he was commissioned in the 8th Hussars in 1824, purchased command of the 15th Hussars in 1832, and was removed for misconduct in 1834. Nothing daunted, in 1836 he purchased command of the 11th Hussars, and in 1837 succeeded to the family title. Cardigan's notoriety rests with his command of the light cavalry brigade in the *Crimean War, particularly the '*Charge of the Light Brigade' at Balaclava in 1854. He gave his name to the woollen 'Cardigan' jacket popularized by the war.

**Cardiganshire** A west-coast county of Wales bordering the Irish Sea. In 1974 it became the district of Ceredigion in the county of *Dyfed, but in 1996 was reconstituted as a county, retaining the name Ceredigion. That name, from which Cardigan is derived, is supposedly after Ceredig, the son of *Cunedda, a leader of the *Votadini. After its conquest by Edward I in 1277, it was created one of the shires of the principality by the statute of *Rhuddlan in 1284. At the Act of *Union with England in 1536 it was retained as a county and has remained as such to the present, apart from the period 1974–96. Its western location has meant that it has been a bastion of the Welsh language.

**Cardwell, Edward** (1813–86). Son of a Liverpool merchant, educated at Winchester and Balliol College, Oxford, Cardwell became a Conservative MP in 1841. He followed the Peelite free traders after the party split of 1846. In ministerial posts under *Aberdeen and *Palmerston, including colonial secretary, he stood out as an administrative reformer. *Gladstone's secretary at war from 1868, he ended flogging in the army and undertook major reforms. Infantry regiments were given territorial designations and linked to reserves, short service was introduced, and the commander-in-chief's office was brought under clearer ministerial authority. The abolition of purchase of commissions was controversial; when the 1871 Army Regulation Bill was blocked by the Lords, the change was implemented by royal warrant.

**Carey, George** (b. 1935). Archbishop of Canterbury. Born and educated in Essex, after national service in the RAF, Carey graduated from the London College of Divinity and King's College, London. He was successively curate in Islington, theological college lecturer, vicar of St Nicholas's, Durham (1975), principal of Trinity College, Bristol (1982), bishop of Bath and Wells (1987), and archbishop (1991). Originally an evangelical, he nurtured tolerance within Anglicanism and progress towards unity with Rome and eastern orthodoxy. He retired in 2002.

**Carey, Henry** See HUNSDON, 1ST BARON.

**Carham, battle of,** 1018. *Malcolm II of Scotland with his ally Owain of Strathclyde took advantage of *Cnut's efforts to establish himself as ruler of England to invade Northumbria. He inflicted a severe defeat on the Northumbrians at Carham, south-west of Coldstream. It meant a significant shift in the balance of power in the north, helping to establish the Tweed as the border.

**Carlisle, Charles Howard, 3rd earl of** (1669–1738). Though twice 1st lord of the Treasury, Carlisle's political career was inconsequential, and his lasting achievement was the building of *Castle Howard. He succeeded to the earldom in 1692. William III showed him favour, making him 1st lord of the Treasury in December 1701. But on Anne's succession in 1702, he was dismissed. He was reappointed 1st lord in May 1715 by George I, giving way to Walpole in October. Increasing gout and his love for Castle Howard made him reluctant to leave Yorkshire. He was buried in the vast mausoleum at Castle Howard designed by *Hawksmoor.

**Carlisle, diocese of** The see, created in 1133, was conterminous with Cumbria until the 19th cent. Initially it had a complex history, for, though ecclesiastically always under the metropolitan jurisdiction of York, it fell politically under the Scottish kings for 21 years (1136–57). The cathedral, originally founded as an Augustinian priory in 1102, is noted for its fine 14th-cent. curvilinear east window.

**Carlyle, Thomas** (1795–1881 Historian and man of letters. Born in Ecclefechan, the son of a presbyterian stonemason, and educated for the kirk at Edinburgh University, Carlyle earned a living as a tutor, schoolmaster, and journalist, developing a deep interest in contemporary German literature; his *Life of Schiller* appeared in 1823, his translation of *Wilhelm Meister* in 1824. His marriage to Jane Welsh Carlyle marked the beginning of a long, celebrated, and difficult marriage. By the late 1820s he had become a noted reviewer, his collection *Sartor resartus* appearing in 1833–4. He abandoned Edinburgh for London in 1834 and began a career as a historian and political moralist. His essays on *Chartism* (1839) and *Past and Present* (1843) dramatized the moral demands subjects make on their rulers. His *French Revolution* (1837), his edition of Cromwell's speeches (1845), and his enormous study of Frederick the Great (1858–65) are imaginative accounts of the moral power of political leadership.

**Carmarthenshire** County of south-west Wales. It was part of the early Welsh kingdom of *Dyfed and its core became the heart of the later kingdom of *Deheubarth. At the Norman Conquest, a royal lordship was created about the borough of Carmarthen. The shire was created at the statute of *Rhuddlan. At the Act of *Union with England, other royal lordships and sublordships were added to the county. In 1974 Carmarthen became a district in the county of Dyfed, but in 1996 it was restored as a county within its traditional bounds.

Carmarthenshire is a county of rich Welsh tradition. The name, an Anglicization of the Welsh Caerfyrddin, is derived from the Welsh name of Merlin. Welsh is spoken by 58.0 per cent in the district of Carmarthen, rising to 66.5 per cent in Dinefwr and falling to 46.5 in Llanelli. The population of the new county was 169,000 in 2000, of whom 44,000 live in Llanelli.

**Carmelites** were originally established as a monastic order in Palestine in the mid-12th cent., claiming descent from early hermits on Mount Carmel. Several communities were established in England c.1242. Shortly afterwards the Carmelites were reorganized as mendicant *friars (the 'white friars'). They remained especially popular in England, where there were nearly 40 friaries at the *dissolution.

**Carnatic wars** The Carnatic region in south India witnessed the initial struggle of the British and French for power. Rivalry between Chanda Sahib and Mohammed Ali to be nawab of Arcot became entangled with rivalry between the English and French *East India Companies. The French backed Chanda Sahib, the English Mohammed Ali. In 1760, the English won a decisive victory at the battle of *Wandewash. However, English hegemony was challenged by Hyder Ali and Tipu Sultan of Mysore, and south India was not fully secured by the British until Wellesley's (*Wellington) victory over Tipu in 1799.

**Carnegie, Andrew** (1835–1919). Philanthropist. Carnegie was born in Dunfermline but brought up in the USA. He made a vast fortune, mainly in railroads and the iron industry, retiring in 1901 to supervise the 'wide distribution' of his wealth. He had already begun in 1882 with the gift of a library to Dunfermline and he followed it with endowments to hundreds of libraries in Britain, the USA, and Canada.

**Caroline of Brandenburg-Anspach** (1683–1737), queen of George II. Daughter of John Frederick, margrave of Brandenburg-Anspach, Caroline married in 1705 George Augustus, electoral prince of Hanover and, from 1727, king of Great Britain. Her life in England from 1714 was far from tranquil. Her husband was testy and choleric. Relations between him, as prince of Wales, and his father George I were bad, and in turn George and Caroline quarrelled bitterly with their son *Frederick, prince of Wales. She did not particularly resent her husband's attentions to other women which, at least, kept him occupied. Her influence over the king, which was considerable, was exercised in favour of Sir Robert *Walpole. A woman of intelligence and learning, she was a benefactress of the Queen's College, Oxford.

**Caroline of Brunswick** (1768–1821), queen of George IV. Caroline's marriage to her cousin George, prince of Wales, in March 1795 was a spectacular disaster. Intimacy was confined to the first night, and the couple separated after the birth of their daughter Princess *Charlotte in January 1796. Thereafter, Caroline spent much time on the continent with a strange entourage, which led to much gossip. A 'delicate investigation' in 1806 cleared her of adultery but declared that she had been indiscreet. When George became king in 1820, Caroline returned to England to claim her place as queen. Her cause was taken up by George's not inconsiderable number of enemies and she won a good deal of popular support. But when Caroline appeared at Westminster abbey in July 1821 at George's coronation, demanding to be let in, she overplayed her hand. She died a fortnight afterwards.

**Carr, Robert, 1st Viscount Rochester, 1st earl of Somerset** (c.1587–1645). Carr, a royal favourite, began his career as page to James VI of Scotland. He acquired political significance only after the death of James's chief minister Robert *Cecil in 1612, acting as the king's secretary. His main alliance, with Henry *Howard, the pro-Spanish and pro-catholic earl of

Northampton, was reinforced when he fell in love with Northampton's relative Frances Howard, wife of the earl of *Essex. James set up a tribunal which annulled the marriage, and in 1613 Frances married Carr, now earl of Somerset. Meanwhile Carr's former friend Sir Thomas Overbury, who had opposed the match, was removed from the scene when James sent him to the Tower, where he died, apparently of natural causes. Only in 1615 did James become aware that in fact Overbury had been poisoned by Frances. Carr and his wife were tried for murder, and although Carr protested his innocence, they were both found guilty. Saved from execution by James, after a few years' comfortable imprisonment they retired into private life.

**Carroll, Lewis,** pseudonym of Charles Lutwidge Dodgson (1832–98). Author and mathematician. Brought up in a country parsonage, excelling in mathematical and classical studies at Oxford, Dodgson was appointed lecturer in mathematics at Christ Church (1855–81). Shyness and a stammer were forgotten in the company of children, whom he amused with stories, puzzles, and riddles; some of these, invented for Dean Liddell's daughters, were recast and immortalized in *Alice's Adventures in Wonderland* (1865) and its sequel *Through the Looking-Glass* (1871). Dodgson also published mathematical works, verse, and pamphlets on university affairs, all combining logic and humour, and was a fine photographer.

**Carson, Sir Edward** (1854–1935). Carson is still seen as the arch-opponent of *Irish Home Rule but was a more complex figure than traditionally depicted. Of middle-class southern protestant background, he became a successful lawyer and Unionist politician. In 1893 he moved his political and legal career to London, becoming solicitor-general for both Ireland and Britain. Carson was elected leader of the Unionist Party in 1910, and associated with Ulster resistance to the third Home Rule Bill. He reluctantly accepted the need for partition by 1914. A member of the war cabinet, he played a significant role in the removal of *Asquith from office in 1916. Attorney-general 1915–16, and 1st lord of the Admiralty 1917–18, his administrative ability was heavily criticized. His denunciation of the Anglo-Irish treaty was

more heartfelt than his welcome of the Northern Irish government.

**Carteret, John, 2nd Baron Carteret, 1st Earl Granville** (1690–1763). Carteret achieved prominence through Baltic diplomacy, 1719–20, and became secretary of state in 1721. *Walpole's and *Townshend's jealousy led to his demotion to the lord-lieutenancy of Ireland in 1724 and dismissal in 1730, whereupon he became a leader of the Whig opposition. Upon Walpole's fall in 1742, Carteret was appointed secretary of state for the northern department. He became George II's favourite minister, developing complex diplomatic schemes to assist Austria, Britain's ally in the War of the Austrian Succession. In November 1744 Granville (as he had become) was forced to resign. After some years of semi-retirement, Granville was persuaded by *Newcastle in 1751 to become lord president. An accomplished classicist, linguist, and wit, Granville's career was restricted by underestimating the power of the Commons.

**Carthusians** Part of an 11th-cent. revival of Egyptian solitary 'desert life', they were founded as a group of hermits near Grenoble, later La Grande Chartreuse (1084), by Bruno (d. 1101). As penance for *Becket's murder, Henry II established the first English house at Witham, Somerset (1178): six more houses followed (1342–1414), including London (1371) and the largest, Henry V's foundation at Sheen. Never relaxing their austerity, nor ambitious to proliferate, they were noted for their holiness. The last prior of the London charterhouse, John Houghton, and his monks were martyred at the *dissolution.

**Cartimandua,** British queen of the *Brigantes. Cartimandua was queen in her own right. In AD 51 she handed over to the Romans *Caratacus, the leader of the Welsh resistance. Her treaty relationship with the Romans provided them with a friendly native state on the northern frontiers of the new province. However both personal and political differences with her consort Venutius led to considerable instability. Venutius' ambitions were initially thwarted by Roman intervention in support of Cartimandua, but during the civil wars of AD 69 he seized the kingdom. The queen was rescued by Roman cavalry, but never regained her throne.

**Cartwright, Edmund** (1743–1823). Inventor. A younger brother of John Cartwright, the parliamentary reformer, Edmund Cartwright was an Anglican clergyman. In 1785 he patented a loom driven by water, which he developed later in a factory near Doncaster. In 1789 he invented a wool-combing machine, which saved labour and caused great agitation among the workers. Cartwright was obliged to abandon his own factory, but his inventions were widely adopted, and in 1809 he was awarded a grant of £10,000 by Parliament.

**Cartwright, Thomas** (1535–1603). A leading early presbyterian, Cartwright was born in Hertfordshire and graduated from St John's College, Cambridge. Expelled on Mary's accession, he returned as fellow of Trinity (1562), but disputes over surplices and church government led him to depart for Ireland (1565–7). After his return as Lady Margaret professor of divinity (1569) his advocacy of presbyterian church government brought him into conflict with *Whitgift, master of Trinity. Deprived of his professorship (1570) and his fellowship (1571), he emigrated to Geneva. Intellectually the leading puritan of his day, he refused to associate with the *Brownists and *Barrowists.

**Carvetii** A British tribe and *civitas*. The Carvetii are one of the many smaller tribes that made up the *Brigantian confederation of northern England. Their name means 'the Deer Men'. They occupied the extreme north-west corner of Brigantian territory comprising Cumberland and part of Westmorland. A capital was established at Carlisle, known to the Romans as Luguvalium.

**Casablanca conference** On 14–24 January 1943 *Churchill and Roosevelt met in Morocco to determine allied strategy. Stalin refused to attend as he was overseeing operations around Stalingrad. The prospect of opening a second front in northern France was discussed but the British considered it premature.

**Casement, Sir Roger** (1864–1916). Humanitarian and Irish hero. As British consul in the Congo Free State and then on the Amazon, Casement uncovered European atrocities against natives which earned him a knighthood in 1911. He then returned to his Irish roots, and collaborated with Britain's enemies during the *First World War, for which he was hanged in 1916 after landing from a German submarine near Tralee to help the *Easter Rising.

**Cashel, archiepiscopal diocese of** The Irish archbishopric of Cashel was established by the Council of Raithbressail (1111), with oversight of the twelve dioceses of Leth Moga (southern half of Ireland). The Council of Kells-Mellifont (1152) further restructured Ireland into four provinces, reducing Cashel's authority to the south-west by the creation of the *Dublin province. Cashel is still a catholic archiepiscopal see, but in 1838 the Anglican see was united with Dublin.

**Casket Letters** The contents of a small silver casket, uncovered in 1567, allegedly incriminating Mary Stuart in the murder of her second husband Lord *Darnley. Surviving copies suggest that, while not outright forgeries, the material was clumsily doctored by Mary's opponents.

**Cassivellaunus** British chief or king. Cassivellaunus is known only from the war diaries of Julius *Caesar and Dio Cassius' later derivative account of Caesar's invasions of 55 and 54 BC. Nevertheless, he may have been a key figure in south-eastern Britain before the Roman conquest. His territory is described as beginning some 75 miles from the sea, and on the far side of the Thames. This places him in the Chilterns and suggests that he may have founded a kingdom there under the tribal name of the *Catuvellauni. His abilities as a leader are confirmed by his selection by the British to lead the opposition to Caesar.

**Castillon, battle of,** 1453. On 17 July 1453, the English lost Gascony, which they had held for 300 years. An Anglo-Gascon attack on a fortified artillery park on the right bank of the Dordogne was probably launched without knowledge of the strength of its defence. The assault was repulsed, the English overrun, and *Shrewsbury, their legendary 65-year-old commander, killed in the rout. Only *Calais was left to the English.

**Castle Howard,** near Malton (Yorks.), is one of the grandest houses privately built, comparable with *Chatsworth. It was commissioned by the 3rd earl of *Carlisle, who began in 1699 to transform the sprawling hamlet of Henderskelfe. The main house was designed by *Vanbrugh. The three great features are a superb south front, the imposing dome, and an extensive park, dominated by Vanbrugh's Temple of the Four Winds and *Hawksmoor's sombre mausoleum.

## Castlereagh, Robert Stewart, Viscount, 2nd marquess of Londonderry

(1769–1822). Castlereagh outgrew his background in Ulster politics and became an advocate of the union between Britain and Ireland, a capable war secretary, and finally a distinguished foreign secretary. He entered the Irish House of Commons in 1790, soon felt drawn to the policies of the younger *Pitt, and was elected to the Westminster Parliament in 1794. Castlereagh sympathized with reform in France but was unhappy about the decline of the French Revolution into violence, and was anxious about the impact of Jacobin ideas in Ireland through the secret society the *United Irishmen. He supported the war against France, became prominent in the suppression of the *Irish rebellion of 1798, and bore the main burden in carrying the Irish Act of *Union in Dublin. He supported *catholic emancipation, and resigned with Pitt when George III thwarted it. He served however in *Addington's administration from 1802 and in Pitt's second ministry in 1804. On the death of Pitt he left office but became war secretary in the *Portland ministry. The *Peninsular War was supported by Castlereagh from the start and he took the initiative in bringing Wellesley (*Wellington) forward. The failure of the *Walcheren expedition meant that Castlereagh left the war department as the scapegoat. The decision to withdraw was a bitter one, the more so because Canning was eager to ensure that Castlereagh carried the responsibility for failure. The result was the collapse of the Portland ministry and the duel with Canning, which relegated both men to the back benches for several years.

Castlereagh's great opportunity came when he was appointed foreign secretary and leader of the House of Commons on the formation of *Liverpool's ministry in 1812. He built up the final coalition against Napoleon, and at Vienna did much to frame the peace settlement. He was committed to regular meetings of the powers in congress not in order to perpetuate the status quo, but to enable peace to be preserved by adjustment to inevitable change. Castlereagh became alienated from Metternich and by 1820 had dissociated Britain from the *Holy Alliance, which he had condemned as 'a piece of sublime mysticism and nonsense'. Although his distrust of Russian expansion in the Near East drew Castlereagh closer to Metternich over the Greek revolt, he seriously contemplated the recognition of the independence of the Spanish American colonies. In 1822, worn out by overwork, he suffered a nervous breakdown and committed suicide.

**castles** developed first in France in the 10th cent. The first castles in England were built in Edward the Confessor's reign by his Norman followers, and were strongly resented by the English, as foreign imports. Lordly residences in late Saxon England appear to have been enclosed with a palisade and a ditch, but the defences were slight. Castles were an introduction into England and a direct consequence of the Norman invasion of 1066.

Orderic Vitalis, a Norman historian, said that the English fought bravely but lost because they lacked castles. William secured his first landing in England with a wooden castle, and on entering London, after the battle of Hastings, one of his first acts was to order the creation of a castle to control the city: the *Tower of London. William used castles to secure his new kingdom; the nobles to whom he granted estates did the same in taking control of their new lands. The castles built immediately after the Conquest, whether by the king or his followers, were generally rapidly constructed of earth and timber. In form, they were either a fortified enclosure surrounded by a ditch (known as a ringwork) or a motte and bailey, that is an earth mound topped with a fortification and surrounded by a ditch connected to a further lower fortified enclosure. Large castles like *Windsor, *Dover, or Richmond seem to have been conceived from the first as residences as well as fortresses. The White Tower built by William I to subdue London incorporated two large suites of rooms, a grand chapel, and extensive storage space. During the Conquest all Norman barons, great or small, seem to have built castles; however, the wooden fortresses were not very durable and their owners were soon forced to decide whether they should be replaced in stone. Further, the castle's importance in warfare meant that its design was constantly being refined so that to maintain its military efficiency meant a constant outlay. Many smaller landowners ceased to be castle owners, preferring instead a fortified manor house. Castles became the prerogative of the wealthy baronage and the crown. Thus the castles which are notable monuments today are those which were rebuilt and updated in the 12th cent. and later. Amongst the most developed examples in Britain are the castles built for Edward I in north Wales, for example, Conwy, *Caernarfon, and *Harlech. Despite the introduction of gunpowder, castles retained their importance. Late examples, such as Raglan (Monmouthshire), were designed to include cannon as part of their defences. Castles were again important in the English Civil War, when large numbers were refortified and held for the king. In recognition of the part that castles had played in the war, the majority of surviving buildings were slighted by the victorious parliamentarians.

**Cat and Mouse Act,** 1913. Exasperated by the tactics of militant suffragettes in going on hunger strike, *Asquith's government passed the Prisoners' Temporary Discharge for Ill-Health Act, known commonly as the Cat and Mouse Act (3 Geo. V c. 4). Prisoners could be released and subsequently rearrested.

**Cateau-Cambrésis, treaty of,** 1559. Mary Tudor's marriage to Philip of Spain dragged her into a disastrous war against France in 1557 in the course of which *Calais was lost. When Elizabeth succeeded in November 1558, she was anxious for peace. The treaty was signed on 3 April 1559. The French ceased to support the claims of Mary, queen of Scots, to the English throne, and the English, by implication, gave up hopes of regaining Calais, since the French were to retain it for eight years and then restore it on conditions certain to be broken.

**cathedrals** are the chief churches of a diocese, where the archbishop or bishop has his throne (*cathedra*). The fabric and worship of the church itself is the responsibility of the dean. The oldest dioceses of the Church of

England are Canterbury (597), London (604), Rochester (604), York (625), Norwich (631), Lincoln (Lindsey) (634), Durham (Lindisfarne) (635), Lichfield (656), Hereford (676), and Worcester (680). The newest are Birmingham (1905), Southwark (1905), Chelmsford (1914), Bury St Edmunds (1914), Coventry (1918), Bradford (1920), Derby (1927), Guildford (1927), Leicester (1927), and Portsmouth (1927).

**Catherine of Aragon** (1485–1536), 1st queen of Henry VIII. Catherine was a victim of dynastic politics. The daughter of Ferdinand and Isabella of Spain, she was sent to England in October 1501 to marry Prince *Arthur, eldest son of Henry VII. The young couple were sent to Ludlow, where Arthur died five months after the marriage. Catherine stayed in England and in 1503 it was arranged that she should marry Arthur's younger brother Henry. Henry VII was in no haste to expedite the matter and for some years Catherine was in an unpleasant position. But on Henry VIII's accession in 1509 he hastened to fulfil the agreement. The marriage was at first affectionate, though not until 1516 was a living child, Mary, born. By 1526, for a mixture of public and private reasons, Henry was thinking of divorce, it having belatedly occurred to him that he had married his brother's wife. From this time forward, the fate of her marriage was out of Catherine's hands, though she continued to protest and refused to enter a nunnery. In July 1531 Henry left her and never saw her again. Her later years were spent at Buckden and Kimbolton, comforted by her faith, deprived of her title as queen, and forbidden to see her daughter. She died in January 1536 and was buried in Peterborough abbey.

**Catherine of Braganza** (1638–1705), queen of Charles II. Daughter of John, king of Portugal, Catherine's marriage to Charles II on 21 May 1662 was regarded by English merchants as 'the most beneficial that ever our nation was engaged in'. Her dowry included Bombay and Tangier. Dark-haired, petite, and amiable, Catherine was badly educated. She had, however, some charm and Pepys thought her 'mighty pretty' when he saw her with the king in 1663. Tension inevitably arose between her and Charles's mistress Lady Castlemaine. Catherine miscarried several times and had no live children. This fuelled suggestions of a divorce, but Charles stood by her. After his death in February 1685, she moved to Somerset House before returning to Portugal.

**Catherine Howard** (1520–42), 5th queen of Henry VIII. Catherine, niece of the duke of *Norfolk, was 19 when Henry became interested in her. The annulment of his marriage to *Anne of Cleves on 9 July 1540 was followed a fortnight later by his marriage to Catherine. She was tiny, pretty, and vivacious. Henry showered her with gifts but by the end of 1541 he had heard rumours of her adultery, before and after marriage. Pre-marital affairs with Francis Dereham and her cousin Thomas Culpeper were the basis for a charge of treason. Catherine was placed under house arrest at Syon House, and beheaded on 13 February 1542.

**Catherine Parr** (1512–48), 6th queen of Henry VIII. Daughter of Sir Thomas Parr of Kendal, Catherine was well educated with protestant sympathies. She was 31 and had been twice married when she attracted Henry's attention. The marriage was performed at Hampton Court on 12 July 1543. She provided something of a home for the royal family, and interested herself in Mary and Elizabeth. On Henry's death in 1547 she married the ambitious Thomas *Seymour, a former admirer, and promoted Baron Seymour of Sudeley. She died on 7 September 1548 shortly after the birth of a daughter.

**Catherine of Valois** (1401–37), queen of Henry V. Youngest daughter of Charles VI of France, her marriage to Henry on 2 June 1420, after bitter warfare between France and England, was an affair of state. At the same time, the treaty of *Troyes was signed, whereby Henry was to become Charles's heir. A son, later Henry VI, was born in December 1421 at Windsor. Catherine accompanied Henry to Harfleur, and returned a widow in May 1422 when Henry died of dysentery. She subsequently made a secret marriage with Owen *Tudor. The grandson of this marriage took the throne as Henry VII. Catherine died in February 1437, was buried in the Lady Chapel, Westminster abbey, and later placed alongside Henry V.

**Catholic Apostolic Church** This millennialist denomination derived from meetings held from 1826 at Albury Park, the Surrey home of the London banker and Tory politician Henry Drummond (1786–1860). Among those attending was Edward *Irving, minister of Regent Square Scottish Church, London, then at the peak of his wayward genius. Excluded from Regent Square in 1832, Irving established a congregation in Newman Street. This became the first Holy Catholic Apostolic Church. Liberally supported by Drummond, the new body developed a hierarchy of apostles, prophets, evangelists, and pastors. Since only apostles could ordain, the Church, which claimed 6,000 members in 1851, lost its impetus after the last apostle's death in 1901.

**Catholic Association,** 1823–9. Daniel *O'Connell's Catholic Association, founded in Ireland in 1823, was one of the most successful pressure groups of the 19th cent. Its object was to persuade or force the British government to grant *catholic emancipation, allowing catholics to sit in Parliament. It organized petitions, held monster meetings, collected the 'catholic rent' of a penny a month, and was accused of drilling and intimidation. When O'Connell (unable as a catholic to take the oath) was returned to Parliament at the Co. Clare by-election in July 1828, *Wellington gave way rather than risk civil war.

**catholic emancipation** was achieved by an Act of Parliament of 1829, enabling Roman catholics in Britain to participate fully in public life by abolishing the *Test and *Corporation Acts. O'Connell's electoral success in the Co. Clare by-election convinced *Wellington that there was no means of controlling Ireland, other than to accede to the demands of the majority. English catholics played little part in the campaign. By splitting the Tory Party, with the ultra Tories regarding the actions of Wellington and *Peel as a gross betrayal, it prepared the way for the Whig victory of 1830 and for the decade of reform which followed.

**catholicism** The word derives from the universality of faith in the Christian church, but since the 16th cent. has referred to the portion of Christianity accepting papal authority. It delineates the distinctive post-Reformation communities in Britain which rejected the assertion of royal supremacy over the church in England. These communities survived legal proscription by *penal laws, eventually lifted in the late 18th and early 19th cents. That process can be understood in a series of phases, beginning with the period of survival as *recusant communities during the 17th cent. Up to 1688, catholics launched a missionary campaign to maintain catholic life and worship. The sacramental nature of catholicism meant that the congregations were dependent on priests who had to be trained in missionary seminaries in Europe. The first of these was founded by Cardinal William *Allen at Douai in Flanders and in Rome in the 1570s. The priests, subjected to the law of treason, went in fear of their lives and depended on the protection of lay families, mostly gentry. Lay and clerical catholics were executed up to the 1680s. The extent to which the penal laws were imposed varied according to the circumstances of the day and in some areas catholicism flourished unmolested. Parts of Lancashire, the north-east, and the midlands became relatively safe territory. In Ireland, catholics formed the great majority outside Ulster, and in Scotland were strong in the Highlands and Islands.

In these areas it became possible, in the second phase from 1688 to the mid-18th cent., for catholic life to establish its existence. The mood of the early 18th cent. turned against religious persecution and few of the laws were enforced. By the mid-18th cent., catholic practice was largely tolerated and life for the small congregations, served by travelling missionaries or gentry chaplains, fell into a pattern of quiet independence.

The final defeat of the *Jacobite cause in 1745 removed the political animus against catholicism, though not until 1829 was the prohibition on catholic MPs lifted. In the 1740s catholics were a negligible fraction of the population of England and Wales, but from that time they entered a new phase of modest growth. The drift to the towns began and urban catholicism in London, the midlands, and parts of the north emerged. Chapels and schools, though still technically illegal, began to appear. Numbers were increasing rapidly, from around 80,000 at the end of the 18th cent. to nearer 700,000 in the 1851 religious census. This growth was partly endogenous and partly due to massive migration of impoverished Irish catholics. Clerical training had been forced back onto British soil by the French Revolution and clerical numbers, organization, and ecclesiastical authority were increasing.

The restoration of the catholic hierarchy to England and Wales in 1850 gave English catholicism a sense of belonging fully to the universal church under papal authority. The task after 1850 was to rebuild English catholicism in the image of European catholicism and to create the churches, schools, devotions, and loyalty which built the powerful, close-knit catholic culture characteristic until the middle of the 20th cent.

**Catholic University of Ireland** Though from 1793 catholics could take degrees at *Trinity College, Dublin, few did so, and in 1844 *Peel proposed the establishment of undenominational colleges at Cork, Belfast, and Galway. The Irish catholic community split in response, the majority condemning them as godless, and the Synod of Thurles in 1850 warned catholics not to attend. Archbishop *Cullen then presided over a committee to set up a catholic university. It opened in 1854 with 20 students but could make little progress without government assistance. Augustine Birrell, chief secretary in the Liberal administration of 1906, introduced the major reconstruction of 1908, which established the National University, with component colleges at Dublin, Cork, and Galway. Though formally undenominational, it was under catholic control.

**Cato Street conspiracy** A plot to murder Lord *Liverpool's cabinet at dinner in February 1820 was led by Arthur Thistlewood, a follower of the agrarian communist Thomas *Spence. The plotters were betrayed by a government spy and arrested as they assembled in a stable in Cato Street. Thistlewood and four fellow-conspirators were executed on May Day, 1820.

**Catterick, battle of,** 6th cent. *Aneurin's poem *Gododdin* relates how the North Britons from Edinburgh were defeated at Catterick by the men of *Bernicia and *Deira. The battle was probably in the late 6th cent., and was an important step in the development of Northumbria as a strong Saxon power.

**Catuvellauni** A British tribe and *civitas*. The Catuvellauni first appear in Dio Cassius' account of the Claudian invasion of AD 43, where they led the opposition to the Roman forces. We can trace the tribal kingdom back at least three generations to a king called Tasciovanus by the coins issued by him and his successor *Cunobelinus. In fact, it seems likely that the chief called *Cassivellaunus who had opposed Caesar in 54 BC had already begun to carve out the Catuvellaunian kingdom. The *civitas* which the Romans created in the mid-70s reflects this expansion. The *civitas* capital was at *Verulamium, the original capital of Tasciovanus' kingdom.

**Cavalier Parliament,** 1661–79. This Parliament succeeded the *Convention, which had summoned Charles II back from exile. Though its members were overwhelmingly loyal they were by no means prepared to yield Parliament's rights. The Anglican majority was less willing to forgive and forget than the king. It began by ordering that the *covenant be burned by the public hangman, supported a fierce penal code against dissenters, and forced Charles II in 1673 to withdraw his *Declaration of Indulgence.

**cavaliers** Nickname for the royalists who fought for Charles I during the civil wars. Like 'roundhead', 'cavalier' originated as a term of abuse. Stemming from the Spanish word *caballero*, it was meant to connote catholicism, foreignness, and immorality. Rather than reject the nickname, the royalists redefined it for their own purposes. They saw themselves as well-born men who out of loyalty and conscience had chosen to defend their king.

**Cavell, Edith** (1865–1915). The daughter of a Norfolk vicar, Edith Cavell was a governess in Brussels before training as a nurse. In 1907 she became matron of the hospital of St Gilles, Brussels, and remained there at the outbreak of war in 1914. She set up escape routes for hundreds of Belgian and allied fugitives and was arrested by the Germans in August 1915. Court-martialled on 7 October, she was shot on 12 October, dying with dignity and courage. The reaction world-wide to her death elevated her to the status of martyr. Her body was later reinterred in Norwich cathedral. A memorial was erected to her in St Martin's Place, off Trafalgar Square, London.

**Cavendish, Lord Frederick** (1836–82). The second son of the 7th duke of Devonshire, Cavendish entered Parliament as a Liberal in 1865. His wife was the niece of Mrs Gladstone and Cavendish became Gladstone's private secretary. In 1882, when W. E. *Forster resigned, Cavendish was sent to Ireland as chief secretary to replace him. Arriving in Dublin on 6 May he walked in Phoenix Park with T. H. Burke, the under-secretary, and was stabbed to death by a gang known as the Invincibles. Cavendish's murder caused a sensation. He was buried at *Chatsworth at a funeral attended by 300 MPs, brought from London by special train.

**Cavendish, Henry** (1731–1810). A nephew of the 3rd duke of Devonshire, he studied in Cambridge and in Paris, before living as a recluse in London. He worked in the new field of pneumatic chemistry, isolating 'inflammable air' (hydrogen) and proving that water was not an element but a compound. The Cavendish Laboratory in Cambridge was founded in his memory.

**Cavendish, William** See DEVONSHIRE, 4TH DUKE OF.

**Cawnpore (Kanpur)** saw a bitter struggle during the *Indian mutiny. Its British garrison was obliged to surrender to Nana Sahib who, on hearing of the approach of Sir Henry *Havelock's relieving army, ordered all prisoners to be killed. Havelock retook the town and his forces wreaked a fearful revenge. However, the garrison he left behind proved unable to hold on and Tatya Tope, Nana Sahib's general, effected a reoccupation. It was not until December 1857 that Sir Colin *Campbell's army achieved the final reconquest.

**Caxton, William** (*c.*1420–*c.*1492). A prominent merchant from Kent, Caxton established the first successful press in England. He learned printing in Cologne and the Low Countries, producing the first printed book in English—his own translation of *Le Receuil des histoires de Troye*—in Bruges *c.*1473–4. His press at Westminster, established in 1476, printed nearly 100 volumes, including works by *Chaucer, *Gower, John Lydgate, and *Malory.

**Ceawlin** (d. *c.*593), king of the West Saxons (560–91). Ceawlin, who began to reign in 560, fought against the Britons. At the battle of *Dyrham in 577 he is reported to have defeated three kings and to have taken Gloucester, Cirencester, and Bath, thus separating Britons in the south-west from those north of the Bristol channel. Dissatisfaction may have produced another king or subking, Ceol, in 591, and in 592, after a defeat at Wodnesbeorh, Ceawlin was expelled. He 'perished' the following year. *Bede listed him as the second *bretwalda.

**Cecil, Sir Robert** (1563–1612). Jacobean statesman. He was the younger son, but political heir, of Elizabeth I's chief minister William Cecil (*Burghley). Small in stature, humpbacked, and frail, he entered Parliament in 1584. Knighted in 1591, he was already acting secretary of state, though not formally appointed until 1596. In the last decade of Elizabeth's reign the Cecils' hold on power was challenged by a faction around Elizabeth's young favourite, the earl of *Essex. Fortunately for the Cecils, Essex overreached himself and was executed. This left Cecil without rival as the queen's chief minister after the death of his father in 1598. Only the prospect of James VI's accession threatened him, but Cecil neutralized this by opening secret communications with the Scottish king. He remained in office after James became king of England in 1603. James relied on Cecil, his 'little beagle', for the day-to-day business of government. Cecil was a staunch protestant but, like the king, took a relatively tolerant attitude towards catholics. He loved peace, and in 1604 brought the long war with Spain to a close. In 1608, when he was earl of Salisbury, James appointed him lord treasurer. Cecil's major attempt to refinance the crown, the *Great Contract, came close to success in 1610, but its eventual collapse diminished his influence. Although not yet 50, his health was in decline, and in 1612 he died. He had inherited the princely mansion called Theobalds, but its situation in good hunting country made James covet it. Cecil, ever the perfect courtier, therefore exchanged Theobalds for the ruinous palace at Hatfield, some miles away, where he built the palatial house in which his descendants still live.

**Celtic church** This term, which describes the Christian church as it developed in Wales, Ireland, and Scotland, recognizes that church practice in all three countries had many features in common, but should not disguise the fact that there were very real differences between them. In particular, the concept of the territorial episcopal diocese was based on the administrative divisions of the Roman empire, with which Ireland had no formal link, and consequently the diocesan system had difficulty in taking root there. At the time of the Roman withdrawal much of Wales and Scotland was still heathen, and the earliest exact date for the presence of Christians in Ireland is a reference in 431 to Palladius, bishop to 'the Irish who believe in Christ'. Ireland was evangelized largely from Britain, its most famous British missionary being St *Patrick, in the early and mid-5th cent. The diffusion of the cult of Patrick, and the growth in the status of *Armagh, the ecclesiastical centre most closely associated with him, parallels that of St *David in Wales, while the arrival of the Irish saint *Columba in *Iona (Scotland), in 563, marked the start of a lengthy period of Irish missionary activity in Britain and the continent.

**Celts** From the 5th cent. BC, Greek ethnographers described the Celts as one of the major ethnic groups of central and western Europe, locating them inland from Marseilles. Caesar in *De bello Gallico* states that only the Gauls of central and southern Gaul called themselves Celts, with Belgae living in the north of Gaul and Aquitani in the south-west.

Interest revived in the Celts during the Renaissance. In 1582 George Buchanan claimed that the former inhabitants of Britain were Celts or Gauls on the basis of similarity in ancient place-names in Gaul and Britain. The term 'Celt' was thus extended to refer to speakers of these languages—Bretons, Celts, Cornish, Welsh, Irish, Manx, and Scottish.

To identify the ancient Celts, 18th- and 19th-cent. scholars turned to archaeology, describing certain objects and burial rites as 'Celtic'. Kemble and Franks, as early as 1863, had referred to objects from Britain decorated in a distinctive curvilinear art style as 'Celtic'. This art style was also found on the objects fished out at La Tène on Lake

Neuchâtel in Switzerland. By the late 19th cent. the La Tène culture became that of the Celtic peoples, and La Tène art became 'Celtic' art. It was also assumed that there was a close correlation between ethnicity, language, art, and material culture. Scholars such as Powell (1958) and Filip (1962) used archaeology to seek the origin and spread of the La Tène culture. On the evidence of the continuity of burial rites from the preceding Hallstatt period, and of a concentration of richly decorated early La Tène art objects, the centre of origin was identified as northern France–western Germany, more specifically in Champagne. From these areas it was claimed the Celts expanded in the 4th and 3rd cents. BC by migrating into southern and western France, Britain, and central Europe.

This explanation has come under increasing criticism. It does not account for Celtic-speaking groups in Iberia where La Tène objects are rare; the supposed invasion of Britain in the 4th–3rd cents. BC corresponds with the period when insular–continental contacts were at their lowest; and continuity from the early to the late Iron Age is seen as the norm in virtually all areas where the archaeological record is sufficiently complete (e.g. Britain). The supposed 'expansion' of the Celts is largely a product of misinterpretation of the archaeological record. This revised, and still disputed, view of the Celts is forcing us to adopt new models for the diffusion and adoption of language, material culture, and art styles, independent of one another. The naming of the language group as 'Celtic' is seen as an arbitrary choice by 17th-cent. scholars—it could have equally been Britannic, Belgic, or Gallic. If we accept that there were never any Celts in antiquity in Britain, it follows that terms such as the 'Celtic' church, Celtic art, or indeed the description of the Welsh, Irish, and Scots as 'Celts' are without historical foundations.

**Census Act,** 1800. In 18th-cent. Britain there was much uncertainty about the size of the population. In 1753 Thomas Potter moved in Parliament for an annual census. His opponents retorted that it would give valuable information to enemies, and complained of the affront to British liberty. The bill was lost in the Lords. The 1800 bill, which carried the day, was introduced at the sug-

gestion of John Rickman. There was no opposition and the first census of Great Britain was carried out on 10 March 1801. The population of England and Wales was returned as 9.168 million and Scotland as 1.599 million, revealing an upwards trend. Contemporaries were struck by the size of London which, at 1 million, was as big as all the other towns together. The census was a milestone in the provision of statistical data and has subsequently been held at ten-year intervals.

**Central** An administrative region of Scotland, created in 1973 from Clackmannanshire, parts of Perthshire, most of Stirlingshire, and the Bo'ness area of West Lothian. It was divided into three districts—Clackmannan, Falkirk, and Stirling. In April 1996 Central region was abolished, and all local government functions taken over by the previous districts.

**Cenwalh** (d. 672), king of Wessex (642–5, 648–72). Cenwalh was driven out by his powerful Mercian neighbours in 645 for repudiating his wife, sister of the Mercian king. He sought refuge at the court of East Anglia, where he was baptized, but returned in 648. His main successes were against the Britons, gaining victories at Bradford on Avon (652), Peonnan (658), and Posbury (possibly Pontesbury near Shrewsbury) in 661. Against the Mercians he was less successful and in 661 lost parts of Hampshire to Mercia, which granted them to *Sussex.

**Cenwulf** (d. 821), king of Mercia (796–821). Cenwulf became king after the brief reign of Ecgfrith, son of the great *Offa, doubtless by a coup. He took over Offa's extensive authority in southern England. In 798 he repressed a revolt in Kent, brutally. His authority there was diminished by a bitter dispute with Archbishop Wulfred of Canterbury, appointed in 805.

**Ceolwulf** (d. 764), king of Northumbria (729–31, 731–7). Such Anglo-Saxons of his day who can claim immortality owe this to *Bede. So with Ceolwulf. Bede dedicated his *Ecclesiastical History* to 'the most glorious King Ceolwulf'. In the same year (731) Ceolwulf was, an annalist says, 'seized, tonsured, and restored to rule'. Six years later he was deposed for good. He lived long as a monk at *Lindisfarne.

**ceorl** is one of the terms used in the early (7th- and 9th-cent.) English laws for the lowest class of freeman. Thus in Wessex his blood-price was 200 shillings: that of other free classes was 600 and 1,200. In Kent his status was higher. Even the West Saxon ceorl appears as the head of a free peasant household, owing military service, capable of owning slaves, and with significant legal status. In the 11th cent. the status of free peasants often fell and by 1300 the word was acquiring its modern sense of disparagement.

**Cerdic, House of** By the late 9th cent., when the *Anglo-Saxon Chronicle* was compiled, Cerdic was regarded as the ancestor of *Alfred and all previous kings of the West Saxons; however, the reality is hard to ascertain. The arrival of Cerdic and his son Cynric is recorded in the *Chronicle* annal for 495, but the entries concerning them are riddled with inconsistencies.

**Ceylon** *See* SRI LANKA.

**Chad (Ceadda), St** (d. 673). One of four Northumbrian brothers who were 'famous priests', Chad studied in Ireland and was a disciple of *Aidan. In 664 he succeeded his brother Cedd as abbot of Lastingham and was nominated to the see of Northumbria by King *Oswiu. Informed by Archbishop *Theodore that his consecration (c.665) was irregular, he resigned the see. He became (fifth) bishop of the Mercians, the Middle Angles, and the people of Lindsey in 670, his seat at *Lichfield.

**Chadwick, Edwin** (1800–90). Reformer. John Stuart *Mill called Chadwick 'one of the organising and contriving minds of the age'. He was born in Manchester and became a lawyer. In 1832 he was appointed to the Poor Law Commission and the following year to the commission on children in factories. His influence on both reports was great and he was appointed secretary to the Poor Law Commission in 1834, a post which brought him savage criticism. Another of his abiding interests was sanitary reform and from 1848 to 1854 he served as a commissioner on the new Board of Health. He was then rather pointedly pensioned off and his public career closed. He was hard-working and determined, but also tactless, unhumorous, impatient, dogmatic, and over-confident.

**Chalgrove Field, battle of,** 1643. Prince *Rupert disrupted *Essex's advance on Oxford in the summer of 1643 with a series of brilliant sorties. On 17 June he set out with nearly 2,000 men, mainly cavalry, and surprised several parliamentary garrisons. On the way back the following day, he turned on his pursuers at Chalgrove, between Watlington and Oxford, and inflicted a severe defeat. Fatally wounded in the battle was John *Hampden, of ship money fame.

**Chamberlain, Sir Austen** (1863–1937). Though he failed to obtain the premiership, Austen Chamberlain enjoyed a ministerial career of distinction. His rise owed much to the patronage of his father Joseph. Chancellor of the Exchequer under Balfour (1903–5), he strongly supported tariff reform. During the First World War he accepted responsibility for the failure of the Mesopotamian campaign, resigning as secretary of state for India in 1917. But he was soon recalled to the Exchequer, and remained a leading supporter of *Lloyd George's coalition until its fall in October 1922. He succeeded Bonar *Law as Conservative leader in 1921, but lost his chance of the premiership through loyalty to Lloyd George. As foreign secretary under *Baldwin (1924–9) he is best remembered for the *Locarno treaties of 1925.

**Chamberlain, Joseph** (1836–1914). Radical and imperialist. Chamberlain made his fortune as a screw manufacturer, which enabled him to retire at the age of 38. He dedicated the rest of his life to politics, first on the Birmingham city council, where he rose to be mayor in 1873–5, and then as a Birmingham MP. He was an advanced social reformer, clearing slums, building houses for the poor, setting up free public libraries and art galleries, and taking the gas, water, and sewage systems of Birmingham into municipal ownership. He also had sharp views on the aristocracy, which he regarded as useless ('they toil not, neither do they spin').

He rose to cabinet rank in 1880. But he was not comfortable in the *Liberal Party, because of his patriotic views on national issues. These were sorely tested by *Gladstone's limp policies on South Africa and Egypt, which caused him to break formally with the Liberal Party over *Irish Home Rule in 1886. The new *Liberal Unionist group he attached himself to never made it up with the rest of the Liberal Party, and eventually allied with the *Conservatives, providing Chamberlain with his next major platform, as colonial secretary in *Salisbury's government of 1895.

As colonial secretary Chamberlain proved as radical as he had on the domestic scene, advocating the development by central government of what he called Britain's 'imperial estates'. He also believed in their extension, particularly in southern Africa, where he was instrumental in trying to bring the Afrikaner republics to heel, first clandestinely (the *Jameson Raid) and then by helping to provoke the second *Boer War. But he was an unusual imperialist. He sought to extend the empire, but worried about its *over*-extension. With this in mind in 1898 he tried to fix a protective alliance with Germany behind Salisbury's back. He also wished to consolidate the colonies. In 1903 he came out publicly in favour of *imperial preference as a means of achieving this, resigning from the cabinet in order to press it at the next election (1906). The result was to split the Conservative Party, and give the Liberals a landslide victory. He may have been right. In July 1906, however, he suffered a disabling stroke. Without his energy behind it the tariff reform campaign wilted.

**Chamberlain, (Arthur) Neville** (1869–1940). Prime minister. Chamberlain was born in Birmingham, a son of Joseph *Chamberlain. Educated at Rugby and Mason College, Birmingham, he seemed destined for a business career, but his election to the city council in 1911 provided an opportunity to display his talents as a municipal reformer. His record in local government led to appointments first as a member of the control board established to oversee the liquor trade during the First World War, and then as director-general of national service (1916).

In 1918, at the late age of 49, he was elected as a Conservative MP for Birmingham. Chamberlain had conceived a healthy dislike for *Lloyd George, but supported the coalition government (1918–22). In 1922 his half-brother Austen tried unsuccessfully to persuade the Conservative Party to maintain the coalition, but Neville agreed with *Baldwin and Bonar *Law that it had outlived its usefulness. In 1922, Chamberlain joined Bonar Law's gov-

ernment as postmaster-general, becoming minister of health in 1923, chancellor of the Exchequer 1923–4, and returning to the health portfolio in Baldwin's second government (1924–9).

Chamberlain's years at the Ministry of Health established his claim to be one of the greatest social reformers in Britain in the 20th cent. At his urging the cabinet agreed to finance a widows', orphans', and old-age pensions bill in 1925. He initiated the great Local Government Act of 1929, which abolished the Poor Law Guardians, transferring the institutions they administered to the counties and county boroughs. Meanwhile, he was able to bring about a partnership between private builders and local authorities to build almost 1 million houses for the working classes.

At the general election of 1929 Baldwin's government was voted out. Chamberlain agreed to Baldwin's suggestion that he undertake a reorganization of Conservative central office, establishing a research department, but he used this period (1929–31) to work strenuously for the abandonment of free trade. During Baldwin's absence abroad Chamberlain represented the Conservative Party in the negotiations which led to the formation of the *National Government and he held office in that administration as chancellor of the Exchequer.

Neville Chamberlain's years at the Treasury, coinciding with the depression of the 1930s, were years of challenge. In 1932 he persuaded the cabinet to agree to the abandonment of free trade: a general duty of 10 per cent was placed on almost all imports, except those from within the British empire. In 1934 he was able to restore earlier cuts in unemployment pay, and in 1935 to lower income tax. This policy of financial good housekeeping was blown off course by the need to rearm in the face of the Nazi menace, but his budgets assisted economic recovery, and put the nation's finances into a position whereby they were able to meet the demands of war in 1939.

In May 1937 when Baldwin resigned the premiership, Chamberlain's succession was automatic. Almost exactly three years later he resigned in a welter of criticism, triggered by Britain's withdrawal from Norway but largely informed by public disenchantment with his pre-war foreign policy. Chamberlain's policy towards Nazi Germany is commonly associated with '*appeasement'. But there was widespread agreement that Germany had been treated badly at Versailles in 1919. He saw it as his mission to prevent war with Germany and, if that could not be achieved, to postpone hostilities as long as possible. But he had been unable to prevent Italian intervention in the Spanish Civil War, and Hitler's so-called 'invasion' of Austria caught him off guard. His policy during the Czech crisis (September 1938) was undermined by the unwillingness of the French to fulfil their treaty obligations towards the Czechs. None the less, Chamberlain's dramatic airline flight to Berchtesgaden (15 September), to meet Hitler, was tremendously popular at home, and his second visit, to sign the Munich agreement, was at the time hailed as a triumph.

In 1939, in relation to the British guarantee of Poland's borders, Chamberlain saw that appeasement was at an end. He was then seen as a gullible English gentleman totally outmanœuvred by a ruthless Führer. In May 1940 he resigned to make way for Winston *Churchill, and died shortly afterwards.

**Chanak crisis,** September–October 1922. Turkish nationalists under Mustapha Kemal were unhappy about the loss of territory to Greece under the Sèvres treaty of 1920. They expelled the Greeks from Smyrna by force in August 1922 and threatened to cross the Dardanelles. Britain feared for the security of the Straits. *Lloyd George reinforced British positions in Chanak, thus blocking the Turks. Conflict was averted by an agreement settled on 11 October. Eastern Thrace and Adrianople were returned to Turkey in return for recognition of the neutral zones of the Dardanelles.

**chancellor of the Exchequer** This office is held by the head of the *Treasury. The critical changes were embodied in resolutions passed by the House of Commons in 1706 and 1713 that it would only consider proposals for public expenditure which came from the crown, endowing the executive with the sole authority to instigate financial initiatives. The subsequent growth of public expenditure and taxation, and the enhanced economic responsibilities assumed by governments, greatly increased the importance of the office.

**Chancery, Court of** The Chancery (*cancellaria*) began life as the royal secretariat during the Norman period. Its task was to draw up royal charters and writs under the authority of the great seal, which was in the possession of the chancellor. By the 14th cent. common law had become the ordinary law of the land administered through courts independent of the crown, yet the king retained the power to administer justice outside the regular system. Petitions were presented to the king in council asking for relief. However, by the end of the 14th cent. petitions began to be addressed to the chancellor direct and by the end of the 15th cent. he was sitting alone to hear them.

The rules of common law were bound by tradition and statute. The chancellor was not bound by such rigid procedures. The Chancery could sit anywhere, at any time. It was quick and inexpensive justice which especially benefited the poor and the weak. Business increased steadily and by the 16th cent. the court was overwhelmed with petitions.

The chancellor's form of justice acquired the name of 'equity'. At first equity was not seen as a rival to common law, but resentment arose over the growth of Chancery business. In 1616, clashes over jurisdiction occurred between *Coke, chief justice of King's Bench, and Chancellor Ellesmere. Gradually equity became bound by precedent and Chancery litigation became expensive and slow, often taking 30 years by the 19th cent. The backlog of cases grew acute under Chancellor *Eldon (1801–27). The 1873 Judicature Acts reduced the Court of Chancery to a division of the new High Court of Justice and judges were empowered to administer both law and equity.

In Ireland a chancellor presided over a separate court of equity. In Scotland a chancellor existed from the 12th cent. and largely performed the same functions as his English counterpart. However, the chancellor became the chief administrator of law and not of a separate equitable system.

**Channel Islands** All that remains to the monarchy of its extensive possessions in France, retained when John lost the rest of *Normandy in 1204. They consist of the four larger islands of Jersey, Guernsey, Alderney, and Sark, with a number of smaller islands. The population of Jersey in 2001 was 87,000, Guernsey 60,000, Alderney 2,300, and Sark 591. Jersey, the largest of the islands, is some 10 miles from east to west and 5 from north to south; its capital, St Helier, is on the south coast. The official languages are English and French, with some Norman-French patois still in use. The queen appoints a lieutenant-governor as her representative. During the Second World War, the islands were occupied by German troops and liberated on 9 May 1945.

**Channel Tunnel** The earliest detailed proposal for a tunnel dates from the peace of *Amiens in 1802, suggesting two tunnels with horse-drawn vehicles and stabling facilities. Mercifully it was not built. The invention of railways made the project more practical. The London, Chatham, and Dover Company made some exploratory digs and an English Channel Company was formed in 1872. In 1966, the prime ministers of France and Britain pledged themselves to have the tunnel built. Work began in December 1987 and the tunnelling was completed by June 1991. The official opening by President Mitterrand and Queen Elizabeth II was in May 1994. After a series of embarrassing and entertaining mishaps, the first travellers passed through in November 1994.

**chantries** Founded either by individuals, guilds, or corporations, chantries were endowments for offering masses for the soul's repose in purgatory. Wealthy men invested heavily. By the Reformation there was a total of about 3,000 chantries. Ostensibly to rid the church of superstitious practice, chantries were dissolved in 1547.

**Chaplin, Charles** (1889–1977). Film actor and director. London-born of music-hall performers, with a wretched childhood, Chaplin learned vaudeville techniques with the Fred Karno Company before being signed by the Keystone Company (Hollywood) in 1913. He gained fame in silent films through portrayal of a baggy-trousered, moustachioed tramp, softening the original character with sentiment and pathos (*The Kid, The Gold Rush, City Lights*). He made few films after the introduction of sound, but received a special Academy Award in 1972 and was knighted (1975). Chaplin's personal life was frequently stormy, and he left America in 1952 because of political hostility, to settle permanently in Switzerland.

**chapters and chapter houses** The chapter house of a monastery, cathedral, or collegiate foundation was second only to the church in importance. Here the community assembled daily in pre-Reformation times for prayer, for the reading of a chapter in the rule (hence the name), and for the transaction of business. There are outstanding examples in England and Wales, including the ruins at *Rievaulx in Yorkshire, Margam in Glamorgan, and Wells in Somerset.

**Charge of the Light Brigade,** 1854. During the battle of *Balaclava (25 October 1854) Lord *Raglan ordered Lord *Lucan to advance his cavalry to stop the Russians removing captured cannon from the Causeway Heights. Confusion led to Lucan mistakenly sending the Light Brigade to attack strong Russian positions at a different location, North valley. About one-third of the 673-strong brigade, commanded by Lord *Cardigan, became casualties. Thanks partly to *Tennyson's poem, the action has become a symbol of military stupidity and blindly obedient courage.

**charity schools** Although the practice of establishing charity schools for the poor by private donors had begun in Elizabethan times, a great increase in numbers occurred towards the end of the 17th cent. The main object was religious and moral, as well as enabling the poor to earn a livelihood. The *Society for Promoting Christian Knowledge (SPCK), at its first meeting in 1699, considered how best to establish 'Catechetical Schools' in every parish in London. Children between the ages of 7 and 12 were admitted. Teaching was from 7.00 to 11.00 in the morning and 1.00 to 5.00 in the afternoon. However, by 1760 the charity school movement was faltering.

**Charles I** (1600–49), king of England, Scotland, and Ireland (1625–49). Charles was the second son of James VI. Born in Scotland, he moved to England in 1604 after his father ascended the English throne. He developed into a somewhat reserved, scholarly boy, who hero-worshipped his elder brother Prince *Henry. Only after Henry was struck down in 1612 did Charles, as heir apparent, move centre stage. In 1621 he attended the House of Lords as Parliament considered whether England should intervene on the protestant side in the Thirty Years War. James, a leading protestant ruler, hoped to heal religious divisions by concluding a marriage between Charles and the Infanta Maria, sister of 'the most catholic king' of Spain.

Charles persuaded his father to let him make an incognito romantic journey to Spain, setting off in February 1623, accompanied by the royal favourite, *Buckingham. Two weeks' hard riding through France brought them to Madrid, where Charles received a royal welcome. The growing realization that the infanta was merely a pawn in a power game opened the eyes of Charles to the fact that the expansion of Spanish power threatened England. When he returned home in September, without the infanta, he began constructing an anti-Spanish coalition. The adhesion of France was essential, and Buckingham therefore arranged a marriage between Charles and Louis XIII's sister *Henrietta Maria.

James remained committed to peace, but was persuaded to call Parliament in 1624. Charles and Buckingham co-operated with its leading members in preparing the ground for war, but only became free to act in March 1625, when the death of James brought Charles to the throne. The new king promptly summoned Parliament, but suspicion of Buckingham led the Commons to make only a token grant of money. When the 1626 Parliament impeached Buckingham, following the failure of an expedition against Cadiz, Charles dissolved it. He then levied a *forced loan to pay for another expedition, this time in support of the French protestants. When this also ended in defeat a further clash with Parliament seemed inevitable. But Charles's acceptance of the *petition of right in 1628 defused the situation, and Buckingham, the bone of contention, was removed by assassination in August of that year.

When Parliament reassembled in 1629 Charles expected harmony, but the religious issue came to the fore. Charles was a high churchman and promoted *Arminians, but members of Parliament were predominantly low church. The Commons drew up a resolution against Arminianism, and when Charles tried to prevent its discussion by

dissolving Parliament, *Eliot and his associates held the Speaker down in his chair. Charles responded to this outrage by imprisoning the offending members and dispensing with Parliament altogether. His personal rule was far from an *'Eleven Years Tyranny', but Charles's continued patronage of the Arminians—in particular Archbishop *Laud—outraged public opinion. So also did his resort to non-parliamentary taxation. Nevertheless, the personal rule was not threatened until the dèbâcle of the *Bishops' wars left Charles with no choice but to summon Parliament. So weak was his position by late 1640 that he had to accept Acts severely curtailing his power. He also had to permit the impeachment and subsequent execution of Laud and his chief minister, *Strafford. However, conservative opinion began rallying round him when Parliament broke with convention by trying to deprive him of control over the army.

Charles had transformed himself into the guardian of the constitution, but in January 1642 he yielded to pressure from his wife, who advocated tough measures. Going down to the House of Commons, with an armed guard, he entered the chamber, and demanded the arrest of five of his opponents. But, as Charles quickly noted, 'the birds are flown'. He decided to leave the capital and appeal for support to the country. In August 1642 he raised the royal standard at Nottingham, and shortly afterwards established his headquarters at Oxford. During the civil war that ensued, Charles showed qualities of endurance and decisiveness. But royalist resources were sufficient only for a short war, and Parliament had the longer purse. Yet even in defeat the king was still a key figure. The parliamentary army was so concerned that in June 1647 it sent a troop of musketeers to remove the king from parliamentary guardianship and bring him closer to London. He was held captive at Hampton Court until November, when he escaped and took refuge in Carisbrooke castle on the Isle of Wight.

The political situation was now chaotic, with Parliament, the army, and the Scots all putting proposals to Charles. Confronted by this disunity among his enemies, Charles took the risky course of playing them off against each other. The spring of 1648 saw a series of violent outbreaks called the second civil war. These convinced the army that a permanent peace settlement depended on removing him. In December 1648 they 'purged' Parliament of its conservative members, leaving the remaining 'rump' free to set up a high court to try the king. Charles refused to plead, insisting that he was accountable only to God. He was sentenced to death and beheaded, in front of the Banqueting House in Whitehall, on 30 January 1649.

Charles had many good qualities. He loved the arts, and assembled a collection of paintings among the best in Europe. He loved his wife and children, and he loved God. But his exalted view of the kingly office and his autocratic tendencies opened a chasm between him and his subjects which swallowed up the monarchy he struggled to preserve.

**Charles II** (1630–85), king of England, Ireland, and Scotland (acceded 1649, restored 1660–85). Charles received his practical education in 1648–51 when he learnt how to adapt to rapidly changing circumstances, and trust no one. He commissioned *Montrose to raise the Scottish Highlands, but withdrew his support to conclude an agreement with the more powerful *covenanting party, who defeated and hanged Montrose (April 1650). Invited to Scotland by *Argyll, he took the covenant and publicly condemned the religions and policies of his father and mother. When *Cromwell's army advanced he took the gamble of invading England. After a disastrous defeat at *Worcester (September 1651) he made a romantic escape to France. Divisions among the republican factions brought about his 1660 *Restoration, which was unconditional. It was old cavaliers who in 1661–2 imposed conditions by restoring strict Anglican religious uniformity and making Charles abandon his *Declaration of Indulgence (1662). In his first years Charles was advised by his principal minister, *Clarendon, to rule within the laws. After the failure of the *Anglo-Dutch War of 1665–7 he abandoned Clarendon and initiated a new line of policy.

Charles, his brother James, and the *cabal ministers concluded treaties with France because it was the strongest European power. Victory in a new Dutch war would be assured. French subsidies and increased revenues from expanded trade would reduce, or even eliminate, dependence on Parliament. Charles, James, and *Clifford also thought that they could become catholics and institute religious toleration: in the secret treaty of *Dover (1670) Louis XIV promised military aid if a rebellion resulted. In the event, unlike the other two, Charles delayed his conversion until his death-bed in 1685. For the first time no parliamentary session occurred in 1672, and had the Dutch War succeeded Charles would have been able to dictate from a position of strength. But stalemate at sea enabled Parliament to make Charles withdraw his Declaration of Indulgence and assent to the *Test Act barring catholics from office, forcing James and Clifford to resign. In 1673–4 Parliament refused to vote money, compelling Charles to desert France and make peace.

Charles also retreated in domestic politics, allowing his new lord treasurer *Danby to return to upholding the interests of the church, enforcing the penal laws against catholics and dissenters. Danby was alarmed at the increase in French power and wished to balance it by championing William of Orange, furthering this policy by negotiating the marriage of William to James's daughter and heir Mary. Charles allowed the marriage in order to put up the price that Louis would pay for English neutrality, but Louis found it cheaper to bribe the opposition and give them secret papers incriminating Danby. This forced Charles to dismiss Danby and dissolve Parliament. At the same time 'revelations' broke of a *Popish plot to murder Charles. James's catholicism and absolutist and French sympathies made him seem the obvious beneficiary. By sending James into exile Charles raised doubts whether he would steadfastly resist the Whig bill to exclude James from the succession.

However Charles saw *exclusion of the rightful heir as changing the monarchy from a hereditary, divinely appointed institution into an elective, limited office. He stopped the first Exclusion Bill by dissolving Parliament (July 1679). When Charles fell ill and James returned from exile to defend his right, Charles sent him to rule Scotland. In 1680 Charles blocked exclusion by encouraging the Lords to reject a second bill, and in March 1681 he dissolved the third Whig Parliament which he had ordered to meet at

*Oxford. No further meetings of Parliament were allowed, Charles being financially secure with a new secret treaty with France giving him subsidies.

Charles had two constructive achievements to his credit. He successfully resisted intense cavalier pressure in the early 1660s to go back on the Act of Indemnity that was intended to heal the divisions caused by the civil wars. Secondly his personal tolerance, ineffective in trying to suspend religious persecution, found full play in his protection of intellectual freedom, although he did little more in science than observe the experiments of the *Royal Society.

Charles's irregular private life resembled that of his French grandfather Henri IV. It seldom affected politics: the only politically active and influential mistress, the duchess of *Portsmouth, worked in the French interest. The barren Portuguese queen, *Catherine, counted for nothing.

**Charles, prince of Wales** (b. 1948). Prince Charles was 3 when his mother succeeded to the throne as Queen Elizabeth II. He was sent to Cheam School, Gordonstoun, Geelong Grammar School in Australia, Trinity College, Cambridge, and University College, Aberystwyth, where he studied Welsh. Created prince of Wales in 1958, he was invested in *Caernarfon castle in 1969. He then entered the armed forces and pursued a vigorous training programme—flying a supersonic jet, qualifying as a helicopter pilot, catapulting from the deck of *Ark Royal*, training in minesweepers and submarines, and commanding a mine-hunter. His private pleasures included not only painting, music, and acting, but surfing, sailing, skiing, fishing, shooting, riding, and playing polo to international standard. His reward for these strenuous activities was to be increasingly portrayed in newspapers as a 'crank', 'a young twerp', and a 'wimp', who admitted talking to flowers and showed an interest in alternative medicine. His public utterances on matters like the environment, modern architecture, and the preservation of natural resources, on which he feels strongly, were greeted with indignation by interested groups. In 1981 the prince married Lady *Diana Spencer in St Paul's cathedral. Two sons, Prince William and Prince Henry, were born in 1982 and 1984, but disharmony in the marriage was increasingly the subject of com-

ment, and the royal couple separated in 1992 and divorced in 1996. After the death of Princess Diana in Paris, the Prince married Camilla Parker-Bowles (duchess of Cornwall) in 2005.

**Charleston, battle of,** 1780. In 1779 the British decided to concentrate on the southern states in America in order to encourage the loyalists. *Clinton took a strong expedition from New York to Georgia and moved north to besiege Charleston. After heavy fighting, the defenders surrendered on 12 May 1780. But the political response was disappointing.

**Charlotte Augusta, Princess** (1796–1817). The daughter of George, prince of Wales, and Caroline of Brunswick, Charlotte bore the brunt of the hatred between her parents. Much of her childhood was spent with little access to the outside world. In December 1813 she was betrothed to William, prince of Orange, but broke off the engagement, not wishing to live in Holland. Her stubbornness momentarily united her warring parents, her father dismissing her entire household and her mother refusing to receive her. When, in 1816, Leopold of Saxe-Coburg proposed, Charlotte readily accepted and the marriage took place on 2 May. Charlotte died giving birth to a stillborn child on 5 November 1817.

**Charlotte of Mecklenburg-Strelitz** (1744–1818), queen of George III. Though Charlotte was chosen unseen from lists of German princesses in 1761, her marriage to George III proved a great success. She was considered by many to be rather dull and distinctly plain, but George was devoted to her. She cared for her husband during his long slide into insanity, though terrified by his occasional outbursts of violence. She predeceased him and was buried in November 1818 in St George's Chapel, Windsor.

**charters** are grants of privilege. They are of fundamental importance to students of medieval legal, constitutional, and municipal history. But they need to be used with great caution since spurious charters are by no means uncommon, interpolations were frequently made, and contemporary phrases can be difficult to render precisely. The oldest charters appear to be grants made to the church in Kent during the reign of *Æthelbert in the 600s. Grants of land to individuals became common and the phrase 'bookland' indicated an estate held by charter. Next came charters to towns, giving them the right to hold markets or fairs, to collect tolls, or to elect their own officials. Charters as regular instruments of royal policy seem to have been introduced into Scotland from 1095 during the reign of Edgar. The 'coronation charters' of Henry I, Stephen, and Henry II were rather different in character and more like political manifestos, since they promised good government in accordance with the traditional laws of the realm. Though the promises were not always kept, the charters implied some limitation on royal authority and paved the way for *Magna Carta in 1215, itself constantly confirmed. Later came charters to guilds and to trading companies. The sanctity of charters was regarded as the very bedrock of property. Consequently the campaigns by Charles II and James II after 1681 to call in the charters of parliamentary boroughs and remodel them roused fierce opposition.

**chartism** (1837–54) was the first attempt to build an independent political party representing the interests of the labouring sections of the nation. For many of its followers chartism was basically 'a knife and fork question'. Yet its programme was a series of political demands. The chartists were so named because they formulated their demands in a six-point charter: universal (manhood) suffrage, annual parliaments, vote by (secret) ballot, abolition of property qualifications for MPs, payment of MPs, and equal electoral districts. The object was to make the charter the law of the land by legal, constitutional means if possible, or by force if necessary. Great efforts were made to collect support for a petition to the House of Commons, but on each occasion the House rejected its demands. Alternative methods were therefore advocated. There were plans for making the central body of chartist delegates the national convention, a people's parliament which would bypass Westminster; a general strike ('national holiday') was attempted in August 1839; and local riots, and perhaps an abortive insurrection (the *Newport rising) in November 1839, showed that 'physical force' might not be ruled out.

In its origins chartism was an umbrella movement which drew together many strands of radical grievance. In London and the provinces Working Men's Associations were formed in 1837; in Birmingham, the movement at first was closely allied with middle-class radicals and currency reformers; in Leeds, *Owenite socialists combined with middle-class radicals and physical-force militants. In other towns of the West Riding and the industrial north local grievances included the 1834 New Poor Law. Attempts to build a national organization repeatedly fell apart; and the most effective link between chartists was the widely read chartist newspaper the *Northern Star*. The chartists failed to achieve their six points which, with the exception of annual parliaments, were realized later.

**Chatsworth House** (Derbys.). Country seat of the Cavendishes, dukes of Devonshire. The Elizabethan house, begun by Sir William Cavendish in 1552 and completed by his widow Bess of Hardwick (Lady *Shrewsbury), was replaced by the present building which has south and east fronts by William Talman (1687–96) and a north front by Thomas Archer (1704–7). Chatsworth has painted ceilings by Verrio, Thornhill, and Laguerre, furniture by William *Kent, sculpture by Cibber and Canova, and paintings by Rembrandt, Frans Hals, *Van Dyck, Tintoretto, and *Lely. The formal parterres at Chatsworth were designed by George London and Henry Wise, whilst the cascade has a classical temple at its top by Thomas Archer (1702). From 1761 Capability *Brown made major changes in the grounds, incorporating new planting and a bridge by Paine (1760–4). During the 19th cent. the 6th duke of Devonshire and his gardener Sir Joseph Paxton devised a system of cascades, fountains, and pools, culminating in the Emperor Fountain of 1843.

**Chaucer, Geoffrey** (c.1343–1400). Chaucer's enduring fame reflects the range and quality of his poetry and prose, but also the accessibility of his midlands-based London English. His impact on the English language through the absorption of French words, ideas, and forms is considerable.

Born into a family of prosperous vintners, Chaucer served as page then esquire to various aristocratic households, including that of

Richard II. Chaucer's specific assignments included fighting in the *Hundred Years War c.1359, undertaking trade and diplomatic missions to Italy and France, and acting as customs controller at the port of London and clerk of works at Westminster. Chaucer's situation on the periphery of aristocratic circles perhaps underlies his self-presentation as a bystander at life's games of power and love. A courtly audience seems implied, for instance, by *The Book of the Duchess*, probably a consolation for *John of Gaunt at the death of his duchess Blanche c.1369, while the ballade 'Lack of Steadfastness' offers advice to the king.

Apart from the brilliant five-part tragedy *Troilus and Criseyde*, the poems are mainly small to medium scale, while in the broken ending of *The House of Fame* we perhaps see Chaucer losing his direction in an ambitious experimental project. Solemnity rarely goes unpunctured, yet Chaucer is also 'the noble philosophical poet of love' (Usk). Notable is Chaucer's ability not only to impersonate other voices (from the coy hen falcon in *The Parliament of Fowls* to the blustering Host in the *Canterbury Tales*), but also to articulate different world-views with apparent impartiality. The only direct mention of 14th-cent. events is the jocular reference in the *Nun's Priest's Tale* to Jakke Straw, a leader of the 1381 *Peasants' Revolt, but the contemporary problems of religious charlatanry and the misuse of money and power are treated in the *Canterbury Tales* with pervasive irony.

**Chaumont, treaty of,** 1814. Even after Napoleon's defeat at Leipzig in 1813 he remained dangerous, and Castlereagh, Britain's foreign secretary, was concerned lest he succeed in signing a separate peace with one of the eastern powers. In March 1814 Castlereagh negotiated the treaty whereby Britain, Russia, Prussia, and Austria agreed to put 150,000 men each in the field, and to guarantee Europe against French aggression for 20 years.

**Cheke, Sir John** (1514–57). Cambridge-born protestant Greek scholar and educator, Cheke was fellow of St John's College from 1529. As regius professor 1540–51, he was supported by his friends Sir Thomas *Smith and Roger *Ascham in introducing the new 'Erasmian' pronunciation of Greek. Under Henry VIII, Cheke was tutor to Prince Edward who, as Edward VI, gave him land, a knighthood, and the provostship of King's College, Cambridge; he was also member of Parliament, clerk to the council, and secretary of state. A supporter of Lady Jane *Grey, he was imprisoned under Mary 1553–4 but allowed to migrate to Basle, before being enticed to Brussels by Mary's agents in 1556 and again imprisoned in London. Securing release by renouncing his religion, he died soon after.

**Chelmsford, diocese of** The present see, created in 1914, is conterminous with Essex. In 604 *Augustine consecrated *Mellitus bishop of London to convert the East Saxons, but success was short-lived. In c.650 *Oswiu, king of Northumbria, sent Cedd as bishop of the East Saxons. The Essex see was independent until 675, when Bishop Eorcenwald moved to London. After that Essex remained within the London diocese until the 19th cent. In 1845 Essex was removed from the London diocese and united with *Rochester, only to be transferred to the new see of *St Albans in 1877. With the creation of the see of Chelmsford, Essex again had a bishop of its own.

**Chelsea hospital** (London) was founded by Charles II for veteran soldiers. The pensioners wear an 18th-cent. uniform and celebrate the founder on Oak Apple Day (29 May). The buildings were by Christopher *Wren and the foundation stone was laid in February 1682.

**Chequers,** in the Chilterns near Wendover (Bucks.), was given in 1917 by Lord Lee of Fareham as a country residence for the prime minister. Lee, a Conservative MP first elected in 1900, was an admirer of Lloyd George, served as director-general of food production in 1917, and moved to agriculture in 1919 and to the Admiralty in 1921. The house has a Tudor core, with Victorian additions and substantial remodelling by Lee 1909–12.

**Cheriton, battle of,** 1644. After *Roundway Down, *Hopton and *Waller continued their struggle in Wessex, manœuvring for possession of Winchester. On 29 March they met at Cheriton. The royalist cavalry suffered heavily when caught in deep rutted lanes and Hopton was obliged to retreat.

**Cheshire,** a lowland county in north-western England, resembles a hammock slung between the south-west Pennines (east) and Flint–Denbighshire uplands (west). The Romans had established a legionary fortress at Deva (*Chester), as a base for advances into Wales, but place-names reflect subsequent traces of early Celtic influence and Scandinavian invasions. Initially part of *Mercia and 'shired' in the 10th cent., the county boundaries conformed to roughly their present extent by the 12th cent. *Palatinate from 1237 when the earldom passed to the crown, Cheshire was not rich in castles despite its border position; large country houses, characteristically half-timbered, were its greater glory.

Long known for its salt and cheese, Cheshire remained only moderately important agriculturally until specialization encouraged expansion of its dairying. Under the influence of the expanding cotton industry, Stockport and other towns in north-east Cheshire grew rapidly; Birkenhead then developed around Cammell Laird's shipyard. As population quadrupled during the 19th cent., canals took coal and salt all over England; railway networks radiated from Crewe and Chester and a tunnel under the river Mersey linked Birkenhead with Liverpool (1886). The emergence of the chemical industries, concentrated on Northwich (salt), Runcorn, and Port Sunlight (soap), lessened the dependence on textiles. Much of northern Cheshire has become a dormitory area for nearby Lancashire urban centres.

**chess** The origins of chess have been much discussed but remain obscure. It seems to have begun in India or China about the 6th cent. AD and to have been adopted in Persia, where it was known as *shat-ranj*. It spread to the West through the Arabs and the Vikings, and a Viking ivory chess set, discovered in the Hebrides in 1831, has been dated to the 12th cent. The medieval game was slow and was speeded up in the 16th cent. by giving the queen and bishop greater powers. The game is controlled, with some difficulty, by the World Chess Federation, founded in 1924.

**Chester** Known to the Romans as Deva, was founded in the 70s as a legionary for-

tress, originally for *legio II Adiutrix*. From the 80s it became the long-term base of *legio XX Valeria Victrix*. In the later Roman period the intensity of occupation declined, though was probably still military. After the Norman invasion of 1066, William marched north to subdue the rebellious native population, particularly the Welsh; the castle was commenced and a hereditary earldom created, though this title reverted to the crown in 1237. Although Chester prospered as an administrative centre, the port was no longer viable by 1600 because of silting.

Granted a royal charter in 1506, Chester was severely affected by the Civil War since city and county supported opposing factions. By mid-18th cent., it had recovered into quiet country-town prosperity. The continuous, first-floor arcades of the medieval rows are unique, but many of the black-and-white half-timbered restorations are Victorian.

**Chester, battle of,** *c.*616. *Æthelfryth of Northumbria defeated the Britons of Powys, killing their leader, Selyf. According to *Bede, the battle was preceded by a massacre of monks from Bangor-is-y-Coed (near Wrexham), who were praying for a British victory. The Saxon victory was part of a westwards expansion which ultimately drove a wedge between the Britons of Strathclyde and those of Wales.

**Chester cathedral** The Benedictine abbey of St Werburgh was founded in 1092 on the site of an Anglo-Saxon foundation. It produced the earliest of the Chester mystery plays, and the *Polychronicon* of Ranulph Higden (d. 1364) was its main contribution to medieval learning. After the dissolution of the monasteries, the abbey was reconstituted in 1541 as the cathedral, in the newly formed diocese. The abbey buildings are among the best-preserved monastic remains in Britain. The carved choir-stalls (*c.*1390) are particularly fine, though five misericords were destroyed by Dean Howson for being 'very improper'.

**Chesterfield, Philip Dormer Stanhope, 4th earl of** (1694–1773). Politician and diplomat. Chesterfield owed his entrée into politics in 1714 to his kinsman James *Stanhope. Inheriting his father's earldom in 1726, he served as ambassador to The Hague, 1728–32, but after his return joined the opposition to *Walpole. After Walpole's fall he made his peace in 1745 with the *Pelhams, and accepted office as lord-lieutenant of Ireland. In 1746 he was appointed secretary of state (northern department), but found his senior colleague *Newcastle difficult, and in 1748 resigned. Chesterfield's *Letters to his son*, famously described by *Johnson as exhibiting 'the morals of a whore and the manners of a dancing master', were published the year after his death.

**Chester-le-Street, diocese of** Created in 883, when the monks of *Lindisfarne, evicted in 875, settled here with *Cuthbert's relics. The cult of the saint made it the centre of power in the north-east until the see was moved to *Durham in 995.

**Chesterton, Gilbert Keith** (1874–1936). Chesterton and his friend Hilaire Belloc (1870–1953) were the best-known catholic writers of Edwardian England—*Shaw dubbed them 'Chesterbelloc'. Busy journalists, they engaged in public controversy, particularly with Shaw, *Kipling, and *Wells. Chesterton's best works are probably *The Napoleon of Notting Hill* (1904), *The Club of Queer Trades* (1905), and *The Man who was Thursday* (1908), though his most popular books were the Father Brown detective stories from 1911. Chesterton's 'cheese and good ale' stance grows tedious at times, and the deep nostalgia which he shared with Belloc is perhaps best captured in the latter's poem 'Ha'nacker Mill'.

**Chevy Chase, battle of** *See* OTTERBURN.

**Chichele, Henry** (*c.*1362–1443). Archbishop of Canterbury. The son and brother of prominent London merchants, Chichele was an original fellow of New College, Oxford. From 1406 he was in royal service as an ambassador, earning the bishopric of St Davids, and in 1414 promotion to Canterbury from Henry V. In 1438 he founded the college of All Souls, Oxford.

**Chichester** (Roman). The *civitas*-capital of the *Reg(i)ni; its Roman name was Noviomagus. The Roman town developed early. This can be ascribed to the influence of the pro-Roman king *Cogidubnus, mentioned on two exceptionally early Roman inscriptions from the town.

**Chichester, Arthur, 1st Baron** [I] (1563–1625). Lord deputy of Ireland. Chichester came from a Devon family. In 1604 he was made lord deputy in succession to *Mountjoy and held the post for a remarkable eleven years, retiring in 1615. There were two prominent features of his administration—to weaken the loyalty of the native Irish to their chiefs, which resulted in the *Flight of the Earls in 1607, and to encourage Scottish and English immigration to Ulster.

**Chichester, diocese of** The diocese was created by the transfer of the see from *Selsey under the terms of the Council of London (1075), and is roughly conterminous with Sussex. The cathedral, built between *c.*1091 and 1305, is Norman in origin, but was largely rebuilt between 1191 and 1210 in a style reminiscent of Canterbury.

**Chichester-Clark, James, Lord Moyola** (1923–2002). Prime minister of Northern Ireland. Chichester-Clark was from a landed background. He was Unionist chief whip in the Stormont Parliament (1963–6), leader of the House of Commons (1966–7), and minister of agriculture (1967–9). He deftly united support among both the allies and opponents of the prime minister, O'Neill, when he resigned from the cabinet in April 1969 in opposition to the new local government franchise: he succeeded O'Neill on 1 May. The emergence of the more militant Provisional IRA in early 1971 forced Chichester-Clark to demand a new security initiative from London; and when this was not forthcoming, he resigned, taking a life peerage.

**children** The proportion of children in British society has varied over time. In 1801, the proportion of children under 15 years was estimated to have been one-third of the total, increasing to almost 40 per cent by the mid-19th cent. By 1991 the proportion of children had decreased to about a quarter of the total population. Although many children were born, infant mortality rates were high until the improvements in health care in the last quarter of the 19th cent. Official statistics indicate that the number of children per family varied little between social classes until the 1870s, when contraception was taken up by the better-off. Access to contraception spread to all levels of society during the 20th cent., particularly after the introduction of the female contraceptive pill in the 1960s.

Attitudes to children have varied over time. The concept of childhood drawn from the doctrine of original sin required that children be saved from the devil by a sound inculcation of Christian values beginning with the sacrament of baptism. The image of a child was not of innocence but of an imp, likely to commit sin unless corrected. It was accepted that all children at every level of society needed religious education. The care of children was normally the task of parents but, amongst the wealthy, care was the responsibility of special servants, such as nursemaids or 'nannies'. In the later Middle Ages, the sons of the aristocracy were sent as pages into another noble household at about the age of 12 years. Later, children of the upper classes were educated at home by a resident tutor or governess, while the middle classes sent their sons away from home to boarding schools.

A dramatic challenge to accepted ideas about children and childhood emerged in the 18th cent., expressed at its most controversial in *Émile* by J. J. Rousseau. The English edition appeared in 1763. Rousseau argued that children were born innocent and would continue so unless corrupted by adults. Although this remained a minority view for many years, it helped to modify some severity towards children. In addition, this new view of children stimulated the development of special toys and pastimes to help them learn. A major innovation, led by the publisher John Newberry in the later 18th cent., was literature specifically designed for child readers.

The enjoyment of leisure in the ways suggested in the debates about childhood was completely outside the experience of most children. In rural areas, children of the less well-off had always performed household and other tasks. This pattern was continued in urban and industrial areas with children as young as 3 years being employed in textiles, mines, and other occupations. Charles *Kingsley's account of the London chimney sweeps in *The Water Babies*, and many of *Dickens's novels, drew attention in fiction to the reality of life for many children. During the 19th cent. there was increasing involvement of the state to protect children by controlling working practices and, eventual-

ly, to finance and regulate full-time education. State intervention continued in the 20th cent., raising the age at which children might leave compulsory full-time education and giving access to a range of educational opportunities.

**Chiltern hundreds** Members of Parliament cannot resign directly and must therefore, if they wish to retire, apply for an office of profit under the crown, which disqualifies them. By convention this is the stewardship of the Chiltern hundreds.

**Chimney Sweeps Act,** 1875. The plight of small boys sent up to clean chimneys had been raised as early as the 1760s by the philanthropist Jonas Hanway. Legislation to ensure decent treatment was largely ineffective. Lord *Shaftesbury took up the matter towards the end of his life. The 1875 Act (38 & 39 Vic. c. 70) laid down that chimney sweeps should be registered by the police and certificates withheld if they disregarded safety.

**China wars,** 1839–42 and 1856–60. Otherwise known as the 'Opium wars'. Opium was grown in British India and was one of the few commodities that China was prepared to trade. In 1839 the imperial Chinese government attempted to block the trade. The resulting war was an unequal conflict, with the Chinese having no answer to British firepower. The treaty of *Nanking gave Britain *Hong Kong. China then collapsed into a brutal civil war known as the Tai Ping rebellion (1850–64). Other powers took advantage of this, and in 1857 British and French forces occupied Canton. Although repulsed at the Taku Forts in June 1859, the Anglo-French force captured them next year, and founded the naval base at Port Arthur (modern Luda). After the convention of Peking had ceded Kowloon to Britain, the Imperial Summer Palace at Peking was destroyed in reprisal for Chinese barbarities.

**Chippendale, Thomas** (1718–79). Cabinet-maker and designer, the son of a Yorkshire joiner, he set up business in London about the 1750s. Chippendale designed an extensive range of furniture, carpets, wallpapers, and brassware, from the elaborate yet delicate for the homes of gentry, to the simple and unpretentious for their servants' quarters. In 1754 he published *The Gentleman *and Cabinet-Maker's Director* which influenced style in Europe and America.

**Chippenham, battle of,** 878. *Alfred's Wessex forces were encamped at Chippenham in Wiltshire on 6 January 878 when they were routed by a surprise attack from a Danish army, led by *Guthrum. Alfred was forced into hiding in the marshes of Somerset.

**Chippenham, treaty of** *See* WEDMORE.

**chivalry** The French precursor of this term, *chevalerie*, indicates that this code of behaviour derived initially from the special status of the mounted warrior. Developments in warfare *c.*800–1100 elevated this type of soldier in both a military and social context. Thus was generated a moral, religious, and social code, which over the centuries became more closely defined through the conduct of *tournaments, laws of war, orders of chivalry, and *heraldry. The church, too, was keen to encourage the proper conduct of the warrior élite, and the crusades helped to shape 'the distinctive Christian strand in chivalry'. Historians of chivalry debate whether art and literature reflected realities or were intended to shape them. Although chivalry was to some degree institutionalized in the later Middle Ages it remained a nebulous concept. It was important in creating a social bond between the crown, nobility, and gentry, and in generating the code of behaviour expected of a gentleman, demanding personal honour, generosity, loyalty, and courage. Thus it survived well beyond the era of the mounted knight.

**cholera,** an acute diarrhoeal disease transmitted by faecal contamination of water supplies and food, escaped from Bengal in 1817 to initiate the first of several world-wide pandemics. Asiatic cholera eventually appeared in England in October 1831 in Sunderland. It soon arose in Newcastle, Edinburgh, and London, before reaching France. It caused some 31,000 estimated deaths in England and Scotland, and a further 20,000 in Ireland. A second outbreak commencing in London in 1848 was even more serious, with some 65,000 deaths in England, Wales, and Scotland and 30,000 in Ireland. The last two outbreaks of 1853–4 and 1866 were milder. Despite its shock value, it was surpassed by tuberculosis and the fevers

as a cause of death, but local government reorganization facilitated progress in public health, and few cases occurred in Britain after 1893.

**Christadelphians** A Christian sect founded by John Thomas (New York, *c.*1848), but with adherents in Britain. Originally called Thomasites, the name Christadelphian ('Brother of Christ') was adopted during the American Civil War to justify objection to military service. The core belief is millennialist, with Christ expected to return and rule from Jerusalem.

**Christianity,** derived from Judaism to become the dominant religion of western Europe, has underpinned much of Britain's cultural heritage for fourteen centuries. Urban Christianity was sufficiently vibrant to send three bishops (London, York, Colchester) to the Council of Arles (314). *Paganism, despite a brief revival 360–80, was in decline as the century ended, when historical figures such as *Ninian and *Patrick began to emerge. On the arrival of Anglo-Saxon invaders with their gods Woden and Thor, British Christianity was virtually extinguished except for the western Celtic fringes. *Monasticism had reached the Celts at a formative stage in their Christianity, and monks rather than bishops led the church. Patrick (*c.*390–461) evangelized Ireland, Ninian (*c.*360–*c.*432) the Picts of Galloway, and Kentigern (d. 612) Strathclyde; Illtud (d. *c.*540) and *David (*c.*530–*c.*589) worked in Wales, *Columba settled in *Iona (*c.*563), whence *Aidan brought Christianity to *Lindisfarne (635). When Roman missionaries under *Augustine arrived in Kent (597), divergences between the two strands arising from differences in organization and disagreement about the date of Easter led to clashes unresolved until the Synod of *Whitby (664), when Roman customs prevailed. Conversion had sometimes been slow, though helped when a ruler embraced the new faith (*Æthelbert of Kent, *Edwin of Northumbria), but a brief golden age followed statesman-archbishop *Theodore's reorganization of dioceses, which produced scholars such as *Bede, and missionaries like *Boniface of Crediton. Attacks from *Viking raiders during the 9th cent. destroyed religious houses but did not totally destroy the church.

For two centuries after about 1050, sustained attempts were made to apply gospel principles and canon law to society generally, through Gregorian reform, clergy discipline, and then modification of lay life. The Norman Conquest, which joined England politically and ecclesiastically with Europe's main states, led to a revival of religious life. *Edward the Confessor had already rebuilt the abbey church at *Westminster, but ecclesiastical administration was reorganized, cathedrals commenced, and the cathedral school at Oxford grew into a university. Monasticism again flourished, but with changed structure: diverging from the original *Benedictines were *Cluniacs, *Cistercians, and *Augustinians. A redemptive religion, one of Christianity's attractions was its promise of an afterlife. Since the prospect of punishment was more dramatic than that of paradise, the threat of eternal damnation was used to enforce ethics. By the 15th cent. explorers, merchants, and colonizers had started to spread Christianity beyond Europe. Empire-building not only involved colonization and trade, but active and purposeful extension of religion; the cross followed the flag, sometimes vice versa. Nevertheless, with late 20th-cent. decolonization, Christianity, far from dying in these newly independent territories, has become more vigorous, especially in Africa.

The principal sacraments (or 'mysteries') recognized by all Christians, except *quakers, are the eucharist and baptism. Other sacraments, not universally acknowledged, are confirmation, marriage, ordination, confession, and anointing of the sick. The Bible is an important primary written source for most Christians, taken literally by some, but regarded as no more than a history book by others. The greatest challenges to Christianity have been the doctrinal upheavals that led to the *Reformation (and the English church's rupture from Rome) and *secularism. The Census Report on Religious Worship (1851–3) caused alarm by its revelation that nearly 40 per cent of the population were unwilling or unable to attend a place of worship. While Christianity remained Britain's established religion at the end of the 20th cent., the challenge from secularism has increased, compounded by the ethnic mix from immigrants with their own religions, and a growing interest in cults.

**Christian socialism** *See* SOCIALISM, CHRISTIAN.

**Christmas** Literally Christ-Mass, the liturgical commemoration of the birth of Christ. There is evidence of its observance on 25 December at Rome by the early 4th cent. There is no evidence to support the theory that this was the actual birth-date of Christ. The choice was rather dictated by well-established pagan celebrations on that day. Many of the features of modern Christmas, such as Christmas trees, cards, and boxes, are Victorian rather than earlier.

**Church Army** Founded in 1882 by the Revd Wilson Carlile, a 35-year-old Church of England curate in Kensington, its organization was consciously modelled on that of Booth's *Salvation Army. Like the Salvation Army, Carlile's Church Army was dedicated to evangelism among the poor.

**church commissioners** *See* ECCLESIASTICAL COMMISSIONERS.

**churches** *See* ABBEYS; CATHEDRALS; PARISH CHURCHES.

**Churchill, Lord Randolph** (1849–95). An MP from 1874, after the Conservative defeat of 1880 he joined a small ginger group known as the *Fourth Party undermining the leadership of *Northcote. Churchill exploited the discontents of the provincial associations in the National Union and claimed to speak for a 'Tory Democracy' derived from *Disraeli. Audacious in language and style, Churchill was a young man in a hurry, perhaps knowing that syphilis would shorten his career. His deal with *Salisbury in 1884, abandoning the National Union in return for admittance into the collective leadership, ended Northcote's chances of the premiership. Secretary for India in Salisbury's 1885 government, Churchill had Burma annexed. Though he flirted with Parnell's nationalists, once *Gladstone had proposed *Home Rule Churchill hoisted unionist colours: 'Ulster will fight and Ulster will be right.' Chancellor of the Exchequer and leader of the Commons in 1886, he became impatient with cabinet colleagues and, seeking tactical alliance with *Chamberlain's wing of the Liberal Unionists, he began to challenge Salisbury's leadership. When Churchill, frustrated over cutting the services estimates, offered a tactical resignation, Salisbury called his bluff and accepted. Harassed by health and financial worries, Churchill never recovered politically.

**Churchill, Sir Winston Leonard Spencer** (1874–1965). Prime minister. Churchill was born at Blenheim palace in 1874, the elder son of Lord Randolph *Churchill. His mother was the American heiress Jennie Jerome. Educated at Harrow and Sandhurst, he served with the 4th Hussars and rode in the lancers' charge at *Omdurman. Between 1899 and 1900 he was a war correspondent in South Africa, where he was captured by the Boers but escaped. He saw active service in the trenches for a few months in 1916.

In 1900 he entered the House of Commons as a Conservative but crossed the floor within four years to join the Liberals on the issue of free trade. Returned as a Liberal at the next election, he gained his first ministerial experience under *Campbell-Bannerman as under-secretary for the colonies. *Asquith brought him into the cabinet at the age of 33 as president of the Board of Trade (1908) and moved him to the Home Office before he had reached the age of 35 (1910). By now Churchill had married Clementine Hozier (1908) who provided him with a stable emotional base for the rest of his life. Meanwhile, along with *Lloyd George, he played a major part in laying the foundations of the welfare state by establishing labour exchanges and social insurance. His tenure of the Home Office, on the other hand, is remembered for the myth that he sent troops to Wales to crush the striking miners of Tonypandy (1910).

In 1911 he became 1st lord of the Admiralty and a figure of significance. Completing the work of Admiral *Fisher, he replaced dreadnoughts with super-dreadnoughts, established a naval air service, and began the conversion of the fleet from coal to oil. Having the fleet ready was one of Churchill's contributions to the British war effort between 1914 and 1918. Another was the part he played in the development of the tank. However, he was remembered most of all for conceiving the 1915 Dardanelles campaign, designed to shorten the war by removing Turkey and allowing the western allies to link up with Russia. The attack on Gallipoli failed due to naval delays. In its wake, Asquith was forced to form a coalition with the Conservatives, who loathed Churchill as a renegade, and had him transferred to become chancellor of the duchy of Lancaster. Lacking any influence over the course of the war, Churchill resigned and took command of a battalion of the Royal Scots Fusiliers in France. A few months later he was recalled by Lloyd George to become minister of munitions. Between 1918 and 1920 he was secretary of state for war and air, in which capacity he was responsible for running down the planned post-war Royal Air Force from 154 squadrons to 24, with only two for home defence. His attempts to persuade his colleagues to overthrow the Bolsheviks in Russia were unsuccessful.

In 1921 he became colonial secretary and made a treaty with the *Irish Free State. He also negotiated a peace settlement with the Arabs, advised by T. E. *Lawrence. Although he opposed Lloyd George's policy towards the Turks, he gave his prime minister vociferous support over the *Chanak crisis of 1922. When the coalition fell a few months later, he was defeated in the 1922 election and began work on his history of the First World War, the first volume of which was published in 1923. A friend quipped: 'Winston has written an enormous book about himself and called it *The World Crisis.*'

Returning to the Commons in October 1924, he was offered the chancellorship of the Exchequer by *Baldwin and rejoined the Conservative Party. In 1925 he put Great Britain back on the gold standard, unfortunately at the pre-war parity of £1 = $1, which was of little help to British exporters. Three years later he introduced the 'ten-year rule', whereby the service estimates would be prepared on the assumption that no war was likely for the next ten years. Meanwhile, he was only prevented from running down the navy as he had already run down the RAF by the threatened resignation of the entire Board of Admiralty. In the General Strike of 1926, he took overall command of the government newspaper the *British Gazette*. Churchill's star, however, was set to wane. With the fall of Baldwin's government in 1929, he was out of office for the next ten years.

Churchill himself turned the 1930s into his wilderness years. His attacks on constitutional progress in India and his defence of

Edward VIII found little response. Nor was Churchill able to capture the public imagination as the foe of fascism. He admired Mussolini and sympathized with Franco during the Spanish Civil War. Finally, on the great economic questions of the day—unemployment, protection, recovery—he had little to say.

Churchill did however take up the cause of resistance to Nazi Germany. There were many obstacles to this. The Treasury in particular opposed rearmament: after a year of war, Britain, it predicted, would be bankrupt. The Foreign Office asked just who our allies were going to be. America was neutral, the dominions unpredictable, and even if the Soviets could be brought in, an alliance with them might push Franco into the arms of the axis and close off the Mediterranean. The appeasers, therefore, had a good case. Churchill did not believe that war was inevitable and knew that Hitler wanted Britain as an ally. However, he believed that a grand alliance against the dictator would make him moderate his plans. If not, perhaps he could be overthrown before it came to war. But if Germany would not see reason, then war it would be. He envisaged that war, however, as one in which Britain would make her contribution with sea and air power. He thought a continental army a mistake.

When war came, Churchill returned to the Admiralty, although he acted as if he were already prime minister. Almost immediately he became involved in a madcap scheme to send an expeditionary force to Norway, ostensibly to help save Finland from the Russians, but in practice to cut off Swedish iron ore from the Germans. The lack of air cover meant that the campaign was a disaster. Ironically, *Chamberlain was blamed and Churchill became prime minister at the head of a national government.

As war leader, Churchill was a mixture of ruthlessness and impetuosity. Determined to do everything possible to win the war, in practice he had few means of doing so. Still, he did what he could, which meant the bombing offensive, plus the Mediterranean campaign. Determined to have action, he prodded and sacked his generals and made many mistakes—sinking the French fleet at Oran, invading Greece, defending Crete, neglecting the Far East. Yet his position as prime minister was secure, since he had be-

come in the summer of 1940 the spirit of British resistance incarnate, defying the Nazis with speeches of supreme eloquence. His real hope of victory depended on the entry of the USA, and when that happened, Churchill persuaded the Americans to make Europe the primary theatre of the war and to participate in the north African campaign. When Hitler attacked Stalin, he immediately offered aid to the Soviets. Towards the end of the war, in October 1944, aware of US plans to send their troops home once the war was over, he signed the Percentages agreement with Stalin, dividing the Balkans into spheres of influence and saving Greece from communism.

As war leader, Churchill had little time for the home front. Nor was he much interested in post-war planning. When the *Beveridge Report was published in 1942, he doubted whether a bankrupt Britain would be able to afford it. In any case, he had left domestic affairs to *Attlee and his Labour colleagues, which proved a mistake. For it was to them that the electorate turned in July 1945 once victory had been secured. Churchill was still respected, but the voters guessed that he was not the man for post-war reconstruction. But as leader of the Conservative Party and of the opposition, he was more politically secure than he had ever been before in peacetime. His voice continued to be heard in international affairs and, just as he had warned against the rising threat from Hitler, he now warned against the 'iron curtain' which was descending over Europe. He also spoke out in favour of a united Europe, although he never meant that Britain should be part of it.

In 1951 he returned as prime minister. He was now 77 years old, had suffered two strokes, and would suffer two more. Yet his government was highly successful. *Eden shone as foreign secretary, *Macmillan built a record number of council houses, and nothing was done to undermine the welfare state, inherited from Labour. In April 1955 he agreed to retire as prime minister, completing a career without equal among democratic politicians. He died in 1965, soon after retiring from the Commons, was given a state funeral, and was buried in Bladon churchyard.

**Church in Wales** The Church in Wales within the Anglican Communion came into being in 1920, when the Act of 1914 disestablishing the Church of England in the principality came into force. The four ancient Welsh dioceses of Bangor, St Asaph, St Davids, and Llandaff became a self-governing church, with the bishop of St Asaph, Alfred George Edwards, as the first archbishop of Wales.

**Church Missionary Society** Founded in 1799 for missions in Africa and the East, the society became the Church of England's first effective body for such work despite far earlier establishment of the *Society for Promoting Christian Knowledge and the *Society for the Propagation of the Gospel. Consistently evangelical in its theology, it continues to sponsor Bible translations.

**Church of England** Though, as an Erastian institution, the Church of England dates only from the 16th cent., *Christianity in these islands originated with merchants, administrators, and soldiers in 2nd- and 3rd-cent. Roman Britain. The present English church dates from the reintroduction of Celtic Christianity into Northumbria by *Aidan (635) and Roman Christianity into Kent by *Augustine (597). Though medieval kings exercised considerable authority over the church, it was the break with Rome (1534) which fully established royal supremacy, from which date the established Church of England (*Ecclesia Anglicana*) can be said to exist. The Act of *Supremacy (1534) declared Henry VIII to be 'the only supreme head of the Church' in place of the pope, which Elizabeth's Act (1559) moderated to the less offensive 'Supreme Governor'.

Apart from this the church remained legally and administratively much the same. The church courts and their penalties, diocesan administrative systems, the authority of bishops and archdeacons all continued. The non-monastic cathedrals survived as before. Ecclesiastical law remained unchanged. Though now under royal control the *convocations of Canterbury and York survived. The church after Henry VIII was thoroughly Erastian, its officials little more than agents of the crown. Indeed post-Restoration clergy were also agents of royalist propaganda, parsons thundering from their pulpits the doctrines of *divine right, *non-resistance, and passive obedience.

Though Henry VIII made virtually no theological or liturgical break with the past, there was under Edward VI a considerable influx of continental reform and innovation from Bucer, Zwingli, and Calvin. After a brief reversion to catholicism under Mary, the church moved towards a comprehensive settlement under Elizabeth. Enshrined in the Acts of *Supremacy and *Uniformity, the *Book of Common Prayer, and the *Thirty-Nine Articles, this attempted to reconcile the diverse shades of English opinion. Provided citizens fulfilled the royal injunction to weekly church attendance, there was to be no test as to conscience, 'no windows into men's souls'. Presbyterianism and adherence to Rome were unacceptable. Most accepted, but minorities existed, some still adhering to Rome, others to presbyterianism or more extreme protestant views. After the heyday of the sects in the *Interregnum (1649-60), compromise became impossible. The Restoration settlement refused to recognize those already ordained non-episcopally, and demanded tests. A thousand incumbents were ejected—and thus became *nonconformists. From that time the church ceased to be the church of the whole nation.

After 1689 church life remained turbulent but settled down from 1714. Eighteenth-cent. ecclesiastics' reputation for idleness and rationalist indifference is undeserved. Nevertheless liturgically the church was deadening. Eighteenth-cent. Prayer Book liturgy and weighty preaching was unsuited to a mainly illiterate, uneducated people. The preaching of the *Wesley brothers thus fell on ready ears, but it was to the church's shame that these two devoted Anglican priests, both high churchmen, were rejected.

Though there is evidence of both evangelical and Caroline high-church strands in the 18th cent., the full *evangelical revival spilled over into the 19th cent. and, with the *tractarian movement, invigorated church life. Evangelicalism produced many of note, clergy like *Simeon and laymen such as *Wilberforce and *Shaftesbury. Tractarianism, led by *Keble, *Newman, and *Pusey, initially traced Anglicanism's traditions back to Augustine, but developed later into a powerful movement to restore fully the church's catholic wing.

As the British empire spread throughout the world in the 18th and 19th cents., the church followed—or in some cases led the way. Two overseas dioceses in 1800 increased to 72 in

1882, and to 450 dioceses (in 28 provinces) in the 1990s. The *Ecclesia Anglicana* from having been merely the church of the English people became a world-wide communion of many nations. To provide cohesion and consensus, the first Lambeth conference with 67 bishops met in 1867, to be followed at Archbishop Tait's inspiration by the second in 1878. The archbishop still presides at the Lambeth conference each decade.

Twentieth-cent. developments include women's ordination to the diaconate and the priesthood (in England 1987 and 1994), making the Anglican church the first episcopal church to take this step. Ecumenism, so much a part of 20th-cent. church life, has extended to dialogue with non-Christian faiths, which are now prominent in the English scene. During the archiepiscopate of Rowan *Williams the Church has had difficulties in relation to advocates of 'gay liberation'.

**Church of Ireland** Building on 4th-cent. traces, *Patrick evangelized Ireland (*c.*432) and developed a distinctively Celtic Christianity, but with the partial Anglo-Norman conquest of Ireland the church again joined mainstream western Christendom. Though Henry VIII established the Church *of* Ireland after his break with Rome (1536), the Reformation was less popular than in England. The monasteries continued in Gaelic areas, friars pursued their ministry, and Jesuits arrived (*c.*1545). The Reformation largely failed. Gaelic, which most Irishmen spoke, was forbidden in worship and the established church was inextricably associated with the colonizing offices of state. After 1580 missionary priests poured in, but Anglo-Scottish colonization of Ulster (*c.*1610) made it the bastion of protestantism, *Ussher's 104 Irish Articles (1615) were Calvinistic in ethos, and *Cromwell further antagonized Irish opinion by confiscating catholic land and allowing protestants economic predominance. William III's promise of toleration (1691) was a dead letter until 1791. After the Anglican archbishoprics were reduced to two and bishoprics by eight (1833), the church, always predominantly evangelical, was disestablished (1869). Today with two archbishoprics and twelve dioceses, it has a total membership (2000) of 375,000 (281,000 in the North and 94,000 in the Republic).

**Church of Scotland** The church claims continuity from *Ninian and *Columba. Although the Scottish Reformation's first impact was *Lutheran, the return of John *Knox from Geneva in 1559 led to the church's reconstruction on *presbyterian, lines, a process not completed until 1690. In between kirk and crown battled as to whether Scotland's ecclesiastical system should be presbyterian or *episcopalian. Presbyterianism was advanced by the first *General Assembly (1560). Its popular status was affirmed by the National Covenant (1638), the *Solemn League and Covenant (1643), and the *Westminster Assembly (1643–52). Episcopalianism was advanced by the Stuart monarchs' steady preference, the imposition of the Prayer Book (1637), and the restoration of episcopacy (1660). The conflict was resolved by the revolution of 1688: all ministers must subscribe to the Westminster confession. In the 18th cent. the now dominant church was weakened by secession; the growth of two parties, one favouring the rights of patronage in ministerial settlements, the other favouring congregational rights, led to the formation of the *Free Church. The seceders formed the United Presbyterian Church in 1847; the United Presbyterian and Free Churches became the United Free Church in 1900. At the same time patronage was abolished (1874), there was a significant liturgical revival, and the Church of Scotland Act (1921) paved the way for union with the United Free Church (1929). The General Assembly was now equally composed of ministers and elders, and women were admitted to both eldership (1966) and ministry (1968).

**churchwardens** are representatives of the parish meeting or the vestry. From the 12th to the middle of the 16th cents. churchwardens were primarily responsible for providing and maintaining all that was necessary for public worship in their parish church. A subsidiary duty was that of presentment to the ecclesiastical courts of moral misdemeanours of the laity and clergy of the parish. Their accounts, presented annually to the parish meeting, are a major source of information about parish life.

**Cinque Ports** A maritime confederation in Kent and Sussex. Their privileges from the crown, in return for naval service, go back at least to the 12th cent., and they remained a formidable maritime power until Tudor times. The original 'Five Ports'—Hastings, New Romney, Hythe, Dover, and Sandwich—were later joined by Rye and Winchelsea. The office of lord warden remains a distinguished honour in the gift of the sovereign.

**Cintra, convention of,** 1808. Concluded on 30 August after a British victory over the French at *Vimeiro early in the Peninsular War. The terms negotiated by Sir Hew Dalrymple were ridiculous. All French troops, equipment, and loot were to be transported back to France in British ships. The news of the treaty caused uproar in London and led to an official inquiry, which relieved Dalrymple of his command.

**Cirencester** *Civitas*-capital of the *Dobunni, Corinium grew to be one of the most considerable towns of Roman Britain. The town developed on the site of two successive forts on *Fosse Way. A 4th-cent. inscription mentioning a *Rector* (governor) of Britannia Prima, one of the four late Roman provinces of Britain, suggests that Cirencester may have been a provincial capital. Though there is no evidence for occupation after *c.*400, Cirencester is one of three former Roman towns mentioned in the *Anglo-Saxon Chronicle* entry for 577.

**Cistercians** ('white' monks) were a monastic order established in 1098 by Robert of Molesme at Cîteaux (Burgundy) in reaction to the perceived laxity of contemporary *Benedictine monasticism. Their constitutions aimed at a literal observance of the Benedictine rule. Their estates were organized in self-contained 'granges' staffed by lay brothers ('conversi') who, while not monks, followed a rule and wore a distinctive habit. After initial difficulties the Cistercians enjoyed phenomenal success, particularly during the life of St Bernard, who entered Cîteaux in 1112 and was abbot of its daughter house of Clairvaux.

In England and Wales the first abbey was founded at Waverley (Surrey) in 1128, followed shortly afterwards by *Tintern and *Rievaulx. By 1152 there were about 40, as well as communities in Scotland (such as *Melrose) and Ireland.

**civil law** The term has two meanings: **1.** It is used as synonymous with Roman law, which was accepted in most of the countries of Europe. With the fall of the Roman empire, the Roman or civil law which survived was heavily influenced by custom. Thus Roman law came to have two aspects—the pure classical Roman law and the bastardized Roman customary law which applied in the many barbarian and post-barbarian societies of western Europe.

English law was undoubtedly influenced by civil law, though it never 'received' or adopted Roman law. There was little evidence of survival of Roman law from the Roman occupation of Britain, but the Norman Conquest brought England close to continental traditions, especially through the influence of *canon law. The author of *Glanvill clearly had a sound grounding in Roman law, though the book makes it clear that English law is by no means the same. *Bracton is commonly acknowledged to be heavily influenced by Roman law. But civil law was never a serious threat to the common law in England. **2.** The other meaning of civil law is as distinct from criminal—i.e. the law relating to the adjustment of legal disputes between individuals. The common law was mainly civil law since the work of the courts of common law was primarily the development of the writ system to enable individuals to litigate in the king's courts.

**civil list** The civil list is the grant made by Parliament for the monarch's personal support and for that of the household. It was started in the reign of William and Mary and fixed at £700,000 p.a., out of which the monarchs had to pay pensions and salaries. *Walpole's desire to retain office in 1727 led to George II receiving an extremely generous settlement. The civil list provoked criticism. Victoria, a secluded widow for many years after Albert's death in 1861, spent very little and was repaid with a pamphlet entitled *What does she do with it?* Postwar inflation in the 1960s brought the issue to the surface again in the reign of Elizabeth II. A select committee in 1971 recommended that any savings should return to the public purse and that there should be regular reviews of the civil list award.

**civil service** Despite repeated campaigns to reduce numbers, the civil service remains one of the great growth areas of modern Britain. In the 17th cent. the civil service—i.e. persons directly employed by the government—was tiny. The two secretaries of state had a staff of about fifteen.

The growth of the civil service in the 19th cent. was moderate and hardly kept pace with the rise in population. In 1815 there were 25,000 civil servants; 39,000 by 1851; 54,000 by 1871; and 79,000 by 1891. Some reforms were introduced piecemeal by departments. In the Treasury, North had launched the concept of promotion by merit (1776), Shelburne had inaugurated fixed salaries (1782), and in 1805 an assistant secretary was appointed, the forerunner of the permanent secretary. A comprehensive review waited for the Northcote–Trevelyan Report of 1854, which recommended a division of labour between graduate policy-makers and humble administrators; entry by competitive examination; transfer between departments; and promotion by merit based on assessment. A Civil Service Commission, to supervise recruitment, was set up in 1855.

The vast expansion of the civil service in the 20th cent. is not easy to calculate. Definitions are troublesome and one commentator has referred to the 'statistical conjuring tricks'—e.g. recategorizing thousands of civil servants—to give the impression that numbers are falling. By 1939 the numbers had risen to 387,000 and by 1979 to 730,000. These developments were accompanied by further reports. *Haldane in 1918 was concerned that senior civil servants had little time to think. Plowden in 1961 complained that the Treasury had no adequate system for controlling expenditure—a rather worrying observation—and the Fulton Committee in 1968 deplored the survival of the cult of the amateur gentleman. One consequence was the establishment of a Civil Service College in 1970 to conduct research and training.

Though the public image of the civil servant may remain a pin-striped bowler-hatted Whitehall mandarin, most civil servants work outside London and half of them are women. Of the non-industrial civil service, the large employers are the Ministry of Defence, the Department of Work and Pensions, the Board of Revenue and Customs, the Department of Education and Skills, the Department for Environment, and the Home Office.

**civil wars,** 1642–51. In 1629 Charles I dismissed Parliament, resolving never to call another. He might have succeeded but for the problem of the multiple kingdoms. During the 1630s he decided to bring Scottish religious practice into conformity with English by abolishing presbyterian worship and substituting an Anglican service. The Scots revolted, and Charles's two attempts to subdue them—the *Bishops' wars of 1639 and 1640—were abject failures. At the insistence of the nobility he summoned Parliament. Once convened, the Commons refused him the taxes he needed, and set about dismantling the apparatus of prerogative government, abolishing ship money, the courts of *Star Chamber, *High Commission, *Wards, and others; passing a Triennial Act, depriving church courts of their punitive powers, and attainting Charles's chief minister *Strafford. Charles ratified these changes, but with such ill grace that many doubted whether he would keep his word. Trust became a critical issue upon the outbreak of rebellion in Ireland in the autumn of 1641. Exaggerated reports of atrocities perpetrated against the protestant settlers in Ireland inflamed English opinion. It was accepted that an army should crush the rebellion, but there was no agreement about entrusting the king with command. Charles's attempt to arrest five of the parliamentary ringleaders contributed to the deepening distrust of him. Mistrust was compounded by fear that the king could not be counted on to defend England against the threat of international catholicism. Thus legal and constitutional arguments about taxation, the rights of Parliament, and the extent of royal power were inflamed by religious panic.

Despite its control of the midlands, the east, and the south-east including London, there was nothing inevitable about Parliament's victory. Charles almost overthrew his foes at *Edgehill (October 1642), while in 1643 there were a number of royalist victories. For all the efforts of John *Pym to hold together the parliamentary coalition, parliamentary fortunes reached their nadir in that year.

What turned the tide against Charles I was again the reality of multiple kingdoms. In return for a promise to uphold presbyterian church government and impose it in England, the Scots came to Parliament's aid with an army of 20,000. This bargain was sealed in the *Solemn League and Covenant of 1643, and the Scots army entered England early in 1644. The joint armies dealt a crushing blow to the king's forces at *Marston Moor, near York (July 1644). However, this victory was almost frittered away by Essex when he allowed his army to become trapped by Charles at *Lostwithiel in Cornwall (September 1644). Completely disenchanted with the aristocratic leadership of Parliament's armies, the win-the-war faction under Sir Henry *Vane and Oliver *Cromwell purged the armies of their noble and parliamentary leadership, creating the *New Model Army. Led by Sir Thomas *Fairfax, and knit together by regular pay and religious indoctrination, this army quickly put the royalist forces to flight at *Naseby (June 1645), *Langport (July 1645), and Bristol (September 1645). By May 1646 Charles had handed himself over to the Scots.

Refusing to accept the verdict of the battlefield, Charles dragged out peace negotiations with Parliament, attempting to exploit the rift between army and Parliament and redoubling his efforts to persuade the Scots to assist him. Early in 1648 royalist risings erupted in Kent, Essex, Wales, and the navy in anticipation of a Scottish intervention on behalf of the king. But the Scots were late, and the New Model Army had no difficulty crushing the revolts. When the duke of *Hamilton crossed the border in July, he attracted little support, and Cromwell destroyed his forces between *Preston and Uttoxeter (August 1648). Everywhere triumphant in battle, the army found that Parliament was still intent on negotiating with the king. To prevent such an outcome it occupied London, purged the House of Commons of those who favoured negotiation, and engineered the trial and execution of the king. Once the *Rump Parliament had abolished monarchy and the House of Lords, it launched invasions of Ireland (1649) and Scotland (1650). In spite of Cromwellian ruthlessness at *Drogheda and Wexford, Ireland took three years to subjugate. The Scots were devastated at *Dunbar (September 1650), but continued to resist, to the point of invading England a year later under Charles II. His forces scattered at *Worcester (September 1651), the hapless king fled to the continent. Although the king, lords, and

Church of England were brought back in 1660, prerogative government was not. The constitutional changes of 1641 were preserved, while the legacy of the civil wars in religious liberty and parliamentary domination of the state re-emerged in the '*Glorious' Revolution of 1688–9.

**clans** The Gaelic word *clann* means primarily children. Clans are referred to in the reign of David I (1124–53) in the *Book of Deer*, where there are references to the toiseachs of the Clans Morgan and Canan. A toiseach was a royal official. Mackintoshes are *Clann an Toiseach*, literally 'the toiseach's children'.

Clans Canan and Morgan did not survive. Continual flux, constant rise and fall seems to have been typical of Scottish clans. Most Highland clans were in origin Gaelic communities onto which feudal structures were grafted. Especially in the province of *Moray, there were also feudal groups, such as the Frasers, Chisholms, Grants, and Rosses, which adopted clanship.

From feudalism a clan chief gained the concept of absolute ownership of land, and succession by primogeniture. Female heirs, or wardship by a superior of a male minor, could threaten the tribal identity. Control of the marriage of a female heiress by the cadet branches of the chiefly house, and the office of tutor or guardian within the clan, were partial answers. Kinship was largely bogus for the bulk of a clan, who only began to use surnames very late.

After the forfeiture of the lordship of the *Isles in 1493 broke the Clan Donald into smaller MacDonald clans, three great clans dominated Highland history. These were the Gordons in the north-east, the Mackenzies in the northern Highlands and Hebrides, and Clan Campbell in the west. Highland clans became deeply distrusted after a century of bloody intervention in Lowland politics between 1644 and 1746. After the last *Jacobite rebellion legislation destroyed them as military, jurisdictional, and cultural units. Market economics and clearances completed the job.

**Clapham sect** An influential evangelical network whose activity in the early 19th cent. found a base in Clapham. The name was popularized and perhaps coined by Sir

James Stephen in the *Edinburgh Review* (1844). The banker Henry Thornton (1760–1815) provided the Clapham core but the 'sect's' dominant figure, their kinsman William *Wilberforce, also lived there (1797–1808). The original group, ranging from Granville *Sharp, the oldest, to Thomas *Clarkson, the last survivor, provided some 60 years of public service. Their greatest victories were the abolition of the *slave trade (1807) and of slavery itself in the British empire (1833).

**Clare, Gilbert de** (d. 1230). *See* GLOUCESTER, 4TH EARL OF.

**Clare, Gilbert de** (1243–95). *See* GLOUCESTER, 6TH EARL OF.

**Clare, Richard de** (d. 1176). *See* PEMBROKE, EARL OF.

**Clarence, Albert Victor Christian Edward, duke of** (1864–92). Clarence was the first son of Edward, prince of Wales. He seems to have been congenitally handicapped: at the age of 5 he was described as 'languid and listless'. At 13 he went to Dartmouth Naval College. He spent some time at Trinity College, Cambridge, though one tutor described his faculties as 'abnormally dormant'. The university obliged with an honorary degree. He was next placed in the army where the commander-in-chief reported that even elementary drill movements were beyond him. Known in the family as 'Eddie', he remained wayward and what vigour he did possess was devoted to sexual encounters of various kinds. 'His education and future', wrote his father in 1890, 'has been a matter of considerable anxiety to us.' Matrimony was, of course, suggested. In 1891 Princess *Mary of Teck, his cousin, accepted him, but he died of pneumonia on 14 January 1892, a month before the wedding. In due course his younger brother married his fiancée and succeeded as George V. The more lurid stories connected Clarence with the Ripper murders.

**Clarence, George, 1st duke of** (1446–78). Reputed to have been drowned in a butt of malmsey, Clarence was the younger brother of Edward IV. He was enticed by a promise of the crown to support *Warwick the King-

maker (whose daughter Isabel he married) against his brother. After Henry VI had been restored in 1470, Clarence abandoned Warwick to help Edward IV recover the throne. In the early 1470s he was high in Edward's favour, but his truculence and insubordination exasperated the king. Arrested in 1477, he was executed secretly in the Tower, by means never officially revealed.

**Clarendon, Assize of** An assize (set of instructions for the king's judges) issued on Henry II's orders at Clarendon in 1166. It required grand juries to name ('present') suspected criminals so that the sheriff could have them brought for trial before royal judges in the county courts. The assize was an important step in the development of machinery for the public prosecution of crime.

**Clarendon, constitutions of** A statement of Henry II's view of his customary rights over the English church. It was issued at a council held at Clarendon in 1164 in an attempt to settle the issues at stake in the king's quarrel with *Becket. He required the bishops to promise to obey these customs, but since some of the constitutions, including one perceived as undermining *benefit of clergy, seemed to threaten the liberty of the church and in consequence were condemned by Pope Alexander III, the dispute escalated.

**Clarendon, Edward Hyde, 1st earl of** (1609–74). In the first session of the *Long Parliament, 1640–1, Hyde led the attack on Charles I's prerogative courts, but in the second he perceived John *Pym's policies as an equal threat to constitutional liberties. He co-authored Charles's declarations, joining him at York in May 1642. In 1643 as privy counsellor and chancellor of the Exchequer he persuaded Charles to convoke a parliament at Oxford. Similarly as adviser to the exiled Charles II he counselled him not to owe his restoration to foreign intervention.

In 1660 he became earl and lord chancellor. His pregnant daughter *Anne's marriage to James, duke of York, provoked charges that he dominated the royal family. He opposed the second *Anglo-Dutch War. But when the war ended in failure, Charles abandoned him, encouraging his impeachment. Clarendon fled to France, where he completed his monumental *History of the Rebellion*.

## Clarendon, Henry Hyde, 2nd earl of

(1638–1709). Clarendon was the son of the lord chancellor, and brother of Anne Hyde, mother of Queen Mary and Queen Anne. On the accession of his brother-in-law James II in 1685, Clarendon and his younger brother *Rochester were given high office. From 1685 to 1687 Clarendon held the privy seal and was lord-lieutenant of Ireland. But as a protestant he was increasingly anxious at James's headlong catholicizing policy. In January 1687 both brothers were dismissed. At the revolution, Clarendon joined William. Nevertheless he refused to swear allegiance to the new monarchs and had two spells in the Tower in 1690 and 1691.

## Clarendon, George Villiers, 4th earl of

(1800–70). Whig Politician. Clarendon served under such diverse leaders as *Aberdeen, *Palmerston, *Russell, and *Gladstone (1853–8, 1865–6, and 1868–70). The Tory leader, *Derby, twice offered him a place in government. A good linguist, he was an acknowledged expert on foreign affairs. Clarendon had learned the skills of diplomacy as minister in Madrid during the Carlist wars and later as lord-lieutenant in Ireland (1847–52). As foreign secretary in 1853 he had the misfortune during the *Crimean War to be in a divided cabinet. Clarendon's biggest opportunity to distinguish himself occurred during the Congress of *Paris in 1856 when he resisted the more extreme demands of Palmerston in London.

## Clarendon code

The title given, inaccurately, to the statutes passed after the Restoration re-establishing the Church of England. They embodied the vindictiveness of the cavalier majority in Parliament rather than the judgement of Lord *Clarendon, Charles II's chief minister. The *Uniformity Act (1662) required clergy to have episcopal ordination and use only the Book of Common Prayer. The *Conventicle Act (1664) penalized all religious meetings outside the church. The *Five Mile Act (1665) banned dissenting ministers from corporate towns.

## Clarkson, Thomas

(1760–1846). Antislavery campaigner. Born in Wisbech (Cambs.), Clarkson was educated at St John's College, Cambridge, where he became concerned about slavery. In 1787 he helped found a committee for the suppression of the slave trade and lectured on abolition until his health collapsed in 1794. He resumed lecturing in 1805 until the ending of the trade in the British empire in 1807. With William *Wilberforce he was a vice-president of the *Anti-Slavery Society (founded 1823), and after the Act was carried in 1833 for the abolition of slavery in the British empire, he retained his concern for wider abolition.

## class

is about power. The concept of social class has been used by historians to understand the experience, social relationships, and social conflicts of past and present. By the 1960s, historians had established the major outlines of this story. Sometime in the late 18th-early 19th cent., the way in which the British people began to think about their own society began to change. Eighteenth-cent. society was a hierarchy of ranks and orders held together by relationships of deference and patronage. The new relationships and consciousness of class were associated with economic change, with the dominance of capitalist relationships, and, above all, with the reorganization of work through the division of labour and new machine-based technologies. Early conflicts were associated with trade unionism and the new technologies. The 1830s and 1840s were decades of conflict associated with constitutional change. There were key periods of industrial conflict in the 1880s and the quarter-century before 1926.

Behind this interpretation lay a series of assumptions. British writing was dominated by a three-class model, loosely related to the three factors of production identified by *Ricardo in 1817. The aristocracy were rent takers, the middle class were profit takers, and the working class wage earners. A rigid Marxist presentation assuming an increasingly divisive conflict between capital and labour was rare, but the notion of a potential conflict was central to the story. Class was related to market position and hence involved privileges of education as well as property.

This story has been questioned. Eighteenth-cent. historians have identified a 'middling sort' not least in patterns of consumption. The re-examination of the political events of the 1830s and 1840s yields little evidence of self-aware conflict groups based upon economic relationships. The closer study of work revealed a lack of homogeneity of experience within the major social classes. Divisions within classes, of gender, party, religion, region, ethnicity, were seen as providing identities more dominant than class itself.

***Classis Britannica*** was the name of the Roman fleet which policed the Channel. Its main base was at Boulogne, with an important installation at Dover. Bricks and tiles stamped *CL BR* are widely distributed in Kent and East Sussex.

**Claudius** Roman emperor AD 41–54. After the assassination of Caligula, the middle-aged Claudius was unexpectedly proclaimed emperor. To reward the army and prove his prowess, Claudius decided to resume the work of his ancestor Julius *Caesar with an invasion of Britain in 43. The emperor himself came to Britain for the formal entry into Camulodunum (*Colchester). Having spent sixteen days in the new province, Claudius returned to Rome, where he celebrated a triumph.

**Cleveland** was one of the new non-metropolitan counties created by the English local government reforms of 1972. It straddled the border of the river Tees between Yorkshire and Co. Durham. Middlesbrough and Stockton had been united in Teesside county borough (1968–74), and the town of Hartlepool, and the Yorkshire districts adjacent to Middlesbrough, were added to form Cleveland county. Many people in these areas failed to identify with it and in 1996 the county was abolished.

**Clifford, Thomas Clifford, 1st Baron** (1630–73). Clifford was a Devon gentleman determined to make a mark after the Restoration. Elected in 1660, he spoke frequently and in December 1660 was appointed a gentleman of the privy chamber. Bitterly opposed to the Dutch, he urged the second war in 1664. In 1666 he became comptroller of the household, held the post of treasurer 1668–72, and 1672–3 was lord high treasurer with a peerage. But as a member of the *cabal, his judgement seems less good than his spirit. He advocated the secret treaty of *Dover with Louis XIV, which involved Charles II in great embarrass-

ment; suggested the stop on the Exchequer, a short-term expedient of doubtful wisdom; and pushed hard for a third Dutch War. When the *Test Act passed in 1673, he resigned all offices as an avowed catholic.

**Clitherow, St Margaret** (1556–86). Catholic martyr. Daughter of a sheriff of York and a butcher's wife, she became a catholic (1574). She was tried at York for harbouring Jesuits and priests and hearing mass in her house. She refused to plead, was condemned and pressed to death. A fine example of recusant courage and the brutality of the age, she was canonized in 1970.

**Clive, Robert** (1725–74). Soldier-statesman who helped to secure British control over India. Born in Shropshire, he joined the *East India Company in 1743. Eight years later, when war broke out between Britain and France in India, he volunteered for military service and, against all the odds, seized and held the city of Arcot. In 1756 he moved to Bengal, where the French-supported Siraj-ud-Daula had taken Calcutta. Clive organized a small force to recapture the city in January 1757, but Siraj was still a major threat. Clive marched inland with no more than 3,200 troops to face Siraj's army of 50,000 at *Plassey. The battle was fought on 23 June 1757; for the loss of only 23 men, Clive routed the enemy.

By now the undisputed master of Bengal, Clive returned to England in 1760, where he was raised to the Irish peerage as Baron Clive of Plassey (1762). He returned to India in 1765 as governor of Bengal, and introduced a series of reforms to company administration. Corruption remained, however, and in 1772 he was forced to defend himself before Parliament. Although exonerated, he committed suicide on 22 November 1774.

**Clogher (Clochar mac nDaimine), diocese of** The Irish see of Clogher in the province of *Armagh was established by the Council of Raithbressail (1111). There were usually Irish, not Anglo-Norman, bishops until the 16th cent. Since the Reformation there have been both catholic and Anglican bishops of Clogher.

**Clontarf, battle of,** 1014. *Brian Boru claimed the high kingship of Ireland, though resisted by Leinster and by the Norse kingdom of Dublin. On 23 April 1014 just outside Dublin, battle was joined. Brian Boru was too old to fight and his troops were led by his son Murchad. Though the Norse were defeated, Brian Boru, inadequately guarded, was killed.

**club-men** Not all Englishmen were keen to fight in the Civil War and by 1644 the depredations of each army had become unbearable. Groups of country folk, particularly in the royalist south and west, began to band together against troops from either side. Armed mainly with clubs, scythes, and spades, they were still formidable, and local commanders tried to enlist their help.

**clubs** The decades after the Restoration saw a proliferation of clubs and societies in London and the main provincial cities, many of them meeting in taverns or coffee-houses. Though the most famous club, to which *Johnson, *Burke, and *Gibbon belonged, was literary, the majority were dining clubs, or political or gambling clubs. The Athenaeum (1824), founded by J. W. *Croker, was literary; the Carlton (1832) was established to restore the fortunes of the Tory Party after its shattering election defeat; the *Reform Club (1836) was a Whig and radical riposte to the Carlton's success. The heyday of the gentlemen's club was late Victorian and Edwardian England, with clubs offering overnight accommodation and libraries as well as good dining facilities. At the other end of the social scale were working men's clubs, where the drink was beer and the entertainment a local comedian, sing-song, or dominoes.

**Cluniacs** were *Benedictine monks from the monastery of Cluny (Burgundy) founded by William, duke of Aquitaine, in 909. Under the leadership of its early abbots, especially Odo (927–42), Odilo (994–1048), and Hugh (1049–1109), Cluny enjoyed considerable prosperity, and exercised a wide influence on monastic reform elsewhere in Europe. The first English Cluniac priory was founded by William de Warenne in 1077 at Lewes. His, the largest community, was joined by some 30 more. Though initially subject to Cluny's authority and hence regarded as 'alien priories', most purchased national identity as 'denizens'.

**Clwyd** A Welsh county created under the Local Government Act of 1972 and extant from 1974 to 1996. It was made up of the former counties of *Denbighshire and *Flintshire, with the Edeyrnion rural district in the south-west, transferred from *Merioneth. It had little in the way of common historical identity, although there was some industrial inheritance, since it included the whole of the North Wales Coalfield. In 1996 it was divided into three new unitary authorities, Denbighshire, Flintshire, and Wrexham, whilst Colwyn on the western border of Clwyd was joined with Aberconwy.

**Cnut** (d. 1035), king of England (1016–35). Cnut, the younger son of the Danish king *Sweyn Forkbeard, campaigned in England by the side of his father, 1013–14. Sweyn forced King *Æthelred into exile and received the submission of all England but died in February 1014. His son took his army back to Denmark after an act of savage brutality when he mutilated his hostages before putting them ashore at Sandwich. He returned in September 1015 and after hard battles with Æthelred's son *Edmund Ironside (d. Nov. 1016) conquered England. For close on 20 years Cnut gave the kingdom a period of substantial peace and prosperity. At a great assembly at Oxford in 1018 he promised to adhere to the laws of King *Edgar. In 1019 he succeeded his elder brother as king of Denmark, and he also gained mastery of Norway in 1028. Cnut made, primarily for political reasons, a Christian marriage to Æthelred's widow *Emma of Normandy, and relied heavily on many of Æthelred's principal advisers, notably Wulfstan, archbishop of York and bishop of Worcester (1002–23). Wulfstan was chiefly responsible for the framing of Cnut's law codes. Local government continued to operate in shires, hundreds, and wapentakes. Cnut exploited to the full the wealth of a basically prosperous England: the regular exaction of geld from the country provided the king with the means to set up stable government. The sophisticated coinage that Cnut had inherited from his predecessors continued to be struck to a high standard. His piety was much more than skin deep and on an impressive visit to Rome in 1027 to attend the coronation of the Emperor Conrad, Cnut took the opportunity to negotiate favourable terms for English traders and pilgrims *en route*. The reputation of Cnut suffered in one respect from sheer biological accident. He died relatively young in 1035. His two sons *Harold Harefoot (by Ælfgifu) and *Harthacnut (by Emma) both died in their early twenties. The return of the ancient dynasty to England in the person of *Edward the Confessor (1042–66) left Cnut with no great apologist among English historical writers. There can be no doubt, however, that medieval Scandinavian historians were well justified in referring to him as 'Cnut the Great'.

**Coalbrookdale** in Shropshire was the site of the great development of the iron industry in the 18th cent. by the Darby family, using local raw materials and the river Severn for transport. The museum complex based on Ironbridge is one of the finest in the country.

**Cobbett, William** (1763–1835). Radical journalist whose *Political Register* (1802–35) was the most influential radical paper of its time. Week after week Cobbett thundered against the political system ('Old Corruption'). Born and raised on a Surrey farm, Cobbett enlisted in 1784, served in Nova Scotia, and was promoted serjeant-major. On returning to England in 1791 he tried unsuccessfully to expose financial corruption in the regiment, and had to flee to France and then to America. In Philadelphia (1792–9) Cobbett patriotically defended Great Britain, and when he returned to England in 1800 was welcomed as a Tory supporter. However, he soon became disenchanted with what he called 'The System' and from 1806 demanded parliamentary reform. Sentenced in 1810 to two years in Newgate gaol for seditious libel, Cobbett was henceforth regarded as a dangerous radical, and when habeas corpus was suspended in 1817 he fled to America. On his return home in 1819 he resumed farming and also wrote some of his finest pieces, published as *Rural Rides*. He was MP for Oldham in the reformed Parliament of 1833.

**Cobden, Richard** (1804–65). A British radical politician, Cobden was devoted to free trade and international peace, and hostile to aristocratic rule. After the successful campaign for the incorporation of Manchester, he joined the *Anti-Corn Law League. Cobden became MP for Southport in 1841 and proved a competent speaker both in and out of Parliament. He was largely responsible for the League's increasing prominence. In 1846 he received from *Peel an exaggerated tribute as the man primarily responsible for repeal of the Corn Laws. Thereafter, Cobden remained a prominent reformer, but opposition to the *Crimean War and *Palmerston's popular foreign policy reduced his influence. In 1859–60 he negotiated an important commercial treaty with France.

**Cochrane, Thomas, 10th earl of Dundonald** [S] (1775–1860). Cochrane had a long and colourful life. In 1793 he joined the navy, in which his uncle was serving. During 1800–1 he commanded the *Speedy*, preying upon Spanish shipping. Next he took up politics, was returned to Parliament in 1806 for Honiton, and then Westminster as partner to Sir Francis Burdett. They formed a radical pair, urging parliamentary reform. In 1814 Cochrane was involved in a Stock Exchange fraud, sentenced to a year in prison, and expelled from Parliament. His Westminster constituents returned him again, but he failed to become a second Wilkes. In 1818, abandoning Parliament, he left for South America, where Spain's colonies were in rebellion, and performed deeds of heroism on behalf of Chile, Peru, and Brazil. He was employed once more 1848–51 as commander-in-chief West Indies and promoted admiral. Cochrane was a vigorous and brave leader of men, but a bad subordinate. An uncomfortable national hero, he was buried in Westminster abbey.

**Cockburn, Henry** (1779–1854). Scottish advocate, judge, and diarist, whose *Memorials of his Time* (1856) remains one of the most vivid accounts of Scottish politics and Edinburgh society. A well-connected Whig who spent his whole life in Edinburgh, a successful and talented criminal advocate, Cockburn was a founder member of the *Edinburgh Review. He became solicitor-general for Scotland in 1830, drafted the Scottish Reform Act, and was promoted to the Scottish bench in 1834. His strongly topographical *Circuit Journeys*, written while he was a circuit judge, is a neglected masterpiece.

**cock-fighting** A ferocious blood-sport, probably introduced by the Romans, in which intensively trained gamecocks with metal or bone spurs were set to fight, usually to the death, on a stage in a circular pit. Mains (matches) were variously structured, with rules, the rowdy spectacles generally accompanied by heavy betting. County competition first showed itself in this sport, usually as three-day events and often associated with race meetings. Opposition grew in the early 19th cent., but although banned in 1835 and 1849, it persisted in coal-mining areas, and may still occur secretly.

**Codrington, Sir Edward** (1770–1851). Codrington was of the Gloucestershire family of baronets and entered the navy in 1783. He served with distinction at the *Glorious First of June in 1794. At *Trafalgar he captained the *Orion*. In 1827 he was given a difficult command in the eastern Mediterranean, where the Greeks were in rebellion against the Turks. His squadron was intended to enforce an armistice but on 20 October an accidental clash with a Turkish fleet led to the Turks' annihilation in *Navarino Bay, on the southwest of the Morea. The British government, while praising Codrington, explained the battle as an 'untoward event'. He was promoted admiral of the blue in 1837 and commanded the Channel fleet from 1839 to 1842.

**coffee-houses** Coffee, tea, and chocolate became available through the *East India Company (founded 1600) and the first coffee-houses, as alternatives to taverns or alehouses, appeared in Oxford (1650) and London (1652). They developed as centres for the exchange and distribution of domestic and foreign news, intelligence, and gossip. Initially they worked in conjunction with the Post Office for the delivery of letters, but by 1700 the well-organized arrangements of the coffee-men were costing the Post Office much revenue.

The class and type of customer varied according to locality, trade, and fashion. They soon became political headquarters, the Cocoa-Tree a famous Tory haunt, Ozinda's for Jacobites, and the Smyrna and St James's coffee-houses for Whigs. They were also used for educational purposes, lodge meetings, assignations, planning robberies, and occasionally for selling slaves. They were beginning to outlive their usefulness by 1830. The remaining coffee-houses reverted easily to taverns or wine-houses, or developed into clubs.

**Cogidubnus,** British king of the *Regni (Regnenses). It is possible that Cogidubnus was a prince of the *Atrebates, for his kingdom included the southern part of the old Atrebatic kingdom. Tacitus records that he was a loyal friend of Rome, and this is confirmed by his forenames—Tiberius Claudius—which reflect Claudius' grant of Roman citizenship. He appears to have been installed in a newly created kingdom by the Romans and to have provided them with a safe base at *Fishbourne on Chichester harbour. The palace built over the site of the Roman camp is likely to have been erected by Cogidubnus, although he may not have lived to see it completed in the late 70s.

**coins and currency** The king's coinage was one of the most visible manifestations of royal authority. The number of mints was carefully controlled and permission to subjects to strike coins granted sparingly. Counterfeiting or clipping the coinage was regarded as a heinous crime. In 1350 Edward III declared counterfeiting to be high treason. As late as 1742 gilding shillings to pass as guineas was made treason. Nor were these idle threats. Phoebe Harris was burned before 20,000 people in 1786 and Christian Murphy in 1789.

At the time of Caesar's invasion in 55 BC coins were circulating in southern England. They were largely imitations of Gaulish coins. Tasciovanus, king of the *Catuvellauni, minted gold, silver, and copper coins (c.20 BC). After AD 43 the Romans substituted their own imperial coinage and by c. AD 430 the import and use of coins seems to have ended.

The peoples who penetrated the Roman empire—Vandals, Visigoths, Lombards, Franks, Angles, and Saxons—soon began to issue their own currency. At first the coins imitated Roman specimens, but later kings substituted their own names and images. In England, gold thrymsas and silver sceats appeared around AD 600. The earliest coins to be struck by an identifiable king came from the short-lived *Peada of Mercia (656). King *Ecgfrith of Northumbria had his name on coins soon after (670–85). In the 750s, Pepin assumed the kingship of the Franks and introduced a completely new silver coinage, using the Latin term 'denarius'. When this was borrowed by the English, they used the name penny but retained the symbol *d.*: twelve denarii made one solidus, and twenty solidi one pound or libra, giving the term £.*s.d.*, which survived until decimalization in 1971. Within a few years *Offa of Mercia was issuing his own silver pennies, which were the main form of currency for the next 600 years. *Edgar carried out a great reform of the coinage (*c.*973), with a system for calling in worn coins for reissue.

There was little alteration in the design of the silver penny in the two centuries following the Norman Conquest. A continuing problem was that of change. With only one denomination, pennies were cut to provide halves and quarters. The *Anglo-Saxon Chronicle* reported in 1124 that a man who took a pound of pennies (240) to market might find only twelve accepted. The coinage was at its worst during the civil war of Stephen's reign, when rival coins circulated, many of them crude.

The later Middle Ages saw a great increase in trade. Edward I carried out a grand recoinage in 1279–80, minting new coins, silver halfpennies and farthings, to remove the need to cut. The innovation of Edward III's reign was the introduction in 1344 of gold coins—a florin (6 shillings), half-florin, and quarter-florin. They were augmented by nobles (80 silver pennies), half- and quarter-nobles. Representations became more interesting. The half-florin had a rather benign leopard (which gave the coin its popular name): the noble had an elaborate scene of Edward III in a two-castled ship, perhaps commemorating his naval victory at *Sluys in 1340. The noble was replaced during the reign of Edward IV by a coin of the same value, a noble-angel, which had a representation of the archangel Michael. It was accompanied by a ryal (from French *royaux*), valued at 10 shillings and with a large Yorkist rose—hence its popular name, rose-noble.

Tudor coinage was marked by three features—fluctuations in the value of the currency; the introduction of a great number of new coins; and the appearance of lifelike representations of the monarchs. Despite the political upheavals of the previous decades, Henry VII inherited a stable currency. But Henry VIII's systematic debasement of the currency from 1526 onwards drove up prices. Elizabeth brought the situation under control with some difficulty. The new coins included a magnificent golden sovereign by Henry VII in 1489 and a half-sovereign; a gold Crown of the Rose at 5 shillings by Henry VIII and a half-crown which settled down later as a silver coin and ran until the 20th cent.; and a George noble in 1526 on which the patron saint made his first appearance. Henry VII's silver shilling carried a good likeness of the king, known as the testoon (from French *tête*). Henceforth the national coinage carried some remarkable portraits—Henry VIII aged on a Bristol groat (1544–7); Edward VI's silver shilling (1550–3); an imperious Elizabeth gold pound (1561–82); a stylish Charles I shilling (1638–9), and a saturnine Charles II crown (1663).

James I celebrated the union of his two kingdoms in 1604 with a gold crown called 'unite' or 'unit', bearing the title 'King of Great Britain' and the legend 'I will make them one people.' But a more important development of his reign was the introduction of copper coinage. Lord Harington in 1613 was given a patent to produce copper farthings, known colloquially as Haringtons, with an intermediate status between coins and tokens.

The Civil War produced some desperate expedients, particularly 'siege-money', made out of any metal to hand and cut into strange shapes. The Commonwealth issued its own coinage, with inscriptions in English: one legend 'God with us' prompted cavaliers to the obvious retort that 'the Commonwealth was on one side and God on the other'.

As soon as he returned from his travels in 1660, Charles II tackled the question of the currency. An innovation was the use of Guinea gold from Africa, which settled at 21 shillings and was called a guinea. The need for small change remained a problem and thousands of tradesmen's tokens circulated. To meet this, Charles introduced copper halfpennies and farthings in 1672: on the new coins, Britannia made her appearance for the first time.

Charles was also king of Scotland and of Ireland. The Scottish coinage dated from David I's reign in the early 12th cent. But the number of coins struck was small, and there were mints only at Edinburgh, Berwick, and Roxburgh. Scottish coins had their own peculiarities. Their international standing was undermined in the 15th and 16th cents. by persistent debasement. At the union of the crowns in 1603 the Scottish pound was fixed at only one-twelfth that of the English. The falling value of the Scottish currency derived in part from the practice of mixing silver with alloy to produce the base metal billon. James I introduced a billon penny and halfpenny: James III followed with a billon plack (from French *plaque*) valued at first at threepence and later at sixpence, a half-plack, and a copper farthing (1466); in James V's reign the bawbee (1½*d.*) and half-bawbee were issued, and in Mary's the hardhead was issued. The billon coinage was discontinued after 1603, but twopence pieces in copper called hardheads, bodles, or turners continued to be issued until the Act of Union.

The earliest known Irish coins were minted by Sihtric Olafsson in the Viking kingdom of Dublin after 990 and were copies of English silver pennies. No regular coinage was issued until after the Norman Conquest when John introduced coins stamped with a harp. There were no gold coins and, as in Scotland, silver was heavily alloyed. In the Tudor period the Irish coinage suffered great debasement, as did the Scots and English. In 1689 James II issued a bronze currency known as 'gun-money' which, after his defeat at the Boyne, was bought in at metal value—less than 3 per cent of its face value. The fury caused by *Wood's halfpence in 1723 had less to do with the coins, which were of respectable quality, than the state of Anglo-Irish relations.

In Wales, no coins were struck until after the Norman invasion. Coin hoards have been found in Wales dating to the 9th, 10th, and 11th cents., but the coins were foreign, mainly English, Viking, or Arabic. *Hywel Dda's silver penny (*c.*940) was minted at Chester, copied an English coin, and may have been a presentation piece.

One persistent problem was the weight of coins. Individual merchants and financiers had long issued personal bills of exchange, from which developed the cheque and the banknote. The earliest extant cheque, dated 1659, is preserved in the Institute of Banking Library and is for £400. Paper credit expanded rapidly and by the end of the 17th cent. it was calculated that England and Wales had £11.6 million circulating as coins, but tallies, banknotes, and bills worth £15 million. The Bank of England began issuing large-denomination printed notes in 1725.

At the time of the great recoinage of 1696 bimetallism was still the basis of the British currency, silver and gold providing the main-

stay. Later in the 18th cent. declining production of silver made it excessively expensive and the currency went over to gold almost completely. There was continuing difficulty about small change. Some of George III's copper coins ('cartwheels') were too heavy to be practicable since they were intended to contain their own value in copper. The result was that the country was again flooded with token coins.

Four developments in the 20th cent. may be noted. Substantial inflation, particularly after the Second World War, caused several coins to be abandoned: the farthing, beloved of haberdashers, was withdrawn in 1960, and the halfpenny, which survived decimalization in 1971, succumbed in 1984. Secondly, in 1971 the whole coinage was decimalized in preparation for Britain's entry into the EEC. Thirdly, there was fierce debate in the 1990s whether Britain should join a European currency. Fourthly, the spread of credit cards and electronic banking meant that coinage played a smaller part in financial transactions, heralding the day when money would be carried only for sundry purchases like sweets and newspapers.

## Coke, Sir Edward

**Coke, Sir Edward** (1552–1634). Lawyer, judge, and parliamentary figure. Coke was called to the bar in 1578. In 1592 he became recorder of London and later that year solicitor-general. In 1593 the queen appointed him Speaker of the House of Commons and then attorney-general. Coke conducted a number of famous prosecutions for the crown, with unfeeling harshness, including the trials of *Essex (1601), Sir Walter *Ralegh (1603), and the Gunpowder plot conspirators (1605). In 1606 he became chief justice of Common Pleas. Coke held that the royal prerogative was defined by law and could not be arbitrarily extended. In 1613 he was transferred to the King's Bench, a post with more prestige but less influence. Then in 1616 Coke was removed from office altogether. In 1621 Coke re-entered Parliament where he opposed monopolies. His last major political act was his role in drafting the *Petition of Right in 1628.

**Coke, Thomas William, 1st earl of Leicester** (1754–1842). 'Coke of Norfolk' was an assertively Whig MP for Norfolk for over 50 years. He is remembered as an agricultural improver. New crop rotations raised production: turnips (winter food for sheep) preceded grain, followed by sown grass (summer food for sheep) leading again to grain; sheep fertilized for wheat and barley. Publicity for Coke's work has caused neglect of the agricultural improvements of his great-uncle Thomas Coke (1697–1759), earl of Leicester (1744).

**Colchester** First 'capital' of Roman Britain. Camulodunum was the site of the most important late Iron Age *oppidum* of southern Britain, seat of *Cunobelinus (Cymbeline). After its surrender in AD 43 a legionary fortress was planted. A temple to the deified Claudius was under construction when the entire town was burned to the ground in the revolt of *Boudicca. Town and temple were reconstructed.

**Cold War** The antagonism between the USA and USSR lasting from the late 1940s until the late 1980s, 'cold' because it was waged through diplomatic and ideological means rather than force. Britain was allied to the USA. The Cold War came to an end with the collapse of Soviet power, largely as a result of its intervention in Afghanistan, and its progress towards democracy.

**Coleridge, Samuel Taylor** (1772–1834). Poet and polymath whose collaboration with *Wordsworth laid the foundations for English Romanticism. Their *Lyrical Ballads* (1798) opened with his 'Rime of the Ancient Mariner'. Dogged by ill-health and self-doubt, his poetic career was brief and littered with unfulfilled projects: the incomplete 'Christabel'; 'Kubla Khan' famously interrupted by 'a person from Porlock'. Though no friend to *Pitt's ministry, his 'baby trumpet of sedition' was already muted, and his last substantial work, *On the Constitution of Church and State* (1830), finds him staunchly defending them as 'two poles of the same magnet'.

**Colet, John** (1467–1519). Colet, a cleric and educator, was born in London and probably attended Cambridge University before travelling to Paris and Orléans, and to Italy. About 1496 Colet began to teach in Oxford, gaining a reputation for his exposition of the meaning of the Pauline Epistles. Colet's piety and eloquence impressed Erasmus from their first meeting in 1499; he was later Erasmus'

patron and helper. As dean of St Paul's from 1505 to his death of the sweating sickness in 1519, Colet refounded and endowed St Paul's School (1509).

**College of Arms** Established in 1484 by Richard III to bring order into the approval of heraldic designs. Garter king-of-arms has precedence though his concerns are mainly with his order. Clarenceux king-of-arms looks after the area south of the Trent, Norroys king-of-arms the area north and Ulster. Scottish heraldry is the responsibility of the Lyon Office under Lord Lyon king-of-arms.

**Collingwood, Cuthbert, 1st Baron** (1750–1810). The Newcastle upon Tyne-born Collingwood had no influence behind him, unlike *Nelson, when he joined the navy in 1761. In dauntless courage Collingwood was unquestionably Nelson's equal, but a natural stoicism assisted Collingwood to more balanced judgements. Present at the '*Glorious First of June' battle 1794, and at *Cape St Vincent in February 1797, Collingwood ruefully accepted not being within Nelson's command which resulted in victory at the *Nile; and admiral rank only came in February 1799. At *Trafalgar Collingwood commanded the *Royal Sovereign*, devastatingly opening the action at midday, and taking command of the fleet on Nelson's death at 4.30 p.m. Raised to the peerage, Collingwood died at sea in March 1810, but was buried close to Nelson in St Paul's.

**Collins, Michael** (1890–1922). Collins is the best-known 20th-cent. Irish revolutionary leader. From a west Cork farming background, he moved to London at 15. He played a background role in Dublin during the *Easter Rising. After internment, Collins became the key figure in the reorganized Irish Volunteers/*Irish Republican Army. Against his will, he was a negotiator at the Anglo-Irish conference of October–December 1921, revealing his pragmatism by signing the *Anglo-Irish treaty. As chairman of provisional government January–June 1922, Collins presided over the establishment of the new state while striving to appease anti-treaty former colleagues. While visiting pro-treaty troops as commander-in-chief, he was killed in a west Cork ambush on 22 August 1922.

**Colonial Office** The changes in the status and structure of the Colonial Office mirror the vicissitudes of the British empire. For most of the 17th cent., while the American colonies were being established, there was no co-ordinating body at Westminster. Not until 1696 was a Board of Trade and Plantations established under a president, working through the Privy Council. In 1768 a third secretaryship was created for the colonies, usually known as the American secretary. By 1782, with the rebellious colonies almost gone, both the third secretaryship and the Board of Trade were abolished, though the latter was revived in 1786. Colonial affairs went to the home secretary. In 1794, a third secretaryship was re-established under Henry *Dundas, with responsibility for war and the colonies. Indian affairs meanwhile fell to the Board of Control, set up in 1784. These rather makeshift arrangements sufficed until 1854, when a fourth secretary of state with special responsibility for the colonies was created. A further reorganization took place in 1925 when a new Dominions Office was created with its own secretary of state. The extraordinarily rapid decolonization in the 1960s left the Colonial Office with few territories to administer. The secretaryship was abolished in 1966 and the Colonial Office merged with the Commonwealth Relations Office. They were both integrated into the Foreign Office in October 1968.

**Columba, St** (d. 597). Founder, in 565, of the monastery of *Iona, which contributed to conversion in Northumbria, Mercia, and Pictland. Born between 519 and 522 into the Cenél Conaill of Donegal branch of the northern royal Uí Néill, Columba had founded Derry in the 550s before his condemnation at the Synod of Teltown (Co. Meath), for involvement in the battle of Cúl Drebene (561), prompted him to be pilgrim-exile in the southern part of *Dalriada. There King Conall gave him Iona (574). His political eminence may explain why he was regarded as one whose prayers gained victory for favoured kings, including *Oswald.

**Columbanus, St** (c.543–615). Born in Leinster (Ireland), Columbanus entered religious life as a young man. Fired with missionary zeal, he left the monastery at Bangor c.590 with twelve companions. He greatly influenced the spread of monasticism in Gaul, attracting many followers. Driven out of Burgundy in 610 by Queen Brunhilde for criticizing her grandson's immorality, Columbanus settled in Lombardy, founding his great monastic centre at Bobbio, where he died.

**Combination Acts**, 1799–1800. These Acts were directed against trade unions (combinations of workmen) when the government feared unrest and even revolution. They failed to crush the unions, but did force them to operate circumspectly or secretly. Repeal of the Acts came in 1824–5 after a campaign master-minded by *Place and presented by Joseph *Hume, and was followed by an upsurge in trade union activity.

**'commercial revolution'** This preceded major industrialization by two centuries and encompassed great upsurges in overseas trade. There were three long periods of growth, separated by virtual stagnation. Between 1475 and 1550 existing markets for English broadcloths and other woollens grew rapidly, because the importing regions became more prosperous. In the second period, 1630–89, two general circumstances aided expansion. South European markets were won by the English and the Dutch in competition with one another. The second circumstance was the rise of virtually new trades because cheaper English re-exports of sugar, tobacco, and calicoes created fresh markets. The third period, 1730–60, was linked to the growth of American and West Indian populations, production, and purchasing power.

In the first period English woollen cloth exports were the bulwark of overseas trade, the wool trade declining sharply after 1510. In a period of inflation the quantity of cloth exported more than doubled by 1550; London gained at the expense of provincial ports, as trade with Antwerp grew and was controlled by the Company of *Merchant Venturers.

The second expansion in the 17th cent. can be largely attributed to the growth of exports to southern Europe. Demand increased in Spain and was supplemented from Portugal and Italy. Light cloths or 'New Draperies' were attractive to these markets and increasingly beat Dutch competition.

Several new imports in the period 1500–1750 provided exceptional profit margins. In the 16th cent. the chief imports were luxuries, especially French wine, but in the following century Spain and Portugal became important suppliers. Apart from wine, most imports were manufactures, bought in the Netherlands but produced in many parts of Europe. The gradual growth of British industry reduced the dependence on foreign manufactures in the 17th cent. Trade with the Baltic became more direct because of the activities of the *Eastland Company (1579). In years of bad harvests Baltic corn was a standby, but after 1650 new raw materials were much more important. Amounts of timber, potash, tar, pitch, flax, and hemp increased as the navy and merchant marine grew, and Swedish iron also became important after 1650.

Trade with countries beyond Europe, insignificant before the Civil War, grew rapidly by 1700 when America and Asia accounted for a third of England's imports. The discoveries that Virginia could grow tobacco plants and that Brazilian sugar cane would flourish in the West Indies were fundamental to the later development of the Atlantic economy and of the triangular trade with Africa. The *East India Company (1600) began trading principally in pepper and then in cotton cloth. Trade in slaves, sugar, coffee, tobacco, pepper, and oriental cottons underpinned the third great era of expansion in the 18th cent. before industrialization had proceeded far. Liverpool, Bristol, and Glasgow benefited most from these developments.

The Atlantic trade was controlled by merchant partnerships. If journeys were long or large capitals were required, the company form of organization was preferable. Once trade was established the return to trading by partnerships was general. The *Russia Company (1555), the *Levant Company (1581), and the *Royal Africa Company (1672) all succumbed to this pattern; only the *Hudson's Bay Company (1670) retained control over its territory. The East India Company also survived and was much the most important in terms of trade and capital employed.

The 'commercial revolution' was important for its effects upon the British economy and the British state. It was buttressed by protective mercantilism, especially by the navigation laws; its result was the accumulation of capital from foreign trade. Foreign produce brought profits to distributors involved in inland trade. Merchant investment in land was probably more important than capital flows to industry, but the growth of London was exceptional in Europe.

**Commius** was a Gallic noble who allied himself with Julius *Caesar and was rewarded with the kingship of the Gallic *Atrebates. In 55 BC he was sent by Caesar to win over British tribes prior to the invasion, but was taken prisoner. Released at the end of the 55 BC invasion, he participated in the 54 BC invasion. In 52 BC he sided with the revolt of Vercingetorix in Gaul, and on his defeat fled to Britain, founding a new dynasty of the Atrebates.

**common law** The origins of the common law lay in the justice of the king, exercised through his *curia regis, rather than the customary law exercised in the old communal courts of shire and hundred, or the feudal law exercised by the lord in relation to his own vassals. As overlord of all subjects, the king had a residual right to give justice to all, and as feudal lord of the tenants-in-chief he had the right and the duty to sit in his curia regis to hear their disputes. Until the reign of Henry II, royal justice was available to subjects who were not tenants-in-chief only in exceptional cases. However, in the reign of Henry II, access to the king's justice was extended by the enactment of a principle that 'no man need answer for his freehold land without the king's writ being obtained'. As these royal writs became popular with litigants, they increasingly sought the justice of the king's courts rather than the local or feudal courts, which slowly declined.

The king's justice was dispensed by the itinerant justices of the curia regis. When the courts of Common Pleas, King's Bench, and Exchequer developed as separate entities, the law they applied was the common law. By the time of Edward I there was in existence a 'common law'—the law administered in the king's courts throughout the land and therefore 'common' to the whole kingdom.

The term 'common law' came to be used of the English legal system and, generally, to describe a system where the law is built up through the decisions of the courts. The term is therefore used to describe rules of law which have been established by the courts as against laws which are formally enacted by Parliament (statute law).

**Common Market** *See* EUROPEAN ECONOMIC COMMUNITY.

**Common Pleas, Court of** One of the three courts of common law. The Court of Common Pleas was an offshoot of the *curia regis, the court which followed the king on his travels around the country. The insistence of *Magna Carta led to a court being established in one place. The court was based at Westminster Hall. In the Middle Ages it was the busiest of the common law courts. Over the centuries this position declined as other courts encroached on its jurisdiction. In the Judicature Act of 1873 the Court of Common Pleas along with the courts of Queen's Bench and Exchequer all became divisions of the High Court of Justice. Ultimately, they were all merged into the Queen's Bench Division in 1880.

**Commons, House of** From modest beginnings, the House of Commons has progressed until it shares effective sovereignty with the prime minister. Commoners were summoned to Parliament at first less for their advice than for their consent to taxation. Knights of the shire were first called to Parliament in 1254 and in Simon de *Montfort's Parliament of 1265 they were joined by representatives from certain boroughs and cities. Early usage was extremely fluid, with committees and groups joining for plenary sessions. From the early 14th cent. the Commons began to meet as a separate house. The knights stayed with the citizens rather than joining the baronage, with whom they had much in common, adding great weight to the Commons house. The lesser clergy, who had been represented in some early parliaments, dropped out after 1340 and used *convocation, making it easier for the Commons to cohere as a body.

The Commons soon began to act as a channel for receiving petitions and took the lead in legislating to remove grievances. Their chief weapon was control of taxation and as early as 1395 the formula was in use that the grant was made 'by the Commons with the advice and assent of the Lords'. The use of Parliament by the Tudors to regulate the succession to the throne and to reform the church enhanced the standing of that body. Two further developments helped to confirm the Commons' identity. In 1547 they were granted St Stephen's chapel as their meeting place and stayed there until the great fire of 1834. At the same time, the House began a formal record of its own proceedings, the *Journals of the House of Commons*.

The result of the great struggles of the 17th cent. was to increase the power of the Commons at the expense of the Lords. Indeed, when the Commons in 1649 galloped out of control, Lords and monarchy were abolished as 'dangerous and useless'. Though the pendulum swung back after 1660, the strengthened position of Parliament after 1688 helped the Commons, particularly by limiting the power of the crown to govern without Parliament or to retain a complaisant Parliament. In addition the Commons reasserted its sole right to decide matters of taxation. Though the House of Lords retained considerable influence, the balance was further affected by the extensions of the franchise from 1832 onwards, which increased the Commons' claim to speak for the nation, and by a slow loss of faith in the hereditary principle.

The starting-point of any discussion of the modern House of Commons is two related features—the near dominance of the executive and the ever-present power of the political parties. Among the functions of the House of Commons, that of legislation would be given pride of place. But legislation bears the stamp of the executive: most important bills are introduced by the government of the day. Popular criticism of the modern role of the House of Commons focuses on the alleged rigour of party control over the backbenchers, and tends to overlook the advantage the executive would have, even if the House were composed of 659 genuinely independent members.

Note first the long-standing rule that increases in taxation can be imposed only on the proposal of the crown. Any private member who sponsors a bill that would increase public expenditure must either obtain the backing of the government or impose the new duties on local councils. More recent procedural changes allocate most of the time of the House to the government. Private members are allotted ten days a year for the discussion of their bills and the privilege of being awarded a day is decided by ballot.

A second element of the strength of the executive lies in its near monopoly of knowledge. Ministers are backed by an experienced and informed department: the backbencher has only his personal resources. In the 1960s, the House made fitful attempts to form specialized select committees to inquire into particular areas of government activity, and these arrangements were made permanent in 1979. Service on these select committees certainly makes for more informed backbenchers. But the select committees do not themselves examine legislation: this remains the province of the transient and unspecialized standing committees.

The third feature is party loyalty and party organization. Virtually every member (bar the Speaker) is elected as the candidate of a party, and members most of the time vote in the House with their party. Many explanations have been offered for the strength of party cohesion in the British Parliament. The whips cannot in themselves deny reselection to a dissident member, though withdrawal of the whip can rouse difficulties with the member's constituency association. In both parties the hope of office, and in the Conservative Party the thirst for honours, may prompt the potential rebel back into line.

The government then is the dominant force in the legislation passed by the House. But in exercising these and other powers it is accountable to the House. Traditionally this accountability has been exercised most obviously through question time. The value of question time, however, is greatly exaggerated. The Labour government of 1997 curtailed it to one period a week, usually dominated by 'sound-bites' from the prime minister and the leader of the Opposition. The ordinary process of debate is another way in which members can highlight blunders or mismanagement. But members may well be inhibited from embarrassing a minister of their own party by the delight it affords their opponents. Today, the select committees, with all their limitations, are becoming the chief means by which ministers are made accountable to the House. Even though they do not debate legislation, they enable the House to scrutinize the work of departments, and the publicity given to their reports is a salutary check upon ministerial evasion and bureaucratic complacency.

**Commonwealth** The Commonwealth took its origins from a vote by the *Rump Parliament on 4 January 1649, 'That the people are, under God, the original of all just power', and that they, the Commons, possessed supreme authority as the people's representatives. Two days later they set up the High Court of Justice which tried Charles I. The abolition of the monarchy and the House of Lords followed, and another brief Act on 19 May formally declared England to be a Commonwealth. From February, executive authority was vested in a *Council of State, accountable to the Rump, elected annually by it, and drawn mainly from its own members.

The Commonwealth expanded to include Scotland and Ireland after the army's conquest of those countries. The Rump's materialist outlook and evident aversion to 'a godly reformation' brought it under increasing pressure from the army during 1652 to make way for a successor. Eventually it did introduce a bill for a new parliament to meet in November 1653, but its contents (which do not survive) left the army unsatisfied, and Cromwell in a rage expelled the Rump on 20 April. The brief experiment of a nominated assembly ('*Barebone's Parliament', July–December 1653) ended in its own abdication, and on 16 December the Commonwealth gave way to the Cromwellian *Protectorate. It was briefly restored in May 1659, after a coup by the army against Richard *Cromwell, but renewed quarrels between the officers and the Rumpers soon exposed the political bankruptcy of both. General *Monck was enthusiastically acclaimed when he opened the way to the Restoration by readmitting the members 'secluded' in Pride's Purge on 21 February 1660.

**Commonwealth of Nations** The present Commonwealth comprises Britain and most of her old empire: 53 states, scattered over all the inhabited continents, with a population estimated (in 2008) at 1.9 billion. Mozambique, not a former British colony, was admitted as a special case in 1995.

The term 'commonwealth', in this context, dates from the early 20th cent., and grew out of the realization that several of Britain's older-established colonies were already self-governing in all essential respects. To call them 'colonies', or an 'empire', appeared to undervalue their real independence, and the new word was felt by some to express better the form the empire would take: a federation of equal nation states. This development was not to everyone's liking, however. Enthusiasts for the 'commonwealth ideal' had generally envisaged the dominions taking an equal share in the formulation of policies that would then be common to them all: instead it came to mean that they would have equal rights to separate policies of their own.

This privilege was established in the early 1920s, after disputes within the Commonwealth over the Washington naval conference of 1921–2 and the *Chanak affair in 1922. In 1923 Canada became the first dominion to conclude a treaty with a foreign power (the Halibut Fish treaty) without reference to Britain; and the pattern for the future was set. It was formalized by an important pronouncement of the 1926 imperial conference, defining dominion status; and by the 1931 statute of *Westminster, which confirmed the dominions' legislative autonomy. For the moment this only applied to colonies of European settlement, and not to the 'non-white' colonies. That changed in 1947, when the newly independent nation of India was admitted to the Commonwealth. That established the multiracial character of the Commonwealth as it exists today.

As *decolonization progressed, other ex-colonies followed. Many old imperialists regarded this process with pride. Some of them saw the new Commonwealth as the culmination of the empire. In a way it was, for there had always been a strong tradition of what was called 'trusteeship' in British imperial thought. The idea that the Commonwealth could be a kind of empire-substitute, however, was soon shattered. The newest members regarded their hard-won national independence jealously, and there were sharp clashes between members, especially over the issue of apartheid, which forced South Africa to leave in 1961. So the Commonwealth became much less than the united 'third force' in the world that the imperial optimists had envisaged.

As it stands now, it is totally unlike any other international organization of states. It has a secretariat, and a secretary-general (set up in 1965), but little else in common. It has

no power, no united policy, no common principles, and no shared institutions. Most member states are parliamentary democracies, but not all. Most have retained English legal forms, but not all. Most play cricket, but not all. The single constitutional feature common to all member states is that they acknowledge the British monarch as symbolic head of the Commonwealth, but fewer than half recognize her or him as the head of their own states. It was once thought of as an economic unit, a potential free (or preferential) trade area, but that was never convincing, and collapsed when Britain joined the *European Economic Community in 1973.

Nevertheless the Commonwealth still serves a purpose, as a forum for informal discussion and co-operation between nations of widely disparate cultures. That function is served by a host of specialist Commonwealth institutions (the Commonwealth Institute in London, the Commonwealth Parliamentary Association, the Association of Commonwealth Universities, the Commonwealth of Learning); and by biennial conferences of Commonwealth heads of government. The ideal it represents still flickers, albeit fitfully.

**Common Wealth Party** Formed in 1942, Common Wealth was a merger of a movement Forward March, formed by the Liberal MP Sir Richard Acland, and the 1941 Committee of the playwright J. B. Priestley. An idealistic, socialist party, its membership was heavily middle class. The major parties had an electoral truce during the war, which gave a great fillip to Common Wealth. Once the electoral truce was over, Common Wealth suffered the fate of most new parties in Britain. After the election of 1945, Acland called upon the party to dissolve and for its members to enrol with Labour as individuals.

**Communist Party of Great Britain**
The success of the Bolshevik Revolution produced a realignment of the left and the Communist Party was founded in 1920. It gained two MPs in 1922, one of them under Labour colours. Such strength as the new party had was largely in south Wales and industrialized Scotland. Modest success came in 1935 when Willie Gallacher won the West Fife seat. The party pursued a grimly Stalinist

line and the outbreak of the Second World War produced vigorous intellectual gymnastics. The anti-fascist conflict to be won at all costs in September 1939 became an 'unjust and imperialist' war a month later when Stalin, now in alliance with Hitler, made it clear that his British comrades had made a false diagnosis. The German attack on the Soviet Union in 1941 produced another reappraisal. No great breakthrough followed, and the development of the Cold War forced it onto the defensive. The collapse of the Soviet Union in 1989 produced another reappraisal. One group resolved to change its name to the Democratic Left: their opponents retained the old name. At the general election of 1997 the five Communist candidates polled one-eighth of the collective vote of the Monster Raving Loony Party.

**commutation** was the change from meeting feudal obligations in labour or in kind to cash payments. It had obvious advantages for the lord, since serf labour was often grudging and unenthusiastic, while the serf knew more precisely what his obligations were and could plan his time. A process which began in the 12th cent. accelerated in the 14th, and was almost completed by the 16th cent.

**companies, trading** Trading companies monopolized overseas trade, made great fortunes, and played a part in the history of imperialism. The state supported their power and the companies made the state rich. The most important early English example was the Merchants of the *Staple which ran the wool trade from the 12th to 14th cents. It was followed, at the end of the 15th cent., by the *Merchant Venturers of London, monopolists of the expanding cloth industry's overseas trade. In the last quarter of the 16th cent. English overseas trade boomed. The French, Spanish, Russian, Barbary, Levant, and Eastland (Baltic) companies all date from this time. However the development of an effective navy at the end of the 17th cent. put an end to the need for monopoly trading in Europe; only those companies that went across the world, such as the East India Company (1600), still needed to protect themselves.

**Compton, Henry** (1632–1713). Bishop of London. Royalist son of the earl of North-

ampton, Compton served in the new Horse Guards (from 1661), before graduating from Queen's College, Oxford (1666). Following ordination he was successively canon of Christ Church (1669–74), and bishop of Oxford (1674–5) and of London (1675–1713), where he was also responsible for the education of Princesses Mary and Anne, James's protestant daughters. James II suspended him (1685). He was one of seven inviting William to England (1688). Restored to his see, he briefly acted as primate, crowning William and Mary (April 1689), during *Sancroft's suspension.

**compurgation** or law-wager was an Anglo-Saxon defence against an accusation by bringing a number of persons to testify to one's innocence as character witnesses. The laws of King *Ine laid down rules for the status of the compurgators. The practice gradually fell into disuse after the Norman Conquest.

**Comyn, John** (d. 1303), known as the 'Red Comyn'. A guardian (regent) of Scotland during the interregnum between Alexander III's death (1286) and John Balliol's accession (1292). He helped to negotiate the treaty of *Birgham and subsequently supported Balliol, his brother-in-law, as king of Scots. He submitted to Edward I in 1296, but had joined William *Wallace by December 1297.

**Comyn, John** (d. 1306), the 'Red Comyn'. Son and heir of John *Comyn, he was a leading Scottish patriot. A devoted supporter of his uncle King John Balliol, he remained steadfastly loyal after Balliol's enforced abdication, and served from 1298 as a guardian or regent of Scotland in Balliol's name. His murder by Bruce in the Franciscan church, Dumfries, was probably provoked by his refusal to desert Balliol and support Bruce's bid for the throne.

**Confederation of British Industry (CBI).** The CBI emerged in 1965 from a group of older employers' organizations, the Federation of British Industries, the British Employers' Confederation, and the National Association of British Manufacturers, and like its predecessors aimed to influence economic decisions taken by governments. It is the most powerful lobbying group on behalf of employers.

**Congregation, Lords of,** 1557. A group of Scottish nobles who pledged their lives to maintain, set forward, and establish the reformed religion in Scotland. Signed by the earls of Argyll, Glencairn, and *Morton, Lord Lorne, and Erskine of Dun, this 'Common Band' was a protestant response to the increasing domination of Scotland by France during the regency of *Mary of Guise.

**congregationalists** were one of the main protestant dissenting sects. Since they believed strongly in the autonomy of each congregation, they were also known as independents or separatists. The first congregations were established in the late 16th cent. and increased rapidly during the Civil War period. Another great expansion took place in the early 19th cent. and at the time of the religious census of 1851 they were said to have 3,244 churches in England and Wales—more than the *baptists though less than a third of the *methodists. The Congregational Union, formed in 1831, was necessarily a loose federation: in 1972 it joined with the Presbyterian Church of England to form the United Reformed Church.

**Congress system** Formally set up by article VI of the *Quadruple Alliance, signed with the second treaty of *Paris (20 November 1815). It had been foreshadowed in the treaty of *Chaumont of March 1815, when the principal allies against Napoleon—Austria, Great Britain, Prussia, and Russia—resolved to remain united after the war to safeguard the peace. Congresses met four times, at Aix-la-Chapelle (1818), Troppau (1820), Laibach (1821), and Verona (1822). The Congress system broke down because of the divergent aims of its members, the eastern powers wishing to use it to 'police' Europe, Britain insisting that it was intended only to secure the peace settlement. But it foreshadowed the peacekeeping efforts of the *League of Nations and the *United Nations in the 20th cent.

**Congreve, William** (1670–1729). English poet and playwright. Educated at Kilkenny School and Trinity College, Dublin, Congreve quickly gave up law for literature. After *Incognita* (1691) Congreve found his *métier* in witty comedy, establishing his reputation with *The Old Batchelour* (1693), *The Double Dealer* (1693), *Love for Love* (1695), and *The Way of the World* (1700). Disappointed by the recep-tion of this last play, Congreve gave up writing for the stage.

**Connacht (Connaught),** taking its name from the mythical Irish figure, Conn of the Hundred Battles, was, by the 8th cent., dominated by the Uí Briúin dynasty. Their hegemony was threatened by Anglo-Norman colonization in the 13th cent., led by the de Burgh family. The establishment of the presidency of Connacht in 1570 and the shiring of the province thereafter led to piecemeal plantation, and in the aftermath of the rebellion of *1641 surviving catholic landholders were transported there, a process summed up in the aphorism ascribed to *Cromwell 'To hell or Connacht!' It played a significant part in the *1798 rebellion, witnessing the landing of the French General Humbert at Killala, and Connacht was also the scene of much activity in the Land Wars of the late 19th cent., most memorably in the incident involving the land-agent Captain Boycott.

**Connolly, James** (1868–1916). Author and union leader, Connolly was the most important Irish socialist. Though unsuccessful in an attempt to reconcile socialism and nationalism, he remains a great influence in Ireland and Scotland. Born in Edinburgh, Connolly joined the British army. Self-educated, he became a socialist organizer in Belfast and Dublin, founding the Irish Socialist Republican Party 1896 and 'the Workers' Republic' 1898. In 1910, he organized the Irish Transport and General Workers' Union with James *Larkin and led the strike following a lock-out in 1913. Badly wounded in the *Easter Rising, he was executed strapped to a chair.

**Conrad, Joseph** (1857–1924). Writer. Conrad was born in the Ukraine, son of a revolutionary who was sent into internal exile. He went to sea, first visiting England in 1878 and becoming a British citizen in 1886. Though he never spoke English fluently, he wrote in it, publishing *Almayer's Folly* in 1895. It was followed rapidly by *An Outcast of the Islands* (1896), *The Nigger of the 'Narcissus'* (1897), *Lord Jim* (1900), and *Nostromo* (1904). Conrad drew on his own experiences at sea to write adventures with a moral dimension. In *Lord Jim*, Jim, chief mate of the *Patna*, 'eaten up with rust', abandons ship unnecessarily, is disgraced, and redeems himself by sacrificing his life.

'Heart of Darkness' (1902), a long short story, based on Conrad's time in the Congo, is, among other things, a sharp critique of imperialism.

**conscription** In 1914 Britain was the only great power which relied upon volunteers to man its army. This tradition was continued until January 1916, by when nearly 2.5 million men had volunteered. But by the summer of 1915 the flow of volunteers was failing to keep pace with the anticipated rate of casualties. Asquith compromised. In January 1916 legislation was passed conscripting single men, followed in May by a second Act conscripting married men. In 1939, conscription was introduced at once.

**Conservative Party** The less reformist of the (normally) two main parties in British politics. It has a longer history than any other political party, perhaps anywhere, with an institutional continuity under that name from the early 1830s, though it drew upon older traditions including a church and king *Toryism. The matrix of 19th-cent. Conservatism lay in the younger *Pitt's government, a cause given wider appeal and sharper focus by its resistance to the *Jacobinism of revolutionary France. A long near-monopoly of government ended only in 1830 when issues like *catholic emancipation and parliamentary reform broke up old solidarities. The Reform Bill struggle of 1831-2, though a defeat, was a crucible of party development and the newly named Conservative Party set itself to limit further damage to established institutions.

The party operated in competition with the Whig Party, which, with its radical allies, developed into the *Liberal Party. The disintegration of the Liberals in the early 20th cent. meant the Conservatives' main challenge came from the trade union-based Labour Party mobilizing the working-class vote. That change also involved a shift in the dominant issues. The Victorian Conservative Party had been identified with the defence of the constitution and the interests associated with it: the monarchy and House of Lords, the established churches, the Union with Ireland, landownership, property rights and inheritance, a limited franchise. From around the Great War these traditional causes were largely superseded by socio-economic issues. The main threats identified

by the party were now trade unionism, egalitarianism, redistributive welfare, socialism, and Bolshevism. The Conservatives became more a party of business and more clearly the party of middle-class interests. Its leaders now came to be drawn from the business and professional classes rather than the landed and titled. At the same time nearly a third of the working classes has usually supported the Conservatives for reasons of patriotic identity, resentment of immigrant groups, hostility to catholics or dissenters, or just a sense of economic interest.

The Conservatives spent most of the period 1830-86 in opposition. Only two general elections, 1841 and 1874, were won. Franchise extensions and advancing urbanization and industrialization handicapped the party and its 1846 split over the *Corn Laws left long-term damage. It then benefited from the comparable Liberal split over *Irish Home Rule in 1886 and was maintained in office by the *Liberal Unionists for most of the next 20 years. Though hit by the Parliament Act removing the absolute veto of the Conservative-dominated House of Lords in 1911 and by the progress of Home Rule, the Conservatives gained from the Great War, which brought them back into government and divided the Liberals again. After the war, the Conservatives, who gained most of the disintegrating Liberal vote, established themselves as the dominant party, and controlled the *National Government coalition from 1931. The Second World War undermined this position: it brought Labour into government and to the management of the 'home front', and the 1945 general election was lost decisively by the Conservatives. The 1945-51 Labour government established a 'post-war consensus' around a mixed economy, the welfare state, and a commitment to full employment. Conservative governments from 1951 to 1964 were founded on acceptance of this legacy. What was left of the colonial empire was liquidated. The party had come to terms with full democracy. With the breakdown of this domestic consensus by the 1970s under pressure of rising inflation, labour disputes, increasing unemployment, and declining economic competitiveness, the party turned (perhaps returned) sharply towards the free-market economics represented by the *Thatcher government of 1979-90. This tenure of office and four successive general election victories were assisted by divisions within the Labour Party. Though the 20th cent. stands more than the 19th as 'the Conservative century', Conservative dominance of government owed much to the fragmentation of the political left.

The Conservative Party has never had a clear ideological identity: its political practice has generally been pragmatic, geared to the needs of electoral success and office-holding. Three heavy election defeats (1997, 2001, 2005) forced the Conservative Party into a reappraisal of its political position and led to a rapid procession of party leaders (John *Major, William *Hague, Iain *Duncan Smith, Michael *Howard, David *Cameron). The most recent policy aims at presenting a softer image of the party. Though the Conservatives have made much progress in restoring their position in local government, their relative weakness in Wales and Scotland remains a severe handicap.

**consistory courts** The consistory court was the court of a bishop for his diocese and was the normal forum for deciding serious cases of defamation and matters relating to wills of personal property. Where the consistory court found the defendant guilty of defamation it could impose penance. The court was normally presided over by the chancellor, a layman, and appeal lay from its decision to the court of the archbishop.

**constable** One of the great medieval offices of state, derived from *comes stabuli*, count of the stables. The first lord high constable was a supporter of the Empress *Matilda, who made him earl of Hereford. It then passed to the Bohuns, on to *Thomas of Woodstock, and to his descendant Edward, duke of *Buckingham, executed by Henry VIII in 1521. It had acquired responsibility for the mobilization of the army, for the enforcement of martial law, and for adjudication on matters of chivalry. Scottish constables commanded the army and from the time of Robert I the office became hereditary in the Hay family, earls of Erroll.

**Constable, John** (1776–1837). Landscape painter, born at East Bergholt (Suffolk), the son of a miller. At first intended for the church, then to follow his father, eventually Constable was allowed to go to London to study at the Royal Academy Schools. Encouraged by Benjamin *West, Constable

rarely painted outside the genre of landscape: 'my art is to be found under every hedge.' In 1819 he became ARA, but a further ten years elapsed before he was elected a full academician.

**Constantín, son of Fergus** (d. 820), king of Picts (from 790) and of Scottish *Dalriada (from 811). Constantín was the first king to rule by right over both Picts and Scottish Gaels. After defeating a rival in 789, he reigned first as king of the Picts, only in 811 taking the kingship of Dalriada, which his father had held 778–81. His power base was the central Pictish territory of *Fortriu.

**Constantine** (*c*.274–337), first Christian Roman emperor (306–37), known as 'the Great'. Born at Naissus (now Nis), Constantine was the son of *Constantius I by Helena. In 305 Constantius succeeded as *Augustus* (senior emperor) of the West. Constantine fled from the court of Galerius, eastern *Augustus*, in time to be at his father's death-bed at York in 306. He was illegally proclaimed *Augustus* by the army there. In 312 he invaded Italy and defeated Maxentius near Rome. By 324 Constantine was sole *Augustus*. Constantine promoted Christianity financially, legally, and theologically, being baptized on his death-bed in 337. He probably revisited Britain in 312 and 314, taking the title *Britannicus* in 315.

**Constantine III** (d. 411). Usurper, proclaimed emperor by Roman troops in Britain. At the beginning of the 5th cent. AD Roman Britain was not heavily defended, *Stilicho having withdrawn troops in 401–2 to help defend Italy against German invaders. In AD 406 Marcus seized power in Britain, but after a few months was replaced by the equally short-lived Gratian. The next usurper, Constantine III, was more effective, managing to take substantial territories in Gaul and Spain. Eventually he was defeated by the forces of the western emperor Honorius: in 411 he was captured and executed.

**Constantine I** (d. 877), 'king of the Picts' (862–76), anachronistically regarded as third king of Scotland. Son of *Kenneth I, he succeeded his uncle Donald I. His career was chiefly consumed in a desperate struggle for survival against Scandinavian incursions. In 866 the Norwegian king of Dublin devastated

Pictland and in 875 Halfdan the Danish king of York inflicted a crushing defeat on Constantine at *Dollar. Constantine was killed in 877 by the Danes at 'Inverdufata' (unidentified).

**Constantine II** (d. 952), king of 'Scotland' (900–940/5). His father was *Æd (d. 878). Constantine II laid the foundations of the kingdom of Scotland. His victory over the Danes at Strathearn in 904 represented a turning-point in its struggle against Scandinavian aggression, and after another victory at (probably) Corbridge (west of Newcastle) in 918 he initiated a policy of *rapprochement* with the Danes cemented by the marriage of his daughter to the Danish king Guthfrith. This was designed to support Danish York in its struggle for survival against kings of Wessex. The kings of Wessex began to threaten Scotland itself when *Athelstan invaded as far as Dunnottar in 934, and in 937 an invasion of England mounted by Constantine and the Danes from Dublin led by Guthfrith's son *Olaf ended in disaster at the battle of *Brunanburh.

**Constantine III** (d. 997), king of 'Scotland' (from 995). He reigned for only a year and a half following the assassination of *Kenneth II. He was a son of King *Cuilén, and the last of the descendants of King *Æd (d. 878) to hold the kingship. He was killed by *Kenneth III, a member of the rival branch of the royal dynasty.

**Constantius I** (Constantius Chlorus) (d. 306), *Caesar* (deputy emperor) and then *Augustus* (emperor) of the western Roman empire (AD 292–306). In 293 Constantius wrested power from the usurper *Carausius. Carausius was assassinated by Allectus who in turn usurped imperial power. Constantius' forces attacked Allectus in Britain; Allectus was killed and Constantius made a triumphal entry into London. In AD 305–6 Constantius, then co-emperor with Maximian, conducted a campaign in northern Britain. His son *Constantine joined him, and was declared emperor when Constantius died at York.

**constitution** A constitution is a body of rules, formal or informal, which regulates the government of a state. The distribution of power between the various organs of government, the limits of governmental authority, and the methods of appointing or electing those who govern form the staple of a constitution.

The existence of a constitution implies that there are some restraints upon those who govern. If decisions, for instance, depend upon the whim of an absolute monarch, or the fancy of a dictator, it is hard to speak of a constitution. Most states, and many private associations, have written constitutions—a code of written rules binding those who govern, together with any amendments which have been made in accordance with the procedures laid down in the constitution. Thus the US constitution is the document accepted in 1787, together with the 27 amendments which have been passed subsequently.

A contrast is sometimes made between written and unwritten constitutions. Britain, it is said, has an unwritten constitution. But the distinction is overdrawn. Britain is unusual in that there is no single document which can be called the formal constitution. The constitution in Britain is scattered through hundreds of Acts of Parliament and judicial rulings. But the description of Britain as having an unwritten constitution usually focuses on another attribute—the importance of conventions. Some of Britain's most important constitutional rules are in fact, *conventions*. There is a convention that the monarch acts on the advice of his or her ministers: there is no direct legal compulsion on the monarch to do this, but he or she invariably does. By convention, a government clearly defeated on a vote of confidence in the House of Commons either resigns or holds a general election.

The absence of a written constitution has prompted some people to suggest that a bill of rights is needed to protect British citizens, particularly since the 1689 *Bill of Rights is concerned mainly with governmental structures. There is already European legislation on human rights. A British bill of rights would certainly lead to increased legislation, and some citizens would undoubtedly devise more rights. Consequently others have counter-proposed that any bill of rights should be accompanied by a formal statement of duties.

**Conventicles Act,** 1664. This Act (16 Car. II c. 4) was one of the fiercest provisions of the *Clarendon code, which aimed at restoring Anglican supremacy after the Restoration. It forbade attendance at any meeting of more than five persons for religious purposes other than Church of England ceremonies.

**Convention of Estates,** 1689. The flight of James VII in 1688 made it impossible to summon a legal Scottish Parliament. It was therefore decided to fall back upon a Convention of Estates, which had often been summoned in emergencies, and which met on 14 March 1689 in Edinburgh. By the Claim of Right it declared that James VII had been deposed.

**Convention of royal burghs** Meetings of the royal burghs in Scotland went back to the 14th cent. and in 1487 a statute authorized annual sessions. The conventions were in addition to the representation of the burghs in the Scottish Parliament and, after 1707, the British Parliament. The same commissioners often served in both bodies.

**Convention Parliaments** The constitutional crisis of the 17th cent. produced two occasions when there were impediments to the summoning of a lawful parliament. The first was at the Restoration. On 25 April 1660, a month after the *Long Parliament had dissolved itself, a convention assembled and declared that the government should be in king, lords, and commons. Its first act was to declare itself a genuine parliament, 'notwithstanding any defect or default whatsoever'. A similar procedure was adopted in 1689 after James II's flight meant that the calling of a lawful parliament was impossible. The Assembly which gathered at Westminster on 22 January was a parliament in all but name, and its first act, using the exact words of the 1660 measure, was to declare itself a parliament.

**conversion of England** *See* CHRISTIANITY.

**convocations of Canterbury and York** These provincial assemblies, originally of bishops, date from Archbishop *Theodore (668–90), though York's, smaller and historically less significant, only developed separately *c.*733. Representatives (proctors) of cathedrals, monasteries, and parochial clergy attended later (13th cent.). Initially

sitting together, bishops and lower clergy split into upper and lower houses (15th cent.). Convocations normally legislated by canons, until compelled by Henry VIII to limit their powers drastically (Acts of *Submission 1532/1534). Acrimonious altercations between the Whiggish upper and Tory lower house of the Canterbury convocation (1689 and 1700–17) led the crown to suspend both convocations. They met only formally until the *evangelical and *tractarian revivals inspired them to resume discussion (1852 and 1861).

**Conway, treaty of** *See* ABERCONWY.

**Cook, James** (1728–79). Usually referred to as Captain Cook, he was perhaps the greatest ever maritime explorer. He established much of the basic geography of Australasia and the Pacific region, disposed of the myth of the southern continent, and learned how to keep his men free of scurvy. He used Harrison's chronometer and lunar distances to calculate longitudes accurately.

Cook was born in Yorkshire and apprenticed to a Whitby shipowner. In 1755 he entered the Royal Navy. Soon, his charts helped General *Wolfe up the St Lawrence. Recognized as an expert navigator, he was chosen leader of the expedition in the *Endeavour* which took scientists to Tahiti to observe the transit of Venus in 1769. He also sought the reputed southern continent, circumnavigated the New Zealand islands, and explored the whole eastern coast of Australia. In the *Resolution* in 1772–5, Cook sailed round Antarctica and also discovered Tonga and the New Hebrides. A third major expedition in 1776–9 was to the North Pacific to find the end of the North-West Passage. He did not, but he did discover the Hawaiian Islands, where on a second visit he lost his life in a fracas with some natives over a stolen boat.

**Cooper, Samuel** (1609–72). English miniaturist who enjoyed a European reputation. He was active before, during, and after the English Civil War and his patrons included *Cromwell and Charles II, *Milton and *Monck. Cooper regarded the miniature as a painting, not a piece of the jeweller's art; with his use of light and shade, combined with superb draughtsmanship, he broke away from his predecessors, especially *Hilliard.

**Co-operative movement** The Co-operative movement is often identified solely with retailing, and its foundation ascribed to the '*Rochdale Pioneers' who set up the first store to pay dividends to members on the basis of how much they had purchased. It originated in the ideas of Robert *Owen, the factory owner and social thinker of *New Lanark. During the 1820s and 1830s many groups of people started on the road to creating an alternative society based on mutual assistance rather than competitive individualism, the 'New Moral World' whose superiority would drive out capitalism. The first step was to set up a shop, whose surpluses could then be applied to manufacturing and ultimately farming. The Rochdale Pioneers system rendered Co-operation attractive to those who sought to save as they spent. After the Pioneers began in 1844 the movement spread rapidly, making a distinctive virtue of refusing credit. Co-operation was especially popular in the textile towns of Lancashire and west Yorkshire in the mid-Victorian years. Societies were locally based, but the Co-operative Wholesale Society co-ordinated purchasing and then manufacturing for the whole movement from 1863. Although most members came to view the dividend as the most important aspect, the Co-op never lost its idealism completely, providing classes and libraries, supporting strikes, and (through its Women's Guild) offering political confidence to working-class women. The societies were democratically run and in 1918 a Co-operative Party was set up, which ran in harness with the Labour Party. After 1945 the movement faced difficulties. Societies amalgamated, local identities were lost, the dividend itself was abandoned, and the Co-op seemed to many to have lost its way. Its position in the retail trade was eroded by competition from large and enterprising supermarkets.

**Coote, Sir Eyre** (1726–83). Coote was born at Limerick and joined the army during the Jacobite uprising of 1745. His most distinguished service came in India where he fought under *Clive at *Plassey in 1757. On 22 January 1760 he commanded at *Wandewash when the French threat to southern India was extirpated. Posted to *Calcutta, he rapidly quarrelled with members of the Bengal Council and left for England in 1762. In 1769 he returned as commander-in-chief of the Bengal army but resigned again for the same reason. In 1779, he came back once more as C.-in-C. under Warren *Hastings and led the army in the second Mysore War. But he was defeated by Hyder Ali, the Mysore sultan, at Porto Nuovo in 1781. Coote died at Madras in 1783.

**Copenhagen, battle of,** 1801. This encounter with the Danish fleet was fought on 2 April in the narrow 3-mile-long King's Channel, which bounded the eastern defences of the Danish capital. These consisted of the formidable Trekronor fort, flanked to the north by 5 moored warships and to the south by a redoubtable line of 7 unmasted warships and 10 floating batteries. The British under Sir Hyde Parker with *Nelson as his second had 15 ships. Following a daring navigation, the British attacked in line and broke the Danish defence. Nelson 'turned his blind eye' to Parker's premature signal to withdraw.

**copyhold** Rack rents, or leasehold rents, in which the tenant pays an economic rent to the landlord, only became common across the country in the later 19th cent. Until then large parts of England, particularly in the north and west, had a variety of arrangements offering more (or less) security to the tenant. These included copyhold, customaryhold, lifeleasehold, three-life, and 99-year leases, which gave the tenant virtual rights of ownership. Copyhold literally meant 'by copy of the court roll', in other words by an agreement entered into the court rolls of the manor. By the 19th cent. the traditional rents were so out of line with real values that landlords sought to convert them to rack rents.

**copyright** is the ownership of and right of control over the means of reproducing works of literature, art, drama, film, sound, and computer technology. Until the 18th cent. authors had little protection against pirate publication of their works. An important step forward was a statute of 1709 'to encourage learned men' (8 Anne c. 19) by granting the author sole right of publication for fourteen years, with the possibility of a further extension of another fourteen years. Copyright now lasts 70 years after the death of an author. Under the terms of the Public Lending Rights scheme, introduced in 1983, authors can receive royalties on the use of their books in libraries in Britain and elsewhere.

**Coram, Thomas** (1668–1751). Coram, a successful sea-captain, was an active philanthropist in the Walpole period, supporting the foundation of the colony of Georgia in America as a haven for debtors. Concerned at the plight of tiny children abandoned in the streets of London, he was the driving force behind the establishment of the Foundling hospital in 1739. *Hogarth, who painted a fine portrait of Coram, gave his support and *Handel conducted performances of *Messiah* to raise funds. Though the hospital was demolished in 1928, the entrance lodges still stand in front of Coram's Fields, largely given over to children's playgrounds.

**Corbeil, treaty of,** 1326. On 26 April 1326 Robert I Bruce and Charles IV of France agreed to a treaty of mutual aid against the English. This was an early step in the formation of the *Auld Alliance between Scotland and France.

**Corbridge** Coriostopitum was a major Roman military base in the valley of the Tyne where the east–west road (the Stanegate) met the north–south road (Dere Street). Inscriptions attest the continuing military importance of Corbridge whenever the Romans campaigned northwards. The town consisted of buildings suggesting commercial activity tied to the military and the local populace.

**Coritani** A British tribe and *civitas*. It occupied the territory between the rivers Welland and Humber, fringed on the west by the southern Pennines. The impression of the tribe at the time of the Roman conquest is that it was not yet united into a single powerful kingdom. This may explain the rapid Roman advance through their territory, culminating in the foundation of a legionary fortress at *Lincoln *c.* AD 60. The pacified tribe were awarded local self-government as a *civitas* a decade or two later, with *Leicester, known as Ratae Coritanorum, as its administrative centre.

**Cork (Corcach már Muman), diocese of** The Irish see of Cork was established in the province of *Cashel at the Council of Raithbressail (1111). As part of a policy of Anglicization to establish sees in royal cities and so subordinate the Irish to English rule, Cork was eventually merged with Irish Cloyne (1411). This catholic diocese remained together until 1747, when Cork became separate again. Similarly the Anglican diocese of Cork has at times been held with Cloyne and Ross. There are cathedrals at all three sites.

**Corn Laws** First passed in 1815, these were always controversial. Britain's fast-growing population was making the country a food importer rather than exporter as before. The French wars had forced up domestic prices and encouraged agricultural investment, so there was fear of a post-war collapse of prices. Parliament prohibited the importation of wheat until the domestic price reached 80 shillings a quarter. In 1828 a sliding scale was introduced, which meant that duties would reduce as prices rose and vice versa. *Peel modified this in 1842 to a lower level of duties. Despite this trend to easier importation, the Corn Laws came under fierce attack from the *Anti-Corn Law League, which blamed recurrent industrial depressions on agricultural protection. Peel, alarmed by the industrial crisis of 1842 and fearing the conjunction of high food prices with league agitation and mass unemployment, concluded that political stability required a sacrifice of the Corn Laws. Using the Irish potato famine of 1845 as an excuse, he proposed total repeal. This betrayal of party commitments and the landed interest produced a revolt of Conservative backbenchers and though Peel carried repeal in 1846, he split his party into a free-trading minority and a protectionist majority. The main effect of repeal was delayed until the 1870s when cheap transatlantic grain flooded in and produced both sharp falls in food prices and acute agricultural depression.

**Cornovii** British tribe and *civitas*. The Cornovii are a surprisingly obscure tribe, given that they lay well within the boundaries of the Roman province and their *civitas*-capital was one of the largest towns in Britain. The *civitas* encompassed the modern counties of Shropshire, Staffordshire, and Cheshire. More or less at the heart of this territory lay the *civitas*-capital of Viriconium (Wroxeter), which may have replaced, and borrowed the name of, the nearby Iron Age hill-fort on the Wrekin.

**Cornwall** The oldest of English duchies (from 1337, though first a Norman earldom *c.*1140) has dimensions other than its peninsularity: the south-flowing Tamar forms the county boundary with Devon. As the distant part of 'civitas *Dumnonia' the Romans may not have colonized Cornwall, but they monopolized its tin production. For Cornish people England is entered by crossing the Tamar, and in the Civil War, though Cornish levies defended the crown within the county, they could not be brought to do so further east. Cornwall has a place in western prehistory at least as far back as the 3rd millennium BC, and in the 5th–6th cents. AD a church coloured by Irish and eastern Mediterranean practice; in later centuries it had a role not only in trade but in pilgrimage routes to southern Europe. In the 5th cent. AD Brittany received an immigration from Dumnonia (Britons), and the disused Cornish language may still be studied in Breton schools. Cornwall has had its share in the evolution of the Atlantic world. The Falmouth mail service developed a proud record on its American run 1688–1850, and in the 19th cent. Cornish miners worked, and died, in the mines of South America and South Africa; in 1901 Marconi, in Newfoundland, received the first transatlantic radio transmission from Poldhu near the Lizard. Back home, it had taken all Brunel's genius to bridge the Tamar at Saltash 1857–9, and so bring the railway, and a holiday industry, to Cornwall.

In antiquity tin from Cornwall's streams, increasingly deep-mined by the later 16th cent., was the region's life-blood. As ingots the metal was exported far and wide, but the earliest traders appear to have used the two north coast havens, St Ives-Hayle and the Camel estuary: no place in Britain is so rich in the remains of 5th–6th-cent. Mediterranean pottery as is Tintagel. Few, if any, British sites have more romance and mystery than this inhospitable headland: its history prior to the cliff-hanging castle built there by Earl *Richard of Cornwall in the 1230s is elusive, and associations with 'King *Arthur' are solely attributable to the chronicler *Geoffrey of Monmouth. At the time of *Domesday Book (1086), in which neither Tintagel nor tin receive mention, Cornwall was evidently underpopulated. In 1346, however, Fowey was able to send over 40 ships to aid Edward III at Calais; in Armada year (1588) the port had only one ship in Queen Elizabeth's service, though Cornwall had become one of the most populous of southern counties. Its present-day population is some 480,000, the most concentrated urban area being Redruth–Camborne. Truro (18,000) only became a centre in the early 19th cent., its cathedral, built 1890–1910, marking Cornwall as a diocese independent of Exeter for the first time.

The special status of the tin-miners may have been established before the Conquest. When, in 1201, King John granted them their first charter confirming exceptional legal autonomies, in the Court of the *Stannaries, agriculture in Cornwall needed to give way to the territorial requirements of the tin-streamers; with the dukedom's establishment in 1336 their rights came under royal wardenship, though the court itself was only formally wound up in the mid-19th cent. By the 16th cent. the leading county families, Rashleighs, Eliots, Godolphins, formed closely knit groupings to which the Tudor monarchs responded by granting enfranchisement to some fifteen additional boroughs, including Bossiney and Penryn, famed respectively for their slate and granite quarries. Their political evanescence may, however, be gauged by the *Great Reform Act of 1832 which disfranchised almost all of them. But great houses, Lanhydrock, Cotehele, Trerice, still attest to aristocratic pride. Today, though the pilchard no longer thrives along their coasts and their deep mines are derelict, the Cornish retain their cultural richness. Britain and the wider world would be poorer without their artists and potters, their cream, and Mr Lemon Hart's rum.

**Cornwall, duchy of** From the Norman Conquest onwards, Cornwall has had close links with the crown. William the Conqueror gave large estates there to his half-brother Robert; John's second son *Richard was earl of Cornwall, but his line became extinct by 1300. In 1337 Edward III created his son, *Edward the Black Prince, duke of Cornwall— the first English dukedom. Henceforward the duchy belonged to the prince of Wales, reverting to the crown when there was no prince. It is administered from Lostwithiel. It is a private estate, provides the prince of Wales with most of his income, and has property outside Cornwall. The annual income from the duchy was estimated in 1996 as £4.5 million, but since 1993 the prince of Wales has paid standard income tax.

**Cornwallis, Charles, 1st Marquis Cornwallis** (1738–1805). Soldier and administrator. Cornwallis served during the American War of Independence and from 1780 commanded the British forces in South Carolina. Though an able general, he was cut off at *Yorktown by American forces. He was forced to surrender on 19 October 1781 thus ending the war. In 1786–93 Cornwallis acted as governor-general and commander of the army in Bengal. He introduced the permanent settlement, concerning landownership, and judicial and revenue reforms. He also gained victory over Tipu Sahib of Mysore at the battle of Arikera (13 May 1791). In 1798 Cornwallis left for Ireland as lord-lieutenant and succeeded in subduing the *Irish Rebellion. He presided over the Act of *Union (1800) but resigned a year later after the government's refusal to grant catholic emancipation. Cornwallis died at Ghazipur shortly after resuming his former post in India.

**coronations** Though the monarch succeeds automatically on the death of his predecessor, the coronation is a public avowal of his new position. Indeed, earlier tradition held that he was not really king until he had been crowned. Consequently, coronations followed accessions very swiftly, particularly if there were rival candidates, allowing little time for elaborate preparations. Harold II was crowned on the very day of Edward the Confessor's burial. The ceremony was, essentially, religious—a dedication to God's service. But the political opportunities were soon apparent. Monarchs wished for a widespread demonstration of their acceptance, especially by the most eminent in the land, with the chance to remind their subjects of the need for obedience: subjects found in the ceremony a chance to remind monarchs of their own rights. Hence, the evolution of the ceremony registers the ebb and flow of political power.

The English ceremonial which developed was more religious and more elaborate than that in Scotland or Ireland. The first recorded instance in England of a ceremony reflects both its nature and its limitations. In 787 Ecgfrith, son of *Offa of Mercia, was publicly anointed to ensure his succession: in the event he survived for only six months before he was overthrown by a cousin, *Cenwulf. The coronation of *Edgar at Bath in 973 suggests the development of considerable ritual: a ring, sword, and sceptre were delivered as tokens of authority and the anthem 'Zadok the Priest' chanted. *Edward the Confessor was crowned at Winchester in 1043, but all later coronations have taken place at Westminster.

The central features of the ceremony have remained. The monarch is first presented, usually by the archbishop of Canterbury; takes a series of oaths; is anointed with holy oil; is crowned, receives the regalia, and accepts homage. Most of the ancient regalia of the crown was sold off after the execution of Charles I. The spoon and ampulla, in the shape of a golden eagle, survived. The ampulla was believed to contain holy oil, said to have been given by the Virgin Mary to Thomas *Becket and rediscovered in time to assist Henry IV at his coronation in 1399. The rest of the regalia now consists of replicas fashioned in 1660 for Charles II, or later additions. A copy of the crown believed to have been worn by Edward the Confessor was made at the Restoration, and a lighter crown produced for Victoria in 1838. The coronation chair was made for Edward I, again on the pattern of Edward the Confessor's, and until 1996 included the stone of *Scone, brought back from Scotland in 1296. Two swords of state were made in 1660, one of which subsequently went missing: a third was made in 1678. The sword of offering was made in 1821. An orb was introduced in the 15th cent. to reinforce the monarch's imperial claims to the throne of France. A bible was added to the ceremony in 1689. Of the ritual, the 'vivat' by Westminster boys dates from 1625 and *Handel's setting of 'Zadok the Priest' has been used since 1727.

Politically, the alterations to the oath are instructive. The original oaths were fervent but vague. Mistrust of Edward II led in 1308 to a new oath being added, to maintain the laws as chosen by his subjects. After the experience of James II's reign, the oath for William and Mary was intended to bolt the door against catholicism and despotism, obliging the monarchs to observe 'the statutes in parliament agreed on' and to maintain 'the Protestant reformed religion established by law'.

In practice coronation ceremonies have frequently had difficulty in living up to the solemnity of the occasion. William the Conqueror's coronation was marred by a massacre of his new Saxon subjects, whose shouts of acclamation were mistaken by nervous Norman guards as the signal for a rising. The pageantry of the royal champion has often caused problems. In 1377 Richard II's champion appeared at the abbey during mass and had to be told to go away. In 1685 James II's champion fell flat on his face, which suggests that it was just as well that the challenge was not taken up. In 1559 Elizabeth I complained that the holy oil was greasy and smelled unpleasant. In 1727 Queen *Caroline had to borrow jewels since George I had given the rest to his mistress. A special hazard at the coronation of George IV was the arrival, in the middle of the ceremony, of his estranged wife, demanding to be let in. Victoria's own account tells of the pain she suffered when the archbishop pushed the ring on her wrong finger, and George VI's account of 1937 was that the archbishop juggled so much with the crown that he never did find out if it was on the right way.

The coronation of Scottish monarchs remained much simpler. Until the 13th cent. it was a ceremony of inauguration, usually at Scone, involving the elevation on a stone or chair. But later ceremony was restrained by the fact that so many Scottish monarchs succeeded as infants or children and could not sustain a demanding role: James III, for example, was inaugurated at Kelso, aged 8, a week after James II's death outside Floors castle in 1460. The last Scottish coronation, that of Charles II in 1651, was a hasty business in the midst of adversity: Charles was required to swear to the covenant, and anointing was dropped as a superstitious and popish practice.

**Coronel, battle of,** 1914. At the outbreak of the First World War, the German Pacific squadron, commanded by Admiral von Spee, steamed across the Pacific with the intention of returning to Germany. On 1 November 1914 von Spee was intercepted by a British squadron commanded by Rear-Admiral Sir Christopher Craddock off Coronel on the Chilean coast. The Germans had more modern vessels armed with heavier guns and within an hour they had sunk most of Craddock's ships. They were themselves destroyed at the battle of the *Falkland Islands in December.

**coroner** The coroner was an official appointed by the king to 'keep' or enrol the pleas of the crown for the county and thus to safeguard the rights of the crown. The office was first referred to in 1194 though it probably existed before that time. Under the Norman and Angevin kings the pleas of the crown were noted by the sheriff and any fines due to the king from these offences were collected by him. The coroner was appointed to keep a check on the sheriff. In addition, the coroner held an inquiry or 'inquest' into certain matters which were of special interest to the king. These included inquiries into the cause of unexplained death, treasure trove wrecks, and finding of sturgeon. The coroner still has an important role, holding inquests in cases of sudden or unexplained death.

**Corporation Act,** 1661. This statute (13 Car. II c. 1) was the first part of the '*Clarendon code' and set out to reassert Anglican supremacy after the Restoration. Persons holding municipal office were obliged to qualify by taking communion with the Church of England. It remained a bone of contention throughout the 18th cent. and was not repealed until 1828.

**corporations** A large number of economic activities are so complex or costly that they can only be undertaken by the combination of many individuals. It is not surprising, therefore, that all economic systems have been characterized by the development of large institutions such as the state or the firm. Early forms of large-scale undertakings were found in the trading *companies whose business took them to the Baltic or Mediterranean. Major companies, trading ever further afield, were granted monopoly rights by the crown. The most famous was the *East India Company, chartered in 1600 for a single voyage, and eventually established as a continuous operation in 1657. By 1617 the

East India Company had 36 ships and 934 stockholders. These large organizations, the precursors of modern corporations, proliferated with royal charters granted to the *Bank of England in 1694 and, early in the following century, to the *South Sea Company, the *Royal Exchange Company, and the London Assurance. The government took an opportunity in granting charters to secure promises of loans from the beneficiaries.

**corresponding societies** The initial welcome for the French Revolution in Britain came largely from middle-class and dissenting groups, but its ideas soon gained wider popularity through the spread of Painite radicalism, disseminated especially by corresponding societies. In 1792 the most famous of all the radical societies of the period—the London Corresponding Society—was founded by Thomas Hardy, a Scottish shoemaker, with the intention of corresponding with provincial radicals to promote the cause of parliamentary reform. The government, thoroughly alarmed, arrested the leaders and clamped down heavily on the LCS. By 1797 the corresponding societies had collapsed or been driven underground.

**Corrichie, battle of,** 1562. When Mary, queen of Scots, returned from France as a widow in 1561, great influence was wielded by her half-brother Lord James Stuart, illegitimate son of James V. He pursued a pro-English and pro-protestant policy. Early in 1562 he was made earl of *Moray, which was also claimed by the 4th earl of *Huntly, a leader of the catholics. Huntly was forced into rebellion and then captured by Lord James on 28 October at Corrichie, near Aberdeen. Huntly died that night, being 'gross, corpulent, short of breath'.

**Corrupt Practices Act,** 1883. Electoral corruption continued after the Reform Act of 1832 and was not eradicated either by the Corrupt Practices Act of 1854, or by *secret ballot in 1872. The 1883 Act (46 & 47 Vic. c. 51) strengthened the previous Act by laying down the limits of electoral expenditure. Corruption was not eliminated but the growing size of the electorate and the disfranchisement of many small boroughs reduced it.

**Cort, Henry** (1740–1800). Cort was born at Lancaster, son of a mason. His interest in the production of iron developed after the Russians had raised their prices. By 1784 he was able to patent an invention for 'puddling' iron to make it malleable. With Adam Jellicoe he entered into large naval contracts, but Jellicoe's death in 1789 revealed fraud, which brought Cort down. During the last years of his life, he existed on a small pension.

**Corunna, battle of,** 1809. In October 1808 the British, under Sir John *Moore, pushed into northern Spain to draw the French from Madrid. Outnumbered and inadequately supplied, they were in danger of being cut off. Moore skilfully retreated through the mountains towards the coast, closely pursued by the French under Marshal Soult. At Corunna on 16 January 1809 Soult attacked with 20,000 men. Moore with 15,000 men repulsed the French, allowing the British to evacuate safely by sea, but was himself fatally wounded.

**Cotman, John Sell** (1782–1842). Architect, draughtsman, landscape and water-colour painter. The son of a prosperous silk-mercer in Norwich, Cotman was intended for his father's business, but preferring art, went to London to study in 1798. He exhibited at the Royal Academy 1800-6, before returning to Norwich in 1807 to open a school for drawing and design. He joined the Norwich Society of Artists, becoming president in 1811. He is now seen as a most original artist, with the water-colour *Greta Bridge* (1805) probably his masterpiece.

**Cottington, Francis, 1st Baron Cottington** (*c.*1579–1652). Cottington, from Somerset, was first employed by James I in Spanish matters, knew the country well, and spoke the language. In 1622 he became secretary to Charles, prince of Wales, was given a baronetcy in 1623, and brought into Parliament. A shadow fell over his progress when he quarrelled with *Buckingham, but after the duke's murder Cottingham forged ahead. In 1629 he became chancellor of the Exchequer and held the post until 1642. When war broke out he joined the king at Oxford, acted as lord high treasurer, and on the surrender in 1646 went into exile. He died a catholic in Spain in June 1652.

**Council, Great** *See* GREAT COUNCIL.

**Council for Wales in the Marches** Edward IV had large estates as earl of March in the Welsh borders and in the 1470s established a council at Shrewsbury. Henry VII, Welsh by birth, followed the example. After a period in abeyance, the council seems to have been revived by Thomas *Cromwell. A statute of 1543 established a council in Wales and in the border counties of Shropshire, Herefordshire, Worcestershire, and Gloucestershire. Much of its business was judicial and petitioners were saved a long journey to London. Unlike the *Council of the North, the Council in Wales was not abolished by the *Long Parliament. Reconstituted in 1660, the council never regained its former importance and was abolished in 1689.

**Council of State,** 1649–60. After the execution of Charles I and the abolition of the monarchy, the *Rump Parliament in February 1649 gave executive power to a Council of State of 41 members. It contained three peers, a number of lawyers including *Bradshaw, and senior army officers such as *Cromwell, *Fairfax, and Philip Skippon. When Cromwell became lord protector in December 1653 he was given a council of 21 under the *Instrument of Government. Though it had less power than its predecessor, Cromwell complained that he was in toils.

**Council of the North** The chief arm of government in the turbulent northern shires of Yorkshire, Durham, Cumberland, Westmorland, and Northumberland in the Tudor and early Stuart period. As duke of Gloucester in Edward IV's reign, Richard III had shared power in the north with the earl of *Northumberland. Having seized the crown in 1483, he appointed Northumberland warden of the marches but created a separate council at York. Its importance in Elizabeth I's reign is indicated by the fact that, after the dangerous rising of the *northern earls in 1569, the presidency was held by Lord *Huntingdon, the queen's cousin, from 1572 until 1595, and by Lord Burghley, elder brother of Sir Robert *Cecil, from 1599 until 1603. In 1628 Charles I appointed *Strafford to be president. He retained the office while he was lord deputy in Ireland but in 1641 was attainted and executed. The council was abolished by the *Long Parliament shortly afterwards. From the

dissolution of the monasteries to its abolition, the council met in the King's Manor at York, the residence of the lord president.

**counties** The county (otherwise the shire) was the main unit of provincial government in England from before the Norman Conquest until modern times. *Domesday Book (1086) describes 32 shires. Five of these were subdivisions of the former kingdom of Wessex. Of these, Hampshire already existed in 757; the others may be as old. Five shires derive from former kingdoms absorbed into Wessex (Kent, Sussex, Essex, and East Anglia (divided into Norfolk and Suffolk)). The shires of the midlands were nearly all created in the 10th cent. The only additions to the system were Westmorland, Cumberland, Lancashire, Durham, Northumberland, and the anomalous Rutland. The Domesday shires had, to a remarkable extent, the boundaries which they retained for many centuries. By 1066 each shire (sometimes pairs of shires) had an official, the *sheriff, responsible for the royal lands and the exercise of aspects of royal authority. The *county court, meeting twice annually, was a principal forum for justice both civil and criminal.

After the Norman Conquest the principal changes were the construction of shire castles and a great increase in the frequency with which the shire courts met. Although the importance of these courts diminished, the most important new judicial authorities, the *justices of the peace, were organized on a shire basis. The justices acquired many powers as time went on; their *quarter sessions were the principal organs of local government until the establishment of *county councils by the Local Government Act of 1888.

The only major innovation in the centuries before 1888 was the creation of the office of *lord-lieutenant in 1549, whose function was to command the shire levies. Shire associations of regular regiments were made standard and universal by an act of 1881. This was an expression of the greater shire-consciousness of the later 19th cent., expressed also in the associations of archaeological societies, cricket clubs, and agricultural societies. An Act of 1972 brought major changes in county organization. Some historic shires were merged and new ones without historic antecedents created. Further changes were made in 1996. Central government has usually shown little affection for counties, the general public more so.

**country houses** The country house was the focal point and symbol of the ascendancy of the gentry in the period between the Glorious Revolution and the First World War. It no longer had military significance. It was large enough to accommodate the family and its dependants, and the bevy of servants who supported them. Ideally it could give hospitality to a considerable number of guests since it often served as a political headquarters. It stood in its own park, with a lodge and a drive, partly to give privacy, partly to impress or even overawe visitors.

Country house does not seem the right term for Tudor residences. The great palaces—Hatfield, Longleat, Burghley, Hardwick—were too grand: 'prodigy houses' has been suggested. Many of the rest were modest, often in the middle of a medieval village, squalid rather than picturesque. One of the objects of *enclosures in the 18th cent. was often to round off a park, or eliminate an irritating footpath.

Most of the land released by the *dissolution of the monasteries in the 1540s found its way into the hands of the gentry and nobility and many of the estates were future country houses, betraying their origins as Woburn abbey (Beds.) or Hitchin priory (Herts.). Good examples of the modest 17th-cent. manor house are Washington Old Hall, south of Newcastle upon Tyne, and Woolbridge Manor (Dorset). On a grander scale are Capheaton, Northumberland (1668), Milton, Oxfordshire (1670), and Uppark, Sussex (1685–90). With *Chatsworth, Derbyshire (1687), *Castle Howard, Yorkshire (1699), Stowe, Buckinghamshire (1720), and Mellerstain, Borders (1725) we are moving towards palaces.

The mid-18th cent. was an age of improvement. A large number of country houses were rebuilt in classical style and much money spent on embellishing parks. At Kedleston, Milton, Chippenham (Cambs.), Nuneham Courtenay, and Wimpole, whole villages were removed to give greater privacy. The internal arrangements were remodelled to give much greater privacy and comfort than had existed in the semi-communal house of medieval times, with its great hall.

Though the 18th cent. was the heyday of the country house, more were built in the 19th cent. than ever before. *Disraeli, who surprisingly became leader of the Tory Party, had no country house of his own and had to borrow money from the Bentincks to buy Hughenden Manor in Buckinghamshire. Sir William *Armstrong, the north-eastern armaments king, built himself an extraordinary country retreat at Cragside in the Northumbrian hills, where elegance gave way to comfort. The Rothschild family covered the vale of Aylesbury with large and ornate country houses—Aston Clinton (1840), Mentmore (1852–4), Tring (1873), Ascott (1874), Waddesdon (1880), and Halton (1884).

The decline in the later 19th cent. had a variety of causes. Country gentlemen no longer dominated politics, and the country house lost its *raison d'être* as a political centre. The agricultural depression after the 1870s struck the landed interest hard and for decades land ceased to be an attractive investment. The cost of running households escalated just as *death duties and discriminatory taxes were beginning to bite. Though many country houses survive, others have been transformed into hideous parodies of former greatness, and serve as conference centres, reform homes, cult headquarters, and even fun-fairs and amusement parks.

**County Councils Act,** 1888. The *Municipal Corporations Act of 1835 had given elected corporations to the large towns but rural administration remained in the hands of the justices of the peace. In the Act of 1888, Lord Salisbury's government created 62 county councils in England and Wales, some of the larger shires being subdivided. Sixty-one towns of over 50,000 inhabitants were given county borough status and London was given its own county council. In England there was great continuity of personnel, many JPs being elected, and several lords-lieutenant becoming chairmen. But in Wales, nonconformist liberals swept the board at the expense of the gentry.

**county courts** The shire or county courts were the most important of the communal courts which governed all aspects of local life in Anglo-Saxon and Norman England. The shire court gradually declined with the growth of the common law courts and the development of Parliament in the 13th cent. By the 19th cent. there was no legal forum available to the would-be civil litigant whose means were small. In 1846, to meet this criticism, the County Courts Act set up a network of new 'county courts' within each area. These courts became and remain civil courts of limited jurisdiction.

**Courcy, John de** (d. 1219). Conqueror of Ulster. De Courcy's parentage is unknown, though he probably came from Somerset. He is said to have visited Ireland in 1171 with Henry II, who promised him Ulster if he could acquire it. Returning in 1176 with a small but well-organized force, he moved north from Dublin and succeeded in gaining the lands east of the Bann. From 1185 to 1190 he was justiciar in Ireland.

**court** The institution known as the court has changed its meaning over the centuries. In early medieval times, the court, or household, was the centre of government. The monarch, with counsellors and great officers in attendance, would do business, receive petitions, and dispense justice. As public business increased, various functions were delegated: much administration was left to the council, and justice to the specialized law courts. But as long as political power remained with the monarch, the division between public and private could never be absolute. It has been suggested that, as a result of the 'Tudor revolution in government', the court from the 1530s took on a purely ceremonial role. That is premature. All through the Tudor and early Stuart period, careers could be made or broken at court—*Wolsey, *Leicester, *Essex, *Rochester, *Buckingham. But after the Glorious Revolution, as power drained away to Parliament and the cabinet, the importance of the court began to diminish. By George II's reign, court life was routine and placid, save for a few grand occasions. Monarchs still wielded considerable influence but in direct consultation with ministers in private or in correspondence rather than through the court. The Edwardian court in the 1900s saw a brief social revival, partly because of the novelty of a visible monarch after Victoria's protracted seclusion. But it was an Indian summer and went down in the trenches of 1917.

**court and country party** Names employed for government and opposition in the late 17th and early 18th cents. The term 'country party' had obvious advantages. It was much broader than Tory or church party and avoided the divisive names of Whig and Tory at a time when many were combining to overthrow *Walpole. It hinted at massive support in the nation at large. It called to mind a golden past when squire and countryman had lived in harmony before the new moneyed interest bore everything down. 'Court', on the other hand, suggested a clique subservient to the monarch, wallowing in patronage and corruption.

**Courtenay, William** (*c*.1342–96). Archbishop of Canterbury. Courtenay's aristocratic connections carried him rapidly up the ladder of preferment. Of the Devon family, he graduated in law at Oxford and was chancellor in 1367. In 1370, he became bishop of Hereford, transferring to London in 1375. His tenure there saw the *Peasants' Revolt, in which Simon *Sudbury, the archbishop of Canterbury, was murdered. Courtenay replaced him and for a short while held the great seal as chancellor. His relations with the young king, Richard II, were turbulent. In 1385 they quarrelled violently when Courtenay attempted to rebuke him for his wild way of life, yet the archbishop supported the statute of *Praemunire (1393), which curbed papal authority.

**Court of Session** In 1532, partly at papal suggestion, James V established a Court of Session, or College of Justice. There were to be fifteen members. The arrangements were confirmed by the Act of *Union, though the number of justices has been increased to deal with the growth of litigation. The justices are accorded the courtesy title Lord, though they do not sit in the House of Lords, and the title is not hereditary.

**courts leet** were originally held as a form of franchise by the lord of the manor. Such a grant entitled the lord to hold the hundred court, dealing with all minor criminal matters within the district, and to receive the fines paid to the court. Courts leet declined with the advent of the *justices of the peace but some became the kernel of a new local government for the growing boroughs which incorporated an existing manor.

**courts martial** Strictly these are courts administering military law, i.e. the rules applicable to members of the armed forces. However, the term has also been used to describe courts administering '*martial law'. As early as the Wars of the Roses, powers were exercised by military commanders to try and to punish offenders in areas of conflict. In so far as there is any such principle as 'martial law', it can only be that necessity may on occasion be a defence.

**covenanters** As supporters of the Scottish National Covenant (1638) they sought to preserve *presbyterianism in Scotland. After defeating Charles I in the *Bishops' wars (1639–40), they forced him to accept presbyterianism in Scotland. Though after Charles I's execution Charles II signed the covenant (1650), *Cromwell's victorious army forced the Scots to tolerate sectarianism. Revival of Scottish episcopacy (1662) was unpopular; presbyterianism was restored (1690).

**Covent Garden** (London). Anxious to restore his dilapidated estate (land belonging to the convent of Westminster prior to the *dissolution of the monasteries), the 4th earl of Bedford commissioned Inigo *Jones as architect. Influenced by study in Italy, Jones created a piazza surrounded by St Paul's church and three terraces of tall houses. The houses became highly sought after, but the expansion of the fruit, flower, and vegetable market (established 1670) made them less fashionable. Shops and coffee-houses proliferated, and its first theatre (now the Royal Opera House) opened in 1732.

**Coventry** Cathedral city in Warwickshire. It developed around an important priory, founded in 1043 by Earl *Leofric and Countess Godgifu ('Lady *Godiva' of Coventry folklore). In the 14th cent. the city rose spectacularly through cloth-manufacturing to become the fourth largest English town. It declined equally spectacularly in the 16th cent., but found renewed industrial prosperity from the 18th cent. It was heavily bombed in the Second World War.

**Coventry, diocese of** The modern see, created in 1918, is roughly conterminous with Warwickshire. In Anglo-Saxon and early Norman times the Mercian church had been centred on *Lichfield, then on

*Chester, and eventually, after 1102, on Coventry abbey. In 1836 Coventry and its neighbourhood were put under *Worcester, but the massive increase in population in the midlands necessitated the foundation of the *Birmingham diocese in 1905 and Coventry in 1918. St Michael's parish church served as the cathedral, until it was destroyed by bombing in 1940. The new cathedral, designed by Basil *Spence, is dominated by the great tapestry of *Christ in Glory* by Graham *Sutherland.

**Coverdale, Miles** (1488–1568). Augustinian friar turned secular priest, popular preacher, and early reformer, Coverdale spent most of the time between 1528 and 1548 in exile, producing the first complete translation of the Bible into English, whilst abroad, in 1535. Prior to this, he may have worked with William *Tyndale, upon whose New Testament translation he relied. Meanwhile, Thomas Cromwell initiated an official translation for use in every parish church, entrusting the revision to Coverdale. The 'Great Bible' was published in 1539. Coverdale was appointed bishop of Exeter in Edward VI's reign, deprived, but escaped persecution under Mary Tudor.

**Cowes regatta** Cowes week is held early in August and is the climax of the yachting season. Cowes castle, built by Henry VIII, has been the headquarters of the Royal Yacht Squadron since 1856. East and West Cowes lie on either side of the estuary of the river Medina in the north of the Isle of Wight.

**Cowper, William, 1st Earl Cowper** (1664–1724). Politician and lawyer. Called to the bar in 1688, Cowper proved a brilliant lawyer, entering the Commons in 1695. He was appointed lord keeper in 1705, becoming a peer in 1706, and lord chancellor in 1707. In 1710 he presided over the trial of Dr *Sacheverell, and later that year resigned with his party. Reappointed lord chancellor by George I in 1714, he promoted the *Riot and *Septennial Acts. By 1718, however, he was voting increasingly with the Tories, and resigned a month after receiving an earldom.

**Crabbe, George** (1754–1832). Born in Aldeburgh (Suffolk), Crabbe began training as a doctor before taking holy orders. But his love was poetry and, moving to London, he was fortunate enough to be taken up by *Burke, *Johnson, and the Manners family. His poem *The Village* (1783) is a gloomy description of poverty and toil, intended as a contrast to *Goldsmith's idealized *Deserted Village*. It brought Crabbe considerable reputation and much clerical preferment. His other major work was *The Borough* (1810), which described his home town, and included the story of Peter Grimes, a sadistic fisherman, used by Benjamin *Britten.

**Craftsman, The: or, The Countryman's Journal** Best-selling newspaper which, from 5 December 1726, spearheaded the opposition to Sir Robert *Walpole. Backed by *Bolingbroke and William *Pulteney, the paper's avowed aim was to expose political craft. 'Country' rhetoric was employed in the attempt to create a political platform strong enough to accommodate the opinions of Tories and dissident Whigs.

**Craig, James, 1st Viscount Craigavon** (1871-1940). First prime minister of Northern Ireland. Craig, the son of a millionaire whiskey distiller, was elected as Unionist MP for East Down in 1906. With *Carson he led the Ulster Unionist resistance to the third *Home Rule Bill. He held junior ministerial office as parliamentary secretary to the Ministry of Pensions (1919-20) and as financial secretary at the Admiralty (1920-1): he influenced the Government of *Ireland Act, successfully pressing for a six-county partition scheme. Despite his standing at Westminster, he accepted the premiership of the newly created Northern Ireland in 1921, holding office until his death in 1940.

**Cranfield, Lionel, 1st earl of Middlesex** (1575-1645). Cranfield, competent and industrious, became lord treasurer under James I. He was a successful *Merchant Venturer and when in 1613 he was appointed surveyor-general of the customs, it was a case of poacher turned gamekeeper. In 1614 he became a member of Parliament, and attached himself to the royal favourite, George Villiers, later duke of *Buckingham. In 1621, when he became lord treasurer, he found that reform was needed in 'every particular'. Cranfield made spending cuts, and courtiers lost their pensions and allowances. He soon fell, brought down by Buckingham, his former patron. He was impeached, found

guilty of corruption, fined, and briefly imprisoned in the Tower. He was pardoned in 1625, and for the rest of his life lived in retirement.

**Cranmer, Thomas** (1489-1556). Archbishop of Canterbury. Cranmer played a greater role than any other single churchman in shaping the Church of England. He was born to a gentry family in Nottinghamshire and studied at Jesus College, Cambridge. He rose to sudden prominence in 1529 on the strength of his suggestion that the universities of Europe be asked to provide opinions on the legitimacy of Henry VIII's first marriage. On an embassy to Germany in 1532 he met and married the niece of the Lutheran church leader of Nuremberg, Andreas Osiander, whom he later brought secretly back to England. When Archbishop William *Warham died in that year Cranmer was proposed as his successor. Clement VII provided the papal documents for his consecration early in 1533. Cranmer then presided over the court which annulled Henry and *Catherine's marriage. He was also used, later on, to decree the nullity of Henry's marriage to *Anne Boleyn and to celebrate, and end, the marriage to *Anne of Cleves.

During *c.*1535-8 it is hard to separate Cranmer's role from that of Thomas *Cromwell in the shaping of religious policy. He was clearly opposed to the Act of *Six Articles in 1539 (which forced him to send his wife away) but, unlike Latimer, did not resign his see in protest.

On the accession of Edward VI, Cranmer issued definitively protestant works, above all the first *Book of Homilies*, a set of official model sermons. In contrast, his first version of the *Book of Common Prayer of 1549 was painfully conservative, to the glee of catholic opponents and the embarrassment of Cranmer's allies. In 1549 Cranmer welcomed a galaxy of German and Italian protestant stars into England. They helped guide Cranmer into formulating his most explicitly anti-catholic liturgical document, the second version of the Book of Common Prayer (1552) and the Forty-Two Articles of Religion (1553), the basis for the Prayer Book of 1559 and the *Thirty-Nine Articles of 1563 respectively.

Cranmer offered no resistance to Mary I's accession despite her known catholicism. He and other protestant bishops regarded her coming as a divine test. An attainder for treason was set aside in favour of a show-disputation at Oxford in April 1554, in which Cranmer defended himself less vigorously than Nicholas *Ridley. He was kept in prison and eventually persuaded to sign recantations in which he accepted key catholic doctrines. He later withdrew these and was burned for heresy on 21 March 1556.

**Cravant, battle of,** 1423. In the summer of 1423, the earl of Salisbury with his Burgundian allies marched to relieve Cravant on the river Yonne in France. The besiegers, led by the earl of Buchan, constable of France, were caught on 1 August between the garrison, making a sortie, and Salisbury's men, and badly defeated.

**Crécy, battle of,** 1346. The first great English land victory of the *Hundred Years War. Edward III landed unexpectedly in Normandy, and marched northwards. At Crécy in Ponthieu, the English prepared for battle on 26 August with knights and men-at-arms dismounted, flanked by archers. The French first sent forward Genoese mercenary crossbowmen, whose weapons proved no match for the English longbows. Cannon, used for the first time in a major battle, helped to terrify the French, their cavalry charging through their own retreating crossbowmen. The final stages of the battle witnessed moments of pointless chivalric heroism from the French, notably when the blind king of Bohemia was led into the mêlée, his knights bound to him by ropes. All were slain. After the victory, Edward laid siege to Calais, which surrendered in August 1347, giving the English a vital line of communication to the continent.

**Crediton, diocese of** Carved out of the *Sherborne bishopric in 909, it initially covered all Devon and Cornwall, though from 931 to 1027 *St Germans was the separate see for Cornwall. In 1050 Leofric moved the bishopric to *Exeter.

**cricket** is not mentioned in James I's *Book of Sports* (1617) but was certainly well developed before the end of the century. An eleven-a-side match for 50 guineas was played in Sussex in 1697 and in 1709 Kent played Surrey at Dartford. Bowling was underarm and the bat was a heavy curved club. In 1744 there was an attempt to formulate agreed rules and the same year an All England XI played the men of Kent at the Artillery Ground, Finsbury. A meeting at the Star and Garter in 1774 drew up new rules, with 22-yard pitches, 4-ball overs, stumping, and no-balling: 'the wicket-keeper should not by any noise incommode the striker.' In 1787 Thomas Lord opened his new ground at Marylebone and in 1788 the Marylebone Cricket Club issued revised rules, prohibiting any attempt to impede a fielder while making a catch. The club moved to its present ground in 1814.

The most important change in the rules in the 19th cent. was the introduction of overarm bowling in 1864 after vehement controversy. The Gentlemen v. Players match was first held in 1806 and was annual after 1819; Oxford v. Cambridge dates from 1827. By 1864 enough cricket was being played for John Wisden, himself a celebrated bowler, to launch his *Cricketers' Almanack*. The first test match was played at Melbourne in 1877, when Australia won, and when they won again at the Oval in 1882, the *Sporting Times* declared that the ashes of English cricket would be taken to Australia. Though county teams competed from early days, the county championship did not start until 1889, and was dominated in its early years by Nottinghamshire, Surrey, Yorkshire, and Lancashire. Gloucestershire, for whom the great W. G. *Grace played, had been strong in the 1870s. Grace, probably the best known of all Victorian figures, gave cricket a national following.

The two main developments of 20th-cent. cricket were the spread of international competition, as the West Indies, India, Pakistan, Sri Lanka, and others came in to join England, Australia, New Zealand, and South Africa, and the introduction after the Second World War of limited-over cricket at the highest level. Limited-over cricket was not quite the innovation sometimes suggested, since village, club, and northern league cricket had always been played on that basis. It was made necessary because gate money could no longer support the traditional county championship in the face of alternative leisure attractions.

**crime** Anglo-Saxon law codes suggest a restitutive system, essentially a regulation of the feud. Post-Conquest England experienced a growing criminal justice system, the reign of

Henry II (1154–89) providing the most durable elements. Interpreting the level and nature of medieval crime is difficult. There were criminal gangs who at times indulged in outright banditry, but criminal prosecutions in the 14th cent. suggest a more modern criminality in some areas, with theft as the most prominent offence.

Record survival permits more systematic work from the 1550s, which has centred mainly on the study of felony (a category which includes serious offences such as homicide, burglary, theft, rape, and arson). Prosecution of these offences reached peaks in the late 1590s (a period of bad harvests) and the 1620s, a decade which experienced severe social and economic problems. When the running of criminal courts was resumed after the civil wars, however, levels of prosecuted felonies were low, and remained so until the mid-18th cent., when a resumption of population growth and the economic dislocation which attended the arrival of the industrial revolution caused them to rise.

During the early 19th cent. levels of crime rose alarmingly. Mass demobilization of soldiers and sailors after 1815 caused a crime wave, and this continued as industrialization and urbanization burgeoned. It was in the early 19th cent. that crime was identified as a social problem in the modern sense. The period saw the origins of criminology as a discipline, the introduction of national crime statistics, the emergence of such concepts as juvenile delinquency, professional police forces, and prison as the standard punishment for serious offenders. With the emergence of improved living standards among the working classes, levels of prosecution dropped slightly in the late Victorian and Edwardian periods. From the 1950s, however, levels of prosecution increased, and continued to do so alarmingly over the 1980s and 1990s.

Criminals have always shown ingenuity in inventing new crimes. The introduction of motor cars in the early 20th. cent. led to car theft, drunken driving, and insurance evasion. Two disagreeable developments in the early 21st cent. were the proliferation of computer crimes, involving hacking into bank accounts, and an increase in 'street crime', particularly the theft of cameras, handbags, and mobile phones. By 2007 British prisons were so full that the reintroduction of prison hulks was seriously mooted.

**Crimean War,** 1853–6. Known to contemporaries as 'the Russian War', this arose from long-term Russian ambitions to expand westward and southward. The immediate cause was a petty struggle between Russia and France over rights in Ottoman Turkey. This produced an ultimatum from Russia to Turkey in March 1853, followed by Russian occupation of the Ottoman Danubian provinces (modern Romania) and a naval victory over Turkey at Sinope on 27 November. Britain and France (later joined by Sardinia as well as Turkey) issued their own ultimatum against Russia on 27 March 1854.

The Black Sea theatre dominated contemporary perspectives of the war. Britain supplied a field army of about 28,000, which, with a French contingent of equal size, landed in May 1854 at Varna to defend it against Russian forces crossing the Danube. When this threat failed to materialize, the allied armies were transferred to the Crimean peninsula, landing north of the main Russian naval base of Sebastopol on 14 September. Their first victory, at the *Alma six days later, enabled them to continue south around Sebastopol to Balaclava, so establishing a partial siege of the base.

Through the autumn the Russians tried to break the siege of Sebastopol, the major attacks being at *Balaclava in October and *Inkerman in November. After surviving a bad winter, the allies launched naval expeditions against the smaller Russian bases of Kerch in May and Kinburn (near Odessa) in October 1855. Meanwhile, the Russians made one final attempt to relieve Sebastopol in August at the Tchernaya. Repeated British and French attacks on Sebastopol finally led to the base becoming untenable and the Russians abandoned it in October.

Modern historical study pays as much attention to the naval campaign fought in the Baltic as to the Crimean theatre. The end of the war came about not through the fall of Sebastopol but through the British victory in August 1855 in destroying the Russian dockyard at Sweaborg (outside modern Helsinki). Rather than face the loss of Cronstadt as well as Sebastopol, the Russians agreed to moderate peace terms in the treaty of *Paris of 30 March 1856, with the Black Sea declared neutral and the Danube an open waterway.

The result of the Crimean War has been much debated. By pursuing a limited aim the allies held Russia in check for a generation, rather than destroying themselves by marching on Moscow. Equally, although British performance in the Crimea was a contemporary byword for incompetence, it is recognized that by the winter of 1855 most of its problems were solved.

**criminal law** In Anglo-Saxon and Norman England, there was no distinction between criminal and civil law. Violence, or the causing of damage or harm to another's person or property, was subject to savage penalties if the offender was caught red-handed, but other cases, including homicide, were dealt with by a system of compensation whereby, according to a tariff, wrongs were recompensed by money payments.

Certain offences which were especially serious were the 'pleas of the crown', declared by the Anglo-Saxon kings to affect the king's interests especially, such as a breach of the king's peace. The Normans adopted these notions and extended the pleas of the crown, as well as introducing the concept of felony. These pleas came to be dealt with by the king's own justice—i.e. by the king or his justices.

In the Assizes of *Clarendon and *Northampton (1166 and 1176), Henry II introduced a system under which twelve men of each hundred were to present to the justices of the *curia regis those suspected of serious crime. Some see this as the beginning of a true 'criminal law', since it acknowledged that it is the role of government in the person of the king to ensure that crime is dealt with. Those presented might then be put to the ordeal to ascertain their guilt or innocence. When the clergy were forbidden to participate in ordeals by the Lateran Council of the church in 1215, the justices turned to the verdict of a jury to decide.

Lesser offences were presented to the sheriff at the periodic session of the *hundred court (held four times a year), which was known as the 'sheriff's tourn'. Where the lord of the manor held a *court leet, the jurisdiction of the hundred was exercised in that court, and the fines collected were payable to the lord. Later, after the introduction of the *justices of the peace, lesser offences were tried by the JPs in *petty sessions or *quarter sessions.

The 18th and 19th cents. saw the introduction of large numbers of capital offences. The so-called 'bloody code' imposed savage penalties for many offences and, even when transportation was introduced as an alternative to the death penalty, punishments remained severe. The severity of the penal system was to some extent modified by the use of fictions, especially the undervaluing of goods stolen at less than a pound; by the use of benefit of clergy to enable a defendant who had been found guilty to evade the death penalty; by the reluctance of juries to convict; and by the very widespread use of the power of pardon. Gradually, under the influence of reformers such as *Bentham, *Romilly, *Mackintosh, and *Peel, the ferocity of the penal code was mitigated.

This system of criminal justice remained until the 19th cent. and was little changed until the 1971 Courts Act, which abolished assizes and quarter sessions. Serious criminal cases are now tried in the crown court with a jury. Less serious cases are dealt with summarily by magistrates sitting without a jury, or by a stipendiary magistrate.

**Cripps, Sir Stafford** (1889–1952). Cripps was a successful barrister before he was appointed Labour solicitor-general in 1930. The economic crisis converted Cripps to socialism and he took the leadership of the Socialist League. His energetic advocacy of the 'Popular Front' made Cripps prominent but earned him expulsion from the Labour Party in 1939. During the war, Cripps rose to the fore after the success of his ambassadorship to Russia. In 1945 Attlee appointed him president of the Board of Trade (1945–7) and then chancellor of the Exchequer (1947–50). These jobs he carried out with his characteristic emphasis on self-sacrifice and austerity. Poor health forced his resignation in 1950, and he died soon after.

**Croker, John Wilson** (1780–1857). An Irish lawyer, educated at Trinity College, Dublin, Croker had two separate though related careers as politician and as man of letters. He entered Parliament in 1806 and was taken up by *Canning, becoming a strong Tory supporter, though sympathetic to both *catholic emancipation and a measure of *parliamentary reform. He was on close terms with both *Peel and *Wellington. In 1809 he helped to found the *Quarterly Review*, in which most of his essays appeared. *Perceval appointed him secretary to the Admiralty in 1809, a well-paid post which he held for 22 years. But his upwards progress faltered after 1820 when his only child, a 3-year-old son, died, He went out with the Tories in 1830 and played a prominent part in opposing the Whig Reform Act. But after the passage of the bill, he gave up his seat, devoting the rest of his life to his literary work, though staying on close terms with Peel until his conversion over the Corn Laws, which Croker thought had 'ruined the character of public men'.

**Crome, John** (1768–1821). Landscape painter, born in Norwich where he spent almost all his life. The son of an innkeeper, Crome had little education and was apprenticed early to a sign-writer. He supplemented his income by giving drawing lessons, and became the drawing master at the local grammar school in 1801. In 1803 he helped found the Norwich Society of Artists, of which he became president in 1808.

**Crompton, Samuel** (1753–1827). Inventor. One of the men who revolutionized the Lancashire textiles industry, Crompton was born near Bolton. His 'spinning mule', invented in 1779, improved upon *Hargreaves's jenny. It was a cross between the jenny and *Arkwright's water frame and produced yarn of high quality.

**Cromwell, Oliver** (1599–1658). General and lord protector. It is still difficult to appreciate the unique character of Cromwell's career. In a country governed by custom, precedent, and the common law, Cromwell completely changed the ancient frame of government, reforming Parliament and imposing a written constitution. By conquest he incorporated the separate kingdoms of Scotland and Ireland into a single commonwealth with England. He remains the only British statesman whose entire career depended on the control and use of military power. Yet his achievement proved to be totally ephemeral.

A provincial gentleman from Huntingdon of modest means, Cromwell first became prominent in the second session of the *Long Parliament (1641–2). Cromwell urged Parliament to assume control of both the army destined for Ireland and the home mi-

litia, and soon became identified with the war party. He made the forces maintained by the *Eastern Association the most formidable of the parliamentarian armies. Cromwell's men contributed decisively to the victory at *Marston Moor (July 1644).

Cromwell deplored the failure to follow up this victory effectively, denounced his own neighbour and superior officer, Lord *Manchester, and helped pass the *self-denying ordinance. This barred peers and MPs, with exceptions of whom Cromwell was one, from commands and set up a central army, the *New Model, of which he became second in command. At *Naseby, Cromwell annihilated Charles's field army (June 1645). He next emerged as the chief military politician, eclipsing his superior, Lord *Fairfax. Cromwell took the lead, first in representing army grievances, but soon in a wider sense claiming to speak and act as the embodiment of the 'cause' for which it had fought the war. In July 1647 the army issued the *Heads of the Proposals, a manifesto for a new constitutional settlement, which it discussed with Charles. The manifesto did not go far enough to satisfy the more radical officers and men. Influenced by *Leveller ideas, the radicals published an *Agreement of the People: this was discussed in the *Putney debates of the army council, a body representing all ranks and units.

During this period of rapid change Cromwell developed the techniques which enabled him to keep control over the army for the rest of his life. He could not depend on politicized radicals obeying orders. He had to break up networks of officers that could develop into challenges to his authority, he had to balance the factions—ambitious opportunists (like *Lambert), religious fanatics (Thomas Harrison), professionals (*Monck, Montagu). He learned that neglect of the interests and grievances of ordinary soldiers led to their politicization. Above all he knew that army unity must be maintained.

Early in 1648 royalist risings broke out and a Scottish army invaded on Charles's behalf. Cromwell and Fairfax reacted with great speed, annihilating enemy forces. Opinion in the army now accepted that as a 'man of blood' the king had to be punished. Cromwell clearly inspired the action that followed. Colonel Pride, backed up by armed soldiers, prevented MPs who were unacceptable to the army from entering the Commons. The purged House that subsequently worked with the army was known as the *Rump. By killing the king the regicides made any future compromise impossible.

In 1649-51 Cromwell was almost continuously on campaign away from Westminster. His militarily successful Irish campaign of 1649-50 has been universally condemned for its ruthlessness, especially for the massacres at *Drogheda and Wexford. Cromwell's methods represented a revival of those used in Elizabeth's Irish wars and he saw them as a reprisal for atrocities committed by the Irish rebels in 1641. In 1650-1 he was engaged in war against the Scots, who crowned Charles II king of Scotland. Cromwell defeated them at *Dunbar and finally *Worcester in successive Septembers, 1650 and 1651.

Cromwell's second major coup, his ejection of the Rump on 20 April 1653, opened the way for an experiment to create a form of government that would be in accord with what he took to be God's will. He and the army council named a constituent body to draft a godly constitution, *Barebone's or the 'Nominated' Parliament. The fanatics in Barebone's Parliament disappointed Cromwell by wanting the abolition of tithe and universities, seeing a salaried and learned ministry as unnecessary. After moderates dissolved the 'Parliament' Cromwell infuriated the fanatics further by ending the Dutch War, giving the defeated enemy lenient terms (March 1654). After Barebone's Parliament came a written constitution, the *Instrument of Government (December 1653), introducing a form of government based on a balance of power between a reformed single-chamber parliament elected by a new representative system, an elected council, and the executive, Lord Protector Cromwell. This constitution was superseded in 1657 by the *Humble Petition and Advice which established an upper house in Parliament and empowered the lord protector to designate his successor. Neither constitution gave the impression of a governmental system built to last. This explains Cromwell's reluctant refusal in 1657 to assume the familiar title of king.

In the short term Cromwellian government worked. He maintained army discipline and unity but he could not eradicate all potential radical activists. Quakers as well

as catholics and Prayer Book Anglicans were excluded from toleration. The costs of maintaining the army, aggravated by a Spanish war that began in 1655, produced an accumulation of debt that would have ended in an insoluble crisis. But the greatest change brought about by the institutionalization of the Protectorate was the erosion of the 'cause' which Cromwell embodied, the establishment of a form of government in which the godly, not a monarch, wielded power. Previous rulers—even Elizabeth—had failed to undertake and complete all the tasks required of a godly prince. Cromwell's missionary cause was to create a godly nation, but by 1658 few still shared his zeal.

**Cromwell, Richard** (1626-1712). Lord protector (1658-9). Son of Oliver *Cromwell, he held no important position until 1657. Under the *Heads of the Proposals, Oliver could nominate his successor. Despite inexperience, Richard initially provided stability, settling army discontent and calling a parliament elected on the traditional constituencies. His eventual failure was caused principally by problems which he inherited. Accumulated debt worsened by the Spanish War could not be tackled because the main cause was expenditure on the army and navy. Even more fatal was the revival of radical political activism in the army. In April 1659 Richard tried to use Parliament to gain control over the military: this drove the generals into the radical camp and they forced him to dissolve Parliament. Richard was never deposed; his authority was no longer recognized. Thereafter he lived privately, in exile from 1660 to 1680.

**Cromwell, Thomas** (*c.*1485-1540). Thomas Cromwell was the second great minister to whom Henry VIII gave much trust and the one most personally associated with the programme which made Henry VIII supreme head of the church in England. The son of a Putney cloth-worker, he somehow acquired a broad education including some knowledge of business and law. He sat in the 1523 Parliament and entered the service of Thomas *Wolsey. Though he stayed with Wolsey longer than most after his disgrace, he escaped the wreck to join a group of administrators who were working on plans for Henry VIII to escape from the impasse in his divorce negotiations.

Cromwell became master of the king's jewel house in 1532 and principal royal secretary in 1534. Though he was thereafter to accumulate other offices including chancellor of the Exchequer, master of the rolls, lord privy seal, and great chamberlain, it was on his role as royal secretary that his power rested. It is not certain what role Cromwell played in the birth of Henry VIII's campaign for supremacy over the church. The arguments used to justify this campaign antedated Cromwell's rise to influence. Nevertheless, it seems likely that Cromwell drew the strands together, and recognized that parliamentary statute offered the most authoritative way to announce the new changes. Cromwell is thought to have been responsible for drafting the Supplication of the Commons against the Ordinaries in 1532. He certainly took charge of the drafting of the Act in Restraint of *Appeals to Rome (1533) and the Act of *Supremacy (1534).

Just as important was Cromwell's ruthless treatment of high-profile opponents of the policy. The long examinations of Sir Thomas *More, and his eventual trial and conviction for refusing the oath of supremacy, testify to Cromwell's anxiety to be seen to observe the forms of law. Cromwell gave away a hostage to fortune by his efforts to propel Henrician religious policy in a moderately protestant direction. As royal vicegerent in spirituals from 1535 Cromwell was responsible for the Ten Articles of 1536 and the royal injunctions of 1536 and 1538, which systematically attacked catholic teaching. On a wider front, Cromwell patronized ideas for social reform, especially improvements to poor relief.

Thomas Cromwell never enjoyed the sort of ascendancy held by Cardinal Wolsey and the last four years of his life were a constant struggle to overcome rivals. Using parliamentary Acts of attainder he secured the judicial killing of *Anne Boleyn (1536), and the Courtenay and Pole families (1538). By this period Cromwell was seeking an alliance with pro-protestant princes in Germany. In 1540 he brought about the disastrous marriage of Henry and *Anne of Cleves in pursuit of this policy. Political and religious enemies led by the duke of *Norfolk and Bishop Stephen *Gardiner gained the king's ear and convinced Henry that Cromwell was a traitor and an ultra-prot-

estant 'sacramentarian' heretic; he was condemned untried by the weapon of parliamentary attainder which he had himself used so often, and executed on 28 July 1540.

**Cropredy Bridge, battle of,** 1644. While waiting for news of *Rupert's attempt to relieve York, Charles I's southern army clashed with *Waller at Cropredy bridge, near Banbury (Oxon.), on 29 June. Waller, seeing the royalist army strung out on the march, hoped to punch a hole between van and rear by taking Cropredy bridge. But he found himself facing a battle on two fronts and was fortunate to extricate himself with the loss of some light guns. Cropredy sustained royalist morale until the news from *Marston Moor came through.

**croquet** may have originated in France, since most of the terms are French in origin, and seems to have been played in England in the 16th cent. Like many games, it became standardized in the Victorian period, and an English tournament was organized at Evesham in 1867. Simple versions are played in many private gardens, with unexpected hazards, but the national game is administered by the Croquet Association at the Hurlingham Club.

**Crotoy, battle of,** 1347. In 1346 Edward III laid siege to *Calais with a naval blockade. On 25 June 1347 a French fleet of some 40 vessels bringing relief was scattered at Crotoy, at the mouth of the Somme. Calais surrendered on 3 August and remained in English hands for more than 200 years.

**Crowley, Sir Ambrose** (1658–1713). Crowley was a remarkable industrial magnate. He came from a quaker family of Worcestershire and his ancestors were blacksmiths. He built up an enormous iron enterprise, first establishing a foundry at Sunderland, where coal was cheap, transport to London quick, and the Tyneside shipbuilders needed nails. In 1691 he transferred his business to Winlaton, west of Newcastle.

**crown** See MONARCHY.

**Cruikshank, George** (1792–1878). Caricaturist and book illustrator. Born in London of Scottish parents, apprentice in his father's print factory, Cruikshank rapidly became *Gillray's successor as leading political caricaturist, but from about 1824 turned to book illustration. As Regency exuberance yielded to Victorian gentility, he began to outlive his popularity.

**crusades** The crusades constituted the most popular mass movement of the later Middle Ages. They may be defined as a species of holy war, authorized by the pope; a just war, that is a defensive reaction to aggression towards Christian people or territory, their participants enjoying a set of privileges offered by the pope and enshrined in canon law. Such a definition, crucially, did not require a crusader to fulfil his vow in the Holy Land, nor did it postulate Muslims as the normative object of crusading. Crusades came to be deployed against a variety of opponents—against Moors in Spain, Mongols in eastern Europe, pagan Slavs in north-eastern Europe, heretics in Bosnia and in southern France, and a variety of papal political opponents.

Many of these various applications were controversial at the time. The same is true of the very notion of crusade, from the time that Pope Urban II made his call to the First Crusade at the Council of Clermont in November 1095. In protestant Britain, crusades have been harshly judged for centuries. This train of thought was famously stated by David *Hume: 'the most signal and durable monument to human folly that has yet appeared in any age or nation.' Such a tradition has militated against serious consideration of the significance of the crusades in British history. Were the crusades not a terrible distraction, deflecting the king from his primary concerns at home? Were they not a deplorable squandering of resources?

Times and attitudes have changed. One recent trend has been a move towards thorough investigation of the impact of the crusades upon the societies in which they were preached, and it is now apparent that the crusades affected vast areas of life. The heyday of crusading was in the 12th and 13th cents., at least so far as English participation is concerned, but as an institution the crusade only finally withered in the later 16th cent. Every king of England between 1154 and 1327 took the cross, though only one, Richard I, fulfilled it in person.

**Crystal Palace** Designed by Sir Joseph Paxton to house the *Great Exhibition in Hyde Park in 1851, it was itself the greatest success of the Exhibition. Paxton based it upon the lily house he had built at *Chatsworth for the duke of Devonshire—a vast glass conservatory, dubbed the Crystal Palace by *Punch. In 1852 the building was removed to Sydenham, where it was destroyed by fire in November 1936.

**Cubitt, Thomas** (1788–1855). Builder. Son of a Norfolk carpenter removed to London, Cubitt set up as master carpenter. After the London Institution (1815) he moved into speculative building, progressing from Highbury villas to Bloomsbury and Belgravia. According to Queen Victoria (for whom he altered *Osborne), 'a better, kinder-hearted man never breathed'.

**Cuilén** (d. 971), king of 'Scotland' (from 966). Son of *Indulf, Cuilén became king following Dub's death fighting the men of Moray. He had challenged Dub in 965, but had been defeated at Duncrub (west of Perth). He was killed by Rhydderch son of King Dyfnwal of Strathclyde in a battle fought in Lothian.

**Culloden, battle of,** 1746. Fought on Wednesday, 16 April, south-east of Inverness. The retreating Jacobites occupied Inverness in February 1746. An attempted night attack on the advancing army of the duke of *Cumberland failed on 15 April, and Charles *Stuart offered battle on the bare boggy Drumossie Moor above Culloden House. The Jacobites could assemble only 5,000 men. Cumberland had 9,000 men including many Scots. Cumberland's field guns decimated the Jacobite ranks for 20 minutes. Charles, in command for the first time, fatally delayed the order to charge. When the Jacobite right was launched, gallantry could not match discipline. The Macdonalds on the Jacobite left rightly pulled back at first in good order, pursued by cavalry. Retreat became rout.

**Cumberland** consisted of the western part of the Lake District, a surrounding coastal plain, and two outlying areas, a hilly district to the east towards Alston, and fertile lands north of *Hadrian's Wall towards the Scottish border. Carlisle grew as a bridge over the Eden, where an east-west route from Newcastle towards Ireland intersected with two major north–south routes, an ancient road through Tebay, and an old route from York-shire across Stainmore.

Cumberland was one of the last shires to take shape and for centuries was disputed between England and Scotland. In Caesar's time it was in the territory of the *Brigantes, but that was a loose confederation and the local tribe were the *Carvetii. The Romans were interested in the area for strategic and economic reasons. In the end, their boundary with the Scots settled along the line of Ha-drian's Wall. Carlisle (Luguvalium) was a major Roman town, and there were important forts at Hardknott (the worst posting in Roman Britain), and at Maryport, Penrith, Netherby, and Bewcastle. Ravenglass, where the Mite, Irt, and Esk meet, was a superb natural harbour until it silted up. The local mineral resources were also exploited—silver and lead from the Alston region, copper, coal, and iron elsewhere. After the Roman period, the orientation of the region was towards Scot-land and Ireland rather than the south. It was a meeting-place of peoples and cultures. The basic stratum was Welsh or British, and the name, Cumberland, means the land of the Cumbri—the Welsh. But the Saxons pene-trated across from Northumbria and later there were settlers from Ireland and the Isle of Man, who left Norse place-names—Aspa-tria, Cleator, Ennerdale, and Borrowdale. Roman and Celtic Christianity also competed here. St *Ninian's mission at Whithorn was only the other side of Solway Firth and St Kentigern certainly evangelized in the 6th cent. from Strathclyde. After *Æthelfryth's vic-tory at *Degsastan in 603, the region fell under Saxon rule and became part of *Northumbria.

But it was hard for any power to keep a firm grip on the area and as Northumbrian influ-ence waned, that of Wessex rose. In 926 *Athelstan, king of Wessex, met the kings of Strathclyde and Scotland at Eamont bridge to dictate terms, and reasserted his authority in 937 with a crushing victory at *Brunanburh. But Wessex control of so distant a territory can only have been fitful.

By this time the term Cumbria was coming into use. The Normans did not at first occupy the area and neither Cumberland nor West-morland was included in the *Domesday survey in 1086. But in 1092 William Rufus brought a large force there and began build-ing the castle at Carlisle and in 1133 Henry I established Carlisle as a bishopric. The Scots

had by no means abandoned their claims. David I of Scotland took advantage of the confusion of Stephen's reign to occupy the area and died at Carlisle in 1153. Henry II reconquered it in 1157 and it stayed part of England. Westmorland was hived off to form a separate county and by the end of the 13th cent. Cumberland, like the other counties, sent two knights of the shire to Parliament.

Though Cumberland was now firmly at-tached to England, it remained a border county. The tide of war rolled backwards and forwards. The Scots besieged Carlisle in 1296; Robert I Bruce did homage in the ca-thedral in 1297; and Edward I died at Burgh campaigning against the Scots in 1307. Dur-ing the Civil War, in 1644-5, Carlisle stood a siege from the Scots who destroyed much of the cathedral. The last serious fighting on English soil occurred in the county during Prince Charles *Stuart's retreat in 1745, when he left a forlorn hope in Carlisle castle.

Although not a large town, Carlisle domi-nated the county. Penrith had military im-portance because of the junction of two major routes, and the market towns of Brampton, Wigton, Cockermouth, and Kes-wick had local significance. Travellers avoided the area if they could. But the char-acter of the county began to change with the industrial revolution, which created an urban fringe to west Cumberland, and the revolution in taste, which brought visitors in search of Romantic scenery of lakes and hills. Local landowners were vigorous in ex-ploiting mineral resources and opening up ports. The Lowthers sponsored Whitehaven, which exported coal to Dublin, the Curwens did the same for Workington. The chief ben-eficiary or victim of Romanticism was per-haps Keswick, on the shore of Derwentwater, which changed from a small market town into a fashionable Victorian resort and thence into a tourist trap. By the local gov-ernment reorganization of 1972 Cumberland was united with Westmorland and the Fur-ness district of Lancashire to form Cumbria.

## Cumberland, Ernest Augustus, duke of (1771–1851). Ernest Augustus, fifth son of George III, had an eventful life. At 15 he was sent to the University of Göttingen in Han-over and in 1790 was commissioned in the Hanoverian army. A brave cavalry com-mander, he was severely wounded in 1794,

losing one eye. In 1799 he was created duke of Cumberland, took his seat in the Lords, and spoke frequently as a protestant Tory. In the crisis of 1828–32, Cumberland became the spokesman for those opposed to the repeal of the *Test and Corporation Acts, *catholic emancipation, and the *Reform Bill. On becoming king of *Hanover in 1837, he cancelled the liberal constitution granted in 1833 by his brother William IV, substituting a more limited one three years later. The Hanoverians, delighted to have a resident monarch once more, admired him greatly and he survived the year of revolution in 1848 without difficulty.

**Cumberland, William Augustus, 1st duke of** (1721–65). Cumberland was the second surviving son of the prince of Wales, later George II. Made duke of Cumberland in 1726, he was promoted lieutenant-general in 1744, after fighting at *Dettingen. Recalled in October to deal with the *Jacobite rebellion, he finally crushed it at *Culloden in April 1746.

At the start of the *Seven Years War, he virtually ran the British war effort but was destroyed by defeat against superior French armies in Hanover. The convention of *Kloster-Zeven, which he signed with the French, was repudiated. He retired from the army, but remained a powerful political influence into the early years of George III.

**Cumbria** The new county of Cumbria was established by the Local Government Act of 1972, which joined the traditional counties of Cumberland and Westmorland, and added that section of north Lancashire to the south of the Lake District.

**Cunedda** Leader of the *Votadini tribe of southern Scotland in the late Roman period. Cunedda and the Votadini migrated from southern Scotland to north Wales. The contention that the British leader *Vortigern arranged the migration of the Votadini in order to strengthen north Wales against the Irish must be treated with caution.

**Cunningham, Andrew, 1st Viscount Cunningham** (1883–1963). Sailor. Cunningham spent the First World War as captain of the destroyer *Scorpion*. The outbreak of the Second World War found him an acting Admiral as commander-in-chief Mediterranean. This became a post of supreme importance when Italy entered the war in 1940. In November 1940 an air attack on the harbour at *Taranto forced the Italian fleet to withdraw northwards and in March 1941, in a night attack, Cunningham won a decisive victory over an Italian force off Cape *Matapan. He was appointed 1st sea lord and chief of the naval staff in 1943.

**Cunobelinus** succeeded Tasciovanus as king of the *Catuvellauni around AD 5. By AD 10 he had overrun the kingdom of the *Trinovantes and had moved his own capital from *Verulamium (St Albans) to Camulodunum (*Colchester). He became the most powerful monarch in Britain and the Roman historian Suetonius described him as 'Britannorum rex'—king of the Britons. He reigned for more than 35 years, dying a year or two before the Claudian invasion of AD 43.

**curia regis** *See* GREAT COUNCIL.

**Curragh mutiny** In March 1914, 57 officers of the 3rd Cavalry Brigade, stationed at Curragh near Dublin, informed the commander-in-chief that they would accept dismissal rather than help to impose the Irish Home Rule Bill on Ulster. They succeeded in obtaining a written assurance that they would not be expected to do this.

**Curzon, George Nathaniel, 1st Marquis Curzon** (1859–1925). Curzon became an authority on the East through travelling extensively in the 1880s. He was sent to India as viceroy in 1899, where he worked hard to further the interests of both Britain and the natives, and in some splendour. He also quarrelled with his army commander, Lord *Kitchener; and with most of the population of Bengal by partitioning the province in 1905. His resignation later that year was accompanied by recrimination, and followed by exclusion from public life, until the *First World War resurrected his career in 1916. After the war he was foreign secretary (1919–24), but again quarrelsome; and was disappointed at not becoming prime minister in 1923.

**customs and excise** Monarchs and governments have traditionally levied customs and excise duties, but they became more important as the expense of government increased, particularly during the 17th cent. Historically, customs and excise duties have been objects of popular resistance. *Ship money, for example, was only one of several imposts introduced by Charles I which caused widespread resentment. Later, the 1707 *Union of England and Scotland, though highly contentious, embodied a customs union, including an enhanced malt tax, which caused riots in Scotland. In 1733 Walpole was nearly brought down by the *Excise crisis.

By the late 18th cent. the customs and excise had become increasingly efficient. In the 19th cent. growing belief in *free trade persuaded governments to reduce customs duties where possible, but increasing international competition produced calls for protective tariffs which, articulated by Joseph *Chamberlain, split the Conservative Party in 1903. Protectionist arguments made progress after the *First World War, but one of the objects of the *European Economic Community was to reduce customs duties between member states. Customs and Excise was merged in 2005 with Inland Revenue under the Revenue and Customs Board.

**custos rotulorum** The officer charged in the 14th cent. with keeping the records of the county sessions, though the name did not come into use until the 15th cent. Later the office became identified with the *lord-lieutenancy.

**Cuthbert, St** (d. 687). Probably of aristocratic Anglo-Saxon origin, and born in Northumbria c.635, Cuthbert was prompted by a vision of the soul of *Aidan to enter the monastery at Melrose. With Abbot Eata, he entered Alchfrith of Deira's new monastery at Ripon (late 650s), but returned after refusing to accept Roman practices. Cuthbert became prior in 664 and undertook teaching tours in Northumbria. After the Synod of *Whitby (664), Eata removed to Lindisfarne. Cuthbert followed and became prior, but had some difficulties managing the monks. He retreated to Farne Island (c.676) but was, reluctantly, made bishop of part of Northumbria under Archbishop *Theodore (685). His seat was at Lindisfarne. He retired in 686 and died in 687, on Farne. In 698, in promotion of his cult, his remains, buried at Lindisfarne, were exhumed and enshrined, in which process they were found to

be incorrupt, and for which the Lindisfarne Gospels may have been produced. Scandinavian incursions having caused the community to move, his coffin reached Durham in 995, where a new shrine was established in 1104. The 698 decorated coffin survives, in fragments, now displayed with his pectoral cross and some Anglo-Saxon gifts to his shrine in the cathedral.

**Cuthred** (d. 756), king of Wessex (c.740–56). When Cuthred succeeded, King *Æthelbald of Mercia dominated the southern English kingdoms. In 743 the two kings are recorded as combining against the Welsh, whom Cuthred was fighting again some ten years later. In 752, Cuthred defeated Æthelbald at *Burford. This victory apparently brought independence to Wessex, but it seems to have reverted to Mercian dependency soon after Cuthred's death in 756.

***Cutty Sark*** The last and most famous tea clipper, launched in 1869 from Dumbarton (the figurehead's 'cutty sark' = short chemise). She plied the Australian wool trade until 1895. Now restored, she lies at Greenwich. Badly damaged in a fire in 2007, the vessel is once again being renovated.

**cycling** A primitive wheeled cycle was exhibited at Paris in 1791 but had to be pushed with the feet, as were the hobby-horses of the 1810s. In the 1860s a front-wheel-drive machine was manufactured—the bone-shaker—and in subsequent decades the front wheel became larger until the penny-farthing had developed. The Rover safety model, built at Coventry from 1885, had a rear-wheel chain drive and from 1888 pneumatic tyres could be fitted. Cycle races began early and special tracks were built in the 1880s. The National Cyclists' Union was founded in 1878 and the Cyclists' Touring Club the same year.

**Cynegils** (d. 643), king of the West Saxons (c.611–43). Cynegils extended his frontier by defeating the Britons at Beandun, probably Bindon, east Devon, but suffered setbacks. Expansion was slowed by conflict with expanding Mercian neighbours, and it seems likely that Wessex lost lands gained in 577, in the lower Severn valley, to *Penda of Mercia. In 635, Cynegils was baptized by the recently arrived missionary Birinus. He became the first Christian king of Wessex.

**Cynewulf** (d. 786), king of Wessex (757–86). Cynewulf deposed his predecessor, Sigeberht. In 757 he attended the Mercian court, witnessing one of *Æthelbald's charters, suggesting that Wessex was again a Mercian dependency. He appears to have lost lands to Offa after defeat at *Benson (*c.*777). The *Anglo-Saxon Chronicle* account of his death reads like a heroic saga. After a long reign, he was attacked and killed by Cyneheard, the deposed Sigeberht's brother, when visiting his mistress. His few attendants fought to the death. The next day, Cynewulf's remaining force confronted his killer. Loyal to their lord they refused offers of money, slaying Cyneheard and his followers.

**Cyprus** is the third largest island in the Mediterranean. It was Arab from AD 647 for 500 years, then an independent Frankish kingdom for about 300 years, before falling briefly into Egyptian hands until 1489, when it was occupied by the Venetians. In 1571 it was conquered by the Ottoman Turks. In 1878 administration of the island was taken over by Britain and on the outbreak of war with Turkey in 1914 it was annexed. Pressure for independence or union with Greece ('Enosis') developed after the Second World War and in the 1950s EOKA began a guerrilla campaign. Independence was declared in 1960 with Greek Cypriot Archbishop Makarios as president and a Turkish Cypriot, Dr Küçük, as his deputy. In 1974 an EOKA coup to replace Makarios prompted a Turkish invasion and the occupation of northern Cyprus. Despite occasional negotiations, the two communities remain implacably apart. Cyprus joined the European Union in 2004.

**Dafydd ap Gruffydd** (d. 1283), prince of Wales (1282–3). The third son of Gruffydd ap Llywelyn of Gwynedd, he was the last prince of Wales. Ambitious and disloyal to his elder brother *Llywelyn, he allowed himself to be manipulated by English kings. In 1263 he joined Henry III, though when Llywelyn was recognized as prince of Wales (1267) Dafydd was restored to land and position and swore fealty to Llywelyn. In 1274 he plotted Llywelyn's death, after which he fled to Edward I. After Llywelyn's defeat (1277), Dafydd married the king's relative, Elizabeth Ferrers. Dissatisfied with his treatment, he attacked Hawarden (21 March 1282) and Llywelyn was drawn into the war. After Llywelyn's death (December), Dafydd held out and styled himself prince of Wales. He was betrayed by Welshmen and executed for treason (3 October 1283.

**Dafydd ap Llywelyn** (c.1208–46), prince of Gwynedd (1240–6). The only son of *Llywelyn ab Iorwerth, prince of Gwynedd, and Joan, daughter of King John, he was declared heir to his father's principality. Dafydd's elevation alienated his illegitimate elder brother Gruffydd; in 1239 Dafydd deprived Gruffydd of some lands and imprisoned him. When Llywelyn died (1240), Henry III determined to curb Dafydd's ambitions. At Gloucester (15 May) he was knighted by the king, who received his homage; but Llywelyn's acquisitions outside Gwynedd were withheld and the homage of other Welsh nobles was reserved to the king. After Gruffydd died (1 March 1244) while trying to escape from the Tower of London, Dafydd resolved to resist the king: he gained support from Welsh nobles, sought endorsement from the pope, styled himself prince of Wales, and resumed his father's policy of creating a modern, feudal principality. Henry III launched an expedition against him (1245),

but it was Dafydd's sudden death at Aber (25 February 1246) that halted his ambitions.

**Dáil Éireann** is the Lower House of the Parliament of Eire. Its first meeting in the Mansion House at Dublin was in January 1919 after *Sinn Fein had won 73 seats at the general election, boycotted the Westminster Parliament, and proclaimed themselves the Parliament of the Irish Republic. The prime minister is the taoiseach.

***Daily Telegraph*** This newspaper has come to embody the ideology of conservative, middle-class, middle England. Its origins were far from this, being a pioneer of 'popular' journalism in 1855, with its selling price of 2 pence later dropping to 1 penny. By 1888, its sales of 300,000 had left *The Times*'s 60,000 far behind. In the 20th cent., Lord Camrose reshaped it successfully in its middle-class mould.

**Dalhousie, James Andrew Broun Ramsay, 1st Marquis and 10th Earl** (1812–60). Born at Dalhousie castle, Scotland, he was the son of a commander-in-chief of the Indian army. After serving at the Board of Trade from 1843–5, he was appointed governor-general of India in 1848. His period in office was distinguished by its aggressive westernization, which contributed to the *Indian mutiny of 1857. He resigned exhausted in 1856, the victim of overwork and ill-health.

**Dalriada, kingdom of** Dalriada, or Dal Riata, started as an Irish kingdom on the coast of Antrim, but migrated to the west coast of Scotland in the 5th cent. This brought it into contact with the kingdom of the *Picts to the north-east and *Strathclyde to the south-east. *Ædan of Dalriada clearly had wide ambitions, raiding in Orkney and Man, and waging war against Picts and Northumbrians. An attack on the Northumbrians c.603 ended in severe defeat for Ædan at *Degsastan. Norse pressure to the west in the early 9th cent. might have squeezed Dalriada, but the reverse happened. The line of advance was apparently perceived as eastwards and in 843 *Kenneth MacAlpin, king of Dalriada, took over Pictland. Dalriada henceforth merged into the kingdom of *Alba.

**Dalrymple, John, 1st earl of Stair** [S] (1648–1707). Lawyer and statesman. Like his father, Dalrymple was in disfavour during the early 1680s and was twice imprisoned in Edinburgh castle. But in 1687 James VII appointed him king's advocate [S] and the following year lord justice clerk [S] and a lord of Session. Nevertheless he gave strong support to William of Orange and was reappointed king's advocate 1689–92. From 1690 he was also secretary of state in Scotland, but was obliged to resign his offices for authorizing the massacre of *Glencoe. Anne promoted him to the earldom of Stair in 1703, and he took an active part in bringing about the Union.

**Dalton, John** (1766–1844). Chemist. Dalton's first interests were in meteorology and in colour blindness: being colour blind himself, he made the first scientific study of the phenomenon. From 1794 he worked at the Manchester Literary and Philosophical Society, taking private pupils to augment his income. He concluded that each chemical element has distinct atoms, and began to work out structures of compounds, using simplicity rules.

**dame schools** Before the *Education Act of 1870, many young children were taught by unqualified women in their own homes. The dame schools were privately supported and fees were charged. The curriculum was narrow and concentrated on reading and writing.

**Damnonii** A tribe of central Scotland. This tribe may well have been called the Dumnonii, but the spelling used by Ptolemy is retained here. There is no known connection between them and their namesakes of southwest England. They are known only from Ptolemy's *Geography*. If his identifications are correct, they place the tribe firmly in the central Lowlands.

**Danby, Thomas Osborne, 1st earl of, marquis of Carmarthen, and duke of Leeds** (1632–1712). Danby did not come from a leading family and at first acted as lieutenant to the 2nd duke of *Buckingham. Appointed lord treasurer in 1673 to restore royal finances after the collapse of the *cabal he secured himself in office by reversing previous unpopular policies. He made Charles II realize that without money the *Anglo-Dutch War must be abandoned. He rallied the bishops and clergy, out of royal favour since 1663, renewing prosecutions of catholics and dissenters. He defeated all attempts to force the dissolution of Parliament or his dismissal. Danby negotiated the marriage of the later William III and Mary II but failed to commit Charles to war against France. By releasing incriminating papers to MPs, Louis XIV drove Danby from office. Under impeachment he was confined in the Tower from 1679 to 1684. During the *Glorious Revolution, Danby seized York and Hull for William. Lord president of the council (1689), he resumed his activities as a political manager and fixer, becoming identified as the leading Tory.

**Danegeld** The term is often wrongly applied to tribute payments made to the *Vikings in the reign of *Æthelred II (978–1016); these payments are known as *gafol* in the *Anglo-Saxon Chronicle*. In 1012 Æthelred introduced an annual land tax to pay for a Scandinavian force led by Thorkell the Tall which he had recruited to fight for him. The levy was continued by *Cnut and his sons to pay for their own forces. It was this tax which Norman administrative documents called 'Danegeld'.

**Danelaw** When during the 10th cent. the *Viking settlers of eastern England recognized the authority of the English kings, they were allowed to follow their own laws. By the 11th cent. the term 'Danelaw' was being used to indicate the geographical area in which customary law was influenced by Danish practice, defined in 12th-cent. documents as comprising all of eastern England between the Thames and the Tees.

**Darby, Abraham** (1677–1717). The founder of the great Shropshire iron industry, using local supplies of coal and iron. He was born in Worcestershire of a quaker family, apprenticed in Birmingham, and set up as a brass founder in Bristol. In 1709 he leased a furnace in *Coalbrookdale. Two successive Abraham Darbys developed the business and in 1779 the *Iron Bridge at Broseley advertised the company to the world.

**Dardanelles campaign** *See* GALLIPOLI.

**Darien venture** Previous Scottish attempts to establish colonies had been small scale, but the Company of Scotland, established in 1695, had grand ideas. It aimed at raising £400,000—perhaps half the capital in Scotland. Five ships were equipped, 1,200 men enrolled, and the expedition sailed in July 1698. After a difficult voyage of three months, the ships reached Darien on the isthmus of Panama, found some friendly Indians, and began building New Edinburgh. But what appeared at first sight an earthly paradise was in reality a fever-ridden swamp. On 22 June 1699 the colonists evacuated. A second expedition found deserted huts and hundreds of graves. After four months they surrendered to a Spanish force. The disaster for a small country was shattering.

**'Dark Ages'** A term deployed in the 17th and 18th cents. to indicate the intellectual darkness which was believed to have descended on Europe with the ending of the Roman empire until new light was provided by the *Renaissance. In the field of British history is sometimes applied just to the 5th and 6th cents., which many historians would prefer to designate as sub- or post-Roman.

**Darling, Grace** (1815–42). One of nine children, Grace Horsley Darling was born on 24 November 1815 at Bamburgh (Northd.). From 1826 her father was lighthouse-keeper of the Longstone Light on the Farne Islands. She became a national heroine when, with her father, she rescued nine passengers from the steamship *Forfarshire* when it struck rocks during gales on 7 September 1838. She continued to live with her parents until her death from tuberculosis on 20 October 1842.

**Darnley, Henry Stewart, Lord** (1545–67). The son of Matthew Stewart, 4th earl of Lennox, and grandson of *Margaret Tudor, Darnley's place in the English succession was second only to that of Mary Stuart. Darnley was born and brought up in England. His arrival in Scotland in 1565 was swiftly followed by their marriage by catholic rite on 29 July 1565. The marriage incensed Elizabeth but provoked in Scotland only a minor rebellion. But Darnley's good looks masked a meretricious personality and his relations with the queen soon soured. Mary's refusal to grant him the crown matrimonial drove him to ally with disaffected nobles who carefully implicated him in the *Rizzio murder of March 1566. The future James VI was born on 19 June. It remains unclear who murdered Darnley at Kirk o' Field, Edinburgh, on 10 February 1567, and whether Mary was party to the deed. Her precipitate marriage to Bothwell, however, handed the Lennox Stewarts a gift-wrapped opportunity to gild Darnley's memory at Mary's expense.

**darts** evolved from throwing spears or shooting arrows. Hand arrows were a useful weapon, known as 'dartes', and this was one of the few games that medieval and early modern governments did not feel obliged to prohibit. The standard clock-face became established in the late 19th cent., and paper flights to fit the darts were patented in 1898. In the 20th cent., two world wars (with much killing of time) followed by the spread of television helped to popularize the game.

**Darwin, Charles** (1809–82). Intended for medicine, Darwin took courses at Edinburgh, but dropped out unable to bear surgery. He went on to Christ's College, Cambridge, took a pass degree, and became a clergyman. In 1831 he was offered a place as companion to the captain on HMS *Beagle* surveying Cape Horn. On the five-year voyage round the world, Darwin became a great descriptive scientist and collector. Thinking about nature's diversity, he hit upon the idea of natural selection. Animals and plants produced more young than could survive: those better adapted to their surroundings would be 'selected' by nature and their offspring would diverge, inheriting characteristics. Darwin spent over 20 years collecting and marshalling evidence before publishing the *Origin of Species* in 1859. Despite furious controversy, his theory prevailed, and by the end of his life he was universally recognized.

**David I** (*c.*1085–1153), king of Scots (1124–53). An outstanding monarch, he was the youngest son of *Malcolm Canmore and Queen (later St) *Margaret, and succeeded his brother *Alexander I. Educated at Henry I's court he drew on his experience of the Anglo-Norman world to bring the Scots kingdom within the mainstream of European development. The 'Davidian revolution' involved the settlement in Scotland of Anglo-Norman nobles, who established powerful local lordships defended with castles and supplied knights to the king's army. The monarchy was strengthened by an extensive programme of church reform. He also developed the economic basis of the kingdom by founding burghs (notably Berwick, Edinburgh, and Aberdeen) and by introducing the first Scottish *coinage.

Quintessentially, however, David was as much a conventional Celtic ruler as a new-style 'feudal' monarch, preferring to work with traditional power structures. He continued to use the ancient centres of royal authority; loyal native lords kept their prominence as members of the governing élite alongside the Anglo-Norman incomers; the existing pattern of administrative offices coexisted with the sheriffs, justiciars, and other new officers; the taxation system remained based on the old levies of cain and conveth ('tribute and hospitality'); and customary methods of military recruitment retained fundamental importance. His Scottish power base was confined largely to the Lowlands; but the reality of growing royal might was firmly demonstrated when he led vast armies in wars of territorial conquest against the embattled King Stephen, and from 1141 he ruled the 'English' north to the rivers Ribble and Tees as an integral part of an enlarged Scoto-Northumbrian realm. But in 1152 David's only surviving son Henry predeceased him. When David himself died, he was therefore succeeded not by a mature and experienced heir, but by a boy-king, his grandson Malcolm IV; and in 1157, at Henry II's insistence, the Scots were obliged to withdraw from Northern England.

**David II** (1324–71), king of Scots (1329–71). He succeeded to the throne at the age of 5; and within three years his realm was invaded by Edward *Balliol and Edward III of England. With his young wife *Joan, sister of Edward III, he had to take refuge in France. Not until 1341 was he able to return; and in 1346 he was captured at the battle of *Neville's Cross, near Durham, spending eleven years in captivity before his release in 1357.

After his return to Scotland in 1357, David's government proved efficient. He was able to impose heavy taxation to meet the cost of his ransom. He dealt firmly with a baronial revolt in 1363 and with opposition from individual barons. His main weakness lay in his personal affairs. His first wife seems to have abandoned him after 1357, returning to England. David above all required an heir. By 1363 he had formed an attachment to *Margaret Logie, whom he married in that year. When no heir was forthcoming by 1370, he divorced her and was planning to marry Agnes Dunbar, when he himself died unexpectedly, early in 1371.

**David (Dewi), St** (d. *c.*601). Bishop of Menevia (St Davids), and patron saint of Wales. All accounts of him are based on the *c.*1090 biography by Rhygyfarch (Ricemarch). According to the legend David's birth was predicted by St *Patrick. David was born in Ceredigion to St Non, a nun who had been ravished by Sant (David's father), and there is a tenuous connection to the *Cunedda family. He became a pupil of Paulinus (possibly St Paul of Leon), and is reputed to have worked miracles. He finally settled at Mynyw (St Davids) and began a life of intense austerity. After a pilgrimage to the Holy Land, David attended the Synod of Brefi, and was elected primate of the Cambrian church with his see at Mynyw. His cult was well established by the 11th cent. and at least 60 churches were dedicated to him by 1200. David was canonized in 1120.

**Davies, Emily** (1830–1921). Born in Southampton, Emily Davies began by helping Elizabeth Garrett *Anderson to obtain her medical training. In 1862 she joined a committee to lobby for access to university examinations for women and then moved on to help organize a women's college. This opened at Hitchin in 1869 with five students and transferred to Girton in 1873, with fifteen. Davies served as mistress from 1873 until 1875. She was also a strong advocate of women's suffrage and organized J. S. *Mill's petition to Parliament in 1866.

**Davis, John** (c.1550–1605). One of the English navigators who sought the North-West Passage, Davis obtained backing from *Walsingham for three expeditions in 1585–7. Following *Frobisher's example, he sailed south and west of Greenland, but then penetrated much further north to about 73° in the strait that bears his name. Later in his life, Davis sailed to the Magellan Straits, fought the Spanish Armada, and died in a skirmish in the East Indies.

**Davitt, Michael** (1846–1906). Irish nationalist. Born in the famine period, Davitt lost his right arm in an accident in a Lancashire cotton-mill when he was 12. He joined the *Fenians and in 1870 was sentenced to fifteen years in gaol. Released after seven years, in October 1879 he formed the *Irish Land League, with Parnell as president. He took a hostile line to Parnell after the divorce scandal and was returned to Parliament in 1895. Though his early belief in violence moderated, Davitt alienated many supporters by his anticlerical views and his collectivist attitude towards land questions.

**Davy, Sir Humphry** (1778–1829). Cornish chemist and applied scientist. Davy's apprenticeship to an apothecary was interrupted when he was invited to Bristol to a clinic where oxygen and other gases were given to those with tuberculosis. He met S. T. *Coleridge, and with him discovered the properties of laughing gas. In 1801 he was appointed to the *Royal Institution in London, where his eloquence made his lectures fashionable. In 1815, his help was sought in controlling mine explosions; he came up with the lamp made him the obvious candidate to succeed Sir Joseph *Banks as president of the *Royal Society in 1820.

**D-Day,** 6 June 1944, was decisive in the war on Germany. D-Day, though cloudy and windy, justified Eisenhower's decision to accept a comparatively hopeful weather forecast. *Montgomery, in command of ground forces, dispatched five infantry divisions, to five separate Normandy beaches, plus three airborne divisions, landing over 150,000 men on the first day. On one American beach, Omaha, against a good German division, casualties were high. The British and American air forces virtually stopped German movement of troops by day and made impossible a co-ordinated German counter-attack.

**deacon** The rank in the Christian ministry below that of bishop and priest or presbyter. The order has its New Testament warrant from Acts 6. Today the diaconate, open to men and women, has become little more than a preparatory step to priesthood.

**dean** The title is most commonly associated with the priest who presides over the life and work of a cathedral. Originally it evolved from the Latin 'decem' (ten) as descriptive of one who had authority over, or the supervision of, a group of ten others. The statutes governing most English cathedrals give the dean and chapter together a considerable degree of independence from episcopal control.

**death duties** The taxation of inheritance provided a source of government revenue in Roman times. A death tax was introduced in Britain in 1694 but the modern framework dates from 1779–80. Since 1894, when Sir William Harcourt introduced a new system in the teeth of fierce opposition, death duties have mainly been in the form of estate duties (on property left at death).

**Declaration of Independence,** 1776. Conflict in America was well advanced when Congress on 4 July 1776 adopted the Declaration of Independence. Primarily the work of Thomas Jefferson, a principal objective was to facilitate an understanding with France. The celebrated 'self-evident truths' of life, liberty, and the pursuit of happiness were followed by a fierce denunciation of George III as 'a tyrant unfit to be the ruler of a free people'. The declaration concluded that 'all political connection between them and the state of Great Britain is, and ought to be, totally dissolved.'

**Declaration of Rights,** 1689. In February 1689, the *Convention drew up a Declaration of Rights, which it presented to William and Mary in the Banqueting House at Whitehall. It related the misdeeds of James II, begged William and Mary to accept the throne, and laid down an oath of allegiance. William accepted on their behalf and they were proclaimed king and queen. *See* GLORIOUS REVOLUTION.

**Declarations of Indulgence** Charles II disliked the penal laws against protestant and catholic dissenters and in 1672 issued a Declaration of Indulgence. The House of Commons protested vehemently: 'no such power was ever claimed or exercised by any of Your Majesty's predecessors.' Charles climbed down and withdrew it. James II issued another declaration in 1687, repeated it in 1688, and compounded matters with a foolish preface declaring, 'we cannot but heartily wish, as it will easily be believed, that all the people of our dominions were members of the Catholic Church.'

**Declaratory Act,** 1766. This asserted parliamentary sovereignty against the claims of the American assemblies. It was designed to win the consent of king, Lords, and Commons to the modification, or repeal, of the *Stamp Act.

**decolonization** The origins of British decolonization may be found in the grant of responsible government to self-governing settler colonies in the Canadas, Australasia, and southern Africa from the 1840s onwards. But later policies feeding into decolonization in the 20th cent. were by no means intended as an abrupt abandonment of British preponderance. The formal empire experiment with the method of dyarchy, especially in India following the 1919 Government of India Act, whereby some branches of public affairs were reserved for the imperial government while others were to be gradually devolved, reflected the same spirit.

The Second World War cannot be said to have led to any coherent vision of decolonization—if anything the reverse. Although Prime Minister *Churchill joined in the *Atlantic charter (August 1941) which affirmed the right of peoples to determine the governments under which they lived, his subsequent statement that he 'had not become His Majesty's Chief Minister to preside over the liquidation of the British Empire' is just as well known. Some possessions—principally *Malaya and *Burma after December 1941—were overrun, but planning for their reconquest got under way immediately.

It was in south Asia after 1945 that decolonization took shape. During the events leading up to the independence of *India and *Pakistan (August 1947) the Labour government's essential requirements were that British prestige should not be impaired, that the process should take place on an agreed basis, and that no important political, strategic, or economic interest of the United Kingdom should be harmed. It was convenient for all concerned in 1947 that the position of the crown remained at first untouched, though in 1949 the expressed wishes of India and Pakistan to become republics were accommodated within a multiracial *Commonwealth, of which the British monarch became head. Meanwhile Burma's statehood (January 1948) outside the Commonwealth, and *Ceylon's independence (February 1948), constituted the two poles of British decolonization on the margins of the subcontinent.

The transition in south Asia, however, did not necessarily set precedents for other parts of the British empire. No British colonial territory became independent during the peacetime premiership of Churchill (October 1951–April 1955). Although subsequently *Sudan became the first country in British Africa to attain statehood (January 1956), it did so as part of the unravelling of the old Anglo-Egyptian Condominium. Both the Gold Coast (January 1957), renamed *Ghana, and Malaya (August 1957) acquired independence having met certain political and financial requirements, though whether the same tests would be applied to other territories remained uncertain.

The second phase of British decolonization followed the re-election of Harold *Macmillan's Conservative government in October 1959, and especially his speech before the South African Parliament on 3 February 1960, warning of the 'winds of change'. *Nigeria became independent during 1960, Tanganyika (*Tanzania) and *Sierra Leone in 1961, *Uganda in 1962, *Kenya and *Zanzibar in 1963, *Zambia and *Malawi in 1964, the *Gambia in 1965, *Lesotho in 1966, and *Swaziland in 1968. More or less simultaneously the British Caribbean provided a footnote to African decolonization, *Jamaica and *Trinidad opting in August 1962 for independence apart from the ill-fated West Indian Federation. The emergence of the Republic of Cyprus (August 1960) had already signified that smallness was no longer a constraint on the application of self-determination.

If British governments ever pursued a distinct *policy* of decolonization, it was in the

Afro-Caribbean world between 1960 and roughly 1966. The lack of alternatives to this outcome meant that any controversies between, or within, the main British political parties remained limited. More polemic surrounded the scuttle from *Aden (November 1967) and the abandonment of contractual obligations to Gulf rulers—this was the real 'swansong of empire'. By far the most complicated and dangerous 'unfinished business' of decolonization in the later 1960s and 1970s was *Rhodesia, where a white settler rebellion was not quelled and the territory brought back into the mainstream of legitimate independence-making till the emergence of Zimbabwe in April 1980.

During the prolonged run-up to the last great British decolonization, that in *Hong Kong (30 June 1997), the preoccupation of the British government and its representative, Governor Patten, was to establish beyond dispute the commitment to democracy and the welfare of the local population. The speech before the joint British Houses of Parliament by the greatest living 'freedom-fighter', President Nelson Mandela of South Africa, on 5 July 1996, in which he legitimized Britain's moral standing abroad from the ending of colonial slavery through to the granting of African 'freedom' by Harold Macmillan, testified to the final triumph of the British version of decolonization. *See* BRITISH EMPIRE; IMPERIALISM.

**De facto Act,** 1495. The name is misleading since the statute, 11 Hen. VII c. 1, does not appear, contrary to much commentary, to distinguish between kings *de facto* and kings *de jure*. Henry VII, victorious at *Bosworth, faced a series of challenges to his throne. To buttress his position, this statute declared that a person performing his duty to the king could be 'in no wise convict of high treason' and that any subsequent legislation to the contrary would be null and void.

**Defenders** were Irish catholics who banded together to combat the protestant *Peep o' Day Boys. They began to organize in the 1780s and in the 1790s merged with the *United Irishmen. The spread of catholic disaffection culminated in the *Irish rising of 1798.

**Defoe, Daniel** (*c.*1660–1731). Prolific English writer. Educated at a dissenting acade-

my, Defoe was pardoned for fighting for *Monmouth, and gaoled for bankruptcy in 1692, before becoming William III's unofficial apologist in the best-selling *True-Born Englishman* (1701). Imprisoned and pilloried for seditious libel for his satire on high-church bigotry, *The Shortest Way with the Dissenters* (1702), Defoe was recruited as a propagandist by Robert *Harley. Having finally made his peace with the Whigs, Defoe published *Robinson Crusoe (1719), the first of a series of fictional autobiographies, including *A Journal of the Plague Year* (1722), *Moll Flanders* (1722), and *Roxana* (1724). In the 1720s Defoe undertook a series of journeys, interested particularly in commercial matters, and published in his impressive *A tour through the whole island of Great Britain*.

**Degeangli** Indigenous British tribe of the Iron Age and Roman periods whose territory covered much of northern Wales. They were the northern neighbours of the *Ordovices. The tribe was incorporated into the province of *Britannia* and became a *civitas* (tribal administrative district).

**Degsastan, battle of,** 603. This was apparently a severe defeat for *Ædan, king of *Dalriada, at the hands of *Æthelfrith of Northumbria. The site of the battle is probably Dawston Rigg in Liddesdale.

**De heretico comburendo,** 1401. This statute was directed against the *lollards, 'a certain new sect', who were causing dissension 'under the cover of dissembled holiness'. It threatened them with the stake. Strong action against the heresy was pushed by Archbishop *Arundel (1399–1414) and by the new king, Henry IV.

**Deheubarth** ('the south part'), one of Wales's larger medieval kingdoms. Formed during the reign of *Hywel Dda (died 949/50) by combining, through marriage, *Seisyllwg and *Dyfed, it covered the west and southwest of Wales and sometimes extended into *Brycheiniog. Its capital, Dinefwr, acquired legendary status, but, unlike Dyfed and Ceredigion, the name has not been revived.

**Deira, kingdom of** Anglo-Saxon kingdom lying north of the Humber and south of the Tees. The Deiran dynasty appears well established by the end of the 6th cent. when Ælle was ruling. The last member of the Deiran royal house to rule was Oswin (644–51) who was murdered by Oswiu of Bernicia. During the reign of *Ecgfrith (670–85) Deira was fully integrated with Bernicia to form the kingdom of *Northumbria.

**deism** A term derived from Latin *deus*, meaning belief in a Supreme Being and used to describe the system of natural religion first developed in the late 17th cent. The classical exposition of deism was John Toland's *Christianity not Mysterious* (1696), which argued against the supernatural. Deists asserted the supremacy of reason and denied the validity of miracles, prophecy, and a literal, fundamentalist interpretation of the Bible. The term deism was little used after the 18th cent., when the term free thinkers came in.

**Delius, Frederick** (1862–1934). Composer. Born in Bradford (Yorks.) of German descent, Delius spent most of his life abroad yet his music often evokes a sense of the English landscape. His most popular pieces are short and idyllic, such as *On Hearing the First Cuckoo in Spring* or *Brigg Fair*. In his final years he was blind and paralysed but was able to continue composing through the assistance of Eric Fenby, his musical amanuensis.

**demesne** was a legal term to describe land and property worked for the direct benefit of the owner. During the Middle Ages the importance of such holdings varied: at times it was more valuable for owners to work the land themselves, whilst at others it was more profitable to rent the land to tenants. When demand for agricultural produce was high and profits good, demesnes expanded. When the costs of production rose, as after plague during the 14th cent., many magnates leased demesnes to tenants for cash rent, keeping the part near to residences to meet household needs.

**Demetae** Indigenous British tribe of the Iron Age and Roman periods whose territory covered Pembrokeshire and much of Carmarthenshire in south-west Wales. The tribe was incorporated into the province of Britannia and became a *civitas* with the capital at Carmarthen (Moridunum Demetarum).

**democracy** In Britain, the transition from oligarchy to democracy was piecemeal. The civil wars and Glorious Revolution of the 17th cent. confirmed the supremacy of Parliament, but an unreformed electoral system restricted effective participation to a small minority. What public opinion existed could be expressed only spasmodically. The proliferation of newspapers in the 18th cent. and the publication of parliamentary debates after 1770 widened the scope of opinion, but not until the Great Reform Act of 1832 was the system itself substantially modified, with the introduction of a standard franchise and the grant of representation to great towns like Manchester, Birmingham, Sheffield, and Leeds. Further extension of the franchise in 1867 and 1884 gave most adult males the vote, secret ballot in 1872 reduced the influence of the gentry, and the Corrupt Practices Act of 1883 curtailed bribery. Two further reforms of 1918 and 1928 gave the vote to women, and the voting age was reduced to 18 by an act of 1969.

Democracy affords voters the opportunity to change their government, but the extent to which the opinions of ordinary people are effective in other matters remains a subject of debate, and it is arguable that specific interest groups carry more weight than the casting of a vote (often for a losing candidate) once every four or five years. In local government, where the influence of the individual might be expected to be greatest, the effect has been reduced by powerful strides towards centralized decision-making, and by the domination of many councils by one party. Participatory democracy, accepted in principle by almost everybody, is not easy to practise in a large country, where issues are many and complex.

Democracy has been hailed as a formula which would establish world stability and peace, but its appeal, in the face of alternative religious or national enthusiasms, has proved dispiriting. Voters sometimes seem obstinately attracted to strong-arm presidents, to religious fanatics, or even to military dictatorships. The extent to which democracy can be exported, as opposed to growing indigenously, must remain doubtful.

**Democratic Unionist Party** (DUP). Formed in 1971 to challenge the position of the Ulster Unionist Party and represent traditional loyalist working-class opinion. Its platform is a mixture of uncompromising unionism and social and economic populism. Massively dominated by its leader Ian *Paisley, its support extends far beyond the Free Presbyterian Church. The party has always been suspicious of peace initiatives and it rejected the Downing Street declaration in 1993. At the election of 2005, the DUP replaced the Unionists as the largest Ulster party and in 2007 Paisley took office as First Minister in the power-sharing government.

**Denain, battle of,** 1712. Marshal Villars, leading a French army of 24,000 troops, surprised an Anglo-Dutch force of about 10,000 men under Albemarle close to Denain on 24 July. Allied reinforcements under Prince Eugene tried to come to Albemarle's assistance but could not cross the Scheldt river. Fewer than 4,000 of Albemarle's men escaped.

**Denbighshire** A county of north-east Wales created in 1536 at the Act of *Union with England. Its core was Perfeddwlad, east of the Conwy, together with Dyffryn Clwyd. These, after the Norman Conquest, constituted the lordships of Denbigh and Ruthin. In 1974 it became part of the county of *Clwyd and the former county was divided into three districts—Colwyn, Glyndŵr, and Wrexham Maelor. In 1996 it was reconstituted as a county, but without Wrexham, which became a county borough in its own right.

**Derby** Described by Disraeli as 'the Blue Riband of the Turf', the Derby is the top event in the flat season's racing calendar. First run on 4 May 1780, the race is named after its founder, the 12th earl of Derby. It is a race for 3-year-olds, run on Epsom downs.

**Derby, diocese of** The see, roughly Derbyshire, was created in 1927 out of the diocese of *Southwell, where the ecclesiastical union in 1884 of Nottinghamshire and Derbyshire had not been a success. The cathedral is the former parish church.

**Derby, Edward Stanley, 14th earl of** (1799–1869). The longest serving of Conservative leaders. Heir to an ancient title (the main estates in south Lancashire around Knowsley), Stanley, after Eton and Christ Church, Oxford, was a Whig MP by 1822. After minor office under *Canning, he served

in *Grey's cabinet. As chief secretary for Ireland he introduced the Irish Church Temporalities Bill and a measure for popular education and as colonial secretary the abolition of colonial slavery, all in 1833. Alienated by *O'Connell and his Irish and by his Whig rival *Russell, Stanley led the resigners from the cabinet in 1834 (the *Derby Dilly). He and most of his followers moved into the Conservative Party. Colonial secretary in Peel's government of 1841, he opted for a peerage in 1844. *Lytton saw him as 'frank, haughty, rash, the Rupert of debate'. In 1845 Stanley was the only cabinet minister to hold out against Peel's policy of Corn Law repeal and left the government, seeing it as an issue of honour. Though his efforts to stop repeal failed, he became leader of the protectionist rump of the divided party in July 1846. By 1849 Stanley had appointed *Disraeli leader in the Commons.

Derby (he inherited the earldom in 1851) was prime minister of three governments (1852, 1858–9, and 1866–8). Throughout that period the Conservatives remained a minority party in the Commons. In the second ministry Derby attempted a measure of parliamentary reform and displayed a more progressive stance than previously. After the defeat of 1859 he decided to prop up *Palmerston's moderate Liberal government against radical challenges and settled for opposition. In 1866 after Palmerston's death the Conservatives overturned Russell's Liberal government over parliamentary reform and Derby became premier again. He determined to pre-empt any further Liberal measure with a reform measure of his own; the second Reform Act (he called it 'a leap in the dark') was his initiative, though handled by Disraeli in the Commons. He retired because of ill-health in 1868, Disraeli succeeding as premier.

Derby never realized the early promise of his career. Disarmingly open in manner, especially in sporting contexts, he was also acutely aware of his social standing, and aristocratic stiffness handicapped his dealings with middle-class politicians.

**Derby, Edward Stanley, 15th earl of** (1826–93). Educated at Rugby and Trinity College, Cambridge, and an MP from 1848, Stanley was closer to *Disraeli than was his father in the 1850s. He was colonial and

Indian secretary in 1858–9 and foreign secretary in 1866–8 and, after inheriting the earldom in 1869, again from 1874. During the Eastern Question crisis he conducted an independent policy and, having fallen out with Disraeli, resigned in 1878. As colonial secretary under *Gladstone from 1882 he was disinclined to a 'forward policy'. In 1886 he broke with Gladstone over *Home Rule and led the *Liberal Unionists in the Lords until 1891.

**Derby, James Stanley, 7th earl of** (1607–51). Derby was lord-lieutenant of Lancashire, lord of the *Isle of Man, and a leading royalist peer during the *civil wars. In 1642 he raised over 6,000 men in the county for the king. He spent most of the next seven years on the Isle of Man, emerging in 1644 to fight at *Marston Moor. In 1650 he declared for Charles II and brought a small contingent to the mainland, but was defeated at Wigan Lane (25 August 1651). Derby fought at *Worcester (September 1651), was captured, and beheaded at Bolton, a town which he had sacked in 1644, killing 1,600 civilians.

**Derby, Thomas Stanley, 1st earl of** *See* STANLEY, THOMAS.

**Derby Dilly** *O'Connell's belittling phrase for the moderate Whigs who, led by four cabinet ministers including Edward Stanley, heir to the *Derby earldom, seceded from the reformers in 1834 and began a restructuring of parties. Dilly was slang for a diligence or rapid stage-coach.

**Derbyshire** is a heart-shaped county in the heart of England. It has been little altered by boundary changes, but since 1974 borders Greater Manchester.

The Romans, chiefly interested in its lead and the springs at Buxton, established a number of forts and roads. Christianity came with the first religious house in Mercia built at *Repton in 656 (where the Saxon crypt survives).

Throughout the medieval period Derbyshire remained sparsely populated. The county suffered grievously from the plague, the final outbreak occurring famously in 1665 when six-sevenths of the population of Eyam died. By the 17th cent., the Cavendishes had established themselves as the premier family, mostly due to Bess of Hardwick (countess of

*Shrewsbury) (1520–1608). In addition to the building of great country houses, such as Chatsworth, Kedleston, and Calke abbey, the 18th cent. saw the development of cotton-mills in Derbyshire (notably by *Arkwright at Cromford, 1771), impressive growth in coal-mining and iron production around Bolsover and Chesterfield, and framework-knitting at Belper, Ilkeston, and Heanor in the east. The railways profoundly changed Derbyshire. By the mid-19th cent., Derby had become the railway centre of the midlands. Today, although coal has ceased to be of economic significance, quarrying (especially limestone) is still important, as are textiles and engineering, most famously at *Rolls-Royce's aero-engine factory in Derby. In addition, the Peak District (Britain's first national park) attracts vast numbers of visitors.

Derby is by far the largest town in the county, with 235,000 inhabitants in 1999, but culturally it has suffered from its proximity to larger Nottingham. Additionally, the city's southern location reinforces the county's diffuse nature, with the north-east looking to Sheffield, and the north-west to Manchester. The county's administrative headquarters are at Matlock, a fine spa town, its first bath built in 1698, and its dramatic cliffs drawing visitors ever since. But it was Buxton, England's highest market town, that prospered most from its hot waters; its sumptuous Crescent, built by the Cavendishes 1780–6, is said to have cost £120,000 and the town retains a sense of Georgian elegance. In the east and north, where iron, cotton, and coal dominated, runs the M1 motorway, past Ilkeston and Alfreton. Above them is Chesterfield, with its celebrated twisted spire atop an exceptional Gothic church. The north-west tip of Derbyshire is the least populated part and contains the Ladybower reservoir, opened in 1945; its largest town, Glossop, retains the appearance of a Victorian mill town.

**Dermot MacMurrough** (*c.*1110–71), king of Leinster. Dermot is said to have been large, violent, and voluble. He plunged into fierce fighting but in 1166 was forced into exile and begged Henry II to assist him. He was joined in Ireland in 1170 by Richard de *Clare, 'Strongbow'. Together they recaptured Dublin, and Strongbow married Dermot's daughter Eva (Aoife). Dermot died the following year and five months later Henry himself led an expedition which laid the foundation for the Anglo-Norman acquisition of Dublin and the *Pale.

**Derry, diocese of** Derry had been a bishopric from 1254 and was continued at the Reformation as a diocese of the Church of Ireland. The bishopric of Raphoe was joined to Derry in 1834. The medieval cathedral was destroyed by an explosion in 1566. The new cathedral was built between 1628 and 1633 and extensively remodelled in Victorian times. St Eugene's Roman catholic cathedral was completed in 1873 and a spire added in 1903.

**Despenser, Hugh, 1st earl of Winchester** (1261–1326). Despenser's father had been a member of the baronial opposition to Henry III, and was killed with de *Montfort at *Evesham. Despenser was an ardent supporter of Edward II and his closest companion after the death of *Gaveston. He and his son received many estates and incurred great unpopularity. In 1321 Edward was forced to exile him, but the death of his great enemy *Thomas of Lancaster at *Boroughbridge the following year seemed to have secured his position. But he was speedily overthrown in 1326. Edward's queen *Isabella led an invasion, and Despenser was captured at Bristol and executed. His son was taken a few days later with the king and hanged at Hereford. The king himself was deposed two months later.

**Dettingen, battle of,** 1743. Britain entered the War of the *Austrian Succession on the side of Maria Theresa and placed an army in the field in Germany under Lord Stair. In June 1743 it was trapped near Hanau by a superior French force. It succeeded in fighting its way to safety on the 27th mainly because of the musket fire of the infantry. George II led his troops into battle, sword in hand, with remarkable courage.

**Deusdedit,** archbishop of Canterbury (655–64), was the sixth man to hold that office and the first Englishman to be appointed. He was a West Saxon whose English name seems to have been Frithuwine. He died on 14 July 664 in the great plague.

**de Valera, Eamon** (1882–1975). The dominant figure in Irish politics for over 40 years despite his aloof, ascetic personality. De Valera was born in New York, reared in Co. Limerick, and was originally a mathematics teacher. He came to advanced nationalism through the Irish Language Movement. His rise to leadership was due to his being the last surviving commandant of the *Easter Rising. Following release from internment in early 1917, he led a broad-based Sinn Fein coalition. Arrested May 1918, de Valera escaped from Lincoln gaol in February 1919, and became president of the Dáil. After the truce in July 1921, de Valera became chief negotiator in Dáil ranks but controversially absented himself from the peace conference. Opposing the *Anglo-Irish treaty, he advanced external association as an alternative. Splitting from Sinn Fein and the IRA and their Dáil abstentionist policy, he formed Fianna Fail Party, entering the Dáil in 1927. After winning the 1932 election he followed a treaty reform policy, abolishing the oath of allegiance to the British crown. The constitution of 1937 epitomized his social and cultural conservatism. De Valera followed popular neutrality policy in the *Second World War. Defeated in elections 1948 and 1954, but taoiseach again 1951–4 and 1957–9, he withdrew to the presidency 1959–73. De Valera himself said: 'I was meant to be a dyed-in-the-wool Tory or even a Bishop, rather than the leader of a Revolution.'

**devolution** A form of delegation of power which was advocated as a means of giving citizens a sense of more immediate or direct control of decision-making. Northern Ireland had a devolved government from its establishment. Taken up by the Labour Party, it was expected to head off progress by *Plaid Cymru in Wales and the *SNP in Scotland towards total independence. After a 'Yes' vote in a Scottish referendum, a Scottish parliament opened in Edinburgh in May 1999. In Wales the proposal for devolution had been heavily defeated in 1979 but won a narrow majority in a second referendum in 1997: a National Assembly opened in Cardiff in 1999. The outcome has scarcely been what the advocates of devolution had hoped for. The SNP emerged from the 2007 elections as the largest party in the Scottish Parliament and were able to form a minority government, pledged to bring in a proposal for independence. In

Wales the progress of Plaid Cymru enabled it to share government with Labour. The result has placed the structure of the United Kingdom in some jeopardy and former sponsors of devolution have begun to rediscover the value of 'Britishness' and the advantages of maintaining the Union.

**Devon** was the third largest of the old counties. Having two sea-coasts, it was orientated in different directions, the northern shore along the Bristol channel, the south shore along the English channel. Dartmoor in the south, Exmoor in the north, and the Blackdowns in the east are the highest points, but much of the county is hilly, with deep valleys. The name first appears in the *Anglo-Saxon Chronicle* in 851 as Defensascir, which appears to be derived from the *Dumnonii, the Celtic tribe inhabiting the area. In Roman times, *Exeter (Isca Dumnoniorum) was an important base and port.

In post-Roman times, the British kingdom of *Dumnonia embraced both Devon and Cornwall: it survived at least until the early 8th cent. The eastern part of the region had fallen to the Saxons after *Cenwalh's victory at *Penselwood in 658 and much of the western part by the end of the century. It then formed part of the kingdom of *Wessex. *Ine established a bishopric for the area at *Sherborne in 705, moved to *Crediton in 909, and to Exeter itself in 1050. By the 11th cent. it had taken shape as a shire. In the *Domesday survey of 1086 Exeter was by far the largest town.

Though Exeter was the county town and of national importance, it did not dominate in so large a shire. Consequently, Devon developed as a county of seaports—Barnstaple, Bideford, Brixham—and of market towns of largely local significance, Okehampton, Tavistock, Tiverton, Torrington, Newton Abbot, Honiton, and Ashburton. Until the growth of the cloth industry in the later Middle Ages, it was wholly dependent upon agriculture and fishing, with a little mining. *Plymouth developed as a naval base as vessels grew larger and its superb harbour was more needed, replacing Plympton. Charles II built the citadel and William III established the royal dockyard in 1692.

The reputation of the county was for unintelligible speech, turbulence, and independence. In 1549 there was a formidable rising

on behalf of the old religion and Exeter was threatened. Later, protestant dissent made much progress. During the Civil War there was heavy fighting. Exeter was held for the king but Plymouth, a fiercely puritan town, proved a thorn in the royalists' side. The county gave some support in 1685 to *Monmouth, who landed at Lyme, and more in 1688 to William of Orange, who came ashore at Brixham in November.

Improvements in roads and the coming of the railway made Devon less inaccessible: Brunel's lines reached Exeter in 1844 and Plymouth in 1848. Exeter grew from 17,000 in 1801 to 47,000 by the end of the century but was surpassed by Plymouth, more than 100,000 in 1901. Even more remarkable was the growth of the resorts as the habit of seaside holidays caught on. Ilfracombe, on the north coast, rose to well over 8,000 by 1901: Torquay, a hamlet of only 800 at the beginning of the century, was a town of 33,000 by 1901, and the new borough of Torbay had a population of 132,000 in 2004 as against 115,000 in Exeter.

**Devonshire, Spencer Compton Cavendish, 8th duke of, marquis of Hartington** (1833–1908). Heir to the Cavendish family's dukedom and a Palmerstonian Whig, Hartington was an MP at 24 and a cabinet minister at 34. Elected Liberal leader in the Commons after *Gladstone's retirement in 1875, he was undermined by the latter's political comeback and, when offered the premiership after the Liberal victory of 1880, recommended Gladstone instead. He broke with Gladstone over *Home Rule in 1886 and, as the leader of the *Liberal Unionists, maintained *Salisbury's Conservatives in power until 1892. In 1895 Devonshire, as he had become, joined Salisbury in a unionist coalition and served as lord president. In 1904 he resigned from *Balfour's government in protest at Joseph *Chamberlain's campaign for imperial preference.

**Devonshire, William Cavendish, 1st duke of** (1641–1707). Devonshire backed the right horse in 1688 and prospered exceedingly, founding one of the great Revolution families. A page at Charles II's coronation, he saw naval service, and served as MP for Derby 1661–81, succeeding as 4th earl in 1684. A zealous Whig and keen supporter of *exclusion, he was one of the seven who invited William of Orange over in 1688 and took up arms at Derby. In the new reign, he was at once made lord steward and, in 1694, a duke. He began the building of *Chatsworth in 1687.

**Devonshire, William Cavendish, 4th duke of** (1720–64). Cavendish came from a highly political Whig family. He entered Parliament at the age of 21 for Derbyshire, and succeeded as duke in 1755. After serving as master of the horse 1751-5, he was made lord-lieutenant of Ireland. In the crisis of 1756, conciliatory and trusted, he became 1st lord of the Treasury with *Pitt as the driving force. When Pitt was obliged to come to terms with *Newcastle, Devonshire was moved to be lord chamberlain 1757-62. In the new reign he and his Whig colleagues resented the ascendancy of *Bute. After Newcastle resigned, Devonshire refused to attend councils and in November 1762 was dismissed by George III and his name removed from the Privy Council. Devonshire's early death robbed the Whigs of a future leader.

***Dialogus de Scaccario*** The *Dialogue of the Exchequer* is the earliest administrative handbook in English history and a prime source for historians of royal finance. Written in the 1170s it gives an account of Exchequer practice in the form of a dialogue between pupil and master. Its author, Richard *FitzNigel (*c.*1130-98), was rewarded in 1189 by being made bishop of London.

**Diamond Jubilee,** 1897. By 1897 Victoria had surpassed George III as the longest reigning British monarch. The celebrations were restricted by her age and infirmities and the centre-piece, on 22 June, was a short service outside St Paul's, while the queen sat in an open carriage.

**Diana, princess of Wales** (1961–97). Lady Diana Spencer was the third daughter of the 8th Earl Spencer of Althorp (Northants). Her father had been equerry to George VI 1950-2 and to Queen Elizabeth 1952-4. Lady Diana was educated at Riddlesworth Hall. Her marriage to Charles, prince of Wales, in 1981 attracted enormous public interest. Her two sons, William and Henry, were born in 1982 and 1984. Soon afterwards there were rumours that the princess was

unhappy and in 1992 it was announced that she and Prince Charles were to separate. Divorce followed in 1996. Princess Diana was the subject and sometimes the victim of massive press coverage, but her attitude towards it often appeared ambivalent. She was killed in a car crash in Paris in 1997 and buried at Althorp.

**Dickens, Charles John Huffam** (1812–70). Novelist, born at Portsea, Portsmouth. His father's transfers to Chatham and ultimately to London were to influence the settings of his work. A fictionalized Chatham, its neighbouring city of Rochester, and the landscapes around them figure prominently in *Pickwick Papers, Great Expectations*, and in the unfinished *The Mystery of Edwin Drood*. It was, however, London which became the main focus of Dickens's work. It figures as an often confusing and exhilarating setting for the earlier fiction, but, from *Bleak House* (1852-3) onwards, London seems to assume a new darkness, mystery, and drabness. Dickens used his popularity to campaign for the reform of British institutions (e.g. the 1834 Poor Law, the prison system, the civil service, the law). In his *American Notes* (1842) he gave a vivid account of his visit to the USA, which offended many Americans.

***Dictionary of National Biography*** The brainchild of the publisher George Smith. The work began in 1882 with Sir Leslie Stephen as editor and the last volume appeared in 1900. Supplements and updates have followed and Oxford University Press's new edition appeared in 2004.

**Diggers** Small communistic groups, active in 1649-50, sometimes calling themselves True Levellers. Their prophet Gerrard *Winstanley taught that God made the earth to be a common treasury; property and man's subjection to man were results of the Fall. A pioneering group began digging the commons on St George's Hill (Surrey), in April 1649. The *Council of State ordered General *Fairfax to disperse them, but it was angry locals who finally destroyed their cabins.

**Dilke, Sir Charles** (1843–1911). Liberal politician. Dilke is supposed to have ruined his chance of becoming prime minister by his involvement as co-respondent in a famous divorce case (*Crawford* v. *Crawford*) in 1885–6; but he probably would not have made it anyway. Before this happened he was better known as a radical, a close ally of Joseph *Chamberlain, an early propagandist for the *British empire, and one of the most boring speakers in the House of Commons.

**Dillon, John** (1851–1927). Irish nationalist. Dillon was born at Blackrock (Co. Dublin) and educated at the *Catholic University. He took a degree in medicine and entered politics as a supporter of John Mitchel in 1875. In 1880 he was returned to Parliament and served until 1918. After the Parnell split he joined the anti-Parnell group, becoming leader when Justin McCarthy resigned in 1896. Four years later he gave way to *Redmond as leader of the re-united party. Dillon lost his seat at the general election in December 1918 to *de Valera.

**Disestablishment** The 19th cent. saw the questioning of the right of a church which represented only a minority of Christian believers to be the established church, its clergy maintained by parishioners who did not belong to it. The Irish church was the first to be disestablished, by Gladstone in 1869. In Wales, where nonconformists accounted for 80 per cent of worshippers, a similar campaign was waged. Several parliamentary bills from 1870 onwards failed, until one was passed in 1914. The First World War delayed its implementation, but it came into force in 1920. The 1869 Irish disestablishment left the Church of Ireland a shadow of its former self, particularly in the overwhelmingly catholic rural areas. In Wales the delay saw a different outcome. By 1920 nonconformity itself was losing its dominant place in Welsh life, and the Church in Wales was able to maintain a widespread presence throughout the principality. Disestablishment of the Church of England has been frequently mooted, sometimes from within, but has failed to become a dominant issue.

**dispensing power** was the prerogative or discretion claimed by the monarch of exempting from the operation of statutes in particular cases. The *Long Parliament, in its *Nineteen Propositions, accused Charles I of making excessive use of it. James II used it to exempt catholic army officers from the *Test Act. After James had fled in 1688, the *Bill of Rights abolished the *suspending power outright and the dispensing power 'as it hath been assumed and exercised of late'.

**Disraeli, Benjamin, 1st earl of Beaconsfield** (1804–81). Conservative statesman and novelist. Of a Christianized Jewish upper middle-class family, his father a distinguished man of letters, Disraeli led an early life that handicapped his political career. Egotistical, raffish, self-publicizing, he combined recklessness in financial and sexual matters with a talent for scrambling up lifelines. Helped by his patron *Lyndhurst, Disraeli became a Conservative MP in 1837. Desperate for office, he was ignored by Peel in 1841. More notice was gained by his novels, which he wrote partly for money but which also developed social and political ideas then current. *Coningsby* (1844) explored the nature of aristocratic party politics and *Sybil* (1845), a 'condition of England' novel, deplored the gulf between the 'Two Nations' of rich and poor; *Tancred* (1847) completed the trilogy. Disraeli had belonged to the otherwise aristocratic *Young England group of political romantics and his growing hostility to *Peel expressed itself in the House over *Maynooth and the *Corn Laws in 1845–6. Disraeli's devastating mockery of Peel gave him prominence for the first time. The shortage of talent on the protectionist front bench made Disraeli indispensable and by 1849 Stanley (the future earl of *Derby) had accepted him as leader in the Commons. Disraeli gained in experience and weight through the long service, and also benefited from his marriage in 1839 to the wealthy and older Mary Anne, widow of a Conservative MP. Never a protectionist on principle, Disraeli had to be restrained by Derby from jettisoning protectionism with indecent haste (it was abandoned after the 1852 defeat). Hungry for office, he deplored Derby's rejections of opportunities in 1851 and 1855. His biography *Lord George Bentinck* (1852) repaid a considerable personal debt; the Bentincks also provided the money to set Disraeli up as a country gentleman at Hughenden in Buckinghamshire.

Disraeli served as chancellor of the Exchequer and leader of the Commons in the three Derby minority ministries of 1852, 1858–9, and 1866–8, though a major triumph came only in 1867 when his cynical handling of the government's Reform Bill divided the Liberals and enabled the Conservatives to cling to office long enough to pass a measure. Scarcely 'democratic' in intention, it minimized the damage a Liberal measure would have done to Conservative interests. Disraeli succeeded Derby as premier in 1868 ('I have climbed to the top of the greasy pole') and, in opposition after electoral defeat, survived party discontent. By 1872, when he made major speeches at Manchester and Crystal Palace proclaiming a supposedly distinctive Conservative philosophy, *Gladstone's Liberal government was disintegrating. The election victory of 1874, the party's first since 1841, owed more to Gladstone than Disraeli, but it gave the latter the prolonged period of office he sought. Disraeli's platform in 1874—stability at home and the patriotic assertion of national interests abroad—was pure *Palmerston.

Disraeli's name rests mainly upon his ministry of 1874–80. Its social legislation was the work of Richard Cross at the Home Office and had no obvious link with the social theorizing of the premier's Young England past. Only the trade union legislation of 1875 went markedly beyond what any government might have passed. This phase was over by the time an ageing Disraeli moved to the Lords as earl of Beaconsfield in 1876. More significant was his forwardness in foreign and colonial matters. Disraeli seized the chance to buy a controlling interest in the Suez canal, sent the flamboyant *Lytton to India as viceroy, and his 1876 *Royal Titles Act proclaimed Victoria empress of India. Over the Eastern Question, the struggle between Russia and Turkey in the Balkans, a dramatic confrontation developed between Beaconsfield and the former Liberal leader Gladstone: at the expense of cabinet resignations, the government decided to intervene to sustain Turkey. Beaconsfield's reward was a personal triumph at the Congress of *Berlin, a Balkan settlement that suited Britain ('Peace with Honour'), and the cession of *Cyprus by Turkey. But colonial wars in Afghanistan and southern Africa went less well and gave Gladstone the chance to attack 'Beaconsfieldism' in his *Midlothian campaigns. A new nationalist mood in Ireland and economic depression also contributed to the heavy electoral defeat of 1880, which put Gladstone back in office. Though not retiring as party leader, Disraeli was depressed by developments, and his death in 1881 came at a low ebb of party fortunes.

Soon Randolph *Churchill and the *Primrose League were active in cultivating a mythology of Disraelian 'Tory Democracy'. In fact the substance of Disraeli's politics was more orthodox than romance suggested: a matter of upholding the 'aristocratic constitution', the monarchy, the Union with Ireland, property rights, and social stability. His foreign policy helped to claim a patriotic and imperial identity for the Conservative Party. But none of this matched the rhetoric, wit, and phrase-making that Disraeli brought to politics. What distinguished him was his immense stamina, his great loyalty to the Conservative Party, and his unquenchable thirst for office, power, and patronage. He was a great *arriviste*.

**dissent** (nonconformity). Though dissenting sects could trace some of their doctrines to well before the Reformation, for example to the *lollards, pre-Reformation heterodoxy is usually termed schism or heresy. The term dissent is reserved for those who did not conform to the Church of England and, though this included catholics, it is usually confined to protestant groups.

The seed time for nonconformity was the Civil War. The confused situation gave dissenting sects the opportunity to establish themselves. The independents or *congregationalists dissented from the dissenters, disliking the rigour of presbyterian rule and demanding toleration; the *baptists split between the general baptists and the particular baptists, who were closer to *Calvinism; George *Fox founded the 'Children of Light', later known as *quakers; Thomas Harrison looked for the imminent establishment of Christ's *Fifth Monarchy and the triumph of the saints.

In the declaration of *Breda (April 1660) Charles II offered 'a liberty to tender consciences' in religious matters. But the *Cavalier Parliament, elected in March 1661 to replace the Convention, was much less inclined to forgive and forget, and a new Act of Uniformity (1662) led to some 2,000 puritan clergy leaving their livings. The '*Clarendon code' waged war against the nonconformists, and the *Test Act of 1673 barred dissenters, protestant and catholic, from public office, including membership of Parliament. The reigns of Charles II and James II were difficult for the dissenters, fierce bursts of persecution alternating with efforts to woo them. At the crisis of 1688, the majority of protestant dissenters heeded the warning from *Halifax that 'you are to be hugged now only that you may be the better squeezed at another time'.

After the Glorious Revolution, the *Toleration Act of 1689 granted freedom of worship, provided that dissenters took a simple oath of allegiance. At the same time a new schism arose when 400 Anglican clergy decided that they could not swear to the new regime and formed the *non-juring church. The acceptance after 1688 of an avowedly presbyterian church order in Scotland, confirmed by the Act of *Union in 1707, was proof that the Church of England no longer had an official monopoly in the British Isles.

Under these comparatively relaxed conditions, the dissenting groups might have been expected to flourish. In practice toleration proved more damaging than persecution. Some of the more prosperous dissenters conformed for social or political reasons, but the dissenters also suffered from internal convulsions. The development of the *methodist movement from the 1730s onwards led to a vast increase in dissent, though during *Wesley's lifetime his followers remained in the Anglican church. By the 1770s the dissenters had arrested their decline and were growing more confident, fortified by the success of nonconformity in America. This led many of them to oppose the American war, bringing them renewed unpopularity. The support of many dissenters for the French Revolution in its early stages kindled fresh bitterness and *Priestley's house in *Birmingham was burned in 1791 in church and king riots. In 1828, the long wars safely over, repeal of the Test and Corporation Acts went through with surprising ease. Though nonconformists retained substantial grievances, especially over marriage and tithes, they had at least achieved formal civil equality.

It transpired that they had achieved a good deal more. The early years of the 19th cent. witnessed a remarkable upsurge in support for dissent. The methodists pointed the way to other sects. At the time of Wesley's death in 1791 they numbered some 56,000: by 1836 there were 360,000 in the different methodist churches. Congregationalist membership

increased from some 20,000 in 1760 to 127,000 by 1838, baptists from 11,000 to 100,000.

The effect of these changes was a transformation of the religious scene recorded by the religious census of 1851. First the census showed that nearly 40 per cent of those eligible to have attended church on 30 March had not done so. Secondly, it revealed that Anglican attenders scarcely outnumbered the dissenting sects—3,773,000 against 3,487,000, of whom methodists were 1,463,000, independents 793,000, baptists 587,000, catholics 305,000, unitarians 37,000, and quakers 18,000. Dissenters were in a comfortable majority in many northern towns like Sheffield, Leeds, and Bradford, and formed a great majority in Wales.

Anglicans braced themselves for another attack on the established position of the church. Tithes went in 1868; the Irish *church was disestablished in 1869; the Welsh church in 1920. But the Church of England held out until the tide of religious belief was clearly ebbing. Meanwhile the influence of dissent was all-pervasive. The *Municipal Corporations Act of 1835, which set up elected councils in the large towns, had brought hundreds of dissenters into local government. The nonconformist conscience was a powerful political force, as Charles *Dilke and *Parnell discovered. The influence of dissent may be seen most clearly in the *Liberal Party. *Bright and W. E. *Forster were quakers, Joseph *Chamberlain a unitarian, *Asquith from a congregationalist family, *Lloyd George from a baptist home. The Parliament of 1905, which gave the Liberals their biggest majority ever, contained over 180 protestant dissenters. But both dissent and the Liberal Party were poised for eclipse. The removal of many of their grievances by the Liberals persuaded some dissenters to move to the political right, while the new *Labour Party offered alternative accommodation to those who remained radical.

Dissent itself was also in decline. From 1918 onwards there was a marked falling-off in membership of both the Church of England and the dissenting denominations. There was increasing difficulty in recruiting clergy. The Church of England had 20,000 clerics in 1900, 10,000 by 1984; the methodists, with 4,700 ministers in 1950, had 2,500 by 1993. The churches responded in a variety of ways—by merging parishes, by abandoning unwanted churches, by institutional amalgamations, and by ordaining women ministers and priests. Though religious issues still surfaced in public life, politics, except in Northern Ireland, was largely secularized.

**dissenting academies** The Act of *Uniformity (1662) excluded dissenting ministers from their posts. Many, out of necessity, became teachers. Dissenting academies were particularly popular in Devon, Lancashire, London, and Wales, some of the most distinguished being at Tewkesbury, Northampton, and Warrington. They were much used by nonconformists who could not take the oaths at Oxford or Cambridge.

**dissolution of the monasteries** of England and Wales occurred between 1536 and 1540. Profoundly controversial to contemporaries, this was an unparalleled secular spoliation of ecclesiastical property. By the 16th cent. most English monasteries were in some decline, but remained wealthy, and hence tempting to Henry VIII. The full-scale valuation of ecclesiastical income, the *Valor ecclesiasticus* (1535), had revealed the extent of monastic revenues. The desire to appropriate these potently combined with the king's continuing onslaught on the ecclesiastical establishment. Royal visitations revealed convenient scandals and in 1536 all monasteries with an annual income of less than £200 were suppressed. In 1539 all surviving greater monasteries were dissolved. Monks were given annual pensions; a number became secular priests. Ex-nuns were more harshly treated and were not permitted to marry till the reign of Edward VI. Monastic lands, administered through the Court of Augmentations, largely fell into the hands of the aristocracy and gentry.

**distraint of knighthood** Post-Conquest military obligations attached to knighthood were increasingly avoided. In theory landowners of a certain status were required to present themselves at coronations to be knighted. Henry III began campaigns to oblige freeholders with estates worth £20 p.a. to take up knighthoods, issuing writs of distraint. At this stage, the motive was primarily military but later monarchs were more interested in the revenue they could raise by allowing subjects to compound or pay fines. Charles I, in his search for extra-parliamentary revenue, recommenced distraining. Considerable revenue was raised and even more considerable animosity.

**divine right of kings** It was taken for granted in early modern Europe that monarchs derived their authority from God. James VI of Scotland, the protestant son of a catholic mother, defended his own authority against the claims of both *presbyterians and *Jesuits. But his insistence that kings were gods in their own right, above the law in theory, alarmed his English subjects after 1603. Charles I overrode property rights through prerogative taxation, and political liberties by ruling without Parliament. The divine right of kings apparently died with him but was resuscitated during the later Stuart period. Only after the *Glorious Revolution did it become irrelevant.

**Dobunni** A British tribe and *civitas*. The Dobunni were centred on Gloucestershire. According to the Greek historian Dio Cassius, early in the Claudian invasion in AD 43, some of the Dobunni deserted the British cause and came to terms with the Roman invaders. Subsequently, around AD 70, the tribe was granted *civitas* status and *Cirencester (Corinium) became its capital.

**Dogger Bank, battle of the,** 1915. The battle of the Dogger Bank was fought in the North Sea on 24 January 1915. A raiding force of German battle-cruisers was intercepted and pounded by *Beatty's battle-cruiser squadron. The action convinced the German Admiralty that they were right to pursue a cautious strategy.

**Dollar, battle of,** *c.*875. The battle, east of Alloa, Scotland, was a crushing defeat for *Constantine I of Alba by the Norsemen, led by Halfdan of York. The whole northern part of Scotland was conceded to the invaders.

**Domesday Book** was the result of the great survey commissioned by William the Conqueror at Gloucester at Christmas 1085. Domesday Book's name shows that it was a source of awe and wonder. It is fundamental for all types of historical enquiry and is important for geographers, lawyers, and linguists. It is primarily a record of landholders, both in 1086 and in the time of Edward the Confessor, and of the manors which they held. The survey's purpose and the method of its compilation are subjects of debate. The current emphasis is on a financial purpose, since it seems to be primarily concerned with resources and assessments. However, its value as a register of title must not be overlooked. Computer-based studies of Domesday Book's contents are starting to yield impressive results.

**domestic service** refers to paid employment as servants in the households of others. In all periods of history both men and women sought such employment. However, fewer men than women became servants after 1780, when a tax was imposed on all adult male indoor servants.

Domestic service was the most important type of employment for women until after the start of the First World War in 1914, when women took on the jobs of men who joined the services. In upper-class households there was often a hierarchy of servants 'below stairs', ranging from the butler to kitchen skivvies. Frequently these servants remained with the household for many years, some holding positions of intimacy and trust. Amongst the lower middle class only a 'maid of all work' was employed, often enduring long hours and little prestige. Her lot was superior only to the 'daily' helping with the 'rough work'.

**domestic system** The organization of production in the homes of workers. The method began in the Middle Ages when almost all manufacturing was carried out within the home. However, when markets grew rapidly, some production was concentrated in factories. For some products, such as textiles, gloves, boots, and shoes, the system of subcontracting remained. The domestic or putting-out system had many advantages for the master or capitalist manufacturer. The work often required little training. Workers were paid only for their output, and employers did not have to bear the cost of lighting and heating. The masters employed 'bagmen' to distribute raw materials and to collect finished items. The payments for work done depended on the quality of the product and disputes often arose between agents and workers.

The decline of the domestic system was a consequence of the *industrial revolution. Growth in mass markets, combined with the development of textile machines, gave dominance to factory production. During the 20th cent. the domestic system or home working survived, usually associated with low-paid work by women, who rarely joined trade unions or organized to obtain adequate pay and conditions. Home working continues in a wide range of contexts, from the making of exclusive high-fashion knitwear for the fashion industry to new developments in teleworking and networking from home using computers.

**Dominica** is the most northerly of the Windward Islands in the eastern Caribbean. It has been an independent state within the Commonwealth since 1978. Sighted and named by Columbus in 1493, it was disputed in the 18th cent. between France and Britain.

**Dominicans** ('black' or 'preaching' *friars) were a mendicant order founded by a Spanish *Augustinian and preacher, St Dominic, to combat the Albigensian heresy in southern France. The order was confirmed by Pope Innocent III in 1215, and its rule codified by 1221. The Dominicans were dedicated to educational activity and quickly established themselves at the forefront of intellectual life with friaries found in virtually every university town in the medieval West. They first settled in England in Oxford and London in 1221 and by their *dissolution in 1538–9 there were over 50 English friaries.

**dominion status** was the term chosen to describe the position of the self-governing member states of the inter-war *Commonwealth. They were to be regarded, proclaimed the 1926 imperial conference, as 'autonomous communities within the British Empire, equal in status, in no way subordinate one to another'. That was necessary to their self-respect. After 1947, however, when India entered the club, the word 'dominion' was quietly dropped, as implying—despite Britain's disavowals—a certain subordination to her.

**Donald I** (d. 862), 'king of the Picts' (858–62), anachronistically regarded as second king of Scotland, brother of *Kenneth I, whom he succeeded. He presided over an assembly of the Gaels at the royal centre of Forteviot. He died (probably) at 'Rathinveramon'—perhaps a fort near Scone.

**Donald II** (d. 900), king of 'Scotland' (889–900). Donald is the first king to be referred to as '*rí Alban*', 'king of Scotland'. 'Scotland' in this period, however, was only the eastern region north of the Forth. Donald was son of *Constantine I. His family had lost power between 878 and 889, but monopolized the kingship thereafter for 145 years. Donald's reign, like his father's, was plagued by Scandinavian incursions.

**Donald III** (d. *c.*1100), king of Scotland (1093–4, 1094–7), known as Donald Bane. He seized the kingship on the death of his brother, *Malcolm III. His first rival was *Duncan II, Malcolm's eldest son. Duncan, supported by William II of England, dislodged Donald from the kingship in 1094, but was soon defeated and killed in battle. Donald was restored to the throne. In 1097 William II gave military backing to another of Malcolm and *Margaret's sons, *Edgar. Donald was again defeated. In 1099 he was blinded by Edgar and died.

**Donne, John** (1572–1631). Metaphysical poet and churchman. Having been a volunteer on the 1596 Cadiz expedition, he became secretary to Sir Thomas Egerton, but marriage to Anne More (1601) led to dismissal and unemployment. He had by then written much of his passionate, witty poetry and begun to reject catholicism. Even as an Anglican, his deep, personal religious struggle continued. He was ordained in 1615. Preferment was then rapid and he became famous for his powerful sermons. Despite uncertain health, he was installed as dean of *St Paul's cathedral (1621).

**Dorchester** (Dorset). *Civitas*-capital of the *Durotriges. Lying near the Iron Age hill-fort of *Maiden castle, Durnovaria may have succeeded a base of *legio II Augusta*. A large bath-house lay in the south-eastern part of the town and the amphitheatre lay to the south, reusing the site of a Neolithic henge monument, Maumbury Rings.

**Dorchester-on-Thames, diocese of**
First created in *c.*635 as the see of Birinus for Wessex, it was transferred to *Winchester

*c.*663. A Mercian bishopric existed here twice, 675–85, and again following the 8th-cent. Danish invasions. The see was moved to Lincoln *c.*1072.

**Dorset** is one of the oldest and most beautiful shires. The county is largely the basin of the river Frome. For centuries it was the quietest of rural counties, with small market towns like Shaftesbury, Beaminster, and Blandford, and quiet harbours like Wareham, Lyme, and Bridport. The balance of the county was transformed from 1850 onwards by the sudden growth of the coastal towns. In 1801, no town in the shire had above 5,000 people. But by 1931, when Dorchester had reached 10,000, Poole had grown to 57,000 and Weymouth 22,000. The boundary changes of 1972 reinforced this shift by bringing in Bournemouth and Christchurch from west Hampshire. Bournemouth's growth was amazing. In 1841 it boasted 26 dwellings. But after the coming of the railway in 1870, it gained county borough status by 1895, and was well over 163,000 by 2004. Since by 2004 Poole had grown to 137,000, nearly half of the county's population was tucked into the south-east corner.

At the time of the Roman invasion in AD 43 the local tribe was the *Durotriges. Their fortress of *Maiden castle was stormed by *Vespasian's second legion, and nearby *Dorchester developed as the Roman town of Durnovaria. *Sherborne was established as a bishopric as early as 705, and remained one until 1075 when it was removed to Old Sarum. The region formed part of the kingdom of *Wessex.

The *Domesday survey of 1086 identified four boroughs—Shaftesbury, Dorchester, Wareham, and Bridport—the latter having difficulty in sustaining its position because of the vulnerability of its sea defences. In the later Middle Ages and Tudor period, the coastal towns suffered greatly from French and Spanish reprisals and from Algerine pirates. Wareham gradually silted up, losing its prosperity to Poole. Bridport manufactured hempen ropes. The demand for Portland stone increased vastly from the 17th cent. onwards, with the *Banqueting House, *St Paul's, and *Greenwich palace being made of it. Purbeck marble was also much in demand. Inland, cloth manufactures

flourished—silk at Sherborne, lace at Blandford, linen at Gillingham, baize at Sturminster.
But the mainstay of the county was the sheep
on the chalk downs around Dorchester and
the cattle in the vale of Blackmoor to the north.

After 1731 one fortunate result of a disastrous fire at Blandford was a complete rebuilding, making it one of the most
charming Georgian towns in the country.
Another rebuilding was at Milton Abbas,
where Joseph Damer pulled down the old
town and employed Capability *Brown to
build a new model village. The county remained remote and little known. Visits by
George III helped to encourage Weymouth
as a resort.

The 20th cent. produced a vast urban build-
up between Poole and Bournemouth and a
diversification of industry—an atomic energy
station on Wynfrith Heath, oil drilling off the
coast. The hinterland remains largely unspoiled and boasts villages like Sixpenny
Handley, Ryme Intrinsica, Okeford Fitzpaine,
Toller Porcorum, and Hazelbury Bryan.

**Douglas, Archibald Douglas, 3rd
earl of** [S] (d. 1400), known as 'the Grim'.
Douglas rose to prominence as a supporter
of David II. David made him constable of
Edinburgh castle (1361), warden of the west
marches (1364), and lord of Galloway (1369).
He bought the earldom of Wigtown (1372),
received Bothwell by marriage, and inherited
the earldom of Douglas (1388), creating the
Douglas power that dominated Scotland
until 1455.

**Douglas, Archibald Douglas, 4th
earl of** [S], **lord of Galloway and Annandale, duke of Touraine** (c.1372–
1424). Son and heir of Archibald 'the Grim',
3rd earl of Douglas [S], and later nicknamed
'the Tyneman' (the Loser), perhaps because
of his presence in so many battles on the
losing side. Earl Archibald was none the
less a magnate of immense influence, and
one of the triumvirate (with *Albany and
Mar) who controlled the country during the
captivity of James I. Latterly Douglas supported the cause of Charles VII of France
against the English. Created lieutenant-general of the French army, Douglas was killed
in battle against John, duke of *Bedford's
forces at Verneuil (August 1424).

**Douglas, James Douglas, 2nd earl of**
[S] (c.1358–88). Son of William, the 1st earl,
whom he succeeded in 1384. Douglas was
one of several Scottish earls who took advantage of the expiry of truce, and the domestic
troubles of Richard II, to invade England
(1388). His force met with Henry (Hotspur)
*Percy at *Otterburn (August 1388). In the
ensuing battle Percy was captured, the English defeated, but Douglas killed. He was
commemorated as 'doughty Douglas' in the
ballad 'Chevy Chase'.

**Douglas, William Douglas, 8th earl
of** [S] (c.1425–52). Eldest son of James 'the
Gross', 7th earl of Douglas. Douglas grew up
to become the most powerful magnate in
Scotland. Lieutenant-general for the young
James II from 1444, with his brothers James
(who succeeded him), Archibald (earl of
Moray), Hugh (earl of Ormond), and John,
Lord Balvenie, Douglas dominated Scottish
politics between 1444 and 1452. During William's absence abroad, the adult James II
plundered the Douglas lands of Wigtown
and Selkirk. A reconciliation followed in
1451, but in 1452 a bond between Douglas,
Crawford, and Ross provided the excuse for
the earl's murder by James II at Stirling.

**Douglas, Sir James** (d. 1330). One of the
most successful leaders in the Scottish Wars
of Independence. In 1306, Douglas rallied
immediately to Robert Bruce. His forte was
the daring surprise attack. Early in 1307, he
wiped out the English garrison of his family's
castle at Douglas; in 1308 he helped Bruce
gain his victory at the pass of Brander by
climbing the slopes of Ben Cruachan to attack the enemy in the rear. In 1314, he recovered Roxburgh by a night attack; led one
of the brigades at *Bannockburn; and repeatedly thereafter raided into England.

**Douglas cause** On the death of the 1st
duke of Douglas in 1761, the estates were
disputed on behalf of his cousin, the duke
of Hamilton, aged 5, and Archibald Stewart,
claiming to be a nephew, aged 13. In 1767
the Court of Session decided against the
nephew but in 1769 the House of Lords reversed the verdict. Since Stewart's mother
would have been 51 at the time of his birth,
the Lords' verdict was received with some
surprise.

**Dover, treaty of,** 1364. This agreement between Edward III and Louis de Mâle, count of Flanders, on 19 October 1364, was intended to lead to the marriage of Edward's fourth son, Edmund, with the count's daughter and heiress, Margaret. The marriage would have led to English dominance on the northern fringes of France. Charles V of France therefore put pressure on Pope Urban V not to allow a dispensation, and negotiated instead Margaret's marriage to his own son Philip.

**Dover, treaty of,** 1670. Louis XIV's attack upon the Dutch in 1667 had been halted by the *Triple Alliance of Holland, Sweden, and England. To prepare for a decisive victory, Louis needed to smash the alliance and in 1669 began negotiations with Charles II. The treaty of May 1670 pledged the two powers to a joint attack on the Dutch and not to make a separate peace. A secret clause committed Charles to declaring himself a catholic and Louis to providing him with an army if disaffection followed. Suspicions of Charles's sincerity were an important factor in allegations of a *Popish plot in 1678.

**Dover castle** is the gateway to England. Dover was one of the harbours of the *Saxon Shore and the base for the Roman fleet, *Classis Britannica*. Its Roman lighthouse probably dates from the 1st cent. AD. The present castle was started in the reign of Henry II and ready for use in 1185. The keep is similar to that at Newcastle upon Tyne, and by the same master builder, Maurice the Engineer.

**Dowding, Hugh, 1st Baron Dowding** (1882–1970). Air chief marshal. Dowding was born in Dumfriesshire and went to Winchester. He joined the army, and just before the First World War qualified as an RFC pilot. He finished the war as brigadier-general and transferred to the new RAF. In 1936 he was made commander-in-chief of Fighter Command. He thus held a crucial post during the Second World War and in May 1940 he begged that no more fighter planes be sent to France. Dowding was in personal control all through the Battle of *Britain which followed. In his victory broadcast of May 1945, Churchill paid a special tribute to Dowding.

**Down** was one of the six counties of Northern Ireland before the local government reorganization of 1973. Its boundary to the north is the Lagan; to the south, with the Irish Republic, Carlingford Lough. The Mountains of Mourne are in the south-west corner.

**Down (Dún Lethglaisse), diocese of** The Irish bishopric of Down was listed at the Councils of Raithbhressail (1111) and Kells-Mellifont (1152) as a diocese in the province of *Armagh. It was united with Connor 1441–1944, and with Dromore since 1842. The Catholic bishopric is Down and Connor.

**Downing Street** was built by Sir George Downing in the 1680s. Only three of the original houses remain, on the north side—no. 10 used by the prime minister, no. 11 by the chancellor, and no. 12 by the whips. Sir Robert *Walpole accepted it from George II in 1732 for the prime minister of the day.

**Downs, battle of the,** 1652. A clash on 18 May which helped to precipitate the first Anglo-Dutch War. Robert *Blake with fifteen vessels was attacked by a superior fleet under Martin Tromp. The encounter was not decisive but the Dutch lost two ships.

**Downs, battle of the,** 1666. A heavy naval engagement on 11–14 June during the second *Anglo-Dutch War. Albemarle (*Monck), with some 56 vessels, left the Downs and encountered a large Dutch fleet under de Ruyter, Cornelis Tromp, and de Witt. *Rupert brought up reserves on the fourth day enabling Albemarle to retire into the Thames estuary but the English losses were heavier.

**Doyle, Sir Arthur Conan** (1859–1930). Author. Educated at Edinburgh University, Doyle qualified as a doctor but gave up medicine for writing. He published his first novel, *A Study in Scarlet*, in 1887, which introduced the detective Sherlock Holmes. In 1891 Doyle began to write short stories under the title 'The Adventures of Sherlock Holmes' for the *Strand Magazine*. Doyle was an avid imperialist, serving as a physician during the *Boer War (1899–1902). In later years he was absorbed by the subject of spiritualism.

**Drake, Sir Francis** (*c*.1543–96). In legend the greatest of the Elizabethan 'sea-dogs'. A skilled seaman and naval tactician, an inspiring leader of men, he was, nevertheless, capable of greed, disloyalty, and poor judgement as a naval strategist. Though of yeoman stock, Drake became closely associated with a predatory aristocracy ready to sanction piracy against the French, Portuguese, and, above all, the Spanish. The contests also had a religious edge as Drake was a determined protestant.

Originally from Devon, Drake learned seamanship on a coastal bark plying from the Thames, but in the 1560s joined a kinsman, *Hawkins, on ventures to Spain and the Caribbean. He made at least three more piratical expeditions to the Caribbean, with that in 1572 capturing 30 tons of silver. In 1577 Drake embarked on a circumnavigation of the globe financed by the queen. Drake's expedition was the second to circuit the globe and led to his claiming California for Elizabeth. On the return of the *Golden Hind* in 1580, Drake, rich and famous, was knighted.

There followed further raids on Spain and, most notably, assaults on key Spanish positions around the Caribbean in 1585–6 and Cadiz in 1587. These actions, combined with the defeat of the Spanish Armada in 1588 with Drake second in command, ended Spain's supremacy at sea. In 1589, Drake led an expedition against Lisbon before settling into involvement in the life of Plymouth, becoming its MP. He was encouraged to resume a privateering career in 1595 but the attacks in the West Indies failed and Drake died at sea.

**dreadnought** is the name given to a type of battleship introduced into the principal navies after the experiences of the Russo-Japanese War. The chief innovations were higher speed and a main armament of heavy guns. The first to enter service was HMS *Dreadnought* in December 1906.

**Drogheda** is north of Dublin at the mouth of the river Boyne. It was the first garrison to be attacked by *Cromwell when he invaded Ireland in 1649. When Sir Arthur Aston refused to surrender, Cromwell blasted two holes in the wall and on 10 September sent his men into the breach. Only after the second assault did the parliamentarians overrun the town, at which point he ordered 'any that were in arms' put to the sword. Cromwell's intention was that the example of Drogheda would bring Irish catholic resistance to a speedy end. Events proved him wrong.

**druids** A priestly caste in British tribal society. The Greek geographer Strabo accused them of mass human sacrifice. Although they are not specifically identified as the instigators of the slaughter which accompanied the capture of Camulodunum (*Colchester) by *Boudicca's rebels, there can be little doubt that both Tacitus and Dio Cassius held them responsible for the atrocities. Pliny confirms the important role of sacred groves in druidic religion, particularly those of oak trees. He was also responsible for linking the druids to mistletoe, white robes, golden sickles, and herbal medicines.

**Drumclog, battle of,** 1679. John Graham (*Dundee) of Claverhouse, attempting to disperse a rising of *covenanters on 1 June, was sharply repulsed in a skirmish at Drumclog, near Strathaven. The engagement was described by *Scott in *Old Mortality*.

**Drury Lane** (London) takes its name from Sir Thomas Drury, who had a house there in Elizabeth I's reign. The first theatre opened in 1663 and Nell *Gwyn made her début in 1665. The theatre, burned down in 1672, was rebuilt by *Wren. *Garrick made his début there in 1742, became manager, and passed it on to *Sheridan in 1776. His new theatre, built by Holland in 1794, was burned down in 1809. The replacement, by Benjamin Wyatt and much restored, is the present building.

**Dryden, John** (1631–1700). English poet, playwright, and critic. Dryden's influence on political poetry was marked. Educated at Westminster School and Trinity College, Cambridge, Dryden came from a 'middling' landed family. After commemorating Oliver *Cromwell's death in *Heroic Stanzas* (1658), Dryden turned to celebrating the Restoration of Charles II in *Astraea Redux* (1660), *To His Sacred Majesty* (1661), and *Annus Mirabilis* (1667). Appointed poet laureate in 1668 and historiographer-royal in 1670, Dryden continued to support the king, most notably at the height of the *Exclusion crisis with

*Absalom and Achitophel* (1681). Dryden converted to catholicism on the accession of James II, writing a religious allegory, *The Hind and the Panther* (1687). Stripped of his offices in 1688, he returned with success to the theatre.

**Dub** (d. 966), king of 'Scotland' (962–6). Son of *Malcolm I. He succeeded on the death of *Indulf at the hands of Norwegian raiders. He beat off a challenge for the throne by Indulf's son *Cuilén in 965, at the battle of Duncrub. Dub was vanquished by the men of Moray at Forres.

**Dublin** takes its name from the Irish *Duibhlinn,* 'black pool'. Duibhlinn was an ecclesiastical centre seized by the *Vikings in 841. It quickly became the main Viking military base and trading centre in Ireland and its Hiberno-Norse rulers exercised power over its hinterland. After the victory at Clontarf (1014), Irish rulers established themselves as kings of Dublin and by the time Ireland was invaded by the Anglo-Normans in 1169 Dublin was effectively the country's capital. It fell to Anglo-Norman arms in 1170 and remained the headquarters of the English colony in Ireland. Georgian Dublin flourished and the abolition of its parliament in 1800 did little to lessen the city's expansion. Opposition to the *Union led to the *Easter Rising in the city in 1916, followed by the establishment of the *Irish Free State in 1921, with Dublin as capital and the home again of an Irish parliament.

**Dublin (Áth Cliath), archiepiscopal diocese of** Originally a Norse city-state, *Dublin was one of the first regular episcopal sees in Ireland subject to *Canterbury. There developed a strong link between Dublin and Canterbury, and 12th-cent. bishops were usually monks from the Canterbury province. Soon to be the centre of Henry II's colonial administration, Dublin became an archbishopric at the Council of Kells-Mellifont (1152). In 1238 Dublin unsuccessfully challenged the primatial claims of Armagh. It is still the see of both catholic and Anglican archbishops.

**Dublin, kingdom of** Established by the *Vikings in 841, the kingdom of Dublin survived until the execution of its last Hiberno-Norse king, Asgall Mac Turcaill, by invading Anglo-Normans in 1171. After the defeat of King *Olaf Cuarán (Sihtricsson) at the battle of Tara in 980 Dublin's kings came increasingly to feel the domination of the Irish provincial kings, most spectacularly in the defeat of Olaf's son, Sihtric Silkbeard, at the hands of *Brian Boru at *Clontarf in 1014.

**Dublin, treaty of,** 1646. In the early months of 1646 Charles I's position deteriorated sharply. On 28 March 1646 the *Kilkenny Confederates reached an agreement in Dublin with *Ormond, the lord-lieutenant. But when Ormond published the peace terms in July, they were repudiated by the Confederates as inadequate. Ormond was accordingly forced to open negotiations with the English Parliament and in June 1647 a parliamentary army reached Dublin.

**Dublin castle** The *Viking town of Dublin was, by the 10th cent., dominated by a fortress which was captured by Anglo-Norman invaders in 1170. In 1204 King John ordered the construction of a castle, which became the administrative headquarters of the English colony in Ireland, housing the main organs of government.

**Dudley, Edmund** (*c.*1470–1510). Dudley came of Sussex gentry stock. He was employed with Sir Richard *Empson to raise revenue for Henry VII and was Speaker of the House of Commons in 1504. His work on the king's behalf made him many enemies and at the outset of Henry VIII's reign he was sent to the Tower and executed the following year on an implausible charge of high treason.

**Dugdale, Sir William** (1605–86). Dugdale married at 18 and devoted the rest of his life to history and antiquities. Friends found him a place in the Herald's Office and he became Garter king-at-arms in 1677, and was knighted. In 1655, he published the first volume of *Monasticon Anglicanum,* documents relating to the English monasteries. His *Antiquities of Warwickshire,* one of the first and greatest of county histories, came out in 1656.

**duke** The title of duke, derived from the latin 'dux', is the highest in the peerage and until 1448 was restricted to members of the royal family. In that year, Henry VI created

William de la Pole, who had fought in France on many campaigns, duke of Suffolk. After the Glorious Revolution, Whig grandees were promoted to dukedoms in quick succession—Bolton, Shrewsbury, Leeds, Bedford, Devonshire, and Newcastle. George II and III resumed the policy of restraint. The first non-royal Scottish dukedom was Montrose (1488) and the first Irish, Ormond (1661).

**Dumfries and Galloway** has since 1973 been a local authority region of Scotland comprising the counties of Dumfries, Kirkcudbright, and Wigtown. Till 1996 it shared local government activities with its districts of Annandale and Eskdale, Nithsdale, Stewartry, and Wigtown, but now has sole responsibility.

**Dumnonia, kingdom of** After the Roman withdrawal, Cornwall became part of the kingdom of Dumnonia, which also included Devon (the name derived from Dumnonia). Its geographical position enabled it to survive for centuries. Dumnonia was sufficiently part of the known world for *Aldhelm, bishop of Sherborne, to address a letter, c.705, to its king Geraint, putting him right on the date of Easter, and though Geraint was defeated by *Ine of Wessex c.710, the kingdom survived. *Egbert of Wessex completed the conquest of the area in 814.

**Dumnonii** British tribe and *civitas*. The Dumnonii seem to have occupied the whole of the south-west peninsula, and parts of southern Somerset. They appear to have accepted the Roman conquest without resistance, the town of *Exeter (Isca Dumnoniorum) becoming their administrative centre.

**Dunbar, battle of,** 1296. In 1292 Edward I found in favour of John *Balliol as king of Scotland. Three years later, relations between the two had broken down. In the spring of 1296 Edward captured Berwick and laid siege to Dunbar. A relieving army was defeated on 27 April and the castle capitulated. Edward then proclaimed himself king of Scotland.

**Dunbar, battle of,** 1650. Dunbar was *Cromwell's greatest victory, won against severe odds. The royalist army was led by David *Leslie. On 2 September Cromwell's army, weakened by sickness, was bottled up at Dunbar. Cromwell chose to attack the following day and destroyed Leslie's force, taking 10,000 prisoners. 'God made them as stubble to our swords,' Cromwell reported to Parliament.

**Dunblane, diocese of** This see in Perthshire was named after Blane (d. c.590), a saint who preached in Scotland. Dunblane became a bishopric (1162) under David I and the cathedral was built on the site of Blane's monastery.

**Duncan I** (d. 1040), king of Strathclyde (possibly before 1034) and king of Scotland (1034–40). On the death of *Malcolm II the male line of the royal dynasty was extinguished. The vacuum was filled by Duncan, son of Crínán, abbot of Dunkeld (d. 1045), and Bethóc, daughter of Malcolm II. Far from being Shakespeare's old man, he is likely to have been in his twenties. His prime concern was apparently Northumbria, where he found his wife and where he mounted a disastrous campaign in 1039. This gave *Macbeth an opportunity to challenge for the throne. Duncan went on the offensive and led an army into Moray, where he was killed.

**Duncan II** (d. 1094), king of Scotland (1094), was the eldest son of *Malcolm III. He was given as a hostage following Malcolm III's submission to William I at Abernethy in 1072, and remained a captive in England until freed by William II in 1087. William II gave him military backing in a bid to oust his uncle *Donald III from the kingship in 1094. He was killed by Mael Petair, *mormaer of the Mearns, and his uncle restored to the kingship.

**Duncan, Adam** (1731–1804). Born at Lundie (Dundee), Duncan was a Scot of prodigious strength and height. In the American War he served under *Rodney at the first relief of Gibraltar 1779 and under *Howe at the second in 1782, attaining the rank of admiral in 1787 when he was 56. Duncan's most celebrated command was in the North Sea in 1797. His defeat of the Dutch off *Camperdown was testimony to Duncan's resource and leadership. He was created Viscount Duncan of Camperdown.

**Duncan Smith, Iain** (b. 1954). Politician. After seven years in the Scots Guards (1975–81), Duncan Smith moved into industry before election in 1992 for Chingford. In 1997 he became Conservative spokesman for social security and in 1999 for defence. On the right of the party, he was a strong opponent of further *EEC integration. After the resignation of William *Hague in 2001, he was elected leader, but struggled to impose his authority on a party demoralized by crushing election defeats in 1997 and 2001. Dissatisfaction with his parliamentary performance led to his replacement as leader in November 2003 by Michael *Howard.

**Dundalk, battle of,** 1318. Edward *Bruce's short-lived kingdom of Ireland ended in October 1318 when he was defeated and killed at Dundalk by an Anglo-Irish army under John de Bermingham.

**Dundas, Henry, 1st Viscount Melville** (1742–1811). Scottish politician, son of Robert, Lord Arniston, president of the Court of Session. Dundas followed his family tradition and in 1766 was appointed solicitor-general for Scotland. He was MP for Midlothian 1774–90 and for Edinburgh 1790–1802 when he was created Viscount Melville. A burly figure and a forthright speaker with a broad Scots accent, he became successively lord advocate [S] 1775, joint keeper of the signet [S] 1777, privy counsellor, treasurer of the navy 1782–3 and 1784–1800, home secretary 1791–4, president of the India Board of Control 1793–1801, secretary of state for war 1794–1801, keeper of the privy seal of Scotland 1800, and 1st lord of the Admiralty 1804–5. The list testifies to his indispensable value to *Pitt, and Dundas became his right-hand man as well as his friend and drinking companion.

**Dundee** Situated on the Firth of Tay, and already a thriving centre with trading connections throughout northern Europe when granted burghal status c.1191, Dundee prospered through textiles, guns, and its role as an entrepôt port until the mid-17th cent. Past renown for shipbuilding, 'jute, jam, and journalism' has yielded to economic and social insecurity.

**Dundee, John Graham, 1st Viscount** [S] (1648–89). John Graham of Claverhouse

was heir to a small estate near Dundee. A conservative royalist and episcopalian, he made a career in internal security duties against presbyterian radicals. Politically, he allied with James, duke of York (later James II). After 1685 Claverhouse was made provost of Dundee and a viscount. After the Glorious Revolution, he rebelled against the provisional government of Scotland in 1689. He could only raise a small army, mainly Highlanders, but routed his Williamite opponent at *Killiecrankie. Dundee died in the battle and his army disintegrated.

**Dunes, battle of the,** 1658. On 14 June Turenne, commanding the French forces with the help of an English contingent, attacked a Spanish army defending Dunkirk. The Spaniards, under Don John and Condé, were badly beaten.

**Dunfermline abbey** (Fife). On the foundations of a pre-Conquest Celtic church, a Benedictine monastery church was erected by David I (1150). The burial place of royalty during the 11th–15th cents., it became one of the richest and most influential abbeys in Scotland, used for meetings of the Scottish Parliament, and election of bishops. After 1587 all remaining properties were annexed to the crown. The monastery guest-house was enlarged as a residence for royalty, and was the birthplace of Charles I (1600).

**Dungeness, battle of,** 1652. A sharp naval action during the first *Anglo-Dutch War. Tromp, on convoy duty in the channel, attacked *Blake off Dungeness on 30 November. Blake was obliged to break off the encounter and the Dutch convoys went through unscathed.

**Dunkeld, battle of,** 1689. The death of their leader *Dundee deprived the Jacobites of the advantage they had gained at *Killiecrankie in July 1689. Mackay, leading the Williamite forces, was able to regroup. On 21 August, the Jacobites attacked a small force under William Cleland at Dunkeld. Though Cleland was killed, his men repulsed the attack with such vigour that the Jacobite force was routed.

**Dunkeld, diocese of** The first monastery at Dunkeld ('fort of the Celts') may have been founded by St *Columba. *Kenneth I

MacAlpin made it his capital jointly with Scone. The see was revived by *Alexander I (1107–24), ruling jointly with his brother David I (1107–53), who may have founded the cathedral (1127) on the site of the monastery. A new one was built between 1312 and 1464 in Norman and Gothic styles. The Anglican see was merged with St Andrews (1842).

**Dunkirk** North-eastern French port, whence 27 May to 4 June 1940, 200,000 British troops were brought back to England. On 10 May 1940 German troops attacked the Netherlands, Belgium, Luxembourg, and France. On 20 May German units reached the English Channel, splitting the allied forces. On 25 May Gort, commanding the British Expeditionary Force, gave up attempts to cut the German corridor and ordered British retreat to the coast. Churchill's view that Britain should continue the war, whatever happened to France, was reinforced by a promising start to the Dunkirk evacuation. The drama of the evacuation, including the part played by small civilian pleasure boats, raised British morale.

**Dunnichen Moor, battle of** See NECHTANSMERE.

**Dunning's motion** On 6 April 1780 John Dunning carried by 233 votes to 215, in the face of Lord *North's protests, a motion that the influence of the crown had increased, was increasing, and ought to be diminished. This was the high spot of the opposition's campaign for *economical reform. But the *Gordon riots of June 1780 gave North's administration a reprieve.

**Duns Scotus, John** (c.1265–1308). Duns Scotus is said to have been a Franciscan, born at Duns in Berwickshire, and to have studied at Oxford and Paris. He wrote extensively on grammar, logic, philosophy, and theology, concerned primarily with the nature of God, but distinguished between faith (theology) and reason (philosophy). If his concerns were still essentially medieval, his methodology was modern. Duns Scotus was greatly admired for the rigour of his thinking, yet, when medieval scholastic philosophy fell into disfavour in the 16th cent., his name was borrowed to coin the word 'dunce'.

**Dunstan, St** (c.909–88). Dunstan was born into an aristocratic family related to the royal house of Wessex. His early career owed much to family and royal patronage with special support from King *Edmund, who appointed him abbot of Glastonbury c.943. He was made bishop of Worcester (957), of London (959), and finally archbishop of Canterbury (959–88). From his Glastonbury base he was largely instrumental in the introduction of reformed *Benedictine observance into England. As archbishop, Dunstan was immensely influential in secular and ecclesiastical affairs during the reign of Edgar (959–75). In 973 he established the *Ordo* for Edgar's coronation at Bath, which remained the basis for English coronation ritual. Popular opinion accorded him sainthood with a commemorative day on 19 May.

**Dunwich, diocese of** Felix from Burgundy converted the East Angles in the 630s and established his episcopal seat at Dunwich, then a thriving port on the Suffolk coast. In c.673 *Theodore divided the see into two, placing Norfolk under the see of *Elmham. After the Danish invasions in the 9th cent. Dunwich was not revived.

**Dupplin Moor, battle of,** 1332. Edward *Balliol, supported by Edward III, claimed the throne of Scotland after the death of Robert I Bruce. On 11 August 1332 he was victorious at Dupplin Moor outside Perth over a force led by Donald, earl of Mar, regent for the young David II. Mar was killed and Balliol crowned at Scone the following month.

**Durham** was one of the last shires to be fully incorporated into the English political and legal system, because for centuries it was a *palatinate under the jurisdiction of the bishop. It did not receive parliamentary representation until as late as the 17th cent. Geographically the county is of two halves and three rivers. The western half is hilly, the eastern half flat. It has always been mining country, with iron and lead in the hills and coal in the coastal plain. The northern boundary is the river Tyne and its tributary the Derwent; the southern is the Tees. Through the middle flows the Wear from Bishop Auckland to Sunderland.

In Roman times the area formed part of the territory of the *Brigantes. After the Saxon occupation, it was part of *Berni-cia, the northern half of the great kingdom of *Northumbria. The county owed its pre-eminence largely to one man, St *Cuthbert, who died in 687 on the Farne Islands and was first buried on *Lindisfarne. In 875 the monks were forced by Viking raids to abandon the place and, taking Cuthbert's coffin with them, established themselves at *Chester-le-Street. In 995, in the face of fur-ther raids, they fled once more, taking the coffin first to Ripon, then to Durham, where it has remained. There it attracted the great wealth on which the power of the later bishops depended. The name—Dun-holm, the island on the hill—reflected the nature of the place, a rocky promontory, almost completely sur-rounded by a loop of the river Wear.

The region was not included in the *Do-mesday survey and offered fierce resistance to the *Norman Conquest. When finally it was subdued, the bishop was given palati-nate powers, partly to deal with the local population, partly to resist Scottish incur-sions. The castle at Durham was begun by William in 1072, blocking the neck of the peninsula: the great cathedral was started in 1093.

Although the coal measures had been worked since the 13th cent., Durham remained thinly populated. Defoe visited the county in the 1720s and was not greatly im-pressed: Darlington had 'nothing remarkable but dirt', and Chester-le-Street 'an old dirty, thorough-fare town'. But the industrial, mining, and shipbuilding developments of the 19th cent. acted as a magnet, and by 1891 the county had well over 1 million people. Darling-ton had grown from a town of 5,000 to 36,000; Gateshead from 8,000 to 85,000; South Shields from 8,000 to 97,000; Stockton from 4,000 to 51,000; and Sunderland, which established it-self as a major industrial centre of shipbuilding, pottery, and glass, from 12,000 to 156,000.

Nineteenth-cent. prosperity was not main-tained and the collapse of shipbuilding, mining, and the steel industry led to massive unemployment. The industrial base of the county has diversified, with chemicals at Bill-ingham, car manufacture at Sunderland, and light industry in the Team valley south of Newcastle.

**Durham, city of** Though small, Durham is one of the great cities of Britain. It is best

seen from the 1857 railway viaduct to the west of the town, which looks down on the great loop of the river Wear, across to the cathedral and the castle. The first settlement was probably at Elvet, where Pehtwine was consecrated bishop of Whithorn in c.762: the church is dedicated to St *Oswald (d. 642), suggesting a 7th- or 8th-cent. foundation. But the arrival of the remains of St *Cuthbert in 995 drew pilgrims and the diocese was transferred from *Chester-le-Street. After the Norman Conquest, building of the castle was ordered by William I in 1072 and the foundation stone of the cathedral laid by *William of St Carilef in 1093. Durham devel-oped into an important regional capital and administrative centre.

**Durham, diocese of** The bishopric, con-terminous with the old county of Durham, was created in 995, when *Aldhelm moved the see from *Chester-le-Street. The conse-quent translation of St *Cuthbert's bones to Durham benefited the new see spiritually and financially. The prince-bishops of the Middle Ages were people of influence in both church and state. Today the bishops of Durham still hold seniority, with London and Winchester, second only to the arch-bishops of Canterbury and York. The original Anglo-Saxon cathedral of 995 was replaced by the present magnificent Norman cathe-dral. The tombs of Cuthbert and *Bede are in the Galilee chapel.

**Durham, John Lambton, 1st earl of** (1792–1840). A wealthy Durham landowner, Lambton became one of the county's MPs from 1813, advocating reforms and acquiring the nickname 'Radical Jack'. He was created Baron Durham in 1828. When his father-in-law *Grey became premier in 1830, Durham joined the cabinet and helped to draft the ministry's Reform Bill. He was promoted earl of Durham in 1834. From 1835 to 1837 he was ambassador to Russia. After a rebel-lion in Canada in 1838, he was sent there and produced the *Durham Report. Although tal-ented, he was difficult, proud, short-tem-pered, and easily offended.

**Durham, treaties of,** 1136, 1139. In the struggle between Stephen and Matilda for the throne of England, David I of Scotland supported the latter, his niece. He occupied Northumberland but reached a settlement at

Durham with Stephen in 1136. The agreement soon broke down but, despite a defeat in 1138 at the battle of the *Standard, David negotiated similar terms in 1139, retaining Northumberland, save for Newcastle and Bamburgh.

**Durham Report** John Lambton, earl of *Durham, was appointed governor-in-chief of Canada in January 1838 following rebellions in Canada. He recommended the union of Upper and Lower Canada (now Ontario and Quebec) with local self-government. Durham's *Report* was hailed by late 19th-cent. enthusiasts as the Magna Carta of the empire.

**Durotriges** British tribe and *civitas*. Centred in Dorset, the Durotriges seem to have been a loosely knit confederation at the time of the Roman conquest. Their coinage carries the names of no kings, and there were many occupied hill-forts which were probably the strongholds of local chieftains. At the time of the Roman invasion the Durotriges put up spirited opposition and they were almost certainly one of the two tribes which Suetonius records fighting against *Vespasian. The *civitas* of the Durotriges had its capital at Durnovaria (Dorchester).

**Dussindale, battle of,** 1549. *Kett's rebellion in Norfolk in 1549 posed a formidable threat to the government of Protector Somerset. One relief force under William Parr, Lord Northampton was driven out of Norwich. In August Lord Warwick (*Northumberland) was dispatched with a sizeable force, stiffened by German mercenaries. After heavy fighting on 27 August, Warwick offered pardon, which most of the peasants accepted.

**Dyfed** County of south-west Wales, extant between 1974 and 1996. The name given to the new county under the Local Government Act of 1972 was derived from that of the post-Roman kingdom. At the statute of *Rhuddlan in 1284, the county of *Cardiganshire was created, and by the Act of *Union with England in 1536, *Pembrokeshire and *Carmarthenshire. It was not until 1972 that these were united as a new county and given the name Dyfed. The county had little in the way of contemporary common interest and in 1996 authority reverted to the former three counties and Dyfed as a formal administrative area ceased to exist.

**Dyfed (Demetia), kingdom of** The land of the *Demetae people at the time of the Roman invasions. The kingdom may have been founded by Irish immigrants, the Deisi, in post-Roman times; its royal dynasty lasted until Llywarch ap Hyfaidd's death (904), when his daughter's husband *Hywel Dda, son of the king of neighbouring *Seisyllwg, succeeded; Dyfed then became part of the larger *Deheubarth.

**Dyrham, battle of,** 577. The *Anglo-Saxon Chronicle* recorded that at Dyrham, east of Bristol, *Ceawlin, king of Wessex, defeated and killed three British kings, and went on to occupy Bath, Cirencester, and Gloucester. There is little doubt that this was a major victory in the Saxon advance.

**Eadgyth** (*c.*1022–75), queen of *Edward the Confessor. Eadgyth was the eldest daughter of Earl *Godwine, the most powerful nobleman of his day, and sister of *Harold II. She married Edward in 1045 soon after his succession. There were rumours that the marriage was never consummated and certainly there were no children.

**Eadwig** (d. 959), king of England (955–9). The elder son of King *Edmund, Eadwig succeeded at about 15 on the death of his uncle *Edred. Rivalry at court may explain opposition to his marriage to Ælfgifu, his cousin, and their separation in 958 on the grounds of consanguinity. Ælfgifu's brother Æthelweard in his *Chronicon* says Eadwig was known as 'All-Fair' and that he 'deserved to be loved'.

**Ealdgyth,** wife of Harold II. Daughter of the Mercian earl Ælfgar, she was previously married to the Welsh king *Gruffydd, defeated by Harold in 1063, and slain by his own men. Harold probably married her to ensure the allegiance of her brothers, the earls of Mercia and Northumbria. Ealdgyth bore him a son after his death.

**ealdorman** in early usage could indicate a patriarch, prince, or ruler. In the laws of King *Ine, *c.*700, the ealdorman appears as a functionary, in charge of a *scir* (shire). In another context such men would probably appear as *subreguli* (under-kings). From the early 11th cent. the Scandinavian term '*earl' is used for such potentates. But the general sense of 'ealdorman' gave the term lasting life, in particular in towns.

**Eardwulf** (d. *c.*810), king of Northumbria (796–*c.*810). Before his accession Eardwulf was an *ealdorman. He became king at a disturbed period in Northumbrian politics and within four years had defeated an attempted coup. He attacked *Cenwulf of Mercia in 801 for harbouring his enemies. In 806

or 808 he was forced into exile, but returned with help provided by the Frankish king Charles the Great; not long afterwards he was succeeded by his son Eanred.

**earls** Though earl is the oldest peerage title, it has been overtaken by duke and marquis. In early Saxon England it was merely the general name for noble. Administrative responsibility in shires belonged to *ealdormen. But the name earl gradually merged with the Danish jarl and, after the reign of *Alfred, earls took over the responsibilities of ealdormen. Since they supervised several shires or provinces, administration passed increasingly to the shire reeve. After the Conquest, earldoms tended to become hereditary.

**East Anglia, kingdom of** Anglo-Saxon migrants settled in East Anglia in the late 5th cent. Its difficult western boundary in the Fens ensured a degree of independence and the East Angles preserved in what became the two shires of *Norfolk and *Suffolk their own social customs. Their ruling dynasty, the Wuffingas, appears to have had some affinity with Sweden. The greatest of their early rulers, *Rædwald, who died *c.*625, was probably the king commemorated in the ship-burial at *Sutton Hoo. In the 8th cent. the East Angles fell increasingly under Mercian control. East Anglia bore the main brunt of the Danish invasions in the 9th cent. Its last king, St *Edmund, was martyred in 870, and for a period East Anglia was governed by Scandinavian kings. On its recovery by *Edward the Elder and *Athelstan, it was absorbed into the shire system of England

**Easter**—the uniquely English word is derived from the Teutonic goddess Eostre— is the primary Christian feast celebrating Christ's resurrection. Its dating has always presented a problem. While the gentile church, stressing the resurrection element, celebrated it on a Sunday, the province of Asia followed the Jewish Passover date in the lunar calendar. At the Council of Nicaea (325) Easter was settled as the Sunday following the first full moon after the vernal equinox. Another revision (6th cent.) caused divergence between the Celtic church and Rome, thus creating animosity when the 6th/7th-cent. Roman missionaries arrived in Britain until resolved at the Synod of *Whitby (664).

**Eastern Association** Consisting of Norfolk, Suffolk, Cambridgeshire, Hertfordshire, and Essex, this was the only one of the parliamentary county associations to enjoy any permanence in the Civil War. While its chief function was to protect the eastern counties, the army later ventured further afield, most notably at *Marston Moor (July 1644). The Eastern Association army was absorbed into the *New Model in the spring of 1645.

**Eastern Question** This was the problem created by the slow collapse of the Ottoman (Turkish) empire. Turkey's weakness became apparent in a series of wars with Russia in the late 18th cent. The British feared that, if the Turkish empire broke up, Russian power would threaten the British empire in India. The *Crimean War of 1854–6, in which Britain, France, and Turkey fought Russia, was the result of miscalculations, arising from France and Russia's over-vigorous championing of the rights of Turkey's catholic and orthodox Christians respectively, and Britain's fears that Russia wished to seize Constantinople (Istanbul). Nationalist feelings in the Balkans grew and the problem flared up again in the 1870s. The Bosnians rose in 1875, followed by the Bulgarians in 1876. Russia declared war on Turkey but the other powers thought the treaty of San Stefano (1877) too favourable to Russia and amended it at the Congress of *Berlin (1878). European opinion wavered over the next 30 years between the comparative stability provided by the Ottoman empire and the volatility of the emerging Balkan states. It can be argued that the Eastern Question caused the *First World War. Austria angered Serbia by annexing Bosnia in 1908. Russia helped to organize the Balkan League of Serbia, Bulgaria, Macedonia, and Greece, which

went to war with Turkey in 1912. Militarily they were successful but then fought between themselves. The situation was still unstable when the heir to the Austrian throne was assassinated in the Bosnian capital, Sarajevo, in 1914. The Austrians blamed the Serbs: Russia backed them. War followed within weeks.

**Easter Rising** (1916). The Easter Rising was planned by the *Irish Republican Brotherhood's military council to take advantage of British participation in the world war. The plans collapsed due to British intelligence discovery of American links and confusion over time of arrival of arms from Germany. The leaders of the IRB went ahead with the rebellion by taking over various buildings in Dublin. Outside the General Post Office, their GHQ, Pearse read out the provisional declaration of an Irish Republic; five days later, the rebels surrendered. Leaders were executed in stages, and over 2,000 interned. While there was little overt support for the rising at the time, British actions gave it a retrospective significance.

**East India Company** The first English East India Company was formed in 1599 to compete with the Dutch for the trade of the spice islands. However, following the *Amboyna massacre of 1623, it abandoned the East Indies to concentrate on the Indian subcontinent. The company began to acquire a territorial empire in India after the battle of *Plassey in 1757, and the defeat of the Maratha empire in 1818 gave it undisputed supremacy. Territorial conquest, however, brought about more direct parliamentary control through the Regulation Act of 1773 and the India Act of 1784. It survived as a quasi-department of the British state until the *Indian mutiny of 1857, whereafter it was abolished and its powers vested in a secretary of state for India.

**Eastland Company** One of the great trading companies, chartered in 1579, and trading with the Baltic. The foreign residence was first at Elbing, then at Danzig. The company imported timber and tar, flax and linen, and corn, and exported mainly cloth.

**East Saxons, kingdom of** See ESSEX.

**East Sussex** See SUSSEX, EAST.

**Ecclesiastical Commission,** 1686. The Court of *High Commission, to impose uniformity in the church, was abolished in 1641 by the Long Parliament. Nevertheless, in 1686 James II named seven ecclesiastical commissioners, who summoned Henry *Compton, bishop of London, to explain why he had not suspended Dr Sharp for preaching an anti-catholic sermon. Compton challenged the commission's authority but was himself suspended, and in 1688 was one of the 'seven' who appealed to William of Orange for help. James's commission was declared 'illegal and pernicious' by the *Bill of Rights in 1689.

**ecclesiastical commissioners** were established in 1836 as a permanent body to supervise the financial management of the Church of England. In 1948 they were merged with the administrators of *Queen Anne's Bounty and are now known as the church commissioners.

**ecclesiastical courts** have existed alongside secular courts from the Norman Conquest, though their activities were much diminished after the Glorious Revolution of 1688. In addition to supervising clerical discipline, the courts had important jurisdiction over matrimonial disputes, probate, and wills, and a general responsibility for the behaviour of the laity. In the 12th cent. the boundaries between royal and ecclesiastical jurisdiction and the extent of *benefit of clergy were hotly disputed and contributed much to the conflict between Henry II and *Becket. Until the Reformation the hierarchy of courts was archdeacons' courts, bishops' (consistory) courts, archiepiscopal courts, and the papal court. Above the archiepiscopal court for Canterbury was the Court of Arches: above York, the Chancery Court.

**Ecclesiastical Titles Act,** 1851. In 1850, Pope Pius IX, encouraged by Nicholas *Wiseman, announced the restoration of a Roman catholic hierarchy in England with English territorial titles, such as archbishop of Westminster. This provocative move caused one of the final bouts of English anti-popery. Lord John *Russell, the prime minister, encouraged protests by his 'Durham letter' and by passing in 1851 the Ecclesiastical Titles Act, which forbade Roman catholics from using English place-name titles. The Act

was a dead letter and was repealed by Gladstone in 1871.

**Ecgfrith** (d. 685), king of Northumbria (670–85). During the reign of Ecgfrith *Northumbria reached the peak of its power. He extended the range of lordship of his father Oswiu, even sending a strong military expedition to Ireland. In his attempts to stabilize his northern frontier he subdued the British kingdom of Strathclyde, but he overreached himself on campaign against the Picts and was killed at *Nechtansmere in 685.

**economical reform** Christopher *Wyvill's *Yorkshire Association was launched in 1779 when taxation was biting as a result of the *American War. A programme of retrenchment was taken up by the *Rockingham opposition, partly to embarrass *North's ministry, partly to weaken the influence of the crown. The triumph of the campaign was the carrying in April 1780 of *Dunning's motion that the influence of the crown 'ought to be diminished'. The Rockinghams achieved a modest measure of reform when they came to power in 1782. *See also* PLACE ACTS.

**Eden, Anthony, 1st earl of Avon** (1897–1977). Prime minister. After Eton, Eden fought with distinction on the western front. With a first at Oxford he entered Parliament in 1923 for the safe seat of Warwick and Leamington. At this stage Eden showed few signs of distinction or originality, but he rose rapidly and as parliamentary private secretary to Austen *Chamberlain 1926–9 began a lifelong association with foreign affairs.

It was as junior Foreign Office minister after 1931 that Eden's career prospered. He was seen as the champion of collective security through the *League of Nations. Eden became lord privy seal in January 1934 and minister for League of Nations affairs in June 1935. In December 1935, after Samuel *Hoare's resignation in the wake of the Hoare–Laval Pact, he emerged as foreign secretary, aged 38. Despite calling for accelerated rearmament, there is little evidence that he ruled out an accommodation with Hitler. It was ostensibly over relations with Italy that Eden resigned in February 1938, though the increasing interventions of the new prime minister, Neville *Chamberlain, were contributory factors. Nevertheless, his resignation secured his reputation as an anti-appeaser.

With the outbreak of war Eden became dominions secretary and was promoted to the War Office in May 1940. That December Eden returned to the post of foreign secretary where he established an effective partnership with *Churchill. He was often called upon to restrain Churchill's fertile but over-exuberant brain and from 1942 was Churchill's designated successor.

After the Conservatives' electoral defeat in 1945, Eden endured a further difficult decade as heir apparent. Churchill was frequently absent from Parliament, effectively leaving Eden to act as leader of the opposition. In 1951 Eden returned again to the Foreign Office. By now his relationship with Churchill had deteriorated. None the less his final period as foreign secretary was distinguished. Britain, through Eden, cut an impressive figure on the world stage which belied the decline in her intrinsic power even since 1945.

Churchill finally retired in April 1955 and Eden began his premiership on a wave of goodwill. Despite an impressive general election victory in May, the prime ministerial honeymoon was soon over. Colleagues became increasingly conscious of weaknesses which perhaps made him unsuited for the highest office of state—irritability, vanity, hyper-sensitivity, and an inability to place sufficient trust in subordinates. Into this unpromising scenario broke the crisis created by Nasser's nationalization of the Suez canal in July 1956. Eden was handicapped by Britain's inability to take immediate military action. Nasser refused to provide him with the pretext for military intervention. After a secret agreement, which Eden tried desperately to erase from the historical record, Britain and France entered Egypt, ostensibly to separate the Israeli and Egyptian combatants. It was a paper-thin deception. Under the pressure of world opinion, Britain was compelled to accept a cease-fire on 6 November. Above all, Eden had grossly misjudged the response of the USA to Britain's actions. Eden was compelled by his doctors to resign the premiership and withdraw from public life in January 1957. With the patient care of his second wife, Clarissa, Eden lived for a further 20 years.

**Eden, William, Lord Auckland** *See* AUCKLAND, 1ST BARON.

**Edgar** (943–75), king of England (959–75). The reign of Edgar marks an important stage in the development of the English monarchy. His coronation at Bath in 973, when the king was in his 30th year, had strong ecclesiastical as well as secular implications, and indeed the ceremony contained elements that formed the basis for all future coronations. Edgar's early years were not easy. He and his elder brother Edwy were the sons of King *Edmund (939–46), and on the death of their uncle *Edred (946–55) Edwy succeeded to the throne. He proved incompetent, and a revolt in 957 by the Mercians and the Northumbrians resulted in a partition which left Edwy ruling Wessex, but Edgar (still only 14) as king in the north. Civil war was averted by the death of Edwy in 959, and Edgar ruled thereafter a reunited kingdom. In the secular field he was remembered for his good peace, and for his laws in which he recognized the validity of Danish social and legal customs where they had settled. Late in his reign, *c.*973, he was responsible for a massive reform of the coinage. In religious matters he worked closely with St *Dunstan, whom he had appointed as bishop of Worcester, then of London, and finally as archbishop of Canterbury. Immediately after his coronation, Edgar sailed to Chester, where he received formal pledges of loyalty from a number of rulers drawn from the Welsh, Scottish, Cumbrian, and Scandinavian communities. Later historians tell of a ceremonial rowing on the river Dee, with the king at the helm and the other rulers at the oars.

**Edgar** (*c.*1074–1107), king of Scotland (1097–1107). Edgar inherited the throne in 1093 when both his father *Malcolm Canmore and his elder brother Edward were killed at *Alnwick. Driven out by Malcolm's half-brother *Donald Bane, Edgar re-established himself in 1097 with the help of William Rufus. He relied considerably on his English allies and in 1100 his sister *Matilda married Henry I.

**Edgar the Atheling** (*c.*1052–*c.*1125), a grandson of *Æthelred the Unready, was proclaimed king by the English gathered in London after the battle of *Hastings. His claims to the succession were brushed aside by William the Conqueror. After 1066, Edgar intermittently played the role of pretender and was deeply involved in the English revolts of 1069–70. Reconciled with William in 1074, he thereafter lived as a courtier.

**Edgecote, battle of,** 1469. In July 1469 Edward IV was in Nottingham when *Warwick marched against him. Reinforcements for the king led by the earl of Pembroke and the earl of Devon reached Banbury on 25 July. Next day, Pembroke's Welsh force was continuing its march when it was overwhelmed at Edgecote by a force of Warwick's supporters. Pembroke was captured and beheaded. On hearing the news, Edward's army deserted and he became Warwick's prisoner.

**Edgehill, battle of,** 1642. Edgehill was the opening battle of the English Civil War. After raising his standard at Nottingham in August, Charles I embarked on a recruiting march in the west midlands, while Parliament gathered an army under *Essex to face him. Charles began an advance towards London. Essex shadowed him. The royalists slipped past but on 23 October turned to fight on the steep slopes of Edgehill, outside Banbury. Prince *Rupert's cavalry had the better of the exchanges, but the parliamentary infantry stood firm. The road to London was open for the king but his leisurely advance gave his opponents time to regroup.

**Edinburgh,** the capital of Scotland, is an ancient settlement, archaeological evidence pushing its history back over 4,000 years. A fine defensive site, the growth of the city stretched from the castle to Canongate and the abbey of Holyrood. The 'Old Town' by 1700 was teeming with people, its population huddled in great tenements. The building of a 'New Town' across the deep troughs was a consequence of further population growth. The wealthy were the first to move into a neoclassical grid-square suburb with wide streets and magnificent Georgian houses. Linked by bridges (1772–1857), the 'New Town' became a major shopping area. In 2004 the city's population numbered 453,000.

Employment in the 21st cent. is increasingly dominated by the service sector. Scottish banks, investment trusts, building societies, and insurance companies provide jobs in financial services; the supreme courts of Scotland—the *Court of Session (1532) and the High Court of *Justiciary—are located in the Old Parliament House (1640); the universities (including Heriot-Watt (1964) and Napier (1992)), the merchant company, and private and public schools serve a wide constituency. As the capital, Edinburgh is the administrative centre of Scotland, and the Scottish Parliament has met there since 1999. Since the 1950s leisure and tourism have become major civic industries, the International Festival being a particular attraction.

**Edinburgh, Philip, duke of** (b. 1921). The duke of Edinburgh is the son of Prince Andrew of Greece and Denmark, and nephew of Earl *Mountbatten, who was killed in 1979. After school at Gordonstoun, Prince Philip entered the navy in 1938, served throughout the Second World War, and was mentioned in dispatches at Cape *Matapan. His family connections brought him into contact with the royal family, and his engagement to Princess Elizabeth was announced in June 1947. Before the marriage in November, he was given the Garter and a dukedom. Since 1952 Prince Philip has filled the difficult role of royal consort. Of the many societies and causes which he supports, the duke of Edinburgh's scheme for young people (1956) and his concern for the protection of wild life rank high. He retains much of the briskness and forthrightness of his early naval career.

**Edinburgh, St Giles** Founded 854, formally dedicated 1243, rebuilt in stone after burning by Richard II (1385), St Giles was created a collegiate church in 1467. On *Knox's return from Geneva, it became involved militantly in the new reformed church's activities. Under presbyterian rule, 19th-cent. reconstruction of the 'high kirk' has been enhanced by the Thistle chapel (1911).

**Edinburgh, treaty of,** 1328. The treaty set the seal on the achievements of Robert I Bruce. Edward III recognized the full independence of Scotland, and relinquished his claim to Berwick and the borders. Though the treaty was intended as a 'final peace', it unravelled as soon as Robert died the following year.

**Edinburgh, treaty of,** 1474. The first firm Anglo-Scottish alliance of the century was concluded by Edward IV and James III. The Scottish king's infant son and heir James, duke of Rothesay, was formally betrothed to Edward IV's daughter Cecilia. The proposed marriage was never solemnized and war soon resumed.

**Edinburgh, treaty of,** 1560. The treaty has been claimed as a turning-point in Anglo-Scottish relations. Elizabeth had succeeded in England in November 1558. At Edinburgh, French and English negotiators agreed on 6 July to withdraw all troops from Scotland. Though Mary, queen of Scots, returned to Scotland in 1561 after the death of her husband Francis I in December 1560, the French had no longer the same incentive to support her, and the outbreak of the French wars of religion greatly weakened their position.

**Edinburgh castle** stands on Castle Rock dominating the city of Edinburgh and is approached across the Esplanade, the site of the annual military tattoo. It houses the crown jewels (*Honours) of Scotland, and occupies a special place in Scots history: in 1566 Mary, queen of Scots, gave birth there to Prince James, later King James VI of Scotland (1567) and James I of England (1603).

**Edinburgh Review** Founded in 1802 by Henry Erskine and Francis Jeffrey, the latter as editor for the first 26 years, it followed a radical Whig line and its contributors included Henry *Brougham, Francis *Horner, Sydney *Smith, *Macaulay, and Thomas *Carlyle. 'To be an *Edinburgh Reviewer*', wrote *Hazlitt, 'is, I suspect, the highest rank in modern literary society.' It survived until 1929.

**Edington, battle of,** 878. After the disaster at *Chippenham in January 878, Alfred was reduced to guerrilla warfare from the marshes around Athelney. By May he was ready to attack again and encountered *Guthrum's Danes at Edington, near Westbury. His decisive victory forced Guthrum to sue for peace and give hostages. 'Never before', wrote

*Asser proudly, 'had they made peace with any one on such terms.'

**Edmund** (d. 870), king of East Anglia, known as 'the Martyr'. More famous in legend than in life, Edmund was killed by the Danes on 20 November 870. Stories quickly grew concerning his refusal to forswear Christianity, and his death (tied to a tree and shot to death by arrows). His burial place at Bury St Edmunds became a shrine, and the great abbey founded there helped to perpetuate his memory.

**Edmund I** (*c.*922–46), king of England (939–46). Edmund succeeded his brother *Athelstan in 939. His prestige as a young warrior-prince who had fought at *Brunanburh (937), and the evidence of his law codes, suggests potential greatness, but at only 24 or 25 he was murdered by a private enemy at Pucklechurch (Glos.) on 26 May 946.

**Edmund II** (d. 1016), king of England (1016), known as 'Ironside'. After the death of *Æthelred in April 1016, his son Edmund, then in his early twenties, was recognized as his successor and took command of the forces resisting *Cnut. A season of hard campaigning produced varying fortunes. Cnut failed in his efforts to take London, but Edmund was defeated in the autumn at *Ashingdon in Essex. Cnut was content to come to terms and reached an agreement near Deerhurst to partition the kingdom, leaving Edmund in possession of Wessex. However, Edmund himself died on 30 November 1016, and Cnut was received as king throughout England.

**Edmund,** son of *Malcolm Canmore by *Margaret, daughter of *Edward the Atheling, is said to have shared the throne of Scotland with his uncle *Donald III from 1094 to 1097. They were then ousted by Edmund's brother *Edgar.

**Edred** (d. 955), king of England (946–55). The third of *Edward the Elder's sons to succeed to the West Saxon kingship, Edred was confronted during the greater part of his reign by an independent Scandinavian kingdom of York. Only in the last year of his life did Edred rule over a united kingdom of England.

He was a devout Christian and a close friend of Abbot *Dunstan of Glastonbury.

**Education Acts** Starting in the 19th cent., a series of Education Acts have signalled the reorganization of all aspects of education. The 1870 Act, steered through Parliament by the Liberal W. E. *Forster, established a system of elementary schools in England and Wales. Locally elected school boards were to provide schools where there was a deficiency by the denominational bodies. This Act was the beginning of the so-called 'dual system', which still exists. An 1880 Act imposed universal compulsory schooling under the age of 10.

The 1902 Act, the work of the Conservative A. J. *Balfour, set up a co-ordinated national system of education, administered by a central Board of Education. School boards were abolished and replaced by local education authorities. Grammar schools were established and free places provided for pupils from elementary schools.

The 1944 Act, introduced by Conservative R. A. *Butler, stipulated that education should be organized in three stages—primary, secondary, and further—and divided into grammar, technical, and modern. The Board of Education was replaced by a Ministry of Education and provision was made for raising the school-leaving age from 14 to 15: it was raised to 16 in 1972. The Act remained in force for the next four decades, but selection for the different schools caused difficulty. Labour governments from 1964 encouraged comprehensive schooling.

**Edward** (d. 924), king of England (899–924), known as 'the Elder'. Up to 910 when he won a decisive victory against the Danes at *Tettenhall in Staffordshire, Edward was involved first in suppressing a revolt led by his cousin Æthelwold, then in efforts to keep the peace with Danish forces. Tettenhall left Edward in effective command of all England south of the Humber. His success was possible partly because of the readiness of Danes, settled into the countryside, to submit to a strong legitimate king who could offer peace, and partly due to co-operation between the West Saxons and the Mercians. Edward worked well first with his brother-in-law *Æthelred, ealdorman of Mercia, and after his death in 911 with his widow, Edward's own sister *Æthelfleda, the formidable 'lady

of the Mercians'. An outstanding feature of their campaigns was the implementation of a 'burghal' policy, setting up fortified defences at towns manned by forces drawn from surrounding estates. Burhs were built or repaired (where existing fortifications already existed) at places such as Hertford, Witham, Buckingham, Bedford, Maldon, Towcester (specially defended by a stone wall), Tempsford, and Colchester by Edward, and at Bridgnorth, Tamworth, Stafford, Warwick, and Runcorn by Æthelfleda.

At various points in his reign Edward also had his overlordship recognized by Welsh princes, Scottish rulers, by the Britons of Strathclyde, and by Northumbrian noblemen exercising authority at Bamburgh, but his major contribution to the ultimate achievement of English unity rested on military and institutional success south of the Humber.

**Edward** (d. 978), king of England (975–8), known as 'the Martyr'. On the sudden death of *Edgar, 8 July 975, parties formed around his two sons, Edward, aged about 13, and Edward's half-brother *Æthelred, probably only 7 or 8. Edward was eventually accepted as king. Later authorities speak of him as unstable and violent, but all was overshadowed by the manner of his death. On a visit to his young brother and stepmother at Corfe in Dorset on 18 March 978 (just possibly 979) he was stabbed to death in cold blood by his brother's retainers.

**Edward** (c.1005–66), king of England (1042–66), known as 'the Confessor'. Edward was born at Islip (Oxon.), the first recorded child of *Æthelred's second marriage: his mother was *Emma, daughter of Richard I, count of Normandy. During the Danish conquest of England, Edward took refuge in Normandy, initially in 1013. Emma married King *Cnut in 1017, and seems to have been influential in Edward's recall from the long exile in 1041 in the reign of *Harthacnut, her son by Cnut. In the following year Edward succeeded his half-brother on the throne. He proved far from the pious nincompoop portrayed by some historians, and should be given credit for keeping his kingdom intact in troubled time, for reconciling the English and Danish elements in the aristocracy, and for accustoming England to regular cultural and political contact with continental Europe. His reign was dominated by his relationship with one of the most extraordinary families in English history, that of Earl *Godwine of Wessex, whose daughter *Eadgyth married Edward in 1045. Godwine's five sons, *Sweyn, *Harold, *Tostig, Leofwine, and Gyrth, all achieved the rank and office of earl, and Harold succeeded his brother-in-law as king in 1066. In 1051, as a result of quarrels, Edward enforced the exile of the whole Godwine family, and although they returned under arms in the autumn of 1052 they did not do so unconditionally. In their absence Edward had indulged in a degree of Normanization. Godwine's return prompted reaction. *Robert of Jumièges, whose promotion to the see of Canterbury in 1051 had caused disaffection, was replaced by *Stigand. Godwine himself died in dramatic circumstances at Easter 1053, not long after his return. After Godwine's death, Edward affirmed his overlordship in spectacular fashion, sending Harold on an embassy, and recalling from Hungary his own nephew and namesake *Edward the Atheling, presumably as a possible heir. The last decade or so of Edward's reign was a period of relative prosperity. Local government functioned effectively and urban life flourished, notably in London and Winchester. Tax systems and coinage were advanced, sophisticated, and efficient for the age. An outbreak of rebellion in Northumbria in October 1065, resulting in the exile of Tostig, caused the king much grief and seems to have precipitated his final illness. He had spent much treasure on the rebuilding of *Westminster abbey, but was too sick to attend the dedication on 28 December. He died in the first week of 1066, on 4 or 5 January, and was buried in the abbey. In the 12th cent. Edward became something of a symbol of reconciliation between Norman and English. His reputation as a lawgiver, largely unmerited, became great, and his personal piety exaggerated. In 1161, he was canonized by Pope Alexander III. The by-name 'the Confessor' persisted, as one who suffered for his faith, though initially it was given merely to differentiate him from his half-uncle *Edward the Martyr.

**Edward I** (1239–1307), king of England (1272–1307). When Edward came to the throne he was already an experienced general and politician. He had played the major role in the defeat of Simon de *Montfort in

1265 and had taken a leading role in his father's council before departing on crusade in 1270. The first 20 years of the reign were remarkably successful, marked by a great series of statutes, which largely proceeded in response to the grievances of his subjects. These same years also saw Edward's scotching of Welsh independence, following his campaigns of 1277 and 1282–3.

The early 1290s proved the turning-point in the reign and in Edward's fortunes. It culminated in the crisis of 1297, but it is a measure of Edward's authority that although rebellion threatened, none actually rose in revolt.

On his tomb in Westminster abbey Edward is described famously as the 'hammer of the Scots'. But this is far from the truth. He acted as arbitrator between the claimants to the Scottish throne (the *Great Cause of 1291–2), as feudal overlord of the kingdom. The throne was adjudged to John *Balliol, and Edward's attempts to secure Balliol and exercise his overlordship proved to be the beginning of the long-drawn-out *Scottish War of Independence. The campaign of 1296 was intended to be as decisive as the conquest of Wales. Edward was victorious, and symbolically removed the 'stone of destiny' from *Scone to Westminster abbey. But it was only a temporary settlement. He lived to see Robert Bruce crowned king in 1306, and it demonstrates his dogged determination that he should die leading yet another expedition to Scotland in 1307.

Edward 'Longshanks' was physically impressive. He stood head and shoulders above most men. As a young man, in particular, he was conspicuous for his enthusiasm for tournaments, and his devotion to the crusading cause is especially notable. But he could be cruel, as when he imprisoned Bruce's sister Mary, the countess of Buchan, in apparently inhuman conditions in 1306. Yet he was devoted to his family. In particular, his love and fondness for his first queen, *Eleanor of Castile, is legendary and the marriage was both happy and fruitful. He grieved for her deeply, and in the famous *Eleanor crosses Edward constructed the most elaborate series of monuments ever created for an English queen or king.

**Edward II** (1284–1327), king of England (1307–27). Tall and good-looking, Edward II had the right physical attributes for kingship, but few other qualifications. Contemporaries ridiculed the pleasure he took in rowing and working with craftsmen. His predilection for favourites, whether or not based on homosexual attraction, was politically disastrous.

The main issue in his first years on the throne was the role of Edward's favourite Piers *Gaveston, exiled in 1308, to return in 1309. He was exiled once more by the *Ordainers in 1311. When he returned, the king was unable to protect him from a baronial opposition increasingly dominated by *Thomas of Lancaster, and Gaveston was savagely executed in 1312. The next twist in the saga came when the government was discredited by the defeat by the Scots at *Bannockburn in 1314. That placed the earl of Lancaster in a dominant position, but he proved no more capable of effective rule than the king.

The earl of Gloucester had been a notable casualty at Bannockburn. He left three sisters, and the competition between their husbands for the lion's share of the inheritance was of major political significance. Above all, the ambitions of one of them, Hugh *Despenser the Younger, husband of Eleanor, provided a new and divisive element. A political settlement of sorts was reached in the treaty of Leake of 1318, but by 1321 civil war had broken out in the Welsh marches. An alliance was struck between the marcher lords and the earl of Lancaster. The Despensers, father and son, were forced into a brief exile, but in the autumn of 1321 an astonishingly successful revival of royal and Despenser power took place. A brief campaign shattered the power of the Welsh marcher lords, and Lancaster marched north, only to be defeated at *Boroughbridge and executed at Pontefract. An unprecedented bloodbath of his supporters followed.

The royalist triumph at Boroughbridge marked the start of one of the most unpleasant regimes ever to rule in England. The war with Scotland went badly. An ineffective English march as far as Edinburgh in 1322 was followed by a Scottish raid into England, in which the king himself was nearly captured. Conflict with France over Gascony in the War of Saint-Sardos of 1324–5 further discredited the English. The queen, Isabella, was sent to France to assist in negotiating peace, but went into exile in Paris, where she took

as lover Roger *Mortimer, one of the rebels of 1321, who had succeeded in escaping from the Tower.

In the autumn of 1326, Isabella invaded with a small force. The Despenser regime collapsed like a house of cards. Edward and his associates fled to Wales, where they were captured. The Despensers were executed with barbaric ritual; Edward was removed from the throne by Parliament in January 1327, and murdered in Berkeley castle.

**Edward III** (1312–77), king of England (1327–77), claimant to the French throne (1340–60 and 1369–77). Edward came to the throne in 1327 in unpropitious circumstances, with the government in the hands of his unscrupulous mother *Isabella and her lover Roger *Mortimer. Yet he must rank as one of the most successful English kings. His war with France saw the great victories of *Crécy and *Poitiers. The king of France and the king of Scots were both captured and held for huge ransoms. The Order of the *Garter epitomized the glittering chivalric glamour of courtly and military circles.

Edward's first independent political action was in 1330, when he led the coup against his mother and Roger Mortimer at Nottingham. In 1333 he took a major gamble, supporting Edward *Balliol's cause in Scotland, and reopening a war which had appeared concluded. The battle of *Halidon Hill in 1333 was a triumph, but succeeding campaigns achieved little, partly because of French support for the Scots. War with France began in 1337. A new element was provided by Edward's claim, through his mother, to the French throne.

The French war dominated Edward's reign. It saw the great triumphs at Crécy in 1346 and Poitiers ten years later, but also the disappointment of the 1359 campaign, which brought an unsatisfactory truce until 1369. Edward showed himself to be a great commander, taking great care in the planning of his campaigns, and inspiring his men. How far he planned the strategy which led to the great success at Crécy is a matter for debate, but it is clear that arrangements were made for additional supplies to be brought from England, and that a march northwards was always intended.

The war was extremely expensive. By 1339 the king was effectively bankrupt. Political crisis came in Parliament in 1340-1, with the king's former chief councillor and chancellor, John Stratford, leading opposition to the crown. Edward rolled with the punches, accepting the new statutes imposed on him in Parliament, only to repeal them once Parliament had been dissolved. He was even ready to concede on the question of military service in 1352, in the knowledge that he would have little difficulty in recruiting troops by means of contracts with the main commanders. Parliament's demands were also accepted in 1352 over the question of treason, Edward agreeing to a considerable narrowing of the definition of treason in the interests of political peace. By 1376 the power of the Commons was dramatically displayed in the *Good Parliament, with the impeachment of Lord Latimer, the chamberlain, many royal officials, and even the king's own mistress, Alice Perrers. Yet, as in 1340-1, Edward knew that once Parliament was dissolved, it would be possible to regain the lost ground.

Edward was extremely successful in his dealings with his own family, and with the magnates. He was able to provide adequately for his sons, so that he never faced the internal family problems that had beset Henry II. The creation of six new earldoms in 1337 was a courageous move which could have aroused hostility from the established nobility. In practice, Edward skilfully manipulated the chivalrous feelings of his followers, patronizing tournaments and founding the Order of the *Garter. He did not attempt to curb the authority of his nobles as Edward I had done, and though it can be argued that the crown's control over them was in theory diminished, in practice the results of royal policy prove the wisdom of the king's approach.

**Edward IV** (1442-83), king of England (1461-70, 1471-83). The tall and handsome 'Rose of Rouen', born in that city, the eldest son of Richard, duke of *York, gained the throne of England in March 1461 when he was only 18. Possession confirmed on the field of *Towton a few weeks later, he was crowned in June. His reign, however, was interrupted in 1470 by his deposition and the temporary restoration of Henry VI.

During his first reign Edward was never fully secure. It took three years for him to eradicate Lancastrian opposition. In these early years he owed much to the earl of *War-wick. No sooner had Lancastrian resistance been brought to an end, however, than his secret marriage to *Elizabeth Woodville, and the promotion of her family, led to a rift between them. The Lancastrian exiles in France offered a convenient rallying-point for dissidents, the option Warwick finally took in the summer of 1470. When Warwick invaded England, Edward fled precipitately to the Netherlands. Here he received the backing of the duke of Burgundy, his brother-in-law. In March 1471 a small fleet put Edward ashore at Ravenspur. He successfully evaded the forces opposing him in Yorkshire, and defeated Warwick at *Barnet. He then rapidly marched west to intercept and overwhelm a Lancastrian army at *Tewkesbury. With Warwick and *Edward of Lancaster dead, and Henry VI promptly murdered on royal orders, he was secure.

Edward began his second reign determined to secure reconciliation through war against France. Parliament voted generous taxation; a triple alliance with Brittany and Burgundy was forged and a truce with Scotland concluded. In 1475 a large army crossed the Channel. But at the eleventh hour, Edward came to terms with Louis XI at *Picquigny, accepting a generous pension. For the remainder of his reign Edward sought to enjoy the fruits of success. In 1477, however, he turned on and destroyed his brother Clarence, who was executed in 1478. Two years later, largely through the pressure of his younger brother Richard of Gloucester, he became embroiled in war with Scotland. Moreover, the treaty of Arras, concluded between France and Burgundy in 1483, left his foreign policy in tatters.

Edward died peacefully after a short illness on 9 April 1483. Historians have always found it hard to judge his achievement. The earliest admired the manner in which he restored peace and prosperity in his second reign, but admiration gave way to disapproval in the 19th cent. when his personal morals coloured interpretation. Impressed by innovations in government, the recovery of royal finances, and the determination with which he imposed his will after 1471, later historians saw him as the progenitor of the revival of royal authority, developed further by Henry VII, and known as 'New Monarchy'. But it is a misjudgement to see novelty in Edward's kingship. Indeed it was backward-looking. Rule through a band of mighty subjects was no foundation upon which to lay a permanent recovery of the monarchy. Edward IV aimed low: like Charles II two centuries later, his principal objective after 1471 was never to go on his travels again. Contemporaries attested to Edward's personal charm and ease of manner. He was a brilliant general, victorious in all his battles. In his youth he was callow and inexperienced, and even when he was older, he was not capable of sustained attention to business. It is probable that his excessive lifestyle contributed to his early death.

**Edward V** (1470–c.1483), uncrowned king of England (1483). Eldest son of Edward IV and *Elizabeth Woodville, Edward was brought up at Ludlow under his maternal uncle Earl *Rivers. On the death of his father in April 1483, the 12-year-old prince of Wales left Ludlow to be proclaimed king in London, but at Stony Stratford his attendants were arrested by his paternal uncle Richard of Gloucester, claiming a conspiracy to deprive him of the protectorship. Edward was transferred in mid-May to the royal apartments at the Tower as part of the coronation preparations. He was joined by his younger brother Richard in mid-June, when they were seen playing in the garden, but at length they ceased to appear altogether. The rumours that ensued have been followed by continued controversy over the reliability of contemporary accounts, the manner of the presumed death of the princes, and the degree of involvement of Richard of Gloucester, who had declared himself king as Richard III.

**Edward VI** (1537–53), king of England (1547–53). Since Edward was 9 years old when he succeeded Henry VIII in 1547, he was in tutelage for the greater part of his reign, with *Somerset as his governor until 1549 and *Northumberland thereafter. His mother Jane *Seymour died when he was born. Edward's chronicle, which he kept from the age of 12, is largely factual and reveals little of character, save perhaps reserve. Contemporaries saw much in him to admire. In 1552 the imperial ambassador reported him 'a likely lad, of quick, ready and well-developed mind'. Less sentimentally, G. R. Elton summed up: 'Edward had a marked intellectual ability, which an appall-

ing schooling had turned into a precocious passion for protestant theology—a cold-hearted prig.'

The religious policy must have been that of his two chief ministers, though with Edward's growing approval. A series of measures during Edward's reign pushed England into the protestant camp. Catholic bishops were replaced by reformers. The new *Prayer Book of 1549, though not going far enough for many protestants, shocked Devon and Cornwall catholics into revolt. In 1552 the young king had measles and smallpox and by the beginning of 1553 the signs of pulmonary tuberculosis were evident. Edward's last significant action was an attempt to head off any catholic revival by a 'devise of the crown', switching the succession from Mary. The plan to bring in Lady Jane *Grey, of the blood royal, hastily married to Northumberland's son, was not as hare-brained as the ultimate fiasco made it seem. The last weeks of Edward's life were grim as the illness took hold and diplomats speculated on his survival in terms of days, then hours. He died at Greenwich palace on 6 July. The settlement of the succession, which had meant so much to him, lasted barely a fortnight.

**Edward VII** (1841–1910), king of Great Britain and Ireland, emperor of India (1901–10). The success of Edward VII's reign would have amazed his parents. His uncommon laziness, wrote *Albert when the poor youth was only 18, 'grieves me when one considers that he might be called on at any moment to take over the reins of government'.

His disadvantages were considerable. He was not particularly intelligent and was easily bored. His temper was untrustworthy as a small boy and did not much improve. His liaisons were numerous, his taste raffish, and his set fast. While prince of Wales, he was subpoenaed in one divorce case and was involved in an unpleasant legal action about cheating at baccarat.

Nevertheless, he had certain assets. He enjoyed company and had a gift for making graceful impromptu little speeches. He had a good memory for names and faces and an excellent command of both French and German. Not least of his assets was his Danish wife *Alexandra, an excellent foil to Edward's flamboyance, whom he married in 1863.

At the start of his reign in 1901 he indicated that he would be his own man, announcing that he wished to be known, not by his first name Albert, but as Edward—thus frustrating the deepest hopes of his fond parents. Over the years, Edwardian England has acquired the image of a golden age of tranquillity before the horrors of the Great War. It was in fact turbulent. There was a marked increase in industrial unrest. The militant phase of the women's suffrage movement began in 1905 when Sir Edward *Grey was shouted down at Manchester. The rise of the *Labour Party, returned in numbers at the general election of 1906, heralded a move towards class politics, which the king greatly deplored. The Liberals, after their great election victory, were pushed leftwards by Labour and the Irish. The rejection of Lloyd *George's budget in 1909 by the House of Lords drew the king into the political arena. Edward made it clear that he was unwilling to create 500 Liberal peers to carry the Parliament Bill, regarding it as a shabby manœuvre. He died in the middle of the crisis, leaving *Asquith to wring a grudging promise from his inexperienced son George V.

Internationally, the reign was marked by the abandonment of isolation, splendid or otherwise, which had proved so uncomfortable during the *Boer War. First, an alliance was reached with Japan in 1902; next, in 1904 the *Entente was formed with France, and lastly an attempt was made to bury differences with France's ally, Russia. By the time of the king's death, Britain was firmly in the Entente camp, ranged against the Triple Alliance of Germany, Austria, and Italy.

In two respects, his influence was of consequence. He took a keen interest in the armed forces, supported *Fisher's naval reforms, and encouraged *Haldane's overhaul of the army. Secondly, he raised the profile of the monarchy. Any ruler who succeeded to an 81-year-old widow was bound to have a residue of goodwill to draw on.

Edward was carried off by severe bronchial illness, exacerbated by a lifetime devoted to cigars and good living. He was fortunate to die when he did. His reign was brief and he did not overstay his welcome. The crowned heads of Europe—kings, emperors, tsars, and kaisers—still entertained each other at regattas, manœuvres, weddings, and funerals. The king was still head of society and there was society still to be head of. Great shooting parties assembled for long weekends at country houses. The landed aristocracy had not yet gone down before the twin perils of the Great War and penal taxation. Behind the gun-carriage which conveyed Edward to his resting-place at Windsor marched nine kings.

**Edward VIII** (1894–1972), king of Great Britain and Ireland, emperor of India (1936). Edward was the eldest son of George, duke of York, later King George V. A brief period at Oxford was followed by non-combatant but arduous service in the British Expeditionary Force in France. As heir to the throne he was not permitted to serve in the front line, but none the less courted danger, visiting the troops, sharing their cigarettes, and listening to their stories. In 1919, he undertook a tour of Canada and the USA; in 1920 he visited Australia and New Zealand, and toured India and the Far East in 1921–2; in 1925 and 1931 he journeyed to South America. All these trips were resounding successes.

Edward was a notorious 'ladies' man', engaging in a succession of sexual liaisons with married women, one of whom, Lady Furness, introduced him to Mrs Wallis *Simpson, with whom he became infatuated. He also revelled in his assumed role as the champion of the common man, making it his business to visit the depressed areas. Edward's infatuation with Mrs Simpson was not reported in the British press, but within ruling circles was a matter of common knowledge. Edward was determined to make her his wife. Mr Simpson acquiesced in a divorce, which was granted nisi, at Ipswich, at the end of October 1936.

By then Edward had been on the throne for nine months. His brief reign was dominated by 'the King's matter'. Stanley *Baldwin, the prime minister, advised that a marriage to Mrs Simpson would not be popular. It was not so much that Mrs Simpson was a commoner: rather, she was an American, twice-divorced commoner. Rank-and-file Conservatives were reminded, too, of his embarrassing political interventions. During a visit to south Wales, in mid-November 1936, the king fuelled this prejudice by remarking, in relation to the unemployed, that 'something must be done to find them work'—an innocuous comment widely interpreted as an attack on Conservative economic policy. Baldwin was not prepared to countenance a morganatic marriage. On 10 December Edward signed the instrument of abdication, and ceased to be king the following day, when he and Wallis travelled to France, where they were married.

The new king, Edward's younger brother George, agreed to confer on him the title duke of Windsor, but Wallis was not permitted officially to call herself HRH. Relations between Edward and the royal family were, and remained, bitter. Edward's much publicized visit to Hitler (October 1937) was not so much sinister as naïve. None the less, when Edward and Wallis fled to fascist Spain after the fall of France, Churchill, now prime minister, packed them off to the Bahamas, of which Edward became governor. But when, following his death in Paris, he was buried in the royal mausoleum at Frogmore, Wallis was permitted to be present at the interment.

**Edward, duke of York** *See* YORK, DUKE OF.

**Edward, prince of Wales** (1330–76), known as the 'Black Prince' was one of the great chivalric heroes. The eldest son of Edward III, he was made earl of Chester in 1333, duke of Cornwall in 1337, and prince of Wales in 1343. In 1362 he became prince of Aquitaine, becoming a virtually independent ruler there. His military career began at *Crécy, where he fought bravely, and the notable victories of *Poitiers in France (1356) and *Najéra in Spain (1367) marked him out as one of the best medieval commanders. Disease forced him to return to England in 1371. In 1376 he predeceased his father, leaving his young son Richard as heir to the throne.

**Edward, prince of Wales** (1453–71). The heir of Henry VI and in exile in France, Edward's prospects were transformed in 1470 by the restoration of his father. Six months later, he returned to England only to find that Henry VI had been deposed once more by Edward IV. The prince's army was defeated at *Tewkesbury on 4 May. He was probably killed in flight from the field.

**Edward, prince of Wales** (1476–84), was the only child of Richard III by his marriage to *Anne Neville. He was born at Middleham castle (Yorks.), and at Richard's second coronation at York in September 1483 was created prince of Wales. In April 1484, he died at Middleham, and was buried at Sheriff Hutton in Yorkshire.

**Edward the Atheling** (d. 1057), known as 'the Exile'. Mystery surrounds the return of Edward the Atheling to England in 1057. The son of King *Edmund Ironside (d. 1016), he was forced into exile as an infant by *Cnut's conquest of England. He was well treated in Hungary, and married a royal princess, Agatha. Negotiations were set on foot for his return by an embassy sent out in 1054, but he died soon after his arrival. One version of the *Anglo-Saxon Chronicle* has the laconic and sinister entry, 'we do not know for what reason it was brought about that he was not allowed to look on (the face?) of his kinsman, King Edward'.

**Edward Balliol** *See* BALLIOL, EDWARD.

**Edward Bruce** *See* BRUCE, EDWARD.

**Edwin** (d. 633), king of Northumbria (617–33). The son of Ælle, king of Deira, Edwin was driven into exile during the reign in Northumbria of *Æthelfryth. With East Anglian aid he defeated and killed Æthelfryth in 617. His marriage to a Kentish princess in 625 brought a Christian mission to Northumbria led by *Paulinus. According to *Bede, Edwin gained authority over the whole of Britain, excluding Kent, but including Anglesey and Man. In 633 he was defeated and killed by *Penda, king of Mercia, and *Cadwallon, king of Gwynedd, at *Heathfield.

**Egbert** (d. 839), king of Wessex. Egbert succeeded to the West Saxon throne in 802. He was descended from Ingild, the brother of King *Ine (688–726). In the 820s, he took advantage of Mercian weakness, winning one of the decisive battles in Anglo-Saxon history at *Ellendun in 825. The *Anglo-Saxon Chronicle* records that he conquered Mercia and was recognized as a *bretwalda (overlord). It is misleading, however, to regard Egbert as the first king of a truly united England. He concentrated personally on the western heartlands of his kingdom, winning a substantial victory in 838 against the Danes and their Cornish allies at *Hingston Down. His permanent memorial proved to be the achievement of West Saxon mastery over England south of the Thames, ending all hopes of a Mercian supremacy.

**Egypt** British interest in Egypt arose from concern to protect the route to India. Napoleon's occupation in 1798 was terminated by the peace of *Amiens three years later, when the country was restored to the Ottoman empire. The opening of the Suez canal in 1869 increased the strategic importance of Egypt, and British troops occupied the country in 1882. A British protectorate was declared in 1914 when Germany's alliance with the Ottoman empire posed a new threat. Nominal independence, under a constitutional monarch, was restored in 1922, but Britain maintained a military base until Gamal Abdel Nasser seized power in 1952 and in 1956 nationalized the canal.

*Eikon basilike* or King's Book was one of the most successful books ever published and established Charles I's reputation as a martyr. It came out within hours of the king's execution in January 1649 and was a strange mixture of prayer and political commentary. Perhaps the greatest impact was made by a woodcut as frontispiece showing Charles at his devotions.

**eisteddfod,** meaning a session or congress, is a competition of Welsh bards and minstrels. The institution is of great antiquity since the laws of Hywel *Dda (d. 950) describe arrangements for chairing the bard. A strange commission by Elizabeth in 1568 suggested that the principality was crawling with bards—competent bards were to be recognized by experts, 'the rest not worthy to return to some honest labour'. In the 18th cent. there was a marked increase of interest in Welsh culture, with the Society of Cymmrodorion set up in 1751. Revivals of local eisteddfodau followed, with meetings at Corwen and Bala in 1789. 'The first of the great modern eisteddfodau' was held at Carmarthen in 1819. The National Eisteddfod Association was formed in 1880 and holds an annual gathering.

**El Alamein, battle of,** 1942. Fought in Egypt, El Alamein was the first decisive, irreversible British victory over German ground forces, which were forced to retreat 1,500 miles to Tunisia. Rommel, short of fuel and against British air superiority, could not fight a mobile battle to balance *Montgomery's superiority in combat troops. The 8th Army had nearly 200,000 men, more than half from Britain, against about 100,000 Italians and Germans. The battle caused silenced church bells in Britain to be rung in celebration and made Montgomery a national hero.

**Eldon, John Scott, 1st earl of** (1751–1838). Lord chancellor. The son of a Newcastle coal merchant, Scott rose rapidly in his profession. He entered Parliament in 1783, and became solicitor-general 1788 and attorney-general 1793. He was appointed lord chief justice of Common Pleas in 1799, becoming Baron Eldon, and lord chancellor in 1801. He served in the cabinets of *Addington, *Pitt, *Perceval, and *Liverpool until 1827. Eldon came to symbolize political obscurantism but was an exceptionally able lawyer and in private life good-natured and even-tempered.

**Eleanor of Aquitaine** (c.1122–1204), queen of Henry II. Heiress to the vast duchy of Aquitaine, Eleanor first married Louis VII of France in 1137, but they were divorced in 1152, largely because Eleanor had produced only daughters. Aquitaine accordingly reverted to Eleanor. In 1152 she married Henry of Anjou, soon to be king of England. Their marital relations deteriorated, however, and this played a part in Eleanor's decision to rebel against him in 1173 in support of her sons. She was captured by Henry, and kept in close confinement. On Richard I's accession, she renewed her political life, playing an important role during Richard's absence on crusade.

**Eleanor of Castile** (c.1242–90), queen of Edward I. The daughter of Ferdinand III, Eleanor married Edward I in October 1254, when they were both children, bringing with her Gascony. The couple were unusually close and Eleanor accompanied him on several crusades. Edward was devoted to her and mourned her death deeply. He commissioned a series of twelve stone crosses, known as the *Eleanor crosses, to mark the stopping-places of her funeral cortège from Harby to Westminster abbey.

**Eleanor of Provence** (1223–91), queen of Henry III. Daughter of Raymond Berenger IV, count of Provence, Eleanor married in 1236. The queen and her Provençal relatives were not popular. She raised funds for her husband during the baronial wars and gathered troops on his behalf. She died at Amesbury on 25 June 1291 and was given a full burial by Edward I, her son.

**Eleanor crosses** were monuments erected by Edward I at Lincoln, Grantham, Stamford, Geddington, Northampton (at Hardingstone), Stony Stratford, Woburn, Dunstable, St Albans, Waltham, West Cheap in the city of London, and at Charing between 1291 and 1294 to commemorate the progress of the funeral cortège of his queen *Eleanor of Castile from Harby where she died to Westminster abbey. Those at Waltham, Geddington, and Hardingstone still survive.

**'Eleven Years Tyranny'** (1629–40). After the tumultuous end to the 1629 session of Parliament (*see* ELIOT, SIR JOHN) Charles I broke with convention by ruling without Parliament for eleven years. Financial needs were met through prerogative levies, the most notorious of which was *ship money, and the prerogative court of *Star Chamber supervised the maintenance of order. This was hardly a tyranny, for Charles had no police force or army to compel obedience. Charles's own misjudgement in the *Bishops' wars brought the 'Eleven Years Tyranny' to an end.

**Elgar, Edward** (1857–1934). Born at Broadheath, west of Worcester, in the shadow of the Malvern hills, and largely self-taught, his early life was spent as a local musician, conducting bands and choirs and teaching the violin. His breakthrough came with the Enigma Variations (1899), commemorating his friends in the area. *Sea Pictures* (1899) was followed by *The Dream of Gerontius* (1900), the First Symphony (1908), the Violin Concerto (1910), the Second Symphony (1911), and the darker Cello Concerto (1919). Honours were heaped upon him—a knighthood (1904), the Order of Merit (1911), mastership of the king's musick

(1924), and a baronetcy (1931). His palm-court pieces and the extraordinarily popular 'Pomp and Circumstance' marches gave him a reputation at variance with reality. With the appearance of a retired colonel and often accused of jingo patriotism, Elgar was, in fact, a deeply sensitive man, easily hurt.

**Elgin marbles** These were part of the frieze and pediment of the Parthenon of Athens, sent to England by the 7th earl of Elgin. While British ambassador in Constantinople, he obtained authority from the Turks first to study, then to remove some of the antiquities. In 1816 Elgin received £35,000, much less than his expenses, and the marbles were placed in the British Museum. The Greek government has at times requested their return.

**Eliot, George** (1819–80). Novelist whose real name was Mary Anne (later Marian) Evans. Born in Warwickshire, the landscapes and rhythms of daily life in the towns of the English midlands are reflected in much of her work, notably in her two novels set at the time of the first Reform Bill, *Felix Holt, the Radical* (1866) and the masterly *Middlemarch: A Tale of Provincial Life* (1871–2).

**Eliot, Sir John** (1592–1632). Eliot, a parliamentarian, was initially a client of the royal favourite *Buckingham, but turned against him, and in 1626 took part in the impeachment proceedings. For this, Charles I imprisoned him in the Tower. Further imprisonment followed in 1627, when Eliot refused to pay the *forced loan. In 1629 he led the Commons' attack on *Arminianism and prerogative taxation, and organized the coup on 2 March when the Speaker was held down in his chair to prevent him foreclosing debate. Eliot was again sent to the Tower, where he spent the rest of his life.

**Eliot, T. S.** (1888–1965). Poet. Born in St Louis, after Harvard he studied in Europe, in 1927 becoming a British citizen. *The Waste Land* (1922) is usually seen as a commentary on the western civilization which collapsed in the Great War. For others, the religious poetry of *Ash-Wednesday* (1930) and *Four Quartets* (1943) is his most profound response. Attempts to restore poetic drama to the West End stage had mixed success, though *Murder in the Cathedral* (1935) has endured.

**Elizabeth I** (1533–1603), queen of England (1558–1603). Her mother was *Anne Boleyn, Henry VIII's second wife. Elizabeth was born at Greenwich in September 1533 five months after her parents' marriage had been announced. In May 1536 her mother was executed and a new Act of Succession declared Anne's marriage void, Elizabeth illegitimate, and recognized Henry's third marriage to *Jane Seymour as 'without spot, doubt or impediment'. The birth of her half-brother Edward in October 1537 made her chances of succeeding to the throne appear remote. A third Act of Succession in 1543 reinstated her, declaring that if Edward died without heirs, the throne would pass to Mary and then Elizabeth.

She spent most of her girlhood at Hatfield. She received a high-powered classical education which left her in command of Latin and Greek and speaking French, Spanish, and Italian 'most perfectly'. She was on good terms with *Catherine Parr, Henry's last wife, and when, after his death, Catherine married Lord *Seymour, Somerset's younger brother, Elizabeth moved into the household. The arrangement ended when Seymour made playful advances to Elizabeth which were not totally unwelcome. After Catherine died in childbirth, Seymour suggested marriage to Elizabeth, who replied prudently that such a matter should be laid before the council. Seymour was arrested in 1549 on a charge of treason and Elizabeth closely questioned.

When Edward was dying in 1553 and could not bear the thought of a catholic succession, he bypassed Elizabeth and named Lady Jane *Grey, *Northumberland's daughter-in-law, as his successor. During the ensuing crisis, Elizabeth stayed at Hatfield on the plea of illness. She was not well rewarded for her acquiescence in Mary's triumph. Within a month Mary was urging her to attend mass and Elizabeth, in floods of tears, real or simulated, begged for time to study the question.

In February 1554 *Wyatt's rising against Mary's Spanish marriage brought Elizabeth to the brink of disaster. Summoned urgently to court, she pleaded more illness, then reluctantly obeyed. In March she was sent to

the Tower while the conspirators were racked to provide evidence against her. 'She will have to be executed,' wrote the emperor's envoy Mendoza briskly. Ultimately she returned to Hatfield, attended mass regularly, and refused all offers of marriage. 'She is too clever to get herself caught,' Renard, the imperial ambassador, told the emperor.

In the event, Elizabeth's accession, on 17 November 1558, passed off without incident. Even Mary, in her last weeks, had conceded its inevitability. Elizabeth was faced at once with the same problems that had confronted Mary on her accession five years before—the religious question and her own marriage. The outlines of her religious policy were signalled at an early stage when she placed two of Mary's bishops under arrest for intemperate sermons, and in her first Parliament took back the governorship of the church. It would have been surprising had she done anything else. To adopt a catholic posture would have meant accepting her own bastardy and admitting that she had no right to the throne. The famous *via media* was to a great extent forced upon her.

The second problem, marriage, had already caused trouble. The political objections to marriage were overwhelming and her council and Parliament urged in vain. A foreign husband would drag the country into continental disputes and reawaken religious animosities: marriage to a subject would be an act of condescension and a formula for faction. Though her reasons for virginity were largely negative, she turned it to her own advantage, declaring that she was married to her people.

Two other decisions could not be delayed—her choice of advisers and her attitude towards the war with France which she had inherited from her sister. On the very first day of her reign she appointed as secretary William Cecil, (*Burghley), whom she had employed as her estates surveyor.

Elizabeth was anxious to wind up the war against France, but dared not risk alienating her ally Philip, lest the nightmare possibility of a grand catholic coalition of Spain, France, and Scotland should come into existence. Nor could she easily reconcile herself to losing *Calais and in the end a face-saving formula had to be devised. No sooner had she escaped from one conflict than another emerged—in Scotland where she was persuaded to intervene in 1560 on behalf of the protestant lords against the French. Though the assault on the French-held Leith castle was a dismal failure, the death of Mary of Guise took the heart out of the French resistance and by the treaty of *Edinburgh they agreed to withdraw.

The next developments in foreign affairs were on a totally different scale—no limited interventions, but the great crisis of her reign. Three problems ran together in the 1570s and 1580s—the international religious question, the problem of Mary, queen of Scots, and the developing rift with Philip over the revolt of the Low Countries. Immediately after the failure of the rising of the *northern earls, Pius V, far less moderate than his predecessor Pius IV, issued in 1570 a bull deposing her. The result was a series of plots against Elizabeth's life—*Ridolfi 1572, *Throckmorton 1584, Parry 1585, and *Babington 1586. The second element of the worsening storm was the decision of Mary, queen of Scots, after her disastrous marriages to *Darnley and *Bothwell, to flee her country in 1568 and place herself under Elizabeth's protection. She was soon under close arrest. Despair at ever being released led Mary to dabble in plots and each plot produced fresh demands from ardent protestants for her execution. For many years Elizabeth resisted but the Babington plot sealed Mary's fate and she was executed in 1587. The third factor was that relations with her erstwhile ally Philip broke down and from 1585 Elizabeth sent help to the Dutch rebels. Philip's retort was to begin planning the invasion of England and in July 1588 the great *Armada left Corunna. At Tilbury, Elizabeth delivered the most famous of all her speeches, 'not doubting that we shall shortly have a famous victory over those enemies of my God, of my Kingdom and of my People.'

The defeat of the Armada turned her into a living legend and the most famous of all English monarchs. Philip launched more attacks and the centre of anxiety moved to Ireland, where *Tyrone's rebellion had Spanish support. Many of her counter-measures were unsuccessful and Essex's foolish behaviour in Ireland, followed by his abortive insurrection, darkened her last days. But she died still in charge, capable of putting on performances and, at the end, naming 'our cousin of Scotland', James VI, as her successor.

**Elizabeth II** (b. 1926), queen of Great Britain and Northern Ireland (1952– ). When Princess Elizabeth was born to the duke and duchess of York in 1926 there was little reason to expect that she would succeed to the throne. Her uncle, the prince of Wales, was only 31 and was being urged to marry: it was also quite possible that her parents would have a son who would take precedence. But the abdication of her uncle in 1936 brought her father to the throne as George VI.

Princess Elizabeth grew up pretty, cheerful, and obedient. Her strong sense of duty called to mind her grandfather George V and Queen Victoria. Most of the war was spent at Windsor castle. At the age of 18, and with the war coming to a close, Elizabeth was allowed to join the ATS and went each day to Aldershot to take a driving and vehicle maintenance course. She was already devoted to her cousin Philip Mountbatten, a naval officer. They were married in November 1947. Their first child, Prince Charles, was born a year later. In 1952 she succeeded her father on the throne at the age of 25.

The coronation of 1953 was a great success, a splash of colour and ceremony in a still austere post-war Britain. Excitable journalists wrote of a New Elizabethan Age to come. In fact criticism developed rather quickly. Though not shy, the queen had reserve. In 1957 when Lord Altrincham complained that she sounded like a 'priggish schoolgirl', he was predictably threatened with horsewhipping. Political clouds also rolled in quickly. Britain found it extremely hard to shake off recurrent financial and economic crises and the *Suez fiasco of 1956 was a reminder that the country had neither its former strength nor its confidence.

The early years of her reign were dominated by the painful process of economic recovery and withdrawal from empire. By 1953 the crippled economies of Europe were beginning to recover and Germany, in particular, proved a formidable competitor. This was followed by the rise of the Far Eastern economies, Japan, Hong Kong, and Korea. Several of her governments ran onto the rocks of balance of payments difficulties, inflation, unemployment, and runs on the pound: traditional industries declined and their replacements were slow to emerge.

The Suez crisis was only one of the more dramatic episodes in the retreat from empire. The withdrawal from India had taken place in 1948 before Elizabeth came to the throne. It was followed into independence by Malaya (1957), Ghana (1957), Nigeria (1960), Sierra Leone (1961), Tanganyika (1961), Uganda (1962), Jamaica (1962), Trinidad (1962), Zambia (1964), and Aden (1967). The withdrawals were effected with relatively little rancour, though there was fighting in Malaya (1948–60), in Aden (1963–73), a protracted crisis over Southern Rhodesia (1965–80), and an unpleasant and tedious campaign in Kenya against *Mau Mau from 1952 to 1955. The queen and the royal family played an active role in efforts to transform the empire into a commonwealth of equal states. But most of the newly independent countries opted to become republics and although the queen remained head of the Commonwealth, her role was largely social.

The later years of her reign have seen considerable economic progress. Macmillan's remark of 1957—'most of our people have never had it so good'—was premature, but the gross national product continued to grow. This was partly because the sharp rise in world oil prices was offset by North Sea oil from 1975 onwards.

As the empire shrank and economic performance faltered, Britain's relationship with Europe emerged as a major issue. It had implications for the monarchy since the more advanced schemes for a federal Europe would affect sovereignty. Britain's first two applications to join the *European Economic Community were vetoed by de Gaulle in 1963 and 1967, before Edward *Heath's government gained acceptance in 1972. In the 1980s, as what was at first envisaged as a trading community moved towards political integration, the question of 'Europe' moved steadily to the front of the political agenda.

Of more immediate concern to the queen was probably the role of the monarchy itself and the vicissitudes of the royal family. The first indications that the royal road might be bumpy came in 1953 when the queen's sister wished to marry a distinguished airman, Group Captain Peter Townsend, who was in

the process of divorcing his wife. The princess was persuaded not to marry him. When she did marry Anthony Armstrong Jones in 1960, it ended in divorce. These were no more than the drops of rain that preceded the deluge. The marriages of three of the royal children who embarked on matrimony ended in divorce. In November 1992 at the Guildhall, the queen referred ruefully to a year which had seen one divorce, two marital breakdowns, and a devastating fire at Windsor castle as 'not a year on which I shall look back with undiluted pleasure ... an *annus horribilis*'.

It is too soon for any informed assessment of the queen's constitutional role. Though her prime ministers have enthusiastically published their memoirs, they have been bland in their references to the sovereign. There was some criticism of the procedure in 1957 when *Eden was forced by ill-health to resign and was succeeded by Macmillan rather than *Butler. But the lord chancellor and the lord president of the council (Kilmuir and *Salisbury) were asked to sound the cabinet, and its strong preference for Macmillan was confirmed by the chief whip, the chairman of the 1922 committee, the chairman of the Conservative Party, and Sir Winston *Churchill. The queen certainly did not act against advice. Nor did she in 1963 when the choice of Lord *Home to succeed Macmillan caused surprise. She acted on the advice of Macmillan himself, whom she visited in hospital. Changed arrangements in the Conservative Party in 1965 for electing its leader make it unlikely that this royal prerogative will cause awkwardness in future.

There is no doubt that, from the 1980s onwards, there has been increased criticism of the royal family, though not of Elizabeth herself. The decline in respect is a general phenomenon and applies to many other institutions—to the church, the law, Parliament, and, not least, to the press itself. A policy of openness, inaugurated by the film *Royal Family* (1966), has evident dangers. Satire, which in the 1960s was refreshing and witty, may become coarse and spiteful. 'The Palace' has often had to ponder the balance between over- and under-exposure. That the latter has its risks is demonstrated by the example of Queen Victoria's unpopularity during her seclusion after Albert's death. But the problems caused by under-exposure are more easily remedied.

The most recent decade of her reign has been one of the most stable, despite long-running conflicts in *Iraq and *Afghanistan and the onset of international *terrorism. Until 2007 the economy prospered and the incessant gaze of public attention was mitigated by the increasing role of her son, Prince Charles, and her two grandsons, Princes William and Harry. The jubilee of her accession, in 2003, was marked by widespread celebrations and in 2007 Elizabeth became the oldest reigning monarch, surpassing the 81 years of Queen Victoria.

**Elizabeth of Bohemia** (1596–1662). The eldest daughter of James VI and I and sister of Charles I, she married in 1613 Frederick of the Palatinate. Five years later, the Bohemians elected Frederick as king in defiance of the Habsburgs. In the wars that followed, they were driven out of their new kingdom and the Palatinate overrun. She spent only October 1619–November 1620 at Prague and hence was known as the 'Winter Queen'. She was the mother of Prince *Rupert and through her daughter Sophia the Hanoverians came to the throne of Britain in 1714.

**Elizabeth Bowes-Lyon** (1900–2002), queen of George VI and queen mother. Perhaps the most remarkable member of the royal family in modern times, Elizabeth was born at St Paul's Waldenbury (Herts.), daughter of the 14th earl of Strathmore in the Scottish peerage. Her childhood was extremely happy, mainly because of the high spirits of her mother. When she was 19 she met Prince Albert (duke of York and future George VI) and in 1923, after some hesitation, agreed to marry him. Their daughters Elizabeth and Margaret Rose were born in 1926 and 1930. The abdication of her brother-in-law Edward VIII in 1936 brought her husband to the throne and made her queen. During the Second World War the royal couple played a prominent role and their decision not to leave London was an important boost to national morale. George VI's death in 1952 at the age of 56 left her facing a long widowhood. She took the title Her Majesty Queen Elizabeth the Queen Mother. Into advanced age she carried out numerous public duties, and her 100th birthday was celebrated in August 2000 with great public affection.

**Elizabeth Woodville** (c.1437–92), queen of Edward IV. Elizabeth was a widow with two children when she married Edward IV secretly on 1 May 1464. She was the daughter of Earl Rivers. Almost certainly a love match, the unwise marriage to a woman considered beneath the king's dignity caused political tension, and later allowed Richard III to claim that their children were illegitimate. In truth she was far more sinned against than sinning, by both her unfaithful husband and ambitious brother-in-law. After Bosworth, although her daughter *Elizabeth became queen, she was excluded from court and retired to Bermondsey abbey.

**Elizabeth of York** (1465–1503), queen of Henry VII. Henry set the seal on his great victory at *Bosworth in August 1485 by his marriage in January 1486 to Elizabeth, daughter and heiress of Edward IV, thus uniting the houses of York and Lancaster. She died soon after the birth of her last child in the Tower on 11 February 1503 and was buried in Henry VII's great new chapel at Westminster abbey.

**Ellendun, battle of,** 825. *Egbert's victory over Beornwulf at Ellendun marks the transfer of overlordship within the Anglo-Saxon kingdoms from Mercia to Wessex. Fought just south of Swindon, it gave Egbert mastery of the critical strategic area leading into the middle Thames valley.

**Elmet, kingdom of** British kingdom based in the south-west of Yorkshire, including the area around Leeds; modern place-names with the suffix 'in-Elmet' delineate its eastern border. Before the end of the 7th cent. it had been incorporated into Deira.

**Elmham, diocese of** The see of Elmham, conterminous with Norfolk, was created c.673 by *Theodore's division of the East Anglian bishopric of *Dunwich. The see was moved to Thetford in 1072 and soon afterwards to *Norwich.

**Ely, diocese of** The see, now roughly conterminous with Cambridgeshire, was created in 1109. King *Edgar and *Æthelwold founded a monastery here in 970 to replace the double monastery, established in 673, but destroyed by the Danes in 870. When the see of *Dorchester was transferred to *Lincoln in 1072, the abbot's request for a bishopric was not granted until 1109, when Henry I carved the Ely diocese out of the vast see of Lincoln. Based on a rich abbey, Ely was in the first league of wealth and power. But the town for centuries had a reputation as a squalid and unhealthy place, though the cathedral, begun c.1083, rose majestically above the fens, a landmark for miles.

**Elyot, Sir Thomas** (c.1490–1546). Humanist, administrator, and political theorist, Elyot was educated at Oxford and the Middle Temple. Clerk to the justices of assize (1511–26) and to Henry VIII's council (c.1523–30), he retired in 1530, being knighted in the same year and made ambassador to Charles V in 1531–2. Elyot's *Book Named the Governor* (1531) advocated a monarchical 'public weal' for England and described the education necessary to prepare Englishmen to help the king rule it. His use of English was intended to show how the vernacular could be effective in encouraging wise conduct.

**Emma of Normandy** (d. 1052), queen of *Æthelred II and of *Cnut. Emma played an important role in the confused succession to the English throne between 1016 and 1066. Early in life she became the second wife of Æthelred II (1002). Her first son, *Edward, succeeded to the English throne in 1042: her great-nephew was William the Conqueror. After the death of Æthelred in 1016 she married Cnut. On his death in 1035, Emma tried to obtain the kingdom for their son *Harthacnut, who was then about 16. In 1037 she was obliged to take refuge in Flanders but returned with Harthacnut in 1040. When he died two years later, her first son, from whom she was alienated, took the throne. Henry of Huntingdon called her 'the gem of the Normans'.

**Emmet, Robert** (1778–1803). Irish patriot. Emmet, a middle-class protestant republican, came to prominence after the failure of the 1798 rising. He was influential in reactivating the United Irish movement in 1799, and in 1801 journeyed to Paris in order to revive French support. After March 1803 Emmet and other United Irish veterans began to prepare a second revolt. This oc-

curred in a haphazard fashion on 23 July in Dublin, and was swiftly suppressed. Emmet escaped into the Dublin mountains, but was captured in August, and tried for treason. He readily accepted his guilt, was convicted, and hanged.

**Empson, Sir Richard** (d. 1510). Empson and his colleague and neighbour Edmund *Dudley were the first victims of Henry VIII's ruthlessness. Empson came from Towcester, took a legal training, represented Northamptonshire in the Parliament of 1491, and was elected Speaker. In 1504 he was knighted and appointed chancellor of the duchy of Lancaster. His zeal in collecting taxes on behalf of Henry VII made him extremely unpopular. On the second day of Henry VIII's reign he was arrested on a trumped-up charge of treason. He was executed with Dudley on Tower Hill.

**enclosures** The process of 'enclosing' land into 'private' holdings goes back many centuries, and was a development from the system of open field farming. Enclosure changed agricultural practices which had operated under systems of co-operation in communally administered landholdings. Instead, agricultural holdings were created which were non-communal, and within man-made boundaries which separated one farm from another.

In the 16th cent. landlords tried to enclose their land in order to keep more sheep. This process was condemned by the church and opposed by the government. By the 1630s government opposition was breaking down, and a good deal of 'by agreement' enclosure took place in the period c.1630–c.1750.

From 1750 Parliament began to pass bills to allow for the enclosure of the land under certain clearly defined conditions. As a result, between 1750 and 1830 in England more than 4,000 enclosure Acts were passed. The process continued through the 19th cent. until there were hardly any open fields remaining. Only in the Nottinghamshire village of Laxton does a common field system continue to operate to this day.

Enclosure in Scotland occurred primarily in the 18th cent., in the Lowlands in the 1760s and 1770s and in the uplands at the end of the century.

***Encyclopaedia Britannica*** A typical product of the Enlightenment, when there was a vast amount of new knowledge to be disseminated and a rapidly growing reading public. It was a riposte to the French *Encyclopédie* and was published between 1768 and 1771 by a consortium of Edinburgh printers. It is now in its fifteenth edition (1992).

**Engagement,** 1647. Charles I gave himself up to the Scots in 1646 and began negotiations. In December 1647 he signed a secret treaty or engagement, whereby *presbyterianism should be established in Scotland, and in England for three years. In exchange, the Scots promised an army. The result was the second civil war in 1648. But the Scottish army under *Hamilton which invaded England was routed by *Cromwell at *Preston in August 1648.

**Engels, Friedrich** (1820–95). Engels was the lifelong collaborator of Karl *Marx. Son of a German textile manufacturer, Engels worked in a family-owned cotton-mill in Manchester. He met Marx in 1842, and together they wrote the *Communist Manifesto* during the revolutionary unrest of 1848. Engels, who gave Marx generous financial help, was closely involved with all of Marx's writings, and functioned as the authentic voice of Marxist views after Marx's death. In addition, Engels contributed a distinctive dimension to Marxist ideology—what has been termed 'dialectical materialism'.

**England, kingdom of** The kingdom of England was created by its monarchs. Successive rulers, sometimes from ambition, sometimes from fear, strengthened their armed forces, extended their boundaries, imposed law and order on their quarrelling subjects, introduced standardized coinage and administration, and encouraged one religion. There were moments when the kingdom seemed in danger of being washed away or disintegrating—in the 9th cent. when the Vikings overran most of the country, or during the great Civil War when the nation seemed about to destroy itself.

The evolution of the kingdom of England had, therefore, two aspects, its relations with other peoples—Britons, Vikings, French, Scots, Welsh, Irish—and its development as an effective political and military organism. Many of the characteristics of the English kingdom which emerged derived from the circumstances of the Anglo-Saxon settlements. The settlers came largely from Schleswig-Holstein. The fact that much of the north and west of the mainland was mountainous influenced the ultimate division between Saxon and Celt. The mountains of Wales and Scotland provided refuges: they were also less attractive to settlers and less worthwhile to conquer.

The English settlers were divided into a number of kingdoms, waging constant warfare. The enmities between them invited Celtic counter-attack if it could be organized. But the Celts were also divided and, though they were able to inflict sharp defeats on the Saxons, they were not able to drive them out. While the small kingdoms of East Anglia, Kent, Essex, Mercia, Northumbria, and Wessex struggled for supremacy, a kingdom of England remained a long way off. But in the title of 'bretwalda'—overlord of Britain—may be seen aspiration, even if the substance was shadowy and fleeting. Had Northumbria been able to consolidate its 7th-cent. superiority, a more northerly based English kingdom might have come into existence. But with the decline of Northumbria, the struggle was between Mercia and Wessex and the probability was that any English kingdom would be southern.

From the incessant warfare of the Saxon settlement emerged the kingdom of Mercia. In the later 8th cent., *Offa (d. 796) overran Kent and Essex, including London, pushed back the Welsh, and confined Wessex to south of the Thames. At one stage he took the title Rex Anglorum. But Mercia's supremacy depended essentially on Offa's personal prestige and his country was in decline before the Viking raids commenced in the 9th cent. By 878, the north and midlands, including Mercia, had fallen to the Danes, and *Alfred of Wessex was hanging on precariously in the Somerset marshes.

For some time it looked as if the British Isles might become part of a grand Scandinavian empire. But, in the event, the Vikings promoted the emergence of a kingdom of England. First, by destroying Northumbria and Mercia, they cleared the way for the supremacy of Wessex. Secondly, the effort required to throw back the invaders gave Wessex a new vitality. Alfred's counter-attack was so vigorous that he was able to divide the country between Wessex and the Dane-law, and his successors built upon his achievements. *Edward, his son, and *Æthel-fleda, his daughter, began the reconquest as far as the Humber, and before his death in 924 Edward had received the submission of northern England. *Edgar was said to have been rowed on the Dee at Chester in 973 by British, Welsh, and Scottish kings, though whether this was alliance or homage is not clear.

It follows therefore that when the Normans conquered in 1066 the existence of the kingdom of England was not in jeopardy. Though there was an almost total change of top personnel, there was no mass settlement and the small number of Normans was bound to be absorbed before long. But the ruthless rule of the Norman kings meant that the kingdom was less likely to disintegrate than ever. The main effects were twofold. First, Englishmen and the English language were under a cloud for several generations. Secondly, the country found itself in the wider context of western Europe, as part of an empire which included, at times, most of France.

But the kingdom soon recovered its English character. The Conqueror's youngest son, Henry I, was born in England in 1068, and spoke the language. Within three months of succeeding in 1100 he had married an English princess, the great-granddaughter of *Edmund Ironside. The English language, which had given way in court circles and administration to Norman French or Latin, took longer to recover, partly because of the international utility of Latin. But in 1362 Parliament was opened with a speech in English and the law courts were instructed to hear cases in the English tongue.

In succeeding to the Anglo-Saxon state, the Normans succeeded to its neighbours in the British Isles. The north of England had never been fully integrated into the Anglo-Saxon kingdom. William I's answer was the fearsome harrying of the north in 1069 and 1070. Against Scotland, William achieved a temporary supremacy with a campaign in 1072 as far as the Tay. Of more lasting consequence were the Norman advances against Wales and Ireland. The foundation for the eventual conquest of Wales was laid by the creation of the marcher earl-

doms. In 1171 Henry II landed at Waterford, and received the submission of many of the Irish chiefs.

The transformation of the small Wessex kingdom into a kingdom of Britain was built on these foundations. The conquest of Wales was completed by Edgar I, and the principality was brought into the English political and administrative system in 1536 by the Act of *Union. The conquest of Ireland proceeded by fits and starts, according to English preoccupations elsewhere. Henry VIII declared himself king of Ireland in 1541. Later, the Elizabethan settlements, the influx into Ulster from Scotland, and the Cromwellian land redistributions strengthened the English position.

Scotland was a different matter. There were repeated attempts by the English to unite the two countries, by diplomacy or conquest. Edward I's gains were cancelled by the disaster which overtook his son at *Bannockburn in 1314. A plan to marry Edward VI to Mary, queen of Scots, came to nothing. Unification came as a consequence of Elizabeth's preference for virginity: the marriage of Henry VIII's sister *Margaret in 1503 paid off 100 years later when her great-grandson, James VI, succeeded as James I of England.

A governmental union of his two kingdoms was top of the agenda for James. A combined flag was designed and the name of Great Britain put forward. To a glum Parliament, James outlined the advantages: 'do we not yet remember that this kingdom was divided into seven little kingdoms, besides Wales . . . And hath not the union of Wales to England added a greater strength thereto?' It was to no avail. 'We should lose the ancient name of England, so famous and victorious,' retorted his opponents. The project foundered.

Where James's arguments failed, Cromwell's sword succeeded. After his victories over the Scots at *Dunbar and the Irish at *Drogheda, the Scottish and Irish parliaments were wound up. The *Instrument of Government in 1653 instituted one Commonwealth Parliament, with 30 MPs each from Scotland and Ireland. The arrangement lapsed at the Restoration, for while the case for union remained strong, Charles II was unwilling to build with Cromwell's bricks.

With the great war against Louis XIV from 1688 onwards and the risk of subversion from a Jacobite Scotland, the matter became urgent. William III was still pushing it when he died. In 1702 more negotiations followed, and when they broke down, relations between the two countries reached their lowest point since the 1540s. The Union of 1707 was essentially a Whig move to secure the Hanoverian succession. Scotland obtained access to English markets, while preserving its own legal, educational, and ecclesiastical system. England gained a greater measure of military security.

The new state was to be known as Great Britain and strenuous efforts were made to persuade all subjects to abandon old animosities. For many years such appeals fell upon deaf ears. Londoners, who had jeered at the Welsh in *Pepys's day, jeered at the Scots in *Wilkes's. The Union is usually discussed from a Scottish point of view—'the end of an auld song'. But many of the English looked at it sourly. They objected that Scotland was not paying its fair share and mistrusted its retention of a *presbyterian form of church government.

The push towards British unification continued. The next great crisis, when the new British state faced the French Revolution, brought the Union with Ireland in 1801, and yet another change of name to the United Kingdom. Wessex, having swallowed its neighbours in England, had now swallowed its neighbours in Britain. But Ireland proved hard to digest. Whereas the unions with Wales and Scotland undoubtedly contributed to British power, that with Ireland was a dubious asset. In 1916, when Britain was in great peril, it was not possible to apply conscription to Ireland. It is a strange union which the government cannot call upon its people to defend. The breaking away of the *Irish Free State suggested that the process of more than 1,000 years was in reverse. How far it would go remains unanswered. The policy of *devolution, which some believed would head off Welsh and Scottish nationalism, has seen both *Plaid Cymru and the *SNP obtain a share in government, while still maintaining their objective of national independence.

But even should events push the kingdom of England back whence it came, two results of Wessex's supremacy will last for some time. The great imperial expansion of the 17th and 18th cents. produced America, Canada, Australia, and New Zealand and spread the practice of parliamentary government throughout the world. The second was that for centuries to come the language of international diplomacy and communication will remain that of *Hengist and Horsa, *Ælle and Cissa.

**Englefield, battle of,** 871. The battle at Englefield, near Reading, in early 871 marks the opening of the bitter struggle between the West Saxons and the Danes. Æthelwulf, the ealdorman of Berkshire, was killed in the failure of the West Saxons, commanded by King *Æthelred and his brother *Alfred, to dislodge the Danes. The failure led directly into the so-called 'year of battles' in the course of which the king died, to be succeeded by Alfred.

**English Heritage,** the Historic Buildings and Monuments Commission for England, was set up under the National Heritage Act, 1983. A wide variety of sites are in the care of English Heritage and are presented with informative displays, exhibitions, and occasional re-enactments of historic events.

**Englishry** To afford some protection to lone Normans in the tense period after the Conquest, William I declared that if a murdered man could not be proved to be English, he would be presumed to be Norman, and the hundred fined. By the time of Richard I, it had fallen into disuse, as the nations merged, though it was not formally abolished until 1341.

**entail** The growth of landed estates in England from the mid-16th cent. until the 1880s was partly a product of the system of 'entailing' property. Until the mid-17th cent., the available forms of entail were restricted, but thereafter the courts agreed to permit an owner to tie up his estate to the second and third generation, through a process of 'contingent remainders'. It was once held that as a result great estates were kept together, but modern research holds that the system of entailing property was introduced partly to protect the financial interests of younger children, that entailed estates could be partially or completely freed, and that the consolidation of estates was due to factors other than entail.

**Entente cordiale** Friendly relations between England and France, stopping short of a formal alliance. The term was coined at Haddo House, the country home of the 4th earl of *Aberdeen, by the French chargé d'affaires, the comte de Jarnac, in 1843. It was revived to describe the relationship inaugurated by the agreements of 1904, which eventually brought Britain into the *First World War on the side of France and Russia.

**Eochaid,** king of the Picts (877/8–885/889). Eochaid, son of Rhun (king of Strathclyde) and a daughter of *Kenneth I, is mentioned only once as king, and even there it is noted that 'others say that *Giric . . . reigned at this time'. The same source claims that Giric may have been Eochaid's guardian, and that both were expelled in June 885.

**Episcopal Church of Scotland** Scotland had no territorial episcopate before the 12th cent. and no archbishoprics before the late 15th cent. Although the church assumed an increasingly *presbyterian accent after the Reformation, bishops remained a lively issue in the conflicts bedevilling church and crown between 1560 and 1690. Thereafter Scotland's remaining episcopalians formed links with English *non-jurors, participating in 1711 in a joint consecration of bishops. An Act of Toleration (1712) gave them legal standing provided their ministers took the oath of allegiance to Queen Anne. The 19th cent. saw substantial reconstruction: seven dioceses by 1837, a doubling of churches and clergy by 1857, a Church Council since 1876, and a Consultative Council on Church Legislation since 1905, the whole later enhanced by a General Synod.

**episcopalianism** is the form of church polity in which the chief authority is exercised by bishops, as opposed to *presbyterianism, in which it is exercised by ministers and elders, and *congregationalism, in which it is exercised by gathered fellowships of believers. The system, normal among Christians by AD 200, became dominant in Christian Europe. Since the Reformation the term has usually been applied to episcopal churches not in communion with the Roman catholic church, and is particularly applied to the Anglican Communion.

**Epstein, Sir Jacob** (1880–1959). Sculptor, painter, and draughtsman. Born in New York, he studied in Paris before settling in London in 1905 and becoming a British citizen. From his first commission in 1907/8, eighteen figures for the BMA headquarters in the Strand, which were attacked as obscene, his work was surrounded by controversy. His Oscar Wilde memorial in Père Lachaise cemetery, Paris (1910–11), was at first banned as indecent. Two of the best-known monumental sculptures are *Christ in Majesty* (1954/5) in Llandaff cathedral and *St Michael and the Devil* (1955/8) at Coventry cathedral.

**Erik Bloodaxe** (d. 954), king of York (947–54). Erik was the last Scandinavian ruler of the short-lived kingdom of *York. Son of Harold Fairhair of Norway, he was a typical battle-leader. Expelled from his native land, he made himself master of York in 947, and was welcomed for the protection he offered against the West Saxons. He was soon dispossessed by *Edred but returned in 952. Significantly his coinage for Jorvik (York) shows an unsheathed sword. In 954 he was killed at *Stainmore, possibly making for the Norse kingdom of Dublin or for the Isles.

**Ermengarde de Beaumont** (d. 1233), queen of William I of Scotland. Married to William the Lion on 5 December 1186, she was chosen for him by Henry II, then overlord of Scotland. Her father was one of Henry's French vassals, Richard, vicomte of Beaumont-sur-Sarthe. During her long widowhood from 1214 she founded the Cistercian abbey of Balmerino (Fife), where she was buried.

**Ermine Street** was the Roman precursor of the Great North Road, running from London via Lincoln to York. The name is from the Anglo-Saxon *Earninga Stræt* meaning 'the street of the ?eagle's people'.

**Erskine, Thomas** (1750–1823). Erskine was the son of the earl of Buchan [S]. After serving in the navy and the army he entered Trinity College, Cambridge, and was called to the bar. He achieved fame as defence counsel in a series of important 'political' trials, such as those of Baillie, Stockdale, Tom *Paine's *The Rights of Man*, and Hardy, who supported parliamentary reform. He twice served as MP for Portsmouth, was for a time attorney-general to the prince of Wales and, from 1806-7, lord chancellor. He enjoyed immense popularity when opposing repressive legislation, and again when he defended Queen *Caroline in 1820.

**Essex** originated as a kingdom. *Cunobelinus moved the capital of the *Catuvellauni from Verulamium to Colchester, subduing the *Trinovantes before Caesar's invasion. The Romans took over the site and made it the provincial capital, Camulodunum, sacked in *Boudicca's rebellion in AD 61. In the 5th cent. the area fell to the Saxons, and a kingdom of the East Saxons was in existence by the early 7th cent. It maintained a somewhat precarious existence, and by the 9th cent. had become a client state, first of Mercia, then of Wessex. In the late 9th cent. it was overrun by the Danes and allotted to them at the peace of *Wedmore in 878. It was reconquered by *Edward the Elder, and shired. The county town was Chelmsford rather than Colchester, perhaps because it was more central.

For centuries Essex remained something of a backwater. Colchester was a sizeable town, the centre for a vigorous cloth trade, but most of the other towns—Saffron Walden, Thaxted, Braintree, Romford, Waltham Abbey, Dunmow, Halstead, and Ongar—were of only local importance. The shire provided London with fresh vegetables, but for many years the marshes remained a barrier to urban expansion. As late as 1907, the *Victoria County History* could write that Essex was 'one of the purely agricultural counties of England, depending almost entirely upon tillage for its prosperity'.

The chief characteristic of the shire was religious nonconformity. Proximity to the continent made for easy access to reforming ideas in the Tudor period and the Essex towns provided a number of protestant martyrs during Mary's reign. Its puritan sympathies made it come down heavily in the 1640s for Parliament against the king. In 1698 Celia Fiennes noted that Colchester was 'a town full of dissenters, besides Anabaptists and Quakers'.

Economic transformation came in the 19th cent. with the overflowing of London, first along the docks of the Thames, then following the railway from Shoreditch to Romford in 1839, which built an important junction and repair works at Stratford. Dockers and railwaymen replaced farmers in the streets of south-west Essex. In 1801, Dagenham, Barking, Ilford, Walthamstow, East and West Ham were still separate villages or small towns. But for a time the increase in population was the fastest in the whole country. West Ham had fewer than 5,000 inhabitants in 1801 but 267,000 in 1901, dwarfing the county town, which had 13,000. The taste for sea-bathing gave prosperity to Southend, which became Londoners' favourite resort. The arrival of the Ford Motor Company at Dagenham in 1929 created a great new borough. Though suburban growth declined after the Second World War, the new towns at Harlow and Basildon and the airport at Stansted kept numbers increasing, while Epping, Braintree, and Chelmsford became commuter towns, disgorging into Liverpool Street. In the 1980s the concept of 'Essex man', upwardly mobile, fast-driving, Tory-minded, brought the shire back into national consciousness.

**Essex, Arthur Capel, 1st earl of** (1631-83). In 1670 Essex was sent to Denmark on a diplomatic mission and from 1672 to 1677 was lord-lieutenant of Ireland. Two years later, he was treasurer for six months. He resigned in November 1679, gave strong support to the *Exclusion Bill and moved closer to *Monmouth. In 1683 Essex was arrested in connection with the *Rye House plot but was reported to have cut his throat in the Tower while awaiting trial.

**Essex, kingdom of** Essex was formed in the 6th cent. by Saxon settlers. The ruling dynasty claimed descent from an obscure Saxon deity, Seaxneat. In the early 7th cent. London was regarded as part of the kingdom. Final conversion to Christianity took place in the 650s under Bishop Cedd from Northumbria. After Cedd's death episcopal authority passed to the bishop of London though political control of the city rested in other hands. Indeed, while retaining its own kings until the 9th cent., Essex played a minor role. When dominance passed to the West Saxons after their victories over the Mercians in 825 and 829, the subordinate role of Essex was further emphasized, and from that point onwards it was governed by *ealdormen not by kings. The boundary drawn up by *Alfred and the Danes after 878 left Essex in the *Danelaw, though there is no evidence of Danish settlement in depth. Essex was reabsorbed into the English kingdom in the early 10th cent.

### Essex, Robert Devereux, 2nd earl of

(1566–1601). Courtier. Essex served under his stepfather *Leicester at *Zutphen in 1586 and was knighted for gallantry. From 1587 he was Elizabeth's master of horse and was given the Garter in 1588. After his capture of Cadiz in 1596 his success seemed assured. But a second expedition in 1597 was unproductive, and his short spell as lord-lieutenant of Ireland in 1599 was disastrous. Instead of subduing *Tyrone as he had vowed, Essex met him for private negotiations. When Essex returned to England in express defiance of Elizabeth's orders, he was disgraced. His half-hearted attempt at a palace coup in 1600 led to his execution.

### Essex, Robert Devereux, 3rd earl of

(1591–1646). Essex was the son of Elizabeth I's favourite. He was appointed parliamentary commander-in-chief as soon as war came, fighting prudent defensive campaigns at *Edgehill and *Turnham Green in 1642. In September 1644 he led the ill-advised foray into Cornwall which ended in disaster at *Lostwithiel. Essex resigned in accordance with the self-denying ordinance in 1645 and died the following year.

### Étaples, treaty of, 1492.

In October 1492 Henry VII invaded France in support of the Bretons and to induce Charles VIII of France to repudiate Perkin *Warbeck. The French offered terms which he accepted on 3 November. France was to pay financial indemnities and agreed not to assist Warbeck. Henry's campaign of one month proved highly profitable.

### Eton College

Founded by Henry VI in 1440, the school was modelled on the foundations of *Winchester and New College, Oxford, set up by *William of Wykeham.

### European Communities Act, 1972.

Act of the British Parliament giving effect to the legislation of the European Communities, effectively confirming Parliament's acceptance of British entry.

### European Economic Community

was the title of the EEC, which Britain joined on 1 January 1973, also known as the Common Market, later as the European Community; after the treaty of *Maastricht, as the European Union.

Britain stayed out of the EEC's forerunner, the European Coal and Steel Community (ECSC), formed in 1952. This was a French initiative designed to ensure continuing influence over the German Ruhr's coal and steel production. The Labour government had just nationalized Britain's coal industry and faced trade union opposition to 'handing it over to foreign capitalists'. The members of the ECSC agreed in 1955 to explore further economic and atomic co-operation. Britain declined to send a representative and therefore had no influence on the treaty of *Rome that established the EEC. *Macmillan's application in July 1961 was vetoed by French President de Gaulle in 1963, as was a second application, made by *Wilson in 1967. De Gaulle's downfall in 1969, coupled with French economic weakness, cleared the way for the success of Britain's third application to join, under *Heath in 1970–1. Unfortunately for Britain, the EEC had come to agreements in 1970, detrimental to Britain's future membership, on the Common Agricultural Policy (CAP), and budget contributions.

The early *Thatcher years from 1979 were dogged by arguments over Britain's EEC budget contribution. Opinion varies on how far Thatcher's behaviour was responsible for the favourable deal eventually at the Fontainebleau European Council in June 1984, but the whole row reinforced Britain's reputation for obstructiveness. With the budget row settled, Britain went on to play a positive role in the mid-Thatcher years. A new, more subtle approach enabled Britain to work with others to guide the eventual Single Market proposals towards the aim of trade liberalization with minimal institutional reform. The Single European Act, signed in Luxembourg on 17 February 1985, was the result, coming into force on 1 July 1987. Majority voting in the Council of Ministers was extended to ease the passage of European legislation.

However, Thatcher was still to be found in isolation. She was hostile to participation in the Exchange Rate Mechanism (ERM), or European Monetary Union (EMU), which led to the resignation of cabinet ministers

Lawson and Howe. Others ridiculed the idea that national identities were threatened by European integration. Thatcher's opposition to these views was famously articulated in her Bruges speech of 20 September 1988: 'Europe will be stronger precisely because it has France as France, Spain as Spain, Britain as Britain, each with its own customs, traditions and identity . . . We have not successfully rolled back the frontiers of the State in Britain only to see them reimposed at a European level with a European superstate exercising a new dominance from Brussels.' Divisions within the Conservative government of John *Major from 1990 were damaging. In September 1992 his government was forced to withdraw from the ERM, and in August 1993 he carried the Maastricht treaty, which he had struggled to renegotiate, only after making it a confidence vote. The Labour government of 1997 began with warm intentions towards Europe, but became markedly less enthusiastic as the Euro, the new single currency introduced in January 1999, went into embarrassing decline. Meanwhile a policy of *devolution within the UK sat oddly with the avowed ambition of many European spokesmen to seek ever further integration, which would inevitably increase the power of Brussels.

**European Free Trade Association (EFTA).** The idea of an intergovernmental organization to reduce tariffs on trade between the non-communist European countries was put forward by Britain in 1956. The Swiss government invited those countries who would not join the EEC (Iceland, Norway, Britain, Denmark) or, because of Soviet disapproval of the EEC and considerations of neutrality, could not (Finland, Sweden, Switzerland, Austria) to negotiations which resulted in the Stockholm convention setting up EFTA (3 May 1960). Finland became an associate member and Portugal joined the others as full members, who managed to eliminate mutual tariffs by the end of 1966. Yet Britain applied to join the EEC in 1961. In the 1990s EFTA reached agreements with the EEC, but by 2000 only Norway, Switzerland, Iceland, and Liechtenstein remained members.

**Eustace, Prince** (c.1127–53). Eustace was the second son of King Stephen, but the death of his elder brother Baudouin c.1135 made him heir apparent. After Eustace's death on 10 August 1153, Stephen came to terms with his great rival *Matilda, accepting her son Henry as his successor.

**evangelicalism** A predominantly Anglican movement stemming from the mid-18th cent., originally with links to *Whitefield and *methodism, its characteristics were Calvinistic with a literalist interpretation of the Bible, sabbatarianism, conversion-preaching, reform of the heart, human sinfulness, and personal salvation. The second generation was wealthy and close to political power; William *Wilberforce, his cousin Henry Thornton, John Venn, vicar of Clapham, and Charles *Simeon formed the *Clapham sect, whose aims were the reformation of manners and the abolition of slavery (see ANTI-SLAVERY). Hannah *More, a great propagandist with her *Thoughts on the Manners of the Great* (1787), and Wilberforce's Proclamation Society called not only for a moral reformation, but respect for government, orderly society, and hard work. World-wide mission was another aim, for which the *Church Missionary Society (1799) and the British and Foreign Bible Society (1804) were founded.

**Evelyn, John** (1620–1706). The second great diarist of his time, less self-revelatory than Samuel *Pepys, though his diary covers a far longer time-span, 1641–1706. A fervent royalist, he spent the Civil War years touring in Europe, but after 1660 he was commissioner for sick and wounded in the *Anglo-Dutch War of 1665–7 and for the mint. Evelyn was a founding fellow of the *Royal Society.

**Evesham, battle of,** 1265. After his victory over the forces of Henry III at *Lewes in May 1264, Simon de *Montfort took possession of king and government. But Prince Edward, Henry's son, escaped in May 1265 and raised an army in the west. De Montfort marched to Evesham, hoping to link up with his son Simon. He was intercepted by an overwhelming royalist force and on 4 August, just north of Evesham, de Montfort and his supporters were butchered, 'for battle none it was'.

**Exchequer** Financial institution. The term is derived from the chequered cloth, similar to a chess board, which was placed over a table to assist in the counting of sums due to the crown. Its function is first described in the *Dialogus de Scaccario* (*Dialogue of the Exchequer*, *c*.1179): the Lower Exchequer received and issued money, the Upper Exchequer was essentially a court of account where royal revenue was managed, accounts audited, and disputes dealt with. The Exchequer thus exercised a judicial as well as financial competence. By the later 12th cent., the Exchequer was permanently based at Westminster. In the 16th and 17th cents., the *Treasury developed as a separate department, so that the administrative functions of the Exchequer declined. The Treasury is now a ministerial department headed by the chancellor of the Exchequer, although the prime minister is technically its 1st lord.

**Excise crisis,** 1733. In 1733 Sir Robert *Walpole, George II's first minister, was anxious to conciliate the country gentlemen by reducing the land tax to 1 shilling in the pound. He therefore proposed the substitution of excise duties for customs duties on tobacco and wine, to maximize revenue and discourage smuggling. However, a full-scale outcry was raised in London and many provincial towns. In the Commons Walpole's majority almost collapsed, and he withdrew the measure.

**Exclusion crisis** A period of intense political strife during 1679–81 generated by the attempt to bar Charles II's catholic brother James, duke of York, from the succession. Widespread apprehension that James would inaugurate a catholic 'absolutist' monarchy was aroused in 1678 by Titus *Oates's revelations of a *Popish plot. In the three parliaments called between 1679 and 1681 discontented 'Whig' groups exploited their majority in the Commons, but were each time defeated when the king used his prerogative to close proceedings.

**Exeter** Isca Dumnoniorum was successively fortress of *legio II Augusta* from the mid-50s to the mid-70s then *civitas*-capital of the *Dumnonii. Some houses have been excavated, but comfort and degree of Roman culture do not seem to have been high. Exeter was refounded as a fortified town (burh) by *Alfred. It rose to be one of the leading English towns of the 10th–12th cents., acquiring a bishop's see (1050) and, after a rebellion against the Normans, a castle (1068). It never really industrialized, and has remained a modest-sized regional centre.

**Exeter, diocese of** The see, now conterminous with Devon, was created when Leofric, bishop of *Crediton, moved his seat to Exeter in 1050. For 800 years it comprised Devon and Cornwall, but in 1877 Cornwall was hived off to form the new diocese of *Truro. The cathedral, rebuilt between 1260 and 1307, is a fine example of the Decorated period.

**Exeter, John Holand, 1st duke of** (1395–1447). Henry V, in his policy of reconciliation, restored Holand in 1416 to the earldom forfeited in 1400 by his father. He earned restitution by service in the French war from 1415 to 1421, when he was captured at *Baugé. Holand was again fighting in France from 1429, a joint warden in the Scottish marches in 1435–6, and finally lieutenant of Gascony for six years from 1439. Henry VI created him duke in 1444.

**exploration** The notion of Europeans discovering other peoples and telling them who they were and where they lived is now suspect. Exploration has been linked with the exercise of political and economic power and sometimes religious evangelism. Britain's increasing domination of exploration broadly accompanied the rise of the English and then the British state to world power after 1500.

Explorers became the pattern for heroes of boys' adventure stories and subjects for numerous biographers. *Hakluyt began with his *Principall Navigations . . .* of 1589. The great 18th-cent. travel collections continued the tradition and in 1846 William Desborough Cooley founded the Hakluyt Society to publish historical accounts of voyages.

Despite Hakluyt, the English contribution to primary exploration in the great age of maritime discovery was modest. John and Sebastian *Cabot, English by adoption, contributed to the discovery of the Americas in 1497 and 1509, but most English maritime adventurers in the Tudor period merely followed the Portuguese and Spanish and attempted to steal some of their treasures. This was true of *Drake although his circumnavigation of 1577-8 involved the discovery of California. But the English did try to open up new routes to the Orient—the North-East and North-West Passages with the voyages of Willoughby and Chancellor to Russia in 1558 and the contemporary travels in central Asia of Jenkinson matched by the voyages to the west of *Frobisher in 1576 and *Davis in 1585-7. *Hudson reached the bay bearing his name in 1607-11.

The Pacific attracted much British attention in the 18th cent. with Dampier's *New Voyage round the World* of 1697 and the circumnavigations of *Anson in 1740-4. *Cook's first voyage of 1768-71 revealed New Zealand and eastern Australia but the second voyage of 1772-5 effectively disproved the existence of a southern continent. Cook's third voyage was to the northern Pacific, so completing the greatest series of scientific expeditions ever undertaken. *Banks had been on the first voyage and then came to dominate British exploratory activity, being instrumental in founding the African Association in 1788. This aimed to do for the interior of Africa what Cook had done for the Pacific. Mungo *Park reached the upper Niger in 1795-6. Government took over the organization of expeditions by Clapperton and others and in 1830 Lander solved the vexed question of where the Niger debouched into the sea. The mantle of the African Association was taken on by the Royal Geographical Society, founded in 1830, which sent explorers especially to eastern and central Africa and to the Polar regions. *Livingstone, *Burton, *Speke—who reached the source of the Nile—Cameron, *Stanley, and Thomson were the great African explorers, while the old obsession with the North-West Passage led to the expeditions of Parry, and especially of *Franklin whose disappearance after 1845 led to no fewer than 40 search expeditions. In the south polar region, *Ross, *Bruce, *Shackleton, and *Scott are the great names.

**Eyre** The General Eyre, which probably dates from the reign of Henry I and is believed to derive its name from the Latin *iter*, was a commission issued by the king to officials of the *curia regis, who travelled round the kingdom every few years. The powers given to the justices under the Commission of the General Eyre were extremely wide. Although not at first oppressive, the General Eyre became unpopular and in the 14th cent. faded away.

**F**

**Fabian Society** The Society took its name from the Roman dictator Fabius, nicknamed 'Cunctator', or delayer. It was founded in 1884 by a group of middle-class intellectuals to further 'the reconstruction of Society in accordance with the highest moral principles', but *gradually*. Its first pamphlet, *Why are the Many Poor*, made it plain that the highest principles were socialist. Shortly afterwards Sidney *Webb and Bernard *Shaw, its most famous members, joined. It survives, the most senior of all Britain's socialist organizations.

**Factory Acts** were introduced to protect working people from employers who permitted dangerous practices in workplaces. The first Acts of 1809 and 1823 failed to include effective enforcement clauses. In 1833 Lord Ashley (later earl of *Shaftesbury) introduced the first effective law, establishing an inspectorate with powers to enter premises and require compliance with restrictions on the employment of women and children. A coherent law relating to safety at work was not achieved until 1969 when the Health and Safety Executive was set up.

**factory system** The 'factory system' has been an important element in the accelerating processes of industrialization known as the *industrial revolution. As British industrial enterprises expanded in the 18th cent., it became important to develop a more tightly organized form of production than the traditional method of employing workers in small workshops or their own homes—as in the '*domestic system'. The solution was the construction of large manufacturing establishments, in which the work-force could be closely controlled and strict conditions of time-keeping maintained. In this way employers were able to minimize the loss of raw materials by theft, and to install powerful prime movers (water wheels or steam-engines) to drive their machines.

From the employers' point of view, this factory system had such manifest advantages that it was widely adopted, especially in the textile industries, where the Lombe silk factory in Derby was a marvel of the age. Indeed, the factory system became the dominant form of industrial organization throughout the 19th cent., and remained important in the 20th cent. However, the introduction of electricity and road haulage has made possible a significant dispersal of industry, and the 'information revolution' of modern electronics has enabled an increasing number of people to work at home.

Architecturally, the factory system developed through several phases. Early factories were solidly built to accommodate the necessary machines and sources of power. Many factories became well-built structures with decorative flourishes such as ornate chimneys. Idealistic entrepreneurs, such as Robert *Owen or Titus *Salt, provided good housing and public amenities for their workers. Modern 'industrial estates' are typically composed of a series of temporary boxes of little architectural distinction.

**Fairfax, Sir Thomas** (1612–71). Fairfax was probably the best commander on the parliamentary side in the civil wars. His career started inauspiciously in March 1643 when he was beaten by *Goring at Seacroft Moor in Yorkshire, but he turned the tables on Goring in May 1643, capturing him at Wakefield. He then gained an impressive string of victories at *Winceby, *Nantwich, *Selby, and *Marston Moor. In the winter of 1644 he was busy training the *New Model Army to unprecedented standards of efficiency. In the spring of 1645 he replaced *Essex as commander-in-chief and his two great victories at *Naseby in June and

*Langport in July knocked the heart out of royalist resistance.

**fairs,** as periodic gatherings for the sale of goods and services developed in the Middle Ages. They brought together traders from much greater distances than the markets held weekly or more frequently in many towns and villages. Fairs were held at regular intervals for a fixed number of days. They were licensed by charter, usually from the crown. In turn, they were highly profitable to magnates and corporations through stall rents. Some fairs became famous for their specializations, Stourbridge (Cambs.) for dried fish and cloth, St Ives (Cambs.) for wool, hides, and cloth, and Boston (Lincs.) for wine and wool.

Fairs continued for seasonal agricultural trade in grain, cattle, and sheep into the 19th cent.; and the custom of hiring workers also persisted. However, these features declined as railways made deliveries of farm produce to major markets reliable and other forms of labour recruitment became the norm. The emphasis was increasingly on entertainment.

**Falaise, treaty of,** 1174. Earliest Anglo-Scottish treaty whose terms are known in full. It was imposed by Henry II on the captive William the Lion at Falaise in Normandy in December 1174, and ratified at York in August 1175. To secure his release from custody, William explicitly recognized Henry as feudal overlord of Scotland.

**Falkirk, battle of,** 1298. *Wallace's victory at *Stirling Bridge in 1297 had shaken the English hold on Scotland. Edward I assembled a large army and on 22 July 1298 defeated William Wallace's men near the river Carron.

**Falkirk, battle of,** 1746. After the Jacobite retreat from Derby in December 1745, it was not Charles *Stuart's intention to abandon the enterprise but to consolidate in Scotland. *Cumberland handed over the pursuit to General Hawley. On 17 January at Falkirk the Highland charge once more carried the day, inflicting a sharp defeat on the Hanoverians. Cumberland returned to Edinburgh to take over.

**Falkland, Lucius Cary, 2nd Viscount** [S] (1610–43). Falkland was educated in Ireland, where his father was viceroy, but settled at Great Tew, outside Oxford. This became, in the words of *Clarendon, 'a university bound in a lesser volume'. Elected to Parliament in 1640, Falkland condemned arbitrary rule, but opposed radical change. In January 1642 he accepted office as secretary of state, in the vain hope of closing the gap between the king and Parliament. This 'incomparable young man', as Clarendon called him, found a welcome death in battle in September 1643.

**Falkland palace** Royal home and hunting lodge, Fife. After Falkland castle (home of the earls of Fife and dukes of Albany) came into the possession of James II, his 1450s extension became the north range of the palace. James IV renovated the north range's great hall (1502) and added the east and south ranges, which were embellished by James V: his French craftsmen transformed them in the 1530s into the first Renaissance building in Scotland, now regarded as among the finest work of its period in Britain and marking the height of the 'Auld Alliance'.

**Falklands, battle of the,** 1914. After dispatching Craddock's squadron at the battle of *Coronel, von Spee's ships rounded Cape Horn and on 8 December 1914 attacked Port Stanley in the Falkland Islands. However, the Germans found themselves fighting a much stronger British squadron under Vice-Admiral Sturdee, who sank all but one of von Spee's ships.

**Falklands War** (1982). The Falkland Islands had been under British control since 1833, but Argentina had become increasingly anxious to acquire them. On 19 March 1982 a group of Argentine scrap metal merchants landed on South Georgia, and this was followed on 2 April by full invasion. The British government acted swiftly, assembling a task force consisting of 10,000 troops and 44 warships. It was dispatched 8,000 miles to the South Atlantic, using Ascension Island as a forward base.

British troops, under aerial attack, landed on the Falklands at San Carlos on 21 May. After fierce fighting the settlements at Darwin and Goose Green were retaken and on 14 June the Argentine garrisons surrendered. The war cost the lives of 236 British and 750 Argentine soldiers. It was the turning-point in the fortunes of the Thatcher Conservative government, but in Argentina, General Galtieri's military junta fell from power a year later.

**family history** From earliest times, tracing ancestors and establishing proof of relationship had practical importance for the wealthy and privileged and, in particular, for the sovereign. Records of the aristocracy and royal families had always been maintained by the earl marshal and, in Scotland, by Lyon king-of-arms. However, in 1484, the *College of Arms was incorporated as a permanent institution comprising heralds, who had the task of investigating descent and establishing incontestable rights to titles. Recognition of property rights guaranteed social status and acceptance. After the civil wars of the mid-17th cent. both aristocracy and gentry supported the publication of detailed histories of counties in England and Wales, which included family histories. These county histories focused on the wealthier residents of each county, giving little information about other levels of society.

In the 20th cent. interest in family history became widespread. Tracing family history is a popular activity, as a recognition of the importance of family at all social levels. By 1960 county record offices had been established in all areas of England and Wales, providing readily available sources such as parish records, ancient wills, and, where they existed, family papers.

**famine** may be defined as the occurrence of serious food shortages resulting in significant rises in the death rate. Mortality during famines was rarely caused solely by starvation but from related diseases like dysentery, typhoid, and typhus.

What has been described as the worst famine in England in the last millennium occurred in 1315–18, after a century of population growth. After the arrival of plague in 1348, however, England's agrarian economy was able to feed its much reduced population, and famine mortality disappeared until population growth accelerated again in the 16th cent.

England's Celtic neighbours experienced more severe famines for far longer. Scotland suffered spectacularly in 1623–4 when death rates in some areas increased eightfold. Greater specialization on pastoral agriculture in the 18th cent. seems to have increased vulnerability. Scotland suffered severe famine mortality in the 1690s which may have killed 15 per cent of its population, Lowland areas were hit in 1740–1, and parts of the Highlands suffered famine late into that century. Famines were experienced in Ireland in the 1620s, 1640s, and 1650s. As the diet of its poor increasingly became dominated by the potato, Ireland became more rather than less famine-prone. Serious mortality occurred in 1727–9 and the 1740–1 scourge killed some quarter of a million people. Famines occurred again in 1744–6, 1800–1, and 1817–19 but these were dwarfed by the last Great *Famine in Ireland, caused by potato blight which ravaged the staple potato, 1845–8. Recent estimates put the number of deaths attributable to this disaster at one million.

**Famine, Irish** (1845–51). The famine originated with the recurrent failure of the potato crop: around 1 million died in Ireland as a result either of starvation or—more commonly—disease. The origin of this demographic cataclysm lay with a fungus, *phytophtora infestans*, which destroyed half the Irish potato crop of 1845, and brought a near total crop failure in 1846. A partial recovery in 1847 was offset by a greatly reduced area under cultivation, so that although there was a good yield per acre sown, the total harvest was poor. The potato crop failed almost totally in 1848.

The Conservative administration of Sir Robert *Peel initially tackled the blight with some success, buying Indian meal and establishing food depots. Peel's government fell in June 1846, to be replaced by a more doctrinaire Whig administration. The Whigs relied at first on an extensive scheme of public works, but this was abandoned in 1847, being replaced by soup-kitchens. The limited crop recovery in 1847 persuaded the government that the emergency had ended, and all special relief programmes were abolished. This apparent British complacency fired later 19th-cent. Irish nationalism.

**Faraday, Michael** (1791–1867). Chemist and pioneer of electromagnetism. As a bookbinder's apprentice, he went to Humphry

*Davy's lectures at the *Royal Institution and asked to be taken on as his assistant. By 1820 he was himself a prominent chemist, famous for his experimental skill. He isolated benzene in 1825, and when Davy died in 1829 he worked on the nature of electricity, magnetism, and light.

**Farington, Joseph** (1747–1821). English landscape painter and draughtsman, Farington studied at the Royal Academy from its foundation in 1768. In 1921 his copious diary was discovered and revealed Farington as an authority on matters artistic, literary, social, and political. A friend to many in Parliament and well informed on politics in France, Farington's work is rich in anecdote about many leading politicians.

**Fascists, British Union of** *See* BRITISH UNION OF FASCISTS.

**Fashoda crisis,** 1898. In 1893 France, irritated by Britain's continued hold over Egypt, decided to go for Fashoda, on the White Nile to the south. An expedition was sent under Colonel Marchand, who arrived on 10 July 1898. On 18 September a British army under *Kitchener met him there. All that happened was that the two men sat down, cracked open a bottle of champagne, and waited for the respective Foreign Offices to patch things up. In the end (3 November) the French gave in.

**Faulkner, Brian** (1921–77). One of the ablest of Northern Irish Unionist prime ministers, Faulkner was from a commercial rather than a landed background. He became the last Northern Irish premier in March 1971 and won British government support for a stiff security policy culminating in internment. The failure of that policy led him to change stance and accept the power-sharing executive following the Sunningdale agreement of 1973. He became chief executive of the new administration, which collapsed after the loyalist strike of 1974. Faulkner died in a hunting accident.

**Fawkes, Guy (Guido)** (1570–1606). Fawkes was born in York in a family of protestant ecclesiastical lawyers, but became a catholic. In 1604 Robert Catesby and his fellow-conspirators, despairing of obtaining relief for the catholics from James I, brought Fawkes into their plot to blow up the king and Parliament and proclaim the Princess *Elizabeth. Fawkes was put in charge of a cellar which they hired directly under the House of Lords. His task was to light the slow fuse to ignite the gunpowder. After a warning letter to Lord Mounteagle, the cellar was searched and Fawkes taken. He faced torture in the Tower with great coolness but confessed after hearing that his fellow-plotters were captured, and was executed at Westminster on 31 January 1606.

**Fenians** *See* IRISH REPUBLICAN BROTHERHOOD.

**Fens, drainage of** From the 13th cent. the commissioners of sewers in the fenlands of eastern England were responsible for undertaking works designed to prevent inundation. With James I's declaration in 1621 that he was unwilling to allow waterlogged lands to lie waste, a firmer base was created for action, and this arrived in the form of the Dutch entrepreneur Sir Cornelius Vermuyden who in 1626 began draining the fens of Hatfield Chase and the Isle of Axholme. Work resumed after the Restoration, but it was the second half of the 18th cent. before much enthusiasm could be generated. In the 1830s and 1840s the introduction of steam pumps ensured that the risk of flooding had virtually disappeared. *See* BEDFORD LEVEL.

**Fermanagh,** one of the six counties of Northern Ireland until the local government reorganization of 1973, borders on the Irish Republic. Enniskillen, the chief town, was a protestant settlement in the early 17th cent. and sustained a siege in 1689 which took much of the pressure off the Jacobite attack on *Londonderry. The area depends upon tourism, cattle, and fishing, with a little light industry. It has a mixed religious population.

**Fethanleag, battle of,** *c.*584. The site is disputed but possibly at Stoke Lyne, near Bicester (Oxon.), between the West Saxons and the Britons. Although the West Saxon king *Ceawlin is reported to have taken towns and considerable booty, he returned home in anger. It seems likely that the West Saxons suffered a check to their westward expansion.

**feudal aids** Following the Norman Conquest, custom permitted the king, at times of exceptionally heavy expenditure, to take an 'aid' (*auxilium*) from his tenants-in-chief; a lord, similarly, could exact an aid from his free tenants. *Magna Carta (1215) listed three occasions when the king, or a lord, might demand a 'reasonable' amount. These were: the knighting of his eldest son; the marriage of his eldest daughter (once); and the ransom of his own person from captivity.

**feudalism** An abstract term commonly used to highlight those features believed to be characteristic of western European society during the Middle Ages. It is based on the Latin noun *feudum* (or *feodum*) which is now usually translated as 'fief' and understood to mean property held by a tenant in return for service. This notion of feudal tenure was used by 16th-cent. French legal historians as a key to understanding the origins of aristocratic rights in France in the centuries after the fall of Rome. In the 17th cent. Sir Henry Spelman argued that it was imported into England by the Normans. Hence *Maitland's crack that it was Spelman who introduced the feudal system into England. The view that the Normans brought 'feudalism' to England, and that during the next two centuries French and English invaders and settlers took it to Scotland, Wales, and Ireland, remains widely held—and also widely disputed. Since it is clear that rulers before 1066 expected political and military service from their landed élites, those historians who believe that William the Conqueror feudalized England have had to define feudalism in terms of precisely those features which they believe he introduced: castles, the 'feudal quota', and the 'feudal incidents'.

One problem with feudalism is that the 'facts' on which it is said to be based—e.g. that fiefs became hereditary in 9th-cent. France, or that William I introduced 'feudal incidents' and the quota—are themselves contentious. So many different definitions of feudalism have been offered—or, worse, simply assumed—that a degree of confusion has been the inevitable result. The adjective 'feudal' is commonly used to denote almost any social system regarded as being oppressive or backward. In these circumstances it is not surprising that some American and British medieval historians believe that both word and concept are past their sell-by date.

***fidei defensor*** (Defender of the Faith). A title first given (1521) to Henry VIII by Pope Leo X for writing his *Assertio septem sacramentorum* against Luther. After the break with Rome, Parliament authorized it as a royal title (1544), which it has remained and it is still used on coins of the realm.

**fief (or fee).** An estate held by feudal tenure from a lord—in the case of tenants-in-chief the obligation was knight service to the king. In the early Norman period, some 2,500 knights were required. The archbishop of Canterbury was to provide 60, the abbot of Bury St Edmunds 40: Robert of Gloucester was to provide 100, the honour of Totnes some 75. The tenant-in-chief usually subcontracted to his own vassals. As the cost of maintaining horse and armour rose, the complement of the feudal levy declined, and the proportion of hired men increased.

**Field, John** (1782–1837). Field was a piano virtuoso and composer, whose delicate and sentimental nocturnes had considerable influence on Chopin, Mendelssohn, and others. Born in Dublin of a musical family, he was taken to St Petersburg by Clementi, and spent most of his life in Russia.

**Fielden, John** (1784–1849). Factory reformer. A wealthy cotton-spinner, whose mills dominated Todmorden, Fielden was a friend and admirer of *Cobbett. He held that the welfare of labouring people should be the aim of all government. As MP for Oldham from 1832 he tirelessly sponsored bills to regulate minimum wages and hours of child labour in mills. In 1833–4 he collaborated with Robert *Owen in the National Regeneration Society for an eight-hour day. His pamphlet *The Curse of the Factory System* was published in 1836, but it was not until 1847 that his *Ten Hours Bill was finally passed.

**Fielding, Henry** (1707–54). English writer and magistrate. Educated at Eton and Leiden, Fielding wrote numerous plays, including swingeing political satires of *Walpole's government, until the theatrical Licensing Act of 1737. Called to the bar in 1740, Fielding subsequently divided his time between the law and literature, in *Joseph Andrews*

(1742) and his masterpiece, *Tom Jones* (1749). Appointed JP at Bow Street in 1748, Fielding was an energetic advocate of effective measures to reduce crime, corruption, and public disorder. His health undermined by overwork, Fielding travelled to Lisbon after the publication of *Amelia*, his final novel, and died there.

**Field of Cloth of Gold,** 1520. This was an extravagant diplomatic spectacle staged by Henry VIII of England and Francis I of France (1515–47) on 7–24 June 1520 at the Val d'Or, near Guînes. The two kings spent the time jousting, wrestling, and feasting, concluding with a mass and a banquet. Though the meeting was a great cultural spectacle, as a device to foster friendship between England and France it failed dismally.

**Fields, Gracie** (1898–1979). Music-hall artiste and film star. A Lancashire lass, born Grace Stansfield, Fields joined a touring music-hall company (1913) and became a star overnight in the West End (1924). Talented, versatile, and dedicated, she could control her audience with merely a headscarf for a prop, switching easily from 'Ave Maria' to 'The Biggest Aspidistra in the World'. As music-halls declined, 'Our Gracie' moved successfully into film-making. She settled in Capri after the war, and was created Dame (1979).

**field systems** Perhaps the best-known system was the common, or open field, system of farming in which the land of a particular parish was divided into two, three, four, or even more fields depending on local conditions. The system is usually dated to the Anglo-Saxon era, and emerged with the division of land and livestock among a mass of small occupiers. The need for common folding compelled common management of inter-mixed parcels of land.

The common field system was found predominantly in midland England, and other systems were nearly as widespread. In upland regions, and particularly in Scotland, the system of infield-outfield cultivation was found. In Scotland the infield was an area of land under permanent cultivation. The 'outfield' land lay in irregular patches at varying distances from the settlement. They were broken up and cropped on a shift-ing system. Each parcel might be cropped for four or five years and then allowed to rest for five years. *See also* ENCLOSURES.

**Fife** lies on a peninsula between the Forth and Tay estuaries. Its name derives from a Pictish lordship, extending rather further west than the present boundary; the present region is still occasionally called the kingdom of Fife. In the 1973 local government reorganization of Scotland, Fife fought a successful campaign to be a region, and not to be divided between the neighbouring areas (Tayside and Lothian). It has good agricultural land, partly underlain by coal seams, which formerly provided much employment, and, particularly round its coastline, there is a remarkable concentration of small towns.

**Fifteen rising** *See* JACOBITE RISING.

**Fifth Monarchy men** A movement of extreme *millenarians, arising in 1649. Fifth Monarchists interpreted the four beasts in Daniel's dream (Dan. 7) as the four great empires of the ancient world. The fourth, the Roman, had been usurped by the papacy, alias Antichrist, or the Beast in Revelation (Rev. 11–20). The fifth monarchy was to be that of Christ, exercised on his behalf by his saints for 1,000 years (Rev. 20: 3–5), until he returned in person to pronounce the Last Judgement. They disagreed over using force, but the militants attempted risings in London in 1657 and 1661.

**Fiji** The republic of Fiji is a group of small islands in the Pacific, 1,000 miles north of New Zealand. They were first explored by Tasman in the 17th cent., were declared a British colony in 1874, but were granted independence in 1970, within the Commonwealth. The population in 2005 was 893,000.

**financial revolution** This term refers to the extensive changes brought about in the British financial system between the Glorious Revolution of 1688 and the 1720s by the creation of a system whereby a national debt could be accumulated to provide government with spending power beyond the scope of taxation. This became necessary as a result of the extensive military commitments undertaken between 1688 and 1815. At the same time business, in order to expand, required a secure means for making payments, as well as a stable system of credit. There were three main elements to this revolution: the use of the bill of exchange for financial transactions, trade in shares of the capital stock of corporations, and perpetual annuities issued by the government and thus free from the risk of default.

These developments had profound economic results. They provided an institutional framework within which economic activity expanded, not only by creating a means by which provincial business could be transacted and linked to the main financial centre in London, but, perhaps more critically, by integrating London with the main European financial centre, Amsterdam, which by the end of the 18th cent. it had superseded. Secondly they provided a conduit through which investment on an unprecedented scale could be mobilized. Throughout the 18th cent. the principal customer remained the government. The state thus played a major role in stimulating the development of the financial system.

**Finn Barr, St** (d. *c.*623). Bishop of Cork. Finn Barr lived as a hermit by Lake Gougane Barra. Attracting numerous followers, he established the monastery of Etargabail, renowned for its school and centre of his cult. More famous was his foundation around which the city of Cork developed and where he is buried.

**first fruits** A tax, usually of the first year's income, paid to a feudal or ecclesiastical superior. Before the Reformation, first fruits for all clerical benefices went to the pope, together with an annual payment of one-tenth of the income. The Act of *Annates (1532) declared this unlawful, payments were diverted to the crown, and a treasurer and court established to collect them. In 1704 the revenue was diverted to found *Queen Anne's Bounty, to augment the incomes of poor livings.

**First World War** In August 1914 Britain ostensibly went to war against Germany because of the latter's invasion of Belgium. In reality Britain fought the First World War to prevent Germany dominating Europe and, with the help of her Austrian and Turkish allies, threatening the British empire. The men who made British policy wanted a peace settlement which would reduce Germany's power and also ensure that neither Russia nor France could tilt the European balance against Britain or menace Britain's imperial possessions.

In 1914 the *Asquith government believed that the war would reach its climax in 1917. Britain could achieve her objectives at least cost by allowing her allies to carry the weight of the continental land war with only token British assistance. Meanwhile the Royal Navy would undermine the German economy by blockade and Britain would offer financial help to her allies. This policy collapsed because France and Russia were not willing to fight for three years without British military support. By late 1915 the government had reluctantly accepted that if they failed to give their allies large-scale support on the continent, France and Russia might prefer to make a negotiated peace. But it was equally obvious that the cost of increasing Britain's commitment to the continental land war might be self-defeating. The British offensive on the *Somme in 1916 was an enormous gamble. The government was wagering that the Entente could win the war before Britain went bankrupt.

The attack failed, for although both the British and German armies suffered enormously, the Germans had no intention of asking for peace terms. Instead they tried to starve Britain into submission by launching a campaign of unrestricted U-boat warfare against British shipping. This was the strategic situation which *Lloyd George inherited when he became prime minister in December 1916. Lloyd George knew that the people had to be convinced that their sacrifices were reaping tangible victories, and if they could not be won on the western front, they had to be gained elsewhere. One reason why he supported offensives at Salonika in Greece, in Palestine, and in northern Italy was his belief that a victory gained on one of those fronts would provide a much-needed stimulus to British morale.

The new government also knew that victory could only be achieved in co-operation with its allies. But in the spring of 1917 the pillars upon which British strategy had rested began to crumble. In March 1917 the British greeted the first Russian Revolution with cautious enthusiasm, hoping that Russia would follow the same path as France in

1794; from the ruins of the tsarist regime would emerge a new military colossus. But their hopes soon gave way to the fear that Russia would desert the alliance, and that the Germans would move large numbers of troops to the western front. In the meantime a large part of the French army mutinied. At sea German U-boats were sinking so many merchant ships that Britain was close to starvation. The only cause for optimism in the Entente camp was that in April 1917 the USA declared war on Germany.

The debate about the future of British strategy in the summer of 1917 therefore concerned one question: what should be the new timetable for administering the knock-out blow against Germany? One option was to divert troops to northern Italy. The Italians had entered the war on Britain's side in May 1915. If they could defeat the Austrians, they would destroy Germany's ambition of establishing an empire stretching from Hamburg, through Austria-Hungary, Bulgaria, and Turkey, to Baghdad. The alternative was to permit the commander-in-chief, Sir Douglas *Haig, to have his way and mount an offensive in Flanders. Haig believed that he could force the Germans to sue for peace by Christmas 1917. The politicians doubted, but allowed him to try.

The third battle of Ypres in July 1917 was a failure. Haig then launched a second offensive, using massed tanks, at Cambrai, but that also failed. In October Italy suffered a major defeat at Caporetto and in November the Bolsheviks seized power in Russia and soon signed an armistice. The arrival of the American army was even slower than the British had anticipated. Lloyd George decided that Britain must preserve her army and economic staying-power in 1918. The knock-out blow against Germany would be delayed until 1919, when the arrival of the Americans would give the Entente a crushing superiority.

Lloyd George's timetable for victory in 1919 collapsed because in the spring of 1918 the Germans made their own final attempt to win the war. But by June the last German offensive had been stopped, and in July the Entente's armies began a counter-offensive, forcing the Germans back. The way in which the war ended surprised Britain and her allies. As late as mid-October Haig did not think that the German army was so badly beaten that the German gov-

ernment would accept armistice terms. When the armistice negotiations began the British had to consider several conflicting factors. Should they continue fighting into 1919, to invade Germany and inflict a Carthaginian peace upon the German people? Would such a settlement threaten the future peace of Europe by leaving the French too powerful and by making the Germans vengeful? Were the British people willing to fight for another year? It was only after weighing these factors they opted for an early peace and the guns fell silent on 11 November 1918.

**Fishbourne** was an exceptionally early, large, and luxurious Roman villa or 'palace'. One mile west of *Chichester, the site was first occupied by a supply base of the invasion period. In the Neronian period the first stone civil buildings were constructed. The Mediterranean-style complex and decoration (black-and-white mosaics, stuccowork) were unique in late 1st-cent. Britain. The complex declined through the 2nd and 3rd cents., though still a comfortable villa. It was destroyed by fire in the late 3rd cent.

**Fisher, John** (1469–1535). Bishop. Fisher was educated at Cambridge, became fellow of Michaelhouse, and took priestly orders in 1491. Through the patronage of Lady Margaret *Beaufort, he was made reader in divinity in 1502, and two years later bishop of Rochester. At Cambridge he promoted Renaissance humanist studies. He wrote copiously against Martin Luther, his works including the *Assertionis Lutheranae confutatio* (1522/3), the *Defensio regiae assertionis* (1523), and the *Sacri sacerdotii defensio* (1525). When Henry VIII sought to repudiate his first wife, *Catherine of Aragon, Fisher was one of the king's most public opponents, and was imprisoned in 1533. In 1534 he refused the oath of supremacy. In 1535, just after his elevation to the cardinalate by Paul III, he was put on trial and executed on 22 June 1535. He was canonized in 1935.

**Fisher, Sir John, 1st Baron Fisher** (1841–1920). Admiral. 'Jackie' Fisher was the main architect of the fleet with which Britain went to war in 1914. Between 1905 and 1910, when he served as 1st sea lord, he introduced two new classes of warship, the all-big-gun, turbine-propelled *dreadnought class of battleship and the more lightly armoured Invincible class of battle-cruiser. Recalled to serve as 1st sea lord in October 1914, he resigned amidst great acrimony in May 1915 when he lost patience with his political chief, Winston *Churchill, over the navy's growing commitment to the *Dardanelles.

**Fishguard invasion,** 1797. In one of the more bizarre episodes of the Revolutionary War, the French Directory collected 1,200 men, mainly from gaols, and landed them from three frigates and a lugger near Fishguard on 23 February 1797. They surrendered two days later to the local militia under Lord Cawdor. According to legend, the invaders mistook the red coats of the Welsh women for cavalry.

**fishing** *See* ANGLING.

**Fitzgerald, Lord Edward** (1763–98). Irish patriot. Fitzgerald was born into one of the wealthiest families of the Irish aristocracy: his father was James, 1st duke of Leinster. He was MP for Athy in the Irish House of Commons (1783), transferring in 1790 to Co. Kildare. An enthusiastic Francophile, he came to regard Parliament as unreformable, and turned instead to the *United Irish Society. He was eventually arrested and mortally wounded on 19 May 1798.

**Fitzgerald, Gerald, 8th earl of Kildare** [I] (c.1457–1513). Fitzgerald's father, the 7th earl, was a prominent Yorkist and deputy to the lord-lieutenant of Ireland on several occasions. Fitzgerald was continued as deputy by Edward IV, Richard III, and Henry VII, and was effectively ruler of Ireland. In 1487 he and his brother Thomas supported Lambert *Simnel: the earl is said to have crowned him in Dublin and Thomas Fitzgerald was killed fighting for him at *Stoke. Nevertheless, Fitzgerald gained a pardon. In 1505 he was given the Garter, and Henry VIII continued him in his post. Fitzgerald was killed in a skirmish at Lemyvanna, King's County.

**Fitzgerald, Gerald, 9th earl of Kildare** [I] (1487–1534). He was appointed to his father's place as deputy and held the office until 1520. He accompanied Henry to the *Field of Cloth of Gold. Reinstated as deputy in 1524 at the expense of his great

rival Ormond, he was recalled in 1526 and sent to the Tower. He returned once more to Ireland in 1530 and was reappointed deputy in 1532. When he was recalled again in 1534 and imprisoned in the Tower, his son Thomas led a rising. Fitzgerald, who had been wounded in a skirmish the previous year, died in September 1534.

**Fitzgerald, Gerald, 14th earl of Desmond** [I] (c.1533–83). Fitzgerald succeeded his father in the earldom in 1558, in his mid-twenties. In 1565 he was wounded in private warfare with *Ormond and sent to the Tower 1567–70. From 1574 he was in conspiracy against Elizabeth and from 1579 in open rebellion under papal encouragement. He was killed in 1583 and his head stuck on London bridge.

**Fitzgerald, James Fitzmaurice** (d. 1579). Fitzgerald was cousin of Gerald, the 14th earl of Desmond [I]. In 1569 he claimed the earldom for himself and launched a catholic crusade. Forced to submit in 1573, he went to the continent. Pope Gregory XIII encouraged him in an expedition to Ireland and he landed at Dingle in 1579, fortifying Smerwick. But he was killed in an affray and the garrison at Smerwick was butchered by Lord Grey.

**Fitzgerald, Thomas, 10th earl of Kildare** [I] (1513–37). In 1534 Fitzgerald's father, the 9th earl, was recalled as lord deputy to England and imprisoned in the Tower in disgrace. Fitzgerald, then Lord Offaly, began with a show of defiance to Henry VIII which developed into open revolt. In September 1534 his father died and Fitzgerald succeeded to the earldom. William Skeffington's relief army arrived in October, took Fitzgerald's stronghold at Maynooth, killed the garrison, and shattered the revolt. Fitzgerald surrendered, on promise of life, was sent to London, and there executed in 1537 with five of his uncles.

**FitzGibbon, John, 1st earl of Clare** [I] (1748–1802). FitzGibbon was the son of a lawyer and Irish MP from Co. Limerick, attended Trinity College, Dublin, and Christ Church, Oxford, and represented Trinity College, Dublin 1778–83 and Killmallock 1783–9 in the Irish Parliament. In 1783–9 he was Irish attorney-general and from 1789 until his death he was lord chancellor [I]. Created Baron FitzGibbon [I] in 1789, he was advanced to a viscountcy in 1793 and made earl of Clare [I] in 1795. He was one of the leading advocates of the Union, arguing that Ireland would then play her full part in a larger political context.

**Fitzhamon, Robert** (d. 1107). Fitzhamon was one of the leading Norman colonizers of south Wales. He seems to have moved from his holdings in Gloucester to carve out a marcher lordship in Glamorgan, beginning the building of Cardiff castle in 1080.

**FitzNigel, Richard** (d. 1198). Bishop of London (1189–98) and treasurer of England (c.1158–98). A member of the outstanding family who developed the sophisticated 12th-cent. English administrative system, he was son of Nigel, bishop of Ely, treasurer, and nephew of Henry II's justiciar, Roger of Salisbury. He is chiefly remembered for writing the *Dialogus de Scaccario* (*Dialogue of the Exchequer*).

**Fitzosbern, William, earl of Hereford** (d. 1071). Fitzosbern, steward at the court of Normandy, was one of William the Conqueror's most trusted advisers and fought at Hastings. In reward he was given great estates in the west country, the rank of earl, and palatine powers. Much of his energy went into fighting the Welsh and establishing the Norman position in Glamorgan.

**Fitzwilliam, William Wentworth, 2nd Earl** (1748–1833). Fitzwilliam inherited the wealth and vast estates of his uncle Lord *Rockingham in 1782 and became head of the Whig political interest in Yorkshire. He was a lifelong friend of *Fox and in 1782 he also succeeded Rockingham as patron of Edmund *Burke. He reluctantly broke with Fox in 1794 and joined *Pitt's cabinet, being sent to Ireland in January 1795 as lord-lieutenant. Under Burke's influence he attempted to persuade the cabinet to catholic emancipation, but he was dismissed in March. He rejoined Fox and *Grenville after 1802 and was lord president of the council under Grenville in 1806.

**Five Knights' case,** 1627. After the 1626 Parliament had been dissolved without granting subsidies, Charles I raised money by various means, including *forced loans. In 1627 five knights, imprisoned for refusal to contribute, appealed to *habeas corpus. Lord Chief Justice Hyde denied bail. As a means of alienating the propertied classes, Charles's policy was highly successful.

**five members,** 1642. On 4 January 1642 Charles I, exasperated at the opposition of the House of Commons, attempted in person to arrest five of its leaders—John *Pym, John *Hampden, Denzil *Holles, Arthur *Haselrig, and William Strode. Forewarned, they made their escape, leaving the king to mutter, 'I see that my birds have flown.' Within a week he had left London, never to return as a free man.

**Five Mile Act,** 1665. 17 Car. II c. 2 was part of the '*Clarendon code', which aimed at restoring Anglican supremacy. Clergymen and schoolmasters were forbidden to live within 5 miles of any city or parliamentary borough unless they took an oath not to endeavour to alter the government in church and state.

**fives** The game of fives, in a rough form, dates back to Tudor times, though the derivation of the name is unclear. The essential ingredients are a hard ball, gloves to protect the hands, which are used instead of rackets, and a wall or court.

**Flambard, Ranulf** See RANULF FLAMBARD.

**Flamsteed, John** (1646–1719). Flamsteed was the first astronomer-royal. Handicapped by ill-health, he began astronomical observations and in 1675 was placed on a panel to investigate claims to ascertain longitude at sea. The same year he was appointed by Charles II to supervise the new royal observatory at Greenwich. In 1677 he was elected to the Royal Society. In 1707, after many difficulties, Flamsteed's first catalogue of observations was published.

**Flaxman, John** (1755–1826). English sculptor, designer, and book illustrator. He studied at the Royal Academy Schools, before working as a designer for Josiah *Wedgwood. In 1787 Flaxman travelled to Italy to study. During the seven years he spent there, he drew illustrations for the *Iliad*, the *Odyssey*, and works of Dante and Aeschylus, which earned him an international reputation. On his return to England he was immediately in demand as a sculptor of monuments and figures.

**Fleet prison** (London) was in use from the time of the Norman Conquest until the reign of Queen Victoria. It held those who owed money to the crown.

**Fleet Street** (London) was for centuries the home of the newspaper industry and the name is still used to describe the national press. It ran from the Fleet river, a noisome ditch, to the Strand—strategically between the city and the court. In the 1980s there was a wholesale exodus of newspapers to less-congested sites elsewhere.

**Fleming, Sir Alexander** (1881–1955). Discoverer of penicillin. A farmer's son from Ayrshire, Fleming moved to London at 13 and then went to St Mary's hospital for training in medicine. He was assistant to Sir Almroth Wright, working on bacteria. In 1928 he noticed that a culture of staphylococcus in his untidy laboratory was being attacked by a mould, which he isolated and grew. He had high hopes of it, but it was not until the Second World War with the work in Oxford of H. W. Florey and E. B. Chain that penicillin was purified to be clinically effective. The three shared a Nobel Prize in 1945.

**Fletcher, Andrew** (1655–1716). Politician. Fletcher of Saltoun was taught by Gilbert Burnet, who later described him as 'a most violent republican and extremely passionate'. He represented East Lothian at the convention of estates and in the Scottish Parliament and was in strong opposition to *Lauderdale and James, duke of York (later James II). From 1682 he was in exile in Holland. After the Glorious Revolution he returned to Scotland but was soon in opposition to William III. Returned to Parliament again in 1703, he became a prominent opposition speaker. He was violently opposed to the Act of *Union, proposing a separation of the crowns instead.

**Flight of the Earls,** 1607. *Tyrone and Rory *O'Donnell, who had been in open rebellion against Elizabeth, submitted in 1602. O'Donnell was created 1st earl of Tyrconnel. But increasingly dissatisfied with their posi-

tion, they fled on 4 September 1607 with some 90 family and retainers and took refuge at Rome. Neither saw Ireland again.

**Flinders, Matthew** (1774–1814). Flinders accurately delineated the coasts of Australia and began the practice of using that name for it. After joining the Royal Navy in 1789, Flinders served with *Bligh before surveying the New South Wales coast in 1795. In 1798–9 he and Bass circumnavigated Tasmania. A new scientific expedition led by him 1801–3 mapped the coasts of nearly all Australia.

**Flintshire** County of north-east Wales lying along the estuary of the river Dee. The shire was created at the statute of *Rhuddlan in 1284 and was coincident with the Welsh cantref (hundred) of Tregeingl. It was not modified until 1974 when Flintshire became part of *Clwyd and was divided into three districts, Rhuddlan, Delyn, and Alyn and Deeside. In 1996 the county was reconstituted from the three districts.

The economy is dominated by tourism, extensively developed on the north coast, and industry. The last coal mine, at Point of Ayr, closed in 1996, and iron and steel production has also ceased, although a range of engineering and electronic industry has succeeded. In such a border county, Welsh-speaking proportions are low, ranging from 9.6 per cent in Alyn and Deeside, to 17.8 in Delyn, and 16.2 per cent in Rhuddlan.

**Flodden, battle of,** 1513. While the young Henry VIII was pursuing military glory against the French, his brother-in-law James IV of Scotland, an ally of France, declared war. He crossed the Tweed at Coldstream, and occupied the castles of Norham, Etal, Wark, and Ford. Lord Surrey (*Norfolk), commanding the English forces, marched north from Newcastle to Wooler. The armies met on the 9th, on Branxton Hill, near Flodden. There was little tactical manœuvring, but four hours of desperate hand-to-hand combat. The turning-point was when James himself, in the thick of the battle, was cut down. The Scots sustained the heaviest defeat of their history, the flower of their nobility dying with the king.

**Foliot, Gilbert** (c.1108–87). A learned, austere, and ambitious prelate who became *Becket's most outspoken opponent. He protested when Becket was made archbishop of Canterbury and opposed the archbishop at every turn. When Becket quarrelled with the king Foliot became one of the king's principal advisers. Despite his own highly successful career—prior of Cluny, abbot of Gloucester (1139–48), bishop of Hereford (1148–63), and finally bishop of London (1163–87)—Becket's friends believed that Gilbert had wanted Canterbury for himself.

**Fontenoy, battle of,** 1745. In the War of the *Austrian Succession, the French were besieging Tournai. The duke of *Cumberland attacked a superior French force under Marshal Saxe on 11 May. After heavy fighting, the attack was repulsed, the Irish Jacobite brigade particularly distinguishing itself.

**fools and jesters** Laughter-makers were employed at court in the classical world and in many ancient monarchies. They had various functions—to entertain, to prick solemnity, to defuse awkward situations. The heyday of the court fool seems to have been late medieval and early modern, and the jester's costume—green and yellow patchwork garments, cap, bells, and stick—was introduced in the 15th cent. Most fools had their own specialities—singing, dancing, juggling, tumbling, or mimicry.

**Foot, Michael** (b. 1913). Deputy leader (1976–80) and leader (1980–3) of the *Labour Party. A distinguished left-wing author and journalist, Foot, as editor and managing director of *Tribune*, was a leading *Bevanite in the 1950s and after 1958 prominent in the *Campaign for Nuclear Disarmament. An MP from 1945, he accepted office for the first time as employment secretary 1974–6. Between 1976 and 1979 he was lord president of the council and leader of the House of Commons, before succeeding James *Callaghan as party leader. He led a divided party however, and went down to humiliating defeat at the hands of Mrs *Thatcher in 1983 on a manifesto described as 'the longest suicide note in history'.

**football (soccer).** Medieval football was extremely violent, akin to modern hooliganism. Repeated attempts were made by the authorities to suppress it as dangerous, disruptive, and a diversion from archery practice.

Modern football developed with the growth of large industrial towns. In the early 19th cent. the game declined in popularity, but it survived among public schoolboys and at Cambridge University where, in 1848, a first attempt was made to compile common rules. Previous rules were local, with disagreements about charging and hacking, the size and shape of the ball, and the duration of the game. A further attempt to produce standard rules in 1863 led to the formation of a Football Association, from which some clubs soon seceded to follow a handling code.

At this stage football was strictly amateur. The new Association launched a cup competition in 1872. Wanderers beat Royal Engineers 1–0 at the Oval before 2,000 spectators. Gradually the strength of the game moved towards the midlands and north, where clubs were beginning to pay expenses. A watershed was the 1883 Cup Final, when Blackburn Olympics beat Old Etonians 2–1. In 1885, after protests, professionalism was accepted. Attendances began to edge up. The Cup Final at Manchester in 1893 between Wolves and Everton was watched by 45,000 people. With professional teams dominating the cup competition, an Amateur Cup was instituted in 1893.

In 1888 twelve clubs from the midlands and north, including Preston North End, Accrington Stanley, and Blackburn Rovers, formed the Football League. Over the next four years, sixteen more clubs joined, including Nottingham Forest, Sunderland, and Everton, and a second division was added in 1892. By 1914 the Football League had extended south to bring in Chelsea, Arsenal, Tottenham, Fulham, and Bristol City. The Scottish League began in 1890 and an Irish League the same year.

After the Second World War, recognition of the game was accorded by knighthoods to Stanley Matthews, the Stoke and Blackpool winger, to Alf Ramsay, manager of the World Cup victors of 1966, and to Matt Busby, manager of Manchester United. But by the 1980s attendances were falling in the face of rival leisure activities and a growing distaste for the hooliganism of the terraces. From this parlous state, the game was rescued, largely by television.

The first international football match took place at Partick in 1872 between England and Scotland, ending in a 0–0 draw. FIFA was founded in 1904 but international competition did not make much headway until after the First World War, when the World Cup competition was started in 1930. England did not take part until after the Second World War, and was able to retain a comfortable sense of superiority. This was shattered in 1950 by a 1–0 defeat from the USA, followed three years later by a 6–3 defeat at Wembley from the Hungarians, and was not totally restored by victory in the World Cup at Wembley in 1966. In European competitions, British clubs, often with a good stiffening of foreign players, have done remarkably well, but apart from its triumph in 1966, the English national team has tested the patience of its supporters.

Recent developments towards premier leagues and super leagues have made life difficult for small clubs and a number of them have fallen by the wayside. But underpinning the 90 or so professional clubs in the English league are the semi-professional leagues, and the vast number of amateurs, of all shapes, sizes, and talents, who play on windswept recreation grounds in Saturday or Sunday leagues, where attendances are measured in single figures, and it is not unknown for teams to turn up with nine men.

Four developments have changed the nature of the game radically. The 'Bosman' ruling of 1995 freed players to negotiate their own contracts which, assisted by agents, became lucrative. Secondly the spread of television poured money into the game, at least at the top level, as never before. Thirdly the increase in foreign players, foreign managers and sometimes foreign owners limited opportunities for English players and the national team suffered accordingly. International competition became ever more severe as national teams from Africa and Asia joined those already established in South America.

**forced loans** were non-parliamentary taxes which English monarchs demanded from their richer subjects. The forced loan of 1626 was exceptional in being levied on all taxpayers. This attempt to bypass Parliament provoked intense hostility, and in 1628 such levies were outlawed by the *petition of right.

**Foreign Office** The Foreign Office was created as a separate department in 1782. It was headed by the secretary of state for for-

eign affairs, usually second in authority only to the prime minister himself. He was assisted by two under-secretaries. The permanent under-secretary was a civil servant. In 1841 the rest of the establishment consisted of a chief clerk, six senior clerks, ten clerks, seven junior clerks, eight other clerks attached to particular duties, a librarian, a sub-librarian, a translator, a private secretary, a précis-writer, and a printer. Originally, the staff was recruited entirely by patronage and even qualifying examinations were not introduced until 1856. Limited competition for entry was introduced in 1908. As the Office grew more professional, its influence on policy-making increased. Lord *Palmerston had regarded his subordinates as mere clerks. Even at the end of the century, Lord *Salisbury expected little in the way of 'advice' from the Office.

**foreign policy** As long as monarchs wielded great personal power, it is hardly possible to divorce foreign policy from the individual circumstances and character of each king. Nevertheless, at an early period, certain themes emerged. The connection with France that came about in 1066 was fortuitous, but it introduced a pattern that survived for 500 years. From the days of William Rufus to those of Henry VIII, English monarchs attempted to retain or extend their French possessions. Not until the loss of Calais in 1558 did this aspiration come to an end. This, in turn, had profound effects upon another object of English policy, which pre-dated the Conquest—the ambition to turn a southern English kingdom based upon *Wessex into a kingdom of Britain, which should include the north, Wales, Scotland, and Ireland.

Even within the limits of so general a context, other patterns may be discerned. The principle of supporting one's enemy's enemy is elementary, yet it had important consequences. The Scots, in their long struggle for independence, soon perceived the advantages of an understanding with France, and the 'Auld Alliance' survived from the treaty of *Paris of 1295 until 1560. England pursued a similar policy, supporting Brittany and Burgundy against France. Balance of power came into consideration centuries before the phrase was invented. In the 16th and 17th cents., when Spain and France disputed European hegemony, the choice was which side to take. It was left to the monumental incapacity of Charles I to contrive to be at war with both great powers at the same time.

The rift in Christendom in the 16th cent. introduced a new factor into foreign policy, but one which was rarely decisive. Monarchs certainly supported their co-religionists in other countries, but the co-religionists were well aware that the commitment was fragile. Catholic unity did not prevent the long struggle between France and Spain, nor protestant commitment three wars between England and the Dutch in the 17th cent.

The development of a recognizably modern context for foreign policy dates from the *Glorious Revolution of 1688, when three factors combined to change the nature of diplomacy. First was the steady spread of representation at foreign courts, which made policy more of a regular activity and less of a response to occasional crises. The second factor was the changed importance of Parliament after 1688 which initiated a move away from a personal towards a national foreign policy. The third factor was the growth of empire. In 1600 England had no overseas colonies: by 1700, in addition to the twelve American colonies, there were valuable possessions in India, the West Indies, and Africa to be protected.

The broad outlines of 18th-cent. foreign policy are simple. After the swift collapse of Spanish power and rapid rise of France under Louis XIV, there was no question which was the dominant power in Europe, and the fact that France was also a major colonial competitor helped to bring about what has been called the second Hundred Years War. Between 1689 and 1815 Britain and France were at war for nearly half the time. France's much greater population and resources were a substantial handicap, but to build restraining alliances was far from easy.

These factors dictated Britain's overall foreign policy. It was an accepted point that she must have a continental ally and, on the one occasion when she did not, she lost the American colonies. Indeed, the 1780s, at the end of the American War, were exceptionally difficult. Britain's gains at the end of the *Seven Years War in 1763 had cast her in the role of overmighty power and made the balance of power operate against her: Spain, France, and Holland, at war with Britain in 1780, were supported by Russia, Denmark, Sweden, Prussia, Portugal, and the empire in the *League of Armed Neutrality.

The peace which brought the Revolutionary and Napoleonic wars to a conclusion in 1815 was based essentially on balance of power considerations. France was made to disgorge the enormous gains she had made under Napoleon, but there was no attempt to reduce her to a second-rate power. Austria and Prussia both made substantial territorial gains but it was still considered essential that they should balance each other in Germany.

Victorian foreign policy conjures up a vision of a John Bullish Lord *Palmerston; of Britain dominating world trade; a liberal, constitutional Britain, which supported national and liberal movements on the European continent against the forces of despotism; a Britain which, at the end of the century, was to rule the greatest empire in the world. The picture is not entirely false but it owes too much to the image which politicians like Palmerston and *Disraeli wished to project. Britain had only firmly established her right to be considered a European great power in the 18th cent. and had come close to forfeiting that status as a result of the American War of Independence. In the French Revolutionary and Napoleonic wars, Britain's naval strength had been of enormous importance but her lack of a large standing army had made the other European powers see her as a minor player on the continent.

All those responsible for British foreign policy between 1815 and 1865, Castlereagh, *Canning, Wellington, *Aberdeen, and Palmerston, looked back to William *Pitt the Younger as their mentor. The *Vienna settlement of 1814–15 followed roughly the lines envisaged by Pitt in 1805 and the powers agreed to meet periodically to maintain the peace settlement. Castlereagh felt obliged to withdraw from the resulting *Congress system because he believed it was being perverted from its original purpose of maintaining international peace to the suppression of any subversion which might threaten authoritarian regimes.

The great issues of this period were the Eastern Question—the dangerous vacuum left by the decline of the Ottoman empire—and the rise of liberal and nationalist movements in western and central Europe. Britain reluctantly followed a policy, in the crises of 1840 and the *Crimean War, of propping up the Ottoman empire to prevent Russian advances. The British public had some genuine sympathy with liberal and national movements, especially in Italy, but the government was always extremely cautious in its approach.

By the 1860s the balance of forces was changing. The British navy still commanded the seas but Britain's industrial lead was about to be challenged by other powers, especially the USA and Germany. Palmerston's last ministry saw Britain come close to what might have been a disastrous involvement in the American Civil War and Palmerston's bluff over Denmark was called by Bismarck. Britain stood aside from the Austro-Prussian War in 1866. Disraeli put a brave face on it. Britain's abstention, he said, was the result of increased strength, not decline.

There was a more real clash of ideologies between Disraeli and *Gladstone than between their predecessors. Gladstone had a clear vision of how international affairs should be conducted, with all submitting to the rule of law and disputes settled by arbitration. In Europe he was defeated by Bismarck who created his tight, and dangerous, system of alliances to protect the newly united Germany. Disraeli turned to the empire and made it a Conservative cause.

Britain's acquisition of a new empire in the late 19th cent. is usually seen as defensive, a matter of weakness rather than strength. Britain still had a great empire in India and its defence sometimes required further accretions of territory. Ironically, Britain acquired more of Africa, during the Scramble period, under Liberal than under Conservative administrations. The motive was almost always a challenge by another power, usually France or Germany. The rhetoric of Palmerston, Disraeli, and their successors convinced the public of Britain's greatness. Sober statesmen, Lord *Salisbury, *Balfour, or *Grey, knew the dangers of the situation. 'Splendid isolation' was not glorious. In 1902 Britain, embarrassed by world reaction to the *Boer War, concluded an alliance with Japan. Over the next twelve years she shifted from Salisbury's policy of 'leaning' on the Triple Alliance of Germany, Austria, and Italy to close relations with her two traditional rivals, France and Russia. Britain could not afford to see Germany defeat France again. She fought Germany in 1914 in defence of a balance of power as she had fought Philip II, Louis XIV, or Napoleon—to stop one power dominating Europe.

After 1918 Britain was sated and exhausted. The alliance which had defeated the central powers had begun to disintegrate even before the Great War ended, as Russia collapsed into revolution and civil war. The USA turned to isolationism, the Anglo-Japanese alliance was not continued after 1922, and France, Britain's main ally, was mistrusted in the 1920s as too belligerent and in the 1930s as too defeatist. The inability of the *League of Nations to deal with the Manchurian crisis was an early warning that collective security might offer little protection and was followed in 1933 by the advent to power in Germany of the Nazis. The policy of *appeasement was accompanied by a new search for allies. Though Russia was admitted to the League of Nations in 1934, there was massive mistrust on both sides, and in 1939 Stalin preferred to do a deal with Hitler. Much effort was devoted to wooing Italy, whose strength was overrated. Under these circumstances, British foreign policy lurched. Having abandoned Czechoslovakia in 1938, Britain gave a guarantee to Poland which could scarcely be honoured.

Many of the same themes re-emerged after the Second World War. Foreign policy was dogged by economic and financial weakness. As the shape of the post-war world unfolded, two problems emerged—security in the face of Soviet power and Britain's attitude towards Europe. The first was achieved by the nuclear deterrent, participation in *NATO (1949), and a close understanding with the USA, jeopardized only temporarily by the *Suez crisis. The debate on Europe was governed by three factors. First was that Britain geographically and culturally was half-in and half-out of Europe. The second was that European unity, which began as the simple determination of European powers never to fight each other again, moved through economic collaboration towards political integration. The 'Common Market', which the British voted to join, masked the political aspirations of many of its continental supporters. The third factor was the timing of Britain's application to join. This was vetoed by de Gaulle in 1963 and again in 1967 at a time when a federal Europe was hardly on the agenda. But by the time Britain entered the EEC in 1973, the movement towards political integration was gathering pace. Britain acted as a somewhat ineffective brake, usually doing enough to exasperate enthusiasts for European unity while not satisfying the anti-Europeans. The issue of Britain's relations with Europe was still unresolved when the 21st cent. dawned.

The spread of international *terrorism in the late 20th cent. introduced a new dimension into foreign policy and 'regime change' became one of the objectives for some powers. Enthusiasm for intervention has waned as the conflicts in *Iraq and *Afghanistan dragged on, demonstrating how difficult it can be to graft democracy and the rule of law on to nations still dominated by religious or tribal factions.

**forest laws** Under the Norman kings, the royal forest grew steadily, probably reaching its greatest extent under Henry II when around 30 per cent of the country was set aside for royal sport. The object of the forest laws was the protection of 'the beasts of the forest' (red, roe, and fallow deer, and wild boar) and the trees and undergrowth which afforded them shelter. The definitive form to forest law occurred during Henry II's reign, most notably in the Assize of the Forest (also known as the Assize of *Woodstock) in 1184. None could carry bows and arrows in the royal forest, and dogs had to have their toes clipped to prevent them pursuing game. Savage penalties for any infringements were often imposed. Discontent with the laws ensured that the forest became a major political issue in John's reign. It culminated in the Charter of the Forest (1217), but only in the 14th cent., when large areas were disafforested, did the political issue subside.

**forma regiminis,** or form of government, June 1264, was arrangements after the victory of Simon de *Montfort at *Lewes for a provisional government until a settlement of the dispute with Henry III had been reached. The king was to be advised by a council of nine. But when Prince Edward, who had been a hostage, escaped in May 1265, negotiation was at an end, and de Montfort was killed at *Evesham.

**Formby, George** (1904–61). Comedian. Born in Wigan (Lancs.), Formby followed his father in the old music-hall tradition. His stage character was that of a gormless but good-natured Lancashire lad, with a squeaky voice, toothy grin, and a talent for playing the ukulele. He made his first film, *No Limit*, in 1935 and then made an average of two films a year until 1946. These made Formby the highest-paid entertainer and the top box-office attraction in Britain.

**Formigny, battle of,** 1450. By 1450 Henry VI, beset by disaffection at home, was hard pressed to defend his French territories. A relief expedition under Sir Thomas Kyriel and Sir Matthew Gough was blocked by the comte de Clermont in Normandy on 15 April and badly defeated. The French use of artillery heralded the crushing victory at *Castillon three years later.

**Fornham St Genevieve, battle of,** 1173. *Henry the Young King, eldest son of Henry II, rebelled in 1173. The support of Louis VII of France and William the Lion of Scotland made the revolt formidable. Henry II beat off an attack on Normandy, leaving Richard de *Lucy, justiciar, to defend England. In September Robert, earl of Leicester, landed in Suffolk. De Lucy marched to intercept the rebels. On 17 October at Fornham St Genevieve, north of Bury St Edmunds, he defeated and captured the earl of Leicester.

**Forster, William Edward** (1818–86). Forster was a hard-working politician whose greatest achievement was the *Education Act of 1870. The son of a quaker missionary, he began in the Yorkshire woollen trade at Bradford. In 1861 he was returned for Bradford as a Liberal. He was given office under *Russell in 1865 and in *Gladstone's first ministry put in charge of education. His Education Bill proposed state schools where voluntary schools had not been established, to be administered by elected school boards. The religious difficulty was met by the Cowper–Temple clause, whereby religious instruction was to be undenominational. Forster also guided through *secret ballot in 1872. In 1880 he was appointed chief secretary in Ireland. He resigned in 1882 when Gladstone negotiated the *Kilmainham 'treaty' with *Parnell.

**Fortescue, Sir John** (c.1394–c.1476). Lawyer. Fortescue studied law at Lincoln's Inn, and became lord chief justice in 1442. A staunch supporter of the Lancastrian cause, he fought on the losing side at *Tewkesbury, being captured. He then made his terms with the triumphant Yorkists. His most important writings were *De laudibus legum Angliae*, in praise of the laws of England, and *On the Governance of the Kingdom of England*, probably written after 1470. Fortescue was at pains to distinguish between absolute monarchy ('dominum regale' as in France) and limited or constitutional monarchy ('dominum politicum et regale' as in England). By doing so he helped to encourage pride in the liberal character of English government and, like *Bagehot, Fortescue created the situation he was describing.

**Fortriu** was the Gaelic name of a Pictish region. Fortriu, its people, and its kings are frequently mentioned in contemporary sources from the 7th cent. until 904, when they are last heard of led by *Constantine II winning a battle in Strathearn (Perthshire) against the Danes. It would appear that 'king of Fortriu' was an alternative title for 'king of the Picts'.

**Forty-five rising** *See* JACOBITE RISINGS.

**Fosse Way** was the Roman road from Exeter to Lincoln, exceptional in cutting across the grain of the main road-system radiating from London. The modern name derives from *fossa*, perhaps used for a raised earthwork.

**Fotheringhay, treaty of,** 1482. Anglo-Scottish relations deteriorated in 1480. Unruly Scottish lords raided northern England. In Fotheringhay castle on 11 June 1482, the exiled brother of James III, Alexander, duke of *Albany, undertook to recognize Edward IV as overlord of Scotland if an English army set him on its throne. This army, led by Richard of Gloucester (later Richard III), reached Edinburgh, but Albany renounced the treaty. The castle of Berwick-on-Tweed was Gloucester's only gain.

**Fountains abbey** (Yorks.) was founded in Skelldale in 1132 by a group of dissident reforming monks of *Benedictine St Mary's, York. In 1133 they adopted the *Cistercian rule. The mismanagement of its largely pastoral economy at the end of the 13th cent. brought Fountains close to ruin. Nevertheless, the late Middle Ages saw substantial

building works and at the *dissolution Fountains was still the wealthiest Cistercian abbey in England.

**Fourth Party** was the name given facetiously to a parliamentary ginger group in the Conservative Party in 1880 (the other three being Liberals, Conservatives, and Irish). It consisted of Lord Randolph *Churchill, J. E. Gorst, Sir H. D. Wolff, and, at some distance, Arthur *Balfour. The contempt of the Fourth Party was as much directed at its own front bench as at Gladstone's administration. The main achievement of the group was to launch the spectacular career of Lord Randolph.

**Fox, Charles James** (1749–1806). Educated at Eton and Oxford, Fox entered the House of Commons while still under age in 1768. He held minor office under *North but fell foul of the king over the *Royal Marriages Act. Once in opposition Fox was drawn to alliance with the *Rockinghamite Whigs. He became a critic of the influence of the crown, and an opponent of British policy towards the American colonists. He supported parliamentary reform and repeal of the Test and Corporation Acts.

When North fell in 1782, Fox became foreign secretary under Rockingham. He wanted to recognize American independence in the hope of securing American goodwill during the peace negotiations but finding himself in disagreement with *Shelburne resigned office on Rockingham's death. This proved to be a misjudgement. He was driven to seek new political allies and joined his old foe, North. By defeating Shelburne over the draft peace terms, the coalition forced itself upon the king. When they tried to reform the East India Company, George III procured the defeat of the *India Bill in the Lords, dismissed the coalition, and after installing *Pitt as prime minister in December 1783 saw him win a great victory at the 1784 general election. Fox faced the prospect of long years in opposition.

Even when Pitt was defeated over parliamentary reform and Irish free trade, there was little comfort for Fox. When George III became ill in 1788 Fox expected that the prince of Wales would call him into office once he had become regent. But the king recovered in February 1789 and Fox was blamed by many colleagues for mishandling the regency question. His fortunes were again at a low ebb.

When the French Revolution broke out in 1789 Fox believed that the French were at long last imitating the English Revolution of 1688. But his party split, and by 1794 Fox had only 60 supporters in the Commons. Though disgusted by the excesses of the Jacobins, he opposed war with France. Only after Pitt's death in January 1806 was the king prepared to accept Fox as foreign secretary in Grenville's ministry, and by that time he was in poor health. Attempts to negotiate a peace with Napoleon collapsed ignominiously. The only consolation for Fox in his last days was the condemnation of the slave trade by the House of Commons. In September 1806 Fox died. He became the inspiration for Whig legend. One irony was that the hero of Victorian liberals was so un-Victorian in his private life. In his youth Fox had been a gambler and womanizer. Though he found happiness with his mistress Elizabeth Armistead, whom he married in 1795, he could never manage his private finances.

**Fox, George** (1624–91). Founder of the Society of Friends (*quakers). A Leicestershire man of puritan upbringing, Fox was an apprentice shoemaker who, after religious experiences, found no church satisfying. He began (1647) itinerant preaching, rallying the many small groups of 'Seekers'. Rejecting organized authority and contemporary social convention, even courtesy, and relying not on sacraments or Scriptures, but on mystical 'Inner Light', his followers were called 'Children of Light' and popularly quakers (1654). They became pacifist and non-political only after 1660.

**Fox, Henry** (1705–74). Fox entered Parliament in 1735 and found favour with *Walpole. Walpole's successor Henry *Pelham also regarded Fox highly and appointed him secretary at war in 1746. Fox was a skilled debater, and a talented manager of men and money. He was a secretary of state briefly, 1755–6, but his lack of expertise in foreign affairs as the *Seven Years War began told against him. When his rival William *Pitt formed a coalition with Newcastle in 1757, Fox was 'bought off' with the lucrative but uninfluential office of paymaster-general. His opportunity for revenge came in 1762–3

when *Bute and George III employed him to push the peace of *Paris through the Commons. He was created Lord Holland, but George III regarded his cynical methods with contempt and his career was over.

**Foxe, John** (1516–87). Martyrologist. Born in Lincolnshire, educated at Oxford, he was fellow of Magdalen College (1539). Foxe's reputation rests principally on his *Actes and Monuments* (Latin 1554, English 1563) or *Book of Martyrs*, dedicated to Elizabeth, a best seller which reinforced the concept of England as God's elect nation. It was based on massive, but biased and often inaccurate protestant scholarship.

**Foxe, Richard** (c.1448–1528). Bishop and statesman. Foxe was educated at Magdalen College, Oxford. Henry VII appointed him bishop of Exeter, king's secretary, and lord privy seal. He was greatly employed in diplomatic and matrimonial negotiations. Foxe was translated to Bath and Wells in 1492, to Durham in 1494, and to Winchester in 1501. From 1507 to 1519 he was master of Pembroke College, Cambridge. His influence waned as that of *Wolsey grew in the reign of Henry VIII and he gave up the privy seal in 1516.

**Fox's martyrs** was the facetious description of the 90 or so supporters of the Fox–North coalition who lost their seats in *Pitt's landslide victory at the general election of 1784. It derived its name from John *Foxe's famous book of 1563 of the sufferings of the faithful.

**Fox-Talbot, W. H.** See TALBOT, W. H. FOX.

**franchise** See SUFFRAGE.

**Franciscans** (or 'friars minor' or 'grey friars') were a mendicant order founded by St Francis of Assisi (1181/2–1226), the son of a wealthy merchant, in 1209, when he gave his disciples, like him devoted to poverty, care of the sick. Francis was unwilling to regularize his rapidly growing band of itinerant preachers, and control soon passed from his hands. In 1223 Pope Honorius III confirmed a more institutionalized rule which emphasized total poverty. Thereafter the order expanded rapidly, appealing particularly to urban benefactors, and the Franciscans settled and preached primarily in towns.

The first Franciscans were sent to England by Francis in 1224 and communities founded at Canterbury, London, and Oxford. Thereafter the Franciscans grew rapidly and there were some 60 houses by 1300. At Oxford the Franciscans soon acquired a reputation for their scholarship, and were in the forefront of intellectual activity during the 13th and 14th cents., their number including Roger *Bacon, *Duns Scotus, and *William of Occam. There were more than 50 houses at the dissolution in the 1530s.

**Franco-Scottish alliance** Also known as the Auld Alliance. An offensive and defensive alliance, aimed at crippling England's attempts to conquer Scotland or France by threatening war on two fronts. First agreed at Paris in 1295, the Franco-Scottish alliance was renewed periodically until renounced by Scotland in 1560.

**Franklin, Sir John** (1786–1847). After a distinguished naval career in the wars against Napoleon, Franklin became the most famous British Arctic explorer of his day. Then he became even more of a national figure by disappearing into the unknown. Franklin made his greatest discoveries on two overland journeys of 1818–22 and 1825–7 when he explored vast areas of northern mainland Canada. After a spell as governor of Tasmania from 1834 to 1843, he was chosen to take the Antarctic ships *Erebus* and *Terror* to the Arctic to force the North-West Passage. Having got through sea passages to the west side of King William Island, the ships were frozen in. Franklin died, but his men survived to perish later of scurvy, starvation, and lead poisoning from their tinned foods. Not until 1859 was the nature of the disaster fully established.

**frankpledge** was a form of collective responsibility for good conduct, whereby every member of a tithing, or group of ten, was answerable for the good behaviour of the others, on pain of fine or amercement. Some elements were to be found in Anglo-Saxon and Danish England, but it developed after the Norman Conquest, perhaps to give some security to individual Normans in a hostile land.

**Frazer, Sir James** (1854–1941). Anthropologist. Frazer was born in Glasgow, and was elected to a fellowship at Trinity College, Cambridge in 1879, which he held for the rest of his life. He published *The Golden Bough* (1890), a pioneer work of comparative anthropology, which occupied him until the 1930s. The evolution of society was, Frazer suggested, from magic to religion and then to science. Prodigiously dedicated, he amassed a vast pile of evidence, much of it printed in *Anthologia anthropologica* (1938, 1939).

**Frederick Lewis, prince of Wales** (1707–51). Eldest son of George II and Queen Caroline; father of George III. For most of his life Frederick was at odds with his parents, and by the mid-1730s he had become a willing tool of opposition politicians. Brought up in Hanover, he came to England in 1728. After his marriage in 1736 to Augusta of Saxe-Coburg, he soon established a rival court at *Leicester House which became an important meeting-ground for *Walpole's leading opponents. The 'Leicester House group' made a limited impact in Parliament in the 1740s, and broke up on the prince's sudden death in 1751.

**Free Church of Scotland** This issued from the *Disruption of 1843, when those unable to accept the infringements of the *Church of Scotland's right of self-government which the Auchterarder case (1838–9) highlighted seceded under Thomas Chalmers (1780–1847). Under a powerful Edinburgh leadership, the church steadily moderated its theological conservatism. It affirmed its political liberalism, developed a centralized financial system new to presbyterianism, and united with other presbyterian secessions: the original seceders (1852), the Reformed Presbyterian Church (1876), and the United Presbyterians (1900), thus forming the United Free Church, which joined with the Church of Scotland in 1929. Inevitably each union bred its rump.

**freeholder** Technically any outright owner of land is a freeholder, but the most regular use of the word historically has been in the context of voting rights. Freeholders were those people who owned property worth 40 shillings (£2) a year and were thus entitled to vote in county elections, at least until the franchise extensions of the 19th cent. The 'freeholder' was thought of as an independent voter exercising his legal rights unconstrained by threats.

**freemasons** were originally skilled workers in stone who, in the Middle Ages, travelled from site to site and developed a set of secret signs and passwords for private identification. Later they ceased to have much resemblance to craft guilds and became prosperous social clubs, which claimed to do much charitable work. Lodges were better organized, with regular meetings after 1691, and admitted broader social ranks; the first grand lodge was founded in 1717. The movement prospered, with many lodges owning their own premises, and in 1802 they established themselves as a national organization. Largely because of their secrecy, freemasons attracted much criticism, particularly from the Roman catholic church, which believed freemasonry to be a cover for free-thinking; others suspected secret political influence or accused members of promoting each other's interest by stealth.

**free trade** The basic tenet of the theory is that free trade, which is the absence of any artificial restrictions on the level or composition of trade or the price at which commodities are exchanged, represents the best form of organization in international markets. Free trade assumes a state of perfect competition.

The fact remains that there are very few examples of any country following a complete free trade policy, Victorian Britain constituting a notable exception. The repeal of the *Corn Laws in 1846 brought a shift in political perceptions by removing the protection traditionally given to agriculture in favour of securing cheap imported food for the industrial areas. (See PROTECTIONISM.) In the Victorian period the British economy was heavily dependent on international trade and finance, especially the latter. No other country, before or since, has diverted such a large share of national income to overseas investment. Furthermore, British industry depended heavily on export markets. It was thus in the interests of the British economy that international trade flourished.

The First World War severely undermined the British balance of payments as overseas investments were sold to pay for the war. The 1929–32 depression marked the end of free trade. In 1932 a general tariff was introduced imposing a 10 per cent import tax, but allowing preferential treatment to Commonwealth countries in return for concessions on British exports. But one of the objectives of the *EEC after the 1950s was the reduction of tariff barriers, at least between member countries. *See* EFTA.

**French, Sir John** (1852–1925). Soldier. After leading a cavalry division during the second *Boer War and serving as chief of the imperial general staff, 'Johnnie' French served as the first commander of the British army in France 1914–15. He was ill-suited to this role. A charismatic cavalryman, he had little understanding of staff work or diplomacy. He was dismissed in December 1915 following failure at Loos in September–October 1915. He served 1918–21 as lord-lieutenant of Ireland and was given a peerage in 1922 as 1st earl of Ypres.

**friars** (from Latin *fratres*, i.e. brothers) belonged to the so-called mendicant (i.e. begging) monastic orders. The four most important were the *Franciscans, *Dominicans, *Carmelites, and *Augustinians. The friars emerged in the early 13th cent., partly as a response to the spiritual needs of a changing society, particularly increasing urbanization, partly to combat heresy by teaching and example.

The friars, though frequently following variants of older monastic rules, differed from monks in fundamental respects. Adopting a life of poverty, they refused endowments and property, relying instead on begging; their *raison d'être* was engagement with, rather than seclusion from, the secular world. As orthodox evangelists they placed much emphasis on learning both within their own communities and in the universities, and it is no coincidence that almost all of the leading intellectuals of late medieval Europe, including Thomas Aquinas and *Duns Scotus, were friars.

**friendly societies** of working men can be traced back to the late 17th cent., but their rapid growth began about 1760. In return for a small weekly or monthly contribution paid into a common fund, they provided sickness and funeral benefits. Originally friendly societies were local institutions with seldom more than 100 members. But in the 1830s and 1840s these were eclipsed by the affiliated orders, with their organization into a unity (headquarters), districts, and lodges: the Oddfellows, Foresters, Druids, Ancient Britons, Antediluvian Buffaloes, and Rechabites. From an estimated 925,000 members in 1815 they grew to about 4 million in 1872. After 1875 the insurance aspect of the societies became increasingly important; and under the 1911 National Insurance Act the societies were given a new role as agents in the state scheme of national health insurance.

**Friends of the People** was an association of radical Whig aristocrats and parliamentarians launched in 1792 by Lord John *Russell, Charles *Grey, and their friends. It advocated moderate parliamentary reform as a means of preserving the constitution. Their most important contribution to the reform cause was probably their report on the state of parliamentary representation, corruption, and influence.

**Frobisher, Sir Martin** (c.1535–94). Although notable as an early English sea trader in west Africa and the eastern Mediterranean in the 1550s and later associated with *Drake in the West Indies expedition of 1585–6 and the defeat of the Spanish Armada in 1588, Frobisher is best remembered as an explorer who made three attempts in the period 1576–8 to find the North-West Passage. After more encounters with the Spanish in the 1590s, Frobisher was killed at Brest.

**Fry, Elizabeth** (1780–1845). Reformer. Elizabeth Fry was born into the quaker family of Gurney, bankers of Norwich, and brought up at Earlham Hall. At the age of 20 she married another quaker banker, Joseph Fry, and went on to raise a large family. Elizabeth Fry began visiting Newgate and in 1817 founded an association to help the female prisoners. In 1818 she gave evidence to a parliamentary committee, insisting on the importance of useful work for prisoners. By the 1820s she had acquired an international reputation, though her husband's bankruptcy in 1828 forced her to curtail her activities.

**Fuentes de Onoro, battle of,** 1811. On 3 May 1811 Wellington's Anglo-Portuguese army of 37,000 men tried to halt Marshal Masséna's 47,000-strong French army advancing to relieve Almeida. Masséna's attacks on the village of Fuentes de Onoro were repulsed. Along with *Albuera, Fuentes de Onoro stalemated the situation along the Portuguese border.

**Fulford, battle of,** 1066. Eight months after *Harold Godwineson's succession in January 1066, *Harold Hardrada, king of Norway, launched a major attack, in conjunction with *Tostig, Harold's brother. They sailed up the Ouse to Riccall, south of York. On 20 September, Edwin and Morcar, Harold's brothers-in-law and earls of Mercia and Northumbria, gave battle at Fulford, but were heavily defeated.

**Fursa, St** (d. c.649). Successfully establishing a monastery in Ireland, he left to escape the crowds he attracted, and, crossing to East Anglia c.633, built one near Yarmouth. When he withdrew again, he lived briefly as a hermit before going to Gaul. His monastery at Lagny, east of Paris, was built c.644. Fursa's fame, however, rests upon his visions of the other world.

**fyrd** In theory all freemen of Anglo-Saxon England were under an obligation to serve in the fyrd (army) when called upon. In practice communications were so difficult, crises so sudden, piratical or Viking raids so mobile, that the national militia was rarely summoned. Local raids were dealt with normally by the fyrd in the shires concerned, led by their *ealdormen. Though after the Conquest military provision was reorganized on the basis of knight service, the fyrd remained in existence and was called upon by William I and Rufus. The growing sophistication of weapons made local forces increasingly ineffective and it is perhaps fortunate that the fyrd's later manifestations, the trained bands, militia, or Home Guard, did not have to face a major invasion.

**Gabbard, battle of the,** 1653. An important naval battle towards the end of the first *Anglo-Dutch War. *Monck and *Blake with a large fleet encountered Martin Tromp near the Gabbard shoal, east of Harwich. The fighting lasted 12 and 13 June with the Dutch losing seventeen ships.

**Gaelic,** one of the Celtic dialects, is of the group known as the Goidelic, comprising Irish, Scottish Gaelic, and Manx. Scottish Gaelic and Manx developed through the migrations of Irish speakers in the late 4th cent. From the original settlement of *Dalriada the Gaels spread northwards and eastwards through Scotland cutting through native Pictish resistance. Following the establishment of the Gaelic church on *Iona by *Columba in the 6th cent., the Gaels acquired the means of spreading both their authority and their language. In the 9th cent., Gaels and Picts were finally united under a Gaelic king, probably of mixed parentage. In the 11th cent., *Malcolm Canmore, son of *Duncan, came to the throne with the aid of English forces and began to introduce Anglo-Norman customs and language. His descendants followed this policy and the Gaelic language was gradually replaced by English in state and church administration.

For 1755 it has been estimated that under a quarter of Scotland's population were Gaelic speakers—i.e. some 290,000. By 1971 Gaelic-only speakers numbered no more than 477 out of 5,228,000. Support for the Gaelic language began in the 19th cent., and in 1882 it became possible to study Gaelic as part of a university degree course. Today children can be educated in Gaelic at the primary level and it can be studied at secondary level. Since these efforts to save the language have been in place, the number of speakers has increased.

**Gaelic League** Founded in Ireland in 1893 with Douglas Hyde as first president, its intention was to revive the Irish language. Ostensibly non-political, the League inevitably attracted Irish nationalists. The work of the League ensured that Gaelic was declared the national language in 1922 and Douglas Hyde became first president of Eire in 1938.

**Gag Acts** *See* SIX ACTS.

**Gainsborough, Thomas** (1727–88). Painter. Gainsborough was born in Sudbury (Suffolk), the youngest of nine children. He showed early promise as a landscape artist and at 13 went to London to study. He set up as a portrait painter in 1752, first in Ipswich, then, in 1760, in Bath. Royal patronage and that of artists, aristocrats, and politicians ensured his lasting prosperity.

**Gaitskell, Hugh** (1906–63). As Labour party leader, Gaitskell exercised a more enduring impact on British politics than might be supposed from his brief ministerial career. After Winchester and Oxford, Gaitskell spent eleven years as an academic before taking up a wartime civil service post at the Ministry of Economic Warfare.

Elected to Parliament in 1945, Gaitskell was among the most impressive of Labour's new intake. Conspicuous success at the Ministry of Fuel and Power ensured rapid promotion and he became minister of state at the Treasury after the 1950 general election. Gaitskell was fortunate in the timing of his ministerial ascent. Many of the leading figures in the cabinet had been continuously in office for a decade. Gaitskell, by contrast, seemed to be the coming man of Labour politics. When illness forced the resignation of Stafford *Cripps in October 1950, the 44-year-old Gaitskell was an obvious successor as chancellor.

His only budget in 1951 proved to be controversial. His decision to introduce limited Health Service charges prompted the resignations of Aneurin *Bevan, Harold *Wilson, and John Freeman. *Attlee finally retired from the leadership in December 1955 and Gaitskell easily defeated Bevan and Herbert *Morrison for the succession. His first years as leader were relatively uneventful. He even succeeded in effecting a reconciliation with Bevan. Gaitskell performed effectively in Parliament over the *Suez crisis. With the Conservatives badly shaken by Suez, Labour approached the election of 1959 with confidence.

The result—a third successive Conservative victory and a substantially increased majority—was a considerable personal blow. Gaitskell determined to modernize the party to accommodate the aspirations of middle-class voters. To traditionalists, however, this meant diluting the socialist content of the party's ideology. Such opposition led to Gaitskell's defeat in 1960 over his attempt to remove clause 4 (the common ownership of the means of production) from the party's constitution. But he restored his authority a year later, resisting the left's attempts to commit Labour to unilateral nuclear disarmament.

Gaitskell died suddenly in 1963, having done much to re-establish Labour as a credible party of government—an achievement which benefited Harold Wilson in October 1964.

**Gallipoli/Dardanelles    campaign,** 1915–16. In February and March 1915, following a call for help from their Russian ally, the British and French navies mounted an attack against the Turkish defences on the Gallipoli peninsula. Despite bitter fighting, the British, French, Australian, and New Zealand forces only secured some small beachheads. Ironically the most successful part of the operation was the evacuation of the allied troops between December 1915 and January 1916.

**Galsworthy, John** (1867–1933). Galsworthy went to Harrow and New College, Oxford, began as a lawyer, but took up writing after meeting Joseph *Conrad. In his plays *The Silver Box* (1906), *Strife* (1909), and *Justice* (1910) he showed how heavily the law could bear upon the poor. The first novel of the Forsyte family appeared in 1906 as *The Man of Property*, followed by *In Chancery* (1920) and *To Let* (1921), brought together in 1922 as *The Forsyte Saga*. Galsworthy declined a knighthood in 1918, was awarded the OM in 1929, and the Nobel prize for literature in 1932. His plays lost their topicality, but the novels remained popular and the *Forsyte Saga* had a resounding success when transferred to television in the 1970s.

**Gambia** Formerly a British west African protectorate. Britain became interested in the Gambia in the late 16th cent., concentrating upon the river which gave its name to the territory and provided access to trade. Though something of a geographical anomaly, Gambia became independent in 1965.

**game laws** From the later 14th cent. the right to hunt game, and particularly the edible game of deer, pheasants, rabbits, and partridges, was legally restricted to persons with an income of £40 a year or more. The legal position was strengthened in 1671 in an effort to prevent anyone from hunting hares, partridges, and moor fowl, unless they had freeholds of at least £100 a year. Not surprisingly the laws produced considerable friction in the countryside. Efforts to repeal them began in the 1770s, but came to a successful conclusion only in 1831. However, poaching remained an offence, and as a result an undeclared state of war persisted in the countryside through the 19th cent.

**Gandhi,  Mohandas  Karamchand** (1869–1948), the 'Mahatma' or Great Soul. Born in an Indian princely state, he read for the bar in London. In 1893 he took up practice in Natal but rapidly turned to politics. He unified opposition among the disparate Indian community to the passing of racially discriminatory laws and pioneered the techniques of *satyagraha* (non-violent resistance). From the 1920s to early 1940s he led a series of passive resistance campaigns in pursuit of *Swaraj* (self-rule), which redefined the character of Indian nationalism. He sought tolerance between Hindus and Muslims and the eradication of caste untouchability. He refused to celebrate independence in 1947 and rejected the Pakistan partition. In January 1948 he was assassinated by a Hindu fanatic for his pro-Muslim sympathies.

**garden cities** Planned estates had been built by Robert *Owen and Titus *Salt in the earlier 19th cent., and by the Cadbury family at Bournville in the 1880s. Garden cities were conceived by Ebenezer Howard. His plan was for limited-size cities built on municipally owned low-cost agricultural land. The centre of each city would be a garden, ringed by civil and cultural amenities, city hall, museum, library, and theatre. Howard envisaged clusters of garden cities, linked by railways, and powered by new low-pollution electricity. In 1899 the Garden City Association was inaugurated. Prototype garden cities were built at Letchworth from 1903 and Welwyn from 1919, greatly influencing the new towns built after the Second World War.

**Gardiner, Stephen** (c.1497–1555). Bishop. Gardiner taught at Cambridge until taken up by *Wolsey as a secretary in 1524. Wolsey secured for him the mastership of Trinity Hall in 1525. On Wolsey's fall Gardiner became principal secretary to Henry VIII, and received the wealthy bishopric of Winchester in 1531. He acted on Henry VIII's behalf in his divorce suit and wrote *De vera obedientia* ('On True Obedience') in 1535 in defence of the king's actions. He promoted the Act of *Six Articles in 1539, and worked for Cromwell's fall the following year. From 1542 to 1547 he was one of Henry's leading ministers. On Edward VI's accession Gardiner was outspoken in opposition to Protector *Somerset's Reformation: from summer 1548 he was imprisoned in the Tower of London, losing his bishopric in February 1551. On the accession of Mary I he was restored to all his positions and made lord chancellor in August 1553. Gardiner married Mary and Philip, welcomed Cardinal Pole to England, and played a minor role in the persecution of leading protestants until his death on 12 November 1555.

**Garrick, David** (1717–79). Actor. Reared in Lichfield, he accompanied *Johnson to London (1737), but soon abandoned law studies for the wine trade; the appeal of acting and overnight success as Richard III (1741) led to further change. Having purchased a share of Drury Lane's lease, he set about reforming plays, players, and audiences, with modifications to theatre layout, stage design, and eventual introduction of concealed lighting. A devotion to Shakespeare induced textual reclamation from the Restoration adaptations, not always creditably, and his cherished Shakespeare

Jubilee at Stratford-upon-Avon (1769) was washed out.

**Garter, Order of the** This, the oldest and highest order, was instituted in 1348 by Edward III in imitation of King *Arthur and the great deeds of *chivalry. Membership was limited to the sovereign, prince of Wales, and 24 knights. The headquarters of the order is at Windsor, where St George's chapel was built by Edward IV. The significant decorations are the Star, a garter to be worn below the left knee, and a diagonal blue ribbon.

**Gascony** French region lying between the river Garonne and the Pyrenees. In the 11th cent. it was acquired by the dukes of Aquitaine; the 1152 marriage of *Eleanor of Aquitaine to Henry II meant that it passed into the hands of the kings of England. As a result of military defeats suffered in John's reign, from the early 13th cent. onwards the duchy of Aquitaine generally consisted of little but Gascony. The total disarray of Henry VI's government in 1450 allowed the triumphant Charles VI of France to walk into Gascony virtually unopposed.

**gavelkind** was the practice of partible or equal inheritance, as opposed to *primogeniture. It was predominant in Kent but found elsewhere, particularly in Wales and Ireland.

**Gaveston, Piers** (1284–1312). The most notorious favourite of Edward II was the son of a Gascon knight who served in Edward I's household. Whether his relationship with Edward II was sexual is not clear, but it seems likely that it was. Once Edward II came to the throne he showered his waspish 'brother' with favours, starting with no less than the earldom of Cornwall. Gaveston was forced into exile by the king's opponents in 1309, and again in 1311; he returned to surrender at Scarborough in Yorkshire, and died at the hands of his opponents at Blacklow Hill in Warwickshire in 1312.

**Gay, John** (1685–1732). One of the leading members of the remarkable group of authors in the early 18th cent., Gay was on close terms with *Pope, *Swift, and Arbuthnot. Of Devon dissenting stock, he moved to London, soon abandoned the silk trade, and established himself as a minor poet. His enormous success, *The *Beggar's Opera,* was produced at Lincoln's Inn Fields by John Rich in 1728 and was said to have 'made Gay rich and Rich gay'.

**genealogy,** the study of ancestry and family descent, is an indispensable handmaiden of history. In post-Roman Britain, it was important for monarchs to claim impressive credentials, however unlikely. *Bede insisted that *Hengist and Horsa were descended from Woden. In the Middle Ages, genealogy was related to heraldry and of concern largely to the monarchy and nobility. As the status of the gentry improved, their own interest in genealogy kindled. Richard III established the *College of Arms in 1484 and from the 15th cent. to 1688 the heralds conducted visitations to confirm or deny claims. Genealogical investigation was also a powerful motive behind the foundation of many 19th-cent. local history societies. The Society of Genealogists was founded in 1911. In the later 20th cent. there was a remarkable growth of interest in tracing *family history among ordinary people, using record offices and reference libraries.

**General Assembly of the Church of Scotland** Instituted in 1560 and meeting annually from the 18th cent., its constitution declares it to be the supreme court of a national church. Its national standing is symbolized by the attendance of the lord high commissioner (or the monarch), its freedom of action by that commissioner's place in a gallery outside assembly bounds.

**general elections** have changed over the years. Until the 17th cent., there was no statutory requirement about their frequency, and the *Triennial Act of 1694, which laid down that a general election must be held every three years at most, was the first effective legal provision. In 1716 the *Septennial Act lengthened the period to seven years, an interval which lasted until the *Parliament Act of 1911 reduced it to five years.

Many seats were uncontested right up until the end of the 19th cent. Even in 1900, 165 candidates in Great Britain were returned unopposed, and a further 69 in Ireland. Today it is normal for every seat to be contested.

In the 17th and 18th cents. general elections scarcely merited the term 'general'. They were essentially struggles between magnates and other interests for local paramountcy, and national factors played little part. Indeed, as late as 1830 it was not clear whether the Whigs or the Tories had won the general election, since many MPs sat loose to party. Elections in the 18th cent. did not choose governments, which, with heavy powers of patronage, could normally expect to carry any election. The decline of patronage made this increasingly hard and also created a vacuum which was filled by organized parties. Nowadays, general elections are held to choose a government and the choice of MPs is usually incidental to that decision.

**General Strike,** 1926. The strike arose from the problems of the coal industry. Miners were locked out on 30 April; the TUC negotiated with the government; but Baldwin's administration precipitated the strike by breaking off negotiations when the printers at the *Daily Mail* refused to print a leading article. The strike began at midnight on 3 May, with workers in printing, transport, iron and steel, gas, electricity, and building being called out first. The strike failed because of government preparations which enabled essential supplies and services to be delivered. After nine days the strike was called off, although the miners remained out for many months in the winter of 1926–7.

**general warrants** Eighteenth-cent. secretaries of state claimed a discretionary power in cases of seditious libel to issue general warrants for the arrest of persons unnamed. In 1763 Lord Halifax issued one for the apprehension of all connected with printing or publishing No. 45 of the *North Briton.* Forty-nine persons were arrested, including *Wilkes, author of the offending piece. But in December 1763 Chief Justice Pratt (*Camden) declared general warrants illegal. The House of Commons confirmed the ruling in 1766, and in 1769 Wilkes won £4,000 damages from Halifax for wrongful arrest.

***Gentleman's Magazine*** Issued monthly, the *Gentleman's Magazine* was the brainchild of Edward Cave and achieved a spectacular success. The first issue came out in 1731 and included reviews, essays, songs, births, deaths, and marriages. By the late 1730s Cave was claiming to sell 10,000 copies. In modified form the magazine lasted until 1907 and Cave's premises in Clerkenwell survive.

**gentry** Technically the gentry consists of four separately defined groups, socially inferior or only to the ranks of the peerage. The senior rank is that of *baronet, a position founded in 1611 by James I giving the possessor the hereditary right to be addressed as Sir. The second rank is that of *knight, originally a military honour, but increasingly employed in a secular manner as a reward for service to the crown. The third term 'esquire' originally had connotations with the battlefield. In the 14th cent. it was an honour which could be conferred by the crown, and by the 16th cent. it had a specific Office of Arms definition. Heraldic visitations, which began in 1530, were designed to oblige anyone claiming gentry status to prove their right. Increasingly through the 16th and 17th cents. the heralds found it difficult to enforce their authority, and numbers proliferated, both of esquires and particularly of the fourth gentry rank, that of gentleman. 'Gentleman' emerged as a separate title in connection with the statute of Additions of 1413 and, like esquire, was originally closely defined.

The concept of the gentlemanly way of life was current in the 16th cent., and became increasingly important by the 19th cent. A gentleman was a man who held a social position implying a style of living, usually without manual labour, and with connotations for the defence of honour.

In terms of wealth, contemporary social commentators such as King and Joseph Massie placed the gentry immediately below the peerage, while Daniel *Defoe argued that £100 a year was the minimum income required for a man to be a gentleman. Certainly this was the qualification figure required for JPs and *land tax commissioners. But since there were no automatic channels of admission to the peerage, some very wealthy men remained socially as gentry simply because they had no title. This anomaly is clearest by 1883 when John Bateman's survey of landownership revealed that 186 out of 331 landowners with 10,000 acres or more were gentry in this sense.

Informed estimates suggest that the gentry owned about 50 per cent of the landed wealth of the United Kingdom from the 17th cent. onwards. This position was maintained by the queue of businessmen, merchants, bankers, and industrialists to invest part of their fortune in landed estate. The link with landownership has to be treated with care since contemporaries were by no means clear in their understanding. Increasingly a man was a gentleman depending on his style of life, and without reference to his ownership of landed acres. This has given rise among historians to the concept of urban gentry, people who lived in towns, enjoying a reasonable income but lacking the landed acreage or the mansion associated with the country gentry. Many of these were members of professions—lawyers, doctors, and clergy—rising in status and in numbers during the 18th cent. As a result, the gentry as a social group has traditionally lacked cohesion.

**Geoffrey of Brittany** (1158–86). The trouble-making third son of Henry II and Eleanor of Aquitaine. He became duke of Brittany (initially in name only) in 1166 when his father invaded Brittany and forced Duke Conan to resign and agree to Geoffrey's betrothal to his daughter Constance. The wedding took place in 1181 and she was pregnant with *Arthur when he died. From 1173 onwards, when he joined his mother's revolt against his father, Geoffrey was in the thick of every Plantagenet family quarrel. He was at Paris plotting with King Philip Augustus of France when he was trampled to death in a tournament accident.

**Geoffrey de Mandeville** (d. 1144). An English baron whose stormy career caused controversy both in his own day and since. As keeper of the Tower of London and as possessor of large estates in Essex and East Anglia, he played a central role in the turbulent politics of Stephen's reign. Despite being created earl of Essex by the king in 1140, he joined Matilda in 1141 and was made hereditary sheriff of Essex. Like many others, swiftly disenchanted by her rule, by the late summer of that year he was back in Stephen's camp. Until mortally wounded while laying siege to Burwell, he did much of the damage which created the notion of Stephen's reign as 'the anarchy'.

**Geoffrey of Monmouth** (*c.*1100–55). Geoffrey was raised in Wales. As a young man, he went to Oxford and is thought to have been a canon of St George's church. His principal work, earning him fame, was the *History of the Kings of Britain* (*c.*1136). Written in chronicle form, it proved very popular, particularly in Wales, for the portrayal of a long and glorious Welsh past. It launched the romantic *Arthurian legend in European literature.

**Geoffrey 'Plantagenet'** (1113-51), count of Anjou (1129-51) and duke of Normandy (1144-51), became the husband of Henry I's designated heiress, the Empress *Matilda, on 17 June 1128. His political ambitions seem always to have been restricted to the traditional aim of the counts of Anjou, the conquest of Normandy. He never visited England during the civil war between his wife and King Stephen, which began in 1135, but his eventual conquest of the duchy in 1144 had a huge impact on Britain's history because it laid the foundation on which their son Henry II built the *Angevin empire.

**George I** (1660-1727), king of Great Britain and Ireland (1714-27) and elector of Hanover. George was the eldest son of Ernest Augustus, elector of Hanover (1692-8), and of *Sophia, granddaughter of James I of England, who herself became heir to the British throne by the 1701 Act of *Settlement. She died on 8 June 1714, and George succeeded peacefully on 1 August upon the death of Queen Anne.

George favoured a Whig administration, though he did employ a handful of senior Tories until the Jacobite Rebellion in 1715 led to the proscription of that party. The Whigs won the general election of 1715, and established their supremacy for the next four and a half decades.

George appears to have been diligent in politics, especially in his chosen fields of foreign affairs, diplomacy, and the army. His court was private and he much preferred the company of his German ministers to his British advisers, as well as that of the duchess of Kendal and the countess of Darlington. These two were long thought to have been his mistresses, and indeed Kendal was from 1691. Darlington, however, was his half-sister.

Relations between George and his son, the prince of Wales (later George II), were often strained, and in 1717 a violent quarrel erupted. The prince and his wife were expelled from the court and set up a rival one in *Leicester House. This quarrel coincided with the Whig schism in which *Walpole and *Townshend left the ministry of *Sunderland

and *Stanhope. In April 1720 the royal quarrel was patched up as a cover for the reconciliation of the ministry with the schismatic Whigs.

George frequently returned to Hanover in the summer months. The king's attachment to his electorate and its presumed prominent influence on English foreign policy created a good deal of friction. George, however, was close to some of his English ministers, particularly Stanhope, who looked after foreign policy, and Sunderland. It was the king's attachment to the latter which kept him in power after the bursting of the *South Sea bubble in 1720 (the most serious crisis of the reign) and Stanhope's untimely death in 1721. Sunderland's unexpected death in April 1722 forced George to accept Walpole (whose acumen in salvaging the financial disaster had in effect saved the dynasty) and Townshend as his chief ministers. He died of a stroke on 20 June 1727 at Osnabrück.

**George II** (1683-1760), king of Great Britain and Ireland (1727-60) and elector of Hanover. Best remembered for being the last British monarch to lead troops into battle (1743), George was much more than a soldier, and made sensible use of the still considerable political powers accorded to him by the 18th-cent. constitution.

The king could choose his own ministers. Walpole had served George I for many years and George II soon formed an equally successful relationship with him. He persuaded the king to keep Britain out of the War of Polish Succession and survived the turmoil of the *Excise crisis. Though Walpole fell in 1742, the Whig oligarchy remained and the king gravitated towards *Carteret, the German-speaking former diplomat, but his rivals, the *Pelham brothers (assisted by William *Pitt), forced him to resign in November 1744. The Pelhams reinforced their pre-eminence in February 1746 by threatening to resign unless the king took them into his full confidence. He was furious, but was unable to form a viable alternative government. Gradually George came to appreciate the prudence of Henry Pelham, 1st lord of the Treasury until his death in 1754. Thereafter, a period of instability set in; Pelham's brother, the duke of Newcastle, became 1st lord, but the Commons was restless, with Pitt and Henry *Fox ridiculing the government (of which they were both members). War and expediency brought Newcastle and Pitt together in 1757, to form one of the greatest ministries in British history. George never came to like Pitt, but they worked effectively together; even in old age the king remained at the heart of government and had, usually, the final word.

George II's reputation for parsimony was not restricted to his finances. He was an emotional miser too, having few, if any, close friends. This tendency extended to government. He was notoriously reluctant to 'dilute' the peerage with new creations, despite their political value. The one emotion he displayed liberally was a prodigiously bad temper. He was blunt, rude, and lacked social graces to a surprising degree. George had little interest in cultural or intellectual matters (with the exception of his patronage of *Handel). His wife Queen *Caroline, however, was renowned for her intellectual curiosity and quick wit. George loved her deeply, but it did not prevent him from taking a number of mistresses.

His beloved younger son was the duke of *Cumberland; he was very like his father in his devotion to the military. Cumberland's error of judgement and consequent resignation in 1757 cast a shadow over George's otherwise triumphant final years. The king's pride in Cumberland contrasts with the loathing he (and Queen Caroline) had for their heir, *Frederick, prince of Wales. Frederick's early death in 1751 provided the opportunity for reconciliation between the king and the princess of Wales and his grandson and heir.

During his reign George II demonstrated that his love of the military was not purely ceremonial. His courage in battle was obvious as early as 1708, when as Prince George Augustus of Hanover he fought as a British ally in the War of *Spanish Succession. His courage was required again during the War of Austrian Succession, not just on the battlefield at Dettingen, but in the face of an invasion by Charles Edward *Stuart in 1745. George was certain of victory, even when the Jacobites reached Derby. The *Seven Years War brought momentous British successes in the colonies and in Europe. George supervised military operations and appointments carefully, though preferring elderly commanders to the more enterprising younger officers advocated by Pitt.

**George III** (1738–1820), king of Great Britain and Ireland (1760–1820), and elector of Hanover. The reputation of George III has been revised perhaps to a greater degree than any other British monarch. He was born in England, the first Hanoverian monarch to be a native of his own kingdom. Upon the death of his father Frederick in 1751, George became heir to the throne. The young prince was not on good terms with his grandfather, George II, believing that the old king was the tool of corrupt politicians. A key influence on the formation of this naïve viewpoint was Lord *Bute, tutor to the prince from 1755. When George succeeded to the throne in 1760, Bute rapidly rose from courtier to cabinet minister and, in May 1762, became prime minister. Yet, Bute proved a disappointment and resigned within a year. Ministries followed each other in swift succession: there were four different premiers between the fall of Bute and the appointment of *North in 1770.

The advent of the North ministry inaugurated a period of political stability. The king behaved with impeccable constitutional propriety throughout North's twelve-year premiership. Ministers, not the crown, were responsible for policy. This was particularly the case with regard to America. Yet, once war had broken out, it became necessary for the rebels to describe matters differently and the *Declaration of Independence of 1776 enshrined the king as villain of the piece.

George III took a keen interest in the military struggle and refused to accept that America was lost, even after the disastrous defeat at *Yorktown in 1781. Bowing to Parliament's refusal to continue the war, the king reluctantly parted with North. The king tried to maintain some freedom of manœuvre by playing upon the rivalry between *Shelburne and *Rockingham, the leading opposition politicians who now formed a ministry. When Rockingham died unexpectedly in July 1782, George III appointed Shelburne as his successor. But Shelburne was forced to resign following a concerted attack by the followers of Charles *Fox and Lord North. The king viewed North's actions as personal betrayal, and remained implacably hostile to the coalition. The king's obvious dissatisfaction persuaded the younger *Pitt to negotiate secretly for the overthrow of the coalition, which was accomplished during the *India Bill crisis of 1783. Although the means had been underhand, the king's choice of Pitt proved excellent. Political stability was re-established and no serious threat arose until the king fell ill in the autumn of 1788. The ensuing *Regency crisis was precipitated by the apparent madness of the king. According to modern diagnosis he was suffering from acute intermittent porphyria, a hereditary metabolic disorder. The king recovered despite the treatment he received.

Pitt continued to dominate parliamentary politics, but found it necessary, in the wake of the French Revolution, to strengthen the ministry by incorporating *Portland and the conservative Whigs. The king benefited from a groundswell of enthusiasm for monarchy, becoming a personal symbol of national resistance. But the danger of revolution was not negligible, and rebellion in Ireland convinced ministers of the necessity of parliamentary union. Having achieved this objective, Pitt resigned in 1801 over George III's refusal to countenance the removal of residual penalties against catholics. George considered his coronation oath, with its pledge to uphold the protestant religion, to be absolutely binding. The fall of Pitt led to a period of factional instability, akin to the early years of the reign, but further complicated by fears for the king's mental state. A moderate proposal for relief, by the *Talents ministry in 1807, precipitated a ministerial crisis, during which the king reaffirmed his intransigence.

In 1810 the king suffered a final decline into mental derangement, exacerbated by increasing deafness and blindness. The following year a regency was established under his eldest son, the future George IV. As a hard-working monarch, devoted husband, and sincere Christian, George III compares favourably with his dissolute successor.

**George IV** (1762–1830), king of the United Kingdom of Great Britain and Ireland (1820–30), and king of Hanover. Brought up under strict discipline by his parents George III and Queen Charlotte, he was a high-spirited boy. In 1780 his father had to buy back the letters he had written to the actress Mary 'Perdita' Robinson. George then fell in love with Maria Fitzherbert. They married secretly in 1785 without his father's consent, so that the marriage was illegal under the *Royal Marriage Act, and as she was a Roman catholic it would have prevented his succession to the throne.

George was fascinated by the arts and had a lifelong mania for building. In 1787 he applied to Parliament for additional funds to pay his debts, but had to authorize his friend Charles *Fox to deny in the House of Commons that he was married. His subsequent disclosure of the truth to Charles *Grey resulted in a breach between him and his Whig political allies. They made up the quarrel in 1788 when his father suffered his first attack of mental illness, the Whigs proposing that George should be made regent with full use of all royal prerogatives, hoping that he would change the government in their favour. *Pitt defeated their scheme by proposing limitations on the regent's powers, but the king recovered before the regency came into effect.

When the French Revolutionary War began in 1793, George was again deeply in debt owing to the cost of building and furnishing Carlton House, his London residence, and the pavilion at *Brighton. In return for financial help the king insisted that he should marry a protestant princess, to secure the royal succession. The choice fell upon *Caroline of Brunswick-Wolfenbüttel in 1795. George, however, took an instant dislike to her coarse language, and flighty manner. They separated soon afterwards, though he had managed to father a child, Princess *Charlotte, born nine months after the wedding.

During the Napoleonic War of 1803–15 George was again unsuccessful in obtaining a military command. After Fox's death in 1806 he severed his political connection with the Whigs and in 1810, when his father's illness became permanent and he was appointed prince regent, he confirmed the existing Tory ministers in office. During the later war and post-war years he was very unpopular with his subjects, who contrasted his lavish life-style with the distress of the country. When he became king in 1820 his attempt to divorce his wife by a parliamentary Bill of Pains and Penalties on the grounds of her alleged immoralities aroused a public outcry against him in view of his own infidelities. His popularity sank to its nadir during this period but Caroline's death in 1821 and recovery from the economic recession marked a turning-point. George's love of pageantry, given full rein in the magnificent coronation which he himself designed in 1821, helped to boost his popularity.

George IV attempted to exert authority over his ministers and their policies, but he lacked political skill and persistence and he could always be outmanœuvred or outfaced. He was compelled to accept the repeal of religious discrimination against dissenters and catholics in 1828-9 and his reign witnessed a further decline in the 'influence of the crown'.

**George V** (1865–1936), king of the United Kingdom of Great Britain and Ireland and emperor of India (1910–36). The second son of Edward, prince of Wales (later Edward VII), George was not born to be king. His private education was followed by a naval career, but the death, at the beginning of 1892, of his elder brother, the duke of *Clarence, meant that he was now in direct line of succession after his father. The following year he married Princess Mary of Teck (formerly the fiancée of the duke of Clarence); the couple were, and remained, devoted to each other; there were six children of the marriage. George's naval experience left him with a deep respect for habits of routine and obedience.

When George's father succeeded as king on Victoria's death (22 January 1901), George undertook a strenuous round of international engagements as heir to the throne, visiting Australasia, South Africa, Canada, and Europe. But Edward VII's death in 1910 presented him, as king, with the first of a series of constitutional and political problems, which he handled with propriety.

The refusal of the House of Lords to approve the Liberal government's budget of 1909 had led to a general election (28 January 1910) at which the government was returned with a reduced but still effective majority. George gave an undertaking that, should it become necessary (which it did not), he would agree to the creation of a large enough number of peers to ensure the budget's passage into law. In December 1910 he authorized a second general election in order to test opinion on reform of the powers of the House of Lords; the passage of the *Parliament Act of 1911, destroying the Lords' power of veto over money bills, and severely restricting their ability to delay other bills, owed something to George's own common sense. This crisis was followed by another, over the government's intention to grant *Home Rule to Ireland, and the determination of the Ulster protestants, supported by the Conservative opposition, to take up arms unless Ulster remained part of the United Kingdom. The king did not take sides in this quarrel, but he used his influence with the Conservative leadership in order to moderate the tone of public utterances, and on 21 July 1914 invited representatives of all sides to a round-table discussion at Buckingham palace.

During the Great War, George, mindful of sensitivities over the German connections of the royal family, ordered that German names be replaced by English ones: the house of Windsor was inaugurated. In the years 1918–24 the political topography of Great Britain underwent a fundamental change, the Liberal Party being replaced by Labour as the only credible alternative to the Conservatives. When the first, minority, Labour government of Ramsay *MacDonald took office in January 1924, the king did much to ensure a smooth transition. In 1929, on the occasion of the formation of the second Labour government, he played a similar role. During the crisis of August 1931, which resulted in MacDonald's 'betrayal' of that government and agreement to head a national, all-party administration, the king's role was more controversial. He urged MacDonald to form such an administration, and played a part in persuading the Liberal and Conservative leaders (Herbert *Samuel and Stanley *Baldwin) to serve in it, under MacDonald's leadership.

George was a shy, reserved man, not blessed with an overabundance of intellect, who none the less did his duty in a selfless manner. He went out of his way to bring the monarchy closer to the common people. In 1924 he made the first of a series of radio broadcasts heard throughout the British empire; in 1932 he inaugurated the annual Christmas Day broadcasts by the sovereign. He attended rugby matches at Twickenham, cricket at Lord's, tennis at Wimbledon; but he also presented the trophy at the football Cup Final at Wembley. George V gave to the monarchy a quiet dignity, and in the process made it genuinely national and genuinely popular.

**George VI** (1895–1952), king of the United Kingdom of Great Britain and Northern Ireland (1936–52), and emperor of India. George was born at Sandringham on 14 December, the second son of the future George V and Queen Mary. He was christened Albert Frederick Arthur George, and known in the family as Bertie. As a child Prince Albert lacked close emotional contact with his parents and was often overshadowed by his elder brother, Edward. His subsequent insecurity meant he was intensely shy and developed a stammer.

In 1909–13 he studied at the Naval College at Osborne and then Dartmouth. Prince Albert then spent time at sea on the battleship *Collingwood* but his active career was not a success. He suffered from chronic seasickness and spent long periods on sick leave for gastric troubles, though he served in the battle of Jutland on 31 May 1916.

In 1920 he was granted the title of duke of York. By now he was occupied with official duties. In 1919 he had become president of the Industrial Welfare Society touring industrial areas, showing genuine concern for problems and developing the 'human touch'. He also founded the Duke of York's camp in 1921 to promote better relations between boys of different class backgrounds. At this time he fell in love with Lady Elizabeth Bowes-Lyon, young, spirited, and attractive. She finally agreed to marry him in 1923 and the wedding took place on 26 April at Westminster abbey. She was to be the stabilizing influence in his life and provide him with the love and support he had often been without. They had two daughters: Elizabeth Alexandra Mary born on 21 April 1926 and Margaret Rose born on 21 August 1930. They were devoted parents and formed a close family unit.

The duke and duchess toured the empire, visiting Ireland and East Africa in 1924, and New Zealand and Australia in 1925, opening the new parliament building in Canberra on 9 May. His stammer was still evident and made it difficult to make public speeches. In 1925 he was put in touch with Lionel Rogue, a speech therapist, who over the years helped him become a more assured speaker.

On 20 January 1936 George V died and by the end of the year Edward VIII had abdicated. The duke dreaded the prospect of becoming king, but resigned himself to the task. At the coronation on 12 May 1937 he was crowned George VI in an effort to restore a sense of continuity and stability.

The king and queen refused to leave London during the Blitz, although Buckingham palace was bombed nine times. Thus the royal family shared a sense of common danger with the nation. They toured devastated areas, met civilian workers, and the king devised the *George Cross medal for civilian gallantry. He also shared the grief when his youngest brother George, duke of Kent, was killed in action.

The post-war period was stressful for the king who fretted constantly. With Labour victory in 1945, he was worried at the scope and speed of the new legislative programme. Yet despite being a traditionalist, the king was not averse to social reform when necessary. He watched with great regret the dissolution of the Indian empire. In 1947 he toured South Africa in an attempt to strengthen ties to the Commonwealth, the future of which he was anxious to secure. The strains of war and the post-war period took their toll on his health. On 12 March 1949 he had an operation to remove a thrombosis on his right leg and on 23 September 1951 he had the whole of his left lung removed. Both operations were a success but he fought a losing battle to regain his health, and died in his sleep at Sandringham on 6 February 1952.

**George, St** St George, patron saint of England and of several other countries, is said to have been martyred at Lydda in Palestine in the 4th cent. and began to attract reverence in the 6th cent. The story of the dragon appears as late as the 12th cent. and is presumably a reminiscence of Perseus and Theseus. His adoption as patron saint of England is post-Conquest though a church in Doncaster was dedicated to him in 1061. Crusaders may have brought back accounts of the respect paid him in the Middle East and the red cross may have come from the same source. The cult probably gathered pace after the foundation of the Order of the *Garter in 1348, with the emphasis on chivalry and St George as patron.

**George of Denmark, Prince** (1653–1708), consort of Queen Anne. The younger son of Frederick III of Denmark, George was affable but dull. 'I have tried him drunk,' Charles II once remarked, 'and I have tried him sober and there is nothing in him.' His marriage to Anne in 1683 sealed a diplomatic concord between their respective kingdoms against the Dutch. Though dogged by ill-health, he was the queen's mainstay throughout her many personal and political tribulations.

**George Cross and Medal** The award was instituted by George VI in September 1940 for acts of outstanding heroism, particularly among the civilian population dealing with the *Blitz—firemen, police, ambulance men, and civil defence personnel.

**Gerald of Wales** (1146–1223). Gerald was born at Manorbier in Pembrokeshire with a Norman father and a Welsh mother. After education at Gloucester and at Paris, a promising career in the church (he was arch-deacon of Brecon by 1175) ran into difficulties and he consoled himself with his writing. He failed to become bishop of St Davids because the strong support given to him by Welsh princes may have alarmed the English. His best-known works were his accounts of Ireland and Wales—*Topography of Ireland* (1188), *Conquest of Ireland* (1189), *Journey through Wales* (1191), and *Description of Wales* (1194).

**Germain, Lord George** (1716–85), formerly Sackville. After a promising early career, both as politician and army officer, Sackville was court-martialled for disobeying orders at *Minden in 1759. Stripped of his rank and forbidden the court, he did not rehabilitate himself until the 1760s, eventually becoming American secretary in 1775. A flawed strategist, he must share responsibility for the defeat at *Saratoga (1777), having authorized two separate offensives, mistakenly hoping that each might succeed independently.

**Germanus of Auxerre, St** Soldier, bishop, and church emissary who visited Britain in AD 429 to counter heresy. In the early 5th cent. the teachings of *Pelagius were proving popular in Britain. In 429 the Roman ecclesiastical authorities in Gaul dispatched Germanus to Britain to combat Pelagianism by preaching the true faith—Divine Grace—in British churches and the countryside. Before becoming a bishop Germanus had been a soldier, and he defeated *Picts and *Saxons in a battle where he gave his troops the battle-cry 'Alleluia'.

**Ghana** Formerly the Gold Coast, British west African colony and protectorate. British traders became interested in the Gold Coast in the second half of the 17th cent., attracted by the trade in gold and, increasingly, in slaves for the Americas. It was decided to establish a crown colony in 1874. The development of cocoa as an export crop brought prosperity to the country and made possible the expansion of European education there. The Gold Coast then became the leader in the nationalist movement in British African dependencies and gained its independence, as Ghana, in 1957.

**Ghent, treaty of,** 1815. Peace talks to end the *War of 1812 between Britain and the USA began at Ghent (modern Belgium) in August 1814. A treaty was signed on 24 December. It resolved none of the proclaimed causes of the war. Because of slow communications, a major battle was fought after the conclusion of the treaty, at New Orleans in January 1815.

**Gibbon, Edward** (1737–94). Historian. After fourteen months at Magdalen College, Oxford, which the laziness of the dons made 'the most idle and unprofitable of my whole life', Gibbon converted to catholicism and had to leave. His enraged father sent him to Lausanne (Switzerland), under a Calvinist tutor, where he learned French, reverted to protestantism, and determined to write some great work. In 1773 he began serious work on *Decline and Fall of the Roman Empire*, the inspiration of which was a visit to Rome in 1764, described in his *Memoirs*. The following year he entered Parliament, was given minor office by Lord North, but never spoke: 'the great speakers', he wrote memorably, 'fill me with despair, the bad ones with terror'. The first volume came out in 1776 and established him at once: the work was completed in 1788. The intrinsic merits of his book, its scholarship, silky style, and philosophic detachment, made it an enduring classic.

**Gibbons, Grinling** (1648–1721). Wood-carver and sculptor. Born in Rotterdam and probably trained in Holland, he was in England by 1668. Gibbons's decoration appears in Windsor castle and Hampton Court and also in St Paul's cathedral on the choir-stalls and organ screen. One of the most skilful wood-carvers ever, his garlands of fruit, flowers, small animals, and cherubs led Horace Walpole to say, 'There is no instance of a man before Gibbons who gave to wood the loose and airy lightness of flowers.'

**Gibbons, Orlando** (1583–1625). Jacobean composer and keyboard player who contributed to most musical genres of the time. A chorister at King's College, Cambridge, in 1596, by 1605 Gibbons was a gentleman of the Chapel Royal, later serving as joint organist. He was also organist at Westminster abbey from 1623. Gibbons's madrigals favoured the serious approach of the moralistic 'Silver Swan': 'More geese than swans now live, more fools than wise.'

**Gibbs, James** (1682–1754). As an architect Gibbs was unusual for his time, not because he was Scottish-born or even because he was Roman catholic, but because he spent six years in Rome and studied under Carlo Fontana (1703–9). His thought was unblushingly baroque. Appointed as surveyor for the '50 new churches' legislated for London in 1711, Gibbs built St Mary-le-Strand (1714), but he lost the 'political' surveyorship in 1715. He was appointed architect for the unbaroque St Martin-in-the-Fields (1722–6). Probably his best-known secular building is Oxford's Radcliffe library, the 'Camera', completed 1748; at Cambridge, he built the Senate House and Gibbs's Building at King's.

**Gibraltar** At the southern tip of Spain, 1,270 feet at its highest point, 'The Rock' commands the western entrance to the Mediterranean. The name derives from Djebel Tarik (Mountain of Tarik) after Tarik ibn Ziyad, the general leading the Moorish invasion of Spain in 711. In 1704, during the War of the Spanish Succession, it was captured by an Anglo-Dutch fleet under Sir George *Rooke and ceded to Britain by the treaty of Utrecht (1713). It has remained in British hands ever since.

**Gibson, Edmund** (1669–1748). Bishop of London, scholar and prelate. Educated at Oxford, Gibson produced several translations of major historical works, including *Camden's *Britannia*, before being ordained in 1697. His extensive researches in ecclesiastical law resulted in 1713 in the publication of his monumental *Codex juris*. A high-church Whig, he was appointed bishop of Lincoln in 1716, and in 1723 translated to the see of London. In the early years of his administration *Walpole relied heavily on him in church affairs and patronage. Their association ended in 1736 over Walpole's support for the Quakers' Bill, which Gibson had advised his fellow bishops to oppose. Gibson was passed over for Canterbury in 1737.

**Gielgud, John** (1904–2000). Actor, director, and producer. Great-nephew of Ellen *Terry, sharing her passion for *Shakespeare and the Terry mellifluence of voice, Gielgud devoted himself wholly to the theatre as one of his generation's greatest stage and screen actors. Joining the Old Vic, his portrayal of Hamlet (1929) preceded a series of impressive performances. Ambition to direct was realized in the 1930s (Queen's and Haymarket theatres), followed by wartime productions in Britain and abroad. In the 1950s he seemed happier in classical revivals and solo Shakespeare recitals than new drama—he was knighted in 1953—but his versatility led to acclaim in contemporary works later.

**Gilbert, Sir Humphrey** (c.1537–83). A half-brother of *Ralegh, Gilbert was able to get official support for his interests in overseas activities. After service in Ireland, and as an MP, he was knighted and began expeditions with a patent from the queen to plant colonies in North America. A venture in concert with Ralegh in 1578–9 apparently failed, but in 1583 Gilbert annexed *Newfoundland, though no settlers were left. He and his ship were lost on the return voyage.

**Gilbert, William Schwenck** (1836–1911). Gilbert is one of the rare examples where the librettist is as well known as the composer. His achievement in his partnership with *Sullivan was threefold. Like all good librettists, he stimulated his composer and helped him to produce sparkling music. Secondly, Gilbert spiced his plots with contemporary satire, which helped to sell tickets, had a cutting edge, and has lasted remarkably well. Finally, like all great writers, he created his own world, a world of gentle cynicism, honest simplicity, and legal quibbling, and he peopled it with memorable characters—the reluctant policemen; the decent, patriotic pirates; the philosophical sentry; the modern major-general; the skittish judge in *Trial by Jury*.

Gilbert was born in London and educated at King's College. He spent his early years as an 'impecunious party' practising the law, before turning, with great success, to literature. He met Sullivan in 1871 and *Trial by Jury*, their first success, was produced in 1875. They worked together until 1896 when *The Grand Duke* was a comparative failure. Gilbert's many publications brought him considerable wealth, he was knighted in 1907, and he died after rescuing a woman from drowning in the lake at his home.

**Gilbert and Ellis islands** *See* KIRIBATI.

**Gilbert of Sempringham, St** (*c.*1083–1189). Founder of the *Gilbertines, a purely English order. A wealthy Norman knight's son, Gilbert became incumbent at Sempringham (Lincs.), where (*c.*1131) he allowed a group of devout women to use a building next to the church. Failing to persuade the general chapter of Cîteaux to oversee the order, he was confirmed as administrator by Pope Eugenius III (1147). Growth was so rapid that by his death there were 1,500–2,000 members.

**Gilbertines** St *Gilbert became spiritual adviser to a group of seven anchoresses *c.*1131. His following increased and in 1147 they were organized as an order. It enjoyed considerable success in eastern England, and by Gilbert's death in 1189 there were nine double houses and four for canons only. However, the order never successfully spread outside England and disappeared following the *dissolution of its 24 communities in 1538–9

**Gildas** (fl. some time between *c.*475 and *c.*550). An important British cleric, Gildas is chiefly known for his tract *On the Ruin of Britain*. This work outlines some of the history of 4th- and 5th-cent. Britain. He is the only early author to provide an account of the first Saxon settlements in Britain.

**Gillray, James** (1756–1815). Caricaturist. Abandoning the discipline of reproductive engraving for pungently witty etching, and stimulated by the political satires of James Sayers, Gillray played a key role in the evolution of pictorial journalism by his development of recognizable caricature. Using brightly coloured, almost grotesque distortion of an individual's salient features, Gillray targeted the royal family, politicians, society figures, exquisites, and charlatans.

**Giric,** king of Picts (877/8–885/9). The sources for the succession in what (*c.*900) became the kingship of the Scots are meagre. Two names of possible kings in this period are *Eochaid and Giric. Giric may have been Eochaid's guardian. By the 12th cent., however, he acquired legendary status as liberator of the Scottish church from Pictish oppression and (fantastically) conqueror of Ireland and most of England.

**Girl Guides** Female branch of the Scouting movement founded in 1910. At the first big rally of the *Boy Scouts at Crystal Palace in September 1909 there appeared a large contingent of girls dressed in the Scout hat and scarf. *Baden-Powell was not in favour of incorporating girls into his organization, believing it would discourage boys from joining. The following year his sister Agnes established the Girl Guides and together they wrote the Guide Handbook *How Girls Can Help Build up the Empire*. The Brownies were formed in 1914 for 8–11-year-olds. They were originally called Rosebuds, but the name Brownie was adopted in 1918. Today there are estimated to be around 8.5 million Guides in over 100 countries.

**Gladstone, William Ewart** (1809–98). Statesman and author. Gladstone was in office every decade from the 1830s to the 1890s, starting as a Tory, ending as a Liberal-radical. Born in Liverpool on 29 December 1809, the son of John Gladstone, a merchant from Scotland, Gladstone was educated at Eton and Christ Church, Oxford. Intensely religious, he at first felt drawn to ordination in the Church of England, but not sufficiently to go against his father's objections. While president of the Oxford Union, he strongly opposed the Whigs' proposals for parliamentary reform and was elected to the Commons as a Tory in December 1832. Influenced by both *Coleridge and the *Oxford movement, he published *The State in its Relations with the Church* (1838) and *Church Principles* (1840) arguing that the Church of England should be the moral conscience of the state; *Macaulay, in a savage refutation, called him 'the rising hope of those stern and unbending tories'. In *Peel's government 1841–5 he was vice-president and then president of the Board of Trade. He resigned in 1845 over the *Maynooth grant, returning in 1846 to be briefly colonial secretary and to support repeal of the Corn Laws.

In 1852, as a member of the *Aberdeen coalition, he began the first of his four terms as chancellor of the Exchequer (the others were 1859–66, 1873–4, and 1880–2); his greatest budgets were those of 1853 and 1860. Gladstonian finance emphasized a balanced budget, minimum government spending, the abolition of protective tariffs, and a fair balance between direct and indirect taxes. In his 1853 budget he repealed about 140 duties; in 1860 he repealed duties on 371 articles, many of them as a consequence of the treaty with France which he planned and Richard *Cobden negotiated.

In the 1850s and 1860s Gladstone emerged as a politician of national standing with a reputation for oratory. Though MP for Oxford University from 1847 to 1866, he began to take increasingly radical positions, especially on questions like parliamentary reform. However, the modest Reform Bill proposed by Gladstone and *Russell in 1866 led to the temporary disintegration of the Liberal Party and the resignation of the government. Gladstone responded with increasingly radical demands on other questions, such as the abolition of compulsory church rates and disestablishment of the Irish church. He led the Liberals to win the 1868 election and became prime minister in December 1868: on receiving the queen's telegram of summons, 'My mission is to pacify Ireland.' In his first government, one of the greatest of British reforming administrations, he disestablished the Irish church (1869), passed an important Irish Land Bill (1870), but failed with his Irish University Bill (1873, when the government resigned, only for *Disraeli to refuse to take office). His government also abolished purchase of commissions in the army and religious tests in the universities; it established the *secret ballot and, for the first time, a national education

system in England, Wales, and Scotland (1870–2). Gladstone called and lost a snap general election in January 1874. He then announced his retirement from the party leadership.

Gladstone, 64 in 1874, expected a retirement of scholarship. In his lifetime he published over 30 books and pamphlets and about 200 articles. In his pamphlets of 1851–2 and a stream of subsequent works, Gladstone opposed the 'temporal power' of the papacy. He opposed the declaration of papal infallibility in 1870 and nurtured links between Orthodoxy and Anglicanism as an antidote to Roman catholicism. Not surprisingly, therefore, he was swiftly drawn into the Bulgarian atrocities campaign in 1876. A series of speeches and pamphlets broadened into a general attack on 'Beaconsfieldism' and having fought the *Midlothian campaign 1879–80 he was elected MP for Midlothian. He again became prime minister in 1880. His second government passed an important Irish Land Act (1881) and, after initial rejection by the Lords, the Reform Act of 1884; but it failed to establish elected local government for Ireland or for Great Britain.

Since the 1860s, Gladstone had tried to meet Irish demands. He accompanied the concessionary *Land Act (1881) with coercion, imprisoning *Parnell, and breaking the power of the *Irish Land League. From 1882, disregarding the set-back of the *Phoenix Park murders, he sought to encourage the constitutional character of the *Home Rule movement. His government resigned in 1885, unable to agree on local government for Ireland. Gladstone encouraged Parnell to bring forward a Home Rule proposal and fought the general election of November 1885 on a manifesto which carefully did not exclude it. In January 1886, his son Herbert having flown the *'Hawarden Kite' and Lord *Salisbury having turned down Gladstone's proposal that the Tory government introduce a Home Rule measure with bipartisan support, Gladstone formed his third cabinet. He saw devolution as the best means of maintaining Ireland within the United Kingdom and drew up a Home Rule Bill, providing for a legislature with two Houses in Dublin. This was too bold for his party and the bill was defeated in the Commons in June 1886, many *Liberal Unionists defecting and eventually forming their own party.

In foreign policy, Gladstone stood for an international order governed by morality. His first government submitted the *Alabama* dispute to international arbitration and paid the hefty fine, thus clearing the way for good relations with the USA. In the Midlothian campaign, Gladstone laid out 'six principles' of foreign policy, which recognized the equal rights of nations and the blessings of peace. In office in the 1880s, however, Gladstone found himself intervening in unpalatable ways; to maintain order in *Egypt, he bombarded Alexandria in 1882 and then invaded Egypt in what was intended as a brief occupation. In 1881, war against the Boers in South Africa included the disaster of *Majuba Hill. Order had also to be established in the *Sudan and Gladstone, despite misgivings, failed to prevent Lord Hartington and others sending Charles *Gordon to a Sudanese imbroglio partly of Gordon's own making; Gordon's death in 1885 was a further embarrassment to a beleaguered government.

Gladstone was aged 75 when his first Government of Ireland Bill was defeated. Committed to campaigning for another attempt, he led the Liberal Party in opposition 1886–92, winning the general election of 1892. In 1892 he formed his fourth and last government. In 1893 he successfully piloted his second Government of Ireland Bill through the Commons after 82 sittings; the Lords then brusquely rejected it. His eyesight deteriorating, he finally resigned the premiership in March 1894, aged 84. He died on Ascension Day, 19 May 1898.

Gladstone was an impressive man with a large head and a powerful voice, his fitness maintained by long walks and his legendary tree-felling. Intense sexuality competed with equally intense religious belief, and he had difficulty in balancing the two when he undertook his 'rescue' work with prostitutes. These inner struggles combined with outward confidence to make him a very characteristic Victorian.

**Glamorgan** County of south Wales. It was part of the Welsh kingdom of Glywysing, but in the 10th cent., under Morgan Hen, became known as Gwlad Morgan. Under the Normans it was converted to the lordship of Glamorgan, and remained a lordship of the march until 1536, when it was made into a

shire at the Act of *Union with England. In 1974 it was divided into three—South, Mid, and West *Glamorgan.

The county was best known for the coalfield and the mining villages strung out along the valleys. The iron and steel industry of the late 18th and 19th cents. developed on the northern outcrop in places such as Merthyr Tydfil. The British Steel plant at Margam in West Glamorgan is the contemporary successor. Coal-mining has virtually ceased. Modern industry has collected about the M4 motorway, and north of *Cardiff, which grew as a port and is now the capital of Wales.

**Glamorgan, Edward Somerset, 1st earl of, 2nd marquis of Worcester** (1603–67). Somerset was born at Raglan and in 1642–5 held south Wales for the king. After *Naseby, Herbert was made earl of Glamorgan and sent to Ireland to treat with his fellow-catholics in the *Kilkenny Confederation. His private instructions were to obtain Irish troops at all costs. Victim of Charles I's tricky diplomacy, Glamorgan's secret treaty made such sweeping concessions to the catholics, that the king was obliged to repudiate it. Glamorgan recovered his estates at the Restoration.

**Glamorgan, kingdom of** A medieval Welsh kingdom which emerged from an earlier kingdom called *Morgannwg. It may be equated with the post-Roman kingdom of Glywysing, whose line of kings from Meurig ap Tewdrig lasted until the late 11th cent. From the 1090s Robert *Fitzhamon and the Normans occupied the lowlands and established a marcher lordship called Glamorgan.

**Glamorgan, Mid, South, and West** These three counties were created by the Local Government Act of 1972 and came into operation in 1974. They were in being for only 22 years before being replaced in 1996. In April 1996 eight unitary authorities were substituted. They are, with approximate populations in brackets, Swansea (225,000), Neath and Port Talbot (136,000), Bridgend (130,000), Vale of Glamorgan (122,000), Rhondda, Cynon, Taff (232,000), Merthyr Tydfil (55,000), Caerphilly (171,000), Cardiff (317,000).

**Glanvill, Ranulf** (d. 1190). One of Henry II's most influential legal and administrative experts, though he is no longer regarded as the author of *The Laws and Customs of the Kingdom of England*, the first systematic treatise on English common law. Younger son of a Suffolk baron, he became sheriff of Yorkshire in 1164, made his name as a soldier when he captured King William of Scotland at *Alnwick in 1174, and rose rapidly in Henry II's service. From 1180 he was chief *justiciar at a time of significant development for the English legal system.

**Glasgow,** an ancient burgh (1175–8), first developed as an ecclesiastical centre on a hill near the cathedral. Having a grammar school from the early 14th cent., in 1451 the burgh acquired its university by papal bull and became an archbishopric in 1492. From the mid-17th cent. Glasgow began to develop its overseas trade with Europe and the American colonies. After the *Union of 1707 Glasgow dominated the tobacco trade and the city with about 12,000 inhabitants in 1700 began to grow as a manufacturing centre.

By 1776 Glasgow merchants imported more than half of Britain's tobacco and had lucrative re-export markets in Europe. The improvement of Glasgow harbour and the development of a diversified industrial economy had also progressed; the problems posed by the American War led to the formation of the Glasgow Chamber of Commerce (1783) and the growth of the West Indies trade. Cotton imports became significant, and Glasgow by 1850 had become a manufacturing city with a population of 345,000. Situated in a region rich in coal and iron, Glasgow became a major shipbuilding and engineering centre, the Clyde leading the world for tonnage launched and railway rolling stock and machinery produced. The 20th cent. witnessed the decline of heavy industries. Service industries gradually provided more employment, and consumer industries became more significant.

**Glasgow cathedral** The earliest church, dedicated to the Holy Trinity, was part of a monastic foundation established by St Kentigern (more popularly, St Mungo, d. 603) on ground consecrated by St *Ninian in the 5th cent. This site is now covered by the Blacader aisle. The diocese of Glasgow was re-established by David I and the first stone building consecrated in 1136 in his presence. It is now

crown property, worshipped in by the *Church of Scotland in the reformed tradition, under presbyterian government.

**Glastonbury,** a Somerset market town, is distinguished by a conical hill, Glastonbury Tor. Noted for its Iron Age lake village settlements, its magnificent medieval Benedictine abbey was a centre of pilgrimage, inspired by a complex of legends about *Arthur, Joseph of Arimathea, and the Holy Grail. A monastery existed here at least from the 6th cent. At the abbey's dissolution (1539), Abbot Whiting was hanged on the Tor.

**glebe** was a portion of land allocated to support a priest. Though originally it was intended as the sole support, it soon required substantial augmentation, usually through tithes.

**Glencoe massacre** As part of the pacification of the Highlands after the collapse of the Jacobite rising of 1689–90 a royal order required all clan chieftains to take an oath of allegiance to William and Mary. The chief of the Macdonalds of Glencoe, near Fort William, did so, but only after the time limit of 1 January. The Scottish secretary, Sir John *Dalrymple, used his lateness as a pretext to send a force to Glencoe to exact submission. The officers and men of this force were Campbells, hereditary enemies of the Macdonalds. After being given traditional Highland hospitality, on 13 February 1692 the soldiers massacred some 40 of their hosts, and many of those who escaped perished in winter storms.

**Glenfruin, battle of,** 1603. The clan Gregor in Scotland had long been troublesome. After their attack on the Colquhouns on 7 February 1603 at Glenfruin near Loch Lomond, they were subjected to draconian measures, designed to extirpate them.

**Glenlivet, battle of,** 1594. Throughout the 1580s and 1590s, the catholic lords in Scotland were in touch with Philip II of Spain about an invasion to restore catholicism. In October 1594 Huntly and Erroll joined forces and on the 3rd defeated at Glenlivet a larger royalist force led by the inexperienced Argyll. But the rebels did not pursue their victory, and Spanish troops were not forthcoming.

**Glenshiel, battle of,** 1719. A small Spanish force landed at Loch Alsh in April 1719 to support the Jacobite cause. But they received little local support, and Wightman advanced against them from Inverness. On 10 June the two groups met at Glenshiel. After a short engagement, the Scottish Jacobites fled and the Spaniards surrendered.

**Globe theatre** Built 1598/9 on Bankside in Southwark, by Richard Burbage the actor, its sign showed Hercules carrying the globe on his shoulders. Burned down in 1613, it was rebuilt but closed by the puritans in 1642 and demolished. *Shakespeare was both a shareholder and an actor and several of his plays, including *Romeo and Juliet*, *Othello*, *Lear*, and *Macbeth*, were first performed there. A replica of the first theatre was opened in 1996.

**Glorious First of June,** 1794. An Anglo-French naval battle fought some 400 miles out in the Atlantic from the Breton peninsula, which shelters the French naval base of Brest. Lord *Howe's strategy was to watch Brest from Torbay. The battle's immediate cause was Villaret de Joyeuse's evasion of Howe in order to cover a 117–strong convoy bound for Brest from America with 67,000 barrels of wheat flour for the critically under-provided French capital. By a brilliant chase in foggy conditions, Howe intercepted the French, taking six ships prize and sinking another. But the convoy from America reached Brest unscathed on 15 June.

**Glorious Revolution** Title given to the revolution of 1688–9, which resulted in the 'abdication' of James II and the succession of William III and Mary II. Participants had differing objectives. Tories and Anglican clergy wanted to stop James undermining the church. Whigs aimed to depose James and limit the powers of the crown. Ordinary people detested James for his catholicism. William needed to remove a potential ally of Louis XIV and lead England into the war against France that had just begun.

In June 1688 William instigated an invitation from two Tories, four Whigs, and Bishop *Compton to intervene. The birth that month of an infant prince to James had transformed the political future: he would succeed James in place of Mary (his eldest, protestant daughter, married to William). William's intervention was necessitated by the size of James's professional army. However, William was promised that most of its officers would defect. When this happened soon after William landed at Torbay on 5 November James found that he could not fight a battle. Demoralized, James tried to fly the country but was stopped. A second successful escape to France was the direct result of William's pressure. This left a vacuum. The *Bill of Rights (1689) followed the Whig formula, construing James's flight as abdication, declaring the throne vacant, and William and Mary as joint sovereigns.

**Gloucester** The earliest Roman military site, of *c.* AD 50, was at Kingsholm. The move to the present site took place in the mid-60s with the building of a legionary fortress. This was turned into a *colonia* for legionary veterans under Nerva (96–8). As elsewhere, well-appointed houses became more common at Gloucester in the 3rd and 4th cents. There is no evidence that the town was still in being when it fell to the Anglo-Saxons after the battle of *Dyrham in 577.

Gloucester revived as a royal and ecclesiastical centre in the 7th cent., and as a fortified and planned town (burh) in the 9th. Situated at the lowest point bridgeable on the Severn (until 1966), it was long an important inland port. The medieval town was dominated by St Peter's abbey (created the cathedral in 1541) and the Norman castle: the Norman kings wore their crown at Gloucester annually and the town then ranked among the ten richest in England.

**Gloucester, diocese of** The see, conterminous with Gloucestershire, was founded in 1541 by Henry VIII from part of the *Worcester diocese. The Norman cathedral, previously St Peter's Benedictine abbey church, was partly transformed in Perpendicular style, reputedly the earliest example, by the inflow of money from pilgrims to the shrine of Edward II. The 14th-cent. fan-vaulted cloisters are among the finest in England.

**Gloucester, Gilbert de Clare, 4th earl of** (d. 1230). Gloucester had been one of the barons in opposition to John and was among the 25 appointed in 1215 to see that *Magna Carta was carried out. Consequently he was excommunicated by Innocent III when John did his deal with the papacy. After John's death, Gloucester supported the dauphin's attempt on the throne and was captured at the battle of *Lincoln in 1217. In later years he campaigned against the Welsh.

**Gloucester, Gilbert de Clare, 6th earl of** (1243–95). On succeeding his father in 1262, Gloucester joined de *Montfort's party in opposition to Henry III and fought at *Lewes in 1264 capturing the king. But he soon changed sides, joined Prince Edward, and was prominent in the defeat of de Montfort at *Evesham in 1265. Much of his time was devoted to holding back the Welsh under *Llewelyn and he was responsible for building the great castle at Caerphilly.

**Gloucester, Humphrey, 1st duke of** (1390–1447). The youngest son of Henry IV and brother of Henry V. Created duke of Gloucester in 1414, Humphrey played a prominent role, both in France and at home, during his brother's reign. He became protector of England following Henry's death in 1422, surrendering the office in 1429 when Henry VI was crowned, but continued as president of the minority council until 1437. These years were dominated by his quarrel with Cardinal *Beaufort, which caused disruption in 1425–6, 1432, and 1440. The scandal of his duchess's trial for witchcraft finally discredited him in 1442. In 1447 he was accused of treason, imprisoned at Bury St Edmunds, and died in suspicious circumstances before he came to trial. He bequeathed his substantial library to the University of Oxford, where it forms the nucleus of the Bodleian collection.

**Gloucester, statute of,** 1278. This was an important attempt by Edward I to tighten up royal authority. Writs of *quo warranto were to be issued to anyone claiming territorial franchises.

**Gloucester, Thomas, duke of** (1355–97). Also known as Thomas of Woodstock, from his birthplace. He was the youngest son of Edward III, and uncle to Richard II. In 1376 he was declared constable of England. After serving in France and against the Scots, he was created duke of Gloucester in 1385. He took a prominent part against the royal favourite Michael de la *Pole. In 1387 he

defeated de Vere (*Oxford) at *Radcot Bridge, occupied London, seized the king, and used the *Merciless Parliament against his adversaries. For some years there was an uneasy *rapprochement* with Richard, but in 1397 Gloucester was seized, and taken to Calais, where he died, having apparently been smothered under a feather bed.

**Gloucestershire** is one of the bigger counties, even after losing part of its southern fringe to *Avon in the reorganization of 1972. The balance of the county has been much affected by two great towns. *Bristol was a major city with a mint well before the Conquest and in 1373 was given status as a county in its own right. Consequently it was outside county government. Cheltenham was a mushroom development of the late 18th cent., after the celebrated visit by George III in 1789 had helped to spread the fame of its waters.

Roman Gloucestershire was prosperous. A military base was soon established at *Gloucester (Glevum); *Cirencester (Corinium) became the second largest town in Roman Britain; great villas at *Woodchester and at Chedworth testify to the wealth of some of the inhabitants. The local inhabitants were the *Dobunni tribe. After the withdrawal of the legions, much of Gloucestershire fell to the Saxons in 577, when *Ceawlin of Wessex defeated British chiefs near Cirencester. But Wessex did not long retain the area. In 628, *Penda, pagan king of *Mercia, defeated the Wessex levies, and took possession. The eastern part became the kingdom of the *Hwicce under Mercian overlordship: the western fringes of the Forest of Dean formed part of the autonomous kingdom of the *Magonsaetans. This division was reflected in the ecclesiastical organization. The Hwicce territories became part of the see of *Worcester, while the Magonsaetans fell under the jurisdiction of *Hereford, founded in 676. The area changed hands again, falling once more to Wessex: *Athelstan pushed back the Welsh, with the boundary becoming the Wye rather than the Severn, and died at Gloucester in 940.

After the Norman Conquest, Gloucestershire, first named as a county in 1016, was still a frontier region, and the earl of Gloucester had *palatine powers. The Cotswold pastures had proved ideal for sheep, and a flourishing cloth industry established itself around Stroud and Dursley. The creation of a bishopric at Gloucester in 1541, after the *dissolution of the monasteries, gave a shot in the arm to the county town.

As the cloth industry in the east and mining in the west went into decline, the county's industries diversified—wagon works at Gloucester, aeronautics at Bristol, piano-making, printing, furniture, chemicals, and tourism in the Cotswold valleys. In the 1960s the county was criss-crossed by the M4 running east-west and by the M5 running north–south: the interchange at Almondsbury was briefly a traffic sensation. Even more important was the Severn bridge in 1966 which brought to an end the old Beachley–Aust ferries. A second bridge opened in 1996.

### Glyndŵr (Glendower), Owain (c.1359–c.1415), self-styled prince of Wales. A wealthy landowner in north-east Wales, his father was descended from princes of *Powys and his mother from princes of *Deheubarth. Owain was a well-to-do gentleman and became a retainer (by 1387) of the lord of Chirk, Richard Fitzalan, earl of Arundel. By 1400 conditions in Wales were ripe for rebellion.

Glyndŵr took the lead partly because of personal grievances against Lord Grey of Ruthin and Henry IV. He was proclaimed prince of Wales by friends and relatives on 16 September 1400, and attacked Grey's estates close to the English border. Owain advanced into central and south Wales following a victory in the Plynlimmon mountains (1401); his capture of Lord Grey (April) and the uncle of Edmund Mortimer, earl of March and claimant to the English throne (22 June), was a political coup, especially when the captive Mortimer married Owain's daughter. Owain sought allies among other rebels, especially the Percy family and the earl of March's supporters, though Henry IV's victory at *Shrewsbury (21 July 1403) was a set-back. Owain focused on south Wales, capturing several castles, as well as Aberystwyth and Harlech (1404). He negotiated the treaty of Paris with Charles VI of France (14 July 1404), and he 'and his hillmen' held assemblies at Machynlleth, Harlech, and Pennal (1404–6) where ambitious plans were laid for an independent principality. Although French troops landed in

Milford Sound to assist him, 1405–6 saw significant reverses, and his French and Percy allies faded away. Following a raid in Shropshire in 1410, Owain disappeared; he refused a pardon from Henry V in 1415 and may have died soon afterwards.

### Goderich, Frederick John Robinson, 1st Viscount (1782–1859). Prime minister. Educated at Harrow and St John's College, Cambridge, Goderich sat as a moderate Tory for Carlow in 1806 and for Ripon, 1807–27. He held a number of offices—lord of Admiralty 1810–12, vice-president of the Board of Trade 1812–18, lord of Treasury 1812–13, joint paymaster general 1813–17, president of the Board of Trade 1818–23 and 1841–3, treasurer of the navy 1818–23, secretary of state for war and the colonies 1827, 1830–3, lord privy seal 1833–4, president of the Board of Control for India 1843–6. He was made viscount 1827 and earl of Ripon 1833. His period as chancellor of the Exchequer 1823–7 earned him the nickname 'Prosperity Robinson', yet his premiership September 1827–January 1828 was a dismal failure, distinguished only by cabinet quarrels. 'A transient and embarrassed phantom', was Disraeli's terse comment.

### Godiva (Godgifu) (d. between 1057 and 1086). Wife of Earl *Leofric of Mercia. To obtain her request that Coventry be relieved of a heavy toll, she is alleged to have ridden naked through the market. The legend obscures her reputation as benefactress of religious establishments. She and Leofric were buried in their Coventry church. Roger of Wendover in the 13th cent. first related her ride; 18th-cent. writers embellished it with picturesque detail like 'Peeping Tom'.

### Gododdin, kingdom of the A British kingdom of the 6th cent. in south-east Scotland. *Aneurin's heroic poem tells of a raid by the Gododdin on the Anglo-Saxon kingdoms of *Bernicia and *Deira, and of the battle at *Catterick (c.600). The Gododdin were utterly routed: 'of three hundred, save one man, none returned.'

### Godolphin, Sidney Godolphin, 1st earl of (1645–1712). Prime minister. MP for Helston (1668–79) and St Mawes (1679–81), Godolphin was created baron (1684) and earl (1706). A Tory by inclination, he was the

archetypal bureaucratic politician, who held the offices of a lord of the Treasury (1679), secretary of state for the northern department (1684), 1st lord of the Treasury (1684–5, 1690–6, 1700–1), chamberlain to Queen Mary of Modena, and a commissioner of the Treasury (1687). From the accession of Anne, he and *Marlborough (the 'duumvirate'), ran the government, Godolphin being lord treasurer and, effectively, prime minister (1702–10). His forte was in financial affairs, and he was responsible for raising the money which enabled England to fight 20 years of continental wars.

**Godwin, William** (1756–1836). English writer and novelist. In 1793 Godwin published his anarchist masterpiece *Enquiry Concerning Political Justice*, which caught the public imagination and made his reputation. He argued against the use of coercion of any kind, whether political, ecclesiastical, or military, because it was corrupting and counter-productive. In the ideal society there would be no government and no punishment: individuals would live in harmony because of their mutual grasp of reason.

**Godwine, earl of Wessex** (d. 1053). Godwine rose to prominence in the reign of *Cnut, as one of his chief advisers, and has traditionally been held responsible for the brutal death of Æthelred the Unready's exiled son *Alfred in 1036. When the Danish line ended (1042), Godwine supported the accession of Alfred's brother Edward, who married Godwine's daughter. With his sons established in earldoms, his area of influence was vast. In 1053 Godwine died, his enemies said choking while protesting his innocence of Alfred's murder. Wessex passed to his son *Harold, who died at Hastings in 1066.

**Gold Coast** *See* GHANA.

**Golden Jubilee,** 1887. The fiftieth anniversary of Victoria's accession saw a well-orchestrated outburst of loyalty. The Round Tower at Windsor was illuminated by electrical light, prisoners amnestied, medals struck, statues erected, the fleet reviewed at Spithead, and a thanksgiving service held at Westminster abbey with music by the late Prince Albert. 'And *all* was the most perfect success,' wrote Victoria afterwards.

**Goldsmith, Oliver** (1728–74). Man of letters. Born in Ireland, Goldsmith attended Trinity College, Dublin, before briefly studying medicine in Edinburgh and Leiden. On settling in London from 1756, he supported himself partly as a physician, partly as a hack-writer, and partly by borrowing from friends. But he gradually pulled himself out of Grub Street. His poem *The Traveller* (1764) was well received; a novel *The Vicar of Wakefield* (1766) has remained a minor classic; *The Good-Natured Man*, a comedy (1768), had a respectable stage run; *The Deserted Village* (1770) touched the chord of nostalgia and was much admired; *She Stoops to Conquer* (1773) was a great success. Goldsmith was a strange man, feckless, naïve, unworldly, generous. He died heavily in debt, and Horace *Walpole wrote of him that 'he had sometimes parts, though never common sense'.

**golf** Though the Dutch game of *kolf* has been claimed as the origin, the first undoubted reference to golf was in 1457 when the Scottish Parliament deplored its popularity, since it took young men away from archery practice. But the great development of the game was in the later 19th cent. The handful of golf clubs in the early decades had risen to a dozen by 1870 and well over 1,000 by 1914. The British governing body is the Royal and Ancient Club at St Andrews, founded in 1754.

**Good Parliament** (1376). This Parliament saw the first use of *impeachment by the Commons, and the emergence of the office of Speaker. There was widespread discontent with an ineffective and apparently corrupt government. Charges were brought against the chamberlain, William Latimer; the king's mistress Alice Perrers; the steward of the royal household, John Neville, and others. The Commons' triumph did not last long; the government, guided by *John of Gaunt, undid most of their work in the following year.

**Gordon, Charles George** (1833–85). British soldier and Christian mystic. After serving with distinction in the *Crimean War (1853–6), Gordon gained public acclaim by his exploits in China (1860–5) where he showed great talent as commander of irregular troops in the defence of Shanghai during the Taiping rebellion. Seconded to the service of the khedive of Egypt as governor of Equatoria (1873–6) and then as governor-general of the Sudan until 1880, Gordon mapped the upper reaches of the White Nile. He returned to the Sudan in 1884 to evacuate Egyptian troops threatened by the forces of the Mahdi, a Muslim revivalist. A relief force failed to arrive in time and Gordon was killed in Khartoum in January 1885.

**Gordon, Lord George** (1751–93). Soon after his election to Parliament in 1774 Lord George, third son of the 3rd duke of Gordon, began to exhibit signs of religious mania. On 2 June 1780, as president of the Protestant Association, he presented a monster petition denouncing concessions to the catholics. Six days of rioting and looting followed and Gordon was tried for treason. It was argued on his behalf that he had not intended violence and he was acquitted. He subsequently converted to Judaism and, convicted of libel, spent the last five years of his life in comfortable confinement in Newgate prison. *See also* GORDON RIOTS.

**Gordon riots,** 1780. The greatest outburst of civil disorder in modern British history. They lasted for six days from 2 to 8 June and did enormous damage in London. They began with the presentation by Lord George *Gordon of a petition to Parliament against recent concessions to the catholics, but violent and criminal elements soon took over. Many members of the mob lost their lives, shot by the military, engulfed by flames, or buried in rubble. In all, 135 were put on trial, 59 capitally convicted, and 26 hanged, including a Jew, a negress, a one-armed man, and 'a poor, drunken cobbler'.

**Goring, George** (1608–57). Royalist commander in the Civil War. Despite being universally disliked, George, Lord Goring, rose high in the king's service. He was first under *Newcastle in Yorkshire and gained a notable victory over Sir Thomas *Fairfax at Seacroft Moor in March 1643. At *Marston Moor, in 1644, he commanded the left wing of the royalist army. After *Naseby, Goring was forced to give up the siege of Taunton by the approach of Sir Thomas Fairfax's army. Despite the tactical brilliance with which Goring deployed his men at *Langport, they were easily vanquished in July 1645. Goring

then fled the country and joined the service of Spain, where he died.

**Goschen, George Joachim, 1st Viscount** (1831–1907). A front-rank and long-serving politician in his day, Goschen is now remembered chiefly in one phrase. Grandson of a Leipzig publisher, his father settled in London in 1814. Goschen was sent to Rugby and Oxford to get an English education, took first-class honours in classics, and was president of the Union. He entered the Commons in 1863 as the Liberal member for London, and remained in Parliament all his life. Given junior office by *Russell in 1865, he was brought into the cabinet the following year as chancellor of the duchy of Lancaster, and served as president of the Poor Law Board 1868–71, 1st lord of the Admiralty 1871–4 and 1895–1900, and chancellor of the Exchequer 1887–92. After the Home Rule crisis of 1886, he joined *Hartington in leading the *Liberal Unionists. When Lord Randolph *Churchill resigned dramatically from Salisbury's government in 1886, expecting to be recalled, his place was filled by Goschen, and not a dog barked. 'I forgot Goschen,' explained Lord Randolph ruefully.

**Gower, John** (*c.*1330–1408). Poet. A friend of *Chaucer, Gower was probably born in Kent. His main work, *Confessio Amantis* (*c.*1386), contained 141 examples and stories of love in a conversation between a lover, Amans, and a priest of Venus, Genius. By the time the lover had understood the nature of love, he was too old and tired to care. Highly thought of in the Tudor period, Gower's lack of humour led to Chaucer overshadowing him.

**Gowrie, William Ruthven, 1st earl of** [S] (*c.*1541–84). The Ruthven estates were in Perthshire and the family, protestant by religion, formed part of the English interest. He was the leader in 1582 of the *Ruthven raid and held the king prisoner for ten months. An ill-judged reconciliation with *Arran in 1584 led to his downfall and he was executed at Stirling. His sons were involved in the *Gowrie conspiracy in 1600, both being killed.

**Gowrie conspiracy,** 1600. James VI of Scotland mistrusted the Gowrie family. The 1st earl of *Gowrie had held James captive after the *Ruthven raid in 1582. On 5 August 1600, while hunting, James was urgently invited by Alexander Ruthven to Gowrie House in Perth, according to the king to investigate a mysterious stranger with a pot of gold. No stranger materialized and after a meal James repaired to an upper turret with Ruthven. James's version was that Ruthven then reproached him with the execution of the 1st earl and told him to prepare to die: James wrestled free and cried 'Treason' from a window, whereupon his followers rescued him and killed both Ruthven and his elder brother, Lord Gowrie. If the brothers were conspirators, looking for a repeat of the Ruthven raid, they are among the most incompetent in Scottish history.

**Grace, W. G.** (1848–1915). Grace was probably the greatest sporting hero of late Victorian and Edwardian Britain, his bulky form and black beard instantly recognizable. He was by profession a Bristol surgeon. Before he was 17 he had appeared for the Gentlemen against the Players at the Oval and at Lord's. In 1870 he launched the Gloucestershire side. In all he made 126 centuries and took 2,876 wickets, playing his last first-class game in 1908, at the age of 60.

**Grafton, Augustus Henry Fitzroy, 3rd duke of** (1735–1811). Prime minister. Grafton became secretary of state in the first *Rockingham administration, but resigned in April 1766 after the failure to negotiate Pitt's entry into the ministry. Grafton returned to office in July, when Pitt (now earl of Chatham) succeeded Rockingham as prime minister. Although Grafton became 1st lord of the Treasury, Chatham headed the ministry as lord privy seal. This unusual arrangement did not achieve its object of preserving Chatham's precarious health. Grafton gradually emerged as *de facto* prime minister during 1767 and officially led the ministry after Chatham finally resigned in October 1768. The Grafton ministry was plagued with serious problems, such as the *Wilkes case and the *Townshend duties crisis; Grafton himself was ridiculed in the press by *Junius. Unable to withstand the pressure, Grafton resigned in January 1770. He never returned to the front rank of politics, but served as lord privy seal in 1771–5 and 1782–3.

**Graham, Sir James** (1792–1861). Heir to an important border landed estate, Graham was educated at Westminster School and Oxford. He joined the Whig opposition in Parliament, supporting *catholic emancipation and parliamentary reform. In 1830 he became 1st lord of the Admiralty in *Grey's cabinet, and was one of the four ministers who drafted the Great Reform Act. At the Admiralty he introduced administrative reform, before resigning in 1834 over proposals for reforming the established Irish church. He became home secretary and Peel's right-hand man in the 1841–6 ministry, resigning with him in 1846. After Peel's death, Graham remained a prominent Peelite politician, returning to the Admiralty in *Aberdeen's coalition ministry of 1853–5.

**Grampian** (named because the eastern Grampian mountains lie within it) was from 1973 to 1996 a local authority region of Scotland. From April 1996 the new all-purpose local authorities for the former Grampian region are: Aberdeen, Aberdeenshire, and Moray. Over 40 per cent of the region's population live in *Aberdeen, Scotland's third largest city.

**Granby, John Manners, marquis of** (1721–70). Granby, heir to the dukedom of Rutland, became a national hero after brilliant cavalry actions at *Minden (1759) and Warburg (1760), during the *Seven Years War. He was elected to Parliament before he was 21 and remained in the Commons all his life. From 1763 to 1770 he was master of the ordnance, and commander-in-chief from 1766. In January 1770 he resigned office, having changed his mind on the *Wilkes issue: 'he recanted a vote he had not understood,' wrote Horace *Walpole, 'for reasons he understood as little.' He died unexpectedly at the age of 49. *Reynolds painted his florid, bald, ruddy countenance many times, and for decades less distinguished portraits swung outside countless taverns.

**grand jury** The Assize of *Clarendon provided that twelve men of each hundred were to present on oath to the travelling justices those suspected of serious crimes. From the late 14th cent. the grand jury had the task of scrutinizing indictments to examine whether or not the accused should be sent for trial.

**Grandmontines** This monastic order was founded by the hermit St Stephen (*c.*1054–1124) of Muret, near Limoges. It was an ascetic community of choir and lay brothers which, after Stephen's death, established itself at Grandmont and followed a strict version of the *Benedictine rule. Three small priories were founded in England but only one of these (Grosmont, Yorks.) survived till the *dissolution.

**Grand National** The most famous jumping race in the world. First run in 1839, it is a handicap for horses 6 years old and upwards, run near the end of March at Aintree, Liverpool. The course of 4 miles and 856 yards includes 30 jumps, such as the Canal Turn Fence, Valentine's Brook, and the notorious Becher's Brook.

**Grand National Consolidated Trade Union** Founded in 1834 by delegates of societies nation-wide in response to calls of Derby artisans and labourers 'locked out' for belonging to 'combinations'. It was associated with Robert -*Owen, who became president only after the trial of the *Tolpuddle martyrs in March. Handicapped from the outset by meagre funds, the GNCTU's demise was precipitated when the treasurer absconded with its finances in December 1834.

**Grand Remonstrance,** 1641. This lengthy petition was part of *Pym's campaign to retain the initiative in his parliamentary struggle against Charles I. A long indictment of the misdeeds of the reign was carried on 18 November by 159 votes to 148. It demanded that in future the king should employ such counsellors as Parliament 'may have cause to confide in'. Charles replied that in the 'choice of our counsellors . . . it is the undoubted right of the crown of England to call such persons . . . as we shall think fit'.

**grand tour** A standard part of the education of the English aristocracy between the Restoration and the outbreak of the Revolutionary and Napoleonic wars in 1789, though since it could take two or three years, it was extremely expensive and only a few could afford it. It therefore tended to be limited to elder sons. It had several objectives—to broaden the mind, to introduce the tourist to classical civilization, to encourage social grace, to improve the command of languages, to establish useful personal and diplomatic links, and to enable wild oats to be sown at a distance. Many commentators, such as *Smollett, *Johnson, and *Gibbon, disapproved, arguing that the tour encouraged habits of dissipation and that the noblemen were too young to have much appreciation of what they saw. The advent of railways in the early 19th cent. meant that the journeys could be made in a few weeks and the tour did not survive in its traditional form.

**Grantham, Thomas Robinson, 1st Baron** (1695–1770). Robinson's father was baronet of Newby Hall, east of Ripon. His first parliamentary seat in 1727 was Thirsk. At Westminster School he formed a friendship with Henry *Pelham and the duke of *Newcastle, who looked after him for the rest of his life. Until the conclusion of the peace of *Aix-la-Chapelle in 1748 his career was diplomatic. From 1749 to 1754 he held minor government posts. He was thrust into prominence in 1754 when Henry Pelham died unexpectedly and Newcastle needed a spokesman in the House of Commons. But his months as secretary of state were a torment, assailed by *Fox and *Pitt, often in tandem. In 1755 he was replaced by Fox and held only minor office subsequently. But his compensation as a discard was substantial—a handsome pension and a barony in 1761, when even his minor post was needed for someone else.

**Granville, Granville George Leveson-Gower, 2nd Earl** (1815–91). Politician. Son of the 1st Earl Granville, he was educated at Eton and Oxford. A lifelong Whig, he was MP for Morpeth (1836–41) and Lichfield (1841–6) before succeeding to the title. He was under-secretary for foreign affairs 1840–1 and succeeded Lord *Palmerston as foreign secretary 1851–2. Granville was considered a possible prime minister in 1859 and 1865 but tended to hold honorific offices until he became colonial secretary (1868–70), foreign secretary (1870–4, 1880–5), and colonial secretary (1886) under *Gladstone. An urbane and well-liked man, he was not an energetic politician.

**Grattan, Henry** (1746–1820). Statesman. Grattan was educated at Trinity College, Dublin, and called to the Irish bar in 1772. Returned to the Irish Parliament in 1775 for Charlemont, he rapidly gained a reputation as an orator and became a leader of the patriot group, pressing for Irish legislative independence, granted in 1782. In 1790 he founded the Irish Whig club and was elected for Dublin, denouncing parliamentary corruption and advocating concessions to the catholics. He was in England for the 1798 rebellion but was elected to the Dublin Parliament in 1800 in time to protest against the Act of *Union. In 1805 he was persuaded to enter the Westminster Parliament for *Fitzwilliam's borough of Malton and from 1806 to 1820 represented his old seat in Dublin. He declined office and strove continuously for *catholic emancipation, his hopes remaining unrealized.

**Gray, Thomas** (1716–71). Gray led a sheltered existence: 'a life so barren of events as mine', he wrote. Educated at Eton, he went to Peterhouse, Cambridge, and returned after a grand tour as a fellow-commoner. In 1756 he transferred across the road to Pembroke College, having found his Peterhouse neighbours boisterous. In 1768 he was made professor of history and, characteristically, did not lecture but worried about it. His poetic fame came in 1750 when his 'Elegy in a Country Churchyard' was published. It touched many of the themes that tormented the 18th cent., particularly the vanity of human wishes: 'the paths of Glory lead but to the grave.'

**Great Britain** The geographical term Great Britain was used to distinguish the largest of the British Isles from Brittany, or Little Britain. When James I succeeded Elizabeth in 1603 he proposed that the union of the crowns should be followed by a governmental union and suggested the name Great Britain. Though the English Parliament could not be brought to agree, James adopted the name by proclamation and used it on his coinage. It was given statutory authority by the Act of *Union with Scotland in 1707. This usage lasted until the Act of Union with Ireland in 1801, which substituted the term 'United Kingdom of Great Britain and Ireland'.

*Great Britain* was the second of three highly innovative steamships designed by I. K. *Brunel. It was intended by the Great Western Steamship Company as a sister ship to Brunel's *Great Western*, which had been launched in Bristol as a wooden-hulled paddle steamer in 1837. But Brunel conceived a much bigger vessel, the first large iron ship and the first large screw-propelled ship. Launched in Bristol by the Prince Consort on 19 July 1843 (3,270 tons, compared with 1,340 for the previous ship), the *Great Britain* entered service between Liverpool and New York in 1845. She was eventually abandoned in the Falkland Islands in 1886, but survived to be brought home to Bristol in 1970, where she is on show.

**Great Cause** The disputed Scottish succession which arose when Alexander III died in 1286 leaving only a young granddaughter, the Maid of Norway, who herself died in Orkney in 1290. Edward I was called in to adjudicate between the twelve 'competitors', chief of whom were John *Comyn, John *Balliol, and Robert *Bruce. The complex proceedings culminated in Edward claiming the throne of Scotland for himself.

**Great Contract,** 1610. By the time James I ascended the throne of England royal finances had been undermined by inflation. In 1610 Lord Treasurer Robert *Cecil proposed that Parliament should vote the king a regular annual income. In return, the crown would abandon its deeply resented right to make wards of under-age heirs of landowners and sell control of their estates to the highest bidder. The contract was duly formalized, but during the parliamentary recess members were made aware that their constituents were implacably opposed to it. Since James had become convinced that it would leave him no better off, the contract was abandoned, amid general recriminations.

**great council and king's council** Elementary prudence dictated that medieval monarchs should seek the advice of their greatest subjects and should be seen to have their support. Anglo-Saxon monarchs had the *witan. Norman and Plantagenet monarchs had their council, under various names. As business became more complex, councils tended to divide into specialized bodies. Two bodies have been suggested, the great council and the king's council (curia regis). The great council began as a meeting of the tenants-in-chief and barons and was largely advisory. Consequently a more specialized council developed, consisting of household officers. This was the king's council, though it was not formally an institution with defined functions until the later 13th cent.

The king's council survived and coped with an ever-increasing volume of business. In the 16th cent. it threw off the *Star Chamber to take over more judicial work, and in Henry VIII's reign developed into the *Privy Council, with a small membership of hard-pressed administrators, meeting most days. For a hundred years it was the main engine of executive government, but after the Restoration it began to lose ground to the *cabinet.

**Great Eastern** After the *Great Western* and the *Great Britain*, I. K. *Brunel went on to design his third and largest steamship, the *Great Eastern*. This was a huge vessel of 18,915 tons, the largest ship built before the 20th cent. She was launched sideways into the Thames in January 1858. The *Great Eastern* failed to establish herself as a successful passenger ship, but performed a valuable service in laying the transoceanic cables across the Atlantic and Indian Oceans.

**Great Exhibition,** 1851. Master-minded by *Albert, the Great Exhibition was the largest trade show the world had ever seen. Joseph Paxton's *Crystal Palace, spanning 19 acres within Hyde Park (London), was accepted after 233 other plans had been rejected. Some 6 million people between 1 May and 11 October 1851, many of them on railway excursions, visited 100,000 exhibits. Queen Victoria, always keen on her husband's achievements, visited 34 times. Profits secured land in Kensington, future sites for the Victoria and Albert Museum, the Science Museum, and the Natural History Museum.

**Great Reform Act,** 1832. The first major reform of the representative system since the time of *Cromwell. Lord *Grey saw reform as a means of satisfying the desire of the respectable middle classes for greater representation and the character of the Act was accordingly moderate. The principal changes were: 1. Redistribution of constituencies. Boroughs with a population of less than 4,000 were either disfranchised, or reduced to one member instead of two. Some seats were added to the rural counties and others to towns such as Birmingham and Manchester. 2. Changes in the electoral qualifications: long leaseholders were added to the '40s. freeholders' in the counties and in the boroughs a uniform franchise, vested in householders occupying property valued at £10 or more for local rates, was established. 3. Rules were established for the conduct of elections. The Act satisfied the middle classes in general but agitation for more radical reform continued among the working classes, though no further general changes were made until 1867.

**Great Schism,** 1378–1417. After the papacy's stay from 1309 at Avignon, an enclave in southern France, the Roman populace in 1378 demanded an Italian pope and the conclave, intimidated, elected Urban VI. Within three months, his conduct had alienated many supporters, who elected Clement VII. The rival pope established himself once more at Avignon. The rift perpetuated itself and the Council of Pisa in 1409, summoned to restore church unity, merely succeeded in electing a third pope, Alexander V. Not until the Council of Constance in 1417 was unity restored with the election of Martin V. The king of France supported the Avignon popes, who were more likely to be under French influence. The English, bitterly opposed to France, recognized the Roman popes. The Scots, allied to France, joined in acknowledging Avignon.

**great seal** The seal originated in the reign of Edward the Confessor as an imitation of the emperor's seal and was about 3 inches in diameter. The king is depicted in majesty, bearing sceptre and orb. The Norman rulers continued its use and the custody of the seal was given to the *chancellor. The seal is broken at the start of a new reign and a fresh one made. Since the great seal was heavy, the practice developed of employing a privy seal and later a signet. The great seal is used for proclamations, writs, letters patent, and treaties. A separate seal for Scotland, authorized by the Act of *Union in 1707, is in the custody of the secretary of state for Scotland.

**Great Yarmouth,** on the Yare estuary in Norfolk, developed in the 11th cent. as a fishing town, especially for North Sea herring. From then until the First World War it was a major port, one of the largest towns in England.

**Greene, Graham** (1904–91). One of the most versatile, prolific, and popular writers of the mid-20th cent., Greene was born at Berkhamsted (Herts.), where his father was headmaster of the public school, and educated at Balliol College, Oxford. He converted to catholicism at the time of his marriage in 1927. Greene published a book of verse, *Babbling April*, in 1925, and followed with a historical novel, *The Man Within*, in 1929. Next he produced a series of thrillers ('entertainments') starting with *Stamboul Train* (1932) and continuing to *The Third Man* (1950), made into a remarkable film. Increasingly Greene explored the world of catholic guilt in *Brighton Rock* (1938), *The Power and the Glory* (1940), *The Heart of the Matter* (1948), and *The End of the Affair* (1951). His themes of ambiguity, betrayal, and seediness reflected and appealed to his own times.

**Green Party** The British Green Party started life in 1973 as an environmental pressure group called 'People'. Two years later it became the Ecology Party. In the 1983 general election the party fielded 108 candidates but mustered barely 1 per cent of the vote. In 1985 it changed its name to the Green Party in line with similar international environmental movements. However it never managed to emulate the success of its continental counterparts. Its biggest success came in winning 15 per cent of the vote in the European elections in June 1989, but in the 1997 election 88 Green candidates polled under a quarter of one per cent of the poll. In the election of 2005 the Greens polled 258,000 votes, giving them one per cent of the total. The party has suffered from the working of the electoral system for the Westminster Parliament but has two members in the European Parliament.

**Green Ribbon Club** An important Whig venue in London, formed in the mid-1670s and named from the colours its members wore in their hats. Based at the King's Head in Chancery Lane, it played a major part in staging rowdy pope-burning processions during the *Exclusion crisis.

**Greenwich, treaty of,** 1543. On 1 July 1543, after their defeat at *Solway Moss the previous year, the Scots made peace and agreed to a marriage between the infant Queen Mary and Prince Edward, Henry VIII's heir, which would lead to a union of the kingdoms. The terms were repudiated by the Scottish Parliament in December and fighting resumed the following year.

**Greenwich palace** began life as Bella Court, built by Humphrey, duke of *Gloucester, brother of Henry V. After passing to *Margaret of Anjou, the palace came to Henry VII, who built extensively: Henry VIII and his daughters Mary and Elizabeth were born there. James I gave it to his wife Anne of Denmark, who employed Inigo *Jones to begin building the Queen's House. It passed next to *Henrietta Maria, but during the civil wars fell into decay. Charles II began a major reconstruction, but did not complete it, though the observatory on the hill dates from 1676/7. William III decided in 1694 to employ *Wren to build a great new hospital for seamen.

**Grenada,** the southernmost of the Windward Islands in the Caribbean, became independent in 1974. It is a constitutional monarchy with the queen as head of state, within the Commonwealth.

**Grenville, George** (1712–70). Prime minister. After training as a lawyer, Grenville entered Parliament in 1741 and held a number of junior posts from 1744. He was not offered high office until October 1761, when he became leader of the Commons. Soon afterwards he accepted cabinet office, becoming northern secretary in May 1762, but was moved to the Admiralty in October after clashing with Bute over patronage and policy. Grenville, therefore, was not a leading candidate for the premiership after Bute's resignation in April 1763, but when Henry *Fox declined he became 1st lord of the Treasury virtually by default. As prime minister he was responsible for the *Stamp Act of 1765, which provoked rioting in America. In Britain there was no significant opposition to this legislation until after the Stamp Act crisis. American affairs had played no part in Grenville's fall in July 1765. The prevailing atmosphere of political suspicion left by Bute's resignation, exacerbated by

Grenville's propensity to lecture the king, jeopardized political stability. Having avoided dismissal in the spring of 1765, Grenville determined to extort public proof of his mastery, insisting upon the removal of Bute's brother from the Scottish privy seal, thereby forcing George III to break his promise of granting the office for life. Unable immediately to retaliate, the king rid himself of Grenville at the first opportunity. Grenville spent the remainder of his political career in opposition, doggedly defending both his conduct as prime minister and his policy towards America.

**Grenville, Sir Richard** (1542–91). Of a landed family, Grenville was born at Buckland abbey, between Tavistock and Plymouth, which he sold to Francis *Drake in 1581. A relative of *Ralegh, Grenville was much involved, both as MP and man of action, in transatlantic settlement, especially during 1585–6 at Roanoke Island (North Carolina). In 1588 he fitted out ships against the Spanish Armada, and in 1591, under Lord Thomas *Howard's command, Grenville sailed to the Azores to intercept the Spanish treasure fleet. In *Revenge*, Grenville confronted alone a force of over 50 Spanish warships. Sinking one and damaging others before surrendering, Grenville died of his wounds and *Revenge* foundered shortly afterwards. Grenville's last fight became a legend.

**Grenville, William Wyndham, 1st Lord** (1759–1834). Prime minister. The third son of George *Grenville, prime minister 1763–5, he was educated at Eton and Christ Church, Oxford, where he became a distinguished classical scholar. He entered Parliament in 1782 and cast in his lot with his cousin the young William *Pitt. *Shelburne appointed him chief secretary in Ireland in 1782 and under Pitt he was paymaster of the forces 1783–9.

In January 1789 Grenville became Speaker of the House of Commons but he craved a cabinet post and when the Regency crisis was over was appointed home secretary. In 1790 he was elevated to the Lords. Translated to the foreign secretaryship in 1791, for ten years he was responsible for British policy in the French Revolutionary War. In 1801 he resigned with Pitt over the king's refusal to grant catholic relief, but unlike Pitt he

determined not to take office again unless the king withdrew his veto. Accordingly he did not return with Pitt in 1804 but formed an alliance with the Foxite Whigs, with whom he served in the 'Ministry of All the *Talents' in 1806–7.

As prime minister, Grenville achieved little beyond the abolition of the slave trade. The government collapsed when George III thwarted their attempt to smuggle concessions to the Irish catholics past his protestant conscience. For the next ten years Grenville and *Grey, Fox's successor, led the opposition to *Portland, *Perceval, and *Liverpool. The alliance ended in 1817 when they disagreed over the government's suspension of *habeas corpus to deal with radical agitation. Grenville then retired from political life, devoting his remaining years to classical scholarship.

**Gresham, Thomas** (1519–79). Second son of Sir Richard Gresham, he became a banker, merchant, and royal agent or king's factor. As adviser to Queen Elizabeth I he was an advocate of sound monetary policy, seeking the re-minting of base money, a reduction in debt, and prompt payment by the crown. He is credited with 'Gresham's Law', that 'bad money drives out good'. He founded the *Royal Exchange in London.

**Grey, Charles, 2nd Earl Grey** (1764–1845). Prime minister. Son of General Sir Charles Grey of Fallodon, Northumberland, Grey entered Parliament in 1786 as a member for Northumberland. Grey inherited Howick in 1808, from which he could rarely be tempted to attend to his duties as leader of the Whig Party after *Fox's death.

A headstrong young man, Grey was attracted to Fox and his circle and joined the opposition to *Pitt. He distinguished himself from the outset as a brilliant orator in the House of Commons, but in 1792 he committed himself to parliamentary reform, helping to found the Association of the *Friends of the People. He hoped to use the reform movement to advance his career but the step split the Whigs, aristocratic grandees like the duke of *Portland and Earl *Fitzwilliam being frightened by the prospect of the spread of the French Revolution. They joined Pitt in 1794, while Fox and Grey led the rump of the party in opposition.

After the peace of *Amiens and the subsequent resumption of war against Napoleon the Whigs formed a coalition with the group led by Lord *Grenville, but their conservatism meant that Grey had to give up active support of reform. In the 'Ministry of All the *Talents' (1806-7) Grey served as 1st lord of the Admiralty and after Fox's death succeeded him as foreign secretary. After the fall of the 'Talents', Grey tried to steer a middle course between radicalism and conservatism.

In 1807 Grey inherited the peerage which, to his dismay, *Addington had conferred on his father in 1802. For the remainder of his life he sat in the House of Lords, where his oratorical gifts were less effective. Though he never quite abandoned the position of leader of the Whig opposition, the party suffered from a lack of direction. He consistently advocated *catholic emancipation and gave important assistance to *Wellington in achieving it in 1829.

In 1830 George IV's death removed the royal veto on Grey and at the same time the demand for parliamentary reform revived. Wellington's refusal to consider it broke up his administration and William IV sent for Grey, at the age of 66, to form the ministry which was to pass the *Great Reform Act. This was Grey's major achievement. He proposed it on the same principles which he had professed in 1792, the need to satisfy the demand of the respectable classes for greater representation while denying power to the mass of the people. He was able to persuade William IV to maintain a reluctant support for the measure and, finally, to promise to create enough new peers, if necessary, to force the bill through the House of Lords. His cabinet was a coalition of interests rather than a united party, and in 1834 when its divisions over the Irish church question became public Grey resigned, with relief at ending his burdensome duties. He spent the rest of his life in retirement at Howick.

**Grey, Sir Edward** (1862-1933). Foreign secretary. Grey has been described as curiously 'suspended between the world of high politics and rural isolation', a man who sought refuge from the toils of office in fishing and ornithology. Behind the reserve lay a very determined and tough politician. He was among those Liberals who supported the *Boer War, and was involved in the attempt to compel *Campbell-Bannerman to move to the Lords on becoming prime minister in 1905. But it was as foreign secretary (December 1905–December 1916, the longest continuous tenure of that office) that he has attracted the interest of historians.

He gained his first experience in the Foreign Office under Lord *Rosebery in the mid-1890s. As foreign secretary himself Grey quickly dispelled fears that a Liberal government might weaken Britain's role in the world. In the Moroccan crisis with Germany (1905-6), he went further than his predecessor by agreeing to precautionary military staff talks with France. He also overcame the doubts of some cabinet colleagues to push through the entente of 1907 with Russia.

As Europe stumbled towards war in July 1914 cabinet divisions prevented Grey from unambiguously signalling that Britain would fight in defence of France. Grey himself threatened to resign rather than abandon France, but it was German infringement of Belgian neutrality which ensured that most of the cabinet opted for war on 4 August.

**Grey, Lady Jane** (1537-54). Jane was the eldest daughter of Henry Grey, marquis of Dorset, later duke of Suffolk, and a cousin of Edward VI. The duke of *Northumberland planned to use her to seize the succession when Edward should die. Against her own wishes, she was married on 21 May 1553 to Guildford Dudley, fourth son of Northumberland. After Edward's death on 6 July 1553, she was proclaimed queen. Mary Tudor's supporters rallied and on 19 July Jane's father admitted defeat. Lady Jane's reign had lasted a mere nine days. She was held in the Tower and executed on 12 February 1554.

**greyhound racing** as an organized sport developed in the USA, though greyhounds had been bred and raced for centuries. The sport owed its appeal to the oval course, which makes for tactical running, and to betting. The National Greyhound Racing Club was established in 1928.

**Griqualand, East and West** Griqualand West, an arid region occupied by the Griqua people, was annexed to Cape Colony in 1871 after diamonds had been found there. The chief town is Kimberley. It now forms part of

Cape Province (South Africa). Griqualand East was annexed to Cape Colony in 1880, but is now divided between the Transkei and Natal.

**Grosseteste, Robert** (*c*.1170–1253). Scholar and bishop. Of a humble Suffolk family, Grosseteste went to Cambridge and later lectured at Oxford. He held archdeaconries for Wiltshire, Northampton, and Leicester before election in 1235 to the vast diocese of Lincoln. He plunged into reforming the discipline of the see and into the quarrels that preoccupied him for the rest of his life. A man of great learning, Grosseteste wrote innumerable translations and commentaries. The combination of pugnacity and piety, more common in the 13th cent. than today, persuaded Powicke to classify him as the 'church militant'.

**Grub Street** is a derogatory term for bad writing. Its figurative use was commonplace by the early 18th cent. and Jonathan *Swift referred to a paper he was involved with as 'a little upon the Grub-Street'.

**Gruffydd ap Cynan** (*c*.1055–1137), king of Gwynedd (1081–1137). He was the son of Cynan ab Iago, a descendant of *Rhodri Mawr but an exile in Ireland. With Viking and Norman aid, he returned to re-establish Rhodri's line in Gwynedd (1075), but failed to overcome rivals. In a second foray (1081), again with Viking aid, he allied with *Rhys ap Tewdwr in *Deheubarth, but was betrayed to the Normans and imprisoned. He took part in the major uprising of 1094, but by 1098 was again in Ireland. Only with Norman agreement did he return permanently (1099) and rule in Anglesey, whence he consolidated his control of Gwynedd, and created a stable, prosperous kingdom.

**Gruffydd ap Llywelyn** (d. 1063), king of Gwynedd and Powys (1039–63). The son of Llywelyn ap Seisyll, king of *Gwynedd, and Angharad, the king of Deheubarth's daughter, Gruffydd created a personal dominion over much of Wales in alliance with English and Scandinavians. He won Gwynedd and *Powys in battle (1039) and defeated the Mercians on the river Severn. His conquests in *Deheubarth took longer (1040–55), during which he slew two of its kings. His alliance with Earl Ælfgar of Mercia, whose daughter he married, sustained a long struggle with *Harold Godwineson (later Harold II). Harold's attack on Gruffydd's court at Rhuddlan (1062) caused him to flee, and soon afterwards (5 August 1063) he was killed by his own men.

***Guardian*** Newspaper which has come to embody the ideology of liberal, middle-class, regional, and metropolitan England in popular perception. From its founding as the weekly *Manchester Guardian* in 1821, it was a radical voice, demanding liberal economic and political reform. It became a daily from 1855, but did not drop its 'Manchester' prefix until 1959.

**Guildford, diocese of** The see comprises most of Surrey. The massive increase in commuter population in the early 20th cent. necessitated the creation of a new bishopric which was carved out of the *Winchester diocese (1927). The cathedral, designed by Sir Edward Maufe and built between 1936 and 1961, is in a simplified Gothic style.

**guilds** The guild was one of the most characteristic organizations of the later medieval period and an instrument of local urban monopoly operated by a particular craft or by the market guild. Major towns had specialized guilds for different trades and London had a great variety of both mercantile guilds, such as grocers, goldsmiths, and vintners, and manufacturers like tailors and saddlers. The purpose of the guild was to regulate the local market. This took the form of control of the price and quality of goods. Membership conferred substantial advantages. Members of Southampton's guild were exempt from local tolls and customs and enjoyed the right of the first option to purchase goods brought to the town.

**Guild Socialists** advocated workers' control of industry by transforming trade unions into monopolistic producers' guilds. These guilds would form one part of a pluralist power structure with the state, which would represent the individual as consumer on equal terms. Guild Socialism developed partly as a reaction to *Fabian 'state socialism'. Hilaire Belloc feared that state intervention would make workers 'well fed instruments of production' whilst maintaining 'wage slavery'. Peaceful change was advocated by the gradual

g

encroachment on the role of employers by union representatives. But the practical achievements of Guild Socialists were meagre.

**Guilford courthouse, battle of,** 1781. As late as the spring of 1781 British forces in America were capable of inflicting sharp defeats on the rebels. To follow up his victory at *Camden in August 1780, *Cornwallis moved northwards towards Virginia, impeded by Nathaniel Greene's forces. At Guilford courthouse on 15 March Greene gave battle. Cornwallis had scarcely 2,000 men and was heavily outnumbered, but carried the day, capturing the American guns.

**Gulf War,** 1990–1. On 2 August 1990 Iraq invaded the tiny neighbouring state of Kuwait, giving the Iraqi dictator Saddam Hussein control of about 15 per cent of the world's oil. The almost defunct Soviet Union did not block a strong American response, which employed the United Nations Security Council to denounce Iraq's action. President George Bush assembled a coalition of 29 countries against Iraq. Britain's policy was to support the USA completely, to demonstrate both her reliability as an ally and her importance as a second-ranking power.

The coalition forces took several months to assemble in Saudi Arabia. Iraqi strategy was to prevent a coalition forming by playing on pan-Arab sentiment, in particular over past American support for Israel. On 29 November the United Nations Security Council set a deadline of 15 January 1991 for Iraqi withdrawal from Kuwait. Early on 17 January 1991, the coalition began with a massive air bombing attack against Iraq, which responded by attacking Israel (which had taken no military action) with long-range missiles. Critically for coalition solidarity, Israel refused to retaliate. The coalition launched its ground offensive to clear Kuwait on 24 February. This revealed that the Americans had greatly overestimated the Iraqi army, which offered only token resistance.

With the liberation of Kuwait dissident groups within Iraq, notably the Kurds of the north, rose in rebellion. Over the next year Saddam gradually reasserted his rule, and survived in power. But a second Gulf War began in 2003 when coalition forces, including Americans and British, invaded Iraq.

Saddam was overthrown quickly, tried by an Iraq court and hanged in 2006, but full pacification and reconstruction proved to be protracted.

**Gulliver's Travels,** Jonathan *Swift's best seller, appeared on 28 October 1726. Purporting to be an autobiographical account of Gulliver's 'Travels into Several Remote Nations of the World', contemporaries interpreted Swift's work as a political allegory on the administration of Sir Robert *Walpole. Although Swift's scathing portrait of the bestial Yahoos outraged Victorian sensibilities, *Gulliver's Travels* endured as a children's classic.

**Gunpowder plot,** 1605. Soon after becoming king of England in 1603, James I relaxed the penal laws which subjected catholics to fines, imprisonment, and even death. However, the ensuing uproar in Parliament persuaded him to backtrack, leaving the catholics feeling betrayed. A band of young catholic hotheads decided to seize the initiative by destroying the entire English government. They smuggled barrels of gunpowder into the cellars of Parliament, and Guy *Fawkes stood ready to ignite these on 5 November 1605, when the king, Lords, and Commons were assembled. The plot was betrayed, however, and the conspirators captured, tried, and executed. It etched itself upon the collective English memory, and bonfires and 'burning the guy' have remained traditional features of Bonfire Night celebrations.

**Gurkhas (or Gorkhas)** were the ruling clan of the Kathmandu valley who, in the 18th cent., expanded their empire over much of Nepal. They were defeated in 1814–16 by Lord *Hastings. However, their fighting qualities—especially with the *kukri* knife—earned much respect. The king of Nepal was invited to supply Gurkha contingents to the British Indian army. Gurkha batallions served with distinction in many colonial engagements, including the *Indian mutiny, and in the First and Second World Wars.

**Guthrum** (d. 890). Viking leader, king in East Anglia, and major opponent of King *Alfred. Guthrum probably first appeared in England as leader of the 'great summer army' which joined the forces commanded by Halfdan at Reading in 871. When the army split up in 875, Guthrum returned with his contingent to Wessex. In 878 he nearly succeeded in capturing Alfred at *Chippenham, but was defeated by Alfred at the battle of *Edington later the same year. Guthrum was subsequently baptized with Alfred as his godfather and took the new name of Athelstan. He retired with his forces to rule East Anglia and issued coins there in his baptismal name.

**Guyana,** an independent republic within the Commonwealth since 1970, was the only British colony on the South American mainland. The population in 2005 was an estimated 765,000 and the capital is Georgetown.

**Gwent** County of the south-east Wales border, which has had a singularly complex administrative history. Its basis was the Welsh kingdom of Gwent. It was quickly seized by the Anglo-Normans moving west after 1066 and a series of lordships created in both upper (Gwent Uwchcoed) and lower (Gwent Iscoed) Gwent. These were merged in 1536 to form the new county of Monmouthshire. After the Local Government Act of 1972, Wales was defined formally to include Monmouthshire, which was renamed Gwent. The county town was moved from Monmouth to Cwmbran. In 1996, in yet another reorganization, Gwent was divided into four new unitary authorities, Blaenau Gwent, Torfaen, Monmouthshire (reviving the old name), and Newport. *See also* MON-MOUTHSHIRE.

**Gwent, kingdom of** A post-Roman kingdom situated between the rivers Wye and Usk that took its name from the Roman town of *Caerwent, and lasted until Norman incursions in the late 11th cent. From 1070 the Norman conquerors quickly created several marcher lordships in more accessible parts; native dynasties survived elsewhere, even acknowledging the overlordship of the lord *Rhys of *Deheubarth and, in the 13th cent., of the princes of *Gwynedd.

**Gwyn, Nell** (1650–87). Born in 1650 in Hereford, Nell first worked as a barmaid and then as an orange-seller outside the Theatre Royal, Drury Lane (London), before attracting the attention of Charles II. She became his mistress though sharing his affections with others. Charles was infatuated by her physical appeal and her natural wit. The birth of two sons, Charles Beauclerk, later earl of Burford and duke of St Albans, on 8 May 1670 and James on 25 December 1671, ensured that she remained in favour. Following Charles's death in 1685, she was given Bestwood Park near Nottingham, where she lived until her own death following a stroke on 16 November 1687.

**Gwynedd** A county of north-west Wales created by the Local Government Act of 1972 and extant in its initial form from 1974 to 1996, when it was modified by the removal of *Anglesey (Ynys Môn), which became a separate unitary authority. It was based upon the post-Roman and medieval kingdom of Gwynedd which, after conquest by Edward I, had been divided by the statute of *Rhuddlan in 1284 into the counties of Anglesey, Caernarfonshire, and Merionethshire.

**Gwynedd, kingdom of** The kingdom was based upon Snowdonia and Anglesey, extending at its height to include territory to the east of the Conwy. It was one of the immediate post-Roman kingdoms of the 6th cent., ruled by Maelgwn (Maelgwn Gwynedd), said to be a descendant of *Cunedda. From the outset Gwynedd was one of the most significant of the Welsh kingdoms, with claims to overlordship, and pursuing an expansionary policy. Its downfall came from overambition on limited resources. Gwynedd took advantage of English divisions during the reign of Henry III to reassert itself and the treaty of *Montgomery in 1267 gave it substantial territorial gains. But after the campaigns of Edward I in 1277 and 1282–3 it became part of the principality under the control of the English crown and was eliminated as a political entity.

**habeas corpus** Before Magna Carta, the writ of habeas corpus constituted a command in the king's name to have a defendant brought physically before the court. It had then no libertarian function. In the 17th cent. it was employed to challenge arbitrary arrests by the royal government. In Darnel's case in 1627, the judges refused to allow bail to a person detained 'at the special command of the king'. The *petition of right (1628) protested at the practice, but opponents of the crown such as Sir John *Eliot and John *Selden (1629) continued to be committed for political purposes.

When the king lost control of the situation in 1640, his adversaries moved to defend habeas corpus. The Act of 1641 which abolished *Star Chamber declared that the writ could ensure that a person imprisoned by king and council should be brought before the court without delay with the cause of imprisonment shown.

After the Restoration, the struggle was resumed. The Habeas Corpus Act of 1679 blocked up many of the loopholes and improved the mechanism of enforcement. In Scotland, the equivalent to habeas corpus was obtained by an Act for Preventing Wrongous Imprisonments in 1701.

**Haddington, Thomas Hamilton, 1st earl of** [S] (1563-1637). Hamilton studied law at Paris and at 29 became a lord of Session as Lord Drumcairn. He was appointed by James VI one of the Octavians to control royal finances and in 1596 became king's advocate. Knighted in 1603, he was created Lord Binning (1613), earl of Melrose (1619), and earl of Haddington (1627). He was secretary of state [S] 1612-26, president of the Court of Session from 1616 until 1626, and lord privy seal [S] 1627-37. James's nickname for him—taken from the Edinburgh street—was 'Tam o' the Cowgate'.

**Haddington, treaty of,** 1548. The response of *Mary of Guise and the pro-French party to intimidation by the English *'rough wooing' of 1544-8 was the treaty of Haddington of 7 July 1548. Mary, queen of Scots, then aged 5, was to marry the dauphin. The following month Mary was sent to France to be brought up. The marriage took place in April 1558.

**Hadrian** Roman emperor 117-38. Publius Aelius Hadrianus was born in 76, probably at Italica near Seville. Related by marriage to Trajan, he became a ward of the future emperor. During Trajan's reign he progressed through a series of military and civil offices, succeeding Trajan in 117. In the early part of his reign he toured his empire, coming to Britain in 122. Here he commanded the building of the wall which bears his name.

**Hadrian IV** *See* ADRIAN IV.

**Hadrian's Wall** was a Roman frontier work of the early 2nd cent. running 70 miles from the Tyne near Newcastle to the Solway west of Carlisle. Commenced at the behest of *Hadrian on his visit to Britain in 122, the wall was originally to consist of a running barrier fronted by a ditch (except on the crags of the central sector), with a gateway defended by a fortlet every mile (milecastle) and two watchtowers (turrets) between each pair of milecastles. Apparently a frontier, it was designed to supervise not to deny movement. The line could not have been held against a concerted attack; in the event of a crossing Roman forces would concentrate to the south to expel invaders.

**Hague, William** (b. 1961). Politician. Hague's meteoric rise to the leadership of the Conservative Party was assisted by the shattering defeat of 1997, which removed from Parliament a number of potential rivals. President of the Oxford Union (1981), he was returned for Richmond (Yorks.) in 1989. He served as minister for social security 1994–5 and secretary of state for Wales 1995–7. From 1997 his political task was to restore morale and credibility to a battered and divided party. He became a redoubtable Commons performer, quite capable of bruising the Labour prime minister, Tony Blair. But after the Conservatives failed at the general election of 2001 to make any progress, Hague resigned immediately. From 2005 he has served as shadow Foreign Secretary.

**Haig, Sir Douglas, 1st Earl Haig** (1861–1928). Soldier. Before 1914 Haig was recognized as one of the outstanding soldiers of his generation. In December 1915 he replaced Sir John *French as commander-in-chief of the British armies in France. He fought two of the most costly and controversial battles in British history, the *Somme (1916) and third Ypres (1917), convinced that the German army would run out of soldiers if he continued to attack. Haig remains a figure of great controversy. Despite attempts by some historians to portray him as an 'educated soldier', his popular image remains that of a callous butcher.

**Hailsham, Quintin Hogg, 2nd Baron** (1907–2001). Conservative politician and lawyer. Hogg entered Parliament at the Oxford by-election of 1938, a supporter of appeasement. He turned against *Chamberlain before the latter's fall in 1940. Elevated to the Lords in 1950 on his father's death, he anticipated a career as a barrister. But Hailsham was recalled to government by *Eden and enjoyed high office under *Macmillan, including a successful period as party chairman. He renounced his peerage in 1963 to contest—unsuccessfully—the party leadership, returning to the Commons. He anticipated becoming home secretary under *Heath in 1970 but, ennobled with a life peerage, served instead as lord chancellor. Hailsham showed his adaptability by retaining frontbench status under Margaret *Thatcher, becoming lord chancellor again in 1979.

**Hakluyt, Revd Richard** (*c*.1551–1616). In 1589, 'for the honour and benefit of this commonwealth wherein I live and breathe', Hakluyt published the *Principall Navigations, Voiages, Traffiques and Discoveries of the English Nation*. He wished to persuade the English to embark on enterprises in the wider world. Later a canon at Westminster, he became a publicist for the North-West Passage idea, and adviser to the new *East India Company in 1600.

**Haldane, Richard Burdon, 1st Viscount Haldane** (1856–1928). The son of a Perthshire landowner, Haldane became a successful Chancery barrister in London. In 1885 he was elected to Parliament for East Lothian and remained an MP until he left the Commons for the Lords in 1911. Haldane took office in *Asquith's 1905 Liberal government as secretary for war. His reforms of the army earned him considerable respect. In 1911 he was created viscount and he became lord chancellor in 1912. In 1914 he returned to the War Office but his affection for Germany caused public suspicion and he was dismissed by Asquith in 1915. He served briefly as lord chancellor in the first Labour government under Ramsay *MacDonald.

**Halidon Hill, battle of,** 1333. For years after the great victory of *Bannockburn in 1314 Scotland was in a powerful position. But the death of Robert Bruce in 1329, leaving a young son David II, encouraged Edward III to intervene once more, supporting the claims of Edward *Balliol. In the spring of 1333 Edward besieged Berwick in person. Sir Archibald Douglas led a large Scottish army to the rescue. The armies met at Halidon Hill on 19 July. The Scots attacked up the hill and suffered severely from English arrows. Their heavy losses included Douglas. Balliol was reinstated as king of Scotland.

**Halifax, Charles Montagu, 1st earl of** (1661–1715). Though of aristocratic background, Montagu achieved political recognition through matchless powers of oratory and a measure of machiavellian trickery. Entering Parliament in 1689, he soon achieved prominence as a court manager, becoming a Treasury commissioner in 1692, chancellor of the Exchequer in 1694, and 1st lord of the Treasury in 1697. Accusations of malversation forced his resignation in 1699, but in the year following he was created baron. An attempt to impeach him in 1701 failed. Throughout Anne's reign he was a *Junto leader in the Lords, and at George I's accession (1714) was reappointed 1st lord and made an earl.

**Halifax, George Savile, 1st marquis of** (1633–95). Politician and essayist. Halifax both epitomized and advocated the 'middle path' in politics—'The Trimmer'. A wealthy Yorkshire baronet, he entered politics in the 1660s and was made a viscount in 1668. Initially hostile towards *Clarendon, he was then critical of the pro-catholic policies of the *cabal, and then of the Anglican reaction of *Danby. He emerged by 1679 as a firm opponent of '*exclusion', was reappointed to the Privy Council, and in 1682 was created a marquis. As lord privy seal, however, he was increasingly unhappy in the enclaves of high Toryism and in 1685 James II dismissed him. Although in 1688 he threw aside his neutrality and supported William of Orange, he soon found himself out of favour and retired in 1690. *See* TRIMMER.

**Halifax, Edward Wood, 1st earl of** (1881–1959). A Conservative politician, Halifax made some progress as viceroy of India (1926–31) towards constitutional change in talks with the nationalist leader Mahatma *Gandhi. As foreign secretary (1938–41) he searched for an accommodation with Nazi Germany until September 1939, when he displayed mixed feelings during the Munich crisis (1938), and argued early in 1939 for tougher policies, including faster rearmament. In the leadership crisis of May 1940 he was favoured by some to succeed *Chamberlain as prime minister. Between 1941 and 1946 this tall, aloof aristocrat served with surprising success as ambassador in Washington.

**Halley, Edmond** (1656–1742). Astronomer, remembered because his name is attached to a comet. Leaving Queen's College, Oxford, without a degree in 1676, he went to St Helena to map the southern stars. After a famous meeting with *Wren and *Hooke, he visited *Newton in Cambridge, and hearing about his work on gravitation, persuaded him to publish it. In 1703 he became professor of astronomy at Oxford, and in 1720 astronomer-royal. He computed the orbits of several comets, and deduced that those of 1456, 1531, 1607, and 1682 were periodic returns of the same body.

**Halsbury, Hardinge Gifford, 1st earl of** (1823–1921). Conservative lawyer. Son of the editor of the Conservative *Standard* newspaper, Gifford was trained up to both the law and party politics. He was solicitor-general under *Disraeli in 1875 even before he had become an MP. He was prominent in the Conservative harassment of *Bradlaugh. Lord chancellor in all Conservative or Unionist governments from 1885 to 1905—seventeen years in all—Halsbury made many political appointments to the judicial bench. A productive legal reformer, he oversaw the production of the digest of *The Laws of England* (1905–16) which bears his name.

**Hamilton, William Douglas, duke of** [S] (1634–94). A younger son of the 1st marquis of Douglas [S], he was created earl of Selkirk in 1646. In 1656 he married the daughter of the 1st duke of *Hamilton, who was duchess in her own right. At the Restoration he was created duke for life. Favourable to *presbyterianism, Hamilton spent much of Charles II's reign in rivalry with *Lauderdale. James II favoured him. He was given the Garter in 1682, made a commissioner of the Treasury [S] 1686–9, and appointed to the English Privy Council in 1687. But he joined the Williamite cause in 1688 and presided over the Convention which met at Edinburgh in 1689 and offered the throne to William and Mary.

**Hamilton, Emma** (1765–1815). Born in the Wirral as Amy Lyon, Emma's sensational beauty became celebrated through the art of an early mentor, George *Romney (1734–1802). Mistress of Sir Harry Fetherstonhaugh, and then in 1782 of Charles Greville, Emma fell deeply in love with him. But in 1786 he passed her on to his widower uncle Sir William Hamilton (1730–1803), British representative at the court of Naples and Sicily. Hamilton delighted in Emma's theatrical flair, and in 1791 he married her. An intimate of Queen Maria Carolina, Emma was able to bring timely sustenance to Nelson's ships before the Nile battle in August 1798. From this time on Nelson's infatuation with her moulded her future and dramatized Nelson's. Defiant in self-induced adversity, after her mother's death in 1810 Emma Hamilton degenerated beyond redemption. She died in Calais.

**Hamilton, James Hamilton, 1st duke of** [S] (1606–49). Charles I's adviser on Scottish affairs during the civil wars.

Educated at Exeter College, Oxford, Hamilton became a privy counsellor under Charles I and fought for the protestant cause in Germany during the 1630s. He failed to pacify the Scottish religious disturbances of the late 1630s, or to wrest control of Aberdeen from the *covenanters in 1639. Fleeing Scotland in 1644 for the king's court in Oxford, he was arrested and imprisoned. Freed in 1646 he laboured to persuade the Scots to support a royalist-presbyterian uprising in England. When the rising did occur in 1648, Hamilton did not arrive with his promised army until July. His cavalry strung out in a thin line more than 20 miles long, he was easy prey for Cromwell's hardy veterans at *Preston (August 1648). Hamilton surrendered at Uttoxeter and was executed on 9 March 1649.

**Hamilton, James Hamilton, 4th duke of** [S] (1658–1712). Hamilton's grandfather had been executed in 1649 as a royalist and his great-uncle had been killed fighting for Charles II at *Worcester. His mother, duchess in her own right, surrendered her title to him in 1698. Though his father supported William of Orange at the Glorious Revolution, Hamilton was long suspected of Jacobitism. After taking his seat in the Scottish Parliament in 1700, he became leader of the party which brought about the confrontation with England caused by the Act of *Security of 1703. But he switched in 1705, moving that the queen should appoint the commissioners to treat for Union. He was not included in the commission and opposed the terms of Union vehemently. After the Union, he served as a representative peer 1708–12 and was given the dukedom of Brandon [GB] in 1711. The House of Lords refused to allow him to take his seat. In 1712 his fortunes seemed to have recovered: he was appointed master-general of the ordnance and given the Garter, but perished in a duel in Hyde Park (in which his opponent Lord Mohun was also killed).

**Hamilton, William Hamilton, 2nd duke of** [S] (1616–51). Scottish royalist leader in civil wars. Hamilton was educated at the University of Glasgow, created earl of Lanark in 1639, and made secretary of state for Scotland the following year. He was regarded with suspicion by English royalists on account of his links with the *covenanters. In

1646 he regained the king's confidence and worked throughout 1647 for a treaty with the Scots, the *Engagement, to restore the king to his throne in exchange for establishing presbyterianism in England. He played a leading part in preparing the invasion of England in 1648, led by his brother, the 1st duke. After inheriting his brother's title in 1649, he joined the second invasion of England in 1651. 'To go with a handful of men into England', he wrote, seems 'very desperate'. He was right. Wounded at *Worcester, he died a few days later and was buried in the cathedral.

**Hamilton, John** (c.1511–71). Archbishop of St Andrews. Hamilton was an illegitimate son of the 1st earl of Arran. He became a Benedictine monk as a boy. After study at Paris, he used his influence with his half-brother, the Regent *Arran, on behalf of the old religion and was appointed lord privy seal in 1543. He was made bishop of Dunkeld in 1544 and three years later, after the murder of Cardinal *Beaton, was translated to the archbishopric of St Andrews and primacy. Captured in 1571 after Mary's cause had collapsed, he was accused of complicity in the murders of *Darnley and of *Moray, and hanged at Stirling.

**Hamilton, Sir Thomas** See HADDINGTON, 1ST EARL OF.

**Hampden, John** (1594–1643). Hampden, a parliamentarian, sat in every Parliament from 1621 until his death. He was imprisoned in 1627 for refusing the *forced loan and became a close friend of Sir John *Eliot. He rose to national fame by providing the test case of the legality of *ship money (1637–8), and in the Short and Long Parliaments his reputation was second only to *Pym's. He raised his own foot regiment in his native Buckinghamshire, fought at *Edgehill, and was mortally wounded in a skirmish with *Rupert's horse at *Chalgrove Field.

**Hampden clubs** (1812–17), named after the 17th-cent. parliamentarian, marked a new era of agitation for parliamentary reform after the radicalism of the 1790s. Founded by Major John Cartwright, the clubs spread rapidly in the provinces among the working classes. A national convention was held in

1817; whereupon the clubs were immediately suppressed by government legislation.

**Hampshire** was essentially the hinterland of the great port of *Southampton from which it took its name, plus the *Isle of Wight. At the time of the Roman occupation, the region was inhabited by the *Regni in the south-east, the *Belgae towards the south-west, and the *Atrebates in the north. The Roman advance, undertaken by *Vespasian, was early and occupation thorough. There were two major towns, each probably of pre-Roman origins—Silchester (Calleva Atrebatum) in the north, *Winchester (Venta Belgae) in the south.

Saxon settlement was relatively easy and Winchester became the capital of *Wessex, though Silchester was abandoned. The Isle of Wight and the eastern valley of the Meon were areas of Jutish settlement and for a while formed part of the kingdom of *Sussex. By the 8th cent., a harbour of Hampton had developed near the site of the small Roman port of Bitterne Clausentum. Under 755, the *Anglo-Saxon Chronicle* referred to Hampton-shire, though we cannot be sure what area was intended. As Wessex flourished, Winchester became the capital of England: *Edward the Confessor was crowned there and many kings, including *Alfred and *Cnut, buried there.

In the course of the 12th cent., the capital was removed from Winchester to Westminster, but Winchester retained importance as a bishopric: the new cathedral, the longest in Europe, was begun in 1079. The connection with Normandy and the continent enhanced Southampton's trade. In the west of the county, the New Forest was appropriated by William I as a game reserve.

In the *Domesday survey of 1086, Winchester and Southampton were clearly important towns, and Basingstoke, Christ-church, and Stockbridge were of local significance. *Portsmouth is not mentioned by Domesday but was granted a charter in 1194. Its prosperity rose with the establishment of the Royal Navy. By 1801 it was the ninth largest town in England with more than four times the population of Southampton. Andover developed as a centre for the north-west of the shire and Basingstoke for the north-east: each was far enough from Southampton and Portsmouth to have its own sphere of influence.

Though relatively little touched by the industrial revolution, the shire changed considerably in the 19th and 20th cents. The popularity of seaside holidays produced the extraordinary growth of Bournemouth. The Isle of Wight also profited, partly no doubt because of the publicity given to *Osborne House. An equally spectacular growth was in the north-east of the county. The army began building barracks at Aldershot in 1854, transforming a hamlet into a sizeable town, and Basingstoke, chosen for urban development in 1963, grew from 25,000 to nearly 155,000.

**Hampton Court conference,** 1604. Although Elizabeth I established a protestant church in England in 1559, it offended *puritan opinion by retaining many catholic practices. In 1603 at the accession of James I the puritans presented him with the *millenary petition. James, who relished theological debate, responded by summoning a conference of puritans and bishops to Hampton Court in January 1604. Discussions produced considerable convergence on minor matters, but the only major achievement was the authorization of a new translation of the Bible—the 'King James version'.

**Hampton Court palace** (Middx.). Royal residence, situated on the banks of the Thames, south-west of London. Started by Cardinal *Wolsey in 1514, Hampton Court was confiscated in 1529 by Henry VIII, who subsequently added the great hall and a new court where the present Fountain Court is, and remodelled the Chapel Royal and the Clock Court. From 1689 Sir Christopher *Wren started work on the new Fountain Court, with its east and south frontages to the garden, and on a new range of the Clock Court. Wren's buildings are classical essays in brick and stone. William III's Privy Garden was restored in the 1990s.

**Handel, George Frideric** (1685–1759). German-born composer who took English nationality. Initially cathedral organist in his native Halle, Handel played violin and harpsichord at the Hamburg opera-house, where his first two operas were produced in 1705. In 1710 Handel was appointed Kapellmeister to the elector of Hanover (later George I of England), although within a few months he was in London. Here the colourful arias and magnificent stage effects of his opera *Ri-

*naldo* (1711) created a sensation, and by 1712 he had settled permanently in England, acting 1717–19 as resident composer to the future duke of Chandos at Cannons (near Edgware).

Although Handel continued composing operas until 1741, increasing financial pressures encouraged him to turn to a new dramatic medium, the English oratorio. *Esther* (1732) initiated a series of oratorios. The oratorio gradually displaced opera in the public's interest, forming the basis after Handel's death for a lasting English choral tradition centring especially on *Messiah* (1742).

**Handley, Tommy** (1892–1949). Comedian. Handley's heyday was the Second World War when, with much entertainment suspended, radio predominated. Born in Liverpool, Handley began as a commercial traveller and singer in variety shows, with modest success until the launch of the radio programme *ITMA* (*It's That Man Again*) in 1939. The weekly programme attracted vast audiences to the gallery of comic characters—Mrs Mopp, Colonel Chinstrap, Mona Lott, Funf—and repetitive catch-phrases. The show was still running when Handley died at 57.

**Hanover** was in personal union with Britain from 1714, when George I succeeded Queen Anne under the terms of the Act of *Settlement, until 1837 when the Salic Law prevented Victoria from retaining Hanover and it passed to her uncle, Ernest Augustus, duke of *Cumberland. In 1714 it had a population of just over 500,000 and was rather bigger than Yorkshire. The chief town, Hanover, had about 10,000 inhabitants. In 1719, the acquisition of Bremen and Verden at the expense of Sweden gave the electorate access to the North Sea.

The connection with Hanover was regarded by most Britons with distaste or at best as a necessary evil. The Act of Settlement had indicated a marked distrust. The new monarch could not appoint Germans to any post in Britain, could not declare war to help Hanover without parliamentary consent, and could not even visit his native land without parliamentary approval. Though the last condition was soon dropped, as personally offensive to the sovereign, suspicion remained. In December 1742, William *Pitt gained great popularity by declaring that 'this great, this powerful, this

formidable kingdom is considered only as a province of a despicable electorate'.

After 1760, British hostility to Hanover declined. The declaration by the new king, George III, that 'born and educated in this country, I glory in the name of Britain' played the nationalist card to some effect, and the swarms of Scots who clustered around *Bute gave the English new people to hate. George III never visited Hanover, though at moments of crisis he mused on retiring there.

**Hanseatic League** The league was a trading alliance which, at its height, included 200 towns, of which the most important were Lübeck, Hamburg, Bremen, Cologne, and Danzig. Founded in the 13th cent., it survived until the 17th and exercised great naval and diplomatic, as well as economic, power. The German word *hanse* meant a guild or company. Its London base, the Steelyard, was just west of London bridge, until closed by Elizabeth I in 1598.

**Harcourt, Simon Harcourt, 1st Viscount** (1661–1727). Of an Oxfordshire gentry family, Simon Harcourt studied law and, returned for Abingdon in 1690, supported the Tories. His fortunes closely followed those of his schoolfriend Robert *Harley. In 1702–8 he was solicitor-general and then attorney-general, resigning with Harley. In 1710 he defended *Sacheverell at his impeachment, speaking to great acclaim. During the subsequent Tory ministry he was lord keeper and then lord chancellor, obtaining a barony in 1711. On George I's arrival, he was dismissed.

**Harcourt, Sir William Vernon** (1827–1904). Liberal politician. Harcourt probably regarded himself as a failure. He was a brilliant lawyer, politician, and polemicist, who rose to be home secretary (1880–5) and chancellor of the Exchequer (1886, 1892–5), and expected to succeed *Gladstone as premier, but was passed over when the latter retired (1894) in favour of *Rosebery. Harcourt's main contribution to British history was his introduction of death duties in the budget of 1894, and the claim 'We are all socialists now' that went with it.

**Hardie, James Keir** (1856–1915). Socialist politician. Born in Lanarkshire, Hardie grew up in extreme poverty. While working as a journalist he organized the Lanarkshire and Ayrshire miners, becoming secretary of the Scottish Miners' Federation in 1886 and, in 1887, chairman of the Scottish Labour Party. In 1892 he was elected as an independent Labour MP for South West Ham; the following year he established the Independent Labour Party. Hardie was a thoroughly class-conscious socialist, outraging Westminster opinion by wearing a cloth-cap and tweed jacket in the Commons. He deliberately downplayed his socialist creed in order to persuade the Trades Union Congress of the need for the foundation (1900) of the Labour Representation Committee, forerunner of the Labour Party.

**Hardwicke, Philip Yorke, 1st earl of** (1690–1764). As the longest-serving lord chancellor of the 18th cent., Hardwicke had significant legal achievements to his credit, particularly in clarifying the laws of equity. He was solicitor-general at the age of 29, chief justice and a peer at 42, and lord chancellor at 46 (1737). An austere man, he had the lifelong friendship of the duke of *Newcastle and, though resigning as lord chancellor in 1756, he remained a member of the 'effective cabinet' until 1762.

**Hardy, Thomas** (1840–1928). Novelist and poet, Hardy initially trained as an architect. He left his native Dorset, the 'Wessex' of his books, for London where he lost his faith under the influence of *Darwin and *Huxley. His famous pessimism developed early and coloured everything to come. In the 1870s he caught the taste of an increasingly urbanized England for accounts of a vanishing world with *Under the Greenwood Tree* (1872) and *Far from the Madding Crowd* (1874). An unrivalled observer of the countryside, he found no Wordsworthian solace there, nor in his own unhappy marriage. His major novels tackled the social issues of the day, the double standard in *Tess of the D'Urbervilles* (1891), the unfairness of the divorce laws in *Jude the Obscure* (1895), the hostile reception they encountered prompting a return to his first love, poetry.

**Hargreaves, James** (1720–78). Inventor. Hargreaves was a largely self-taught weaver from Lancashire, who invented the spinning jenny in 1764 and patented it in 1770. *Kay's flying-shuttle had greatly speeded up the process of weaving and Hargreaves's jenny, using several spindles at once, enabled spinning to keep up.

**Harlech castle** was built for Edward I as one of a series of fortifications intended to secure his conquest of north Wales. Begun in May 1283, it was largely completed in seven years and is one of the greatest achievements of its architect, Master James of St George. In the Welsh rising of 1400–13, Harlech fell to Owain *Glyndŵr, became the residence of his court and his family, and may have been the place where he was crowned prince of Wales.

**Harley, Robert, 1st earl of Oxford and Earl Mortimer** (1661–1724). Prime minister. From a puritan Herefordshire family, Harley was MP for Tregony (1689–90) and New Radnor Boroughs (1690–1711), and in the 1690s a leader of the new country party, as well as twice Speaker of the Commons. He was again Speaker (1702–5), and in 1704 was appointed secretary of state for the northern department in the *Godolphin ministry. His growing Toryism and reputation for deviousness led to his resignation in 1708. His revenge was to gain the confidence of Queen Anne and to engineer the fall of the ministry in 1710, becoming chief minister for the next four years.

Though leader of an essentially Tory ministry, Harley wanted to establish a government above party. He failed as a result of increased extremism in the Tory Party. One week before she died, Anne dismissed Harley from office. He was impeached in 1715, largely for his part in the peace of *Utrecht which George I had opposed, and remained in the Tower until 1717 when proceedings were dropped.

**Harmsworth, Alfred, 1st Viscount Northcliffe** (1865–1922). Newspaper proprietor. The eldest son of a Dublin barrister who moved to London in 1867, Northcliffe was largely self-educated. Attracted to journalism, he discovered that he had a natural aptitude for the profession. In 1887 he formed his own publishing house, which he ran with his brother *Harold. The business acquired first the *Evening News*, later the *Daily Mail*, the *Daily Mirror*, the *Observer*, and, in 1908, *The Times*. He was created baron (1905) and viscount (1918).

**Harmsworth, Harold, 1st Viscount Rothermere** (1868–1940). Newspaper proprietor. Younger brother of Alfred *Harmsworth, Viscount Northcliffe, Harold eschewed the public limelight enjoyed by Alfred, but in 1917 accepted *Lloyd George's invitation to take charge of the Air Ministry. Meanwhile he had increased the scope of his own newspaper proprietorship, producing the *Sunday Pictorial*, London's first Sunday picture newspaper, in 1915. Created baron (1914), he was advanced to viscount (1918). On his brother's death in 1922 Harold assumed control of Associated Newspapers, and used this opportunity to write forceful articles for the *Daily Mail* in praise of Hitler and Mussolini.

**Harold I** (*c*.1016–40), king of England (*c*.1035–40), known as 'Harefoot', was a son of *Cnut, by Ælfgifu of Northampton, his first wife. In 1035, on Cnut's death, he claimed the throne of England in opposition to his half-brother *Harthacnut, whose mother was *Emma, Cnut's second wife. Since the sons were young, the probability is that they were pawns in the hands of formidable mothers. By 1037 he had established himself as king of the whole realm. Harthacnut prepared to invade but Harold's death at Oxford in 1040 allowed a peaceful succession.

**Harold II (Harold Godwineson)** (*c*.1022–66), king of England (1066), was defeated and killed by William the Conqueror at the battle of *Hastings. Along with the rest of his family, Harold rose to increasing prominence in England during the reign of *Edward the Confessor, receiving the earldom of East Anglia in 1044 and succeeding his father *Godwine as earl of Wessex in 1053. He was subsequently the most powerful man in the kingdom after the king. There is nothing to suggest that Harold was being groomed for the succession or that he coveted it, until he was designated as his successor by the dying Edward. The most probable explanation of Harold's career between 1053 and 1066 is that he was a careful politician who did not take risks. Edward's death-bed bequest of succession to the English kingdom was probably a recognition that Harold was the only man likely to be accepted with anything resembling unanimity by the English. After his coronation on the day immediately following Edward's death, Harold's efforts to defend his kingship against his rivals were effective and courageous. The support he received during the great campaigns of 1066 must indicate that he was widely accepted as king. His march north to win the battle of Stamford Bridge was a remarkable military feat, as was the return to confront William the Conqueror. The length and hard-fought character of the battle of Hastings suggests that the English were both well led and well organized. Harold's death occurred late in the battle.

**Harold Sigurdsson** (d. 1066), king of Norway. Harold, the half-brother of St Olaf, was the last great Viking invader of England. Nicknamed 'Hardrada'—stern in council—and a man of great stature and strength, he joined forces in 1066 with *Tostig, *Harold II Godwineson's exiled brother. Harold Hardrada claimed the throne of England and Tostig was to be restored to his earldom of Northumbria. The local earls, Edwin and Morcar, were defeated at *Fulford, just outside York, but five days later the victorious Norsemen were attacked at *Stamford Bridge by Harold, who had led a forced march from the south. After bloody fighting, Harold Hardrada and Tostig were killed.

**Harrington, James** (1611–77). Political philosopher. His *Commonwealth of Oceana* (1656), though dedicated to *Cromwell, implicitly censured the *Protectorate. Its central doctrine was that the distribution of property in a state determined its form of government. Where one ruler disposes of all the land, absolute monarchy results; where an aristocracy holds most of it, mixed monarchy is the natural form; but where property is widely distributed, only a republic can provide stable government.

**Harrington, William Stanhope, 1st earl of** (*c*.1683–1756). Stanhope was a younger son who, with good connections, built a distinguished career. Queen Anne complained of his 'insipid sloth', Lord *Hervey of his 'infinite laziness'. But the earls of Chesterfield were distant cousins and James *Stanhope, commander in Spain and briefly first minister, was another cousin. William Stanhope served in the army in Spain, and was soon given a regiment, rising to full general. In 1715 he was returned to Parliament for Derby and began a diplomatic career as ambassador to Spain. In 1730 he joined *Walpole's cabinet as secretary of state, receiving a barony. His connections were with the duke of *Newcastle and he survived Walpole's fall, gaining promotion to an earldom in 1742 and serving as lord president of the council 1742–5. In 1744 he resumed as secretary of state and finished his career as lord-lieutenant of Ireland between 1746 and 1750.

**Harris, Sir Arthur Travers** (1892–1984). Marshal of the Royal Air Force, famous as commander-in-chief, RAF Bomber Command, 1942–5. Harris repeatedly claimed that wrecking large German towns would win the war. British 'strategic bombing' killed and maimed civilians, destroyed beautiful buildings, and sacrificed many bomber crews, but did not win the war. Harris resisted 'precision bombing' but his favoured methods failed to reduce war production as he planned. He was not engaged in 'genocide', nor was he a 'war criminal'. Nevertheless, he did not get a peerage and there were hostile demonstrations when a statue to him was erected in London in 1992.

**Harris, Howell** (1714–73). A founder of Welsh Calvinistic methodism. Born at Trefecca, Talgarth, near Brecon, and educated locally, Harris hoped for Anglican ordination, but started teaching (1730). Following a conversion experience, he began studies at Oxford (1735) but soon returned home. Though an Anglican until his death, he began itinerant open-air preaching (1737) so effectively that by 1739 he had aroused much of Wales. He had close contacts with Selina, countess of *Huntingdon, and *Whitefield.

**Harrowby, Dudley Ryder, 1st earl of** (1762–1847). Harrowby was elected on the family interest at Tiverton in 1784 at the age of 21, supported *Pitt, and worked his way up the ladder. He was made under-secretary at the Foreign Office in 1789, served as paymaster 1791–1800, was foreign secretary 1804–5, and chancellor of the duchy of Lancaster 1805–6. He succeeded his father as 2nd baron in 1803 and was raised to the earldom in 1809. From 1812 until 1827 he served

under Liverpool as lord president of the council and in December 1827 was offered the premiership, which he declined on grounds of ill-health. He played an important role during the reform crisis of 1831–2 as a leader of the waverers, who ultimately voted for the bill.

**Harrow School** was founded by John Lyon, a yeoman in the neighbouring village of Preston, in 1571 as a free grammar school for the education of 30 poor children. After a period of decline, the school's fortunes were restored largely by the eminent headmaster Dr Charles Vaughan (1816–97).

**Harthacnut** (c.1019–42), king of England (1040–2), was a son of *Cnut by his second wife *Emma of Normandy, widow of *Æthelred II. At his father's death in 1035 he was in Denmark, but his mother put forward his claim to the throne of England against his half-brother *Harold Harefoot. On the latter's death in 1040 Harthacnut succeeded. In 1042, at the wedding-feast of his standard-bearer Tofig the Proud, he 'died as he stood at his drink and suddenly fell to the ground with a horrible convulsion'.

**Harvey, William** (1578–1657). Physician. After Cambridge, Harvey went to the great medical school at Padua. Back in England, he settled down to successful practice in London, becoming physician to Charles I and a staunch royalist. The structure of the heart and vein valves convinced him that, contrary to received physiological opinion, blood must circulate round the body, rather than ebb and flow.

**Haselrig, Sir Arthur** (c.1600–61). Haselrig, a Leicestershire baronet, was a leader of the parliamentary cause throughout the civil wars. A staunch puritan, educated at Cambridge and Gray's Inn, he was a close associate of *Pym. He served for his native county in the *Short and *Long Parliaments and his strong opposition to *Strafford and *Laud led to his being one of the *five members 'named' by Charles I in January 1642. He was an active cavalry commander during the first civil war, at the head of his regiment of 'lobsters', and was made governor of Newcastle upon Tyne in 1647. He refused to serve on the High Court which tried the king and quarrelled with *Cromwell when the *Rump

Parliament was dismissed. After quarrelling with *Lambert, he threw in his lot with *Monck. At the Restoration he was stranded and though Monck saved his life, he spent his last months in the Tower.

**Hastenbeck, battle of,** 1757. *Cumberland, the hero of *Culloden, commanded the Army of Observation in the *Seven Years War. On 26 July, on the Weser near Hameln, Cumberland was attacked by a superior French force under Marshal d'Estrées, and was forced to retreat. Acting on private instructions from his father George II, he retired in good order to Stade, where he negotiated the convention of *Kloster-Zeven, disbanding his forces. The British government repudiated the convention.

**Hastings, battle of,** 1066. Fought on 14 October at what is now Battle (Sussex). The core of Harold's army had marched south in under three weeks after its victory at *Stamford Bridge. The two armies were probably almost evenly matched numerically, but William's contained cavalry. A mixture of genuine and feigned retreats by William's army appears to have disrupted the packed English forces by drawing them down from their defensive position on the ridge. Harold's death, late in the day, ensured that the battle would be decisive.

**Hastings, William Hastings, 1st Lord** (c.1430–83). Hastings was the lifelong confidant of Edward IV. In the last years of the reign he was one of the half-dozen men on whom the king relied. Unquestionably loyal to the dynasty, he gave his total support to the young Edward V in the early summer of 1483. Because of his antipathy towards the Woodvilles, he was prepared initially to support Richard of Gloucester in his bid for power. But he himself became a victim when he was suddenly seized and executed on 13 June.

**Hastings, Francis Rawdon-Hastings, 1st Marquis, and 4th Baron Moira** (1754–1826). Hastings was born in Ireland and educated at Harrow and Oxford. In 1771 he joined the army and served in the American War of Independence 1776–81. Thereafter he held appointments mainly at home until he was made governor-general of India in 1813. His period in office was marked by major military conquests, which consolidated British power. He retired from India in 1823 and was appointed governor of Malta 1824–6.

**Hastings, Warren** (1732–1818). Hastings joined the *East India Company in 1750. He rose quickly in its service, being a member of the Bengal Council by 1757 when Robert *Clive achieved his first military victories. In 1764 he retired to England with a large fortune which he rapidly lost. He returned to India in 1769 and, three years later, was appointed governor of Bengal. In 1773, he became the first governor-general of India. In office, he reformed the company's revenue and commercial systems and extended its influence across the Ganges valley. He retired with a second fortune, but was impeached for murder and extortion. The prosecution was led by Edmund *Burke and the proceedings lasted from 1788 until 1795, when Hastings was acquitted, but left impoverished.

**Hatfield, Council of,** 680. The council arose out of concern over the Monothelite heresy, significant in the East, and finally condemned at the Council of Constantinople, 680–1. At Hatfield (Herts.), the bishops and teachers united in their declaration of the orthodox catholic faith.

**Hatton, Sir Christopher** (1540–91). Lord chancellor. Of Northamptonshire gentry stock, his good looks and graceful dancing brought him to Queen Elizabeth's attention. Despite total devotion to her, his governmental career was slow to develop. He was appointed lord chancellor in 1587, when any shortfall in legal training was outweighed by impartiality, common sense, and Star Chamber experience.

**Havelock, Sir Henry** (1795–1857). Havelock was born in Sunderland and took an army commission in 1815. He served with distinction in the first *Burmese War (1824–6), the first *Afghan War (1838–42), and the first *Sikh War (1845–6). He was a member of Sir James Outram's expedition to Persia in 1857 but returned to India after the outbreak of the *Indian mutiny. Although winning several victories, he failed to hold *Cawnpore or lift the siege of *Lucknow. He had to await Sir Colin *Campbell's army before success could be achieved. He died of dysentery at Lucknow in November 1857, shortly after its relief.

**'Hawarden Kite'** After the general election of 1885 Gladstone's Liberals with 333 seats were balanced by 251 Tories who had an understanding with *Parnell's 86 Irish MPs. In December 1885 Gladstone's son Herbert leaked to the press that his father had a scheme for Home Rule. The Conservative government was defeated and resigned, and Gladstone formed his third administration, splitting his party on the Irish question. The satirical name given to Herbert Gladstone's initiative was taken from Hawarden in Flintshire, where Gladstone had made his home.

**Hawke, Sir Edward** (1710–81). The son of a barrister. Hawke was captain at 24 and rear-admiral at 37. His chance came towards the end of the War of the *Austrian Succession when the commander of the Channel fleet, Sir Peter Warren, fell ill and Hawke took over. Off *Cape Finisterre in October 1747 he won a decisive victory, taking seven out of nine enemy vessels. Hawke was again employed in the *Seven Years War. An expedition against Rochefort in 1757 was a dismal failure but in 1759 he blockaded Brest and in November his brilliant victory at *Quiberon Bay ended all chance of a French invasion.

**Hawkins, Sir John** (1532–95). Hawkins began his career as an ally of the Spanish, to whose West Indies and South American colonies he carried west African slaves between 1562 and 1569. *Drake was with him when relations with Spain became hostile on the last expedition. He was subsequently an MP and comptroller of the navy, which he developed. Further active commands followed—against the Armada, on an expedition to Portugal in the following year, and the disastrous association with Drake on the West Indies anti-Spanish expedition of 1595, when he died off Puerto Rico.

**Hawksmoor, Nicholas** (c.1661–1736). 250 years after his death some critical opinion hailed Hawksmoor as the most daringly original architect England has produced. Hawksmoor, self-schooled in the architecture of the classical world, built seven London churches during the twelve years 1712–24,

revealing a profoundly original control of mass, if not of the play of light, over complementary broken surfaces.

**Haydon, Benjamin Robert** (1786–1846). A historical painter, born in Plymouth, the son of a painter and publisher, Haydon is now chiefly remembered for his *Autobiography and Memoirs*, published in 1853.

**Hazlitt, William** (1778–1830). The son of a unitarian minister, Hazlitt grew up in Wem (Shropshire). Religious doubts preventing him following his father's profession, he started as a painter, and then began literary work for periodicals. But he was cantankerous—'I have quarrelled with almost all of my old friends'—his two marriages failed, and he was frequently in financial distress. Hazlitt is at his best as an occasional essayist—his piece on the bare-knuckle fight between Neate and the Gas-man is in many anthologies. His best work is *The Spirit of the Age* (1825), with vivid and caustic sketches of contemporaries.

**Heads of the Proposals,** 1647. In June 1647 the army had taken custody of Charles I and, in the course of July, *Lambert and *Ireton worked out a basis for negotiation. The monarchy was to continue and to retain its veto; episcopacy was confirmed, though the bishops were to lose their coercive authority; there were to be guarantees of religious toleration; the militia was to be under the control of Parliament for ten years; parliaments were to be biennial and were to be elected on a reformed system. There was to be a council of state. Though these proposals were remarkably conciliatory in the aftermath of civil war, Charles rejected them out of hand.

**Heath, Sir Edward** (1916–2005). Prime minister. Heath went to Balliol College, Oxford, where he secured an organ scholarship and became president of the Union. The *Second World War deepened Heath's conviction that European reconstruction and unity represented the greatest challenge facing his generation. He was among the impressive new Conservative MPs elected in 1950, joining the 'One Nation' group of Tories who took a particular interest in social policy. His maiden speech was on the subject of

Europe—the most consistent theme in his career.

Heath enjoyed good relations with both *Eden and *Macmillan; under the latter his career prospered. After the 1959 general election he became minister of labour. In 1960, however, Macmillan decided to make Lord *Home foreign secretary with a second cabinet minister (Heath) in the Commons. This proved a turning-point in Heath's career. In 1961 the government determined to seek membership of the Common Market and Heath had the delicate task of negotiating the terms of entry. Though the mission was doomed, Heath won widespread applause for his handling of the discussions.

The choice of Home as a short-term leader in 1963 suited Heath since he was himself not yet ready to stake a claim. In the last year of Conservative government, Heath, as president of the Board of Trade, surprised many by introducing controversial legislation to abolish retail price maintenance. As shadow chancellor in 1965 Heath further impressed. With his commitment to the tasks of opposition he stood in marked contrast to his leading rival for the succession, Reginald Maudling. When Home suddenly resigned in July, Heath secured a narrow victory over Maudling. But Heath never had the subtlety or political skills to compete effectively with Wilson, the Labour leader. His popularity lagged behind that of the prime minister even when the Conservatives were running well ahead. None the less Heath prepared assiduously for government. A major policy review emerged in the document 'Putting Britain Right Ahead'. It spoke of encouraging a competitive economy, moving from direct to indirect taxation, greater selectivity in the social services, and taking Britain into Europe.

Heath's defeat in the 1966 election had been widely expected. But his comfortable victory in June 1970 surprised most commentators. Whatever Heath's true intentions, his government seemed more right-wing than any since the war. It was certainly beset by bad luck. The chancellor, Iain Macleod, died within a month of the election; Northern Ireland provided unlooked-for difficulties; world economic problems, especially the quadrupling of Arab oil prices in 1973, distorted domestic politics and fuelled inflation. None the less, it is hard to escape the conclusion that Heath's government was

a failure. Its one lasting achievement was to take Britain into the EEC, though on terms which ensured that this would remain a contentious issue.

Rising unemployment initiated an abrupt change in policy by the end of 1971. Heath's government then became one of the most interventionist since the war. By 1972 he had re-embraced the notion of an incomes policy. Industrial relations policy proved a disaster. The government finally collapsed in the wake of the miners' strike of 1973–4, to which Heath responded with a three-day week and finally a general election. The campaign was mishandled. A minority Labour government took office after Heath failed to negotiate a deal with the Liberals.

Further defeat followed in a second election in October. By now Heath had succeeded in alienating many of his own backbenchers. Challenged by Margaret *Thatcher, he withdrew from the leadership contest after failing to win the first ballot in February 1975. Heath never reconciled himself to these events, and time failed to heal or even soothe his wounds. Heath remained an MP throughout Thatcher's premiership, devoid of his earlier charm. He stayed in the Commons until 2001, becoming father of the House.

**Heathfield** (Haeth felth, Hatfield Chase), **battle of,** 633. On the Lindsey-Elmet border, north of the Idle on Hatfield Chase, died *Edwin of *Deira, king of Northumbria, in circumstances which enabled his promotion as a saint. He was defeated on 12 October by the allies *Penda of Mercia (pagan) and *Cadwallon of Gwynedd (Christian), both threatened by Northumbrian expansion.

**Heathfield, George Augustus Eliott, 1st Baron** (1717–90). A younger son of a Scottish baronet of Roxburghshire, Eliott attended the University of Leiden and served in the Prussian army before joining the Horse Grenadiers, his uncle's regiment, in 1739. He was promoted lieutenant-general in 1765, served as commander-in-chief in Ireland 1774–5, and became general 1778. In 1776 he was appointed governor of *Gibraltar, a post he held for the rest of his life. During the War of *American Independence, Gibraltar resisted a four-year siege, 1779–83, against Spanish and French forces. Eliott inflicted enormous losses on the Spanish floating batteries in September 1782 with red-hot shot and the following month *Howe raised the blockade.

**Heavenfield, battle of,** 634. Fought near Hexham. *Oswald of Northumbria defeated and killed *Cadwallon of Gwynedd, who had been ravaging the province after slaying Osric of Deira and Eanfrith of Bernicia (brother of Oswald) the year before. Through this victory Oswald secured his own position as king of both Bernicia and Deira and ensured that Northumbria would return to Christianity after a year of apostasy.

**Hebrides** *See* WESTERN ISLANDS.

**Hedgeley Moor, battle of,** 1464. Despite her crushing defeat at *Towton in 1461, Queen *Margaret retained a following in the north of England and was given assistance by the Scots. In the spring of 1464 they raised a substantial force under the duke of Somerset and Sir Ralph Percy. Montagu, *Warwick's younger brother, defeated it on 25 April at Hedgeley Moor, between Alnwick and Wooler. Sir Ralph Percy was killed but the duke of Somerset survived to offer battle three weeks later at *Hexham.

**Heligoland Bight, battle of,** 1914. In a confused naval encounter on 28 August 1914, *Beatty's battle-cruisers sank three German light cruisers and one destroyer. The action, though fierce, was limited, any victory when the Germans were still advancing on Paris was welcome.

**Henderson, Arthur** (1863–1935). Labour politician. Brought up on Tyneside and apprenticed as an ironfounder, Henderson, then a Gladstonian Liberal, moved slowly to the view that the political future of the working classes lay in separation from Liberalism. Elected for Barnard Castle under the auspices of the Labour Representation Committee in 1903, Henderson became secretary of its successor, the Labour Party, in 1911. Unlike Ramsay *MacDonald, Henderson approved of the war in 1914; he succeeded MacDonald as leader of the parliamentary Labour party, and in 1915 agreed to serve in Asquith's government, becoming a member of Lloyd George's war cabinet the following year. In 1917 he resigned from the government over

his support for a negotiated peace. He was foreign secretary in the second Labour government.

**Hengist and Horsa** Reputed founders of the kingdom of *Kent and its royal house. *Bede was the first to identify the two brothers as the leaders of Germanic forces invited to Britain by *Vortigern in 449; fuller accounts are provided in the 9th-cent. *Anglo-Saxon Chronicle* and *Historia Brittonum*.

**Henrietta Maria** (1609–69), queen of Charles I. Charles married Henrietta Maria, youngest daughter of Henri IV of France, in May 1625 after his Spanish marriage plans had come to naught. She was aged 15, small and vivacious, with dark curly hair, large brown eyes, and protruding teeth. Her husband was rather solemn and there was a very sharp quarrel in 1626 when he sent all her servants packing. But her relations with her husband became close, particularly after the death of *Buckingham in 1628. The 1630s she looked back on as halcyon days but increasingly Charles's political troubles darkened their lives. She fled to Holland in February 1642 with the crown jewels to raise men and money. Returning in July 1643 she joined Charles at Oxford. Heavily pregnant, she fled once more in 1644, giving birth to her youngest daughter at Exeter in June *en route* for France. She never saw her husband again. During the Cromwellian years she remained in France, returning to England at the Restoration in 1660. She left England for good in 1665.

**Henry I** (1068–1135), king of England (1100–35) and duke of Normandy (1106–35), was the youngest son of William the Conqueror. He played an intermittent role in the struggle between his elder brothers *Robert Curthose and William Rufus for control of the Anglo-Norman realm and seized the opportunity provided by the latter's death in 1100 to take over the English kingdom. Henry moved quickly to consolidate his coup, issuing a coronation charter which promised to renounce the supposed abuses of William II's rule, recalling Archbishop *Anselm from exile, and marrying *Matilda, the niece of *Edgar the Atheling and the daughter of *Malcolm Canmore, to create a dynastic link with the Old English ruling house and an alliance with the kingdom of Scots. By 1101 he was sufficiently powerful to resist Robert's invasion of England and to agree terms with him which confirmed Henry's kingship in England. In 1105-6 he invaded Normandy and completed his conquest of the duchy by defeating Robert in 1106 at the battle of *Tinchebrai, thereby recreating William the Conqueror's Anglo-Norman realm. Henry ruled both England and Normandy for the rest of his life, but his control over Normandy was always threatened until the death of Robert's son William Clito in 1128. Marriage alliances were used to secure useful allies, such as the one between his nephew, the future King Stephen, and *Matilda, heiress to the county of Boulogne. The death of his only legitimate son in the *White Ship increased Henry's problems and his failure to obtain an heir through his second marriage to *Adela of Louvain forced him into marrying his daughter, the Empress *Matilda, to Count *Geoffrey Plantagenet of Anjou in 1128.

The frequent warfare in northern France had an impact on England because Henry was obliged to raise money. His administration, supervised by Bishop Roger of Salisbury, had a reputation for efficiency and has been regarded by historians as being notably innovative. Other developments, such as the more frequent interventions of royal justices in the localities, can also be regarded as opportunist centralization because they relied fundamentally on the existing structure of shire courts and were not regular visitations after the pattern later established in Henry II's reign. Despite enduring problems, Henry was a very successful ruler. England was at peace after the early years of his reign and Normandy was kept secure. He dominated Wales as no predecessor had done and maintained good relations with his nephew, David I of Scotland. He experienced problems with the church in his early years, most notably when Archbishop Anselm of Canterbury took a stand over the practice of lay investiture of bishops and went into exile in 1103. Henry and the papacy reached a settlement in 1107 and thereafter Henry's relations with the church were generally good. He was a great patron of monasteries, most notably of Reading abbey, in which he was buried. Despite his many successes in war, diplomacy, and government,

Henry I's legacy was a disputed succession and almost inevitable civil war.

**Henry II** (1133-89), king of England (1154-89). The first of the *Plantagenet kings of England was one of the most successful of this country's monarchs. His achievements are the more remarkable since his responsibilities encompassed not just England, but also two-thirds of France, for Henry was also duke of Normandy, count of Anjou, and, by right of his wife Eleanor, duke of *Aquitaine. England was but part of the vast *Angevin empire. In England, Henry inherited in 1154 a realm severely affected by the political disintegration in Stephen's reign. He proceeded to restore, and then further develop, the governmental structure inherited from his grandfather Henry I. But to restore the crown's overall position, including the recovery of lands, offices, and castles lost in Stephen's reign, Henry needed the co-operation of the greater magnates. Equally, from this same group of men Henry demanded the restoration of the crown's rights—a seemingly impossible task. While bending the magnates to his will, he also succeeded in placating them and finding a place for them in his regime. Hence the remarkable general political stability of England during Henry's reign. Only in 1173-4 did serious unrest occur, in connection with the so-called Great Rebellion in England and France, and even then only a handful of English nobles were involved.

This political settlement helped provide the stable context for a notable extension of the crown's activities, especially through the introduction of the famous assizes. A far greater positive role was being taken by the crown than hitherto, whereby the king's law was becoming truly national in scope. Some measures concerned trade and commerce, such as the assizes of wine, ale, bread, and measures, whilst the Assize of *Arms dealt with the defence of the realm. But the most significant assizes were those which transformed both civil and criminal law. The grand jury, established by the Assize of *Clarendon, would be fundamental in the prosecution of crime until the establishment of the director of public prosecutions in 1879.

Stocky, of medium height, Henry was robust in his prime, fat in his later years. In the 1180s, it seems, he was aged beyond his actual years, worn out by constant travelling and exertion. When not on the move around his dominions, he seldom sat still for long, except to eat or play chess. Even at mass, he scribbled memoranda or whispered business to courtiers. He was a man of violent passions, easily moved to anger. He was capable of hatred, most notoriously revealed in his struggle with Thomas *Becket. But much of the threatening side of his nature was deliberately cultivated to get his own way. There was another side to his character that enjoyed simple, good-hearted fun.

One problem he never satisfactorily resolved—the partition of the Angevin empire between his sons. The issue blighted the last twenty years of his life, and poisoned relations within the family. He died vanquished, defeated by his son Richard and Philip II of France over that very issue.

**Henry III** (1207–72), king of England (1216–72). Henry was one of the most cultured monarchs ever to sit on the English throne, inspired by artistic beauty for its own sake, judging by his payments for a wide range of objects—silver, gold, and enamel work, hangings and embroideries, and frescos for the royal palaces. Equally, he chose to sink large sums into works of art to give visual expression to his heightened conception of monarchy. Nowhere is this more apparent than *Westminster abbey, which he established as the royal necropolis. Huge sums were spent on its rebuilding after 1245, despite an ever-worsening financial position. He deliberately promoted the cult of Edward the Confessor, having his own tomb in Westminster abbey placed within the aura of sanctity of Edward's tomb.

His conception of monarchy looked back to the period before *Magna Carta when kingship was unlimited, in theory if not in practice. The traumatic experiences of his early years—the bringing down of his father, King John, French invasion and civil war, tutelage by baronial regency council—probably propelled him in this direction as well. This attitude contributed to the crises which characterized his reign after his personal rule began in 1232. It culminated in the demand for radical reform in 1258 and the imposition of the provisions of *Oxford, the prelude to the so-called Barons' War that tore the country apart until the defeat of Simon de *Mont-

fort at the battle of *Evesham (1265). But it was by no means only, even chiefly, constitutional issues that were at stake. Protest against his hated half-brothers, the Lusignans, who came to England after 1247, lay at the heart of the baronial confederacy of 1258.

Henry was particularly vulnerable in 1258 because he faced imminent excommunication if he did not meet the gigantic debt he owed to the papacy, incurred when he accepted the grant of the kingdom of Sicily to his son Edmund in 1254. This was the culmination of a foreign policy ever more grandiose. At first, Henry's chief goal was the recovery of those parts of the *Angevin empire lost under John. This was entirely reasonable. But the odds stacked against Henry steadily rose as the power of Louis IX of France and his brothers increased. His failure led him into a wider European strategy that involved a network of foreign allies, including Emperor Frederick II, who married Henry's sister Isabella in 1236, and the Savoyards, the powerful kinsmen of *Eleanor of Provence, whom Henry himself married in 1236. When Frederick was deposed by Pope Innocent IV in 1245, Henry was drawn into an attempt to secure the different parts of the imperial inheritance.

None of these schemes came to anything, and the huge costs incurred in the pursuit of Sicily forced him to abandon them. In 1259, too, he finally accepted reality and agreed to the treaty of *Paris, whereby he renounced his French claims as well. Henry's capacity to play for very high stakes, and yet lose, is truly remarkable.

**Henry IV** (1366–1413), king of England (1399–1413). The eldest son and heir of *John of Gaunt, duke of Lancaster, he was born at Bolingbroke (Lincs.) in the same year as his cousin Richard II, whom he deposed in 1399. Returning from exile with the declared intent only to recover his inheritance, within three months he usurped the throne. Although descended from Edward III, his claim to the throne was weak.

The first seven years of Henry's reign were years of crisis. He faced his first rebellion in January 1400 from a group of Richard II's excluded courtiers. Its principal victim was Richard himself, who died in custody at

Pontefract shortly afterwards. Other baronial rebellions followed, especially those of the Percys who had been Henry's principal supporters in 1399. In 1403 *Hotspur, heir to the earl of *Northumberland, was killed at *Shrewsbury. In 1405 the earl himself fled to Scotland after a failed rising; he was finally killed in an invasion in 1408. More serious to king and kingdom was the rebellion of the Welsh under Owain *Glyndŵr in 1400, which, despite annual English campaigns, led to the complete liberation of Wales by 1405. In addition war with Scotland, a running war at sea and constant threats to the remaining English possessions in France left Henry beleaguered. The cost of defending the throne led to frequent parliaments, frequent requests for taxation, and a hostile Commons, especially in 1401, 1404, and 1406.

That Henry survived these torrid years was due to several factors; his own determination and energy; the strength of his supporters; and his own pragmatism. He was also helped by the divisions in the ranks of his enemies, especially the development of civil war in France. As a result, by the end of 1406 the worst of his difficulties were over. But the strain ruined his health. In the spring of 1406 Henry had the first of a series of strokes, which by 1410 left him incapacitated. Yet at no time was Henry's throne threatened, and when he died in 1413 there was no challenge to the succession of his charismatic son.

**Henry V** (1386/7–1422), king of England (1413–22). Eldest son of Henry IV and his first wife Mary Bohun, Henry was born at Monmouth, most probably on 9 August or 16 September 1386 or 1387. He was thrust into prominence by his father's usurpation of the throne in 1399. From then on Henry took a prominent part in affairs. Between 1400 and 1408 he was mostly in the west, concerned with the war against the Welsh. On 21 July 1403 he was with his father at the battle of *Shrewsbury, where the English rebels under Henry *Percy, 'Hotspur', were defeated. Between 1410 and 1413 there seems to have been tension between the king and the prince. It is possible that the king was asked to abdicate in favour of the prince on the grounds of ill-health, but refused to do so. In the last fifteen months of the reign the prince seems to have taken little part in government. Henry succeeded his father on 20 March 1413.

The start of Henry's reign was seen by contemporaries as a new beginning. Henry lived up to these expectations, providing dynamic leadership that fired widespread enthusiasm, and appealed to feelings of nationalism and nationhood. Henry encouraged the keeping of the festivals of English saints and promoted the use of English. He used the war with France to promote the idea that England was a nation blessed by God. The general enthusiasm for the war is evidenced by the large number of the nobility who followed him to France, and by the generous grants of taxation made by Parliament before the first campaign. The contemporary *Agincourt carol commemorated the battle as a famous English victory.

Henry did not at first claim the French throne but began by pressing for the implementation of the treaty of *Calais of 1360 in which the French had ceded Aquitaine, and to which he added further claims to Normandy, Touraine, and Maine. It is not clear whether Henry really expected to gain his ends by diplomacy, for he had made extensive preparations for war. The subsequent campaigns for the conquest of France were well organized. Henry's diplomacy secured the early neutrality of John, duke of Burgundy, and after Agincourt the whole-hearted support of the Emperor Sigismund. The first campaign brought the capture of Harfleur in September 1415, and victory at Agincourt on 25 October 1415. Further campaigns were aimed at the conquest of Normandy, during which Rouen fell in January 1419. Henry's success forced the French to agree to the treaty of *Troyes in May 1420, by which Henry was recognized as heir to the throne of France. The treaty was cemented by Henry's marriage to the Princess *Catherine, which took place on 2 June. After this Henry continued his campaigns to reduce areas of the country still loyal to the deposed dauphin, Charles. During the sieges of Melun and Meaux his health began to fail and he died, probably of dysentery, at Bois de Vincennes on 31 August 1422, leaving, as his heir to both crowns, his son Henry, less than a year old.

**Henry VI** (1421–71), king of England (1422–61 and 1470–1). Henry VI was the youngest king of England ever to ascend the throne; the only one ever to be crowned king of France; and arguably the worst, who inherited two kingdoms and lost both. His reign is divided into three parts. The first is his minority (1422–37); the second is his active majority (1437–53); and the third is the period of his mental incapacity (1453 until his death). Given the inherent dangers, Henry's minority was remarkably successful. Fifteen years later not only was Henry still on the throne (he was crowned king of England in 1429, king of France in 1431), but his kingdom was not unduly lawless, the crown was solvent, and a substantial part of Henry V's conquests in France remained in Lancastrian hands.

It was a cruel trick of fate to provide Henry V with a son who was the very antithesis of the martial traditions of the house of Lancaster. Henry VI proved to be improvident, malleable, vacillating, uninterested in the arts of government, and, above all, antipathetic to the chivalric world his ancestors had adorned. The defining moment came in 1440 when at 18 he had the opportunity to take the field in Normandy. Instead he sent his cousin the duke of *York as his lieutenant, devoting himself to the foundation of *Eton College. Within ten years the government of the kingdom had fallen into the hands of an unscrupulous court faction led by William de la Pole, duke of Suffolk, royal debts were mounting, and Normandy was lost. In 1450 the regime was shaken by *Cade's revolt, the most widespread popular rising since 1381.

Henry VI fell into a coma in August 1453. He recovered his senses just before Christmas 1454, but was permanently impaired. By 1459 royal government was almost totally powerless, the administration of the law had collapsed, and the crown was bankrupt. In the civil war that erupted Henry was a passive onlooker. In 1461 he became the victim when he was deposed by the victorious Edward IV. But his life was spared. There was no sentiment in this. Throughout the 1460s the hope of his cause was carried by his only son and heir *Edward, in exile in France; killing Henry would only have promoted a more plausible Lancastrian claimant. In 1470 he was restored to the throne for six months. Coming out of the Tower for rare public appearances, he was a pitiful sight. But the death of the prince of Wales at *Tew-

kesbury in 1471 sealed his own fate, and a few days later he was done to death.

**Henry VII** (1457–1509), king of England (1485–1509). Though the belief that Henry VII was a new kind of ruler at the head of a new kind of monarchy has long been abandoned, he was certainly an unusual ruler. Despite the fact that he was a competent soldier, he did not hanker after military glory. Secondly, he seemed to take positive pleasure in the detail of government and administration, while many monarchs left the hard work to ministers. Thirdly he seems to have wished to amass money rather than spend it.

The weakness of Henry's claim to the throne has been exaggerated. Henry's father was a half-brother of King Henry VI; his grandmother had been queen to Henry V and a princess of France; his great-great-grandfather was John of Gaunt, son of Edward III. Nevertheless, Henry's early life was inauspicious. His father Edmund Tudor, earl of Richmond, died three months before Henry was born at Pembroke castle. His young mother Lady Margaret *Beaufort remarried. His grandfather Owen *Tudor was beheaded at Hereford after the Lancastrian defeat at *Mortimer's Cross in 1461, and his uncle Jasper *Tudor, earl of Pembroke, was forced to flee. On the brief restoration of Henry VI in 1470 he was reunited with his uncle, but after the crushing defeat at *Tewkesbury, they both fled to Brittany. Not until Richard usurped the throne in 1483 did Henry's prospects brighten. In secret negotiations with Edward IV's widow, it was agreed that Henry should marry her daughter *Elizabeth, thus uniting the houses of Lancaster and York. But an attempt on the throne in 1483 proved premature. His ally *Buckingham was captured and beheaded, and Henry's own expedition to the south coast was scattered by gales. In 1484 Richard put pressure on Brittany to hand over Henry, who escaped to France in the nick of time. Thence he sailed with 2,000 men to Milford Haven in 1485 on the journey that brought him to *Bosworth and the throne.

He needed to learn very quickly since his nomadic existence before Bosworth had left him short of experience in government. He learned early not to be too trusting. Lord *Lincoln, who had fought against him at Bosworth, was forgiven, taken into employment, and attended the council to decide how to deal with Lambert Simnel—before riding off to join the rebels. But Henry became a good judge of men, and was well served by John *Morton, archbishop of Canterbury from 1486, and by Richard *Foxe, who finished as bishop of Winchester.

His main objectives were to secure his own position, to found a dynasty, and to establish a stable government. Of his four predecessors as kings, two had been murdered, one had died in battle, and the fourth (Edward IV) had been driven ignominiously from the kingdom in the middle of his reign. The foundation of Henry's success was the marriage to Elizabeth of York. The first challenge from Yorkist irreconcilables came in April 1486, was headed by Lord Lovel and the Hastings brothers, and was put down without difficulty. It was followed by the Simnel plot in 1487. Simnel claimed to be Edward, earl of Warwick, despite the fact that Warwick was in the Tower. His supporters, strengthened by German mercenaries, were subdued at *Stoke near Newark only after hard fighting. Simnel, a mere boy, was given a place in the royal kitchens and lived out a long life in safe obscurity. Perkin Warbeck, claiming to be Richard, duke of York, was received by James IV of Scotland as Richard IV, captured in 1498, but executed with Warwick the following year.

Under these circumstances, Henry's foreign policy could hardly be very ambitious. He was unable to save Brittany from annexation to France but the task was impossible once the duchess of Brittany herself had married the French king. The short war with Scotland 1496–7 was not of Henry's making but arose from James IV's support for Warbeck. Henry stood on the defensive and used the large parliamentary subsidy to emerge with a handsome profit. By the end of his reign, England's standing in Europe had been greatly enhanced. At home the nobility was kept in check less by legislation against livery and maintenance than by large financial bonds hanging over them. Financial security, which had the advantage of allowing Henry to do without parliaments for much of his reign, was built up by the patient exploitation of the opportunities and dues open to the crown. Their zeal on Henry's behalf made his servants *Empson

and *Dudley the most hated men in the kingdom and they were instant victims of Henry VIII's new reign in 1509.

**Henry VIII** (1491–1547), king of England (1509–47). Henry was born on 23 June 1491 at Greenwich, the third child and second son of Henry VII and Elizabeth of York. On the death of his elder brother *Arthur in April 1502 he became heir apparent; a few days after the death of his unpopular father, he was proclaimed king on 23 April 1509. Despite being only 17, Henry acted as king in his own right at once. Shortly after his accession he solemnized his fateful marriage to *Catherine, daughter of Ferdinand and Isabella of Spain and widow of his brother Arthur. However, apart from sacrificing Richard *Empson and Edmund *Dudley, his father's two most detested servants, he made few changes among his leading advisers. He began to play the European game of military alliances almost at once: a disastrous campaign in the Pyrenees in 1512 was followed in 1513 by the more successful seizure of Tournai and Thérouanne and the earl of Surrey's demolition of the Scottish aristocracy at *Flodden. Peace was made in 1514.

The political scene was transformed by Thomas *Wolsey, who used his position as royal chaplain and almoner to build up a formidable collection of church and government posts, becoming lord chancellor in 1515 and papal cardinal-legate *a latere* in 1518. With the accession of Francis I of France (1515–47) Henry found a rival whom he both disliked and imitated. For several years he manœuvred in the diplomatic game, until in 1518 he and Wolsey stage-managed the great European peace treaty of *London (1518). The next year another charismatic leader, Charles V of Austria, Burgundy, and Spain, became Holy Roman emperor, and Henry began meddling in the endless duel between Charles and Francis. He attacked France in 1522–3, but withdrew from the alliance just too soon to profit from Francis's defeat and capture at Pavia (1525).

During the 1520s Henry's marriage to Catherine had deteriorated. After bearing a princess (the future Mary I) in 1516, the queen had suffered a series of miscarriages and still-births which reawakened Henry's early misgivings about the marriage. By early 1527 an annulment of the marriage was openly discussed. However, in that year Charles V's troops sacked Rome and forced Pope Clement VII to seek protection from Charles V. While in the emperor's hands, the pope would not shame his captor's aunt by annulling her marriage. Wolsey tried unsuccessfully to persuade the pope to allow him to resolve the issue in England. When the final failure of this effort became apparent, Wolsey was stripped of his offices; he only escaped treason charges by his own death (1530).

The king's belief in his status as God's representative now became a potent political factor. It was exploited by a group of political theorists managed by the new rising minister, a former client of Wolsey, Thomas *Cromwell (1485–1540). In the Act in Restraint of *Appeals (24 Hen. VIII c. 12, 1533), the preamble enunciated Henry's claim to 'imperial' authority, without earthly superior, over clergy and laity alike. Henry secretly married *Anne Boleyn in January 1533, and was formally separated from Catherine the following May. Having then been excommunicated by the pope, however, Henry's regime enacted further statutes up to 1536, which cut all fiscal, legal, and spiritual ties to Rome and left the English church in schism.

Having broken with the papacy, the question of doctrine could not be evaded. Henry had a queen, Anne Boleyn, an archbishop of Canterbury, Thomas *Cranmer, and a leading minister, Cromwell, all of whom were in varying degrees Lutheran sympathizers. Henry's personal detestation of Luther, with whom he had exchanged polemics in the 1520s, and his horror of what he called 'sacramentarian' heresy left religious policy the plaything of factions. Nevertheless, enough innovations, both religious and fiscal, were introduced to bring about the revolts known as the '*Pilgrimage of Grace' in autumn 1536. The regime survived these by biding its time and retaining the loyalty of the nobility and the south. However, the Act of *Six Articles of 1539 marked a reaffirmation of certain traditional shibboleths and a hunt for 'heretics'. Meanwhile, the regime plundered the church, taxing the seculars heavily while abolishing the regular orders entirely and confiscating their wealth (1536–40).

Instability in official doctrine was matched by sanguinary feuds at court. In May 1536,

after the birth of a daughter (the future Elizabeth I) and a miscarriage, the temperamental Anne Boleyn, with her brother and several of her attendants, were executed for alleged acts of treasonable adultery. By the end of the month the king had married *Jane Seymour, who bore him his only son, the future Edward VI, on 12 October 1537 and died twelve days afterwards. Court rivalry and religious instability combined in the king's search for a fourth wife. Despite the reactionary strain then evident in religious policy, Henry was cajoled into a marriage-contract with *Anne, sister of the duke of Cleves, a reforming sympathizer. Henry accepted her on the strength of a flattering portrait, and married her, with evident distaste, on 6 January 1540. Thomas Cromwell survived this disastrous marriage for only a few months.

In his final years the king became more unpredictable and vulnerable. *Catherine Howard, niece of the duke of Norfolk, whom Henry had married on the day of Cromwell's execution, proved unfaithful. Her fall and execution on 13 February 1542 left the king devastated. He threw himself once more into diplomacy and war. A successful campaign in 1542 by Lord Wharton in Scotland left Scotland's army broken and accelerated the death of its king, but Henry did not follow up the victory. Instead he made fresh overtures to Charles V and in June 1544 invaded France again, capturing Boulogne at huge cost shortly before Charles V made a separate peace with Francis I. In these final years Henry wavered between a campaign against 'heresy', which reached peaks in 1543 (when it threatened Cranmer) and 1546 (when it briefly threatened Henry's last queen, *Catherine Parr), and periods when Henry allowed Cranmer to embark on cautious, partial reform of the old liturgy. In the dying months of the reign the reformers, led by the earl of Hertford (*Somerset), secured the near-total defeat of the conservative Howards; the duke of *Norfolk was awaiting execution when the king himself died on 28 January 1547. The education of the young Edward VI had been committed to reforming humanist tutors, so the old king's conservative legacy did not last into the new reign.

Few kings of England set out so consciously to glorify the style of the monarchy. Henry was the first to be addressed as 'Majesty' and the first defender of the faith and supreme head of the church. He had great athletic strength, a talent for music, and an enthusiasm for theology. In this light, the impression is of advantages squandered. He came to the throne rich and bequeathed debts, a corrupt coinage, and roaring inflation. His impact on the history of his time was colossal; yet nearly every part of his legacy was either disowned or significantly reinvented under his successors.

**Henry, prince of Wales** (1594–1612). Eldest son of James VI and I and Anne of Denmark. Following his father to England in June 1603, he impressed the crowds by his fine horsemanship and erect bearing. His promise and popularity occasioned jealousy in James; championship of *Ralegh, dislike of the royal favourite *Carr, and naval and military interests further increased tension. Marriage plans were overtaken by his sudden death from typhoid fever, leaving his less gifted brother Charles as heir.

**Henry, the Young King** (1155–83), was the eldest surviving son of Henry II and *Eleanor of Aquitaine. At Montmirail (Maine) in January 1169 Henry II announced his intentions for the division of his vast dominions, the Young Henry, as eldest son, to receive England, Normandy, and Anjou, Henry II's own inheritance. In May 1170 the young king was duly crowned joint king of England, but remained powerless since Henry II had no intention of abdicating. Young Henry, though, remained feckless and irresponsible, utterly uninterested in the serious business of government. This led him into revolt in 1173. Relations between father and son never fully recovered and he rebelled again in 1183, shortly before his death.

**Henry of Grosmont** (*c.*1300–61) was a cousin of Edward III and the king's right-hand man. His father was earl of Lancaster and Leicester. He was born in Grosmont, created earl of Derby in 1337, and succeeded his father as earl of Lancaster in 1345. In 1349 he was created earl of Lincoln and in 1351 duke of Lancaster. He was also created earl of Moray in Scotland in 1359. When the Order of the *Garter was instituted, he was next to the prince of Wales. Henry fought constantly against the French and the Scots and was with the king at the naval victory of

*Sluys in 1340 and at the surrender of *Calais in 1347. His palace at the Savoy was sumptuous. His younger daughter and ultimate heir married *John of Gaunt, for whom the dukedom of Lancaster was revived.

**Henry Stewart** *See* DARNLEY, LORD.

**Hepplewhite, George** (d. 1786). Cabinet-maker and furniture designer, Hepplewhite linked the ornate style of *Chippendale and the severer lines of *Sheraton. He was apprenticed to Robert Gillow of Lancaster, then opened a business in London about 1760. His reputation rests with *The Cabinet-Maker and Upholsterer's Guide* published two years after his death.

**heptarchy** The description of 7th-cent. England as a 'heptarchy' probably derives, ultimately, from the historian Henry of Huntingdon, writing in the earlier 12th cent. The idea was that there were seven kingdoms, Northumbria, Mercia, East Anglia, Essex, Kent, Sussex, and Wessex. Reality was more complicated. But the formulation was a useful one and had a long life.

**heraldry** The use of personal distinguishing marks on shields and banners seems to have developed in England and Scotland in the second half of the 12th cent. and in Wales in the 13th cent. Such devices rapidly became consistent and hereditary, and were used in a wide range of contexts, such as seals, surcoats, architectural features, and stained glass. The original purpose of identification was never lost, but the bearing of arms developed a further, social significance in denoting those of noble or gentle birth and status. Such a complicated and socially sensitive subject required increasing scrutiny; this was provided by heralds, who make their first official appearance in English royal records under Edward I. The office of Lord Lyon in Scotland appears in 1318, and that of Garter king-of-arms in 1417, with the full incorporation of the *College of Arms by Richard III in 1484. Tudor and Stuart heralds embarked upon visitations of counties 'to remove all false arms', and 'to take note of descents'.

**Herbert, George** (1593–1633). Poet. Grounded in classics at Westminster School, then graduate of Trinity College, Cambridge, Herbert obtained the post of university orator (held 1620–7) as a preliminary to public service. But by 1625 his 'Court-hopes' had faded with his patrons' deaths, so he turned to the church, finally being ordained in 1630 and inducted at Bemerton, near Salisbury. Herbert concentrated his remaining years on the parish and church repair—'Holy Mr Herbert' was a contemporary assessment. He is best known for his sacred poetry (*The Temple*, posthumously 1633), portraying his spiritual conflicts.

**Herbert, Sidney, 1st Baron Herbert of Lea** (1810–61). Politician. Herbert was educated at Harrow and Oxford. He entered the Commons as a Conservative in 1832, being in office in 1834–5 and 1841–6. In 1845–6 and 1852–5 he was secretary of war, being less blamed than others by the Roebuck Commission of 1855 for the poor organization of the army during the Crimean War. He returned to the War Office in 1859 and began an energetic programme of reform; overwork and Bright's disease caused his early death.

**Herbert, William, 3rd earl of Pembroke** (1580–1630). Herbert succeeded to the earldom at the age of 21 in 1601. He was under a cloud at Elizabeth's court for getting Mary Fitton, one of the maids of honour, pregnant. He fared better with James I, and from 1615 served as lord chamberlain. In 1626 he became lord steward. He was often at odds with royal policy and on bad terms with *Buckingham, favourite to both James I and Charles I. Nevertheless, his wealth and amiability gave him standing, he was chancellor of the University of Oxford, and Pembroke College was refounded in his honour.

**Hereford, diocese of** Around 679 *Theodore created the bishopric, conterminous with Herefordshire and south Shropshire, for the *Magonsaetan tribe, out of the Mercian see. Hereford was vulnerable to the Welsh, who sacked the cathedral in 1055 and killed the bishop, Leofgar. William I strengthened the region's defences by making it (until 1076) a Norman palatine earldom. The cathedral, dedicated jointly to the Virgin Mary and Æthelbert, the martyred East Anglian king (753), is mostly Norman and its 15th-cent. College of Vicars is still intact.

**Hereford and Worcester** This was a new county, formed under the Local Government Act of 1972. It included the county borough of Worcester, the old county of Hereford, and all of Worcestershire, save for Dudley, Halesowen, and Stourbridge, hived off to West Midlands. There was considerable opposition from Herefordshire, the smaller of the counties, complaining that it had little in common with the industrialized parts of north Worcestershire. But in accordance with the Banham Commission recommendation of 1994 the two counties were separated once more in 1998.

**Herefordshire** is a small border county, full of castles, running from the Black Mountains in the west to the Malverns in the east. Hereford itself was for centuries a stronghold against the Welsh, holding the crossing of the Wye.

In the pre-Roman period, Herefordshire was part of the territory of the *Silures, to whom *Caratacus appealed in his fight against the Romans. In the mid-7th cent. it fell to *Penda, pagan king of the Mercians. Soon after his death in battle, Hereford was founded as a diocese (676). A hundred years later Offa's Dike marked the limit of Mercian expansion, running through the west of the county from Kington, through Hay, to White Castle.

In the reign of *Athelstan Welsh princes did homage at Hereford, but the county remained vulnerable. Almost all the towns were on the east side, out of reach of the Welsh—Hereford, Leominster, Bromyard, Ross, Ledbury. Hereford itself was sacked by *Gruffydd ap Llywelyn in 1055 and the new cathedral destroyed. The next bishop of Hereford was a fighting man, Leofgar, who lasted a mere eleven weeks before he was slain. The Normans took the border in hand. William *Fitzosbern was given palatine status as earl of Hereford and began the building of a formidable castle there. The shire was only just held against *Llywelyn the Great in the early 13th cent. and threatened again by *Glyndŵr in the early 15th.

The industrial revolution touched Herefordshire lightly and it remains a quiet rural county. In the local government reorganization of 1972, Herefordshire, the fourth smallest county in population, was merged, despite much protest, with its larger eastern neighbour, Worcestershire. But the forced union was abandoned on 1 April 1998, and Herefordshire reconstituted.

**heresy** is the holding of religious views regarded or defined as unacceptable by the church. The first notable British heretics were *Pelagius and Celestius in the early 5th cent., who argued, against Augustine, that man's own efforts could steer him towards salvation. Condemned by Pope Innocent I, Pelagianism continued to find support in Britain and St *Germanus was sent over in 429 specifically to deal with it. Heresy was hardly a problem in the Anglo-Saxon church and only a handful of cases can be identified. Concern over heresy dates from *Wyclif's challenge to the doctrine of transubstantiation and his attacks upon the wealth of the church. Though Henry IV's act *De heretico comburendo passed in 1401 it was only after Oldcastle's *lollard rebellion in 1414 that systematic persecution of heresy began. There was a marked revival of lollardy in the early 16th cent., which merged with the Lutheran heresy. Henry VIII repealed De heretico comburendo in 1533 but retained the right to burn heretics. Edward VI then repealed all statutes against heresy, though it remained an offence at common law. Mary at once revived the previous statutes and Elizabeth abolished them again in 1558. In Scotland the laws against heresy were repealed by the Reformation Parliament in 1560.

Though persecution of laymen for heresy ceased, the careers of clerics and academics (in holy orders) could still be jeopardized by charges of heresy, and the offence of blasphemy remained dangerous. James Nayler, a quaker, was whipped, branded, and had his tongue bored for blasphemy in 1656/7, and Thomas Aikenhead, a mere youth, was executed in Edinburgh in 1697. William Whiston, Newton's successor at Cambridge, was deprived of his chair in 1710 for Arianism. Later prosecutions included the publishers of *Paine's The Age of Reason (1797, 1812, 1819), and the publisher of *Shelley's Queen Mab (1821). Existing legislation against blasphemy protects Christianity only and there has been pressure to extend it to cover Islam and other religions.

**Hereward** (11th cent.), known as 'the Wake' ('the watchful one'), was the leading figure in the fenland revolt against William the Conqueror. In 1070, the appearance of a Danish fleet in the waters of Ely raised hopes of resistance among Englishmen of that district, many of whom had Danish blood. Hereward, leading a band of outlaws and Danish allies, sacked and plundered the monastery at Peterborough. In 1071 William attacked with ships, constructing a causeway for his main force. Hereward escaped by water, after which nothing certain is known of him.

**heriot** is derived from the Anglo-Saxon word for 'war-gear' (in Scotland, *hereyeld*). This was a feudal obligation due to a lord on the death of a tenant. Originally the tenant's heir returned armour and weapons lent to him, but it developed into a claim by the lord to the best beast or chattel. It was, in effect, a kind of death duty, though its incidence varied widely. By the 14th cent. it was becoming common for the heriot to be commuted to a money payment.

**heritable jurisdictions** In the Scottish legal system before 1747, many of the king's subjects were not under the jurisdiction of royal courts either at local or at central level. Instead, they were answerable to a complex of hereditary or franchise jurisdictions in the hands of the feudal nobility. High treason alone justified royal intervention. Though resented by the crown, the system provided cheap, quick local justice. It was abolished after the 1745 *Jacobite rising by the Heritable Jurisdictions (Scotland) Act of 1747.

**Herrick, Robert** (1591–1674). Poet. Son of a Cheapside goldsmith, initially apprenticed to the trade but graduating at Cambridge (1617), Herrick was ordained in 1623. Returning to London and in contact with other writers (especially Ben *Jonson), musicians, and court wits, he established himself as a poet, and was admitted to the living of Dean Prior (Devon). Here he spent most of the rest of his life. Herrick's poetry was widely appreciated, appeared in miscellanies, and was set to music.

**Herschel, John** (1792–1871). The most eminent physicist of early Victorian Britain. His father *William was a famous astronomer, and John went to Cambridge where with Charles *Babbage he reformed the mathematics course. After toying with law, he turned to physics, working on optics as the new wave theory was coming in, and to astronomy. In 1833 he sailed to the Cape to observe the southern stars (results published 1847).

**Herschel, William** (1738–1822). An astronomer, he added the planet Uranus to the list known since antiquity. He came to England from Hanover as a musician. Taking to astronomy, he made his own reflecting telescope: with it in 1781 he saw the planet, which he had at first thought a comet. He named it *Georgium Sidus*, after George III.

**Hertford, Synod of,** 672. Convened by *Theodore, archbishop of Canterbury, to reorganize the church following the Synod of *Whitby (664), when Celtic Christianity gave way to Roman traditions, the synod was the first general assembly representing the whole English church. The Roman dating of Easter was affirmed. The precedence of one bishop over another was determined by seniority of consecration.

**Hertfordshire,** though a small county, has little geographical unity. The southern parts are within the orbit of London and discharge commuters into Euston, St Pancras, King's Cross, and Liverpool Street. The north retains quiet spots like Gaddesden in the west and Wyddial in the east.

The area was one of the earliest to be occupied by the Saxons and formed at first part of the diocese of London, established in the early 7th cent. to minister to the East Saxons. There was subsequently an ecclesiastical reorganization since, until the foundation of the new diocese of St Albans in 1877, most of Hertfordshire was in the vast diocese of Lincoln. In the 8th cent. the region formed part of the kingdom of Mercia. In the 9th and 10th cents., Danes and Saxons fought for control. The boundary between the territories of *Alfred of Wessex and *Guthrum was settled by the treaty of *Wedmore in 878 as the line of the river Lea. *Edward the Elder, in his counter-attack in 913, fortified Hertford as a strong point and it became the nucleus of the emerging county. The first reference to Hertfordshire by name is in the *Anglo-Saxon Chronicle* for AD 1011. In the 13th cent. Hertford and St Albans established their right to parliamentary representation.

Hertford, slightly off centre, never dominated the shire as some county towns did, and a considerable number of small market towns grew up, serving their immediate locality— Ashwell, Buntingford, Royston, Baldock, Hitchin, and Hoddesdon. St Albans was always bigger than Hertford and when the first county council was set up in 1889, it met alternately in the two towns.

The county remained rural until late. There were plenty of open fields surviving well into Victoria's reign, and tributes to the beauty of the shire continued to pour in. In 1801 no town in the county had as many as 4,000 inhabitants. But by 1901 the shape of the 20th cent. was becoming clear. Watford had increased to 32,000, twice the size of the next town, St Albans; and Cheshunt (12,000) and Barnet (7,000), on the fringes of London, had moved up. Two years later, a development which cast a long shadow took place. The first garden city was started at Letchworth, chosen in the main for its nearness to London. It was joined after the First World War by the second garden city at Welwyn. The success of the garden cities prompted governments to look to Hertfordshire for sites for the new towns. Stevenage was the first to be set up after the Second World War, followed by Hatfield and Hemel Hempstead, and Welwyn was taken over as a new town. The effect upon a small county of five in such close proximity was predictable. Increasingly it was reduced to quiet pockets and enclaves, though within the network of motorways and junctions, fragments of an old county survive.

**Hervey, John, Lord** (1696–1743). The second son of the 1st earl of Bristol, Hervey was elected to represent Bury St Edmunds (1723), supported Walpole, and was rewarded with the posts of vice-chamberlain and privy counsellor. A favoured companion of Queen *Caroline, Hervey had considerable influence at the court of George II, which furnished ready material for his cynical and witty *Memoirs*, a superb and sustained piece of writing.

**Hexham, battle of,** 1464. The duke of Somerset, campaigning on behalf of Henry VI, was defeated at *Hedgeley Moor in April 1464, but rallied his forces at Hexham the following month. They were trapped by Montagu, *Warwick's younger brother, and cut to pieces on 15 May. Somerset was executed after the battle.

**Hexham, diocese of** The see was created in 678 for part of Northumbria. *Theodore unsuccessfully tried to persuade *Cuthbert to be bishop, who, though consecrated, refused. The bishopric collapsed under the Danish invasions (c.821) and was not revived.

**hides** In *Domesday Book (1086), every village and estate in southern and western England was assessed in terms of hides. (In large areas of the north and east the corresponding unit was the 'carucate'.) The system of assessment was comprehensive, related to the levy of tax and military and naval service. It was normal, in some shires, for almost every village to be assessed at 5 hides. In others, somewhat larger areas were assessed at, say, 20 hides. The etymology of this word indicates a connection with the idea of a household. The Burghal Hidage (c.900), shows how hidage assessments were used to allocate responsibility for fortress maintenance. By the 13th cent. its use was residual and local.

**high church** Within the Church of England, the high-church party stresses continuity with the pre-Reformation church and holds a 'high' concept of the authority of the church, bishops, and sacraments. High churchmen flourished under the later Stuarts because of their insistence on the *divine right of kings. Their theological and ecclesiastical opinions survived, to be rediscovered by the *Oxford movement of the 1830s.

**High Commission, Court of** Known as such from c.1570, it emanated from earlier ecclesiastical commissions (after 1547), was given statutory authority (1559), reconstructed (1583), and exercised the ecclesiastical appellate and original jurisdiction of the crown as supreme governor. Extensively used by *Whitgift, *Bancroft, and *Laud, its inquisitorial methods, swift and secret in action, were more efficient than diocesan courts. Feared and detested universally, its abolition with *Star Chamber (1641) was not revoked (1661), though James II revived it briefly in modified form as the *Ecclesiastical Commission (1686–8).

**high kings of Ireland** *See* IRELAND, HIGH KINGS OF.

**Highland** An administrative region of Scotland, created in 1973 from the counties of Caithness, Nairn, Sutherland, Inverness (except the Outer Hebrides), Ross and Cromarty (except Lewis), and a northern part of Argyll. Between 1973 and 1996 it was a region, sharing local government activities with its eight districts, but now exercises all local government functions. Farming by crofting is still significant in the north and west and the islands, and tourism for the whole region.

**Highland clearances** were evictions which eliminated the bulk of the Gaelic-speaking population from the Highlands and Islands of Scotland. Between 1763 and 1775 thousands of Highlanders migrated to colonial British North America motivated by resentment at higher rents and consolidation of farms. Next, large-scale sheep-farming came to the Highlands, based on the replacement of the small indigenous sheep by commercial breeds such as the black-faced Linton. By the early 19th cent. this revolution had reached the vast Sutherland estates north of Inverness. Tenants were resettled on the coastal areas to combine fishing with farming and ancillary activity such as gathering kelp to make commercial alkali. After 1860, tenants were cleared to create deer forests.

**Highland games** were originally meetings of clans. They developed into more formal gatherings under the influence of the revival of interest in Scottish antiquity fostered by *Scott and others in the 1810s. At Invergarry in the 1820s the games included not only piping, tossing the caber, hammer-throwing, wrestling, and running, but twisting the four legs off a cow. Modern gatherings are held usually in late summer.

**Highland Land League** Scottish crofters in the 1870s watched the success of the Irish in obtaining concessions, and had 'a mind to turn rebels themselves'. The Highland Land League was formed in 1882 and returned four sympathetic MPs at the election of 1885. Results were gratifyingly swift. *Gladstone's Crofters' Act of 1886 gave security of tenure and *Salisbury, the same year, established a separate secretary of state for Scotland.

**highwaymen** are more picturesque in fiction and retrospect than they were in reality. The heyday of the highwayman was from the Restoration, when coaches began to appear on the roads in large enough numbers to make the occupation profitable, to the end of the 18th cent., when stage-coaches travelled with armed guards and policing was better. Because of the density of traffic, the outskirts of London were particularly frequented by robbers, and Finchley Common, Hounslow Heath, Bagshot Heath, and Blackheath all acquired a bad reputation. Highwaymen soon became popular heroes. Their exploits sold well, often accompanied by a woodcut of the final gallows scene.

**Hilda, St** (614–80). Baptized in 627 with her kinsman, the Northumbrian king *Edwin, at 33 Hilda became a nun, joining a community on the banks of the Wear. A year later she became abbess at Hartlepool, and in 657 founded the double monastery at Streanaeshalch (Whitby). Kings and princes sought her advice, and, representing Celtic traditions, she was an important figure at the Synod of *Whitby.

**Hill, Octavia** (1838–1912). Social reformer. Early influence from her grandfather, the sanitary reformer Dr Southwood Smith, persuaded Hill of the need for better housing for the poor. A loan from John *Ruskin (1865) enabled purchase of squalid property in Paradise Place, Marylebone (London), for which she demanded both prompt rent payments and cleanliness, with profits directed to repairs and improvements. The experiment was so successful that the scheme spread. Her passionate belief in preserving open spaces for public use led to co-founding the *National Trust (1895).

**Hill, Rowland, 1st Viscount Hill** (1772–1842). Soldier. Hill was a younger son of Sir John Hill, baronet, of Shropshire. He was wounded near *Alexandria in 1801, and was promoted major-general in 1805. Later he served in Portugal and was again wounded at *Talavera (1809). On Napoleon's return from Elba, Hill hastened to Brussels and was in action at *Waterloo, where he had a horse killed under him.

**Hill, Sir Rowland** (1795–1879). Inventor of penny postage. Hill was born in Kidderminster, son of a schoolmaster. He took over his father's school but abandoned teaching, and in 1835 became secretary to a commission to colonize south Australia. He then became interested in the postal service, which was so prohibitively expensive that revenue was falling in a period of rapid population growth and commercial expansion. Hill suggested prepayment, a standard delivery charge irrespective of distance, and the use of an adhesive stamp. Hill was put in charge but met with vast obstruction from within the Post Office and was dismissed in 1842. Reinstated by *Russell in 1846, he held office until 1864.

**Hillary, Sir Edmund** (1919–2007). A New Zealander, Hillary's reputation as a mountaineer and, in particular, his experience of Himalayan climbing led to an invitation to join the Everest expedition of 1953. The leader, Sir John Hunt, selected him and Sherpa Tenzing to make the assault on the summit, and in May 1953 they became the first two men to reach the top of the world's highest mountain. Hillary also explored the Antarctic, reaching the South Pole in 1958. He devoted much of his later life to helping the Sherpa community.

**Hilliard, Nicholas** (1547–1619). The greatest of English miniaturists. In 1570 he was appointed to the court, where his jeweler's skills suited Elizabeth I's desire for a painted image of splendour. About 1600, he wrote a treatise *The Arte of Limning*, in which he recorded that his method of painting without the use of shadow was in agreement with the queen's taste, 'for the lyne without shadowe showeth all to a good Iugment'.

**Hingston Down, battle of,** 838. For decades the Britons of Cornwall (*Dumnonia) had been resisting the growing pressure of *Wessex. In 838 they joined with a Viking force, possibly from Ireland, but were defeated at Hingston Down, between Callington and the Tamar, by *Egbert. Cornwall was then incorporated into the Wessex empire.

**Hoadly, Benjamin** (1676–1761). Bishop. Born in Kent and educated at Catharine Hall, Cambridge, Hoadly held livings in London and successively the bishoprics of Bangor (1716), Hereford (1721), Salisbury (1723), and Winchester (1734). A Whig polemicist in conflict with *Atterbury after 1705, he was rewarded by becoming George I's chaplain, but his appointment to Bangor shocked even supporters. His sermon (1717) advocating private judgement and sincere conscience in preference to ecclesiastical authority challenged both high churchmen and the established church. It thus provoked the bitter *Bangorian controversy and consequent suspension of *convocation.

**Hoare, Samuel, 1st Viscount Templewood** (1880–1959). Educated at Harrow and New College, Oxford, Hoare entered Parliament in 1910 as a Conservative and sat for Chelsea until given his peerage in 1944. He took office under Bonar *Law in 1922 as secretary of state for air and again under *Baldwin. In 1931 he became secretary of state for India in the National Government and carried the Government of India Bill, advancing towards self-government. Baldwin, in 1935, moved him to the Foreign Office. Hoare was plunged straight into the crisis over Italy's designs on *Abyssinia. In December 1935 he drew up with Pierre Laval, French foreign minister, a plan which would have dismembered Abyssinia. The public outcry forced his resignation. Though he was brought back as a minister in 1936, and served as 1st lord of the Admiralty, home secretary, lord privy seal, and secretary of state for air, his career limped. After resigning with *Chamberlain in 1940, he served for four years as ambassador to Spain, at a very critical juncture.

**Hobbes, Thomas** (1588–1679). Philosopher. Hobbes is without doubt the greatest political philosopher to have written in the English language. After graduating from Oxford, he devoted his very long life to private tutoring and study. In 1651 he published in English *Leviathan, his masterpiece, in which he set out systematically an ingenious social contractarian case for an authoritarian government. Hobbes argued that the state of nature (i.e. the pre-political condition) was a condition of 'war of all against all', since humans are by nature moved by competitiveness, fear, and pride to coerce others. They would contract together to establish an absolute ruler, since that was the only way in which their security could be guaranteed.

**Hobson, John Atkinson** (1858–1940). An economist with unconventional views, Hobson earned his living through part-time lecturing and journalism. Two of his books launched revolutions. *The Physiology of Industry* (1889) undermined *laissez-faire* economics by arguing that its tendency was to over-produce; and *Imperialism: A Study* (1902) attributed colonial expansion to the resulting surpluses of goods and capital. In this way he sowed the seeds of two of the most powerful ideologies of the 20th cent.: Keynesian economics, and the Leninist interpretation of imperialism.

**hockey** claims a very ancient pedigree since there are tomb-drawings and classical reliefs showing men hitting a ball with curved sticks. Like most games, it was formalized and regulated in the 19th cent. Blackheath had a hockey club before 1861 and Teddington introduced the hard ball into the game in the 1870s. The National Association was formed in 1886, mainly by London clubs. The Federation of International Hockey was established in 1924.

**Hogarth, William** (1697–1764). Artist. London-born, Hogarth set up as an illustrator, largely self-taught, before producing 'conversation pieces', engraving scenes of contemporary life, and history painting. Pugnacious, provocative, and a passionate believer that honest naturalism was preferable to the sterility of formal training, he suffered for his attempts to ridicule the deeply entrenched, Renaissance-based theories of good taste. Underrated as a painter, he is best remembered for his moral and satirical engravings (*Rake's Progress*, *Marriage à la Mode*, and *Gin Lane*).

**Hogue, La, battle of** *See* LA HOGUE, BATTLE OF.

**Holbein, Hans** (c.1497–1543). Painter. It is hardly an exaggeration to suggest that our visual image of Henry VIII and his courtiers is derived from Holbein's portraits. Born the son of an Augsburg artist, Holbein paid two visits to England, a short one 1526–7 and a longer one 1532–43. On the first occasion he brought with him introductions from Erasmus to Sir Thomas *More, and painted a celebrated More family portrait. On his next visit his patron More was in disfavour, but Holbein received many commissions, and entered the service of the king, for whom he painted a family reconstruction, showing Henry, his parents, and *Jane Seymour. An early commentator wrote of Holbein: 'he is not a poet but an historian.'

**Holinshed, Raphael** (*c.*1520–*c.*1581). Holinshed was the author and compiler of *Chronicles of England, Scotlande and Irelande*, published in 1577. He had little method or sceptical approach but his eclecticism made him a valuable quarry for historical playwrights. *Shakespeare made use of the *Chronicles* in several plays, including *Lear*, *Macbeth*, and *Cymbeline* and the later historical plays.

**Holles, Denzil** (1599–1680). Holles, a parliamentarian, achieved notoriety on 2 May 1629 when, acting with *Eliot, he held down the Commons' Speaker. Punished by a brief spell in prison, he was re-elected to Parliament in 1640. Though included by Charles I among the five members threatened with impeachment in January 1642, Holles advocated a negotiated settlement. This brought him into collision with the army, and in December 1648 he fled to France. *Cromwell permitted him to return to England in 1654, but he took no part in political life until the restoration of Charles II, who made him a baron.

**Holst, Gustav** (1874–1934). Of German/Swedish ancestry, he was one of the most original English composers of his day and an influential teacher. Holst studied composition with Stanford at London's *Royal College of Music alongside his lifelong friend *Vaughan Williams, with whom he shared a passionate interest in folk-song. The sparse economy of his later works, together with their adventurous harmonies and use of bitonality, was regarded by many contemporaries as excessively cerebral. *The Planets* (1914–16, first performed 1919), however, was an immediate and lasting success.

**'Holy Alliance'** was the derisive name given to the declaration at Paris in September 1815 by Alexander I of Russia, Frederick William III of Prussia, and Francis I of Austria that they would govern and collaborate in accordance with Christian principles. The driving spirit was the tsar in the midst of a devout phase. Britain, pleading her constitutional position, did not sign, though the prince regent expressed personal approval. *Castlereagh, then foreign secretary, dismissed it privately as 'a piece of sublime mysticism and nonsense'. No mechanism was included in the declaration and disagreements between the signatories soon appeared.

**Holyrood** (Edinburgh). Holyroodhouse stands at the foot of the Canongate in the Old Town of Edinburgh, in the lee of Arthur's Seat. Holyrood abbey was built for *Augustinian canons. The palace of Holyroodhouse, the official residence in Scotland of the reigning monarch, was started in the reign of James IV of Scotland and extended by James V. It is set around the four sides of a courtyard, and although the interiors are in an Anglo-Dutch style, the character of the exteriors is French. After a period of neglect, royalty came back to Holyroodhouse in 1745 in the person of Prince Charles Edward *Stuart (Bonnie Prince Charlie), but it was not until after George IV's visit in 1822 that it was restored.

**homage** was the formal and public acknowledgement by a vassal of his allegiance and obligations to a lord of whom he held land or whose overlordship he accepted. By making an act of homage, the vassal's own rights were deemed to be confirmed by his lord. The ceremony of homage involved the vassal kneeling before his lord, the clasping of hands, the uttering of certain key words which acknowledged lordship, and the kissing which symbolized accord. Homage by the peers of the realm remains part of the *coronation service.

**Home, Sir Alec Douglas-Home, 14th earl of** [S] (1903–95). Prime minister. Douglas-Home succeeded to the earldom in 1951 but relinquished it in 1963 to re-enter the Commons as prime minister, in succession to Harold *Macmillan. In 1974 he returned to the House of Lords as Lord Home of the Hirsel. He was first elected in 1931 and served as private secretary to Neville *Chamberlain (1937–40), minister of state at the Scottish Office (1951–5), Commonwealth secretary (1955–60), and foreign secretary (1960–3). He also served as deputy leader (1956–7), then leader of the House of Lords and lord president of the council (1959–60).

An immensely sincere and straightforward figure, he appeared to be out of touch with political realities as prime minister. A poor public speaker and television performer, he was unfortunate to encounter Harold *Wilson as leader of the opposition. His upper-class, 'grouse moor' image was another drawback, while the refusal of both Iain Macleod and Enoch *Powell to serve under him undermined his credibility. He clearly resented the attacks on his upbringing. In a famous speech, he pointed out that if he was the 14th earl of Home, Mr Wilson was 'the fourteenth Mr Wilson'.

None the less, after a year of almost non-stop electioneering, Sir Alec, who concentrated on foreign and defence affairs, lost the 1964 election to Labour by the most slender of margins. Given the legacy of economic problems and scandals he had inherited from Macmillan, this was no small testament to his character.

After the controversy about the way in which he had become prime minister, and given that the queen could not choose a Tory leader while the party was in opposition, Sir Alec arranged that his successor as party leader should be elected. This turned out to be Edward *Heath under whom he served as foreign secretary between 1970 and 1974. Relations between them were smooth, unlike those between Heath and his successor a decade later. As foreign secretary, Sir Alec was one of those who helped take Britain into the Common Market in 1973.

**Home Guard** A volunteer organization founded by Anthony *Eden, the secretary of state for war, in May 1940. Originally called the Local Defence Volunteers, its task was to assist in the defence of Britain against a possible German invasion. By 1943 over 2 million men served in the Home Guard in their spare time. The Home Guard was disbanded on 31 December 1944 but was immortalized in the television series *Dad's Army*.

**Home Office** Until 1782 the two secretaries of state divided their responsibilities into southern and northern Europe, dealing with the catholic and protestant powers. Domestic duties needed little attention: the justices of the peace looked after most problems of law and order and the secretary at war was at hand if troops needed to be called in. In 1782, when the Rockinghams took office, a new division was agreed: one secretary took domestic and colonial affairs, the other foreign affairs. The first home secretary, Lord *Shelburne, had two under-secretaries, a chief clerk, and ten other civil servants. But in the 19th cent. business increased dramatically as the office picked up responsibility for aliens, prisons, and police supervision. In 1833 the Home Secretary was empowered to appoint factory inspectors. By the 20th cent. the post of home secretary had become one of the most senior and difficult in the government.

**Home Rule** See IRISH HOME RULE.

**Homildon Hill, battle of,** 1402. The clash at *Otterburn in 1388 was followed by a ten-year truce on the Anglo-Scottish border. In June 1402 *Hotspur got the better of a small skirmish at Nisbet Moor, in Berwickshire. *Glyndŵr's rising in Wales gave the Scots a chance of revenge and in September 1402 a large force under *Douglas pillaged Northumberland. Hotspur cut off their retreat near Wooler, and Douglas fought at Homildon Hill. The Scots were badly deployed, the English archers kept up a hail of fire, and Douglas was captured.

**Hong Kong** island was used by the British as a staging-post for the opium trade and was taken by them as a free port during the *Opium War (1839–42). Their occupancy was ratified by the treaty of *Nanking. In 1860 the Kowloon peninsula was added to the port and in 1898 the New Territories were received from China on a 99-year lease. Growth was rapid during the 1930s when many Chinese fled the civil wars and Japanese invasion on the mainland and the population doubled to 1.6 million. Hong Kong itself surrendered to the Japanese on Christmas Day 1941 and was not liberated until 30 August 1945. During the 1960s, the colony became a major manufacturing centre and its population reached over 4 million by 1991. The lease for the New Territories ended in 1997, whereupon the whole colony reverted to the People's Republic of China.

**Honours of Scotland** The Scottish crown jewels, consisting of a sceptre given to James IV (1488–1513) by Pope Alexander VI (1494), a sword from Pope Julius II (1507), and a crown made for James V (1513–42) in 1540. Buried in Kinneff kirk (1652–60) to avoid Oliver *Cromwell's attentions, the Honours were feared lost following the Union (1707). They were found hidden in Edinburgh castle by Sir Walter *Scott (1818), and remain there today.

**Hood, Alexander** (1726–1814). Admiral. The younger brother of Samuel *Hood, Alexander had an active naval career of 54 years, first commissioned in 1746 and still commanding at the blockade of Brest in 1800. In 1755 he served under Saunders in North America, in 1759 was at *Quiberon Bay with *Hawke, and in 1761, off Belle Île, retook the *Warwick* from the French in a fierce contest. He served under Keppel at Ushant in 1778, and took part in the second relief of Gibraltar in 1782. In 1794, at the Glorious First of June action, he was second in command to *Howe, and was subsequently created Lord Bridport in the Irish peerage.

**Hood, Samuel** (1724–1816). Admiral. Born of Dorset clerical stock, Hood and his brother Alexander entered the navy at the same time. Given a commission in 1746, Hood served throughout the Seven Years War and was present at *Quiberon Bay in 1759. In 1767, still a captain, he was appointed commander-in-chief in North America; subsequently from 1771 to 1780 he was stationed at Portsmouth. A baronet (1778) and rear-admiral (1780), Hood was *Rodney's second at the battle of the *Saints (April 1782), and was severely critical of Rodney's failure to pursue the French.

**Hooke, Robert** (1635–1703). Hooke made the microscope well known as a scientific instrument, publishing his *Micrographia* in 1665. Its splendid engraving of the flea made a tremendous impression. Previously, Hooke had worked with Robert *Boyle on the air pump, and in 1662 had been appointed curator to the *Royal Society, with the duty of performing experiments at the meetings.

**Hooker, Richard** (1554–1600). Theologian and political theorist. Educated at Oxford, Hooker became a fellow of Corpus Christi College and master of the Temple before 'retiring' to a country living to write his masterly defence of the Elizabethan system of government *The Laws of Ecclesiastical Polity*. He argued that in England there was

an essential unity between church and state, which were different aspects of a single community, both subject to the authority of the monarch. Hooker supplied the most effective statement of the theoretical foundations of Anglicanism, and greatly influenced the ideas of later political theorists such as John *Locke and Edmund *Burke.

**Hooper, John** (d. 1555). Bishop of Gloucester and Worcester. Born in Somerset and educated at Oxford, Hooper probably took Cistercian vows at Gloucester. After the *dissolution he returned to Oxford to study reformed theology, but fled abroad in disguise and eventually settled in Zurich (1547–9). He returned to London as Protector *Somerset's chaplain. When offered the see of Gloucester (1550), his disagreement with Cranmer over vestments led to brief imprisonment before he agreed to consecration fully robed (1551). In Mary's reign he was imprisoned, deprived (1554), and burned at Gloucester.

**Hopton, Sir Ralph** (1596–1652). One of the most successful royalist commanders during the Civil War, Hopton was given a barony in 1643. In the *Long Parliament, he initially opposed the king, voting for *Strafford's attainder in 1641. The following year he joined the royalist cause. A west countryman by birth, he spent almost all his time campaigning in that region. He had a good record of success, winning at *Braddock Down (January 1643), *Stratton (May 1643), *Lansdowne (July 1643), *Roundway Down (July 1643), before being beaten by *Waller at *Cheriton in March 1644. Beaten again by *Fairfax at *Torrington (February 1646), he was forced to capitulate and went into exile.

**Horner, Francis** (1778–1817). Horner had an influence and standing out of all proportion to his career or achievements. Born and educated in Edinburgh, he was called to the bar in 1800. Two years later he joined Francis Jeffrey and Sydney *Smith in launching the *Edinburgh Review* as a radical Whig journal. He was brought into Parliament in 1806 and made a reputation as a financial expert, chairing an important committee on bullion. He left England at the end of 1816 in search of health and died in Italy aged 38.

**Horne Tooke, John** (1736–1812). A man of many parts (clergyman, philologist, and wit), Tooke carried the radicalism of the 1760s into the early 19th cent. His legal and organizational talents were first apparent in his vigorous championing of *Wilkes. His subsequent support for the American colonists led to a prison sentence. In 1781 he joined the *Society for Constitutional Information, which he soon dominated; and in 1792 assisted in the formation of the London *Corresponding Society. He was tried for high treason in 1794 and acquitted.

**horse-racing** consists of flat racing or jumping, 'over the sticks'. Racing became popular during the 16th cent. and the first race-course with an annual fixture was established on the Roodee at Chester in 1540. Racing received support from successive monarchs. James I established a hunting stable at Newmarket and Charles II made it fashionable. Racing expanded with courses springing up at Doncaster (1595), York (1709), Ascot (1711), Epsom (1730), Goodwood (1801), and Aintree (1827). In 1750 the Jockey Club was founded to regulate the sport. Lord George *Bentinck (1802–48) devised the flag start, race card, paddock parade, and much of modern race-course practice. Highlights of the flat season include the *Derby, Oaks, and St Leger.

Steeple-chasing derived from horses racing each other cross-country to the nearest church steeple. The concept of a course with artificial fences originated at the Newmarket Craven meeting in 1794. A Grand Annual Steeplechase began at Cheltenham around 1815. In 1866 the Grand National Hunt Steeplechase Committee was formed to establish rules and the first Calendar appeared in 1867. It became the National Hunt Committee in 1889. Highlights include the *Grand National and the Cheltenham Gold Cup.

**Hospitallers** Originally established at the end of the 11th cent. to care for Jerusalem pilgrims, following the success of the First Crusade the Hospitallers' role expanded, with papal support, to include care of the sick and protection of pilgrims. During the 12th cent. the order spread rapidly both in the crusading states and in western Europe. The first English priory was founded c.1144 at Clerkenwell. The order's English properties were confiscated in 1540.

**Hotspur** *See* PERCY, HENRY.

**housecarls** were the immediate bodyguard of Danish and late Saxon kings, the nucleus of the army. They were introduced by *Cnut and were similar to Saxon thegns. They were men of some rank, with a strong code of honour and service.

**household** Originally not merely the domestic residence of the monarch but the place from which the kingdom was governed. No rigid distinction was made between its different functions. But as administration grew more complex and requests for justice more common, offices became specialized. At first the whole household moved from place to place, with only a skeleton staff left behind: when the king was absent in Normandy officers left in England had to possess some discretionary authority. The peripatetic nature of the household became increasingly inconvenient and in clause 17 of *Magna Carta in 1215 it was declared that *common pleas would be heard in one place. At length the household and its offshoots settled at Westminster. A permanent headquarters allowed more comfort and more ceremonial and the household developed into the *court.

**Housman, A. E.** (1859–1936). Poet and classicist, whose failure at Oxford only delayed a career taking him to chairs of Latin at London and, in 1911 at Cambridge. His emotional life went into his poetry, *A Shropshire Lad* (1896) and *Last Poems* (1922). Shropshire, over the border from his native Worcestershire, became 'the land of lost content', where the beauty of nature was no defence against betrayal and death. He is buried at Ludlow.

**Howard, Charles, 2nd Baron Howard of Effingham and 1st earl of Nottingham** (c.1536–1624). Howard took advantage of his high birth to sustain a long and distinguished career. *Anne Boleyn was his first cousin. He was a grandson of the 2nd duke of *Norfolk, the hero of *Flodden; he went on to serve Mary as lord high admiral and Elizabeth as lord chamberlain. In 1569 he accompanied Hunsdon on the campaign which crushed the northern rebellion and in 1575 was given the Garter. In 1585 he was appointed lord high admiral for life, holding the position until he was 83: he held supreme command when the *Armada was destroyed in 1588. In 1596, with *Essex, he stormed Cadiz to forestall another Armada. The following year he was created earl of Nottingham and served as lord high steward until 1615.

**Howard, Henry, 1st earl of Northampton** (1540–1614). Howard's father Lord Surrey was executed when he was 7. In Edward VI's reign, he was tutored by John *Foxe, the protestant martyrologist, but at Mary's accession a catholic bishop took over. The indiscretions of his elder brother the 4th duke of *Norfolk blighted his prospects in the 1570s. Not until 1600 did Elizabeth consent to receive him at court. By that time, he was cultivating James VI of Scotland and advising him by correspondence. It paid off handsomely. In 1604 he was created earl of Northampton, given the Garter in 1605, and became lord privy seal in 1608.

**Howard, John** (1726–90). Prison reformer. Howard was born in London and owned a small property at Cardington (Beds.). He was an independent in religion, worshipping at the chapel *Bunyan had served, a teetotaller, vegetarian, and a man of austere habits. In 1773 he was appointed sheriff of Bedfordshire and discovered that prisoners who had been acquitted were unable to leave gaol unless they could pay the gaoler's fee. This led Howard to embark upon an extraordinary life of prison visits throughout the British Isles and ultimately most of Europe. His *State of the Prisons in England and Wales* (1777) exposed the squalor and brutality of many gaols. He died of typhus on a visit to Russia and was buried there.

**Howard, Michael** (b. 1941). Politician. The son of Rumanian immigrants of Jewish faith (surname: Hecht), Howard was educated at Llanelli grammar school and Peterhouse, Cambridge. He began a legal career but entered Parliament for Folkestone in 1983. After junior office, he became Minister of State, Department of Environment (1987–90), Secretary of State for Employment (1990–2), for the Environment (1992–3), and for the Home Department (1993–7). In Opposition he was shadow Foreign Secretary (2001–3). His reputation was then as a right-wing Tory and a Eurosceptic. His powerful performances in the House of Commons made him an unopposed choice to succeed Iain *Duncan Smith as leader of the Conservative Party in October 2003. His party gained seats at the general election of 2005 but did not threaten the Labour majority and Howard resigned the leadership at once.

**Howard, Thomas, 1st Baron Howard de Walden and earl of Suffolk** (1561–1626). Howard's father, the 4th duke of Norfolk, was executed in 1572 when Thomas was 11 for conspiring to rescue Mary, queen of Scots. His mother was heiress to Baron *Audley of Walden, Henry VIII's lord chancellor, and he inherited Audley End. In 1584 he was restored in blood and four years later was knighted for gallantry against the Armada. He served at sea in the 1590s and was given the Garter in 1597. He was in favour with James I, who made him earl of Suffolk and employed him as lord chamberlain 1603–14. From 1614 to 1618 he was lord high treasurer. His building programme at Audley End was on a lavish scale and pushed him heavily into debt. In 1619 he was imprisoned in the Tower and fined £30,000 for peculation.

**Howard, William, 1st Baron Howard of Effingham** (*c.*1510–73). Howard was a younger son of Thomas, 2nd duke of *Norfolk, who died in 1524. He was great-uncle to Princess Elizabeth. In the 1530s he served as ambassador to Scotland and to France but was in danger in 1542 when his niece *Catherine Howard was executed. For the last 20 years of his life he held high office continuously as lord high admiral 1553–8, lord chamberlain 1558–72, and lord privy seal 1572–3. He gained some displeasure by protecting the Princess Elizabeth, and on her succession in 1558 he was in high favour. His son Charles commanded the fleet against the Spanish Armada.

**Howe, Richard** (1726–99). Descended through his mother from a half-sister of George I, Howe was commissioned in the navy in 1745, seeing active service through to 1758, when he succeeded his elder brother as 4th viscount in the Irish peerage, becoming also MP for Dartmouth until 1782. Promoted admiral in 1770, Howe's professional standing and conciliatory disposition saw him given wide powers in 1776 to try to negotiate peace in America. After two indecisive years and lacking the ministerial support he expected, Howe gave up in disillusion. Raised to a British peerage in 1782, he relieved Gibraltar that October, and from 1783 to 1788, when he became an earl, was 1st lord of the Admiralty. His standing was further enhanced by the '*Glorious First of June' victory (1794), and his reputation proved important in quelling the *Spithead mutiny in spring 1797, in which year he received the Garter.

**Howe, William** (1729–1814). Younger brother of Richard *Howe, William served in the army in Flanders 1747–8, and with distinction in Canada and Cuba 1759–62. Between 1758 and 1780 he was MP for Nottingham, where there was a family interest. Having previously refused to serve in America at the outbreak of rebellion, he arrived in Boston in May 1775, and after *Bunker Hill was appointed KB. Promoted full general in 1793, Howe became governor of Berwick-on-Tweed and, in 1805, of Plymouth, where he died.

**Hudson, Henry** (d. 1611). Though clearly an accomplished navigator, Hudson's life is obscure. However, by 1607 he was employed by the *Muscovy Company in whose service he reached Svalbad (Spitsbergen). After another northern expedition, he was recruited by the Dutch, for whom he explored Chesapeake and Delaware bays following the Hudson river as far inland as Albany in a vain search for the North-West Passage. Hudson returned to English service in 1610, again to search for the passage to India, and entered the bay now bearing his name. But he and his son were cast adrift by a mutinous crew, who returned home without them.

**Hudson's Bay Company** The company was founded on 2 May 1670 under the patronage of Prince *Rupert after a voyage in 1668 had proved that access to the fur trade could be established through Hudson Bay. The company fought the French for control of the bay until 1713. Its territorial rights were sold to the dominion of Canada in 1869, but the company continued to trade.

**hue and cry** Early English common law process of pursuing felons 'with horn and with voice' (*hutesium et clamor*). The outcry could be raised by peace-officer or private citizen, whereupon everyone was duty bound to search and pursue on horse or foot. The main statutes and amendments (1285, 1585, 1735) were repealed in 1827, though the element of 'citizen's arrest' has persisted.

**Hugh of Lincoln, St** (1140–1200). Bishop. Born in Burgundy and educated in a convent at Villard-Benoît, Hugh was ordained deacon at 19 and subsequently made prior of a smallholding at Saint-Maximin. He became a *Carthusian in 1160 after visiting the Grand Chartreuse. Known for his holiness, in 1175 he was asked by King Henry II to become abbot of the first Carthusian monastery in England at Witham (Som.). In 1186, Hugh was elected to the see of Lincoln, beginning the rebuilding of the cathedral soon after. He is said to have had remarkable concern for lepers, tending them with his own hands and often sharing a meal from the same dish. Hugh condemned the persecution of the Jews which spread throughout England in 1190–1. Twenty years after his death he was canonized by Pope Honorius III, the first Carthusian saint.

**Hugh de Puisset** *See* PUISSET, HUGH DE.

**Huguenots,** a term of uncertain origin, were French-speaking (and some Walloon-speaking) protestants of *Calvinistic temper, who fled from two centuries of persecution to seek asylum in countries more sympathetic to Reformation practices. After the St Bartholomew's Day massacre (1572), the first wave of refugees to Britain were received at already established French churches in London, Canterbury, and Norwich. Relative quiet in France lasted only until 1661, when there commenced a steady erosion of privileges, culminating in the Revocation of the Edict of Nantes (1685), after which the trickle of émigrés became a flood, then a torrent. Some 40,000–50,000 Huguenots are estimated to have settled in England, the majority in London. They proved highly motivated, productive, and a considerable economic asset to their new host nation. Today only one French church remains in London, but Huguenot names such as Courtauld and *Olivier are familiar to all.

**Hull, Kingston upon** *See* KINGSTON UPON HULL.

**'humanism'** is the term conventionally used to describe a set of moral and literary values and techniques chiefly associated with the *Renaissance of the 15th and 16th cents. It embraced enthusiasm for the Greek and Latin classics; preference for rhetoric over logic to persuade; the belief that a literary education would produce better people; and optimism about mankind's dignity and worth.

Renaissance 'humanism' originated in Italy. It was through literary and church contacts with Italy that humanism spread to England in the first half of the 15th cent. At first, some English patrons paid Italian secretaries and scribes to prepare for them manuscripts of ancient and more recent texts. Humphrey, duke of *Gloucester (1390–1447), youngest brother of Henry V, employed such writers as Tito Livio Frulovisi, Antonio Beccaria, Lionardo Bruni, and Pier Candido Decembrio to prepare texts for him.

By c.1500 the teaching of rhetoric, poetry, and those classical writers neglected in the Middle Ages had become appreciated at both Oxford and Cambridge universities. William Grocyn (c.1449–1519) introduced Greek studies to Oxford on his return from Italy in 1491. The royal physician and Oxford academic Thomas Linacre (c.1460–1524) wrote works on Latin composition and also encouraged good medical practice. In 1511–14 John *Fisher recruited the famous Netherlands humanist Desiderius Erasmus (c.1466–1536) to teach Greek at Cambridge.

The apogee of English humanism was reached in the first four decades of the 16th cent. John *Colet (1467–1519) learned Greek in Italy and taught at Oxford from c.1497; as dean of St Paul's from 1504 he refounded St Paul's School with a curriculum based on the new classical learning. Thomas *More (1478–1535), unusually for humanists a lay lawyer rather than an ecclesiastic, cultivated the friendship of Erasmus and produced the most bewildering literary fantasy of the movement, *Utopia* (1516). Sir Thomas *Elyot (c.1490–1546) in *The Book Named the Governor* produced an English equivalent of the many treatises on education and politics current in Europe at the time.

By the mid-16th cent. it becomes impossible to speak of 'humanism' as a distinct entity, because its influence was spread so widely. Renaissance techniques for learning classical languages and editing classical texts became generally accepted. The belief that exposure to vast quantities of Greek and Latin literature, combined with vigorous physical exercise, would produce healthy, moral youg men survived until the later 20th cent.

**Humberside** was a new county established by the Local Government Act of 1972. It was built around the county boroughs of Hull and Grimsby, with a substantial hinterland taken from the East Riding of Yorkshire, from parts of Lindsey in Lincolnshire, and Goole, previously part of the West Riding. There was much opposition to the change, particularly from people in north Lincolnshire, who voted by more than 2:1 against the proposal. The Humber bridge, intended to knit the two parts together, was opened in 1981. Humberside was abolished in 1996.

**Humble Petition and Advice** The second written constitution of the *Protectorate, formulated by its second Parliament early in 1657. Originally, its main purpose was to make *Cromwell king, but it also proposed a new second chamber ('the other house'), to be nominated by him. Cromwell was much drawn to a constitution bearing Parliament's authority, the *Instrument of Government having only the army's, but he was asked to accept all of it or none, and he did not want the crown. Skilfully, he protracted negotiations for six weeks, until Parliament agreed to let him have the new constitution with the old title. The succession problem was settled by empowering him to name his own successor.

**Hume, David** (1711–76). Philosopher and historian, the younger son of a strict presbyterian laird, Hume lost his Christian belief at Edinburgh University in the 1720s. His *Treatise of Human Nature* (1739–40) provided a devastating critique of contemporary metaphysics, which cleared the ground for a genuinely empirical account of human understanding. His massive *History of England* (1754–63) is a neglected masterpiece, which remained a best-seller for more than a century. In general, Hume wanted to recommend a 'sceptical Whiggery' to his contemporaries as an antidote to party zealotry and an ally of commerce.

**Hume, Joseph** (1777–1855). The archetypal middle-class parliamentary radical. A confirmed *Benthamite, Hume was an indefatigable speaker in Parliament and organizer of committees, pressure groups, and alliances designed to promote advanced liberal causes. Among these were repeal of the Combination Acts, catholic emancipation, Poor Law reform, disestablishment of the Church of England, repeal of the Corn Laws, free trade, extension of the suffrage, retrenchment in government spending, reform of municipal corporations, and the establishment of London University.

**hundreds** were the principal subdivisions of most English shires from before the Conquest and for many centuries afterwards. Their approximate equivalents in Northumberland, Durham, and Cumberland were called 'wards', in six Danelaw shires 'wapentakes'. Hundreds are first mentioned by name in the laws of *Edmund (c.940); it is likely that they derive from a somewhat earlier reorganization of local government. Through most of the Middle Ages, the jurisdictional function was predominant. The hundred court usually met every three weeks and exercised petty civil jurisdiction. Hundred courts had a long decline until Victorian legislation (especially an Act of 1867) dismantled them.

**Hundred Years War** This term for the Anglo-French hostilities of 1337–1453 was coined in the 1860s but has enjoyed universal acceptance ever since. When the last descendant of the main Capetian line died in 1328, Edward III had a claim to the French throne through his mother. The war which broke out in 1337 arose largely out of Edward's tenure of *Aquitaine as a fief of the French crown, but was fuelled by dynastic ambition and by English annoyance at French involvement in Scottish affairs. Only in January 1340, however, did Edward adopt the title king of France, initially, it seems, to win Flemish rebels to his cause. He proved militarily successful in France but when war resumed in 1369, the French had the upper hand until Henry V's victories (1415–19). By the treaty of *Troyes he became both heir and regent to Charles VI. From 1420 to 1435 the English controlled much of northern France, and Henry VI was crowned king in Paris in 1431. The successes of Joan of Arc and the defection of the duke of Burgundy after the Congress of *Arras weakened the English position, leading to their expulsion from Normandy in 1450 and Gascony in 1453. *Calais remained English until 1558, but English kings continued to call themselves kings of France until 1802.

**Hunsdon, Henry Carey, 1st Baron** (1526–96). Hunsdon's mother was Mary Boleyn and he was therefore Elizabeth I's first cousin. Since Mary Boleyn was Henry VIII's mistress for a time, it was suggested that he was also Elizabeth's half-brother. At Elizabeth's succession he was given a barony, followed by the Garter in 1561. Appointed governor of Berwick in 1568, he won an important victory the following year near Carlisle over Sir Leonard Dacres, one of the leaders of the rising of the *northern earls. At the crisis of the Armada in 1588 he commanded the troops at Tilbury.

**Hunt, Henry** (1773–1835). Radical reformer. 'Orator' Hunt was a Wiltshire gentleman farmer, who became convinced of the need for a thorough reform of the existing political system, based on universal suffrage, annual parliaments, and the ballot. In 1816–17 he headed three huge anti-government demonstrations in Spa Fields, London. He was arrested for his part at *Peterloo and imprisoned for 2½ years in Ilchester gaol. After several unsuccessful parliamentary contests, he was returned for Preston in 1830, and opposed the 1832 Reform Bill as a half-measure which did nothing for the working class.

**Hunt, William Holman** (1827–1910). Painter. The eldest son of a warehouseman, he entered the Royal Academy Schools in 1844, where he met *Millais and *Rossetti, with whom he founded the Pre-Raphaelite Brotherhood. Hunt devised the technique of the brotherhood, using bright colours with no strong contrasts of light and shade. Among his best-known works were *The Light of the World* and *The Hireling Shepherd*, reproduced in great numbers in Victorian Britain.

**hunting** *See* BEAGLING.

**Huntingdon, Henry Hastings, 3rd earl of** (1536–95). Huntingdon was of royal blood and briefly within reach of the throne. His great-grandmother was a daughter of the duke of *Clarence and a niece of Edward IV. Huntingdon was summoned to Parliament in 1559 in his father's barony and succeeded him in 1560. Two years later, when the queen was believed to be dying of smallpox, Huntingdon, as a protestant, was discussed as a monarch to keep out Mary, queen of Scots. Elizabeth recovered and Huntingdon became a trusted servant.

**Huntingdon, Lady** (1707–91). Foundress of the Countess of Huntingdon's Connexion, Selina Shirley, daughter of the 2nd Earl Ferrers, married the 9th earl of Huntingdon (d. 1746) in 1728. Despite her aristocratic background, her fortune was slender and her marriage a love match. She was converted by her sister-in-law, Lady Margaret Hastings, and joined the methodist society in Fetter Lane in 1739. Coming to know the *Wesleys, the Welsh evangelist Howell *Harris, and George *Whitefield, she built a number of chapels in such places as Brighton (1761), Bath (1765), Tunbridge Wells (1769), Worcester (1773), and Spa Fields, London (1779), served by ministers trained after 1768 at the college which she instituted at Trevecca, near Talgarth. Many of her sixty chapels, like her college, long survived her.

**Huntingdonshire** was the third smallest of English counties in population until merged with Cambridgeshire in 1972. The origins of the county almost certainly derive from the establishment of a Roman settlement at the point where two roads, from Cambridge and Sandy, joined Ermine Street, just before it crossed the river Ouse. Godmanchester, which arose on that site, was for centuries part mother, part rival to the town of Huntingdon, which developed just north of the bridge. The area passed into the kingdom of the East Angles but was taken over by Mercia. In the later 9th cent. it was overrun by the Danes. Reconquered in 920 by *Edward the Elder, king of Wessex, it was fortified by him and had both a mint and a market by the mid-10th cent. The earliest mention of the shire is in the *Anglo-Saxon Chronicle* for 1011, when it was once more overrun by the Danes. By the time of the *Domesday survey, Huntingdon was one of the largest towns in the kingdom.

The county remained overwhelmingly rural. Drained by the Ouse, the western parts were good arable land, the eastern good grazing land. *Cobbett in 1822 echoed *Camden in the 1580s in admiring the meadows around Huntingdon—'the most beautiful that I ever saw in my life'. Godmanchester and Kimbolton slowly stagnated, but the existence of several other flourishing market towns seems to have inhibited the growth of Huntingdon—St Ives and St Neots remain comparable in size, and Ramsey, in the north-east, is considerably bigger.

**Huntly, George Gordon, 4th earl of** [S] (1513–62). Gordon's mother was an illegitimate daughter of James IV of Scotland. Huntly won a success against the English at Hadden Rigg in 1542, was a regent after the death of James V, but was captured by *Somerset at *Pinkie Cleugh in 1547. In 1546–9 he was chancellor [S] and again in 1561, but lost favour with Mary after her return from France. When she gave the earldom of Moray, which he claimed, to her illegitimate brother Lord James *Stewart, Huntly rose in rebellion. His troops were defeated at *Corrichie and he died immediately after the battle, being 'gross, corpulent and of short breath'.

**Huntly, George Gordon, 2nd marquis of** [S] (1592–1649). Huntly played a curiously ineffective role in Scotland during the Civil War. He spent much of his early life at the court of James I and then in France. In 1632 he was created Viscount Aboyne [S] and succeeded his father as 2nd marquis in 1636. His vast influence in the north-east made Charles I appoint him king's lieutenant in the north. But he was proud, moody, and irresolute. In the skirmishes of 1639 he was overwhelmed by *Montrose, then acting for the *covenanters. The hatred Huntly entertained for Montrose seriously weakened the royal cause in Scotland. He was arrested in 1647 and beheaded in March 1649.

**Huskisson, William** (1770–1830). Huskisson's father was a country gentleman from Staffordshire, and Huskisson had a career to make. He was in France at the outbreak of the Revolution and became acquainted with Lord Gower, the ambassador and a Staffordshire man. On their return to England in 1792, Huskisson was employed to help French refugees and became known to *Canning, *Pitt, and *Dundas. In 1795 he was made under-secretary for war and was brought into Parliament in 1796. Though not a ready speaker, he built a reputation as an administrator. He went out of office with Canning in 1809 and returned in 1814 to the comparatively humble post of commissioner of woods and forests, which he held until 1823. Next he became president of the Board of Trade, and on Canning's death *Goderich made him colonial secretary, with the leadership of the Commons. Huskisson was now a leader of the liberal Tories. He stayed in office under *Wellington, but with increasing friction, especially over parliamentary reform, and his offer of resignation in May 1828 was eagerly accepted. In September 1830, at the opening of the Liverpool to Manchester railway, he was run down and killed, 'seeming like a man bewildered', by the engine *Rocket*. A shy, awkward man, Huskisson was a strange fish in what was still an aristocratic pond—a man of business of more than common talent.

**Huxley, T. H.** (1825–95). Biologist, *Darwin's bulldog, essayist, public figure, and sage, Huxley was one of the most prominent Victorian scientists. After sketchy schooling, he studied medicine in London on a scholarship, and became a naval surgeon. Serving on HMS *Rattlesnake* surveying in Australian waters, he dredged, described, and classified marine invertebrates. Leaving the navy, he sought academic posts, and was appointed to the School of Mines, an ancestor of Imperial College, London. After 1859, he became famous defending Darwin's *Origin of Species*.

**Hwicce, kingdom of the** An Anglo-Saxon kingdom conterminous with the diocese of Worcester. The royal house of the Hwicce, whose earliest recorded kings Eanhere and his brother Eanfrid belong to the second half of the 7th cent., may have been established with Mercian help. Five generations of rulers are known, with several instances of joint rule by brothers. The Hwicce seem to have come increasingly under Mercian domination and the last independent Hwiccian rulers appear as subordinates in the charters of *Æthelbald and *Offa of Mercia.

**Hyde, Anne** (1637–71). Though she did not survive to become queen herself, two of Anne Hyde's daughters, Mary (b. 1662) and Anne (b. 1665), became queen. The daughter of Edward Hyde, earl of *Clarendon, lord chancellor to Charles II, Anne met James, duke of York, while she was maid of honour to Mary, princess royal and princess of Orange. Marriage did not take place until September 1660, when Anne was eight months pregnant with a son, who died an infant. Though Pepys thought the new duchess very plain and she rapidly grew fat, by 1668 he remarked that 'the duke of York, in all things but in his codpiece, is led by the nose by his wife'.

**Hyde Park riots,** 1866. Soon after the death of *Palmerston, Lord *Russell's government introduced a second Reform Bill, extending the franchise. Opposition by discontented Liberals led to the fall of the government in June 1866 and a minority Conservative administration took office under Lord *Derby. On 23 July a large *Reform League meeting called for Hyde Park found it closed. The crowd broke down the railings and clashed with police inside the park. Lord Stanley, a member of the cabinet, commented that there was 'more mischief than malice, and more of mere larking than either', though a policeman was killed. Nevertheless, when there were further disturbances in 1867 the home secretary, Spencer Walpole, was forced to resign.

**Hyndman, Henry Mayers** (1842–1921). Socialist. Born into riches, Hyndman was converted to Marxism by reading *Das Kapital*. In 1881 he published a kind of précis of it under the title *England for All*, which he distributed to delegates at the first *(Social) Democratic Federation conference in order to convert them to socialism. From 1884 he edited the leading British Marxist journal *Justice*. A committed anti-imperialist, he opposed the *Boer War, but then supported the First World War, which estranged him from most of his fellow-socialists.

**Hywel** (d. 949/50), king of much of Wales (c.904–49/50), known as Hywel Dda ('the Good'). The grandson of *Rhodri Mawr, king of *Gwynedd, he and his brother inherited *Seisyllwg from their father Cadell. He extended his authority into *Dyfed c.904, when he married Elen, probably the daughter of its last king; Gwynedd and *Powys fell into his grasp when their king was killed by the English in 942. Faced with Viking threats,

Hywel acknowledged the English kings *Edward the Elder (918) and *Athelstan (927) as his overlords. Like King *Alfred he visited Rome (928), and Alfred's example may have inspired the codification of Welsh law which tradition attributes to Hywel. The earliest surviving texts of 'The Laws of Hywel Dda' date from the early 13th cent., but parts seem older and may have been codified by Hywel.

**ice hockey** was pioneered by McGill University in 1880 and spread rapidly throughout Canada and the USA. A small English league was formed in 1903 and the first Scottish game was played in 1908. A British Ice Hockey Association was formed in 1914 and the sport was introduced into the Olympics in 1920.

**Iceni** British tribe and *civitas*. The tribal coinage, which carries the name ECEN or ECENI, suggests that the tribe were restricted to Norfolk and parts of Suffolk and Cambridgeshire. Their first mention is probably in Caesar's account of his British expeditions, where he refers to a tribe called the Cenimagni. Initially their contacts with the Roman invaders were not unfriendly, and the Icenian king Prasutagus became a client-king of Rome. On his death, however, his kingdom was incorporated into the Roman province and this, and other alleged abuses, led to the Icenian revolt, led by Prasutagus' widow *Boudicca. No doubt this set back plans for the Iceni to be given self-governing status as a *civitas*, but eventually that was accorded the tribe and their capital was established at Caistor St Edmund (Venta Icenorum).

**ice-skating** in its simplest form dates back many centuries, with skates made out of animal bones. It became fashionable in the 18th cent. and a London Skating Club was founded in 1842. Speed skating held its first international competition at Hamburg in 1885 and was admitted to the Olympics in 1924. Ice rinks were built in large numbers after one was opened in Manchester in 1877.

**Icknield Way** A trackway which runs from the central Thames, through the Chilterns, and northwards to the Wash near Hunstanton. Though claims are made for a prehistoric origin, it is doubtful that such long-

distance trackways existed, at least as a single entity, until the Iron Age at the earliest.

**Ida** (d. *c*.559), king of Bernicia (c.547–c.559). Founder of the *Bernician royal house from whom all subsequent Bernician and, after the reign of *Oswiu, Northumbrian kings with genealogies surviving claimed descent. *Bede believed that Ida came to the throne in 547 and ruled twelve years. In Northumbrian tradition Ida is associated with the conquest of the area around *Bamburgh.

**Idle, River, battle of the** *See* RIVER IDLE, BATTLE OF THE.

**impeachment** was a trial by the House of Lords at the instigation of the House of Commons, which presented articles and arranged the management. The first clear example was the presentation in 1386 of Michael de la *Pole, earl of Suffolk, but the practice became common in the 17th cent. with the struggle between crown and Parliament, when a number of royal ministers—*Bacon, Middlesex (*Cranfield), *Strafford, and *Danby—were impeached. The impeachment of Warren *Hastings, which went on for seven years and ended in acquittal, helped to discredit the process and the impeachment of Henry *Dundas, Viscount Melville, in 1806 for peculation was the last.

**imperialism** was not used in its modern sense until the later 19th cent. Before then it usually referred to the aggression of Napoleon Bonaparte. That does not mean of course that it cannot be used retrospectively, to describe the origins and growth of the *British empire in Stuart and Hanoverian times, for example; but the convention is to call these 'colonization'. It has also taken on a wider meaning. It usually refers to territorial acquisitions, but can also cover extensions of power or influence which fell short of that. 'Economic imperialism', for example, means the process by which an economy extends its financial control over others.

It has been explained in various ways. Missionaries used to attribute Britain's imperial successes to the will of God. 'Social Darwinists' thought they proved the British race was 'fittest' to survive. The favourite theories, however, are economic. At the root of imperialism lay Britain's phenomenal commercial expansion following her industrial revolution. That gave her world-wide material interests, which needed to be secured. Later, according to J. A. Hobson, the Marxists, and some capitalists (like *Rhodes), that need grew desperate, as capitalism began 'over-producing', and the industrialized countries began competing with each other for outlets. That, however, is controversial.

At its height, around 1900, imperialism also took on a domestic character. Britons forgot the old Napoleonic connotations, and took pride in their imperialism. At its crudest, this pride manifested itself in *jingoism; but it also had a more responsible side. All the main political parties—even Labour—sprouted imperialist wings.

By 1902 it was clear that the empire was stretched about as tight as it could be without bursting, and imperialists turned away from expansion to consolidation. An imperialist became someone who wished to federate the empire: economically (through *imperial preference), militarily, and even politically. Many of these imperialists were highly idealistic, and even liberal in their vision of a great multiracial empire, which would bring peace and civilization to the world. Some of them hoped that the post-Second World War *Commonwealth might achieve all this, only to be disappointed in the longer run.

**imperial preference** This was a favourite nostrum of late 19th- and early 20th-cent. imperialists to bind the empire together by levying lower tariffs on colonial imports than on others. Joseph *Chamberlain championed it from 1903. But there was a snag. Britain still adhered to *free trade. You cannot grant more preferential tariffs than none at all. Chamberlain wanted a tax on imported corn, to make this possible, but that was rejected at the election of 1906 because it would mean dearer bread. So the imperialists had to wait until 1932, when food import tariffs were introduced generally again. Imperial trade increased thereafter, though that may not have been wholly due to this. After the Second World War the policy slowly declined, as a result of American pressure, the General Agreement on Tariffs and Trade (1947), and Britain's adhesion to a rival trading unit—the *European Economic Community—in 1973.

**Imphal, battle of,** 1944. In March 1944 the Japanese 15th Army under Mutaguchi advanced over the river Chindwin into India towards Imphal. *Slim's 14th Army was taken by surprise, but three divisions were able to take up defensive positions around the town of Imphal on 4 April. The Japanese besieged Imphal on the following day, but it was relieved on 22 June after bitter close-quarter fighting. Japanese offensive power was severely damaged at Imphal, and they were forced to fall back to Burma.

**impositions** Tudor sovereigns received lifetime parliamentary grants of customs duties called *tonnage and poundage, but as inflation reduced the royal revenue they had recourse to impositions—additional prerogative levies on imports, first collected under Mary I. The Commons never accepted the validity of these non-parliamentary levies, and they were a cause of constant friction with both James I and Charles I. They were finally declared illegal by the Tonnage and Poundage Act of 1641.

**impropriations** Impropriation was the assignment of a benefice to a lay proprietor, as distinct from appropriation to a monastery. When the monasteries were dissolved, many appropriated monastic benefices were impropriated, causing Matthew *Parker, for instance, great difficulty as primate in curbing Elizabeth's rapacious courtiers. Lay impropriators, as *Tenison noted (1713), were known for seeking cheap and often indifferent curates. An effective Whig 1830s reform insisted on incumbents being resident.

**Inchiquin, Murrough O'Brien, 1st earl of** [I] (c.1614–74). Inchiquin, a protestant, was one of several commanders who played a semi-independent role in the confused situation that followed the Irish rising of 1641. He took up arms against the catholic

Confederation and inflicted several defeats upon it in Munster. Passed over by Charles I for the presidency of Munster, which he expected, he joined the parliamentary side in July 1644 and working with *Monck won an important victory over the Confederation troops at Knockmanus near Mallow in 1647. But the following year he rejoined the royalists. Driven into exile when *Cromwell landed, he was raised to the earldom by Charles II in 1654, converted to catholicism, and fought for the French. At the Restoration he was given back his Irish estates with substantial compensation.

**income tax** was introduced in 1799 by William *Pitt's government to fund the war against the French. The need for a new tax arose from unprecedentedly high expenditure on the British armed forces and on subsidies to the allies. Many supposed that income tax would be a temporary expedient of war and in fact Parliament repealed the tax in 1816 and ordered the commissioners for the affairs of taxes to destroy their records.

Raising revenues continued to present problems to chancellors of the Exchequer. In 1842 Sir Robert *Peel proposed that 'for a time to be limited, the income of the country shall be called upon to contribute to remedying this growing evil [the deficit]'. No chancellor since 1842 has removed income tax.

Although *Disraeli proposed, in 1853, the abolition of income tax by 1860, the expense of the *Crimean War encouraged *Gladstone to keep it. Government expenditures on defence continued to rise and after 1906 the cost of defence and social welfare increased rapidly. David *Lloyd George's 'People's Budget' of 1909 imposed, for the first time, income tax with rates varying according to the ability to pay. During the First World War alterations in the rates of tax on incomes offset some costs of warfare. The highest personal rate was known popularly as 'supertax' and the prosperity of firms involved in wartime activities incurred Excess Profits Duty.

Although changes in the rates of income tax occurred between the two world wars, the *Second World War required both more revenue and limits on demand inflation. This latter threat arose from higher wages seeking inadequate quantities of goods and services. The year 1941 saw the introduction of a new type of levy, reimbursable post-war credits, at the rate of 10*s*. (50p) in the pound, to enforce savings. Repayment was slow; many taxpayers waited as long as 20 years for their money. Simultaneously the surtax rate increased to 19*s*. 6d. in the pound.

Since 1945 reductions in the standard rate have occurred, although rates have always remained above those of peacetime in earlier periods.

**Indemnity and Oblivion, Act of,** 1660. Restorations after long exiles usually disappoint the loyalists since there are so many claims to be rewarded. In the declaration of *Breda, Charles II had promised a general amnesty and the Act of 12 Car. II c. 11 put it into effect, 'to bury all seeds of future discords'. But the many changes in landownership which had taken place during the Commonwealth were ignored, leading royalists who had suffered severely to jeer that it was indemnity for enemies, oblivion for friends.

**Independent Irish Party** The forerunner of the *Irish National Party put together by Isaac *Butt and *Parnell. It was formed by about 40 Irish MPs in 1852 to assist the *Tenant League campaign and to obtain the repeal of the *Ecclesiastical Titles Act. But it split badly between catholics and protestants, sympathizers of the Liberals and of the Conservatives, and those who gave priority to land reform over the religious question. The latter were known to their admirers as 'the Irish brigade', to their detractors as 'the Pope's brass band'.

**Independent Labour Party (ILP).** The party was established in 1893 at a conference in Bradford, composed of 120 delegates largely drawn from the industrial north and Scotland and chaired by Keir *Hardie. Chronic lack of union funding and modest successes at local and parliamentary elections led the ILP to take the initiative in forming the Labour Representation Committee in 1900. With the outbreak of war in 1914, a significant number of ILP members including Ramsay *MacDonald adopted a pacifist stance. Some became involved in the *Union of Democratic Control, thereby strengthening contact between Labour and left-wing Liberals.

Disappointment over the second Labour government (1929–31) accelerated the leftward drift of the ILP and made many of its members rebellious in Parliament. As a result the party, under the Clydeside firebrand Jimmy *Maxton, disaffiliated from Labour in 1932. By 1935 the ILP, which assumed a neo-Marxist character, had fewer than 5,000 members, only a quarter of the previous figure.

**India,** or Hindustan, was named by the Greeks after the Indus valley. Its dominant civilization was Hindu and Buddhist but, from the 11th cent., it was subject to conquest from the Islamic north. The most famous of its conquerors were the Mughals, who established their empire in 1526. In the age of exploration, the first Europeans to arrive were the Portuguese who developed a sea-borne empire centred on Goa. In the early 17th cent., the Dutch displaced the Portuguese, but India was peripheral to their principal interests in Java. The English *East India Company established its presence from the 1610s and the French arrived in the 1660s. From the 1720s, the power of the Mughal empire started to decline. In Europe, France and England found themselves at war in this period and their respective companies carried on the conflict by constructing alliances with the successor states. At first, the French under Dupleix had the upper hand. But, from the late 1740s, the English company's fortunes began to turn as Robert *Clive won a series of military victories. The major threat posed by the French was eliminated after the battle of *Wandewash in 1760. For the next 30 years, there was some hesitancy in British circles at building on these foundations. But, during the Revolutionary and Napoleonic wars, the opportunity was seized and by 1818, with the defeat of the Maratha empire, the East India Company had gained supremacy. After the *Indian mutiny of 1857, however, the company was abolished and sovereignty passed to the British crown. In the 19th cent., India was undoubtedly Britain's most important colony. After the First World War, both its military and economic status began to decline and a mass nationalist movement emerged under the leadership of Mahatma *Gandhi. As early as 1920, the British began to clear the way for 'responsible self-government' and, by 1935, had drawn up plans for India's eventual conversion into a dominion. However, the Second World War cut short this programme of devolution and promoted an extremely hasty retreat. British India was partitioned into the separate states of Pakistan and India, which became independent on 15 August 1947.

**India Bill,** 1783. An abortive reform of the *East India Company, drafted largely by Edmund *Burke and introduced by the Fox–North coalition. Opponents expressed exaggerated fears that the patronage thus created would give the coalition a stranglehold on power. The cause of the bill's defeat in the Lords in December 1783 was the resentment of George III against his ministers and the underhand pressure he brought to bear by letting it be known that anyone voting for the bill would henceforth be treated as a personal enemy. Secret and prior negotiations with *Pitt allowed the king summarily to dismiss the coalition.

**Indian mutiny** On 10 May 1857, sepoys of the Bengal army shot their British officers and marched on Delhi to restore the aged Mughal emperor, Bahadur Shah, to power. Existing 'loyalist' forces were unable to quell the rebellion and reinforcements had to be called from China. It took until December 1857 for Sir Colin *Campbell's army to reoccupy the key strategic points along the Ganges valley. The causes of the mutiny lay in attempts to impose British-style army discipline—the celebrated issue of cartridges greased with animal fat being symptomatic of wider problems. The events of 1857 marked a watershed in Indo-British relations. Afterwards, the British came to doubt the possibilities of a rapid social transformation and treated their Indian subjects with increasing suspicion. The army was reorganized to improve British surveillance.

**Indulf** (d.962), king of 'Scotland' (954–62). His father was Constantine II and his mother was (probably) Danish. He succeeded Malcolm I, and extended the kingdom's territory south across the Firth of Forth to include Edinburgh. His reign witnessed a resurgence of Scandinavian incursions. A fleet of Vikings was defeated in Buchan, and Indulf himself perished in battle against a Norwegian force at 'Invercullen'.

**indulgences** Arising in crusading times—first in 1063—from Roman law concepts, they became an integral part of every late medieval crusader's—and pilgrim's—commitment. After sacramental confession, absolution, and penance, the church, on God's behalf also, granted the sinner remission of 'temporal penalties' still inevitable after sin. Later, widespread abuse, often financial, made religious commitment mechanistic, and indulgences vulnerable to attack from 16th-cent. reformers.

**Industrial Relations Act,** 1971. The Act, designed by a newly elected Conservative government to weaken the bargaining powers of trade unions, had its origins in the problems encountered by earlier administrations, such as excessive wage demands, unofficial strikes, and inter-union disputes. Unions had to register to keep their legal privileges; before a strike, they had to hold secret ballots of their members, effectively a cooling-off period.

**industrial revolution** In 1837 Louis-Auguste Blanqui used the phrase to describe the changes Britain had undergone during the previous half-century in her social and economic life. Widespread use of the term followed from Arnold Toynbee's *Lectures on the Industrial Revolution of the Eighteenth Century in England* published in 1884. Debates about the precise period and its meaning reflected efforts to identify what brought about the transformation from a predominantly rural society, whose major source of livelihoods derived from the land, to a rapidly urbanizing country whose wealth came from commerce and manufacturing.

Symbolic of the industrial revolution was the use of coal as a source of energy. The conversion of coal to coke made cheaper iron ore smelting possible and simultaneously produced town gas, used from the early 19th cent. for lighting. Coal-fuelled boilers provided steam-power for mines drainage, factory machinery, and locomotives, making speed and repetitive activities less arduous and greatly augmenting output. Particularly associated with such changes were cotton textiles, made cheaply in large quantities.

Social changes occurred simultaneously. Many new jobs were created between the later 18th and the mid-19th cent. from the ever widening applications of technical innovations such as in gas-making, in the chemical industry, in canal and railway transport, and in textiles. New methods of industrial production also required many people to move to urban locations. Some existing towns such as *Manchester expanded very rapidly, whilst new towns emerged, such as St Helens (Merseyside). Rapid urban growth posed many unforeseen problems of overcrowded houses, inadequate sanitation, and law and order.

Many historians, geographers, and political economists have sought to explain the origins of the changes during the second half of the 18th cent. and why they should have occurred in Britain. The search for one main underlying cause has led to elaborate and careful studies of both economic activities and social developments, including geographical determination, religious discrimination against nonconformists, technological innovations in sources of power, and the rise of literacy.

In contrast other historians have challenged the very concept of an industrial revolution. For example, econometric techniques applied by N. F. R. Crafts and others indicate slow rates of change in British economic life. Innovations in technology and in organization occurred piecemeal in different parts of the economy, suggesting that the image of revolution seems inappropriate.

**Ine** (d.726), king of Wessex (688–726). The reputation of Ine rests on two foundations, legal and ecclesiastical. He reigned from 688 for a very long period, 37 years, and was confident enough to resign his throne to younger men, making his way as a pilgrim to Rome where he died. His laws were impressive. Alfred (871–99), who was descended from Ine's brother, used Ine's decrees when he drew up his own statement of just law. In the ecclesiastical field Ine himself presided over the first synods known to have been held among the West Saxons, and founded the bishopric at *Sherborne to serve his people west of Selwood. Internal evidence within the law code betrays a deep concern with ecclesiastical law. Heavy penalties were imposed on failure to see that a child was baptized or to pay proper dues to the church. His laws also show a significant concern with the status of Welshmen assimilated to the kingdom. The Welshmen of the code of laws clearly referred to the British inhabitants of the west country taken over and governed according to Germanic law by the West Saxon king. Ine was also from time to time busy in the south-east. In 694 he compelled the Kentishmen to pay an immense compensation for the murder of the West Saxon prince Mul, the brother of Ine's own predecessor. But his main efforts and achievement lay in the heartlands of Wessex and the south-west. Scholarship flourished under the inspiration of *Aldhelm, abbot of Malmesbury, and then first bishop of Sherborne (705–9). Ine's master achievement was to complete the political conquest of Devon, following on a generation or so of steady Saxon migration and agrarian settlement under arms in the fertile valleys of the south-west.

**Inkerman, battle of,** 1854. In November 1854 an Anglo-French force was besieging Sebastopol in the Crimea. On 5 November a Russian army under Menshikov attacked at Inkerman. Despite having superior numbers, perhaps 50,000 to 15,000 allies, the Russian attacks were badly co-ordinated. The arrival of allied reinforcements eventually forced the Russians to withdraw, having lost about 12,000 men to the allies' 3,400.

**Inns of Court** Legal institutions of medieval origin situated in London and responsible for the education of barristers. They were first used as accommodation and were a cross between the college, the club, and the trade union. Originally around 20 Inns were known to have existed of which only four survive: Inner Temple, Middle Temple, Gray's Inn, and Lincoln's Inn. In the 15th cent. the Inns gradually assumed responsibility for the education of students and today anyone wishing to become a barrister must first join one of the Inns. When students are considered qualified for the profession they are 'called' to the bar by their Inn and entitled to practise in the higher courts of law.

**inoculation** *See* VACCINATION.

**Instrument of Government** The written constitution under which Oliver *Cromwell became lord *protector on 16 December 1653. Its author was Major-General

*Lambert. Like the army's earlier *Heads of the Proposals, which he had helped to draft, the Instrument was a prescription for limited monarchy, and it originally named Cromwell as king. Cromwell declined the crown, but eventually accepted authority as protector under the instrument's terms.

These were that he should govern by the advice of a council, whose members it named. On his death the council was to elect his successor. Legislative power was vested in a single-chamber parliament representing England, Wales, Scotland, and Ireland and elected at least every three years on a property franchise. A national church was to be maintained, but with freedom of worship for protestant dissenters.

**intercursus magnus and intercursus malus** were treaties between Henry VII and the Archduke Philip of Burgundy, primarily for the encouragement of trade between England and the Low Countries. By the first (1496) Philip agreed not to support Perkin *Warbeck, pretender to the English throne, to limit tolls, and to provide for speedy redress for merchants. Difficulties continued and the second treaty in 1506 allowed English cloth exports without duty. It was not ratified and a third treaty, in 1507, returned to the terms of the 1496 agreement.

**interdict** A papal prohibition which could operate at various levels. A general interdict could be imposed only by the pope. Pope Alexander III placed Scotland under an interdict when William the Lion rejected the papal nominee to the see of St Andrews in 1178, and Innocent III issued an interdict against England when John in 1206 refused to accept Stephen *Langton as archbishop of Canterbury. The Scottish interdict ended in a compromise after ten years. Innocent's interdict forbade all ceremonies save baptism of infants and confessions for the dying. John resisted strongly but in 1213, beset by baronial opposition, he surrendered completely, agreeing to hold his kingdom as the pope's vassal. The interdict was lifted in 1214.

**Interregnum** is the name sometimes used for the period between the abolition of the monarchy in February 1649 and the restoration of Charles II in May 1660. Royalists insisted that Charles II had become king as soon as his father was executed.

In Scotland, two interregna followed the death of Queen *Margaret, the Maid of Norway, in September 1290. The first lasted until the nomination of John *Balliol in November 1292. The second followed his deposition by Edward I in July 1296 and lasted until the coronation of Robert I, the Bruce, in March 1306.

**'Intolerable Acts',** 1774. These Acts were the British government's response to the *Boston Tea Party. The Boston Port Act, the Massachusetts Government Act, and the Massachusetts Justice Act temporarily closed the port of Boston, replaced an elective council by a crown-nominated one, and allowed capital trials of soldiers and officials to be transferred outside Massachusetts.

**Invergordon mutiny** Severe pay cuts imposed by the National Government in 1931 led sailors of the British Atlantic fleet at the naval port of Cromarty Firth, Scotland, to refuse to go on duty. The cuts were revised slightly. The mutiny ringleaders were discharged from the navy.

**Inverlochy, battle of,** 1645. *Montrose's victory at *Aberdeen in September 1644 was but a raid and he was soon on the move again, pursued by superior forces under *Argyll himself. When the covenanters retired for the winter, Montrose was persuaded to an insolent incursion into the heart of Campbell country around Inverary. On 2 February 1645, under the shadow of Ben Nevis, Argyll's forces were cut to pieces at Inverlochy.

**Inverurie, battle of,** 1308. A decisive victory of Robert I, king of Scots, over John *Comyn, earl of Buchan, probably on 23 May. After his escape at *Slioch, Robert was able to capture strong points on the coastal plain of Moray and in the Black Isle before returning to Buchan, where, near Inverurie, he routed the earl's forces. The battle gave Robert control of the north.

**Investiture contest** Name given by historians to the conflicts which ensued when 11th-cent. church reformers, popes like Gregory VII (1073–85) at their head, tried to free the church from its subordination to the secular world. To reformers that subordination was symbolized by the investiture ceremony in which a new bishop or abbot received the staff or ring of office from the hands of the lay ruler, who had in practice appointed him. In Germany and Italy the quarrels took on the dimensions of a great 50-year struggle between empire and papacy. In England the contest between kings and church reformers such as *Anselm was a relatively brief one and was ended in 1107 by a compromise. Henry I renounced his right of investiture but, as before, prelates continued to be chosen in accordance with royal wishes and swore homage to the king.

**Iona** The monastery founded by St *Columba in 563 soon became the centre for Celtic Christianity, sending out missionaries to Scotland and Northumbria. Although the ravages of Viking raids before and after 800 made Iona a more dangerous place to live, its prestige continued well into the 9th cent. Scottish kings, according to tradition, continued to be buried there, and *Margaret, wife of Malcolm III, king of the Scots, held the monastery in favour.

The building of a new Benedictine monastery in 1204, followed by an Augustinian nunnery, spelled the return of Iona's fortunes. Closely linked to the Lords of the Isles from the 14th cent. onwards, and the seat intermittently of the bishop of the Isles, Iona in the later Middle Ages was a great centre of sculpture. Only with the forfeiture of the lordship in 1493 and the Reformation did Iona's decline set in in earnest.

**Ipswich** Suffolk town, on the Orwell estuary. It was one of the earliest post-Roman towns in Britain, originating in the 7th cent. as a trading port (wic). Large and wealthy from *c.*650 to 850, it was less important in the high and later Middle Ages. Under the Tudors and Stuarts it enjoyed a second heyday as a port and cloth town, and was one of the half-dozen largest English provincial towns.

**Iraq,** which formed part of the Turkish empire, was the scene of heavy fighting in the First World War, the British capturing Baghdad in 1917. At the end of the war the territory became a *mandate under the *League of Nations. From 1921 until 1958, when Faisal II was assassinated, the country was a monarchy. The second Labour government gave notice in 1929 that it would relinquish the mandate in 1932 and in that year Iraq entered the League of Nations as an independent country. The mandate was replaced by an Anglo-Iraq treaty which gave Britain military bases, held until after the Second World War. The attack on Kuwait in 1990 by Saddam Hussein, who had come to power in 1979, led to the *Gulf War, in which Britain sent troops under United Nations auspices. A second war in 2003, undertaken by Britain and America, overthrew Saddam in three weeks, but the move to a stable, peaceful, and democratic Iraq proved very difficult.

**Ireland, Government of, Act,** 1920–1. The first major constitutional reform since the Act of *Union 1800–1 resulted from the need for an alternative to the third Home Rule Bill, suspended 1914, which no longer had the backing of Southern Irish nationalist opinion. It aimed to establish two devolved governments for the six counties of the north-east and the 26 counties of the south and west. Essential powers were to be retained at Westminster, proportional representation was to be used at elections, and a Council of Ireland was to be established. The Dáil rejected the Act, which was supplanted by the *Anglo-Irish treaty of 1921. For 80 years the Act has provided the legal basis for Northern Ireland's existence.

**Ireland, high kings of** Despite the popular perception of the importance of the 'high kingship' of Ireland, early medieval Ireland did not possess a monarch whose rule was effective over the entire island. Nevertheless, the most powerful dynasty, the Uí Néill, who dominated the northern half of the island, were often able to compel most of the other province kings to submit. *Brian Boru, however, destroyed the Uí Néill monopoly and in the 11th and 12th cents. Ireland generally only had a high king 'with opposition', the last of whom was Rory *O'Connor, high king at the time of the Anglo-Norman invasion in 1169.

**Ireland, lordship of** Ireland first emerges into the light of history with the introduction of Christianity in the 5th cent. in documents ascribed to the British missionary St *Patrick. Thereafter it developed a highly literate society, which has left us a substantial corpus of Latin and vernacular literature. The 7th–8th-cent. law tracts,

heavily influenced by the Scriptures, portray a society that was intensely hierarchical.

At the highest rung of the ladder stood the kings, around whom society revolved. Ireland was a land of many kings, the law tracts defining three grades: kings of petty local kingdoms, overkings ruling several of these, and 'kings of overkings' who effectively ruled a whole province. Although the laws rarely refer to a *high king of all Ireland, it is clear that for several centuries the leading dynasty, the Uí Néill (based in the northern half of the country), did claim, and were occasionally able to enforce, supremacy throughout the island. Their primacy was smashed by the upstart *Munster king *Brian Boru (d.1014).

*Viking incursions in the late 8th cent. for a time seemed likely to overwhelm the country. Certainly, the Vikings increased the intensity of warfare, and by developing towns at *Dublin, Waterford, Limerick, Wexford, and Cork, they added to the wealth of what was otherwise a largely pastoral economy. In time, the Viking enclaves were assimilated into the Irish political superstructure, and those Irish kings who succeeded in asserting dominance over them gained an advantage over their rivals in the race for the high kingship. This was especially true in the case of Dublin, overlordship of which was, by the late 10th cent., generally asserted by successful claimants to the high kingship.

What might have been the evolution of a national monarchy was cut short in the mid-12th cent. by the Anglo-Norman invasion. The invaders were led by Richard de Clare, earl of *Pembroke, better known as Strongbow. At this point, late in 1171, Henry II (who had received a papal licence to invade Ireland) came to Ireland himself, the first English king ever to do so, and established the English lordship. A widespread process of colonization then began, which involved the introduction to Ireland of English common law and institutions. By the end of the 13th cent., English rule was effective over perhaps two-thirds of the island.

At this point a gradual decline began to take place in the fortunes of the English colony. This was accompanied by a dramatic revival in the power of the native Irish lords, whose culture many of the settlers had begun to adopt, in spite of frequent attempts by the Irish *Parliament to legislate against it. Costly military campaigns in the second half of the 14th cent., two led by Richard II, failed to turn the tide. A preoccupation with the war with France meant a curtailment in the English commitment to the government of Ireland in the 15th cent., resources being channelled into a cordoned enclave surrounding Dublin known as the *Pale.

A growing separatist tendency among the Anglo-Irish community, culminating in a declaration of parliamentary independence in 1460 (though checked by the passage of *Poynings's Law in 1494), led to the emergence of the earls of Kildare as effective masters of the Pale, though nominally the king's deputy. The Kildare ascendancy continued until the rebellion by Thomas *FitzGerald, son of the 9th earl, in 1534, which was used by Henry VIII as a pretext for destroying Kildare power. The Irish 'Reformation Parliament' convened in 1536 declared Henry supreme head of the church, while that of 1541 gave the English monarch for the first time the title of king (as opposed to lord) of Ireland, in the process bringing the medieval lordship to an end.

**Ireland Act,** 1949. Following the Irish Free State government's declaration of a republic in September 1948, the Act gave guarantees that the constitutional status of Northern Ireland would not be changed without the consent of the Parliament of Northern Ireland. That assurance has been reiterated at frequent intervals since 1969 although rephrased as: no change without the consent of a majority of the electorate. It has, however, never completely managed to reassure unionist opinion, constantly fearful of a British sell-out.

**Ireton, Henry** (1611–51). Ireton was plunged into the Civil War, since he was appointed by Parliament to command the horse at Nottingham two months before Charles I raised his standard in the same town. He fought at *Edgehill and in the first battle of *Newbury, where he was wounded, and rapidly became one of *Cromwell's most trusted lieutenants. In 1646 he married Cromwell's daughter Bridget. Bulstrode Whitelocke described him as an excellent man of business with a great influence over Cromwell. He took a prominent part in the *Putney army debates of November 1647, ardently defending the rights of property against radical and egalitar-

ian proposals. The second civil war persuaded him that no deal with Charles was possible and in January 1649 he signed the king's death warrant. He accompanied Cromwell to Ireland and remained in charge when Cromwell returned to England in May 1650. The following year he died of fever.

**Irish Constabulary/Royal Irish Constabulary** (after 1867). The Irish Constabulary was created in 1836 with an initial strength of around 7,500: this figure rose to 12,358 in 1850, before settling at around 10,000. The force was distinct from its English counterparts, being armed and centrally controlled. The prefix 'Royal' was granted in 1867 in recognition of the constabulary's conduct during the *Fenian rising. The RIC bore the burden of the *Irish Republican Army onslaught of 1919–21, sustaining around 416 killed and just under 700 wounded. The force was disbanded in 1922 after the ratification of the *Anglo-Irish treaty in London and Dublin.

**Irish Famine** *See* FAMINE, IRISH.

**Irish Free State,** 1922–48. The state was formed by the *Anglo-Irish treaty of December 1921, which granted dominion status, with defence safeguards, to 26 counties of the south and west of Ireland. Its first months, December 1922–April 1923, saw the completion of a bitter civil war. The tactics used by the Free State government, especially executions, ensured long-term acrimony. Thereafter the Free State proved remarkably stable, thanks to an overwhelmingly catholic agrarian population and the exclusion of the north-eastern counties. Both Cumann na nGaedheal (1922–32) and Fianna Fail (from 1932) governments adopted protectionist economic policies and catholic hierarchy-approved social policies. *De Valera's government of the 1930s successfully widened the treaty settlement by abolishing the oath to the crown and removing the governor-general. The constitution of 1937 established a virtual republic and independence in international affairs was confirmed by neutrality during the *Second World War. A republic was finally declared by the coalition government at a press conference in Ottawa in September 1948.

**Irish Home Rule** From the formation of the Home Government Association, led by

Isaac *Butt, in 1870, Home Rule became the ill-defined term representing the demands of the constitutional nationalists. Its origins lay in Daniel *O'Connell's Repeal Movement of the 1840s: like O'Connell, Home Rulers between 1870 and 1918 never made clear precisely what form amendment of the Act of *Union 1800–1 should take. There was agreement that the movement's tactics should be based on winning concessions from the British Parliament by influencing British MPs and by building up effective Irish representation in the Commons. Butt's embryonic party and his leadership, however, proved ineffective during the 1870s. From 1881 the movement entered upon its most successful period under the charismatic and autocratic leadership of Charles Stewart Parnell. Through his leadership of the *Irish Land League, Parnell was able to provide mass popular backing for Irish MPs. Parnell took advantage of *Gladstone's dependence on the Irish Party for the survival of his government to influence him to introduce the first Home Rule Bill 1886. The bill allowed for only limited devolution: the British government was to retain control over security, foreign policy, and financial institutions. Though the bill failed to pass the Commons, it represented a triumph for Irish nationalism and an acknowledgement that Ireland could govern itself. From 1886 and with the advent of a new Conservative government, Parnell's party lost much influence and unity collapsed over Parnell's involvement in the O'Shea divorce case in 1890. In 1893 Gladstone introduced a second Home Rule Bill, which was soundly defeated in the House of Lords. Between 1893 and 1910 more limited forms of self-government were considered by Tory and Liberal governments and the growth of cultural nationalism in Ireland challenged the hegemony of the parliamentary party. A constitutional crisis, caused by reform of the House of Lords 1910–11, resulted again in a minority Liberal government, dependent on the Irish Parliamentary Party, and led to the introduction of a third Home Rule Bill. The years 1912–14 produced a great test for the Home Rule cause in British politics, with fierce Ulster resistance, backed up by the Tory Party. By 1914 and the final stages of the bill, civil war threatened with the option of partition, temporary or permanent, as the only alternative.

When the First World War intervened, the Home Rule Bill was on the statute book, but was suspended for the duration of the war. Following the *Easter Rising, *Lloyd George made another attempt to achieve a settlement, which again foundered on the partition question. By the end of 1918 the situation was transformed by the collapse of the Irish Parliamentary Party and Sinn Fein's demand for a settlement considerably in advance of Home Rule. The Government of *Ireland Act 1920–1 attempted a Home Rule settlement, with separate north-east and southern parliaments: ironically it was the loyalist Northerners who accepted the offer. The consequences of Home Rule's failure are still felt on both sides of the Irish Sea.

**Irish Land League,** 1879–82. The league was formed during the agrarian depression to demand tenant rights, including fair rents and security of tenure. It spread through much of the south and west of Ireland, unifying the interests of large and small farmers, provincial town and countryside. Its adoption of the boycott tactic towards rack-renting landlords pressurized *Gladstone to introduce his *Land Act in 1881, granting many of its demands. *Parnell, president of the league, in accepting a revised Land Act and rejecting further agitation by the *Kilmainham treaty 1882 effectively terminated the movement.

**Irish National Party (Irish Parliamentary Party).** Beginning from 1870 under Isaac *Butt's Home Government Association, it only became a disciplined successful party under *Parnell 1880–90. It split into contending factions over Parnell's fall 1890–1 and unity was only restored in 1900 under John *Redmond. Appearing close to success when the third Home Rule Bill was introduced in 1912, it suffered from the effective opposition in Ulster and in the Conservative Party to that bill. By supporting the British government in the First World War, it was blamed for the war's increasing unpopularity, and was obliterated by Sinn Fein in the 1918 general election.

**Irish rebellion,** 1798. The 1798 rising occurred in the summer, and involved between 30,000 and 50,000 insurgents and around 76,000 government troops. The intellectual leadership came from the Francophile

*United Irish movement (1791), originally middle class and urban and in favour of constitutional reform. As the possibility of non-violent reform diminished in the 1790s, the militancy of the United Irish movement developed. The revolt was precipitated by the government's brutal efforts, especially in April–May 1798, to suppress sedition and conspiracy. There were two main centres of rebellion: in eastern Ulster, where the insurgents were decisively defeated at Antrim and at Ballynahinch; and in south Leinster, where the critical rebel defeat occurred at *Vinegar Hill (Co. Wexford) on 21 June. A French landing, at Killala (Co. Mayo) in August, came too late. The rising further discredited the Irish government with William *Pitt, and reinforced his sympathy for a constitutional union between Britain and Ireland.

**Irish rebellions,** 1641, 1848, 1867, 1916. *See* KILKENNY, CONFEDERATION OF; O'BRIEN, WILLIAM SMITH; IRISH REPUBLICAN BROTHERHOOD; EASTER RISING.

**Irish Republican Army (IRA).** The Irish Volunteers, formed in 1913/14 and reorganized along conventional military command lines after the *Easter Rising, became known as the IRA from 1919. During the Anglo-Irish War, 1919–21, it became the dominant military arm of the Dáil government. Divided over the *Anglo-Irish treaty of December 1921, the minority formed the Provisional Government/Free State Army, while the majority armed against the new state in the civil war 1922–3. Defeat was implicit in the ceasefire of April 1923. The *raison d'être* of the organization remained because of partition and the allegiance to the British crown. The outbreak of violence in Derry and Belfast from 1969 found the movement wanting in its traditional protective role for the catholic minority: graffiti claimed IRA stood for 'I ran away'. A split occurred between the Belfast-based traditional nationalist Provisional IRA and the Marxist Official IRA, with the latter shrinking and splintering into smaller republican organizations. The Provisional IRA waged a high-profile terror campaign, which was instrumental in the collapse of *Stormont in 1972 and in power-sharing initiatives, but it lost support and momentum as a result of an unsuccessful truce 1974/5.

Gaining considerable support from the hunger strike crisis of 1981, the movement adopted a more political strategy with Sinn Fein Armalite and ballot policy. Its refusal to begin effective disarmament jeopardized the peace process in the early 21st cent. The IRA would not disband but agreed to put its weapons out of use and in 2005 declared the armed struggle to be at an end.

**Irish Republican Brotherhood** Better known as the *Fenian movement. A secret society, organized along cell lines, it became the long-term agency for the planning of Irish insurrections. It was behind the abortive uprising in Ireland in 1867 and the equally unsuccessful 'invasions' of Canada between 1867 and 1870. Its military council planned the *Easter Rising; many advanced nationalists blamed the IRB for the rising's failure and argued that its usefulness was over.

**Irish Volunteers** *See* VOLUNTEER MOVEMENT.

**Ironsides** was a nickname given to Oliver *Cromwell by Prince *Rupert after the battle of *Marston Moor (July 1644). The title was derived 'from the impenetrable strength of his troops, which could by no means be broken or divided'. Later the term was extended to the soldiers themselves—the double regiment of cavalry which Cromwell had raised in East Anglia at the outbreak of the Civil War, and known both for its discipline and its religious radicalism.

**Irving, Edward** (1792–1834). Religious leader. Born in Annan, educated at Edinburgh University, Irving was successively master of Kirkcaldy Academy, assistant at St John's, Glasgow, and minister at Hatton Garden chapel, London (1822), where his extravagant preaching moved many. Convinced of Christ's imminent second coming, he encouraged 'speaking with tongues' and translated a Spanish Jesuit's *The Coming of the Messiah in Glory and Majesty* (1827). After returning to Scotland (1828), he was charged with heresy and removed from Regent Square (1832). His congregation mostly followed him to found the *Catholic Apostolic Church (or Irvingites).

**Irving, Henry** (1838–1905). Actor and theatre manager. Born John Henry Brodribb, Irving emerged as a leading actor, with a gift for the macabre, in 1871. On becoming lessee and manager of the Lyceum theatre (London), he mounted elaborate, sumptuous productions, paying much attention to detail and hiring leading designers and composers. After heavy losses in a fire and serious illness (1898), the struggle to maintain the Lyceum company ended in 1902.

**Isabella of Angoulême** (*c.*1188–1246), queen of King John. Isabella was the second wife of King John and was about 12 at the time of their marriage in August 1200. The alliance seems to have been a mixture of passion and diplomacy on John's part, since Angoulême lay in the heart of *Aquitaine, which John was seeking to retain. Their first child, the future Henry III, was born in 1207. After John's death, Isabella returned to France and in 1220 married Hugh de Lusignan, comte de la Marche, to whose father she had previously been betrothed.

**Isabella of France** (1292–1358), queen of Edward II. The daughter of Philip IV of France, Isabella married Edward II at Boulogne in January 1308, soon after his accession. Infatuated by Piers *Gaveston, Edward neglected her. Nevertheless, they produced four children. The future Edward III was born in 1312. The influence of the *Despensers estranged her from her husband and in 1325 she took refuge in France. In 1326 she joined her lover, Roger *Mortimer, in an invasion which easily swept away Edward's power. London rose in her favour, the Despensers were executed, Edward deposed in January 1327 and murdered at Berkeley castle in September 1327. For three years she and Mortimer ruled the country on behalf of the young Edward III. But in 1330 they were overthrown by a coup at Nottingham. Mortimer was at once executed, Isabella lived in comfortable retirement before entering a convent for her last years.

**Isabella of France** (1389–1409), queen of Richard II. The second daughter of Charles VI of France, Isabella became second wife of Richard II in November 1396. She was only 7 at the time but commented: 'they tell me that I shall be a great lady.' Richard showered his child-bride with gifts and seemed to be genuinely fond of her. But in May 1399 he left for Ireland and on his return was deposed by Henry of Bolingbroke. Richard's successor, as Henry IV, had some idea of marrying Isabella to Henry, prince of Wales, but she was returned to France in 1401. She married her cousin Charles, count of Angoulême, in 1406 but died in childbirth in September.

**Isabella of Gloucester** (d.1217), queen of King John. Isabella, also known as Avice or Hawisa, was the youngest daughter and co-heiress of William, 2nd earl of Gloucester. She was betrothed to John, son of Henry II, in 1176 when he was only 9, presumably to provide him with estates. The marriage did not take place until 1189, when John's brother Richard had succeeded. It is doubtful whether they ever lived together. Isabella was not crowned when John became king in 1199 and the following year they were divorced on the grounds that, as cousins, they were within the prohibited relationships. John married his second wife, *Isabella of Angoulême, almost at once. Isabella of Gloucester remained a wealthy heiress and seems to have lived in honourable confinement. But in 1214 she was given as a bride to *Geoffrey de Mandeville, presumably as a favour, and on his death in 1216 she married, very shortly before her death, Hubert de *Burgh.

**Isandhlwana** Hill, located 75 miles north of Pietermaritzburg (South Africa), site of an important battle in the *Zulu War. Part of the centre column of a British invasion of Zululand was surprised by a Zulu army on 22 January 1879. Disciplined rifle fire enabled the column to hold its own until it ran short of ammunition. Then it was overrun and almost completely wiped out.

**Isle of Man** The Isle of Man in the Irish Sea is 48 miles from Anglesey, 38 miles from the Irish coast, and only 20 miles from Scotland. It is some 30 miles from north to south and 10 east to west—i.e. rather smaller than Anglesey but larger than the Isle of Wight. The population in 2001 was 76,000, many of them retired people. From AD 800 it formed part of the Norse empire, though the control of the king of Norway was fitful. The representative institutions reflect the Norse influence. In 1266 it was ceded to Scotland after the battle of

*Largs, but did not stay long in Scottish possession. The island was disputed between Scots and English until 1333, when Edward III annexed and retained it. The bishopric of *Sodor and Man, founded in 1134, continued under the supervision of the archbishopric of Trondhjem but was placed in the archdiocese of York in the 15th cent. From 1406 the island belonged to the Stanleys, earls of Derby, who ruled it as lords of Man, and held it until 1736. It then passed to the dukes of Atholl, but in order to curtail smuggling the British government purchased it in 1765 and took full control in 1828.

The island is a crown possession with wide independent powers under a lieutenant governor. There is a two-chamber assembly, the *Tynwald, the lower house of which is the House of *Keys. The emblem of the island—the three legs of Man—is an ancient design, possibly going back to the Norse period. The Manx language, basically Celtic, was widely spoken until the 19th cent., but is now an acquired tongue. The largest town and capital is Douglas (25,000), followed by Ramsey (7,000), Peel (3,800), and Castletown, the old capital (3,000).

**Isle of Wight** Known to the Romans as Vectis, the Isle of Wight is largely chalk, some 22 miles across by 13 north–south. At the end of the Roman period it was settled by the *Jutes and for a time had its own kings. But it was difficult to stand against the kingdoms of Sussex, Mercia, and Wessex. *Cædwalla of Wessex took it c.687 and gave a quarter of the land to St *Wilfrid for the church. It was used as a base by the Danes in 998, and in 1371 Newport was sacked by the French. In the 1840s the building of *Osborne House for the queen and the establishment of the Royal Yacht Squadron at Cowes nearby in 1856 did much to popularize the island. The population grew from just over 20,000 in 1801 to over 80,000 by Victoria's death in 1901, and to 138,000 by 2004. From Saxon times the island formed part of the county of *Hampshire and fell under the authority of the bishop of *Winchester. It was

given a county council in 1890 and is now a unitary authority.

**Isles, kingdom of the** The origins of the kingdom of the Isles can be sought as far back as the 840s. It was apparently the successor kingdom in western Scotland to *Dalriada (last mentioned in the Irish annals in 839). It developed in the power vacuum left by the departure of *Kenneth MacAlpin, king of Dalriada and 'conqueror' of the Picts, to *Fortriu in 842. Kenneth may have had a hand in its inception, because its first king appears to have been his ally, and possible father-in-law, Gofraid mac Fherghusa, described on his death in 851 as *Toisech* or *Rí Innse Gall*, 'king of the Isles'. The extent of the kingdom is unclear, but by the late 10th cent. it included the *Isle of Man.

After a period of complete obscurity, from the 930s a close relationship developed between the Isles and Dublin. In 937, a *Rí Innse Gall* called Gébennach was slain at the battle of *Brunanburh, fighting against *Athelstan, the Anglo-Saxon king, apparently as a subordinate of *Olaf Godfreyson (or Guthfrithsson), king of Dublin.

In addition to a continuing close relationship between the Isles and Dublin, the kingship of both being held on occasion by the same figure, the 11th cent. apparently saw a conquest of the Isles by *Thorfinn the Mighty, jarl of Orkney, from the 1040s until his death c.1065. However, the most important event for the future history of the Isles was the reign of Godfrey Crovan. Godfrey was a capable warrior who had taken part in the battle of *Stamford Bridge as a mercenary. He conquered Man with a force of Hebrideans and took the kingship c.1079. His descendants were the kings of Man and the Isles for the next 200 years. By the treaty of *Perth (1266) Man and the Isles, which had fallen under a shaky Norwegian overlordship, became part of the kingdom of Scotland. The lordship of the Isles was vested in the Scottish crown in James IV's reign in the 15th cent.

**Jacobins** were originally a faction in Paris who met in the old Dominican convent at the church of St Jacques, and opposed the more moderate Girondin group. The name was soon borrowed in England and applied indiscriminately to radicals and reformers. It was exploited by *Canning and his friends in their *jeu d'esprit* the *\*Anti-Jacobin*, which came out in 1798/9.

**Jacobite risings** were attempts after 1689 to reverse the expulsion of the senior branch of the Stuart family. Supporters of the exiled dynasty were known as Jacobites from the Latin form of the name James which is *Jacobus*. James VII and II fled from England in December 1688. He landed in Ireland in March 1689, with French troops, but left when defeated at the *Boyne in 1690.

The first Jacobite rising was in Scotland in 1689 led by Viscount *Dundee. Large clans and great magnates were inactive, apart from the Campbells, whose chief, *Argyll, was restored by the events of 1688–9. Dundee died in victory at the battle of *Killiecrankie in July 1689, and the Jacobite army was finally routed at the Haughs of Cromdale in May 1690.

Not until the passage of the *Union of 1707 did outraged Scottish national sentiment make another rising thinkable. In March 1708 James Francis Edward *Stuart, after his father's death in 1701 the Jacobite claimant, was off the coast of Fife with a French expedition, but the French fled north at the sight of Royal Navy ships.

Queen Anne's death in 1714 was followed by the smooth accession of the protestant Hanoverian dynasty. The Whig coup at the accession of George I drove many Tories to despair, some to rebellion. After failing to get a job from George I, the earl of *Mar started a Scottish national rising. There was also a small English rising in Northumberland. The Scottish rising failed due to the action of *Argyll, and Mar's incompetence. An attempt to raise the Lancashire catholics was foiled at *Preston on the same day (14 November) that Mar failed to sweep Argyll aside at *Sheriffmuir.

The next Jacobite rebellion was a fiasco cynically sponsored by a Spanish government which was quarrelling with the British over Mediterranean issues. The main invasion force was intended to strike at the west of England, but was scattered by storms. A purely diversionary force did invade the north-west Highlands, only to be crushed by General Wightman at *Glenshiel in June 1719.

By 1744, war had broken out between France and Britain, and the French brought Prince Charles *Stuart, elder son of James Stuart, to France to front an invasion. Then they dropped the idea. The arrival of Charles in the west Highlands in the late summer of 1745 was designed to reverse the French decision by seizing a poorly defended Scotland and then invading England to provoke French intervention. With the help of the Camerons and smaller central Highland clans, Charles occupied Edinburgh before shattering government forces under Cope at *Prestonpans. The invasion of England in late 1745 was agreed to reluctantly by many Jacobite Scots. Even the field commander, Lord George *Murray, regarded it as a reconnaissance to test English willingness to restore the Stuarts. By Derby, it was clear there was none, and retreat in the face of superior armies was brilliantly executed. A victory over the pursuing Hanoverian army under General Hawley at *Falkirk in January 1746 merely postponed the day of reckoning which came on 16 April at *Culloden east of Inverness, where the Jacobites were totally routed by the duke of *Cumberland, a younger son of George II.

**Jacobitism** was a series of political movements which supported the restoration of the exiled house of Stuart after James II had been ousted from the throne at the Glorious Revolution in 1688 and had fled to France. Jacobites continued to support the claims to the throne of James's son James Francis Edward *Stuart (the Old Pretender or 'James III') and his two grandsons Charles Edward *Stuart (the Young Pretender or 'Charles III') and Henry *Stuart (the cardinal duke of York or 'Henry IX').

Jacobitism had a religious, as well as a political, dimension. James II and his son and grandsons were catholics, whose refusal to convert to protestantism made their restoration virtually impossible other than by armed invasion. However, most of their supporters were protestants, and a great many were nonjurors, who had refused the oaths of loyalty to William and Mary, and consequently had lost their secular or religious offices. In Scotland, where Jacobitism was strongest, the episcopalian church had been disestablished at the Glorious Revolution, and subsequently many episcopalians became Jacobites. Jacobitism in Scotland also became a refuge for many who opposed the Union with England in 1707.

That Scotland was central to Jacobitism is shown by the two main risings which took place in 1715 and 1745. Many Highland chiefs and clansmen, who did battle for the Stuart cause, paid for their loyalty with their lives. Few English Jacobites came out in support of either rebellion. Jacobitism was largely crushed as a political force after the retreat from Derby by the forces of the Young Pretender and the defeat at *Culloden in 1746. Thereafter the romantic and cultural aspect of the movement, which had always been a potent factor in attracting supporters, became dominant.

**Jamaica,** immediately to the south of Cuba, is the third largest of the Caribbean islands. It was sighted by Columbus in 1494 and the name is of Amerindian origin. Under Spanish occupation, the Arawak population was decimated. During *Cromwell's regime, it was seized by the English under William *Penn in 1655. Becoming independent in 1962, it is a constitutional monarchy with the queen as head of state, and a member of the Commonwealth.

**James I** (1394–1437), king of Scots (1406–37). James was the third son of Robert III (1390–1406), and was born in July 1394. By the age of 7, he was the sole surviving male and heir to the throne. In 1405-6 the country was racked by civil war, with the rump of Robert III loyalists supporting the young Prince James against a formidable Albany/Douglas faction. Early in 1406 events came to a head when James took ship for France, only to be captured at sea (22 March) and delivered to Henry IV of England. Less than a fortnight later Robert III died (4 April), and James became king at the age of 12, uncrowned and in English hands for the next 18 years.

These were the formative years of James I's life, instilling in him an admiration for English royal government. Already suspicious of the Albany Stewarts, James had his fears of Albany ambitions further fuelled by the release of Duke Robert's son and heir Murdac (*Albany) from English captivity in 1416. The king had to wait a further eight years for his own release.

James re-entered Scotland in April 1424, in his 30th year, bringing with him an English wife, *Joan Beaufort. Having taken part in English wars in France, on occasion against his Scottish subjects, he can hardly have been popular; and he was saddled with a ransom of £40,000 sterling.

Despite this inauspicious start, James possessed virtues which earned him praise. Abbot Bower describes his many accomplishments, including prowess in sports, music, and literary pursuits: the king was the author of the autobiographical love poem 'The *Kingis Quair'. He was, untypically for the Stewarts, a faithful husband, and Queen Joan responded loyally by producing twin sons and a string of daughters.

In his efforts to increase the authority, resources, and security of the crown, James launched pre-emptive strikes against members of his nobility. The Albany Stewarts were all but annihilated in 1425. The earl of Douglas was suddenly arrested in 1431, the earl of March in 1434. James's failure at the siege of Roxburgh (August 1436) was followed by Sir Robert Graham's abortive attempt to arrest him during a general council, and his murder at Perth (20-1 February 1437) by Walter Stewart, earl of *Atholl. Ultimately the king was the victim of his own methods; Atholl, seeing his influence in Strathearn threatened by the king, responded with his own pre-emptive strike.

**James II** (1430–60), king of Scots (1437–60).
James II is the first Scottish king of whose
appearance we can be fairly certain. He is
portrayed as a confident young man, his
hands on a dagger at his belt, with the whole
of the left side of his face disfigured by a livid
vermilion birthmark. In a short life—he died at
29—he followed the path taken by his father,
broke the power of the greatest magnate
house, the Black Douglases, secured a sizeable increase in royal power at home and a
formidable reputation abroad.

James was the younger of twin sons born
to James I and *Joan Beaufort at Holyrood in
October 1430. (The elder twin, Alexander,
died in infancy.) His father's assassination
at Perth in 1437 thrust James into the kingship aged only 6 and necessitated a long
minority (1437–49). The disappearance of
many major noble families, and the political
imbalance which resulted from this caused
an enormous concentration of power in the
hands of the Black Douglas family, with its
head, the young William, 8th earl of *Douglas, becoming lieutenant-general for James
II (probably in 1444).

In July 1449 James II married *Mary of
Gueldres, only daughter of Duke Arnold of
Gueldres and niece of Philip the Good of
Burgundy. The Scottish king threw off the
frustration of being under tutelage with confidence and ruthlessness. James II's target
was the Black Douglases. The outcome was
an attack on Douglas estates followed by the
great crime of the reign, James's murder of
Douglas at Stirling castle on 22 February
1452, after a two-day conference which Douglas attended under a royal safe conduct.

Civil war followed, with the 9th earl of
Douglas pitted against a determined James
II. The king was lucky to escape from Stirling with his life when the Douglases arrived to confront him a month after the
murder. Thereafter the situation improved.
A male heir was born to Mary of Gueldres
at St Andrews (May 1452); a royalist Parliament justified the Douglas murder; and the
king walked the political tightrope of satisfying his own supporters and negotiating
with the Douglases until he was strong
enough to deliver the killer punch. In 1455
the king's sieges of Abercorn and Threave,
and a skirmish at *Arkinholm on the river
Esk, completed the ruin of the Black Douglases.

James II's five remaining years reveal no
let-up in the king's energy and aggressive-
ness. He died as he had lived, the eternal
warrior, mortally wounded by the explosion
of one of his own guns at the siege of Roxburgh castle in August 1460.

**James III** (1452–88), king of Scots (1460–88).
The eldest of the three sons of James II and
*Mary of Gueldres, James was born at St An-
drews in May 1452. His father's death at the
siege of Roxburgh (August 1460) was swiftly
followed by the coronation of the 8-year-old
James III at nearby Kelso abbey. The ensuing
minority (1460–9) had its difficulties, but
under the wise guidance of Mary of Gueldres
(d. 1463) the Scots secured the cession of Berwick from the refugee Lancastrians (1461),
and then changed horses to back the victorious Yorkists. The late king's marital and territorial schemes finally came to fruition in the
1468 treaty of Copenhagen, by which James III
was to marry *Margaret, daughter of Christian
I of Denmark-Norway. Christian's inability to
afford his daughter's dowry resulted in his
pawning the earldom of *Orkney, then the
lordship of *Shetland; both were annexed to
the Scottish crown by 1472. Thus, by the early
years of James III's personal rule, the Scottish
kingdom had reached its widest territorial extent.

The view of James III which has come
down to us is largely that of late 16th-cent.
writers. These portray the king as something
of a recluse who ignored the counsel of his
nobility in favour of that of low-born famil-
iars; he disliked war. This later legend is
broadly unconvincing. The unwarlike king
is difficult to discern in a ruler who proposed
annexations or invasions of Brittany,
Gueldres, and Saintonge between 1471 and
1473, and this view may draw its relevance
only from James's alternative policy of peace
and alliance with Yorkist England. Again,
complaints of neglect of his magnates may
reflect James's failure to reward support, as
in the classic case of the earl of Huntly in
1476, whose invasion of Ross and capture of
Dingwall castle for the king merited only a
gift of 100 marks' worth of land.

In fact, James III's failure may be explained
largely without reference to the later legend.
He was a static king, rarely moving out of
Edinburgh during his adulthood. Successive
parliaments criticized him repeatedly for this

failing. Furthermore, James may have been unfortunate to have adult brothers as potential rivals, though his treatment of them was appalling. Alexander, duke of *Albany, fled to France in 1479, while John, earl of Mar, was arrested later that year and died mysteriously in custody shortly afterwards. The return of Albany in 1482, backed by Edward IV, prompted a great Stewart family crisis, with the seizure of James III at Lauder, the permanent loss of Berwick to the English, Albany's temporary acquisition of the office of lieutenant-general, the king's incarceration in Edinburgh castle, and his subsequent release and recovery of power through the timely intervention of loyal north-eastern nobility.

However, crown–magnate mistrust persisted, and the king's wide-ranging Treasons Act (1484) showed that he had learned nothing from the warning of 1482. When his eldest son James, duke of Rothesay, a youth of 15, moved against him in the spring of 1488, no armed assistance was forthcoming from the former loyalists of the north; and on 11 June James III, bearing Robert Bruce's sword and a black box full of money and jewels, succumbed to his son's army on the 'field of Stirling' (*Sauchie Burn).

**James IV** (1473–1513), king of Scots (1488–1513). The eldest son of James III and *Margaret of Denmark, James IV was born at *Stirling castle on 17 March 1473. The successful rising against his father in 1488 associated his name with an act of regicide and patricide, and he undertook elaborate penances to atone for his role in James III's death. Yet the young king benefited greatly from the manner of his accession, for he was assisted by many magnates who had found his father's rule unacceptable, and who had no choice but to support him. And at the outset of James IV's personal rule, in the spring of 1495, there was no violent political upheaval, but a smooth transition.

In almost every respect, King James's government affords a sharp contrast with that of his father. The king was a tireless traveller, driving the justice ayres in the south and north-east, intervening in major feuds, and he placed himself at the centre of a glittering court. His expenditure on building, especially on *Holyrood palace and the King's House and great hall at Stirling castle, was large, his lavishing of money on a royal navy spectacular. An insight into James's court is provided not only by the treasurer's accounts but also by the poetry of William *Dunbar and Robert Carver's astonishing nineteen-part motet 'O bone Jesu'.

Recognizing that parliaments were often a focus for criticism of the crown, James IV called only three in the seventeen years of his adult rule. The money he needed for his navy, his building programmes, above all for his wars, was acquired through rigorous exploitation of feudal casualties, by income from profits of justice, by taxation of a loyal clergy, by the imposition of two Acts of revocation (1498 and 1504), and perhaps above all by setting royal lands in feu-farm in the later years of the reign.

In foreign affairs, James IV adopted a high-risk policy which proved broadly successful. His invasions of Northumberland (1496–7), ostensibly in support of the Yorkist pretender Perkin *Warbeck but in fact to utilize the military talents of the Scottish nobility and put pressure on Henry VII, provoked the English king into furious retaliation. But the Cornish rising of 1497, born partly out of resentment at heavy taxation to support the Scottish war, put an end to Henry's efforts to chastise the Scots; and the eventual alternative was the treaty of *Perpetual Peace of 1502, as a result of which James IV married Henry's daughter *Margaret Tudor (August 1503).

This union of the Thistle and the Rose did little to improve Anglo-Scottish relations. The real Scottish understanding was with Louis XII of France, who from 1502 to 1513 provided James IV with shipwrights, soldiers, ships, money, and munitions. A naval race with the English resulted in the construction of the Scottish *Margaret* followed by the English *Mary Rose*; and in October 1511 James attended the launch at Newhaven of the *Michael*, briefly the largest warship in northern Europe. When the young Henry VIII sought to renew the *Hundred Years War in 1512–13, James made a formal treaty with Louis XII, invaded England, and took Norham castle by storm. However, on 9 September 1513 James rashly committed himself to battle against the earl of *Surrey at *Flodden and was killed, together with no fewer than nine of his earls, a striking if tragic reflection of his popularity in Scotland.

**James V** (1512–42), king of Scots (1513–42). Born on 10 April 1512, James inherited the throne when barely 18 months old on the death of his father James IV at *Flodden. The protracted regency which ensued witnessed the kind of power struggle which had dominated the minorities of successive Stewart monarchs. In this case, however, the conflict between James Hamilton, 1st earl of *Arran, and Archibald Douglas, 6th earl of *Angus, was aggravated by the latter's marriage in 1514 to the queen mother, *Margaret Tudor, sister of Henry VIII, and the involvement of the king's French-born kinsman John Stewart, duke of *Albany. While Albany was regent from 1515 to 1524, it was Angus who came to dominate the regime and from whose clutches the 16-year-old king engineered his own escape in May 1528.

The vindictive pursuit of his former Douglas captors is often seen as the leitmotif of James's personal rule. However, while Angus was forced into English exile in 1529, the king's justifiable suspicion of the Douglases hardly amounted to a relentless vendetta. Likewise, the charge that a paranoid fear of his nobility led to the ruthless expropriation of their lands is exaggerated.

Lawyers like Erskine may well have lent juridical weight to the authoritarian style of kingship suggested by James's fascination with the most potent contemporary symbol of royal power: the closed 'imperial' crown. If so, the clergy had as much reason to fear the king as the nobility. Although James's former tutor, Gavin Dunbar, archbishop of Glasgow, remained chancellor throughout the reign, the clergy's monopoly of legal and administrative expertise was steadily eroded. James exploited both the weakness of his own ecclesiastical hierarchy and the papacy's fear that he might follow his uncle Henry VIII in repudiating Rome altogether. Thus, with papal blessing, he was able to consolidate royal control over appointments to major benefices, milk the revenues of the religious houses, and levy the heaviest tax on clerical income which the *ecclesia Scoticana* had ever experienced. Determined to establish a court-life befitting a Renaissance prince, the king spent lavishly on maintaining a large royal household and on creating the architectural settings at *Falkland, *Linlithgow, and *Stirling in which the full majesty of his kingship could best be displayed.

Even with greatly augmented revenues, however, James was hardly in a position to compete with contemporary princes like Henry VIII, Charles V, or Francis I. Nevertheless, the intense rivalry between France, England, and the empire lent the Scottish king unwonted diplomatic weight. His shrewd exploitation of the marriage market led to his securing first the hand of Francis I's eldest surviving daughter *Madeleine, and then on her death that of *Mary of Guise. Despite Henry VIII's attempts to sever them, Scotland's traditional ties with France and Rome remained intact. Yet the alliance with France came at the price of war with England—and a military reversal from which the king's reputation never recovered. Although a Scottish army was beaten at *Solway Moss on 24 November 1542, it was neither a personal humiliation for the king (who was not there) nor the result of noble disaffection. In fact, James had substantial support for his war policy and, when he died on 14 December 1542, preparations were already in train for a further English campaign. As this suggests, the king's death was hardly the result of shame or despair. More probably, and prosaically, it was the plague or cholera which brought his vigorous rule to a premature end.

**James VI** (1566–1625), king of Scotland (1567–1625) and, as **James I,** king of England (1603–25), was the son of Mary, queen of Scots, whose enforced abdication brought him to the throne when he was not 2 years of age. James was educated by a succession of formidable tutors, including George *Buchanan, whose insistence that kings were servants of their people provoked his pupil into believing the opposite. James's assumption of power in 1585 marked a turning-point, for he brought the nobles to heel at the same time as he involved them in government. His main adversary was the presbyterian church, or kirk, which claimed that its authority, deriving directly from God, was superior to his own. James skilfully outflanked the kirk's leaders by encouraging the moderates and reviving the office of bishop. He also used his learning to buttress his position. *The Trew Law* and the *Basilikon doron*, both written in the 1590s, proclaimed that kings were the images of God upon earth and should be venerated as such.

Deprived of female company during his formative years, James found an outlet for his deepest emotional needs in male favourites, of whom Esmé Stuart, created duke of *Lennox by the boy king in 1581, was the first of a long line. But James was also capable of relations with the opposite sex, as he showed in 1589 when he crossed the seas to Norway to bring back *Anne of Denmark as his wife. The marriage began well and produced a number of children, of whom two sons, *Henry and Charles (later Charles I), and a daughter, *Elizabeth, survived into adult life.

In 1586 James concluded a treaty with Elizabeth I which provided him with a substantial pension and acknowledged his right to succeed to the English throne. When, in early 1603, news came of Elizabeth's death, James was impatient to quit his impoverished kingdom, but he was not ashamed of his Scottishness. On the contrary, his major objective once he was established in England was to complete the union of crowns by a union of states. Debates on the union, the principal business of the Parliament which James summoned in 1604, revealed the depth of English prejudice against the Scots. They also revealed that James's subjects were acutely suspicious of his intentions. In his writings and speeches, he used the language of absolutism, and he was not familiar with the very different English political tradition based on *Magna Carta and the common law.

James's open-handed generosity, particularly towards his Scottish companions, won him few friends among the English. Nor did the spread of corruption in public life, including the sale of titles and offices, much of which was generated by royal favourites such as *Carr and *Buckingham. Conviction that James would squander any money grants brought about the collapse of the *Great Contract. James's resort to non-parliamentary taxes like *impositions made matters worse and led to the failure of the *'Addled' Parliament. Matters improved considerably after 1620, when he appointed a merchant-financier, Lionel *Cranfield, to the Treasury, but by then the damage was done.

In the sphere of religion James was more successful, not least because his protestantism was unquestionable. After the *Hampton Court conference he came to realize that English *puritans were far less dangerous than Scottish presbyterians, and in 1610 he pleased them by appointing the low-church

George *Abbot as archbishop. James also remained tolerant towards his catholic subjects, even after the *Gunpowder plot. The problem for James was that religion and politics were inextricably intertwined. In hopes of acting as a European peacemaker, he married his daughter to a leading protestant prince and planned a match between his son and the daughter of the king of Spain. This ecumenical approach to international politics baffled and outraged his subjects, who believed that England's place was at the head of a protestant crusade.

Fortunately for James, he died in March 1625, before war broke out. He was not deeply mourned; undignified and conceited, long-winded and short-tempered, he caused offence without realizing it. But he kept his kingdoms in peace at home and abroad, he preserved the powers of the crown, and he held the church firmly to a middle course.

**James VII** (1633–1701), king of Scotland and, as **James II,** of England (1685–8). James's formative years before 1660 were spent in the French and Spanish armies. His experiences in exile permanently distanced him in sympathies from most Englishmen. As duke of York under his brother Charles II he developed a career as lord admiral, defeating the Dutch off *Lowestoft (1665) and commanding at Sole Bay (*Southwold) (1672). James advocated wars against the Dutch with the objective of strengthening royal power, particularly by reducing its dependence on Parliament and the militia.

After 1667 James constantly worked for an alliance with France. Around 1672 he became a catholic, refusing in 1673 to take the Anglican sacrament as required by the *Test Act and resigning as lord admiral. He had urged Charles to veto the Test, to dissolve Parliament, and continue the third Dutch War in alliance with France. When he remarried to a catholic Italian, *Mary of Modena, opposition politicians began to exploit a growing impression that James was unfit to succeed Charles. In 1678 'revelations' of a *Popish plot to murder Charles so as to place James on the throne led *Shaftesbury and the Whigs to lead a parliamentary and popular movement to exclude James from the succession. This issue dominated three parliaments in 1679, 1680, and 1681. James feared that Charles would abandon his right, but the king resisted all Whig pressure and after concluding a subsidy treaty with France ruled for his last four years without Parliament. James succeeded without opposition in February 1685.

A Tory Parliament voted revenues which, with foreign trade expanding, freed James from his predecessors' dependence on parliamentary grants. *Monmouth's rebellion was easily crushed. Anglicans generally acquiesced in non-enforcement of the penal laws against catholics. But James aimed to free the crown from any dependence on its subjects. The *Ecclesiastical Commission, set up to discipline Anglican clergy who attacked catholicism, suspended the bishop of London. James used his *dispensing power to put catholics in offices. The militia was run down, the professional army expanded. James ineffectively canvassed peers and MPs to pass legislation granting catholics equality of civil and religious rights. Their refusal led him to suspend discriminatory statutes by the *Declaration of Indulgence (April 1687), provoking fears that this asserted and dubious royal power could be used to terminate any law that restricted the actions of the crown. Sweeping changes in Ireland, where catholics replaced protestants in government, army, law, professions, and corporations, seemed to indicate such an intention. In England James initiated a political campaign to manipulate elections to a future parliament. This involved purging the justices and deputies in the counties and the urban corporations.

Some Whig and Tory notables established clandestine contacts with William of Orange, but most people believed that James could not live long. His protestant daughter Mary, married to William, would then reverse James's policies. The queen's pregnancy and the birth of a prince (June 1688) dashed these hopes. These developments led to the invitation sent to William by Whig and Tory leaders to intervene (30 June). Army and navy officers defected, the provinces declared for William, and even the Anglican clergy stood neutral. Broken psychologically, James fled to France. Louis XIV sent him to Ireland under French supervision. Defeated at the *Boyne (July 1690) he lived as Louis's client at Saint-Germain praying for another restoration.

**Jameson Raid,** 1895. At the time (29 December 1895) this was presented as a brave attempt by cavalry led by Dr Leander Starr Jameson, the British South Africa Company's representative in *Rhodesia, to rescue English women and children persecuted by a wicked Boer government in the *Transvaal. It turned out, however, to be a sordid conspiracy by Cecil *Rhodes, almost certainly with the British colonial secretary Joseph *Chamberlain's prior knowledge, to seize the Transvaal for the *British empire. It failed ignominiously, and sullied Rhodes's, Chamberlain's, and the empire's reputations.

**Jane Seymour** (c.1509-37), 3rd queen of Henry VIII. Jane Seymour was a lady-in-waiting to *Anne Boleyn in 1534 when she began to attract Henry's attention. From a Wiltshire gentry family at Wolf Hall, she was said to be quiet and amiable, while Anne was growing more highly strung and imperious. By May 1536 Anne was under arrest and Jane's marriage took place soon after her execution. A new Act of *Succession disinherited the Princesses Mary and Elizabeth in favour of Jane's offspring. In October 1537 she gave birth to the future Edward VI but died twelve days later.

**Jeffreys, George** (1648-89). Notorious as the judge who presided at the *Bloody Assizes, Jeffreys was a career lawyer who became conspicuous as an aggressive prosecutor and partisan judge. Attached to James II since 1677, he became lord chancellor in 1685 and as Baron Wem acted as Speaker of the Lords. The other judges involved in the Bloody Assizes allowed Jeffreys to incur responsibility for the brutal treatment of Monmouth's rebels. Consequently Jeffreys was cast as scapegoat after the *Glorious Revolution, but died soon after being arrested.

**Jehovah's witnesses** An exclusive millennialist sect developed out of Charles Russell's International Bible Students Association (founded in Pittsburgh, 1872), now worldwide. Russell's successor, Judge Rutherford, sought to affirm Jehovah as the true God and developed the concept of a 'theocratic Kingdom' which will emerge after Armageddon. Baptized by immersion, witnesses insist on high moral probity, oppose blood transfusions on scriptural grounds, write and publish prolifically (chief periodicals: *The Watchtower* and *Awake!*), and, after training, preach enthusiastically on doorsteps.

**Jellicoe, Sir John** (1859–1935). Admiral. As commander-in-chief of the Grand Fleet until December 1916, Jellicoe knew that a single wrong decision could cost Britain the war by losing command of the seas. His handling of the Grand Fleet at *Jutland was marked by excessive caution and he forfeited any chance of decisively defeating the Germans. He was a tired man in December 1916 when he was transferred to the Admiralty as 1st sea lord. He was dismissed in December 1917, and received his earldom, belatedly, in 1925.

**Jenkins, Roy** (1920–2003). Chancellor of the University of Oxford; previously deputy leader (1970–2) of the Labour Party and leader (1982–3) of the *Social Democratic Party. Author, bon viveur, and quintessential establishment figure, he became Lord Jenkins of Hillhead in 1987. His political appointments included minister of aviation (1964–5), home secretary (1965–7, 1974–6), chancellor of the Exchequer (1967–70). From 1977 to 1981 he was president of the European Commission. His main political achievements were to facilitate the 'moral revolution of the 1960s' as home secretary (defending the 'permissive society' as 'the civilized society'), to give strong support to the move into Europe, and to help keep the Labour Party out of power in the 1980s and 1990s.

**Jenkins's Ear, War of** Although Captain Jenkins's ear was cut off by the Spanish in a skirmish in 1731, the war between Spain and Britain did not begin until October 1739. Domestic pressure for war with Spain marked the beginning of the end for *Walpole's premiership. From December 1740 the War of Jenkins's Ear was subsumed into the War of the *Austrian Succession.

**Jenner, Edward** (1749–1823). Vaccination pioneer. As John Hunter's first housepupil and dresser at St George's hospital (London), Jenner shared Hunter's belief in experimentation, but chose to practise at home at Berkeley (Glos.). He became obsessed with the idea that inoculation of cowpox matter was a better protection against smallpox than using exudate from smallpox lesions. An initial paper having been rejected, he published privately *An Inquiry into Cow-pox* (1798), and very slowly the idea of 'vaccination' was popularized.

**Jervis, John, 1st earl of St Vincent** (1735–1823). Promoted earl following his triumph over the Spanish fleet in February 1797, Jervis, son of a crooked Staffordshire lawyer, had an inauspicious and impoverished start in life. Jervis served with *Wolfe at Quebec in 1759, and subsequent service in the North Sea and Mediterranean endorsed his talents as a seaman. He was present at *Keppel's indecisive action off *Ushant in July 1778, while at home he became MP 1783–94. Promoted admiral in 1787 he combined well with the army in the West Indies in 1793, but it was his command in the Mediterranean 1795–9 which established his fame, together with his affectionate tutelage of his subordinate *Nelson. In 1801, as 1st lord of the Admiralty, St Vincent prosecuted an inquiry into theft in the dockyards which contributed to Lord *Melville's impeachment in 1806 for malversation of funds.

**Jesuits** The Society of Jesus was founded by Ignatius Loyola and approved by Pope Paul III in 1540. It offered total obedience to the papacy and was prominent in the effort to recover ground lost to the church by the Reformation. Mary Tudor, though a devoted catholic, mistrusted the order and did not invite it to England. But the deterioration of relations between Elizabeth and the papacy, culminating in the bull of excommunication of 1570, changed the situation. William *Allen had already founded a seminary at Douai and about 100 catholic priests had made their way back to England by 1580, living an undercover existence, hiding in priest holes, and protected by the old catholic gentry. In that year, two Jesuit priests landed—*Campion and *Parsons. Their mission lasted only a few months but gave an important boost to the morale of English catholics. Campion was soon apprehended and executed in December 1581: Parsons left for the continent and never returned. The events of the rest of the decade—powerful French and catholic influence in Scotland, plots against the queen's life, the threat of the Armada—combined to strengthen anticatholic feeling in England. But the culminating disaster for English catholics was the *Gunpowder plot of 1605, which resulted in the capture of Henry Garnett, Jesuit superior in England for nearly 20 years. Though he claimed that he knew of the plot only through the confessional, he was executed as a traitor. For decades, 'Jesuitical' became a term of abuse, signifying mental reservation, prevarication, and casuistry. But, in the long run, the Enlightenment proved more damaging to the order than downright persecution. The Jesuits were accused of undue pliability in their zeal to proselytize and the order was wound up by Pope Clement XIV in 1773 after France, Spain, and Portugal had all moved against it. Though reconstituted in 1814 by Pope Pius VII, the circumstances which had made Jesuits so hated were no longer in existence. The English province of the order was re-established in 1829. Although fierce bursts of anti-catholic feeling were still possible, particularly at the time of 'papal aggression' in 1850, the role of the Society of Jesus was no longer a national bugbear.

**Jevons, W. S.** (1835–82). Distinguished neoclassical economist. Jevons was born in Liverpool, and educated in Liverpool and London. After studying chemistry at University College London, and working as an assayer in Australia, he returned to University College in 1859 to study political economy, philosophy, and mathematics. From 1863 he was tutor, lecturer, and then professor at Owens College, Manchester, moving in 1876 to a chair at University College London (until 1880). His principal contribution is his work on the marginal utility theory of value (*Theory of Political Economy*, 1872), the introduction of marginal analysis marking 'the true dividing line between classical theory and modern economics'.

**Jewel, John** (1522–71). Bishop. Born in Devon and educated at Merton College, Oxford, Jewel became a fellow of Corpus Christi College, Oxford, but was deprived at the accession of Mary and fled to the continent. He returned in 1559 after Elizabeth's accession and was made bishop of Salisbury. In 1562 his *Apologia pro Ecclesia Anglicana* defended the Church of England from the charge of heresy.

**Jews** Though there must have been individual Jews in Anglo-Saxon England, there is no evidence of settled communities. But after the Norman Conquest, hundreds of Jews entered the country, mainly from Normandy where there had been settlements. As their numbers increased and they moved outside London into provincial towns, tensions rose. As early as 1144 the accusation of ritual murder was made against them, with the charge that they had killed a small boy in Norwich, 'St William'. Severe restrictions were placed upon them. They were confined to Jewries, from 1218 were obliged to wear badges, and in 1232 a *domus conversorum* was opened in London for proselytizing. Fresh hostility came with the crusading movement. At the accession of Richard I in 1189—a notable crusader—there were attacks on Jews in London, which spread to the provinces, and culminated in the slaughter of 150 Jews in the castle at York. Religious zeal was reinforced by greed and envy. Some of the Jews were already very wealthy—Aaron of Lincoln in the 1170s dealt with kings, archbishops, municipalities, and monasteries.

The difficulties of the Jews continued in the 13th cent. The story of William of Norwich was repeated in 1255 with the account of Hugh of Lincoln—another boy said to have been butchered, and again given saintly status. In 1290, in exchange for a large subsidy from Parliament, Edward I expelled all Jews from the kingdom, giving them three months to leave.

Between 1290 and the 1650s there were no Jewish communities of any size, though individuals slipped through, sometimes professing conversion. When approached in the 1650s, *Cromwell was more sympathetic than his council, perhaps because he had made use of some Jews in espionage and diplomacy. There was no dramatic reversal of policy but Jews were allowed in once more. Their numbers and status built up and the financial and commercial revolutions of the early 18th cent. gave them enhanced possibilities. Sir Samuel Gideon was prominent in assisting the government with loans in the crisis of 1745, and his son was given an Irish peerage in 1789. But old hatreds died hard and when the Pelhams brought in a modest measure to facilitate naturalization in 1753, the public outcry was so great that they were forced to repeal it.

Catholic emancipation in 1829 left the Jews as the only religious group suffering under severe disabilities. Yet the progress of Jews in society was unmistakable. David Salomons was made sheriff of London in 1835 and lord mayor in 1855; Francis Goldsmid was the first practising Jew to be given a baronetcy in 1841. When first Lionel *Rothschild (1847) and then Salomons (1851) were elected to Parliament, only to be kept out by their inability to take the oath as a Christian, the plight of the Jews was dramatized, and the law was changed in 1858. The first government minister of Jewish faith was appointed in 1871, the first judge in 1873. The obstacles facing Jews remained substantial, but they were personal and social rather than legal.

**Jex-Blake, Sophia** (1840–1912). Pioneer of women in medicine. Sophia Jex-Blake was mathematics tutor at Queen's College, London (1859), but an American friendship drew her to medical studies, initially in New York but then in Edinburgh, until increasing hostility prevented clinical training. She responded by founding the London School of Medicine for Women (1874). Gaining MD, Berne, then the Dublin licentiate, but too stormy for the LSMW (who appointed Elizabeth Garrett *Anderson as dean), she returned hurt to Edinburgh, where she founded her own medical school for women (1886). This did excellent work but foundered through her own intransigence. Jex-Blake finally admitted defeat (1899) and retired to Sussex.

**jingoism** The word comes from a music-hall song popular at the time of the 1876–8 Eastern crisis: 'We don't want to fight, but by jingo if we do . . .'. Later it was used to describe other manifestations of popular bellicosity during foreign wars.

**Jinnah, Mohammed Ali** (1876–1948). Jinnah, 'the father of Pakistan', was born in Karachi and trained as a barrister. Initially, he was sympathetic to the Indian National Congress and did not join the Muslim League until 1913. He helped to organize the Lucknow pact (1916) and the Khilafat movement (1919–22), by which the Muslim League ran campaigns of anti-British resistance parallel to those of the Congress. However, he became suspicious that, especially under *Gandhi's leadership, Congress was being taken over by a narrow Hindu nationalism. In 1934 he became president of the Muslim League and chaired its 1940 conference at Lahore when the demand for a separate Pakistan state was first made. In the 1946–7 negotiations, he stubbornly resisted proposals that India should be granted independence as a unitary nation state. Pakistan proclaimed its independence on 15 August 1947 with Jinnah as its first governor-general.

**Joan (Joanna)** (1210–38), queen of Alexander II of Scotland. Eldest daughter of King John and sister of Henry III, her marriage to Alexander at York on 19 June 1221 helped to reinforce the Anglo-Scottish peace which lasted from 1217 to 1296.

**Joan, Princess** (d. 237). An illegitimate daughter of King John, Joan was married 1205/6 to *Llywelyn ab Iorwerth of Gwynedd, prince of North Wales. Thereafter, she was a wise counsellor to her husband and a peacemaker in the fluid and often belligerent relations between England and Wales. He founded a Franciscan monastery to her memory at Llanfaes (Anglesey), where she is buried.

**Joan Beaufort** (c.1400–45), queen of James I of Scotland. Daughter of John Beaufort, earl of Somerset, Joan was married to James I of Scotland at Southwark in February 1424, a match celebrated in James's poem 'The *Kingis Quair'. A target for King James's assassins in 1437, the wounded queen escaped to head her infant son's administration.

**Joan of Kent, princess of Wales** (c.1328–85). Joan was a daughter of Edmund, earl of Kent (d. 1330), and succeeded as countess in 1353. While considerably under age, she secretly married Thomas Holand. In his absence in Prussia, she soon contracted a second marriage with the earl of Salisbury; this was annulled nine years later, in 1349. Within a year of Holand's death, this reputed beauty married *Edward the Black Prince and accompanied him to Gascony, where their sons Edward (d. 1370) and Richard (II) were born.

**Joan of Navarre** (c.1370–1437), queen of Henry IV. A daughter of Charles the Bad, king of Navarre, Joan married John IV, duke of Brittany, in 1386. After his death in 1399, she acted as regent for Duke John V until his inauguration in 1401. Henry (IV) had visited the Breton court during his exile. Joan was crowned in 1403; the marriage was childless.

j

She chose to remain in England after Henry's death. Relations with her stepson Henry V were amicable until 1419, when she was accused of plotting his death by witchcraft. She was confined without trial until 1422, but restored by Henry's death-bed wish.

**Joanna of the Tower** (1321–62), queen of David II of Scotland, was the youngest daughter of Edward II and born in the Tower of London. In 1328 when she was 7 she was married to David Bruce, son and heir of Robert I of Scotland, who succeeded in 1329. In 1346 David was captured by the English at *Neville's Cross and taken to London. Joanna visited him but soon after his release in 1357 she left him, and spent the rest of her life at the court of her brother Edward III.

**John** (1167–1216), king of England (1199–1216). As every schoolboy knows, John was a monster and a tyrant. It is a reputation with deep historical roots, culminating in the judgements of Victorian historians such as J. R. Green. The Victorian view of John stemmed from a perspective from the high moral ground, and drew its support almost entirely from contemporary chroniclers, responsible for so many of the notorious anecdotes concerning him.

More recently, the unreliability of many of these chronicle sources has been exposed. John has come to appear in a new light as a capable administrator with great powers of organization and application. No one would now doubt that John was an intelligent and able man. The system of continental alliances that he built up against Philip II of France prior to the disaster at *Bouvines (1214) reveals diplomatic skill and a sure grasp of strategy. His surrender of England as a papal fief in 1213 was a brilliant piece of manœuvring, at a stroke dividing the pope from the conspiracy developing against John in France and England.

Yet modern scholarship has also strengthened some of the traditional charges against him. Perhaps the most infamous charge, that he murdered—or caused to be murdered—his own nephew, *Arthur of Brittany, now seems virtually certain. Other acts of cruelty are also proven, his hanging of 28 hostages, sons of rebel Welsh chieftains, in 1212, or the starving to death of William de *Braose's wife and son in

a royal prison. The consensus has grown that although men of his age could be excessively cruel, John overstepped the mark.

He did not live up to contemporary expectations of a king. In contrast to his brother Richard I, he seemed incompetent in warfare. Particularly damaging was the epithet 'Softsword' applied to him as early as 1200. Again, he took the business of dispensing justice seriously, but often his subjects could complain that the judgment rendered was unfair and partial.

Had John succeeded in regaining his lost lands, Magna Carta would almost certainly not have occurred and the legend about him would never have developed. But he lost, and paid a posthumous penalty as well. And one of the chief reasons that he lost lay in his appalling handling of his greater subjects. Whatever John's technical competence as a ruler, it was constantly compromised by his suspicious nature towards them, his jealousy, unpredictability, and caprice. None could live easily with such a ruler. Rule by fear might keep them in check, but in the long run, John's regime was unstable. John remains baffling and enigmatic. As Lewis Warren put it so succinctly, 'He had the mental abilities of a great king but the inclinations of a petty tyrant.'

**John, Augustus Edwin** (1878–1961). British painter. John was born in Tenby (Wales), the son of a solicitor. A brilliant student, he trained at the Slade School, then went to Liverpool as an art instructor. In the first decade of the 20th cent. he was at the height of his powers, expressing in art and life an independent and rebellious nature.

**John, lord of the Isles** *See* MACDONALD, JOHN.

**John Balliol** *See* BALLIOL, JOHN.

**John Bull** The character of John Bull was invented by John Arbuthnot in a series of pamphlets, *Law is a Bottomless Pit*, published in 1712. Bull's sturdy honesty contrasted with the wily Frenchman Lewis Baboon. He became popular with cartoonists in the early 19th cent. and acquired the Pickwickian squat top hat and the Union Jack waistcoat.

**John of Gaunt, 1st duke of Lancaster** (1340–99). The third surviving son of Edward III, born in Ghent, and England's greatest territorial magnate following the death of his father-in-law *Henry of Grosmont. As earl of Richmond (1342–72), he was engaged in the French war from 1355. He also had commands on the Scottish border. His wealth enabled him to form the largest baronial retinue of knights and esquires. From 1372 he assumed the title of king of Castile in right of his second wife, which he renounced—profitably—after campaigning there in 1386–7. His patronage of *Wyclif and hostility to the bishop of London roused riots; his Savoy palace was sacked in 1381. Despite allegations of treason by hostile courtiers, Gaunt's backing was invaluable to Richard II. His son seized the throne in 1399 and reigned as Henry IV.

**John of Salisbury** (c.1120–80). Scholar and clerical author. Born at Salisbury, a student at Paris (1136–46) in the days of Abelard, in his *Metalogicon* he defended the value of logic as an intellectual discipline. As political secretary to Archbishop Theobald (1147–61) of Canterbury he used his friendship with *Adrian IV to promote Canterbury's interests at the papal curia. He acted as adviser to *Becket during his quarrel with Henry II and then promoted the cult of the murdered archbishop.

**Johnson, Samuel** (1709–84). Johnson was the son of a bookseller in Lichfield (Staffs.). He attended local schools before spending just one year at Pembroke College, Oxford, 1728–9. His early attempts at teaching failed, but he married the widow Elizabeth Porter (1735). The hard life of Grub Street in London beckoned him next. Johnson wrote his fine poem *London* at this time (1738), containing the line 'Slow rises worth, by poverty depressed.' In 1746–55 Johnson worked on his *Dictionary*, the first full collation of the English language and a masterpiece of prose. He composed *The Vanity of Human Wishes* in 1749 and lost his wife three years later. To pay for his mother's funeral, Johnson wrote *Rasselas* (1759) in one week; it is possibly his finest work, a profound novel upon 'the choice of life'. Between the larger works Johnson composed periodical moral essays under the title of the *Rambler*,

the *Idler*, and the *Adventurer*. In 1762, Lord *Bute bestowed upon Johnson a pension of £300 a year, ending his financial difficulties. After receiving his pension Johnson's literary output was smaller, but he produced his masterly edition of Shakespeare (1765), *Journey to the Western Islands of Scotland* (1775), and *Lives of the Poets* (1779–81).

Much of Johnson's fame comes from his personality. To list his friends is to list many of the leading cultural figures of the 18th cent., painter Sir Joshua *Reynolds, novelist Oliver *Goldsmith, politician Edmund *Burke, and actor David *Garrick. All were members of the celebrated Literary Club, of which Johnson was a founder; many of the splendid discussions that took place there were recorded by Boswell in his incomparable *Life of Johnson* (1791). To many Samuel Johnson has become the personification of the 18th cent.

**Jones, Inigo** (1573–1652). Masque designer, architect, and courtier, Jones's architectural legacy only fructified in the early 18th cent. through the neo-Palladian movement. Yet Jones personally remains frustratingly elusive, for all his arrogance and engrossing power as surveyor of the king's works (1615–44). Apart from entrancing scenic and costume designs, only seven of Jones's 45 architectural works survive: the most notable are the Whitehall *Banqueting House, Queen's chapel at St James's, Queen's House at *Greenwich, and, by no means least because of its Carolean town-planning context, St Paul's church, *Covent Garden.

**Jones, Sir William** (1746–94). Oriental scholar. Educated at Harrow and University College, Oxford, Jones was a gifted linguist, eventually mastering 13 languages and knowing 28 others. Called to the bar in 1774, he was knighted and appointed a judge in the High Court of Calcutta in 1783. He remained in India until his premature death, founding the Bengal Asiatic Society (1784) and developing an appreciation of Indian law and culture unusual in a European.

**Jonson, Ben** (1572–1637). English Renaissance poet and playwright, the most forthright and politically conservative of his contemporaries. His writing—poetry, drama, and opinions—is a curious blend of disciplined classicism and carnival grotesque. His best-known plays are *Volpone* (1605), *The Alchemist* (1610), and *Bartholomew Fair* (1614). Socially and culturally aspirant, Jonson attracted royal patronage, creating a series of court masques (in collaboration with Inigo *Jones) and receiving a life pension from James I.

**Jordan,** previously known as Trans-Jordan, was part of the Turkish empire in 1914 but after the First World War became a British *mandate under the *League of Nations. In 1946 the independence of Jordan was declared and a kingdom established under the Amir Abdullah. During the *Gulf War of 1990 Jordan maintained a precarious neutrality.

**Jowett, Benjamin** (1817–93). Scholar. Jowett held the regius chair of Greek at Oxford for nearly 40 years and was master of Balliol College for more than 20 years. He became professor of Greek in 1855 and began a successful series of lectures in Greek philosophy, while devoting much time to individual students. Elected to the mastership in 1870, his four-volume translation of Plato appeared in 1871, followed by Thucydides (1881) and Aristotle's *Politics* (1885). Waterhouse's rebuilding of the Broad Street front of Balliol was finished during Jowett's mastership and under his influence the college became pre-eminent in the university.

**Joyce, James** (1882–1941). High priest of modernism and most uncompromising of novelists. The short stories of *Dubliners* (1914) chapter the moral history of his country 'in a style of scrupulous meanness'. In *A Portrait of the Artist as a Young Man* (1916) he set an ironical distance between himself and the catholicism and aestheticism of his youth. The major work *Ulysses* (1922) chronicles a single day in June 1904 but was eight years in the writing and passed the censors only in 1933. In the still more experimental *Finnegans Wake* he goes where few readers follow.

**Julian of Norwich** (1342–*c*.1416). Anchoress and mystic, probably educated by Benedictine nuns. After nearly dying (1373) she had a series of sixteen religious experiences, 'shewings', and decided to become a recluse and spiritual counsellor in an anchorage attached to St Julian's church, from which she took her name. Twenty years later, she wrote *The Revelations of Divine Love*, meditations on her 'shewings', the first book known to have been written by a woman in English.

**Junius** was the pseudonym adopted by the unknown author of 69 letters to the *Public Advertiser* between 1769 and 1772. After an unspectacular start, they became a political sensation, boosting the sales of the paper and being widely reproduced. Junius moved from an exchange with Sir William Draper to repeated attacks upon the first minister, the duke of *Grafton, and at length to a celebrated and offensive letter to the king himself. Dozens of people have been suggested as possible authors, but the evidence points strongly to Philip Francis, then a senior clerk in the War Office.

**Junto** was the name given to the Whig allies in the later part of William III's reign and that of Anne. They were particularly strong in the Lords, where the leaders included *Somers, *Halifax, *Orford, *Sunderland, and Wharton.

**jury system** The origins of the jury system are disputed. The name means a body of persons sworn to make a statement on a matter. Although it has been suggested that the jury has Germanic-Anglo-Saxon origins, it is more likely that the institution of a body of men giving an answer, under oath, to a specific question originated in the Frankish inquest. The first juries in the common law were juries instituted by Henry II to make presentment of serious crimes to the travelling justices.

The 'trial jury' originated when, in 1215, the Lateran Council forbade clergy to participate in ordeals, which were, at that time, the means of deciding guilt. Deprived of the ordeal, the justices resorted to the use of sworn bodies of neighbours to decide whether the accused person was guilty. Gradually the 'trial jury' of twelve developed after a number of experiments.

In 1670 it was decided in Bushell's case that a jury could no longer be attainted for reaching a verdict contrary to the evidence or the wish of the court. Majority voting was introduced in the 20th cent. and the complexity of some trials, particularly in matters of fraud, led to suggestions that the use of juries should be reviewed.

**justice Eyre** *See* EYRE.

**justices of the peace** The forerunners of the justices of the peace were the conservators of the peace, first appointed in the reign of Richard I. In the 13th cent. conservators of the peace, consisting of knights and gentry of the county, served on the commissions of *assize, *oyer and terminer, and gaol delivery. In the reign of Edward III, they were given powers to punish offenders and in 1344 to hear and determine criminal cases. A new function was entrusted to the conservators when, after the *Black Death had decimated the population, the statutes of *Labourers provided for the fixing of wages by the justices.

From that time onwards, the legislature increasingly extended the role of the justices of the peace. Their judicial function remained a vital part of the administration of criminal justice. In addition to their judicial and peacekeeping duties, they were used to administer the *Poor Laws and, through the quarter sessions, to oversee the whole of local government. The magistrates' courts remain a vital part of the administration of criminal justice in England and Wales, trying most criminal cases.

**justiciar** The frequent absences of Norman kings on the continent necessitated a competent viceroy or regent in England. This function became associated with the justiciar, who acted as chief minister, performing a great variety of duties, including campaigning, as well as presiding over the *curia regis. *Ranulf Flambard and Roger of Salisbury acted in this capacity under William Rufus and Henry I, without having the title: later the office was held by men of the calibre of Richard de *Lucy, Ranulf *Glanvill, Hubert *Walter, Peter des *Roches, and Hubert de *Burgh. After de Burgh's overthrow by Henry III in 1232, the office lapsed. The legal duties were taken over by the chancellor or the lord chief justice.

**Justiciary Court** (Scotland). The High Court of Justiciary is the supreme criminal court in Scotland. It was established in 1672, and consisted of the lord justice general, the lord justice clerk, and five of the lords of Session. The court has jurisdiction over serious crimes in Scotland and also acts as a court of appeal.

**Justus, St** (d. *c.*627). Sent, according to Bede, by Pope Gregory I with *Mellitus to Kent in 601, and consecrated bishop in Rochester by *Augustine in 604, Justus was associated with Archbishop *Laurentius' exhortations to follow Roman practices. The accession of pagan kings in Kent and over the East Saxons prompted all three to decide to return to Rome, but after a year awaiting developments in Gaul, Justus and Mellitus, whom Justus succeeded as fourth archbishop of Canterbury in 624, were recalled to England.

**Jutes** Bede's account of the Jutes is highly specific—that they were a Germanic people who inhabited a region north of the Angles and that their settlements in England had been in Kent, the Isle of Wight, and on the mainland just north of the Solent. Their leaders had been *Hengist and Horsa. Modern research has modified these suggestions, holding that the differences between Angles, Saxons, and Jutes was smaller than assumed and that the Jutes are less likely to have come from south Schleswig than from Frisia or even the mouth of the Rhine. The pattern of settlement has also been queried. There is evidence from burial practices and place-names of a variety of cultures in Kent, including strong Romano-British survival, and the settlements in the west are seen as secondary migrations rather than direct from the continent.

**Jutland, battle of,** 1916. The war in the North Sea was a frustrating experience for the Royal Navy. The Grand Fleet never gained the overwhelming victory over the German High Seas Fleet for which it yearned. The best opportunity the British had to fight a second Trafalgar was on 31 May 1916 when *Beatty succeeded in luring the High Seas Fleet under the guns of the Grand Fleet. But the outcome only served to demonstrate the weakness of the British fleet. The Grand Fleet's range-finders were deficient, its target-plotting machinery prone to error, and its gunnery computers, staff work, and armoured protection defective. The British suffered greater losses of both ships and men, proof of the excellence of German gunnery and ship construction. But although Jutland was a tactical victory for the Germans, it was a strategic victory for the British. The allied naval blockade of Germany, which was doing so much to strangle its economy, remained unbroken.

**Juxon, William** (1582-1663). Juxon, a bishop and statesman, came to prominence through the favour of *Laud, who persuaded Charles I to make him bishop of London in 1633 and, three years later, lord treasurer. Juxon's unwavering commitment to Anglican values brought him close to the king, and he acted as Charles's spiritual adviser until the very end, standing beside him on the scaffold. Thereafter he lived quietly in the countryside until the restoration of Charles II in 1660, when he was appointed archbishop of Canterbury, but old age made him little more than a figurehead.

**Kames, Henry Home, Lord** (1696–1782). Judge and man of letters. Son of a petty laird, Kames became a lord of Session in 1752. He was a prominent member of the Edinburgh literati and an important patron whose protégés included Adam *Smith and John *Millar. His *Elements of Criticism* (1762) was an early and influential textbook, widely acclaimed in the Anglo-Saxon world.

**Kay, John** (1704–c.1780). Engineer and inventor. Born in 1704 near Bury (Lancs.), Kay patented his flying-shuttle for a loom in 1733. It produced a great speeding-up in the process of weaving, but Kay experienced considerable difficulty in exploiting his invention. His house was destroyed in 1753 by a mob concerned about unemployment, while the Leeds manufacturers banded together to indemnify each other against legal proceedings to enforce Kay's patent.

**Kay-Shuttleworth, Sir James Phillips** (1804–77). Administrator. Educated at Edinburgh University, he graduated as a doctor in 1827. Working in Manchester, Kay (Shuttleworth was added after his marriage) interested himself in sanitary and educational reform. He was appointed assistant Poor Law commissioner in 1835 in the eastern counties and London area. His opportunity to develop national education came in 1839 when he was appointed secretary to the Committee of the Privy Council. For the next ten years, until his health broke down, he worked with great zeal to establish a public system of elementary education, supervised by a national body of inspectors.

**Kean, Edmund** (1787–1833). Actor. Son of an itinerant actress, Kean was exploited as an infant prodigy. The impassioned delivery of his appearance at Drury Lane (1814) as Shylock rapidly replenished the theatre's coffers. Barely average height, his flashing, some-

times demoniac approach, which so contrasted with the measured Kemble school, made him one of the most controversial of the early 19th-cent. actors. Famous for his tragic roles of Richard III, Shylock, and Othello, youthful irresponsibility quickly evolved into recklessness, vanity, intolerance of rivals, and drunken debauch.

**Keats, John** (1795–1821). Poet and sometime surgeon's apprentice, his early work suffered by association with Leigh Hunt and the 'Cockney School'. Most richly sensuous of Romantic poets, with a Schubertian sensitivity to love and death, the 'indescribable gusto' which *Arnold found in his writing continues to attract. A severe self-critic, he introduced *Endymion* (1818) with apologies and abandoned the over-Miltonic *Hyperion* the following year. His best work is contained in the *Odes* of 1819.

**Keble, John** (1792–1866). Credited with launching the *Oxford movement with his Assize Sermon of 1833, which was provoked by the moderate reform of the Irish Church Temporalities Act. To Keble it represented a sacrilegious interference with church order by the secular power. At Oxford he was regarded as a brilliant intellect and was professor of poetry (1831–5) until he married and left Oxford for the parish of Hursley in Hampshire, where he spent the rest of his life.

**Kells, Book of** A Latin copy of the four Gospels and some preliminaries, possibly late 8th cent., but first recorded at the monastery at Kells (Co. Meath) in 1007 after its theft and loss of covers. In 1654 the town governor sent it to Dublin for safety from Cromwellian iconoclasm, following which it was presented to Trinity College.

**Kelvin, William Thomson, 1st Baron** (1824–1907). Pioneer of thermodynamics and one of the greatest of classical physicists. Educated in Belfast, Glasgow, and Cambridge, he was in 1846 chosen professor of natural philosophy at Glasgow. He remained there for 50 years, and on retirement signed on as a research student. The leading physical scientist in Britain, he was made a peer in 1892.

**Kemble, Charles** (1775–1854). Actor and manager. Youngest son of actor-manager Roger Kemble, Charles abandoned the post office for the stage, first appearing in the provinces (1792), then Drury Lane, London (1794). Often performing with his brother John Philip and sister Sarah (Mrs *Siddons), he had an extensive repertoire but excelled in comedy. His management of Covent Garden commenced 1822/3, but it was saved from bankruptcy only by the début in 1829 of his daughter Fanny.

**Kemp, John** (d. 1454). Archbishop of York and Canterbury. Like *Chichele, Kemp was an Oxford DCL who began his career in church courts. After an embassy to Aragon, he was a member of Henry V's council in France, as chancellor of Normandy and keeper of the privy seal. He was one of Henry *Beaufort's supporters in the council of Henry VI's minority and appointed chancellor of England in 1426. By then he had risen through the episcopate as bishop of Rochester (1419), Chichester (1421), and London (1421), to the archbishopric of York (1426). Duke Humphrey of *Gloucester removed Kemp from Chancery in 1432, but he remained a councillor, occasionally an ambassador. When the regime of William de la Pole, duke of Suffolk, collapsed in 1450, Kemp was recalled to be chancellor. From 1452 he was archbishop of Canterbury. His death, while Henry was insane, was a loss from which the Lancastrian government never recovered.

**Kempe, Margery** (c.1373–c.1440). The manuscript of her memories, which she had dictated in the later years of her life, was discovered in 1934, first published in 1947, and is now considered to be the earliest English autobiography. After the birth of her first child, Kempe, daughter of a prosperous burgess of King's Lynn (Norfolk), suffered a spiritual crisis. In later life she became deeply religious and undertook many pilgrimages to the Holy Land, Rome,

and Santiago de Compostela, amongst others.

**Ken, Thomas** (1637–1711). Bishop of Bath and Wells. Educated at Winchester and New College, Oxford, Ken was chaplain to Morley, bishop of Winchester (1665), and to Princess Mary (later Mary II) at The Hague (1679–80). He became bishop of Bath and Wells (1684) and attended *Monmouth on the scaffold (1685). As one of the seven bishops petitioning James II to withdraw the *Declaration of Indulgence he was imprisoned in the Tower (1688), but acquitted. Nevertheless, a man of conscience, he refused to recognize James's abdication or William's accession, was deprived of his see (April 1691), and lived at Longleat until his death.

**Kenilworth castle** (War). combined strong fortifications with palatial residential accommodation. The effectiveness of the defences was demonstrated when supporters of Simon de *Montfort held the castle for a year against Henry III after the battle of *Evesham and were able to surrender on terms in December 1266. Robert Dudley, earl of *Leicester, undertook major building work at the castle, to which Elizabeth was a visitor; one such visit is vividly described in *Scott's *Kenilworth*.

**Kennedy, Charles** (b. 1959). Politician. Born in Inverness and educated at Fort William, Kennedy studied politics at the University of Glasgow. He was elected to Parliament as an *SDP member in 1983 for Ross, Cromartry, and Skye at the age of 23. He joined the *Liberal Democrats when the SDP merged and became leader in 1999, succeeding Paddy *Ashdown. A lively and engaging speaker, his party did well at the general elections of 2001 and 2005, but in 2006 he admitted to alcohol problems and resigned the leadership.

**Kennedy, James** (d. 1465). Provided to the bishopric of Dunkeld by his uncle, James I (1437). Support of Queen *Joan in James II's minority, and opposition to the Basle conciliarists, enabled his promotion to bishop of St Andrews (1440). His foundation of St Salvator's College at St Andrews (1450) is his most enduring legacy. Abroad on James II's death (1460), Kennedy was overlooked in *Mary of Gueldres's distribution of minority government offices. He finally gained possession of James III on her death (December 1463), and acted as royal guardian until his own death in May 1465.

**Kenneth II** (d. 995), king of 'Scotland' (971–95). His father was *Malcolm I and his brother King *Dub. He succeeded *Cuilén to the kingship, but faced competition from Cuilén's brother Olaf, whom he killed in 977. He repeatedly raided northern England and attacked the Britons of *Strathclyde, who defeated him at 'Moin Uacornar' (unidentified). His rule over *Lothian was recognized c.975 by *Edgar, king of England. He met his end at Fettercairn (30 miles south of Aberdeen), assassinated by the daughter of the earl of Angus in revenge for killing her only son.

**Kenneth III** (d. 1005), king of 'Scotland' (997–1005). He was son of King *Dub and became king by killing *Constantine III in battle at 'Rathinveramon' (probably a few miles north of Perth). This engagement represented the final victory of Kenneth's branch of the royal dynasty over its rivals, the descendants of *Æd (d. 878). Kenneth faced competition for the kingship from his own branch of the dynasty, however, and was killed in battle at Monzievaird (15 miles west of Perth) by *Malcolm II, his first cousin.

**Kenneth I MacAlpin** (d. 858), king of Dal Riata (c.840/1–58) and 'king of the Picts' (842/3–58). Kenneth is anachronistically regarded as first king of Scotland because he is deemed to have unified the *Picts (north of the Firth of Forth) with the Gaels (in Latin, *Scoti*) of *Dalriada (Argyll). 'Scotland' (*Alba in Gaelic) did not emerge until 900, however, and is likely to have begun as a much smaller area than the united territories of the Picts and Dalriada.

Kenneth's ancestors were probably kings of Dalriada and his father Alpin may have been king before him. Both Dalriada and the Picts were suffering from the first large-scale Scandinavian incursions which, in 839, wiped out the Gaelic dynasty which had ruled the key Pictish region of *Fortriu since 789. By 849, Kenneth had secured his grasp on the kingship. Whatever his attitude to the Picts may have been, he clearly looked to Gaeldom for support, and in 849 erected a church in *Dunkeld which housed relics of St *Columba, implying that Kenneth sought to cultivate the enormous influence of the Columban network of monasteries.

Kenneth raided Northumbria repeatedly, but his kingdom suffered assaults from the Britons of *Strathclyde as well as Scandinavians. He died of a tumour on 13 February 858, at Forteviot (5 miles south-west of Perth).

**Kensington palace** is architecturally one of the more modest royal residences, but historically it is full of interest. It began life as a private residence of the Finch family and was purchased by William III in 1689 since it provided fresh air but was near to London. *Wren, surveyor of the works, was employed to rebuild extensively, but the scale was moderate, partly because there was lavish building at *Hampton Court. The delightful orangery by *Vanbrugh was added during Anne's reign. Much of the later internal decoration, including the king's staircase, was by William *Kent, and the gardens were laid out and redeveloped by George London, Henry Wise, and Charles *Bridgeman. The Round Pond and the Serpentine were finished during the reign of George I.

**Kent** is one of the oldest counties, having been a kingdom in Saxon times. (*See* KENT, KINGDOM OF.) It has always been of great importance because of its strategic position as gateway to the continent.

In pre-Roman times, the inhabitants were the *Cantiaci, a group of tribes who offered serious resistance to *Caesar's two expeditions. The main Roman port was Richborough (Rutupiae), where there remains a remarkable Roman lighthouse. A major road ran from the port to *Canterbury (Durovernum) and crossed the Medway at Rochester (Durobrivae), before reaching London. It was later known as *Watling Street.

In the middle of the 5th cent., the area was overrun by *Jutish settlers and a kingdom established. *Æthelbert pushed Kentish power to its height, occupying London and taking control of the East Saxons. He converted to Christianity and founded the sees of Canterbury (597) and *Rochester (604). Later kings of Kent found it difficult to sustain their independence against powerful neighbours and fell under the domination, first of *Mercia, then of *Wessex.

Kentish society had a number of unusual features. The shire was divided into five large divisions or lathes and then into more than 60 small hundreds. The local custom of *gavelkind supported equal inheritance and Kentish men had a reputation for independence. The east–west division of the shire, hinted at by the establishment of two bishoprics, continued strongly. There was a convention that representation in Parliament should be shared between east and west and JPs normally exercised their authority only in their own half. Quarter sessions were at Canterbury for east Kent, Maidstone for west Kent.

By *Domesday in 1086, Dover had developed as an important borough, along with Canterbury and Rochester. Also of significance were Romney, Hythe, and Sandwich, subsequently recognized among the *Cinque Ports, and given special privileges in exchange for heavy defence responsibilities. The close association with the continent after the *Norman Conquest brought the shire considerable prosperity, and more came with the development of the royal dockyards. By 1801 the largest towns in the shire were Deptford (17,000), Greenwich (14,000), and Chatham (10,000). Production for the ever-growing London market encouraged orchards, market gardens, hop-fields, and the rearing of sheep and cattle. As the remorseless growth of London continued, the balance of population in the county shifted to the north-west. Lewisham with 4,000 people in 1801 had 174,000 in 1921; Deptford had risen to 119,000, Plumstead to 76,000, Bromley to 68,000. Another rapid development was Gillingham with 95,000. In 1888 Kent lost a slice of London suburbia to the new London County Council, and in 1965 Erith, Bromley, Bexley, Chislehurst, and Orpington were moved out into the Greater London Council.

**Kent, kingdom of** Kent was founded, according to tradition, in the middle of the 5th cent. by two brothers of Jutish origin, *Hengist and Horsa, who came to Britain to protect the native inhabitants against the Picts and Scots, turned against their paymasters, and won a kingdom for themselves. Kingship was not always unitary, and there were two clear-cut divisions within Kent along the Medway, the men of Kent and the

Kentishmen. There are also vestiges of survival of Roman administrative divisions. Under Æthelbert (d. 616), Kent reached the height of its political power, falling back later in the 7th cent. as overlordship passed briefly to East Anglia, and then to Northumbria. Æthelbert's chief claim to fame is his acceptance of Christianity, and with the help of the mission led by St *Augustine he framed laws to accommodate the new church. But politically Kent had no high aspirations, and was overshadowed in the 8th cent. by Mercia, and after 825 by Wessex. There were no independent kings in Kent after 825, though Canterbury preserved its special prestige as an archbishopric.

**Kent, William** (1685–1748). Architect, painter and landscape architect. In 1719 Kent was brought back from Rome by Lord *Burlington, and together they became the leading proponents of *Palladianism in England. In 1727 Kent published *The Designs of Inigo Jones*. Although Kent designed the Horse Guards, the Royal Mews, and the Treasury buildings, most of his architecture was for private clients. A notable instance of this was his collaboration with Burlington at Holkham Hall, Norfolk (1734), with its dramatic apsidal entrance hall with columns, coffered ceiling, and grand staircase. Significant too are Kent's garden buildings and landscaping at Chiswick, Rousham, Stowe, and Claremont.

**Kenya** Former British protectorate and colony in eastern Africa. A British protectorate was declared in 1895. The development of the agricultural resources by white settlers was made possible by the administration's need to generate income and by the construction of the Uganda railway from 1897. The change in Britain's attitude towards colonial dependencies in the 1950s led to Kenyan independence under African rule in 1963.

**Kenyatta, Jomo** (c.1894–1978). Kenyan nationalist statesman. Kenyatta's involvement in politics began in 1922 when he campaigned for the restoration of land lost by his Kikuyu tribe to white settlers. In 1929 he went to London to plead the case of the Kikuyu and stayed in Europe. Returning to Kenya in 1946 he was elected president of the Kenya African Union in 1947. In 1952 he

was found guilty of master-minding the
*Mau Mau rebellion although the evidence
was far from conclusive. He was released in
1961 and became prime minister in 1963
when the country achieved independence,
then president in 1964 when Kenya became
a republic.

**Keppel, Arnold Joost van, 1st earl of
Albemarle** (c.1670–1718). Dutch confidant
of William III. Born in Holland, Keppel attended William of Orange to England in 1688
as a page of honour. He rose quickly in the
king's favour, and was appointed groom of the
bedchamber in 1691 and master of the robes
in 1695. Gossip inevitably spoke of an improper relationship, while in parliamentary opinion he (together with *Portland) was regarded
as a sinister Dutch influence. After the king's
death in 1702 he returned to Holland and was
a commander of the Dutch forces in the allied
campaigns against Louis XIV.

**Kett, Robert** (d. 1549). Kett showed more
organizational skill than is usually found in
peasant risings. He was a tanner and small
landowner, holding the manor of Wymondham (Norfolk). Residual resentment over the
*dissolution of the monasteries, local feuds,
and anger over enclosures sparked a riot in
the town in the summer of 1549 which developed into a major rising. The insurgents set up
camp for six weeks on Mousehold Heath, notable for the discipline which Kett imposed.
After he had occupied Norwich, the government gathered a force under Lord Northampton, which the rebels routed. Three weeks
later, a second force, stiffened by mercenaries,
cut the insurgents to pieces at *Dussindale.
Kett was hanged at Norwich, his brother William at Wymondham.

**Kew Gardens** (Surrey). Location of the
Royal Botanical Gardens, which contain a
vast collection of herbs, trees, and shrubs
gathered from all over the world. Kew Gardens evolved from two adjoining 18th-cent.
royal estates: Richmond Gardens, belonging
to George II, and Kew House, the residence
of his son Frederick, prince of Wales. Charles
*Bridgeman assisted in the laying out of
Richmond Gardens, where William *Kent
designed the Hermitage (1730) and Merlin's
Cave (1735). At adjacent Kew, following the
death of Frederick in 1751, the Dowager
Princess Augusta employed Sir William

Chambers to lay out the grounds and to
embellish them with a variety of temples
and garden buildings, including the orangery
(1757–61), the Alhambra (1758), the Temple
of the Sun (1761), and the pagoda (1761–2).

**Keynes, John Maynard** (1883–1946).
Arguably the foremost economist of the
20th cent., Keynes was born in Cambridge
and combined a successful academic career
with that of civil servant and government
adviser. His *Treatise on Money* (1930) and
*The General Theory of Employment, Interest
and Money* (1936) heralded the Keynesian
revolution, which regarded government control of spending as the key to providing full
employment.

**Keys, House of** The elected chamber of
the *Tynwald, parliament of the *Isle of Man.
Dating back to Nordic times, when the island
was the centre of a western sea empire, it
claims to be the oldest parliament in continuous existence. From early times there have
been 24 members. The name is probably an
English imitation of the Manx Yn Kiare-as-
feed, the *four and twenty*.

**Kilkenny, Confederation of,** 1642. The
Irish rebellion of 1641 was not a spontaneous
peasant rising but a planned insurrection.
The rebels, while protesting their loyalty to
Charles I, took steps to organize the large
areas under their control. An assembly or
parliament summoned at Kilkenny in October 1642 adopted a provisional constitution,
with a general assembly choosing a supreme
council. The new Confederation raised
armies for the four provinces, imposed
taxes, and confirmed the privileges of the
catholic church. Charles I's policy was to
offer terms to the Confederation that would
enable an army to be sent over to England to
turn the scales in the Civil War, and as his
position worsened, the terms improved.
Many of the confederates were prepared to
wait until Charles was forced to offer not
merely relaxation of the penal laws against
catholics but their total removal, and they
were strengthened when the papal nuncio,
Rinuccini, who arrived in November 1645,
took an intransigent line. Charles's diplomacy was characteristically convoluted, but to
no avail, for Chester surrendered in February
1646 and there was nowhere left for Irish
reinforcements to land. The confederates

now found the English Parliament a much more formidable opponent than Charles had been and their forces were routed at *Rathmines by Michael Jones. *Cromwell's campaigns of 1649 and 1650 restored English supremacy.

**Kilkenny, convention of,** 1341. The English crown was too preoccupied with Wales and Scotland in the reign of Edward I, and too insecure in the reign of Edward II, to give much attention to the English Pale in Ireland. Edward III was forced to pay attention in 1341 by a Parliament which began in Dublin and adjourned to Kilkenny when the royal ministers lost control. The Anglo-Irish protested vigorously against the decision to revoke all grants since 1307, demanded action against English ministers who knew nothing of the country, and warned that much territory had been lost to the native Irish. Edward returned a conciliatory answer and dismissed most of the ministers. The condition of the Pale continued to give concern.

**Kilkenny, statutes of,** 1366. Lionel, duke of Clarence, second son of Edward III, was appointed the king's lieutenant in Ireland in 1361. In 1366 he summoned a parliament at Kilkenny, which passed a number of statutes intended to buttress the position of the English. They were not to use the Irish language, or intermarry with the Irish; they were not to sell horses or armour to the Irish; they were forbidden to play hurling but told to practise archery. The statutes, though frequently repeated, did not prevent the Anglo-Irish from becoming Irish-speaking.

**Killiecrankie, battle of,** 1689. *Dundee's campaign for James VII in the spring of 1689 led to a chase through the glens between his small force and a slightly larger Williamite army under Hugh Mackay. On 27 July Mackay's men were caught in the pass of Killiecrankie, near Pitlochry, and badly beaten. But Dundee was shot in the side and killed. The Jacobite campaign disintegrated after the check at *Dunkeld in August.

**Kilmainham 'treaty',** 1882. In October 1881, Charles Stewart *Parnell was arrested and imprisoned in Kilmainham gaol (Dublin) 'on reasonable suspicion' of encouraging violence. In April 1882 Gladstone opened negotiations with him. In exchange for his release and a government promise to help with tenants' arrears of rent, Parnell agreed to denounce violence. The Irish chief secretary, W. E. *Forster, resigned in protest. His replacement, Lord Frederick *Cavendish, was murdered in Phoenix Park the day he arrived.

**Kilmore (Cell Mór), diocese of** This Irish see was first named Ardagh and then Kells at the Council of Kells-Mellifont (1152). Later, when the bishop of Kells was expelled (c.1185) by the bishop of Meath, the see of Kells was abolished. The territorial struggles between lordships confused loyalties so that in c.1453 the pope agreed to the parish church of Kilmore being raised to cathedral status. Later the see was merged with Elphin and Ardagh (1841). It is still a diocese in both catholic and Anglican churches.

**Kilsyth, battle of,** 1645. Six days after Baillie had been beaten by *Montrose at *Alford, outside Aberdeen, in July 1645, a covenanting parliament assembled at Stirling. Montrose moved southwards to harass it. Baillie faced him at Kilsyth, south of Stirling on 15 August. The covenanters were caught while still deploying and suffered very heavy casualties. But it was the last of Montrose's victories.

**Kilvert, Robert Francis** (1840–79). Kilvert, a young Victorian curate, kept a diary in the 1870s when he served at Clyro, near Hay-on-Wye, and assisted his father at Langley Burrell, near Chippenham. His simple and direct style and his keen interest in the country people he met on his walks make his diary a vivid and moving account of the period. Kilvert died of peritonitis four weeks after his marriage, and is buried at Bredwardine, his last living.

**Kilwardby, Robert** (c.1210–79). Dominican scholar, archbishop of Canterbury, and cardinal. Educated at Paris, Kilwardby taught grammar and logic before becoming a Dominican friar (c.1240). Later by upholding traditional scholasticism against the new Aristotelianism he was Aquinas's foremost opponent, though a fellow-Dominican. Appointed archbishop by the pope in 1272, he was the first English friar to hold high office, but, little involved politically, he was on good terms with Edward I. To move him from

Canterbury, the pope elevated him to the curia as cardinal-bishop of Porto (1278). He died at Viterbo.

**Kimberley, John Wodehouse, 1st earl of** (1826-1902). A Whig politician, Kimberley served in all of Gladstone's ministries. At the Colonial and India Offices he acquired the reputation of an 'imperial handyman'. Some thought him irresolute during the first *Boer War in 1880-1, but he concluded that a military victory would not give Britain real control of the Transvaal. Self-government under British suzerainty followed. He also accepted the need for *Irish Home Rule. As foreign secretary in 1894-5 he recognized that Britain could not respond to popular demands for intervention against the savage Turkish repression of an Armenian uprising.

**Kimberley, siege of** Episode during the second *Boer War (1899-1902). Kimberley was a diamond town of 50,000 inhabitants. From November 1899 it was defended by about 1,000 troops under Colonel R. G. Kekewitch with 3,800 irregulars, and besieged in haphazard fashion by about 7,500 Boers. The relief of Kimberley was finally accomplished in spectacular fashion by the cavalry division under Major-General John *French on 15 February 1900.

**'Kingis Quair'** A poem now generally accepted to have been written by James I of Scotland following his return from imprisonment in England (1424). Written in Scots, with English influences, it is an autobiographical account of the king's incarceration, his love for his future queen, and their eventual marriage.

**King's Bench, Court of** One of the three courts of common law. The Court of King's Bench evolved from the *curia regis, the itinerant royal court which dealt with the administration of the realm. Its origins have been traced back to 1178 when Abbot Benedict of Peterborough recorded that Henry II ordered five judges of the curia regis to sit permanently to hear complaints from his subjects. In 1268 King's Bench was appointed its first chief justice. It had unlimited criminal jurisdiction throughout the realm. The Judicature Act of 1873 unified the courts

system and transferred jurisdiction to a single High Court of Justice.

**King's College chapel** (Cambridge). Eton and King's College, Cambridge, were founded by Henry VI to celebrate his majority (aged 15) in 1437, before his reign had disintegrated into defeat in France and civil war at home. King's began in 1441 as the College of St Nicholas and the name was changed in 1443. Henry laid the foundation stone of the chapel on 25 July 1446. The chapel was not completed until 1515 and for many years afterwards totally dominated the site, since Gibbs's building, which helps to balance it, was not started until 1723 and the King's Parade neo-Gothic façade by Wilkins was only begun in 1824. The fan-vaulting (the most striking feature of the interior), the stained glass, and the screen all date from the reign of Henry VIII.

**king's counsel** *See* QUEEN'S COUNSEL.

**king's evil, touching for** *See* TOUCHING FOR THE KING'S EVIL.

**king's friends** The term gained credence with *Burke's *Thoughts on the Present Discontents* (1770), which explained the lack of success of the Rockingham party by the machinations of royalists, manipulating policy through a 'double cabinet'. No such organized, sinister, and servile corps existed. But George III's desire for a non-party administration appealed to many, the advent of a young monarch could hardly fail to strengthen royal influence, and the abandonment by the Tories of fruitless opposition meant a corresponding stiffening of governmental resolve.

**Kingsley, Charles** (1819-75). Vicar of Eversley (Hants), social reformer, novelist, and 'muscular Christian'. Influenced by F. D. *Maurice and Thomas *Carlyle, Kingsley became a leading spirit in the *Christian socialist movement of 1848-54, and under the pseudonym 'Parson Lot' contributed to *Politics for the People* (1848) and *The Christian Socialist* (1850-1). His novels *Yeast* (1848) and *Alton Locke* (1850) were sympathetic middle-class descriptions of working-class life.

**King's Lynn,** on the estuary of the Great Ouse (Norfolk), was for centuries one of England's major ports. It was developed by the first bishop of Norwich in the 1090s, and enlarged by the third bishop, each sector with its own church and market. Its trade was international in the Middle Ages, but mainly domestic from the 16th cent.

**Kingston, treaty of,** 1217. Immediately after the defeat of his supporters at *Lincoln in May 1217, Louis, dauphin of France, began peace negotiations. They broke down in the summer but a further naval defeat at *Sandwich persuaded him to agree terms. In exchange for a large indemnity, he renounced his claim to the crown of England. (*See also* LAMBETH, TREATY OF.)

**Kingston upon Hull** Yorkshire port at the junction of the river Hull with the Humber, usually called just 'Hull'. It originated as a monastic wool-exporting port, but was acquired and renamed by Edward I (1293). By 1800 it was the third British port after London and Liverpool. The city (as it became in 1897) was hard hit by Second World War bombing, and by the collapse of its fishing industry in the 1970s.

**Kinnock, Neil G.** (b. 1943). Leader of the Labour Party (1983–92), European commissioner from 1995. Kinnock was born in Tredegar and elected to Parliament in 1970 for Bedwellty. Having lost two general elections in a row to the Conservatives (1987, 1992), Kinnock disarmingly confessed to being a failure. His left-wing views (particularly support for the *Campaign for Nuclear Disarmament) alienated many voters, while his rhetorical style was considered verbose even by many of his own supporters. Though he demonstrated courage in facing up to left-wing extremists in his party, dropping unpopular policies, and beginning the process of modernizing Labour, the impression remained that he lacked the *gravitas* required of a prime minister. He resigned the leadership immediately after the election of 1992 and was made a life peer in 2005.

**Kinsale, battle of,** 1601. Around 4,000 Spanish troops sent to assist Hugh *O'Neill, earl of Tyrone, against Elizabeth I landed in September 1601 at Kinsale, where they were besieged by Lord *Mountjoy, who had taken over from *Essex. On 24 December an attempt to relieve the town failed and the Spaniards surrendered on terms.

**Kipling, Rudyard** (1865–1936). Kipling is often thought of primarily as the trumpet of empire, but his writings were more varied than that suggests and he was far from triumphalist in tone. Kipling was born in Bombay, where his father had a chair in architecture. His first name is derived from Rudyard Lake, near Leek (Staffs.), where his parents had met. After United Services College in Devon, he returned to India as a journalist and rapidly acquired a reputation. At 24 he settled in London. *Life's Handicap* (1891) launched him as a London figure and he followed with *The Jungle Book* (1894/5). His poem 'Recessional' for the *Diamond Jubilee of 1897—'lest we forget'—made him a national figure. *Stalky and Co.* (1899) drew on his schooldays and *Kim* (1901) on India. He published the *Just So Stories*, one of the few children's books that children enjoy, in 1902 when he moved into Bateman's in Sussex, and *Puck of Pook's Hill*, set in the post-Roman period, in 1906. Kipling declined national honours but was awarded the Nobel prize for literature in 1907. His only son was killed in the Great War in 1915.

**Kiribati,** formerly the Gilbert Islands, is an independent republic within the Commonwealth. It lies to the north-east of Fiji, and became independent in 1979.

**Kitchener, Horatio Herbert, 1st Earl** (1850–1916). Soldier and imperial statesman. Kitchener saw extensive service as a soldier and imperial administrator in Egypt, South Africa, and India. Amongst his achievements were the reconquest of the Sudan (1898) and the imposition of British peace terms on the Boer republics (1902). But his greatest service to the British empire was between 1914 and 1916, when he served as secretary of state for war. Far from being merely a great poster, as *Lloyd George claimed, he was a prescient strategist. To ensure that Britain emerged victorious he expanded the small regular army by raising a huge new army of volunteers. He was drowned when HMS *Hampshire* was sunk off Orkney by a German mine.

**Kit Kat Club** An early 18th-cent. London dining club which took its name from Christopher Cat, who kept the tavern in which it first met. Although not a political club, its members were prominent in the Whig

Party. Kneller was commissioned to paint portraits of the members. All but one of the 42 pictures are now in the National Portrait Gallery.

**Kloster-Zeven, convention of,** 1757. After *Cumberland's defeat at *Hastenbeck in July, he withdrew to Stade and opened negotiations with the French. He interpreted his orders from his father, George II, as authority to preserve his army at all costs and on 8 September signed the convention of Kloster-Zeven, arranging for it to be disbanded. George II repudiated the convention. Cumberland, hastening to Kensington palace, was greeted with 'Here is my son who has ruined me and disgraced himself.' He resigned all his military offices in protest and never held command again.

**Kneller, Sir Godfrey** (c.1646–1723). A native of Lübeck, Kneller came to England c.1676. He became court portraitist to William and Mary, Anne, and George I, enjoying a reputation which evidently eclipsed *Van Dyck's. Kneller's more notable works include the eight 'Hampton Court Beauties' commissioned by Mary II, and his '*Kit Kat Club' portraits, executed between 1697 and 1721.

**knights** In continental Europe from the 10th cent. onwards, the term *miles* (knight) was applied to a mounted warrior usually dependent on a greater lord. *Domesday evidence suggests that this definition is appropriate for the knights of Norman England. Over the next two centuries, knights were enfeoffed with land, becoming more fully involved in landed society. Although the term never lost its military connotation, it had become by the late 14th cent. a social rank below the nobility, but above the squirearchy. By the mid-15th cent., knights numbered only a few hundred. The decline has usually been explained in terms of personal preference: men of the requisite social standing resisted the crown's attempts to force them, by *distraint of knighthood, to take up the rank because they feared the additional expense and burden of responsibility. Most knights were knights bachelor; the title was not hereditary, nor did it give noble status, so that knights were represented in Parliament in the Commons. The knight banneret emerged in the early 13th cent. as a senior rank, probably relating, in its initial stages, to special military significance. The

creation of *baronetcies, which were hereditary, in the early 17th cent. brought about a further decline in the status of knighthood. Though the link with military service did not totally disappear and successful admirals were often knighted, 18th-cent. knights were just as likely to be diplomats, lord mayors of London, or wealthy merchants.

**Knollys, Sir Francis** (1512–96). Knollys was a prominent courtier and parliamentarian during Elizabeth I's reign. His career took off after he married the daughter of Mary Boleyn, first cousin to Princess Elizabeth. Most of Queen Mary's reign he spent abroad, but on Elizabeth's accession he was made a privy counsellor and vice-chamberlain. His accumulation of estates and a large family gave him a powerful electoral interest: six of his seven sons sat in Parliament and Knollys was a leading government spokesman in all the Elizabethan parliaments. In 1567 he became treasurer of the chamber, in 1570 treasurer of the household, and in 1593 was given the Garter.

**Knox, John** (c.1514–72). Scottish protestant preacher. Born at Haddington and educated at St Andrews University, Knox was ordained a catholic priest before being called to the protestant ministry in 1547. In 1549, following two years' imprisonment on a French galley, he settled in England, where his powerful preaching and extreme reliance on biblical authority established his radical credentials. Driven into continental exile by Mary Tudor's accession in 1553, his radicalism developed a powerful political edge, culminating in his diatribe against female rule, *The First Blast of the Trumpet against the Monstrous Regiment of Women* (1558). On Elizabeth's accession, Knox returned to Scotland where in 1559 his iconoclastic preaching triggered a protestant rebellion against the regent, *Mary of Guise. The reformed settlement of 1560, however, was jeopardized by the return to Scotland in 1561 of the catholic Mary Stuart. While Knox denounced her idolatry from his Edinburgh pulpit, politically he was marginalized and played no significant role in Mary's subsequent downfall.

**Korean War,** 1950–3. On 25 June 1950 the communist North Korean army attacked the Republic of South Korea, crossing the 38th

Parallel, which acted as the artificial boundary. The army of the South was forced to retreat. On 27 June the United Nations voted to provide military aid and the USA led a fifteen-nation task force to the peninsula. On 15 September the UN gained the initiative by launching an amphibious assault on Inchon and pushed north capturing Pyongyang, the North Korean capital. However, by January 1951 the communists, massively reinforced by China, were marching south again. A cease-fire came into effect on 10 July. The two Koreas remained implacably opposed until the 21st cent.

**Kruger, Paul** (1825–1904). Boer (Afrikaner) statesman and devout Calvinist. Kruger spent most of his life trying to escape British rule. As a boy he accompanied his parents on the Great Trek away from Britain's Cape Colony. He was present at the signing of the *Sand River convention in 1852 and was a founder of the South African Republic (Transvaal) in 1856. When Britain annexed the republic in 1877, he led the resistance to British administration which culminated in the first Anglo-Boer War (1880–1). His diplomacy resulted in two conventions (*Pretoria 1881 and London 1884) which recognized the internal autonomy of the Transvaal and in 1883 he became president of the republic. Renewed British designs on the Transvaal led to the second Anglo-Boer War (1899–1902). The elderly Kruger sought help in Europe and died there in 1904.

k

**labour aristocracy** Top 10–15 per cent of manual wage earners in the 19th cent., characterized by relatively high and regular earnings, membership of a trade union, and respectable life-style. This élite of skilled artisans—engineers, cabinet-makers, printers, cotton-spinners—set the tone of working-class leadership between the 1840s and the 1890s. Some historians have suggested that a labour aristocracy with a conservative ideology and a stake in the status quo helps to account for the social stability of mid-Victorian Britain. However, the labour aristocracy maintained a distinctive working-class ideology through its unions, and also provided the leadership in some radical reform movements.

**Labourers, statute of,** 1351. The statute was an early attempt at a wage freeze, rarely a popular policy. The scourge of the *Black Death led to an acute shortage of labour. When Parliament met in 1351 there were complaints that 'out of singular covetise' wages had risen, and the statute (25 Edw. III s. 1) was passed. Men were to work at pre-1349 wage levels, and masters were forbidden to offer more. Persons below the age of 60 not in employment were not to refuse offers of work. Resentment played a part in the grievances leading to the *Peasants' Revolt in 1381.

**Labour Party** Labour has been the principal progressive alternative to the Conservative Party since the 1920s, forming governments in 1924, 1929–31, 1945–51, 1964–70, 1974–9, and 1997. The Labour Representation Committee was established in 1900 by a conference of trade unionists and socialists orchestrated by Keir *Hardie. Although it won only two seats in the 1900 'khaki' election, the secret electoral pact with the Liberal Party negotiated by Ramsay *MacDonald in 1903 helped the rechristened

Labour Party enjoy a tally of 30 MPs after the 1906 election.

The First World War proved to be Labour's turning-point. Arthur *Henderson (parliamentary chairman after MacDonald's resignation on the outbreak of war) entered the cabinet on the formation of the wartime coalition in 1915 and from August 1917 worked with Sidney *Webb in devising a new constitution. In 1918 Labour became formally committed to the socialist objective of 'public ownership of the means of production' (clause 4).

Under conditions of manhood suffrage, the 1918 'coupon' election awarded Labour 63 seats. In 1922 Labour gained 142 seats to become the official opposition. Following the inconclusive 1923 election, it briefly formed the government with 191 MPs between January and October 1924, which demonstrated Labour's competence. However the second MacDonald government exposed the financial orthodoxy of ministers in the face of mounting unemployment and the financial crisis of 1931. The resignation of the Labour cabinet in August and the subsequent formation of the *National (coalition) Government by MacDonald (with the support of only a handful of Labour figures such as *Snowden and J. H. Thomas) caused lasting bitterness within the Labour Party. After the disastrous 1931 election (which reduced Labour from 288 to 52 seats), Labour began a gradual recovery and won 154 seats in 1935 on 38 per cent of the vote. The unassuming Clement *Attlee was elected leader before this election. The participation of Labour in *Churchill's coalition government from May 1940 rebuilt its image with voters and *Bevin, *Morrison, and *Cripps played highly visible roles on the 'home front'. The year 1945 heralded an unexpected landslide victory for Labour, which won 393 seats with 48 per cent of the vote. This strong administration, with

Bevin at the Foreign Office, Dalton and then Cripps as chancellor, and 'Nye' *Bevan at Health, was Labour's 'finest hour'. Despite economic headaches, by 1950 the 'Attlee consensus' of a mixed economy with a welfare state was firmly established.

Despite achieving its highest ever poll in 1951, Labour began thirteen years of opposition. The period witnessed faction fighting between left-wing 'Bevanites' and right-wing followers of Hugh *Gaitskell, elected leader in 1955. In response to three successive (and widening) election defeats, Gaitskell unsuccessfully attempted to persuade the conference to abandon 'clause 4' in 1959. The following year, Labour's anti-war tradition resurfaced in conference support for unilateral nuclear disarmament (reversed in 1961).

However, a tottering economy together with Harold *Wilson's invigorating leadership allowed Labour to squeeze back into office in October 1964 by a four-seat majority. An easy victory in the 1966 'follow-up' election gave Labour a majority of 97. Despite positive achievements in the field of education and liberalizing social legislation, Wilson's government struggled to cope with the legacy of Britain's relative economic decline and was humbled by the 1967 devaluation of sterling and consequent policy U-turns.

In opposition again after 1970, Labour divided over Britain's entry into the EEC and the left's call for more extensive public ownership. Wilson's two further narrow election victories in 1974 obscured a weakening of Labour's appeal since the 1960s. Left-wing alienation from the government's (under *Callaghan from 1976) deflationary response to mounting unemployment and inflation came to a head after Labour began a further lengthy spell in opposition after 1979.

In 1980 and 1981 Tony Benn's supporters won constitutional changes which precipitated the defection of right-wingers to form the *Social Democratic Party. Subsequently, Michael *Foot led Labour to heavy defeat in the 1983 election. Under Neil *Kinnock (1983–92) and John *Smith (1992–4) a slow revival of Labour's fortunes occurred as the party shifted back towards the 'centre' and purged itself of militant infiltration. Tony *Blair's 'New Labour' strategy from 1994 accelerated this trend, and, with Major's Conservative govern-

ment in disarray, secured a massive win at the 1997 general election. It retained large majorities at the elections of 2001 and 2005. Blair resigned in 2007 and was succeeded as prime minister by Gordon *Brown.

**labour services** were tasks undertaken by tenants as part of their obligations to landowners for the right to farm or use land. These duties came to be seen as part of the rent paid by tenants under the *'manorial system' during the Middle Ages. Precise statements of labour services owed by landholders were set out in 'custumals', documents produced in manorial courts under oath. During the 14th cent. landowners found it profitable to commute labour services for fixed cash payments. A few labour services survived in economically underdeveloped areas until the early 18th cent.

**Ladysmith** Town in northern Natal, besieged by Afrikaner forces during the second Anglo-Boer War. Ladysmith became the main British military supply base in Natal in 1897. When the Boers advanced into the colony at the outbreak of war in 1899 the British commander, Sir George White, was heavily defeated and found himself surrounded in Ladysmith. Fortunately for White, the Boer commander, Joubert, did not exploit his success and the town was relieved at the end of February 1900.

**Lagos, battle of,** 1693. On 17 June 1693 off Lagos in southern Portugal, Sir George *Rooke, escorting a convoy of 400 vessels to the Mediterranean, was attacked by the French admiral de Tourville with a vastly superior force. One hundred English and Dutch merchantmen were lost.

**Lagos, battle of,** 1759. In the summer of 1759 the nucleus of a French invasion fleet under de la Clue left Toulon and slipped past Edward Boscawen's squadron at Gibraltar. A running fight developed and on 18 August four French vessels sought refuge in Lagos Bay in southern Portugal. They were attacked, two captured and two burned, and de la Clue killed. The Portuguese protested at the violation of their neutrality.

**La Hogue, battle of,** 1692. Control of the Channel, lost by the defeat off *Beachy Head in 1690, was restored in May 1692 by the victory of La Hogue, near Barfleur. De Tourville, the French admiral, had orders to engage while still awaiting reinforcements from the Mediterranean. This gave Edward Russell (\*Orford) an advantage of nearly two to one. The French were badly beaten. James II, on shore with a French invasion force, watched the destruction of his hopes.

**lairds** The Scots word 'laird' is a shortened form of 'laverd', an older Scots word deriving from an Anglo-Saxon term meaning lord. By the 15th cent. it was widely used of lesser landowners holding directly of the crown and therefore entitled to go to Parliament, but lairds were clearly distinguished from the higher aristocracy or lords of Parliament. In the 16th and 17th cents. it was commonly applied to the chief of a Highland clan with no other title, as in 'the laird of McGregor'. Lairds were therefore a numerous class in rural Scotland, though decreasing relative to the higher nobility over time. They were not a homogeneous class: Orkney and Shetland produced merchant-lairds.

*laissez-faire* The transition from the medieval to the modern economy was characterized by the progressive removal of restrictions on individuals and groups in favour of the operation of market forces. The balance between complete unrestriction and some control is still strenuously debated. In reality the state of complete *laissez-faire* has never existed. John Stuart \*Mill defined what has become accepted as the minimum level of state intervention. Amongst such interventions for the greater good, he included the power to enforce contracts and secure property rights, the administration of justice, the right to tax in order to provide public goods such as transport systems, sanitation and public health, and state-supported education.

While the notion of *laissez-faire* is usually associated with the decline of the medieval and mercantilist economic regimes, it has an enduring modern counterpart in the views of the neoclassical and new classical economists, who may use different terminology, but whose essential view is that individual freedom to function within untrammelled markets, with little involvement from government, represents the best type of economic organization. All these strands of thought assert the right of the individual and depict state involvement in the economy as ineffectual or malign.

**Lamb, Charles** (1775–1834). Lamb was born in London, spent his 'joyful schooldays' at Christ's Hospital, and earned his living as a clerk in the East India House. Much of his life was devoted to caring for his sister Mary, who killed their mother in a fit of madness. His most successful works were the *Tales from Shakespeare* (1807) for young readers, and the *Essays of Elia* (1823, 1833).

**Lambert, John** (1619–83). Lambert was a good cavalry commander in the first civil war, and a leading general in the second, serving with \*Cromwell at \*Preston. He added to his military reputation at \*Dunbar in 1650 and at \*Worcester in 1651. He was largely responsible for the \*Instrument of Government setting up the Protectorate in 1653, and was widely tipped as Cromwell's successor. In 1657 however he went too far in opposing the \*Humble Petition and Advice and was stripped of his military and civil appointments. Triumphantly reinstated when the army overturned Richard Cromwell in 1659, he looked like a \*Monck in the making. But his position collapsed speedily. When Monck in Scotland threatened to intervene on the Rump's behalf, Lambert marched north to face him, but his troops melted away. He was captured and put in the Tower. Lambert spent the remaining 23 years of his life in captivity, mainly in the Channel Islands.

**Lambeth, treaty of,** 1217. After John's death in 1216, the supporters of his young son Henry III defeated Louis of France's men at \*Lincoln. On 20 September 1217 the treaty of Lambeth ratified terms agreed at \*Kingston upon Thames. Louis abandoned all claims to the English throne and retired to France but was given 10,000 marks in compensation.

**Lambeth palace** Lambeth and its manor house was bought by \*Baldwin (*c*.1185). Known as Lambeth House until 1658, it is conveniently near the administrative centres of Westminster and Whitehall for archbishops as 'Primates of all England'.

**Lancashire** Isolated by dense forests, this north-western area of England remained remote and desolate even at *Domesday. Fully recognized as one of the English shires by 1194 and a county *palatine since 1351, the palatine rights were subsequently vested in the sovereign as duke of Lancaster.

Cloth-manufacturing was initially a subsidiary employment in the upland farms, encouraged by the soft water and mild, moist climate. The invention of machines for spinning (*Hargreaves's spinning jenny, *Arkwright's water frame, *Crompton's mule) and development of steam-power in the later 18th cent. encouraged exploitation of the coalfield and a move from a domestic to a factory system, with increasing concentration on the more easily worked cotton. Aided by improved communications and transport, and growth of *Manchester as a business centre and *Liverpool as an Atlantic port, the expansion in cotton enabled Lancashire to dominate the British textile industry. Commerce, cotton, chemicals, and engineering generated industrial development, massive growth in population, and local wealth, but at the expense of scarring the valleys. Glass, soap, and shipping still prospered, but as textiles and mining declined, unemployment, urban decay, and out-migration accelerated. Cricket and association football retain passionate support, but, despite its regional distinctiveness, the county (shorn in 1972 of Merseyside, Greater Manchester, and its southern Lakeland fringe) continues to drift back to its former position on the periphery.

**Lancaster, duchy of** The duchy originated in the desire of Henry III to provide for his youngest son Edmund Crouchback, after the failure of a scheme to make him king of Sicily. He was granted many of the estates of Simon de *Montfort, killed at *Evesham, and in 1267 was given all the royal estates in Lancashire, assuming the title of earl. Edmund's grandson, *Henry of Grosmont, was created duke by Edward III in 1351, with considerable *palatine powers. Henry left a daughter who married *John of Gaunt, Edward III's younger son. When John's son Henry seized the throne as Henry IV in 1399, the dukedom of Lancaster was merged with the crown.

**Lancaster, Joseph** (1778–1838). Founder of the Lancasterian system of education. The son of a nonconformist, Lancaster opened a school at Borough Road, south London, in 1798, offering free education to those unable to pay. He divided the pupils into small classes; a group of these classes was supervised by a head monitor. Recognition came in 1805 when George III met Lancaster and promised his support. A Royal Lancasterian Society, later the *British and Foreign School Society, was set up in 1808, but Lancaster quarrelled with the trustees and emigrated to America.

**Lancastrians** The three kings of England between 1399 and 1461 (Henry IV, Henry V, and Henry VI) were so named because they were descended from *John of Gaunt, duke of Lancaster. The term is also applied to their retainers, identifiable in many effigies by the wearing of the Lancastrian collar of SS, and to those who supported Henry VI in the Wars of the *Roses.

**Land Acts** is a collective term applied to Irish land reforms enacted between the end of the 19th and early 20th cents. This legislation was an attempt to defuse the increasingly assertive peasant nationalism which was threatening the stability of British rule in Ireland. The legislation generally had two aspects: first, the immediate improvement of the tenant's contractual position, and, second, the gradual encouragement of a peasant proprietorship. *Gladstone's Land Act of 1870 sought to give legal force to the *Ulster custom, and to give tenants enhanced security of tenure. Conservative legislation developed these Gladstonian precedents, although the principle of land purchase (a secondary feature of the Act of 1870) was much more prominent: the 'Ashbourne' Land Purchase Act (1885) provided £5 million in order to fund sales of property to occupying tenants. This measure provided a precedent for the much more lavishly funded and successful Wyndham Land Act (1903). The Acts effected a social revolution in Ireland long before the Anglo-Irish War of 1919–21.

**Landen, battle of** *See* NEERWINDEN.

**landscape gardening** The 18th-cent. English landscape garden or park was a major contribution to European art. It replaced the earlier fashion for highly formal gardens and presented an effect of natural, rolling grassland coming right up to the house, with distant clumps of trees.

The expansiveness of such landscapes undoubtedly encouraged a sense of power and superiority in the minds of their aristocratic owners, although they were also held to demonstrate the spirit of British liberty. Pioneers of the new taste in gardening, favoured by the poet Alexander *Pope, were Stephen Switzer (1682–1745), Charles *Bridgeman (fl. 1709–38), the latter credited with the invention of the 'ha-ha', and William *Kent (1685–1748). Such schemes often had complex, symbolic 'programmes' based on literary or political allusion, as at Stowe (Bucks.). The extensive gardens there were laid out mainly from 1713 by Viscount Cobham and his successor Earl Temple. Again, the scheme was initiated by Bridgeman and developed by Kent; a process of simplification and enlargement was begun by Lancelot *Brown, c.1749.

The final phase of the English landscape garden began late in the century, Picturesque theorists having rejected what they saw as the repetitive, over-formulaic approach of Brown. Thus Humphry *Repton (1752–1818) adopted a more varied approach, involving the effect of 'accidents' of nature and a more organic relationship between buildings and landscape.

**Landseer, Sir Edwin** (1802–73). English painter, sculptor, and engraver of animal subjects. Of precocious talent, Landseer first exhibited at the Royal Academy when he was 13, became ARA at 24, and an academician five years later. In 1865 he declined the presidency of the academy. Capitalizing on an upsurge of Scottish Romanticism, Landseer painted many Highland subjects, notably *The Stag at Bay* and *The Monarch of the Glen*. He also sculpted the lions at the foot of Nelson's Column in London.

**land tax** is an indirect tax levied on the value of land and often forms part of wider property taxation. Local government relied upon land taxes (in the form of rates) for much of their revenue from the mid-17th cent. until the 1980s. Throughout the whole of the 18th cent. the land tax was the main source of government revenue. Introduced in 1693 to pay for the French wars of William III's reign, it sufficed until 1799 when the cost of the Revolutionary War forced *Pitt to the even more drastic expedient of income tax. It

was an object of *Walpole's government in particular to avoid involvement in war so that the land tax could be kept down and the gentry content.

**Lanfranc** (c.1010–89), archbishop of Canterbury (1070–89), was an Italian from Pavia, who moved to northern France in the 1030s, and rose in *Normandy before 1066 to be William the Conqueror's chief ecclesiastical adviser. After 1070 his influence was widely pervasive throughout the Normanized church in England. He asserted Canterbury's primacy over York and, as a result, was able to preside over synods of the entire English church which gave a central direction to the efforts of the new Norman bishops. His close and harmonious co-operation with William the Conqueror assisted the Norman settlement of England.

**Lang, Cosmo Gordon** (1864–1945). Archbishop of Canterbury. Lang was a native of Scotland. After a short ministry at the university church in Oxford, he became (1896) vicar of Portsea. At the age of only 37 he was nominated as suffragan bishop of Stepney, and then promoted (1908) to be archbishop of York. Here he proved a contrast to the more conservative, cautious, and diplomatic Randall Davidson, his fellow-Scot who was archbishop of Canterbury. Lang succeeded Davidson at Canterbury in 1928, but his work as primate was overshadowed by criticism for his part in the *abdication crisis of 1936. He resigned in 1942.

**Langham, Simon** (d. 1376). Archbishop of Canterbury, chancellor, and curial cardinal. Born in Rutland, Langham entered the Benedictine monastery at Westminster (c.1335), and was successively prior and then abbot (1349), then treasurer of England (1360), bishop of Ely (1362), chancellor (1363), and archbishop (1366–8). After a brief spell as archbishop, Edward III forced him to resign, whereupon he accepted a cardinalate without royal permission, thus becoming a valued diplomat in the papal curia at Avignon (1368). When the Canterbury monks re-elected him archbishop (1374), the pope would not spare him.

**Langland, William** (1330s–90s). Author of *Piers Plowman*. Little is known about Langland beyond what can be surmised from his great allegorical poem: that he was a cleric in minor orders, married to one Kit, that he originated in the south-west, had connections with Malvern, and lived for a period in London.

**Langport, battle of,** 1645. After his defeat at *Naseby in June 1645, Charles had few resources left in England. He managed to raise another army, largely of Welsh recruits, and *Goring was still pursuing a rather desultory siege of Taunton. *Fairfax moved against him and at Langport, on 10 July, inflicted a severe defeat. News of the surrender of Carlisle and of *Montrose's defeat at *Philiphaugh completed a disastrous summer for the royalists.

**Langside, battle of,** 1568. On 2 May 1568 Mary, queen of Scots, imprisoned for nearly a year in Lochleven castle, made her escape and raised support. Her troops, under the earl of *Argyll, confronted a smaller force under the regent, *Moray, on 13 May near Glasgow. The issue was decided by a cavalry charge and Mary's supporters broke.

**Langton, Stephen** (c.1156–1228). Biblical scholar and ecclesiastical politician who helped in the making of *Magna Carta. Educated at Paris, Langton stayed on to teach theology there. Pope Innocent III made him a cardinal in 1206 and next year consecrated him as archbishop of Canterbury against the wishes of King John. John's refusal to allow Langton into England led to a quarrel between king and pope that lasted until John submitted in 1213. Once in England, Langton's concern for lawful government made him an important mediator between the king and his baronial enemies. During the minority of Henry III his moderating presence and co-operation with Hubert de *Burgh did much to keep the peace, until he withdrew from politics in the year before his death.

**Lansbury, George** (1859–1940). Christian socialist and pacifist. Lansbury came from working-class stock, and identified himself with socialist politics. In 1921 he and other members of Poplar Borough Council suffered imprisonment rather than authorize the payment, to the London County Council, of monies which they claimed impoverished London boroughs could not afford. Lansbury was excluded from the 1924 Labour govern-

ment, but in 1929 he became first commissioner of works. In 1931 he was elected Labour leader in the Commons. His obsession with pacifism led him to oppose sanctions against Italy following Mussolini's invasion of Abyssinia, and in a dramatic gesture he resigned the leadership at the 1935 Labour conference.

**Lansdowne, battle of,** 1643. This Civil War encounter was part of the early manœuvring for control of the west country, and fought between two old friends, Sir William *Waller and Sir Ralph *Hopton. Hopton's royalists attacked Waller on 5 July, trying to drive him from the Lansdowne ridge, 5 miles north of Bath. In hand-to-hand fighting, Hopton's men pushed their way up the wooded slopes and, during the night, Waller made an orderly retreat. There is a memorial on the field of battle to Sir Bevil Grenville, the Cornish leader killed in the attack.

**Lansdowne, William Petty, marquis of** See SHELBURNE, 2ND EARL OF.

**Lansdowne, Henry Petty-Fitzmaurice, 3rd marquis of** (1780–1863). Statesman. Lansdowne was a Whig grandee and for decades Bowood in Wiltshire and Lansdowne House in London were headquarters of Whiggism. His father, better known as *Shelburne, was prime minister 1782–3. Lansdowne succeeded as marquis in 1809, having been chancellor of the Exchequer in the Ministry of All the *Talents at the age of 26. He supported *Canning's brief ministry in 1827, and was home secretary in *Goderich's administration 1827–8. He served as lord president of the council in Whig ministries 1830–4, 1835–41, and 1846–52, and remained in the cabinet without portfolio 1852–8, as guardian of the Foxite tradition.

**Lansdowne, Henry Petty-Fitzmaurice, 5th marquis of** (1845–1927). A Liberal politician, Lansdowne resigned from *Gladstone's government over Irish land reform in 1880. After serving as governor-general of Canada and viceroy of India, he joined *Salisbury's 1895 cabinet. As foreign secretary from 1900, he did much to satisfy those who believed that Britain could no longer afford the so-called policy of *'splendid isolation'. In 1901 he resolved Britain's outstanding disputes with the USA. An alliance with Japan followed in 1902. An entente with France in 1904 resolved various imperial differences—notably over Morocco and Egypt. As leader of the Unionist peers from 1903 to 1916, he was much criticized for his conduct in opposition to *Asquith's Liberal government. Initially a strong supporter of the war against Germany, he wrote a highly controversial letter to the *Daily Telegraph* in November 1917 putting the case for a compromise peace.

**Largs, battle of,** 1263. Throughout the reign of Alexander III of Scotland there were disputes about the Western Isles, under the sovereignty of Norway. In the autumn of 1263 Haakon IV of Norway assembled a large fleet, raiding and raising revenue. Early in October, some of his ships were driven ashore near Largs. It was not clear who had the better of the fighting, but after Haakon had returned to Kirkwall, where he died, negotiations began for the Isles to be ceded to Scotland.

**Larkin, James** (1876–1947). Larkin was the nearest thing to a revolutionary leader that the modern trade union movement has thrown up. He wished, on *syndicalist lines, to use trade union power not merely to obtain concessions but as a battering ram to destroy capitalism. Born in Liverpool of Irish parents, he went to Ireland to organize the dock workers. His first task was to persuade protestants and catholics to work together. In 1908 he founded the Irish Transport and General Workers' Union. In the autumn of 1913 a strike on the Dublin trams led to a long confrontation with the employers and gave Larkin his finest hour. Threatened with arrest, he whipped off a false beard on the balcony of the Imperial hotel, O'Connell Street, to encourage his men. The strike dribbled away with little gained and there were other matters to preoccupy Ireland.

**Larkin, Philip** (1922–85). Poet, librarian, novelist, and, it has been said, 'unofficial laureate of post-1945 England'. The discovery of *Hardy's poems helped him find his own distinctive voice, first heard in *The Less Deceived* (1956). With the responsibility for a large university library at Hull, writing was pushed to the margins and only two more collections followed: *The Whitsun Weddings* (1964) and *High Windows* (1974). A reclusive figure, he alternated between self-deprecation and self-dislike, and the publication of

his letters in 1992 produced criticism of some of his attitudes and prejudices.

**Latimer, Hugh** (*c.*1485–1555). Bishop. One of the 'Oxford martyrs', Latimer was also one of the most celebrated and effective preachers of the Tudor church in the early years of the Reformation. The son of a Leicestershire yeoman, he was educated at Cambridge, ordained priest, and in 1522 licensed as one of the university's preachers. In 1535, after the break with Rome, he was appointed bishop of Worcester. As bishop he demonstrated the concern for the poor. He resigned his see in 1539 in protest against the Act of *Six Articles and was twice imprisoned in the 1540s. On Edward VI's accession he was released, resuming his career of energetic and fashionable preaching. On Mary I's accession he was summoned to London, declining opportunities to escape into exile. He confronted catholic spokesmen in the Oxford disputation of April 1554; after two examinations for heresy in 1555, he was burned at Oxford on 16 October 1555, alongside the former bishop of London, Nicholas *Ridley.

**latitudinarianism** was a reaction against the theological controversies and civil wars of the 17th cent., placing little emphasis on precise points of doctrine and arguing for toleration. High-church opponents retorted that tolerance could slide into deism, as it did with *Locke, or into downright indifference, their charge against *Hoadly.

**Laud, William** (1573–1645). Archbishop of Canterbury. Laud has always been a controversial character. Born at Reading, a graduate of St John's College, Oxford (1594), he was successively chaplain to the earl of Devonshire (1603), president of St John's (1611–21), dean of Gloucester (1616), bishop of St Davids (1621–6), Bath and Wells (1626–8), and London (1628–33), and archbishop (1633–45). Historians have regarded his use of the Court of *High Commission and especially his supposed attempt to enforce the English Prayer Book on Scotland (1637) as the watershed of the reign. Impeached by the *Long Parliament (December 1640), committed to the Tower (1641), and tried (1644), Laud was beheaded on 10 January 1645. Past historians have evaluated him either as a secret papist who corrupted the church or as the martyr of true Anglicanism.

Modern research, however, based on his own writings reveals a different picture; Laud aimed not to provoke, but to heal, controversy. Not a theologian, he was unconcerned by doctrinal minutiae; far from encouraging popery his one known theological work is a stout defence of the church against catholicism. The Scottish Prayer Book was not the work of Laud, but of the Scottish bishops, backed by Charles.

**Laudabiliter,** *c.*1155–60. The authenticity of this papal bull, granted by Adrian IV and recognizing Henry II as lord of Ireland, has been much debated. The balance of scholarly opinion finds in its favour, but there is, in any case, little doubt that the papacy supported Henry's pretensions. Alexander III, Adrian's successor, praised Henry's attempt to subjugate 'this barbarous and uncouth race which is ignorant of divine law'.

**Lauder, Sir Harry** (1870–1950). Entertainer. A genial if thrifty Lowland Scot, Lauder progressed from amateur concerts to small music-halls before appearing at Birkenhead as an Irish comedian. Risking Scottish songs in London (1900), he soon became one of vaudeville's greatest box-office attractions, tirelessly entertaining the troops in both world wars (earning a knighthood, 1919). 'The Laird of the Halls' drew on traditional airs to produce simple attractive lilts ('I love a lassie'), and could carry his audience easily from trifles to more serious ballads.

**Lauderdale, John Maitland, 2nd earl of** [S] (1616–82). Born to a Lowland territorial base, Lauderdale subscribed to the Scottish National *Covenant in 1638. His record through the Civil War—he was prominent in negotiating the *'Engagement' with Charles I in December 1647 and in persuading Charles II to go to Scotland in 1650—demonstrated Lauderdale's Scottish royalism; and he suffered imprisonment in England and severe material loss during the Republic. His strangely enduring hold upon Charles II ensured a dominant role in Scottish government throughout the 1660s and 1670s, earning him the fear and detestation of compatriots.

**Lauffeld, battle of,** 1747. After subduing the Jacobites in 1746, William, duke of *Cumberland, was placed in charge of an allied army in the Low Countries, commanding

English, Hanoverian, Dutch, and Austrian troops. On 2 July 1747 he was attacked at Lauffeld, just west of Maastricht, by a large French army under Marshal de Saxe. After heavy fighting, Cumberland was forced to retreat. Peace negotiations to conclude the War of the *Austrian Succession began soon afterwards.

**Laurentius (Lawrence)** (d. 619). Second archbishop of Canterbury. Named Lawrence 'the priest', he landed in Kent with *Augustine in 597. At Augustine's request he returned to Rome (601) to fetch a new body of missionaries and the pallium, the archiepiscopal insignia, for Augustine. Before his death Augustine consecrated him as his successor (*c.*604). When *Æthelbert of Kent died (616), there was likelihood of reversion to paganism under Eadbald, but, unlike Mellitus and Justus, Laurentius stayed and converted him.

**Lausanne conference,** November 1922–July 1923. The conference was held to negotiate a treaty with Turkey to replace the unratified and disputed treaty of Sèvres (1920) imposed following the First World War. Turkey renounced all claims to territories of the former Ottoman empire occupied by non-Turks but recovered eastern Thrace in Europe.

**Law, Andrew Bonar** (1858–1923). Prime minister. Described on his death as the 'Unknown Prime Minister', Bonar Law was a modest and melancholy figure, who appeared content to remain as second in command to *Lloyd George from 1916 to 1921.

Law's Ulster-Scottish parentage and stern presbyterian upbringing reinforced his rather dour personality. He joined the family ironmasters' business in Glasgow and worked for the Clydesdale Bank. This meant that as an MP from 1900 onwards he possessed—unusually—a personal understanding of business. His excellent memory and aggressive style soon made him a useful orator at a time when tariff reform was becoming central to the party's policy.

But Law did not appear to be heading for the top until, after *Balfour's enforced resignation in 1911, the Tory Party split evenly between Walter *Long and Austen *Chamberlain. Energetically promoted by Max Aitken (*Beaverbrook), Law emerged as a compromise candidate. However, he had almost no experience of government, enjoyed few powers of patronage, and led a party subject to bitter divisions over tariffs. As a result he encouraged his own extremists to pursue their attack on *Irish Home Rule in the belief that this was best calculated to restore party unity.

While the outbreak of war in August 1914 resolved one dilemma, it created another. In May 1915 he reached a private agreement with Asquith to join a coalition. Remarkably Law failed to insist on a major position for himself and accepted the Colonial Office. When Asquith resigned in December 1916, Law had an opportunity to seize the premiership. Instead he served under Lloyd George as chancellor and member of the war cabinet. A remarkable period of co-operation ensued, and as leader of the House he played a vital role in keeping the coalition majority intact.

In 1918 Law judged that the Conservatives' best interests lay in keeping the coalition in being and fighting the election under Lloyd George's leadership. Eventually ill-health forced him to retire in March 1921. However, by this time many Conservatives were restless, and at a meeting in October 1922 they voted to sever relations with Lloyd George. Law indicated his willingness to return as party leader. As a result he succeeded at last to the premiership and won an immediate general election. Though obliged by poor health to withdraw after a few months, he had the satisfaction of having guided his party through a dangerous period, detaching it from Lloyd George before it suffered serious damage.

**Law, Edward, 1st Baron Ellenborough** (1750-1818). Lawyer. Law was called to the bar in 1780 and practised successfully on the northern circuit. He was leading defence counsel in the impeachment of Warren *Hastings and through his success acquired a lucrative London practice. He accepted office as attorney-general under *Addington and entered Parliament in 1801, becoming lord chief justice of Common Pleas a year later. He spoke forcefully in the Lords and in 1806 he was brought into the cabinet to strengthen Addington's numbers. He was 'a remorseless cross-examiner', too severe and intolerant to be popular, but an entertaining table companion.

**Law, Edward, 1st earl of Ellenborough** (1790-1871). Law succeeded his father in 1818. Elected to Parliament in 1813 as a Tory, he had a long and varied political career. He held the privy seal in *Wellington's government 1828-9; was president of the Board of Control for India 1828-30, and on three later occasions for short periods; governor-general of India 1841-4; and 1st lord of the Admiralty in 1846. His term of office as governor-general was dominated by the first *China War, the winding-up of the ill-fated *Afghan campaign, and the annexation of Sind.

**Law, John** (1671-1729). Scottish financial genius, banker, and gambler. In 1716 the French regent gave him permission to set up his own bank in France, which was suffering from Louis XIV's wars and deeply in debt. In 1719 his Mississippi Company gained the monopoly of all French overseas trade. Its stock was placed on the market, demand was high, speculators made fortunes. In the mean time Law had become director-general of the Banque Royale (previously his Banque Générale) and issued paper notes to match the share issues of the company. Holders of paper money began exchanging it for coin, of which there was insufficient to redeem all paper; a decree to halve the notes' value led to loss of confidence, panic, and crash (1720). Law fled and spent the remaining years of his life in England and Italy.

**Law, William** (1686-1761). Law, one of the most influential religious writers of his age, came from a modest family at King's Cliffe, near Stamford, and was elected to a fellowship at Emmanuel College, Cambridge. But in 1714 he refused to take the oaths of loyalty to George I and was deprived of his fellowship. His most famous work, *A Serious Call to a Devout and Holy Life* (1728), preached a quiet and meditative Christianity, restrained, humble, and charitable. *Johnson spoke of the great effect it had upon him as a student and *Wesley and *Whitefield were also much influenced. In 1732 he published *The Case of Reason*, arguing faith against deistical scepticism. From 1740 he established at King's Cliffe a devout household, including the widow of Archibald Hutcheson, MP, and Gibbon's aunt Hester.

**lawn tennis** evolved from real (royal) tennis in the 1870s. Among the pioneers was Major Walter Wingfield who introduced Christmas guests in 1873 to Sphairistike, which contained the ingredients of tennis. The MCC tried to draw up standard rules in 1875 and championships were first staged at Wimbledon in 1877, the crowd at the final numbering 200. The scoring system, of crucial importance, probably derived from clock quarters.

**Lawrence, D. H.** (1885–1930). Nottinghamshire miner's son destined for notoriety as the author of *Lady Chatterley's Lover* (1928). His autobiographical *Sons and Lovers* (1913) sketches the background from which he escaped, first to London and then the continent. With him went Frieda von Richthofen, their early struggles recorded in his poem sequence *Look! We Have Come Through!* (1917). The frankness of his approach led to prosecution of *The Rainbow* (1915). *Women in Love* (1920) rivals Joyce's *Ulysses* as the greatest novel of the century.

**Lawrence, Sir Henry** (1806–57). Soldier. Henry Lawrence was the elder brother of John *Lawrence, later viceroy of India. Commissioned in 1822 in the Bengal artillery, he took part in the expedition to Kabul in 1842 after the disastrous retreat, and fought in the *Sikh War of 1846. From 1849 he administered the Punjab but resigned in 1853 after a disagreement with his brother John. He was in *Lucknow when the Indian mutiny broke out in May 1857. In June Lucknow fell to the mutineers and Lawrence was forced back to the residency. There he was struck by shellfire and died after two days.

**Lawrence, John Laird Mair, 1st Baron** (1811–79). Lawrence was born in Yorkshire, educated at Haileybury School, and joined the East India Company service in 1830. He achieved celebrity during and after the *Sikh wars (1845–6 and 1848–9). As the first commissioner of Jullundur district, he laid the foundations of 'the Punjab school' of administration which identified closely with the interests of the peasantry and sought to preserve traditional forms of society and law. He was viceroy of India from 1864 to 1869, and was given his barony on leaving office.

**Lawrence, Sir Thomas** (1769–1830). Painter. Lawrence was born in Bristol, the son of an innkeeper, and almost completely self-taught. In 1791 he was elected ARA, made a full academician three years later, and president in 1820. A portrait of Queen Charlotte, painted in 1790, led to enormous success and his appointment as painter to the king on the death of *Reynolds in 1792. Fellow-artist Benjamin *Haydon, less successful, said of him, 'Lawrence . . . was suited to the age, and the age to him. He flattered its vanities, pampered its weaknesses, and met its meretricious taste.'

**Lawrence, T. E.** ('Lawrence of Arabia') (1888–1935). Born in north Wales, educated at Oxford High School and Jesus College, Oxford, Lawrence's interest in medieval military architecture led to a fellowship to excavate in the Middle East. In 1914 his rare expertise in Arab affairs resulted in intelligence work in Egypt. He was not the only British officer involved in the Arab rebellion, but his guerrilla attacks, particularly on communications, distracted Turkish troops remarkably effectively. Demobilized as a colonel, he was appointed adviser on Arab affairs to *Churchill in the Colonial Office (1921), and worked on his war memoir *Seven Pillars of Wisdom*. Lawrence then enlisted as an RAF aircraftsman, changing his name to Ross, then Shaw by deed-poll (1927). In 1935 he was killed in a motorcycling accident. His RAF experiences were published in 1955 as *The Mint*.

**lead-mining** took place in Britain before the Roman invasion and archaeological remains of mining occur in the Mendip Hills in Somerset, Devon, Cornwall, the Pennines, and Wales. Demand for lead grew during the Roman occupation when the metal was used for various purposes including making water-pipes. Lead-mining continued after the Romans left. Lead was used for many purposes such as roofing churches and castles, fixing decorative glass in windows, and in the manufacture of pewterware and paint.

Miners secured separate special jurisdictions and regulated their mining activities and social life. These legal privileges remained in being until most of them were superseded by the formation of commercial mining companies during the 16th cent. or later. These organizations became necessary to pay for the equipment needed for extracting ores at greater depths. But mining in Britain became less worthwhile once cheaper supplies of lead from overseas became available and British mining dwindled rapidly in importance after 1850.

**League of Armed Neutrality** The league was founded in 1780 during the American War of Independence to resist Britain's blockade of the rebels. The founding members, Sweden, Denmark, and Russia, were joined by the Dutch, the Holy Roman empire, Prussia, and Portugal. At issue was the right to search neutral vessels and the league retorted by arming convoys. A second league was formed in 1800 during the Napoleonic War and included Denmark, Sweden, Russia, and Prussia. The British response was the attack upon the Danish fleet at Copenhagen by Lord *Nelson.

**League of Nations** The League of Nations was formally established on 10 January 1920 with a permanent headquarters at Geneva. It was very much the brainchild of President Woodrow Wilson. As a peacekeeping body, the League suffered from two handicaps which proved insuperable. First, some of the most important world powers were not members: Germany was excluded until 1926, the Bolshevik government in Russia denounced it as a capitalist club and did not join until 1934; worst of all, Wilson failed to persuade the US Senate to ratify the treaty and the most powerful nation of the world was therefore absent. Secondly, the League had no armed force of its own and member states were reluctant to provide troops: it was therefore obliged to rely upon economic sanctions, which were difficult to enforce and slow to take effect.

The League had some modest successes in its early days. Its specialized agencies did much to encourage international co-operation against slavery, drugs, and disease, and the Permanent Court of International Justice, set up by the League in 1920, resolved a number of minor disputes. In December 1925 at *Locarno, Britain, France, Germany, Belgium, and Italy reaffirmed their commitment to peace, a prelude to Germany's entry into the League in 1926.

The League's first major test came in 1931 when the Japanese invaded Manchuria. The

League retorted with a condemnation of Japan's violation of the covenant, and the Japanese promptly withdrew from the League in March 1933. A second challenge came in October 1935, when Mussolini's Italy invaded Ethiopia. This time the League did attempt to enforce economic sanctions, though the invasion was completed before sanctions could bite. But, in any case, the rise of Nazi Germany presented a challenge on a far larger scale. Hitler had always made clear his contempt for the League of Nations as a talking shop and a tool for the Versailles victors. He lost no time in withdrawing Germany. The remilitarization of the Rhineland, the anschluss with Austria, the dismemberment of Czechoslovakia, and the invasion of Poland followed in quick succession, with the League helpless. The council met only once after the outbreak of the Second World War, on 8 April 1946 when it handed over its powers to the new *United Nations.

**Lear, Edward** (1812–88). Artist. Commencing his career as an illustrator for others, particularly of birds, he depicted the earl of Derby's private menagerie at Knowsley in 1832–7, when he entertained his patron's grandchildren with humorous verses, tales, and sketches. These subsequently developed into the engaging books of nonsense for which he is today chiefly remembered. Travelling widely in Mediterranean countries, indefatigable and productive, he earned a living as a topographical landscape painter in both water-colour and oils.

**Leeds** The earliest mention of Leeds is in Bede's *Ecclesiastical History* as the region of Loidis in the 7th cent. It developed with the cloth trade from the 14th cent. onwards, less as a manufacturing centre than as a market for the surrounding villages. Charles I gave Leeds a charter in 1626 and its assessment for ship money in the 1630s suggests a town of importance—£200 as against £520 for York and £140 for Hull. In 1698 Celia Fiennes found Leeds 'esteemed an excellent town of its bigness in the count(r)y, its manufactures in the woollen cloth, the Yorkshire cloth in which they are all employed, and are esteemed very rich and very proud'. Communications were improved by the opening of the Leeds and Liverpool canal, in stages, between 1770 and 1816. The first railway, in a complex network, was the Leeds to Selby line in 1834, followed by lines to Derby (1840), Manchester (1841), and Thirsk (1849). By 1801 Leeds was the fifth largest provincial town with a population of 53,000. In the 20th cent., as the cloth trade moved to *Bradford, Leeds diversified, with engineering, chemicals, banking, and services becoming important. The construction of the M1 and M62 motorways in the 1970s preserved its importance as a great commercial centre, the crossroads of the north–south and east–west highways.

**Leeds, Francis Godolphin Osborne, 5th duke of** (1751–99). Leeds was known as Lord Carmarthen till 1790, but sat in the Lords as Baron Osborne from 1776. A supporter of Lord *North, he shifted to opposition and was punished, in 1780, with dismissal from his lord-lieutenancy (Yorkshire, East Riding). Reinstated in 1782, he supported *Shelburne after Charles *Fox's resignation. Shortage of available talent led to his appointment as foreign secretary under William *Pitt in December 1783. An active, but never illustrious, foreign secretary, Leeds resigned in April 1791, when Pitt refused to back his aggressive policy towards Russia.

**Leeward Islands** The Leeward Islands in the Caribbean form part of the Lesser Antilles, lying to the east of the Dominican republic. They include the *Virgin Islands, *St Kitts and Nevis, *Antigua and Barbuda, *Montserrat, and Guadeloupe.

**legions, Roman** *See* ROMAN LEGIONS.

**Le Goulet, peace of,** 1200. On Richard I's death in 1199 a struggle over the succession broke out between King John and his nephew *Arthur of Brittany. Philip II 'Augustus' of France lent Arthur support and invaded Normandy and Maine, but he was obliged to consider peace. John also needed breathing space to establish himself securely. The two met at Le Goulet (southern Normandy) and sealed a treaty (22 May 1200). Philip recognized John as Richard's successor, receiving his homage, and abandoned Arthur. But John had to pay a heavy price, consenting to pay the enormous sum of 20,000 marks as relief (succession duty) to Philip as his overlord.

**Leicester** was the Romano-British *civitas*-capital of Ratae Corieltavorum (formerly Coritanorum). In the reign of *Hadrian a forum/basilica complex was constructed, and slightly later a set of public baths in the *insula* (block) to the east of the forum. Relatively little is known of the development of private buildings in the town, but in the *insula* north of the forum was a major 2nd-cent. private house with exceptional wall-paintings. Next a Mercian town, Leicester became one of the Danish five boroughs until captured by the English in 918. Under the Normans it was a seigneurial town, its lords the earls of Leicester based in the castle. Lordship then passed to the earls and dukes of Lancaster, and in 1399 to the crown: the end of the castle as a ducal residence was a blow to Leicester's prosperity. The town revived through hosiery from the 17th cent. and later through footwear; by 1901 it was the fifteenth largest English town, a city from 1919 and a diocesan see from 1926.

**Leicester, diocese of** The modern see, created out of the *Peterborough diocese in 1926, comprises Leicestershire without Rutland. The see's existence began in 737, when it was one of six, planned by *Offa for his projected archbishopric of *Lichfield. But when the 9th-cent. Danish invasions made Leicester untenable, the diocese was moved to *Dorchester (*c.*870).

**Leicester, Robert Dudley, 1st earl of** (*c.*1532–88). Son of John Dudley, duke of *Northumberland, Dudley became one of Elizabeth I's most prominent courtiers. Until his death in 1588, he was master of the queen's horse and a privy counsellor. He was appointed general of the English forces in the Netherlands in 1585, where his conduct angered Elizabeth greatly.

Leicester was a controversial figure. He was involved in his father's plan to crown Lady Jane *Grey and was sentenced to death in January 1554, but pardoned in October of that year. Any hopes he might have had of marrying Elizabeth were destroyed by the suspicious manner of the death of his first wife, Amy Robsart, in 1560. Later there were plans for a marriage to Mary, queen of Scots, and he was created earl in 1564 to make him a more acceptable husband. In the end, his second wife was Lettice Knollys, widow of the 1st earl of Essex (1578). He died in September 1588 soon after taking charge of the army at Tilbury against the Spanish Armada.

## Leicester House opposition

Leicester House, built in the 1630s, was leased in 1718 by George, prince of Wales, and became a focus of opposition to his father's ministers. Twenty-five years later, his own son *Frederick, prince of Wales, set up in opposition there and, after his death, the tradition was continued by his widow Princess Augusta, and his son, the future George III. Though Leicester House politics was often factious, it was free from the taint of Jacobitism and helped make the concept of opposition acceptable.

## Leicestershire

was one of the most regularly shaped shires, with Leicester itself almost exactly in the middle, on the river Soar. The western boundary with Warwickshire ran along the line of *Watling Street, the north-west between Derbyshire and Nottinghamshire was the angle formed by the Soar joining the Trent, and the southern border with Northamptonshire followed the rivers Avon and Welland.

Leicester was not far from the intersection of two great Roman roads, Watling Street and the *Fosse Way. It became an important town of some 2,000–3,000 people, Ratae Corieltavorum, the tribal capital of the *Coritani. In the course of the 6th cent. the area was occupied by Anglo-Saxon settlers and became part of the kingdom of Mercia in the 7th cent., under the episcopal jurisdiction of Lichfield. Leicester became one of the five boroughs when the Danes overran the region in the late 9th cent., and though it was reconquered by *Æthelfleda on behalf of Mercia in 918, Danish influence remained substantial. The shire was divided into wapentakes rather than hundreds, and many of the place-names—Ingarsby, Scraptoft, and Barkby Thorpe—are of Scandinavian origin.

Throughout the medieval period, Leicester remained an important town, granted a charter during John's reign. The de *Montfort family in the 13th cent. took its earldom from the shire. *Wyclif, the morning star of the Reformation, was vicar of Lutterworth in the later 14th cent. Parliament met at Leicester in 1414 and 1426 and it was to Leicester that Richard III summoned his troops in August 1485 before marching out to fight his last battle at Bosworth.

The north-west of the shire around Charnwood Forest was still heavily wooded, but the open country to the east of the Soar was ideal for rearing sheep. Local wool became the basis of a flourishing textile industry, and though the county was rather thinly populated, Loughborough, Melton Mowbray, Market Harborough, Hinckley, and Ashby de la Zouch developed as small market towns. *Camden, in Elizabeth's reign, described Leicestershire as 'champain country, rich in corn and grain'.

*Defoe visited the shire in the 1720s and thought the sheep the best in England for wool, and commented that 'the whole county seems to be taken up in country business'. But the character of parts of the county began to change in the later 18th cent. Attempts to overcome the liability that the main river, the Soar, was not navigable had been made since the early 17th cent. But improvements in turnpike roads, canals, and then railways fastened the shire into a national network of communications. The dramatic reduction in the cost of conveying coal led to the opening of a number of pits in the north-west.

The growth of industry and population in this period was extraordinary. The domestic system of textiles production gave way rapidly to a factory system. Leicester itself, some 17,000 in 1801, was 60,000 by 1861, and 211,000 by 1901: it continues to dominate the shire, with nearly half the population in 1951. Coalville was an almost overnight growth. In 1801 it was not in existence. The opening of the Whitwick colliery in 1824 led to 1,200 people by 1846, 15,000 by 1901, and 25,000 by 1951. Hinckley and Loughborough also grew rapidly. By the local government reorganization of 1972 Leicestershire took over the neighbouring county of Rutland, but it was restored in 1995.

## Leighton, Frederic

(1830–96). Painter. Born in Scarborough, the son of a doctor, Leighton studied art in Frankfurt, Rome, and Paris. Talented and personable, he soon had several wealthy patrons. Leighton was elected ARA in 1864 and made president in 1878. Among his best paintings are a portrait of Sir Richard *Burton (1875) and *The Garden of the Hesperides* (1892). He suffered increasingly from poor health and was given a barony on his death-bed: this unique peerage lasted only one day.

**Leinster,** which takes its name from a people known as the Laigin, was, in the early medieval period, dominated by two dynasties, the Uí Dúnlainge and the Uí Chennselaig. By the time of the Anglo-Norman invasion the latter, who had come to exercise overlordship of the Viking town of *Dublin, were dominant, and were led by *Dermot MacMurrough, who initiated the invasion in an effort to recover his kingship. Dermot's daughter married the leader of the invaders, Strongbow (*Pembroke), who succeeded to Leinster after him, making it the heartland of the new Anglo-Norman colony in Ireland, with Dublin as its capital.

**Leland, John** (c.1506–52). Leland, a distinguished antiquarian, was born in London, and educated at St Paul's and at Christ's College, Cambridge. He took holy orders, served the duke of Norfolk, and was appointed royal librarian by Henry VIII. In 1533 he was made king's antiquary and spent much of the next ten years on a remarkable tour of cathedrals and churches. He was given considerable encouragement, but became insane before his collections could appear in print. His notes were scattered but were used by John Stow in his work on London and by William *Camden in his *Britannia* (1586). The *Itinerary* was not published until 1710, when Thomas Hearne produced an edition at Oxford.

**Lely, Peter** (1618–80). Portrait painter. Born Pieter van der Faes, 'Lely' was a nickname borrowed from his family home at The Hague. He seems to have come to England in the early 1640s as an aspiring landscape artist. His natural enterprise procured him patronage from the Commonwealth government, and by the time of Charles II's restoration Lely enjoyed high repute as a portraitist. Within two years he had become naturalized and in receipt of a royal pension.

**Lennox, Esmé Stewart, 1st duke of** [S] (1542–83). Lennox was a comet who blazed across the Scottish sky and was gone. His father was a brother of Matthew Stewart, earl of *Lennox and regent 1570–1. He held the seigniory of Aubigny in France,

to which his son succeeded in 1567. In 1579 Lennox arrived in Scotland, an exotic visitor from the court of France, and captivated the 13-year-old James VI. He was created earl of Lennox, and in 1581 was promoted to duke. Meanwhile he had announced his conversion to protestantism and brought down the regent, *Morton. In 1582 James was seized by *Gowrie and other lords in the *Ruthven raid and forced to order Lennox to leave the kingdom. He died shortly afterwards.

**Lennox, Margaret Stewart, countess of** (1515–78). The daughter of Lady *Margaret Tudor by her second husband Archibald, earl of *Angus, Lady Margaret was niece to Henry VIII. If Elizabeth was bastardized, the countess was near the throne. In 1544, at St James's, Westminster, she married Matthew, earl of *Lennox, a great-grandson of James II of Scotland. During Mary's reign, as a catholic, the countess was in high favour and given precedence over Elizabeth. In 1565, when her son married Mary, queen of Scots, she was sent to the Tower. Lady Lennox played for high stakes and, in the shape of her grandson James VI and I, gained a posthumous victory.

**Lennox, Matthew Stewart, 13th earl of** [S] (1516–71). The great-grandmother of Lennox was a daughter of James II of Scotland. Lennox spent some years in France and was hostile to the English interest until Henry VIII gave him his niece Lady Margaret Douglas in marriage in 1544. The double royal connection made him a person of some consequence. During Mary's reign, he and his wife, both catholics, were in high favour, but Elizabeth regarded them with suspicion. He was confined to the Tower in 1562 and was again in disgrace after 1565 when his son Lord *Darnley married Mary, queen of Scots. Elizabeth allowed him to return to Scotland and in 1570 had him elected regent for his grandson, but took the precaution of keeping the countess in England. Civil war in Scotland ensued and in 1571 he was stabbed in Edinburgh by a partisan of Mary.

**Leofric, earl of Mercia** (d. 1057). Leofric rose to power in the reign of *Cnut, as one of three great earls involved in governing England. In 1051, when Godwine defied Edward the Confessor, Leofric and Siward supported the king with matching strength. A number of foundations were enriched by his gifts, not least the monastery and church he built with his famous wife Godgifu (*Godiva).

**Leslie, Alexander** (*c.*1580–1661). Leslie was a good professional soldier, who served for many years in the Swedish army and fought alongside Gustav Adolf at Lützen in 1632. When the Scottish presbyterians began armed resistance in 1639, Leslie was placed in command of the covenanting army. In 1640 he brushed aside royalist resistance at *Newburn and occupied Newcastle. He remained at the head of the Scottish forces in alliance with the English Parliament and fought at *Marston Moor. When Charles II, after the execution of his father, reached an understanding with the Scottish presbyterians, Leslie once more commanded their forces, but was badly beaten by *Cromwell at *Dunbar in 1650.

**Leslie, David** (*c.*1600–82). Like his namesake Alexander *Leslie, David Leslie also fought alongside Gustav Adolf of Sweden. He returned to Scotland in 1640 and commanded the Scottish cavalry at *Marston Moor in 1644. He was then recalled to Scotland to deal with *Montrose, whom he defeated at *Philiphaugh in September 1645. When Charles II accepted the covenant in 1650, David Leslie had effective control, under Alexander Leslie, of the Scottish forces resisting *Cromwell, but they were heavily defeated at *Dunbar. He commanded the royalist advance into England, was beaten at *Worcester, and subsequently captured. He remained a prisoner until the Restoration, when he was created Lord Newark [S].

**Lesotho, kingdom of** Former British crown colony of Basutoland. Threatened by the Boers of the *Orange Free State, Mshweshwe, the ruler of the Basuto, sought British protection in 1843 and in 1869 agreed to the annexation of his country. Basutoland was administered by its traditional rulers under British supervision until it became independent in 1965.

**Levant Company** The company, granted a charter by Elizabeth in 1581, had the sole right to trade with the Ottoman empire. A new charter in 1592 increased the number of traders and added Venice to its sphere. It was commonly known as the Turkey Company.

**Levellers** A popular democratic movement which emerged fully in 1647, though its leading pamphleteers, John *Lilburne, Richard Overton, and William Walwyn, had campaigned earlier for specific rights and reforms. The Levellers' basic principle was that all men and women are born equal, and are rightfully subject to no authority except by agreement and consent. By 1647 the *New Model Army was defying Parliament's threat to disband it, so the Levellers set about indoctrinating its newly elected agitators. They persuaded six cavalry regiments to bring a revolutionary '*Agreement of the People' before the army's general council in the famous *Putney debates. Implying the abolition of monarchy and the House of Lords, the agreement proposed that biennial, popularly elected parliaments should wield supreme authority. They suspended their opposition during the second civil war, but when the *Commonwealth was established their leaders (Walwyn excepted) denounced it virulently in *Englands New Chains Discovered*. They also raised a new and more serious mutiny in the army but after its suppression they lost coherence as an organized movement.

**Leviathan** (1651) was the masterpiece on political philosophy written by Thomas *Hobbes to justify absolute sovereignty. Hobbes held that the greatest threat to human security was the anarchy of the 'State of Nature', and that to avoid that horrific condition, where life was 'solitary, poor, nasty, brutish, and short', men must contract to establish a sovereign power with sufficient authority to enforce laws and maintain order.

**Lewes, battle of,** 1264. In the early hours of 14 May 1264, before sunrise, the army of Simon de *Montfort advanced on Lewes (Sussex), where Henry III's forces lay. Although outnumbered, Montfort won a complete victory. Montfort's protectorate, that lasted until his death at Evesham (1265), was established.

**Lewis, C. S.** (1898–1963). Lewis was a fellow of Magdalen College, Oxford, from 1925 to 1954, and then took the chair of medieval and Renaissance English at Cambridge until a few months before his death. His most significant scholarly book was *English Literature in the Sixteenth Century* (1954). His influence with the wider public came from broadcasts during the war, from his Christian apologetics *The Problem of Pain* (1940) and *The Screwtape Letters* (1942), and from his heavily allegorical and highly successful Narnia books for children, beginning with *The Lion, the Witch and the Wardrobe* (1950).

**Lexington, battle of,** 1775. The first serious encounter in the American conflict occurred when General Gage dispatched on 18 April a force of 700 men from Boston to Concord, some 20 miles, to recover arms and ammunition. By the time they reached Concord to conduct a search, the Americans were in arms and heavy fighting took place. On the retreat back to Lexington, the British forces were harassed by snipers, but were met in the town by a sizeable relief party under Lord Algernon Percy.

**Libel Act,** 1792. Prior to 1792 the jury in a libel case only had power to determine the facts of publication and was not permitted to decide whether the matter in question was libellous—that decision being reserved to the judge. In May 1791 Charles *Fox argued that civil liberty would be safeguarded by extending the jury's competence to the whole question of libel. The measure was not opposed by the prime minister, William *Pitt, and duly became law the following year.

**Liberal Democrats** British political party founded in 1988 from the merging of the *Social Democratic Party (SDP) and *Liberal Party, following the disappointing performance of the two parties' alliance at the 1987 general election. The increasing popularity of party leader Paddy *Ashdown enabled the Liberal Democrats to recoup much of the support that had been lost. The party, with a strong commitment to Europe, won 46 seats at the general election of 1997, 52 in 2001, and 62 in 2005. The leadership passed in turn to Charles *Kennedy, then to Sir Menzies Campbell, and in 2007 to Nick Clegg.

**Liberal Imperialists** were a faction of the Liberal Party around 1900, who disapproved of their leaders' lukewarm line over the *Boer War. The leaders of the 'Lib Imps' were *Rosebery, *Grey, and *Haldane.

**Liberal League** A political organization within the Liberal Party, founded in February 1902 with Lord *Rosebery as president and including H. H. *Asquith and Sir Edward *Grey among its vice-presidents. It succeeded in retaining within the Liberal Party some who considered leaving it over the party's cautious attitude to the Boer War. It was well represented in the Liberal government of 1905 (though not by its president).

**Liberal Party** Before 1868 the Liberal Party had been an uneasy coalition of Whigs and radicals. The broadening of the suffrage in the boroughs in the *Reform Act of 1867 strengthened the radicals and the *Gladstone government of 1868–74 ranks as one of the great reforming administrations of modern times. Whig disquiet grew, especially during the second Gladstone government of 1880–5. There was a slow drift of Whigs to the Conservatives but Gladstone's *Home Rule Bill of 1886 was the catalyst for the realignment of parties which had long been prophesied. Ninety-three Liberal MPs voted against its second reading in June 1886. Despite the loss of Chamberlain and his closest colleagues, the effect of the schism was to radicalize the Liberal Party: it also fractionalized it.

More important than the Whig secession was the change in the character of radicalism. Until 1868 radicalism was an individualist creed. The mid-century Liberal slogan —'Peace, Retrenchment and Reform'— summed up radical aspirations. The mid-century radicals were conspicuous champions of *laissez-faire*. The radical programme was negative in character. It called for the disestablishment of the Church of England and for the redress of other nonconformist grievances. It sought to limit the power of government and demanded that government should not intervene in economic and social affairs.

After 1868 there was a gradual but major change in the nature of radicalism. Radicals began to address the problems of industrial society. Thus, Joseph Chamberlain as mayor of Birmingham embarked on a major programme of social reform in that city.

In the 1890s a new cleavage developed. After Gladstone gave up the leadership, some of the most prominent Liberals, such as *Rosebery, his successor as prime minister, demanded a reorientation of party attitudes. The Liberal Party must show that it could be trusted with the administration of a great empire. *Liberal Imperialism ranged itself against Little Englandism. *Asquith, *Grey, and *Haldane, all to hold high office in Liberal governments after 1906, were among the leaders of the new organization, the *Liberal League. The onset of the *Boer War dramatized and made more acute the division of the party.

In the end, the mistakes of the Unionists restored the unity of the Liberal Party. The *Education Act of 1902 upset the religious balance achieved by the Liberal Education Act of 1870. Nonconformists were outraged and many of those who had deserted the party in 1886 came back. More important, in 1903, Chamberlain, now one of the leading figures in the Unionist government, repudiated free trade, an article of faith to both parties for over 50 years. The Education Act and tariff reform healed the rift in the Liberal Party which, in 1906, won a landslide victory.

Liberal hegemony lasted until 1915. During those nine years the party largely completed the unfinished agenda of Victorian radicalism, restricting the powers of the Lords, introducing *Irish Home Rule, and disestablishing the Church of England in Wales. At the same time it looked forward, with the introduction of old-age pensions in 1908, the Trade Boards Act of 1909, and the National Insurance Act of 1911, to the collectivist agenda of the 20th cent.

There were two general elections in 1910, both bound up with the problem of the House of Lords. The Liberals, now led by Asquith, lost their overall majority and their continuance in office depended on the recently founded *Labour Party and on the Irish nationalists. The next few years were a period of bitter political conflict over Irish Home Rule and a dangerous division between the two main parties was averted only by the outbreak of the First World War in 1914. A coalition government under Asquith was formed in 1915; dissatisfaction with Asquith's leadership led to the formation of a new coalition with Asquith's rival, *Lloyd George, as premier. Asquith, still party leader, went into opposition, with the Conservatives and a section of the Liberals following Lloyd George. At the general election at the end of the war in 1918, Lloyd

George and his Liberals allied with the Conservatives against Asquith's independent Liberals and Labour. The result was a triumph for Lloyd George and a disaster for the Liberals. Even the two wings added together could muster only 170 MPs.

The early post-war years provided the most encouraging backcloth that Labour could have had. Heavy unemployment contributed to the unpopularity of the governing coalition which Labour, with more MPs than the Asquithians, could exploit. In 1922 the Conservatives broke with Lloyd George: a purely Conservative government was formed and called an early general election. The Liberals fought as rival sections. Their combined total fell to 115 while Labour more than doubled its representation to 142. This was a decisive victory, for Labour now became the official opposition in Parliament and henceforth the alternative to the Conservatives. Two years and two elections later, the reshaping of the party system was confirmed. In 1924 the Liberals, though reunited, were reduced to 40 MPs.

The Liberal Party split again in 1930 over the question of supporting the minority Labour government, a split made permanent in 1932 when more than half the party's MPs decided to support the *National Government, under the title of National Liberal. The independent Liberals soldiered on but elected only nineteen MPs at the general election of 1935: after the Second World War the decline continued until the party was reduced to five MPs in 1957.

There then began the first of the post-war Liberal revivals. Those of 1958 and 1962 soon petered out; but another revival in the early 1970s was followed by a remarkable Liberal performance in the two elections of 1974, when in October the party polled one-fifth of the votes and elected 13 members. The schism in the Labour Party in 1981 led to the formation of the Liberal-SDP alliance: in 1983 it won 25 per cent of the votes (2 per cent behind Labour) and elected 23 MPs, the best showing for the Liberals since 1929. Strains within the alliance led to a merger of the two parties in 1987 under the name *Liberal Democrats. It, and its predecessor the Liberal Party, has been the most consistently pro-European of all three parties. At the general election of 1997, the Liberal Democrats gained 46 seats and 62 in 2005. As party leader, *Ashdown was followed by

Charles *Kennedy who resigned in 2006. Its future seems still to depend upon its ability to effect proportional representation.

**Liberal Unionists** The Liberal government's proposal for Irish Home Rule and land reform in 1886 caused substantial opposition within the party and the fall of the government in June 1886. The opponents of Gladstone's Irish settlement, known to themselves as Liberal Unionists, believed Home Rule would lead to separation. After the 1886 election, when about 55 Liberal Unionists were elected, and the failure of talks in 1887, several returned to the Liberal Party. In the 1890s the Liberal Unionists became more closely linked with the Unionists, Chamberlain and *Devonshire entering *Salisbury's government in 1895. They split over tariff reform in the 1900s, some following Chamberlain into protection, others forming, with some Tories, the Unionist Free Food League. The Liberal Unionists fused with the Conservative Party in 1912 and their members were admitted to the *Carlton Club.

**Lib-Labs** were working-class MPs who, whilst prepared to speak out on 'labour' issues, accepted the Liberal whip. In 1874, Thomas Burt (Morpeth) and Alexander Macdonald (Stafford) became the first two such MPs. The decision of the miners to join the *Labour Party in 1908 dealt a fatal blow to the Lib-Lab creed, notwithstanding the handful of Liberal working-class MPs who persisted until 1918.

**Licensing Act,** 1662. A feature of the Commonwealth period was the unprecedented proliferation of pamphlets and broadsheets. In 1662 Charles II's government moved to curb them, 13 & 14 Car. II c. 33 condemning 'the general licentiousness of the late times'. Henceforth, publications were to carry the name of printer and author and were to be submitted for approval to a licenser. After 1688 the matter became even more contentious. A Whig licenser, Fraser, was forced to resign: a Tory licenser, Bohun, was dismissed. In 1693 the Act was continued for two years only and in 1695 it was not renewed at all. Within a decade of the Act lapsing, the London and provincial newspaper press had established itself.

**Lichfield, diocese of** There were Celtic bishops from 656, but no formal see until c.669, owing allegiance to *Lindisfarne, not Canterbury. *Theodore of Canterbury nominated *Chad as first bishop (d. 672). Lichfield became briefly (788–803) an archiepiscopal see, while *Offa, as *bretwalda, was in conflict with Canterbury. The creation of the separate Chester diocese in 1541 reduced Lichfield's significance, and in 1836 Coventry came under the *Worcester diocese, further reducing Lichfield's influence. The 12th–13th-cent. cathedral of red sandstone with three spires was badly damaged in the Civil War, restored in the 1660s, and again in the 19th cent.

**Lilburne, John** (1615–57). Leveller leader. Of minor Durham gentry stock, he was apprenticed to a London clothier. In 1638 he was hauled before *Star Chamber, flogged, pilloried, and imprisoned for distributing illegal anti-episcopal literature. *Cromwell secured his release in 1640, and he rose to lieutenant-colonel in Cromwell's Eastern Association cavalry, but left the service in 1645. Combative, indomitable, and self-dramatizing, he was the leading spirit of the *Leveller movement from 1647 onward, and broke with Cromwell. In 1649 he denounced the newly established *Commonwealth in *Englands New Chains Discovered*, fostered a serious army mutiny, and publicly demanded Cromwell's impeachment. He died a quaker.

**'Lillibullero',** which 'sang a prince out of three kingdoms', was a doggerel ballad, attributed to Lord Wharton, with a tune by *Purcell. It purported to be the native Irish welcoming James II's lord-lieutenant *Tyrconnel in 1687 to 'cut the Englishmen's throats'. The refrain 'Lillibullero' is probably a nonsense-jingle.

**Limerick (Luimnech), diocese of** The Irish see of Limerick was first named as such at the Council of Raithbressail (1111), though its first bishop Gilli was elected in 1106. It is now the seat of both Catholic and Anglican bishops.

**Limerick, treaty of,** 1691. The treaty concluded the siege of Limerick and the Jacobite war and was signed on 3 October. The military articles were generous, allowing the besieged army to migrate in French and English ships to join the forces of Louis XIV. The Irish Parliament, which reluctantly ratified the treaty only in 1697 in a maimed form, later wholly defied its spirit of toleration by passing penal laws.

## Limited Liability Act

This legislation was introduced in the United Kingdom in the 1850s and consolidated in an Act of 1862. Prior to this anyone owning a share in a commercial activity was responsible for any debts incurred in the case of bankruptcy without limit and this was an obvious deterrent to potential investors. The legislation limited the extent of this liability to the amount initially invested.

## Lincoln

was a legionary fortress, then the *colonia* of Lindum, where the river Witham flows east through the ridge of the Lincoln Edge. The gates, including the surviving Newport Arch, were impressive. In the 4th cent. Lincoln may have become a provincial capital; a bishop may have attended the Council of Arles in 314. After five centuries of near-desertion Lincoln was revived by the Vikings as a river port. The Normans planted a castle and cathedral in the upper city (the Roman site); the commercial centre spread downhill, where it still is. Lincoln's heyday was the 12th and 13th cents., when it was one of the six largest English towns, with 47 parish churches and a thriving textile industry. It declined spectacularly in the 14th and 15th cents., and revived only modestly as a social centre in the 18th cent. and as an industrial town in the 19th.

## Lincoln, battle of,

1141. Stephen, besieging Lincoln castle, held by supporters of *Matilda, the rival claimant to the throne, was himself attacked by a relief force under *Robert, earl of Gloucester, Matilda's half-brother. After heavy fighting in the streets on 2 February, Stephen was captured and taken to Bristol for imprisonment.

## Lincoln, battle of,

1217. The opponents of King John called in Louis, dauphin of France, to assist them. He continued his campaign in 1217 after John's death. On 20 May 1217 his supporters besieging Lincoln castle were themselves attacked by a relief force under William *Marshal, regent for John's young son Henry III. The comte de

la Perche, commanding the French troops, was killed and resistance melted away.

## Lincoln, diocese of

Now merely conterminous with Lincolnshire, this was one of the largest medieval sees, founded *c.*1072. After the reconquest of the Danelaw (10th cent.) the see of Dorchester extended from the Thames to the Humber. In 1072 it was moved to Lincoln. The vast diocese was reduced in size by the creation of the sees of *Ely (1109), *Peterborough (1541), and *Oxford (1542). The cathedral, begun in 1192 by St Hugh, stands magnificently on its hill, a superb example, the epitome perhaps, of 13th-cent. cathedral-building.

## Lincoln, John de la Pole, 1st earl of

(*c.*1462–87). Pole's mother was Edward IV's sister Elizabeth: his father, John de la Pole, 2nd duke of Suffolk. Under Richard III he was in high favour. He served Richard as president of the Council of the North and fought for him at *Bosworth. Lincoln and his father submitted to Henry VII but, with *Warwick in the Tower and a boy of 10, was the strongest Yorkist claimant to the throne. In 1487 he suddenly fled the country and returned with an invading force supporting Lambert *Simnel's claim to be Warwick. He was killed at the battle of *Stoke.

## Lincolnshire

is the second largest English county but one of the most thinly populated. The greater part of the county is flat but there are three parallel north–south ridges. *Lincoln stands at the gap in the western ridge, the Lincolnshire edge, Louth at the gap of the eastern.

At the time of the Roman invasion, the region formed part of the territory of the *Coritani. The Romans established a legionary base and then a *colonia* at Lincoln (Lindum) where the Fosse Way and Ermine Street intersected. Caistor was another Roman town of significance, possibly a spa. There were few obstacles to early Saxon settlement except in the south where salt marshes rendered the land impenetrable. *Lindsey, in the northern part, may have formed a subkingdom, disputed between Mercia to the west and Northumbria to the north.

From the 870s onwards, the area formed part of the *Danelaw, Lincoln and Stamford being two of the five boroughs. Many of the place-names are of Danish origin—Grimsby,

Saxby, Beckby, Swinthorp. The area was divided into three trithings—Lindsey, Kesteven, and Holland—and the largest, Lindsey, was further divided into three ridings. The smaller divisions known elsewhere as hundreds were in Lincolnshire called *wapentakes. The shire itself seems to have been formed after 1016. The *Domesday survey treated it as one unit.

In 1066 Lincoln was one of the leading towns in the country, with a population of about 5,000. Castles were built at Lincoln and Stamford and in 1072 the diocese was transferred from Dorchester to Lincoln. Barton did not long retain its importance, partly because the Great North Road diverted to the west from Ermine Street, bypassing the shire completely, partly because *Hull took much of its river traffic. Boston, however, not mentioned in Domesday, developed rapidly and by 1204 was second only to London in subsidy payment. Louth and Sleaford, under the jurisdiction of the bishop, were just outside Lincoln's pull at 26 and 17 miles, and developed as local centres.

In the later Middle Ages a slow decline began. Stamford and Lincoln suffered much from the *Black Death in 1349. A number of small harbours suffered from silting up of the coast. With the growth of colonies in the New World the whole axis of trade shifted towards western ports. *Camden in 1586 wrote of the county largely in terms of past glories.

Tudor and Stuart Lincolnshire was little known or visited—a quiet county of small market towns. Its participation in the *Pilgrimage of Grace in 1536 provoked Henry VIII to denounce its inhabitants as 'the most brute and beastly of the whole realm'. Celia Fiennes in the 1690s noted that Lincoln's waterways were choked up, and 20 years later *Defoe, while admiring the minster and the countryside, dismissed the town as 'an ancient, ragged, decay'd and still decaying city'—if, indeed, it could be called a city.

The industrial developments of the 19th cent. helped to diversify the shire. Improvements in transport—turnpikes, canals, railways—helped to knit the shire together but did comparatively little to integrate it with the rest of the nation. Schemes for a main railway line north through Lincoln came to nothing and in the end the main line followed the Great North Road, almost bypassing the county. But the growth of an agricultural industry brought employment to Lincoln, Gainsborough, and Grantham. Grimsby opened its new dock in 1800 but its spectacular expansion followed the arrival of the railway in 1848, which benefited the fish trade. By 1901 it had overtaken Lincoln as the largest town in the shire. The discovery of iron in the north-west of the county led to the development of a steel industry and the town of Scunthorpe came into existence: by 1961 it was the third largest town with 67,000 people. Rail transport and the cult of seaside holidays produced Cleethorpes, Skegness, and Mablethorpe with holiday camps and caravan sites.

### Lindemann, Frederick, 1st Viscount Cherwell

(1886–1957). Lindemann is one of the comparatively small band who have combined science and politics. Lindemann was educated in Germany, took his doctorate in 1910, and stayed on to do research in low-temperature physics. In 1919 he was elected to a chair at Oxford, reorganized the Clarendon Laboratory, and was attached to Wadham College, though living in Christ Church. A strange creature in the aristocratic world which his wealth allowed him to frequent, he was known as 'the Prof.' When war broke out, Churchill leaned upon his scientific knowledge, got him a barony in 1941, and made him paymaster-general. In 1951, when Churchill formed his second administration, the Prof. was promoted viscount and resumed as paymaster until 1953. Confident and overbearing, as a wartime adviser he was a doubtful asset.

### Lindisfarne

(Holy Island) is a small island off the coast of Northumbria south of Berwick-on-Tweed. It is connected to the mainland by a causeway which is inaccessible at high tide. It was the seat of sixteen bishops from 635 to 883, the most famous of them being St *Aidan, who was brought from *Iona by *Oswald to Christianize the north, and later St *Cuthbert, who took charge of the Romanized see after the Synod of *Whitby. After the island had been ravaged in the 8th and 9th cents. by Vikings, the religious community removed to seek a new sanctuary, eventually settling at Durham.

### Lindisfarne, diocese of

The bishopric, originally based on the island monastery founded by *Aidan (c.635), became the spiritual springboard of Celtic Christian mission in England. *Cuthbert became bishop in 685, but died in 687. After the island had been sacked twice by the Danes in 793 and 875, the monks fled with Cuthbert's relics and the *Lindisfarne Gospels to *Chester-le-Street and then to *Durham.

**Lindisfarne Gospels,** now British Library, Cotton MS Nero D.iv. A Latin text of the Gospels, with a later Anglo-Saxon translation or gloss, which was made at the monastery of Lindisfarne by Eadfrith, who was bishop of Lindisfarne 698–721. It is an elaborately decorated book. It is likely that the manuscript was made for the elevation of the relics of St *Cuthbert in 698.

**Lindsey, diocese of** *Theodore carved this bishopric out of the Northumbrian diocese of *York *c.*677 to serve part of modern Lincolnshire. It collapsed under the Danish invasions *c.*873 and was not revived.

**Lindsey, kingdom of** Lindsey was one of the smaller kingdoms of early Anglo-Saxon England and its existence must always have been rather precarious. Bordered in the north by the Humber and the east by the North Sea, it followed the Trent in the west, taking in the Isle of Axholme, and the Witham in the south, including Lincoln itself. A list of the kings of Lindsey has survived, though Stenton called it 'the obscurest of English dynasties'. It starts, conventionally, with Woden and ends with Aldfrith, probably in the 8th cent. An area of heavy Scandinavian settlement, it became one of the ridings of the later county of Lincolnshire and was itself divided up into ridings. These divisions lasted and Lindsey was given its own county council in 1888, the county town being Lincoln.

**Linlithgow, Victor Alexander John Hope, 2nd Marquis** (1887–1952). Linlithgow was born in Scotland and educated at Eton. His connection with India developed through his chairmanship of the Royal Commission on Agriculture in India (1926–8) and the Select Committee on Indian Constitutional Reform (1930–2). He was appointed viceroy of India in 1936. His period in office witnessed the growth of mass support for the Indian National Congress, the withdrawal of Congress co-operation for the Second World War, and the Quit India movement of 1942. His harsh response to the Quit India movement helped to spread guerrilla resistance to British rule. He resigned in 1943.

**Linlithgow palace** (Lothian). Initially a royal manor house beside the loch, and lodging for Edward I who strengthened it (1301–3), it was rebuilt in stone by James I of Scotland after the 1424 fire. Birthplace of James V (1512), it remained empty after the death of James IV at Flodden (1513) until the 1530s, when work was resumed reflecting James V's tastes, as at Falkland. Birthplace also of Mary, queen of Scots (1542), the palace fell into disrepair after the accession of the infant James VI (1567). Charles I was the last monarch to sleep there (1633).

**Lister, Joseph** (1827–1912). Surgeon and pioneer of antisepsis. Having qualified at London, then teaching at Edinburgh, he was appointed (1860) as regius professor of clinical surgery at Glasgow, where he was one of the few to pursue the implications of Pasteur's recent work on fermentation and the beginnings of the germ theory. Recognition led to chairs at Edinburgh and London, the presidency of the *Royal Society, and a barony (1897). His work improved public confidence in both hospitals and surgery, and stimulated the infant science of bacteriology.

**Liverpool,** created a borough by royal will (1207) as a convenient place of embarkation for Irish campaigns, fluctuated in prosperity until the early 17th cent. when Irish industries developed and Chester declined (from silting). Continuing to control the larger share of the Irish trade, Liverpool gained impetus from lucrative commerce with the plantations (sugar, tobacco, cotton) and the rapid development of Manchester's textile industries. Involvement in the slave trade brought riches and an unsavoury reputation. Despite extensive reconstruction of the business quarters after severe bomb damage in the Second World War, the subsequent de-industrialization of Liverpool has led to its being better known for its football teams, pop music groups, and comedians. Liverpool was European city of culture during 2008.

**Liverpool, Charles Jenkinson, 1st earl of** (1729–1808). Tory politician. Jenkinson was a 'man of business', serving Lord *Bute as private secretary and under-secretary of state, 1761–2, and holding similar second-rank offices through to 1782. During Lord *North's administration he was believed to be influential 'behind the scenes' and the secret agent of George III in the ministry. He left office on the fall of North but returned under *Pitt in 1784, becoming president of the Board of Trade 1786–1804 and chancellor of the duchy of Lancaster 1786–1803. He was made Lord Hawkesbury in 1791 and promoted earl of Liverpool in 1796.

**Liverpool, Robert Banks Jenkinson, 2nd earl of** (1770–1828). Liverpool was a capable and intelligent statesman. He entered the Commons while under age in 1790 and supported the war with France after 1793. After gaining experience at the India Board, he served *Addington as foreign secretary, had two spells as home secretary, and between 1809 and 1812 proved himself as an efficient war secretary. When he became prime minister in 1812 the prospects for his ministry were uncertain but Liverpool soon showed that he was in command. The war against Napoleon was turning in favour of the allies. Liverpool was adroit in handling the prince regent: by 1820 he had the advantage of knowing that his colleagues would follow him out of office if he had to resign. It was Liverpool who insisted that the prince regent could not accede to the *Holy Alliance in a personal capacity. Liverpool was protective towards the landed interest, but though he favoured a corn law he was compelled to accept a fixed duty in 1815 because his supporters were not prepared to accept a sliding scale. He opposed parliamentary reform, but was eager to find some compromise on the catholic question short of full emancipation. Liverpool was determined to maintain public order but had no desire to strengthen the powers of central government. Lacking a police force he had to rely on the local magistrates for law and order. At the time of the *Peterloo affair in 1819 Liverpool criticized the Manchester magistrates in private but defended them in public. After 1820 the situation improved. The economy revived and Liverpool allowed his ministers greater freedom in reducing duties and stimulating trade. He appointed *Canning as foreign secretary and gave more scope to *Peel, *Huskisson, and Robinson (*Goderich). The extent to which the government depended upon him was revealed when a stroke compelled his retirement in 1827.

**Liverpool cathedrals** Giles Gilbert Scott (1880–1960) was only 22 when his design in a Romantic Gothic style won the competition for the proposed Anglican cathedral. The foundation stone was laid in 1904 by Edward VII. Consecrated in 1924, the cathedral was finally completed in 1978. Set on raised ground, and having the highest interior of all English cathedrals, it dominates the Merseyside skyline and awes worshippers.

The metropolitan cathedral was originally designed by Edwin *Lutyens but only the crypt completed. Frederick Gibberd's prize-winning design (1959) has resulted in a circular building whose radial buttresses and glass-walled central tower have prompted a number of affectionate nicknames. It was consecrated in May 1967.

**livery and maintenance** *See* BASTARD FEUDALISM.

**livery companies** were organizations of master tradesmen which developed in the city of London during the Middle Ages. Their purpose was to control the numbers and character of new entrants. Originally livery referred to the special clothing of retainers and servants, but later the term became associated with distinctive costumes for grand occasions. Prosperous companies erected their own guildhalls and endowed churches dedicated to the patron saint of their crafts, with chapels for their use. They have retained their independence to the extent that, currently, members of a company have the status of freemen of the city of London. By 1979 there were 84 livery companies.

**Livingstone, David** (1813–73). Scottish missionary and explorer. Livingstone arrived in South Africa in 1841 to assist in the work of the *London Missionary Society. He was soon attracted northward in the hope of spreading the gospel in central Africa. His travels took him first to the Atlantic coast and then across the continent to the Indian Ocean. His discoveries brought him fame in Britain and won him the support of the Royal

Geographical Society. The circumstances of his death in the interior of Africa in 1873, during a final journey, proved to be the decisive factor in stimulating British action against the east African slave trade.

**Llandaff, diocese of** Llandaff cathedral looks to the 6th-cent. saints *Teilo and Euddogwy as its founders, and the shrine of the former was a place of pilgrimage until the Reformation. Work on the building of the present cathedral, and the definition of the territorial boundaries of the see, were however the responsibility of the first Norman bishop, Urban, early in the 12th cent. The diocese, the most populous in Wales, originally encompassed most of the counties of Glamorgan and Monmouth (Gwent), though the latter became a separate bishopric in 1921.

**Lloyd, Marie** (1870–1922). Music-hall artiste. Born Matilda Wood, but quickly rejecting the stage-name 'Bella Delmare' for 'Marie Lloyd' when first appearing in music-hall aged 15, she was soon performing in London's West End. Despite some pantomime roles, her forte was music-hall, where she specialized in character songs imbued with vitality, sauce, and gesture.

**Lloyd George, David, 1st earl Lloyd-George** (1863–1945). Prime minister. Lloyd George laid the foundations of what later became the welfare state, and put a progressive income tax system at the centre of government finance. In 1918 he was acclaimed, not without reason, as the 'Man Who Won the War'. Yet until the appearance of a spate of sympathetic books in the 1970s his reputation remained remarkably low.

He grew up in a modest, but not poor, home in north Wales. Once he had qualified as a solicitor, he was able to use the firm's income to build his political career. In 1890 he won a by-election as a Liberal in the marginal Conservative seat of Caernarfon Boroughs which he retained until 1945. After nearly a decade as a lively backbench rebel, he became a national figure as a result of his courageous opposition to the South African War (1899–1902). In December 1905 his talents were recognized by *Campbell-Bannerman, the new Liberal premier, who made him president of the Board of Trade.

Lloyd George's real breakthrough came in 1908 when *Asquith promoted him as chancellor of the Exchequer. As he felt politically disadvantaged by his lack of a large private income, he was apt to grab an opportunity to make a quick profit; hence his involvement in the *Marconi scandal. But Asquith had correctly seen that Lloyd George possessed the necessary political flair to be chancellor. His famous 'People's Budget' of 1909 solved the government's problems by levying extra taxes on a few large incomes and on items of conspicuous consumption like motor cars. This enabled them to pay for both *old-age pensions *and* *dreadnought battleships. When his budget was rejected by the peers Lloyd George grasped the opportunity to attack the Conservatives for trying to preserve a privileged élite. This restored the initiative to the Liberals and enabled them to retain their working-class vote in two general elections in 1910. Subsequently Lloyd George maintained his radical credentials with the 1911 *National Insurance Act which introduced both health and unemployment insurance for millions of people.

After the outbreak of war he stood out as the only minister whose reputation rose significantly. This was largely attributable to his success as minister of munitions from May 1915. However, his brief spell as secretary of state for war proved less happy because he found himself trapped by the conservative thinking of the military men. His frustration led him to join with Bonar *Law in putting pressure on Asquith to streamline the war machine. The result was Asquith's resignation in December 1916. Lloyd George managed to put together a government based on Conservative support plus a majority of the Labour members and a minority of the Liberals. He made an immediate impact on the war effort by instituting a five-man war cabinet serviced by a cabinet secretariat under Sir Maurice Hankey. New ministries were created—Food, Shipping, Air, National Service, Pensions, Labour—to deal with the problems thrown up by the war, and non-party experts and businessmen such as Sir Eric Geddes were often appointed to them.

None the less, Lloyd George's premiership remained a precarious affair. Most Tories neither liked nor trusted him. The sudden military victory in November 1918 gave Lloyd George immense prestige and, thus, a degree of bargaining power. Instead of returning to the Liberal Party he decided to organize his own Lloyd George Liberals and to fight the election in co-operation with the Conservatives.

As a result of his government's overwhelming victory in 1918 he retained office until 1922. Although restricted by the numerical dominance of the Conservatives he had major achievements to his credit: the parliamentary reform of 1918 which enfranchised women, the 1918 Education Act, the 1919 Housing Act, the settlement of the Irish question in 1921, and, of course, the treaty of *Versailles. But in time both Liberal and Tory followers grew dissatisfied. Controversy over the huge funds the prime minister accumulated by the sale of honours undermined him; knighthoods were freely offered for £12,000 and baronetcies for £30,000. Finally at a meeting in October 1922 the Conservatives voted to cut their links with Lloyd George. He resigned immediately and never took office again.

Though he spent much of the 1920s engaged in Liberal Party infighting, he still made an impact on politics by means of his collaboration with J. M. *Keynes and others over a detailed strategy for tackling unemployment. He was too ill to join the National Government in 1931. Though widely expected to serve in Churchill's coalition after 1940, Lloyd George was not keen to do so, and the invitation never came.

**Lloyd's of London** From the late 1600s to the late 1700s London coffee-houses were the centre of social and business life. From the 1690s merchants, bankers, and seafarers met in Edward Lloyd's coffee-house in Lombard Street, where they undertook shipping business. Merchants prepared to take a share of a marine risk would write their names on a policy one beneath the other, becoming 'underwriters'. From the late 1970s Lloyd's experienced turbulent times: claims, particularly from natural disasters, became much larger, and there has been incompetence, fraud, theft, and resignations.

**Llywelyn ap Gruffydd** (d. 1282), prince of Wales (1246–82). Known as Llywelyn 'the Last', his ambition to create a permanent, independent Welsh principality came close to realization. The grandson of *Llywelyn ab Iorwerth, he may have been designated the

heir of his uncle *Dafydd ap Llywelyn. After Dafydd's death (1246) and the treaty of *Woodstock with Henry III (1247), Llywelyn was restricted to *Gwynedd west of the river Conwy. By 1255 Llywelyn had defeated his brothers and restored his uncle's dominion: he advanced east of the Conwy, exploiting divisions in England. Most Welsh lords regarded him as overlord (1258) and Llywelyn took the title of prince of Wales. At *Pipton (1265) Simon de *Montfort acknowledged his status and promised Llywelyn his daughter in marriage. At *Montgomery (1267) Henry III conceded recognition. Llywelyn misjudged Edward I in refusing to fulfil his obligations as the king's vassal. The war of 1276–7 was a disaster for Llywelyn, who was confined once more to west Gwynedd by the treaty of *Aberconwy (1277). The uneasy peace was shattered by his brother Dafydd's assault on Hawarden (1282) and, in the renewed struggle with Edward, Llywelyn was killed near Builth on 11 December.

**Llywelyn ab Iorwerth** (1173–1240), prince of Gwynedd (1195–1240), known as 'the Great'. The son of Iorwerth 'Flatnose' and Margaret, princess of *Powys, Llywelyn spent most of his life restoring and enhancing the hegemony of his grandfather *Owain Gwynedd. Good relations with King John brought recognition and his marriage to John's natural daughter *Joan. But his aggression towards Powys made John retaliate (1210–11) and Llywelyn then allied with the French. He planned to perpetuate his principality by securing recognition from king and pope (1220–2) of his son *Dafydd as his sole heir. He took the evocative title of prince of Aberffraw and lord of Snowdon (1230), and he compared himself to the king of Scots.

**Locarno, treaties of,** 1925. These treaties (1 December 1925) briefly raised hopes that Europe was at last settling down after the First World War. They confirmed the inviolability of the frontiers between France, Belgium, and Germany, and the demilitarization of the Rhineland. German entry to the *League of Nations followed in 1926.

**Locke, John** (1632–1704). Perhaps the most influential English-language philosopher and political theorist, Locke is regarded as the founding thinker of liberalism. Locke lived in the household of *Shaftesbury the

Whig leader and like him had to go into exile. His *Letter Concerning Toleration* (1689) contains two fundamental assumptions: that religion is a matter for each individual, and that churches are voluntary associations. His arguments lead logically to the principle and practice of separation of church and state. The *Two Treatises of Government* bases government on the consent of the governed, who need an authority to defend their property. A ruler who turns himself into a tyrant, as Charles II and James II had been doing, forfeits his authority and may be resisted. One of Locke's most influential publications was *Some Thoughts concerning Education*, which argued for a broader syllabus and a more humane attitude towards children.

**lollardy** Described recently as 'the premature reformation', lollardy developed originally from *Wyclif's teaching. Lollards (from middle Dutch *lollaerd*—a mumbler) were a motley group lacking theological coherence. Lollardy also attracted influential men, close to the court, some driven by genuine puritanism, some anticlerical, some selfishly cynical with eyes on clerical wealth. Providing havens for writing and copying texts, they patronized lollard preachers, which alarmed the government, who enacted the statute *De heretico comburendo* (1401) to arrest unlicensed preachers and sometimes hand them over for public burning. After Sir John Oldcastle's abortive revolt (1414) and death (1417), aristocratic lollardy was a spent force. Chased from university and aristocracy, lollardy embraced local artisans and yeomen farmers, who held negative, often simplistic, views. Though the authorities feared lollards as dangerously articulate with a backbone of literacy, their negative ideas had little popular appeal except for emphasis on Bible-reading.

**London** (Roman). Londinium was the provincial capital of Roman Britain from *c.* AD 60 onwards. Roman remains have been located at the confluence of the rivers Thames and Fleet. London's status appears to have been enhanced after *Colchester (the original provincial capital of Roman Britain) was destroyed during the Boudiccan revolt of AD 60. A tombstone of the new procurator, Gaius Julius Classicianus, dating to the after-

math of the revolt, suggests that London had now become the seat of administration.

**London, diocese of** The senior see after the two archbishoprics, it comprises Greater London and part of Surrey north of the Thames. Though a British bishop from London attended the Council of Arles in 314, *Augustine did not establish a diocese for the East Saxons until 604. The true succession of London bishops restarts with Wine in 666, for Cedd, Celtic bishop of the East Saxons (654–64), was never based in the city. The medieval St Paul's was destroyed in the Great Fire of 1666. The present cathedral (1675–1710) by Christopher *Wren is in Renaissance style and miraculously survived the London Blitz (1940–1).

**London, fire of,** 1666. The blaze that started in Thomas Farriner's bakehouse in Pudding Lane, near London bridge, in the early hours of Sunday, 2 September, has become known as the 'Great Fire'. A driving east wind fanned the flames across firebreaks, and, despite the efforts of parish officials and the lord mayor, they soon became uncontrollable. The wind persisted until Tuesday night, but it was not until Friday that the firefighters and county militia could assess the devastation. The Tower of London (to the east) had survived, but Old St Paul's cathedral, the Guildhall, Royal Exchange, 87 parish churches, 52 company halls, markets, gaols, and 13,200 houses had succumbed. Charles II, who had placed his brother in control of the city to maintain order and discourage looting, rapidly introduced measures for recovery. To commemorate events, the Monument was erected near the site of the outbreak (1677); to the inscription, the words 'But Popish frenzy, which wrought such horrors, is not yet quenched' were added in 1681 and not removed until 1830.

**London, government and politics**
The exceptional size and resources of London gave it military significance in addition to its political importance as the capital. William the Conqueror granted London a charter, confirming its previous privileges, but also began building the White Tower, nucleus of the *Tower of London, as a strong point. London did not replace the old Wessex capital of *Winchester until the 12th cent.

Before the Conquest, Saxon rulers had granted London remarkable privileges—a folk moot which met three times a year; the husting (Danish: *hus-ting* (house assembly)) which met every week; aldermen to supervise justice in the ward moots. In 1018 London had paid one-seventh of the national tribute to *Cnut and in the decades before the Conquest the *witan had met there more often than anywhere else. When representatives of the boroughs began to be summoned to Parliament in the late 13th and early 14th cents., London usually returned four members rather than the standard two.

The government of the city consisted of a Court of Aldermen, chosen for life; a Common Council of some 200 members, chosen annually by the wards; a Common Hall of some thousands, representing the liverymen; and ward moots or parish meetings. The executive was the mayor (after 1283 increasingly referred to as the lord mayor), the two sheriffs, a large number of paid officers, of whom the recorder and town clerk were the most important; and a host of lesser officials, paid and unpaid, down to precinct level, including scavengers, constables, night-watchmen, and rate-collectors. There was a constant struggle for power between the component parts, the Common Council and even more the Common Hall tending to radical disenchantment with the national government, the aldermen, consisting of the senior and wealthy merchants, often on close terms with the government of the day. Great influence was also exerted by the *livery companies which developed from the medieval guilds: the Weavers' charter was granted in 1155, Fishmongers' 1272, Goldsmiths', Merchant Taylors', and Skinners' 1327, Drapers' 1364, Mercers' 1394, and Grocers' 1428.

On several occasions London was in the hands of rebels—Wat *Tyler in 1381, Jack *Cade in 1450, Thomas *Wyatt in 1554—attempting to seize or intimidate the government. These incursions were rarely successful, partly because there was little government to seize, partly because it was difficult for rebel leaders to control their men once they had entered the city. Of more consequence were the occasions when the city itself acted with unity and resolution. Londoners, with their close financial and trading links with the Low Countries, were very receptive

towards reformed doctrines in the early Tudor period and London became the spearhead of the English *Reformation. One hundred years later, it was in the forefront of the opposition to Charles I, and the Civil War may, in one sense, be seen as London versus the rest. In the later 19th century London radicalism was less evident, partly because new towns like Birmingham, Manchester, and Sheffield had taken up much of the running.

The growth of London also placed great strain on its governmental institutions. London itself had long before expanded beyond the city limits, taking in Southwark in 1550. By 1811, only one-tenth of the capital's population lived within the city's jurisdiction. What administration there was outside the city was left largely to parishes and vestries, supported by a patchwork of trusts, commissions, and charities. A leap forward in co-ordination came in 1829 with the Metropolitan Police Act. Not until 1888 was the London County Council established. A second tier of 28 borough councils operated beneath, sharing responsibilities. The London County Hall, on the south bank of the Thames, was opened in 1922 as a headquarters for the new authority. London was once more reorganized in 1965, partly for party advantage, partly because Greater London had outgrown the LCC area. The Greater London Council supervised 31 boroughs and the cities of London and Westminster. Dislike of its left-wing politics and jealousy of any rival source of authority caused the Thatcher government to abolish the GLC in 1986, leaving London as the only capital city with no overarching authority. The 1997 Labour government responded by giving London an elected mayor as chief executive, though the post went to Ken Livingstone, not their favoured candidate.

**London, growth of** London was Britain's biggest settlement as early as the 7th cent. It began a phase of rapid growth in the late 10th cent., in 1100 its population may have numbered 25,000. Recent research suggests that the city numbered between 80,000 and 100,000 people by 1300. London's population contracted after the *Black Death (1348): its population still numbered only about 50,000 in 1500.

Sixteenth-cent. London grew more rapidly than England. The first well-grounded estimates suggest a population of about 75,000 in 1550, 200,000 in 1600, 400,000 in 1650, and over half a million by 1700. The 18th cent. saw an initial slowdown of metropolitan growth but the first *census in 1801 revealed the population of London to be about 1,117,000. Its population doubled again by 1851, and by 1901 it comprised a metropolis of some 6,586,000 inhabitants. London's growth peaked at about 8,700,000 on the eve of the Second World War.

London's early growth owed much to its development as a seat of government in the 13th and 14th cents., and to its increasing share of the nation's overseas trade. Disproportionate growth thereafter occurred because it was a world city, not merely a national capital. The development of its financial institutions in the late 17th cent., and its role as a colonial and then imperial capital in the 18th and 19th cents., are vital in explaining its phenomenal expansion.

**London, treaty of,** 1357. David II of Scotland was captured at *Neville's Cross in 1346 and taken to the Tower of London. Negotiations for his release came to nothing until the treaty of London of May 1357. The Scots paid a large ransom and gave hostages. The treaty was confirmed at *Berwick in October.

**London, treaty of,** 1358. Draft treaty. Edward III's diplomatic hand was strengthened by the capture of John II of France at *Poitiers. This treaty would have given Edward Aquitaine, Poitou, Ponthieu, and Calais in full sovereignty, as well as a ransom payment of 4 million *écus*, yet without obliging him to drop his claim to the French throne. It was never ratified, and Edward subsequently increased his demands to include Normandy, Anjou, and Maine. It may be that he had set his demands deliberately high so that the inevitable French refusal would justify the renewal of war.

**London, treaty of,** 1423. Anglo-Scottish agreement finalizing the terms of James I's release from English custody. King James was to pay 60,000 marks, 10,000 of which would be remitted as the dowry of his queen, *Joan Beaufort.

**London, treaty of,** 1474. In 1473 Edward IV was preparing an attack upon Louis XI of France but having difficulty mustering allies.

In July 1474, by the treaty of London, Charles of Burgundy agreed to recognize Edward as king of France and join his campaign.

**London, treaty of,** 1518. The victory of Francis I, the young king of France, over the Swiss at Marignano in 1515 threatened the balance of power in western Europe. *Wolsey and Henry VIII began constructing an anti-French alliance. In 1518 they switched policy to a *rapprochement* with Francis and the treaty of London followed. Tournai, captured by the English in 1513, was to be handed back; Mary, Henry's 2-year-old daughter, was to marry the dauphin; France was not to support the anti-English party in Scotland; there was to be a treaty of universal peace and a crusade against the Turks. Though endorsed by the meeting of Francis and Henry in 1520 at the *Field of Cloth of Gold, the peace did not hold and the *rapprochement* did not prosper.

**London, treaty of,** 1604. When James I succeeded Elizabeth, he found his new kingdom at war with Spain in support of the Dutch. After lengthy negotiations, a suspension of hostilities was converted into peace. James refused to recall 'volunteers' in the Dutch service but agreed that they should not be recruited in his dominions. Englishmen in Spain would not be harassed by the Inquisition provided that they caused no public scandal. Reconciliation with Spain remained a major objective with James for the rest of his reign.

**London, treaty of,** 1827. This was an attempt by Canning in company with Russia and France to protect British interests during the Greek revolt against Turkish rule. The three powers demanded an immediate armistice, and an allied fleet under Admiral *Codrington was sent with vague instructions to prevent further fighting. In the event the Ottoman navies were destroyed at *Navarino in October 1827. The treaty was a step on the road to an independent Greece in 1832.

**London, treaty of,** 1831. The settlement of the Belgian question was the first test for *Palmerston on becoming foreign secretary in Lord *Grey's administration. Belgium, previously the Austrian Netherlands, had been reunited with Holland in 1815 to form a barrier to French expansion, but had rebelled in August 1830 and declared itself independent. A conference of the great powers in London in February 1831 recognized Belgian independence and, when the Dutch refused to submit, French troops marched in. When they proved reluctant to leave, Palmerston dropped hints of war. By the treaty of November 1831 Belgian independence and neutrality were guaranteed.

**London, treaty of,** 1840. This was concluded with Russia, Austria, and Prussia to secure the ultimate return of Syria from Egypt to Turkey. While it provided for the closing of the Straits to all warships, it ended whatever unilateral advantages Russia had enjoyed under the treaty of Unkiar-Skelessi (1833).

**London, treaty of,** 1871. The treaty of Paris, at the end of the Crimean War, declared the Black Sea to be neutral and demilitarized. In 1870, during the Franco-Prussian War, Russia took the opportunity to repudiate the clause. Since there was nothing a conference in London could do, it passed a pious resolution that states could 'rid themselves of their treaty engagements' only with the consent of the other signatories.

**London bridge,** for centuries the sole thread across the Thames, saw both ceremonial entries into the city and rebellious challenges; the gruesome custom of displaying traitors' heads above the gatehouse, commenced with William *Wallace (1305), was discontinued in 1661. *Rennie's 1831 stone bridge was sold in 1969 and re-erected in Arizona.

**Londonderry** was until 1973 one of the six counties of Northern Ireland. It is dominated by Londonderry itself, near the mouth of the Foyle, with a population of nearly 100,000. In 1610 the city of London took over the area for colonization and began building the walls. In 1689, as a protestant bastion, it withstood the famous siege by James II's troops. Later it became a centre for linen manufacture and in the 20th cent. diversified into chemicals and light industry. Civil rights demonstrations in the city in 1969 were the beginning of the renewed troubles that have haunted Northern Ireland.

**Londonderry, siege of,** 1689. When William of Orange landed at Brixham, Lord-Lieutenant *Tyrconnel, to furnish Irish troops for England, had weakened his Ulster garrisons. In December both Londonderry and Enniskillen shut their doors against fresh garrisons. In April James II himself advanced against Londonderry. Governor Robert Lundy was prepared to surrender, but was overthrown by a popular rebellion and replaced by the Revd George *Walker. The town was in extreme distress before a Williamite supply ship broke the besiegers' boom on Lough Foyle on 28 July.

**London Missionary Society** Founded in 1795 as a non-denominational body to proclaim 'the glorious gospel of the blessed God' abroad, it adopted the name London Missionary Society (1818) and became mainly *congregationalist. Brief success in Sierra Leone was followed by lasting success in South Africa, where its most celebrated missionary was David *Livingstone.

**London University** was founded largely on the initiative of Lord *Brougham. Opening in 1828, University College had no religious entrance requirements and became known as 'the godless institution of Gower Street'. In the following year, in contrast, King's College was founded to promote 'the doctrines and duties of Christianity'. In 1900 a federal structure was adopted. London has a vice-chancellor and a principal, and consists of schools of the university, medical schools, and senate institutes. Senate House and a nucleus of colleges were built in Bloomsbury in the late 1930s.

**Long, Walter** (1854–1924). Conservative statesman. After holding junior office, Long entered the cabinet in 1895. He was a contender for the Conservative leadership in November 1911, but—with Austen *Chamberlain—withdrew in favour of Bonar *Law. He was appointed president of the Local Government Board in the first wartime coalition in May 1915, and became colonial secretary when the Lloyd George coalition was formed in December 1916. He was 1st lord of the Admiralty, his last ministerial post, between January 1917 and February 1921.

**Longchamp, William** (d. 1197). Bishop and statesman. Longchamp was born in

Normandy and was taken up by Richard, heir to Henry II, who appointed him chancellor of Aquitaine. When Richard succeeded in 1189, Longchamp was made chancellor of England, given the see of Ely, and became a papal legate. In the long absences of Richard, he was the most powerful man in the kingdom. Richard's brother John acted as a rallying-point for opposition to Longchamp; his seizure of Geoffrey, archbishop of York, scandalized many; and in 1191 he was forced into exile on the continent.

**Long Parliament,** 1640–60. Charles I's defeat by the Scots in the *Bishops' wars diminished both his reputation and his financial resources, leaving him with no option but to summon Parliament in November 1640. But the initiative was seized by his critics, who impeached his chief minister, *Strafford, and pushed through a bill forbidding the dissolution of Parliament without its own consent. Further Acts, in mid-1641, abolished the instruments of prerogative rule, such as *Star Chamber, outlawed prerogative taxation, and provided for triennial parliaments, thereby restoring the traditional constitution.

From 1648 England was governed by the '*Rump' of the Long Parliament, which executed the king, abolished the monarchy and House of Lords, and declared a republic. Cromwell called in troops to expel the Rump in February 1653. The Long Parliament remained in abeyance until 1659, when the army generals briefly recalled the Rump. But not until early 1660, when *Monck ordered the readmission of the excluded members, did the full house reassemble. In March 1660 the Long Parliament voted to dissolve itself.

**lord advocate** The post dates from the 15th cent. when the lord advocate quickly became a prominent officer of the Scottish crown. From 1746 the lord advocate was largely responsible for the management of the Scottish administration until the department of the secretary for Scotland was established in 1885. Today the lord advocate advises the government on Scottish legal matters.

**lord chancellor** *Edward the Confessor first created the post of chancellor, which has always remained one of the leading offices of state. The chancellor was keeper of

the great seal and acted as chief secretary to the king, drawing up charters and writs. In the 14th cent. the chancellor entered the legal system when he began to hear appeals from subjects unable to obtain justice from the common law courts. From this it evolved that the chancellor became a judge in his own court, the Court of *Chancery. He presided over the highest court of appeal in the country, the House of Lords. In 2005, as part of a highly controversial remodelling of the functions of the Lord Chancellor, the chairmanship of debates in the Lords was given to the Lord Speaker, while the Lord Chancellorship, together with the Secretaryship of State for Justice, went to a member of the House of Commons.

**lord chancellor of Ireland** The earliest chancellor of Ireland was Stephen Ridel, appointed in 1189. An Irish Chancery was established in 1232 and granted to the chancellor of England. Since 1922 there has been one lord chancellor for the whole of the United Kingdom, who is always chosen from the English bench or bar.

**lord chief justice** The second highest post in the judicial ranking. Since the days of Sir Edward *Coke, the chief justice of King's Bench has informally used the title of lord chief justice. Unlike the lord chancellor, the lord chief justice has no political role and remains in office after a change of government.

**lord high steward** Originally purely a household officer, the task of the steward, or seneschal, was to place dishes on the royal table, but like many comparable offices it gathered other duties and rose in prestige. Eventually, as lord high steward, he performed at coronations and presided over the trial of peers. In Scotland, the office became hereditary in the 12th cent. in the Stewart family, who became monarchs in the 14th cent.

**lord justice clerk** Scottish legal post. Originally the lord justice clerk of Scotland was clerk and assessor to the *Justiciar's Court. The court, usually presided over by peers, had professional lawyers as clerks. Gradually the post increased in importance and by the late 16th cent. the holder was always a member of the Privy Council. By the late 17th cent. he had become one of the judges in the court itself. Today the lord justice clerk is the holder of the second highest judicial office in Scotland.

**lord justice-general** Scottish legal post. From the 15th cent. the lord justice-general was recognized as the supreme judge of criminal cases in Scotland, superseding the post of *justiciar. In 1830 the Court of Session Act declared that after the death of the existing office-holder, the 3rd duke of Montrose, the office of lord justice-general would be merged with that of the lord president of the *Court of Session.

**lord keeper** The great seal of England was normally in the custody of the *lord chancellor. But an office of vice-chancellor or sealbearer in the 12th cent. developed into the separate office of lord keeper. The lord keepership seems to have been used when the holder did not have the standing necessary for the chancellorship.

**lord president of the council** A regular member of the cabinet for much the same reasons as the *lord privy seal—it is useful to the prime minister to have ministers whose duties are small and who can be asked to undertake special responsibilities or fill the role of elder statesmen. The office originated in Tudor times when the *Privy Council was evolving from the medieval council.

**lord privy seal** The privy seal developed early in the 13th cent. when the use of the *great seal was too cumbersome. From 1275 there was a keeper of the privy seal and the office was upgraded in 1487 when Bishop *Foxe was designated lord privy seal. The use of the privy seal was finally abolished in 1884 but by that time the lord privy seal had long established his position as a member of the cabinet. Being without portfolio, he is now available to take on special governmental responsibilities.

**Lords, House of** The upper chamber of the British Parliament. Originally part of the *great council or the king's council of the Norman and Plantagenet monarchs, the Lords became separated from the Commons in the reign of Edward III. It has been in continuous existence since, except between 1649, at the end of the English Civil War,

when it was abolished by a unanimous vote of the Commons, and 1660. Before the Reformation the spiritual lords (who then included abbots and priors) were in a majority. After 1529, when the abbots and priors were removed, the House was dominated by the lay peers, whose numbers expanded enormously. Life peerages were introduced in 1958, and the Labour government of 1997 removed the right of hereditary peers to attend, while postponing a comprehensive review of the composition of any second chamber. Reform might strengthen the House of Lords or merely add to the influence of the government of the day.

The House of Lords is the highest court of appeal, a function developed since the late 13th cent. when Parliament was regarded as the highest court of royal justice. The appeals were heard by the whole House and any member could take part. An increased work-load led to the problem of finding judicial personnel, and eventually led to the creation in 1876 by the Appellate Jurisdiction Act of the modern judicial powers and practice of the House. These included salaried 'lords of appeal in ordinary', who were to hold peerages only during their terms of office. A further Act of 1887 allowed the lords of appeal to retain their peerages for life.

Over the years the powers of the House of Lords *vis-à-vis* the House of Commons have been severely curtailed. This process probably began in 1407 when Henry IV agreed that money grants were to be initiated in the Commons. The rejection by the Lords of the Finance Bill in 1909, which contained *Lloyd George's 'People's Budget', led to a major constitutional crisis which was resolved by two general elections and the promise of a massive creation of peers given by King George V to *Asquith. The Lords backed down and the resulting Parliament Act of 1911 drastically reduced the powers of the Lords to those of limited delay. A money bill could receive the royal assent after one month even though the consent of the Lords had been withheld, while other public bills could only be delayed by two years (reduced to one year by the Parliament Act of 1949).

**Lord's cricket ground,** home of the Marylebone Cricket Club and of the Middlesex County Cricket Club, was opened in 1787 by Thomas Lord in Dorset Square, near Regent's Park. The first match was between Middlesex and Essex. In 1809 he was obliged to move to St John's Wood. The first test match on the ground was between England and Australia in 1884.

**lords-lieutenant** came into existence at a time of considerable unrest after the death of Henry VIII. Protector *Somerset appointed the earl of Shrewsbury in 1547 to be his lieutenant in the counties of Yorkshire, Lancashire, Cheshire, Derby, Shropshire, and Nottinghamshire and to muster the levies. The system was extended in 1549 when there was widespread rioting. The lord-lieutenant became the chief royal representative in each shire. The growth of a standing army and the reforms of 1871 deprived the lord-lieutenant of most of his military responsibilities, but social prestige remained.

**Losecoat Field, battle of,** 1470. Soon after his capture by *Warwick's supporters after the defeat of his troops at *Edgecote, Edward IV regained some freedom of action. In the spring of the following year, Warwick gave covert support to a Lancastrian rising in Lincolnshire, led by Sir Robert *Welles. Edward defeated the rebels without difficulty on 12 March 1470 near Empingham, 5 miles west of Stamford. In the rout the rebels tore off their incriminating coats and badges.

**Losinga, Herbert de** (*c.*1054–1119). First bishop of Norwich (*c.*1094–1119). Possibly a Lotharingian by descent but English-born, Losinga was educated at Fécamp (Normandy), where he became prior, before moving to Ramsey (Hunts.), as abbot (*c.*1088) and buying the bishopric of Thetford (1091). Sensitivity forced him to resign on grounds of simony, but Pope Urban reinstated him. Losinga moved the see to flourishing Norwich (1094), where he started building the impressive cathedral (1096).

**Lostwithiel campaign,** 1644. Charles I's stunning success at Lostwithiel rescued the royalist cause when almost at its last gasp. *Marston Moor in early July 1644 had been a devastating blow to the king. He was given respite through *Essex's ill-conceived excursion into Cornwall. Unsurprisingly, Charles took the opportunity to pursue Essex and cut off his retreat. His cavalry managed to break out, and Essex himself abandoned his troops, but 6,000 of the infantry were forced to surrender on 2 September.

**Lothian** is the name applied to the tract of land bounded by the Forth and Tweed rivers, which was absorbed into *Northumbria in the 7th cent. and became firmly part of Scotland in the 10th cent. From 1977 until 1996 it formed an administrative region of Scotland. The region was abolished in 1996 and its territory divided between four all-purpose councils, Edinburgh, East Lothian, Midlothian, and West Lothian. The number and strength of the institutions based in Edinburgh cannot fail to ensure that the area round Edinburgh retains the leadership which it acquired when medieval kings of Scotland made it their capital and when ships at the quayside at Leith unloaded French claret and Calvinist theology.

**Loudoun, John Campbell, 1st earl of** [S] (1598–1662). Loudoun played a dexterous part in the tortuous politics of mid-17th-cent. Scotland. Loudoun was raised to the earldom in May 1633 but, since he opposed Charles I's policies, the promotion was not confirmed until 1641. In the meantime, he had become a prominent member of the *covenanting party. Bereft of friends, Charles I was obliged to appoint him chancellor of Scotland and 1st commissioner of the Treasury in 1641. He supported Scottish intervention in the Civil War and was a member of the team which negotiated with the king at *Uxbridge in 1645 and Carisbrooke in 1647. He was on the losing side at *Dunbar, took part in Charles II's coronation at Scone in 1651, but surrendered to *Monck in 1655. At the Restoration, he was deprived of the chancellorship and fined.

**Loudoun Hill, battle of,** 1307. After the defeat at *Methven in 1306, Robert I Bruce fled and his followers were savagely treated. He resumed campaigning the following spring and on 10 May inflicted a sharp defeat on a superior force under Aymer de *Valence at Loudoun Hill, near Kilmarnock.

**Louisbourg** on *Cape Breton Island was the keystone of 18th-cent. French strategy in the North Atlantic. Massive fortifications were commenced in 1719–20, and completed shortly before a British and American colonial force captured it in 1745. Restored to France in 1748, it was again captured after heavy bombardment in 1758, and razed by the British in 1760.

**Louviers, treaty of,** 1196. When Richard I left the Third Crusade and was imprisoned in Germany, Philip Augustus of France launched an attack on Normandy. Once Richard was released he began a successful counter-attack. At Louviers, in January 1196, Richard recovered most of the territory that had been lost. But after John's accession, the whole of the duchy of Normandy was lost in 1204.

**Lovett, William** (1800–77). Chartist. Born in Newlyn, Lovett migrated in 1821 to London, where he became a cabinet-maker. In 1836 he founded the London Working Men's Association, from which emerged the *chartist movement. Helped by Francis *Place and J. A. *Roebuck, Lovett drafted the People's Charter, and from 1838 was a national chartist leader. Lovett was arrested in 1839 following riots in Birmingham and spent a year in gaol. On his release he concentrated on 'knowledge chartism', emphasizing education, self-help, and alliance with the middle class.

**low church** As against the *high-church view of the Church of England, low churchmen minimized continuity with the medieval past and the role of bishops and sacraments. Their views were often described in the late 17th and 18th cents. as '*latitudinarian'. The term passed out of use until the 19th cent., when it was recovered in contrast to the high-church views of the *Oxford movement. By then it had taken on some of the characteristics of the *evangelical revival and shed its lukewarm latitudinarianism.

**Lowe, Robert** (1811–92). Liberal politician. An albino and a sharply sarcastic debater, Lowe cut a distinctive political figure. Of Anglican clerical family and educated at Winchester and Oxford, as a Liberal MP he gained a reputation for anti-democratic views, apparently sharpened by Australian experience. As vice-president of the Privy Council and responsible for popular education, he introduced the 1862 'revised code' linking government grants to examination results in basic subjects. Out of office Lowe

fronted the Whig '*Adullamite' revolt against the 1866 Reform Bill, bringing down *Russell's government and putting the Conservatives in office. When they passed a comparably 'democratic' measure, Lowe concluded it was necessary 'to compel our future masters to learn their letters'. Chancellor of the Exchequer in *Gladstone's 1868 government, Lowe had to withdraw his 1871 budget and was moved to the Home Office in 1873.

**Lowestoft, battle of,** 1665. A heavy engagement in the second Anglo-Dutch War between the English fleet, commanded by James, duke of York (later James II), *Sandwich, and Prince *Rupert, and a Dutch fleet under Jacob van Opdam, on 3 June. Opdam was killed when his flagship blew up and the Dutch losses were severe. 'A great victory, never known in the world,' was Pepys's summary.

**Lucan, George Charles Bingham, 3rd earl of** (1800–88). Born into an aristocratic family, George Bingham became an officer in the British army by purchase in 1816. He relinquished his command in 1837, succeeding to the title of Lord Lucan two years later, but in 1854 was appointed to command a cavalry division for service against the Russians. Landing in the Crimea, the cavalry accompanied the rest of the army in an advance on Sebastopol; on 25 October, during the battle of *Balaclava, Lucan's poor relations with Lord *Cardigan contributed to the '*Charge of the Light Brigade' under Cardigan's command. Lucan rose to the rank of field marshal in 1887.

**Lucknow** or Luknau was the capital of Awadh annexed by the British in 1856. During the *Indian mutiny, the British residency was subjected to a siege beginning in June 1857. Sir Henry *Lawrence, the chief commissioner, was killed in August and the town was not relieved until 16 November.

**Lucy, Richard de** (d. 1179). Justiciar. De Lucy was one of the chief props of Henry II's reign. He originally supported Stephen and by the treaty of *Winchester of 1153, which arranged the succession, he was put in charge of the Tower. He was joint justiciar with the earl of Leicester until 1168 and sole justiciar until 1178. He supported the king against Thomas *Becket, who excommunicated him as 'a promoter of royal tyranny'. In the great crisis of Henry's reign in 1173–4, when the king was campaigning on the continent, de Lucy was the mainstay at home, driving back William the Lion of Scotland and defeating the rebel earl of Leicester at *Fornham St Genevieve.

**Luddites** Machine-breakers, so called after a mythical leader, General Ludd. In 1811–16 textile workers in the east midlands, south Lancashire, and west Yorkshire met secretly in public houses or on the moors, took oaths, and smashed the machinery of mill-owners who refused their demands. At a time when trade unions were illegal, Luddism may be interpreted as collective bargaining by riot: frame-breaking in the east midlands was an attempt to coerce employers rather than hostility to machines as such. Eventually the Luddite bands were tracked down and the reputed leaders executed or transported.

**Ludford Bridge, battle of,** 1459. After *Salisbury's victory at *Blore Heath, he marched to Ludlow to join his allies *Warwick and *York. Confronted by a large Lancastrian force, the Yorkist leaders fled, leaving their troops to surrender.

**Ludlow, Edmund** (c.1617–92). Ludlow was one of a group of austere republicans that included *Vane and *Haselrig. Ludlow joined *Essex's army in 1642 and fought throughout the war, mainly in Haselrig's cavalry. Returned for Wiltshire in 1646, he signed the king's death warrant in 1649. In 1651–5 he served in Ireland, though disapproving *Cromwell's Protectorate. Returning to Parliament in 1659, he opposed Richard *Cromwell and, after his fall, joined Haselrig in the *Council of State. At the Restoration in 1660 he escaped to the continent. In 1689 he misjudged the situation in England, returned to London, and was obliged to flee again when a proclamation was issued for his arrest.

**Ludlow castle** (Shropshire), standing on a cliff above the river Teme, has long been regarded as a romantic and picturesque ruin, attractive to artists and writers. Founded soon after the Conquest by the de Lacy family as a strong point in the turbulent march area, the castle and town remained important throughout the Middle Ages. In 1473, when Edward IV sent his son to Ludlow, the castle became the headquarters of the nascent *Council of the Marches, which between 1534 and 1641 was the focus of government for the Welsh border.

**Lugard, Sir Frederick, Baron Lugard** (1858–1945). Colonial administrator. Lugard started as a soldier and adventurer. Then he helped the Royal Niger Company in the west, and when its charter ran out became British commissioner in northern Nigeria. While there he devised a new way of governing 'natives', called 'indirect rule', or ruling them according to their own customs rather than by imposing alien ones. He later justified this philosophically, in a seminal book called *The Dual Mandate in British Tropical Africa* (1922). That made Lugard an obvious choice for the League of Nations Permanent Mandates Commission, on which he sat from 1922 to 1936.

**Lulach** (d. 1058), king of 'Scotland' and Moray (1057–8). His mother Gruoch married *Macbeth after the death of Lulach's father Gille Comgáin, king of *Moray, in 1032 at Macbeth's hands. He probably allied with *Malcolm Canmore against Macbeth, and became king of Scotland when Malcolm killed Macbeth in 1057. Four and a half months later Lulach was himself Malcolm's victim, slain 'by treachery' at Essie (west of Aberdeen), probably on 17 March 1058.

**Lumphanan, battle of,** 1057. On 15 August 1057 *Malcolm Canmore defeated and killed *Macbeth. The version given in Shakespeare's play runs together several encounters in different places.

**Lutheranism** While the views of Calvin were largely expounded in one treatise, his *Institutes*, those of Martin Luther (1483–1546) had to be gleaned from a number of tracts and sermons. Luther took the Bible as the ultimate authority for Christians and his main belief was justification by faith alone: it was therefore essential for Christians to understand the Bible and Luther made his own celebrated translation into German. He recognized three sacraments: baptism, the eucharist in both kinds, and penitence. He was as committed to predestination as Calvin, finding no freedom for the human will.

Lutheranism's greatest success was in north Germany and in Scandinavia. In England, his reputation was marred by a sharp theological exchange with Henry VIII, to whose *Defence of the Seven Sacraments* (1521), which had won from the papacy the title 'Defender of the Faith' for the king, Luther replied with *Against Henry King of England* (1522). Many English churchmen thought it wise to distance themselves from Luther and to insist that the English Reformation was autonomous and independent. After Luther's death, the influence of Calvin and Geneva on the English clergy, and certainly on the Scottish, was much greater than that of Lutheranism.

**Lutyens, Sir Edwin Landseer** (1869–1944). English architect. Starting in 1896 with Munstead Wood (Surrey) for the gardener Gertrude Jekyll (1843–1942), Lutyens's early houses include Deanery Gardens, Sonning, Berks. (1899–1902), Tigbourne Court, Witley, Surrey (1899–1901), and Folly Farm, Sulhamstead, Berks. (1905). All demonstrate his ingenious planning and his imagination, sensitivity, and wit in the use of brick, tile, stone, and other traditional materials. Lutyens's commitment to classicism is best seen in such London office buildings as Britannic House (1920–4) and the Midland Bank (1924–37), and in his design for the Roman catholic cathedral, Liverpool (1929–44). Lutyens's Cenotaph in Whitehall (1919–20) lacks the eerie grandeur of his memorial to the missing of the Somme at Thiepval, near Arras, France (1927–32).

**Lyndhurst, John Singleton Copley, 1st Baron** (1772–1863). Lord chancellor. Born in Boston (Mass.), son of J. S. Copley, the portrait painter, he came to England, attended Cambridge University, and was called to the bar in 1804. He was appointed solicitor-general in 1819 and prosecuted the *Cato Street conspirators and in the 'trial' of Queen Caroline. He became attorney-general in 1824, master of the rolls 1826, and Tory lord chancellor 1827–30, 1834–5, and 1841–6. A leading opponent of the Reform Bill, and a tower of strength to the Conservative Party in the Lords after 1830, he was a vigorous and effective speaker even in his later years.

**Lytton, Edward Robert Bulwer-Lytton, 1st Earl** (1831–91). Son of the historical novelist, Lytton was educated at Harrow. He enjoyed a successful career in the diplomatic service and became attached to the Conservative Party interest. He was appointed viceroy of India in 1875 by *Disraeli and organized the great 'durbah' proclaiming Victoria queen-empress in 1877. His administration was principally distinguished for its aggressive external policies which, in 1878, brought about the second *Afghan War. In 1887 Lytton was appointed ambassador to Paris by Lord *Salisbury.

**Maastricht, treaty of** Popular name for the treaty on European Union, signed on 7 February 1992 at Maastricht in the Netherlands by the twelve EEC members. The treaty amended the treaty of *Rome and Single European Act, increasing the competence of the European Union (EEC), and giving the European Council (meetings of heads of government) greater powers in the fields of defence and immigration. John Major, the British prime minister, obtained opt-outs for the social chapter and single currency and claimed the negotiations as a triumph.

**McAdam, John Loudoun** (1756–1836). Road surveyor. Returning as a loyalist from New York in 1783, McAdam settled in Ayrshire, and managed the British Tar Company. His travels turned interest into profession, as he covered nearly 19,000 miles in 1,900 days on the road, 1798–1814, making the observations that formed his 'principles': employing small stones direct onto the subsoil as the method of making effective roads largely impermeable to water. McAdam secured appointment as surveyor-general of the Bristol roads from 1816, and unpopularly consolidated his dynasty across Britain: McAdam, three sons, four grandsons, and a brother-in-law held 136 surveyorships in England and 8 in Scotland, 1816–61. His fame led to the use of the term 'macadamize' as early as 1824.

**Macartney, George, 1st Earl Macartney** (1737–1806). Born in Ireland and educated at Trinity College, Dublin, Macartney had a varied career. He was envoy to St Petersburg (1764–7); a chief secretary for Ireland (1769–72); and captain-general of the Caribbee Islands (1775–9). In 1780 he was appointed governor of *Madras. The Madras Council was riddled with corruption and Hyder Ali, the sultan of Mysore, stood at the gates threatening to drive the English into the sea. Macartney re-established internal order

and engaged Mysore in a truce. After returning to England in 1786, his most important office was as first British ambassador to the court of Peking (1792–4). His final office was that of governor of the Cape of Good Hope (1796–9).

**Macaulay, Thomas Babington, 1st Baron** (1800–59). Poet, historian, and politician. Of Scottish presbyterian ancestry, he was the son of Zachary Macaulay, the evangelical anti-slaver and co-founder of the *Clapham sect. Educated at Trinity College, Cambridge, he acquired an early reputation as a Whig orator and a later reputation as a formidable contributor to the *Edinburgh Review*. A Whig MP for Calne, Leeds, and Edinburgh, he became secretary at war, paymaster-general, and was involved in drafting a new penal code for India. His *Lays of Ancient Rome* appeared in 1842, four years after he had projected the future *History of England*. Originally intended as a history of England since 1688, Macaulay had only reached 1702 by the time of his death. It set the terms of a new Whig historiography which survived until the middle of the 20th cent.

**Macbeth** (d. 1057), king of Moray (1032–57) and king of 'Scotland' (1040–57). Macbeth's reputation as a tyrannous usurper is, of course, anachronistic. He became the only person from northern Scotland to rule the Scottish kingdom for more than a few months, and the only king of Scotland to visit Rome (in 1050) where, we are told, 'he scattered money like seed to the poor'. So strong was his position that he retained the Scottish throne in 1054, despite defeat at Dunsinnan (north of Perth).

Macbeth's family was riven by a feud that claimed the life of Macbeth's father in 1020, which Macbeth avenged in 1032 by burning his cousin Gille Comgáin, king of Moray. He married Gille Comgáin's widow Gruoch, perhaps in an attempt at reconciliation. In 1040 he killed *Duncan I (probably) at Pitgaveny (near Elgin) and in 1045 reached his zenith when he crushed Duncan's father. After Dunsinnan, however, he was forced to accept the return of Duncan's son *Malcolm Canmore from exile, and in 1057 was killed at *Lumphanan (25 miles west of Aberdeen) by Malcolm.

**Macclesfield, Thomas Parker, 1st earl of** (1667–1732). Parker was the son of a Staffordshire attorney and educated at Trinity College, Cambridge. Returned for Derby as a Whig MP in 1705, he took a leading part in the prosecution of Dr *Sacheverell in 1710. From 1710 to 1718 he was lord chief justice of Queen's Bench and was made Baron Parker in 1716. He removed to the lord chancellorship in 1718 and became earl of Macclesfield in 1721. In 1725 he was accused of peculation and forced to resign.

**MacCormick, John MacDonald** (1904–61). A Glasgow lawyer and son of a sea-captain, MacCormick was a leading founder of the National Party of Scotland in 1928. In 1934 the National Party merged with the Scottish Party to form the *Scottish National Party. MacCormick lost control of the party in 1942 to more radical leaders, who opposed the war. He then formed a Scottish Convention which summoned a 'Scottish National Assembly' in 1947 to call for devolution.

**MacDonald, Flora** (1722–90). Born on South Uist, but educated in Edinburgh, Flora's help was enlisted during a visit to the island of Benbecula for Charles Edward *Stuart's escape to Skye, after *Culloden. She crossed the Minch with a manservant and 'an Irish spinning maid, Betty Burke'; the party then travelled from Kilbride to Portree for a boat to take Charles to Raasay.

**MacDonald, James Ramsay** (1866–1937). Prime minister. Between 1900 and 1929 Ramsay MacDonald contributed more than any other individual to building the Labour Party into a credible, national party of government. Throughout his career he retained a clear vision of a democratic socialist movement which would unite middle-class radicalism with working-class votes. As prime minister and foreign secretary in

the first Labour government of 1924 he went a long way to demonstrating Labour's fitness to govern. Yet under pressure, defects of temperament undermined his effectiveness as an executive leader. Basically a shy and insecure man, his loneliness made him vulnerable to friendships in aristocratic circles later in life. This was all the more natural when the failures of his second government led to his participation in the *National Government in 1931. This decision immediately destroyed his standing on the left; and he has been regarded as a traitor ever since.

Born into poverty in Lossiemouth on the north-east coast of Scotland, MacDonald was the illegitimate child of a servant girl and a farm labourer. But by the 1890s he had become a leading figure in the new *Independent Labour Party. By 1900 he was sufficiently well known and respected to be invited to serve as secretary to the new Labour Representation Committee which became the Labour Party in 1906. In 1903 he negotiated an electoral pact with Herbert Gladstone, the Liberal chief whip, which meant that the Liberals would refrain from running candidates in 29 of the 50 constituencies contested by Labour at the 1906 general election. In 24 of the 29 seats Labour candidates subsequently proved successful, including MacDonald himself, elected for Leicester.

As an MP his oratorical powers and capacity for mastering legislative detail made him the outstanding parliamentarian on the Labour bench and in 1911 he became chairman of the parliamentary party. Up to 1914, it appears that he intended to maintain the pact. The First World War interrupted both this strategy and MacDonald's steady rise. By opposing British entry into the war he put himself in a minority and gave up the party chairmanship. In the chauvinistic mood of the 1918 election MacDonald suffered a heavy defeat at Leicester.

He achieved his comeback in 1922 when he became the member for Aberavon. Now that opinion had turned against the pre-war arms race and wartime casualties, he gained much credit for the principled stand he had taken in 1914. In the contest for the party leadership he narrowly defeated J. R. Clynes.

MacDonald deserves credit for the skill with which he played a difficult hand in the aftermath of the 1923 election. With only 191

MPs he was invited to form a government. He deliberately avoided any deal with the Liberals, so as to prevent a return to the client relationship Labour had enjoyed before 1914. He strengthened his administration with former Liberal and Conservative ministers and, as foreign secretary, played a constructive role in reducing German reparations. Although the government was defeated in Parliament after nine months, MacDonald had largely succeeded in his object of establishing Labour as a competent governing party.

During the next five years the inability of the *Baldwin government to tackle unemployment helped Labour to a further advance. In 1929 they won 288 seats. But this time MacDonald's conventional economic policy proved inadequate. As unemployment mounted the prime minister seemed indecisive and self-pitying—the 'Boneless Wonder' in *Churchill's phrase. By August 1931 the balance of payments deficit obliged the cabinet to attempt to restore confidence by balancing its budget. But it split over proposed cuts in unemployment benefit. MacDonald astonished his colleagues by accepting the king's invitation to lead a *National Government with the Liberals and Tories. Though originally seen as a temporary expedient, the National Government rapidly assumed a permanent form by holding a general election in October 1931. MacDonald thus retained the premiership until 1935 and continued in office until 1937.

**MacDonald, John, 4th lord of the Isles** (1434–1503). He succeeded his father Alexander, 3rd lord, in 1449, aged 15, and was almost immediately involved in efforts to defend his huge inheritance—which included not only the Hebrides and western coastline from Lewis to Kintyre, but also the earldom of Ross. MacDonald's rebellion of 1451 put him on the wrong side in the James II–Black Douglas civil wars of the 1450s. In 1462 he made the treaty of *Westminster-Ardtornish with Edward IV of England, an abortive pact which envisaged the tripartite division of Scotland among MacDonald, his cousin Donald Balloch, and the forfeited 9th earl of Douglas. Summoned for treason, MacDonald finally forfeited his earldom of Ross in 1476, and lost his credibility in the Isles at the same time. The forfeiture of the

lordship (1493) left John MacDonald a pathetic pensioner of the crown until his death in January 1503.

**Mackenzie, Sir George** (1636–91). 'Bloody Mackenzie' was a nephew of the 2nd earl of Seaforth [S], briefly secretary of state [S] to Charles II in exile. A lawyer by profession, he opposed the rule of *Lauderdale at first but in 1677 was appointed king's advocate [S]. In this capacity he harassed the *covenanters, particularly after the skirmish at *Bothwell Bridge in 1679. His use of torture earned him his nickname and the 1680s were known in covenanting circles as 'the killing time'. He took no part in public life after the Glorious Revolution.

**Mackenzie, William Lyon** (1795–1861). Mackenzie was born in Dundee and emigrated to Upper Canada (now Ontario) in 1820, where he became a newspaperman and radical politician. In 1834 Mackenzie became first mayor of Toronto, but in 1836 reformers were routed in Assembly elections. During 1837 Mackenzie organized armed demonstrations, but lost control of events. Rebellion broke out on 4 December. Mackenzie escaped to the USA, but an amnesty enabled him to return to Canada in 1849.

**Mackintosh, Charles Rennie** (1868–1928). Scottish architect and designer, a leading exponent of the Glasgow School of art nouveau. He designed a number of houses in and around Glasgow at the turn of the century but his best work was the designs for the Glasgow School of Art. His furniture and interior designs are characteristically art nouveau while avoiding florid excess.

**Mackintosh, Sir James** (1765–1832). Scottish philosopher, historian, lawyer, and politician. A man of many talents, Mackintosh read philosophy at Aberdeen University, qualified in medicine at Edinburgh in 1787, and was called to the bar in London in 1795. He contributed to literary journals, and wrote a celebrated critique of *Burke's *Reflections on the Revolution in France*, entitled *Vindiciae Gallicae* (1791). Mackintosh became recorder of Bombay in 1804, and returned to England to take up a parliamentary seat in 1813, speaking in defence of civil liberty against the authoritarian policies introduced by the post-war Tory administration.

**Maclise, Daniel** (1806–70). Historical and portrait painter and caricaturist. Born in Cork, the son of a Scottish soldier, Maclise became a student of Cork Academy when it opened in 1822, and of the Royal Academy Schools in London in 1828. In 1840 he was elected RA but later declined the presidency and a knighthood.

**Macmillan, Harold** (1894–1986). Prime minister. Anglo-American by birth, Macmillan proceeded from Eton to Balliol College, Oxford, where he secured a first in classical moderations. During the war he was badly injured. After the war he served as ADC to the governor-general of Canada before going into the family publishing firm.

Macmillan was elected as member for Stockton at his second attempt in 1924. In Parliament he associated himself with a group of progressive Tories, styled the YMCA, but his career suffered a blow when he lost his seat in the 1929 general election. He won it back in 1931. The publication of *The Middle Way* in 1938 showed Macmillan's commitment to a mixed economy and considerable government intervention. Macmillan was also at odds with the foreign policy of the National Government and resigned the Conservative whip for the last year of *Baldwin's premiership.

When *Churchill became premier in May 1940 Macmillan's ministerial rewards were initially small. But in 1942 he made his first major political advance with his appointment as minister of state for north Africa. Macmillan took easily to his new authority and struck up a good working relationship with General Eisenhower.

Macmillan lost his Stockton seat again in the general election of 1945, but was soon returned to Parliament following a by-election in Bromley. As minister of housing after 1951 Macmillan achieved credit as the man who fulfilled the Conservative pledge to build 300,000 houses in a single year. He served briefly as minister of defence, but became foreign secretary when Eden succeeded to the premiership in 1955. Too forceful in this post for Eden's liking, he was transferred to the Exchequer after six months.

An ardent proponent of the *Suez adventure in 1956, its failure provided Macmillan with his opportunity. Though it was he who pressed the financial necessity of bringing the operation to an end, his earlier enthusiasm ensured the backing of the Conservative right. To the surprise of many he was preferred to Butler when ill-health forced Eden's resignation in January 1957.

As prime minister Macmillan displayed political skills which few had anticipated. Against the odds, he restored party morale after Suez and led the Conservatives to a third successive electoral victory in 1959. By 1960 Macmillan stood at the height of his power. The nickname 'Supermac' encapsulated the public's acclaim. But then problems arose. The collapse of the summit conference of 1960 was a particular blow which helped persuade Macmillan to seek British admission to the European Common Market. This quest ultimately met with the veto of General de Gaulle. Meanwhile difficulties mounted on the domestic front. Many sensed panic when Macmillan dismissed a third of his cabinet, including the chancellor, in the famous 'Night of the Long Knives' in July 1962. Thereafter the government was beset by a series of sex and spy scandals. Illness precipitated Macmillan's resignation at the time of the Conservative Party conference in October 1963.

Macmillan was a complex individual. An external self-confidence was matched by inner doubts, exacerbated no doubt by his wife's long-standing affair with Robert Boothby. The years of his premiership remain controversial. For some they represent a period of unprecedented prosperity; for others a time when a blind eye was turned to underlying problems in the British economy.

**Macready, William** (1793–1873). Actor. Macready had a long and successful career in the age of Mrs Siddons and Kean. The son of an Irish actor settled in London, he took up the stage when his father's ventures collapsed, appearing at Birmingham in 1810 as Romeo. He first appeared on the London stage at Covent Garden in 1816, but not until his Richard III in 1819 was his popularity firmly established.

**McTaggart, William** (1835–1910). Painter. McTaggart was born in Kintyre (Strathclyde), in a poor labouring family. He studied in Glasgow and Edinburgh, meeting his expenses by painting portraits, and first exhibited in 1856. He became a regular exhibitor at the Royal Academy and Royal Scottish Academy. He decided early on to concentrate on landscapes, and by the 1870s the sea and boats were the most recurrent themes of his work.

**Madeleine of France** (1520–37), queen of James V of Scotland. The eldest surviving daughter of Francis I of France, Madeleine married James V in Paris on 1 January 1537. Madeleine herself favoured the match, despite warnings that her fragile health would not survive the Scottish climate, and sailed for Scotland in May 1537. She died only weeks later on 7 July.

**Madog ap Maredudd** (d. 1160), prince of Powys (1132–60). The Welsh princes took advantage of the civil war in England during the reign of Stephen to rebuild their position after the reign of Henry I. Madog inherited Powys from his father Maredudd ap Bleddyn in 1132 and had to deal with the expansionary ambitions of *Owain, prince of Gwynedd, on his northern border.

**Madras (Chennai)** as founded by Francis Day of the English *East India Company in 1639. It stood on a strip of the Coromandel coast famous for its textiles. A fortification (named after St George) was built and became the headquarters of company activities. The city became the capital of a presidency in the 19th cent. but suffered economic stagnation.

**Mael Snechta** (d. 1085), king of Moray (c.1058–c.1078). A son of *Lulach, it is likely that he succeeded his father as king of *Moray after his death at the hands of *Malcolm III. Mael Snechta himself suffered a serious defeat by Malcolm III which may have broken his power. He died peacefully in 1085.

**Mafeking** is a small town in the north-east corner of Cape Province (South Africa), where a British garrison was besieged for seven months during the second *Boer War, before being relieved on 17 May 1900. That gave rise to a display of *jingoism back in Britain, for which a new word—'mafficking'—was coined.

**Magersfontein, battle of,** 1899. As Lord Methuen, commanding a British division, advanced to relieve the Boer siege of *Kimberley, he approached the Magersfontein heights. A Boer force under General Cronje lay in wait, and when Methuen's Highland Brigade tried to turn the enemy flank on 11 December, the Boers inflicted heavy punishment.

**Magna Carta** was sealed by King John on 15 June 1215 at Runnymede (Berks.). It followed a period of intense political and military activity after John's defeat at *Bouvines. Magna Carta was the product of long and hard negotiation. It was designed to be a negotiated peace, bridging the extreme rebels on the one hand, and John and his supporters on the other. But in this it was a total failure for John had no intention of adhering to Magna Carta, agreeing to it only to gain time. In September 1215 civil war began in earnest. The charter's achievement and significance lie elsewhere, for it laid down standards to be observed in the future by the crown, for the first time in written law establishing defined limitations to royal rights. With the reissues of 1216 and 1217, and the definitive version of 1225 (much briefer than the original), the charter became a statement of law.

**Magnus, St** (c.1075–c.1117). Magnus was the victim of his ambitious cousin Haakon, who intrigued with the Norwegian king Magnus Barefoot to bring about the downfall of their fathers, ruling earls of the Orkney Islands. When the Norwegian king died, Haakon returned to rule the Orkneys. Magnus claimed his share of the earldom, but within a few years Haakon determined to dispose of his rival. Magnus, with a few retainers, was invited to meet and confirm a covenant of peace, but was confronted by Haakon and a large armed retinue. Offering no resistance, he accepted his death. Kirkwall cathedral is dedicated to him.

**Magonsaete, kingdom of the** Although the Anglo-Saxon kingdom which was conterminous with the diocese of Hereford is usually referred to as the kingdom of the Magonsaete, the name is not recorded until the 9th cent. The people of the province may originally have been known as the West Angles. The first element of 'Magonsaete' is possibly derived from Magnis, the Roman town of Kentchester. The earliest recorded king is Merewalh, who is described as a son of *Penda of Mercia. The last known ruler Mildfrith, son of Merewalh, died *c.*735 and it would appear that the province became a Mercian ealdormanry after that date.

**Maiden castle** is perhaps the most spectacular Iron Age hill-fort in Britain. However, this 50-acre hilltop 3 miles south of Dorchester has a longer history stretching back to the neolithic. The Iron Age fort, initially enclosing 25 acres, was built over the neolithic camp around 600–500 BC. The defences were gradually elaborated by the addition of further ramparts, finally achieving their present form around 100 BC. It was defended against Roman attack around AD 43–5, as skeletons with wounds from sword cuts and ballista bolts were found buried in the east entrance.

**Maidstone, battle of,** 1648. Although the Kentish royalists in 1648 had assembled an army of 11,000 men, they dispersed them among several towns, leaving just 2,000 in Maidstone. Sir Thomas *Fairfax, after assembling a 4,000-strong parliamentary force, attacked the town on 1 June. Under heavy rain the defenders were eventually overpowered.

**Main plot,** 1603. Regarded by the government as the principal conspiracy to distinguish it from the *Bye plot. The Spaniards were said to have encouraged a scheme to replace James I by his cousin Arabella *Stuart in the hope of obtaining peace.

**Maitland, Frederick William** (1850–1906). Historian. By common consent, Maitland was one of the great British historians, with remarkable influence after a comparatively short academic career. Educated at Eton and Trinity College, Cambridge, he began as a lawyer but switched to history. His most famous book was a *History of English Law* (1895) of which his co-author, Sir Frederick Pollock, wrote only a fraction.

**Maitland, John Maitland, 1st Baron** [S] (*c.*1545–95). Maitland succeeded his father in 1567 as keeper of the privy seal [S]. He and his elder brother Sir William Maitland were strong supporters of Mary, queen of Scots. But when James VI came of age, Maitland found himself in favour. In 1584 he was

knighted and made secretary of state for life, and from 1587 until his death he was lord chancellor [S].

**Major, John** (b. 1943). Prime minister. Major entered the House of Commons in 1979 after a career in banking and during the next decade had a meteoric rise to power. His parliamentary career began in the whips' office (1983–5), and then in the Department of Health and Social Services (1985–7). He became chief secretary to the Treasury in 1987 but two years later, still a political unknown, was chosen by Mrs *Thatcher to replace first Sir Geoffrey Howe as foreign secretary, then Nigel Lawson as chancellor of the Exchequer. In 1990, on Mrs Thatcher's resignation, Major defeated Douglas Hurd and Michael Heseltine for the leadership, attracting support as Thatcher's political heir. In 1992 he won the general election against the odds.

Relations with Europe were at the heart of Major's difficulties as prime minister. The Tory Party was split on the issue, yet in 1992 he agreed to sign the treaty on European unity at *Maastricht, which laid down a timetable for a single currency and established majority voting in almost every area of policy. The concessions Major gained in the negotiations appeared cosmetic and it was not easy to understand how he could claim to have won 'game, set and match'.

Major's popularity, based in part on the contrast he offered to his predecessor, declined sharply. A 'back-to-basics' initiative, intended to improve the moral climate of the nation, foundered amid Tory scandal and sleaze. In 1994 Major attempted to recapture the initiative by tackling the Irish problem, although it involved, contrary to previous assurances, negotiating with the *Irish Republican Army. In spite of a considerable economic recovery, Tory divisions over Europe continued to fester, although in 1995 Major beat off a challenge to his leadership from John Redwood, representing the anti-Europe sceptics. Major postponed a general election until the last possible moment. In May 1997 his party suffered a severe defeat and he resigned immediately, though remaining in the Commons as an elder statesman. Widely regarded as honest and well intentioned, and considerably more popular than his party, Major's years as leader were dogged by misfortune and he rarely seemed in advance of events.

**major-generals, rule of the** The division of England into twelve military districts, each under the direct rule of a major-general, was in part a consequence of the breakdown of the *Instrument of Government, in part *Cromwell's response to *Penruddock's rising in March 1655. The emergency measure was deeply resented by many of the local gentry, the natural rulers of the shires, and the major-generals were bitterly attacked as men of low birth.

**Majuba Hill, battle of,** 1881. Majuba Hill was the only major battle of the first *Boer War (1880–1), which arose from the British annexation of the Republic of the *Transvaal in 1877. In December 1880 the Boers rose in revolt, laying siege to isolated British garrisons. At Majuba Hill the British were driven off with 287 casualties compared to 7 Boers. By the convention of *Pretoria of 5 April the Transvaal regained its independence.

**Malachy, St** (*c.*1094–1148). Malachy was a great reforming bishop in Ireland, when hereditary succession linked church with clan, sacraments were neglected, and old customs frequently prevailed over canon law. His own nomination as archbishop of *Armagh, 1129, was strongly opposed by his predecessor's kin and took several years to resolve.

**Malawi** Former British central African protectorate of Nyasaland. The missionary explorer David *Livingstone led the first group of Britons to the region in 1859 and after initial set-backs Nyasaland became a thriving centre of missionary activity. A British protectorate was declared in 1893. Nyasaland became independent as Malawi in 1964 and a republic in 1966.

**Malaysia,** or the Malay archipelago, was long famous for its trade. English interest began in 1786 with the foundation of Penang and increased in the 1820s with the development of the Straits Settlement. The settlement became a crown colony in 1867. It was amalgamated with other sultanates, previously held as protectorates, to form the Federation of Malaya in 1948. In 1957 the Malaysian Federation became independent.

**Malcolm I** (d. 954), son of *Donald II, was king of 'Scotland', ousting the aged *Constantine II in the 940s. He led a victorious army into *Moray, raided northern England as far as the Tees, and in 945 won *Edmund, king of Wessex's recognition that the kingdom of *Strathclyde/Cumbria lay within his sphere of influence. He was killed by the men of the Mearns at Fetteresso (south of Aberdeen).

**Malcolm II** (d. 1034), king of 'Scotland' (1005–34). Son of *Kenneth II, Malcolm was known to later generations as 'the most victorious'. His career was not always so, however. He became king in 1005 by killing his first cousin Kenneth III at Monzievaird (west of Perth), and in the following year invaded northern England as far as Durham, but was thoroughly defeated. Despite this reverse he successfully re-established control over *Lothian by a famous victory at *Carham (west of Berwick) in 1018. He could not escape the power of *Cnut, however, and submitted to him in 1031/2.

**Malcolm III** (d. 1093), king of 'Scotland' (1058–93). Malcolm 'Canmore' ('big head' or 'great leader') was the son of *Duncan I and was still a child when his father was killed by *Macbeth in 1040. Malcolm found refuge in England, and was backed by *Siward, the Anglo-Danish earl of Northumbria, who led an army into Scotland in 1054 defeating Macbeth at Dunsinnan (north of Perth). On 15 August 1057 Malcolm killed Macbeth at *Lumphanan (west of Aberdeen), but *Lulach, Macbeth's stepson and cousin, won the kingship. After only eighteen weeks Lulach was killed 'by treachery' by Malcolm at Essie (west of Aberdeen). Malcolm's grip on the kingship was only secure, however, after he defeated Lulach's son Mael Snechta, king of *Moray, in 1078.

Malcolm's struggle against *Mael Snechta made him an ally of Moray's traditional foe, the earl of Orkney, whose close relative Ingibiorg he married. Malcolm was already a widower, however, when the Anglo-Saxon royal family fled to Scotland in 1070, and he took *Edgar Atheling's sister *Margaret as his second wife. His attention now focused on Northumbria, which he raided repeatedly despite submitting to William the Conqueror in 1072 at *Abernethy (south-east of Perth).

In August 1093 he laid the foundation stone of Durham cathedral; two months later he was killed on a raid at *Alnwick.

**Malcolm IV** (c.1141–65), king of Scots (1153–65), later known as 'the Maiden'. Grandson and successor of David I, his uncontested enthronement in 1153 at the age of 12 reflects the contemporary strength and prestige of the Scottish monarchy. He and his advisers continued to implement David I's Normanizing policies, despite mounting native opposition. After the crisis of Stephen's reign, Henry II swiftly restored English royal might, and at Chester in 1157 Malcolm had to surrender the northern English counties in return for the earldom of Huntingdon.

**Maldives** The Maldive islands lie 400 miles south-west of Sri Lanka. The Portuguese briefly established a settlement 1518–28 but in 1887 the British government placed them under a direct protectorate.

**Maldon, battle of,** 991. In August 991 Byrhtnoth, ealdorman of Essex, was killed by a Danish force led by Guthmund and Olaf Tryggvason at Maldon on the river Blackwater in Essex. Byrhtnoth's heroic death was commemorated in the great Anglo-Saxon battle poem, *The Battle of Maldon.*

**Malory, Sir Thomas** (d. 1471). The identity of Malory, author of *Le Morte Darthur*, is not certain. The most likely suggestion is Sir Thomas Malory of Newbold Revel (War.). If it is correct, he had been knighted in 1445, served in Parliament for Warwickshire the same year, and was a follower of *Warwick the Kingmaker. Malory's famous volume was a compilation from various sources, mainly French, and was printed by Caxton in 1485.

**Malplaquet, battle of,** 1709. As allied (British—imperialist) forces under *Marlborough and Prince Eugene laid siege to Mons, a French army under Marshal Villars moved towards them. When the allies attacked on 11 September they faced heavy opposition, and although the French were forced to retreat, the costs to both sides were horrific.

**Malta** The island of Malta, of great strategic significance, lies 60 miles south of Sicily: it is 17 miles in length and 9 across. Malta was acquired by Britain at the end of the Napoleonic wars in 1814. From 1940, when Italy entered the Second World War, it was subjected to constant bombing until 1943 and received the George Cross as a tribute. It became independent in 1964 and was declared a republic in 1974. Malta has been a member of the European Union since 2004.

**Malthus, Thomas Robert** (1766–1834). Malthus was born near Guildford, his father having private means. After attending Jesus College, Cambridge, he was elected to a fellowship (1793), took holy orders, and became a curate in Surrey, and from 1805 taught at the East India Company College at Haileybury. His most celebrated work, the *Essay on Population* (1798), was directed at the facile optimism of Condorcet and *Godwin. Malthus argued that while population, unchecked, would increase geometrically, subsistence would increase only arithmetically. Consequently any improvement in the standard of living would soon be wiped out. His theory was seized upon by those who wished to argue that progress must be an illusion, and his condemnation of the Poor Laws for encouraging breeding had important consequences.

**Man, Isle of** *See* ISLE OF MAN.

**Manchester** Sited where natural routes crossed and bridges could be maintained, the Roman military station Mamucium or Mancunium controlled the *Brigantes, while acting as a supply base. Encouraged by the moist atmosphere, soft water, and nearby coal supplies, local textile industries so flourished that Manchester became their chief commercial centre as well as a manufacturing and finishing site. Crowded, makeshift dwellings and dangerous sanitary conditions underlay a strong working-class radical movement and the so-called '*Peterloo massacre' (1819), but unemployment and *Luddism were tempered by the rise of trade unionism and methodism. Belief in free trade prompted *Cobden and *Bright to push for the repeal of the Corn Laws, and the city's political temper began to harden into Liberalism. Home of the *Manchester Guardian*, Victoria University, and the Hallé Orchestra, it was a city of enormous vitality in its cultural and intellectual life.

**Manchester, diocese of** The rapid population expansion of the industrial north led the ecclesiastical commissioners of 1835 to recommend that Chester diocese be relieved by the creation of two new sees of Ripon and Manchester. Covering Lancashire, except for Liverpool district, Furness, and Cartmel, the initial archdeaconries of Manchester and Lancashire were augmented by those of Blackburn (1877) and Rochdale (1910); Blackburn became a separate diocese in 1926.

**Manchester, Edward Montagu, 2nd earl of** (1602–71). Parliamentary commander during the Civil War. Manchester was sympathetic towards *presbyterianism and a leading opponent of the king before the outbreak of war. He fought in the opening battle at *Edgehill and was in command at *Marston Moor and at the second battle of *Newbury. In November 1644 *Cromwell launched a fierce attack upon him, accusing him of lethargy and of hankering after compromise. He was forced to resign by the *self-denying ordinance in 1645. He survived to help bring about the restoration of Charles II, and held high court office for the rest of his life.

**Manchester, Greater** A term first used in 1914 to describe a commercial rather than municipal focus in north-west England, but now applied to the major conurbation which was created a metropolitan county after local government reform (1972). Of the six such counties created, it is the only one to be named after its central city.

**Manchester martyrs,** 1867. On 18 September an attempt was made to rescue *Fenian leaders Thomas Kelly and Timothy Deasy from police custody in Manchester. During the attempt, Police Sergeant Charles Brett was killed, causing strong anti-Irish feeling. Three Fenians, William Allen, Michael Larkin, and Michael O'Brien, were executed for the murder on 23 November. There was widespread indignation in Ireland and the 'martyrs', as they became known, were given a public funeral attended by over 60,000 people.

**Manchester School** This provided a convenient label to identify many of the 19th-cent. advocates of *laissez-faire and, in particular, *free trade. Widespread support for free trade developed amongst the manufacturers of the cotton industry in Lancashire and Cheshire. The intellectual focus for this movement included Richard *Cobden and John *Bright. The initial case for removing mercantilist regulations of trade had been made by Adam *Smith in *The Wealth of Nations* (1776).

**mandates** After the First World War, the colonial territories of the defeated powers were distributed to the victorious allies, under the general supervision of the *League of Nations, which set up a Permanent Mandates Commission. It was insisted that the mandated territories would move towards self-government. Britain acquired Iraq, Trans-Jordan, and Palestine from Turkey, and Tanganyika, West Togoland, and South Cameroons from Germany. South Africa took German South West Africa, Australia became responsible for New Guinea, and New Zealand for Western Samoa. Iraq became independent in 1932. After the Second World War, a United Nations trusteeship replaced the mandate scheme and the territories moved rapidly towards independence.

**Mann, Tom** (1856–1941). Socialist and trade union leader. Born near Coventry and apprenticed as an engineer in Birmingham, Mann moved to London in 1877 and was active in the *Social Democratic Federation from 1885. He achieved notoriety as a leader of the London dock strike of 1889, and was elected first secretary of the *Independent Labour Party in 1893.

**Manners, Society for the Reformation of** These societies, which sprang up in the 1690s in London and the larger provincial towns, were a mixture of evangelicalism and social control. The church courts were no longer keen to enforce morality and sabbath observance. The societies brought prosecutions against vice and protested against lewd plays and lascivious entertainments, such as masquerades.

**Manning, Henry Edward** (1808–92). Cardinal. Manning was born in Hertfordshire, son of a wealthy banker and MP. Educated at Harrow and at Balliol College, Oxford, he was president of the Union in 1829. An enigmatic and complex figure, he was an Oxford high churchman and gained ecclesiastical preferment rapidly, becoming archdeacon of Chichester in 1840, where he remained until his conversion to catholicism ten years later. He voiced strong support for the papal states and was the chief proponent of papal infallibility at the first Vatican Council (1869–70). From 1865 Manning was the second cardinal-archbishop of Westminster.

**manorial courts** After the Norman Conquest the system of feudal landholding required the lord of the manor to provide a court for his tenants. Such 'seigneurial' courts were the court of the honour and the court baron, for free tenants, and the court customary for unfree tenants or villeins. The court baron was attended by all free tenants who were both its suitors and its judges. The court customary (or hallmoot) was the court for unfree tenants or villeins and was presided over by the lord's steward or bailiff.

Eventually the court baron faded into oblivion and the court customary survived as a court for free and unfree tenants alike.

**manorial system** A term used by historians to describe the method of estate management of landowners in the Middle Ages and in Tudor and Stuart times. Landowners whose estates embraced the major part of a village or a whole cluster of small villages found it convenient to administer such property by establishing a manor. In some places where a large village was divided in ownership among several landowners, there were several manors.

By the 13th cent. most manorial lords had established two courts, *leet and baron, which met at the same place. These had a senior officer of the lord or even the lord in the chair and all tenants were required to attend these meetings whether they were free or bond in status. Between them these courts dealt with all matters relating to the maintenance of boundaries, preservation of property, and changes in tenure. They regulated the pattern of agriculture, for example the rotation of crops in the common fields, and the manorial market. Where the lord of the manor had a demesne farm, the court appointed a *reeve to supervise the farming activities, using labour services and collecting rents.

**Mansfield, William Murray, 1st earl of** (1705–93). Judge. In 1742 Mansfield became solicitor-general with a seat in Parliament for Boroughbridge. *Newcastle relied heavily on Mansfield and was reluctant to see him become chief justice of King's Bench in 1756. However Mansfield remained in the cabinet until 1763 and was attacked by *Junius for being a 'political judge'. He twice refused the lord chancellorship, preferring the security of a non-political post.

**Maori wars,** (New Zealand) 1844–72. The treaty of *Waitangi in 1840 was not accepted by all chiefs. The Maoris were a warlike people and clashes continued between Maori and settlers. The first period of warfare began in 1844 at Kororareka and remained small scale, since most Maori tribes held aloof. The second conflict developed after repeated incidents in Taranaki, beginning in 1860 and continuing as a guerrilla war until 1872. One thousand settlers and colonial troops lost their lives, and perhaps twice that number of Maoris.

**Mar, John Erskine, earl of** [S] (c.1510–72). Mar succeeded his father as Lord Erskine in 1555 and was recognized as the rightful earl of Mar in 1565. A member of the reforming party, he had custody of the infant James VI. In 1571–2 he was regent, though real power was in the hands of *Morton.

**Mar, John Erskine, 11th earl of** [S] (1675–1732). Mar entered politics in 1696 as placeman in the court party in Scotland, led by the duke of *Queensberry until his fall in 1704. Mar rejoined him in office in 1705, helping him push the Act of *Union through the Scots Parliament in 1707. Elected to Westminster as a representative Scots peer, by 1713 he was supporting a motion for repeal of the Union. Having failed to attract the favour of George I, he sailed for Scotland to raise the standard of Jacobite rebellion. The national response was spectacular, but Mar ruined the enterprise by sheer incompetence.

**marches of Scotland** The Anglo-Scottish border. The border lands of both England and Scotland were divided into two or three marches. Northumberland with Berwick-on-Tweed was the east march 'towards Scotland' and Cumberland and Westmorland the west march. In both kingdoms, wardens were commissioned to restrain inhabitants of their marches from cross-border crime in times of truce, and to mobilize them in wartime. Magnates with lands in the marches, and therefore tenants, were normally appointed. Percy and Neville wardens led their private armies of marchmen against the king and each other. The wardenships were abolished in 1603, when the two kingdoms came under the personal union of James VI and I.

**marches of Wales** *See* WALES, MARCH OF.

**Marconi scandal** An Edwardian political-financial controversy. The scandal arose out of a contract between the English Marconi Company and the British government for the construction of a chain of wireless stations. *Lloyd George (chancellor of the Exchequer) and Alexander Murray (Liberal chief whip) bought shares at £2 each in the American Marconi Company before they went on sale to the public at a price of £3.50. This led to the appointment of a House of Commons select committee. Though it exonerated the ministers, its verdict was a party political one, for Murray had purchased additional shares for Liberal Party funds.

**Margaret** (1283–90), queen of Scots (1286–90), known as 'the Maid of Norway'. Daughter of Eric II of Norway, she succeeded her grandfather Alexander III at the age of 3 in 1286. Her betrothal to Edward of Caernarfon (the future Edward II), agreed by the treaty of *Birgham, was intended to perpetuate Anglo-Scottish peace through dynastic union. But she died at Kirkwall in Orkney on her way from Bergen to Scotland. This tragedy led to a disputed succession in Scotland, to Edward I's ill-judged interventions in Scottish affairs, and to the *Scottish Wars of Independence.

**Margaret, St** (*c.*1045–93), queen of Malcolm III of Scotland. Mother of Kings Edgar, Alexander, and David. Her father *Edward, son of *Edmund Ironside, was exiled from England by *Cnut, and ultimately found refuge in Hungary. She returned with her father to England where he died soon after. The Norman conquest of England in 1066 left Margaret's brother *Edgar as the last hope of the English royal dynasty; but, following

an unsuccessful rising in 1070, he and his family took refuge in Scotland, where Margaret was soon espoused to Malcolm III. Her posthumous significance was that she gave inspiration as well as prestige to the Scottish royal dynasty.

**Margaret of Anjou** (1430–82), queen of Henry VI. The daughter of René of Anjou, her marriage to Henry VI was part of the terms of the truce of *Tours. Her life was made more difficult by her husband, whose mental health failed in 1453 when she was pregnant with her only child. After his birth she began to play an active part in politics and by 1456 was the leader of the court faction. In the event the thing she most feared came about when Edward IV usurped the throne. Her invasion in 1471 ended in disaster when her son was killed at Tewkesbury and her husband murdered a fortnight later. Portrayed by Yorkist propaganda as a ruthless virago, her reputation has suffered because of the fatal combination of being French and on the losing side.

**Margaret of Denmark** (1457–86), queen of James III of Scotland. Daughter of Christian I of Denmark-Norway (1448–81). The royal marriage took place at Holyrood in July 1469. The queen bore her husband three sons, James (IV), James (duke of *Ross), and John (earl of Mar).

**Margaret of England** (1240–75), queen of Alexander III of Scotland. Eldest daughter of Henry III, she married Alexander III at York on 26 December 1251. Her early married life was disrupted by the factional quarrels of Alexander's minority (1249–60), and Henry III was frequently concerned for her welfare. By 1284 her three children were dead, which left as heir to the Scots throne her granddaughter Margaret, 'the Maid of Norway'.

**Margaret of France** (*c.*1282–1318), queen of Edward I. Edward's second wife, whom he married in 1299, was some 40 years younger than her husband. The marriage was the result of diplomatic moves in the aftermath of the war of 1294–7 between England and France; Margaret was a daughter of Philip III of France by his second marriage. She bore Edward a son, Thomas, in admirably short order. A second son, Edmund, and a daughter, Eleanor, followed.

**Margaret Logie** (d. *c.*1375), queen of David II of Scotland. Daughter of Sir Malcolm Drummond and widow of Sir John Logie. After the death of David II's first wife in 1362, Margaret Logie was openly recognized by the king as his 'beloved'. The two were married in 1363. There were however no children of her marriage to David and in 1370 the king divorced her, probably to leave him free to marry again.

**Margaret Tudor** (1489–1541), queen of James IV of Scotland. Elder daughter of Henry VII of England, Margaret was married to James at Holyrood on 8 August 1503, and bore her husband six children, of whom only one, Prince James (James V), born in April 1512, survived. After James IV's death at *Flodden (1513), Margaret threw her energies into politics during the magnate struggles of her son's minority (1513–28). She married Archibald Douglas, earl of *Angus (1514), but divorced him in 1526 to marry Henry Stewart, Lord Methven. She took a prominent part in James V's coup of June 1528, and died at Methven (1541).

**Marischal, George Keith, 10th Earl** [S] (*c.*1693–1778). Marischal succeeded to the earldom in 1712. The title carried with it the hereditary marshalship of Scotland. In 1715 he joined in the earl of *Mar's rising on behalf of the pretender, fought at *Sheriffmuir, and was attainted. With his brother James he embarked on the abortive rising of '19 and was wounded at *Glenshiel. Thereafter their lives were spent largely abroad, mainly in the service of Frederick the Great. In 1763 he returned to his native Scotland and recovered many of the family estates, but found the climate disagreeable, preferring that of Prussia, to which he returned.

**markets.** During the Middle Ages lords of manors established markets at the centre of settlements on their estates or at crossing points on major routes. Until the industrial revolution and the development of permanent shops, markets were the usual way of trading in everyday goods; exceptional items were bought at fairs or in very large towns. Manorial lords levied a rent on each stallholder in exchange for the right to trade on

a particular day of the week. Markets usually served the population within about 10 or 12 miles, which was as far as a laden horse-drawn cart could journey in a day, whilst allowing time to trade. However, some markets became famous for the sales of special produce, drawing merchants from further afield.

**Marlborough, John Churchill, 1st duke of** (1650–1722). The most successful general of his age, Marlborough was from 1704 until 1710 the leading European statesman. From page he became confidential emissary to the duke of York (the future James II) and in 1685 after playing a decisive part in defeating *Monmouth's rebel army he became a major-general. After 1683 he and his wife Sarah also developed a lasting connection with the future queen Anne.

Churchill made a massive contribution to the success of the *Glorious Revolution by organizing a network of officers who defected to William. As reward he became earl of Marlborough. He organized and led a combined operation that took Cork and Kinsale in southern Ireland (1690), but by championing Anne against her sister Mary he provoked his dismissal from all posts (1692).

After 1700, faced with an impending European war, William designated Marlborough to command the British forces in the Low Countries. In 1702 Marlborough manœuvred the French out of territories bordering on the Dutch Republic. Anne made him duke. But in 1704 French armies in Bavaria threatened to force the German allied princes to capitulate, isolating Britain's other major ally, the emperor. Marlborough marched his army to the Danube where at *Blenheim (13 August) he inflicted the greatest defeat the French had suffered for 150 years.

In 1705 Marlborough failed in an invasion of France up the Moselle valley, but in 1706 he won a second massive victory at *Ramillies. In 1708 he totally defeated a French counter-offensive at *Oudenarde, took the fortress of Lille, and planned a final invasion of France. The expensive victory of *Malplaquet (September 1709) prevented this and convinced a war-weary Britain that Marlborough was committed to an endless war. Dismissed by the Tory government in December 1711 Marlborough exiled himself. Reinstated by George I as captain-general, he supervised suppression of the Jacobite rebellion in 1715.

**Marlborough, statute of,** 1267. It arose from the king's quarrels with the baronial opposition and was based upon the provisions of *Oxford (1258) and the provisions of *Westminster (1259). It confirmed *Magna Carta but its primary purpose was to regulate wardship and to prevent persons outside the lord's jurisdiction being forced to attend his court.

**Marlowe, Christopher** (1564–93). English playwright, poet, and spy. Born in Canterbury, he was educated at Corpus Christi College, Cambridge. His plays, beginning with *Dido, Queen of Carthage* (c.1587), are energetic, restless, generically daring explorations of selfhood. Success came with his two-part epic of ambition and war, *Tamburlaine* (1587-8), and between 1588 and 1593 he wrote four more plays: *The Massacre at Paris, The Jew of Malta, Doctor Faustus,* and *Edward II.* Shortly after a warrant for his arrest was issued in May 1593 on charges of atheism and Marlowe was killed, apparently in a pub brawl.

**Marprelate tracts** In 1588-9, six books and a broadside, published under the pseudonym of Martin Marprelate, were a severe indictment of the episcopal hierarchy and associated press censorship. Their rollicking irreverence incensed Elizabeth, the Privy Council, and the establishment. Despite the execution of John Penry and the death in prison of Nicholas Udall, the most probable author is now regarded as the puritan extremist Job Throckmorton.

**marquis** The title of marquis, second to duke in rank, was the last to be introduced into the peerage and was slow to catch on. The first marquis, Robert de Vere, earl of *Oxford, was made marquis of Dublin in 1385 by Richard II, but within a year had been promoted duke of Ireland. The next, John Beaufort, earl of Somerset, was promoted marquis of Dorset in 1397, degraded in 1399, and offered reinstatement in 1402: he declined, explaining that the title had a foreign flavour. In 1714 there were still only two marquises in the English peerage, compared with 22 dukes and 74 earls.

**Marriage Act,** 1753. Sometimes known as Lord Hardwicke's Act (26 Geo. II c. 33), this was a fundamental reform of English marriage law. Before 1753 a free exchange of vows between a couple could create a perfectly valid marriage. The Act stated that only weddings conducted in church, according to the rubric of the English Book of Common Prayer, and with banns called, were valid. Not until the Dissenters' Marriage Act of 1836 were nonconformists permitted to marry in their own chapels or by a civil contract.

**Married Women's Property Acts,** 1870, 1882. Prior to these a woman's property became her husband's upon marriage. Whilst recognizing the principle that, in certain circumstances, women should retain and control their own property, the 1870 Act was regarded as a 'feeble compromise' and the Married Women's Property Committee pressed for greater reform. The 1882 Act, allowing wives to acquire, hold, use, and dispose of their separate property, was a major victory.

**marshal** One of the great medieval offices of state. The marshal developed as deputy to the *constable and had responsibility for the horses. He then picked up a number of additional duties, including keeping records of military service and adjusting disputes over precedence. From these duties derived the supervision of heraldry and of the *College of Arms, and the organization of coronations, which remain among the duties of the earl marshal.

**Marshal, William** (c.1147–1219). William the Marshal began life as the fourth son of a minor lord. From such modest beginnings, he rose to become earl of Pembroke (from 1189), through marriage to the heiress Isabella, and ultimately regent of England (1216-19) at the time of Henry III's minority. The secret of his success lies in his service to Henry II and his sons, their patronage propelling him to great power. Great wealth came only with his marriage of 1189. From then on, he was one of the crown's leading subjects. He was estranged from John, but rallied to his cause during the civil war that followed Magna Carta. After John's death, William saved England for the Plantagenets following French invasion.

**Marshall, Alfred** (1842–1924). Born in Bermondsey (London), and educated at St John's College, Cambridge, Marshall took the mathematics tripos (1862–5). By 1868 he was college lecturer in moral sciences at St John's College, with particular responsibility for teaching political economy. His reputation as the greatest British economist of his time was founded upon his *magnum opus*, *Principles of Economics* (1890).

**Marston Moor, battle of,** 1644. In the early summer of 1644 Charles I's forces in the north were pressed between the Scots under Alexander *Leslie, Lord Leven, and parliamentary armies under *Fairfax and *Manchester, moving into south Yorkshire. The marquis of *Newcastle fell back upon York, heavily fortified. In June *Rupert set out from Lancashire to relieve the city. On 2 July he gave battle at Marston Moor, in flat pasture land west of the city, with roughly 18,000 men against 27,000. Rupert's defeat was severe and he was said to have been forced to hide in a bean-field.

**Martello towers** On 8 February 1794 the English, with great difficulty, took a small fort at Cape Mortella on Corsica. It was little more than a pill-box but the British government was greatly impressed and in 1804, when facing an invasion threat from Napoleon, began a building programme of similar forts on the south coast. They were designed to mount one gun and to have a garrison of 1 officer and 24 men. Since, like the pill-boxes hastily erected in 1940, they were never put to the test, we shall never know how effective they would have proved.

**martial law** The term has been used in two senses which may cause confusion: 1. The rules which apply to military discipline and related matters. 2. The rules and discipline which exist at times of public emergency, displacing the ordinary principles of the law. This notion has been of greater constitutional importance. It was one of the grievances objected to in the *petition of right and the *Bill of Rights.

The prevailing legal opinion is that there is no such thing as 'martial law' except in so far as the crown must have certain powers to act in the case of emergency, e.g. to put down a rebellion. This is not a special code of law but rather an example of the principle of necessity.

**Marvell, Andrew** (1621–78). Satirist and poet. Son of a Yorkshire clergyman, Cambridge-educated, Marvell tutored Lord *Fairfax's daughter and a ward of *Cromwell's before being eventually appointed (1657) as assistant in the Latin secretaryship to *Milton. Despite having served the Protectorate, he was able to accept the Restoration. He was elected MP for Hull in 1659 but, despite being moderately active in Parliament, was ineffective in the country party. Regarded by contemporaries as a political satirist, Marvell is now generally remembered as a metaphysical poet, eclectic but lyrical and delighting in nature.

**Marx, Karl** (1818–83). German revolutionary socialist. Born in the Rhineland to Jewish parents, Marx was educated in law, history, and philosophy at the universities of Bonn and Berlin before obtaining his doctorate on Greek philosophy at Jena in 1841. A radical young Hegelian, he turned to journalism, editing the liberal *Rheinische Zeitung* in Cologne until it was suppressed by the Prussian authorities in 1843. From then on Marx became virtually an exile, fleeing first to Paris where he began his lifelong partnership with Friedrich *Engels, then to Brussels to meet workers' groups, where he and Engels wrote the *Communist Manifesto* (1848) as a rallying call for the proletarian class to overthrow the bourgeoisie. In 1849 he was tried for sedition, and though found not guilty, he was exiled once more, and made his home in London, studying and writing in the British Museum, and living off Engels's generous allowances. His most important book was *Capital* in which he set out to expose the flaws in classical political economy by showing how capitalism was not a neutral economic system, founded on timeless laws of supply and demand, but a highly exploitative system, characterized by contradictions that would eventually undermine and destroy it.

**Mary** (1542–87), queen of Scots (1542–67). The sole legitimate heir to James V, she inherited the throne on 14 December 1542 when only 6 days old. The ensuing minority was dominated by the conflict between France and England for control of Scotland through the promise of the infant queen in marriage. Initially betrothed to Henry VIII's son Edward, the Scots' rejection of the match led to war with England and Mary's removal in 1548 to France and an eventual marriage to the Dauphin Francis.

The maintenance of French catholic interests in Scotland was the prime aim of the queen mother, *Mary of Guise. Her daughter's marriage to Francis in April 1558 bound Scotland to a French monarchy heavily influenced by the militant catholicism and dynastic ambition of the young queen's Guise relatives. When Henri II died on 10 July 1559, the new French monarchs, Francis II and Mary, united a dynastic inheritance encompassing potentially not just France and Scotland but also England and Ireland.

The potential was never realized, however, for the death of Francis on 5 December 1560 left Mary a childless widow. Her decision to return to Scotland in August 1561, where in 1559–60 a protestant revolution had seen the defeat and death of Mary of Guise and the establishment of an English-backed administration led by Mary's half-brother Lord James Stewart, was driven by the desire to pursue her dynastic ambitions within Britain.

Yet the stability of Mary's rule depended on a delicate balancing act which the explosive issue of her marriage was always likely to upset. Mary's catholic marriage to *Darnley on 29 July 1565 was a love-match, but the problems posed by the rapid breakdown of relations with Darnley proved insoluble. Embittered by the now pregnant queen's refusal to grant him the crown matrimonial, Darnley joined the *Rizzio conspiracy of March 1566. Mary gave birth to a son on 19 June 1566 and the future James VI was baptized a catholic on 17 December.

Mary's complicity in Darnley's murder on 10 February 1567 cannot now be established with certainty. However, her marriage on 15 May to the leading suspect, the earl of *Bothwell, handed her opponents the chance to destroy her. Moves to 'liberate' her from Bothwell led in July 1567 to her enforced abdication. Although defeated at *Langside, it was her ill-considered flight to England which sealed her fate. Characteristically, Elizabeth prevaricated endlessly over signing her dynastic rival's death-warrant. But Mary's incessant plotting led finally to her execution at Fotheringhay on 8 February 1587.

**Mary I** (1516–58), queen of England (1553–8). Few lives can have been sadder nor few reigns more disastrous than that of Mary Tudor. From birth she was a pawn in the diplomatic game and in 1518, at the age of 2, was betrothed to the dauphin of France. But two years later there was a marriage treaty with the Emperor Charles V and by 1523 rumours that she was to marry James V of Scotland. By this time the shadow of her father's possible divorce was falling across her.

The effect of the annulment of her parents' marriage in 1533 was shattering. In the hard dynastic world of 16th-cent. Europe, her matrimonial prospects plummeted. Worse followed. The execution of Anne *Boleyn and her father's remarriage to Jane *Seymour brought no respite, since the king continued to demand that she acknowledge that her mother's marriage had been invalid. But in June 1537, with the assistance of Thomas *Cromwell, she submitted, was granted her own household again, and restored to precarious favour. The birth of a half-brother Edward in October 1537 appeared to remove any chance that she would ever be queen.

The remaining years of Henry's life were quieter for Mary and she was on good terms with his last wife, *Catherine Parr. In 1543 a statute restored Mary to the succession, after Prince Edward and any children Catherine Parr might have. From 1547 Edward VI's reign brought new trials. The king's two chief advisers, *Somerset and *Northumberland, promoted protestant doctrines and the young king grew up an eager reformer. When the Act of *Uniformity of 1549 forbade the use of the mass, Mary continued to hear it and was warned. In March 1551 Edward summoned her before the council, declared that he 'could not bear it', and was told in reply that 'her soul was God's and her faith she would not change'. Her release from this stalemate came with the first signs of the illness that killed Edward on 6 July 1553.

Even then, Mary's succession was by no means certain. Edward had declared Lady Jane *Grey his heir and on 9 July she was proclaimed queen. Mary had already fled to Kenninghall in East Anglia and on 10 July proclaimed herself queen. Northumberland's support collapsed within days and on 7 August Mary entered London to begin her reign. She was 37. She had triumphed against all odds and she attributed it to her steadfastness in her faith and to the help she had received from her co-religionists in Europe.

Mary had, as the imperial ambassador Renard pointed out, no experience of government at all. She turned at once to Renard for advice. The twin objectives of her reign were to restore the catholic faith and to negotiate a marriage which would hold out some hope that the succession would not pass to her half-sister the Princess Elizabeth.

Healing the breach with Rome was not simple. The mass could be celebrated and certain protestant bishops were soon suspended. But many of the ecclesiastical changes had been introduced by statute and would require a parliament to abrogate them. Mary's first Parliament in the autumn of 1553 made a beginning by declaring her mother's marriage legal and by repealing most of Edward VI's religious legislation. But the gentry and aristocracy showed little enthusiasm for disgorging the monastic estates they had acquired.

In view of her age and the need for an heir, marriage had to be arranged at once. When the Emperor Charles V suggested his son Philip, who had just become a widower, Mary was attracted by the Spanish connection and agreed readily. *Wyatt's rising against the Spanish marriage—part of a wider conspiracy which misfired—threatened for a moment, but Mary stood firm and it collapsed. At first the marriage seemed to have fulfilled its main purpose. In 1554 Mary announced herself pregnant. In the summer of 1555 an ornate cradle was prepared and rockers appointed. But no child arrived and in August 1555 Philip left for urgent business in the Low Countries.

Meanwhile the work of reconciliation to Rome went on. It was a joyful day for Mary in November 1554 when Pole returned at last from the continent and pronounced absolution from the sin of schism, and in March 1556 he succeeded Cranmer as archbishop of Canterbury. The supreme headship of the church was revoked by Parliament in December 1554 and acknowledgement made of the authority of the pope. Mary's instincts at first had been for patience towards protestants. But as opposition developed, her attitude stiffened. A first victim, John *Rogers, a

London preacher, went to the stake at Smithfield in February 1555, and some 300 others followed. Moderate catholics were dismayed: 'haste in religious matters', wrote Renard to Philip, 'ought to be avoided. Cruel punishments are not the best way.'

Though the articles of marriage forbade England going to war to assist Spain, that was the intention, and in June 1557 Mary declared war on France. In January 1558 the French seized the initiative and besieged Calais. The great outpost of empire, English for more than 200 years, surrendered within a week.

There was little comfort in the short time remaining to Mary. Philip's second and last visit in 1557 lasted a bare three months. But in January 1558 Philip was told by Mary that she was once more pregnant and the arrival of the child imminent. This time she deceived nobody but herself. By the summer she was obviously ill and more and more people were paying their respects to Elizabeth. In October Mary added a sad codicil to her will, 'as I then thought myself to be with child'. She died on 17 November 1558, twelve hours before Cardinal Pole.

Mary's failure was total and she died with no earthly hope. Modern historians have pointed to the constructive achievements of her reign—reform of the currency, attention to the navy, reorganization of the customs. Mary herself would have counted them as nothing against the collapse of her grand design. The burnings discredited the church she loved, sowed a harvest of hatred, and dogged the catholic cause for centuries to come. Mary did more than anyone else to make England a protestant nation.

**Mary II** (1662–94), queen of England, Scotland, and Ireland (1689–94). Mary was the elder daughter of James, duke of York, by his first wife Anne *Hyde, daughter of the earl of *Clarendon, Charles II's first lord chancellor. Her parents did not convert to catholicism until the end of the 1660s, and she and her sister Anne (born 1665) were brought up as protestants. Their protestant faith remained central to the sisters' lives. Mary was tall, of striking beauty and winning charm. Her marriage to her cousin William of Orange in 1677 initially filled Mary with misgivings; and it proved childless. But she overcame her reservations, and though William was unfaithful to her they shared a taste for simple domesticity.

Mary's willing submission to William ensured that he held the executive power in the joint monarchy. Her relations with Anne were cool owing to Anne's intense resentment at William being joint monarch. Mary acted as regent during William's prolonged absences in Ireland and on the continent 1690–4. Her death from smallpox in December 1694 was widely mourned, not least by the king himself.

**Mary Bohun** (c.1370–94), wife of Henry Bolingbroke, later Henry IV. Mary, Henry's first wife, was the younger daughter and co-heiress of Humphrey Bohun, earl of Hereford (d. 1373). In 1380 she married Henry, earl of Derby, who thus became earl of Hereford. Their surviving children were Henry (later Henry V), Thomas, John, and Humphrey (later dukes of Clarence, *Bedford, and *Gloucester), Blanche, who married Lewis (IV), later elector of the Rhine Palatinate, and Philippa, who married King Eric VII of Denmark. Mary died in childbirth.

**Mary of Gueldres** (d. 1463), queen of James II of Scotland. Daughter of Duke Arnold of Gueldres, Mary became James's queen in July 1449, and bore him at least seven children. After a decade of producing children, Mary took control of government after her husband's death at Roxburgh (August 1460), and showed herself an able diplomat, negotiating first with the Lancastrians (to obtain Berwick in 1461), and then switching sides to the victorious Yorkists.

**Mary of Guise** (1515–60), queen of James V of Scotland. The daughter of Claude, duke of Guise, Mary married James in June 1538. By him she bore two sons, who both died in infancy, and a daughter, Mary, who was barely a week old when her father died on 14 December 1542. In the ensuing minority, the dowager queen staunchly upheld French catholic interests in Scotland. In 1548 her daughter was contracted to marry the Dauphin Francis and in 1554 Mary was formally appointed regent. While this marked a tightening of French control, Mary pursued a conciliatory religious policy to ensure the acquiescence of the protestant nobility in the French marriage. The onset of more repressive policies sparked an inconclusive

protestant rebellion in May 1559, whose outcome was determined by external factors. France was unable to counter England's intervention on the protestants' behalf. Her forces besieged at Leith, Mary fell ill and took refuge in Edinburgh castle, where she died on 11 June.

**Mary of Modena** (1658–1718), queen of James II. Mary of Modena was the second wife of James II, whose first wife Anne *Hyde died in 1671. She reinforced James's catholic zeal, and after a shaky start, when she burst into tears at the sight of James, the marriage developed into one of affection. After a visit to Bath in 1687, she gave birth to a son in June 1688. Protestants regarded the birth with suspicion and despair, and it was a factor in precipitating their appeal to William of Orange. In December 1688 she and her infant son fled to France, and were followed by James. Mary remained at Saint-Germain after his death in 1701.

**Mary of Teck** (1867–1953), queen of George V. Mary of Teck, known before her marriage as Princess May, had a difficult task as queen in following *Alexandra, who had been extremely popular. But her natural dignity, verging on stiffness, and a strong sense of duty, made her fill the role well. She was the only daughter of the duke of Teck, her mother being a granddaughter of George III and first cousin to Queen Victoria. At the age of 25 she was engaged to Albert Victor, duke of *Clarence ('Eddie'), and after his sudden death married in 1893 his younger brother George, created duke of York.

**Mary Tudor** (1495–1533), queen of France and duchess of Suffolk. Mary Tudor was Henry VIII's younger sister and from her descended the claim of Lady Jane and Lady Catherine *Grey to the throne. In 1514, she was married to the elderly king of France, Louis XII. She was queen of France for three months, her husband dying on 1 January 1515. She had previously claimed from Henry the right to choose for herself should she be widowed and within a few weeks had made a private marriage to Charles Brandon, duke of *Suffolk. Her brother's wrath was assuaged by gifts of money and jewels.

**Marylebone Cricket Club** The world's premier cricket club. The MCC was founded in 1787 by a group of noblemen and based at Thomas *Lord's ground in Dorset Square, London. It replaced the Hambledon Cricket Club as the country's leading club and governed the game for 182 years until control passed to the Cricket Council in 1969.

**Mary Rose** Built between 1512 and 1514, the *Mary Rose* was one of the finest vessels of Henry VIII's navy. On 19 July 1545, watched by the king, she sailed from Portsmouth to join in an engagement with the French fleet. Not far from the shore, while setting sail, she sank with the loss of hundreds of men, including the vice-admiral. The Mary Rose Trust, founded in 1979 with the support of the prince of Wales, succeeded in recovering the hull on 11 October 1982.

**Maserfield, battle of,** 642. *Penda of Mercia defeated and killed *Oswald of Northumbria. Penda is said by *Bede to have removed Oswald's head and hands and to have hung them on stakes, perhaps as an offering to a pagan god of war. The site of the battle is uncertain. It has sometimes been identified as Oswestry ('Oswald's tree') in Shropshire, but somewhere closer to the Northumbrian-Mercian border is more likely.

**master of the king's (queen's) music** The title of the director of the monarch's private musicians. Inaugurated by Charles I in 1625 and first held by Nicholas Lanier, the post developed during the Restoration to include the direction of Charles II's band of 24 violins. Nowadays, however, the duties merely involve composing occasional works for state or royal events.

**master of the rolls** One of the senior judges whose responsibilities include preserving the records of Chancery and who was custodian of the Public Records until 1958, when they were transferred to the *lord chancellor. He also serves as president of the civil division of the Court of Appeal.

**Matapan, battle of,** 1941. At a time when Britain was standing alone against the axis powers, victories were scarce. In the Mediterranean, however, the Italian fleet was poorly led. On 28 March 1941, a British fleet under Vice-Admiral Pridham-Wippell encountered the Italians off Cape Matapan. In an action characterized by the use of carrier-borne air-

craft and radar, the British sank three of Italy's latest cruisers and two destroyers.

**Matilda** (*c.*1030–83), queen of William I and duchess of Normandy. The daughter of Count Baldwin V of Flanders, her marriage to William *c.*1050 was initially prohibited by the papacy on grounds of (unspecified) consanguinity. The couple made amends by founding two abbeys at Caen. The marriage seems to have been an exceptionally successful one, and she frequently acted as regent during William's absences from Normandy.

**Matilda** (*c.*1080–1118), queen of Henry I and duchess of Normandy. First wife of Henry I and daughter of *Malcolm Canmore, king of Scotland, and his queen St *Margaret, sister of Edgar the Atheling. Her marriage to Henry in 1100 was clearly intended to reinforce the legitimacy of his kingship by establishing a link with the old English royal house. She is said to have kept a splendid, but pious, court and was a generous patron of artists and musicians.

**Matilda (Maud)** (d. 1131), queen of David I of Scotland. Widow of Simon de Senlis and daughter of Earl Waltheof of Northumbria and his wife Judith, William the Conqueror's niece, she married the future David I in 1113. This marriage brought the Scottish royal house the earldom of Huntingdon (Waltheof's other earldom), and a deep involvement in English society.

**Matilda (Maud), Empress** (1102–67). Matilda was the daughter of Henry I. When she was just 8 years old she left England for Germany to marry the Emperor Henry V, and she only returned on his death in 1125. Matilda was designated as Henry I's successor in England and Normandy in 1127 since she was now his sole surviving legitimate offspring, Prince William having died in the wreck of the *White Ship* (1120). Her second husband, whom she married in June 1128, was *Geoffrey of Anjou, only 14 years old. It was a very unhappy marriage, but the awaited heir, the future Henry II, was born in 1133. But when Henry I died in 1135, his nephew Stephen of Blois staged a coup and took the English throne. Matilda landed in England in 1139 in pursuit of her right. She came closest to success in 1141, when

Stephen was captured, but the crown eluded her, partly because of her mismanagement of the situation. She occasionally acted as Henry II's viceregent and he relied on her counsels in a number of important matters.

**Matilda of Boulogne** (*c.*1103–52), queen of Stephen. Matilda was a doughty supporter of Stephen's cause in the civil war against the *Empress Matilda. She played a central role in disrupting the empress's plans during Stephen's imprisonment in 1141–2. Stephen's cause declined quite rapidly after her death.

**Matthew Paris** (*c.*1200–59) entered the monastery of St Albans in 1217 and spent most of his life there writing history. He composed the *Gesta abbatum*, recording the history of his monastic house. His greatest work, the monumental *Chronica majora*, for which he is renowned, was the most comprehensive history yet written in England.

**Matthews, Sir Stanley** (1915–2000). Footballer. Born at Hanley in the Potteries, Matthews made his début for Stoke City in 1932 and his first appearance for England in 1934. From 1947 to 1961 he played for Blackpool, returned to Stoke from 1961, and retired at the age of 50. He was knighted on his retirement.

**Mau Mau rebellion** The violent, grassroots resistance movement launched by the Kikuyu against the British colonial government in Kenya in the 1950s. It had its origins in the sense of deprivation felt by the Kikuyu, who had lost much of their land to white settlers.

**Maurice, Frederick Denison** (1805–72). Anglican theologian and social reformer. Ordained in the Church of England, Maurice became professor of theology at King's College, London, but was forced to resign in 1853 because of his unorthodox views on eternal punishment. He was deeply moved by the political events of 1848 and declared himself a *Christian socialist. In 1854 he founded the Working Men's College in London and became increasingly recognized as a leader of Christian social reform.

**Mauritius** was long known to the Arabs. It was discovered by the Portuguese but settled by the Dutch who named it after Maurice of

Nassau. The British captured it in 1810 and kept it as their own crown colony. Representative government was established in 1947 and Mauritius became independent within the Commonwealth in 1968.

**Maxton, James** (1885–1946). Socialist agitator. The son of a Glasgow schoolteacher, Maxton joined the *Independent Labour Party (ILP) in 1904 and acquired a well-deserved reputation as a fiery but witty orator in the socialist cause. In 1919 Maxton became an ILP organizer, succeeding to the chairmanship of the party in 1926; meanwhile he had been elected as ILP MP for Glasgow Bridgeton (1922–46). Jimmie Maxton was ever a rebel, the leading member of the Clydesiders.

**Maxwell, James Clerk** (1831–79). Maxwell was a mathematical physicist particularly eminent for his work on electromagnetism, and on the theory of gases. After holding chairs in Aberdeen and in London, he was in 1871 appointed to the professorship at Cambridge founded in memory of Henry *Cavendish. He oversaw the building of the Cavendish Laboratory, where J. J. *Thomson and Lord *Rutherford were to work.

**Mayflower** The *Mayflower*, an unremarkable ship of about 180 tons, has been immortalized, since it carried the first Pilgrims to New England and because the Mayflower Compact of 21 November 1620 was agreed on board. An early exercise in self-government, it was later followed by the formal election of a governor and assembly.

**Mayne, Cuthbert** (*c.*1543–77). Catholic martyr. Mayne was born near Barnstaple and became an Anglican minister early in life. Through the influence of *Campion he converted to catholicism, attended the seminary at Douai, and was ordained priest in 1575. In April 1576 he was sent to Cornwall but was captured within three months. Mayne was executed as a traitor at Launceston in November 1577, being the first seminary priest to suffer martyrdom.

**Maynooth seminary** When catholic seminaries in France were closed by the Revolution, the Irish hierarchy asked to open one in Ireland. The British government approved, since it might remove young Irish priests from the contamination of foreign revolutionary doctrines. The government provided an annual grant. In 1845 *Peel, as part of his reorganization of Irish higher education, increased the grant again. Peel's action was seen by the unbending Tories as yet another betrayal and there was massive petitioning against the bill.

**mayors** The word (*major*='greater') was used in the post-Roman West for officials with supervisory responsibilities, and was taken up by the elected heads of revolutionary town governments in northern France. In imitation of them, the Londoners elected a mayor when they formed a sworn association about 1190, and King John recognized the London mayoralty in 1215. In the later Middle Ages most leading English towns followed London's example. Municipal reform since 1835 has allowed the multiplication of towns with mayors and lords mayor but has diminished their real power: they have become simply chairmen or chairwomen of their councils, and are expected to devote much time to ornamental and ceremonial functions. But under the Local Government Act of 2000, some boroughs have opted to have elected mayors, armed with executive powers.

**maypoles** Ancient fertility emblems, brought in ceremonially from the woods on May Day, erected on village greens, and decorated with flowers as central features during festivities. Reviled by puritans because of associations with paganism and immorality, maypoles were forbidden in 1644, but reappeared after the Restoration for May Day or Oak Apple Day (29 May) celebrations.

**Meath (Mide), diocese of** The Irish see of Meath in *Armagh province was created in 1216 by the amalgamation of the dioceses of Clonard, Kells, and Duleek. There are still dioceses of Meath in both the Catholic and Anglican churches, with cathedrals at Trim and Kildare.

**Meath, kingdom of** Meath (Mide, 'middle province') became the fifth province of Ireland along with Ulster, Leinster, Munster, and Connacht after the Uí Néill established their supremacy over central and north Ireland in the 5th cent. However, in the 8th cent. the kingdom of Meath collapsed and a separate kingdom of Brega was formed.

Though the two were reunited in the 11th cent, Meath never regained its former importance.

**mechanics' institutes** Following the foundation of the London Mechanics' Institute (later Birkbeck College) in 1823, these adult education institutions spread rapidly, especially in the industrial areas of the north and midlands. Their original aim of providing science for artisans, however, proved impracticable and by 1840 they were frequented by lower middle-class clerks and tradesmen and a few better-off artisans. From the 1860s mechanics' institutes acquired a new role as night schools for the Society of Arts and the Science and Art Department, thus becoming forerunners of technical colleges.

**Medina del Campo, treaty of,** 1489. In 1489 Henry VII was attempting to prop up Brittany against French encroachment and also pursuing a marriage between his heir *Arthur and the infant Catherine, daughter of Ferdinand of Aragon and Spain. In March 1489 the treaty of Medina del Campo confirmed the marriage arrangements and concluded an alliance against France. But in 1491 the duchess of Brittany married Charles VIII of France and the realms were united. The marriage of Catherine and Arthur was postponed until 1501 and within five months Arthur had died.

**Medway, battle of,** AD 43. A major battle of the Roman invasion campaign, it is identified only as having taken place at a river between the beachhead and the Thames, almost certainly the Medway. Auxiliary troops swam across and killed the British chariot horses, and legionaries under the future emperor *Vespasian forced a crossing.

**Medway, Dutch attack in the,** 1667. One of the most brilliant of all naval exploits, the Dutch attack upon the Medway anchorage was on 10–14 June, as the English were attempting to recover from the Plague and the Great Fire of London. The Medway was protected by difficult access, sunken ships, and a boom, but the Dutch penetrated the defences and caused consternation. The *Royal Charles* was towed away to Holland, and the *Royal James*, the *Loyal London*, and the *Royal Oak* sunk.

**Melba, Nellie** (1859–1931). Opera singer. Born of Scottish parents as Helen Porter Mitchell, near Melbourne (Australia), it was only after marriage to Charles Armstrong that her gifts were developed. After study in Paris came a brilliant début in Brussels (1887) as 'Mme Melba', clearly derived from her birthplace. World-wide acclaim followed. Immensely popular and honoured as 'Dame' because of her work for war charities, she bade farewell at Covent Garden in 1926.

**Melbourne, William Lamb, 2nd Viscount** (1779–1848). Prime minister. In some respects Melbourne was an essentially 18th-cent. figure: his idea of government was static, if not negative—the maintenance of law and order, conduct of foreign relations, and the implementation of those changes that could neither be postponed nor avoided.

To appearances he was an archetypal old-fashioned Whig—lounging, aristocratic, amiable, amateurish. But appearances were deceptive. Though Melbourne's attitude of ironic unconcern was not a pose, he was capable of hard and sustained application. At the age of 26 he was unlucky enough to marry Lady Caroline Ponsonby, whose indiscretions, scenes, and tantrums reinforced Melbourne's horror of unpleasantness and confrontation, which she adored. Their only child was retarded.

He grew up in a large, high-spirited cliquish family, went to Eton and Trinity College, Cambridge, and spent a year at Glasgow under Professor John *Millar. His fortunes changed abruptly in 1805 when the death of his elder brother left him as heir to the peerage. He abandoned the legal career upon which he had started and began a political one. He joined the Whig opposition but was on the right of the party, and had much in common with *Peel, *Huskisson, and the liberal Tories. He was 48 before, in 1827, he held office in *Canning's ministry as chief secretary for Ireland, and within a year he was out again, resigning with the Huskissons.

This limited service was of consequence since the Whigs, when they took office in 1830, were short of experience and Melbourne became home secretary in Grey's government. He showed unexpected firmness in dealing with the *Swing riots in 1831 and the *Tolpuddle martyrs in 1834. He was the obvious choice to succeed Grey in 1834. William IV mistrusted the government, and after six months, the king turned out the ministry, bringing in the Tories. Peel dissolved, failed to win a majority, and Melbourne returned, taking the opportunity to drop Brougham, one of the more impossible ministers.

It cannot be said that Melbourne's second administration made much of a mark. It was dependent upon Irish and radical votes and the Tory House of Lords killed off several of its measures. Melbourne soldiered on, swearing, jesting, despairing. But the succession of Victoria in 1837 changed everything. He experienced an Indian summer in which he basked in royal favour, the young queen hanging on every word, enjoying every joke. She and Melbourne were hissed at the races and 'Mrs Melbourne' was a vulgar taunt. The *Bedchamber crisis of 1839, when Peel failed to form a ministry in the face of the queen's evident hostility, gave Melbourne's government two more years. But in 1841 he went to the country and was defeated. The following year he suffered a stroke and well before his death in 1848 he was a figure from the past. 'Not a good or firm minister,' was Victoria's cool judgement on a man she had once adored.

**Mellitus** Bishop of London (604–19), archbishop of Canterbury (619–24). Mellitus was one of the missionaries sent from Rome in 601 to reinforce *Augustine's original mission of 597. In 617, when the Christian king of Essex was succeeded by pagan sons, Mellitus was driven from London. A (temporarily) pagan king succeeded in Kent at much the same time, and Mellitus was exiled in Gaul before returning to become archbishop.

**Melun, treaty of,** 1593. Elizabeth and Henri IV of France pledged themselves at Melun not to make a separate peace with Spain. When Henri concluded a settlement in 1598 at Vervins, Elizabeth was indignant.

**Melville, George Melville, 1st earl of** [S] (1636–1707). Melville succeeded to his father's barony when he was 7. An ardent presbyterian from Fife, he was implicated in the *Rye House plot and gave support to the *Monmouth rising. In exile he joined William of Orange. He was raised to the earldom in

1690 and his family had great influence in Scotland during William's reign. Melville himself was secretary of state [S] 1689–90, lord privy seal [S] 1690–6, and lord president of the council [S] 1696–1702.

**mercantilism** This general term, coined in 1763 by Mirabeau, is usually applied to the system of economic policy which flourished between the 16th and 18th cents. Mercantilists were concerned to increase the power of the nation state by competition with hostile rival nations. Most characteristic were their ideas about trade and gold. Wealth was defined exclusively in terms of gold bullion reserves, so that a positive trade balance became a prime aim of policy to increase the currency reserves. Such notions supported the acquisition of colonies to provide necessary imports which, otherwise, would have to be bought from rivals in exchange for bullion. The *Navigation Acts introduced in the 17th cent. by the English government represented a typically mercantilist attempt to manipulate the costs of trade by stipulating that goods in the colonial trade must be carried in English ships.

Modern economic thought gives little support to the basic ideas of mercantilism. Current theory regards the restriction of trade as damaging to economic growth. Similarly monopolistic control and the regulation of economic activity are perceived as sources of inefficiency.

**Merchants, statute of,** 1285. This statute made at Westminster (13 Edw. I s. 3) strengthened the provisions in the statute of Acton Burnell for the swift recovery of debts in the interest of promoting trade. Debtors could be at once imprisoned on default, and were liable to lose all their lands.

**Merchant Venturers** One of the greatest trading companies. The London Merchant Venturers were closely associated with the Mercers' Company, sharing Mercers Hall until the Great Fire in 1666, and rivals of the Staplers' Company, which specialized in wool export. Henry VII granted them a charter in 1505, establishing a governor and 24 councillors. They defended their cloth monopoly against numerous rivals and enemies. Abroad they struggled against the *Hanseatic League and against the vagaries of foreign diplomacy. In 1689, immediately after the *Glorious Revolution, the export of cloth was opened up to all subjects, thus depriving the Merchant Venturers of their monopoly.

**Mercia, kingdom of** Mercia dominated Anglo-Saxon politics in the late 7th and 8th cents. The name 'Mercians' means 'the borderers' and is thought to derive from their position between the Anglo-Saxon settlements of the east coast and British kingdoms of the west. The middle Trent valley was the heartland of the Mercian kingdom. Within this area lie the Mercian episcopal centre of *Lichfield (founded 669) and the important royal centres of *Repton and Tamworth.

The first Mercian king who is reliably attested is Cearl, whose daughter Cwenburh married *Edwin of Deira in the early 7th cent. It is usually assumed that it was *Penda (c.626–55) who established Mercia as a major Anglo-Saxon kingdom. He and his son *Wulfhere (658–75) followed an aggressive military policy which enabled them to collect tribute from the southern Anglo-Saxon kingdoms, Northumbria, and probably some British kingdoms as well.

The 8th cent. was dominated by two very powerful kings *Æthelbald (716–57) and Offa (757–96), both of whom claimed descent from Penda's brother Eowa. They attempted to extend Mercian control to eastern parts of Wales, East Anglia, and provinces south of the Thames. *Kent and *Sussex became Mercian provinces. *Wessex remained independent, but lost territory south of the rivers Thames and Avon to Mercia. The extended boundaries of Mercia were maintained by *Cenwulf (796–821), but increasing discontent with Mercian dominance in Kent, East Anglia, and Wessex weakened Mercian hegemony. When *Egbert of Wessex defeated Beornwulf of Mercia at the battle of *Ellendun in 825 he was able permanently to detach Kent, Sussex, Surrey, and the East Saxons from Mercian control.

However, West Saxon successes did not really threaten the main Mercian province. It was the 'great Danish army' which shattered the kingdom in 874. The area became increasingly dependent on Wessex for survival and *Æthelfleda of Wessex, a daughter of Alfred who had married Ceolwulf's successor *Æthelred, was ruler of the province in the early 10th cent. When Æthelfleda died in 918, her brother *Edward the Elder, who was already winning parts of eastern Mercia from Viking control, annexed western Mercia as well.

**'Merciless' Parliament,** 1388. The lords *appellant, having defeated their opponents at Radcot *Bridge in December 1387, dominated the Parliament which met from February to June 1388. Suffolk (Michael de la *Pole) and *Oxford had escaped to France, but many of their supporters were put to death. Richard II reasserted his power the following year.

**Merionethshire (Meirionydd).** County of north Wales deriving its name from Meirion, one of the sons of *Cunedda, who supposedly moved from Strathclyde in late post-Roman times with his people, the *Votadini, in order to offset the threat of Irish invasion. It was probably an early kingdom but became part of the kingdom of *Gwynedd. The annexation of the lands of the last *Llywelyn by the crown under Edward I led to the creation of the shire in 1284.

Merionethshire has 65.4 per cent of its population able to speak Welsh. Merioneth was once again linked to Gwynedd in 1974 when it became part of that new county, and with *Caernarfonshire constituted a reformed Gwynedd in 1996.

**Merit, Order of** The order was established by Edward VII in June 1902, limited to 24 persons in the armed forces or of distinction in art, science, or literature. It was based upon Frederick the Great's *Pour la mérite* and is in the personal gift of the sovereign.

**Merlin** was famous in myth as the soothsayer and magician at King *Arthur's court. Fragmentary evidence of early oral traditions suggests Merlin's earliest incarnation was as the mythical Welsh poet-madman Myrddin. This figure's transformation into Merlin was probably the work of *Geoffrey of Monmouth (*c*.1100–54), who welded Merlin onto the Arthurian myth.

**Merseyside** Conurbation in north-west England, centred on Liverpool, made a metropolitan county after local government reform in 1972. A distinctive local dialect ('scouse') and wry humour contribute to a regional identity, with Liverpool as the main cultural focus. The metropolitan council was abolished by the Local Government Act of 1985 but the term 'Merseyside' remains in use as a geographical expression.

**Merton, statute of,** 1236. As much a discussion document as a statute, it arose from an assembly at Merton (Surrey) in January 1236 in Henry III's reign, and was an attempt to clarify a number of miscellaneous points of law. Among the many issues, including rights of widows, heirs, and pasturage, was a difference between canon law and common law: canon law held that a subsequent marriage legitimated natural children, common law did not. Despite an earnest appeal by Robert *Grosseteste, the barons refused to change the laws of England.

**Merton, Walter de** (d. 1277). Clerical statesman. Educated at Oxford, Walter became a clerk in Chancery and amassed a large number of livings. In 1261–3 he was chancellor but was forced out by de *Montfort's party and not reinstated after the royal victory at *Evesham. But he acted as chancellor once more 1272–4 after Henry's death and while Edward I was absent on crusade. For the last three years of his life he was bishop of Rochester. He was the founder in 1264 of Merton College, Oxford.

**Mesopotamian campaign,** 1914–18. Following Turkey's entry into the *First World War in November 1914, a small Anglo-Indian force landed in Mesopotamia. Encouraged by early victories, the British advanced towards Baghdad, but were halted by the Turks in November 1915. A considerable British force was besieged at Kut and surrendered in April 1916. Prestige demanded that this defeat be avenged and in March 1917 the British finally occupied Baghdad.

***Messiah,*** Handel's most famous and frequently performed oratorio, was written in just over three weeks and first performed in Dublin on 13 April 1742. It was a great success, raising £400 for charity. The gentle lyricism of arias like 'I know that my redeemer liveth' and the jubilant grandeur of the 'Hallelujah' chorus have survived countless rearrangements and doubtful performances.

**Metcalf, John** (1717–1810). Road-builder, known as 'Blind Jack of Knaresborough'. Blinded by smallpox at the age of 6, Metcalf proved extraordinarily adaptable, and became successively travelling fiddler and horse-dealer, recruiting for *Cumberland's army in 1745; he was present at both *Falkirk and *Culloden. He set up a stage-wagon to York (1754), and traded in horses and provender, before securing his first road-building contract in 1765, eventually constructing 180 miles in northern England, and employing at peak 400 men.

**methodism** began as a religious revival in the 18th cent. and grew to become the largest of the nonconformist churches. Under the leadership of John *Wesley, societies for cultivating religious fellowship were set up, intended originally as auxiliary to the established church, but soon forced into independence by the hostility of the clergy. The movement grew rapidly from the 1740s and developed distinctive institutions, notably the weekly class meeting of ten to twelve members and an itinerant body of lay preachers, who visited the societies, preaching in the homes of members and in the open air. By 1850 membership was about half a million and an estimated two million persons (one-tenth of the total population) were under direct methodist influence.

Socially methodism was a transforming force. Most of the 18th-cent. 'people called methodists' were of humble origin without advantages of education, wealth, or social position. However, their puritan virtues brought them worldly prosperity and, by the 1830s and 1840s, the big Wesleyan chapels in northern towns were dominated by wealthy mill-owners and businessmen. Yet underneath there was a more liberal and democratic spirit. The breakaway churches (such as the methodist New Connexion, *primitive methodists, *Bible Christians, protestant methodists, Barkerites, Wesleyan reformers) were characterized by differences of organization and personalities, not doctrine. Around the chapel there developed an intense world of personal and social relationships, which lasted into modern times In 1932 three of the largest groups united to form the Methodist Church of Great Britain.

Methodism made an important contribution to the leadership of working-class move-ments like *trade unionism and *chartism by providing opportunities for self-education and training in leadership and organization in running the chapel. The general culture of methodism was toward respectability through living a temperate, thrifty, hard-working life. Indeed, historians have argued (somewhat exaggeratedly) that it was methodism that prevented revolution in Britain during the revolutionary decades 1789–1848.

**Methuen treaty,** 1703. When the War of the *Spanish Succession broke out in 1701, the assistance of Portugal was essential. The political alliance was followed in December 1703 by a commercial treaty, negotiated by John Methuen. The Portuguese agreed to allow in English woollen goods while the English offered a preferential duty on Portuguese wines.

**Methven, battle of,** 1306. On 19 June 1306 a small force under Robert I Bruce was routed at Methven, near Perth, by an army commanded by Aymer de *Valence, earl of Pembroke, acting for Edward I. But within a year Bruce regained the initiative.

**Middle Angles, kingdom of** In Book 1 of his *Ecclesiastical History* *Bede includes the Middle Angles among the major peoples of Anglo-Saxon England, but the only known king of the whole Middle Angles is *Peada of Mercia. It was during his rulership that the Middle Angles were officially converted to Christianity through a mission from *Northumbria. The lack of any corporate history before their domination by Mercia had led some historians to doubt whether the Middle Angles had any prior political unity and to see them instead as a Mercian administrative creation.

**Middlesex** was one of the smallest, oldest, and strangest of counties. In Roman times it formed part of the territory of the *Trinovantes and their competitors the *Cassivellauni. Very soon after the Roman arrival, Londinium developed as by far the largest town and this dictated the subsequent history of the area. That part of the territory which survived as Middlesex was probably too small to sustain an independent kingdom, unlike *Sussex, *Essex, and *Wessex. But the existence of *Surrey (the south land) suggests a brief Middle Saxon kingdom straddling the Thames. By the 6th cent. the area seems to have formed a province of Essex, and by the 8th it had been taken over by Mercia. In the later 9th cent., after the struggle between Alfred and the Danes, the region became part of Wessex. By then it was a recognized shire.

The development of Middlesex as a county was stunted by the influence of London. It fell naturally into the diocese of London, founded in 604. In the 12th cent. the city of London was given the right to appoint the sheriff of Middlesex and the assizes were held at the Old Bailey. The influence of London was so overwhelming that few Middlesex towns grew to any size. Economically too, the shire was totally dependent upon London, and from an early period became a scene of market gardens and gentlemen's parks, of which Hampton Court (royal), Sion House (Northumberland), Osterley (Child), and Cannons (Chandos) were the most celebrated.

By 1700, London had half a million inhabitants, by 1800 nearly a million. At that time the largest towns in the shire were Enfield with 6,000 people and Isleworth with 4,000, Uxbridge 2,100, Hendon 1,900, Staines 1,700, and Brentford 1,400.

The political absorption of the county by London gathered pace in the 19th cent. In 1888 a considerable portion of south-east Middlesex, including Highbury, Hampstead, and Hammersmith, was sliced off to form part of the new county of London. In 1965, in another reorganization, Middlesex disappeared altogether, most going to Greater London.

**Middleton, Charles Middleton, 2nd earl of** [S] (c.1650–1719). Middleton succeeded to the peerage in 1673, was secretary of state in Scotland 1682–4 and in England 1684–8, despite adhering to protestant views. One of James II's chief supporters, he joined him in exile at Saint-Germain in 1693 and was then attainted. After 1688 he was one of the leading Compounders, who urged compromise on James.

**Middleton, John Middleton, 1st earl of** [S] (c.1608–73). From Kincardineshire, Middleton was a soldier of fortune and joined the Scottish covenanting army in 1639. He transferred to the service of the

English Parliament and was active during the Civil War. Returning to Scotland, he fought against *Montrose at *Philiphaugh. Next he changed sides and fought for the king at *Preston, where he was taken prisoner, and at *Worcester (1651), where he was wounded. In 1654 he joined with the earl of Glencairn in the Scottish royal rising but was defeated by *Monck. At the Restoration he was created earl and served in Scotland as commander-in-chief and as commissioner to the Parliament. But his political career was less successful and in 1663 he was dismissed at the instigation of *Lauderdale. In 1668 he was made governor of Tangiers, where he died.

**Midlothian campaign,** 1879–80. Unhappy in his Greenwich constituency, and retired from the Liberal Party's leadership, *Gladstone accepted the invitation in May 1878 to contest the constituency of Edinburghshire (as Midlothian, the county around the Scottish capital) at the 1880 election against Lord Dalkeith, the Tory candidate and son of the powerful duke of Buccleuch. Gladstone made a series of highly effective nationally reported speeches, attacking what he dubbed 'Beaconsfieldism' (the policies of Disraeli's government). He won the seat with ease and resumed as leader of the Liberal Party and prime minister.

**militia** The British regionally based volunteer armed forces (from the Latin *miles*, a soldier). Of Anglo-Saxon origin or earlier, the militia was established as an obligation for all freemen by the Assize of *Arms of 1181. Although militarily negligible throughout its existence, the militia was intended to repel any invasion, to secure order locally, and as a regional 'constitutional force' to balance royal control of the standing army. The 1907 *Territorial and Reserve Forces Act abolished the militia by amalgamating all volunteer forces into the Territorial Force, renamed the Territorial Army in 1921, which continues in existence.

**Mill, James** (1773–1836). Utilitarian philosopher. Son of a Scottish shoemaker, educated at Edinburgh University, Mill became an itinerant preacher but lost faith and came to London in 1802 to work as a journalist. He fell under the influence of Jeremy *Bentham and developed his ideas into a coherent philosophy, substituting strict puritanical morality for Bentham's hedonism. Mill rather than Bentham formulated the distinctive '*philosophical radicalism' of the 19th-cent. British utilitarians.

**Mill, John Stuart** (1806–73). Utilitarian and liberal philosopher. The son of James *Mill, a disciple of Jeremy *Bentham, Mill was converted to Benthamite utilitarianism at the age of 15, but later rejected its egoistic psychology and mechanical concept of pleasure. He was employed for 35 years by the East India Company, afterwards serving as an independent member of Parliament for Westminster (1865–8), arguing for radical measures such as votes for women. In *On Liberty* (1859) Mill wrote the most celebrated defence of individual freedom to appear in the English language.

**Millais, John Everett** (1829–96). Painter and book illustrator. A scion of an old Norman family, settled in Jersey since the Conquest, Millais was a prodigy. He entered the Royal Academy Schools in 1840 and first exhibited there at 16. In 1848, with Holman *Hunt and D. G. *Rossetti, he founded the Pre-Raphaelite Brotherhood, of which he was the most technically brilliant. After moving away from the Pre-Raphaelite style, he became a fashionable painter of portraits and costume history.

**Millar, John** (1735–1801). Millar was born in Lanarkshire, son of a minister. Educated at Hamilton Grammar School and Glasgow University, he became a lawyer and in 1761 accepted the regius chair at Glasgow, which he held for the rest of his life. The Glasgow Law School flourished under his supervision and his pupils included Lauderdale and *Melbourne. Most influential was his *The Origin of the Distinction of Ranks* (1771). Heavily influenced by Montesquieu and Hume, it was a pioneering work in comparative sociology.

**millenarianism** Belief in a future millennium (1,000 years) either preceding (premillennialism) or following (postmillennialism) the second coming of Christ, when he will reign on earth in a kingdom of his saints. Contemporary events were interpreted by reference to biblical prophecies or divine revelations concerning the imme-

diate arrival of Christ on earth. Millenarian hopes and visions surfaced at the time of the *Peasants' Revolt (1381) and again among 17th-cent. sects such as the *ranters, *Muggletonians, *Fifth Monarchy men, and some early *quakers. Later millenarian sects included *seventh-day adventists, *Plymouth brethren, and *Jehovah's witnesses.

**millenary petition,** 1603. Elizabeth I, having authorized the establishment of a protestant church in England, stood firm against any further changes. This angered those of *puritan inclination, who believed that it preserved too many catholic vestiges in its structure and worship. They presented James I in 1603 with a petition, said to have 1,000 signatories, setting out their position. James responded by summoning the *Hampton Court conference.

**Milner, Alfred** (1854–1925). British administrator and ardent imperialist. After serving in Egypt (1889–92) and as chairman of the Inland Board of Revenue (1892–7), Milner became high commissioner in southern Africa and governor of Cape Colony in 1897. Convincing himself of the incompetence of the government of the neighbouring Boer South African Republic (Transvaal), he undertook a campaign of criticism which led directly to the second Anglo-Boer War (1899–1902). He was created baron in 1901 and viscount in 1902. Returning to England in 1905 he took office again as a member of Lloyd George's war cabinet (1916–21).

**Milton, John** (1608–74). Milton was intended for the ministry by his father, a well-to-do London scrivener, and was educated at St Paul's School and Christ's College, Cambridge. He became increasingly dedicated to poetry, however, nurturing a vocation to write a great Christian epic. But he put this aside soon after the *Long Parliament met, because he believed that England was on the brink of a great new reformation and that he must serve it with his pen, in prose. *Areopagitica* (1644), a plea for a free press, presented a vision of England as 'a noble and puissant Nation rousing herself like a strong man after sleep, and shaking her invincible locks'. The establishment of the *Commonwealth brought him fresh hope, however, and his *Tenure of Kings and Magistrates* eloquently justified the trial of Charles I.

Gratefully, the *Council of State appointed him as its secretary for foreign tongues. Besides various diplomatic duties, this entailed writing (with the last of his eyesight) lengthy defences of the Commonwealth in both English and Latin. He eulogized Cromwell's *Protectorate too, but gradually turned against its ecclesiastical policies and monarchical tendencies. He was briefly imprisoned at the Restoration, but was spared to complete the epic masterpieces *Paradise Lost, Paradise Regained*, and *Samson Agonistes*, whose composition he had postponed for so long.

**Minden, battle of,** 1759. Ferdinand of Brunswick, commanding a force of 54,000 Hanoverian, British, and Prussian soldiers, tempted a French army, 64,000 strong, out of seemingly impregnable positions at Minden. On 1 August, a brigade of British and Hanoverian infantry, misinterpreting orders, launched a frontal assault on French cavalry in the centre and held firm when counter-attacked. Unfortunately the British cavalry, commanded by Lord George Sackville (*Germain), failed to exploit, and the French, having lost over 7,000, retreated.

**Mines Act,** 1842. In the 1830s a number of investigations into coal-mines revealed the extent of truck payments (i.e. payments in food and kind), employment of women and children, and disregard of safety. The first report on the employment of children in 1842, graphically illustrated, caused a sensation. Lord Ashley (*Shaftesbury) took advantage of the indignation to steer through the Mines Act (5 & 6 Vic. c. 99) which forbade the employment of women underground, and of boys below the age of 10.

**Minorca** is a Balearic island of strategic importance, with Port Mahon a fine harbour. It was taken by the British in 1708. At the outbreak of the *Seven Years War in 1756, Admiral *Byng's failure to prevent the French from capturing it brought down *Newcastle's ministry and led to his own execution. It was returned to Britain again in 1763 by the treaty of *Paris. Lost to a combined French and Spanish force in 1782 it was ceded to Spain in 1783, and though the British once more took the island in 1798, it was given back to Spain at the peace of *Amiens in 1802.

**Minto, Gilbert Elliot-Murray-Kynynmound, 1st Earl** (1751–1814). Minto was called to the bar in 1774 and entered Parliament in 1776. He was a close friend of Edmund *Burke and assisted him in the impeachment proceedings against Warren *Hastings. He was appointed governor of Corsica in 1794, envoy to the court of Vienna from 1799 to 1801, and president of the Board of Control for East India Affairs in 1805. In 1806 he became governor-general of India. His period in office saw the consolidation of British power in the subcontinent and, in prosecution of the Napoleonic wars, the extension of influence into south-east Asia. He retired in 1813.

**Minto, Gilbert John Elliot-Murray-Kynynmound, 4th Earl** (1845–1914). Minto was educated at Eton and Cambridge and joined the Scots Guards in 1867. A Liberal, he was appointed governor-general of Canada 1898–1904, and in 1905 became Viceroy of India. His period in office was distinguished by his work with Secretary of State John *Morley to pass constitutional reforms which introduced the principles of elected representation to the government of India. The Morley–Minto reforms are also remembered for introducing separate Hindu and Muslim 'communal' electorates. He retired in 1910.

**missionary activity** Along with evangelical zeal, an element often present in missionary work has been rivalry between Christian sects. Perhaps the first missionary to post-Roman Britain was *Germanus, sent over in 429 by Pope Celestine I to combat the *Pelagian heresy. Nor was rivalry long in appearing in *Augustine's mission of 597 to reinvigorate Christianity. But within a century the English church was well enough established to send out missionaries of its own, *Willibrord to the Frisians, *Boniface to the Germans.

The Reformation renewed rivalries by formalizing the divisions of Christianity and the earliest post-Reformation missionaries were the *Jesuit priests from Douai who strove to maintain the faith in Elizabethan England. Protestant counter-activity took at first the form of hunting them down, but later in the 17th cent. the considerable success of the Jesuits in America, India, Japan, and China stimulated protestant missions. In 1698 Thomas Bray, an Anglican clergyman, drew up plans for the *Society for Promoting Christian Knowledge to supply libraries and missionaries to the colonies, and three years later the missionary work was handed over to the *Society for the Propagation of the Gospel. As the methodists gathered strength, they also turned to missionary work. The Methodist Missionary Society was set up in 1786 and the Baptist Missionary Society in 1792. The *London Missionary Society was established in 1795, the *Church Missionary Society in 1799, and the British and Foreign Bible Society in 1804. Later in the century, there was much missionary interest in Africa, partly as a consequence of the fame of David *Livingstone, who began working for the LMS in 1841. Slowly the attitude of missionaries and their supporters changed. It was increasingly argued that missions should lead to a self-governing autonomous local church. An ecumenical landmark was the holding of a World Missionary Conference in Edinburgh in 1910 which established an International Missionary Council. This, in 1961, was integrated with the World Council of Churches, started in 1948.

**'Model' Parliament** was the name given by Stubbs to Edward I's assembly at Westminster in November 1295 on the grounds that it was the first to include both knights of the shire and burgesses. But the phrase is inappropriate. Writs found later demonstrate that previous parliaments had a similar composition. Nor was the 1295 composition subsequently followed, since the lesser clergy gradually ceased to be summoned and made do with *convocation.

**monarchy** If we accept Cerdic as founder, the English monarchy dates back to about 519. The Scottish monarchy may be dated from *c.*843, when *Kenneth MacAlpin of *Dalriada united Picts and Scots to form the kingdom of *Alba. The role of the monarch was essentially that of battle-leader. As a consequence, strict primogeniture was slow to establish itself, since it could result in a child or a simpleton on the throne. Few monarchs lasted long enough for old age to be a problem. With expectation of life short, it was unlikely that the eldest son would be old enough for the task. *Edgar's eldest son

Edward was only 13 when chosen in 975 but the innovation was hardly encouraging since he was murdered within three years.

Apart from waging war—admittedly at times a demanding business—early kings had little to do. They attempted very few of the activities of the modern state. Justice was dispensed by landowners themselves; the king did not make law, though he might declare what it was; there was little revenue to collect, though he was entitled to support and hospitality. There was no economic or education policy to supervise.

But the great effort needed to push back the Danes in the 9th and 10th cents. produced important developments in the institutions of Wessex. Burhs, erected as strong points, had to be built and garrisoned, naval vessels commissioned and manned, and all had to be paid for. By the reign of *Athelstan a much more complex governmental structure is apparent and the kingdom of England has emerged. Indeed, by the reign of Edgar, one can see the outlines of a claim to British sovereignty, with the monarch rowed on the Dee in 973 by kings from Scotland, from Wales, and of the British.

With the Conquest in 1066 the kingdom was once more in alien hands. The first three Norman rulers were powerful. Their significance is seen more in relations with the other rulers in the British Isles than in domestic reform. Scotland felt the change quickly. William I paralleled the expedition by Cnut in 1031 with his own march to the Tay in 1072, which brought about the submission of Malcolm Canmore. His son William Rufus reoccupied Cumberland in 1092. Into Wales, the incursion of Norman lords began, particularly in the south, as early as one year after *Hastings. The Norman attack upon Ireland was postponed until the 12th cent. and the reign of Henry II.

Since medieval government centred on the king, its efficacy varied greatly. Under strong rulers, the monarchy advanced, royal justice was extended, revenue increased, local government reorganized. Under weak rulers, control became slack and important concessions were made to subjects—*Magna Carta in 1215, even if the immediate beneficiaries were the barons. Monarchs were frequently in danger since they were still expected to lead in battle: Edward II, Richard II, and Henry VI were deposed and killed,

Edward V murdered, Richard III killed on the battlefield. Success in war, on the other hand, gave the king a strong, if not impregnable, position—William I, Edward I, Edward III, Henry V.

The prestige and standing of the monarchy was enhanced in a variety of ways. The *coronation ceremony became more elaborate and more dignified. Some early coronations were so hasty that rehearsals could hardly have been possible. Henry I apologized to *Anselm for his coronation three days after succeeding Rufus, explaining that 'enemies would have risen up against me'. Monarchs were competitive. The kings of France were proud that, at the coronation of Clovis, an angel had appeared bearing holy oil: fortunately the balance was more than restored when the Virgin Mary herself presented *Becket with holy oil, which was quickly incorporated into the English coronation ceremony.

It was also of value to a monarch to be associated with great buildings and great deeds. The Confessor built Westminster abbey, consecrated just before his death, and Henry III rebuilt it. Rufus built Westminster hall and Richard II embellished it. David I of Scotland founded the abbeys of Holyrood and Dunfermline, later turned into royal residences. Edward III's institution of the Order of the *Garter was supported by a new chapel at Windsor, completed by Edward IV, and deliberately echoed the legendary deeds of King *Arthur.

The Tudor period is usually regarded as the apogee of the English monarchy. Certainly it was stronger than in the 15th cent., when the Wars of the *Roses produced frequent changes of ruler. Yet lawlessness and rebellion were not easily stamped out. Several of their policies returned to haunt their successors. The take-over of church powers added greatly to the patronage of the monarch but also involved him more directly in religious disputation at a time when the waves of controversy were beginning to run high. The Civil War, after all, began with Charles I's dispute over religion with his Scottish subjects. The vast proceeds of the *dissolution of the monasteries were not merely squandered by the crown but finished up with the nobility, helping to strengthen its position. Henry VIII's use of Parliament to effect the *Reformation, and

Mary and Elizabeth's use to adjust it, gave it confidence to challenge the monarchy in the following century.

Though at one level the Civil War was disastrous for monarchy—the king beheaded, the institution abolished—in the end it may have helped its survival. The role of the army in the 1650s and the social upheaval of the Commonwealth period sobered the gentry and nobility and prepared the ground for the peaceful restoration of Charles II in 1660. The complex negotiations of the early 1640s, in which Charles I had described the role of the crown as a balancing one, pointed the way to a compromise between crown and Parliament. From the melodrama of James II's reign, the monarchy emerged strengthened—limited certainly in its formal powers and prerogatives, but more in touch with the wishes of the nation.

From 1688 onwards, though the monarchy retained fundamental powers, it was in slow constitutional retreat. The *Bill of Rights removed the suspending power and the dispensing power as it had been employed. The right of veto fell into abeyance after Anne's reign. Though the choice of ministers remained an important prerogative it was increasingly limited by the growth of party loyalty, and the fiasco of Lord *Bute at the start of George III's reign suggested that royal favourites would no longer serve. Even the granting of honours fell largely into the hands of the prime minister and new orders had to be invented so that the monarch could retain some personal control.

But there were compensations in the changing role and the crown's retreat opened the way for a more national function. After the first three Georges, who had revealed little desire to show themselves to their subjects, George IV introduced a new note, with well-publicized visits to Scotland and Ireland. Though Victoria was not a battle-leader, she undoubtedly became a symbol of the nation and of the empire, as her *Golden and *Diamond Jubilees in 1887 and 1897 demonstrated.

The 20th-cent. British monarchy survived when most others were swept away because it came to terms with democracy. The dangers that awaited it were, in the end, not red revolution or republican egalitarianism, but the more insidious difficulty of knowing what image to present in an age of rapidly changing standards, and how to do it. The abdication of Edward VIII in 1936 appears in retrospect less a grave constitutional issue than an early warning of the problems that would arise if the monarch, or members of the royal family, were not prepared to do their duty. The monarchy was not helped by the growth of a vulgar, censorious, and meretricious press. Universal education produced a nation of critics, less respectful than their 7th-cent. ancestors.

**monasteries,** or religious communities of men or women living apart from secular society, had their origin in the early church in Egypt where hermits (the word monk is derived from the Greek *monos*, one alone) came together to live a life of contemplation and work under the direction of an abbot (from Aramaic *abba*, father). The first monasteries in the British Isles were established in the 5th cent. in Ireland, probably from Gaul. Thereafter communities spread throughout Celtic Britain, notable centres being at *Iona under St *Columba, at St *Davids, and later at *Lindisfarne (or Holy Island). Monasticism was introduced into Anglo-Saxon England by *Augustine of Canterbury, himself a monk, the first community being St Augustine's, Canterbury (c.598). By c.650 many monasteries had been founded throughout Britain: some were communities of men and women, the most famous being *Whitby ruled by its abbess, *Hilda. They followed a variety of rules and customs. Attempts to standardize these under the rule of Benedict were made by *Wilfrid of Ripon and Hexham, *Benedict Biscop of Jarrow-Monkwearmouth, *Theodore of Canterbury, and others, but were not wholly successful. The Viking raids that began in 787 and continued for over a century destroyed all the northern and eastern houses, while in areas less affected most fell under the control of secular lords, who appropriated their property and appointed members of their family as lay abbots. Recovery accompanied Anglo-Saxon political recovery under the Wessex dynasty. By 1066 there were some 35 male houses and 10 nunneries. Virtually all were concentrated in the old kingdom of Wessex, the West Midlands, and the Fens.

The Norman Conquest resulted in the seizure of some monastic lands by the invaders, but generally set-backs were temporary and monasticism was invigorated by new foundations such as Chester, Shrewsbury, St Mary's York, and Durham. The late 11th and 12th cents. also saw an increase in the number of houses for women, some of which belonged to new orders, such as the *Gilbertines. In 1128 the first *Cistercian community in Britain was established at Waverley (Surrey).

Thereafter monastic foundations declined markedly. Ecclesiastical patronage was directed at the new mendicant orders of *friars, and *chantries, frequently established in cathedrals and other churches to pray for the souls of donors and their families, tended to replace monasteries in the pious affections of the laity. The spiritual and intellectual condition of the late medieval monasteries is controversial, but there is little doubt that there was decline from the 'golden age' of the 12th and 13th cents., as friars took the lead in theological debate and universities began to replace monasteries as educational centres. By the time of the *dissolution (1536–40) many monasteries were finding it difficult to attract sufficient recruits.

**Monck, George, 1st duke of Albemarle** (1608–70). Monck, a stolid and taciturn soldier, played a crucial part in bringing about the *Restoration of 1660. In the 1630s he was in the Dutch service but at the outbreak of the Civil War joined the king. After a year in Ireland fighting against the rebels, he was captured at *Nantwich in 1644. At the end of the war, he returned to Ireland on the parliamentary side, fought a difficult campaign, and was captured by royalist forces in 1649. When released, *Cromwell took him to Scotland, where he commanded the regiment that became the Coldstream Guards. On Cromwell's death, Monck's potential role as king-maker was obvious to all. Monck marched his men across the Tweed, reopened negotiations with Charles II, effected his restoration, and met him on the beach at Dover. Next day he received the Garter and a week later his dukedom. He was again at sea in the second *Anglo-Dutch War and served as a figurehead lord of the Treasury from 1667.

**Monmouth, diocese of** The diocese was created out of the ancient see of Llandaff in

1921, and is virtually conterminous with the county of *Gwent. It is the smallest in the Church in Wales, few parishes being more than 25 miles from the cathedral. When the diocese was formed, there was no obvious choice for a cathedral. In the event, the parish church of St Woolo in Newport, the most populous town, was chosen.

**Monmouth, James Scott, 1st duke of** (1649–85). Charles II's eldest and most favoured illegitimate son, Monmouth gained experience with the French army in 1672–4. Becoming an English general in 1678, he defeated the Scottish rebels in 1679. His political ambitions began to soar when *Shaftesbury, in his campaign to exclude the future James II from the succession, exploited the story that Charles had been secretly married to Monmouth's long-dead mother, Lucy Walter. Implicated in the Whig *Rye House plot to assassinate Charles and James he fled to Holland, from where he launched his disastrous invasion after James succeeded Charles. After defeat he was executed under an Act of attainder.

**Monmouth rising** While in exile in Holland radical Whigs persuaded the duke of *Monmouth to invade England while *Argyll invaded Scotland. Landing at Lyme in Dorset on 11 June 1685 with 80 followers only, but arms for 2,000, Monmouth depended on the Whigs rallying to him. Promised diversionary risings in London and Cheshire failed to occur. However Whig rank-and-file supporters, mostly artisans in the depressed textile industry, formed an army of about 3,000 untrained infantry. Aware that this force was no match for the royal professionals, Monmouth conducted an irresolute campaign. He proclaimed himself king in place of James II. Having lost the initiative, he gambled on a night attack (5–6 July) at *Sedgemoor, outside Bridgwater in Somerset. His men were routed. Monmouth was captured (8th) and executed in London a week later.

**Monmouthshire** was the most border of all counties, straddling England and Wales throughout its 400 years' history.

In pre-Roman times, the area was part of the territory of the *Silures. It was rapidly brought under Roman control, the remains at *Caerleon and *Caerwent being among the most impressive in the country. It stayed

British after the Romans left, for some time formed an independent kingdom of *Gwent, and at others was part of the kingdom of *Deheubarth.

The Normans began systematic colonization after 1066, constructing castles at Chepstow, *Raglan, Usk, Monmouth, White Castle, Skenfrith, Grosmont, and Abergavenny, as well as protected boroughs like Newport. The remote region was known mainly for the excellence of its archers and for the woollen Monmouth caps which were popular. Henry V was born in Monmouth, where his statue adorns the town hall. The advent of the Tudors, a Welsh dynasty, changed the status of the area. By the Act of *Union of 1536, the territory was incorporated into England, joining with land to the west of the Usk to form the new county of Monmouthshire. Its peculiar position was reflected by the fact that, like English counties, it was given two knights of the shire, but Monmouth had only one member and shared the representation with six contributory boroughs on the Welsh pattern.

The western parts of the county were little developed, though *Camden noted in 1586 that they were 'not unserviceable to the industrious husbandman'. The large-scale exploitation of the coal and iron resources of Monmouthshire began in the early 19th cent., transforming the economic and political balance. Monmouth, the largest town in 1801 with 3,300 inhabitants, was by 1871 outstripped by Abergavenny, Pontypool, Blaenavon, Tredegar, and Newport. Politically the county became first a Liberal, then a Labour stronghold. By the mid-20th cent. the Welsh language had retreated and the opening of the Severn bridge in 1966 suggested that Monmouth was being pulled back into the English economic orbit. The Local Government Act of 1972 moved the county back into Wales, restoring the name of Gwent, and Monmouth lost its position to Cwmbran, a new town just north of Newport. Even this was not the last throw, for in 1996 a further reorganization of local government divided Gwent into four unitary authorities, one of which was to be called Monmouthshire.

**monopolies** Strictly, monopolies exist when there is a single supplier in a market. Adam *Smith, in the *Wealth of Nations, provided a sustained attack on monopolies but thought of them more as multi-firmed industries with statutory protection along the lines of the medieval guilds.

Attitudes towards monopolies have changed over time. Monopolies granted to courtiers by Elizabeth I and James I caused bitter resentment and there were fierce protests in Parliament. Conferring monopoly power has also been a traditional way of stimulating investment—the *turnpike system for roads. At the international level, monopoly trading power formed a key element in colonial development with singular powers being conferred on bodies such as the *East India Company (1600).

Modern concerns about the effect on consumers from the exploitation of monopoly power have led to state regulation of monopolies—through price controls or profit limits. Mergers which create monopolies are subjected to scrutiny. The large-scale state ownership of monopolies is a relatively modern phenomenon stemming back to the nationalization programme of the Labour government of 1945–50. More recently (since 1979) there has been a return to regulated private monopolies.

**Montagu–Chelmsford Report** The First World War both increased Britain's need for Indian men and *matériel* and presented the Indian national movement with an opportunity to demand constitutional reform. Edwin Montagu, the secretary of state, was sent to India in 1917 and, together with Viceroy Lord Chelmsford, prepared the report which was to lead the country towards 'responsible self-government'. However, the reforms, which were extremely cautious, proved a grave disappointment to Indian national opinion.

**Montfort IV, Simon de, earl of Leicester** (1208–65). Earl Simon has been the subject of controversy ever since his death at the battle of *Evesham (1265). Then, the victorious royalists dismembered his body in revengeful exultation; a detested traitor had met his end. But his followers found solace in the rapid emergence of a cult. A 'political' saint was born.

It is as a supposed martyr for justice that Simon has largely attracted both denigration and adulation ever since. Nineteenth-cent.

scholars saw the *baronial movement for reform, which Simon came to lead, as a formative phase in the making of the English constitution, a crucial step on the road to democracy. Powicke reacted sharply, considering Simon to be a fanatic, a moral and political crusader, whose arrogance and stubbornness wrecked the early promise of the reform movement enshrined in the provisions of *Oxford (1258). What does seem clear is that Simon was no great radical or social reformer. Rather, he accepted the social order of his day and took support from whatever quarter he could.

**Montgomery, Bernard** (1887–1976). General and then field marshal (August 1944), Montgomery was the most controversial general of the Second World War. Arrogant, confident, and self-centred, he did not endear himself to equals or superiors, but 'Monty' won the confidence of subordinates and ordinary soldiers. He rose to fame as commander-in-chief, 8th Army, in north Africa in 1942. With stronger forces and unequalled knowledge of his enemy's weaknesses, he directed the victory of *El Alamein, forcing Italian and German withdrawal back to Tunisia. The climax of his career was the command of ground forces in the attack on Normandy in 1944 until September. He aroused controversy after D-Day when his progress in capturing Caen was thought perilously slow. He showed high qualities in making cautious, 'balanced' provision for the unexpected: he claimed, however, that for him nothing was unexpected.

**Montgomery, treaty of,** 1267. After the defeat of his ally Simon de *Montfort in 1265, *Llywelyn came to terms with Henry III at Montgomery. He was recognized as prince of Wales in exchange for homage and 25,000 marks. The treaty was the highest point of Llywelyn's power.

**Montgomeryshire** (Sir Drefaldwyn) Border county of mid-Wales. It was created at the Act of *Union with England in 1536 and was coincident with the Welsh kingdom of southern *Powys. The English name comes from the French home of the early conqueror, Roger de Montgomery.

There was an early woollen industry in the towns of the Severn valley, and its demise, together with the closure of lead-mines and greater capitalization of agriculture, led to extensive depopulation. In response, Newtown was developed from 1967 and has a range of light industry. In 1974 Montgomeryshire became a district in the county of Powys and was incorporated in the unitary authority of Powys in 1996.

**Montrose, James Graham, 1st marquis of** [S] (1612–50). Montrose was the most brilliant commander on the royalist side during the Civil War and a ray of hope for a sinking cause. In 1639 he joined the covenanters but changed sides. He joined the king at Oxford, was raised to marquis in 1644, and appointed to command the king's forces in Scotland, such as they were. His speed of movement, courage, and tactical skill won him a series of remarkable victories—at *Tippermuir (September 1644), *Aberdeen (September 1644), *Inverlochy (February 1645), *Auldearn (May 1645), *Alford (July 1645), and *Kilsyth (August 1645). But no man could defy the odds for ever. At *Philiphaugh in September 1645 he was beaten, and forced to flee abroad. Returning in 1650 with a forlorn hope, he was defeated at *Carbisdale, betrayed, and hanged at Edinburgh in May.

**Montserrat** is one of the Leeward Islands and a British colony. It was sighted by Columbus in 1493, disputed between France and Britain, and finally confirmed to Britain by the treaty of *Versailles in 1783. It relies mainly upon tourism, cotton, and light industry, but was severely damaged by a volcanic eruption in 1995.

**Moore, Henry** (1898–1986). One of the greatest sculptors of the 20th cent. Drawing inspiration from primitive sculptures and Italian frescos, he intended his work to have 'a pent-up energy, an intense life of its own'. Moore taught at the Royal College of Art 1925–32 and at the Chelsea School of Art 1932–9. At about the same time as his first public commission, the *North Wind* relief on the London Transport Building (1928), Moore produced his first reclining figure. This theme, together with that of mother and child, was repeated throughout his life.

**Moore, Sir John** (1761–1809). Soldier and military reformer. Moore entered the army in 1776. In Corsica, on 10 August 1794, he led the storming party at the siege of Calvi. After an expedition against St Lucia in 1796 he was appointed governor of the island for a time. Moore distinguished himself in Egypt during the night-time landing operation at Aboukir on 22 March 1801. In 1808 he assumed command of the British forces in the Peninsular War, but was killed at *Corunna (16 January 1809) after conducting a hazardous but successful retreat.

**Moray, kingdom of** Morayshire, the county centred on Elgin from the 12th cent. to 1975, was only a small part of the kingdom of Moray, which originally extended from the west coast facing the Isle of Skye across to the river Spey in the east. The kingdom was created by the Gaels of northern Argyll, who, with the Norse from Orkney, overcame the Picts in northern Scotland in the 9th cent. Throughout their history the kings of Moray were faced by powerful enemies to the north and south. In the north they struggled to resist the Norse earls of *Orkney. In the south they strenuously resisted the ambitions of Scottish kings, who sought to make Moray part of their realm. The most famous king was *Macbeth, who successfully turned the tables on the Scottish kings in the south and became king of Scots after killing *Duncan I in 1040. Despite conquest, colonization, and expulsion, the leading families of Moray continued to resist the kings of Scots until 1230. But the days were over when Scotland was a patchwork of regional kings.

**Moray, Thomas Randolph, 1st earl of** [S] (d. 1332). Randolph was a nephew of Robert I Bruce. Captured fighting for Bruce at *Methven in 1306, he changed sides but was captured again, this time by Bruce's men. He rejoined Bruce and, after this unpromising start, became one of his trusted allies and most reliable commanders. In March 1314 he seized Edinburgh castle from the English in a brilliant night attack and fought prominently at *Bannockburn. He won more victories over the English at *Myton in 1319 and at *Byland in 1322. On the death of Bruce he acted as regent 1329–32 for the young David II.

**Moray, Sir Robert** (c.1609–73). Moray, the son of a Scottish laird from Perthshire, was soldier, scientist, and politician. He spent many years in the French service, acting as go-between for Charles I. He took part in the earl of Glencairn's rising in Scotland in 1654 before returning again to the continent, where he practised music and chemistry. After the Restoration, Moray took a prominent part in the foundation of the *Royal Society, acted as president, and looked after Charles II's private laboratory in Whitehall.

**Moray, Alexander Stewart, 5th earl of** [S] (1634–1701). Moray was a descendant of Regent *Moray, himself an illegitimate son of James V. He rose to high office after the Restoration. From 1675 to 1676 he was justice-general [S], a lord of the Treasury in 1678, and served as secretary of state [S] from 1680 to 1689. He was deprived of all his offices after the Glorious Revolution.

**Moray, James Stewart, 1st earl of** [S] (1531–70). Illegitimate son of James V and thus half-brother of Mary Stuart. As Lord James Stewart, he played a key role in the protestant rebellion of 1559–60, subsequently dominating the provisional government which negotiated Mary's peaceful return to Scotland in 1561. Rewarded in 1562 with the earldom of Moray, his policy of 'amity' with England was destroyed by Mary's marriage to *Darnley in 1565, which pushed Moray into rebellion and temporary exile in England. On his return in August 1567, he was made regent for the infant James VI. His defeat of Mary at *Langside in May 1568 lent his regime some credibility. In January 1570 he was assassinated by the Hamiltons, staunch supporters of the exiled queen.

**More, Hannah** (1745–1833). One of the best-known polemicists of her day, Hannah More was born at Stapleton, near Bristol, and joined her sisters in running a school. A poem *Sir Eldred* was well received (1776) and her play *Percy* had a good run at Covent Garden in 1777, thanks to David *Garrick's support. Her growing evangelical interest was evident in *Thoughts on the Importance of the Manners of the Great to General Society* (1788). From her cottage at Cowslip Green, near Blagdon, south of Bristol, she started in the 1790s Sunday schools for the Mendip villages. Meanwhile the outbreak of the French Revolution gave her a chance to write simple and didactic tracts, in which

the poor were invited to count their blessings.

**More, Sir Thomas** (1478–1535). More, lawyer, humanist, and amateur theologian, held great intellectual and moral ascendancy over Henrician England, until his defence of the Roman catholic cause brought about his downfall. His legal and political career prospered in the 1510s and 1520s: he became under-sheriff of London (1510), master of requests (1518), and Speaker of the Commons (1523). He was knighted in 1521, and succeeded *Wolsey as lord chancellor in 1529. Meanwhile, More became a celebrated enthusiast of humanism, and friend of Desiderius Erasmus. His *Utopia, which described an imaginary land whose inhabitants shaped their lives by natural reason, made his literary reputation. The king's first marriage-crisis placed More in a quandary. He tried to persuade Henry to take *Catherine back, and to persecute heretics, until failure forced his resignation from office in May 1532. When required to swear an oath to the new royal succession in 1534, More refused. Swiftly tried and condemned on perjured evidence, More finally spoke out in defence of the papacy, and was executed on 6 July 1535. He was canonized in 1935.

**Morgan, Sir Henry** (c.1635–88). Morgan was a buccaneer and adventurer in the Spanish main. Morgan joined an expedition in 1666 led by a buccaneer, Edward Mansfield: when he was killed in action, Morgan was 'chosen' to lead the raiders. They captured Porto Bello, slaughtered the Spanish garrison, and ransacked the town. Next he proceeded to capture Panama despite a pitched battle by its defenders. He gained favour with Charles II, was made lieutenant-governor of Jamaica in 1674, and knighted. He spent the rest of his life there as a stern defender of law and order.

**Morgannwg, kingdom of** The immediate post-Roman kingdom in south-east Wales was Glywysing. It gave way to the kingdom of Morgannwg, which may have been named after Morgan Hen ('Morgan the Old'), who died 974. The area was penetrated by the Normans after 1066 and Robert *Fitzhamon established the lordship of Glamorgan, beginning his castle at Cardiff c.1080.

**Morley, John** (1838–1923). Journalist and politician. The son of a north country surgeon, Morley used free-lance journalism as a stepping-stone to the editorship of the *Fortnightly Review* (1867–82), which became a major vehicle for the propagation of a new species of radical Liberalism. Elected to Parliament in 1883, Morley, now a Home Ruler, broke with Chamberlain over Ireland, serving as Irish secretary in Gladstone's last ministry (1892–4) and under Rosebery (1894–5). Morley denounced British policy in South Africa at the time of the Boer War, but virtually retired to write a much-acclaimed life of *Gladstone. As a member of the Liberal governments of 1905–14 he was responsible for the reform of the British administration of India, resigning in 1914 over the issue of war with Germany.

**mormaers** were provincial rulers in the Gaelic kingdom of Scotland from the 10th to the 12th cents. They raised the men of their province for the defence of the kingdom, collected tribute from the province's peasants, and administered justice, assisted by the lawman of the province. Mormaers are first mentioned in 918, soon after the emergence of the new kingdom of the *Scots. In the 12th cent., chiefly by virtue of adopting primogeniture and 'military feudalism', mormaers developed into provincial earls.

**Mormons,** or the Church of Jesus Christ of Latter Day Saints, result from visions experienced in Manchester, NY, during the 1820s by Joseph Smith (1805–44), enabling him to locate and translate *The Book of Mormon* (1827), a history of American religion from Babel to the 5th cent. AD, written on gold tablets in 'reformed Egyptian' and deciphered by sacred crystals which Smith had to return to the angel Moroni on completion. There followed seventeen years of sectarian vagabondage: founded in 1830, the sect reached Great Salt Lake Valley, Utah, in 1847. In that time twelve apostles were appointed, Smith became first president, received his revelation about plural marriages (1843), and was killed in prison. Mormonism's survival, therefore, owes most to Smith's successor Brigham Young (1801–77), who shaped Utah into a model state (polygamy was abolished in 1890). The whole was expressed in lives of strenuous simplicity and aggressive

missionary endeavour. The first Mormon missionaries reached England in 1837.

**Morris, William** (1834–96). Poet, artist, craftsman, and socialist, Morris was educated at Marlborough and Oxford. At first intended for the church, he became a painter under the influence of *Rossetti. He quickly realized he had no great talent for painting but that he could design, and in 1861 founded Morris & Co. to produce wallpapers, furnishings, and stained-glass windows. He raised the standards of English design and craftsmanship and through his Kelmscott Press, founded 1890, had a similar effect on book design and printing.

**Morrison, Herbert** (1888–1965). Labour Party politician and statesman. After he became secretary in 1915, Morrison's organizational skills accelerated the steady rise of the London Labour Party. Mayor of Hackney 1920–1, London county councillor from 1922, and MP for South Hackney in 1923–4, 1929–31, 1935–45 (and Lewisham 1945–59), Morrison led Labour to victory in the 1934 LCC elections. The culmination of his London-based successes was the 1951 Festival of Britain. After a brief spell as minister of supply (May–October 1940), for most of the war he served as Churchill's popular home secretary (1940–5). In the post-war Labour government, Morrison played a co-ordinating role as lord president and leader of the Commons (1945–51) before an unhappy tenure as foreign secretary (March–October 1951). Despite serving as Attlee's deputy for a decade, Morrison was defeated for the Labour leadership in 1955, as he had been in 1935.

**Mortimer, Roger, 6th Baron Wigmore** (*c.*1231–82). Mortimer was one of the most powerful marcher barons of Henry III's reign and preoccupied with resisting Welsh advance. His mother was a daughter of *Llywelyn ab Iorwerth. In 1258, Mortimer stood with the baronial opposition to Henry III. But de *Montfort's *rapprochement* with *Llywelyn ap Gruffydd, with whom Mortimer was constantly at feud, caused him to change sides. He fought with the losing royal army at *Lewes in 1264 and subsequently helped Prince Edward to escape captivity. He took a leading part in de Montfort's defeat at *Evesham in 1265.

**Mortimer, Roger, 1st earl of March**
(c.1287–1330). A lord of the Welsh march,
Roger Mortimer was one of the rebels who
surrendered to Edward II in 1321. He made a
dramatic escape from the Tower of London
in 1324, and went into exile in Paris; it is
probably there that he became Queen *Isabella's lover. He was at her side during the
invasion of 1326, and after the deposition of
Edward II he, with the queen, dominated
government until 1330. This regime proved
to be as corrupt and incompetent as that of
the *Despensers which it succeeded, and in
1330 the young king, Edward III, with a small
group of followers seized Mortimer at Nottingham. His execution followed trial in Parliament.

**Mortimer's Cross, battle of,** 1461. The
young earl of March (the future Edward IV)
was at Gloucester when his father was defeated and killed at *Wakefield. He marched
north to intercept a strong Lancastrian force
under the earl of Wiltshire and Jasper
*Tudor, earl of Pembroke, whom he defeated
on 2 February at Mortimer's Cross, 4 miles
south of Wigmore. This was Edward's first
important victory. Owen *Tudor, Pembroke's
father and grandfather of the future Henry
VII, was taken prisoner and beheaded in
Hereford market-place.

**Mortmain, statute of,** 1279. Mortmain
refers to property held by a 'dead hand' and
therefore inalienable. Kings and barons objected to persons granting their land to a
religious institution and receiving it back
again, having shed, in the process, their military and other feudal obligations. The provisions of *Westminster (1259) declared
against alienation of land without the lord's
permission. Edward I's statute of 1279 forbade such transfers on pain of forfeiture, to
the chagrin of the clergy.

**Morton, James Douglas, 4th earl of**
[S] (c.1516–81). The position of regent to
young James VI of Scotland was not an envi-
able one. *Moray, the first, was shot in 1570;
*Lennox was stabbed in 1571; *Mar lasted a
year before dying unexpectedly, with poison
rumoured; Morton was the fourth and last,
and had exercised effective power during the
two previous regencies. After Mary's return
from France in 1561, Morton played an increasingly important role, first as chancellor

[S] 1562–6 and again 1567–73. He took a
leading part in the murder of *Rizzio, an
equivocal one in the murder of *Darnley,
but in 1567 led the opposition to Mary and
*Bothwell, defeating their supporters in 1568
at *Langside. He succeeded Mar as regent in
1572. His strong policy antagonized nobles
and kirk alike, and in 1578 he was overthrown by *Atholl and *Argyll. Elizabeth's
intervention afforded him a shaky return
to office, though scarcely to power, until in
1580 he was charged with Darnley's murder
and beheaded in 1581.

**Morton, John** (c.1420–1500). Cardinal.
Morton was one of the greatest ecclesiastical
statesmen of the 15th cent. A useful ecclesiastical lawyer, he advanced rapidly under the
patronage of Archbishop *Bourchier but, as
an adherent of the Lancastrians, fell into disfavour after *Towton in 1461. He escaped to
the continent, returned with *Warwick in
1470, and after the Lancastrian disaster at
*Tewkesbury in 1471 made his peace with
Edward IV. In 1473 he was appointed master
of the rolls and in 1479 bishop of Ely. During
the short reign of Richard III, Morton was
again forced to flee the country, returning
after Henry VII's triumph at *Bosworth.
Henceforth he was the mainstay of the new
regime, becoming archbishop of Canterbury
in 1486 and lord chancellor in 1487. In 1493
Henry obtained for him a cardinal's hat from
Pope Alexander VI. His extraordinary domination prompts comparison with *Wolsey 20
years later.

**mortuary** Formerly a gift of the second-
best beast of a deceased parishioner to the
incumbent of the parish church, later the
second best of the moveable goods from
the estate. The custom persisted sporadically
into the 18th cent.; the term now applies
more usually to a place for the temporary
reception of the dead.

**Mosley, Sir Oswald** (1896–1980). Labour
politician, orator, and fascist. Born into the
landed aristocracy and educated at Winchester, Mosley served with distinction during the
Great War. From 1918 to 1924 he sat as MP
for Harrow, first as a Conservative and then
as an Independent. In 1924 he joined the
Independent Labour Party, and was Labour
MP for Smethwick 1924–31. Mosley epitomized the impatience of post-1918 youth

with conventional party politics, which he felt was incapable of dealing with social and economic problems. His British Union of Fascists (formed 1932) failed to win a parliamentary seat, and was proscribed in 1940, when Mosley himself was interned.

**Mothers' Union** Church of England women's organization, founded in 1876 by Mary Sumner, wife of a Hampshire rector, originally as a parochial body aiming to uphold 'the sanctity of marriage'. Having developed into a diocesan organization by 1885, it spread rapidly, launched its own journal, formed a central council (1895), and was granted a royal charter (1926); the first overseas branch was founded in 1897.

**motor-cycle racing** Daimler's motor-bicycle of 1885 could reach 12 m.p.h. Britain lagged behind France and Germany in the development of racing at first but in 1907 Brooklands was opened and the first Tourist Trophy race in the Isle of Man was held. Speedway racing was introduced into Britain from America in the 1920s and a league started in 1929. After considerable vicissitudes, it is now re-established and organized by the Speedway Control Board.

**motor racing** began soon after Karl Benz invented the petrol-driven car in 1885. The first race took place on 11–13 June 1895 from Paris to Bordeaux. In 1906 H. F. Locke King built a 2.75-mile concrete track at his Surrey estate called Brooklands. It featured long, steeply banked turns to allow cars to corner at speed.

New courses sprang up in Britain: Donnington Park near Derby (1933), Silverstone in Northamptonshire (1948), Brands Hatch in Kent (1949), and Oulton Park in Cheshire (1953). The British Grand Prix was first held in 1948. It was not until the introduction of the World Drivers' Championship in 1950 that Britain made her mark. That year saw the launch of British Racing Motors (BRM) in an attempt to match the European competition. In 1958 Stirling Moss, driving a Cooper, won the Argentine GP.

In the 1950s Moss and Mike Hawthorn became household names. Graham Hill won the Drivers' Championship in 1962 and 1968, Jim Clark in 1963 and 1965, and Jackie Stewart in 1969, 1971, and 1973. James

Hunt and Nigel Mansell followed suit in 1976 and 1992, and Damon Hill in 1996.

**motorways** are segregated roads devoted to trunk motor traffic. The first true motorway was the Preston bypass of 1958, precursor to the opening of the first part of the M1 in 1959. The network grew slowly: by April 1963, only 194 miles were open, reaching 957 by 1973, 1,731 in 1984, and 1,969 in 1994.

Motorways cut journey times, halving the coach journey from Birmingham to London in 1960, and reduced fatal accidents to less than half the level of ordinary roads. They spread the commuting zone, especially around London, and shifted industrial location to such as the 'M4 corridor', and in the cities divided communities in ways unknown since the railway. In the 1990s, toll- and traffic-charged private finance has been employed to escape the constraints of 'public expenditure', a return to the project of 1938.

**Mount Badon, battle of,** c. AD 500. *Gildas, the chronicler of the decline of Roman Britain, attached great significance to this British victory, which he saw as giving 40 years of respite from the Saxon advance. The most likely sites are Badbury near Swindon, or Baydon near Lambourn. Gildas associated the victory with *Ambrosius Aurelianus; *Nennius in the early 9th cent. introduced the name of King *Arthur and dated it 516.

**Mountbatten, Louis Francis Albert Victor Nicholas, 1st Earl Mountbatten of Burma** (1900–79). Naval commander and statesman. Mountbatten was born to a family closely related to the house of Windsor. After a spectacular career in the navy, in April 1942 he was made commander of combined operations against occupied Europe. In August 1943 he became supreme allied commander for south-east Asia and led the campaign to recover Burma and Malaya from the Japanese. In December 1946 he was appointed the last viceroy of India to oversee the transfer of power, which took place on 15 August 1947. He was chief of the defence staff from 1959 to 1965. He was murdered in Ireland by the IRA.

**Mountjoy, Charles Blount, 8th Baron** (c.1562–1606). Charles Blount succeeded his brother in 1594. He had fought in the Low Countries under *Leicester, and commanded a ship in the defeat of the Armada. His big chance came in 1600 after *Essex, a political ally, had so signally failed to subdue *Tyrone in Ireland. Mountjoy was appointed lord deputy and won a crucial victory in 1601 at *Kinsale when the arrival of a Spanish expedition forced Tyrone to abandon guerrilla tactics and give battle. By 1603 Tyrone had surrendered. James I reappointed Mountjoy lord-lieutenant of Ireland, made him master of the ordnance, and promoted him earl of Devonshire. A patron of authors, Blount appeared a coming man, but died of inflammation of the lungs at the age of 44.

**Mugabe, Robert** (b. 1924). Zimbabwean nationalist statesman. Mugabe was a founder-member of the Zimbabwe African National Union (ZANU) in 1963, but was arrested and imprisoned in 1964. He was released in 1975, having become leader of ZANU the previous year. Almost immediately, as joint leader with Joshua Nkomo of the Patriotic Front, he took up arms against the white-minority government led by Ian *Smith. He played a decisive role in the peace negotiation in 1979, and after the elections held in the following year became Zimbabwe's first African prime minister. A convinced Marxist, he hoped to establish a one-party state; however, with the collapse of communism in Eastern Europe he agreed to abandon his plan in 1991 but insisted on redistributing land to benefit Africans. His long rule in Zimbabwe has been characterized by chronic financial and economic decline, and by allegations of vote-rigging, intimidation, and interference with the law courts.

**Muggletonians,** or 'believers in the third commission', were the followers of Ludowicke Muggleton (1609-98) and his cousin John Reeve (1608-58), the recipients in 1651-2 of revelations for which Reeve was to be the messenger and Muggleton the mouthpiece. Their followers survived into the 19th cent. with a reading room in London.

**Munich agreement** 'Munich' (the agreement signed by Neville *Chamberlain and Adolf Hitler) has entered the English language as a synonym for weakness, and historians continue to debate whether it would

have been wiser for Britain to have risked war rather than to require Czechoslovakia to surrender the Sudetenland to Hitler. At the time (30 September 1938), the commonest feeling in Britain was one of relief.

**Municipal Corporations Act,** 1835. A corollary to the 1832 parliamentary reform was local government reform. The Act swept away the existing heterogeneous borough constitutions and replaced them by a standard form of councils consisting of mayor, aldermen, and councillors elected by ratepayers. Provision was made for the establishment of the same system in urban areas like Manchester and Birmingham which were without proper municipal institutions.

**Munster** was ruled by the Eóganacht dynasty from the 7th to the mid-10th cent., who were then overshadowed by Dál Cais, to whom *Brian Boru (d. 1014) belonged. The province was directly affected by the Anglo-Norman invasion of 1169 which saw widespread colonization, the O'Briens and MacCarthys being confined in the far west. A Desmond revolt in 1579 led to its plantation by English protestant settlers, and the defeat of the Irish forces at the battle of *Kinsale in 1601 meant the collapse of the Gaelic ascendancy throughout Ireland. Munster was the focus of much of the guerrilla warfare that characterized the War of Independence, 1919-21.

**Murray, Andrew** (d. 1297). An undeservedly unsung hero of the *Scottish Wars of Independence, he came to the fore in 1297, when most prominent Scots had submitted to Edward I. He master-minded widespread risings in northern Scotland, advanced south with his supporters, and joined forces with William *Wallace. Together they brilliantly exploited English tactical errors at the battle of *Stirling Bridge (11 September 1297). Wallace went on to invade northern England, but Murray was soon dead, apparently from wounds sustained at Stirling.

**Murray, Lord George** (1694-1760). Jacobite general. A younger son of the 1st duke of Atholl, a Whig, but an opponent of the 1707 *Union, Lord George returned from France to fight for the Jacobites in the '15. Escaping to France, he returned to Scotland with the Jacobite invasion of 1719.

He joined Prince Charles at Perth in August 1745. As lieutenant-general, he was the real Jacobite commander. To him goes the credit for victory at *Prestonpans, for the retreat from England in the face of superior cavalry, and for the victories at Clifton and *Falkirk. He fought bravely at *Culloden, while disapproving of offering battle. He died in the Netherlands.

**Murray, James** *See* ATHOLL, MARQUIS OF.

**Muscovy Company** *See* RUSSIA COMPANY.

**Mutiny Act** Before the *Glorious Revolution, James II had collected a large army on Hounslow Heath to intimidate London. The *Bill of Rights in 1689 declared that a standing army in peacetime was illegal without parliamentary consent and the procedure was adopted of passing an annual Mutiny Act which authorized the imposition of military discipline.

**Myddleton, Sir Hugh** (*c.*1560–1631). The sixth son of Richard Myddleton, governor of Denbigh castle, and younger brother of Thomas, the lord mayor of London, Hugh Myddleton was sent to London to train as a goldsmith/banker. Nevertheless he retained his connections with Denbigh and represented the borough in Parliament six times between 1603 and 1628. He is best remembered for his entrepreneurial feat of constructing the *New River, an artificial waterway created to improve London's water supply.

**Mynydd Carn, battle of,** 1081. After 1066 Norman pressure began on north and south Wales, and a period of confused fighting among the Welsh princes ensued. But at Mynydd Carn, near St Davids, *Gruffydd ap Cynan and *Rhys ap Tewdwr defeated and killed their rivals Trahaearn, Caradog ap Gruffydd, and Meilys ap Rhiwallon of Powys, and established the supremacy of *Gwynedd and *Deheubarth.

**mystery plays** Best preserved of the vernacular religious drama which flourished in England in the high Middle Ages, the mystery plays were known as 'the play of Corpus Christi', since originally performed at that festival. They versify and dramatize the biblical and apocryphal narrative of man's fall and salvation, with emphasis on Christ's trial, death, resurrection, and harrowing of hell. The plays offered religious instruction, entertainment, and a boost to civic pride and commercial interests. Their dramatic impact was enhanced by music, special effects, and moments of comedy, and their contemporary relevance by the presentation, for instance, of high priests as bishops, and shepherds as medieval Yorkshiremen.

**Myton, battle of,** 1319. While Edward II was besieging Berwick in 1319, Robert I Bruce sent Sir James *Douglas and the earl of *Moray on a raid, deep into Yorkshire. They were confronted at Myton-on-Swale, just east of Boroughbridge, by a scratch army hastily collected by William Melton, archbishop of York. The Scots routed their opponents and Edward abandoned the siege. So many clerics joined the archbishop that the episode was known sardonically as the Chapter of Myton.

**nabobs,** a corruption of the Urdu *nawab*, a governor or nobleman, was the fashionable term for men who had returned from India with ample fortunes, and often a taste for lavish living and political advancement. They were satirized by Samuel Foote in a highly successful play, *The Nabob*, put on at the Haymarket in 1772.

**Najerá, battle of,** 1367. This engagement, fought in northern Spain, contributed much to the renown of *Edward, the Black Prince. He had intervened in Castile to assist Peter II (the Cruel), deposed by his half-brother, Henry of Trastamara. The victory on 3 April restored Peter to power.

**Namibia** After much missionary activity, South West Africa was annexed by Germany in 1884. After the First World War, the territory was administered as a mandate by South Africa. In 1966 the United Nations ended the mandate but South Africa retained control in the face of an increasing guerrilla war, waged by the South West Africa People's Organization. In 1990 the territory became independent and a SWAPO government was established.

**Nanking, treaty of,** 1842. The first *Chinese War 1839–42 originated when the Chinese authorities seized and destroyed large quantities of opium, which British merchants were importing. After sporadic military and naval actions, the Chinese emperor agreed to open up trade, pay compensation for the loss of the opium, and cede *Hong Kong.

**Nantwich, battle of,** 1644. Throughout the Civil War, Charles I entertained excessive hopes of assistance from Ireland. In the summer of 1643 he negotiated an armistice with the catholic Confederacy, permitting a number of Irish royalists to cross to England. Lord Byron, holding Chester for the king, sought to organize them and in January 1644 was laying siege to Nantwich. He was attacked on 24 January by Sir Thomas *Fairfax, and though he got his cavalry away, lost most of his new infantry.

**Napier, Sir Charles James** (1782–1853). Soldier. Napier was commissioned into the army at the age of 12. He served in the Peninsular War (1808–11) and in the American War (1812–14). From 1819 to 1830 he was a military resident in Greece. In 1839 he was appointed military commander of the north of England during the chartist agitation. In 1841 he accepted a lucrative Indian staff appointment and provoked the conquest of Sind from which he made £50,000 in loot. He announced his victory with the famous signal 'Peccavi' ('I have sinned'). He left India in 1847 but returned in 1849 as commander-in-chief of the Indian army. However, he clashed with the governor-general, Lord *Dalhousie, and resigned in 1851.

**Napier, John** (1550–1617). Mathematician. Napier invented logarithms, greatly simplifying calculations involving multiplying and dividing. As Kepler put it, he doubled the life of astronomers (by halving the time they took number-crunching). Educated in France and then at St Andrews, he published his *Mirifici logarithmorum canonis descriptio* in 1614, with tables and explanations. In 1617, he published *Rabdologia*, describing 'Napier's bones', or rods calibrated logarithmically; as developed into the slide rule.

**Napier, Robert, 1st Baron Napier** (1810–90). Soldier. Napier was born in Ceylon and almost all his career was in India. Entering the Bengal Engineers in 1826, he was twice wounded in the 1840s in the *Sikh wars, and was wounded for a third time while defending *Lucknow in the *Indian mutiny of 1857. He was knighted in 1858.

He served in the *China War and in 1867 commanded an expedition to Abyssinia. Napier was commander-in-chief in India 1870–6, served as governor of Gibraltar 1876–82, and finished as a field marshal in 1883.

**Naseby, battle of,** 1645. The battle in the first civil war that extinguished royalist hopes which, after the defeat at *Marston Moor, had rested largely on *Montrose's brilliant Scottish campaign. In May 1645 Prince *Rupert captured Leicester, forcing the parliamentarians to raise the siege of Oxford. The armies met on 14 June 1645 at Naseby, east of Rugby. After initial success, the royalists were heavily defeated by superior forces.

**Nash, John** (1752–1835). Born in London, the son of a millwright, Nash was the most successful English architect of the early 19th cent. His first public commission was Carmarthen county gaol. Returning to London, Nash quickly built up a large practice, at first in partnership with Humphry *Repton, the landscape designer, then on his own. For most of his life he worked on grand projects for the prince regent, in particular on a most imaginative scheme for a garden city in the heart of London. Much of the work was completed by Nash's death, but now only Regent's Park remains as envisaged.

**Nash, Paul** (1889–1946). Painter and graphic artist. Wounded during the 1914–18 war, he was appointed an official war artist and examples of his work from this time, *We are Making a New World* and *The Menin Road*, are in the Imperial War Museum. Essentially a landscape artist, who saw himself as a successor to *Blake and *Turner, his work was imbued with deep, sometimes prophetic symbolism. In the Second World War, he was again an official war artist; his *Totes Meer* (Dead Sea) and *Bomber in the Corn* hang in the Tate Gallery.

**Nash, Richard** (1674–1762), later known as 'Beau' Nash. Son of a Swansea glassmaker, Nash entered the Inner Temple (1693). Addiction to gaming drew him to Bath (1705), which, although fashionable, had few arrangements for comfort or entertainment. Good organizational skill and energy led to a position as master of ceremonies where he crusaded against overcharging, duelling, and informality. Although 'arbiter elegantarium', he was primarily a professional gamester. Despite his contributions to Bath's prosperity and the establishment of its Mineral Water Hospital, the corporation coldly watched its uncrowned king slide into poverty, but interred him in Bath abbey.

**Natal** Former British colony in South Africa. British traders and missionaries settled at Port Natal (Durban) in 1824. A British colony was declared in 1843 to check the spread of Afrikaner influence. The dismemberment of Zululand in the 1880s and 1890s extended the boundaries of the colony and in 1910 the colonists reluctantly accepted the inclusion of their country within the South African Union.

**national anthem** First published in recognizable form in 1744 (ambiguously as 'God save our Lord the King') but performed at Drury Lane, September 1745, specifically naming King George in response to the Jacobite threat, it was essentially a compilation of loyal phrases set to a recast Tudor galliard. Rapidly gaining widespread popularity, it was known as the national anthem by 1819 despite its anti-Scots references (still balefully resented by some north of the border).

**national debt** Throughout history governments have had difficulty in maintaining the balance between income and expenditure, since the former relies on the raising of taxation, which is seldom popular. The national debt is the excess of expenditure over revenue, often accumulated over many years and financed by borrowing. This debt grew markedly in the 18th cent. as a result of involvement in numerous wars. (*See* FINANCIAL REVOLUTION.) It escalated again in the 20th cent. as a result of war and the increasing state obligations for welfare payments such as social security and pensions.

**National Front** Established from several small extremist right-wing organizations in 1967, the National Front came to prominence in the 1970s after capitalizing on fears of increasing numbers of immigrants. Although never close to winning a seat in Parliament, it had strong support in parts of London, the midlands, and some northern cities. After reaching a peak in early 1977, support declined. In 1982 the chairman,

n

John Tyndall, left to form the *British National Party, which has since supplanted the National Front on the extreme right.

**National Government** The Labour government of Ramsay *MacDonald in 1931 faced a severe economic crisis with more than 2 million unemployed and a run on the pound. It fell in August when the cabinet split on a proposal to cut unemployment benefit. MacDonald consulted *Baldwin, leader of the Conservative Party, and Sir Herbert *Samuel, leading the Liberals during the illness of Lloyd George. Samuel urged a coalition and Baldwin agreed to serve under MacDonald. Intended as a temporary measure, the coalition stayed in power until the Second World War. In the general election which followed in October 1931, the National Government won a landslide victory with 473 Conservative seats, 35 National Liberals, and 13 National Labour, against a Labour opposition reduced to 52 seats. Baldwin replaced MacDonald as prime minister in June 1935, dissolved in November, and won a handsome majority, though Labour went up to 154 seats. Baldwin gave way to Neville *Chamberlain in 1937. In Labour demonology, MacDonald was the arch class and political traitor and the National Government a Tory sham.

**National Health Service** Established in 1948, the NHS grew out of the Second World War's reconstruction planning of social and medical services, after long debate over health-care provision (Dawson Report, 1920; Cathcart Report, 1936; Sankey Commission, 1937). The 1942 *Beveridge Report assumed that a satisfactory social security scheme depended on 'comprehensive health and rehabilitation services for prevention and cure of disease and restoration of the capacity to work'. Aneurin *Bevan established a tripartite administration: local authorities (for existing clinics and new health centres), panel practice, and nationalized hospitals (conceding some private practice for consultants, and giving teaching hospitals special status). Since the new service was entirely free to patients, funding had to come from taxation, but Beveridge's view that costs would lessen as the nation's health slowly improved had not allowed for technological advances such as joint replacements. The introduction of charges for prescriptions, dental, and ophthalmic treatment (1951) led to Bevan's resignation on grounds of principle. Accusations of extravagance proved unfounded (Guillebaud Report, 1956), and hospital-building, application of medical advances, and staff expansion continued to be sustained by economic growth. Total spending continued to rise. As resources were shifted away from patient care into administration, the morale of many NHS employees plummeted. Though the widespread consensus of earlier decades had been shattered by the strains of 1980s' confrontational government, public confidence in the service continued high. But concern at the ever-rising cost of the service has prompted proposals for closer collaboration with the private sector.

**national hunt** *See* HORSE-RACING.

**National Insurance** In 1911 the *Asquith government passed the National Insurance Act—Health and Unemployment, which introduced sickness and unemployment benefits to be paid for out of employers' and employees' contributions. This was the beginning of the contributory, non-means-tested half of the British social security system; in 1925 state insurance for contributory old-age pensions was added.

The 1946 National Insurance Act established a comprehensive national social insurance scheme: employers, employees, and the self-employed were to make contributions, which would make the insured and their families eligible for benefits when they suffered the contingencies insured against—unemployment, sickness, widowhood, and old age.

**nationalism** is a sense of shared identity and loyalty, based upon common history, language, culture, and traditions. Though it has much in common with religious and local loyalties, it may be distinguished since it almost invariably aims to be the basis of government.

The tendency of recent scholarship has been to see the roots of European nationalisms deep in the past rather than regarding them as essentially 19th-cent. phenomena. A sense of English nationalism seems to have developed during the campaigns to drive back the Danes, though for centuries mistrust between Northumbria, Wessex, Mercia, and East Anglia persisted. It was reinforced after 1066 by resentment of Norman-French domination. The thrust of Norman advance into other regions of the British Isles stimulated rival nationalisms in turn. The military campaigns led by *Wallace and Robert I Bruce culminated in the declaration of *Arbroath (1320), and those in Wales led by *Llywelyn ap Gruffydd and *Glyndŵr gained wide popular support because they convinced many people that they fought to liberate Welshmen from English oppression.

From the personal union of England and Scotland in 1603, and more particularly from the governmental union in 1707, strenuous efforts were made to encourage a sense of British nationalism. While accompanied by military success, imperial achievement, and economic growth, it flourished. In the 20th cent., and especially after 1945, as economic and political problems multiplied, the concept of British nationalism faltered and Celtic nationalist parties began to have some success.

Ireland always presented particular problems for the idea of a British people to parallel a British state. The link between protestantism and Britishness made governments reluctant to let the catholic majority in Ireland share the rights upon which popular Britishness became based, while the willingness of some catholics to look to Spain, France, or Germany for assistance encouraged the English to regard them as potential traitors.

Concessions to the Irish catholics after the Act of *Union of 1801 ('too little, too late' is the easy cliché) failed to prevent the growth of a more militant Irish nationalism, which in turn led to the development of protestant resistance to *Home Rule ('loyalism') and ultimately to the partition of Ireland in 1921.

In Wales, the survival of the Welsh language has given a cultural focus to nationalism. In the 19th cent. dissatisfaction with the power of Anglicized landlords and the privileged position of the Anglican church was used by the Liberal Party to mobilize a Welsh-speaking population already undergoing a cultural revival. The Welsh nationalist party, *Plaid Cymru, inhibited at first by the predominance of English-speaking in south Wales, made considerable inroads in the 1990s, returning four MPs to Westminster at the general election of 1997, and claiming twelve seats in the 60-strong Welsh Assembly in 2003. After the election of 2004, Plaid Cymru formed a shared administration at Cardiff with Labour.

Nationalism in modern Scotland emerged as the autonomy of civil society and local government obtained by the Act of Union of 1707 began to be eroded by the increased speed of communications, the integration of the British economy, and the expansion of the Westminster government's powers of intervention. The resentment of Whitehall, found in many regions, could take a nationalist form in Scotland. But although agitation secured the re-establishment of a Scottish secretary in the cabinet (1885) and led to the foundation of a Scottish Home Rule Association (1886), Scottish nationalism did not mobilize the masses. Conservative and Labour lack of interest in Home Rule led to the foundation of the National Party of Scotland (1928), which metamorphosed into the *Scottish National Party (SNP) in 1934.

Increasing dislike of economic and political centralization, and optimism that North Sea oil could provide a rosy future, led the SNP to shock by-election victories at Hamilton (1967) and Govan (1973). At the October 1974 general election, the SNP took 30 per cent of the Scottish vote and eleven seats. Although the SNP's challenge declined after the inconclusive devolution referendum in 1979, the Thatcher years were widely seen in Scotland as government by an English nationalist. The SNP gained six seats at Westminster in the general election of 1997, and 27 seats out of 129 in the Scottish Parliament, elected in 2003. In 2007 it formed a minority administration at Edinburgh under the leadership of Alex *Salmond.

The cross-currents of nationalism in the 21st cent. are confusing. In one perspective the world has become global with companies in many countries and multi-national organizations like the European Union preaching ever-closer cooperation. In another perspective, there has been a striking increase in the number of small independent states as great empires—the Ottoman, Austro-Hungarian, British and Russo/Soviet—have broken into their component parts. There is surely a paradox in a country like Poland which has for centuries struggled manfully to establish its indepependence in order that many of its citizens should choose to live elsewhere?

**nationalization** Although the 1945 Labour government was chiefly responsible for enlarging the public sector of the British economy to over 20 per cent of GDP, coal, railway, and even land nationalization had been advocated by Edwardian socialists and radicals. The First World War boosted the credibility of state intervention in industry and in 1918 the Labour Party committed itself to 'common ownership of the means of production'.

The Second World War gave further impetus to calls for public ownership; the succeeding Labour government followed its 1945 manifesto 'Let Us Face the Future' and nationalized the Bank of England, Cable & Wireless, coal (1946), inland transport, electricity (1947), gas (1948), and iron and steel (1949). Party-political strife over iron and steel (denationalized in 1953 but renationalized by Labour in 1967) scarcely detracted from the acceptance of Attlee's 'mixed economy' by the Conservatives. However, the *Thatcher governments halted the process and began a 'privatization' programme in 1981; by 1996 the public sector of the economy had been virtually eliminated.

**national parks** Proposals for national parks were first heard in the 19th cent. as industrial towns grew ever bigger and suburbs swelled. The *National Trust was founded in 1895, the Society for the Protection of Nature Reserves in 1912, and the Council for the Protection of Rural England in 1926. The issue was taken up again after the Second World War and a National Parks Commission established in 1949, with power to designate national parks, and to identify areas of outstanding natural beauty, outside the parks, but in need of protection. The first parks, established in 1951, were Dartmoor, Snowdonia, the Peak District, and the Lake District, followed by the Pembrokeshire coast (1952), the north Yorkshire moors (1952), Exmoor (1954), the Yorkshire Dales (1954), Northumberland (1956), and the Brecon Beacons (1957). There are no national parks in Scotland, but national scenic areas have been designated and afforded some protection.

**National Schools Society** Because of the success of Joseph *Lancaster in establishing non-sectarian schools, leading to the founding of the *British and Foreign School Society, the bishops of the Church of England were anxious to promote a rival body. In October 1811 the National Society for Promoting the Education of the Poor in the Principles of the Established Church was formed. Dr Andrew *Bell was engaged to organize monitorial schools, teaching both secular and religious subjects. In 1833 government grants were first given towards building the schools and in 1853 towards their maintenance. By 1888 the society's schools were educating 2,300,000 children.

**National Society for the Prevention of Cruelty to Children** Despite late 18th-cent. humanitarianism and philanthropy, there was scant concern about neglect and abuse of children before 1870. Pioneer work in America observed by the Liverpool banker Thomas Agnew (1881) led to the formation of several provincial societies for the prevention of child cruelty 1883–5. The London society amalgamated with some provincial counterparts to form the NSPCC (1889).

**National Theatre** First proposed by Effingham Wilson (1848), the idea of a state theatre received parliamentary approval (1949) but the promised funding was not forthcoming. The National Theatre company was finally incorporated in 1963, with Laurence *Olivier as director, but it was not until 1976, after financial difficulties and criticism, that the company moved into its permanent home, a three-theatre complex on the South Bank (London).

**National Trust** The National Trust was founded in 1895, largely by Octavia *Hill, Sir Robert Hunter, and Canon H. D. Rawnsley of Westmorland. Its object was to preserve buildings or land of historic interest and beauty. The first acquisition was cliffs overlooking Cardigan Bay and the first large appeal in 1901 was to buy Friar's Crag at Derwentwater. The trust is now custodian for more than 350 stately homes and places, and the National Trust for Scotland for another 100.

**NATO** is the acronym for the North Atlantic Treaty Organization, established in Washington, DC, on 4 April 1949 by the USA, Canada, UK, France, and other west European countries. This was the culmination of diplomatic efforts by those, including the British government, who saw a defence alliance as vital to safeguard western Europe against possible threats by the USSR. The signatories committed themselves to taking 'necessary action' to aid any member facing attack. The *Korean War induced the formation of an integrated military command for NATO, which functioned well until the end of the Cold War. Both its length of existence and its role in seeing off the Soviet challenge give NATO a claim to be among the most successful alliances in history. Problems in the 21st cent. suggest however that success can pose its own challenges.

**Nauru** is a small Polynesian island, east of New Guinea, whose economy is based largely upon phosphate. Visited first in 1798, it became a German colony and was occupied by the Australians in 1914. After the First World War, it was administered as a mandate by Britain, Australia, and New Zealand and occupied during the Second World War by the Japanese. It became an independent republic in 1968 and is an associate member of the Commonwealth.

**Navarino, battle of,** 1827. An accidental encounter fought on 20 October between a Turco-Egyptian fleet of 70 vessels, and a British, French, and Russian fleet of 28 ships, heavier than their adversaries. Navarino Bay is a commodious anchorage in the Morea (Greece). The Turkish government had prevaricated in acceding to an armistice with its insurgent Greek subjects negotiated by the tripartite powers. The allied fleet under Sir Edward *Codrington put into Navarino to escort the Egyptian ships to Alexandria and the Turkish to Constantinople. However, a distrustful Turkish commander opened fire, and in the ensuing engagement the Turkish fleet was virtually destroyed.

**Navarrete, battle of** See NAJER.

**Navigation Acts** were intended to protect English (later British) commerce from foreign competition. This assumed that the volume of world trade was finite and that any gain by one country could only be at the expense of another. The great Act of 1651 was aimed at the Dutch carrying trade. It required that all imports should be carried in ships either owned by English subjects or owned by the nationals of the country from which the goods came. The Navigation Acts were abolished in 1849, a final step towards making Britain a free trade economy.

**navy** Britain's place in the 'Viking World' was rendered most definitive through the person of *Cnut (1016–35). King, or overlord, also in Denmark (1019) and Norway (1028), no English monarch had such distant dominions again until Charles II in the later 17th cent. Cnut's navy seems not to have been a personal apanage but an auxiliary. In 1051 it was dispensed with by *Edward the Confessor out of economy. William I had continuous trans-channel ferry needs during his reign, after the first crucial shipment of an army to Pevensey in September 1066; and he, William II, and Henry I may have made some 40 Channel crossings in all. *Portsmouth, a nascent naval base by the reign of John (1199–1216), or *Southampton were their usual destinations. By the end of the 12th cent. the *Cinque Ports had long enjoyed privileges from the crown in return for an annual provision of ships and men. Through the 13th cent. these ports, joined by Winchelsea and Rye, provided the 'drive' for assembling royal fleets. By this time the oared single sail 'long ship' or galley was ceding place to wider-beamed and higher-sided vessels, furnished with fore and stern castles. These were more difficult to manoeuvre than galleys, but they could carry bowmen and projectiles in their castles and were more suitable for boarding an enemy. Edward III's victory over the French at *Sluys in 1340 must have featured such ships; and before the 14th cent. was out there was vital development of the three-masted ship. The age-old side rudder also gave place to the stern-post rudder aligned on the keel, facilitating steering a few points off the wind.

The evolution of the navy in the 15th cent. has to be seen in the context of an ever-increasing volume of trading voyages, to Iceland, the Baltic ports, to the Basque coast and Portugal, and then the Newfoundland Banks. More distant trades made big ships economic. The three great ships of Henry V were each over 550 tons; the *Grace Dieu* of 1420, whose timbers yet lie in the Hamble river, was of over 1,000. But around 170 years later, when England faced the Armada in 1588, only 14 of the 177 private ships enlisted for service were over 200 tons, and only 5 of the 34 'Queen's Ships' exceeded 500 tons. The late medieval small ship had a durable progeny in the navy of the Tudors, the dynasty which truly founded the navy with its yards at Portsmouth, Chatham, Deptford, and Woolwich. In 1546, Henry VIII's last year, the Navy Board was formed from the navy's principal officers: it was destined to serve as the executant of the fleet's construction, maintenance, and supply, the country's largest industrial undertaking until the 19th cent. The critical change in warship design came during the 40 years before 1588, the removal of the medieval 'castles' in favour of a lower superstructure, with ships' sides pierced for guns on wheeled carriages. Through to the coming of the steam-powered 'ironclad' this was the basic character of the warship; the teamwork, ensuring high rates of fire, made a singular contribution to Britain's awesome repute at sea in the century of *Vernon, *Hawke, *Rodney, and *Nelson.

At long last, and following *Trafalgar, the book was closed on one of the most abiding and distracting of Britain's strategic preoccupations: the security of the West Indies possessions had exercised the minds of all thinking naval officers since the age of William III. This concern lay close to the beginnings of Britain's *commercial* empire in the 16th and 17th cents.—the *Levant Company 1592, the Virginia Adventurers 1609, the *Royal Africa Company 1660, above all the *East India Company 1600—all undertakings calling for ships which must dwarf the warships of Elizabeth I. By the time of Pepys's '30 ship' building programme of 1677 there may have been an average burthen tonnage of 1,200 for ships of over 70 guns as against 940 in 1660. The navy finally became 'royal' in name under Charles II.

The first steam-powered vessels in the navy were the paddle-driven frigates or sloops of the 1820s, but the navy's ships in the Crimean War did not look much different from those of 75 years before. Even *Warrior*, Britain's first screw-driven ironclad (1860), retained sail-power after modifications in 1887. During the incipient naval race with Germany in the 1890s there emerged, in the fascinating and powerfully prophetic educator John Arbuthnot *Fisher, the man who drove the navy into the 20th cent. What has to be understood about his 18,000-tons displacement *Dreadnought*, with her 21-knot speed (launched February 1906), is that such a ship was *waiting* to be built: turbine and not reciprocated engine driven, and with

a provision of *uniformly* heavy guns ensuring straddling salvoes of the highest possible accuracy. Yet *Dreadnought* was rapidly overtaken by more powerful and faster sisters, and she herself played little part in the First World War. But at the end of his life (1920) Fisher was convinced that air power was inseparable from sea power in any future conflict, and that the capital ship had had her day—a glimpse of what was to happen in the Second World War to the *Prince of Wales, Repulse,* and *Hood.* The mine, the torpedo, and the submarine had already set the pace of change; and at the Coronation Review of 1953 only one British battleship remained, the 42,000-ton *Vanguard*, which had never seen action. Yet the *Falklands War in 1982 underlined once again the crucial importance of sea-power.

**Nechtansmere, battle of,** 685. Fought at Dunnichen, near Forfar, it was a disaster for Northumbria, which probably held the territory south of the Forth and had established overlordship of the Picts to the north. King *Ecgfrith fiercely attacked the Picts against all advice, including that of *Cuthbert, bishop of Lindisfarne, who had foreseen the king's early death. Lured into a mountain pass, Ecgfrith and his army were slain. The defeat marked the beginning of decline in Northumbrian power.

**Neerwinden, battle of,** 1693. On 29 July Marshal Luxembourg with 80,000 men attacked William III with 50,000 near Liège. William suffered severe losses of men and guns, but retreated in good order and saved Brussels.

**Nehru, Jawaharlal** (1889–1964). Independent India's first prime minister. The son of Motilal Nehru, a prominent lawyer and leader of the Indian National Congress, Nehru was educated at Harrow and Cambridge and trained for the bar. He became politically active during *Gandhi's first non-cooperation movement (1920–2). In 1939 he was Gandhi's choice to displace fellow-socialist S. C. Bose as Congress president. Nehru played a leading role in negotiations for independence in 1946–7 and was prime minister in India's first interim government. He was confirmed in office at three subsequent general elections.

**Nelson, Horatio** (1758–1805). Emphasis should always be placed on Nelson's East Anglian background. Through both his parents (via his mother Catherine née Suckling he was a great-great-nephew of Sir Robert *Walpole) his roots were tenaciously regional, and his father's pastoral duties in his living at Burnham Thorpe, where Nelson was born on 29 September 1758, brought Edmund Nelson's eight surviving children into daily contact with parishioners whose livelihood was wrung from field, marsh, and coast.

His entry to the navy in 1770 was through patronage, that of his uncle Maurice Suckling, comptroller of the navy 1775–8. Through 'pull' in the right quarters Nelson made early voyages to the West Indies and the Arctic, followed by a spell in the East Indies during which he escaped death by malaria only through the care of Captain James Pigot. Examined for lieutenant in April 1777, Nelson immediately returned to the West Indies, and his years there formed him as a naval officer.

Before Maurice Suckling died he had predicted admiralship for his nephew (attained February 1797), while Hood, a friend of Suckling's, noted the young captain's exceptional dedication. His grasp of the essentials in commanding men was allied to administrative exactitude; and the latter quality prompted him to take issue with illicit American trade in the West Indies which, though a justifiable policy, placed his professional future at risk. The attraction he felt towards women suggests strong emotional cravings. Perhaps it was some self-knowledge which brought him to a marriage, grounded only in 'esteem', with Frances Nisbet (née Woolward) in March 1787. The match involved a serious misjudgement of Frances's likely capacities as a naval officer's wife.

If Frances Nelson could not comprehend her husband's professional zeal, neither could she share in his attachment to north Norfolk during his years of unemployment until, in January 1793, he was at length appointed to the 64-gun *Agamemnon*. Nelson assured his wife he would 'come laughing back one day', and although no finality was intended, a marriage which had proved childless was unlikely to bring him back voluntarily. The seven years which ensued in the Mediterranean, broken only by sick leave September 1797 to March 1798, under Hood, Hotham, Jervis, and, least happily, Keith, saw Nelson become a surpassing commander for those who served under him, and a hero to his countrymen and -women. But they were costly, his wounds, as he drily commented, being 'tolerable for one war': a right eye lost at Calvi (Corsica) July 1794, an internal rupture at St Vincent February 1797, loss of his right arm at Tenerife the following July, a head wound at the Nile in August 1798, which almost certainly affected his mental balance and increased his fear of blindness. This may be a charitable explanation, but it is not unconvincing for the intensity of his passion for Emma Hamilton, his intoxication with the honours which fell to him from George III, Naples, Constantinople, Malta, and his flagrant disregard of a superior's orders at Copenhagen. A national hero, yet a flawed one, the last three years 1803–5, which included a further spell in the Mediterranean and the frustrating chase after Villeneuve to the West Indies and back in the summer before *Trafalgar, confirmed Nelson's renown as a leader of men with an almost spiritual power to articulate the national will to resist Napoleon. He was given a barony after his victory of the *Nile and advanced to viscount after the battle of *Copenhagen.

**Nennius** Author of the *Historia Brittonum*, *c.* AD 800, a principal source for the post-Roman period. Much of the *Historia* attributed to Nennius has been described as having 'all the historical reliability of fairy-stories'. Nennius' reference to *Arthur may well fall into this category. Nennius himself wrote in his preface: 'coacervavi omne quod inveni' ('I have made a heap of everything I have found'). The result of Nennius' efforts is a well-intentioned but sometimes bizarre account of Britain in the 5th and 6th cents.

**Nepal,** a kingdom in the Himalayas, was formed in the 18th cent. out of the expansion of the Gurkha clans of the Kathmandu valley. In 1814–16 the kingdom was defeated by Lord *Hastings and brought into tributary relations with British India. Its dynasty, a sacral Hindu kingship, has survived and has only recently accepted constitutional forms of monarchy.

**netball** is derived from basketball, invented in America in 1891 and introduced into Britain in 1895. It made rapid progress since it was particularly suitable for girls at a time of expanding female education. The national game is controlled by the All-England Women's Netball Association, founded in 1926.

**Neville's Cross, battle of,** 1346. In 1346 Edward III resumed campaigning in France and in August won his great victory of *Crécy. The French urged their Scottish allies to put pressure on England and in October David II led a large force across the border. On 17 October he had reached Durham and was confronted by local English forces at Neville's Cross. The Scots suffered severe losses and David II was captured, remaining a prisoner until 1357.

**New Brunswick** was detached from *Nova Scotia to form a separate colony when 14,000 loyalist refugees arrived from the USA in 1784. The economy boomed from 1809 after Napoleon had blocked timber supplies from the Baltic. Self-government was introduced in 1848 and in 1865-6 New Brunswick was the crucial battleground between supporters and opponents of the union of British North America. French-speaking Acadians make up one-third of the population. With considerable misgiving New Brunswick entered the Canadian confederation in 1867.

**Newburn, battle of,** 1640. Though the battle of Newburn was little more than a skirmish, it helped to bring Charles I to the scaffold. The first *Bishops' War in 1639 ended in negotiation, but the following year a large Scottish army, led by Alexander *Leslie, crossed the border and was confronted by Lord Conway's troops, trying to hold the line of the Tyne. At the ford at Newburn, west of Newcastle, on 28 August 1640, the Scots crossed with little difficulty, occupied Newcastle, and dictated such financial terms to the king that the calling of another Parliament was inevitable. The *Long Parliament, the following year, executed *Strafford and declared itself irremovable, save with its own consent.

**Newbury, battle of,** 1643. After relieving Gloucester in September 1643, *Essex was shadowed on his return journey to London by Charles's army. The royalists reached Newbury a few hours before their opponents, cut-

ting off the retreat. The king's army was some 10,000 men, Essex's perhaps a little less. On 20 September battle commenced with an artillery exchange but the fighting, though heavy, was inconclusive. Charles, short of ammunition, was obliged to withdraw to Oxford, leaving Essex free to return to the capital.

**Newbury, battle of,** 1644. Charles I's staggering victory at *Lostwithiel in September 1644 enabled him to take the initiative once more. While the parliamentarians regrouped and re-equipped, Charles moved to relieve Banbury, Donnington castle near Newbury, and Basing House. On 27 October he dug in at Newbury to face a superior force under *Manchester. The parliamentary army was large enough to permit an enveloping move, but the east-west attack was badly co-ordinated and beaten off. Under cover of darkness, the royalists retreated to Oxford.

**Newcastle, William Cavendish, 1st duke of** (1593-1676). Newcastle was one of the leading royalist commanders during the Civil War. A man of vast estates in Nottinghamshire and Derbyshire, he made spectacular progress up the peerage ladder, moving from viscount (1620), to earl (1628), marquis (1643), and finally duke in 1665. He was an almost automatic choice as commander in the north when war came and had success at *Adwalton Moor in June 1643. In 1644 he was forced back to York by the advance of the Scottish army and Rupert's attempt at relief ended in the shattering defeat of *Marston Moor. Newcastle left at once for the continent and did not return until the Restoration.

**Newcastle, Thomas Pelham-Holles, 1st duke of** (1693-1768). Newcastle held important offices of state for over 40 years. The attention devoted to his personal idiosyncrasies, such as his incessant chattering, can lead to the more successful aspects of his career being overlooked.

Created a duke in 1715, Newcastle rose quickly to high office, becoming lord chamberlain in 1717 and secretary of state for the southern department in 1724. He was subordinate to fellow-secretary *Townshend, but his prominence increased when *Walpole edged Townshend out in 1730. As Walpole's own grip on power loosened, Newcastle's loyalty loosened with it. Walpole's fall in

1742 led to *Carteret, George II's favourite, being promoted secretary for the northern department. Newcastle and his brother Henry *Pelham used parliamentary support to overwhelm Carteret's purely personal power and forced George II to dismiss him in 1744. In 1746 the Pelhams won control over the government, after resigning and obliging the king to invite them back.

Though Henry Pelham as 1st lord of the Treasury quickly became the 'prime' minister, Newcastle retained very wide powers over foreign affairs and patronage, particularly in the Church of England. The death of Henry Pelham in 1754 dealt Newcastle a heavy blow. Newcastle took the post of 1st lord, but would not give a minister in the Commons real power and *Pitt and Henry *Fox subjected the government to heavy attack. War with France commenced with a string of disasters, forcing Newcastle to resign in 1756. In an astonishingly short time, however, he returned as 1st lord in a most successful ministry, the Pitt–Newcastle coalition, 1757–61. Pitt directed the war effort whilst Newcastle dealt with patronage and financial matters. The accession of George III in 1760 changed the political situation dramatically, and Newcastle soon followed Pitt out of office as the *Seven Years War drew to a close in 1762.

Although Newcastle returned as lord privy seal in the Rockingham government 1765–6, he was increasingly marginalized. Throughout his career, Newcastle was most effective as deputy to a man of greater ability, be this Walpole, Pelham, or Pitt.

**Newcastle Programme,** 1891. The split in the *Irish Home Rule party in 1890 weakened the likelihood of a successful Home Rule Bill, and *Gladstone did not attend that year's meeting of the National Liberal Federation. At the 1891 meeting in Newcastle upon Tyne he reaffirmed on 2 October the primacy of Home Rule, but associated it with reforms on the mainland by adopting various proposals of the NLF Council, in particular: land reform; reform of the Lords; shorter parliaments; district and parish councils; registration reform and abolition of plural voting; local veto on drink sales; employers' liability for workers' accidents; Scottish and Welsh disestablishment. So de-

tailed a 'shopping list' was innovatory in British politics.

**Newcastle propositions,** 1646. At the end of the first civil war, Charles I surrendered to the Scots, who removed him to Newcastle. Negotiations for a settlement began. In July, Parliament's commissioners demanded that the king should accept the *covenant, institute a *presbyterian form of church government, hand over control of the army for 20 years, and abandon leading royalists to punishment. Though Charles continued discussions, the terms were totally unacceptable to him and his mind turned increasingly to escape.

**Newcastle upon Tyne** A city and port in Northumberland, and the administrative and commercial centre of north-east England. Its urban history starts abruptly with a 'New Castle' begun by *Robert, the Conqueror's son, in 1080, and a borough planted at its gate. Its growing importance was based on coal exports, controlled by the wealthy and powerful Company of Hostmen. Coal-exporting rose further in the 18th cent., followed by shipbuilding and engineering in the 19th; in the 20th it has become part of a huge conurbation straddling the river Tyne. After a period of difficulty when the traditional industries were in evident decline, the fortunes of the city have revived, and its riverside is rejuvenated by imaginative development of the Quayside.

**Newcastle upon Tyne, diocese of** The see was created in 1882 out of the *Durham diocese simultaneously with *Wakefield, *Southwell, and *Liverpool, to provide pastoral care for the rapidly increasing population of industrial Newcastle. It contains *Lindisfarne, the historic springboard of the Celtic mission to northern England in the 7th and 8th cents.

**Newcomen, Thomas** (1663–1729). Dartmouth ironmonger and inventor of the steam-engine. He combined *Savery's independent boiler with the piston in his first 'fire engine' of 1712 at Dudley, applying atmospheric pressure to the top of the cylinder in which steam was condensed to create a partial vacuum and drive down the piston. Its use was confined to pumping water from mines. *Smeaton's improvements allowed such engines to supply most horsepower in use c.1800, and Francis Thompson's patent (1792), effective rotary motion.

**New Delhi** displaced *Calcutta as the capital of British India in 1912. It was selected to stand adjacent to Old Delhi, erstwhile capital of the Mughal empire, to emphasize continuity between the two imperial traditions. Many of its public buildings were designed by Sir Edwin *Lutyens to provide a sense of majesty, yet within 35 years the British had gone.

**New England** was the name given by Captain John Smith in 1614 to the coastline of America north of the Hudson river. Two years later he published a *Description of New England*, claiming at least 25 fine harbours. The *Mayflower* settlers landed at Plymouth in 1620 and the name New England was applied to the colony (later absorbed by Massachusetts), New Haven (later part of Connecticut), Massachusetts, Connecticut, Rhode Island, New Hampshire, and Maine. The New England colonies, with their strong puritan tradition, ultimately became the core of American resistance in the War of Independence.

**Newfoundland** was probably 'discovered' by John *Cabot in 1497. Europeans soon exploited its cod fishery. Although Newfoundland was claimed for England in 1583 by Sir Humphrey *Gilbert, sovereignty was disputed until 1713, and France retained rights of access to the coasts until 1904. An assembly was introduced in 1832 and self-government in 1855. Newfoundlanders rejected union with Canada in 1869. Military bases in the Second World War brought prosperity and in 1948 Newfoundlanders voted to become Canada's tenth province.

**Newgate prison** was founded during the reign of Henry I in a gatehouse of the city of London. It housed mainly serious criminals and from 1783 replaced *Tyburn as the place for public executions. The prison was destroyed and rebuilt twice, once following the Great Fire of *London in 1666 and again after the *Gordon riots of 1780. Newgate finally closed in 1902.

**New Guinea** *See* PAPUA NEW GUINEA.

**New Hebrides** *See* VANUATU.

**New Lanark** (Strathclyde) a factory village, was built by David Dale to exploit the water-power provided by the Clyde in 1784–5. In 1799 Dale sold New Lanark to Robert *Owen, his son-in-law, and the village acquired a reputation as a profitable and contented community.

**Newman, John Henry** (1801–90). Cardinal. Newman was the leading convert of the *Oxford movement. His writings on the Christian church brought ecclesiastical censure and, after a period of reflection, Newman became a catholic in 1845. His published writings, including *An Essay on the Development of Christian Doctrine* (1845), sermons, and *Letters and Diaries*, profoundly influenced the second Vatican Council (1962–5), often called 'Newman's Council'. He was delated to Rome for his views on the laity and the shadow of suspicion was not lifted until he was made cardinal in 1878. *Apologia pro vita sua* (1864) explained his spiritual and religious views. *The Idea of a University* (1852) was a plea for universities to offer a liberal education, for the cultivation of the mind.

**Newmarket** (Suffolk and Cambs.) is the headquarters of flat racing, run on the downs since the reign of Charles II, who founded the Newmarket Town Plate and after whom the 'Old Rowley' mile course is named. It is the home of the Jockey Club, which built a coffee-house at the course in 1752.

**New Model Army** Created by the Long Parliament early in 1645 out of the three existing armies of *Essex, *Manchester, and Sir William *Waller. The new army represented the triumph of Oliver *Cromwell in his political struggle against Essex and Manchester and, under the generalship of Sir Thomas *Fairfax, vanquished the king's forces at *Naseby (June 1645).

**Newport, treaty of,** 1648. The end of the second civil war found Charles I still at Carisbrooke in the Isle of Wight. In September, Parliament resumed negotiations with the king in the town hall at Newport. Charles made substantial concessions over episcopacy and control of the militia, but admitted privately that he negotiated 'merely in order for my escape'. When the negotiations foundered, the king was moved to Hurst castle on the mainland, before being brought to trial.

**'Newport rising',** 1839. Parliament's rejection of the first *chartist petition in July 1839 placed the chartist leadership in a quandary. There was not enough support for a 'sacred month' (general strike), while to begin an even bigger petition seemed daunting. In the Welsh valleys, the situation was enflamed by the imprisonment of Henry Vincent in Monmouth gaol. But the march on Newport led by John Frost on 3 November can hardly have been intended as more than a mass demonstration. Troops opened fire, killing at least fifteen. The 'rising' was a show of strength that went wrong.

**New River** As Elizabethan London grew, the demand for water outstripped supply, prompting Sir Hugh *Myddleton to construct an artificial waterway from Ware in Hertfordshire (1609–13). Its 39-mile meander terminated at the New River Head, near King's Cross Road.

**New Ross, battle of,** 1798. On 5 June 1798 some 30,000 rebels from Wexford (Ireland), led by Bagenal Harvey and Father Philip Roche, launched an attack on New Ross. The defence, numbering 1,500 men under General Henry Johnston, was disciplined and determined. Government artillery inflicted heavy casualties and, after desperate hand-to-hand fighting, the rebels were driven off.

**New South Wales,** a member state of the federal Commonwealth of Australia, was founded 26 January 1788 as a penal colony when Britain annexed over two-thirds of the Australian continent. NSW was later separated into Tasmania (1825, settled 1803), South Australia (1834, settled 1836), Victoria (1851, settled 1834), Northern Territory (1863, incorporated as a federal territory in 1910, yet to achieve full statehood), Queensland (1859, settled 1824), and the Australian Capital Territory (1911).

With its convict heritage, large unionized industrial population, and somewhat left-of-centre political attitudes, as well as its leading role in the export of wheat and wool, and Sydney's position as Australia's major stock exchange and growing importance as a company headquarters city, NSW is politically and economically Australia's most powerful state.

**Newton, Sir Isaac** (1642–1727). Newton was born near Grantham after his father's death, on Christmas Day. He went to Trinity College, Cambridge, in 1661; during the plague year, 1665–6, the undergraduates were sent home, and he is supposed to have thought of the nature of light, differential calculus, and the theory of gravity. In 1669 he was appointed to the Lucasian chair of mathematics at Cambridge, where he divided his time between mathematical sciences, alchemy, and biblical study. In 1672 his first paper went to the *Royal Society, containing his 'crucial experiment' to prove that white light is a mixture of all the colours. Because he believed that refraction inevitably produced coloured fringes, he advocated reflecting telescopes, and made one.

In 1684 Edmond *Halley came to see him after discussing planetary orbits with Hooke and Christopher *Wren, and found that Newton had worked out the laws of motion and of gravity. With Halley as midwife, Newton's *Principia* was published in 1687. It began by setting out the nature of space, time, and motion; then came the laws of mechanics, a proof that whirlpools of ether cannot explain the phenomena, and, finally, the demonstration that gravity and inertia fitted the facts. He represented the university in Parliament, and in 1696 was appointed warden (later master) of the mint in London, where he supervised recoinage. By the time of his death, he was regarded with awe, and came to stand as the symbol of enlightenment.

**Newtown Butler, battle of,** 1689. In the summer of 1689 Enniskillen, second only to Derry in importance in Northern Ireland, still held out against the Jacobite advance. But when Mountcashel was ordered to pinch out the town, its defenders got their blow in first, attacking his troops at Newtown Butler on 31 July. Though heavily outnumbered, the Williamite forces carried the day.

**new towns** *See* GARDEN CITIES.

**New Zealand** The two main islands of New Zealand are larger than the United Kingdom. South Island is rather bigger than North Island, but contains only a quarter of the people. In 2005 the population was 4 million, most of them living in towns. The capital, Wellington, with 341,000 people, is in North Island: Auckland has nearly one million people, and Christchurch 318,000. Mount Cook in the Southern Alps rises to more than 12,000 feet and in North Island there are geysers and hot springs. The economy is still largely based on cattle- and sheep-rearing, but New Zealand wine flourishes, industry increases, and tourism expanded rapidly after the spread of fast air travel.

The first inhabitants were Polynesian people, ancestors of the Maoris, who settled by the 8th cent. Abel Tasman, the Dutch explorer, sighted the west coast of South Island in 1642, but did not land. The Dutch named the country New Zealand but showed no further interest in it.

Not until 1769 was Tasman's initiative followed up when, on his first voyage, Cook circumnavigated both islands. He revisited the country on his second and third voyages, reporting that it would sustain an industrious people. In 1814 a small Christian mission was established, with little success at first. For 50 years, the situation was close to a state of nature. Increased contact brought diseases to which the Maoris were extremely vulnerable and the acquisition of guns allowed them to try to exterminate each other. The native population declined sharply. By 1838 there were some 2,000 Europeans living in New Zealand—the English, in *Darwin's opinion, 'the very refuse of society'. A New Zealand Association in 1837, supported by Lord *Durham and E. G. *Wakefield, was founded to encourage mass emigration. In 1839 an unenthusiastic British government sent Captain William Hobson to propose annexation to the Maoris to protect them from indiscriminate expropriation and in 1840 the treaty of *Waitangi was signed, ceding sovereignty to the British in exchange for promises of security.

The economic development of New Zealand was boosted by the discovery of gold in South Island in the 1850s, and, more enduringly, by the development of refrigeration in the 1880s. Constitutionally it progressed at remarkable speed, despite the protracted *Maori wars which continued until 1872. A federal constitution was granted in 1852, and was followed in 1856 by full representative government. The capital was moved from

Auckland to Wellington in 1867. In 1907 it became a self-governing dominion.

The population of New Zealand rose undramatically at first. The Maori population in 1896 was put as low as 42,000 and extinction seemed a possibility. By the 1990s it was more than 400,000. The total population of New Zealand in 1907 was still less than 1 million, grew slowly in the 1920s, partly as a result of high wartime casualties, and had risen to 1.7 million by 1945. After that it rose quickly, reaching more than 3 million by 1975. As in South Africa, sport has been a bond of the emerging nation—the All Blacks' attempts to terrify their opponents with the Maori haka, and the prominence of Maoris in rugby teams.

**Nigeria** Former British colony and protectorate in West Africa. British missionaries arrived in Nigeria in the 1840s and in 1853 Lagos was annexed as a British colony as part of the campaign to halt the West African slave trade. When the activities of legitimate British traders in the Niger delta region were threatened by French rivals, the British government took responsibility for the conquest of the interior in 1900. The religious and economic differences between north and south resulted in the creation of an uneasy federal system of government when Nigeria became independent in 1960.

**Nightingale, Florence** (1820–1910). Nursing reformer. Named after the city of her birth, she chafed at the restricted opportunities for women of her station. She learned nursing skills from the deaconesses at Kaiserwerth, but her real talents lay in administration. Invited to go out to Crimea (1854), her success in mitigating Scutari's appalling conditions stemmed from organization, discipline, and hard work. On return, exploiting the legend of the Lady with the Lamp and chronically unwell, she undertook reform of the army medical services, then hospital architecture, nursing education, and sanitary reform in India.

**Nijmegen, treaties of,** 1678–9. Though England was not directly involved in the Nijmegen negotiations, since the third *Anglo-Dutch War (1672–4) had been wound up by the treaty of *Westminster, her interests were at stake. Louis XIV had clearly failed in his original intention of crushing the Dutch, yet he was still able to make significant territorial gains, including fifteen frontier towns and Franche-Comté.

**Nile, battle of the,** 1798. The site of this annihilating encounter was the western end of Aboukir Bay, east of Alexandria. close to Rosetta on the Nile delta. In the evening of 1 August 1798, Nelson sighted Brueys's ships there, Napoleon having disembarked the 'Army of Egypt' a month before. In a night action five British ships attacked from the landward side where the French were least prepared for action, and seven from seaward, led by Nelson in *Vanguard*. By midday on 2 August all but two of Brueys's ships had surrendered, at no British loss.

**Nineteen Propositions** In the summer of 1642, Charles I withdrew from London and prepared for war. On 1 June, Parliament sent to him at York nineteen propositions, which demanded complete political and military control. The king's answer, drafted by Colepeper and *Falkland, was a skilful exposition of the case for a balanced constitution. Though mainly a tactical manœuvre for the middle ground, the answer was not forgotten and was much discussed as the basis for some form of limited monarchy.

**Nine Years War,** 1689–97. Also known as 'King William's War' or the 'War of the English Succession'. William of Orange accepted England's throne in 1688 in the hope that the nation's sea power and financial strength could be used against Louis XIV's ambitions in the Netherlands and Germany. The French king's support for the exiled James II made war inevitable, and in May 1689 William formed a Grand Alliance which included England, the Dutch, and the Holy Roman Emperor. In Ireland James's Franco-Irish army was soon defeated at the *Boyne in July 1690 and the rebels finally suppressed in 1691. But England's naval mastery of the English Channel was initially weakened by the French fleet and several times invasion was threatened until in May 1692 the allies overwhelmed the French off *La Hogue. The war ended in September 1697 when the exhausted protagonists signed the treaty of *Ryswick.

**Ninian, St,** An obscure figure mentioned by *Bede and subject of a much later life by Ailred of Rievaulx. Bede says he was a Briton and he appears to have lived around the time of the ending of Roman Britain, probably in the 5th cent. He is linked with south-western Scotland outside the Roman wall by his association with Whithorn (Dumfries and Galloway), in the territory of the Novantae.

**Nkrumah, Kwame** (1909–72). After university education in the USA, Nkrumah helped to organize the fifth Pan-African Congress in Britain in 1945. Returning to the Gold Coast in 1947 he founded the populist Convention Peoples' Party. Imprisoned after organizing a campaign of non-cooperation in 1950, he was elected to Parliament in 1951 and was released from detention, becoming prime minister of the Gold Coast in 1952. He remained in office when the country, renamed *Ghana, gained its independence in 1957, and became president of the Republic of Ghana in 1960. His financial extravagance and increasingly authoritarian rule led to his overthrow in 1966.

**nobility** *See* ARISTOCRACY.

**Nollekens, Joseph** (1737–1823). An English sculptor, Nollekens was the son of an Antwerp painter settled in England. Between 1760 and 1770, in Rome, he laid the foundations of his financial and artistic success. Many of his monuments and busts are in Westminster abbey.

**Nominated Parliament** *See* BAREBONE'S PARLIAMENT.

**nonconformists** *See* DISSENT.

**non-jurors** were the high churchmen of the late 17th-cent. Church of England, who refused the oath of allegiance to William and Mary in 1688. They held to the doctrine of the *divine right of kings and believed, therefore, that the Stuarts remained the legitimate monarchs. Eight bishops (including *Sancroft of Canterbury), 400 priests, and a few laymen refused the oath.

**non-residence** Residence in one's place of ministry has been compulsory since early times for all bishops and beneficed clergy, but absence became a substantial abuse in the later Middle Ages. Non-residence was a major target of the reformers. It was commonplace in the 18th cent. since many livings were too poor in themselves to support a priest.

**non-resistance** The doctrine of non-resistance flourished in the aftermath of the Civil War, holding that monarchs had total jurisdiction and that their subjects owed them total obedience. After the Restoration, the *Corporation Act (1661) and the Act of *Uniformity (1662) insisted on an oath that 'it is not lawful on any pretence whatsoever to take up arms against the king'. But James II's attack upon the Church of England placed many Tories in a dilemma and the majority abandoned non-resistance to support the invasion of William of Orange. In 1689, the statute 1 Wm. & Mar. c. 8 specifically declared that the previous oath against the lawfulness of resistance 'shall not from henceforth be required'.

**Nonsuch, treaty of,** 1585. In August 1585 Elizabeth took a momentous decision. The fall of Antwerp persuaded her that, without aid, the Dutch rebels would be crushed by Philip II of Spain. She agreed, at Nonsuch palace, to place 7,000 men in the field. *Leicester was put in charge. Philip's response was the preparation of a great *Armada.

**Nonsuch palace** near Cheam in Surrey was built on a grand scale round two courtyards by Henry VIII from 1538 onwards, sold by Mary, and repurchased in 1592 by Elizabeth. Charles II gave it to the duchess of Cleveland, who had it demolished in 1682.

**Nore naval mutiny,** 1797. Unlike *Spithead, the Nore was not a fleet station but an assembly point. The noisome conditions in the depot/flag ship *Sandwich* sparked an agitation which was disseminated through the anchorage. Starvation smothered the mutiny; Richard Parker, the leader, and 29 of his confederates, were hanged.

**Norfolk** was the fourth largest of the traditional counties. From Yarmouth in the east to Sutton Bridge in the west is over 70 miles. From Yarmouth round to the Wash is coast, lashed by what *Camden called that 'great, roaring ocean'.

The county takes its name from the Northfolk of the Saxon settlement. In Roman times it was in *Iceni territory. It then became part of the Saxon kingdom of *East Anglia, which retained some independence until the 9th cent., when it fell under Danish control. Despite severe depredations—Thetford and *Norwich were sacked by the Danes in 1004 —the region grew in population and prosperity. Thetford, Yarmouth, and Norwich were flourishing towns by the time of the *Domesday survey in 1086. Thetford gained a temporary advantage in 1072 when the bishopric was moved there from North Elmham, but in 1094 it was transferred again, this time to Norwich, where it stayed. The great cathedral was started in 1096. Bishop's Lynn, which became King's Lynn at the time of the Reformation in 1536, may have existed before the Norman Conquest, but its development as a major port was in the 11th and 12th cents.

Norfolk's prosperity owed much to its geographical position. The long coastline, though hazardous, promised abundant fish. Yarmouth bloaters soon acquired a national reputation and the town remained in the top ten until the later 18th cent. Unlike Northumberland or Herefordshire, Norfolk did not have to face Scottish or Welsh border raids. *Kett's rising in 1549, mainly a protest against *enclosures, did little permanent damage, though Norwich was taken and retaken. In the south-west of the county, schemes of improved drainage turned thousands of acres of fen into good agricultural land. Norwich became one of the great centres of the cloth industry and by Tudor times was the second town in the kingdom.

By 1800, the county's relative prosperity was over. As colonies were established, the ports of the west coast—*Bristol, *Liverpool, and *Glasgow—had the advantage, and, in population, Norwich was surpassed by the new industrial towns of *Manchester, *Sheffield, and *Leeds. Competition from the Yorkshire woollen industry and then from Lancashire cotton was severe.

In the 19th cent., Norfolk became something of a backwater. The growth of seaside holidays brought modest prosperity to Hunstanton, Cromer, and Sheringham and the Broads developed from the 1870s as a playground. But in more recent decades the pace has quickened as industry diversified—Colman's mustard, Matthews's turkeys, the Norwich Union—and the flight from London gathered pace.

**Norfolk, Roger Bigod, 5th earl of** *See* BIGOD, ROGER.

**Norfolk, John Howard, 1st duke of** (d. 1485). Howard was a retainer of the 3rd duke and perhaps on his nomination the first Yorkist sheriff of Norfolk in 1461, shortly before Edward IV knighted him on the battlefield of *Towton. Thereafter he was one of the king's most valuable servants. He became Lord Howard in 1470. In 1483 Howard supported the usurpation of Richard III, who created him duke of Norfolk. He was the only magnate killed fighting for Richard at *Bosworth.

**Norfolk, Thomas Howard, 2nd duke of** (1443-1524). Norfolk had a remarkable political and military career, despite a bad start. His father was a prominent Yorkist, who died fighting at *Bosworth for Richard III. The son was wounded at *Barnet in 1471 and taken prisoner at Bosworth. He spent some years in the Tower before Henry VII restored his title as earl of Surrey and in 1489 made him chief justice in Eyre north of Trent. From 1501 to 1522 he was lord high treasurer. In 1510 Henry VIII made him earl marshal for life and in 1513 he annihilated the Scots at the battle of *Flodden. His reward was the dukedom of Norfolk. In the king's absence in France at the *Field of Cloth of Gold in 1520, Norfolk acted as guardian of England. For a man who started on the wrong side, this was a crowning achievement.

**Norfolk, Thomas Howard, 3rd duke of** (1473-1554). Norfolk's first wife was a daughter of Edward IV; he was uncle to both *Anne Boleyn and *Catherine Howard. After fighting under his father at *Flodden, he was created earl of Surrey when his father was made duke of Norfolk. From 1513 to 1525 he served as lord high admiral, was lord-lieutenant of Ireland 1520-2 and lord high treasurer 1522-47. He helped to bring down *Wolsey and in 1534 presided over the trial of his niece Anne Boleyn. In 1537 he put down the rising of the *Pilgrimage of Grace with severity. In 1540 he succeeded in ousting Thomas *Cromwell. The imprudence of his son Lord *Surrey, in sporting the royal arms, brought a conviction for treason in 1546 and Norfolk escaped execution only because Henry VIII died. Throughout Edward VI's reign, Norfolk remained in the Tower but, as a catholic, was released by Mary, restored to his honours, and served against *Wyatt's rebellion in January 1554.

**Norfolk, Thomas Howard, 4th duke of** (1538-72). Norfolk was grandson of the 3rd duke. His father Lord Surrey was executed when he was 8. He and his grandfather were restored to their honours at the accession of Mary in 1553 and he succeeded as duke the following year. Elizabeth gave him the Garter in 1559 and employed him in Scotland to oust the French party. This proved his undoing. After the death of his third wife in 1567, he conceived a plan to marry Mary, queen of Scots. They had not actually met but went in for a good deal of literary swooning. In October 1569 he was committed to the Tower and in November his brother-in-law the earl of Westmorland led the rising of the *northern earls, on behalf of Mary and the old religion. Norfolk was released in 1570, but allowed himself to be drawn into the *Ridolfi plot to replace Elizabeth by Mary. He was executed in June 1572.

**Norfolk, Thomas Mowbray, 1st duke of** (1366-99). Mowbray was created earl of Nottingham in 1383, and received the title of earl marshal in 1386. He was one of the lords *appellant who prosecuted Richard II's favourites in 1387-8. Subsequently he assisted Richard's despotic ambitions. In 1397 he arrested the duke of *Gloucester and murdered him at Calais. His ducal title in 1397 was a reward. Soon afterwards Norfolk was accused of treason by Henry (later Henry IV), duke of Hereford; in consequence, both dukes were exiled. Norfolk died in Venice.

**Norham, treaty of,** 1209. In August 1209, King John brought a large army to Norham, west of Berwick-on-Tweed. In return for peace, William the Lion promised to pay £10,000 and handed over his two elder daughters for marriage into the English royal house. Although John failed to secure acknowledgement as feudal overlord of Scotland, these agreements emphasized William's dependence on English goodwill.

**Norham adjudication,** 1291-2. Edward I's adjudication of the claims put forward by John *Balliol and twelve others to the vacant Scottish throne, which began at Norham, near Berwick-on-Tweed, on 10 May 1291.

Their claims were scrutinized by a court of 104 'auditors' (assessors), and judgment was given on 17 November 1292 in favour of John Balliol, who was enthroned at Scone on 30 November.

**Norman Conquest** William the Conqueror's victory at the battle of *Hastings in October 1066 was followed by six years of campaigning. In the succeeding decades, the Norman kings and their followers expanded their power into Wales and Lowland Scotland. A massive take-over of English land and resources accomplished within a framework of notional legality was largely complete by 1086, the year when *Domesday Book was made.

On a longer-term perspective, it is arguable that the Conquest itself had relatively little impact on a broader evolutionary process of economy, society, landscape, and language. The newcomers were a small military élite who were gradually assimilated into Britain. On the other hand, it is not unreasonable to think of the Norman Conquest as a decisive shift within this broader process; the England and the Britain which emerged from the Norman military take-over were surely significantly different from the one which would have developed if Harold had won. There can be no doubt that William and his successors governed through mechanisms which were essentially those of the late Old English kingdom. The new aristocracy claimed to exercise the same powers over their peasants as their English predecessors had done. Not everyone, however, would accept this appearance of continuity at face value. William I, William II, and Henry I all intervened with increasing frequency in the shires. It was also the case that the Conquest's creation of the cross-channel Anglo-Norman realm can be linked over centuries to the outbreak of the *Hundred Years War. The new connection with France also established cultural connections which ensured that England's place in the 12th-cent. renaissance was more closely linked to developments in France than it would have been. The Conquest extracted England from the Scandinavian political orbit which had brought about the earlier conquest by *Sweyn Forkbeard and *Cnut. It is doubtful whether Wales, Scotland, and —ultimately—Ireland would have been as intensively colonized from England but for the presence of a new aggressive aristocracy.

**Normandy, duchy of** The origins of the duchy of Normandy lie in a grant of territory around Rouen made early in the 10th cent. by the king of the west Franks to a Viking chieftain named Rollo. This initial grant was supplemented by others and the whole was forged into a coherent political entity during the 10th cent. by Rollo's descendants. By the first years of the 11th cent. Normandy still retained political and economic connections with Scandinavia and Scandinavian settlers in Britain and Ireland. But monasteries were being refounded, bishoprics were recovering, and government was conducted according to patterns which were Frankish. At the same time, Normandy became the centre of an extensive movement of conquest and colonization into southern Europe and Britain which lasted for much of the 11th cent. Why this should have happened is difficult to explain. The great conquests in the Mediterranean and Britain are best interpreted as a Norman-led movement which absorbed the energies of a large number of enterprising individuals from many regions of northern France. Normandy's place at the centre of a colonizing movement came to an end by the early decades of the 12th cent., though its far-flung connections endured much longer. Normandy's history is thereafter dominated by wars with other French principalities. Henry I had to work hard to defend it, it was absorbed into the *Angevin empire after its conquest by *Geoffrey Plantagenet in 1144 and, subsequently, into the French kingdom in 1204 after its conquest by Philip Augustus. Ultimately its history must be analysed in the context of the history of the French kingdom. Many among its aristocracy possessed lands in Normandy and England, but others resided principally in the duchy; their actions assisted the drift to the status of a province of France.

**'Norman Yoke'** The belief that Anglo-Saxon institutions had been essentially democratic until replaced by autocracy under the Normans, despite its implausibility, was held by many radicals in the 17th and 18th cents. The advantage of the theory to the opponents of Charles I was that they could shake off the charge that they were dangerous innovators and insist that they merely desired the restoration of ancient rights.

### North, Frederick, Lord, 2nd earl of Guilford

(1732–92). North was the eldest son of Francis, 1st earl of Guilford. He was returned to the House of Commons in 1754 for the family seat at Banbury, at the age of 22, and soon began moving up the ladder. He was a useful man of business, hard-working, fat, and cheerful. Almost the whole of his life he spent in the Commons, and, according to Gibbon, he became 'a consummate master of debate'. He was brought onto the Treasury Board in 1759 by his cousin the duke of *Newcastle. He remained in office when Newcastle went out in 1762, mainly because he needed the money. He went out with *Grenville in 1765, declined to serve with the *Rockinghams, and came back into junior office in *Grafton's administration in 1766. His great chance came in 1767 with the sudden death of Charles *Townshend, whom he succeeded as chancellor of the Exchequer. When Grafton resigned in January 1770, North took over as 1st lord of the Treasury at the urgent entreaty of the king. He was 37.

His first few years in office were impressive. Government majorities were restored, the Wilkes issue receded, North's reputation climbed. An acknowledged expert in finance, his budgets were received with scarcely a dissentient voice. His *Quebec Act in 1774 was an important concession to the catholics and helped to persuade Canadians in 1776 not to throw in their lot with the American rebels. The American question, which ultimately brought him down, had its roots deep in the past. (*See* AMERICAN WAR OF INDEPENDENCE.) The British, heavily burdened after the war, resented the colonists' refusal to pay taxes. Grenville's *Stamp Act and Townshend's duties brought in little revenue. North's first action was conciliatory—to abandon all of Townshend's duties save that on tea. The American response was the seizure of the revenue cutter *Gaspée*, the intimidation of customs officers, and the *Boston Tea Party. Coercive measures against the colonists were inevitable. But once fighting began, North was marginalized and the military men took over. Repeatedly he begged to resign: time after time the king refused, understanding the value of North's

parliamentary skill in presenting government policy. Only after the surrender at *Yorktown in 1781, with his majority down to single figures, was North allowed to go.

The last ten years of his life were largely a postscript. He returned to office as home secretary in the spring of 1783 in the coalition with Charles *Fox, but was unwell for several months and content to let his more vigorous colleagues make the running. Dismissed in December 1783, he slid gracefully into the role of a premature elder statesman, defending the Church of England from dissenting attacks and the constitution from dangerous innovation.

### Northampton, Assize of,

1176. The Assize of Northampton was an important stage in the enforcement of English law in the reign of Henry II. In the form of instructions to royal justices, it tightened up the provisions of the Assize of *Clarendon ten years earlier and has been seen as the response to a crime wave. Trial was still ordeal by water.

### Northampton, battle of,

1460. The Yorkist leadership fled abroad after its ignominious flight from *Ludford Bridge in 1459, but returned in the summer of 1460. On 10 July *Warwick and the future Edward IV encountered Henry VI's army just south of Northampton, under the duke of Buckingham. The battle was decided quickly when Lord Grey of Ruthyn deserted the king. Henry was captured and his leading supporters, including Buckingham, executed.

### Northampton, treaty of,

1328. On 4 May 1328 Edward III, or more precisely his mother *Isabella and Roger *Mortimer who then controlled the government, recognized Robert I (Bruce) as king of Scotland and did not demand homage from him. Edward III was subsequently determined to overturn this 'turpis pax' and, encouraged by the success of Edward *Balliol against Robert's heir, invaded Scotland in 1333 to restore English lordship.

### Northamptonshire

is one of the quieter English counties, less affected by the industrial revolution than its western neighbours. It covered a great swathe of central England: Brackley in the west seems like a Cotswold town; Eye, east of Peterborough, a fenland village.

In Roman times the region belonged to the *Coritani. Towcester on *Watling Street was a small Roman town and the Nene valley at Castor, on *Ermine Street, was an important pottery centre. In Saxon times the shire was part of the kingdom of *Mercia. *Peada, son of *Penda, founded a great monastery about 657 at Peterborough, which survived sacking by the Danes in 870. The first mention of Northampton is when a Danish army seized it in 917. When the area was recovered by *Edward the Elder a little later, the Danish territory seems to have been the basis for the emergent county.

In the medieval period the shire was fertile and prosperous. Northampton was a town of importance. Its charter dated from 1189 and parliaments were frequently summoned there. The county produced corn and cattle and, according to Camden, was 'overrun with sheep'. Northampton horse fair was of national importance.

Although the industrial revolution came to Northamptonshire, it was gentler than elsewhere. Northampton was slow to tie into the growing canal network, but after the Grand Junction branch opened in 1815, it began to grow into a manufacturing town, specializing in boots. But the London to Birmingham railway bypassed it in 1838, and a loop line to Birmingham was only established in 1872. Peterborough, promoted to a bishopric in Henry VIII's reign, profited from the coming of the railways, became a major junction, and developed heavy engineering. Wellingborough, Kettering, and Rushden all profited from rail links to become boot centres. Corby, no more than a village in 1801, developed as a steel town, exploiting the local iron resources.

The county has suffered considerable boundary changes. In 1888 the soke of Peterborough, which retained special jurisdictions, was given its own county council, and in 1965 was merged with Huntingdonshire, before finding its way in 1972 into a substantially enlarged Cambridgeshire.

**North Briton** was the satirical name John *Wilkes gave to his weekly periodical, launched in June 1762 in opposition to *Smollett's the *Briton*, published in support of *Bute's administration. It included severe attacks on the peace of *Paris and general abuse of Scots. When the government re-

solved in April 1763 to prosecute no. 45 as seditious libel, it let 'Wilkes and Liberty' out of the bottle.

**Northbrook, Thomas George Baring, 1st earl of** (1826–1904). Baring's father was grandson of the founder of the banking firm, served as chancellor of the Exchequer under Melbourne 1839–41, and was created baron in 1866. Thomas Baring sat in the Commons as a Liberal 1857–66, and held a number of minor posts before serving as viceroy of India 1872–6. In India he succeeded Lord Mayo, who had been assassinated. Much of his time was devoted to attempting to deal with the Bengal famine, which he succeeded in holding in check. He was given an earldom on his retirement and served as 1st lord of the Admiralty in *Gladstone's second administration 1880–5. He left the Liberals over Home Rule in 1886 and did not hold office again.

**Northcliffe, Viscount** *See* HARMS-WORTH, ALFRED.

**Northcote, Sir Stafford, 8th baronet, 1st earl of Iddesleigh** (1818–87). Of Devon gentry family and educated at Eton and Balliol College, Oxford, Northcote was *Gladstone's secretary at the Board of Trade, then joint secretary to the 1851 *Great Exhibition and co-author of the NorthcoteTrevelyan Report on the *civil service. An MP from 1855, he was recruited by *Disraeli to the Conservative ministry in 1859 and served in the cabinets of 1866–8. Chancellor of the Exchequer in 1874–80, Northcote succeeded Disraeli as leader in the Commons in 1876, though his unease with the premier's policy over the Eastern Question became evident. He was joint leader of the Conservatives with *Salisbury from 1881, but his emollient centrism brought criticism from his own side, particularly the *Fourth Party *frondeurs*. In 1885 Salisbury, now premier, removed Northcote from the Commons leadership and gave him an earldom and the 1st lordship of the Treasury. Briefly foreign secretary in 1886, Iddesleigh died suddenly.

**northern earls, rising of the,** 1569. This was one of the most serious risings on behalf of the old religion during the Tudor period. Thomas, earl of *Northumberland, and Charles, earl of Westmorland, mustered a rebel army in the northern counties and gained initial success. The rebels carried the catholic banner of the five wounds of Christ, destroyed English bibles and Elizabethan Books of Common Prayer, restored traditional altars, and celebrated mass in Durham cathedral. The rising was suppressed by troops under Lord *Sussex. Westmorland escaped into exile but Northumberland was beheaded.

**Northern Ireland** was formed by the Government of *Ireland Act 1920–1. It comprised the six counties of the north-east of the island: Antrim, Down, Armagh, Londonderry, Fermanagh, and Tyrone. To ensure a protestant majority, the nine counties of the historic province of Ulster were rejected as the boundary. Fermanagh and Tyrone, though possessing small catholic majorities, were included to provide a credible geographical entity.

The circumstances of the province's formation dictated its turbulent subsequent history. The catholic minority, always over 30 per cent of the population, never accepted partition and usually boycotted the Belfast Parliament. The emerging Free State refused to recognize Northern Ireland. The new province established itself along the lines of a protestant state for a protestant people, with a heavy emphasis on security considerations.

After 1925, the province's future seemed more assured. But economic development was retarded by over-dependence on the British Treasury and by over-reliance on declining traditional industries. The government was dominated by narrow landed and commercial interests; all were members of the *Orange order. Sir James *Craig was prime minister 1921–40, Lord *Brooke 1943–63. Unionist confidence was increased by their contribution in supplying bases and ports for Atlantic convoys, contrasting with the Free State's neutrality.

The declaration of an Irish republic in 1948 caused the constitutional status of the province to be clarified in the *Ireland Act of 1949. Terence *O'Neill's attempts, as premier from 1963, to modernize the economy and reform the sectarian basis of the province highlighted all inherent tensions. Police and special constabulary's reaction to civil rights demonstrations resulted in major riots in Derry city and Belfast, and the belated intervention of British troops. The security situation deteriorated rapidly in 1969–72, resulting in the alienation of the catholic population from the British army, and the formation of the Provisional IRA. The British government's declaration of direct rule from Westminster in 1972 was followed by the establishment of a power-sharing executive in January 1974, which was brought down as a consequence of the loyalist strike within five months.

The 1970s and 1980s saw a continuous IRA offensive against both the security forces and the economy; the growth of loyalist paramilitary retaliation; spates of sectarian assassinations and bombings in the province, in Britain, and occasionally in the Republic. Demands for political status for republican prisoners in 1981 led to further catholic alienation and support for *Sinn Fein.

By 1985 and the *Anglo-Irish agreement, attention turned to co-operation between the Republic and the British government. A sense of exhaustion after 25 years of conflict, better Anglo-Irish government communications, European and American concern, and, finally, negotiations between the *SDLP and Sinn Fein leaders, John Hume and Gerry Adams, all contributed to the Downing Street declaration of December 1993, the IRA cease-fire of August 1994, and the loyalist paramilitary one two months later. After a referendum, administration was handed back in 1998 to a Northern Ireland Assembly of 108 members, of which 24 represented SDLP and 18 Sinn Fein. But hopes for the peace process were jeopardized by the refusal of the IRA to begin serious disarmament, and in 2002 the Assembly was suspended and direct rule reimposed. In July 2005 the IRA declared the armed struggle to be over, but suspicion postponed the reinstatement of the Assembly until 2007, when a power-sharing executive was formed by Sinn Fein and DUP. Though resentments remain, there are indications of social and economic progress.

**Northern Ireland Labour Party (NILP).** Founded in 1924, as a socialist alternative to the largely sectarian politics of Ulster. It strove to remain neutral on the partition question, but in 1949—after the declaration of an Irish republic—it came out in favour of the constitutional link between Northern Ireland and Britain. The renewal of communal violence in 1969 heightened sectarianism and put pressure on the NILP electoral base. The establishment of new parties in 1970–1 (the *Social Democratic and Labour Party, *Alliance) eroded different aspects of NILP support. Thereafter it rapidly declined, surviving with minimal electoral following until 1987.

**Northern Rhodesia** *See* ZAMBIA.

**North Foreland, battle of,** 1666. A major engagement in the second Anglo-Dutch War fought on 4 and 5 August in the Thames estuary and off the Suffolk coast, this was a continuation of the battle of the *Downs after each side had repaired and resupplied. Albemarle (*Monck) and Prince *Rupert with 89 warships were confronted by a Dutch fleet of 88 vessels under Cornelis Tromp and de Ruyter. The English had the better of the exchanges but the Dutch made harbour.

**Northumberland** is a large county of ancient origins as an independent kingdom and one of the earliest centres of British Christianity. A great border region, it is full of peel houses and castles. The industrial development of Tyneside is confined to the south-east corner. The rest is a shire of high fells and deep valleys, thinly populated, with small market towns like Corbridge, Haltwhistle, Morpeth, Hexham, Rothbury, Wooler, and Alnwick. *Berwick-on-Tweed is part of Northumberland geographically, though a county in its own right.

The main northern tribe in pre-Roman times was the *Brigantes. The crossing of the Tyne at the Pons Aelium must soon have become a settlement, the nucleus of Newcastle itself. In early Saxon times, the area formed part of the kingdom of *Bernicia, which joined with *Deira to the south in 651 to constitute *Northumbria (the land north of the Humber), which for centuries disputed supremacy with *Mercia and *Wessex. In the late 8th cent. the area began to suffer from Danish raids and in the following century was in conflict with the Viking kingdom of *York. In 920 it submitted to *Edward, king of Wessex, at Bakewell, and subsequent attempts to recover its independence were of no avail.

Northumbrian resistance to the Normans after Hastings led to William I's despoiling of the area in 1069. It was not included in the *Domesday survey, having yet to recover from the devastation. In the later Middle Ages it was the first line of defence against the Scots, the border region being divided up into marches. Vast power was wielded by the local lords, particularly the Percies of Alnwick. The remoter parts of the county like Redesdale, Coquetdale, and Allendale were under fitful control, border raiding was common, and bloody encounters, like *Otterburn in 1388 when Percy fought Douglas, were not uncommon. The union with Scotland in 1603 gave some respite from cattle-raiding. The last spasm of lawlessness was produced by the Jacobite movement. Thomas Forster was supported by a number of shire gentlemen in the '15, though they did little save proclaim the old pretender at Warkworth and occupy Holy Island for one day.

In so large a county, administration was bound to be decentralized. The assizes were held in Newcastle, but the elections for the shire at Alnwick. Quarter sessions were held at Newcastle, Alnwick, Morpeth, and Hexham in turn. But Newcastle had always been by far the most important town and in the 19th cent. it grew disproportionately to its neighbours. From a base of about 28,000 in 1801, it was 87,000 by 1851, and by 1914, having swallowed its surrounding villages, had reached 271,000. The explosion was due, in the main, to coal-mining and shipbuilding. The long-established tradition of shipbuilding was transformed after 1850. *Armstrong's works at Elswick were opened in 1847, *Parsons at Heaton in 1889. The political effect of this economic development was acknowledged in 1974 with the creation of a new county of Tyne and Wear, and although the new authority was itself abolished in 1986, the areas immediately north of the Tyne did not return to Northumberland.

**Northumberland, John Dudley, 1st duke of** (*c.*1505–53). Dudley had a brilliant but brief career at the very top of Tudor politics. His father, Henry VII's financier Edmund *Dudley, was executed in 1510. His mother Elizabeth Grey, daughter of Viscount Lisle, remarried in 1511. Her second husband, Arthur Plantagenet, was an illegitimate son of Edward IV and therefore an uncle of

Henry VIII. John Dudley began as a soldier, made a reputation for jousting, was knighted in 1523, helped to put down the *Pilgrimage of Grace, and became deputy governor of Calais in 1538. In 1542 he was made warden of the Scottish marches, served as lord admiral, was created Viscount Lisle in turn, and in 1544 captured Boulogne from the French. After the death of Henry VIII, he worked closely with *Somerset, Edward VI's uncle, and was advanced to the earldom of Warwick. He fought alongside Somerset at the battle of *Pinkie Cleugh against the Scots and crushed the Norfolk rebels in 1549 at *Dussindale. From October 1549 he supplanted Somerset and for the rest of Edward's short reign held power as lord president of the council. In 1551 he was created duke of Northumberland. But Northumberland's position was rendered precarious by the growing ill-health of the young king and in 1553 he turned to desperate measures to retain power. Northumberland arranged a marriage between his son Lord Guildford Dudley and Lady Jane Grey and on Edward's death declared her queen. The coup failed miserably and he was executed in August 1553 where his father had been.

**Northumberland, John Neville, 1st earl of** (c.1431–71). The third son of Richard Neville, earl of Salisbury, John fought alongside his father at *Blore Heath and was attainted in 1459, but was restored, created Baron Montagu, and appointed Henry VI's chamberlain after the Yorkists won control of government in 1460. Taken prisoner in the second battle of *St Albans, he was freed after Edward IV's victory at *Towton. Thereafter he was Edward's chief lieutenant in the north, defeating Lancastrian forces at *Hedgeley Moor and *Hexham in 1464. He subsequently changed sides, supported his brother Warwick's restoration of Henry VI and was killed at the battle of *Barnet.

**Northumberland, Henry Percy, 1st earl of** (1341–1408). Percy's military career began in France under Dukes Henry and John of Lancaster; he remained a political associate of the latter, *John of Gaunt. He was created earl at Richard II's coronation in 1377. Gaunt's appointment as lieutenant in the marches led to a breach, from which

Northumberland emerged as sole warden in both marches in 1384. He and his son Hotspur won both wardenships in 1399 as reward for their key role in Henry IV's usurpation. Fearing this regional hegemony was threatened, they revolted in 1403. Prevented from joining Hotspur, Northumberland survived to instigate Archbishop *Scrope's rebellion; on its collapse he fled to Scotland and was deemed forfeit. He was killed at *Bramham Moor (Yorks.).

**Northumberland, Henry Percy, 4th earl of** (c.1449–89). Edward IV kept Percy in detention after the death of his father, the 3rd earl, in 1461. He was restored to the earldom in 1470 and appointed warden of the east march. He supported Richard's usurpation in 1483, and obeyed the call to arms against Henry Tudor but remained inactive at *Bosworth Field.

**Northumberland, Henry Percy, 9th earl of** (1564–1632). Northumberland inherited the title in 1585 when his father, confined to the Tower, was found shot. He was given the Garter in 1593 and performed some military services. But his opportunity came with the death of Queen Elizabeth. He had corresponded with James I, urging him to make concessions to the catholics, and was made captain of the gentlemen pensioners. In November 1605 he was arrested on suspicion of complicity in the *Gunpowder plot. Thomas Percy, one of the conspirators, was a distant cousin, and had dined at Sion House with Northumberland the night Guy *Fawkes was arrested. Northumberland protested his innocence, but was kept in the Tower until 1621. The earl played chess, had a good library, a laboratory, and patronized scholars. His scientific interests earned him a nickname, 'the wizard earl'. He was a difficult man and when his release was granted after sixteen years was reluctant to leave the Tower.

**Northumberland, Thomas Percy, 7th earl of** (1528–72). Thomas Percy was restored in blood in 1549, and in 1557, after helping to suppress a rising in the north, was created earl of Northumberland by Mary. He was made warden of the east march in 1558 and given the Garter in 1563. But in 1569 he joined in the rising of the *northern earls, which captured Durham and celebrated mass in the cathedral. On the collapse of the rebellion, he was beheaded at York in 1572.

**Northumbria, kingdom of** From the middle of the 6th cent. to the 870s when the Danes took York, the Anglo-Saxons who dwelt north of the Humber achieved their own institutional life, ruled by kings. The borders of their territories fluctuated widely. At its greatest extent the kingdom of Northumbria stretched from the Humber and the Mersey in the south to the Clyde and the Forth. Its political roots grew from two principal sources, the northern kingdom of *Bernicia based on the gaunt fortress rock of *Bamburgh, and the kingdom of *Deira in the fertile vale of York. In the 7th cent. under a succession of powerful rulers, *Æthelfryth of Bernicia (d. 616), *Edwin of Deira (616–32), the brothers St *Oswald (633–41) and *Oswiu (641–70), Northumbria was a dominant force in English political life. But after the defeat and death of Oswiu's son *Ecgfrith at the hands of the Picts in 685 Northumbria lost aspirations to overlordship and the 8th and 9th cents. provide a sorry tale of unrest and violence at the royal level. Yet the age of *Bede (672–735) saw the flowering of the so-called Northumbrian renaissance when some of the finest literary and artistic work of the early Middle Ages was produced in the northern kingdom in the shape of the writings of the Venerable Bede and the great Gospel Books, of which the *Lindisfarne Gospels is a supreme example. Towards the end of the century a fresh and disastrous new element was introduced into the life of the kingdom with the first *Viking attacks. In June 793 they brutally sacked the monastery at Lindisfarne, an event which sent shock waves throughout western Christendom. Scandinavian control of communications over the North Sea put Northumbria in the front line. When the Danes in the reign of *Alfred (871–99) made their serious attempt to conquer England, the Northumbrian kingdom collapsed, leaving Danish kings after 878 in firm control of York and only vestiges of native English authority under ealdormen in the more northerly parts of the kingdom. The Danes remained in political control of York until 954. Thereafter no attempt was made to revive the kingship of Northumbria which was integrated, though with occasional manifestations of independence, in the kingdom of England.

**North Yorkshire** See YORKSHIRE, NORTH.

**Norton, Caroline** (1808–77). Author and reformer. Caroline married at the age of 19 in 1827 the Hon. George Norton. Her husband, an unpleasant bully, brought an action in 1836 for crim. con. (adultery) against Lord *Melbourne, then prime minister, which was laughed out of court and formed the basis for *Dickens's *Bardell* v. *Pickwick*. Norton continued to ill-treat his wife, preventing her access to her own children and trying to seize her literary earnings. In her defence, Mrs Norton published, claiming the rights of mothers to custody and of wives to independent property. The Custody of Infants Act of 1839 gave the courts discretion to award custody of children up to the age of 7 to their mothers. The right of wives to independent property was introduced by successive Married Women's Property Acts in 1870, 1882, and 1893. Though Mrs Norton's literary reputation has faded, her position as a pioneer of women's rights is secure.

**Norwich** County town of Norfolk, situated on the river Wensum, and a cathedral city since 1094. It is not recorded before 900, yet by 1066 it was one of the three or four most important towns in England, a position it retained until late Georgian times. The Normans transformed the city by building a castle and cathedral, and laying out a new French borough. In the 16th and 17th cents. it overtook its rivals to be the largest and wealthiest English town after London, its economy sustained partly by a massive immigration of refugees from the Spanish Netherlands who introduced the New Draperies. In the late 18th and early 19th cents. the textile industry declined in the face of Yorkshire competition, and Norwich reverted to its traditional function as a marketing and trading town with only modest industries.

**Norwich, diocese of** The see, conterminous with Norfolk, was founded in 1094. Herfast (1070–85) moved the East Anglian see of *Elmham to *Thetford c.1072 to comply with the Council of London, but Herbert *Losinga (1091–1119) moved it again c.1094 to Norwich, where he established a Benedictine monastic community. Norwich cathedral is a fine Norman building, but with 15th-cent. lierne vaulted roofs and spire. The diocese is renowned for its numerous beautiful parish churches.

**Norwich Crusade,** 1383. Led by Henry Despenser, bishop of Norwich (1370–1404), this 'crusade' scandalously mixed ecclesiastical, commercial, and political motives—with disastrous results. Supported by Pope Urban VI (Rome) in his move against Pope Clement VII (Avignon), the cost was borne by ordinary people's alms, with the aim of releasing Philip of Burgundy's stranglehold on the Flemish wool trade. Despite military experience, Despenser was no strategist. Landing in May, he took coastal towns and besieged Ypres, but hastily abandoned all at Philip's approach.

**Nottingham** County town of Nottinghamshire, situated on the river Trent, and a city since 1897. It is first recorded as one of the 'five boroughs' of the Danes, succeeded by an English fortified town (burh) after 921. In the 12th and 13th cents. it became a regional centre with self-government, town walls, and a major fair. After the Restoration the town became a social centre for the county gentry. Industry developed after 1700 with framework-knitting, and later lace-making, and the town grew rapidly. In the 20th cent. it was known for tobacco, bicycles, pharmaceuticals, and a distinguished university.

**Nottingham, Daniel Finch, 2nd earl of** (1647–1730). A Tory politician, the sober and principled Lord Nottingham was the chief standard-bearer of 'high-church' politics during the reigns of William III and Anne. He disapproved of James II's pro-catholic measures, but only when James fled in 1688 did he align with William of Orange. Appointed secretary of state, Nottingham's *Toleration Act (1689) ensured the preservation of Anglican supremacy after the revolution. He lost office in 1693. During his second term as secretary, 1702–4, his independent-mindedness again made him a difficult colleague and his campaign for a bill against *occasional conformity endangered the ministry's war measures in Parliament. Excluded from the 1710–14 Tory ministry, he was made lord president by George I in 1714 but quarrelled with the Whig ministers in 1716 and was dismissed.

**Nottingham, Heneage Finch, 1st earl of** (1621–82). Finch was a barrister, son of one Speaker of the House of Commons and nephew of another, Sir John Finch. He avoided public life during the Commonwealth but after the Restoration his rise was rapid. He was returned as MP for Canterbury in 1660, transferring to Oxford University in 1661. As solicitor-general in 1660 he prosecuted the regicides, was promoted attorney-general in 1670, granted a barony in 1674, and from 1675 to his death was lord chancellor.

**Nottinghamshire** is the county of the river Trent, which flows through it from south-west to north-east, Nottingham was an important river crossing. The Great North Road crossed the Trent at Newark and ran up the eastern side of the county through Tuxford and East Retford to Bawtry. The *Fosse Way ran south-west to north-east, crossing at Newark on its way to Lincoln.

The shire developed in Saxon times around Nottingham itself, where the rock made a strong defensive position. Various derivations of the name have been suggested but the earliest usage was Snotengaham, the settlement of Snot's people: the opening S, being difficult for the Normans to pronounce, was dropped after the Conquest. By the treaty of *Wedmore of 878 it was retained by the Danes and formed one of their five boroughs. Though Danish rule lasted less than 50 years, Danish settlement was strong: there are many Scandinavian place-names—Fiskerton, Gunthorpe, Thoresby, Granby—and the shire was divided, not into hundreds, but into *wapentakes. In the early 920s *Edward the Elder recovered the town, and built fortifications and a connecting bridge.

Nottingham retained its importance throughout the medieval period, its goose fair in October attracting traders from all over the country. East Retford, Newark, Mansfield, and Worksop developed as market towns, but the area remained thinly populated. The *dissolution of the monasteries strengthened the influence of the gentry and nobility. The Stanhopes gained 20 villages that had belonged to Shelford priory; Welbeck abbey found its way to the Cavendish family, Rufford priory to the Saviles, and Newstead abbey to the Byrons. As the gentry

**n**

moved up the social scale, the north of the shire became known as the Dukeries, Newcastle having Clumber, Portland Welbeck, and Rutland Kelham. The duke of Kingston's estate was at Holme Pierrepont, east of Nottingham.

The agricultural character of the shire began to change in the later 18th cent. The Trent had always been a busy thoroughfare, but was augmented in the 1770s by the Trent and Mersey canal; by the Chesterfield canal in 1777 serving Worksop and East Retford; and by the Grantham canal, opened in 1793. The development of a canal network made the transport of coal much cheaper and led to a great expansion of the Nottinghamshire coalfield. The same period saw the development of the textile industry, *Hargreaves and *Arkwright setting up factories in Nottingham. But a severe recession after the Napoleonic wars caused great distress and gave a radical tinge to local politics. Brandreth's *Pentrich rising of 1817 was in part the product of unemployment and low wages; in the reform crisis of 1831 the duke of Newcastle's mansion at Nottingham was burned; and Nottingham was the first town to return a chartist MP when it chose *O'Connor in 1847. In the later 19th cent., prosperity returned and there was a diversification of local industries. *Boot's Pure Drug Company was established in 1883; the Raleigh bicycle company had 800 employees by 1896; and Player's tobacco company employed more than 1,000 by 1898. Coaching towns like Tuxford and Blyth stood still as the railways passed them by, but Mansfield and Worksop expanded at roughly the same rate as Nottingham, and the balance remained the same.

**Nova Scotia** owes its name to a 17th-cent. Scottish attempt at colonization. Halifax was founded in 1749, and an assembly introduced in 1758. In the 19th cent. Nova Scotians exploited their timber resources and Atlantic orientation to create a trading economy based on the sailing ship. Self-government was achieved in 1848. After heated controversy, Nova Scotia joined the dominion of Canada in 1867.

**Nuffield, William Morris, 1st Viscount** (1877–1963). Born in Worcester, Nuffield attended school at Cowley where he became a cycle repairer and, by 1896, a manufacturer. By 1903 he was repairing motor cars, and, in 1909 he was running the Morris Garage which sold various car models and had a hire department. In 1912 he established WRM Motors to sell his own Morris Oxford cars for £150, in 1914 producing 1,000 cars. In 1951 the firm merged with *Austin to become the British Motor Corporation. Nuffield endowed educational and medical activities through the British United Provident Association, the Nuffield Foundation, and Nuffield College of Oxford University.

**nunneries** In the early Anglo-Saxon period, monastic life for women was almost always in double houses, of which *Theodore disapproved. In most of these, monks and nuns shared a church, though at Wimborne (Dorset) each group had its own church. An abbess ruled over the community. She was often of royal or noble birth and for centuries nunneries remained places for aristocratic women.

A number of double monasteries were destroyed during the Viking incursions, and when the monastic revival developed in the 10th cent. single houses were in favour. By 1275 there were ten Saxon nunneries surviving in England and Wales, and another 118 had been founded since the Conquest. Of the total of 138 nunneries between 1275 and 1535, well over half were *Benedictine; there were 28 *Cistercian nunneries, 18 *Augustinian, 4 *Franciscan, 2 *Cluniac, and 2 *Premonstratensian. By the time of the dissolution, there were some 125 English nunneries still in existence, sheltering about 2,000 women.

**Nyasaland** *See* MALAWI.

**Oakboys** in Ireland were the northern and protestant equivalent of the *Whiteboys in 1771, protesting against compulsory service as road-menders. The campaign of intimidation was less violent than in Munster and lasted only a few months.

**Oastler, Richard** (1789–1861). Factory reformer and anti-Poor Law agitator. Born in Leeds, Oastler was educated by the Moravians at Fulneck, but became Church of England when he succeeded his father in 1820 as steward for Thomas Thornhill, the absentee landlord of Fixby Hall near Halifax. He was a romantic Tory, defending old values against utilitarian radicalism and political economy, criticizing the employment of children in Bradford worsted mills in 1830, leading the *Ten Hours campaign for factory reform, and denouncing the New *Poor Law of 1834. His extreme language and immense popularity alienated his employer who had him imprisoned for debt (1840–4). His motto was 'Altar, Throne and Cottage'.

**Oates, Lawrence Edward Grace** (1880–1912). Having entered the army in 1898, Oates saw service in the South African War. His interest in sailing, hunting, and kindred pursuits led him to apply for a post on *Scott's 1910 expedition to the Antarctic. He was chosen as one of the party of five which reached the South Pole in January 1912. On the return journey, Oates, unable to walk properly because of severely frost-bitten feet, decided that he was lessening his companions' chances of survival and on 17 March 1912 walked out into a blizzard saying, 'I am just going outside and may be some time.' His body was never found.

**Oates, Titus** (1649–1705). Perjurer and fabricator of the '*Popish plot'. Despite his status as an Anglican priest, Oates's penchant was for lies and petty crime. Recogniz-

ing by the mid-1670s that the surest way to advancement was to feed the public taste for catholic scare-mongering, he wormed his way into catholic counsels, and became a member of the faith himself in 1677. In 1678, he unveiled to the government his highly wrought tale of a conspiracy to overturn the protestant establishment. A wave of hysteria swept the country, the political impact of which was the *Exclusion crisis, and Oates's accusations resulted in the execution of 35, including nine Jesuit priests. Tried in 1685 for perjury and condemned to life imprisonment, he was pardoned in 1689.

**O'Brien, James (Bronterre)** (1805–64). Dubbed 'the schoolmaster of chartism'. An Irish barrister, O'Brien was the most theoretical of the chartists and might have rivalled *O'Connor for the leadership but for his unstable personality. He advocated revolutionary action, including physical force if necessary. But after imprisonment in 1840 for seditious speaking, O'Brien concluded that force was impracticable, and supported a tactical alliance with middle-class radicals. He broke with O'Connor and elaborated plans for socialism and land nationalization through a National *Reform League (1850).

**O'Brien, Murrough** *See* INCHIQUIN, EARL OF.

**O'Brien, William** (1852–1928). Irish nationalist. A journalist from Co. Cork, O'Brien became editor of *United Ireland* in 1881 and was imprisoned for his *Irish Land League agitation until released under the *Kilmainham treaty. In 1883 he was returned to the Westminster Parliament in which he served until 1918. In the Parnell split he was a moderate and worked for the reunification of the Irish Parliamentary Party in 1900. His passionate opposition to partition led him towards *Sinn Fein. He did not stand for re-election in 1918 and declined nomination to the Senate of the Irish Free State, since he refused to accept the treaty.

**O'Brien, William Smith** (1803–64). Smith O'Brien was an unlikely, unwilling, and unsuccessful Irish rebel. The younger son of a protestant baronet from Co. Clare, with family links to the earls of Thomond, he was educated at Harrow and Trinity College, Cambridge. He served in Parliament 1828–31 and from 1835 when he was returned for Co. Limerick. He moved steadily into a nationalist stance, much influenced by *Young Ireland, and in 1843 declared for repeal of the Union. A rising planned for August 1848 dwindled into a farcical riot at Ballingarry, Co. Tipperary, where O'Brien explained that he did not intend any violence to property. An attack upon 46 policemen, holed up in Widow McCormack's cottage, was unsuccessful. O'Brien was sentenced to death, but pardoned against his will and transported.

**O'Casey, Sean** (1880–1964). Irish playwright and author. His real name was John Casey, but was later changed to the more Gaelic Sean O'Casey. He worked as a casual labourer until the age of 30 when he became involved in Irish politics as a member of the *Gaelic League, the *Irish Republican Brotherhood, Jim *Larkin's Union, the Irish Citizen Army, and the Irish Socialist Party respectively. In 1916 he turned to writing plays, but it was not until 1923 that one of his plays was staged. His three early plays, *The Shadow of a Gunman* (1923), *Juno and the Paycock* (1924), and *The Plough and the Stars* (1926), dealt with the impact of the Troubles on ordinary people.

**Occasional Conformity Act,** 1711. This Act prevented nonconformists from taking communion in an Anglican church to qualify for national and municipal office according to the *Corporation and *Test Acts. Three previous attempts (1702, 1703, and 1704) had failed because the large Tory majority in the Commons (who aimed at depriving the Whigs of the electoral support of the nonconformists) had been frustrated by the Whig majority in the Lords. The Act was repealed in 1719.

**O'Connell, Daniel** (1775–1847). Irish catholic politician. Born into the catholic aristocracy and called to the Irish bar in 1798, by 1815 he was the recognized leader of the movement for *catholic emancipation. In 1823 he started the *Catholic Association to mobilize catholic peasant opinion for emancipation, repeal of the Union, land reform, an end to tithes, and a democratic suffrage. In 1828 he stood successfully for Co. Clare in a parliamentary by-election, although as a catholic he was disqualified. Faced with civil war, *Wellington's government conceded emancipation in 1829. He continued to hold the loyalty of most Irishmen through his National Repeal Association (founded 1841) until *Young Ireland, with its more revolutionary version of Irish nationalism, broke away in 1846.

**O'Connor, Feargus** (1794–1855). Chartist. An Irish barrister, O'Connor was MP (and follower of Daniel *O'Connell) for Cork in 1832 and for Nottingham (as a chartist) in 1847. He was the greatest of the chartist leaders, and for ten years was head of the movement. His influence came from his charismatic, flamboyant style of oratory, and his ownership of the chief chartist newspaper, the *Northern Star*. He was imprisoned in 1840 for seditious libel. O'Connor's appearance at the last great chartist demonstration on Kennington Common on 10 April 1848 marked the end of the mass platform as a pattern of popular radicalism.

**O'Connor, Rory (Ruaidrí Ua Conchobair)** (d. 1198), last *high king of Ireland, became king of *Connacht in 1156, and high king in 1166. He banished overseas the *Leinster king, *Dermot MacMurrough, who returned with Anglo-Norman aid in 1167. Rory did not submit to Henry II during his expedition to Ireland in 1171–2, but reached an accommodation under the short-lived 'treaty' of *Windsor in 1175, which secured his rule over the unconquered parts of the country.

**Octennial Act,** 1768. Until 1768 the Irish Parliament existed for the lifetime of the king and general elections were therefore infrequent. A radical campaign in the 1760s demanded a Septennial Act and the institution of *habeas corpus. In 1768 the English government gave way and accepted an Octennial Act, though refusing habeas corpus.

**October Club** A ginger group of Tory MPs formed after the election victory of 1710 to watch *Harley and the moderates and hound the Whigs. They took their name from October ale, beloved of country gentlemen, and met regularly at the Bell Tavern, Westminster.

**Odo of Bayeux** (c.1036–97) was half-brother to Duke William II of Normandy (later William I of England). He was destined for an ecclesiastical career, receiving the bishopric of Bayeux from William when he was perhaps 13 years old. He participated in the invasion of England in 1066, the *Bayeux Tapestry, almost certainly produced for Odo, exaggerating his role. Thereafter, he acted occasionally as the Conqueror's viceregent and accumulated enormous wealth in England. But in 1082 William stripped him of his English lands and incarcerated him for reasons that remain obscure. Released in 1087, he joined the rebellion against William II 'Rufus' in 1088. This time he was exiled from England for ever and returned to Normandy.

**O'Donnell, Rory, 1st earl of Tyrconnel** [I] (1575–1608). The second son of the chief of the O'Donnells, Rory joined his brother Hugh Roe and *Tyrone in rebellion against Elizabeth from 1598 until 1602. After the disaster at *Kinsale, Hugh Roe fled to Spain and died in September 1602. Rory assumed the chieftainship and submitted to Elizabeth's lieutenant *Mountjoy. After a visit to James I in June 1603 O'Donnell was created earl of Tyrconnel but became increasingly dissatisfied. He joined Tyrone in the *Flight of the Earls in September 1607. He spent his remaining months in Rome, where he died in July 1608, amid suspicions of poison.

**Offa** (d. 796), king of Mercia (757–96), came to the throne after a disputed succession with Beornred following the murder of King *Æthelbald. He continued the expansion of Mercia from its midland base. By the end of his reign Offa had added the provinces of the *Hwicce, the South Saxons, and *Kent and had expelled their royal houses or reduced them to the status of ealdormen. But he also had to deal with strong opposition. Although he had gained control in Kent in 764, the Kentishmen recovered their independence

after the battle of *Otford in 776 and retained it until 785. *Cynewulf of Wessex fought Offa at *Benson c.779 and although he lost some parts of northern Wessex to Offa, remained an independent ruler. Æthelbert of the East Angles presumably offered resistance as well since in 794 Offa had him beheaded. Offa's Dike still stands as testimony to the seriousness of his campaigns against the Welsh and also to his ability to exact military services from his subjects.

Offa was considered sufficiently powerful by his contemporary Charles the Great to warrant bringing into his sphere of influence by the bestowal of gifts. Offa introduced the 'penny' coinage circulating in Francia and copied Frankish usage in including his portrait in the style of a Roman emperor. His wooing of the pope resulted in a grant of archiepiscopal status for the Mercian see of *Lichfield in 787 and the consecration there of Offa's son Ecgfrith as king of the Mercians later the same year.

**Olaf Guthfrithsson** (d. 941), king of Dublin. Olaf succeeded to the throne in 934. His first years as ruler established his position in Ireland. This freed him for an attempt to regain the Viking kingdom of *York, from which his father had been expelled in 927 by *Athelstan. But Olaf's grand coalition was cut to pieces by Athelstan at *Brunanburh (937). After Athelstan's death in 939, Olaf renewed the struggle, occupied York, harried Mercia, sacked Tamworth, and forced *Edmund to concede all the lands north-east of Watling Street. He was killed the following year near Dunbar, and his successors were unable to hold the territories he had won back.

**Olaf Sihtricsson** (d. 981), king of Deira (941–3, 949–52), king of Dublin (945–81). Olaf's father was *Sihtric, king of *Deira. On Sihtric's death in 927, his brother Guthfrith took the throne (Olaf being a child), but was at once dispossessed by Athelstan. *Olaf Guthfrithsson regained it in 939 and on his death in 941 was succeeded by Olaf Sihtricsson, who had married a daughter of *Constantine, king of the Scots. He could not hold the territories regained from *Edmund, Athelstan's successor, and was driven out of his capital, York, in 943. He did, however, recover the throne of the Norse kingdom of

Dublin in 945. At the end of his life he suffered a severe defeat at Tara (980), abdicated, and spent his last months on Iona.

**old-age pensions** were first paid to persons over 70 years of age on 1 January 1909. A regular weekly payment by the state from taxation was preferred to any contributory scheme because of the high administrative cost. Almost half a million people qualified. After 1925 the age for support was lowered to 65 years. Pension entitlement began under the National Health and Insurance Act (1925) when worker, employer, and the state each contributed.

**Old Bailey** This is the popular name given to the Central Criminal Court in London, set up in 1834. It is the successor of the Old Bailey sessions of gaol delivery for *Newgate prison and of *oyer and terminer for the city of London and the county of Middlesex.

**Old Sarum** was the original site of the city of Salisbury, abandoned in 1220 for the situation closer to the river Avon. By Tudor times it was totally deserted. It continued to return two members of Parliament until 1832 and became a symbol of the old regime.

**Olivier, Sir Laurence** (1907–89). Actor and director. Praised by Ellen *Terry in a school play, Olivier became one of his generation's leading actors. Commencing in repertory, he established a reputation with Shakespearian roles and joined the Old Vic; after starring in film versions of *Wuthering Heights* and *Rebecca* in America, he returned to England to serve in the Fleet Air Arm, before helping rebuild the Old Vic after the Second World War. Handsome, charismatic, then youngest stage knight (1947), he directed and acted under his own management from 1950, revolutionized the art of filming Shakespeare (*Henry V, Hamlet, Richard III*), became director of the newly formed National Theatre Company (1962–73), and was the first actor to receive a life peerage.

**Omdurman** Town in central *Sudan which came to prominence when the mahdi, a religious leader who led a holy war against the Egyptian government, made it his capital in 1885. In 1898 an Anglo-Egyptian army led by Sir Herbert *Kitchener advanced into the Sudan. Early in September the battle for Om-

durman took place and the army of the mahdi was completely destroyed.

**O'Neill, Hugh, 3rd earl of Tyrone** [I] (1550–1616). O'Neill was brought up in England in the charge of Sir Henry *Sidney and *Leicester. On the death of his brother Brien in 1562 he succeeded to the earldom. He was sent to Ireland in 1568 after the death of Shane *O'Neill as a counterweight to the influence of Turlough O'Neill, who claimed the headship of the family. But no sooner had he established his supremacy, by 1595, than he was in full-scale rebellion against Elizabeth. He defeated and slew Sir Henry Bagenal at *Yellow Ford in 1598, outmanœuvred *Essex without great difficulty in September 1599, and maintained resistance until crushed by Mountjoy in 1602. He was reconciled to James I but in September 1607 fled abroad with the earl of Tyrconnel. He died in exile in Rome, blind and powerless.

**O'Neill, Owen Roe** (c.1590–1649). O'Neill was the military linchpin of the Confederation, which struggled for control of Ireland after the rising of 1641. He was a nephew of Hugh *O'Neill, 3rd earl of Tyrone. He was not in Ireland at the start of the rising but arrived in July 1642 and took over command of the Ulster army from Sir Phelim *O'Neill. He managed to keep an army together through the extraordinary political vicissitudes of the next few years and in 1646 gained a significant victory at *Benburb over Monro and the Scottish army. But the end of the Civil War in England enabled Parliament to strengthen its position in Ireland. It is doubtful whether he could have put up much resistance to Cromwell, who landed in August 1649, but he died in November of the same year.

**O'Neill, Sir Phelim** (c.1604–53). O'Neill was one of the commanders of the Irish rebels or Confederation. He claimed to be acting on behalf of Charles I but had great difficulty in maintaining his position until assisted by the arrival of Owen Roe *O'Neill. He continued to fight for the Confederation and took part in the victory at *Benburb in 1646, but was forced to capitulate to parliamentary forces in 1650. He failed to make good his escape and was executed in Dublin as a traitor.

**O'Neill, Shane** (*c.*1530–67). The legitimate son of Con O'Neill, he was passed over in 1542 when his father was created earl of Tyrone, and remainder given to an illegitimate son, Matthew. As soon as he grew up he claimed the inheritance, and by 1557 had driven his father and Matthew O'Neill to take refuge in the *Pale. In 1558 he killed Matthew, but at her succession Elizabeth offered to recognize him if he submitted to the lord deputy, *Sussex. The negotiations broke down, but O'Neill held his own against Sussex and in 1562 visited Elizabeth in London, where he and his followers (who spoke mostly Irish) created a sensation. On his return to Ireland, he resumed his warfare with gusto, particularly against the Macdonnells, but was assassinated in June 1567.

**O'Neill, Terence, Lord O'Neill of the Maine** (1914–90). Prime minister of Northern Ireland (1963–9). O'Neill was keen to promote economic development within Northern Ireland, and to address the traditional hostility between unionist and nationalist, and between Belfast and Dublin. However, he alienated hard-line loyalists without offering substantive concessions to Ulster catholics. The rise of the Northern Ireland Civil Rights Association (founded in January 1967) brought further pressure on O'Neill. In November 1968 he conceded a five-point reform programme, but this satisfied neither the NICRA activists nor many of his unionist colleagues. On 28 April 1969, against the background of a splintering unionism and relentless NICRA pressure, he resigned.

***On Liberty*** (1859) was John Stuart *Mill's influential justification of individual freedom. In this book, Mill set out to establish a 'simple principle'—that the only legitimate reason for interfering with someone's action was to protect someone else. Mill based his defence of liberty on utilitarian grounds, not on a natural right to freedom; arguing that on balance people were happier when left to choose their life-styles for themselves. Hailed as a classic, it has also been condemned as facile.

**Opium War** *See* CHINA WARS.

**Oporto, battle of,** 1809. On 12 May 1809 British forces in the Peninsula under Wellesley faced Soult's French army of 11,000 across the Douro opposite Oporto. Soult was taken by surprise when the British used four wine barges to ferry troops across the river. When the French withdrew from the waterfront, the citizens of Oporto took many more vessels across to speed up the crossing. Soult was forced to retreat, and by 19 May the French had been driven out of Portugal.

**Orange Free State** Former British colony in South Africa. Founded as a republic by Boers (Afrikaners) fleeing British rule in Cape Colony in the mid-19th cent., the Orange Free State retained its independent status until 1900 because of the absence of any resources which might attract the cupidity of foreigners. When the Transvaal declared war on Britain in 1899, the Free State's leaders felt bound to assist. The Boers were defeated and the country became the Orange River Colony in 1900. It was incorporated into the Union of South Africa in 1910.

**Orange order** An Irish protestant organization dedicated to the preservation of the protestant constitution and the 'glorious and immortal memory' of King William III, the victor of the *Boyne (1690). The order was founded in Loughgall (Co. Armagh) in September 1795 by the protestant veterans of a sectarian clash, the battle of the Diamond. In the later 19th cent. the order enjoyed a revival, and was one of the foundations of popular unionism in the 1880s. Since 1905 the order has been formally connected with the *Ulster Unionist Party. Its most public face is the highly organized marching season.

**Ordainers** The initial political crises of Edward II's reign culminated in 1310, when the king was forced to agree to the appointment of 21 Ordainers, chosen by a complex system of election. An initial six Ordinances were followed in September 1311 by the main Ordinances, an elaborate programme for reform of government which included a request for the exiling of the king's favourite, Piers *Gaveston. Royal finance and the administration of justice were the subject of many clauses. The Ordinances were repealed in the statute of *York of 1322.

**Orderic Vitalis** (1075–*c.*1142), the great historian of the Normans, was born near Shrewsbury of mixed English and French parentage, but from 1085 lived his entire life at the abbey of Saint-Evroult in southern *Normandy. His greatest historical work, the massive *Ecclesiastical History*, was composed from 1123 onwards and included material on many of the major events of his lifetime, most notably the expansion of Norman power throughout Europe and the *Norman Conquest of England.

**orders in council** In November 1806 Napoleon's Berlin Decree attempted to exclude British trade from the continent. The British government replied with the orders in council, using the emergency powers of the sovereign, approved by the Privy Council. The orders of November and December 1807 declared a blockade of any harbour that excluded British commerce. The USA protested strongly and its resentment was one of the causes of the *War of 1812.

**Ordnance Survey** One of the beneficial results of the '45 rebellion. The difficulties of the *Culloden campaign persuaded Lieutenant-General Watson, deputy quartermaster-general, that better maps of the Highlands were needed. Much of the work, later extended to the Lowlands, was done by William Roy. In 1765 Roy was appointed to survey coastal areas of Britain and to report to the master-general of the ordnance. At the same time the newly formed *Royal Society of Arts offered rewards for county maps. After Roy's death in 1790, the duke of Richmond, master-general of the ordnance, appointed a small team in 1791. They issued in 1801 the first of a series of one-inch maps, the county of Kent. A survey of Ireland was started in 1825.

**Ordovices** Indigenous British tribe of the Iron Age and Roman periods whose territory covered much of mid-Wales. The Ordovices were the northern neighbours of the *Silures and the southern neighbours of the *Degeangli. After the Claudian invasion the Ordovices and the Silures were stirred into rebellion by *Caratacus.

**Oregon treaty,** 1846. The disputed eastern boundary between Canada and the USA was settled by the *Ashburton treaty of 1842. The vast area between the Rockies and the Pacific known as the Oregon Territory was covered by a convention, extended from 1818, whereby subjects of both states had access. In 1845 James K. Polk was elected president on the slogan of '54° 50' or fight' and in his inaugural speech he insisted that America's claim would be pursued by force if necessary. The *Peel government, in its last months, negotiated a settlement on the line of the 49th parallel, which required only minor revision in 1872.

**Orford, Edward Russell, 1st earl of** (1652–1727). Russell was nephew of the 1st duke of Bedford, entered the navy in 1671, and saw much service in the second *Anglo-Dutch War. Alienated from the court by the execution of his cousin Lord *Russell, he signed the invitation to William of Orange in 1688 and landed with him at Brixham. He was promoted admiral in 1689 and gained the victory of *La Hogue over the French in 1692. He served as 1st lord of the Admiralty 1694–9 and again 1709–10. Under George I, he resumed as 1st lord until 1717. He died without issue and in 1742 the title of Orford was revived for Sir Robert *Walpole.

***Origin of Species, The*** Charles *Darwin's book of 1859 set out the development of new kinds of creatures through natural selection, and inheritance with variability. Its readability, and basis in an immense bulk of varied evidence, carried the day, and made evolution scientifically respectable.

**Orkney** A group of islands lying at the north-east tip of Scotland. The islands are rich in archaeological monuments. Skara Brae is a well-preserved prehistoric village, Maes Howe the best of a series of impressive prehistoric burial cairns, and numerous brochs and settlements attest to the islands' Pictish and Viking periods. Orkney, together with Shetland, became part of Scotland in consequence of the marriage of *Margaret of Denmark-Norway to James III of Scotland in 1469.

**Orkney, jarldom of** From the late 9th cent. the fertile Orkney islands were the locus for a Norse jarldom, for centuries the dominant power in northern Scotland. Orkney had been the seat of a Pictish subkingdom in the 6th cent., according to *Adomnán. The first jarl was Røgnvald, also jarl of Møre in western Norway. He passed on the jarldom to Sigurd the Mighty, his brother. Sigurd, in partnership with Thorsteinn the Red from the Hebrides, turned his attention to the Scottish mainland. Together they are credited, in Icelandic tradition, with conquering Caithness, Sutherland, Moray, and Ross.

The jarldom entered its period of greatest power and influence during the late 10th to mid-11th cents., under Sigurd the Stout and his son by a daughter of the 'king of Scots', *Thorfinn the Mighty. During this period, the authority of the jarls spread south down the western searoute towards Dublin. It is unclear whether Sigurd's presence in the Hebrides amounted to conquest, but Icelandic tradition claims he gathered tribute from Man and the Isles. Thorfinn was remembered by the Icelandic historian Snorri Sturluson as 'the ablest jarl of these islands, and has had the greatest dominion of all Orkney jarls'. After his death in 1065, his conquest fell apart.

### Ormond, James Butler, 1st duke of
(1610–88). Ormond, a protestant and a leading member of the Anglo-Irish ascendancy, succeeded to the earldom in 1633. After the departure of *Strafford from Ireland in 1640, Ormond became the mainstay of royal authority, first as commander-in-chief, then as lord-lieutenant. He checked the Irish rebels at Kilrush in March 1642 and again in 1643 at Ross, but the king, hard pressed, constantly urged him to negotiate, in the hope of obtaining troops to turn the scales in the Civil War. But by the time a settlement was reached in 1646, the position in England had been lost. The following year, Ormond left Ireland, handing over Dublin to Michael Jones, representing the English Parliament. In exile until the Restoration, Ormond resumed his position in Ireland under Charles II, acting as lord-lieutenant from 1662 to 1669 and again from 1677 to 1685. He was given an Irish dukedom in 1661 and an English dukedom in 1682. At James II's accession, he retired from public life.

### Ormond, James Butler, 2nd duke of
(1665–1745). Succeeding his grandfather in July 1688, he supported the petition to James for a free parliament, then accepted William of Orange, for whom he fought in Ireland and Flanders. A pillar of the Tory Party and Anglican church, he unsuccessfully commanded the 1702 expedition against Cadiz, and was twice a controversial lord-lieutenant of Ireland. He replaced *Marlborough in 1712, restraining his troops in the field to facilitate Tory negotiations with France. Dismissed in 1714, he was threatened with impeachment by the Whigs. Panicking, he fled to the Jacobite court. He died exiled and insignificant.

### Orthez, battle of, 1814. *Wellington's troops crossed the Bidassoa into France in October 1813 but Soult's army continued to resist strongly, falling back on a series of river lines. On 27 February 1814, Soult tried to hold the line of the Gave de Pau at Orthez, but was badly beaten.

### orthodox church The eastern orthodox church dating from earliest Christian times has its centre at Constantinople (Istanbul), the residence of the ecumenical patriarch, who has primacy of honour over much of the 'intricate tapestry' of the Christian East, including the Greeks, Serbs, Bulgars, Georgians, and Russians. In 1995 there were c.190 million adherents world-wide. British contacts with orthodoxy began with 16th-cent. merchants and Peter the Great's visit to England (1698). Since the 1950s orthodoxy has flourished in England with c.271,000 members (2008).

### Orwell, George (1903–50). Orwell, whose real name was Eric Blair, embodied the hopes of the left in the 1930s, and the subsequent post-war disillusionment. His career began as a policeman in Burma, but in 1927 he returned to England to be a writer. The experience of poverty enabled him to write *Down and Out in Paris and London* (1930); *Burmese Days* (1931) followed. But Orwell's breakthrough came when he was commissioned by Gollancz of the Left Book Club to write a study of poverty in England. The *Road to Wigan Pier* (1937) was a brilliantly emotive impression of working-class life.

The experience of fighting with the POUM militia against fascists in Spain cemented Orwell's socialist ideas. *Homage to Catalonia* (1938) was a graphic description of the Spanish revolution. *Animal Farm* (1945) launched an acerbic satirical attack on Stalinism. His final book, written in solitude on the Isle of Jura, was *1984* (1949), a grim warning of the dangers of totalitarianism.

**Osborne House** (Isle of Wight). Soon after their marriage, Victoria and *Albert looked around for a private residence, where their growing family could enjoy seaside holidays. In 1845 they purchased the Osborne estate near Cowes. Albert, with the assistance of Thomas *Cubitt, builder of Belgravia, designed a large house in the Italian style. It is now open to the public and contains many Victorian memorabilia.

**Osborne judgment,** 1909. Osborne, a Liberal, went to law to stop his union, the Railway Servants, contributing to the Labour Party. The case reached the House of Lords; their judgment that unions could not use their funds to support a political party was a severe blow to the Labour Party.

**Ossian,** son of Fingal, father of Oscar, whose death—so James MacPherson claimed—marked the end of Celtic civilization in Scotland. MacPherson's translations of Ossian's 'poems' (1762–5) caused a literary sensation. In the event they turned out to be a mixture of genuine verses handed down by oral tradition and imaginative translation and pastiche by their editor.

**Oswald, St** (*c.*604–42), king of Northumbria (634–42). Son of *Æthelfryth and Acha, Oswald spent *Edwin's reign in exile amongst the Irish, becoming a Christian. Defeating *Cadwallon of Gwynedd, at *Heavenfield (634), brought him *Bernicia and *Deira. With *Aidan (from Iona) he restored Northumbrian Christianity. Oswald established an overlordship over Wessex (under *Cynegils) and probably the southern Picts and Scottish *Dalriada, and is one of the so-called *bretwaldas. Killed in a campaign against the pagan *Penda of Mercia, at Maserfield, his cult was promoted by his niece Osthryth, queen of Mercia, and by *Wilfrid.

**Oswald, St** (d. 992). Archbishop of York. One of the three great monastic bishops of the 10th-cent. reformation. In 961 he was created bishop of Worcester and continued to hold that see after he was appointed to York in 971. Oswald introduced monks into the Worcester chapter, and founded or

refounded monasteries at Westbury-on-Trym, Winchcombe, and Pershore, as well as at Ramsey in his native East Anglia.

**Oswin** (d. 651), king of Deira (644–51). *Bede describes Oswin as handsome, pleasantly spoken, and courteous, a good and generous lord who ruled prosperously and was much loved. Humility was his greatest virtue. Conflict arose between Oswin and *Oswiu, king of Bernicia. The two Northumbrian armies gathered, but Oswin, realizing Oswiu's greater strength, sent his men home. With one companion, he took refuge in the house of a friend who betrayed his trust. Oswiu had him murdered.

**Oswiu** (d.670), king of Northumbria (642–70). Ruling Bernicia, Oswiu was responsible for the death of the Deiran king Oswin (651), his wife's kinsman. Oswin's successor allied with the powerful Mercian king Penda, who attacked in 655, but was defeated and killed at the battle of Winwæd, near Leeds. Oswiu fulfilled his promise that, if victorious, he would grant twelve estates for monasteries and dedicate his infant daughter to God's service. He used his influence to convert the Mercian prince, Peada, and revive East Saxon Christianity.

**Otford, battle of,** *c.*776. In the later 8th cent., *Kent was struggling to retain its independence against the growing power of *Mercia. According to Henry of Huntingdon, the Mercians were victorious at this battle near Sevenoaks. But Stenton argues that *Egbert of Kent defeated *Offa and that Kentish independence was restored for some years.

**Otterburn, battle of,** 1388. Though little more than a routine border skirmish, Otterburn was rendered remarkable by the number of ballads it inspired, including 'Chevy Chase'. A large Scottish gathering near Jedburgh in the summer of 1388 resolved on a two-pronged campaign, one attack west towards Carlisle, the other across Carter Bar into Redesdale. The eastern army, under James, earl of *Douglas, having ravaged as far as Durham, was pursued in retreat by Henry *Percy ('Hotspur'). Late on 15 August the English caught up at Otterburn and went straight into the attack. As night fell, the battle developed into a series of hand-to-hand single combats. Percy was captured but Douglas himself was killed. The dead from the battlefield were buried nearby at Elsdon.

**Oudenarde, battle of,** 1708. As French forces under the duke of Burgundy and Marshal Vendôme laid siege to Oudenarde, the duke of *Marlborough marched against them at the head of some 78,000 English, Dutch, and German troops. The French offered battle on 11 July, but were badly deployed. As the French right flank collapsed, over 6,000 French soldiers fell. A further 7,000 were captured.

**outlawry** originated as the community's way of dealing with a violent or dangerous wrongdoer. A declaration of outlawry deprived the outlaw of the protection of the king and the law; his property was forfeit to the king and he could be killed with impunity.

**Owain ap Gruffydd (Owain Cyfeiliog)** (c.1130–97), prince of southern Powys. He was the nephew of *Madog ap Maredudd, prince of *Powys, whom he served (from 1149) in the commote of Cyfeiliog, from which he took his name. He resisted advances by *Owain Gwynedd and *Rhys ap Gruffydd of *Deheubarth (though he married a daughter of each in turn); after Madog's death and the murder of Madog's eldest son (1160), he came to terms with fellow-princes of Powys and Henry II to establish his rule in southern Powys, probably from Welshpool.

**Owain Gwynedd** (c.1100–70), king of Gwynedd (1132–70). Noted by contemporaries for his wisdom, prowess, and prudence, his creation of a large feudal principality in *Gwynedd was an inspiration to his successors. The second son of *Gruffydd ap Cynan (d. 1137), king of Gwynedd, he and his brother Cadwallon helped their father to expand Gwynedd's power (1120s). As king (Cadwallon died in 1132), he strengthened his hold on church and state in Gwynedd, exploited the anarchy in England to advance south, and took his authority eastwards to the Dee. By his death (28 November 1170) he was the pre-eminent ruler in Wales.

**Owen, David** (b. 1938). Former leader of the *Social Democratic Party (SDP). After qualifying as a doctor Owen entered politics as a Labour MP. He rose swiftly, becoming foreign secretary in 1977 at the age of 38. With the party's swing to the left, Owen became increasingly disaffected and helped to found the SDP as one of the 'gang of four'. He became leader of the party in 1983 and continued to preside over a rump SDP until the party was wound up in 1990. He retired from the Commons in 1992 and was granted a life peerage. He acted as European Community Peace Envoy to the former Yugoslavia (1992–5).

**Owen, Robert** (1771–1858). Cotton magnate and utopian socialist. Born in Newtown (Powys), Owen became a partner in cotton firms in Lancashire and at *New Lanark (Strathclyde), where he managed the mills and village (1800–25), gaining a reputation as a successful and humanitarian businessman. His experience led him to publish *A New View of Society* (1814–18), in which he argued that character was formed by environment, and that a system of villages of co-operation rather than unplanned large industrial towns was conducive to social progress. Described as the 'Father of British Socialism', Owen could be regarded also as a protagonist of scientific management.

**Owen, Wilfred** (1893–1918). Most gifted of the poets who died in battle, Owen joined up in 1915 but a meeting with Siegfried Sassoon at Craiglockhart military hospital two years later was crucial to his development. The poems he produced over the next twelve months go beyond Sassoon's more straightforward assault on complacency at home. 'I am not concerned with Poetry', he wrote, 'The Poetry is in the pity.' In October 1918 he won the Military Cross and in November he was killed in action a week before the Armistice.

**Oxford, diocese of** The see, now conterminous with Oxfordshire, Berkshire, and Buckinghamshire, was carved out of the vast *Lincoln diocese by Henry VIII in 1542. The last abbot of Osney, Robert King, was the first bishop. Because initially the diocese was small, consisting only of Oxfordshire, and relatively poor, most late 17th- and 18th-cent. bishops were eager for preferment elsewhere. The cathedral, formerly St Frideswide's Augustinian priory church (1158–85), in Norman style, is an integral part of Christ Church college.

**Oxford, provisions of,** 1258. The struggle between Henry III and the baronial opposition culminated in civil war 1264–5. In 1258 the main grievance was Henry's attempt to acquire the kingdom of Sicily for his second son Edmund, and the influence of his Poitevin advisers. A committee of 24 was appointed to meet at Oxford and limit the king's actions. The *justiciarship was revived, a standing council of fifteen appointed, and Parliament was to be summoned three times a year. Though baronial control soon disintegrated, the provisions were a clear attempt to limit royal authority and listen to the opinions of the community.

**Oxford, Robert de Vere, 9th earl of** (1362–92). According to a chronicler, the 9th earl was one of the young men brought up with Richard II who plotted the death of *John of Gaunt in 1384. Richard's favour enriched him; he was raised in the peerage, to marquis of Dublin in 1385 and duke of Ireland in 1386. When Richard was planning to regain control of government in 1387, Oxford raised forces in Cheshire; they were defeated at *Radcot Bridge (Oxon.). He was one of the royal favourites indicted in the *Merciless Parliament of 1388, but had fled and remained in exile.

**Oxford, St Mary the Virgin** University and parish church. Adopted as the centre of the fledgling medieval university, St Mary's was the seat of its government, academic disputation, and award of degrees until the mid-17th cent. It hosted the trials of the Oxford martyrs (*Latimer, *Ridley, *Cranmer) in 1554–6.

**Oxford movement** Founded by a group of clerical Oxford dons in the 1830s and 1840s, who sought to renew the Church of England through rediscovering its catholic inheritance. It was a response to the perceived decline of the Church of England into dangerous liberalism and excessive control by Parliament. Its starting-point is usually taken as *Keble's Assize Sermon of 1833. Between 1833 and 1841 its leaders produced the *Tracts for the Times,* hence the alternative name of '*tractarianism'.

**Oxford Parliament,** 1258. The Oxford Parliament of June 1258 was summoned while there was much discontent with the rule of Henry III. By the provisions of *Oxford, de *Montfort and his supporters set up a council to control the king and supervise government. The experiment failed and led in 1264 to civil war.

**Oxford Parliament,** 1681. The Oxford Parliament was the denouement of the great *Exclusion crisis and established Charles II's supremacy for the last four years of his reign. The Shaftesbury Whigs who opposed him had won three general elections between 1679 and 1681. In April 1681 Charles summoned a parliament to Oxford where the influence of the London radicals would be less. A secret deal with Louis XIV to supply money enabled Charles to dissolve the Parliament after only one week. The Whigs offered no resistance. Three months later, *Shaftesbury was arrested and the power of the Whigs broken.

**Oxfordshire** In Roman times the region belonged to the *Dobunni tribe. It covered the area between the Cotswolds at Chipping Norton and the Chilterns at Watlington and, until modern times, much of it was heavily wooded.

The town of Oxford owed its existence to a ford and later a ferry. It developed early as an important Saxon centre. Councils were held there in the early 11th cent. and in 1066 it was the sixth largest town in the kingdom. As late as 1901, the population of 50,000 was almost double that of all the other towns in the county combined: Banbury had 7,300, Chipping Norton 3,700, Henley 3,500, Thame 2,900, Witney 2,800, and Bicester 2,700.

In the 7th and 8th cent. the area was disputed between *Wessex, south of the Thames, and *Mercia the midlands kingdom. Wessex regained it after *Ellendun in 825. It became a shire in the early 11th cent. when *Edward and *Æthelfleda were reorganizing Wessex's defences against the Danes, who burned Oxford in 1009.

Ecclesiastical organization fluctuated in similar fashion. An early bishopric was established at Dorchester in 634, possibly because it had been a Roman town. But after 680 it was placed under Sherborne, a Wessex diocese. When Mercia regained control, the see was moved to Leicester. Dorchester recovered its position *c.*870, probably because Leicester had been overrun by the Danes. The bishopric stayed at Dorchester until after the Conquest but was transferred to Lincoln in 1072. For five centuries the shire remained a rather remote part of the vast Lincoln diocese, until a new see was created at Oxford itself in 1542.

Despite the intellectual and ecclesiastical importance of Oxford, the shire remained rural and secluded. Those industries which did develop were agriculturally derived and small in scale—cloth manufacture of different kinds at Witney, Chipping Norton, and Banbury, saddles at Burford, lace and slippers at Bicester, leather at Bampton, brewing at Henley, glove-making at Oxford and Woodstock. As late as the 1830s, the shire could be described as having 'no manufactures of any account, being chiefly agricultural'. But in 1901 William *Morris opened a bicycle-repair shop at Oxford—the forerunner of the great car factory at Cowley.

In the Civil War of the 17th cent., Oxford was the king's capital. The parks and quads became encampments, trees and shrubs were cut down, and attendance at lectures languished. Oxford surrendered in 1646 a few weeks after Charles I had fled, disguised as a servant. Politically city and county continued to be royalist in sympathy. In 1681 Charles II summoned Parliament there and routed his Whig opponents.

The Oxford canal, opened in 1790, and the network of railways which developed in the county in the 19th cent. speeded up internal communication, but did little to promote any great industrial growth. The Local Government Act of 1972 extended the shire south of the Thames, bringing in Abingdon, Wallingford, and Wantage—yet another victory for Mercia over Wessex. The M40 bisects the county from south-east to north-west, from Aston Rowant to Banbury. But north Oxfordshire remains peaceful and unspoiled, and *Blenheim, once a Whig bastion in a Tory countryside, is perhaps the finest of all landscaped parks.

**Oxford University** When the quarrel between Henry II and Philip Augustus in 1167 made it impossible for English students to attend the University of Paris, the opportunity for developing a similar institution arose at Oxford. Dominican friars established their main house of study there on arrival in England in 1221 and were followed in 1224 by

the Franciscans. Divinity was constituted as a superior faculty and students were admitted who already possessed an arts degree.

University colleges, endowed by patrons, were gradually formed where students resided during their long courses of study. William of Durham founded University College in 1249. John *Balliol left money which his widow applied to founding Balliol College in 1282. Earlier, in 1264, Walter de *Merton, chancellor of England, devoted most of his fortune to establishing Merton College. Undergraduates were admitted for the first time about 1500. By Elizabeth's reign, there were fifteen colleges. As at Cambridge, they increasingly attracted the sons of wealthy or aristocratic families rather than poor scholars.

Under the influence of Archbishop *Laud, Oxford became associated with high-church views, reinforced after the 1640s when the city was the headquarters of the royalist army during the Civil War. In the early Hanoverian period it was reputed a nest of *Jacobitism, though such disloyalty as there was caused the authorities little more than momentary irritation. More than two-thirds of its graduates entered the Church of England, and the *Oxford movement in the 19th cent. reflected their concerns about priesthood.

The 19th cent. saw the beginnings of change. Degrees were no longer awarded without written examination. Honours degrees in both classics and mathematics were introduced in 1801, creating the 'double first', and a similar provision was made for science and law in 1890. From the last quarter of the 19th cent. the number of Oxford colleges began to increase. The first two colleges for women were Lady Margaret Hall and Somerville (1879), and since 1937 colleges for postgraduate study, such as Nuffield, St Antony's, Linacre, and Wolfson, have been founded. Still attacked as elitist, the University has been active in encouraging more applications from state schools.

**oyer and terminer** After the Assizes of *Clarendon and *Northampton, the commission of oyer and terminer was issued to the travelling justices to visit the shire and to receive the presentments of those suspected of crime in each hundred. They were instructed to hear and determine (oyer and terminer) each case.

**P**

**Pacifico, David** (1784–1854). The case of 'Don Pacifico' provided *Palmerston with a great oratorical triumph. A Portuguese Jew, Pacifico was born in Gibraltar and was therefore a British subject. In 1847, while a merchant in Athens, his house was destroyed in an anti-Jewish riot. The Greek government refused compensation, believing that his claim was inflated, whereupon Palmerston sent a naval squadron to the Piraeus and seized all Greek vessels. Palmerston's stand earned him vast popularity and established his domination of politics for the rest of his life.

**paganism** In the late Roman world a *paganus* was a 'rustic', and the word's shift to mean 'non-Christian' reflects a period when Christianity had spread among the upper classes and within towns, but not to the rural peasantry. Pagans need not share any common ground, but in Britain the Anglo-Saxons and Vikings recognized the same major gods and goddesses, but with slight variations in name (e.g. Woden/Odin), and although the native British had different deities these had responsibility for similar aspects of life such as warfare and fertility. The Romans had no trouble in assimilating the deities of either group with their own pantheon.

One should not envisage either Celtic or Germanic paganism as having structures or doctrines comparable to those of the Christian church. The building of temples and existence of a professional class of priests seems to have been more a feature of Celtic than Germanic practice. What may have mattered far more to the majority of people were localized guardian spirits who might be honoured at natural sites such as a spring, a grove of trees, or a hilltop.

Christianity saw off the major pantheons of gods and goddesses without too much difficulty and major festivals of the pagan year such as midwinter could be replaced with appropriate Christian celebrations like Christmas. What was harder to eradicate was the attachment to local holy places, though healing springs, for instance, were sometimes absorbed into local saints' cults.

**Paine, Thomas** (1737–1809). Radical writer and revolutionary activist. Paine led an uneventful life as a stay-maker and exciseman before emigrating to Philadelphia in 1774, where he became involved in the American independence movement. In *Common Sense* (1776), he argued for American severance from the British empire. As revolutionary forces in France began to gather strength, Paine went to Paris to give his support, publishing The *Rights of Man* (Part I 1791; Part II 1792), defending the Revolution against the attack launched by *Burke in his *Reflections on the Revolution in France*. He was elected to the French National Convention in 1792. However, Paine did not subscribe to atheism, and in his *Age of Reason* (Part I 1794; Part II 1795), while attacking Christianity, he argued for the existence of the deity as a first cause. Narrowly escaping execution in the Luxembourg prison, Paine found life in France under Napoleon intolerable and returned to his adopted America in 1802.

**Paisley, Revd Ian** (b. 1926). The voice of intransigent Ulster unionism and anti-catholicism, Paisley's massive physical presence and booming voice is in the 19th-cent. Ulster evangelical tradition. He co-founded the Free Presbyterian Church (1951), and vigorously campaigned against the ecumenical movement. He led the resistance to the reforms of the *O'Neill government and rallied traditional loyalist support against the civil rights movement from 1967. He became MP in 1970 and formed the *Democratic Unionist Party in 1971 to represent working-class loyalism. His support was well beyond the confines of his church and he challenged the position of the middle-class *Unionist Party.

Paisley supported the Ulster workers' strike in 1974 which destroyed the power-sharing executive; opposed the Sunningdale agreement 1973, the *Anglo-Irish agreement 1985, and the Downing Street declaration 1993. A member of the European Parliament since 1979, Paisley is the most successful electoral vote-winner in the province. In the 1990s he was a vociferous opponent of the 'peace process', denouncing it as a sell-out to terrorism. But, in a surprising about-turn, he agreed in 2007 to join a power-sharing executive with *Sinn Fein, becoming First Minister. He resigned in 2008.

**Pakistan** was created, and achieved its independence, on 14 August 1947 as the result of a partition of British India. It consisted of the former provinces of Sindh, Baluchistan, and the North-West Frontier together with the east of Bengal and the west of Punjab. These were all regions with a Muslim-majority population. M. A. *Jinnah, the leader of the Muslim League, was the principal advocate of Pakistan. Chaotic conditions at the time of partition also led to at least half a million people being killed in ferocious 'communal' violence. Since independence Pakistan has enjoyed a chequered history. Tensions with India have remained high and have led to three wars. East Pakistan seceded in 1971, amidst much bloodshed, to form the independent state of *Bangladesh. Full general elections were not held until 1970 and democratic institutions have remained at risk from military coups. As a leading Muslim country, Pakistan has been in a critical position since the American/British interventions in *Iraq and *Afghanistan.

**palatinates** were border regions where the demands of security dictated that the local rulers should have special powers, particularly to raise troops and to administer justice to all levels. The earldom of Chester, created in 1071, gradually acquired palatinate privileges, its tenants-in-chief holding directly of the earl and paying all taxes to him. But after 1237 the earldom was taken into the crown and became in due course part of the territories of the princes of Wales. The privileges of Durham, the other great palatinate, go back beyond the Conquest to an independent *Northumbria. The palatine powers were exercised by the bishops. The county of Lancaster was granted palatine status in 1351, though its privileges were less than those of Cheshire or Durham. The palatine status remained with *John of Gaunt and then descended through Henry IV with the crown.

**Pale, The** Originally implying a fence, and by inference the area enclosed by it, this was the name given to an area in Ireland in the late Middle Ages similar to the English Pale which developed in the 15th cent. in Calais. Its first recorded usage in Ireland is in a document that dates from 1446–7, when it clearly refers to that part of Ireland to which effective English government had shrunk, the area surrounding *Dublin.

**Palestine,** awarded by the *League of Nations to Britain as a *mandate in 1922, proved an uncomfortable responsibility. *Balfour's declaration in 1917 tried to square the circle by insisting that Britain would support a national home for the Jewish people while doing nothing to prejudice the position of the non-Jewish peoples of Palestine. Persistent Jewish immigration provoked fierce Arab resistance. After the war, British control was shaken by economic difficulties, by Zionist terror groups, and by international sympathy towards Jewish settlement. The United Nations' scheme for a partition of Palestine had little chance of acceptance and civil war had broken out before the British left in May 1948. A Jewish state of Israel was declared at once and immediately recognized by the USA. Since then Palestinians have struggled, with some success, to obtain recognition for an independent Palestine state.

**Paley, William** (1743–1805). Paley wrote standard works on the evidences for Christianity. Senior wrangler at Cambridge, he was ordained and after tutoring at Cambridge moved to clerical posts in Carlisle diocese, and then to Monkwearmouth (Sunderland). His *Evidences* was published in 1794, and his *Natural Theology* in 1802. Extremely successful, with more than 20 editions, they were required reading for undergraduates at Cambridge and at the infant university of Durham.

**Palmer, Samuel** (1805–81). English landscape painter and etcher. The son of a nonconformist bookseller, Palmer's was a learned and religious childhood. He first exhibited at the Royal Academy at 14 and through the painter John Linnell (later his father-in-law) met William *Blake. In Blake's work, Palmer saw the means to express his own mystical tendencies and he became the most outstanding of Blake's followers. In 1826 Palmer moved to Shoreham (Kent). During his seven years there he produced his most exciting and visionary work (*In a Shoreham Garden, The Magic Apple Tree*).

## Palmerston, Henry John Temple, 3rd Viscount

(1784–1865). Prime minister. A pupil of Dugald *Stewart at Edinburgh, he went on to Cambridge University. He was elected in 1807 for a pocket borough in the Isle of Wight and subsequently represented Cambridge University 1811–31, Bletchingley 1831–2, Hampshire South 1832–4, and Tiverton 1835–65.

Palmerston was perhaps the most famous foreign secretary of the 19th cent. He began his long career as a lord of Admiralty 1807–9 and then served in the relatively junior office of secretary at war from 1809 to 1828. In the Commons he largely confined himself to the necessary business of his office. He kept racehorses and was much liked by the ladies. This carefully cultivated image as a man about town however belied the industry which he brought to his office.

Palmerston became a follower of *Canning, and resigned with his fellow-Canningites from *Wellington's administration in 1828 over the question of parliamentary reform. He was not an enthusiastic reformer, however, and when he decided to join *Grey's ministry, it was another example of his ability to spot the winning side. He was a somewhat reluctant supporter of Grey's Reform Bill.

Palmerston modelled his foreign policy on Canning's. He was foreign secretary from 1830 to 1841, excepting only the interlude of *Peel's 'hundred days', and again from 1846 to 1851. His principles were to defend British political, strategic, and economic interests in Europe and overseas, to remain aloof as much as possible from long-term commitments, to mediate in European disputes to preserve peace, and to assert British power when necessary. His first great success was his settlement of the Netherlands crisis of 1830–9, when as chairman of the London conference he secured the independence of Belgium under international guarantee. This prevented

the Low Countries from falling under French control. He saw France as Britain's potential enemy and was always concerned to preserve the *Vienna settlement of 1815 which placed restrictions on future French expansion. Thus he also tried to prevent the Spanish and Portuguese thrones from falling under French influence. He generally supported 'liberal' constitutional movements in Europe, as being more likely to be friendly to Britain than absolutist regimes, but his attitude was wholly pragmatic. He opposed Russia not because of the tsar's absolutism but because of the threat to British interests in southern Europe and Asia. British trade with Turkey increased eightfold between 1830 and 1850. He was less successful in Afghanistan but he followed a policy of extending British control in north-west India.

Palmerston as foreign secretary was outstandingly successful. His popularity as 'John Bull' was sealed by his robust defence in 1850 of a Portuguese merchant named Don *Pacifico who claimed British citizenship and who appeared to have been victimized by the Greek government. His confidence led him too far in 1851, however, when he sent congratulations to Louis Napoleon on his *coup d'état* in Paris without first consulting the queen or his colleagues and he was dismissed. He remained in the government as home secretary but became prime minister by popular demand when *Aberdeen's ministry collapsed during the *Crimean War.

Palmerston's foreign policy gave the Liberal Party a somewhat incongruous electoral appeal but in domestic affairs his attitudes were never particularly 'liberal'. He strenuously opposed further electoral reform. In Europe, his support for 'liberal' movements such as Italian independence, or in the European revolutions of 1848, was always secondary to his concern for national interests which required stability in Europe.

Palmerston was tall and handsome. Nicknamed 'Cupid', he did not marry until he was 55, chiefly because of his attachment to Emily Lamb, wife of Lord Cowper, which began in 1813 and lasted until his death. They had at least four children out of wedlock and he also had children by other women. In 1839, two years after Cowper's death, they married and enjoyed another 25 years of 'unfamiliar married bliss'.

**Pandulf** (d. 1226). Bishop of Norwich. Born in Rome, Pandulf was sent by Innocent III to negotiate an end to the dispute with King John, which had brought England under *interdict. He arrived in 1211 and demanded the restoration of Archbishop *Langton. John refused and Pandulf departed. He was sent back in 1213, by which time John's position had weakened and he sued for terms, doing homage to the pope for his kingdom. Henceforward Pandulf advised John and was created bishop of Norwich in 1215. After John's death, Pandulf took a prominent part in the government of the country during the minority of Henry III, forming a triumvirate with Hubert de *Burgh and Peter des *Roches.

**Pankhurst, Emmeline** (1858–1928). *Suffragette leader. A superb platform speaker with a fine physical presence, Emmeline Pankhurst came to symbolize the women's struggle for the parliamentary vote.

Emmeline acquired radical views from her father Robert Goulden, a Manchester cotton-manufacturer. In 1874 she married the Liberal lawyer Dr Richard Pankhurst and followed him into the *Fabian Society and the *Independent Labour Party. Following Richard's death in 1898 Emmeline fell under the influence of her eldest daughter Christabel, who became increasingly impatient with the failure of the ILP to give priority to women's suffrage. As a result they established the Women's Social and Political Union in 1903, moved to London, and adopted militant tactics. She decided to vary her methods by attacking property: 'the argument of the broken pane of glass is the most valuable argument in modern politics.' After a spate of window-breaking in the West End in March 1912 she was charged with conspiracy to commit damage and awarded a nine-month sentence. In February 1913 she accepted responsibility for a bomb which exploded at *Lloyd George's house at Walton Heath and was sentenced to three years' penal servitude. Under the terms of the '*Cat and Mouse Act' she was rearrested twelve times.

**Papineau, Louis-Joseph** (1786–1871). Papineau, leader of the *patriote* party in Lower Canada (modern Quebec), was the voice of a vocal nationalism, which by 1834 confronted the British government with demands for effective control of the province. In response, the House of Commons in March 1837 authorized the governor to ignore the Assembly. Lower Canada simmered with protest until November, when an attempt to arrest Papineau triggered open rebellion. British forces suppressed the uprising with much loss of life. Papineau went into exile, returning to Canada in 1845.

**Papua New Guinea** is an independent monarchy within the Commonwealth with the queen as head of state. It is formed by the eastern half of the large island of New Guinea together with a number of adjacent islands to the east and north. The western part of the island was claimed by the Dutch and is now part of Indonesia. During the Second World War there was heavy fighting after the Japanese invaded.

***Paradise Lost*** Epic poem by John *Milton (1667) concerning mankind's disobedience and consequent expulsion from Paradise through Satan's agency. It has become the blind poet's best-known work through its panoramic vistas and mastery of language.

**Paris, treaty of,** 1259. By this Anglo-French treaty of 13 October Henry III surrendered his claim to the Plantagenet lands of northern France which his father John had lost in the first decade of the century. In return, his possession of Aquitaine in south-west France was confirmed by Louis IX of France. The treaty clearly stated that Henry should pay liege homage to Louis for his French lands.

**Paris, treaty of,** 1295. In 1292 Edward I placed John *Balliol on the throne of Scotland. Two years later, when war broke out between Edward and Philip IV of France, Edward called on Balliol to give him support. But a number of Scottish barons sent to France and on 23 October 1295 signed a treaty of mutual assistance which became the basis for the long-lasting *Franco-Scottish alliance, the 'Auld Alliance'.

**Paris, treaty of,** 1303. The treaty of 1259 did not end friction over England's possession of Gascony, and war between Philip IV of France and Edward I broke out again in 1294. After negotiations, the treaty of Paris in 1303 confirmed Edward's fealty to Philip for the territory and arranged for the marriage of Prince Edward to the French princess *Isabella. Edward I turned his attention to his last campaign in Scotland.

**Paris, treaty of,** 1727. Philip V of Spain was far from reconciled to the loss of *Minorca and *Gibraltar to Britain after the War of the *Spanish Succession. In 1725 a Spanish-Austrian *rapprochement* forced Britain, France, and the Dutch into a defensive treaty of Hanover and in February 1727 the Spaniards began a siege of Gibraltar. It was beaten off, and in May 1727 a preliminary settlement was agreed at Paris.

**Paris, treaty of,** 1763. Though the treaty of Paris, which brought to an end the Seven Years War, gave Britain great gains, including Canada, supremacy in India, Grenada, St Vincent, Dominica, Tobago, Senegal, and Minorca, it was denounced by the opposition as wholly inadequate and the duke of *Bedford, chief negotiator, was accused of betraying his country. *Pitt complained that we had abandoned our ally Frederick of Prussia and that the treaty 'obscured all the glories of the war and surrendered the dearest interests of the nation'.

**Paris, treaty of,** 1814. The treaty was concluded between France and the victorious allies (Austria, Great Britain, Portugal, Prussia, Russia, Spain, and Sweden) on 30 May. Napoleon Bonaparte had abdicated on 6 April and the allies wished to offer a generous peace to help the restored king, Louis XVIII. France was allowed to keep her frontiers as on 1 January 1792, thus retaining some of the gains of the revolutionary period. With some exceptions, she regained her colonies.

**Paris, treaty of,** 1815. This treaty (20 November), after Napoleon's Hundred Days and defeat at the battle of Waterloo, was more severe than the first treaty of 1814. With a few exceptions, France had to withdraw to the frontiers of 1790. She also had to pay an indemnity of 700,000,000 francs and agree to an allied army of occupation for five years. It had previously been agreed that France would restore the looted works of art to their owners.

**Paris, treaty of,** 1856. This treaty was signed at the end of the *Crimean War by Austria, France, Great Britain, Prussia, Russia, Sardinia, and Turkey. It was meant to strengthen the security of the Ottoman (Turkish) empire and limit the power of Russia. The other powers undertook to respect the integrity of Turkey and admitted her to the Concert of Europe: in return the sultan promised good treatment of his Christian subjects. The Black Sea was to be neutralized, its waters open to the merchant ships of all nations, but closed to warships. This meant dismantling the Russian Black Sea fleet. In 1870 Russia unilaterally abrogated the Black Sea clauses.

**parish churches** There are parish churches of all sizes, ages, and architectural styles, with internal fittings equally diverse. What is common to all of them is that they are buildings at the centres of their communities. The rights and wrongs of how God should be worshipped aroused great passions, and parish churches have been built and rebuilt, furnished and refurnished throughout their history in conformity with these shifting ideals of worship.

The parochial system developed piecemeal from the 10th cent., but was in place by the 13th. From then until the early 19th cent. the priest was supported by a landed endowment, the *glebe; by a tax payable by the parishioners, the *tithe; and by various offerings like *mortuaries. By the early 13th cent. it was established that the rector could only be expected to maintain the fabric of the chancel of the church from his income, the parishioners being responsible for the upkeep of the nave and for the books and vestments needed. The imposition of this collective responsibility resulted in the emergence of a real sense of community in the later Middle Ages, with the people taking a dominant role in the organization of parish life and the form of the church building and its contents, through their elected representatives, the *churchwardens.

There are examples of parish church buildings from all periods, like the Saxon church of Escomb (Co. Durham), the Romanesque church of Kilpeck (Herefordshire), or the great Decorated church of St Mary Redcliffe (*Bristol). The Reformation brought an end to the extensive rebuilding of the later Middle Ages and there are comparatively few churches built between the mid-16th and early 19th cents. The churches built by *Wren after the Great Fire of *London are an exception, and there are fine Hanoverian churches at Stoke Edith (1740–2) and Shobdon (1752–6) in Herefordshire. The 19th cent. saw another massive church-building programme as the Church of England tried to provide for the growing population.

Parish churches may not often have been rebuilt after the 16th cent. but their interiors were often remodelled. The numerous altars, and images of the saints in stone, wood, glass, paint, and needlework, were swept away in the Reformation. In the 19th cent. church interiors were completely remodelled along the lines advocated by the Victorian reformers to provide space for the proper celebration of the liturgy. Thus, whereas parish churches are of very diverse architectural styles, their interior arrangements are generally 19th cent. The sanctuary was screened off and raised above the floor of the nave by steps, the altar was returned to its medieval position near the east wall, railed off and raised on further steps, so that space was created for the parish choir and organ within the east end.

**Parish Councils Act,** 1894 (more properly the Local Government Act). The Act completed the great reform of *local government in the 19th cent. Towns had been given elected councils by the *Municipal Corporations Act of 1835 and *county councils had been established in 1888. There had been considerable pressure in the Liberal Party for parish councils to develop grass-roots democracy and they were included in the *Newcastle programme of 1891. *Gladstone's legislation introduced urban and rural districts, parish councils for villages of over 300 inhabitants, and parish meetings for hamlets. The Act gave women, whether married or not, the right both to vote and serve. The urban and rural districts were swept away by the Local Government Act of 1972, but parish councils survived, save in Wales, where community councils were established.

**parishes, origins of** Traditional theories that the English parish system was the brainchild of Archbishop *Theodore of Tarsus (668–90) are no longer held. English dioceses, geographically much larger than Italian counterparts, could not be administered from the centre. *Paulinus, bishop of York (627–34), built some local churches and so did the 7th-cent. Celtic mission to Northumbria. *Bede (d. 735) mentions houses of prayer. His advice to Archbishop Egbert (734) shows that no organized system then existed; he advised him to seek aid by 'ordaining priests and instituting teachers who may devote themselves to preaching the word of God in the individual villages'. Thus the parish system gradually evolved in the 8th cent. probably by a two-way process, from the diocesan centre outwards and from local private churches towards the centre. Little is known about these local churches because the thegn had no formal charter from the king and his church was simple and wooden, leaving no trace. It was his own property, served by a poor priest in return for glebe land of 2 virgates, twice as much as a ceorl. In addition the priest was allowed fees for baptisms, marriages, or supervising ordeals. Private churches became normal appurtenances for thegns. Others, founded by kings or bishops as their own, were later known as 'peculiars', withdrawn from ordinary diocesan jurisdiction. The parish system developed as churches continued to be built in villages throughout the Anglo-Saxon period and by the Norman Conquest it was for the most part fully developed. In the course of time, governments found the parish a useful administrative unit, particularly for dealing with poor relief. It then became even more necessary to establish the exact boundaries of parishes, and the annual perambulation, or 'beating the bounds', usually done on Rogation Day, became an important event. Nevertheless, until well into the 19th cent. the pattern of the 10,000 parishes remained chaotic, with separated pockets, disputed areas, and countless idiosyncrasies.

**parish registers** Records of baptisms, burials, and weddings were kept in England following an order of Thomas *Cromwell in 1538. Registers began in Scotland in the 1550s and 1560s, although few survive before the 17th cent. Irish parish registers, too, do not normally start before that century and those that do usually cover only the protestant Church of Ireland; few registers recording the majority catholic population start until the 18th cent.

Before civil registration in 1837 parish registers provide historical demographers with the best means of calculating population statistics. The reliability of their results, however, depends on overcoming the many deficiencies of Anglican parochial registration, since registers record church ceremonies, rather than births, deaths, and marriages. Many babies died before baptism, and an increasing proportion of the population deserted the Church of England so that by the 1810s English registers contain only about two-thirds of the nation's births and deaths.

**Parisi** British tribe and *civitas*. The Parisi as their name suggests seem to have ancestral links, betrayed in particular by their unusual 'chariot-burials', to a Gallic tribe of the same name. It is possible that they acquiesced in the Roman occupation of their territory, which lay in the East Riding of Yorkshire. The geographer Ptolemy ascribes one town to them, Petuaria (Brough on Humber), and it is from here that an inscription survives which appears to confirm the existence of the *civitas*. It is likely that Petuaria served as the tribal capital.

**Park, Mungo** (1771–1806). A child of the *Scottish Enlightenment, Park's Edinburgh medical and botanical training and Sumatran experience led *Banks to choose him to explore the interior of west Africa for the African Association in 1795. From the Gambian coast he reached the Niger near Segu, ending long controversy by proving that the river flowed eastwards. A more ambitious expedition for the British government ended in disaster in 1806 when Park was killed at Bussa much further down the Niger.

**Parker, Matthew** (1504–75). Archbishop of Canterbury. Born in Norwich and educated at Corpus Christi College, Cambridge, Parker was successively chaplain to *Anne Boleyn, master of Corpus Christi (1544), vice-chancellor (1545 and 1549), dean of Lincoln (1552), and archbishop. Close to Bucer and a supporter of Lady Jane *Grey, he was deprived under Mary and lived in obscurity. As a diffident, scholarly man, he reluctantly agreed to the primacy at Elizabeth's request. The major architect of the Elizabethan settlement, Parker courageously promoted theological comprehension within liturgical conformity, a middle road between Rome and Calvinism.

**Parkes, Joseph** (1796–1865). Parkes was an early example of the kind of man needed by the politics of lobbying—the parliamentary agent. He was born in Warwick, was much influenced by *Bentham, became a solicitor, and married a daughter of Joseph *Priestley. In 1828 he was secretary to a committee which lobbied successfully for the transfer of East Retford's parliamentary seats to Birmingham, and in the reform crisis of 1832 he acted as go-between for the Whig ministers in their dealings with the *Birmingham Political Union. Parkes's reward in 1833 was to be made secretary to the committee looking into municipal corporations, which, not surprisingly, reported that there was vast dissatisfaction and substantial reform of local government was needed. He continued to work for the Whigs in election matters until 1847, when he was appointed taxing master in Chancery.

## Parliament
### English Parliament
Parliament is a servant which became a master. It originated with three royal needs; the need of monarchs to obtain advice and information; the realization that subjects were more likely to pay taxes if they knew what they were for; and the need to find some way of dealing with grievances and petitions. The third function of Parliament gradually atrophied as, in the Middle Ages, an elaborate network of local and national courts was established, though the concept of the High Court of Parliament survived in the appellate jurisdiction of the House of Lords.

In a general sense, Parliament may be traced back to the Saxon *witan and the Norman *council, each of which included the chief men of the realm. But the development of Parliament as a wider, national body, with a representative element, reflects the incessant demands of government for more money. Feudal dues were intended to be exceptional—for the king's marriage, his ransom, or the knighting of his son—but chronic warfare demanded ever-increasing taxation and made it impossible for the king to 'live of his own'.

In Saxon and Norman times, a good deal of public business was done at crown-wearings, ceremonial occasions at Christmas,

Easter, and Whitsun. Since the great men were expected to attend to show respect, it was easy to consult them. In the course of the 13th cent., these meetings came to be referred to as discussions—*colloquia* or *parliamenta*. But though their purpose was to assist the king, they could also be turned against an unpopular or unsuccessful monarch. In December 1203 John left Normandy to seek urgent help from his barons at Oxford in saving the duchy: they promised obedience but demanded 'the rights of the kingdom inviolate'. In 1257, when Henry III was absent fighting in Gascony, his regents called another council to appeal for money. Though they augmented the barons with representatives of the lower clergy and two knights from each shire, the money was not forthcoming. During the conflict between Simon de *Montfort's party and the king, each side used Parliament in turn: de Montfort's Parliament in January 1265 included both knights and members from certain boroughs.

By this time, Parliament was becoming a familiar institution, but its composition still varied considerably. The lesser clergy, summoned for the first time in 1257, attended irregularly thereafter, and then dropped out, using *convocation instead. Edward I's *'Model' Parliament of 1295 totalled more than 400 members. Though not a model in the sense that its composition was subsequently adhered to, it was very different from a small council of 40 to 50 members.

We must not however exaggerate the importance of Parliament at this stage. Attendances were not always good, partly because travel was difficult, partly because involvement was not always welcome. Sessions were short—sometimes no more than a week. But the Commons were beginning to assert themselves. Taxation, which had been voted jointly, was said in the reign of Henry IV to be by the Commons 'with the assent of the Lords'—a significant change.

The Tudor period saw a great leap forward, the power of Parliament and that of the monarchy advancing together. Henry VIII's use of Parliament to regulate the succession and to reform the church strengthened its authority and the elimination of the abbots from the Upper House left the lay lords in a strong majority. In 1536, the Act of *Union brought the principality of Wales

into Parliament's range. Yet, by and large, it remained under royal control. During Elizabeth's reign there were signs of restiveness, but in the last ten years of her reign, Parliament was in existence for only some seven months.

In the course of the 17th cent. Parliament made a decisive breakthrough. The ineptitude of James I and Charles I led in 1642 to civil war. But the result was stalemate. The restoration of the monarchy in 1660 could be seen as proof that, as kings had always argued, it was the bulwark against anarchy or despotism. Yet Parliament in 1660 was far from discredited. It had demonstrated a remarkable capacity to improvise in government and to wage war, and an important part of Charles II's appeal from exile had been his promise to summon a free parliament. Even so, relations with parliaments during the rest of his reign were often fraught. The balance tipped in 1688. After James II's flight, the House of Commons took advantage of the situation to improve its position in relation to the new monarchs. The financial settlement given William III was deliberately ungenerous: 'when princes have not needed money,' declared Sir Joseph Williamson, with great candour, 'they have not needed us.' Twenty-five years of almost continuous warfare guaranteed annual sessions and assured Parliament of a regular and inescapable place in the machinery of government. Ministers like *Harley and *Walpole learned how to control Parliament through patronage and cajolery and made reputations as managers. They were helped in their task by the Act of *Union with Scotland in 1707 since the 45 MPs and 16 representative peers who arrived at Westminster were, by and large, penurious and purchasable.

In many ways, Parliament after the revolution was at its zenith. The government of aristocracy and gentry, who had a near monopoly of wealth, leisure, and education, seemed natural and inevitable and could boast of notable achievements. The constitution was greatly admired, at home and abroad. The standard of debate was high, with orators like *Pulteney, *Murray, *Pitt the Elder, *North, *Fox, *Burke, *Sheridan, *Pitt the Younger, and *Canning. In 1801, the Act of *Union with Ireland meant that, for the first time, Parliament could claim total sovereignty over the British Isles, though the result was not an unmixed blessing.

**p**

Yet even when Parliament was at its strongest, there were tremors. The breakaway of the Americans in 1776 foreshadowed the time when Canada, Australia, India, New Zealand, Ireland, and the colonies would follow suit. At the same time, Parliament, with great reluctance, allowed reports of its proceedings to appear in newspapers. 'This', Pulteney had once declared, 'looks very like making us accountable without doors for what we say within.' He was right and through that gap public opinion forced an entrance. The movement of population, the growth of great unrepresented towns, and the development of a more critical, utilitarian attitude gnawed at the foundations of aristocratic rule. In 1832 the first great reform took place. As its opponents gloomily forecast, it led, by stages, to full democracy, though not at the speed which they had envisaged. A continuous series of adjustments, many of them piecemeal, changed the nature of Parliament—the abolition of religious tests, more equal electoral areas, payment for MPs, extension of the franchise through to 1948, and the admission of women members in 1918. Though the *Parliament Act of 1911 stripped the House of Lords of much of its remaining power, the introduction of life peerages in 1958 gave it an unexpected and new lease of life.

## Irish Parliament

The Irish Parliament was instituted at much the same time as the English, Sir John Wogan summoning an assembly in 1295 to Kilkenny, which included the lords and two knights from certain counties. Burgesses were added in 1311. The native Irish were excluded as 'not fit to be trusted with the counsel of the realm' Control was exercised through *Poynings's law (1494), which subjected the Irish Parliament to the English Privy Council. More counties and boroughs were brought in during the 17th cent., and after the Glorious Revolution the Commons consisted of 64 knights, 234 burgesses, and 2 representatives from Trinity College, Dublin. There were some 80 peers in the House of Lords.

Though the Irish Parliament had a splendid building on College Green, begun in 1729, real power was in the hands of the lord-lieutenant and the English government.

Debates were often eloquent but they did not engage directly on the levers of power. Until the *Octennial Act of 1768 parliaments lasted the length of the reign: there was no parliament between 1666 and 1692 (save for James II 's Assembly of 1689), and the first Parliament of George II in 1727 lasted until 1760. Sessions were held every other year.

Throughout much of the 18th cent. there were repeated attempts to wriggle free from English control. Not until England began to run into difficulties after the *Seven Years War were concessions forthcoming. The granting of the Octennial Act in 1768 came at a time when the English were anxious to increase the Irish army, and the repeal of Poynings's law in 1782 came when the *Volunteers carried a clear threat in the midst of the American War.

The grant of legislative independence ushered in the final phase of the Irish Parliament, which has been bathed in a golden light as '*Grattan's Parliament'. But in the end the decisive factor was that law and order broke down in the great rising of 1798. Without a union, Ireland would, wrote the lord-lieutenant Camden, be 'dreadfully vulnerable in all future wars'. By the Act of Union of 1801 the Irish Parliament was suppressed and representation transferred to Westminster. The new parliament house in Dublin, no longer required, became the Bank of Ireland.

## Scottish Parliament

The Scottish Parliament differed significantly from its English counterpart. No equivalent of the Houses of Commons and Lords ever existed; instead, the three estates—clergy, barons, and burgh commissioners—assembled in one chamber. Legislation, from the early 15th cent., was drafted by the *lords of the Articles, a smaller committee elected by the estates, before being passed in full Parliament. Parliament was supplemented by the institutions of general council, until the late 15th cent., and from the 16th cent. by the *Convention of Estates, effectively parliaments without judicial powers.

Evolving from the king's council of bishops and earls, Parliament is first recorded in 1235, referred to as a *colloquium*. In the early 14th cent. the presence of knights and freeholders became important, and from 1326 burgh commissioners attended, because of the need to secure their consent for taxation. Called in this period on average more than once a year, Parliament was expected to provide support for many crown policies. However, it could be a dangerous place for a monarch, and James IV (1488–1513) avoided meetings after 1509.

With the Scottish constitutional settlement (1640–1), the royal prerogative was curtailed, and Parliament took control of the executive, a precedent for the English Long Parliament. The *Interregnum saw a union of parliaments (1657), but the Scottish Parliament returned strongly after the Restoration (1660). In 1689 the attendance of clergy was abolished, followed by the Committee of the Articles (1690). Bribery and parliamentary division, rather than dominant unionism, best explain the crown's ability to secure a parliamentary majority in favour of incorporating union with England (16 January 1707). Finally dissolved on 28 April 1707, the Scottish Parliament remained important to Scottish national identity, and in 1999, after a referendum, it was restored. A new Parliament House was opened in Edinburgh in October 2004.

### Welsh Parliament

Though there is no evidence of a Welsh parliament as a regular part of government, there was a tradition of consultation. *Llywelyn called an assembly of magnates at Aberdovey in 1216 to decide on the territorial divisions of south Wales. *Glyndŵr is said to have summoned two parliaments—at Machynlleth in 1404 and at Harlech in 1405. Some representatives from Wales were summoned to the English Parliament in 1322 and 1327 but Wales was not included in the regular representation until after 1536. A Welsh Assembly was instituted in 1999.

**Parliament, Acts of** The procedure whereby a bill becomes an Act of Parliament is lengthy and has evolved over many centuries. The main stages of a bill in the House of Commons are first reading, second reading, committee, report, and third reading. The first reading is purely formal. If the bill is controversial, the second reading debate is likely to occupy a full parliamentary sitting. The debate is about the principle embodied in the bill, not its detail.

After second reading, most bills are sent to a standing committee for detailed discussion. The bill (unless guillotined) is considered clause by clause, amendment by amendment. The inbuilt government majority will ensure that most opposition amendments are defeated, but there are occasional revolts by government supporters.

The bill, as amended, goes back to the full House for its report stage: this is a rather less thorough version of the committee stage. The last stage is the third reading, when the House once again debates the principle of the bill. If, as is likely, it passes at this stage, the bill will go to the House of Lords to undergo a similar process. The main difference is that the committee stage in the Lords will be taken (normally) in the full House. If passed with amendments, the bill goes back to the Commons to consider the changes. For the bill to become law in that session, the two Houses will have to agree on the full text. The bill is then sent to the monarch for royal assent, which is invariably given.

The procedure outlined is that for public bills. Private bills, those relating to a particular corporation, individual, or company, go through a distinct, complex, and semi-judicial process.

**Parliament, Houses of** (London). The competition for the Houses of Parliament was won in 1836 by Sir Charles *Barry in the required 'Gothic or Elizabethan' style. Construction started in 1840, but the building was incomplete when Barry died 20 years later and was finished 1860–70 by his son Edward Middleton Barry (1830–80). Much of the detail, including the richly embellished interiors, is by A. W. N. *Pugin. The House of Commons was destroyed in the Second World War but rebuilt by Sir Giles Gilbert Scott and Adrian Scott in Gothic.

**Parliament Act,** 1911. Though the immediate cause of the Parliament Act was the House of Lords' rejection of *Lloyd George's budget in 1909, the deeper cause was the late 19th-cent. disintegration of the Whig Party which carried the Liberal Unionists into the ranks of the Conservatives, thus confirming a permanent Conservative majority in the Upper House and placing Liberal legislation at the mercy of the peers. The Act declared that a money bill could be presented for royal assent after one month, even without the Lords' consent, and other public bills after two years. The duration of Parliament was changed from seven to five years. It was carried in the Lords by 131:114 only after *Asquith, prime minister, had extracted from a reluctant George V a pledge to create enough Liberal peers if necessary to carry the measure. By the Parliament Act of 1949 the delaying power of the Lords was reduced to one year.

**parliamentarians** was the polite name given to the opponents of Charles I in the civil wars. The pejorative term was roundheads. Charles's decision not to summon his own Parliament at Oxford until 1644 and his evident mistrust of it gave his adversaries some advantage.

**parliamentary reform** is a general term covering a variety of proposals and changes which need to be carefully distinguished. Alterations to the composition, powers, procedure, and structure of Parliament have continued since the first parliaments were summoned in the 13th cent., but a sustained campaign for parliamentary reform did not develop until the 18th cent. After the *Septennial Act of 1716 there were intermittent calls for shorter parliaments, for a reduction in the number of placemen, and for the abolition of some rotten boroughs to give more representation to the counties. These were modest proposals that would have increased the already overwhelming influence of the aristocracy and gentry. More radical suggestions were put forward during the *Wilkes agitation in the 1770s when the case for manhood suffrage was deployed for the first time since the Civil War period. A comprehensive reform programme was put forward by the Westminster Committee, affiliated to the *Yorkshire Association in 1780, calling for manhood suffrage, equal electoral areas, annual parliaments, secret ballot, payment of members, and the abolition of the property qualification for MPs—the six points of the *Charter 60 years later.

Legislative response was at first slow. A few small boroughs were reformed in the 1770s and 1780s for gross corruption but no review of the entire electoral system was undertaken. Statutes against bribery were largely ineffective. But a series of major

changes came 1828–32. Repeal of the *Test and Corporations Acts in 1828 allowed protestant dissenters to become MPs and the following year the same concession was extended to Roman catholics; the *Great Reform Act of 1832 abolished 56 of the smallest boroughs and brought great new towns like Manchester, Birmingham, Sheffield, and Leeds into the representation, introducing a standard franchise for the boroughs. Further legislation in 1867, 1884, 1918, 1928, and 1969 extended the right to vote eventually to all men and women over 18. Religious disabilities were removed when Jews were allowed to become MPs in 1858 and atheists in 1886. The long-standing problem of bribery and intimidation at elections was dealt with by *secret ballot in 1872, reinforced by the *Corrupt Practices Act of 1883.

**Parnell, Charles Stewart** (1846–91). Charismatic Irish constitutional nationalist leader. Born in Co. Wicklow into an Anglo-Irish protestant family, Parnell inherited the Avondale estate, and became MP for Meath in 1875. He led the 'New Departure' of 1878–9, bringing together ex-Fenians, Irish-American nationalists, and advocates of land reform. He became president of the *Irish Land League in 1879, and forced *Gladstone to grant major changes in the 1881 Land Act. To preserve control of an increasingly radical movement, Parnell initially resisted the Act's implementation and was imprisoned. In the *Kilmainham 'treaty', 1882, he agreed to an amended Land Act and to keep to parliamentary opposition only. Skilful manœuvring of support between Conservatives and Liberals culminated in Gladstone's Home Rule Bill 1886, the summit of Parnell's career. Following the bill's defeat, his effectiveness was compromised by the Liberal alliance and his remoteness from Ireland. Accused of association with Fenian violence in *The Times* in 1887, he was proved innocent in February 1889, only to be ruined by being cited as co-respondent in O'Shea's divorce in 1889/90. Parnell wed Katharine O'Shea in June 1891, but died that autumn.

**Parry, Sir Hubert** (1848–1918). Together with Charles Stanford, whose music he detested, Parry inspired what is called the 'English musical renaissance' of the later 19th cent. He produced some fine second-rank works, of which his Fourth Symphony, Piano Quartet, and shorter choral settings are perhaps the best. He is best known for the tune he wrote for *Blake's 'Jerusalem', which was first performed at a patriotic concert in 1916. He succeeded Sir George Grove as director of the Royal College of Music in 1895.

**Parsons, Sir Charles** (1854–1931). Engineer. A son of the 3rd earl of Rosse [I], Parsons grew up at Birr castle in Ireland before going to Trinity College, Dublin, and St John's College, Cambridge. His father was a distinguished chemist and astronomer and Parsons's education was scientific. After Cambridge, he took an apprenticeship at the Elswick works in Newcastle of Sir William *Armstrong, of whom he spoke later with great admiration. He began working on electricity supply and by 1884 had constructed a turbo-dynamo. In 1889 he founded Parsons of Heaton on the Tyne and a power station at Newcastle was operating by turbo-generation by 1890. Parsons then applied turbines to ships, building the *Turbinia*, by far the fastest vessel afloat.

**Parsons, Robert** (1546–1610). Jesuit missionary. Born in Somerset to protestant parents, he resigned his Balliol fellowship and was received into the Roman church at Louvain, before offering himself to the Society of Jesus (1575). He was sent to England with *Campion in 1580, and stayed a year in great danger. For nearly 20 years he was one of the most ardent promoters of the Spanish invasion. After failure of the *Armada, he concentrated on his order's internal affairs. His missionary zeal combined with political intrigue have contributed much to the popular image of Jesuitry.

**partition treaties,** 1698, 1700. The imminent death of Carlos II of Spain, without children, so soon after the end of the *Nine Years War persuaded European powers to try to settle the Spanish Succession without bloodshed. By the first treaty, signed in October 1698 by Louis XIV and William III, the Spanish inheritance was to go to Joseph Ferdinand, electoral prince of Bavaria. The prince of Bavaria died within a few weeks. By a second treaty in 1700, the Archduke Charles was to take the lion's share, with France receiving Naples, Sicily, and Milan, to be exchanged for Lorraine. But when Car-

los II died in October 1700, leaving by will Philip of Anjou, Louis's grandson, as sole heir, Louis abandoned his treaty obligations and accepted. The War of the *Spanish Succession followed.

**Passaro, Cape, battle of** *See* CAPE PASSARO, BATTLE OF.

**Passchendaele, battle of,** 1917. The British army tried to advance from Ypres in southern Belgium towards the Belgian ports of Ostend and Zeebrugge for several reasons. *Haig believed that he could win the war in 1917. The navy supported him because they wanted to drive the Germans away from the Channel ports. *Lloyd George allowed Haig to continue because he feared that, if the British were not seen to be actively fighting, the French might go the way of tsarist Russia and collapse. The battle began on 31 July 1917, but fierce German resistance, heavy rain, and the destruction of the drainage system of the Flanders plain by the artillery meant that the advance literally bogged down in the mud, at a cost of some 260,000 British casualties.

**Paston letters** Private correspondence (15th–17th cents.) of a Norfolk family, that of the 15th cent. in particular providing insights into the social history of the pre-Reformation period. Not only a family saga (Margery's clandestine marriage to their estate manager in 1469 caused consternation), business affairs, property matters, and associated litigation trace the progress of 'new' gentry.

**Patay, battle of,** 1429. After Joan of Arc had relieved Orléans, the English fell back to bridgeheads on the Loire at Meung, Jargeau, and Beaugency. The first two were soon lost, and in attempting to relieve the third, the troops of Lords Talbot (*Shrewsbury) and Scales were overwhelmed on 18 June by the French, in whose company was Joan. Talbot was captured and imprisoned until 1433.

**Paterson, William** (1658–1719). Founder of the *Bank of England. Paterson was born in Dumfries but brought up in England. He made a rapid fortune in trade in America and the Low Countries. A supporter of the Glorious Revolution, he was engaged during the *Nine Years War in government finance and pressed upon the government the establishment of a national bank to help finance the war. In 1694 when the bank was founded, Paterson became a director. He was one of the leading protagonists of the *Darien venture and worked for the Company of Scotland raising investment. He was lucky to survive the first expedition in 1698, in which his wife and only son perished, but continued to be consulted by the government, urging a union with Scotland.

**Patrick, St** (c.389–c.461). Patron saint of Ireland. Born in Britain, in his youth he was seized by raiders and taken to Ireland. In slavery for six years, he was sustained by prayer. Told in a dream of his impending return home, he made his way to the coast and joined a merchant ship, facing many dangers before rejoining his family. In clerical training, he seems to have spent some years in France, where he was probably consecrated by St *Germanus before embarking on his evangelistic work in Ireland. Often at risk, he was fearlessly determined to destroy paganism. Through his tireless efforts, countless numbers were baptized and confirmed, many clergy ordained, and his see established at *Armagh, whence he began to organize the emerging church on Roman diocesan lines.

**patriot king** The concept of a patriot king was largely an opposition device of the early Hanoverian period. It hinted that the first two Georges were more interested in Hanover than in Britain and deplored the exclusive confidence they placed in the Whigs. The concept was most fully worked out in *Bolingbroke's treatise *The Idea of a Patriot King*, written in 1738 for *Frederick, prince of Wales, who was then heading the opposition to *Walpole. The 'essential character' of a patriot king was 'to espouse no party but to govern like the common father of his people'.

**patriots** The name was appropriated by the opponents to *Walpole since it implied that the interests of the nation were neglected by a supine and corrupt government. William *Pitt, in particular, beat the patriotic drum when he inveighed against Britain's subservience to Hanover, a 'despicable electorate'. Ministers, in reply, were scornful of patriotic rhetoric: 'it is but refusing to gratify

an unreasonable or insolent demand,' declared Walpole, 'and up starts a patriot.'

**Paulinus, St** (d. 644). First bishop of the Northumbrians. A Roman monk, tall, dark, thin-faced with an aquiline nose, according to *Bede one of *Mellitus' party sent in 601 by Pope Gregory I to help *Augustine in Kent. He was consecrated by *Justus to accompany the Princess *Æthelburg to Northumbria to marry *Edwin. He preached at Yeavering, Catterick, Lincoln, and elsewhere, and introduced the building of churches in stone. After Edwin's death (633) at *Heathfield Chase, Paulinus fled to Kent and took up the see of *Rochester.

**Peacock, Thomas Love** (1785–1866). Peacock had modest private means but earned his living as an official in the East India Company. He is best known for his novels, *Headlong Hall* (1816), *Melincourt* (1817), *Nightmare Abbey* (1818), *Crotchet Castle* (1831), and *Gryll Grange* (1860–1). Peacock was a friend of *Shelley in his youth and radical in politics, but he grew increasingly independent, and his satirical victims included ardent Romantics as well as 'march of mind' men like Henry *Brougham. The novels are quirky and an acquired taste, with little plot and much conversation, but offer vignettes of Peacock's contemporaries.

**Peada** (d. 656), king of the *Middle Angles (c.653–6), was a son of *Penda of Mercia, who appointed him king. Shortly afterwards Peada married Alhflæd, daughter of *Oswiu of Northumbria, and as a condition of marriage agreed to become a Christian and to allow evangelization by a mission from *Lindisfarne. After Oswiu defeated Penda at the battle of *Winwæd in 655, he appointed Peada king of the southern Mercians, keeping control of the northern Mercians himself, but, according to *Bede, Peada was murdered the following Easter through the treachery of Alhflæd.

**Pearse, Patrick** (1879–1916). Pearse was the son of an English-born stonemason, a non-practising lawyer, dramatist, and headmaster of St Enda's School (Dublin), which he ran on Gaelic Revivalist lines. A leading member of the *Gaelic League, he supported *Home Rule up to 1912: the Ulster crisis caused him to advocate a militant nationalism and to join the *Irish Republican Brotherhood. He became a member of the IRB military council which planned the *Easter Rising. Pearse read the declaration of the Provisional Irish Republic outside the General Post Office on 24 April 1916; gave orders for surrender five days later; and was executed on 3 May.

**peasantry** Medievalists have questioned whether Britain ever had a social group to which the word peasant was applicable, and would certainly question the continued existence of such a group beyond the Middle Ages. In literary sources the term was occasionally used of labourers, implying someone of low birth and inferior standing. The term also acquired romantic overtones, with the peasantry depicted as the humble members of a fast-disappearing rural society, a Hardyesque chorus.

As a result, it has been employed as a useful shorthand term without specific definition. Most historians use the term to mean small landowners and/or small farmers, but it can also be used loosely to include the cottager, the commoner, and the squatter.

The term has also become a catch-all for the social group largely displaced through the economic conditions prevailing in the post-Restoration period, or at enclosure. Some have argued that the term is inappropriate after 1750 because by then England had no peasantry in the continental sense of the word. However, it is accepted that peasants survived in Ireland and in thinly populated parts of Wales and Scotland.

**Peasants' Revolt** This rebellion in 1381 was the first large-scale popular uprising in England. It began in Essex, in the village of Fobbing. Kent soon followed, and the rebels moved rapidly to London. There were also significant risings in East Anglia, Bury St Edmunds, and St Albans. The spark to the revolt was provided by the third *poll tax, which bore particularly hard on the poor. The rebellion took a dramatic and strongly political turn in London, where the rebels took and executed the archbishop of Canterbury, the treasurer, and others. Radical demands were made by Wat *Tyler, one of the peasant leaders, at Smithfield: serfdom was to be abolished; outlawry was to be aban-

doned; lordship was to be divided between all men. There should be only one bishop, and one prelate; the wealth of the church should be distributed among the people. Wat Tyler was killed at this meeting. Resistance elsewhere in the country was short-lived.

**Pecock, Reginald** (c.1395–c.1460). Bishop of Chichester (1450-9). A Welshman, educated at Oriel College, Oxford, Pecock was fellow there (1414-24) and under Humphrey, duke of *Gloucester's patronage became master of Whittington College, London (1431-44), bishop of St Asaph (1444), of Chichester (1450), and a privy counsellor (1454-7). A rationalist himself, he tried to win over *lollards by vigorous argument rather than by burning. His works include *Repressor of Over Much Blaming of the Clergy* (1455), the first theological treatise in English since 1066, his *Book of Faith* (1456) promoting the authority of reason. Arraigned for heresy (1457), he was expelled from the Privy Council and forced to resign his see (1459) after public recantation.

**Peel, Sir Robert** (1788-1850). Prime minister. Peel was born into a family which had recently become wealthy through cotton manufacture. He was educated at Harrow and Oxford. When he was 21, his father bought him a parliamentary seat for the Irish borough of Cashel. He was widely seen as an able man and in June 1809 became under-secretary for war and colonies. In 1812 he became chief secretary for Ireland. He had a strong physique but by 1818 overwork had impaired his health and he resigned. In 1822 Peel became home secretary in *Liverpool's government. He introduced several important measures, including far-reaching reform of the criminal law and the creation of the Metropolitan Police. He also distinguished himself as a leading opponent of *catholic emancipation, increasing his status with many Tories in and out of Parliament. He left office in 1827, refusing to serve under *Canning, who supported catholic emancipation, but returned after Canning's early death. When *Wellington felt obliged to concede emancipation in 1829, Peel skilfully piloted it through the Commons. This earned him the enmity of many of his old admirers. After the Tory government fell in 1830, Peel increasingly emerged as leader of the opposition to the new Whig ministry. He opposed the *Great Reform Act, but tried to keep within bounds the enmity of right-wing Tories towards the Whigs.

Peel began to establish a national reputation for moderation, exemplified by his *Tamworth manifesto, in which he accepted the Reform Act and committed his Conservative Party to a policy of cautious reform. The manifesto was issued for the general election after William IV dismissed his Whig ministers late in 1834. Peel became prime minister with a minority of seats. In the following election his party gained about 100 seats, but not a majority. The Whigs forced Peel's resignation and returned to office, but the 1837 election brought further Conservative gains. Deepening economic and political troubles brought the Whigs in 1841 to propose a more radical financial policy which involved reductions in tariffs, including the *Corn Laws which protected agriculture. Peel then defeated ministers on a no-confidence motion, took office, and dissolved. In the ensuing election he won decisively. Although the country was suffering grave social and economic troubles, he used the winter of 1841–2 to mature plans for recovery and in the 1842 budget scored a major success. He slashed tariffs as impediments to commerce and revised the Corn Laws downwards. Unlike the Whigs, he was strong enough to balance this loss of revenue by enacting direct taxation on incomes. Ensuing years saw further moves towards free trade, and growing restiveness in some Conservative quarters, as Peel's commitment to the preservation of the Corn Laws became doubtful. The *Anti-Corn Law League's agitation increased right-wing anxiety. From 1842 onwards, Peel's Conservative critics had warned that free trade policies would fail, but economic recovery by 1845 seemed to confound them. By then Peel was at heart a free trader. In 1845 the potato crop failed, bringing catastrophe to Ireland. Peel determined to take the opportunity to repeal the Corn Laws. He was unable to persuade his cabinet to back him, and resigned, but when the Whigs failed to form a ministry late in 1845, he returned to office. He introduced his repeal measures cleverly, offering concessions to the landed interest, but failed to preserve his position when the aristocratic Lord George *Bentinck and the political adventurer Benjamin *Disraeli succeeded in organizing protectionist opposition. With his own following among the Conservatives and support from Whigs and radicals, Peel succeeded in repealing the Corn Laws in 1846. At the same time, disaffected Conservatives joined the opposition in defeating an Irish Coercion Bill, in order to bring Peel down. He resigned immediately after this defeat and never held office again. For the remainder of his life he possessed great influence and enjoyed great prestige in the country. His status owed much to the widespread belief that as a minister he had preferred the public good to his own retention of power.

**peel towers** were temporary refuges, often attached to manor houses, farms, or churches, and commonly built in the 15th and 16th cents. They were normally two storeys, the lower one for cattle, with slit windows, if any, in thick stone walls, and a narrow stair or ladder leading to the upper storey. Of little use against regular forces, they offered some protection against border raiders and were mainly to be found either side of the Anglo-Scottish border.

**Peep o' Day Boys** was the name adopted by Ulster presbyterians in the 1780s and 1790s to confront the catholic *Defenders. On 1 September 1795 they routed their adversaries in a pitched battle at the Diamond, near Armagh, killing many of them.

**peerage** The formal body of aristocracy, distinguished by titles and by the right to sit in the House of Lords. Though the rank of earl preceded the Conquest, it was hardly necessary to define the peerage closely until the House of Lords developed as a regular element in Parliament in the 13th cent. To the ranks of baron and earl were added duke (1337), marquis (1385), and viscount (1440). Apart from attendance in Parliament, their main privileges were access to the monarch and the right to trial by the House of Lords. From 1780 the number of peers increased greatly as bankers, industrialists, scientists, and men of letters were ennobled to augment the landed aristocracy. The greatest change however was the introduction of life peerages from 1958. Hereditary peers were deprived of their seats in the Lords in 1999 by the Labour government.

**Peerage Bill** This bill, introduced into the Lords in March1719 by the *Sunderland/ *Stanhope ministry and dropped in April, had three aims: to protect the chief ministers against impeachment should the prince of Wales, who opposed them, succeed to the throne; to settle the unsatisfactory Scottish representation in the Lords; and to maintain the existing peerage's social position, by limiting creations. The bill laid down that the king could create only six more peerages, then further peers only on the extinction of titles; the 16 Scottish elected peers were to be replaced by 25 hereditary ones. The bill was reintroduced in December 1719, easily passed the Lords, but was defeated in the Commons largely due to the opposition of Robert *Walpole.

**peine forte et dure** After the Lateran Council of the church in 1215 forbade the clergy to take part in ordeals, the king's justices had no means of trying the guilt or innocence of suspected criminals. After a number of experiments they developed the trial *jury of twelve men to decide. Under the statute of *Westminster I (1275), Parliament provided that anyone who refused to accept jury trial should be put into a 'prison forte et dure' until he agreed to it. By some error this section came to be interpreted as '*peine* forte et dure', which in turn came to be literally interpreted as the placing of weights upon the hapless prisoner, increasing until he either consented to jury trial or perished. In 1772 the peine forte et dure was abolished.

**Pelagius** Early 5th-cent. Christian theologian of British or Irish extraction. Pelagius travelled to Rome as a monk *c.* AD 400 and was deeply disappointed by the lax moral standards there. He preached that strenuous efforts were needed to attain individual salvation. The theologian *Augustine was appalled by this insistence on the effectiveness of free will. Pelagius twice suffered excommunication, and where and when he died is unknown. The new sect of Pelagianism was denounced by the Roman ecclesiastical authorities as a heresy, and St *Germanus was sent to Britain in 429 to counter its influence in the British church.

**Pelham, Henry** (*c.*1696–1754). Prime minister. Pelham was 1st lord of the Treasury for over ten years (1743–54). But time has faded his reputation between the vividly coloured careers of *Walpole and *Pitt the Elder. Pelham's career began under the wing of his elder brother, the duke of *Newcastle, who brought him into Parliament (MP for Seaford 1717–22 and Sussex 1722–54). Pelham became secretary at war in 1724 and paymaster-general in 1730, though his status, certainly in the 1730s, was higher than his offices suggest.

After Walpole's fall in 1742 he recommended Pelham as his successor to George II, who favoured *Carteret, the new secretary of state for the northern department. However, in obtaining the Treasury in 1743 Pelham had a firm power base and by the end of 1744 Carteret had resigned. In February 1746, following the retreat of the Jacobites, the king considered replacing his ministers. The Pelham brothers and their many followers resigned, forcing the king to accept them back on their own terms.

Though Pelham was now thought of as 'prime' minister, the government was really a triumvirate of Pelham, Newcastle, and *Hardwicke. Newcastle shaped foreign policy, but Pelham controlled the purse strings. Pelham pursued a policy of including as many political factions in government as possible, leading to an era of undoubted calm.

Pelham's common sense and restrained style was important in preventing excessive reprisals against the Highlanders following the Jacobite rising of 1745, in restraining Newcastle's policy of subsidy payments to allied countries during the War of the *Austrian Succession, and in damping down the popular clamour that followed the bill to naturalize Jews in 1753. It was not part of his political philosophy nor his personal inclination to encourage change.

Pelham's death in 1754 surprised his colleagues and marked a decided change of pace in British politics. George II's declaration upon hearing of it, 'Now I shall have no more peace,' would have seemed to Henry Pelham a high compliment.

**Pembroke, Richard de Clare, earl of** (*c.*1130–76), commonly known as 'Strongbow'. A member of the aristocratic Clare family, he inherited his father's earldom of Pembroke in 1148 but, being a supporter of Stephen, forfeited it when Henry II came to the throne. In 1166, still out of favour, he decided to accept *Dermot MacMurrough's offer of his daughter Eva (Aoife) in marriage and the succession to the kingdom of Leinster in return for military assistance against Dermot's Irish enemies. In 1170, in defiance of Henry's wishes, he took a force to Ireland, where he married Aoife. In 1171 he succeeded Dermot as king. Alarmed by this Henry II invaded Ireland, forcing most Irish kings to recognize him. But by the time he left in 1172 he had recognized Richard both as earl and as his representative in Ireland. Strongbow's gamble had succeeded and the English invasion of Ireland had begun.

**Pembroke, William Herbert, 1st earl of** (c.1507–70). William Herbert's grandfather was a Yorkist earl of Pembroke, executed in 1469, but his father was illegitimate. The family estate was at Ewyas Harold, north-east of Abergavenny. He held minor court office but his great chance came in 1543 when his sister-in-law *Catherine Parr married Henry VIII. He was knighted, given the estates of the abbey of Wilton, and appointed a gentleman of the bedchamber. In 1549 he helped to suppress the western rising and was given the Garter. After backing the duke of *Northumberland against his rival *Somerset, he took many of the executed duke's estates and in 1551 was created earl of Pembroke. He did homage to Lady Jane *Grey in 1553, but changed step nimbly and retained Mary's favour. He commanded her forces against *Wyatt in 1554, stayed at court under Elizabeth, and was lord steward for the last two years of his life.

**Pembrokeshire** County of south-west Wales. The county was created at the Act of *Union with England in 1536. The peninsula, part of the Welsh kingdom of *Deheubarth, was conquered by Arnulf de Montgomery c.1090, who established the lordship of Pembroke in the south. Henry I reinforced the occupation of the south by promoting a Flemish immigration. The result was that the county had a distinctive dual character, markedly English to the south, Welsh to the north. In 1974 the county became part of *Dyfed, but was reconstituted in 1996 as a unitary authority.

Pembrokeshire has been pre-eminently an agricultural county, the southern section being one of the few areas of arable land in Wales, its mild maritime climate giving rise to early vegetable- and flower-growing. The whole coast is designated a heritage coast and makes up the Pembrokeshire National Park. The coast is broken by the major sea inlet (ria) of Milford Haven. Once a major fishing port, it is now dominated by oil refineries, developed for supertankers.

**penal laws** The general name given to the enactments against Roman catholicism made between the accession of Elizabeth I and 1700. Rejection of papal authority was imposed by an oath of allegiance in 1563, stating that 'no foreign prince hath or ought to have any jurisdiction, power, superiority, pre-eminence or authority, ecclesiastical or spiritual within this realm'. After the excommunication of Elizabeth I in 1570, the purpose of legislation changed from securing royal supremacy to defeating the new recusant missionary campaign. Priests were executed, particularly after the Acts of 1584–5 which made it treasonable for a priest to enter England.

The laws of the Restoration period, especially the *Test and *Corporation Acts, kept the catholic community on the margins. Catholics suffered for the disastrous reign of the last catholic king James II under laws barring them from carrying arms, inheriting or buying property, sending children abroad for education, or teaching in a school.

Had this massive penal code been enforced, it could have eradicated English catholicism, but local imposition was sporadic and the Hanoverian mind found religious persecution distasteful. The *Jacobite threat disappeared and repeal of the penal laws became possible. This happened in three main relief Acts of 1778, 1791, and 1829.

**Penda** (d. 655), king of Mercia, can in many ways be seen as the anti-hero of *Bede's *Ecclesiastical History*—a resolute pagan, responsible for the deaths of many Christian kings in battle, including that of St *Oswald at *Maserfield (642). Penda first appears in recorded history in 626 battling with rulers of the West Saxons for control of the province of the *Hwicce. The *Northumbrians apparently first encountered him in alliance with *Cadwallon of Gwynedd at the battle of *Heathfield in 633 and he also fought at least two major battles with the *East Angles. Penda's energetic campaigns from his midland base greatly increased the territory under Mercian control. It was *Oswiu of Bernicia's challenge to his authority which led to Penda's death at the battle of *Winwæd in 655.

**Peninsular War,** 1808–14. Provoked by Napoleon's intervention in Portugal and his imposition of his brother Joseph on the throne of Spain, the war in the Iberian peninsula marked a turning point in the Napoleonic War. By closing Spanish and Portuguese ports to British trade Napoleon had hoped to compel Britain to sue for peace, but his intervention aroused massive popular hostility in Spain and Portugal. Although they were often defeated, the Spanish armies continued to defy the French, while Spanish guerrillas held down large numbers of French troops. Under *Wellington the British collaborated effectively with the Portuguese, whose army was retrained by British officers. In the winter of 1810–11 Masséna's attempt to drive the British into the sea was thwarted by the lines of *Torres Vedras, a masterpiece of military engineering. In 1812 Wellington won the dramatic battle of *Salamanca, and in 1813 he exploited British sea power to conduct a brilliant campaign in northern Spain which reached its climax at the battle of *Vitoria. After expelling the French from Spain, Wellington invaded southern France in 1814. The war in Spain sapped the energies of the French military machine and encouraged the Russians, Prussians, and Austrians in their resistance to Napoleon. It established Wellington's renown as a general and restored the reputation of the British army in the field.

**Penn, William** (1644–1718). Penn, son of Admiral Sir William Penn, educated at Oxford and Lincoln's Inn, exhibited an early religious sensibility, rejecting a conventional career to join the *quakers. Their leading legal spokesman, international propagandist, and public witness, his advocacy of liberty of conscience and religious toleration found some support from Charles II and

James, duke of York, and Penn's wealth aided his efforts. Penn gained an extensive American proprietary in 1681, drafting a constitution for Pennsylvania embodying his very liberal political ideas. The colony lost rather than (as he hoped) gained him a fortune; he faced growing opposition there and in England.

**penny post** See HILL, SIR ROWLAND; POST OFFICE.

**Penruddock's rising,** 1655. Soon after Charles II's flight into exile after the defeat at *Worcester in 1651, his supporters began to plan a general rising in England. The schemes, taken up by the royalist conspiracy of the Sealed Knot, were soon known to *Cromwell's government. On 8 March 1655 only 100 supporters turned up to a rendezvous at Marston Moor which was to have seized York, and even fewer near Morpeth for an attack on Newcastle upon Tyne. A small Wiltshire rising under John Penruddock, a local gentleman, got off the ground four days late, but never numbered more than a few hundred. At South Molton they were rounded up by a small cavalry force. Penruddock was executed at Exeter in May 1655. Cromwell's response to the disorders was to introduce the rule of the *major-generals.

**Penselwood, battle of,** 1016. An encounter in the struggle for the crown between *Edmund Ironside and *Cnut after the death of *Æthelred. The place is given in the *Anglo-Saxon Chronicle* as Peonnan near Gillingham and has consequently been identified as in Kent or at Penselwood on the Dorset–Somerset border. A case can be made out for each. The result at Penselwood was inconclusive.

**pensions, old-age** See OLD-AGE PENSIONS.

**Pentecostal churches** believe that the Pentecost experience remains accessible. Consequently they stress baptism in the Spirit, which they distinguish from conversion or water baptism. This conveys power to practise the gifts of the Spirit: speaking in tongues, prophecy, healing, exorcism. The largest British churches are the assemblies of God (formed in the United States in 1914),

p

the Apostolic Faith Church, the Elim churches, and the New Testament Church of God, with its strength among West Indian communities. Their worship is spontaneous, with emphasis on extempore prayer, believers' baptism, and the Lord's supper.

**Pentland rising,** 1666. Support for the *covenant was strong in south-west Scotland and clandestine conventicles continued after the Restoration. In November 1666 an incident at Dalry, near New Galloway, sparked off a rising. The covenanters occupied Dumfries and advanced upon Edinburgh by way of Lanark. But their numbers dwindled in the face of heavy rain and fewer than 1,000 of them were intercepted and dispersed at Rullion Green, near Penicuik in the Pentland Hills. Retaliation was severe with 30 executions and many transportations.

**Pentrich rising,** 1817. Demobilization, rapid industrialization, and agricultural recession made the post-war years miserable. In November 1816 the *Spa Fields riots culminated in an attack upon the Tower and were followed by the suspension of habeas corpus. The march of the *Blanketeers from Manchester followed in March 1817. The east midlands had its own problems of unemployment among textile workers. On 8 June several hundred men assembled at Pentrich and Ripley and began the 14-mile march to Nottingham, where, their leader Jeremiah Brandreth assured them, they would find support. They found none and in heavy rain were easily dispersed by the hussars. Brandreth, who had killed a man on the march, was executed with two others, and 30 rioters were transported.

**Pepys, Samuel** (1633–1703). Diarist, naval official, bibliophile, musician, member of Parliament, president of the Royal Society, twice master of Trinity House, Pepys lived through an epoch when capacity and drive could help a man rise high, especially if assisted by patronage. Pepys's patron was his cousin Edward Montagu, a naval commander under the republic who promoted Charles II's restoration and became earl of *Sandwich. Pepys was appointed clerk of the acts (secretary) to the Navy Board in 1660 when that body effectively ran the navy under James, duke of York. Weathering the disasters of the second Dutch War, Pepys was

appointed the first secretary of the Admiralty in 1673.

For all his contributions to the navy's wellbeing, however, Pepys has become much the best-known Englishman of the 17th cent. through his diary, or 'Journal', kept in shorthand and complete secrecy between January 1660 and May 1669. Sometimes priggish, it is guileless in self-revelation.

**Perceval, Spencer** (1762–1812). Prime minister. Perceval was the seventh son of John, earl of Egmont. At Trinity College, Cambridge, he became associated with the evangelical group led by Isaac Milner. Having to make his own way in the world, he trained for the bar and practised on the midland circuit. His appointment as a commissioner of bankrupts in 1790 enabled him to marry Jane, daughter of Sir Thomas Wilson, MP for Sussex. He came to notice as a junior counsel for the crown in the trials of the radicals Tom *Paine and *Horne Tooke but he declined *Pitt's offer of the chief secretaryship in Ireland in 1795 because the salary would not support his increasing family. His connections from the midland bar helped to secure him election as MP for Northampton, where he was deputy recorder, in 1796.

*Wilberforce thought him the most generous of evangelical Christians: he gave away all that he could spare to the poor, disapproved strongly of gambling and hunting (though he was a steward of Northamptonshire races), and would have made adultery a criminal offence. He refused to transact business on Sundays, held regular family prayers, and was a student of biblical prophecy. He considered the primacy of the Church of England as essential to the security of the state and he was a most determined opponent of *catholic emancipation.

Perceval's forensic skills made him an effective parliamentary speaker and he rose quickly up the political ladder, becoming solicitor-general under *Addington in 1801 and attorney-general in 1802. He agreed to stay on under *Pitt in 1804 only on condition that there should be no concessions to the catholics. In *Portland's ministry of 1807–9 he became chancellor of the Exchequer and was given the chancellorship of the duchy of Lancaster as well, to increase his income. He reluctantly accepted the leadership of the House of Commons as a compromise candidate and, after the duel between Castlereagh and Canning brought about Portland's resignation, he was appointed prime minister in October 1809, with the king's enthusiastic approval.

Perceval was by no means an ineffective prime minister. He survived the crises of the inquiry into the *Walcheren expedition and the Burdett riots in London in 1810 and doggedly supported the expedition to the Peninsula which was to play a major part in the eventual defeat of Napoleon. He modelled his financial policies on Pitt's and at least kept the war effort going. On George III's final relapse into insanity in 1810 he was confirmed in office by the prince regent but his career ended on 11 May 1812 when he was assassinated in the lobby of the House of Commons by an aggrieved and deranged Russia merchant named John Bellingham, who mistook him for Castlereagh.

**Percy, Henry** (1364–1403), known as 'Hotspur'. Eldest son of the earl of *Northumberland, Percy was appointed sole warden of the east march in 1385; Scottish borderers were soon calling him 'Haatspore'. In early August 1388, he was captured at *Otterburn while pursuing a Scottish army, a battle immortalized in verse as 'Chevy Chase'. Soon ransomed, he was warden of the west march for five years from 1390, and from 1396 succeeded his father in the eastern wardenship, continuing there after Henry IV's usurpation, which he had assisted. Father and son defeated a Scottish invasion at *Homildon Hill in 1402; the king's order against the ransom of their prisoners was one reason for their rebellion. Percy was making for Wales to join Owain *Glyndŵr when the king intercepted him near *Shrewsbury; he was killed in the battle.

**Percy, Thomas** (1729–1812). Percy was the son of a grocer from Bridgnorth in Shropshire and educated at Christ Church, Oxford. He took orders, from 1757 to 1782 held the living at Easton Maudit in Northamptonshire, and for the rest of his life was bishop of Dromore in Co. Down. A scholar and antiquarian, he began early in life collecting ancient ballads, having rescued from a friend in Shifnal an old manuscript folio of verse which the maids were using to light the fire. The *Reliques of Ancient English Poetry* came

out in 1765 and was a leap forward in the preservation and understanding of medieval ballads.

**'perpetual peace', treaty of,** 1502. James IV of Scotland gave considerable assistance to Perkin *Warbeck, the Yorkist pretender against Henry VII in the 1490s. But in a change of policy after Warbeck's death he negotiated in 1502 a treaty of perpetual peace with England, guaranteed by the papacy and sealed in 1503 by James's marriage to Henry's eldest daughter *Margaret— *Dunbar's 'Marriage of the Thistle and the Rose'. The treaty itself lasted no longer than most perpetual treaties. By 1513 the two countries were at war and James was slain at *Flodden.

**Perth, treaty of,** 1266. The failure of Haakon IV's great expedition at *Largs in October 1263 led to a vigorous Scottish counter-attack, which subdued the Inner Hebrides. On 2 July 1266 Magnus IV of Norway, Haakon's successor, signed the treaty of Perth with Alexander III of Scotland. In return for four payments of 4,000 marks and a tribute of 100 marks in perpetuity, the Norwegians surrendered sovereignty over all the Western Islands and the *Isle of Man. They retained possession of *Orkney and Shetland.

**Peterborough, Charles Mordaunt, 3rd earl of** (1658–1735). Politician, soldier, and diplomatist. Known until 1697 by his earlier title of earl of Monmouth, Peterborough's cleverness ran to dishonesty and to any ministry was a liability. An opponent of James II, he mixed with Whig radicals and was an early associate of William of Orange. In 1689 he was given the senior Treasury post of 1st commissioner, for which he was totally unsuited, and resigned a year later. In 1696, when he accused *Shrewsbury and *Marlborough of involvement in the Fenwick conspiracy, he was sent to the Tower. In their propaganda the Tories claimed him as their hero after the expeditionary force he commanded captured Barcelona and Valencia in 1705, but his unreliability cost him any further advancement.

**Peterborough, diocese of** The see, now comprising Northamptonshire and parts of Cambridgeshire and Leicestershire,

p

was founded by Henry VIII in 1541 out of the *Lincoln diocese. The cathedral was built between 1118 and 1237 as the Benedictine abbey church. *Catherine of Aragon was buried there.

**Peterloo** The massacre which was derisively dubbed 'Peterloo' took place in St Peter's Fields (Manchester) on 16 August 1819. A radical reform meeting of 60,000–100,000 people was violently broken up by the local yeomanry who were ordered by the magistrates to arrest the speaker, Henry *Hunt. Eleven people were killed and over 400 wounded. The government promptly congratulated the magistrates and rushed through the *Six Acts. It was condemned at mass meetings throughout the country and was commemorated for many years afterwards.

**Peter's Pence** or Rome-scot began in Saxon times as an annual tribute of 1 penny from each household to the papacy. After the Conquest, it became a total payment of about £200 p.a., collected by the bishops. Monarchs could put pressure on the papacy by withholding payment and by Henry VIII's statute of 1533 (25 Hen. VIII c. 21) it was abolished altogether.

**petition of right,** 1628. Charles I's levy of a *forced loan in 1626–7 and his imprisonment of non-contributors led the Commons in 1628 to frame a petition outlawing non-parliamentary taxes and arbitrary imprisonment. Charles gave an ambiguous reply, to which the Commons responded by withholding their offer of a much-needed money grant. The king therefore authorized a second, conventional, reply which turned the petition into law. When it was printed, Charles included only his first response, but in the event he scrupulously adhered to the letter of the petition.

**Petroc, St** (6th cent.). Particularly associated with Cornwall, Petroc allegedly renounced royal responsibilities in Wales for a religious life. With his followers, he went to Cornwall where he founded monasteries at Padstow and Little Petherick. Later accounts of his life include stories of travels and numerous miracles, portraying him as a typical Celtic saint, alternating between community

life and solitude. He died at Treravel and was buried at Padstow.

**Petty, Sir William** (1623–87). Born in Romsey (Hants), his education took him to the Jesuit College, Caen, and later to Leiden, Utrecht, Amsterdam, Oxford, and London, where his studies focused upon medicine. With doctorates in both physics and medicine, he became professor of medicine, then anatomy, at Oxford University (1648), taking a chair in music in 1651 at Gresham College, London, and at the same time acting as medical officer to the English army in Ireland. His best-known and most influential publications were *Political Arithmetic* (1678) and *Treatise of Taxes and Contributions* (1662), two texts in economics.

**petty sessions** These were the regular courts held by the *justices of the peace to try minor criminal offences summarily—i.e. without a jury. These petty sessions (from French *petit* or lesser) were first so called in the first half of the 19th cent. They dealt with most criminal offences and, as the magistrates' courts, they continue to do so.

**Pevensey, battle of,** 491. The *Anglo-Saxon Chronicle*, in remarkable and suspicious detail, records a Saxon attack in 491 led by *Ælle and his son Cissa on Britons entrenched in the old Roman fort of Anderida or Andredes-cester, near Pevensey. The place was stormed and 'there was not even one Briton left there'.

**Pevsner, Sir Nikolaus Bernhard Leon** (1902–83). A German-born art historian, Pevsner came to Britain in 1934 as a refugee from Nazism. He wrote widely on art and architecture, was a founder member of the William Morris and Victorian societies, and Slade professor of fine art at Oxford and Cambridge, as well as professor of the history of art at Birkbeck College, London. Of his many publications, including the Pelican *History of Art* (begun 1953), the best known is *The Buildings of England*, which he began in 1949 and worked on for 21 years.

**Philip II of Spain** (1527–98), consort of Mary Tudor. Philip's marriage to Mary in July 1554 was part of Spain's long struggle against the French. The son of the Emperor Charles V, he was regent of Spain between

1542 and 1548 and king from 1556 until his death. Although he was not crowned, Philip took the style of king of England. Mary was overjoyed with her young husband and bitterly disappointed when the marriage produced no heir. From Philip's point of view the marriage served its purpose by drawing England into the conflict with France.

After Mary's death in 1558, Philip offered himself as a husband to Elizabeth. Though she refused, England needed Spain as a counterbalance to France. There was a sharp anti-Spanish turn in policy in 1569 which set the pattern for the rest of Elizabeth's reign. Philip was involved in plots against her—*Ridolfi and *Babington—and formal invasion plans—the great Armada in 1588, and further scares in 1595, 1596, and 1597. Elizabeth, for her part, sent an army into the Spanish Netherlands in 1585.

**Philiphaugh, battle of,** 1645. *Montrose's brilliant Scottish campaign, which had begun in August 1644, received its first check at Philiphaugh, near Selkirk, when he left the Highlands. Weakened by desertions, his troops were surprised on 13 September 1645 and outnumbered by *Leslie. Though most of the cavalry escaped, the survivors of the Irish infantry surrendered, only to be massacred in cold blood.

**Philippa of Hainault** (*c.*1314–69), queen of Edward III. Edward married Philippa in 1328. Her main achievement was to provide him with at least twelve children, of whom nine survived infancy. She spent more time in the company of her husband than did most queens, even on occasion accompanying him in France. She is probably best known for her intervention in 1347, when she is said to have pleaded with Edward not to execute the six 'Burghers of Calais' when they surrendered the keys of the town to him.

**philosophical radicals** is a loose term for the group of reformers in the early 19th cent. who based their approach to government and society largely on the *utilitarian theories of Jeremy *Bentham, though they were also influenced by *Malthus, *Ricardo, and Hartley. The leading proponents were James and John Stuart *Mill, George Grote, and John *Roebuck, supported by the *Morning Chronicle*, *Westminster Review*, and *London Review*.

Their efforts to construct a radical party in Parliament after 1832 did not succeed: 'they did very little to promote any opinions,' wrote J. S. Mill, 'they had little enterprise, little activity.' But the general influence of utilitarian ideas permeated politics and, particularly in the period 1820 to 1850, produced an 'age of reform'.

**Phoenix Park murders** Late in the afternoon of 6 May 1882 Lord Frederick *Cavendish, newly appointed chief secretary for Ireland, and Thomas Burke, his under-secretary, were walking in Phoenix Park (Dublin) when four men leapt from a cab and stabbed them to death. Soon afterwards newspaper offices in Dublin received black-edged cards, claiming the outrage for a nationalist group called the 'Irish Invincibles'. They were never caught.

**Picton, Sir Thomas** (1758–1815). Soldier. Born in Pembrokeshire, he joined the army at 13, but was put on half-pay at the peace in 1783. In 1794 he volunteered for service in the West Indies and fought with distinction, being appointed governor of Trinidad, captured from the Spaniards, in 1797. In 1810 he was in Portugal with *Wellington and fought gallantly in the *Peninsular campaign. In 1813 he was knighted and promoted lieutenant-general. As soon as Napoleon left Elba, Picton rejoined Wellington, was wounded at Quatre-Bras, but took his post at Waterloo two days later. He was killed by a bullet at the head of his men, roaring them on.

**Picquigny, treaty of,** 1475. Edward IV's campaign in France in 1475 was something of a non-event. Greatly dissatisfied with the help he had received from his Burgundian allies, the king was very willing to make terms at Picquigny near Amiens, on 29 August. There was to be a seven-year truce; free commercial exchange; provision for arbitration of disputes; a marriage between the dauphin and *Elizabeth of York; and a regular payment by Louis XI of France to Edward. In England the payments were seen as tribute, in France as a bribe or retainer. The *rapprochement* did not last and the marriage never took place.

**Pics** An indigenous tribe or group of tribes in Scotland during the Roman and post-Roman periods. They are first mentioned in

AD 297 by Eumenius who calls them 'half-naked enemies' of the Britons. 'Picts' is probably a Latinized word meaning 'painted people'.

It is difficult to determine whether they had a substantive ethnic identity or if 'Picti' was merely a convenient label given by classical writers to all tribal peoples in Scotland in the later Roman period. A Roman poet observes in AD 310 that the Emperor Constantius chose not to acquire the woods and marshes of the 'Caledones and other Picti'.

An important historical attestation of the Picts is provided by Ammianus Marcellinus, who records attacks on Roman Britain by Picts, Scots, Irish, and Saxons culminating in the 'Picts' War' of AD 367–8. *Gildas refers to 'marauding Picts', savages with more hair on their faces than clothes on their bodies, who came by sea from the north and raided post-Roman Britain. According to legend, the last king of the Picts was killed at the instigation of *Kenneth MacAlpin c. AD 842.

**piepowder courts** were the courts attached to fairs and markets and were probably so called because of the dusty feet (*pieds poudrés*) of the travelling merchants. The judges in these courts were merchants. Piepowder courts were popular with the mercantile community, being quick, effective, and not unduly hampered by procedural technicalities. However, by the end of the 16th cent. most had fallen into disuse.

***Piers Plowman*** Late 14th-cent. poem by William *Langland. Cast in the familiar medieval form of a quest, the poem uses a series of dream-visions to trace the tortuous progress of 'Will' from intellectual wrangling to spiritual understanding as he searches for Truth and then for Do-Wel, Do-Bet, and Do-Best.

**pigeon-fancying** Pigeon clubs are usually confined to small areas to ensure equality of weather conditions, but the birds may fly up to 500 miles. The pigeons, which used to be transported by rail, are now taken to the starting-point in specially constructed road vehicles. The performance of each pigeon is very carefully monitored, and breeding and feeding rigorously controlled. They are descended from the rock doves (*columba livia*) and have been used since ancient times for carrying messages.

**Pilgrimage of Grace,** 1536–7. The Pilgrimage was a widespread northern rising against Henry VIII's religious policies. It seems to have been triggered by the *dissolution of the smaller monasteries, began at Louth in Lincolnshire, spreading to Yorkshire and then to Cumberland and Westmorland. The rebels, who took the badge of the five wounds of Christ and called themselves pilgrims, were led by Robert *Aske. Henry's response was to temporize, to offer pardons, and to attempt to split gentry from commoners. By the spring of 1537 most of the rebels had dispersed and he was able to take a bloody revenge on the pilgrims. Aske was executed at York and Lord Darcy, who had surrendered Pontefract castle to the rebels, was beheaded on Tower Hill. The weakness of royal control which the rising had demonstrated led to the establishment of the *Council of the North in October 1537 to reassert authority.

**pilgrimages,** visits to shrines or holy places, were undertaken for a variety of reasons—from piety, as thanksgiving or penance, in hope of a cure, or as a form of holiday. The great and mighty could visit Rome, Jerusalem, or Compostela. Other people visited the great national shrines—*Becket's at Canterbury, *Cuthbert's at Durham, or the Virgin Mary's at *Walsingham. But there were many other shrines with regional or local fame—St *Hugh at Lincoln, St *Guthlac at Crowland, St Joseph at Glastonbury, St *Ninian at Whithorn, St *Chad at Lichfield, St *David in west Wales. The possession of sacred relics was of great spiritual and financial value to religious communities, and to their towns: Walsingham was said by Erasmus to have 'scarcely any means of support except for the tourist trade'. Though protestant reformers disapproved strongly of pilgrimages, the concept of life as a pilgrimage survived in *Bunyan's *Pilgrim's Progress*.

**Pilgrim Fathers** The leaders of the Plymouth settlement on Cape Cod, made under a Virginia Company grant in late 1620. Religious dissidents from Scrooby (Notts.) had exiled themselves to Leiden in Holland, but decided their Englishness could better be preserved in English America, and sailed in the *Mayflower*. After a terrible early mortality and with Indian help, the colonists survived and increased.

***Pilgrim's Progress*** Religious allegory by John *Bunyan, published in two parts (1678, 1684). Widely regarded as a classic in puritan literature, it renders Bunyan's own spiritual progress (recounted in *Grace Abounding*) into a more objective universalized myth, embodied by the solitary pilgrim Christian's search for the Celestial City. Allegorical figures (Giant Despair, Hopeful), satirical portraits of hypocrites or backsliders (Mr Worldly-Wiseman), and realism enliven an episodic series of adventures.

**pillory** Social corrective combining public humiliation and discomfort, occasionally death. The offender's hands and neck were immobilized within a hinged pair of planks attached to an upright post on a platform, erected in open spaces, usually for an hour on market-day. The spectators' mood could vary. *Defoe found them kind (1703), but taunts and pelting with eggs, vegetables, and vermin were more common; if real anger prevailed, stones could prove fatal. The practice was abolished in 1837.

**Pinkie Cleugh, battle of,** 1547. One of the first decisions taken by *Somerset when he became protector for Edward VI in 1547 was to settle the long-running war against Scotland with a decisive blow. The Scots had rejected proposals for a marriage between the young king of England and the infant Mary, queen of Scots, and had formed an alliance with France. The Scottish army, under *Huntly and *Arran, had a numerical advantage on 10 September when the two sides met at Pinkie Cleugh, east of Edinburgh, but superior cavalry and the help of warships gave Somerset victory.

**pipe rolls** The great rolls of the *Exchequer are preserved in the Public Record Office from the reign of Henry II to that of William IV. Their nickname is taken from their tubular appearance. Since they include the accounts of the sheriffs and deal with crown revenue and crown lands, they are a very valuable historical source.

**Pipton-on-Wye, treaty of,** 1265. An agreement between *Llywelyn ap Gruffydd and Simon de *Montfort, the baronial leader who had Henry III in custody. On 19 June Llywelyn capitalized on civil war in England to secure advantageous terms from the barons, consolidating his control of the central marches of Wales. Although Simon was soon dead at *Evesham (4 August), Henry III concluded a similar peace with Llywelyn at *Montgomery (25 September 1267), confirming his title and status of prince, and his right to the allegiance of Welsh nobles. Llywelyn's power was at its height.

**Pitt, William, 1st earl of Chatham** (1708–78), known as Pitt the Elder. In 1735 Pitt launched his belligerent political career by insulting King George II over his son's marriage and was dismissed from the army commission he had held since 1731. Thereafter Pitt quickly established himself as a leading speaker against *Walpole's ministry and its policy of support for *Hanover.

Walpole's fall did not immediately bring Pitt into the government, but after turning his oratorical fire on *Carteret, he was given the post of paymaster-general in 1746. The king's enmity ensured, however, that he remained outside the cabinet. Henry *Pelham, the prime minister, kept Pitt quiet, but upon Pelham's death in 1754, Pitt entered the great struggle between leading politicians. When the *Seven Years War began with the loss of *Minorca and defeats in America, Pitt was seen by many as the country's only hope. With great reluctance George II invited him to form a government with the duke of *Devonshire nominally at its head in December 1756. It soon became apparent that no government would have the combination of skill and numerical strength in Parliament necessary to prosecute the war unless Pitt and Newcastle acted together; thus, in July 1757, Newcastle was appointed 1st lord with Pitt as secretary of state for the southern department.

Pitt unquestionably acted as leader of the war effort. He inspired the military and the country at large and won the confidence of Britain's major ally, Prussia. Pitt's goal was colonial expansion, and by 1761 Britain had driven the French from Canada, India, and most of the Caribbean.

Pitt had won George II's respect, though never his affection, by the time of the king's death in 1760, but when George III's reign commenced his position was less secure.

The new king, encouraged by his tutor *Bute, wanted peace. Pitt disagreed, and after another year of military success, he resigned over the cabinet's refusal to permit attacks upon the Spanish in October 1761. War with Spain soon followed. In the Commons, Pitt condemned the peace settlement but Fox's managerial skills ensured that the treaty was overwhelmingly approved.

The 1760s was a decade of political instability due in no small measure to Pitt himself. He refused to ally with any political faction, uniformly support the king, or retire. His strongest feelings were reserved for America and he bitterly attacked his brother-in-law Prime Minister *Grenville for passing the *Stamp Act. However, he would not agree with the *Rockingham faction either, who repealed the Act.

The king persuaded Pitt to form a ministry in July 1766. Pitt (hitherto popularly known as 'the Great Commoner') took the title of earl of Chatham and the office of lord privy seal (with the duke of Grafton as 1st lord). Within months he had plunged into a state of virtual insanity. Chatham officially resigned in October 1768, but did not regain his senses until late 1769. The final decade of Chatham's life was divided between illness and dramatic appearances in the Lords to attack *North's American policies. He was against American independence, but believed, as late as 1778, that an imperial settlement could be reached. In April 1778 Chatham was escorted to the Lords by his favourite son, William *Pitt the Younger, but during debate collapsed and died on 11 May.

For a man with so many problems, in office for such brief periods, to be regarded as one of the country's greatest premiers testifies to the scale of his achievements.

**Pitt, William** (1759–1806), known as Pitt the Younger. Prime minister. The second son of William *Pitt, earl of Chatham, was educated privately and at Cambridge. From an early age, his father supervised his upbringing, paying particular attention to skill in public speaking. He entered Parliament in 1781 and soon made his mark in the Commons. He was a critic of *North, whom he blamed for the loss of America, and advocated both economical and parliamentary reform. He was keenly interested in financial and commercial questions and knew the

writings of Adam *Smith and Richard Price. When North fell in 1782, Pitt refused a merely subordinate station in *Rockingham's ministry. After Rockingham's death, Pitt became chancellor of the Exchequer under *Shelburne. He deeply resented *Fox's alliance with North, yet was wise enough to refuse George III's invitation to head a ministry after the fall of Shelburne, preferring to bide his time until a more propitious moment. The crisis over Fox's *India Bill gave George III and Pitt their chance. Pitt agreed to become prime minister provided that a public demonstration of George III's hostility towards the Fox–North ministry indicated where the king's confidence lay.

When Pitt took office in December 1783 few thought his ministry would survive. He faced an opposition majority in the Commons. But several factors worked in his favour. He had the unflinching confidence of the king; the Fox–North coalition was unpopular; and he was able to win over opinion in the Commons. At the general election of 1784 Pitt won a decisive victory.

During his peacetime administration he achieved much in the fields of fiscal, economical, and commercial reform. He cut customs duties and stimulated trade, and set up a sinking fund in the hope of paying off the national debt. Having established his mastery in public finance he negotiated a commercial treaty with France and ended Britain's diplomatic isolation by entering into alliance with Prussia and Holland in the aftermath of the Dutch crisis of 1787. But there were disappointments. Pitt's proposals for a moderate reform of Parliament were defeated; he was compelled to drop his scheme for free trade with Ireland; plans to improve the defences of Portsmouth and Plymouth had to be abandoned; the abolition of the slave trade had to remain an open question within the government. His position was threatened in 1788 when the illness of George III presaged a change of government. When the king recovered in 1789 Pitt seemed invincible. He knew when to yield to political pressure, as over the impeachment of *Hastings, and was adept at turning the ideas of others into practicable policies.

When the French Revolution broke out in 1789 Pitt was sympathetic to reform in France but determined to stay out of European complications if possible. As late as February 1792 he affirmed his expectations for fifteen years of peace in Europe. But with the collapse of the French monarchy and the aggressive policies pursued by the French republic his hopes were shattered. The outbreak of war in 1793 was a disaster for Pitt. His hopes for further reform were indefinitely postponed and he became transformed into 'the pilot who weathered the storm'. The war was long, arduous, and inconclusive. Though loyalism was the dominant feeling in Britain there was much economic distress and rebellion broke out in Ireland in 1798. Pitt had tried to appease Ireland by granting civil rights to Irish catholics and enfranchising the catholic freeholders in the Irish counties. Though the rebellion was crushed, Pitt was convinced that the credibility of the Dublin Parliament was destroyed. He carried an Act of Union with Ireland, hoping to follow it with catholic emancipation. He was thwarted on the catholic question, partly by the opposition of George III. He resigned in 1801, giving general support to *Addington's ministry from the back benches and approving the peace of *Amiens when it was signed in 1802.

During his years out of office he was criticized for failing to build up his party. When Addington left office in 1804, Pitt formed another administration. Despite their differences Pitt wanted to bring Fox into a coalition as foreign secretary. George III vetoed this appointment. As a result, the Foxites and Grenvillites refused to serve. Pitt's health was now in decline and the strains of office wore him out. He built up a coalition to defeat Napoleon, but hopes of a decisive end to the war were dashed by Napoleon's victory at Austerlitz in 1805. On 23 January 1806 Pitt died. He left behind him a band of younger men whose talents he had recognized and fostered and a legend which shaped popular Toryism in the early 19th cent.

**Place, Francis** (1771–1854). The 'radical tailor of Charing Cross' was associated with virtually every reform movement from the *corresponding societies to *chartism. He rose from being a journeyman breeches-maker into a prosperous shopkeeper and employer, from Jacobinism to respectability, and became a disciple of *Bentham and *Mill. His skill as a backroom organizer was demonstrated in the London Corresponding Society, the Westminster elections, the repeal of the Combination Acts, the 1832 Reform Bill agitation, and chartism.

**plague** Bubonic plague is a disease of rats, spread to humans by fleas deserting dead or dying rat hosts. Occurring primarily in the summer, it causes fever, vomiting, and inflammation of the lymphatic glands to give the characteristic swellings or buboes. Bubonic plague kills between 60 and 80 per cent of those infected. Still more lethal is *pneumonic* plague, which occurs when the bacillus enters the lungs and is then transmitted by droplet infection.

Plague arrived in England in 1348 as part of a European pandemic that lasted until the early 18th cent. No subsequent plague epidemic had the same ferocious impact as the Black Death. Recent estimates put the death toll at something like 47 per cent of the entire population. After the late 14th cent. plague tended to occur on a regional rather than a national level, although 1413, 1434, 1439, and 1464 were country-wide.

The overall impact of plague on the national death rate, however, diminished progressively. From the late 15th cent., plague increasingly became a disease of towns and cities, where man and rat lived in closest proximity, or hit villages located on lines of communication. Our historical perceptions are coloured by the experiences of those minority of communities which were devastated by plague. Norwich lost a third of its population in 1579. London accounted for one-third of *all* plague deaths that occurred in England between 1570 and 1670. The capital lost at least 25 per cent of its inhabitants in 1563, and a further 20 per cent or so perished in 1603 and again in 1625. The last 'Great Plague' in London in 1665, recorded in *Pepys, killed about 56,000 people. The disease disappeared from Britain after the mid-17th cent. Scotland's last serious outbreak was 1645–9, England's was 1665–6.

## Plaid Cymru (Welsh Nationalist Party).

Plaid Cymru was established in 1925 mainly to campaign for the protection of Welsh language and culture. After the Second World War the organization took on the functions of a political party to tread the parliamentary road to Welsh independence. During the 1960s its policies became more economically motivated, aimed at reducing unemployment, halting the migration of Welsh youth, and replacing declining traditional industries. It had little success until 1966 when it won a by-election at Carmarthen. In the election of February 1974 two seats were gained—Caernarfon and Merioneth. Plaid Cymru exploited the minority position of the Labour government (1974–9) to force discussion on constitutional change. However, the March 1979 devolution referendum was a blow to the party. From a turn-out of 58.3 per cent, only 11.8 per cent voted for a Welsh assembly.

The breakthrough which Plaid Cymru had been looking for came with the referendum of September 1997 which voted, by a narrow majority, to establish a National Assembly. At the subsequent election in 1999, the party won 17 of the 60 seats in the Assembly, making substantial inroads into the Labour vote, taking seats at Islwyn, Llanelli, and Rhondda. After disappointing results in 2003, Plaid Cymru obtained 15 seats in 2007 and joined Labour in a power-sharing executive.

**Plantagenets** The Plantagenet dynasty took its name from the *Planta Genesta*, or broom, traditionally an emblem of the counts of Anjou. Members of this dynasty ruled England from 1154 to 1399. However, in conventional historical usage, Henry II (son of Count *Geoffrey of Anjou) and his sons Richard I and John are normally termed the Angevin kings, and their successors, up to Richard II, the Plantagenets.

**Plassey, battle of,** 1757. Aware that the French-supported nawab Siraj-ud-Daula was intent on further rebellion against East India Company rule, Robert *Clive led a small force to confront him. He found Siraj on 23 June at Plassey at the head of 50,000 men. However, a rainstorm soaked Siraj's artillery powder and Clive, who had kept his powder dry, opened a devastating fire when the nawab's cavalry tried to charge. Siraj fled, leaving Clive in control of Bengal.

**Playfair, William Henry** (1790–1857). Scottish architect who perhaps studied under Wyatt and Smirke in London. He returned to Scotland in 1816 to complete Robert *Adam's building for Edinburgh University, and thereafter made his mark on the Scottish capital with his public build-

ings, notably those on the Mound—the Doric Royal Institution (now the Royal Scottish Academy, 1822–6, enlarged 1832–5), and the Ionic National Gallery of Scotland (1850–7), overlooked by the Gothic towers of Free Church College (now New College, 1846–50). On Calton Hill he designed the City Observatory (1818), and the National Monument, in collaboration with C. R. Cockerell (1824–9, unfinished).

**pleas of the crown** The notion of the pleas of the crown can be traced back to Anglo-Saxon times to describe those wrongs which were the particular concern of the king and for which the king was entitled to take a fine (wite). Later under the Norman kings and their successors the term came to mean those pleas or cases which concerned the king as distinct from pleas between subjects—common pleas.

**Plimsoll, Samuel** (1824–98). Radical MP. Born in Bristol, a congregationalist, Plimsoll was successively a solicitor's clerk, manager of a brewery, and honorary secretary for the *Great Exhibition of 1851. In 1853 he became a coal merchant in London, gaining an extensive knowledge of coastal shipping. Elected to Parliament for Derby in 1868, he proposed a compulsory load line to prevent overloading and obtained a royal commission in 1873. His anger at the greed of shipowners who resisted his plans led to his temporary exclusion from the Commons in 1875, but his persistence was rewarded with the Merchant Shipping Act of 1876 and the load line soon came to bear his name.

**Plunket, St Oliver** (1629–81). Catholic archbishop of Armagh and primate of Ireland (1670–81). Born in Meath, educated in Rome, Plunket was successively professor of theology there (1657–69) and archbishop of Armagh after consecration in Ghent. Threatened with expulsion after the English Test Act he went into hiding (1674), but was arrested in Dublin (1678) and falsely accused of involvement in the *Popish plot. Tried in London on a trumped-up charge, Plunket was convicted of treason and was hanged, drawn, and quartered at Tyburn. His relics are in Downside abbey (Som.). He was canonized in 1975.

**pluralism** is the holding of more than one ecclesiastical benefice with cure of souls simultaneously. Although consistently denounced by the church, there was never a time when pluralism did not take place. There were many reasons for its continuance. The poverty of many benefices often made the holding of more than one a necessity. Shortage of clergy—increasingly a problem in the 20th cent.—was another reason.

**Plymouth** owes its importance to the magnificent estuary into which drain the rivers Plym and Tamar. The original settlement was at Sutton, the name Plymouth being attached to the harbour. By *Leland's time, in the 1530s, it was 'very large' with 'a goodly rode for great shippes'. During the civil wars, Plymouth was of great strategic importance as a parliamentary bastion in a predominantly royalist region and resisted repeated attempts to subdue it. After the Restoration it increased with the growth of the navy. As a vital naval base, within easy bombing range from occupied France, Plymouth suffered heavily in the Second World War, and the subsequent replanning did not command total enthusiasm.

**Plymouth brethren,** Christian brethren, or Darbyites, began in Dublin in the mid-1820s when groups of young men, several from *Trinity College, met for communion regardless of denomination. With no intention of starting a separate movement, they did exactly that, thanks to J. N. Darby (1800–82), a non-practising barrister who had recently resigned his Anglican orders. Despite the division between open and exclusive sections, they remained similar in beliefs and structure: a world-denying pietism; the Bible as their supreme rule; an interest in prophecy and the Second Coming; believers' baptism; weekly breaking of bread; no set liturgy; no ordained ministry, though many full-time evangelists; a congregational polity with no co-ordinating organization. Popularly stamped with the exclusive image, their ideal atmosphere is better seen as one of spiritual and intellectual liberty set in a context of brotherly love.

**poaching** The punishment for poaching in the king's forest in Norman times was severe: Richard I's assize of 1198 threatened deer-stealers with blinding and castration. Though the royal forests were exceptional, and savage punishments were relaxed, poaching, in its various forms, continued as a major irritant until rural society gave way to town life in the later 19th cent. Although in popular mythology the poacher is a solitary operator, organized gangs made an early appearance. During the civil wars of the 17th cent., the relaxation of law and order gave poachers much freedom and after the Restoration, in 1671, there was an effort to tighten up. Game was reserved for freeholders of property worth £100 p.a., copyholders worth £150, and the son and heir of esquires and above: these persons could hunt over other people's land and appoint gamekeepers with right to search. At the same time, improvements in guns prompted landowners to breed game in greater numbers. Poaching was then no longer a question of pinching rabbits from a common but organized attacks upon private property. The poaching war of the later 18th and early 19th cents. saw bloody affrays, with the landowners defending their game with spring-guns and man-traps. *Blackwood's Magazine* wrote in 1827 that there was 'a war raging against the aristocracy', and poaching was an important element in the *Swing riots of 1830. The Game Reform Act of 1831 repealed 27 previous acts, declared a close season for hunting, allowed tenants to hunt and shoot on their own land, and introduced a system of certificates which gave permission to kill game, subject to the law of trespass. But any amelioration in relations was temporary, for further improvements in guns led to vast *battues*, in which 1,000 birds might be shot in one day. Breeding enough birds became a large industry and the crops consumed by the birds caused bitter resentment. Confrontation between gamekeepers and poachers continued until after the Great War when poaching became incidental rather than endemic.

**pocket boroughs** or nomination boroughs were constituencies where the patron could usually control the return of the members of Parliament. They were often, though not invariably, burgage or corporation boroughs with small electorates. The number of seats under patronage has been put at over 250 in 1761 out of a total of 558.

**poet laureate** James I awarded Ben *Jonson a pension in 1616 and he and Sir William

Davenant (1637) were widely recognized as laureates. But the first court appointment of a laureate was in 1668 when Charles II chose *Dryden. Among the more distinguished laureates were *Wordsworth (1843) and *Tennyson (1850): less distinguished were Whitehead (1757), Pye (1790), and Alfred Austin (1896).

**Poitiers, battle of,** 1356. *Edward, the Black Prince's blooding had been at Crécy in 1346. In August 1356 he was before Bourges but threatened by a much larger army under John II of France. The English attempted to retreat but found their way blocked at Poitiers. The Black Prince offered terms, but on 19 September the French attacked. Archers, lying in ditches and behind hedges, broke up the first assaults, and in their last attack the French were taken in the flank. The large number of prisoners included the French king.

**Pole, Margaret de la** See SALISBURY, COUNTESS OF.

**Pole, Michael de la** (c.1330–89). Son of William de la Pole (d. 1366), merchant of Hull and a major financier of Edward III's campaigns in France, Michael served the crown in various military and diplomatic capacities before becoming chancellor of England in 1383. He enjoyed the favour of Richard II, being created earl of Suffolk in 1385. When Richard lost control of the government in 1386, Pole was impeached for supposed malpractices concerning the French war which was going badly. Stripped of all his lands and honours he died in exile in Paris in September 1389.

**Pole, Reginald** (1500–58). Cardinal and archbishop of Canterbury. Pole was a younger son of Margaret, countess of *Salisbury, daughter of George, duke of *Clarence: he was therefore of the blood royal. Intended from the beginning for the church, he spent 1521–7 on the continent in study. On his return he was made dean of Windsor, but, increasingly opposed to the king's divorce policy, he went abroad again in 1532. Asked for his opinion by the king, Pole produced in 1536 a strong counter-statement, placing his relatives in England in acute danger. His nomination as cardinal increased their peril: his eldest brother was executed, his

nephew died in the Tower, his mother was beheaded in 1541. Pole remained on the continent in constant fear of assassination. On Mary's accession in 1553 he came back as legate in November 1554 and in March 1556 succeeded *Cranmer as archbishop of Canterbury. But the return of England to the faith—the object of Pole's life—was fraught with problems. The burning of protestants caused great outrage; the nobility were most reluctant to return church lands; Mary's husband *Philip found himself at war with the papacy and Pole's legatine authority was revoked. He died on the same day as Mary in November 1558.

**police** For years Britons resisted having a proper police force, because they associated it with repression, especially of the French kind. They also feared it would raise their rates. Their only recourse was the army, backed up by tough sanctions. That could be counter-productive. *Peterloo, for example, and the *Cato Street executions set people against the government. A gentler means of public control was required.

Sir Robert *Peel devised his first police bill while chief secretary for Ireland, leading to the creation of the Irish Constabulary in 1822. In 1829 he persuaded Parliament to accept something similar for London, to be called the Metropolitan Police. All policemen were put in a distinctive uniform, so that they could not be taken for 'spies'. They were unarmed, except for short batons. Of its first 2,800 recruits, 2,238 were dismissed from the force, sometimes for simply taking a drink or a nap. But it worked. Other areas of the country called the 'Met' in to help. After 1833 they were permitted to set up their own forces, on the London model. Those which did not were finally made to by Acts of 1856 (England and Wales) and 1857 (Scotland).

A later development was the growth of a plain clothes detective branch. That began in London in 1842, but consisted initially of only eight men. In 1877 a scandal implicated three of the detective branch's four inspectors in a turf fraud they were supposed to be investigating. That provoked a shake-up, out of which the present-day Criminal Investigation Department was born in 1878.

The police's most controversial role has always been its public order one. Its problem was that keeping order in times of civil unrest could be interpreted as acting for the state against the democracy. Strikes were the most difficult case. In general, the British police have successfully maintained their image of being 'consensual', though periodically accused of 'racism'.

In recent years there has been mounting criticism of both the role and the performance of the police. It is widely acknowledged, particularly within police circles, that too much time is devoted to paper work. At the same time, the vast increase in the ownership of cars has meant that a great amount of resources has to be devoted to monitoring driving. As a result there have been complaints that the police seem disinclined to confront crime or deal with disturbances. The independent report by Sir Ronnie Flanagan, former Chief Constable of Northern Ireland, called attention in 2008 to the need for better use of resources and for improved cooperation with local people. It was welcomed by the Home Secretary.

***Political Register*** The best-known radical newspaper in the early 19th cent. Launched by William *Cobbett in January 1802 as a weekly, supported by William *Windham, it pursued a fiercely right-wing anti-French stance. But Cobbett soon moved to a radical position, condemning the Whigs as mere temporizers and calling constantly for reform of Parliament. In 1816 he brought out a cheap edition—the famous 'Twopenny Trash'—which sold in tens of thousands.

**poll tax** A fixed amount of tax per head, or poll. Poll taxes first came to prominence in the late 14th cent. when they were imposed to pay for the war in France (the *Hundred Years War). The *Peasants' Revolt of 1381 arose from that year's tax of 1 shilling per head. Poll taxes were very occasionally used in the 15th to 17th cents., the last time being 1698. However at the end of the 20th cent., Margaret *Thatcher's Conservative government reintroduced the tax, under the name community charge, to replace domestic rates. As in the 14th cent., evasion and riots ensued; and the tax was, in part, the cause of Mrs Thatcher's downfall.

**polo** is derived from the Tibetan word for a willow stick and originated in the East, probably among the horsemen of central Asia.

British tea-planters and cavalry officers adopted it in India. The first game in Britain was held in London in 1871 and the Hurlingham Club, at Fulham, founded in 1875, established itself as the governing body of the sport.

**poor** 'A decent provision for the poor', declared Samuel *Johnson, 'is the true test of civilization.' But identifying the poor with any precision has proved difficult for those wishing to help them and for historians wishing to study them.

Efforts to identify the poor using systematic measurements were attempted from the later 18th cent. onwards. Sir Frederick Eden attempted in 1797 to document the lives of the poor in terms of expenditure on food, fuel, clothing, and shelter, but his studies were criticized as unsystematic. Similar shortcomings were found in *London Labour and the London Poor* published by Henry Mayhew in 1851. Investigators of the London Statistical Society and the Manchester Statistical Society attempted to be more scientific by initiating studies of intakes per head of various commodities of food and drink, but it was not until 1886 that a survey of the budgets of a large sample of the London poor was undertaken by Charles *Booth.

Booth's calculations rested on assumptions about the level of expenditure needed to maintain a healthy life. Even with disciplined expenditure on necessities only, his survey showed that almost 30 per cent of the population of London lived below 'the poverty line'. Using similar criteria to Booth's, Seebohm *Rowntree undertook a survey of the poor in York in 1900 and identified a similar proportion of the population living in poverty. Medical examinations of the men volunteering for military service in the Boer War and those serving in the two world wars provided evidence of the effects of long-term poverty. Such evidence was used to support the arguments in favour of comprehensive social welfare and of the 'welfare state' established during the 1940s.

**poor laws** During the Middle Ages, canon law required each member of the parish to pay a tax of one-tenth, a tithe, of their income to the church. From this income the rector was required to set aside one-third each year for the relief of the poor. This parochial system was undermined when tithe incomes began to be appropriated for other uses. The situation worsened when tithes became a fixed levy rather than a true tenth of incomes within a parish.

The state intervened to make good the shortcomings in the parochial system with the Acts of 1388 and 1391. These legitimized begging and stipulated that the able-bodied poor should look to their birth parish or the parish where they usually lived for support. Poor relief through the allocation of tithe income, where it existed, and begging elsewhere, continued until the Poor Law of 1536. Those who were fit but unemployed could expect no direct help. However, parish funds, where available, could be used to provide employment for them.

Such piecemeal legislation was replaced by a coherent system for England and Wales by the Poor Law Act of 1601. This Act required each parish to be responsible for its own poor. Justices of the peace had the duty of setting up a framework for the administration of the law and, together with the minister of the parish and those householders designated as members of the parish meeting or vestry, had the task of organizing poor relief. The vestry had the authority to raise the necessary money by collecting a rate.

Care of the poor varied from place to place. Some parishes bought cottages to house the homeless or built a house where the poor might live. In small rural parishes relief, in money and in kind, was sometimes provided for the poor in their own home. Such a system assumed a settled agrarian society with few itinerants seeking help. The Act of Settlement of 1662 obliged parish authorities to give poor relief only to those either long resident or born in the parish. All others seeking assistance had to return to their place of origin.

During the 18th cent. there were changes in response to increasing numbers of poor amongst those who had migrated to work in industrial areas. The earlier system continued, but the law was amended to allow Poor Law authorities to attempt novel solutions to the problem of the increasing numbers of those seeking relief. Some parishes combined to form a union, which built a workhouse and required those who were poor but able to work to live within it. The poor who entered the workhouse had to wear a uniform and were referred to as pau-

pers. At the end of the 18th cent. rural poverty in southern England grew so persistently that the Berkshire magistrates met at *Speenhamland and devised a system of poor relief in cash which supplemented inadequate wages. This system was taken up by other authorities and persisted in some places until the Poor Law Amendment Act of 1834.

By the Act of 1834 relief was given only to those poor who agreed to accept the strict regime of the workhouse, where the conditions provided were funded at a level below that affordable by a person in work. In addition, the Act created a commission to supervise the establishment of unions of parishes in England and Wales. These unions were to be administered by boards of guardians comprising magistrates and parish ministers of the Church of England, ex officio, and representatives of parishes elected by ratepayers.

All the evidence from official reports and popular literature shows that the Act was loathed by the poor. However, although the Act was amended on several occasions to make it more appropriate to meet the needs of large urban areas and to respond to the problems of trade depressions and the special needs of children, the basic system remained in place until 1929 when provision for the poor was transferred to county and county borough councils.

**Pope, Alexander** (1688–1744). English poet. Largely self-educated, the son of a Roman catholic draper, and crippled by a tubercular condition, Pope was always an outsider. He made his reputation with his *Pastorals* (1709), the verse *Essay on Criticism* (1711), and the heroi-comical *Rape of the Lock* (1712, 1714). *Windsor-Forest* (1713), at once a paean to peace and a celebration of British imperialism, led to his vital association with *Swift, *Gay, and the Scriblerus Club, and his later involvement in political satire, particularly at the expense of *Walpole, beginning with *The Dunciad* (1728). While the *Moral Essays* (1731–5) and *An Essay on Man* (1733–4) employed moral and philosophical themes to expose contemporary failings, the more strident criticism of the *Imitations of Horace* prepared the way for the apocalyptic revised *Dunciad* of 1743.

**Popish plot,** 1678. Comprising 43 articles deposed by two skilful fabricators, Titus

*Oates and Israel Tonge, before a London magistrate in September 1678, the 'plot' was a tissue of lies. It purported to reveal a Jesuit conspiracy to assassinate Charles II, assuring the succession to the catholic James, duke of York.

**population** Very few conclusions have been agreed about the population of the British Isles before the Norman Conquest. Large-scale migrations of Angles, Saxons, Jutes, Danes, and Norsemen, and substantial movements between Ireland, Scotland, and Wales, make estimates very hazardous. The population of Roman Britain remains highly conjectural with a disturbing divergence of scholarly opinion between 1 million and 6 million for the later 2nd cent. A figure of 20,000 has been proposed for Wales, though there is no way of checking it. Nor is it easier to offer figures for the subsequent Saxon period, since we cannot be sure to what extent devastation and warfare were offset by new arrivals. The consensus puts the figure for England towards the end of the Saxon period at about 1½ million. The most prudent historians of Ireland and Scotland refuse to suggest or endorse any estimates for those countries.

There is little disagreement that the population of England increased greatly between 1066 and the plague disasters of the mid-14th cent. If the estimates for William I's reign, based on Domesday Book returns, are correct, the population was about 1½ million and had more than doubled by 1300 to about 4 million. This was part of a general European pattern, assisted in England after the Conquest by the absence of major invasions and a lessening of internal conflict. Plague then struck four times between 1349 and 1375 with devastating consequences. It seems that over 40 per cent of the population died. The Black Death also visited Ireland, Wales, and Scotland. Only in Scotland does the mortality seem to have been significantly lower, perhaps because the plague was at its most deadly in crowded towns and ports.

Recovery from the Black Death was slow. The population of England may have been reduced to about 2½ million. Not until the middle of the 15th cent. did the rate of increase pick up. But during Tudor times, the population reached its pre-plague position and by the end of the 16th cent. stood at just over 4 million. The population of Ireland was about 1 million, that of Scotland perhaps a little less. Wales was still very thinly populated with about 350,000 people. At over 200,000 London was already the largest town in western Europe and outstripping all its rivals.

From the 17th cent. the sources for demographic study improve. Thomas *Cromwell ordered the keeping of parish registers from 1538, but many incumbents did not at first do so, and some registers have been destroyed by fire, flood, wars, and mice. The high Tudor growth rate was not sustained throughout the whole 17th cent., when emigration, civil war, and plague dampened the increase. The population of England and Wales rose to about 5.4 million by 1656 and then steadied, or even declined slightly. Scotland was affected by plague in the 1640s, heavy emigration to Ulster, and by severe famine in the 1690s. Its population in 1700 was probably little higher than in 1600: Edinburgh, by far the largest town, had between 30,000 and 40,000 people. Despite heavy warfare, the Irish population may have doubled by 1687 and reached well over 2 million by 1700, with Dublin beginning to grow rapidly. London continued to grow disproportionately, had reached half a million by 1700, and was larger than all the other urban centres together.

There were few indications at the beginning of the 18th cent. that the British Isles were on the threshhold of a population explosion. The causes of the acceleration to come have been extensively debated. The establishment of voluntary hospitals and improved methods of combating smallpox were bound to be slow since they did not operate much outside urban areas. Plague at last disappeared. Agricultural yields were improving and the development of turnpike roads and canals later in the century enabled food to be transported more quickly to areas of shortage. But any explanation must have a European dimension since the increase was a general one. The early view that the population rise was largely due to a falling death rate has been increasingly challenged, partly because the increase accompanied widespread urbanization and 18th-cent. cities were by no means healthy places. More emphasis is now placed upon a significant rise in fertility rates, as a result of people marrying earlier, and because a smaller proportion of the population remained unmarried. The move to towns may have freed young men to marry.

Though the causes of the great acceleration are still far from agreed, the consequences are clear. From the 1740s onwards, the population began to rise, not to fall again as it had so often in the past, but a sustained and incremental growth. From 5.7 million in 1750, the population of England reached 8.6 million by 1800 and 16.5 million by 1850. The Scottish population also grew, particularly in the industrial and trading towns of the central region—from 1.2 million in 1750 to 1.6 million by 1800 and 2.8 million by 1850. But the most startling increase was in Ireland, where from about 3 million in 1750, it reached 5 million by 1800, and in 1845, on the brink of the famine, stood at well over 8 million, dangerously dependent on the potato harvest.

The Irish *Famine, from 1845 to 1848, was a unique event in modern European demography. One million people died of starvation and disease, the birth rate fell, and there was a large-scale exodus, mainly of younger people, in the decades after the disaster. Well over a million people left Ireland in the 1840s, another million in the 1850s, and 850,000 in the 1860s—mainly for North America, and especially from Munster and Ulster. The Irish population was down to 6.5 million by 1851, 5.8 million by 1861, 4.4 million by 1901.

In the rest of Britain, the sustained growth was felt in every part of public life. Internationally, it changed Britain's relative position. In 1550 the population of Spain and Portugal was double that of the British Isles: by 1914 the position was reversed. Just before 1914 the population of the United Kingdom passed that of France. Despite Malthus' fears of extra mouths to feed, agricultural improvements meant that fewer farm labourers could support more and more factory workers. The increase provided labour for the industrial expansion and purchasing power to sustain it. The internal balance of England shifted as the great industrial towns of the north developed. In Scotland, Glasgow rose from a town of 10,000 in 1688 to a conurbation of a million in 1901: in Wales, the balance of population moved to the mining areas of the south and Cardiff, a

town of 1,800 people in 1801, had 128,000 inhabitants by 1901.

The population of England and Wales continued to rise in the 20th cent. By 2001, England and Wales totalled 52 million, Scotland 5 million, Northern Ireland 1½ million, and Eire 4 million. England became by far the most densely populated of the major European powers—four times the density of France, and on a par with Holland and Belgium. From this stemmed many social problems: of law and order, bearing in mind that a second-division football match in the 1990s might well attract a crowd twice the size of the second largest city of Stuart England; of traffic jams, road rage, and general transport policy; of noise pollution and broader environmental questions. The slowing down of the birth rate after the Second World War meant an ageing population, with heavy demands on medical care and for pensions. The general movement out of older towns led to the problem of decaying city centres. Though demography is a rarefied and demanding discipline, its implications are profound.

**Porson, Richard** (1759–1808). Scholar. Of comparatively humble family in Norfolk, Porson's youthful promise was so obvious that means were found to send him to Eton. Further contributions sent him to Trinity College, Cambridge, where he was elected to a fellowship. In July 1792, being unwilling to take holy orders, he lost the fellowship, but five months later was elected to the regius chair of Greek. He did not lecture, rarely visited the university, but studied in London, producing a celebrated edition of Euripides.

**Portal, Charles, 1st Viscount Portal** (1893–1971). Portal came from a gentry family of Huguenot ancestry. After Winchester and Christ Church, Oxford, he joined the army in 1914 but in 1915 transferred to the *Royal Flying Corps, and flew more than 900 sorties before 1918. Promoted air marshal in 1939 he took over Bomber Command in 1940, but after six months became chief of the air staff, which he retained until the end of the war. Eisenhower thought Portal the finest of all the war leaders, 'greater than Churchill', and *Churchill himself remarked that Portal 'had everything'.

**Porteous riots,** 1736. In Edinburgh on 14 April 1736 the hanging of a smuggler sparked an angry reaction from the crowd, and stones were thrown at the town guard. The troops then opened fire, though Captain John Porteous always denied that he gave the order. Six were killed and about a dozen more injured. The provost had Porteous arrested; he was tried and sentenced to be executed. But the government granted Porteous a temporary reprieve. On 7 September a mob of 4,000 stormed the Tolbooth prison, seized the captain, and hanged him. A parliamentary inquiry in 1737 resulted in punitive measures against the city, but the episode cost *Walpole much Scottish support in Parliament.

**Portland, battle of,** 1653. Naval engagement in the first Anglo-Dutch War, which developed into a running fight up the Channel from 18 to 20 February. A large fleet under *Blake encountered Martin Tromp's fleet off Portland Bill escorting a convoy. Tromp lost twelve warships but saved most of the convoy.

**Portland, Hans Willem van Bentinck, 1st earl of** (c.1649–1709). Dutch confidant of William III. Entering the household of William of Orange in the early 1660s, Bentinck became the prince's close friend, playing an important diplomatic role in the preparations for William's invasion of England in 1688. On becoming king, William rewarded Bentinck handsomely with English lands and honours, and in April 1689 he was given an earldom. He was impeached in 1701 for keeping English ministers in ignorance of his negotiations with France over the partition of Spain, but was never put on trial. He retired from court following William's death in 1702.

**Portland, William Cavendish-Bentinck, 3rd duke of** (1738–1809). Portland began his career as a follower of *Newcastle and rose to the status of second in command to *Rockingham, succeeding the latter as official head of the Whig opposition in 1782. He shared the leadership with the party's Commons spokesman, Charles *Fox. As nominal premier during the Fox–North coalition ministry, Portland conducted a series of difficult negotiations with the king, which belie his reputation for weakness. The *India

Bill crisis, which precipitated the fall of the coalition, set the pattern of politics for a decade, with Portland and Fox the twin leaders of an increasingly organized Whig opposition. The duke long resisted the pressure to break with Fox, but in 1794 led the conservative Whigs into coalition with Pitt. As home secretary (1794–1801) Portland favoured the use of surveillance and repression to counter the threat of radicalism. He was also a prime mover in the recall of *Fitzwilliam from Ireland in 1795 over the question of catholic emancipation. By the early 19th cent. Portland had ceased to be a party leader, but had become an elder statesman. For this reason the aged and infirm duke became the figurehead prime minister (1807–9) in a ministry that contained the germs of the Toryism that was later to flourish under *Liverpool.

**Portsmouth** is not mentioned in *Domesday Book (1086) but began to develop on Portsea Island as Portchester, on a Roman site, started to silt up. It was granted a charter by Richard I in 1194 and the growth of the navy in the 16th cent. established it as a major town. From the time of Charles II, Portsmouth became the chief naval base. The Royal Naval College was founded in 1720, the *Royal George* went down in the harbour in 1782, and on 15 September 1805 *Nelson hoisted sail in *Victory* for *Trafalgar. By 1801 the town had a population of 32,000, 94,000 by 1861, and 188,000 by 2004.

**Portsmouth, diocese of** The see, comprising south-east Hampshire and the Isle of Wight, was carved, with *Guildford, out of the *Winchester diocese in 1927. The cathedral, the former parish church of St Thomas of Canterbury, originally built c.1190, has an Early English east end and a late 17th-cent. nave and tower (1683–95).

**Portsmouth, Louise de Kéroualle, duchess of** (1649–1734). Of Breton lineage, Louise de Kéroualle accompanied Henrietta Anne, sister of Charles II, to England in 1670; Charles's despair at Henrietta's sudden death and obvious infatuation with Louise encouraged Louis XIV to send her back to England. She rapidly rose to become 'the most absolute of the king's mistresses'. Her son by Charles (1672) was created duke of Richmond and she herself made duchess of Portsmouth in 1673. Universally unpopular as Frenchwoman and catholic, she was mercenary, recklessly extravagant, and haughty to inferiors.

**Post Office** Before the 17th cent., royal ministers had their own king's messengers, but private persons sent letters through servants or friends. Henry VIII had a master of the posts in 1512 but he served only the government. The first attempt at a public system was in 1635 when a service was established to important towns, carrying letters at 2 pence per sheet per 80 miles. In 1680 a London penny post was started and soon taken over by the government; penny posts were established in large provincial towns in the later 18th cent. Two 18th-cent. developments were Ralph Allen's scheme of cross-country services, followed by John Palmer's introduction of scheduled mail coaches. Rowland *Hill's plan of penny postage was adopted in 1840 in the teeth of powerful opposition: prepayment through stamps was introduced and there was no extra charge for mileage. It was followed in the 1850s by the introduction of pillar boxes (a suggestion of Anthony *Trollope). The services offered by post offices proliferated—the introduction of telegrams delivered by messenger boys; the establishment by *Gladstone in 1861 of the Post Office Savings Bank; and the beginning of parcel post in 1883. The start of the use of post offices for a variety of welfare payments was the decision in 1908 to deliver *old-age pensions through them. In the 21st cent., competition and rising administrative costs threatened many small post offices with closure.

**Potsdam conference,** 16 July–2 August 1945. This overlapped a British general election, *Churchill and *Eden being replaced midway by *Attlee and *Bevin (Labour). The Americans and Russians, however, observed no significant change in British policy, with both struck by Bevin's pugnacity. Churchill hoped that the acquisition of the atomic bomb by the USA would increase the bargaining power of the West with the USSR as well as hasten the end of the war with Japan.

**Potter, Beatrix** (1866–1943). Writer and illustrator of children's books. Born in London, she combined her early love of drawing with a keen interest in natural history, copy-

ing flowers and drawing small animals. Illustrated anecdotes about her pet rabbit, sent to amuse a convalescing child, inspired her first published book, *The Tale of Peter Rabbit*, in 1901. It was soon followed by *The Tale of Squirrel Nutkin*, *The Tailor of Gloucester*, and others. Immediately successful, they remain nursery classics with Mrs Tiggywinkle, Jeremy Fisher, and Jemima Puddleduck among many favourite characters.

**Powell, J. Enoch** (1912–98). Educated at King Edward's School, Birmingham, Powell began as a classicist, was a fellow of Trinity College, Cambridge, and then professor of Greek at Sydney. During the war he rose to brigadier. Elected to Parliament in 1950, he was a keen advocate of monetarism and resigned as financial secretary to the Treasury in the *Macmillan government in 1957, though returning as minister of health in 1960. He declined to serve under *Home in 1963 and never held office again. His outspoken hostility to coloured immigration led *Heath to sack him from the shadow cabinet in 1968. He was at odds with his party once more over Europe, bitterly denouncing the loss of British sovereignty, and he retired in February 1974 advising his supporters to vote Labour. Miraculously reborn as an Ulster Unionist in October 1974, he won the Down South seat and held it until 1987, tenaciously defending Ulster's position against encroachment.

**Powys** County of the middle Welsh borderland. The name derives from the Welsh kingdom of post-Roman times. With Norman control it was divided into a series of marcher lordships which were themselves integrated in 1536 into the counties of Denbighshire and Montgomeryshire. It was not until the Local Government Act of 1972 that the name was revived and given to the new county formed by the merging of Montgomeryshire, Radnorshire, and Breconshire. In spite of active campaigning by Montgomeryshire, Powys was retained in 1996 as a unitary authority.

**Powys, kingdom of** A Welsh kingdom that survived the English conquest as part of the march of Wales. The first reference to Powys dates from the 9th cent. Its kings claimed descent from northern Britons, a royal centre at 'Pengwern' (?Shrewsbury), and a role in resisting early English invaders. There does seem to have been a kingdom covering central Wales and modern Shropshire whose eastern part was overrun by Mercians from the mid-7th cent. Powys withstood encroachments from England and *Gwynedd throughout its existence, although the Welsh custom of partible inheritance caused rivalries among the ruling family.

**Poynings's law,** 1494. Sir Edward Poynings served as lord deputy in Ireland from 1494 to 1496. A parliament summoned at Drogheda in December 1494 declared that the English Privy Council must approve the summoning of any Irish parliament and agree to legislation, and that English laws applied to Ireland. Poynings's Act was not repealed until 1782, when the *Rockinghams conceded Irish legislative independence.

**Praemunire statutes** The statutes of Praemunire, the first dating from 1351, were passed to prevent the pope from interfering with the king's rights in relation to clergy benefices in England. The statutes imposed penalties on anyone who invoked papal authority to oust the jurisdiction of the king's courts. This was of great significance in the Reformation period and was one of the principal grounds for arraigning those who sought to appeal to Rome, or to accept the authority of the pope after Henry VIII's break with Rome.

**Pragmatic Sanction** An edict of 1713 attempted to ensure the undisputed succession of the Habsburg lands when Charles VI should die by setting aside the claims of his elder brother's daughters in favour of any daughters he should have. The cause of great diplomatic activity in the 1720s and 1730s, it did not suffice to prevent Maria Theresa being attacked in 1740 by Prussia, France, Spain, Saxony, and Bavaria. Britain came to her assistance and helped to place a pragmatic army in the field.

**Prayer Book** See BOOK OF COMMON PRAYER.

**Prayer Book rising,** 1549. The regime of Protector *Somerset at the accession of Edward VI moved sharply towards protestantism and in January 1549 Parliament ordered the new *Book of Common Prayer in English to be used. The day after it was introduced at *Sampford Courtenay in Devon the villagers demanded that their priest should say the old mass, complaining that the new service was in a language they could not comprehend. Protector Somerset, with *Kett's rising in Norfolk to deal with as well, moved cautiously, but on 17 August at Sampford Courtenay, Lord Russell (*Bedford) subdued the rebels. Somerset's hesitancy helped to undermine his position.

**Premonstratensians** (also known as the 'white canons' or 'Norbertines') were founded at Prémontré (in north-eastern France) in 1120 by St Norbert who, after his conversion, was a canon at Xanten (his birthplace) before becoming a wandering preacher. The early community was strongly eremitical in tone and followed an austere interpretation of the *Augustinian rule, heavily influenced, however, by the *Cistercians. The first house of canons was established in England in 1143 at Newhouse and by the dissolution there were 35 English communities, one in Wales, and several in Scotland, including Dryburgh.

**prerogative** See ROYAL PREROGATIVE.

**presbyterians** were supporters of *Calvinism, preaching the doctrine of the elect and advocating church government by a hierarchy of courts. Ultimate authority was the Bible and services gave great prominence to preaching. The leading exponent of presbyterianism in the Elizabethan church was Thomas *Cartwright, responsible for the *millenary petition to James I in 1603, which objected to surplices, bowing at the name of Jesus, and other ceremonies. They were in strong opposition to Archbishop *Laud, and after his imprisonment dominated the *Westminster Assembly called by Parliament in 1643 to reform the church. Bishops were abolished, statues and pictures removed, ceremonies cleansed. In Scotland, presbyterianism, brought by John *Knox from Geneva in 1559, made rapid progress and was the core of the *solemn league and covenant, adopted in 1643.

After the Restoration, the fortunes of English and Scottish presbyterianism diverged. In England, many of the 2,000 ministers forced out by the Act of *Uniformity in 1662 were presbyterians. Thereafter, presbyterianism formed a declining dissenting sect, vulnerable to *socinian and *unitarian arguments in the early 18th cent. and outdistanced by the *Methodists in the later 18th cent. After severe persecution in the reigns of Charles II and James II, the Scottish presbyterians emerged triumphant in 1690, when their church was recognized as the established *Church of Scotland. Its special position was guaranteed by the Act of *Union of 1707.

**press-gangs** The British crown possessed an ancient right to seize for naval service 'seamen, seafaring men, and persons whose occupations or callings are to work upon vessels and boats upon rivers'. Several attempts to replace this system of arbitrary conscription failed. A 1696 scheme for registering seamen for limited periods of service was abandoned in 1711. Press-gangs hunting seamen came either from individual warships or from the Impress Service which reached its peak during the Napoleonic War. With death rates in the navy very high, particularly in the West Indies, seizure by a press-gang was no light matter.

**Preston, battle of,** 1648. In the spring of 1648 a series of uncoordinated risings heralded the second civil war. In July a sizeable Scottish army under *Hamilton crossed the border near Carlisle, shadowed by *Lambert. Hamilton had substantially more men, but they were badly strung out and were caught still disorganized outside Preston on 17 August. When the royalists withdrew south during the night, a running fight developed. Hamilton's infantry surrendered at Warrington: he and his cavalry were eventually rounded up at Uttoxeter.

**Preston, battle of,** 1715. The Jacobite rising in Northumberland was under the command of Thomas Forster, member of Parliament for the county. He occupied Holy Island for one day, failed to take Newcastle, and then made for Lancashire, where they hoped to find support. At Preston they were bottled up by Hanoverian forces led by Carpenter and Wills, and capitulated on 14 November.

**Prestonpans, battle of,** 1745. Charles Edward *Stuart's first and critically important victory in the '45 rising was gained on 21 September at Prestonpans, east of Edinburgh. The Hanoverian army of some 2,300 men, under the command of Sir John Cope, had been ferried from Inverness to Dunbar to cut off the rebels' advance south. The issue was decided within a few minutes by a fierce Highland charge at dawn.

**Pretoria, convention of,** 1881. This convention ended the first *Boer War, following the British annexation of the Transvaal in 1877. The Boers were given self-government, but the British retained suzerainty and the conduct of foreign relations. This shaky compromise was undermined by the discovery of gold on the Witwatersrand south of Pretoria in 1886.

**Pride's Purge** was a military *coup* by *Fairfax's army, organized by Commissary-General *Ireton and executed on 6–7 December 1648 by Colonel Thomas Pride. Its purpose was to prevent the conclusion of the so-called treaty of *Newport between the Long Parliament and Charles I. Ireton had intended to dissolve the Parliament, but was persuaded by friendly members to purge it instead. Pride prevented 231 known supporters of the treaty from entering the House. What was left became known as the *Rump.

**Priestley, Joseph** (1733–1804). Chemist, clergyman, and political theorist. Priestley was born in Yorkshire and educated at Batley Grammar School and at Daventry dissenting academy. An amateur scientist of great renown, his discovery of 'dephlogisticated air', later named oxygen by Lavoisier, transformed the study of chemistry. As a theologian, Priestley moved from *presbyterianism via Arianism to a unitarian position. His *Essay on the Principles of Government* (1768) was a strong plea for liberty, and he campaigned for the repeal of the Test and Corporation Acts and for the abolition of the slave trade. An incautious phrase in his *Letter to Edward Burn* (1790) caused him to be satirized as 'Gunpowder Priestley', plotting to blow up the British constitution, and brought upon him the wrath of the Birmingham 'church and king' mob. In July 1791 it burned his house, wrecked his laboratory, and destroyed most of his papers. Priestley left England and spent the rest of his life in Pennsylvania.

**prime minister** The modern office of prime minister developed over several centuries. Medieval and early modern monarchs often had chief ministers who wielded vast power—men such as Cardinal *Morton in Henry VII's reign, *Burghley under Queen Elizabeth, and *Buckingham for James I and Charles I. But they depended totally upon the favour of the monarch, as the fate of *Wolsey, Thomas *Cromwell, and *Clarendon demonstrated. The crucial change came after 1688 when it became necessary to summon Parliament every year, and the ability to manage it became a vital political qualification. Robert *Harley, later earl of Oxford, in Anne's reign, had some of the attributes of a prime minister, including a keen understanding of the growing power of the press, but the title of first prime minister is usually given to Sir Robert *Walpole, though the term was derogatory and he denied it. The subsequent development of the office depended upon the gradual development of party, which limited the king's choice of minister; on the growing complexity of public business, which demanded a co-ordinating hand; on the slow decline in the influence of the monarch; and on the development of an organized public opinion, expressed through a reformed electoral system, which substituted the choice of the voters for the choice of the monarch.

As the office grew in stature, the prime minister gradually took over many of the powers of the monarch—the granting and timing of a dissolution of Parliament, the appointment and replacement of ministerial colleagues, and, above all, the granting of honours. Monarchs fought rearguard actions and occasionally won successes, but the general drift was against them. Two heavy blows came in quick succession. In 1832 William IV, with great reluctance, agreed to create enough Whig peers if needed to carry Lord *Grey's reform bill, thus allowing a vital royal prerogative to fall into the hands of a determined prime minister: three years later, when he dismissed Lord *Melbourne, he was obliged to recall him after *Peel had failed to win a majority at the general election.

The powers of the prime minister, though not closely defined, are extensive. He appoints all the other ministers, can transfer them to different offices, or dismiss them altogether. He chairs the meetings of the cabinet and appoints ministers to the numerous cabinet committees. Honours, such as knighthoods, peerages, and other decorations, are awarded on his recommendation. As leader of the government, he exercises a general if not always clearly articulated authority over policy.

In recent years it has become fashionable to describe the office of prime minister as presidential. The official doctrine is that the prime minister is simply the first among equals, and the rule of collective responsibility emphasizes the collegial character of the cabinet. Whenever the post is held by a strong prime minister, the assertion that it has become presidential is propounded, and a contrast is drawn between the office in the 19th cent. and today. The comparison has some force. The urgency of many decisions in the modern world, the increased importance of foreign affairs, media emphasis on the personality of the prime minister, have all tended to enhance the office at the expense of departmental ministers. Yet it is easy to exaggerate the change. The gladiatorial contests between *Gladstone and *Disraeli anticipated the modern concentration on the rival party leaders.

The rule of a prime minister such as Thatcher will always give colour to the image of the prime minister as all-powerful. But though it may be conceded that there is a long-term trend towards the enhancement of the office, there are frequent fluctuations, as dominating prime ministers are followed by more diffident successors. Thus a Thatcher is succeeded by a *Major, a Macmillan by a Douglas-*Home. The bitter price Thatcher paid for her overbearing style suggests that an excessively presidential attitude may exact its own penalties.

**primitive methodists** broke away from the main Wesleyan body and formed their own connexion in 1811, led by Hugh Bourne, a carpenter, and William Clowes, a potter, who had been expelled for holding American-style camp-meetings at Mow Cop (Staffs.). Condemned by the middle-class churches as ranters, the primitive methodists provided a form of evangelism attuned to the needs of labouring people. The 'prims' were noted for their open-air, hell-fire style of preaching, their revivalist, tented camp-meetings, their acceptance of women preachers, and their teetotalism. By the 1850s the primitive methodists had over 100,000 members. In 1932 they helped to form the United Methodist Church.

**primogeniture** The character of the inheritance custom has a great bearing on the social and political evolution of a country. Primogeniture, inheritance by the eldest son, developed in England after the Norman Conquest and had military implications—that the *fief should not be subdivided lest it become incapable of fulfilling its feudal obligation. There were always regions where the custom did not apply—*gavelkind was widespread in Kent and in parts of Wales giving partible inheritance, and the custom of borough English in some places gave inheritance to the younger son. Since primogeniture applied also to titles, it meant that the English nobility was a small group contrasting with thousands of impoverished noblemen to be found in many parts of the continent.

**Primrose League** Victorian Conservative organization. Founded in 1883 by Lord Randolph *Churchill and John Gorst, the Primrose League was intended to enable the Conservatives to adapt to the extension of democracy. The key to its success lay in combining political propaganda with a regular programme of social activities. These included music-hall, dances, teas, summer fêtes, train excursions, and cycling clubs, all available very cheaply. By 1886, 200,000 members had been enrolled, and by 1891 over a million, of whom half were women.

**Prince Edward Island** was ceded by France in 1763, becoming a separate colony in 1769. It was called St John's Island until 1799. Although the dominion of Canada was planned at a conference in Charlottetown, the island's capital, in 1864, Prince Edward Island remained aloof until 1873.

**prince of Wales** The title 'prince of Wales' was not of great antiquity when it was bestowed by Edward I on his 16-year-old son Edward In 1301. *Dafydd ap Llywelyn had taken the title prince of Wales in 1244, though he failed to gain papal recognition, but Henry III was forced to acknowledge *Llywelyn ap Gruffydd in the 1260s. Llywelyn

was killed in 1282. The adoption in 1301 was presumably a gesture of conciliation by Edward I, though the tradition that his infant son, born in *Caernarfon castle, had been shown to the people is a later invention. Of the 21 holders of the title since 1301, 14 have succeeded to the throne.

**prisons** The first use of prisons in England was to detain an accused until trial or to keep a convicted criminal until execution. Under the Anglo-Saxons and the Normans, and throughout the Middle Ages, criminals were punished by fines and, for serious crime, death or mutilation. The first prisons were therefore the local lock-up or the castle keep.

In the sphere of civil law, each central court of common law had its prison (such as the Marshalsea for the Court of *King's Bench). Imprisonment for contempt of court was and still is possible and the Court of *Chancery became notorious for imprisoning those who were deemed to be in contempt. Imprisonment for debt was also common and was not abolished until late in the 19th cent.

During the 19th cent. prison became an important penal sanction though it was not until the 1850s that it became the prevailing form of punishment, especially after the end of *transportation. Overcrowding, dirt, and low hygiene as well as a miserable diet made the prisons breeding places for disease such as typhoid—indeed an illness known as 'gaol fever' was common, and many inmates died in prison.

In the 18th cent. certain reformers became aware of the appalling conditions in English prisons—two of the most famous being John *Howard, the great prison reformer who gave his name to the Howard League for penal reform, and Elizabeth *Fry who worked for the improvement of the lot of women in prison.

In 1865 the principle was introduced of work for prisoners. In 1895 the Gladstone Committee was set up to review the prisons and reform followed. Gradually during the 20th cent. corporal punishment, penal servitude, and hard labour were abolished for prisoners and the rehabilitative aspect of prison re-emphasized. But prison overcrowding in the 21st cent. has led to suggestions for larger units or even for the reintroduction of prison hulks.

**Privy Council** The fate of most councils or committees is to grow too large to be effective and to be replaced by an executive or inner caucus, like a series of Russian dolls. The *council of late medieval times became too big and in the late 1530s a smaller Privy Council was set up. To a considerable extent this was the work of Thomas *Cromwell. In 1540 the Privy Council, with some 20 members, acquired a clerk and a minute book. It became the work-horse of late Tudor government. The Long Parliament replaced it in 1649 by a *Council of State, but Richard *Cromwell restored it, and it was continued by Charles II after 1660. But its great days were by then over. The emergence of the cabal in the 1670s and James II's use of an inner cabinet in the 1680s heralded its fate, and it began to lose importance, first to the cabinet council, then to the cabinet. As the Privy Council continued to grow, its duties became almost purely formal, and by 1994 membership had risen to more than 400.

**pro-Boer** was the misleading name given to those who opposed the government's policy of fighting the *Boer War of 1899–1902. Few of them actually sympathized with their country's enemies. Most were either old-fashioned Gladstonian Liberals, or socialists. *Lloyd George and J. A. *Hobson both forged their reputations as pro-Boers.

**proclamations** were part of the royal prerogative to deal with emergencies or to make enactments while Parliament was not in being. Under the Tudors they dealt with a large variety of matters—the sale of meat, courtesy to the French ambassador, exile for anabaptists, reduced access to Windsor castle, prohibition of the export of leather, and discouragement from playing dice, cards, or tennis. The statute of Proclamations of 1539 reminded subjects that proclamations had the force of statutes, 'as though they were made by act of parliament'. James I's use of proclamations led to a protest in the petition of grievances of 1610 that they were encroaching upon statute and could 'bring a new form of arbitrary government upon the realm'. Charles I made considerable use of them, but they were too necessary to government to be abolished, though their employment after the Restora-

tion ceased to be controversial and they were often exhortatory in nature.

**Promenade Concerts** London's leading concert series. The Queen's Hall Promenade Concerts were established by impresario Robert Newman and conductor Henry *Wood in 1895. Initially they were all given by Wood and the Queen's Hall Orchestra, which was replaced by the BBC Symphony Orchestra in 1930 following the BBC's adoption of the series. After the Queen's Hall was bombed in 1941, the series moved to the Royal Albert Hall, becoming the Henry Wood Promenade Concerts on Wood's death in 1944. Their unique, vibrant atmosphere culminates in the exuberant 'Last Night of the Proms'.

**prorogation** is the royal power, now exercised by the prime minister, to suspend the session of Parliament. Clearly the prerogative of prorogation, like dissolution, could be used tactically, to allow time for negotiation or for tempers to cool. Charles I prorogued Parliament in June 1628 rather than listen to more remonstrances against tonnage and poundage. When he prorogued the 1629 Parliament, the Speaker was held down in his chair to allow protests against innovations in religion.

**prostitution,** the sale of sex for money, predominantly by females with male clients, has always been affected by cultural values. Brothels first sprang up in Southwark where Roman soldiers guarded the Thames crossing, to develop into the Bankside stews that were regulated by Henry II (1162); the church took a pragmatic view since the revenue was highly profitable. With the Reformation, moral rather than health concerns began to prevail, so prostitutes were publicly humiliated and imprisoned for 'correction'. Puritanism merely hardened existing attitudes. During the 19th cent. governments made efforts to regulate the practice, particularly around naval and military garrisons (a third of all sick cases among soldiers were venereal in origin by 1864). Female prostitutes were subject to humiliation and callous treatment under the Contagious Diseases Acts of the 1860s, only repealed in 1886 after the campaigns of Josephine *Butler. Female prostitution is now legally tolerated, though with prohibition of open solicitation, but young women are still forced into the practice by poverty or homelessness. Homosexual male prostitution, particularly in large cities, is increasing.

**protectionism** While international trade has been recognized as a major influence on the growth of the world economy throughout history, virtually all countries at all times have sought to protect either the whole economy, or at least some part of it, from the rigours of international competition by imposing barriers. This has usually taken the form of a tariff, or government levy, on imported goods to bring their price up to or even above the price of home-produced goods. A familiar modern example of protection is the support given to agriculture in the *European Economic Community. This has been so successful that, far from being swamped by a massive tide of cheap food imports as was feared when the Common Agricultural Policy (CAP) was originally devised, farmers in the European Union have become large-scale exporters to the rest of the world.

A tariff imposed on imports raises domestic prices so that consumers are worse off. The government gains tax revenue from the tariff and producers gain from the price increase. The repeal of the *Corn Laws in 1846 redistributed income away from wealthy agriculturalists to manufacturers, although not to any great extent. *Chamberlain's tariff campaign of 1903 was intended to redistribute income to industrialists by protecting sectors like the steel industry from the effects of cheap imports. Protection always entails some loss of efficiency, as compared to free trade, because the lowest price obtainable through competition is replaced by a higher subsidized price. The result is over-production in the home market by suppliers who are less efficient than they would be if exposed to world-wide competition.

**Protectorate** The Protectorate was established on 16 December 1653 when Oliver *Cromwell became head of state as lord protector. Since his power rested on a formidable army, whose officers had devised the Protectorate's constitution, the *Instrument of Government, his regime has often been called a military dictatorship. The description needs to be qualified. The restraints imposed by the Instrument were considerable, and Cromwell welcomed them. Serving officers were always outnumbered by civilians on his council, and formed only a tiny minority among the justices of the peace, to whom local government had been restored.

Cromwell's first Parliament refused to ratify the constitution and proceeded to frame one of its own; he dissolved it in January 1655. Shortly afterwards, *Penruddock's rising gave his military councillors a temporary ascendancy, and the result was the regime of the *major-generals. These officers were much resented, not least for their inferior birth.

The second Protectorate Parliament (1656–8), from which the council excluded over 100 elected members, reflected a growing division between conservative civilians and supporters of the military. Led by the former, it presented Cromwell with a new constitution, the *Humble Petition and Advice, naming him as king and restoring other more traditional ways. His senior officers strongly opposed it, but despite them Cromwell accepted it, though without changing his title of Protector. Cromwell died on 3 September 1658. His son Richard's Protectorate lasted only eight months, not so much because he was personally inadequate as because the disgruntled military 'grandees' were bent on recovering their old political influence. By bringing Richard down, they wrecked the 'Good Old Cause' that they professed to serve.

**protestantism** The term originated with the protest of the reforming minority at the diet of Spires in 1529 against the catholic majority. As a general description of the anti-catholic position, it was adopted with some caution: several of the churches into which the new movement dissolved were strongly opposed to each other, while conservatives were not anxious to stress the role of individual conscience in religious matters. The common protestant ground was rejection of papal authority, emphasis on the Bible, devotion to preaching, clerical marriage, and a more austere ceremonial. The main divisions of protestantism were *Calvinism, *Lutheranism, and Zwinglianism, with the Church of England claiming an autonomous and independent position.

Catholic polemicists argued that the appeal to private conscience must, in the end, lead to religious anarchy. Protestantism was not long in dividing—indeed it was born divided—over the nature of the eucharist, the role of bishops, the importance of good works, and the method of baptism. The fissiparous nature of the movement continued to the 20th cent., with splits, secessions, and schisms in most denominations. In the late 20th cent., falling membership, financial problems, and a more ecumenical spirit prompted a number of protestant reunions, but though relations between protestants and catholics are much warmer than in the 19th cent., reunification has yet to come about.

**Provisors, statute of,** 1351. The papal practice of appointing to benefices (provisions), or granting reversions, was much resented, particularly since many of the clerics were foreign. Edward III was anxious to assert his own rights against both cathedral chapters and papacy. The Parliament of 1351 legislated against the practice (25 Edw. III s. 4), declaring the nominations invalid.

**Prynne, William** (1600–69). Puritan lawyer, antiquarian, and politician. Educated at Oriel College, Oxford, and Lincoln's Inn, Prynne was hauled before the Court of *Star Chamber in 1634 for publishing the *Histriomastix*. This work, a 1,000-page denunciation of female actors and of theatre in general, was interpreted as an attack on Charles I and *Henrietta Maria. Prynne was rewarded with the loss of his ears. His attacks on the bishops landed him a second time before Star Chamber in 1637, where he was sentenced to lose what remained of his ears. After his release by the *Long Parliament in 1640, Prynne was instrumental in securing the conviction and death of his enemy Archbishop *Laud. He continued to write long-winded pamphlets against the republic, popery, and quakerism during the 1650s. When the Long Parliament was recalled, Prynne introduced the bill in March 1660 for its dissolution. As a member of both Convention and Cavalier parliaments, he remained a presbyterian and resumed his attacks on bishops.

**Public Health Act,** 1848. An Act of Parliament for England and Wales (11 & 12 Vic. c. 63) was carried following an agitation organized by Edwin *Chadwick and the Health of Towns Association. It created a General Board of Health in London and local boards of health with wide powers to enforce standards of public hygiene where the death rate exceeded 23 per 1,000 or where 10 per cent of ratepayers petitioned for a local board.

**public schools** During the Middle Ages, the grammar school provided education for poor scholars intended for the church and for the sons of noblemen. This included such schools as *Eton and *Winchester. By the 18th cent. a number of 'Great Schools' had emerged, including *Harrow, *Rugby, Sherborne, and Canterbury. Other changes during the early 19th cent. stimulated the demand for public schools. Reforms in public schools were introduced by heads such as Samuel Butler at Shrewsbury (1793–1836), and Dr Thomas *Arnold at Rugby (1828–42), who were clerics. The school chapel became the focal point of life, discipline was enforced through prefects, and team games emphasized.

Criticism of some of the public schools was so persistent that a royal commission was appointed in 1861, under Lord *Clarendon, to investigate conditions in the nine large public schools—Winchester, Eton, Westminster, Charterhouse, Harrow, Rugby, Shrewsbury, St Paul's, and Merchant Taylors'. Whilst broadly satisfied, the commissioners made a number of recommendations which were embodied in the Public Schools Act (1868). Governing bodies were reformed and schools such as Harrow developed a modern side.

Attempts were made in the 20th cent. to bridge the gap between public schools and the state-provided sector. The Fleming Report (1944) and the first report of the Public Schools Commission (1968) (Newsom) were impracticable. The second report (1970) (Donnison) was more positive, but the advent of a Conservative government avoided further threats. The term public school has now been superseded by independent school.

**Pugin, Augustus Welby** (1812–52). Architect and pioneer of the Victorian Gothic Revival. Before Pugin, 'Gothick' architecture had been largely a romantic plaything of rich dilettantes. He saw something deeper in it. According to Pugin, Gothic was the only

Christian—by which he meant Roman catholic—style. Alton Towers (1836), Scarisbrick Hall (1837), the catholic cathedrals of Birmingham (1841) and Newcastle (1844), and the lush detailing of the new Houses of Parliament (1840–52)—the classicist Charles *Barry did the main plan—are some of the results. They are not the greatest examples of the genre; but Pugin should really be judged by the inspiration he gave to better architects (like *Scott and William Butterfield) after him.

**Puisset, Hugh de** (*c.*1125–95). Bishop of Durham. Puisset was a great aristocratic churchman who held the wealthy see of Durham for more than 40 years. He was a nephew of King Stephen and received his first preferment (an archdeaconry) from Stephen's brother Henry of Blois, bishop of Winchester. Next, another relative, William Fitzherbert, archbishop of York, gave him the post of treasurer in the diocese. In 1153, probably before he was 30, he was made bishop of Durham. A hint at his essentially secular attitude came at the start of Richard I's reign, when the king was raising funds for the crusade. Hugh purchased the earldom of Northumberland and the *justiciarship. He was ousted from the justiciarship by William *Longchamp and surrendered the earldom in 1193. He lived in great style, built lavishly, patronized learning, and fought his corner.

**Pulteney, William, 1st earl of Bath** (1684–1764). Pulteney was Whig MP for Hedon (1705–34) and Middlesex (1734–42), becoming secretary at war in 1714. He supported *Walpole and *Townshend in opposition during the Whig schism from 1717 to 1720, but felt insulted when not offered a post in the reunited Whig administration. Thereafter he became alienated from Walpole and in 1725 joined *Bolingbroke in attacking the ministry in print via the *Craftsman. On the accession of George II in 1727 he was disappointed not to replace Walpole. His greatest triumphs in opposition were the destruction of the *excise scheme in 1733 and his agitation for war with Spain, which eventually brought down Walpole in 1742. But Pulteney refused to take office and was created earl of Bath. Disappointed once more at not being made first minister in 1743, he tried to overthrow Henry *Pelham

in 1746 but failed to form a government. Thereafter he played no part in public affairs.

**Punch,** a satirical weekly periodical, was founded in 1841 under the editorship of Henry Mayhew and Mark Lemon, early contributors including *Thackeray, Hood, and Tenniel. Famous for its cartoons, and a former stand-by in professional waiting-rooms, it closed in 1992 due to debt, but reappeared in 1996 under new ownership.

**Purcell, Henry** (1658–95). The outstanding musician and composer of his time in Britain. Like other 17th-cent. musicians, Purcell's career began in the church, first as a chorister at the Chapel Royal, then as organist at Westminster abbey composing anthems. At court he enjoyed the favour of successive monarchs composing odes on special occasions, but his works for Mary II are the best known, composed when Purcell was reaching the height of his powers, just before his premature death. The music he composed for her funeral is of a truly majestic solemnity and profundity.

**puritans** During the reign of the catholic Mary Tudor (1553–8) many English protestants went into exile on the continent, where they experienced forms of worship which were 'purer' than those prescribed in the 1552 *Prayer Book because they contained virtually no trace of catholicism. Returning to England at the beginning of Elizabeth I's reign, they hoped to create an established church closer to continental models, but the queen insisted on a comprehensive settlement. They were harried by the government, under the name of 'puritans'. The conforming majority, both clerical and lay, shared many of their reservations but were willing, albeit reluctantly, to obey the orders of their royal governor. They were helped by the fact that in its theology, if not its practice, the established church was *Calvinist. This remained the case under James I, despite the failure of the *Hampton Court conference, but the accession of Charles I in 1625 brought the high-church *Arminians to power. By calling all its low-church opponents puritans, the Arminians drove the conforming majority into opposition. This opened the way to the destruction of the established church after the collapse of Charles's rule. Matters were complicated by the proliferation of sects demanding freedom to worship as they pleased. Continuing puritan divisions throughout the Interregnum created a backlash which found expression in the re-establishment of the Church of England after the restoration of the monarchy in 1660. The legislation known as the *Clarendon code imposed severe penalties upon nonconformists, and sporadic persecution of puritans continued until the *Glorious Revolution.

**purveyancing** was the means of supplying the king and his court on progress with the provisions and services they needed at prices to be fixed by royal officers. Consequently the subject was lucky to be paid inadequately, if at all. Since the king could not have palaces and stores everywhere, purveyancing was the only way he could travel his realm. *Magna Carta attempted to regulate it; *Speculum regis* of *c*.1331 declared it a cursed prerogative; the *Ordainers of 1310 moved against it, and it was still a matter of loud complaint in the reigns of James I and Charles I. It was finally abolished during the Civil War.

**Pusey, Edward Bouverie** (1800–82). A leader of the *Oxford movement, Pusey contributed to the series which led to the alternative description of '*tractarians'. He also gave the movement another nickname by maintaining the tradition of the tractarians within the Church of England after *Newman's secession to Roman catholicism. Pusey fought a rearguard action to prevent others following and his supporters became known as 'Puseyites'. He was appointed regius professor of Hebrew in Oxford at the age of 28.

**Putney debates** These occupied the general council of the army from 28 October to 1 November 1647, and were recorded almost verbatim by its secretary William Clarke. The central question was whether to continue seeking a negotiated settlement with the king. Representatives of the *Levellers put before it a revolutionary alternative, an *Agreement of the People, and the ensuing arguments for and against manhood suffrage were memorably eloquent.

**Pym, John** (1584–1643). Parliamentarian. One of the few members of the Commons who realized that poverty was driving Charles I into arbitrary rule, Pym consistently argued the case for restoring the crown's finances. But his attitude towards the king hardened with the conviction that Charles, by patronizing the *Arminians, was opening the door to catholicism. When the *Long Parliament met in November, Pym was the driving force behind the impeachment of Charles's chief minister *Strafford. The revolt of the Irish catholics in 1641 confirmed Pym in his belief that the king was involved in a 'popish plot' to destroy English religion and liberties, and he pushed through the *Grand Remonstrance. Not surprisingly, he was one of the *five members whom the king sought to arrest in January 1642. Pym's major contribution to the parliamentary cause came in 1643 when he persuaded members to impose an excise to meet the costs of war and to accept the *Solemn League and Covenant as the price of Scottish support.

**Pyrenees, battle of the,** 1813. Following *Wellington's offensive in the spring of 1813, Marshal Soult's army of 88,000 men attempted to lift the siege of the French-held towns of San Sebastián and Pamplona in northern Spain. Wellington met Soult at Sorauren near Pamplona on 28 and again on 30 July and won hard-fought victories.

## Q

**Quadruple Alliance** 1. 1718. After the War of the Spanish Succession, Philip V of Spain was anxious to regain territory. France, Britain, and the Dutch formed a defensive *Triple Alliance in 1717, which the Emperor Charles VI joined in 1718. A British naval squadron defeated the Spanish fleet off *Cape Passaro immediately after the treaty had been signed in 1718, and a French invasion of Spain in 1719 forced Philip to come to terms. 2. 1815. At the end of the Revolutionary and Napoleonic wars in 1815, the victorious powers—Britain, Russia, Prussia, and Austria—formed a Quadruple Alliance to hold periodic conferences to consider matters of common interest—the so-called *Congress system. Meetings were held at Aix-la-Chapelle (1818), Troppau (1820-1), and Verona (1822), but differences between the allies were soon apparent. *See* HOLY ALLIANCE. 3. 1834. In the 1830s, the young queens of Portugal and of Spain were challenged by their uncles. Britain and France formed a Quadruple Alliance with Spain and Portugal in 1834 to protect them, as constitutional rulers, against intervention by Metternich.

**quakers,** or Society of Friends, are said to have derived their name either from ecstatic shuddering or from George *Fox's advice to Justice Bennet in 1650 to tremble at the word of the Lord. They originated during the religious tumult of the 1650s, had no formal ministry or service, and professed the principle of the 'inner light', a sense of the direct working of Christ. Their refusal to pay tithes, insistence upon addressing everyone as thou, refusal to doff hats to authority, and the extravagant behaviour of some of their members, shocked a hierarchical society, and they were fiercely persecuted before and after the Restoration. Quakers refuse military service but are often prominent in ambulance and medical corps.

*Quarterly Review* This was the Tory riposte to the very successful *Edinburgh Review*, which had been launched in 1802. It was started in 1809 by Sir Walter *Scott, George Ellis, and John Wilson *Croker, with William Gifford as editor. The early contributors included *Canning and Robert *Southey.

**quarter sessions** The office of *justice of the peace can be traced back to the 'keepers of the peace' in 1195 and 'conservators of the peace' during the reigns of Henry III and Edward I, but the principal statutory provisions establishing the justices of the peace were those of the 14th cent., especially the Justices of the Peace Act 1361. By a statute of 1362, the justices of each county were to meet four times a year and these sessions were therefore known as 'quarter sessions'.

During the 18th cent. the practice arose of reserving the many capital cases for the assizes, and by the Quarter Sessions Act 1842 the jurisdiction of quarter sessions over such offences as treason, murder, felonies punishable with penal servitude for life, and certain other offences was removed. Quarter sessions were abolished by the Courts Act 1971.

**Quatre Bras, battle of,** 1815. After resuming control of France in 1815 on his return from Elba, Napoleon advanced into Belgium, striking with his main force against the Prussians at Ligny. A subsidiary force under Marshal Ney headed towards the vital crossroads at Quatre Bras. Although initially outnumbered, elements of the Anglo-Dutch army defended stoutly until reinforcements, and *Wellington himself, arrived. By nightfall, Wellington had 36,000 men to Ney's 20,000, and was able to fall back to the position at *Waterloo, having won an important strategic victory.

**Quebec, capture of,** 1759. This ended French sovereignty in Canada. Despite fears that the strongly entrenched French, under the brilliant Montcalm, could be dislodged only by a long siege, *Wolfe's troops, with a surprise night manœuvre, followed by a pitched battle, achieved an epic victory.

**Quebec Act,** 1774. This followed but was not part of the *Intolerable Acts. It settled matters relating to the British acquisition of French Canada by recognizing the catholic church, allowing the exercise of French law, denying Quebec an elected assembly, and extending its boundaries to the Ohio. It was fervently condemned in the thirteen colonies, as an attack on protestant and constitutional liberties and on their territorial expansion and as confirmation of the malign intentions of Lord *North's ministry towards America.

**Queen Anne's Bounty** was a product of the strong Anglican resurgence during her reign, caused partly by concern at the apparent progress of dissent since the Glorious Revolution. In 1703 the queen announced that she would devote the income from *first fruits, which had been appropriated from the papacy at the Reformation, to the relief of poor clergy, and trustees were appointed to administer the scheme.

**Queensberry, James Douglas, 2nd duke of** [S] (1662–1711). Douglas (Drumlanrig until he succeeded in 1695) was one of the first to join William at the Revolution, was a gentleman of the bedchamber 1689–1702, lord privy seal [S] 1696–1702, and received the Garter in 1701. As commissioner to the Scottish Parliament, Queensberry played a crucial role in carrying the *Union in Anne's reign. Handsomely rewarded, he was granted a large pension, served 1707–8 as a representative peer, and in 1708 was created duke of Dover in the British peerage. From 1709 he was in charge of Scottish affairs but died early.

**queen's counsel (king's counsel).** These were barristers appointed in the late 16th cent. to assist the law officers of the crown in the conduct of legal affairs. During the 18th cent. they ceased to be closely connected with the crown and the title came to be merely a mark of honour for distinguished barristers. They are said to 'take silk' on appointment, as they then wear a silk gown instead of a 'stuff' gown.

**Queenston Heights, battle of,** 1812. The first major battle of the *War of 1812 occurred when 1,000 New York State militia crossed the Niagara river and scaled the river cliffs. The British commander, Sir Isaac Brock, was killed leading a charge. British reinforcements and Indian allies eventually forced the surrender of over 900 Americans at a cost of 28 British fatalities. Queenston Heights thus became a symbolic Canadian rejection of the USA.

**Queen's University,** Belfast, was founded as Queen's College, Belfast, under Sir Robert *Peel's Colleges Act (1845). The Irish Universities Act (1908) created both a National University of Ireland (binding the colleges of Cork, Galway, and Dublin) and a new Queen's University of Belfast out of the former Queen's College. Queen's now reflects, if still inadequately, the increasing political and economic strength of the catholic community in Northern Ireland.

***quia emptores,*** also known as the statute of *Westminster 1290. This statute of Edward I brought to an end the practice of subinfeudation. The statute provided that where a tenant of land alienated that land, he could not create a new relationship of lord and tenant with the purchaser. The effect was to preserve order, to prevent extending the feudal 'ladder', and to safeguard the lords' interests in their tenants' services.

**Quiberon Bay, battle of,** 1759. This bay lies on the Biscay coast of France. Here, on 20 November 1759, was fought one of the most brilliant engagements in the annals of naval warfare. Britain stood in danger of invasion by France, and Sir Edward *Hawke had blockaded the fleet of Conflans in Brest since the previous May. When the weather blew Hawke off station, Conflans broke out, but early on the 20th Hawke had news that Conflans's 24 ships had entered Quiberon. He risked everything by following the French into this barely known anchorage in fading light and heavy squalls. Six French ships were destroyed in the ensuing action, and many of the remainder suffered irreparable damage.

**q**

**quo warranto proceedings** The *quo warranto* inquiry was instituted by Edward I when he succeeded to the throne in 1272. He instituted proceedings whereby his royal justices investigated the claim of every lord who claimed to have a franchise of a hundred court—a *court leet—inquiring 'by what warrant' the lord made such a claim. The lord had to prove that such jurisdiction had been granted. However, Edward allowed lords to show that they had acquired the franchise by prescription 'from time immemorial'.

**R101 airship** The larger of two rigid airships commissioned by the government in 1924. Designed by Barnes Wallis, it was built to carry up to 50 passengers to India. It set out on its maiden voyage from Cardington on 4 October 1930 with an official party, including the secretary of state for air. At 2 a.m. it touched the ground on its approach to Beauvais, caught fire, and exploded. Only four people survived. The disaster put an end to the use of airships in Britain.

**Radcot Bridge, battle of,** 1387. The accession of a 10-year-old king, Richard II, in 1377 led to baronial rivalry. In 1386 five noblemen, Arundel, Derby (the future Henry IV), *Gloucester, Nottingham, and Warwick, formed an alliance, the lords *appellant, to remove two royal favourites, Michael de la *Pole, duke of Suffolk, and *Oxford. Suffolk was impeached and forced to flee. De Vere, earl of Oxford, raised an army in Cheshire in December 1387 and marched south to join the king. He was intercepted at Radcot Bridge, east of Lechlade, on 20 December and trapped between armies led by Derby in front and Gloucester behind. Oxford fled and joined Suffolk in France.

**Radnorshire** (Sir Faesyfed) County of mid-Wales created at the Act of *Union with England in 1536. It was part of the Welsh kingdom of *Powys but was subject to Saxon attack both before and after the construction of *Offa's Dike. It was rapidly overrun by the Normans, the north becoming Mortimer land, whilst the south was taken by the Braoses. These two areas were eventually formed into the new county, the smallest of the Welsh shires. Incorporated into Powys as a district in 1974, it became part of the Powys unitary authority in 1996.

**Raeburn, Sir Henry** (1756–1823). Raeburn was born and worked all his life in Edinburgh. He was the leading Scottish portrait painter of his day. Largely self-taught, he visited London in 1784 on his way to study in Italy and met *Reynolds, whose style influenced him in a way that his Italian experience did not. In 1812 he was elected ARA and a full RA three years later. In 1822, when George IV visited Edinburgh, he knighted Ræburn, creating him king's limner and painter for Scotland the following year.

**Rædwald** (early 7th cent.), king of the East Angles. Baptized under the influence of King *Æthelbert of Kent, he compromised with his heathen wife, adding a Christian altar in his temple alongside those to pagan gods. Sheltering the Deiran royal exile *Edwin, c. 616, he was under pressure from the Northumbrian king *Æthelfryth to kill him or hand him over. Pre-empting Æthelfryth's threats, he attacked, defeated, and killed him by the *river Idle (Lincs.), securing the Northumbrian kingdom for Edwin. Rædwald's name is often linked with the famous ship-burial at *Sutton Hoo.

**Raffles, Sir Thomas Stamford** (1781–1826). Raffles joined the *East India Company in 1795 and was appointed to Penang, where he rapidly rose to be secretary to the council. In 1810 he was made agent to the Malay states to prepare an invasion of Java, then under the control of the Batavian Republic. He governed Java between 1811 and 1816, instituting far-reaching economic reforms. In 1818 he became lieutenant-governor of Fort Marlborough (Sumatra). Fearing Dutch influence, he persuaded the company to found a settlement at Singapore. He raised the flag there on 2 June 1819 and, by the time of his final return to England in 1824, had established it as an important port.

**ragged schools** were elementary schools for street children pioneered at the beginning of the 19th cent. by John Pounds, a Portsmouth cobbler, 'to chase away ignorance, to relieve distress, and to teach the Gospel'. The Ragged School Union, with the 7th earl of *Shaftesbury as president, was formed in 1844 to further this object.

**Raglan, Fitzroy James Henry Somerset, 1st Baron** (1788–1855). Lord Fitzroy Somerset, eighth son of the duke of Beaufort, was appointed aide-de-camp to the future duke of *Wellington, in 1808. He accompanied the duke throughout his campaigns in the Iberian peninsula (1808–14) and was badly wounded at *Waterloo. In 1852 Somerset was created Baron Raglan, and two years later given command of British forces in the war against Russia. When those forces invaded the Crimea in 1854, it soon became apparent that Raglan was not suited to high command, for although promoted to field marshal, he was widely criticized for orders leading to the '*Charge of the Light Brigade' at *Balaclava on 25 October. He died of dysentery in the Crimea on 25 June 1855.

**Ralegh, Sir Walter** (c.1554–1618). Of Devon gentry stock, Ralegh was half-brother of Sir Humphrey *Gilbert. He spent 1580–1 in Ireland and on his return rose rapidly in court favour under the patronage of *Leicester. Knighted in 1584 and returned to Parliament, he became warden of the stannaries, captain of the queen's guard, and lord-lieutenant of Cornwall. His attempts to promote the colonization of Virginia ended in failure, though they introduced tobacco and potatoes into England. But as the star of *Essex rose at court, Ralegh's waned. In 1595 he led an expedition to the Orinoco in search of gold and in 1596 took part in the attack on Cadiz. His prospects were undermined by the correspondence which Henry *Howard, earl of Northampton, established with James VI of Scotland, which succeeded in discrediting Ralegh. As soon as James succeeded in 1603, Ralegh was stripped of all his offices, tried for treason, condemned to death, and imprisoned in the Tower. Not until 1617 could he obtain release to lead a second Orinoco expedition, which proved a disaster. He brought back no gold and his son was killed. James then had him executed on the original charge. During his long years in the Tower, Ralegh wrote his *History of the World*,

brooding much on time and vicissitudes. It has grand passages and became popular, but Ralegh only reached 130 BC and as a work of history it was old-fashioned before it appeared. John *Aubrey included Ralegh in his *Brief Lives*: Ralegh was a 'tall, handsome and bold man, but damnable proud...he spake broad Devonshire to his dying day.'

**Ramillies, battle of,** 1706. *Marlborough's second major victory in the War of the Spanish Succession, in the Spanish Netherlands (modern Belgium) north of Namur, is regarded as his masterpiece. A bold advance by a French army of about 70,000 under Villeroi was intercepted by a roughly equal number of allied forces (British–Dutch–Danish) under Marlborough, and routed in a battle dominated by tactical subtleties.

**Ramsay, Allan** (1713–84). Portrait painter, born in Edinburgh, son of the poet Allan Ramsay. He studied in Edinburgh, London, Rome, and Naples, settling in London in 1739 and quickly establishing himself as the leading portraitist of the capital. He was particularly successful in painting women. His career as a portrait painter ended in 1773 when he suffered an accident to his right arm.

**Ramsay, Sir William** (1852–1916). Chemist. Ramsay was born in Glasgow and educated at Glasgow University. He developed an interest in chemistry, and studied in Germany. Appointed to the staff at Glasgow in 1874, he moved to Bristol in 1880 to take the chair of chemistry and became principal in 1881. From 1887 until his retirement in 1912 he was professor at University College, London. Ramsay's greatest discoveries were of the inert gases argon, helium, neon, krypton, and xenon.

**Ramsbury, diocese of** Founded in 909 by *Edward the Elder in his reorganization of the *Winchester diocese, Ramsbury comprised Wiltshire and Berkshire. In 1058 it was merged with *Sherborne, which in 1075 was moved to *Salisbury (Old Sarum).

**Ramsey, Michael** (1904–88). Archbishop of Canterbury. Ramsey was born in Cambridge, the son of a Maths don, and was educated at Repton, where the headmaster was Geoffrey Fisher, the man he ultimately succeeded as archbishop. In 1928 he was ordained as a curate in Liverpool, but returned to academic life (1930) when he joined the staff of Bishop's Hostel, Lincoln, training men for the ordained ministry. At the age of 35 he became divinity professor at Durham, and after the war returned to Cambridge as regius professor of divinity. In 1952 he was consecrated as bishop of Durham, becoming archbishop of York in 1956 and finally of Canterbury in 1961. Ramsey was an enthusiastic ecumenist, whose personal relationship with Pope Paul VI was close.

**Ranelagh** was the chief rival as a pleasure garden to *Vauxhall and claimed to be a cut above its competitor. It opened in April 1742 in the grounds of a house built in the 1690s for Lord Ranelagh. The chief attraction was the great Rotunda, demolished in 1803 when the gardens closed. The site was adjacent to Chelsea hospital, where new gardens, still extant, were laid out in the 1860s.

**ranters** An anarchic quasi-religious movement which emerged in 1648 and horrified orthodox puritans. Ranters were never an organized sect, and their writings were so heterogeneous that their very existence as a movement has recently been denied. Contemporaries, however, had no doubt that they existed. Groups of them scandalized the godly by their unbridled dancing, drinking, smoking, swearing, and sharing of sexual partners. Their heyday was short.

**Ranulf Flambard** (*c*.1060–1128). A Norman cleric whose nickname—Flambard meaning incendiary—probably reflects the burning eloquence which he turned against the king's enemies. His role as political and financial adviser to William Rufus made him notorious in church circles. In 1099 he was made bishop of Durham. In 1100 Henry I, in a gesture calculated to win support, threw Flambard into the Tower. Within six months he escaped and made his way to Normandy. He helped to plan Duke Robert's 1101 invasion, yet soon afterwards was back in Henry I's favour and restored to Durham.

**rapes** *Domesday Book shows Sussex in 1086 divided into five secular 'rapes', strips running from north to south, each named after its Norman lord, and containing a castle and a harbour. Each had a sheriff and they seem to have been, in effect, miniature shires.

**rates** are taxes on the occupiers of land and buildings. Various Acts in the 16th cent. provided for a poor rate for the relief of the sick and destitute, but in England 'the rates' date back formally to the Poor Relief Act of 1601, which made the parish the administrative unit for rating. The Rating and Valuation Act (1925) brought in the general rate and made county boroughs, boroughs, etc. the rating authorities and the units of rating. The rates were unpopular because they were mildly regressive and paid by only part of a local electorate. Domestic rates, but not business rates, were abolished in 1989–93, in Scotland, and in 1990–3, in England and Wales, when they were replaced by the community charge or *poll tax.

**Rathmines, battle of,** 1649. In June 1649 Michael Jones and the parliamentary forces were besieged in Dublin by *Ormond. Reinforcements from England enabled him on 2 August to make a sortie and destroy Ormond's camp at Rathmines.

**Ray, John** (1607–1705). Naturalist. The son of an Essex blacksmith, Ray was enabled to study at Cambridge, where he subsequently taught for thirteen years. Supported by prosperous friends, he pursued his career as a naturalist, attempting a systematic description of all living things. Botany remained his first love and he laid the foundation for a system of classification based on all structural characteristics, setting out many of the natural orders now employed by botanists.

**Reading** County town of Berkshire, situated where the river Kennet joins the Thames. A small borough by 1086, it grew partly thanks to Henry I's foundation of a major Cluniac abbey (1121), where he was buried. From the 14th to the 17th cents. it flourished through cloth-making: it was temporarily the eleventh wealthiest English town under Henry VIII.

**Reading, Rufus David Isaacs, 1st marquis of** (1860–1935). After a bumpy start, Isaacs had an unusually varied and distinguished career. The son of a Jewish fruit merchant from the East End of London, he left school at 14 to join the family business. He next turned to stockbroking but was 'hammered' in 1884. His third start was reading law. He was called to the bar in 1887 and quickly established himself. Entering Parliament as a Liberal for Reading in 1904, he was solicitor-general by 1910 and attorney-general the following year. Though singed in the *Marconi scandal of 1912, he was appointed lord chief justice in 1913 and given a barony. Next, from January 1918 until 1919 he was ambassador to the USA at a critical time of the war. Reading resumed his legal career, but in 1921 was sent to India as viceroy, remaining there until 1926.

**Rebecca riots,** 1838–44. These riots in west Wales, coinciding with the *chartist agitation, caused the government much concern. They originated as protests against *turnpikes which imposed heavy burdens on farmers and local people. They took the form of night attacks on toll-houses and -gates, the rioters often well organized, with blackened faces and wearing women's clothes. Their name came from the biblical reference—'the seed of Rebecca shall possess the gates of her enemies' (Gen. 24: 60). The government employed troops, police, and spies to control the situation, but the eventual remedy was an Act of 1844 (7 & 8 Vic. c. 91) to ease and reduce tolls.

**recruiters** In 1641 Charles I gave his consent to a bill which declared that the *Long Parliament could not be dissolved save by its own consent. After 1645 the absentees were replaced by 'recruiters', returned at by-elections, and by March 1647 244 new members had been brought in. By the time of its dissolution, fewer than 100 members of the pre-war House of Commons were in attendance.

**recusants** were catholics who refused to attend church as required by law (1559). Though initially tolerated, Mary, queen of Scots' arrival (1568), the rising of the *northern earls (1569), Elizabeth's excommunication (1570), and the *Ridolfi plot (1571) hardened the government's attitude. The mission of English priests from Douai (1574) and of Jesuits, such as *Campion and *Parsons (1580), strengthened catholicism— there were 400 priests in England by 1603. Recusants faced further penalties; saying or hearing mass was punishable by fine and imprisonment (1581), the recusancy fine

was increased to £20 a month, and being a priest was punishable by death (1585). After temporary alleviation under the *Declarations of Indulgence (1672, 1687, 1688), they were not included officially in the Toleration Act, though afterwards authorities normally turned a blind eye to their worship. Civil disabilities were not removed until the *Catholic Emancipation Act (1829).

**Redmond, John** (1856–1918). Redmond, a lawyer, was born in Co. Wexford. He became clerk of the House of Commons in 1880, and an Irish Parliamentary Party MP from 1881. He led the Parnellites from 1891 and the entire party from 1900. His great opportunity appeared to come with the introduction of the third Home Rule Bill in 1912, but when opposition in Ulster and in the Tory Party mounted, Redmond seemed over-dependent on the Liberal alliance. Redmond failed to react effectively to the British execution of the *Easter Rising's leaders in 1916, and weakened on the partition issue during *Lloyd George's Home Rule negotiations. In 1917, his leadership of Irish nationalism collapsed under Sinn Fein challenge.

**Red River rebellion,** 1869. In 1869 the Hudson's Bay Company sold its territorial rights to the new dominion of Canada. Both parties largely ignored the Métis of the Red River, a French-speaking community of part Indian descent. Led by Louis Riel, they established a provisional government in December 1869. An expeditionary force, commanded by Garnet *Wolseley, reached the settlement in August 1870, after Riel had escaped. The Red River became the province of Manitoba in 1870. Riel was hanged in 1885 after leading a second western rebellion.

**reeve** (Anglo-Saxon *gerefa*). Reeve was the general medieval term for a supervising official and is found in a number of different contexts. The shire-reeve (*scire-gerefa*), appointed by the king, was for centuries the chief royal representative in the counties. The sheriff's deputy was the hundred-reeve, who held the hundred court. The term was also used for the chief officer of a town—a port-reeve or burh-reeve—until overshadowed in the larger towns by the office of mayor or lord mayor. The manorial reeve was one of the most familiar officials for most peasants. He was elected by the tenants but sometimes nominated by the lord, and was responsible for the organization of communal tasks.

**Reflections on the Revolution in France** (1790) by Edmund *Burke exemplified the ideology of conservatism. Part I refuted the claim of Dr Richard Price that the French revolutionaries were following the English revolutionaries of 1688, in demanding a right to determine their own constitutional system. In Part II, Burke enumerated the false principles of the revolutionaries in France, including libertinism, egalitarianism, disrespect for private property, atheism, and, above all, rationalism.

**Reform Acts** The transition from the unreformed system of 1830 to full democracy in the 20th cent. was effected by seven franchise measures—the Acts of 1832, 1867, 1884, 1918, 1928, 1948, and 1969—supported by a number of other reforms.

*Grey's Reform Act introduced a standard franchise of £10 householders in the towns and augmented the franchise in the counties by allowing tenants at will to vote—the Chandos clause. Most of the new voters were middle-class citizens and many of the working classes were disappointed to find themselves excluded. By the second Reform Act of 1867, introduced by *Disraeli after Lord John *Russell's measure had foundered on party disunity, the vote was extended to working-class urban electors on the basis of household suffrage, adding some 938,000 to the existing electorate of 1,056,000. By 1884 natural increase had raised the UK electorate to some 3 million. *Gladstone's Act of that year raised it to 5 million, bringing in large numbers of county voters. With the majority of adult males now enfranchised, the total exclusion of women became more prominent. The First World War did not so much change attitudes as enable politicians to climb down with some dignity and the 1918 measure went through with little disagreement. Even so, the vote was restricted to women over 30, so that they should not form a majority in the electorate, bearing in mind the heavy male casualties during the war. Three more measures brought about almost complete adult suffrage. In 1928 the age limit for women voters was brought

down to 21, giving the vote to 5 million extra 'flappers'. The Labour government's Act of 1948 ended plural voting by taking away the business vote and the special university representation. In 1969, with little controversy, the voting age was lowered to 18, bringing in another 3 million voters.

Of equal importance were accompanying redistribution measures, legislation against undue influence and corruption, and the introduction of democracy into local government. The redistributive clauses of the Great Reform Act of 1832 were probably its most dramatic feature, with the total abolition of 56 'Schedule A' boroughs, including Old Sarum and Dunwich, and the award for the first time of parliamentary representation to great industrial towns like Manchester, Birmingham, Leeds, Sheffield, Bradford, and Wolverhampton. Further redistribution was effected by the 1867 Act, which deprived 38 small boroughs like Honiton and Dorchester of one of their two seats; brought in Burnley, Middlesbrough, Gravesend, and seven other boroughs with one seat (two for Chelsea); and gave an extra third seat to Birmingham, Liverpool, Leeds, and Manchester. An even more drastic redistribution accompanied the 1884 Act. Seventy-nine towns with less than 15,000 population lost both members, and a further 36 with less than 50,000 lost one.

The struggle for purity of elections was laborious throughout the 19th cent. The introduction of the secret ballot in 1872 did not solve the problem. The *Corrupt Practices Act of 1883 made more impact by tightening up control of election expenses.

Local government reform was effected by the *Municipal Corporations Act of 1834, which set up elected councils in the larger towns; by the *County Councils Act of 1888, which replaced the old government in the shires by justices of the peace by 62 elected councils; and by the *Parish Councils Act of 1894, hailed as a great measure of local democracy, but hamstrung by financial limits and watered down by 20th-cent. legislation.

**Reformation** Although 'reform' means many things, 'the Reformation' always denotes the 16th-cent. division of Latin Christendom into protestant and catholic. *Protestantism rejected the catholic belief that salvation comes through grace received in the sacraments; it restricted the church's role to one of proclaiming the unmerited gift of divine forgiveness. The *Church of England, established by statute in 1559, was unambiguously protestant.

The church in England c.1500 was devoutly catholic and loyally papalist. Many parish churches were extravagantly rebuilt, and lavished with vessels and ornaments. Kings and popes usually got on well. The fame of the German Reformation leader Martin Luther (1483–1546) caught the imagination of some English followers in the 1520s. Churchmen including Thomas Bilney (c.1495–1531), Robert Barnes (d. 1540), and the Bible translator and controversialist William *Tyndale (c.1494–1536) reinterpreted the Reformation message. However, their support was confined to young university students and those with foreign connections.

Henry VIII's failure to secure papal annulment of his first marriage led to the break with the papacy during 1532–6. This policy required theoretical justification if the king was to carry such a profoundly catholic nation into schism. Thomas *Cromwell recruited a number of young humanist writers, whose propaganda pieces criticized both the papacy and some aspects of the old cults, such as papal indulgences. Nevertheless, these moves were not avowedly 'protestant': Henry VIII detested Luther. Though Thomas Cromwell's commissioners who toured the doomed monasteries in 1535–6 mocked spurious relics and hunted dissolute monks, the ensuing abolition of the monastic order had no declared religious rationale.

All ambiguity was swept away in the next reign. Revision of the mass-book began almost at once, leading in 1549 to the publication of Cranmer's first *Book of Common Prayer. Meanwhile royal commissioners ruthlessly stripped parish churches of most of the ornaments and furniture associated with the old cult. Distinguished continental reformers such as Martin Bucer and Pier Martire Vermigli settled in the universities and influenced further changes in worship. In 1552 a revision of the Prayer Book simplified the apparatus of worship to the barest protestant essentials.

Mary I inherited religious legislation, in her eyes *ultra vires* and void, which took some eighteen months to reverse. Nevertheless, priests and laity restored the mass at the mere breath of royal suggestion. Once owners of monastic lands were assured of their titles, papal authority was received back with some enthusiasm. The impact of the campaign which burned c.280 heretics between 1555 and 1558 was greater in hindsight (helped by *Foxe's martyrology) than at the time.

Elizabeth, daughter of *Anne Boleyn and legatee of the schism, found the catholic hierarchy much more stubborn than in 1531–3. Re-establishment of the royal supremacy and abolition of the mass required an almost clean sweep of the episcopate. Even the *Thirty-Nine Articles approved by convocation in 1563 were altered by the queen herself, probably to placate conservatives.

The new bishops chosen by Elizabeth from leading reformed clergy in 1559, and most protestant zealots, assumed that the concessions made to tradition were temporary sops. To their increasing horror and bewilderment, they found that the queen obstinately refused to strip away the veneer of ritual. She feared that combative protestant preaching still risked alienating parts of the kingdom and sparking a religious war: the restoration of the mass during the *northern earls' revolt of 1569, and her excommunication by the pope in 1570, lent these fears substance. In the 'puritan' controversies of the 1570s Elizabeth nurtured a faction of clerics led by John *Whitgift (archbishop of Canterbury 1583–1604) which believed with equal zeal in protestant dogma, episcopal church government, and traditionalist ceremonial. So was the peculiar hybrid 'Anglican' church, founded both on Foxe's *Martyrs* and on *Hooker's *Ecclesiastical Polity*, brought to birth by the end of the 16th cent.

**Reform Club** Founded in 1836, the Reform Club was a radical initiative, drawing in Whig support. It was a riposte to the Tory Carlton Club and reflected the desire for better organization, particularly of electoral registration, after the Great Reform Act.

**Reform League,** 1865–9. The Reform League was established in 1865 to press for manhood suffrage and the ballot. It collaborated with the more moderate and middle-class Reform Union and its parliamentary spokesmen included *Gladstone and John *Bright. It gave strong support to *Russell's bill in 1866 and the *Hyde Park riots, a by-product of the mass protest meetings in July 1866, helped to push through *Disraeli's second Reform Act.

**regalia** The English coronation regalia is kept in the jewel house of the Tower of London. The collection of a regalia for coronation purposes added to the solemnity and antiquity of the occasion and seems to have been begun by the monks of Westminster abbey. But almost everything was destroyed during the *Commonwealth as items of superstition. Only a 12th-cent. anointing spoon survived: an ampulla, in the shape of a golden eagle, to hold the holy oil, was made for the coronation of Charles II in 1661. For the Scottish royal regalia, *see* HONOURS OF SCOTLAND.

**Regency** Though there have been several regencies in British history, the term is usually confined to the period 1810–20 when George, prince of Wales, acted as regent on behalf of George III, who had gone mad. It was a time of acute contrasts. Until *Waterloo in 1815 the country was still at war, with bread shortages, *Luddite riots, and severe distress. The post-war years were no better: agricultural depression, widespread unemployment, and the dislocation of early industrialization fuelled radical protest, exemplified at *Peterloo. The fashionable world retained its poise. The prince regent pressed on with his Pavilion at *Brighton until the prime minister, Lord *Liverpool, pointed out what offence it gave at a time of national distress. The radicals—*Cobbett, *Hunt, *Hazlitt, and *Shelley—and the caricaturists—*Cruikshank and *Rowlandson—had plenty to aim at. The prevailing taste in architecture, costume, and furniture was severely classical, aiming at balance and restraint. The finest monument to the period is the Regent Street and Regent's Park complex, built by John *Nash.

**Regency crisis,** 1788–9. In October 1788 George III appeared to have gone mad. It was expected that the prince of Wales would become regent, dismiss *Pitt, and call on *Portland and *Fox to form a ministry. Although a regency bill was prepared, it was not enacted because of the unexpected recovery of the king in February 1789.

**regicides** After the second civil war in 1648, most army leaders despaired of reaching an agreement with the king and resolved to put him on trial. Fifty-nine signed Charles's death warrant in January 1649. At the Restoration, the remains of *Cromwell, *Ireton, and *Bradshaw were taken from Westminster abbey and hanged at Tyburn. Of the 41 regicides still alive, nine were put to death.

**regium donum** (royal gift) originated as a grant of £600 p.a. by Charles II to augment the salaries of Irish presbyterian ministers in 1672 when he was trying to win support for his *Declaration of Indulgence. It was revived by William III, who increased it to £1,200 p.a., but was much disliked by high Anglicans as breaching the principle that only the Church of England should have support from the state. The regium donum became a significant precedent when *Pitt's government decided in 1795 to support the training of Irish catholic priests.

**Regni** A British *civitas*. The *civitas* of the Regni appears to be an artificial creation of the Roman government. It seems to have been based on a kingdom created by them in AD 43 for their client-king *Cogidubnus from the southern part of the territory of the *Atrebates in modern Sussex. Only when Cogidubnus died, perhaps around AD 80, did the kingdom disappear and the *civitas* take its place. The capital of the new canton, however, was located at its southwestern corner, where the major Iron Age stronghold at Chichester was succeeded by the Roman town of Noviomagus.

**Reith, John, 1st Baron Reith** (1889–1971). Reith stamped his image on the first 40 years of the *British Broadcasting Corporation. The son of a minister of the Free Church of Scotland, he was born at Stonehaven in Kincardineshire. He began as a railway engineer and was badly wounded in the First World War. In 1922, he saw an advertisement for general manager of the new BBC and was appointed. Reith created his own vision of an austere, sober, and responsible corporation, with important educational and religious obligations. He stayed until 1938 and then went to Imperial Airways, but at the outbreak of war was brought into Parliament, serving as minister of information, minister of transport, and minister of works. He and *Churchill disliked each other and he was abruptly dismissed in February 1942. A tall, gaunt, impressive, and fierce man, he had no concept of compromise and his diaries are full of unpleasant and savage remarks about colleagues.

**reivers** or moss-troopers were the names given to border raiders. There was little protection against them, save the building of *peel towers and bastle-houses as temporary refuges. Liddesdale on the Scottish side and Redesdale on the English were notorious nests for reivers.

**religious toleration,** a principle accepted without question by most people in the 21st cent., came about more by a process of exhaustion than by the triumph of reasoned argument. Few people in the 16th cent. doubted that state and church had not only the right but the duty to put down religious *dissent. They assumed that religious truth was God-given and absolute; that a country divided in religion would be fatally weakened; that nonconformists were potential traitors; that the exercise of private judgement would, in the end, undermine all authority and produce a shattered and anarchic society, in which everything was permissible.

The *Reformation brought about toleration neither by design nor directly, but as a by-product. None of the great reformers—Luther, Calvin, Zwingli—were tolerant of their opponents. In defence of his own position, Luther was first obliged to challenge papal authority, then to expound the right of the secular ruler to declare the religious policy of his state. That formula was accepted in the Augsburg peace of 1555—*cuius regio, eius religio* (the ruler shall decide religion). Only *catholicism or *Lutheranism were permitted choices and there was no provision for toleration. But in practice political considerations sometimes made rulers embrace toleration. Countries like Prussia, which were chronically short of labour, might find it imprudent to drive out subjects and might welcome refugees from less tolerant states.

In England there had been little need for a hunt after heretics until the late 14th cent., when *Wyclif's teaching combined with social unrest to produce *lollardy. The authorities responded with the act of 1401 *De heretico comburendo*—on the burning of heretics. The seed-time for toleration in England was after the Civil War, when sects multiplied and the victorious parliamentary army demanded from the presbyterians toleration for *baptists, *congregationalists, and independents.

The Restoration in 1660 saw a lurch backwards, with Parliament passing severe legislation against catholics and dissenters. But, again, the exigencies of politics called for tactical behaviour and Charles II and James II both issued *Declarations of Indulgence. In the crisis of 1688, when the dissenters held the balance between the Anglicans and the king, they supported the revolution, and reaped the reward from William III in 1689 in the *Toleration Act, which at least permitted freedom of worship. It was far from complete. Toleration did not apply to catholics, who faced a battery of *penal laws, nor to anti-trinitarians. In Scotland, *episcopalians were persecuted as crypto-Jacobites. Even protestant dissenters did not have full civil rights and could neither sit in Parliament nor on corporations unless their consciences were flexible. But the narrow basis was gradually broadened, with concessions to the *quakers over oath-taking and to the Scottish episcopalians over lay patronage. Underpinning the shift in policy was the start of a change in attitude. In his *Letter on Toleration*, published in 1689, *Locke caught a new mood of calm reason: persecution created, not converts, but hypocrites, 'for no man can, if he would, conform his faith to the dictates of another'.

There remained the problem of civil equality. No catholic and few dissenters could be MPs. Though full emancipation for catholics was held up in 1801 by the refusal of George III to sanction it, it was granted in 1829. Dissenters were allowed into Parliament in 1828 and more concessions on tithes and on marriages followed. In 1858 Jews were allowed into Parliament. At length, in 1886, after the *Bradlaugh case, even atheists were admitted to Westminster. From the beginning of the Reformation, it had taken a mere 350 years.

**Renaissance (rebirth)** characterizes the impulse, initiated in Italy, towards improving the contemporary world by discovering and applying the achievement of classical antiquity. The movement was at its strongest from the time of Petrarch (1304–74) through the 'long 16th cent.' (1450–1625). 'Renaissance' is now generally used to describe the politics, beliefs, philosophy, science, scholarship, discourse, literature, handwriting, printing, painting, engraving, sculpture, architecture, and music of that period.

'Renaissance' was first used alone in the 19th cent., though Giorgio Vasari (1550) saw a 'rinascità delle arti' in his own time, and Voltaire two centuries later a 'renaissance des lettres et des beaux-arts' in Medicean Florence. The concept of an epoch marked by 'the discovery of the world and of man' was taken up in Jakob Burckhardt's *Kultur der Renaissance in Italien* (1860). For Burckhardt the defining emphasis of the Renaissance was secular and individual; the new attitudes he detected in the Italy of that epoch to nature, morality, religion, affairs, art, and literature made him see it as inaugurating the modern era.

The English Renaissance was influenced by the Italian indirectly, through France, Burgundy, and the Netherlands, as well as directly. In its earliest phase, the patronage and book collections of Humphrey, duke of *Gloucester (1390–1447), were important; later, under Henry VII, William Grocyn and Thomas Linacre won a reputation for Greek. From about 1500, however, the chief force in English humanism was the concept of *pietas literata*, or evangelical humanism, associated with Erasmus. The friendship of Erasmus with John *Colet and with Thomas *More was particularly significant; he and More translated Greek together.

England produced no humanist scholar of the first rank during the Renaissance, More's *Utopia* being the finest Latin achievement of its early Tudor phase. Many classical and humanist works were translated into the vernacular, however. A pattern of civility on the Italian model was offered by Sir Thomas *Elyot (*Book Named the Governor*, 1531) and Sir Thomas Hoby (translation of Castiglione's *Courtier*, 1561). Greek studies were notable, from the 1520s especially in association with the Reformation. Erasmus' Greek New Testament with Latin translation (1516–19) was used by Martin Luther for his German New Testament (1521): William *Tyndale used both for his English version (1526–34).

The visual arts and architecture of Renaissance England remained predominantly traditional, in spite of the presence of Italian sculptors and of north European painters such as Hans *Holbein the Younger, Rubens, and *Van Dyck. The first English architect and designer of international stature was Inigo *Jones, the Palladian (1573–1652). Music similarly remained traditional until the flowering of the Italian fashion (1575–1625).

**Rennie, John** (1761–1821). Millwright and civil engineer from Phantassie (Lothian). Rennie learned millwrighting from Andrew Meikle, but added an academic education at Edinburgh, before his first major project, *Watt's Albion Mills in London (1784–8). He continued to advise on mills, but became primarily a civil engineer—of canals, the Kennet and Avon (1810) and Rochdale (1804); bridges, famously Waterloo (1817), Southwark (1819), and London (1831); Bell Rock lighthouse (1810); and numerous dock and harbour works, London (1805), Holyhead (completed 1824), and the massive breakwater at Plymouth (from 1811).

**Repeal Association,** 1840–8. *O'Connell's *Catholic Association was suppressed when catholic emancipation was carried in 1829 but agitation for the repeal of the Union soon recommenced. In 1840, faced with the prospect of a Tory government under *Peel, he responded by organizing the Repeal Association, supported by the 'repeal rent'. It drew up petitions, arranged candidates, sponsored monster meetings, and employed 50 headquarters staff. In 1843 the government banned a meeting at Clontarf and four months later O'Connell was sent to gaol for conspiracy. The Association was replaced in 1848 by a short-lived Irish League.

**representative peers** At the time of the negotiations for Union in 1707, there were more than 130 Scottish peers to 170 English ones. To unite them in one House would have given the Scots disproportionate influence. By the Act of *Union, Scotland was awarded 16 representative peers, to be elected by their colleagues before each session. The practice soon developed of circulating government and opposition lists and, under normal circumstances, the Scottish representative peers were useful allies of government in the House of Lords. A similar formula was adopted at the Union with Ireland in 1801.

**Repton** A 'double monastery', founded in the late 7th cent., it had close associations with the Mercian royal house. The Mercian prince St Guthlac began his monastic career at Repton, and several Mercian kings and princes were buried there including Merewalh, *Æthelbald (d. 757), and *Wiglaf (d. 840).

**Repton, Humphry** (1752–1818). The leading landscape gardener after Lancelot 'Capability' *Brown and a contemporary of Sir Uvedale Price (1747–1829) and Richard Payne Knight (1750–1824). Generally Repton followed Brown, but introduced formal parterres, terraces, and steps near the house, and used arbours, conservatories, lodges, and cottages. Repton's celebrated technique of explaining his designs involved using 'Red Books' with sliding panels indicating the effects 'before' and 'after' improvement.

**republicanism** After the only British experience of a republic, the *Commonwealth of 1649–60, republicanism did not have its own party. Nevertheless, republican sentiment was common among British radicals in the late 18th and 19th cents. Supporters of the American and French revolutions and admirers of Thomas *Paine were usually republicans, as also were the plebeian radicals of the 1820s and 1830s, notably the followers of Richard Carlile, who published the *Republican* from 1819 to 1826. Some chartists were openly republican, as witness two late chartist journals, C. G. Harding's *Republican* (1848) and W. J. Linton's *English Republic* (1851–5). Periods of monarchical unpopularity stimulated republicanism. This was so during the Regency and again in the late 1860s and early 1870s, when a group of Liberal MPs, including Sir Charles *Dilke and Joseph *Chamberlain, revived the republican cause, fuelled by Queen Victoria's withdrawal from public life. At the same time popular republicanism was spread by Charles *Bradlaugh and the secularist movement; and a short-lived journal, the *Republican*, appeared in 1870. The labour and socialist movements of the 1880s and 1890s were republican in principle. But republicanism was only one of the constituents and not a major part of the programme.

**Restoration** The restoration of the monarchy in 1660 was due more to the failure of alternative republican regimes than to the efforts of loyalists. An army junta dispersed the *Rump Parliament in October 1659 but failed to rally civilian support. Dissident garrison soldiers restored the Rump and General *Monck invaded England with the army of occupation in Scotland. He quickly realized that the Rump no longer possessed the consent of the nation; he therefore restored the MPs who had been excluded from the Commons in 1648, on condition that they dissolved Parliament so that new elections could be held. The resulting *Convention invited Charles II to return.

Restoration meant the return of legality, ending arbitrary or 'sword' government and changes enforced by a politicized army. Arbitrary high courts disappeared and Charles I's prerogative courts were not revived. Parliaments were again to be elected on the traditional franchises and by the old constituencies. The Lords returned. Levels of taxation fell sharply as most of the army was disbanded. An Indemnity Act pardoned all except the regicides.

**retainers** *See* BASTARD FEUDALISM.

**Revocation Act,** 1625. When Charles I succeeded his father he already had difficult relations with the Scottish kirk. He increased these in 1625 by a prerogative Act of Revocation, whereby church or royal property which had been alienated since 1540 was taken back by the crown. This greatly alarmed the nobility and raised the spectre of a wholesale attack upon property rights.

**Revolutionary and Napoleonic wars** (1793–1815). Following its defeat of the Prussians at Valmy in September 1792, revolutionary France announced war against the states of the *ancien régime*. In response Britain sent an army under the duke of *York to Flanders in 1793, joining the Dutch and Austrians in the 'War of the First Coalition'. After an inept campaign the defeated Dutch made peace and the remnants of York's army were evacuated from Breda in March 1795. Expeditions against French colonies in the West Indies 1793–6 met with mixed success, although in 1795 the British seized Cape Town and Ceylon from their former Dutch allies. Naval victories over the French in 1794 ('the *Glorious First of June'), the Spanish at *Cape St Vincent in February 1797, and the

Dutch at *Camperdown in October 1797 confirmed Britain's mastery of the seas.

In 1795 Prussia and Spain made peace with France. The defeat of Austria, which made peace by the treaty of Campo Formio in October 1797, ended the first coalition. This was followed by Napoleon's expedition to Egypt in 1798, intended to support Britain's enemies in India, which came to nothing with the destruction of the French fleet at the *Nile in August 1798, the defeat of Tipu of Mysore by an Anglo-Indian army under Arthur Wellesley (*Wellington) in May 1799, and the elimination of the French in Egypt by Abercromby at *Alexandria in March 1801.

Britain formed the 'second coalition', including Austria, Russia, Portugal, Naples, and Ottoman Turkey, in autumn 1798, but a renewed expedition to the Netherlands under York in 1799 again achieved little. Austria was defeated by Napoleon at Marengo in June 1800, and made peace by the treaty of Lunéville in February 1801. Russia also made peace, joining with Sweden, Denmark, and Prussia to form the *League of Armed Neutrality in 1800. This collapsed after the assassination of Tsar Paul and the destruction of the Danish fleet by the British at *Copenhagen in April 1801.

The treaty of *Amiens in March 1802 between Britain and France ended the 'War of the Second Coalition'. But continued French expansion in southern Europe brought a renewed declaration of war from Britain by May 1803. On 2 December 1804 Napoleon proclaimed himself emperor of the French, leading to British treaties with Russia, Austria, and Sweden in the 'War of the Third Coalition'. Despite the failure of Napoleon's plans to invade Britain and the destruction of his fleet by Nelson at *Trafalgar in October 1805, he drove Austria out of the war with victories at Ulm and at Austerlitz, leading to the treaty of Pressburg in December. This was followed by Napoleon's humiliating defeat of Prussia at Jena in October 1806. Russia was also defeated at Eylau and Friedland, and accepted the treaty of Tilsit of July 1807, leaving France dominant in central Europe.

Against Britain, his remaining enemy, Napoleon resorted to economic warfare ('the Continental System'). A French campaign against Portugal, begun in November 1807, was complicated by a Spanish revolt in May 1808, followed by the arrival of a British army under Wellesley in August (the start of the '*Peninsular War'). This became the main British theatre of war, with Wellesley's victories over the French at *Talavera in July 1809 (for which he was made Viscount Wellington), *Fuentes de Onoro in May 1811, Badajoz and *Salamanca in April and July 1812, and *Vitoria in June 1813.

In June 1812 Napoleon attacked Russia, reaching Moscow. Thereafter his army disintegrated through supply problems, disease, Russian attacks, and finally winter. Austria and Prussia rose in revolt, and at Leipzig ('the battle of the Nations') in October 1813 Napoleon was again defeated by a combined Russian-Austrian-Prussian force. In February 1814 Wellington crossed into France from Spain, by March the Prussians had reached Paris, and on 20 April Napoleon abdicated, being exiled to Elba.

The final flourish of the Napoleonic wars was the 'Hundred Days', Napoleon's escape from Elba on 1 March 1815 and return to power in France, culminating in his decisive defeat by a coalition army under Wellington at *Waterloo on 18 June 1815, and his exile to *St Helena.

**Reynolds, Sir Joshua** (1723–92). Portrait painter, born in Devon to a scholarly and clerical family. Educated at his father's school, Reynolds showed early skill in drawing and portraiture and by 1743 was in practice on his own. Almost every person of note in the second half of the 18th cent. had their portrait painted by Reynolds. In 1764 he formed the Club, whose members included Samuel *Johnson, Edmund *Burke, Oliver *Goldsmith, and Adam *Smith. In 1768, on the founding of the Royal Academy, Reynolds was the obvious choice for president. Between 1769 and 1790 he wrote and delivered an influential series of *Discourses* on art.

**Rheged, kingdom of** A 6th-cent. British kingdom round the Solway Firth and southern Galloway, its capital was possibly Carlisle. In Roman times the inhabitants of the area had been the Novantae. Its best-known ruler, Urien, much praised by *Taliesin, was said to have attacked the *Bernicians *c.*580 and to have been killed some ten years later besieging *Bamburgh.

**Rhodes, Cecil** (1853–1902). Imperialist and capitalist. In 1870 Rhodes went to

\*Natal to help his brother grow cotton, but amassed a huge fortune in diamonds and gold. He became prime minister of the Cape in 1890; opened up the country north of the Limpopo, modestly naming it \*Rhodesia; and was involved in the \*Jameson Raid. When he died, his final will provided for a series of scholarships to Oxford.

**Rhodesia** was the name given to an irregularly shaped region of southern Africa, bounded by Bechuanaland, the Congo, German East Africa (Tanganyika), and Mozambique, first exploited by \*Rhodes's British South Africa Company in the 1890s. In 1964 the northern part became the independent nation of \*Zambia, leaving the white minority in Southern Rhodesia to mount a rearguard action against black rule, through a 'Unilateral Declaration of Independence'—independence, that is, from British suzerainty—issued in 1965. Eventually the native peoples won their own battle, helped by international sanctions; and Rhodesia achieved independence as the majority-ruled state of Zimbabwe in 1980. Since then it has been ruled by Robert \*Mugabe and the ZANU–PF party.

**Rhodri** (d. 878), king of Gwynedd, Powys, and Deheubarth (844–78), known as Rhodri Mawr ('the Great'). The son of Merfyn Frych ('the Freckled'), king of \*Gwynedd, and Nest of \*Powys, Rhodri assembled a dominion that inspired others to attempt the same. Rhodri acquired Gwynedd when his father died (844), Powys through his mother and uncle (855), and \*Seisyllwg (modern Carmarthenshire and Cardiganshire) after his wife's brother died.

**Rhuddlan, statute of,** 1284. Sometimes known as the statute of Wales, this was in fact a royal ordinance, not issued by Parliament. It was intended to settle the government of Wales after the execution of \*Dafydd ap Gruffydd in 1283. English criminal law was to be introduced, but Welsh custom and law were to operate in civil proceedings. Six sheriffdoms were established in Anglesey, Caernarfon, Merioneth, Flint, Carmarthen, and Cardiganshire.

**Rhys ap Gruffydd** (1132–97), king of Deheubarth (1155–97), known as 'the Lord Rhys'. The younger son of Gruffydd ap Rhys, king of \*Deheubarth, and Gwenllian,

daughter of \*Gruffydd ap Cynan, king of \*Gwynedd, he married Gwenllian, daughter of \*Madog ap Maredudd, king of \*Powys. He acknowledged the overlordship of Henry II (1158), who tried to limit his dominion; but Rhys rebelled and in 1164–5 seized Cardigan. Henry II respected his power and after Anglo-Norman lords were diverted to Ireland (1169) they came to terms. Richard I was less sympathetic and hostilities marred the years before Rhys's death on 28 April 1197. In the hands of his quarrelsome sons, his kingdom disintegrated.

**Rhys ap Tewdwr** (d. 1093), king of \*Deheubarth (c.1078–93), known later as Rhys the Great. A descendant of \*Hywel Dda, he came to power in 1075, though only at the battle of \*Mynydd Carn (1081), and with \*Gruffydd ap Cynan's aid, did he defeat his rivals and relatives. By then the Norman advances in Wales had begun. William I travelled to St Davids in 1081, probably to assert his authority over Rhys, who may have acknowledged the king's overlordship. After William I's death (1087), Rhys tried to stop further Norman incursions, but was killed near Brecon.

**Ricardo, David** (1772–1823). Born in London of Dutch parents, Ricardo's career 1793–1814 was as a stockjobber. Accruing a reasonable fortune, he bought the country estate of Gatcombe Park in 1814; by 1819 he was elected member of Parliament. Much of his time was devoted to the study of mathematics, sciences, and political economy; this led to *On Principles of Political Economy and Taxation* (1817), where the influence of Adam \*Smith's *Wealth of Nations* is to be seen.

**Rich, St Edmund** (c.1170–1240). Archbishop of Canterbury. Born at Abingdon, he studied at Oxford and Paris where he was a renowned teacher of logic (c.1185–90). As primate (from 1234), he maintained \*Langton's ideals by resisting both royal and papal power. Differences with king, papacy, and his Canterbury monks were such (1240) that he retired to Pontigny, where he died.

**Richard I** (1157–99), king of England (1189–99). Richard has attracted legends in a way that bees are proverbially attracted to the honey-pot. The process began in his own lifetime. Already, by 1199, the epithet Cœur de Lion/Lionheart was being applied.

In the popular imagination today, Richard is a national English hero, the valorous warrior and glorious crusader who struggled against all the odds to come within an ace of recapturing Jerusalem from the equally legendary Saladin on the Third Crusade. The massive bronze statue of Richard in Westminster Palace Yard captures superbly the Ricardian qualities admired for centuries. A powerfully muscular Richard, imposing and magnificent, sits on horseback, in full armour and wearing a crown, his sword triumphantly raised aloft.

Yet English Richard was not, nor even Anglo-Norman. Although born in Oxford, he briefly visited England just twice before his accession in 1189. As king, he spent a mere six months in England. He was born of French parents, Henry II and Eleanor of Aquitaine. Richard spoke no English; he willed his body for burial in Fontevraud abbey (Poitou), his heart for interment in Rouen cathedral (Normandy). He was French through and through.

Yet despite this, most modern historians have judged him from an Anglocentric viewpoint. He might have been a warrior second to none, they argue, but he was an utterly irresponsible king of England, who plundered English wealth in pursuit of his own glory in France and the Holy Land, and who recklessly endangered the security and stability of his island realm.

Modern scholarship is at last beginning to reveal another Richard, one free from the excessive adulation or denunciation of the past, more balanced and credible. This has only become possible by considering him as *not* first and foremost an English king, but rather the lord of the French-based *Angevin empire which he inherited as a whole in 1189. His military reputation remains intact. Indeed, it has been enhanced. The inspired battlefield commander of tradition, and brilliant tactician—as evidenced, for example, by the march from *Acre to Jaffa and the battle of *Arsuf (1191)—is also coming increasingly to be seen as a master of planning and logistics. His crusade, in particular, involving the raising, fitting out, and dispatch of a fleet from northern waters to the east Mediterranean, is a superb example of administrative efficiency.

It has also become apparent that had Richard not been shipwrecked and captured, he would have returned home to find the governmental structure of the Angevin empire intact as he had established it before departure for the crusade in 1190. Far from setting out on crusade without a care for the security of his various dominions, England included, Richard did what he could in the short time available to him.

**Richard II** (1367–1400), king of England (1377–99). Richard became king in 1377 aged 9. There was no formal regency, but the government during his early years was dominated by his uncle *John of Gaunt. The imposition of the third *poll tax was a major cause of the outbreak of the *Peasants' Revolt in 1381; this was the occasion of Richard's first independent political action, when he faced the rebels at Smithfield, witnessed the slaying of Wat *Tyler, and saved the situation by his own intervention. The king's subsequent moves to play a greater political role led to escalating crises. In 1386 the chancellor, Michael de la *Pole, was impeached; Richard infuriated Parliament by declaring that he would not dismiss even a kitchen boy at its request. He provocatively appointed his favourite, Robert de Vere, earl of *Oxford, to be duke of Ireland. The defeat of de Vere at *Radcot Bridge in the autumn of 1387 left Richard defenceless in the face of his aristocratic opponents. The so-called *Merciless Parliament of 1388 conducted a purge of government, using the weapons of appeal and impeachment against a range of royal ministers and favourites, including de la Pole and de Vere.

The return of John of Gaunt from Spain in 1389 brought a renewed sense of purpose and direction to government. The work of the Merciless Parliament was undone, as far as was possible, in 1389, and Richard wisely did not revert to the excesses which had led to crisis in 1387. The final crisis of the reign began in September 1397 when Richard moved against those he regarded as his enemies in a carefully managed Parliament. Archbishop *Arundel was impeached and exiled. Royalist magnates brought appeals against the earls of Gloucester, Arundel, and Warwick. Arundel was executed, Warwick exiled, and Gloucester almost certainly murdered. In 1398 a dispute between Henry Bolingbroke, duke of Hereford (later Henry IV), and the duke of *Norfolk led to the exiling of the two men, after Richard prohibited a judicial duel between them at Coventry. In March 1399 Bolingbroke's Lancastrian inheritance was confiscated. In May the king embarked on a new expedition to Ireland. This was disastrous for, in June, Bolingbroke, now duke of Lancaster after his father's death, invaded England. In the king's absence, there was little resistance. On his return from Ireland, Richard was taken in north Wales, and on 30 September, a broken man, agreed to abdicate, and was deposed in Parliament. Richard did not long survive his deposition, dying at Pontefract, probably early in 1400.

**Richard III** (1452–85), king of England (1483–5). Richard is one of England's most controversial figures, immortalized as evil personified by *Shakespeare, sanctified by a society dedicated to clearing his name. Born at Fotheringhay (Northants), he was the youngest son of Richard of *York and Cecily Neville. He was still a child when his brother Edward IV became king. Stalwartly loyal to his brother, he shared in the triumph of 1471, distinguishing himself on the field of *Barnet. He was handsomely rewarded by Edward IV, who granted him the Neville estates and royal offices in the north of England. With these, and *Warwick's daughter *Anne as his duchess, he made himself even more powerful than the Kingmaker. In 1480 he led the war against Scotland, securing the recovery of Berwick in 1482.

In April 1483 Richard's future was put in doubt by the death of his brother. By a series of palace coups, he seized power, first to secure himself as protector of the realm in the minority of his nephew Edward V and secondly in June to make himself king. He was crowned on 6 July. In September his enemies in the southern counties raised rebellion in the name of Henry Tudor. Even though they were joined by the duke of *Buckingham they were easily dispersed. Richard reigned for two further years in a climate of intensifying crisis as Henry Tudor planned to invade England. The two finally came to blows on 22 August 1485 near Bosworth. Although he fought courageously, Richard was overwhelmed and killed in the mêlée.

Almost every aspect of Richard's career is controversial. The coup of 1483 is interpreted as justifiable self-preservation, or a

skilfully executed usurpation, or a sequence of ill-considered impulsive reactions. His reign has been seen as a valiant attempt to administer justice impartially, or as tyranny in which his northern retainers occupied the south. On the one hand he was genuinely pious, on the other hand he was a cynical hypocrite.

Above all looms the controversy over his crimes. He is probably to be found not proven on the princes in the Tower. Henry VII and the duke of Buckingham have been proposed as alternative culprits. Yet the fact remains that the boys were widely believed to be dead by the middle of September 1483 and Richard himself was believed by contemporaries to have been responsible. It is almost impossible to get to the bottom of all these controversies; partly because insufficient evidence has survived; partly because so much is coloured by propaganda; partly because he divided opinion sharply in his day; and partly because over 500 years the stories of Richard III have taken on their own independent life. Thus Richard III has become a literary figure. This was so from the very beginning, for the supposed peculiarities of his birth and the hunchback, for which he is renowned, were but inventions to signify evil.

**Richard, earl of Cornwall** (1209–72), king of the Romans (1257–72). The younger brother of Henry III, he was granted the earldom of Cornwall (with its tin-mines), which made him the richest man in England after the king. He led the baronial opposition to Henry in the late 1230s, but remained solidly loyal in the years of baronial reform and rebellion (1258–65), suffering the indignity of being captured in a windmill, after the battle of *Lewes (1264). In 1257 he was elected king of Germany, but never fully established his authority over the country before his death.

**Richardson, Samuel** (1689–1761). Novelist. Born in Derbyshire, Richardson settled in London and became a master printer. His first novel *Pamela or Virtue Rewarded* (1740–2) was published when he was 51. *Clarissa Harlowe* and *Sir Charles Grandison* followed in 1744 and 1753. They were instant successes. They dealt with the manners and morals of relatively ordinary people attempting to survive in a naughty world with some degree of happiness and self-respect. They were salacious enough to make excellent reading.

**Richmond palace** began as a manor house at Sheen (Surrey) and was much used by Edward III, who died there. Henry V restored it and, after a disastrous fire in 1497, Henry VII rebuilt it on the grand scale, giving it his own title of Richmond. Mary used it frequently and Elizabeth died there, but during the civil wars it fell into decay.

**riding** is a term indicating a third part. By 1086 Yorkshire was divided into North, West, and East Ridings, all three converging on York. The arrangement may well be of Scandinavian origin. The Yorkshire ridings became independent counties by the Act of 1888; the arrangements being much altered by local government legislation of 1972 and 1996.

**Ridley, Nicholas** (c.1500–55). One of the celebrated 'Oxford martyrs', Ridley played a significant role in shaping the protestant Church of England under Edward VI. A Northumbrian by birth, he studied at Newcastle, Cambridge, Paris, and Louvain, and around 1524 became a fellow of Pembroke College, Cambridge. In 1537 Archbishop *Cranmer chose him as a chaplain; in 1540 he returned to Pembroke as master. Soon after the accession of Edward VI, he was made bishop of Rochester. As bishop of London (1550) Ridley introduced some of the explicitly protestant liturgical innovations which were adopted nationally in the second Book of Common Prayer (1552). He was implicated in the duke of *Northumberland's plot to divert the succession to Lady Jane *Grey; however, it was for heresy rather than treason that Mary I pursued him. At the Oxford disputation of 1554, he defended himself bravely. He was executed by burning at Oxford on 16 October, alongside the former bishop of Worcester, Hugh *Latimer.

**Ridolfi plot,** 1571. Organized by the Italian banker Roberto Ridolfi, this was one of many conspiracies to free Mary, queen of Scots, and promote the catholic cause. Ridolfi began in 1570 to plan Mary's escape, with Thomas, duke of *Norfolk, Philip II of Spain, the Spanish ambassador, and the pope. The plot was uncovered by William Cecil, Lord *Burghley, and led to the execution of Norfolk for treason in 1572. Ridolfi escaped.

**Rievaulx abbey** (Yorks.) was founded in 1131 in the Rie valley by Walter Espec, lord of nearby Helmsley, in consultation with St Bernard, abbot of Clairvaux, and Archbishop *Thurstan of York. It was the second *Cistercian abbey to be established in England. The extensive ruins of the abbey constitute perhaps the finest surviving buildings of any English Cistercian house, and the east end of the abbey church, rebuilt c.1225, is a masterpiece of English Gothic architecture.

***Rights of Man, The*** (Part I 1791; Part II 1792). Thomas *Paine's defence of the French Revolution against the attack launched by Edmund *Burke in his *Reflections on the Revolution in France* (1790). Part I traced the origins of the Revolution and explicated the Declaration of the Rights of Man made by the National Assembly. Part II denounced the hereditary system, prophesied the immediate overthrow of the monarchy, argued that the only defensible form of government was representative democracy, and sketched the outlines of a system of state welfare.

**Riot Act,** 1715. The Riot Act (1 Geo. I s. 2 c. 5) was hastily passed in July 1715 by a Whig Parliament to deal with the threat of Jacobite insurrection. It provided that, if twelve or more persons, tumultuously assembled, refused to disperse within one hour of a magistrate reading a proclamation, they would be guilty of a felony and could face the death penalty. But if the Act was intended to stiffen magistrates, it was a doubtful success. The procedure which became known as 'reading the Riot Act' was difficult to carry out: magistrates were reluctant to read the proclamation and troops even more reluctant to open fire. The proclamation was read for the last time in 1919 but the Act was not repealed until 1967.

**Ripon, diocese of** Though the modern bishopric was not carved out of the *York diocese until 1836, Ripon's early ecclesiastical history is inextricably associated with *Wilfrid. About 650, Celtic monks from Melrose and Iona founded a monastery here, but in 661 Wilfrid, by then in Roman orders,

*Achilles* (both 6-inch guns). Though putting *Exeter* out of action, *Graf Spee* withdrew to Montevideo in the Plate estuary. Captain Langsdorff then blew up and sank *Graf Spee* rather than fight the superior British force he expected and shot himself.

**Rivers, Anthony Woodville, 2nd Earl** (1442–83). The eldest brother of *Elizabeth Woodville, he benefited from the marriage of his sister to Edward IV. Shortly after Edward IV's death, he was seized at Stony Stratford by Richard of Gloucester, whom he had taken to be his ally. On 22 June he was summarily executed at Pontefract. Rivers enjoyed a high reputation among his contemporaries for his chivalry, piety, and learning.

**Rizzio, David** (c.1533–66). Servant of Mary Stuart, brutally murdered in the presence of the pregnant queen by a group of conspirators including Mary's husband *Darnley. Born in Turin, and arriving in Scotland in 1561 in the entourage of the Savoyard ambassador, Rizzio gained Mary's attention through his musicianship, but later acted as her secretary.

**Robert I (Robert Bruce)** (1274–1329), earl of Carrick (1292–1306), king of Scots as Robert I (1306–29). Grandson of Robert *Bruce, the competitor for the Scottish throne in 1291, Bruce never lost sight of his claim to the throne. After John *Balliol's resignation in 1296, Edward I starkly refused any consideration of the Bruce claim. Despite the Scots' continued loyalty to their deposed king Bruce was deeply involved in the rising of 1297, and continued in resistance even after the defeat at *Falkirk (22 July 1298). He served as joint guardian from 1298 probably to early 1300, and remained on the Scottish side till 1302. Then however he made his peace with Edward. Bruce's desertion certainly reduced the chances of Balliol's restoration; and resistance to Edward collapsed in 1304.

Bruce's next move, the coup of 1306, remains very hard to explain. We know that he tried to negotiate with John *Comyn of Badenoch just before he revolted openly early in 1306, and that the result was a quarrel in which Comyn was murdered. Barrow has suggested that Bruce had been biding his time till Edward was close to death, and that in 1306 he judged the time ripe.

Bruce was crowned as Robert I on 25 March 1306; but though Edward was sick

**Ripon, George Frederick Robinson, 1st Marquis** (1827–1909). Son of the 1st earl of Ripon (*Goderich), he was returned to the House of Commons as a Liberal in 1852, succeeding to the title in 1859. He was a loyal *Gladstonite, serving as under-secretary and then secretary of state for war and for India. In 1880, upon Gladstone's re-election, he was appointed viceroy of India to reverse the belligerent Afghan policies of his predecessor, Lord *Lytton. He advanced the causes of Indian education and local self-government. He retired from India with the defeat of Gladstone's government in 1885 but remained politically active into old age. He was colonial secretary in 1892 and lord privy seal 1905–8.

**Ripon, treaty of,** 1640. The treaty of Ripon brought to an end the second *Bishops' War between Charles I and the Scottish *covenanters. Charles had little to negotiate with. By the terms of the armistice, the Scots were left in occupation of the six northern counties and were to receive expenses of £860 a day. The king had lost control of the situation.

**River Idle, battle of the,** 616. According to *Bede, *Edwin, young son of Aelle, king of *Deira, was driven out of the kingdom by Æthelfric, king of *Bernicia, and at length took refuge with *Rædwald, king of East Anglia. Rædwald resisted demands by *Æthelfryth, successor to Æthelfric, to surrender Edwin and accompanied him to the river Idle, west of Gainsborough, where they won a great victory.

**River Plate, battle of the,** 1939. A German 'pocket battleship', *Graf Spee,* heavily armoured, with 11-inch guns, sinking British merchant ships in the South Atlantic, was attacked on 13 December 1939 by three British cruisers, *Exeter* (8-inch guns), *Ajax,* and he was not to be trifled with. Robert himself was defeated at *Methven (19 June 1306) by Edward's newly appointed lieutenant Aymer de *Valence. Robert's supporters and relatives were hunted down and executed; he himself had to go into hiding. He reappeared in Ayrshire in the spring of 1307, and Edward I died in July. Edward II had little energy to spare for Scotland for some years, and this enabled Robert to overcome his internal enemies. The power of the Comyns was destroyed at the battle of *Inverurie. Others, such as the earl of Ross, were won over. By 1314, effective English power was limited to Lothian.

The years from 1308 also saw King Robert's grip over government tightened. In a parliament at St Andrews in 1309, declarations were issued asserting Robert's right to the throne as the lawful successor of Alexander III, and denouncing the aggression of Edward I. Robert I was now widely accepted in Scotland as the rightful king. His authority was confirmed by the decisive victory of *Bannockburn (24 June 1314), following on the recapture of Edinburgh and Roxburgh castles earlier in the year.

In the rest of his reign, Robert I showed himself a masterful king. He was willing to be reconciled with his former enemies, and readily accepted the loyal service of those who were willing to submit. His two chief problems were to secure the succession and to obtain recognition by other rulers. He fell foul of the papacy by his refusal to comply with a papal truce in 1317, as a result of which he was eventually excommunicated in 1320. That excommunication was respited as a result of the appeal usually known as the 'declaration of *Arbroath'; from then on, the pope was prepared at least to give King Robert his proper title. English recognition was more difficult. Edward II would not concede it; and it came only after his deposition. At last in 1328, by the treaty of *Edinburgh/*Northampton, the English government admitted that Robert was king, and agreed to a marriage between his heir and a sister of the young Edward III as an earnest of a settled peace.

Robert died, perhaps of leprosy, on 7 June 1329, having secured both his own position and the independence of his country. Ever since his death, he has been the great hero of the Wars of Independence, the man who foiled Edward I's attempt to assert his authority over Scotland, and who defeated all efforts by Edward II to recover the position which Edward I had lost in 1306.

**Robert II** (1316–90), steward of Scotland (1326–71), earl of Strathearn (1357–69 and 1370–1), the first Stewart king of Scots (1371–90). The birth of a son to Robert I in 1324 left Robert only as heir presumptive failing a direct heir to David II. He was several times king's lieutenant during David's minority and captivity.

Robert was 55 when he eventually succeeded the childless David. For a time he proved more capable than his earlier career would have suggested. Too old to take the field himself, he made good use of the younger nobles to exploit the weakness of English authority during the senility of Edward III and the minority of Richard II. Payment of David's ransom was stopped in 1377; and by the early 1380s most of the lands in English occupation had been recovered. By that time, however, Richard II was emerging as a determined ruler, while Robert II's age was telling. In 1384, as more open war was breaking out, a general council deprived Robert of control of justice, which was given to his son John, earl of Carrick, the future Robert III. He was in turn succeeded in 1388 by the king's second son Robert, earl of Fife, and future duke of *Albany. Robert II died in April 1390, at the age of 74.

**Robert III** (c.1337–1406), earl of Carrick (1368–90), king of Scots (1390–1406). Eldest son of Robert, steward of Scotland, later Robert II. His baptismal name was John, but he took the name Robert when he became king. In his own alleged words, Robert III was 'the worst of kings and the most wretched of men!'

From 1384, the incapacity of his father left John responsible for the administration of justice; but in 1388 he himself was incapacitated by a kick from a horse, and his brother Robert, earl of Fife, was made guardian. Neither Fife nor the king himself proved able to contain the flood of violence, particularly in the north, where Forres was sacked in 1390, and Elgin in 1391 by another of the king's brothers, Alexander, earl of *Buchan, the 'Wolf of Badenoch'.

Robert was faced in 1398 with a struggle for power between the earl of Fife, created duke of *Albany in that year, and the king's 20-year-old son David, created at the same time duke of Rothesay, and appointed in his turn lieutenant for a period of three years. Rothesay proved energetic, but in 1402 he was removed from office in a coup evidently organized by Albany and died in captivity shortly after. Robert III could do nothing to check the power of these nobles, despite the disastrous result of a battle which they provoked against the English at *Homildon Hill (14 September 1402). In 1406 he tried to send his remaining son James (b. 1394) to safety in France, but he was captured off Flamborough Head and taken to captivity in England. Robert's death followed immediately on the shock of the news.

**Robert, earl of Gloucester** (c.1090–1147), was Henry I's favourite from among his many illegitimate sons and was advanced by him to be one of the leading magnates of the Anglo-Norman realm. In 1135 Robert apparently accepted King Stephen's succession, but in 1138 he declared his support for his half-sister *Matilda, and was thereafter the empress's most powerful supporter. His importance to her cause is illustrated by the way in which he was exchanged in 1142 after his capture at Stockbridge for the captive King Stephen, himself taken at the battle of *Lincoln in 1141, and by the fact that Matilda left England very soon after his death.

**Robert Curthose, duke of Normandy** (c.1050–1134), the eldest son of William the Conqueror, was designated as heir to *Normandy before 1066. Any hopes Robert may have had of obtaining England were, however, dashed by his father's death-bed bequest in 1087. Two attempts in 1088 and 1101 to wrest the kingdom from his brothers William II and Henry I failed and in 1106 he was himself ousted from the duchy by Henry after the battle of *Tinchebrai. He was thereafter kept in prison until his death. His heroic contribution to the First Crusade (1096–1100) shows him as a redoubtable warrior capable of prospering in a great military enterprise. His nickname, literally 'Short Boots', is said to have been conferred by his father.

**Robert of Jumièges** (d. c.1052). Archbishop. Born in Normandy, Robert Champart became abbot of Jumièges in 1037 and made the acquaintance of the future Edward the Confessor. He followed Edward to England and was made bishop of London in 1044. In great favour with the king, he was hostile to the powerful *Godwine family. In 1051 the king appointed him archbishop of Canterbury. The Godwines were driven into brief exile, but when they returned in strength in 1052, Robert fled to the continent. Though he gained papal support, he was unable to recover his see and *Stigand, an ally of Earl Godwine, was appointed in his place.

**Roberts, Frederick Sleigh** (1832–1914). Field marshal. Roberts first demonstrated his talents as an army officer during the Indian mutiny (1857–8). During the second *Afghan War (1878–80) he defeated Ayub Khan's army at the battle of Kandahar and was created baron of Kandahar in 1892. From 1885 to 1893 he was commander-in-chief in India and came to prominence once again during the second Anglo-Boer War (1899–1902). The British forces had suffered several humiliating defeats before Roberts arrived in South Africa to take command, when his strategy led to the capture of the two Boer (Afrikaner) republican capitals, Bloemfontein and Pretoria.

**Robin Hood** Along with King *Arthur, Robin Hood is one of the most enduring of legendary heroes. The early versions emphasized Robin's skill with a bow, the later ones that he robbed the rich to help the poor. Maid Marian, who provides the love interest, was a 16th-cent. addition to the story. The earliest reference is in Langland's *Piers Plowman* (c.1377), in which one character remarks that he knows the rhymes of Robin Hood. The stories are set in the 1190s, with King Richard away on crusade and his shifty brother John misgoverning the country. The area of the greenwood is usually taken as Sherwood Forest in Nottinghamshire, or Barnsdale near Wentbridge in Yorkshire, but Barnsdale in Rutland is also a possibility. The many Robin Hood wells and caves are subsequent namings. The original poems were intended for minstrel performance but plays, novels, films, and cartoons eventually followed.

**Robinson Crusoe** This fictional autobiography, published anonymously in 1719 by Daniel *Defoe, has attained the status of myth. Although its indebtedness to the true story of the experiences of Alexander Selkirk has been exaggerated, Crusoe's shipwreck and subsequent desert-island experience is central whether it is approached as traveller's tale, religious allegory, or proto-novel.

**Rochdale Pioneers** is the name given to William Cooper, Charles Howarth, and 26 founders of the *Co-operative movement, whose shop opened in Toad Lane in 1844. They had been encouraged by a lecture from George Holyoake on self-help. It began on a small scale, opened only on Saturday and Monday evenings with the members serving in the shop. The principle was that profits should be redistributed to purchasers by means of a dividend. By 1851 there were 130 similar shops and by 1862 450 co-operative enterprises. As the volume of business expanded, the original social, political, and educational objectives were pushed into the background by commercial considerations.

**Roches, Peter des** (c.1175–1238). A cleric from the Touraine, he entered royal service in the 1190s and was rewarded with the bishopric of Winchester in 1205. He remained loyal to the king throughout John's quarrel with the papacy and was appointed *justiciar in 1213 and then guardian of the young Henry III in 1216. He was a key figure in the minority government, his military skill helping to win the 1217 battle of *Lincoln.

**Rochester, diocese of** Now comprising west Kent, Rochester is the second oldest English see, founded by King *Æthelbert of Kent in 604, with *Justus as first bishop. *Paulinus, the former missionary to Northumbria, expelled in 632, was bishop of Rochester (635–44). Despite its vulnerability to the 9th-cent. Danish invasions, it survived intact. The medieval bishopric had a small population but in the 19th and 20th cents. it became densely inhabited. The cathedral, alongside the 12th-cent. castle, has an impressive late Norman nave, completed in 1130 with additions (1179–1240).

**Rochester, Laurence Hyde, 1st earl of** (1642–1711). Laurence Hyde was the second son of the historian and lord chancellor and younger brother of the 2nd earl of *Clarendon. His sister *Anne married the duke of York (later James II) in 1660 and died in

1671. Hyde served in the House of Commons 1660–81, was employed on diplomatic missions, and was made 1st lord of the Treasury 1679–84 (not the post it later became). When James succeeded in 1685, Rochester and Clarendon, brothers-in-law to the king, carried all before them. Rochester was given the Garter, appointed lord president of the council 1684–5, and then lord treasurer. But James dismissed him in 1686 when he refused to convert to catholicism. A fierce high Tory, he accepted William and Mary after the Revolution, was lord-lieutenant of Ireland 1700–3 and lord president of the council again 1710–11.

**Rochester, John Wilmot, 2nd earl of** (1647–80). Poet and courtier. Wilmot's father fought for the king in the Civil War, was created a baron in 1643, and advanced to the earldom in 1652. Wilmot inherited the title at the age of 11, spent a year at Wadham College, Oxford, fought as a volunteer in the naval battle off *Lowestoft in 1665, and was appointed a groom of the bedchamber the following year. He was a crony of *Buckingham, with a reputation as a wit, debauchee, drunkard, and patron. Some of his poems circulated in manuscript during his lifetime: the collected poems came out in 1680 and 1691. Much of the output is tediously coarse, but there are occasional jewels. His epigram on Charles II is justly famous—'who never said a foolish thing, nor ever did a wise one'.

**Rochester castle** (Kent) stands above the river Medway whose crossing it controlled. The present castle was begun by Gundulf, bishop of Rochester, for William Rufus 1087–9. It was transformed by the addition of a keep built 1127–40, after Henry I had granted the castle to the archbishop of Canterbury. The defensive strength of the castle was demonstrated in 1215 when rebel barons held it against King John. The royal forces took the castle only after they managed to undermine the south-east angle tower.

**Rockingham, Charles Watson-Wentworth, 2nd marquis of** (1730–82). An often underrated politician, Rockingham contributed significantly to the emergence of a distinct Whig ideology. Although his two brief periods as prime minister (1765–6 and 1782) were unhappy, Rockingham achieved much as a party leader. Having held a court appointment from 1751, Rockingham resigned in November 1762 and joined the opposition to Lord *Bute. He was appointed 1st lord of the Treasury in 1765 and successfully orchestrated the repeal of the *Stamp Act in 1766. Rockingham, nevertheless, believed in the subservience of the colonies and repeal was accompanied by a *Declaratory Act, asserting British legislative supremacy. Dismissed in March 1766 because of his continuing suspicions of Bute's influence, he remained in opposition for the next sixteen years. Rockingham and his followers constantly reiterated that they were the only true Whigs and, by force of repetition, a diffuse term was reclaimed: the Rockinghams gradually developed a near monopoly of the title 'Whig Party'. Much was made of the supposedly increased power of the crown and it was argued that the political advantages derived from granting places and contracts ought to be reduced. *Economical reform was favoured rather than parliamentary reform. Rockingham's return to power, in the wake of Lord *North's fall, was irresistible, since his party was the largest in opposition. Rockingham insisted on becoming 1st lord of the Treasury, but his premiership was undermined by the king's insistence on cabinet office for *Shelburne, whom Rockingham rightly mistrusted. Ministers were soon at loggerheads and Rockingham's unexpected death in July 1782 may have simply hastened a looming political crisis.

**Rockingham, Council of,** 1095. *Anselm had become archbishop of Canterbury in 1093 at a time when there were rival popes, Urban II and Clement III. He asked William Rufus for permission to seek the pallium from Urban, and was refused. On 25 February 1095 a council at Rockingham attempted to resolve the question of divided allegiance and urged Anselm to conform to the royal will. Though the conflict was compromised and Rufus recognized Urban, the pope refused to depose Anselm. The archbishop spent the years 1097 to 1100 abroad, returning only after Rufus' sudden death.

**Rodney, George Brydges** (1719-92). Admiral. Always solicitous towards the concerns of the lower deck, Rodney conspicu-

ously failed in his relations with brother officers, and his ill-starred quest for wealth could prejudice his commands out of a greed for prize money. His service spanned the mid-18th-cent. wars and he became well acquainted with the West Indies theatre. Promotion to rear-admiral in 1759 did not afford future financial security, and during 1775-8 Rodney was effectively bankrupt and self-exiled. The American War proved his salvation, and with his relief of Gibraltar (1779) and his saving of Jamaica through his defeat of de Grasse at 'the *Saints' on 12 April 1782, Rodney's lasting fame, though not his fortune, was assured.

**Roebuck, John Arthur** (1801-79). Radical MP for Bath (1832-7, 1841-7) and Sheffield (1849-68, 1874-9). Born in Madras and qualified as a barrister, Roebuck was nicknamed 'Tear 'Em' for his fierce attacks on aristocracy, privilege, and inefficiency. As a *Benthamite and friend of J. S. *Mill, Roebuck proposed a system of state education, supported the New Poor Law, and helped *Lovett draft the Charter. In 1855 he moved for a committee of inquiry into the conduct of the Crimean War, which resulted in the fall of *Aberdeen's government. From the exposure of military inefficiency, Roebuck went on to campaign for administrative (civil service) reform.

**Rogers, John** (c.1500-55). Martyr. Born in Birmingham and educated at Pembroke College, Cambridge, Rogers took holy orders but became a reformer under the influence of *Tyndale, whose English edition of the Bible he prepared for the press. In Edward VI's reign, Rogers was in favour and given London preferments, and immediately after the king's death preached at St Paul's Cross, by order of Lady Jane *Grey's council, warning the people against popery. After Mary had established her claim to the throne, Rogers was sent to prison and in February 1555 burned at Smithfield, dying with remarkable courage, the first of the protestant martyrs.

**Rolls, Charles Stewart** (1877-1910). Rolls was the third son of a wealthy Monmouthshire landowner, who served as Conservative MP for Monmouth 1880-5 and was created Lord Llangattock in 1892. He studied mechanical engineering at Trinity College, Cambridge, where he was a bicycling enthusiast. In 1895 he imported a Peugeot car from France and was stopped by a policeman who pointed out that he needed a man with a red flag to precede him: his journey back to Cambridge took just under twelve hours. In 1905 he joined forces with another engineer, F. H. *Royce, to establish a company producing cars at Derby. Greatly interested in aviation, he made many balloon flights, and in June 1910 crossed the Channel and back non-stop in a Wright brothers aeroplane. The following month he was killed in a flying accident at Bournemouth and buried at Llangattock-Vibon-Avel, near Monmouth.

**Roman Britain** Britain was the Roman province Britannia, AD 43–410. Although there had been increasing contact between Britain and the classical world during the late Iron Age, the first official Roman presence in Britain was that of Julius *Caesar in 55–54 BC. In AD 43 Emperor *Claudius invaded Britain on the pretext of dealing with troublesome tribal princes and druids. The island was subsequently occupied by the Romans, who took advantage of Britain's mineral and agricultural wealth.

Within a generation the British landscape had changed considerably. The Roman army built legionary fortresses, forts, camps, and roads, and assisted with the construction of buildings in towns. A number of important military installations, notably the legionary fortresses, were built close to pre-existing tribal centres (*oppida*) which then became the focus of important Romano-British towns, such as *Colchester. The Romans also brought their particular style of architecture to the countryside in the form of *villas.

*Tacitus tells us that the Romans experienced a number of tribal revolts in the 1st cent. and used the long-established practice of combining treaties with decisive military action to quell unrest. Rome created three client kingdoms: the *Iceni, the *Brigantes, and the *Atrebates. In AD 60 the Iceni rose up under the leadership of *Boudicca, destroying the Roman towns of Colchester, London, and St Albans. The crushing of the Boudiccan revolt was followed by a period of expansion of the Roman province, including the subjugation of south Wales. Between AD 77 and 83 the new governor *Agricola led a series of campaigns which enlarged the province significantly, taking in all Wales, Anglesey, northern England, and southern Scotland.

The 2nd cent. also saw important military and urban developments, particularly under the Emperor *Hadrian. He visited Britain following military disturbances, and in AD 122 ordered the construction of *Hadrian's Wall between the Tyne and the Solway. It was built ostensibly to separate the province from the barbarian north, but probably also acted as an effective customs barrier and a testament to the power of Rome. In AD 139–42 the Emperor Antoninus Pius abandoned Hadrian's Wall and constructed a new frontier defence system between the Forth and the Clyde—the *Antonine Wall—but its use was short-lived and Hadrian's Wall was again the main northern frontier by AD 164.

Roman towns fell into one of three main types: *coloniae, municipia,* and *civitates.* The *coloniae* of Roman Britain were Colchester, *Lincoln, *Gloucester, *York, and possibly *London, and their inhabitants were Roman citizens. The only certain *municipium* was *Verulamium (St Albans), a self-governing community with certain legal privileges. The *civitates,* towns of non-citizens, included the bulk of Britain's administrative centres, such as the tribal capitals of *Silchester, *Winchester, and *Canterbury. Towns usually contained temples, public baths, aqueducts, and an amphitheatre, most acquiring such a range of facilities by the mid-2nd cent.

By the 4th cent. the towns were dominated by stone-built 'mansions', and there were also profound changes in the countryside. Villas grew in size and became more enclosed, exemplified by 'courtyard villas' such as Chedworth. In the early 4th cent. most British villas were embellished with mosaics, an apparent investment in the agricultural basis of the province's wealth in this period. Epigraphic and literary evidence suggests that the Britons adopted Latinized names (e.g. Tiberius Claudius Cogidubnus) and that the élite (at least) spoke and wrote Latin. The indigenous Gaelic or 'Celtic' language of the Roman province Britannia also continued to be spoken; it survives today as Welsh and Cornish.

The end of Roman Britain followed a protracted series of barbarian raids and settlements in north-western Europe such as the 'Picts' War' of AD 367–8. In AD 401–2 troops were withdrawn from Britain by Stilicho to defend Italy, and in AD 408–9 Britain was attacked by Saxons. In AD 410 the Emperor Honorius told the cities of Britain to look to their own defence.

**Roman catholicism** *See* CATHOLICISM.

**Roman legions** formed the core of the Roman army. Each legion of heavily armed infantry consisted of some 5,000 Roman citizen men. The legionary soldier was recruited aged 18–20 for a period of 25 years. Good promotion prospects and a pension of a land grant ensured a constant supply of recruits. The rest of the army—infantry and cavalry—was made up of auxiliaries, who did not have to be Roman citizens.

The legions which invaded Britain in AD 43 under the command of *Aulus Plautius were the *II Augusta, IX Hispana, XIV Gemina*, and *XX Valeria*. With auxiliaries, the force totalled some 40,000 men. Each legion was based in a legionary fortress. The *II Augusta*, for example, was based variously at fortresses in *Exeter, *Gloucester, and *Caerleon.

**Rome, treaty of** Signed by France, Belgium, Italy, the Federal Republic of Germany, the Netherlands, and Luxembourg on 25 March 1957, it established both the *European Economic Community (EEC) and European Atomic Energy Community (Euratom) from 1 January 1958. The EEC treaty set out objectives (such as eliminating mutual tariff barriers and formulating a Common Agricultural Policy) to be achieved within twelve years and outlined the communities' institutions and rules. Britain stayed aloof, disliking the shared sovereignty implicit in the treaty's supranational institutions and expecting that the negotiations would fail.

**Romilly, Sir Samuel** (1757–1818). Legal reformer. Born of a Huguenot family in London, and an initial enthusiast for the French Revolution, he successfully defended John Binns, the Irish radical, on a sedition charge in 1797. In 1800 he became a king's counsel in Chancery and in 1806 Whig solicitor-general. He sat as MP for Queenborough (1806), Wareham (1808), Arundel (1812), and Westminster (1818), opposing the *Corn Law in 1815 and the suspension of *habeas corpus

in 1817, and supporting the abolition of slavery and *catholic emancipation. Romilly wished to reduce capital crimes but most of his time was spent powerless in opposition. He committed suicide four days after the death of his wife in 1818.

**Romney, George** (1734–1802). Painter, mainly of portraits. He was born in Lancashire and worked in the north of England until 1762, when he left his wife and children to go to London. About 1781 he became infatuated with Emma *Hamilton and is probably best known for his many portraits of her. Romney rarely exhibited and never at the Royal Academy. In his later years he became insane and returned to Lancashire to die.

**Rooke, George** (1650–1709). Admiral. One of the most successful naval commanders of his day, promoted admiral in 1690, Rooke was linked, through two of his three marriages, with the prominent Tory earl of *Nottingham, William III's secretary of state (north) and *de facto* navy minister 1689–94. Rooke was at Bantry Bay (1689), *Beachy Head (1690), and *La Hogue (May/June 1692), where he distinguished himself and gained his knighthood. A year later he commanded the ill-fated 300-ship Smyrna convoy, but escaped blame for this débâcle. An MP for Portsmouth 1698–1708, Rooke held a command with the Dutch at the Copenhagen Sound in 1700 which called for prudent diplomacy between Denmark and Sweden. In 1702 he burnt a Franco-Spanish fleet at *Vigo, and in August 1704 commanded at the capture of Gibraltar.

**root and branch petition,** 1640. Charles I's opponents made most of the running in the *Short and *Long Parliaments of 1640. On 11 December, the Commons received a petition from Londoners demanding the destruction of episcopacy, 'root and branch'. A bill to substitute a *presbyterian church government was introduced in 1641 but made no progress. But when the king's position deteriorated rapidly after the attempt to arrest the *five members in 1642, he was obliged in February to consent to 17 Car. I c. 27, whereby the bishops were excluded from the House of Lords.

**Rorke's Drift, battle of,** 1879. Ford across the Buffalo river, north of Pietermaritzburg, South Africa; site of a battle in the *Zulu War. On 22 January 1879 a force of 139 British troops left to guard the ford was attacked by between 3,000 and 4,000 Zulus, who had not been directly involved in the Zulu victory earlier in the day at *Isandhlwana. The British had hastily prepared a strong, defensive position, and the Zulus' tactics proved ineffective when confronted by the courage and disciplined rifle fire of the British troops. No fewer than eleven VCs were awarded among the survivors.

**Rosebery, Archibald Philip Primrose, 5th earl of** (1847–1929). Prime minister. Rosebery seemed destined for a glittering public career, but faults of temperament severely hampered him. He was sent down from Oxford without a degree because he insisted on running his horse in the Derby. This lifelong passion for the turf—his horses won the Derby three times—complicated his relations with strait-laced Liberal nonconformity. It was a sign of Rosebery's diffidence that he refused office from *Gladstone in 1872 and 1880, served from 1881 to 1883 when he resigned, and then declined the Scottish Office in the same year. Yet his political reputation steadily rose. The departure of many Whigs over the *Home Rule issue in 1886 made Rosebery a vital figure in the House of Lords, and he thus became a young foreign secretary in that year.

For a time he enjoyed remarkably wide acclaim. On the one hand he had the confidence of the queen, who chose him as Gladstone's successor in 1894. On the other hand he seemed to many radical Liberals to be better attuned to social problems than Gladstone. One sign of this was his election as first chairman of the London County Council in 1889.

But his chief interest was foreign and imperial affairs. He developed a Liberal vision of the British empire as a 'Commonwealth of Nations', and as chairman of the Imperial Federation League he advocated a structure involving regular colonial conferences and formal colonial representation on the Privy Council. As foreign secretary (1892–4) he resisted party pressure to withdraw from *Uganda and imposed a protectorate on that territory.

On his succession to the premiership in 1894, Rosebery's career collapsed. He fell out with colleagues over the death duties in *Harcourt's budget and his wish to drop Irish Home Rule. On the defeat of his government in the Commons in 1895 he promptly resigned, forcing the Liberals into a disastrous election. A year later he quit as leader. Subsequently he attacked the Liberal position over the South African War and promoted a separate organization of *Liberal Imperialists. However, Rosebery was easily outmanœuvred by *Campbell-Bannerman, and the rest of his career was spent as a crossbencher increasingly out of sympathy with the radical reformism of Edwardian Liberalism.

**Roses, Wars of the** The name is now given to the sequence of plots, rebellions, and battles that took place between 1455 and 1487. They are so called because of the notion that, fought between the dynasties of Lancaster and York, Lancaster was represented by a red rose, York by a white. In fact the idea of the warring roses was invented by Henry VII after he seized the throne in 1485. While the actual phrase 'Wars of the Roses' did not appear until the 19th cent., the idea of the warring roses was rooted in Tudor propaganda.

There were three distinct phases of civil war: between 1455 and 1464; 1469 and 1471; and 1483 and 1487. In the first two fighting for the control of royal government led to outright war for possession of the crown; the third was dynastic from the start. The scale of the fighting and the extent of disorder were much exaggerated by Tudor writers. There was barely more than two years' military activity throughout the 30-year period.

Nevertheless, especially in 1459–61 and 1469–71, there was considerable instability as the houses of Lancaster and York competed for the throne. In 1455 the duke of *York led his supporters in a successful rebellion against Henry VI. In 1459 they rebelled again, were at first defeated, but were victorious at *Northampton in July 1460. Four months later York claimed the throne for himself. Although he was defeated and killed at the battle of *Wakefield, his heir Edward seized the throne and won a decisive victory at *Towton. In 1469 Edward in his turn faced rebellion from *Warwick the King-maker. Warwick resorted to the restoration of Henry VI. Edward IV, however, had the last word, defeating Warwick at *Barnet and a Lancastrian army at *Tewkesbury. The virtual destruction of the Lancastrians seemed to have brought the wars to an end. They were reopened when Edward's brother Richard III made himself king in 1483. It was then that Henry Tudor emerged as a claimant to the throne. Leading an alliance of die-hard Lancastrians and supporters of the deposed Edward V, he swept to power at *Bosworth in August 1485. He brought the wars effectively to an end when he defeated a Yorkist invasion at *Stoke (by Newark, Notts.) in 1487.

**Ross, Sir James Clark** (1800–62). Ross was involved in eight Arctic and Antarctic expeditions after joining the navy in 1812. Those of 1818 and 1829–33 were with his uncle John *Ross, those of 1819–20, 1821–3, and 1824 with Sir William Parry. With Ross he discovered the Magnetic Pole, while with Parry he reached 110 degrees west in Melville Sound. He was appointed in 1839 to lead the navy's first full-scale Antarctic expedition. In specially strengthened ships, the *Erebus* and *Terror*, Ross reached further south than anyone hitherto.

**Ross, Sir John** (1777–1856). Originally with the East India Company, Ross joined the navy in 1805 and became an Arctic explorer. He led the 1818 expedition which sailed into Lancaster Sound from Baffin Bay but inexplicably turned back. The error was retrieved when, in 1829–33, he headed a privately financed expedition employing very inefficient steam vessels for the first time in the Arctic. The ships went under sail through the Strait to explore the Boothia Peninsula and King William Island.

**Ross, James Stewart, 1st duke of** [S] (*c.*1477–1504). Second son of James III. He received more favour from his father than the duke of Rothesay, the future James IV. In particular James III proposed him as part of a marriage alliance with England, but not his elder brother (1486); and made him duke of Ross, an act that precipitated Rothesay into the rebellion that ended with James III's death at *Sauchie Burn (1488). Potential trouble continued. James IV solved this

problem by making Ross archbishop of St Andrews (1497). Chancellor, in name only, from 1501, Ross died shortly before reaching the canonical age for consecration, 27.

**Rossetti, Dante Gabriel** (1828–82). Poet and painter. Rossetti was born in London, the son of an Italian refugee. Taught drawing by *Cotman, he also worked with Ford Madox Brown, before coming under the guidance of Holman *Hunt in 1848. His first major work, *The Girlhood of Mary Virgin*, was also the first to bear the initials PRB (Pre-Raphaelite Brotherhood). He soon moved away from brotherhood principles to follow what *Millais called 'his own peculiar fancies', his best painting being done during his association with the model Elizabeth Siddal, whom he married in 1860.

**Rotary clubs** The first Rotary club was founded in 1905 by Paul P. Harris, a Chicago attorney, to promote service and fellowship among the business community. There was to be a member from each profession or branch of business and meetings were to be held in their rooms in rotation. In 1912 an international association was formed.

**Rothermere, Viscount** *See* HARMSWORTH, HAROLD.

**Rothes, John Leslie, 1st duke of** [S] (1630–81). Leslie's father, the 6th earl, was in high favour with Charles I but died in 1641 at the age of 41. Leslie marched south with Charles II in 1651 and was taken prisoner at *Worcester. At the Restoration, honours were showered upon him. He became president of the council [S] 1660, lord high treasurer [S] 1663, captain-general of the forces [S] 1664. In 1667, through *Lauderdale's influence, he was dismissed from office but made lord chancellor [S] for life. In 1680, when the duke of York was in Scotland, Rothes was created duke [S] but died the following year.

**Rothschild, Lionel** (1808–79). Banker and politician. Rothschild's father, of a family of German Jews, came to England in 1797 to conduct business and was greatly employed in financing the Napoleonic wars. Lionel succeeded to the English business in 1836, supplied loans for the *Crimean War, and provided *Disraeli with £4 million in

1876 for the purchase of the *Suez canal shares. Returned to Parliament in 1847 for London as a Liberal, Rothschild could not take the required oath as a Christian and was not allowed to sit. Though re-elected in 1849, 1852, and 1857, it was not until the law was changed in 1858 that he could take his seat.

**rotten boroughs** was the term used before 1832 to describe parliamentary constituencies where the voters had almost disappeared. A classic example was Old Sarum, which had been deserted since the inhabitants moved down the valley to Salisbury in 1220. But it was close run by other boroughs, such as Gatton in Surrey, which was down to 20 voters at the Restoration and only two 100 years later. Most of them finished up in Schedule A of the *Great Reform Act.

**Roubiliac, Louis François** (*c.*1705–62). French sculptor. Roubiliac settled in Britain about 1732 and made his reputation with a statue of *Handel, now in the Victoria and Albert Museum. His busts show great vividness and energy, conveying character and age.

**Rouen, treaty of,** 1517. The defeat at *Flodden left Scotland with an infant king, James V. The duke of *Albany became regent in 1515 and on 26 August 1517 negotiated the treaty of *Rouen with Francis I of France. Mutual support against England was to be cemented by a French marriage for the young king. The treaty was not ratified until 1522. Albany then launched an attack upon northern England which was a fiasco. The marriage of James to *Madeleine, daughter of Francis, did not take place until 1537.

**'rough wooing',** 1544–8. The birth of Mary, queen of Scots, in December 1542, only a week after her father's death, seemed an ideal opportunity to unite the thrones of England and Scotland. Prince Edward, Henry VIII's heir, was 5 years old and the English pressed for a marriage agreement. By the treaty of *Greenwich in July 1543 Mary was to be betrothed before she was 10. When the Scottish Parliament in December 1543 rejected the treaty, Henry retorted with a punitive expedition led by Lord Hertford (*Somerset), devastating the south-east

border—ironically dubbed the 'rough wooing'. The Scottish reply, by the treaty of *Haddington, was to accept a proposed marriage between Mary and the dauphin and she was taken to France in July 1548.

**roundheads** Scornful nickname coined to describe first the soldiers who supported Parliament during the Civil War. It arose, explained Lucy Hutchinson, 'from the puritans' custom of wearing their hair cut close round their heads', like apprentices, who shortened their hair to demonstrate their contempt for lovelocks. This was in contrast to the flowing tresses of the royalist cavaliers.

**Roundway Down, battle of,** 1643. After Charles I's march on London in 1642 had been halted, the following year developed into a war of manœuvre. After savage fighting on *Lansdowne on 5 July, both sides were badly mauled. *Hopton made off to Devizes, where he was bombarded by *Waller. But reinforcements from Oxford enabled Hopton on 13 July to counter-attack his opponents in rolling chalk downland outside the town. Waller's cavalry suffered severely on steep grassy slopes and he lost all his guns and 1,400 men.

**rowing** Organized competitive rowing, like most sports, developed in the 19th cent., though the Irish comedian Doggett founded his sculling race on the Thames for the Coat and Badge in 1715. The Oxford and Cambridge *Boat Race was first rowed in 1829. Henley regatta was established in 1839, the main events being the Grand Challenge Cup for eights and the Diamond Sculls for single oarsmen.

**Rowlandson, Thomas** (1756/7–1827). Artist. Social commentator rather than caricaturist, Rowlandson's eye for life's comedies led him to favour types rather than individuals. A Royal Academy student, his prodigious output of pen-drawings, watercolours, and prints were so full of gusto that he has been seen as a personification of his age. A friend of *Gillray, he worked for the publisher Ackermann, creating 'Dr Syntax', but technique and vision suffered after 1800 in consequence of his productivity.

**Rowntree, Benjamin Seebohm** (1871–1954). Rowntree, of the York, Liberal, quaker, chocolate-manufacturing family, conducted a local survey of poverty, the first of three during his life, published as *Poverty: A Study of Town Life* (1901). Rowntree concluded that 9.91 per cent of York's population were living in primary poverty and 17.93 in secondary poverty. These combined figures were so close to *Booth's earlier calculations for London as to demonstrate that the problem of poverty was general.

**Rowton Heath, battle of,** 1645. After *Naseby, Charles I's hopes were of reinforcements from Ireland or of a junction with the victorious *Montrose in Scotland. Chester, held by a royalist garrison, was the key to both strategies. In September, Charles moved northwards to Chester, unaware that Montrose's brilliant run of success had already come to an end at *Philiphaugh. On 23 September Charles relieved the garrison but the following day his cavalry was badly cut up by Poyntz's horsemen at Rowton Heath, south of the city.

**Roxburgh, John Ker, 1st duke of** [S] (*c.*1680–1741). Ker succeeded his brother as earl of Roxburgh at the age of 16. When in his twenties he was secretary of state [S] 1704–5, along with the marquis of Tweeddale. A warm advocate of the Union, he was created duke in 1707 and served as a representative peer in the parliaments of 1707, 1708, 1715, and 1727. In 1714–16 he was keeper of the privy seal [S] and fought bravely for the Hanoverians at *Sheriffmuir in 1715. From 1715 until 1725 he was again secretary of state [S]. He lost favour in 1725 when he was suspected of encouraging the Shawfield riots against the malt tax and of favouring *Carteret against *Walpole.

**Royal Academy of Arts** (London) In 1768 the artist Benjamin *West, with the architect William *Chambers, approached George III for his approval of a national academy to foster a school of art, set standards of good taste, and provide for the free exhibition of works of excellence. The first president was Sir Joshua *Reynolds, whose famous *Discourses* laid down the basic concepts of the Academy.

**Royal Africa Company** A number of short-lived charters in particular areas had been granted in the late 16th and early 17th cents., but the Royal Africa Company was not established until 1672. It traded with west Africa for gold and ivory but its main concern was to supply slaves to the West Indian islands.

**Royal Air Force (RAF).** The RAF was formed in April 1918 when the *Royal Flying Corps and the *Royal Naval Air Service were amalgamated to improve co-ordination. After the armistice the new force was drastically reduced, falling to less than 50 aircraft in 1922 for home defence. It also struggled for its independent existence against the army and navy, defended by Lord *Trenchard. Even so, the RNAS was resurrected in 1924 as the Fleet Air Arm, jointly administered until 1937 when it was handed over to the navy. A cadet college was opened at Cranwell in 1920 and a staff college at Andover in 1922. For many years the doctrine that the bomber would always get through, especially when supported by the prime minister, *Baldwin, suggested that defence was useless. But the invention of radar in 1935 and the successful flights of the Hurricane (1935) and Spitfire (1936) tipped the balance back to defence.

At the outbreak of the Second World War in 1939, the Germans had substantial but not overwhelming numerical superiority with some 4,000 planes to Britain's 2,000: the French air force, in poor shape, had some 1,500. But while the British figures included sedate Gloster Gladiators and Hawker Furies (not very furious with a top speed of 223 m.p.h. and introduced in 1931), the Luftwaffe had been completely re-equipped after Hitler's rise to power.

A major problem for the Royal Air Force was its growing commitments, especially after the entry of Italy (1940) and Japan (1941) extended the war to north Africa and the Pacific. From the fall of France in May 1940 the role of the RAF was essentially defensive. During the Battle of Britain its resources were severely stretched, even more in trained aircrew than in machines, with the life expectation for fighter pilots down to four or five weeks. On 8 August 1940, Goering issued an order to 'wipe the British Air Force from the sky'. But his first surprise was that the Stuka dive-bombers, which had spread terror in Poland and France, proved slow and vulnerable to Spitfires and Hurricanes. The Royal Air

Force was not destroyed, Goering switched to softer targets with raids on British cities, and operation Sealion, the invasion of Britain, was called off.

The counter-offensive could now develop. The strategic issue became whether a massive bombing campaign could pound Germany into surrender without the need for a bloody invasion. The great proponent of that view was 'Bomber' *Harris. In June 1942 he mustered a scratch force of just over 1,000 aircraft (including training personnel) for a demonstration onslaught on Cologne, and followed up his success with a memo against 'the disastrous policy of military intervention in land campaigns of Europe'. But the evidence is dubious. *Churchill pointed out that civilian morale is often surprisingly resilient under intolerable suffering and aircraft losses were heavy. Bomber Command lost 55,000 men during the war—more, it has been said, than all the officers killed in the First World War. Until the end of 1944 German production of tanks, guns, and fighter aircraft continued to increase, with factories camouflaged and dispersed.

Since the end of the Second World War, the Royal Air Force has taken part in a number of campaigns—the Berlin Airlift of 1948/9 when 147 planes flew more than 63,000 sorties; the *Suez operation in 1956 when Egyptian airfields were bombed; the *Falklands War of 1982 when the possession of Ascension Island was critical and air cover was provided largely by ship-borne Harriers; the *Gulf War of 1990 when the Tornado squadron in its low-level attacks had a bad first week; the second Gulf War in 2003; and the protracted operations in *Afghanistan. But its main tasks since the 1950s have been to carry the British nuclear deterrent in the V-bomber force and to retain operational efficiency in the face of shrinking resources.

**Royal British Legion** Essentially a product of the Great War, the legion emerged from amalgamation of rival voluntary societies in 1921 as a non-party association of ex-servicemen. Disbursements to alleviate distress (sickness, unemployment), employment offices and schemes, disabled retraining, and increasing preoccupation with pensions followed. Poppy Day (derived from the emblem of Flanders's fields) started cautiously in 1921,

to become the best known of appeals. A royal charter came in 1925, then royal patronage.

**Royal College of Music** London music conservatoire for the training of performers, composers, and teachers. Founded in 1883 and based on the former National Training School of Music, it opened with 50 scholars and 42 fee-paying students under the directorship of George Grove.

**royal commissions** The preferred 18th-cent. method of investigating problems—apart from leaving things alone—was the select parliamentary committee. This had some disadvantages: composed of MPs it was likely to be partisan; few MPs had the time to devote to a thorough inquiry; and it was almost impossible to take the committee round the country to gather evidence. From 1800 onwards, with increasing concern for social questions, royal commissions multiplied—11 in the first decade, 46 in the fourth, 75 in the sixth. The defects of royal commissions are not inconsiderable. They are expensive, slow, and there is no guarantee that action will follow. Indeed, cynics regard them as an admirable way of disposing of awkward issues until after the next general election.

**Royal Exchange** The first Royal Exchange building was erected by Sir Thomas *Gresham in 1565-7 as a bourse where merchants and bankers could meet. Modelled on the Antwerp Bourse, it lay in the city of London between Threadneedle Street and Cornhill. Elizabeth I proclaimed it the Royal Exchange on her visit in 1570. In 1982 its central glass-domed courtyard was refurbished and occupied by the financial futures market.

**Royal Flying Corps** The Royal Engineers experimented with balloons in the 1870s and a small factory was established at Chatham in 1883. Blériot's flight across the Channel in 1909 and the German Zeppelin programme persuaded the army to set up an Air Battalion in 1911 and the RFC was established in April 1912. In 1914, four squadrons went to France with 63 aeroplanes, most of them BE2 biplanes (Blériot Experimental), made at Farnborough. The early role of the corps was scouting, but the build-up of forces and the invention of the synchronized machine-gun, firing through the propeller, led to frequent dog-fights. The corps's defensive capabilities were demonstrated on 3 September 1916 when William Leefe Robinson shot down Zeppelin SL 11 while it was raiding London. In 1918 air warfare was reorganized to assist co-ordination. The RFC amalgamated with the Royal Naval Air Service to form the *Royal Air Force, with its own minister.

**Royal Institution** Founded in 1799 to apply science and technology to the improvement of the lives of the poor. The leading members included *Banks, Count Rumford, Henry *Cavendish, and *Wilberforce. It received a royal charter the following year and moved into the premises in Albemarle Street which it still occupies. Its main activity has been to popularize science through public lectures and its success was assured by Humphry *Davy and then Michael *Faraday, who had started as Davy's assistant in 1813.

**Royal Irish Academy** The academy was founded in Dublin in 1785 and was given royal recognition the following year. Its aims were the exploration and preservation of Irish culture, collecting manuscripts, and publishing transactions. Its first president was Lord *Charlemont and the founder members included *Grattan and Gandon.

**Royal Irish Constabulary** *See* IRISH CONSTABULARY.

**royalists** *See* CAVALIERS.

**Royal Marriages Act,** 1772. Prompted by the unsanctioned marriage of George III's brother Henry, duke of Cumberland, an Act was passed in 1772 making it illegal in future for any member of the royal family under the age of 25 to marry without the previous consent of the monarch, all such marriages to be declared null and void. The Act created problems for the future George IV when he married Mrs Fitzherbert in 1785 at the age of 23, and is still in force.

**Royal Naval Air Service** When the *Royal Flying Corps was founded in 1912 it had a military and naval wing. The latter soon adopted the name Royal Naval Air Service, which was officially recognized in July 1914. It then possessed 39 aircraft, 52 seaplanes, and 7 airships. The RNAS was amalga-

mated with the RFC in 1918 to form the *Royal Air Force. But the special requirements of the navy led to the creation of the Fleet Air Arm, jointly administered until 1937 when it was placed under naval control.

**Royal Navy** *See* NAVY.

**Royal Opera House** (Covent Garden, London). The original Covent Garden theatre was opened by John Rich in 1732; *Handel used it for operas and oratorios, including the first London performance of *Messiah. In 1808 the theatre was destroyed by fire, reopening the following year and from 1847 housing the Royal Italian Opera. It burned down again in 1856; the present building designed by E. M. Barry opened in 1858. The dominant conductor during the first part of the 20th cent. was *Beecham, while more recent musical directors include Solti and Davis. After the Second World War the theatre became home to the permanent Covent Garden Opera Company and Sadler's Wells Ballet (later known as the Royal Opera and Royal Ballet).

**Royal Philharmonic Society** London concert society formed by professional musicians in 1813 to promote primarily orchestral and instrumental music. For the first Philharmonic Society concert, the orchestra was led by the violinist Salomon and directed from the piano by Clementi. Later conductors included Mendelssohn, Sterndale Bennett, *Sullivan, Tchaikovsky, *Wood, *Beecham, and, for a single disastrous season, Wagner. The society was granted its 'Royal' title in 1913.

**royal prerogative** is a term which has changed its meaning considerably. In modern times it mainly refers to a reserve or discretionary power entrusted to the monarch. In the medieval period the term was used largely to describe feudal rights. There was no implication of reserve power since the medieval monarch had massive immediate power, making all important appointments, granting honours, estates, and charters, issuing proclamations, dispensing justice, and declaring war and peace.

The great struggle over the prerogative was decided largely in the 17th cent. At the end of her reign Elizabeth ran into criticism for granting *monopolies by prerogative and promised redress: James I was obliged to give way completely on that issue, the statute of Monopolies of 1624 declaring that they were 'altogether contrary to the laws of this realm'. The House of Commons recorded mournfully in its *Apology of 1604 that 'the prerogatives of princes may easily and do daily grow...the privileges of the subject being once lost are not recovered but with much disquiet'. Eighty years of disquiet reversed that situation. First Parliament attempted to safeguard its own position since, as long as the monarch could dismiss and summon it at will, its power was precarious: an Act of 1641 demanded *triennial parliaments and, though it was modified after the Restoration, it was made effective in 1694. *Purveyancing, the right of the crown to buy at its own prices, was formally abolished in 1660, along with *benevolences, *forced loans, and the surviving *feudal dues. *Habeas corpus in 1679 protected subjects from imprisonment without trial. More prerogatives were removed by the *Bill of Rights after the revolution of 1688—the power to suspend laws, and the power to dispense with laws in individual cases 'as it hath been assumed and exercised of late'.

After 1688 the monarchy retained formidable powers, but over the next 150 years most of its prerogatives either fell into abeyance or were appropriated by the prime minister. The right to veto legislation was not exercised after 1708 and is presumably defunct. The power to call a general election is now exercised on the advice of the prime minister. Choice of ministers remained a tug-of-war throughout the 18th cent. but is now a matter for the prime minister. It is not easy to know what prerogatives are left to the monarch in the late 20th cent. In a crisis, he or she retains a certain power of initiative: George V begged the warring politicians in 1910 and again in 1914 to negotiate but the results were not encouraging.

**Royal Scottish Academy** In the 18th cent. the opportunities in Edinburgh for exhibition did not stop the flow of Scottish painters to London. On the initiative of the artists themselves, the Scottish Academy was founded in 1826 and received its royal charter in 1838.

**Royal Society** The oldest surviving scientific body in the world, the Royal Society was founded in 1660 and obtained its first charter in 1662, for the promotion of natural knowledge. In 1665 Henry Oldenburg, the secretary, began a journal, *Philosophical Transactions*, which evolved from letters to papers, and still continues. Unlike the Paris Academy of Sciences founded soon after, it was and is a kind of club, and it was not until Humphry *Davy was president in the 1820s that a majority on council had published any science. Instead of a group of mostly amateur enthusiasts, the society by the 1870s had become a body of distinguished professional scientists. Since the mid-19th cent. the society has received a parliamentary grant to support research, and increasingly it has advised governments about science. It has a splendid library, but has never had a laboratory.

**Royal Society for the Prevention of Cruelty to Animals** The RSPCA, the largest animal welfare organization, grew out of the humane movement's concern about abuse of working animals, entertainments (cock-fighting), and slaughterhouse conditions. Formed in 1824, Princess Victoria's patronage, royal endorsement (1840), and burgeoning auxiliary societies outside London increased the society's prestige and prosperity.

**Royal Society of Arts** Founded in 1754 by William Shipley, a drawing-master from Northampton, supported by Viscount Folkestone and Lord Romney. Its objective was to 'encourage Arts, Manufactures and Commerce' and the method was to raise funds by subscription in order to award prizes for useful talents and inventions. The early members included *Johnson, *Goldsmith, *Hogarth, *Gibbon, *Pitt, *Chippendale and *Banks. In 1774 it moved into the premises in the Adelphi, built by the *Adam brothers, which it has occupied ever since.

**Royal Titles Act,** 1876. After the Indian mutiny in 1857, sovereignty in India was transferred to the crown and the governor-general became a viceroy. The elevation of Wilhelm I to be Emperor (of Germany) seems to have upset Victoria, who asked her private secretary in 1873, 'why have I never officially assumed this title?' The change of prime minister in 1874 from *Gladstone to *Disraeli enabled the measure to go ahead. By the

Royal Titles Act (39 & 40 Vic. c. 10) the queen became Empress of India.

**Royal Ulster Constabulary (RUC).**
Created under the terms of the Constabulary Act (1922) as a police force for Northern Ireland, the RUC was modelled on the Royal Irish Constabulary (which was disbanded in 1922), being armed and centrally controlled. The initial establishment was 3,000 men, and it was the original intention to allocate one-third of this total to catholic recruits: however this quota was never filled. The force had more than 300 officers killed during the 'troubles' from 1969, and its restructuring, after the Patten report (1999), was an extremely contentious aspect of the peace process in Ulster.

**Royal Victorian Order** The order was founded in 1896 for members of the royal household and is at the personal disposal of the monarch. The chapel of the order is at the Queen's Chapel, Savoy (London).

**Royce, Sir (Frederick) Henry** (1863–1933). Royce was an engineer whose first large commission in 1882 was to install a system of electric street lighting in Liverpool. Two years later he moved to Manchester and established his own electrical engineering firm. With the advent of the automobile he was drawn into this new field and in 1904 produced his first motor car. His early vehicles so impressed the automobile enthusiast C. S. *Rolls that the two men entered into partnership in 1906 as Rolls-Royce Ltd. In the *First World War he responded to pleas from the British government by manufacturing the Eagle aeroplane engine, and he went on to design other aero-engines.

**rugby football** William Webb Ellis is credited with inventing rugby in 1823 by picking up the ball while playing football at Rugby School and running with it. The claim is disputed but there is little doubt that rugby developed at public schools out of a large-scale, few-rules, mauling scrum game. Definition of the code began in 1863 when the Football Association was formed and outlawed handling and hacking. Richmond, Blackheath, and some London clubs stayed with the handling code and in 1871 the Rugby Football Union was formed. As in

soccer, the balance moved in favour of northern clubs and there were accusations of professionalism. In 1895 St Helens, Wigan, and a number of northern clubs formed a breakaway union, which became the Rugby Football League in 1922. The number of players was reduced from fifteen to thirteen and scrums restricted to produce a fast handling game.

The two codes, amateur and professional, treated each other with disdain for many years. But the advent of television after the Second World War led to a gradual thaw. Rugby union introduced a league system, with promotion and relegation, expenses became ever more substantial, and the ban on players returning after playing rugby league was lifted in 1995. Full professionalism followed, together with substantial restructuring of competitions. Place-kicking has become so expert that most games are decided by infringement of the rules and the subsequent addition of points.

**Rugby School** is a boys' public school founded by Laurence Sheriff, a merchant grocer of London, in 1567. The school became unfit for use in 1748 and was rebuilt on its present site consisting of a school house, quad, chapel, and a magnificent playing field. The subsequent high reputation of the school stems from the headmastership of Thomas *Arnold.

**'Rule, Britannia!'** A song with chorus from the final scene of Thomas Arne's masque *Alfred* (words by James Thomson and David Mallett), first performed at the prince of Wales's residence Cliveden in 1740. It was published shortly afterwards as 'The celebrated ODE, in Honour of Great BRITAIN call'd Rule BRITANNIA'.

**Rump Parliament** What remained of the Long Parliament's House of Commons after *Pride's Purge. It assumed full legislative authority, and its early acts (January–May 1649) set up the tribunal that sentenced Charles I to death, abolished the monarchy and the House of Lords, and declared England to be a commonwealth. Eventually it introduced a bill for a genuinely new parliament, but the army remained unsatisfied, and Cromwell forcibly expelled the Rump on 20 April 1653. The army reinstated it in May 1659 after a coup against Richard *Cromwell. Its independent existence finally ended when General *Monck readmitted the members 'secluded' in Pride's Purge on 21 February 1660.

**Runcie, Robert** (1921–2000). Archbishop of Canterbury. After war service as a tank commander, winning the MC, Runcie graduated from Brasenose College, Oxford. He was successively principal of Cuddesdon Theological College (1960), bishop of St Albans (1970), and archbishop (1980–91). A liberal catholic, he developed Canterbury's quasi-patriarchal role by frequent visits overseas. As the first archbishop to propose 'an ecumenical primacy' for Rome, he welcomed Pope John Paul II on the first ever papal visit to Canterbury cathedral (1982).

**Rupert, Prince** (1619–82). Prince Rupert had two military careers, as an army officer until 1646 and as a naval commander thereafter. Son of *Elizabeth, queen of Bohemia, and first cousin to Charles II, he was born in Prague just before his parents were driven out at the start of the Thirty Years War. At the outbreak of the Civil War, he placed himself at the service of his uncle Charles I. For the next four years he was the toast of the royalists, the terror of the roundheads, and the mainstay of the king's war effort. His forte was the cavalry raid, surprising outposts, sweeping down on garrisons, catching the enemy off guard. He took overall command of the royal forces in November 1644 when it was too late and was defeated at *Naseby in June 1645. Sent to hold Bristol, he surrendered in September 1645, causing a bitter breach with the king, who reproached him for 'so mean an action'. Rupert left the country in July 1646.

The next few years were spent commanding small naval squadrons. He took a fleet to Ireland in 1649 but was outgunned by *Blake, and from 1650 to 1652 cruised in the Mediterranean and West Indies, preying on parliamentary shipping. His chance to exercise high naval command came after the Restoration, when he returned to England and shared responsibility in the second and third *Anglo-Dutch wars with *Monck (Albemarle) and James, duke of York. Confronted by tough and experienced Dutch admirals, his triumphs were less heady than on land, though the action off *Lowestoft in 1665 was an important victory.

**Ruskin, John** (1819–1900). Ruskin was the most influential art critic of his time as well as a talented draughtsman and water-colourist. The son of a wealthy wine merchant, he was able to travel extensively after Oxford, developing his artistic knowledge. His large written output gave him enormous influence over public opinion; he successfully defended the Pre-Raphaelites and championed *Turner. In 1870 he was appointed Slade professor at Oxford and endowed the Drawing School there. His house on the shore of Ullswater is preserved for public admission.

**Russell, Bertrand, 3rd Earl Russell** (1872–1970). In his long and complex life, Russell took many roles. After a distinguished mathematics and philosophy course at Trinity College, Cambridge, he was elected to a fellowship. His major early work was *Principles of Mathematics*, written by 1910 but not published until 1930. During the First World War Russell's pacifist activities resulted in the loss of his fellowship. In the inter-war years he lectured and wrote copiously, and was increasingly tempted to set up as sage. In 1938 he took an academic post in America and stayed there for most of the Second World War. His *History of Western Philosophy* (1945) sold well and removed his financial troubles. He was given the OM (1949) and the Nobel prize for literature (1950). From 1954 onwards he took a prominent part in the *Campaign for Nuclear Disarmament. His judgement became foolish and he declared that Harold *Macmillan was worse than Hitler.

**Russell, Lord John, 1st Earl Russell** (1792–1878). Prime minister. A small, cocky man, Russell was the third son of the duke of Bedford and was educated at Westminster and Edinburgh University. He entered Parliament in 1818, sitting for several constituencies until returned for the City of London in 1841, which he represented until his elevation to the peerage as Earl Russell. He first made his mark in taking a leading role in the repeal of the *Test and Corporation Acts in 1828 and he supported *catholic emancipation in 1829. In *Grey's administration he helped to draft the Reform Bill and was prominent in securing its passage through Parliament. Russell used the

r

argument of 'finality' with such enthusiasm that he earned the nickname 'Finality Jack'. During his long career Russell served in many offices of state. He was home secretary and colonial secretary under *Melbourne, leader of the House under *Aberdeen, foreign secretary under first Aberdeen and later *Palmerston. He was twice prime minister: from 1846 to 1852 and again in 1865 to 1866. In 1845 he became a convert to the repeal of the *Corn Laws. Outraged by what he saw as papal aggression he denounced the revival of catholic bishoprics in England in 1850 and introduced the controversial *Ecclesiastical Titles Bill in 1851. Though associated in the public mind with Palmerston, Russell's relationship with his famous colleague was often stormy. Russell had been happy to see Palmerston go after the approval he had given to Louis Napoleon's coup in December 1851. In turn he fell victim to Palmerston's desire for revenge when in 1852 his government was defeated on its militia proposals. Russell was almost as difficult a premier as he was a colleague. In his second premiership he introduced parliamentary reform, which he believed had been thwarted by Palmerston for too long. But he had the mortification of going out of office and seeing *Disraeli carry a Reform Bill which was more advanced than that which he had proposed.

**Russell, Lord William** (1639–83). Russell, son of the earl of Bedford, entered Parliament in 1660 for Tavistock and became a leader of the *Shaftesbury Whigs. In 1678 he moved an address asking Charles II to remove his brother James, duke of York, from his counsels and in 1680 he joined in presenting the duke as a notorious papist. But the court took its revenge. In 1683 Russell was accused of complicity in the *Rye House plot to assassinate James and Charles and was beheaded in Lincoln's Inn Fields.

**Russia Company** The pioneers of a North-East Passage to Russia were rewarded by the English government in 1555 with a trading charter with exclusive rights. The tsar also granted them special privileges. The charter was confirmed by an Act of 1566. Fur and timber were imported, cloth exported.

**Rutherford, Ernest** (1871–1937). Rutherford's work in radioactivity and nuclear physics changed our views of matter. He was born in New Zealand, and won a scholarship to go to Cambridge to work with J. J. *Thomson. In 1898 he went to McGill University in Canada, where he proved that radioactivity was subatomic chemical change. This new alchemy made his reputation. In 1907 he moved to Manchester, and in 1919 succeeded Thomson at the Cavendish Laboratory in Cambridge, where he built up one of the greatest research schools in the history of science.

**Ruthven raid,** 1582. This was an episode during the minority of James VI of Scotland. Resentful of the influence of the king's cousin Esmé Stuart, who led the pro-French and pro-catholic party and had been created duke of *Lennox in 1581, a protestant group, led by the 1st earl of *Gowrie, seized the 16-year-old king and held him captive for ten months. Stuart was forced to return to France but James escaped in June 1583. An insincere reconciliation was followed in 1584 by Gowrie's execution.

**Rutland** was for more than seven centuries a tiny county, some 17 miles across, and only one-fortieth the size of Yorkshire. It had no clear geographical definition but was pleasant, gentle, wooded countryside, hunted from the 1720s by the Cottesmore. There were only two towns, Oakham, the county town, and Uppingham, famous for their schools, founded in 1584.

It had not acquired county status by the time of the Norman Conquest, but was given as their personal property to successive queens. When John granted it to *Isabella in 1204, it was described as a county, and at the end of the century was given two knights of the shire, like the other counties. By the Local Government Act of 1972 the county was merged with Leicestershire, though a vigorous protest movement continued. The protestors triumphed in 1997 when Rutland was restored as a unitary authority.

**Rye House plot,** 1683. This quasi-republican plot was directed against the persons if not the lives of Charles II and James, duke of York. Disclosed to the crown in June 1683, it would have involved intercepting the royal brothers at the Rye House (near Hoddesdon, Herts.) on their return from Newmarket. Charles II was relentless in upholding James's succession rights after '*Exclusion's' failure, and such opponents as *Russell and *Sidney suffered through a wide application of treason law.

**Rysbrack, John Michael** (1694–1770). Flemish-born sculptor, who settled in England about 1720 and was soon making portrait busts for most of the leading men of his day, often using a classical style new to Britain, as in his statue of Sir Robert *Walpole as a Roman senator, in Houghton Hall (Norfolk). Although *Roubiliac overtook him in popularity, Rysbrack remained a formidable rival.

**Ryswick, treaty of,** 1697. In July 1697 the treaty brought to an end the *Nine Years War, in which Louis XIV's France faced a grand coalition of England, the emperor, the Dutch, and Spain. Louis agreed to return most of his territorial acquisitions or *réunions* made since *Nijmegen, but retained the important fortress town of Strasbourg. The Dutch were allowed to garrison barrier fortresses in the Spanish Netherlands. The treaty lasted only four years before the *War of the Spanish Succession broke out.

r

**sabbatarianism** Strict observance of the sabbath (Hebrew *shabath*—to rest) as a rest-day in accordance with the fourth commandment 'Remember the sabbath day, to keep it holy'. Sabbatarianism was uniquely enforced by 17th-cent. English and Scottish presbyterians, especially in the *Interregnum. The evangelical revival made sabbatarianism fashionable, so that on a Victorian Sunday there was no sport or pleasure, not even reading of serious secular literature. In the 20th cent. there was progressive relaxation until Sunday trading was freely allowed.

**sac and soc** Medieval legal phrase, possibly of Danish origin, referring to manorial jurisdiction. Though each word had its original and precise meaning, it became what Stubbs called 'a mere alliterative jingle', which did not bear close analysis.

**Sacheverell riots,** 1710. These erupted in London's West End on the night of 1/2 March 1710 following the third day of the impeachment of Dr Henry Sacheverell. This outspoken high Anglican Oxford don was on trial at Westminster Hall for publishing a sermon condemning the Whig government for its favouritism towards dissenters. Rioters demonstrated their sympathy for the doctor by sacking and burning six prominent dissenting chapels.

**Sacket's harbour, battle of,** 1813. During the *War of 1812, British and American forces struggled for control of Lake Ontario. In May 1813 Sir George Prevost, governor-general of Canada, launched an attack upon the American base at Sacket's harbour, but was repulsed.

**sailing** covers a range of activity from ocean racing to 12-foot dinghy competitions, or merely messing around in boats. At the top end of the sport is the America's Cup, named after the famous yacht which caused a sensa-

tion when it visited Cowes in 1851. The Fastnet race, started in 1925, is from Cowes to Ireland and back to Plymouth. The governing body is the Royal Yachting Association, which organizes Cowes week in August. There is a Dinghy Cruising Association, and local competitions are arranged by clubs, in rivers and estuaries, gravel pits and reservoirs.

**St Albans, battle of,** 1455. The first battle of St Albans on 22 May was little more than a hand-to-hand skirmish. But since it ushered in the Wars of the *Roses, the consequences were important. Richard, duke of *York, had marched south, demanding from Henry VI the dismissal of his rival the duke of *Somerset. The Yorkist victory was largely owing to Richard, earl of *Warwick ('the Kingmaker'). Somerset was killed, Henry VI captured, watching the proceedings.

**St Albans, battle of,** 1461. The second battle of St Albans took place on 17 February 1461. Queen *Margaret hastened south to exploit her crushing victory at *Wakefield and rescue her husband Henry VI, held captive by *Warwick. The Yorkists were again defeated, but Warwick salvaged some troops and joined the future Edward IV from Wales. Henry VI was released by his queen, who failed to follow up her advantage.

**St Albans, diocese of** Now conterminous with Bedfordshire and Hertfordshire, the see was founded in 1877 from parts of the *Rochester diocese (Herts., Essex and north Woolwich). This was a failure, and Essex and north Woolwich were removed in 1914 to form the new see of *Chelmsford; in return St Albans gained Bedfordshire from *Ely, a more natural liaison. The cathedral is the former abbey church, which served the parish after the *dissolution.

**St Andrews** is a city, royal *burgh, and university town in the north-east of the county of Fife in Scotland. It developed from a royal fortress of the Picts situated on the site later built over by St Andrews castle. Never technically part of the medieval burgh, this area fostered the cult of St *Andrew, which became national. Between 1160 and 1318 was built the cathedral which with its 357-foot-long nave was the largest church in Scotland.

A municipality was erected under Bishop Robert around 1140. In 1412–13 Bishop Wardlaw and Pope Benedict XIII incorporated and chartered St Andrews University, the nation's first. St Andrews was a cockpit of the Reformation. John *Knox retired there, while Andrew Melville, father of Scots presbyterianism and bane of King James VI and I, was head of St Mary's College. Uniquely good golfing facilities at the Royal and Ancient club helped the town to become a residential and resort centre from the mid-19th cent.

**St Asaph, diocese of** It is claimed that the church at St Asaph (Llanelwy) was founded by St Kentigern (Mungo), a fugitive from Strathclyde, in the 6th cent. The cathedral, however, bears the name of his successor, Asaph. Later the see approximated to the native Welsh principality of Powys. Many of the popular north Wales coastal resorts, the industrial heartland of Deeside, the populous town of Wrexham, and the largely Welsh-speaking upland farming districts of Merionethshire come within its borders. Most of the church dates from the 14th cent. Severely damaged in the Owain *Glyndŵr revolt, and again under the Commonwealth, it was subject to a major restoration by Gilbert *Scott between 1867 and 1875.

**St Brice's Day massacre,** 13 November 1002. A cardinal blunder committed by King *Æthelred, who is said to have ordered the killing of all Danes in England on that day. This is scarcely credible, considering the numbers involved. Yet some action was taken, probably provoked by Pallig, the Dane who, after taking Æthelred's gifts, broke his pledge of loyalty. The murder of Pallig's wife Gunnhild, sister of the Danish king *Sweyn, may well have provoked Sweyn's invasion in 1003, which was followed by continual onslaught, until in 1017 a Danish king was on the English throne.

**St Christopher and Nevis** are part of the *Leeward Islands in the eastern Caribbe-

an and form an independent republic within the Commonwealth. The islands were visited by Columbus and for some time disputed between Spain, France, and Britain. They were confirmed as a British colony at *Utrecht in 1714.

**St Davids, diocese of** The cathedral of St *David, which still houses the bones of the patron saint of Wales, is one of the outstanding buildings in the principality. Bernard persuaded Pope Calixtus II to canonize David, and also to decree that two pilgrimages to St Davids were equal to one to Rome. The diocese covered the greater part of south-west and mid-Wales, until 1923 when the newly created see of Swansea and Brecon removed Breconshire, Radnorshire, and parts of west Glamorgan.

**Saint-Germain, treaty of,** 1919. Peace treaty with Austria after the First World War, signed on 10 September 1919. Austria lost all the non-German parts of her former empire. South Tyrol went to Italy; Slovenia, Bosnia-Herzegovina, and Dalmatia to Yugoslavia; Bohemia and Moravia to Czechoslovakia; Galicia to Poland; and the Bukovina to Romania. The union of Austria and Germany was forbidden and the Austrian army was restricted to 30,000 men.

**St Germans, diocese of** *Athelstan created this specifically Cornish see by dividing the see of *Crediton in 931. Poverty enforced its reunion with Crediton in 1027. The combined see moved to *Exeter in 1050.

**St Helena,** a volcanic island in the South Atlantic, is 1,200 miles from Africa and 1,800 from South America. With a length and breadth of 10 miles by 6, it is roughly the size of Jersey. The *East India Company took possession of it in 1659 as a port of call and it has been a British colony ever since. The British government, much exercised after *Waterloo to know what to do with their unwelcome guest the Emperor Napoleon, found it more secure than Elba, from which he had escaped without difficulty.

**St James's palace,** though still nominally the headquarters of the British monarchy, since ambassadors are accredited to the court there, is not well known and has been much patched. Originally it was the leper hospital of St James's. Henry VIII purchased the property, still in the fields outside London, in 1532 and began building round four courtyards. The basic pattern is still red-brick Tudor. The palace was greatly used after the Restoration, since *Greenwich had been given up and *Whitehall was burned in 1698. The 'warming-pan baby', later to become the old pretender, was born there in June 1688, when the palace was the residence of James II's wife *Mary of Modena. Gradually *Buckingham palace replaced it for most state occasions, and St James's is now used only occasionally for grand receptions.

**St Kitts** See ST CHRISTOPHER.

**St Leger, Sir Anthony** (c.1496–1559). Lord deputy of Ireland. Of a Kentish family, St Leger married the niece and heiress of *Warham, archbishop of Canterbury, and rose under the patronage of Thomas *Cromwell. In 1540 he succeeded *Grey as deputy of Ireland, with a policy of reasserting royal authority, a first step being Henry VIII's adoption of the title king of Ireland. He was retained in office on Henry's death in 1547 but returned to England in 1548. When his successor died shortly afterwards, St Leger was sent out again but recalled in 1551 as too conciliatory towards Irish catholics. Mary's reign saw him reinstated for the third time (1553) and he served until 1556, when accusations of peculation were brought against him.

**St Lucia** is one of the *Windward Islands in the eastern Caribbean and an independent member of the Commonwealth with the queen as head of state. It became a French colony in the 17th cent., and changed hands frequently in the 18th cent. before being ceded to Britain in 1814.

**St Michael and St George, Order of** The order was founded by the prince regent in 1818 and is reserved mainly for diplomats. Originally it commemorated British rule over Malta and the Ionian Islands, but the scope has been widened.

**St Paul's cathedral** The first cathedral was founded by *Æthelbert, king of Kent, on the site of a former Roman temple (604); destroyed by fire, it was rebuilt in stone (675–

85) by Bishop Earconweald, but was destroyed by Vikings (962). The third building burned down in 1087, and its replacement, known as 'Old St Paul's', outshone anything previously seen in London, the largest church in England and third largest in Europe. Deprived of much of its revenue by the Reformation, structural decay set in; houses and shops were erected against its walls, and the nave became a common thoroughfare ('Paul's Walk') and place for conducting business. Destroyed in the Great Fire of 1666, Wren's new cathedral was completed in his lifetime. It has continued as a focus for state services, surviving the Blitz and retaining a close relationship with the city.

**Saints, battle of** the, 1782. This was the last important naval action in the *American War of Independence. The loss of naval superiority in 1781 forced *Cornwallis to surrender at *Yorktown. The French and Spanish then began picking off British West Indian islands and an invasion of Jamaica was expected. *Rodney left Plymouth in January 1782 with reinforcements and on 10 April 1782 won an important victory over de Grasse at the battle of the Saints in the Leeward Islands.

**St Vincent and the Grenadines** form part of the *Windward Islands in the eastern Caribbean and are an independent state within the Commonwealth. They are believed to have been named by Columbus but became a French colony until ceded to Britain by the peace of *Paris in 1763.

**Salamanca, battle of,** 1812. In July 1812 the French, under Marshal Marmont, with 42,000 men manœuvred to cut *Wellington off from his base in Salamanca. Wellington, with 46,000 men, gave ground and appeared to retreat. On 22 July, Marmont sent his leading division to harass the British. However Wellington was already in position, quickly overcame the division, and then attacked Marmont's centre with a deadly rifle volley and bayonet charge. Marmont was wounded and the French were driven from the field with losses of 13,000.

**Salisbury (Sarum).** Cathedral city in Wiltshire. It originated with an Iron Age hill-fort which housed successively a Roman, Anglo-Saxon, and Norman town. In the 1070s it acquired a cathedral, which in the 12th cent. was a major intellectual centre. In 1219 the bishop moved to a new, level site 1½ miles south; a large cathedral was built in uniform style c.1220–1320, its tower crowned by the tallest surviving medieval spire in Europe. The city flourished through the cloth industry, becoming the fourth largest English town in the 15th cent.

**Salisbury, diocese of** Now roughly conterminous with Wiltshire and Dorset, the see was founded c.1075 when the West Saxon bishopric of *Sherborne, united with *Ramsbury in 1058, was moved to Old Sarum. In 1542 Dorset and some Wiltshire parishes were incongruously assigned to the new Bristol diocese until 1836, when Salisbury regained Dorset. Bristol retains the north Wiltshire deaneries. The Norman cathedral at Old Sarum is now a ruin, but was replaced on lower ground by the present magnificent building, completed c.1258. The exterior is a splendid example of Early English architecture with its slender 14th-cent. spire, the tallest in England, rising 404 feet above the water-meadows.

**Salisbury, Robert Gascoyne-Cecil, 3rd marquis of** (1830–1903). Prime minister. Salisbury was an unlikely candidate for such a long tenure of the premiership. A younger son of an ancient Tory house, he was intellectual (with little taste for aristocratic sports) and unsociable. From 1863, at odds with his family over his non-aristocratic marriage, he supplemented his allowance by journalism (over 600 *Saturday Review* articles and 33 for the *Quarterly Review*), so that we have more of his thinking in print than that of any other prime minister. Though he was an MP for a family borough from 1853 and in *Derby's cabinet in 1866, his prickliness and rigidity made him an awkward colleague. Anti-democratic and anti-populist and long distrustful of *Disraeli as a political mountebank, Cranborne (as he then was) resigned with two cabinet colleagues in early 1867 over the borough franchise proposals in the government's Reform Bill. Out of office he remained a trenchant critic of Disraeli and a standing threat to his leadership. In 1869 he succeeded to the marquisate and the great house at Hatfield, and followed Derby as chancellor of Oxford University and

a foremost defender of its Anglican character. He agreed reluctantly to join the government of 1874, but was clearly a potential dissident in the Eastern Question crisis. Disraeli had, however, worked to cultivate Salisbury, and when Derby and the earl of Carnarvon resigned in the critical moment in early 1878 Salisbury threw in his lot with Disraeli and accepted the Foreign Office. When Disraeli (Beaconsfield) died in 1881, Salisbury became party leader in the Lords and co-leader of the whole party with *Northcote. Angered by Liberal land legislation for Ireland, he played a leading role in the obstruction of Liberal measures in the Lords. Helped by *Churchill's insubordination in the Commons, Salisbury got the better of his rival Northcote, a more emollient figure, and in 1885 he was the premier in the Conservative caretaker government. Once Gladstone had declared for *Home Rule after the election, Salisbury mounted a resolute defence of the Union and skilfully exploited Liberal divisions. By summer 1886 Salisbury was back in office, dependent on the support of the *Liberal Unionists. This uncomfortable position lasted until 1892 and Salisbury had to make various policy concessions (over Irish land purchase, education, and county councils, for example) to conciliate his allies, particularly the demanding *Chamberlain. This made Salisburian government look more progressive than it would otherwise have done. By 1891 Salisbury had installed his nephew *Balfour, who had made his name with a policy of resolute coercion in Ireland, as leader in the Commons. For most of his time as premier Salisbury held the Foreign Office rather than the 1st lordship of the Treasury. In diplomacy he displayed a skill which kept policy on a steady track and away from the alternating extremes of Gladstone and Disraeli earlier. He also kept Britain clear of entangling alliances, though he was a successful negotiator in reconciling differences over colonial claims.

In opposition Salisbury led the Lords in its overwhelming rejection—by 419:41—of Gladstone's second Home Rule Bill in 1893. After the Liberal resignation in 1895 Salisbury brought the Liberal Unionists under Hartington into a formal coalition with the Conservatives and this Unionist government won the election and another in 1900 (the 'khaki' election) when the opportunity of the *Boer War was seized. By now Salisbury's vigour was declining and his policies were looking dated to younger politicians. He resigned the Foreign Office in 1900 and the premiership in 1902.

Though a high aristocrat at a time when events were moving against the aristocracy, he recognized the importance of cultivating middle-class and urban opinion, particularly after the 1885 Redistribution Act. His success owed much to Gladstone's talent for wreaking havoc upon the Liberal Party, and upon the Liberal Unionist Hartington's support from 1886 onwards.

**Salisbury, Robert Gascoyne-Cecil, 5th marquis of** (1893–1972). Conservative politician. Cecil entered Parliament in 1929 and served as junior minister at the Foreign Office. He resigned in February 1938 in support of *Eden's opposition to opening talks with Mussolini. Returning to government under *Churchill, he was spoken of as a possible foreign secretary. He continued to prosper after the war, particularly as a result of his close friendship with Eden. On domestic issues, however, he found himself at odds with the thrust of post-war Conservatism and soon lost sympathy with the premiership of Harold *Macmillan. The occasion of his second resignation was the freeing of the Cypriot leader Makarios from imprisonment in 1957.

**Salisbury, Richard Neville, 5th earl of** (1400–60). Neville was the first son of the (second) marriage of Ralph, 1st earl of Westmorland, and *John of Gaunt's daughter Anne Beaufort. From 1420 to 1436 he was warden of the west march. Royal offices increased his north country dominance. He gained the earldom of Salisbury by marriage to its heiress. Percy opposition to his regional preponderance led to violence and became a reason for Salisbury's breach with the court after 1453 and his alliance with Richard of *York. He was chancellor in York's first protectorate and fought with him at *St Albans; in 1459, at *Blore Heath (Staffs.), he defeated royalist forces opposing his junction with York. Following the Yorkist collapse, he was attainted and took refuge at Calais, returning with his son *Warwick to defeat the royalists

at *Northampton. He was murdered after the battle of *Wakefield.

**Salisbury, Margaret Pole, countess of** (1473–1541). Margaret Plantagenet was a daughter of George, duke of *Clarence, and a niece of Richard III. After the execution of her brother the earl of *Warwick in 1499, she was sole heiress to the dukedom of Clarence and the earldoms of Salisbury and of Warwick, and was granted the title countess of Salisbury in 1513. But after her son Reginald *Pole was made a cardinal in 1536, Henry VIII moved against the Pole family. Her eldest son Lord Montagu was executed in 1539 and her younger son Geoffrey sentenced to death. The countess was executed in the Tower, the executioner bungling the beheading. She was the last of the Plantagenets.

**Salisbury, oath of,** 1086. In August 1086 William I summoned 'landowning men of any account' to attend at Salisbury and swear allegiance to him and to be faithful against all other men. The oath was demanded at a time of crisis when the Conqueror was facing revolt and invasion. There seems little doubt that it was intended as a practical assurance and reminder rather than as a constitutional statement.

**Salisbury, treaty of,** 1289. When Alexander III of Scotland died in a fall from his horse at Kinghorn in March 1286, he left no children, but a granddaughter, *Margaret, 'the Maid of Norway', aged 3. In November 1289 commissioners from Norway, England, and Scotland reached agreement at Salisbury, later confirmed by the Scots at *Birgham. The young queen was to be brought to Scotland within a year and was not to be married without Edward I's consent. But the death of the Maid in September 1290 threw all into confusion.

**Salmond, Alex** (b. 1954). Politician. Born in Linlithgow, Salmond studied History and Politics at St Andrews before working in banking. He was returned to the Westminster Parliament in 1987 as *SNP member for Banf and Buchan and was elected leader of his party in 1990. He campaigned for a 'Yes' vote in the Scottish referendum on devolution in 1997 but stood down as leader in 2000. Re-elected to the leadership in 2004, he returned to the Scottish Parliament and in 2007, with the SNP as the largest party, formed a minority government in Scotland as First Minister. He has been greatly helped by a genial and entertaining manner, which critics hint is simulated, but has maintained the objective of Scottish independence.

**Salt, Sir Titus** (1803–76). Salt, a worsted manufacturer and creator of the model village of Saltaire, entered the wool trade as a stapler and then moved into spinning (1834). A radical Liberal, Salt was a paternalist, who wanted to provide a good environment for his workers; he moved from central Bradford and created Saltaire between 1850 and 1875. Housing and community facilities at Saltaire were excellent.

**Salvation Army** In 1865 William *Booth and his wife launched the 'Christian Mission to the Heathen of our Own Country' in Whitechapel (London), and this mission expanded into the Salvation Army (1878). Its doctrines were those of evangelical revivalism: sin, conversion, justification by faith, hell, and heaven. The officers and soldiers (i.e. members) of the army were themselves working men and women, who had experienced conversion and practised self-denial. From the late 1880s the army turned to social action, establishing slum posts, night shelters, and schemes for assisting the unemployed.

**Sampford Courtenay, battle of,** 1549. The Cornish rebels against the Prayer Book in English in the summer of 1549 declared that they would not accept the new service which was 'but like a Christmas game'. Later in June they crossed the Tamar and laid siege to Exeter. Early in August a punitive force under Lord Russell (*Bedford) drove the insurgents from Clyst St Mary with heavy loss and relieved Exeter. The remainder were routed on 17 August at Sampford Courtenay, near Okehampton.

**Samson, St** (c.485–c.565). Born in Wales, educated and ordained at Llantwit, Samson's missionary endeavours established his renown in Cornwall, the Channel Islands, and Brittany, where he spent his last years. Chief among Breton saints, Samson died at Dol.

**Samuel, Sir Herbert, 1st Viscount Samuel** (1870–1963). Samuel's father, who died when Samuel was 7, was a Jewish banker. After taking a first in history at Balliol College, Oxford, Samuel entered Parliament as a Liberal in 1902. In the Liberal government of 1906 he served as under-secretary for the Home Office and entered the cabinet in 1909 as chancellor of the duchy of Lancaster, transferring to the postmaster-generalship the following year. He was home secretary when *Asquith resigned in 1916, followed him into opposition, and lost his seat at the 'coupon' election of 1918. Samuel returned to Parliament in 1929 and was acting leader of the party (in the absence of *Lloyd George) at the time of the crisis of 1931. He joined *MacDonald's *National Government as home secretary but resigned the following year when it moved towards protection.

**Sancroft, William** (1617–93). Archbishop of Canterbury. Sancroft was a fellow of Emmanuel College, Cambridge (1637), but during the Interregnum moved to Suffolk (1651) and then to Europe (1657). He became master of Emmanuel (1662), dean of York, then of St Paul's (December 1664), where he worked closely with *Wren on the new cathedral. As archbishop (1678), he crowned James II (1685), but refused to sit on his Court of *Ecclesiastical Commission. Leader of the seven bishops petitioning the king against the *Declaration of Indulgence (1688), he was committed to the Tower, tried, but acquitted. After James's departure, Sancroft refused to swear allegiance to William, was deprived of his see (1690), and, as the leading non-juror, lived in Suffolk until his death.

**sanctions** The economic boycott of a country refusing to follow international conventions. Sanctions were the chief coercive method of the *League of Nations under article xvi of the covenant. In October 1935 they were imposed on Italy after her invasion of Abyssinia. However, vital materials were excluded and Italian trade with non-league members was not disrupted. More recently, United Nations mandatory sanctions include trade restrictions placed on *Rhodesia after the unilateral declaration of independence in 1965, on South Africa in the 1980s due to apartheid, and on Iraq following the invasion of Kuwait in 1990. The effectiveness of trade sanctions is questionable as they are easily circumvented.

**sanctuary** Christian sanctuaries were protected under English common law whereby a fugitive charged with any offence except sacrilege or treason could delay punishment by reaching sanctuary, often by grasping the ring or knocker of any church door. He had the choice of submitting to trial or, clad in sackcloth, confessing crime to a coroner and swearing to leave the kingdom after 40 days. Often abused, sanctuary became a source of dispute between church and state. Sanctuary was abolished for criminals (1623) and for civil cases (1723).

**Sandringham House** (Norfolk) is the private country estate of her majesty the queen. Sandringham has been owned by four generations of monarchs, starting with Edward VII who bought it in 1860 when prince of Wales. At first he made only minor alterations, but in 1870 he and Princess *Alexandra started to rebuild the house. The style adopted was Elizabethan, the materials a harsh red brick and stone dressings.

**Sand River convention,** 1852. Appointed governor of Cape Colony and high commissioner in southern Africa in 1847, Sir Harry Smith tried at first to reimpose British authority over the people of Dutch descent (Boers) who had quitted the colony some years earlier. The realization that such a policy might lead to endless strife forced Smith to reconsider his plan and to approve the Sand River convention which recognized the independence of Boers living north of the Vaal river.

**Sandwich, battle of,** 1217. After suffering considerable losses at the battle of *Lincoln (May 1217), Prince Louis of France sent home for further reinforcements in his bid to become king of England. King Henry III's regency council realized that it was imperative to prevent these troops landing and a great sea-battle took place off Sandwich on 24 August 1217. It was a decisive engagement, ending Louis's hopes in England.

**Sandwich, Edward Montagu, 1st earl of** (1625–72). Montagu's cousin, the 2nd earl of *Manchester, was a leader on the parliamentary side during the Civil War. Montagu joined him as a young man and fought at *Marston Moor and *Naseby. He sat in all the Commonwealth parliaments, was a member of the *Council of State in 1653, and took his seat in Cromwell's 'other house' in 1658. He also saw considerable naval action. Early in 1660 he was reappointed general of the fleet and took it over to Charles II's cause. He was rewarded by the Garter and the earldom of Sandwich. In the second *Anglo-Dutch War, he was victorious at the battle of *Lowestoft, but lost his life in the third war in the action off *Southwold Bay in 1672.

**Sandwich, John Montagu, 4th earl of** (1718–92). A politician of considerable achievements and a discerning patron of the arts, particularly music, Lord Sandwich is most frequently recalled as the inventor of the sandwich—popularly supposed to have sustained him during lengthy spells at the gaming table. Sandwich's political ambitions were focused on the Admiralty, where he thrice served as 1st lord (1748–51, 1763, 1771–82), demonstrating administrative ability. He was unjustly blamed for the failings in naval preparedness revealed by the *American War of Independence.

**Saragossa, battle of,** 1710. A mixed force of Austrians, Dutch, British, and Portuguese, under the Archduke Charles, attacked on 19 August 1710 the Spaniards defending Saragossa. *Stanhope commanded the British troops on the left. After a decisive victory, they went on to occupy Saragossa and advanced on Madrid.

**Saratoga, surrender of,** 1777. John Burgoyne's 1777 expedition was over-ambitious and badly executed. The plan to drive south from Canada along the Hudson river to Albany, isolating the New England colonies, sounded plausible. But it was not clear, in an area of dense forest, how the New Englanders would be isolated, what Burgoyne would do when he got to Albany, or even whether he could get there. Burgoyne left Canada towards the end of June and had an initial success when the enemy abandoned Fort Ticonderoga. But in August a large foraging party was annihilated at *Bennington. The march was slow and painful, supplies inadequate, and the enemy vigilant. On 19 September Burgoyne encountered Gates at Bemis Heights and lost more men he could not replace. He fell back on Saratoga and was surrounded. On 17 October Burgoyne and nearly 6,000 men surrendered on terms.

**Sarawak** (north-west Borneo) long had trading links with Siam and China and, in the 15th cent., fell under the influence of the sultanate of *Brunei. In 1841 the sultan offered it as a rajadom to Sir James *Brooke, who had helped to put down a revolt of the local Dayaks and Malays. Sarawak was recognized as an independent state by the USA in 1850 and by Great Britain in 1864. Representative government was established in 1963 and Sarawak joined the *Malaysian Federation.

**Sargent, John Singer** (1856–1925). American painter who settled in England and became the outstanding portraitist of his time. Born in Italy, Sargent studied there and in Paris, where he became a good friend of Monet. In 1885, he settled in London where he remained until his death, although he visited the USA frequently and retained his citizenship. He was an official war artist during the First World War and his powerful *Gassed* hangs in the Imperial War Museum.

**Sark, battle of,** 1448. Renewed border skirmishing saw Henry Percy, future 3rd earl of Northumberland, defeated by Hugh Douglas, earl of Ormond, on 23 October 1448. The encounter took place on the river Sark, near Gretna. Percy was taken prisoner and had to be ransomed.

**Sarsfield, Patrick** (c.1650–93). Jacobite earl of Lucan. Born to a catholic family, Sarsfield entered the Irish army in 1678. He then served in the English regiments which Charles II detached to fight in the army of Louis XIV of France, but returned to England at the succession of James II in 1685, and helped to crush *Monmouth's rising. Sarsfield commanded the Irish troops in England in 1688, but fled to France with James, returning with him to Ireland in 1689.

In the war that followed Sarsfield rose rapidly to major-general. His attacks on Williamite supply lines forced the raising of the first siege of *Limerick but, after defeat at *Aughrim, he concluded the second siege of Limerick on terms which allowed him to sail for France. He was mortally wounded at the battle of *Landen.

**Sauchie Burn, battle of,** 1488. In the summer of 1488, James III of Scotland was faced with a large rebellion, led by Archibald Douglas, earl of *Angus, and supported by the heir to the throne, the 15-year-old Prince James. The king advanced through Stirling to the site of Bannockburn. On 11 June his army was routed and he was killed, possibly in flight.

**Savery, Thomas** (c.1650–1715). Savery was a military engineer who attained the rank of trench master by 1696, and acquired the title of 'Captain'. His inventiveness was perhaps stimulated by his knowledge of tin- and copper-mining in his native Devon. Savery's outstanding achievement was the invention of a machine for raising water by steam pressure, for which he took out a patent (No. 356) in 1698, calling it 'the miner's friend'. His patent was adapted by Thomas *Newcomen in his much more successful atmospheric engine of 1712.

**Savoy conference,** 1661. This was an attempt to reach a compromise at the Restoration between the presbyterians and the Anglicans. Twelve clerics from each side met at the Savoy hospital in April 1661 under the chairmanship of *Sheldon, bishop of London and a future archbishop of Canterbury. The negotiations broke down and in July the delegates reported that 'they could not come to any harmony'. The dream of a comprehensive church had faded.

**Saxons** *See* ANGLO-SAXONS.

**Saxon Shore** A coastal network of late Roman forts stretching from Brancaster to Portchester intended to repel attacks by Saxons. The name 'Saxon Shore' (*litoris Saxonici*) appears only in the *Notitia dignitatum*, a document drawn up c.AD 408. The overall commander of the military network was the *comes*, normally translated as 'the Count of the Saxon Shore'.

**Saye and Sele, William Fiennes, 1st Viscount** (1582–1662). Saye and Sele was a leading member of the radical, win-the-war faction in the House of Lords during the 1640s. As early as the 1620s he was a critic of arbitrary government and illegal taxation. Saye refused to pay *ship money, and declined the military oath imposed by Charles on the nobility at the outbreak of the *Bishops' wars with Scotland. He backed both the *self-denying ordinance of 1645, which excluded the aristocracy from the leadership of the parliamentary armies, and the creation of the *New Model Army. Politically inactive after 1649, Saye devoted himself to religion.

**Scapa Flow** in the Orkneys is a magnificent natural harbour and naval base, commanding the approaches to both the North Atlantic and the North Sea. It was developed immediately before the First World War when the fleet increased in numbers and the vessels in size. The German high seas fleet was escorted to Scapa in 1918 and on 21 June 1919 the 74 vessels were scuttled. The naval base was closed in 1956.

**Scheveningen, battle of,** 1653. Naval battle off the Dutch coast during the first *Anglo-Dutch War. Martin Tromp was ordered to sea to try to break the English blockade under *Monck. Tromp was killed early in the action on 10 August and the Dutch lost eleven vessels.

**Schism Act,** 1714. An extreme Tory measure designed to stamp out *dissent by preventing nonconformists and catholics educating their children in their own schools. Teachers had to apply for licences, which would only be granted if they had taken the Anglican sacrament within the previous year. On the day the Act was due to take effect, Queen Anne died, and her successor, George I, took no steps to enforce it. It was repealed in 1719.

**Schomberg, Frederick Herman, 1st duke of** (1615–90). Schomberg was one of the greatest soldiers of the 17th cent. Born in Heidelberg, he pursued a military career with the Swedes and Dutch before entering French service in 1652 and rising to be a marshal of France. A Huguenot by religion, he left France in 1685 at the revocation of the edict of Nantes and accompanied William of Orange to England in November 1688. After the success of the Glorious Revolution, he

was given the Garter, and created duke of Schomberg. In the summer of 1689 he took over William's forces in Ireland and was killed at the battle of the *Boyne.

**Schools Act (Scotland),** 1696. In 1616 the Scottish Privy Council decreed that in Scotland a school should be established in every parish. This was ratified by the Scottish Parliament in 1633 and a further Act for Founding Schools passed in 1646. It was a further 200 years before a similar system was established in England.

**Schooneveld, battle of,** 1673. In May 1673, during the third *Anglo-Dutch War, it was resolved to attack the Dutch in the Schooneveld, off Walcheren. *Rupert was joined by a French squadron, which gave him some superiority over a Dutch fleet under de Ruyter and Cornelis Tromp. The first engagement on 7 June was inconclusive. On 14 June the Dutch attacked in turn and a running fight developed. Once more the result was inconclusive.

**Science Museums** (Kensington). The museums are the fruit of the *Great Exhibition of 1851. It made a profit and Prince *Albert hoped to establish there a great cultural centre. In 1864 the underground railway station was authorized, and the Department of Science and Arts ran what grew into the Science Museum. In 1881 the Natural History Museum also opened its doors.

**scientific revolution** Herbert Butterfield called attention in 1948 to the tremendous intellectual change he saw taking place during the 17th cent., when the modern scientific world-view was propounded by Francis *Bacon, Galileo, Descartes, and their disciples. This change was reflected in institutions, notably the *Royal Society and the Paris Academy of Sciences, and in publications—especially journals.

Butterfield had seen one revolution, but it might be that science has had several. Thus we have revolutions associated with Galileo, Isaac *Newton, Charles *Darwin, and perhaps Michael *Faraday, Freud, J. J. *Thomson, and Einstein.

Studies of the 19th cent. indicate how many elements of modern science we owe to that epoch rather than to an earlier period, and may make us wonder if it was not the

Age of Science, or the period when science began to revolutionize everyday life. The Royal Society was joined in 1831 by the more open and democratic *British Association for the Advancement of Science, promoting public awareness and local pride. It had earlier been joined by specialized societies dedicated to natural history, geology, and astronomy; and later to chemistry, statistics, and physics. Education began to divide the scientists (a word coined by William Whewell in 1833) from humanists; and as the former divided into chemists and physicists, and then further into organic or physical chemists, so the latter began taking degrees in history or English.

Exponential growth also became evident in the 19th cent., so the question whether there was one scientific revolution or many, or evolution, is open. Clearly, science has been developing in ways that Bacon could only have dreamed of, and it has transformed the way we see the world.

**Scilly Isles** A group of 50 granite islands, five of them inhabited, lying 30 miles off Land's End in Cornwall. The largest islands are St Mary's and Tresco. Piracy, wrecking, and smuggling were not unknown before market gardening and tourism took over.

**Scone, stone of** A block of sandstone, long associated with the inauguration of early Scottish kings at Scone (Perthshire) but seized by Edward I in 1296; since 1308 every anointed English sovereign has been crowned on the special coronation chair built to contain it, thereby claiming overlordship of Scotland. In 1996, 700 years after its seizure, Elizabeth II authorized the stone's return to Scotland.

**scot and lot** was a contribution towards municipal expenses, largely poor relief, scot being the amount and lot the share. In 37 parliamentary boroughs before 1832 the right to vote was restricted to scot and lot payers.

**Scots, kingdom of** In the 9th cent. a new kingdom emerged out of the ashes of the kingdom of *Fortriu and in succeeding centuries became the dominant political force in north Britain. It was born out of the wreckage wrought by repeated Scandinavian incursions in eastern Scotland. Fortriu's heartland

in eastern Perthshire was repeatedly devastated, reaching a nadir of desperation in 875 when Danes inflicted another crushing defeat at the battle of *Dollar (east of Stirling). These Scandinavian attacks were not, however, followed by attempts to colonize eastern Scotland. What brought misfortune to many could also offer the opportunity for a few to refashion political relationships to their own advantage. By the beginning of the 10th cent. a Gaelic lineage—the descendants of *Kenneth MacAlpin—had succeeded in entrenching itself as the rulers of eastern Scotland. For the first time in eastern Scotland kingship was monopolized by a single dynasty. From 900 the kingdom was no longer 'Fortriu' (or 'Pictland'), but *Alba, the Gaelic word for Scotland.

The territory which the first kings of Scots held firmly in their grasp was probably little larger than an 11th-cent. English earldom. Until as late as the early 13th cent. Alba, 'Scotland' (or Albania/Scotia in Latin), was used to refer to the area east of the Grampian mountains stretching north from the river Forth to (approximately) the border with *Moray. In the 13th cent. 'Scotland' came to be used regularly by Scots themselves to refer to the whole of what is now mainland Scotland.

The survival of this new kingdom can be attributed largely to the long reign of *Constantine II. He succeeded his cousin *Donald II, the first recorded 'king of Scotland (Alba)', in 900, and reigned for at least four decades. The emergence of 'Scotland' in this period can, therefore, be compared with other new countries of a similar size, such as Flanders and Normandy, which rose out of the ashes of Scandinavian devastation.

Constantine II's reign was also crucial to the kingdom's survival because he halted the Scandinavian tide of destruction. In 904 a Danish army led by the sons of Ivarr was defeated in battle in Strathearn (southern Perthshire). The kingdom was not attacked again by Vikings for more than 50 years. Constantine's success at keeping the Danes at bay was, however, achieved principally by a policy of *rapprochement*. His daughter married the Danish king of Dublin, while Constantine himself may have had a Danish wife: his son *Indulf bore a Scandinavian name.

When the new kingdom of 'Scotland' emerged in the 10th cent. from its grim struggle for survival it was well placed to expand and dominate north Britain. Its natural rival in the north was the kingdom of Moray, which harnessed the resources of the rich Lowlands surrounding the Moray Firth. The kings of Moray, however, faced constant pressure from the Scandinavian earls of *Orkney. They served, indeed, as a buffer protecting the kingdom of the Scots from the full power of the earls of Orkney. But the greatest danger to the long-term success of the kingdom would have arisen from a rejuvenated *Northumbria stretching from Edinburgh to York. In the 7th cent. Northumbria had established itself as the dominant force in north Britain, but had since imploded into internal chaos and had been largely conquered and settled by Danes. In the late 10th cent. Northumbria south of the Tweed was revived as an earldom and was at times able to match the kings of Scots, but Scottish rule as far as the Tweed was decisively reasserted by *Malcolm II at the battle of *Carham (south-west of Berwick) in 1018. By this time the king of the Britons of Strathclyde (or king of the Cumbrians) had become a client of the king of Scots, and after the accession of *Duncan I, king of the Cumbrians, to the Scottish kingship in 1034 it appears that the two kingdoms were ruled by one line of kings. When *Macbeth, king of Moray, became king of Scots in 1040, Moray, too, became bound into the kingdom of the Scots. By the mid-11th cent., therefore, the kingdom had begun to assume a form recognizable as the Scottish kingdom of the Middle Ages and beyond.

The success of the kingdom of the Scots in this period was second only to that of the kings of *Wessex. The new English realm was undoubtedly more powerful than its northern counterpart. This was already evident in the 930s, which saw on the one hand an English army penetrate deep into Scotland and, on the other hand, the destruction of a combined Scottish, Danish, and British force in England. English kings, however, made no sustained effort to conquer Scotland. Britain's division into two power blocks had begun, and would eventually crystallize into the kingdoms of England and Scotland.

**Scotsman** One of the two daily newspapers which has laid claim to be Scotland's 'national' newspaper, the other being the *Herald* (formerly *Glasgow Herald*). Their competitiveness has symbolized the Edinburgh–Glasgow rivalry for pre-eminence in Scotland. Both were founded as weeklies (the *Herald* as the *Glasgow Advertiser* in 1783, the *Scotsman* in 1817), becoming dailies in the 1850s.

**Scott, Sir George Gilbert** (1811–78). Architect. Scott was the most famous and successful of Victorian Gothic master builders; and also the most correct stylistically, except when it came to railway stations. The most famous of those is St Pancras in London (1865), a kind of Disneyland castle in bright orange brick. His talent was inherited by his grandson, Sir Giles Gilbert Scott (1880–1960), who built Liverpool's Anglican cathedral in his grandfather's favourite style.

**Scott, Sir Robert Falcon** (1868–1912). Scott had entered the navy as a boy in 1880 and by 1897 was a lieutenant and torpedo officer. He was noticed by Sir Clements Markham whose influence led to his appointment as leader of the Royal Geographical Society and Royal Society Antarctic Expedition of 1901–4. Now famous, Scott was chosen to lead an official expedition in 1910 in the *Terra Nova* to get a party to the South Pole. Scott led four others who reached the Pole on 18 January 1912 only to find that Amundsen had preceded them there by just over a month. All five eventually perished on the horrendous walk back to their base.

**Scott, Sir Walter** (1771–1832). Poet, novelist, man of letters. Scott distilled the literary and historical culture of the *Scottish Enlightenment into the first great European works of historical fiction. A patriot and publicist, he placed Scotland on the international tourist map as a land of enlightenment and romance. The son of an Edinburgh lawyer, Scott remained an active lawyer for the rest of his life, becoming latterly sheriff depute of Selkirk and principal clerk of Session. He first made his mark as a poet, collecting, editing, and adapting border ballads and later writing enormously popular narrative poems of which the *Lay of the Last Minstrel* (1805) and *Marmion* (1808) are probably the best. His career as a novelist began in 1814 with the publication of *Waverley*. He built Abbotsford out of his substantial profits, turning it into an extraordinary physical embodiment of his taste for antiquities, real and phoney.

**Scottish Enlightenment** A relatively new term, said to have been invented in 1909 when W. R. Scott described Francis Hutcheson (1694–1746) as the father of the Scottish Enlightenment. It is now used generally to describe the intellectual, material, and moral culture of Scotland during the long 18th cent. It is a culture associated with the middling ranks of Scottish society, with the Scottish universities, and with the clubs, societies, and salons of Edinburgh. Ideologically it was a culture concerned with the defence of the revolution settlement, the Hanoverian succession, the Act of Union, and the presbyterian establishment. It was concerned with the civilizing functions of commerce and culture and with the problems of developing the institutions and manners appropriate to the preservation of a free commercial polity. Philosophers like Hutcheson, *Hume, *Smith, Ferguson, and Reid were interested in the principles of human nature, the meaning of sociability, and the truths of natural religion. Their conclusions made possible the development of a remarkable theory of progress which was instrumental in shaping the political economy of Smith, the histories of Hume and William Robertson, and the historical fiction of *Scott.

**Scottish National Party (SNP).** The SNP was formed in 1934 after a merger between the National Party of Scotland and the Scottish Party. The party is committed to securing an independent parliament for Scotland.

The SNP won their first parliamentary seat in 1945 when Dr Robert McIntyre was returned at a by-election for Motherwell. However the SNP had no great electoral success until the 1960s. In November 1967 Winnie Ewing captured Hamilton from Labour and the SNP had a high profile in the 1968 local elections. By 1974 the SNP had eleven seats in Parliament and polled over 30 per cent of the vote in Scotland. From this point there was a waning in SNP fortunes. In the 1979 general election their share of the poll dropped to 17 per cent and they lost all but two seats.

In 1990 Alex *Salmond became party leader, confirming the SNP as a left-of-centre social democratic party. The SNP accepted the Scottish Parliament as a step towards complete independence, within a European framework. It obtained six seats at Westminster in the general election of 1997, and 35 of the 129 seats in the Scottish Parliament elected in 1999. The following year John Swinney replaced Salmond as party leader but suffered a setback in the 2003 elections. Salmond resumed the leadership in 2004. After the SNP emerged from the 2007 election as the largest party in the Scottish Parliament, Salmond formed a minority government as First Minister.

**Scottish Wars of Independence,** 1296–1357. The name usually given to the prolonged wars between English and Scots after the death of Alexander III of Scotland in 1286. The death of his heir *Margaret ('the Maid of Norway') in 1290 left a number of 'competitors' for the vacant throne, of whom the chief were John *Balliol and Robert *Bruce, grandfather of the future Robert I; in 1292 Edward I, who claimed to be 'Lord Superior of Scotland', awarded the crown to Balliol. Edward however was determined to assert his rights to overlordship; and Balliol found it impossible to maintain the independence of his kingdom against this pressure. In 1295 the Scottish nobles took power out of Balliol's hands, made an alliance with Edward's enemy Philip IV of France, and prepared to defy Edward. A crushing campaign in 1296 forced Balliol to resign the crown.

This was however only the start of a struggle which lasted till 1357. There were three stages: first a 'revolt' against Edward in the name of King John, which was not finally subdued in 1304; secondly, the recovery following the rising of Robert Bruce in 1306, which ultimately secured the recognition of Scottish independence in 1328; and thirdly, the revival of attempts at English conquest under Edward III, which lasted till the treaty of *Berwick in 1357.

The first stage opened with widespread revolts in the early months of 1297, led by William *Wallace in the south, and Andrew *Murray in the north. They joined forces to win the devastating victory of *Stirling Bridge in 1297; but Wallace's defeat at *Falkirk in 1298 left the leadership in the hands of the nobles, who continued to resist Edward till 1304.

Edward's hopes were shattered by the revolt of the younger Robert Bruce in 1306. Bruce was rapidly crowned as Robert I, but as rapidly defeated twice, and by the end of 1306 was in hiding. Edward however died on 7 July 1307, which gave the respite Robert needed. In the next few years he gradually eliminated the English garrisons by a masterly policy of guerrilla warfare. By 1314 few remained; and the decisive defeat of Edward II at the battle of *Bannockburn left Robert secure.

Peace only became possible after Edward II's deposition. By the treaty of *Edinburgh/ *Northampton of 1328, Robert I was formally recognized as king of Scots, and his son and heir, the future David II, was married to *Joan of the Tower, a sister of Edward III. The peace did not last. Robert I died in 1329, when David was aged only 5. The temptation was too great for Edward III. He encouraged the son of John Balliol, Edward *Balliol, to attempt to seize the throne; and the Scottish leaders were forced to confront the invaders in battles, in which the English were twice victorious, at *Dupplin Moor (1332) under Edward Balliol, and at *Halidon Hill (1333) under Edward III himself. Balliol was established as king and much of the south was ceded into English control.

A long guerrilla war gradually wore down the occupiers, and in 1341 David II was able to return. Unfortunately, he continued the policy of raids into England, in one of which he was captured in 1346 and remained a captive till 1357. This led to a renewed English occupation; and parts of southern Scotland remained in English hands for a long time. However, by 1357 Edward III agreed to David's release under ransom. Though the treaty of *Berwick ignored the real issues of Scottish independence, no further attempts at subjection were made till the 1540s, so that the Wars of Independence can be said to have ended with the treaty of 1357.

**Scott Memorial** (Edinburgh). This tribute to the Scottish novelist Sir Walter Scott dominates Princes Street. The design of watercolourist and self-taught architect George Meikle Kemp, it was completed in 1846, two years after Kemp was found drowned in the Union canal.

**Scrope, Richard** (c.1350–1405). Archbishop of York. The third son of Henry, Lord Scrope of Masham, Scrope was chancellor of Cambridge University in 1378 and a doctor of laws. He was appointed bishop of Coventry and Lichfield in 1386. After some diplomatic service to Richard II, he was promoted to York in 1398. He made no opposition to Henry IV's usurpation, but in 1405 *Northumberland apparently prompted Scrope to revolt. Supported by Norfolk, the earl marshal, he published in York a manifesto denouncing Henry's misgovernment, attracting a dangerously large following which assembled on Shipton Moor. Archbishop and earl were enticed to a rendezvous with Ralph Neville, earl of Westmorland, who arrested them. After the king's arrival, they were summarily executed.

**scutage** or shield-money was commutation in lieu of knight service as a fixed levy on the fee. From an early period after the Norman Conquest it became difficult to raise an adequate number of knights to form the royal army, nor was their military prowess necessarily satisfactory. The person holding the fee might be old, infirm, or even a female. There were therefore advantages to both sides in allowing landowners to buy themselves out, and as early as 1100 the term scutage had come into use.

**Sebastopol, siege of** The chief event of the *Crimean War 1853–6. From 27 September 1854 British, French, and Turkish (and later Sardinian) armies maintained the siege of Sebastopol, the main Russian naval base in the Crimea. The French captured the White Tower on 7 June 1855 but the British assault on the Redan on 17 June was a failure. In a joint attack on 8 September the British again failed to hold the Redan but the French captured the Malakov, the key to the town. The Russians evacuated Sebastopol that night, keeping it under fire.

**Second World War** Germany made the Second World War: a necessary condition was a nationalist German government ready, even eager, to use force to secure far-reaching aims. Hitler came to power with the help of German conservatives who combined with the Nazis to resist socialists, in preference to working with socialists to block the Nazis. Until 1939, with British acquiescence, Hitler won success after peaceful success: restoring compulsory military service, creating an air force, remilitarizing the

Rhineland, absorbing Austria, annexing the German-inhabited areas of Czechoslovakia, and then, in March 1939, destroying Czechoslovakia altogether. Hitler's growing support in Germany, as foreign success went with full employment, steadily increased his freedom of action.

In Britain, however, appeasement became unpopular. On 31 March 1939 Neville *Chamberlain pledged Britain to defend Poland, and tried, at last, to build a 'peace front'. But the alliance attempted between Britain, France, and the USSR failed. Stalin thought it safer to make his own bargain with Hitler, took up appeasement, and agreed to help Hitler to destroy Poland. After an attempt to persuade Britain not to interfere, Germany attacked Poland. At dawn on 1 September 1939 began what became the Second World War. On 3 September Britain and France declared war on Germany. As expected, Poland did not last long against German attack and was partitioned with the USSR. Anglo-French strategy was defensive, waiting to build up their armed strength. In May and June 1940 it went badly wrong. France, defeated by a German attack in May 1940, whose main weight was further south than anticipated, surrendered in June. Italy joined Germany, tempted by the prospect of participation in a prospective peace conference. The victory of the *RAF in the Battle of *Britain in 1940 blocked invasion, but in 1941 German submarines nearly defeated Britain; British code-breaking came to the rescue in June.

In 1941 Hitler decided to attack the USSR before the defeat of Britain. His advisers expected success in 1941. It went wrong. Roosevelt, concerned to maintain a world balance of power, gave help to the USSR. Like Churchill he strove to keep the Red Army fighting. The Red Army wore down the German army while the Americans made tanks, aircraft, and ships; hence Hitler's defeat.

In the 20th cent. Japan maintained expanding population by trade, either by cooperating in the international structures or by forceful seizure of raw materials, especially fuel. The Japanese, with the threat from the USSR met by the Germans, decided to seize essential resources. In December 1941, encouraged by Germany, Japan attacked the US Pacific fleet at Pearl Harbor and invaded Malaya, Burma, and the Dutch East Indies.

Hitler, conscious that the USA was already an opponent, and still hopeful of victory over the USSR, clarified the conflict by declaring war on the USA.

The British empire and the USA fought a world war. Both gave priority to defeating Hitler. The main effort against Japan came from the USA. The failure of the Chinese to defend territories from which Japan could be attacked reduced the British role in Burma from the expansion of the line of communications to China to the defence of India and the eventual reassertion of British power in Malaya and Singapore.

In Europe the American army hoped to concentrate all Anglo-American resources in the United Kingdom to invade Europe at the earliest date possible. Churchill and the British thought Germany must first be weakened by campaigns in north Africa and Italy. Thus, British and US ground forces became fully engaged against the German army only after the landings in Normandy in June 1944. By September 1944 the allies had defeated Germany; Anglo-American forces closed to the Rhine, the Red Army had taken Romania, and territorial losses and bombing by overwhelming Anglo-American attack ended German ability to sustain war for much longer. However, SS coercion and fear of the allies, especially the Soviets, enabled Hitler to delay the end until May 1945.

In the Pacific, Japan, too, continued the war long after defeat brought about by attacks by US submarines on transport ships and US bombing attacks on Japanese industry. Japanese authorities, led by the emperor, accepted defeat only after the use of two atomic bombs, developed in time in the USA.

Churchill had foreseen that the gruelling struggle would leave Britain greatly weakened and *decolonization followed at a brisk pace. The USA emerged as the strongest power in the world and, with the collapse of the Soviet Union in the 1990s, perhaps the only super-power.

**secretaries of state** Like many other great offices, the secretaryships of state grew from comparatively modest beginnings. The development from a mere clerk to a policy-maker was largely a 16th-cent. phenomenon. In medieval usage, 'secretary' retained a slightly sinister meaning as one who was privy to secrets. In the reign of Edward IV, a principal secretary holding the signet was appointed, but the jump in status was not until Thomas *Cromwell became principal secretary in 1534. Two years later he added the privy seal and became the engine of government. In the reign of James I the convention was established of appointing two secretaries. After the Restoration, the posts were divided into a secretary of state for the north and for the south—the former conducting diplomacy with the protestant powers of northern Europe, the latter with the catholic powers of southern Europe.

A major reorganization took place in 1782 when the southern secretaryship was converted into the *Home Office and the northern secretaryship into the *Foreign Office. After that there were periodic increases in the number of secretaryships. In the 20th cent., though the foreign and home secretaries have retained their identities and importance, the others have suffered from repackaging according to the vicissitudes of time. The secretary of state for India vanished in 1947 when India became independent. Meanwhile the proliferation of secretaryships illustrated the law that grand titles increase as power diminishes—for industry (1963), education and science (1964), employment (1968), social services (1968), environment (1970), and transport (1976).

The early evolution of the secretaryship in Scotland from the reign of David II followed a similar course to that in England, with the office emerging from the keepership of the signet. In 1558–71 it was held by William *Maitland, in 1661–80 by *Lauderdale, and after 1680 usually by two persons. This arrangement lasted until the Jacobite rising of 1745, after which no secretary of state for Scotland was appointed until 1885. A secretaryship for Wales was set up in 1964. In Ireland, the lord-lieutenant had the main responsibility, but was assisted by a powerful chief secretary. This post lapsed when the Irish Free State was set up in 1922, but a secretary of state for Northern Ireland was appointed in 1972 after direct rule had been imposed on the province.

**secret ballot** was advocated as early as 1656 by James *Harrington in *Oceana*, discussed in pamphlets at the time of the Glorious Revolution, argued by *Defoe in 1708,

and became a persistent radical demand in the 18th cent. Nevertheless, when the reform committee proposed it in 1831 it was struck out by *Grey and the cabinet, to the great relief of William IV. The issue was then taken up by George Grote, and became one of the *chartists' six points. A select committee in 1869 reported in favour and in 1872 *Forster succeeded in carrying the measure against some opposition by the House of Lords.

**sects** *See* DISSENT.

**secularism** was the word adopted by George Jacob Holyoake in the early 1850s to describe a system of morals and social action shaped exclusively by this-worldly considerations, irrespective of religious beliefs. The word was derived from the secular education movement for the complete separation of religious teaching from other forms of education.

Local secular societies were formed in the 1850s, incorporating earlier groups of anti-clerical and atheistic radicals who had supported Richard *Carlile and Robert *Owen. In 1866 these were brought together by Charles *Bradlaugh in the National Secular Society. Ironically, secularism as a movement declined from the mid-1880s partly because society was becoming more secularized, making the campaigns of secularism seem unnecessary.

**Security, Act of** [S], 1704. The Scottish Act of Security was, paradoxically, an important step towards Union. After the failure of the *Darien scheme in 1700, the Scots were bitter towards England. The Scottish Parliament pointedly refused to follow the English Act of *Settlement (1701), which ensured succession to the Hanoverians. Instead, their Act of Security left the Scottish succession to be resolved by Parliament later and declared that the successor in England would not be named if Scottish grievances over religion, liberty, and trade were not met. The two countries were now on collision course and negotiations commenced which resulted in Union in 1707.

**Sedgemoor, battle of,** 1685. Sedgemoor was that most desperate of ventures, a surprise night attack. *Monmouth landed at Lyme Regis on 11 June 1685 and was proclaimed king at Taunton on the 20th.

But he gained little support and his scratch army failed to take Bristol or Bath. He was pursued to Bridgwater by a royal army under Lord Feversham, with John Churchill, the future duke of *Marlborough, as second in command. The royal army drew up east of Bridgwater, behind the line of the Bussex rhine, a waterlogged ditch. On the night of 5 July, Monmouth led out his men in total silence, past the village of Chedzoy, hidden by darkness. But with still a mile to go, the alarm was given. Once the element of surprise had been lost, Monmouth's fate was sealed. As dawn broke, Feversham's men advanced and the fight was over.

**Seditious Meetings Act,** 1795. In the autumn of 1795 high bread prices reinforced a demand for parliamentary reform and the London *Corresponding Society held a mass open-air meeting at Copenhagen House (Islington) on 26 October. Three days later, on his way to open Parliament, George III was hooted and the window of his coach shattered. *Pitt's government responded with the Seditious Meetings Act (36 Geo. III c. 8), which forbade meetings of more than 50 people without prior permission from a magistrate.

**Seisyllwg, kingdom of** An early Welsh kingdom of obscure origin, though it may have been established by Seisyll ap Clydog, king of Ceredigion, by extending his dominion south to the Tywi valley (c.730). Later (904), it was absorbed into the wider kingdom of *Deheubarth under *Hywel Dda.

**Selborne, Roundell Palmer, 1st earl of** (1812–95). Lawyer. Palmer got off to a flying start. He was educated at both Rugby and Winchester, moved on to Christ Church, Oxford, was president of the Union, and gained a first-class degree. He studied law at Lincoln's Inn and entered Parliament in 1847 as a supporter of *Peel. He became solicitor-general in *Palmerston's administration in 1861 and moved up to attorney-general in 1863, holding the post until 1866. A strong churchman, he disapproved greatly of the disestablishment of the Irish church in 1869 and refused *Gladstone's offer of the lord chancellorship. But on the resignation of Lord Hatherley in 1872 with failing eyesight, Palmer succeeded him as lord chancellor, holding office 1872–4 and again 1880–

5. Increasingly uneasy at the radical trend of the Liberals, he parted with them on *Irish Home Rule in 1886, writing sadly in his *Memorials*, 'my idols were broken'. Henceforth he gave independent support to the Conservatives.

**Selby, battle of,** 1644. In the spring of 1644, the royal army in the north, under *Newcastle, was at Durham, to prevent a junction of the Scots with the parliamentary forces under the *Fairfaxes. But on 11 April John Bellasyse, holding Selby, south of York, was badly defeated. York, the king's northern capital, was in imminent danger and as soon as he heard the news, Newcastle moved south to hold the city. Rupert's attempt to relieve York later in the summer led to the crushing royalist defeat at *Marston Moor. Selby was the stone that started the avalanche.

**Selden, John** (1584–1654). Selden, 'the father of English legal history', was one of the most distinguished antiquarians of Stuart England. A lawyer of the Inner Temple, he served as MP for Lancaster (1623), Great Bedwyn (1626), Ludgershall (1628), and in the Long Parliament of 1640 for the University of Oxford. From 1607 he issued a stream of learned works, mainly on legal history, of which a history of tithes (1617) is best known. In the early days of the Long Parliament he was a moderate and there were rumours that he might join the court. But he did not and in 1643 was put in charge of records in the Tower. Meanwhile, Selden continued to publish, including an important treatise on the law of the sea (1636) and another on the privileges of the baronage (1641). The Selden Society was established in 1886 by *Maitland and others to encourage the study of English law.

**self-denying ordinance,** 1645. Growing dissatisfaction in Parliament with the inability of *Essex and *Manchester to finish the Civil War led to a proposal, late in 1644, for a self-denying ordinance, whereby members of both Houses of Parliament could no longer hold commissions. Brought forward again in 1645 after more royalist successes, it passed on 3 April. Essex, Manchester, and *Waller resigned, clearing out the old guard, and paving the way for the *New Model Army under Sir Thomas *Fairfax. *Cromwell was given special exemption from the ordinance.

**Selgovae** A British tribe in southern Scotland. This tribe, whose name is thought to mean 'hunters', is referred to by the Greek geographer Ptolemy. His information places them in the southern uplands of Scotland centred in the upper Tweed basin, sandwiched between the *Votadini to the east and the Novantes to the west.

**Selsey, diocese of** *Wilfrid, formerly of *Ripon and *York, created this see, conterminous with Sussex, in 681. When he returned to *Hexham in 686, Selsey was united with *Winchester until Selsey's revival some years later. After the Council of London (1075), the see moved to *Chichester.

**Senior, Nassau** (1790–1864) Classical economist. Born in Berkshire, the son of a cleric, Senior was one of the most influential economists of his day. His family was of Spanish origins. After Eton and Magdalen College, Oxford, he was called to the bar in 1819. He served twice at Oxford as Professor of Political Economy. Senior played an important part in the enquiry into the poor laws and later into investigations of factory conditions and education. Much influenced by *Malthus and *Ricardo, he was a strong critic of trade unionism, but did not subscribe to the 'iron law of wages' theory, which some used to refuse improvement for the labouring classes.

**Septennial Act,** 1716. This Act prolonged the life of Parliament from a maximum of three years (as the 1694 Triennial Act required) to seven years. Its pretext was the Jacobite uprising in 1715. But by delaying the next election until 1722 the new Whig ministers succeeded in evading electoral judgement until they had consolidated themselves in power and weakened their Tory opponents. The *Parliament Act of 1911 shortened the duration of parliaments to five years.

**Septimius Severus** Roman emperor 193–211. Lucius Septimius Severus was born at Lepcis Magna in north Africa. Consul in 190, he was governor of Pannonia Superior on the Danube when he was proclaimed emperor on the assassination of Commodus. He was opposed by the governor of Britain,

Clodius Albinus, whom he killed at the battle of Lyons in February 197. After a series of wars against the Parthians, Severus' attention was drawn back to Britain by trouble with the Scottish tribes. He took the field with his sons *Caracalla and Geta in 208 and reconquered the Lowlands. Increasing ill-health led to his death early in 211 at York.

**serfdom** is the general term for servitude to a superior, but distinguished from slavery by being regulated by custom. The name masks a great variety of arrangements. There were large areas of England where it had never applied, particularly in Kent, the old Danelaw, and parts of the west country. Though the basic obligation of the unfree was to work for three days a week on the lord's demesne, to assist at harvest time, and to pay certain dues, the details differed from estate to estate. The nearest that serfdom came to being a complete system was in the two centuries after the Norman Conquest. By the 13th cent. the pattern was beginning to unravel as more and more villeins obtained their freedom and became copyholders.

**serjeant at law** The order of serjeants at law, dating at least from the early 14th cent., consisted of the leaders of the legal profession and until 1846 they alone had the right to plead cases before the Court of *Common Pleas. The characteristic of their office was the distinctive 'coif' and they were members of Serjeants' Inn.

**Settlement, Act of,** 1701. This statute, 12 & 13 Wm. III c. 2, is strange and betrays the mixed motives of its authors. The immediate problem was to provide for the protestant succession after the death of Anne's son, the duke of Gloucester, in July 1700. This was done by putting aside more than 50 catholic claimants and offering the succession to *Sophia, electress of Hanover, a granddaughter of James I. But the Tory majority in Parliament took the opportunity to tack on a number of incongruous clauses designed to limit the powers of the monarch, who was not to leave the country or engage in war without parliamentary approval. Royal pardons were not to be issued against impeachments. The clauses devoted to the succession took effect in 1714, when Queen Anne was succeeded by Sophia's son George

I. The other clauses were either repealed or circumvented.

## Settlements and Removals, Act of,

1662. The end of the Civil War period left the Elizabethan *Poor Law arrangements in confusion, since many people had left their native villages and towns. Charles II's *Cavalier Parliament brought in an Act 'for the better relief of the poor of this kingdom' (13 & 14 Car. II c. 12) which governed poor relief until the reform of 1834. The Act of 1662 offered the drastic solution that any persons, not necessarily begging or asking for relief, but only 'likely to be chargeable' might be expelled to their native parishes by a removal order granted by two JPs. In addition to being a gross infringement of personal liberty, the arrangements were bound to lead to disputes between parishes which, according to Rickman in 1822, had become 'the main employment of Quarter Sessions since the Revolution'.

## seven bishops, trial of the, 1688.

Seven bishops, including Archbishop *Sancroft, arrested for petitioning against the public reading of James II's second *Declaration of Indulgence (1688), were tried for 'seditious libel'. The cheering which broke out among James's soldiers on Hounslow Heath when the verdict of acquittal was known was an ominous sign for the king.

## Sevenoaks, battle of, 1450.

In June 1450 Henry VI advanced with a sizeable force into Kent to confront Jack *Cade's rebels. But on the 18th a detachment under Sir Humphry Stafford was routed and the commander killed. Henry left for safer parts and Cade went on to occupy London.

## seventh-day adventists

Largest of a group of sects focusing on the Second Coming—the return of Christ in glory to judge the living and the dead. They originated in the USA in 1831 when William Miller, a baptist farmer, announced the Coming for 1843, recalculated to 1844. The followers observed the sabbath from Friday sunset to Saturday sunset, hence their name, adopted in 1861. They reached England in 1878 with a mission to Southampton.

## Seven Years' War, 1756–63.

In the years immediately after the War of the Austrian Succession, a 'diplomatic revolution' took place in Europe. France and Austria, with support from Russia, Sweden, and Saxony, aligned themselves against Frederick II of Prussia. In 1756 Frederick made a pre-emptive strike into Saxony, followed a year later by an advance into Bohemia. As his enemies responded by threatening Prussia from all sides, Frederick turned to Britain for aid. An 'Army of Observation' under the duke of *Cumberland was deployed to western Germany, but when the French invaded, Cumberland was beaten at *Hastenbeck (26 July 1757) and forced to sign a convention to disband his army. This was countermanded by the British prime minister, William *Pitt (the Elder), who sent British units to reinforce the remains of Cumberland's army, under the command of Ferdinand of Brunswick. A hard-won victory at *Minden on 1 August 1759 allowed the 'Army of Execution' to consolidate its hold over western Germany, but the war was by no means over. Further east, Frederick had managed to survive only by fighting desperate and costly battles at Zorndorf (1758) and Kunersdorf (1759); he had to fight further battles at Liegnitz and Torgau (1760) and at Schweidnitz (1762), to defeat the French, Austrians, and Russians in turn. Only when Russia withdrew from the war on the death of the Tsarina Elizabeth in 1762 did Frederick receive any respite. The war ended in February 1763 with the peace of *Paris.

But the fighting was not confined to Europe. In 1758 Pitt dispatched an expeditionary force of 12,000 men under General *Amherst to capture the fortress of Louisbourg and, when this proved successful, ordered a much more ambitious advance into French-held Canada. On the night of 12–13 September 1759 Major-General James *Wolfe, commanding no more than 3,000 men, mounted a surprise attack on Quebec. The ensuing battle was short and decisive; although both Wolfe and his opponent Montcalm were fatally wounded, the French retreated and Quebec fell. Montreal followed, leaving Britain in control of much of Canada.

By then, the British had also consolidated their power in India, where the pro-French nawab Siraj-ud-Daula was defeated by Robert *Clive at the battle of *Plassey in 1757 to give the East India Company control of Bengal. By 1761, when the French outpost at

Pondicherry surrendered to General Eyre *Coote, this control had been extended into the Carnatic.

**Seville, treaty of,** 1729. In 1727 Spain, with Habsburg support, began a siege of *Gibraltar, held by the British since 1704. It was not pressed with much vigour and an armistice was agreed in 1728. By the treaty of Seville in 1729 Spain restored Britain's commercial concessions while Britain agreed to support Spanish claims in Italy.

**Seychelles** These islands in the Indian Ocean were first marked on Portuguese charts in 1502 but not settled by whites until 1742 when Lazare Picault took possession of them for the French East India Company. In 1810 they were captured by the British and retained at the peace of Paris. The Republic of the Seychelles came into existence on 27 June 1976.

**Seymour, Thomas Seymour, 1st Baron** (1508–49). Seymour played for high stakes and lost. He was the brother of *Jane Seymour, Henry VIII's third wife, and the younger brother of *Somerset, protector to the young Edward VI. His spectacular rise began with his sister's marriage in May 1536. In 1544 he was appointed master-general of ordnance for life and lord admiral. As soon as his nephew became king in 1547 he was created a peer and given the Garter. Within months of Henry VIII's death he had married his widow *Catherine Parr. On her death in childbirth, he seems to have aimed at marriage with Princess Elizabeth, whom he had certainly treated with familiarity. But in January 1549 he was accused of conspiring against his brother, of whom he was envious. Condemned by attainder, he was executed on Tower Hill.

**Shackleton, Sir Ernest Henry** (1874–1922). Almost the antithesis of *Scott as an explorer, Shackleton was impetuous and restless. He successfully applied to join Scott's Antarctic expedition of 1901–4. Sledging with Scott himself, he reached 82 degrees south in 1902. Shackleton raised enough support to take his own expedition back to the Antarctic in 1907–8 where he discovered and named the Beardmore Glacier. Shackleton himself reached 88 degrees south, only 97 miles from the Pole. He was encouraged to lead an official expedition aiming to explore from the Weddell Sea and cross the continent to the Ross Sea. Ordered to go ahead despite the Great War, Shackleton lost his ship *Endurance* when it was crushed by ice in November 1915. With sledges and small boats, he led his men to Elephant Island by the following April, sailed in an open boat to South Georgia, returned to rescue his men, and then visited the Ross Sea. He set out on a third Antarctic expedition in 1921 but died suddenly after reaching South Georgia.

**Shaftesbury, Anthony Ashley Cooper, 1st earl of** (1621–83). Politician. As chancellor of the Exchequer 1661–72, Shaftesbury (then Lord Ashley) was a minor but hard-working and able member of Charles II's early ministries. Promoted to the more prestigious office of lord chancellor in 1672, his deism and attachment to parliamentary government put him at odds with the king's increasingly obvious pro-French and pro-catholic policy and he was dismissed in 1673. He then went into systematic opposition. From 1679 he led the '*Exclusion' campaign to bar the catholic duke of York from the succession, exploiting the *Popish plot to generate anti-catholic feeling. Hounded in his last months on a charge of treason, he died in Holland early in 1683.

**Shaftesbury, Antony Ashley Cooper, 7th earl of** (1801–85). Philanthropist and social reformer. Lord Ashley (as he was styled until 1851) was a strict evangelical who devoted his whole life to promoting a succession of reform causes: the Ten Hour Bill; the 1842 Mines Act; reform of the lunacy laws; abolition of child chimney-sweeping; public health and slum housing; ragged schools; the plight of agricultural labourers; training for destitute children (the Shaftesbury homes). He was motivated by a deep religious faith which was simple, rigid, and exclusive. Shaftesbury was the most active champion of Victorian evangelicalism as applied to all aspects of public life. Politically he was a Tory and opposed all forms of popular democracy.

**Shakespeare, William** (1564–1616). Dramatist and poet. Baptized in Stratford-upon-Avon on 26 April 1564, William was the son of John Shakespeare, a glovemaker and prominent Stratford citizen who became mayor and justice of the peace during William's childhood. He was educated at the Stratford grammar school, and married Anne Hathaway, daughter of a successful local farmer, eight years his senior (and already pregnant at the wedding), in 1582. He started as an actor, continued as a playwright, and developed as an administrator and entrepreneur: by the time of his death, on 23 April 1616, he had established his status as a major shareholder in the King's Men, the principal acting company of his time, and was a successful and wealthy man.

Shakespeare wrote approximately forty-two plays. Quotations from Shakespeare remain an often unwitting part of everyday speech; productions of his plays remain hugely popular, both in theatres and in the cinema. His earliest plays are mostly comedies and histories—*The Two Gentlemen of Verona* and *The Taming of the Shrew* are probably the very earliest. He wrote the first play (known as *2 Henry VI*) in the four-play cycle known as the 'first tetralogy' in 1591, completing it with the best known of his earlier histories, *Richard III*, the following year.

The first tetralogy preceded Shakespeare's attachment to the Lord Chamberlain's Men in 1594; it was for that company, and for their first playhouse, the Theatre, that he wrote the 'second tetralogy', his most popular group of history plays—*Richard II*, *1* and *2 Henry IV*, and *Henry V*. Both tetralogies attest to the lasting impact on English society of the Wars of the *Roses.

The move to the new *Globe theatre in 1598–9 marked a new phase in Shakespeare's writing career and the demise of the Shakespearian history play 'proper'. For the Globe, Shakespeare turned to other genres, writing his mature comedies (*As You Like It* and *Twelfth Night*) and his major tragedies (*Hamlet*, *Othello*, *King Lear*, and *Macbeth*), as well as his later tragicomedies or romances (*Pericles*, *The Winter's Tale*, *Cymbeline*, and *The Tempest*).

The Lord Chamberlain's Men had become the King's Men at James I's accession, and played regularly at court. *King Lear* and *Macbeth*, for example, by depicting dark alternatives, acknowledge the role of James I in reunifying Britain, and both *Lear* and *Cymbeline* delve far back into mythical British history in search of complex political resonances.

Shakespeare wrote at a unique period in the history of the British theatre—for the range of his audiences, for the cultural resonance of theatrical institutions—and his plays cannot fairly be dismissed as 'mere' fiction or entertainment. It is a commonplace of current literary criticism that Shakespearian drama both responded to and shaped public perspectives on history and politics at a time of considerable, and hugely productive, cultural anxiety, 'shaping fantasies' for a developing nation-state.

**Sharp, Granville** (1735–1813). Anti-slavery campaigner. Born in Durham, and grandson of an archbishop of York, Sharp was employed in London as a government clerk when in 1765 he befriended Jonathan Strong, a runaway slave. The ensuing legal disputes culminated in the *Somerset case (1772) in which slavery was declared not to exist in England. In 1783 he formed the idea of an African settlement for freed slaves (*Sierra Leone, 1787), in 1787 he chaired the committee for the abolition of the slave trade, and in 1807 founded the African Institution to work for the total suppression of the trade following its abolition in the British empire.

**Sharp, James** (1613–79). Archbishop. Sharp was educated at Aberdeen University and appointed professor of philosophy at St Andrews. At the Restoration he worked closely with *Monck and was sent to Breda to negotiate with Charles II. He was appointed royal chaplain in Scotland, and made archbishop of St Andrews in 1661. He then began a determined attack upon the presbyterian clergy he had just left. In 1668 he escaped an attempted assassination but in 1679 fell into the hands of a *covenanting group in Fife and was murdered. The incident led to the covenanting rising, suppressed at *Bothwell Bridge.

**Shaw, George Bernard** (1856–1950). Dramatist. Ambitious to write, Shaw left Dublin and his childhood's genteel poverty to join his mother and sisters in London (1876). His novels rejected, he eventually found steady work as literary, music ('Corno di Bassetto'), and theatre critic. Force behind the *Fabian Society, he began to write his own plays, influenced by Ibsen and trying to move the English stage away from affectations to a new *gravitas*: *Widowers' Houses* (1892), considering slum landlordism, and *Mrs Warren's Profession*, on organized prostitution, were radical, unromantic, and offensive to many. *St Joan* (1924) is considered a masterpiece, but *Pygmalion* (1916) remains the most popular.

**Shawfield riots,** 1725. After the *Union of 1707 taxation policy remained a delicate matter in Scotland. The imposition of the malt tax on Scotland by exasperated Tories in 1712 provoked a determined attempt at repeal of the Union and it was not levied. In 1724 a move to raise revenue by 3 pence on every bushel of malt provoked severe riots in Glasgow. Shawfield, the home of Daniel Campbell, MP for Glasgow Burghs, was plundered.

**Sheffield** was a comparatively late developer among the great English cities. Its situation was determined by the river Sheaf joining the Don: William de Lovetot built a castle in the angle in the 12th cent. together with a bridge. As early as the 14th cent. Sheffield had a national reputation for cutlery, since *Chaucer's Miller from Trumpington had a 'Sheffield whittle', a short dagger or knife, in his hose. Its development as a great steel town depended upon local supplies of iron, the water-power of the Loxley, Rivelin, and Porter, as well as the Sheaf and Don, and sandstone for grinding. *Camden's *Britannia* (1580s) found Sheffield 'remarkable, among many other places hereabouts, for blacksmiths, there being much iron digged up in these parts'. The Cutlers' Company was granted a charter under the master cutler in 1624. By 1801, Sheffield, with a population of 31,000, was the tenth town in England. It was given parliamentary representation by the Great Reform Act of 1832, acquired a town council in 1843, and by 1861 was fifth largest, with 185,000 people. It became a city in 1893, gained a university in 1905, and was given cathedral status in 1914.

**Sheffield, diocese of** This see, comprising south Yorkshire, was created in 1914 out of the *York diocese. Though a suffragan see of Sheffield was established in 1901, only the rapid extension of the Doncaster coalfield enabled the passage of the Three Bishoprics

Bill (for Sheffield, *Chelmsford, and *Bury St Edmunds) in 1913. The cathedral is the former Perpendicular parish church (*c.*1430), reconstructed in 1880, with further extensions completed in 1966.

**Shelburne, William Petty, 2nd earl of** (1737–1805). Shelburne was intelligent and able, but deemed untrustworthy by most contemporaries. He entered the army in 1757, became an MP in 1760, and went to the Lords in 1761. Initially a follower of *Bute, he shifted his allegiance to the elder *Pitt (later earl of Chatham) and served under him, from 1766, as southern secretary. Shelburne was frequently at odds with his colleagues and after a disagreement over foreign policy with the *de facto* premier, *Grafton, was marked for dismissal. From his sick-bed, Chatham misread the situation and, believing Shelburne to have been removed, resigned. The net result was the departure of Shelburne and Chatham. After Chatham's death in 1778, Shelburne was the leader of the Chathamites and consequently mistrusted by the *Rockinghamites, who referred to him as Malagrida, an infamous Jesuit schemer. After the fall of *North in 1782, George III played off Shelburne against the Rockinghamites. As home secretary (March–July 1782), he was at variance with the foreign secretary, Charles *Fox, over the peace negotiations, which involved both their departments. Rockingham's death in July 1782 precipitated a cabinet crisis, with the king insisting on Shelburne's succession to the premiership. Fox resigned and then coalesced with the Northites to force Shelburne's resignation in February 1783. Although created marquis of Lansdowne in 1784, Shelburne never regained high office.

**Sheldon, Gilbert** (1598–1677). Archbishop of Canterbury (1663–77). A graduate of Trinity College, Oxford, Sheldon was fellow, then warden (1626), of All Souls. Spiritual adviser to Charles I in the Civil War, he was ejected from All Souls (1648) and briefly imprisoned. He became bishop of London at the Restoration. A keen protagonist of uniformity, he succeeded *Juxon as archbishop (1663). As chancellor of Oxford (1667–9), he had the Sheldonian theatre built at his own expense with *Wren as architect.

**Shelley, Mary Wollstonecraft** (1797–1851). Author. Only daughter of the radical philosopher William *Godwin and early feminist Mary *Wollstonecraft, pretty, bookish Mary eloped with the young Percy Bysshe *Shelley to Europe in 1814, marrying him on his wife Harriet's suicide (1816). Her most famous novel *Frankenstein* (1818) founded the genre of 'scientific Gothick' later exploited by horror-film makers. After the poet's death (1822), Mary returned to England and became a professional writer in order to educate her only surviving child Percy Florence Shelley.

**Shelley, Percy Bysshe** (1792–1822). Son of a Whig landowner, a precocious and unconventional career at Eton and Oxford was followed by a precipitous first marriage and, soon after, elopement to the continent with the daughter of William *Godwin and Mary *Wollstonecraft. Already he had published *Queen Mab* (1813), later revered in *chartist circles. 'Ode to the West Wind' (1819) best represents his impetuous idealism, foreshadowing *Prometheus Unbound* (1820), which imagines a bloodless revolution where 'mankind had only to will that there should be no evil and there would be none'. His life was abruptly ended by an accident at sea off the coast of Italy.

**Sheraton, Thomas** (1751–1806). English furniture designer. Sheraton was born in Stockton-on-Tees, where he learned cabinet-making, probably never returning to this trade after his move to London about 1790. He was principally occupied writing several manuals on furniture design, the most popular, *The Cabinet-Maker and Upholsterer's Drawing Book* (1791–4), including treatises on geometry, architecture, and perspective. Sheraton's many chair-back designs were simple and elegant, employing straight lines and delicate marquetry of animals, flowers, or musical instruments.

**Sherborne, diocese of** The see, carved out of *Winchester in 705 by King *Ine, was further split in 909 by *Edward the Elder; Sherborne retained Dorset, Devon and Cornwall went to *Crediton, Somerset to *Wells, and Wiltshire and Berkshire to *Ramsbury. In 1058 Sherborne was reunited with Ramsbury and in 1075 the combined see was moved to Old Sarum (*Salisbury).

**Sheridan, Richard Brinsley** (1751–1816). The son of an Irish actor, Sheridan achieved fame as both dramatist and politician. Sheridan's major works were all produced before entering Parliament in 1780: *The Rivals* (1775), *The Duenna* (1775), *The School for Scandal* (1777), and *The Critic* (1779).

Sheridan was a superb political orator, achieving fame during the campaign against Warren *Hastings; one memorable speech, on 8 February 1787, lasted an astonishing 5 hours and 40 minutes. For all his ability, Sheridan never attained cabinet rank, and served only as under-secretary at the Foreign Office (1782), Treasury secretary (1783), and treasurer of the navy (1806–7). Mutual antagonism between Sheridan and *Burke contributed to the disintegration of the Whig Party in the 1790s, with Sheridan flaunting his admiration for the French principles Burke despised. He died in straitened circumstances, caused partly by losses incurred from his involvement with Drury Lane theatre.

**Sheriffmuir, battle of,** 1715. Leading the Jacobite rising, *Mar rallied his forces at Perth and commanded 9,000 men: *Argyll, with much smaller numbers, took up position at Stirling. On 13 November the armies did battle at Sheriffmuir, near Dunblane. Argyll retired to Stirling in good order. Mar was unable to follow up his advantage, retreated to Aberdeen, and, at length, took ship for France.

**sheriffs** Reeves were Anglo-Saxon officials, and the king's reeves had special duties to keep order and collect royal dues. By the 11th cent. English kings put each shire under a *scirgerefa* ('shire-reeve', sheriff) who administered justice and collected revenues. Their powers and duties were greatly increased by the Normans, and they became notorious for high-handedness. The crown's long-term solution was to spread the exercise of local administration and justice, especially, from the 14th cent., through *justices of the peace; since the 16th cent. sheriffs have been largely county figureheads.

**Shetland** is a group of islands in the northern North Sea, some 150 miles from the north-east tip of the Scottish mainland. Once annexed by the Vikings and subsequently part of the kingdom of Norway, Shetland (together with Orkney) became part of Scotland in 1469. It is a county of Scotland and has remained a unitary local administrative authority.

**ship money** was an occasional tax on property, traditionally levied in port towns for their protection by the navy. Because Parliament had been dissolved in 1629, Charles I lacked money both for the fleet and for other expenses. In 1634 he therefore levied ship money in London, extending the tax in the following year to the whole country. In 1635, 1636, and 1637 it produced a high yield, but in 1638 it produced only one-third of the assessed amount. John *Hampden, a Buckinghamshire squire, and others refused to pay on principle. In 1641 Parliament declared ship money illegal.

**Shippen, William** (1673–1743). Jacobite parliamentarian. The son of a clergyman, Shippen trained as a barrister. He became a Tory MP in 1707, and, but for one short interlude (1709–10), remained in Parliament for the rest of his life. During the Tory administration (1710–14) he emerged as an outspoken member of the Jacobite wing of the party. With the ostracization of the Tory Party after George I's accession in 1714, Shippen settled into a routine of unrelenting opposition to successive Whig ministries.

**shires** *See* COUNTIES.

**shooting,** as a sport, may be divided into shooting at animals or birds, or shooting at targets in competition. Pheasant- and grouse-shooting reached its peak in the vast country-house gatherings of Edwardian England: game was rigorously preserved and *poaching caused much ill-feeling in rural society. Big-game shooting, largely in Africa and India, was fashionable in the 19th and early 20th cents. Organized target-shooting in Britain dates from the mid-19th cent. The National Rifle Association was founded at Wimbledon in 1860 and transferred in 1880 to Bisley in Surrey.

**Short Parliament,** April–May 1640. The first *Bishops' War ended inconclusively because Charles I was not strong enough to fight the Scots. He summoned Parliament in 1640 in the expectation that it would provide the funds for him to do so. But the

Commons were more concerned with grievances, in particular the growth of *Arminianism and the crown's resort to prerogative taxation such as *ship money. In the end, Charles lost patience and brought proceedings to an abrupt close.

**Shovell, Sir Clowdesley** (1650–1707). Naval commander. Entering the service in 1664 as a cabin boy, Shovell achieved a reputation for unflinching courage and skill during his Mediterranean commands in the 1680s, and was promoted rear-admiral in 1690. In the naval war against the French during the 1690s he proved an effective operational commander, with an important share in the victories at *Beachy Head (1690) and Barfleur (1692). In the early years of Anne's reign he commanded in several Mediterranean actions including the capture of *Gibraltar and the battle off Malaga in 1704. Returning from the unsuccessful Toulon mission in 1707, his flagship was wrecked off the Scilly Isles, and Shovell drowned.

**Shrewsbury, battle of,** 1403. Henry IV learned of the rebellion of Hotspur (Henry *Percy), in league with Owain *Glyndŵr, Thomas Percy, earl of *Worcester, Archibald, earl of *Douglas, and Edmund Mortimer, when he was at Burton. A forced march carried his troops westwards to Shrewsbury to join his son Henry, prince of Wales, campaigning in Wales. Hotspur arrived to find the town in royal hands. Glyndŵr did not join him, and his father, the earl of *Northumberland, got no nearer than Pontefract. Hotspur was outnumbered, but he resolved to give battle rather than risk retreat and disintegration. The early exchanges on 31 July went in favour of the rebels but Hotspur was killed and his followers fled.

**Shrewsbury, Charles Talbot, 1st duke of** (1660–1718). Brought up a Roman catholic, Talbot converted to Anglicanism in 1679, and was one of the 'Immortal Seven' who, in 1688, signed the letter inviting William of Orange to invade. In 1689 he was appointed secretary of state, but resigned in 1690. In 1694 he again became secretary of state and was created a duke. Appointed lord chamberlain in 1699, he resigned on health grounds in 1700. He was appointed lord chamberlain in the Tory ministry (1710–14), and lord-lieutenant of Ireland in 1713. On the dismissal of *Harley, Queen Anne appointed Shrewsbury lord treasurer, thwarting *Bolingbroke's ambition, and upon the queen's death (1 August) he helped to secure the Hanoverian succession. His final office was again as lord chamberlain (1714–15).

**Shrewsbury, Elizabeth Talbot, countess of** (1518–1608). 'Bess of Hardwick' was one of the most remarkable women in Elizabethan England. The daughter of a Derbyshire squire, she gained wealth and status through four increasingly ambitious marriages, the last (in 1567) to George Talbot, earl of Shrewsbury. After the earl's death, Bess, intriguer and termagant, was free to concentrate on her building and furnishing at *Chatsworth and Hardwick Hall.

**Shrewsbury, John Talbot, 1st earl of** (c.1387–1453). Talbot was the most feared in France of the English captains in the last stages of the *Hundred Years War. Having fought briefly under Henry V, he returned to France in 1427, where he served until his death at *Castillon in 1453. A tough, cruel, and quarrelsome man, he came to be regarded as the last of the old chivalric breed.

**shrines** These pilgrimage centres were a central element in medieval life. England could not emulate Jerusalem, the ultimate place of *pilgrimage, Rome with its multitude of relics, or Compostela. Nevertheless, like other countries, England had shrines of great popularity, journeys to which were less arduous and expensive. Before 1066 the most popular included Durham (St *Cuthbert), St Albans, and Bury (St *Edmund), which all faded in the late 12th cent. before the brighter light of Westminster (St *Edward), Worcester (St *Wulfstan), and—by far the most popular—Canterbury (St Thomas *Becket). In late medieval England as elsewhere, as devotion to the Virgin Mary intensified, her shrines at Westminster, Doncaster, Ipswich, and above all at *Walsingham grew in importance.

**Shropshire** is a large and beautiful county. The hilly southern part includes the Wrekin, the Long Mynd, Clee Hill, and Wenlock Edge: the north, adjoining Cheshire, is flatter, with some notable meres. Shrewsbury grew up as an important crossing over the Severn and as a bastion against the Welsh. Whitchurch is the chief town of the northern half, Ludlow, in Tudor times home to the *Council in the Marches of Wales, of the south.

In Roman times, the area fell between the *Cornovii and the *Ordovices. The Roman road *Watling Street ran through the county and Viriconium (Wroxeter), where it crossed the Severn, was an important legionary base. The region was disputed between Britons and Saxons and at one stage much of it belonged to the kingdom of *Powys, whose capital, Pengwern, may have been at Shrewsbury. By the 8th cent. it formed part of the kingdom of Mercia and Offa's Dike runs through the western parts of the shire. By the 10th cent. it was in existence as a shire.

The Normans, finding Saxon pronunciation difficult, called the county Salopescira and studded it with castles, at Shrewsbury, Ludlow, Bishop's Castle, and Clun. Even so, the western parts were defended against the Welsh with difficulty. The county was again at risk during *Glyndŵr's rising in the early 15th cent., when Clun was destroyed, but Glyndŵr's allies, the Percies, were defeated just north of Shrewsbury in 1403 and Henry *Percy (Hotspur) killed.

Until the 18th cent. Shropshire was overwhelmingly an agricultural county, famous for sheep, but the development by the *Darby family of a great mining and iron industry at *Coalbrookdale produced the strange phenomenon of blast furnaces and chimneys amid lush wooded valleys. The Iron Bridge, built in 1777, and now the centre of a splendid museum complex, was for decades regarded as one of the wonders of technological progress.

Shrewsbury retained its primacy as county town without difficulty, hosting the assizes and the parliamentary elections. *Defoe found it 'beautiful, large, pleasant, populous and rich: they speak all English in the town, but on a market-day you would think you were in Wales.' Its central position was enhanced by the coming of the railways in the mid-19th cent., which confirmed its importance as a route centre. The county was not affected by the Local Government Act of 1972, but the balance of population began to change with the development of a new town in the east, absorbing Dawley, Oakengates, and Wellington. It was renamed *Tel-

S

ford, after the great engineer who was county surveyor from 1788 to 1834.

**Sickert, Walter Richard** (1860–1942). British artist. Born in Munich, Sickert's Danish/Irish parents came to England in 1868. After a short career as an actor, he studied at the Slade School before joining the studio of Whistler through whom he met Degas, who became a close friend.

**Siddons, Sarah** (1755–1831). Actress. The eldest of Roger Kemble's twelve children, her early years were spent travelling widely with the family company until marriage to the young actor William Siddons. Her first London season (1775/6) was a failure, but, having established a reputation in the provinces, she reappeared at Drury Lane and rapidly regained recognition. On her farewell at Covent Garden in 1812, she played Lady Macbeth, the role most associated with her.

**Sidney, Algernon** (1622–83). Famous Whig martyr. Sidney fought for Parliament at *Marston Moor, where he was wounded. He refused to serve on the court that tried Charles I but joined the *Council of State in 1652. He disapproved of Cromwell's Protectorate but rejoined the Council of State in 1659. He returned to England in 1677 just as the *Popish plot was about to explode and joined Shaftesbury's Whig opposition. In 1683 he was tried before *Jeffreys for involvement in the *Rye House plot and convicted on shaky evidence. In his statement at the block, Sidney wrote that he died for 'that Old Cause in which I was from my youth engaged'.

**Sidney, Sir Henry** (1529–86). Lord deputy of Ireland. In 1551 Sidney married the daughter of *Northumberland. He backed Northumberland's attempted coup on behalf of Lady Jane *Grey in 1553 but distanced himself in time to avoid disaster. Though Northumberland perished, Sidney still had *Leicester as a brother-in-law and patron. Elizabeth appointed him lord president of the marches in Wales in 1559, and in 1565 he was sent back to Ireland as lord deputy. His first task was to deal with Shane *O'Neill who was in rebellion, but who was assassinated in 1567. By 1571 Sidney had had enough of trying to pacify Ireland and resigned. Fresh rebellions led to his recall in

1575. This time the difficulty was expense, since Elizabeth was unwilling to accept that Ireland could not be subdued on the cheap. He was replaced in 1578.

**Sidney, Sir Philip** (1554–86). Soldier and poet. Educated at Shrewsbury and at Christ Church, Oxford, he was devoted to study. In 1583 he married the daughter of Sir Francis *Walsingham, served in Parliament, and continued to win golden opinions. But in 1585 when *Leicester, his uncle, was given command of the forces against Spain in the Low Countries, Sidney was made governor of Flushing. He volunteered to join Leicester in the attack upon Zutphen, was wounded in the thigh, and died of gangrene nearly a month later. The story that he gave his own bottle of water on the battlefield to a dying soldier was first reported by his friend Fulke Greville many years later, and is suspiciously like a story of Alexander the Great. Sidney left much unpublished work, but his posthumous reputation depended as much upon character and courage as on his poetry.

**Sierra Leone** Former British west African colony and protectorate. British anti-slavery campaigners established a home for freed slaves in Freetown in 1797. The settlement became a British colony in 1808 and a naval base from which the British government could conduct its campaign against the slave trade. The colony became independent in 1961.

**Sihtric (Sigtryggr)** (d. 927). Norse king of York. A grandson of Ivarr the Boneless, Sihtric (nicknamed 'Squinty') joined forces with another grandson, Ragnall, in 917 to recover Dublin, lost in 902. In 920 he left Ireland to succeed Ragnall as king of York. Sihtric refused to acknowledge *Edward the Elder as his overlord, but after his death in 924 proposed an alliance with his successor and in 926 married Eadgyth, a sister of *Athelstan of Wessex. Roger of Wendover reported that Sihtric repudiated both his wife and his new religion. He may have then been dispossessed, since a year later he was dead and Athelstan reigned in York.

**Sikh wars** The wars of 1845–6 and 1848–9 originated over the Sutlej river area of northwest India between the Sikh sect in Punjab and the British. General Sir Hugh Gough defeated the numerically superior Sikh army at Mudki (18 December 1845), Ferozeshah (21 December), and Sobraon (10 February 1846). The Sikhs renounced their claims to the territory. However in 1848 they rebelled. After an initial set-back at Ramnagar on 22 November, Gough defeated the Sikhs at Jallianwalla (14 January 1849) but sustained heavy casualties. Reinforced, he finally broke Sikh resistance on 22 February 1849 at Gujrat.

**Silchester** was a Romano-British *civitas*-capital of the *Atrebates on the present Hampshire–Berkshire border. Development after the invasion was swift, with street-grid, large central timber structures, and possibly the baths. At the centre was the stone-built, Hadrianic forum. Other public buildings included an amphitheatre and temples. Objects indicate occupation into the 5th cent., but thereafter the site was deserted.

**Silures** A British tribe and *civitas*. The Silures are mentioned by several Roman authors, among them Pliny, Ptolemy, and *Tacitus. Tacitus actually described their physical characteristics—swarthy and curly-haired. Their territory was south-east Wales, and for a time in the period around AD 45–57 they led the British opposition to the Roman advance westwards.

**silver jubilees,** 1935, 1977. The success of Victoria's *Golden and *Diamond Jubilees (1887, 1897) persuaded George V's advisers to celebrate his 25 years on the throne with a thanksgiving service, street parties, jubilee mugs, and the like. The silver jubilee of his granddaughter Elizabeth II followed a similar pattern, adding a dash of colour to what had been, in many respects, a sombre reign.

**Simeon, Charles** (1759–1836). A leading evangelical. Born in Reading, Simeon had religious experiences at Eton (1776) and again at King's College, Cambridge. A fellow of Queens' and later vice-provost of King's, he became incumbent of Holy Trinity, Cambridge (1783–1836). Despite initial hostility his pastoral work won people over. He was subsequently a founder of the *Church Missionary Society (1797).

**Simnel, Lambert** (*c.*1475–*c.*1535). Simnel, one of the many pretenders to the throne of Henry VII, was put forward as Edward, earl of *Warwick, nephew of Richard III. He appears to have been the son of an Oxford tradesman. In May 1487 he was crowned as Edward VI in Dublin, and the following month was brought over to England with a formidable invading force. Henry VII met it at *Stoke, near Newark, and was victorious. Simnel, a mere pawn, was pardoned and set to work as a scullion in the royal kitchens.

**Simon, Sir John** (1873–1954). Liberal politician and eminent barrister. Simon's collection of high offices—home secretary, foreign secretary, chancellor of the Exchequer, and lord chancellor—is unique in the 20th cent. Before the Great War he had been appointed solicitor-general (1910) and attorney-general, with a seat in the cabinet (1913). Thereafter his career suffered with the decline of the Liberal Party. But he returned to government in 1931 as foreign secretary at the head of Liberal National MPs. It was a difficult time to hold this office and Simon's reputation declined as first Japan, then Italy and Germany, challenged the authority of the League of Nations. He was more suited to the Home Office (1935–7), playing an important part in the abdication crisis, but as chancellor of the Exchequer (1937–40) his cautious financial control failed to take sufficient account of the need to rearm. In 1940 Churchill sent him to the Lords as lord chancellor, a position for which his legal talents well qualified him.

**Simpson, Sir James** (1811–70). Anaesthetic pioneer. Youngest son of a Scottish village baker, Simpson entered Edinburgh University in 1825, to graduate MD (1832) and proceed rapidly to the chair of midwifery (1839). Excited by the new use of sulphuric ether as an anaesthetic, he self-experimented with other volatile fluids before settling on chloroform (1847). Despite its rapid popularity, its use in natural childbirth led to intense criticism from moralists and theologians until Queen Victoria's delighted approbation after the delivery of her ninth child (1853). A baronetcy followed in 1866.

**Simpson, Mrs Wallis** (1896–1986). Wife of Edward, duke of Windsor. Born into a Baltimore family, Bessie Wallis Warfield first married an aviator, Earl Winfield Spencer, but his fondness for drink led to divorce. On returning to Baltimore she met an English businessman, Ernest Simpson, and in 1928 became the second Mrs Simpson, moving with her husband to London. Two years later an American friend, Thelma, Lady Furness, introduced her to Edward, the prince of Wales. Mrs Simpson lacked beauty, but oozed wit and charm; Edward found in her the feminine sympathy and understanding he craved. In 1936 she divorced Mr Simpson, and Edward gave up his throne in order to marry her. The couple enjoyed a devoted but childless marriage of some 35 years; she is buried next to him at Frogmore.

**Sinclair, Sir Archibald, 1st Viscount Thurso** (1890–1970). Sinclair held the post of secretary of state for air from the formation of *Churchill's government in 1940 until the end of the Second World War. Son of a Scottish baronet, he entered the Life Guards in 1910 and became a close friend of Winston Churchill. Sinclair was returned to Parliament in 1922 as a Lloyd George Liberal. He took office with *Samuel in the National Government of 1931 but resigned a year later on the issue of protection. When Samuel lost his seat in 1935, Sinclair took over as leader of the Liberals. He declined to serve under *Chamberlain in 1939 but accepted Churchill's invitation. He lost his seat in 1945 but Churchill sponsored his viscountcy in 1952.

**Sinn Fein** The Gaelic for 'we ourselves'. Formed as a series of clubs in Ireland at the beginning of the 20th cent., until 1916 Sinn Fein was more important for ideas than organization. From 1917 it was used as an umbrella title for the advanced nationalist party which supplanted the parliamentary party. Following its triumph in the 1918 general election, Sinn Fein formed the Dáil government, but in the Anglo-Irish War it took a back seat and became the political arm of the *Irish Republican Army. Splitting over the *Anglo-Irish treaty, under *de Valera it supported the republican fight in the civil war 1922–3. In 1926 Sinn Fein divided again over the issue of recognition of the Free State Dáil: the minority adhered to an abstentionist policy and retained the Sinn Fein title, the majority formed the Fianna Fail Party. Sinn Fein abandoned its traditional abstentionist policy over the hunger strikes in 1981 and became increasingly popular among the catholic working class. Under the leadership of Gerry *Adams, it took part in the power-sharing executive between 1999 and 2002. By 2005 it had replaced the *SDLP as the larger of the two nationalist parties. After the election of 2007, when Sinn Fein obtained 28 seats in the Assembly, it joined with *Paisley's *DUP in a power-sharing administration, with Martin McGuinness as Deputy First Minister.

**Singapore** was an important trading port between the 11th and 16th cents. In 1819 Sir Stamford *Raffles re-established it as a counterweight to Dutch influence in the region and it became a crown colony in 1867. After the Second World War it remained separate from the Malay Union and was given its own constitution in 1955, which led to self-government in 1959.

**Siward, earl of Northumbria** (d. 1055). Of Danish descent and gigantic stature, Siward seems to have come to England with *Cnut and had been made earl of *Deira by 1026. He subsequently served *Harthacnut and *Edward the Confessor, becoming earl of all Northumbria. In 1054 he led an expedition to Scotland, defeated *Macbeth, and installed *Malcolm Canmore on the throne.

**Six Acts,** 1819. Repressive measures to deal with the radical reform agitation which culminated in *Peterloo. The Acts (a) prohibited most meetings of over 50 people; (b) gave magistrates powers to search private houses for arms; (c) prohibited drilling and military training by civilians; (d) strengthened the laws against blasphemous and seditious libel; (e) limited the right of an accused to adjournment of trial to prepare his defence; (f) increased the stamp duty on newspapers and cheap pamphlets to 4 pence.

**Six Articles, Act of,** 1539 (31 Hen. VIII c. 14). The Act gave legal and penal authority to a set of highly reactionary statements on issues of church belief and practice. The Six Articles upheld (a) the catholic doctrine of transubstantiation; (b) the view that one need not receive both bread and wine in the communion; (c) the obligation of priests to remain celibate; (d) the binding character of vows of chastity; (e) private masses; and (f) auricular confession. Bishops Shaxton of Salisbury and *Latimer of Worcester resigned their sees in protest. The passing of the Act seems to have resulted from a temporary ascendancy in the king's council of conservative opponents of Thomas *Cromwell, especially the duke of *Norfolk and Bishop Stephen *Gardiner. It was repealed in the first Parliament of Edward VI in 1547.

**slave trade** The slave trade of Great Britain, and those of other European countries, transformed the indigenous African and surpassed the Muslim trades. Britain's became the largest national trade. About 75,000 Africans were carried in British ships in the 17th cent.; in 1701–1800 the numbers were about 2.5 million of the 6.13 million slaves exported, reflecting the expanding demand from the British plantations, especially the sugar colonies, as well as exports to Spanish America.

The English trade after 1600 was first conducted by monopolistic chartered companies, of which the Guinea Company (1618) lasted until the 1650s. The Royal Adventurers into Africa (1660, 1663) was succeeded by the *Royal Africa Company (1672–1752). However, private traders were always active, even before the company's quasi-monopoly was ended in 1698.

The trade was critical to the production of major colonial commodities, especially sugar, tobacco, and rice. Its importance for certain British ports is well known. *Liverpool's dominance is clear and Liverpudlians were in the forefront of opposition to reform. Figures for 1750–76 suggest 1,868 ships sailed from there to Africa, 588 from Bristol, and about 260 from London. However, arguments that it provided important investment capital, contributing to the British industrial revolution, are now discounted. *See* ANTI-SLAVERY.

**Slim, William, 1st Viscount Slim** (1891–1970). Soldier. Born in Bristol and brought up in Birmingham, Slim joined the army in 1914, emerging with the rank of major. He spent most of the inter-war years with the army in India and in 1940 was sent with a brigade to Eritrea to fight the Italians. In 1942 he was given a command in *Burma and in October 1943 took over the 14th Army. The following year he won a great victory in repelling a major Japanese offensive and was able to launch a counter-attack

to recover Burma. After the war he served as chief of the imperial general staff from 1948 and was governor-general of Australia 1953–60.

**Slioch, battle of,** 1307. The first of two battles which confirmed Robert I, king of Scots, in his position after the death of Edward I. Probably in October, Robert captured the Comyn castle of Inverlochy and attacked Elgin and Banff. He then fell seriously ill and had to retreat to Slioch, east of Huntly. His enemies, the earls of *Buchan and Atholl, made an unsuccessful attack on Christmas Day.

**Sluys, battle of,** 1340. In 1337 Edward went to war with Philip VI of France who built up a vast armada at Sluys on the Flemish coast for an invasion of England. Edward attacked it on 24 June 1340. A few French vessels made their escape but the armada was totally destroyed.

**Smeaton, John** (1724–92). One of the founders of the civil engineering profession. Born in Leeds, where his father was a lawyer, Smeaton demonstrated a practical aptitude which won him rapid recognition as a craftsman and instrument-maker. He was commissioned to rebuild the lighthouse on Eddystone Rock, 15 miles south of Plymouth, and completed this in 1759 with a remarkably innovative design which set the pattern for all subsequent offshore lighthouses. In 1771 he took the lead in establishing the Society of Civil Engineers, the first professional institution for engineers.

**Smiles, Samuel** (1812–1904). Popularizer of the dominant social values of middle-class Victorian Britain. By profession a doctor, Smiles worked for a time as a radical journalist in Leeds before settling down as secretary (i.e. chief executive officer) to a succession of railway companies. In his leisure time he wrote a series of books, of which *Self-Help* (1859) was the most successful, selling over 250,000 copies during his lifetime.

**Smith, Adam** (1723–90). Famous son of Kirkcaldy (Fife) and educated at Glasgow University, Smith graduated at the age of 14. After six years at Balliol College, Oxford, he became professor of logic, then moral philosophy, at Glasgow University. Although his reputation was founded on *The Theory of Moral Sentiments* (1759), his *magnum opus* was *An Inquiry into the Nature and Causes of the *Wealth of Nations* (1776). It analysed the operation of free market economies where the key players were motivated by self-interest and profit maximization: economic progress would be guided by 'an invisible hand'. Most interpretations have labelled Adam Smith a parent of *laissez-faire* economics, but he was much more interventionist than this.

**Smith, Frederick E., 1st Lord Birkenhead** (1872–1930). Lord chancellor. Educated at Birkenhead and Oxford, Smith made a name for himself as a barrister in Liverpool where (1906) he was elected as a Conservative MP. In 1915 he became solicitor-general and then attorney-general in the wartime coalition government, and in 1919 was appointed lord chancellor; from 1924 to 1928 he served as secretary of state for India. Though a supporter of Ulster's right to opt out of Home Rule, Smith did his best to bring about a compromise in the Irish question, and played a key part in the negotiations which led to the Irish treaty of 1921.

**Smith, Ian Douglas** (1919–2007). Rhodesian politician, advocate of white rule. In 1961 Smith founded the Rhodesian Front, a party which rejected the proposal of the government of the Federation of Rhodesia and Nyasaland to offer more representation for blacks in Parliament. When the federation was dissolved (1963), Smith became prime minister of Southern Rhodesia in 1964. He rejected Britain's plan for black majority rule in the colony and in 1965 unilaterally declared Rhodesia's independence. The civil war subsequently waged by black nationalists forced Smith to take part in negotiations in London, as a result of which black majority rule was introduced in 1979.

**Smith, John** (1938–94). Scottish QC who became leader of the Labour Party (1992–4). Smith was chosen to succeed *Kinnock both as someone who had held office (minister of state, Department of Energy 1975–6; minister of state, Privy Council Office 1976–8; secretary of state for trade 1978–9), and as a political heavyweight who possessed the *gravitas* that Kinnock lacked. His sudden death in

1994 from a second heart attack brought the youthful Tony *Blair as his successor.

**Smith, Sir Sidney** (1764–1840). Admiral. Smith entered the navy in 1777 and saw action in the American War. In 1793 he was posted to Toulon and returned with dispatches after its fall. Smith was given command of the frigate *Diamond* which he used to conduct partisan warfare along the French coast. He was captured in 1796 off Le Havre and imprisoned in the Temple, Paris. Two years later he escaped and returned to command the *Tigre* in Levant. The most famous episode in his career came in 1799 when he undertook the defence of Saint-Jean d'*Acre (3 March–8 May) and heroically repulsed Napoleon.

**Smith, Sydney** (1771–1845). Smith was educated at Winchester and New College, Oxford, where he took orders and became a fellow. After two years in Wiltshire as a curate, he became tutor in 1797 to Michael Hicks Beach and then to his younger brother William. The continent being closed by the war, they settled in Edinburgh. During his stay there, he launched in 1802 the *Edinburgh Review* with his friends *Brougham and Francis Jeffrey and contributed to it for 25 years. From 1806 Smith was rector of Foston near York, which he held until 1829, when he moved to the living of Combe Florey in Somerset. In 1807 his *Peter Plymley* letters, urging religious liberty, had a great success. Smith was an ardent advocate of *catholic emancipation, had a distaste for the excesses of methodists, and his speech at Taunton in 1831 on parliamentary reform ('Mrs Partington and the Atlantic Ocean') became an instant classic. When his Whig friends came to power in 1830, *Grey gave him a canonry at St Paul's, but he was passed over for a bishopric, which hurt him.

**Smith, Sir Thomas** (1513–77). Scholar and statesman. Smith was born in Saffron Walden and educated at Queens' College, Cambridge. In the early 1540s, he plunged into the controversy about the pronunciation of Greek. In 1543 he was made professor of civil law. Under Protector *Somerset he prospered as a protestant. He was appointed provost of Eton, dean of Carlisle, and a secretary of state, and was given a knighthood. He survived Somerset's fall and took a back seat under Mary. Elizabeth restored him to favour and he was involved in negotiating the treaty of *Troyes in 1564. In 1572 he was reappointed secretary of state, using his influence on behalf of the Scottish reformers. His best-known work is his *Discourse on the Commonwealth of England*. It is a description of the mechanics of government in 1565, with a famous, and disputed, account of the role of Parliament.

**Smith, W. H.** A nation-wide chain of retail outlets of books, newspapers, stationery, computers, recordings, games, and other leisure products. William Henry Smith (1792–1865) was born in London where his widowed mother ran a small newspaper business. W. H. Smith extended it, laying the foundations for growth during the second half of the 19th cent. W. H. Smith's son (also W. H.), who entered politics, was satirized by *Gilbert and *Sullivan as 'ruler of the Queen's Navee' when 1st lord of the Admiralty (1877–80).

**Smollett, Tobias** (1721–74). Novelist. Son of a prosperous Dumbarton laird, Smollett became the best-known London-Scottish man of letters of his generation. Much of his literary career was the stuff of hack writing. But he was a cut above the rest. His 'Continuation' of *Hume's *History of England* was not only lucrative but a serious foray into contemporary history. His early picaresque novels *Roderick Random* (1748) and *Peregrine Pickle* (1751) are minor classics. His last novel *Humphry Clinker* (1771) is the first genuinely British novel.

**Smuts, Jan Christian** (1870–1950). South African soldier, diplomat, statesman, and scholar. Having trained as a lawyer in England, Smuts, an Afrikaner, fought against the British in the second Anglo-Boer War (1899–1902). He became one of the main architects of the unification of South Africa within the British empire, but under Afrikaner leadership (1910). During the First World War he commanded British troops in east Africa before serving with distinction in Lloyd George's war cabinet (1916–19) and in the peace negotiations in Versailles. He was not so successful as prime minister of the Union of South Africa (1919–24 and 1939–48) because his attachment to the British empire and Commonwealth angered the Afrikaners.

**Snowden, Philip** (1864–1937). Labour politician. Snowden came from Yorkshire weaving stock, but managed to obtain a junior post in the civil service. He joined the *Independent Labour Party, of which he became (1903–6 and 1917–20) national chairman, entering Parliament in 1906 as MP for Blackburn, later representing Colne Valley. During the 1920s his revolutionary ardour dimmed; he opposed the *General Strike (1926) and resigned from the ILP the following year. Snowden's grasp of fiscal matters led to his appointment as chancellor of the Exchequer in the Labour governments of 1924 and 1929–31, but far from pursuing a socialist economic policy he revealed himself as a devotee of the balanced budget. Following the collapse of the minority Labour government in 1931, Snowden joined Ramsay MacDonald's National Government, retaining his Exchequer portfolio, but the following year (by then a viscount) he resigned on the issue of free trade.

**Soane, Sir John** (1753–1837). English architect. Following successful studies at the Royal Academy, between 1778 and 1780 Soane travelled in Italy on a scholarship awarded by George III. In 1788 he won the competition to design a new Bank of England. Of this, his most important work, only some fine interiors remain. Two houses he designed for himself show his mature style; Pitshanger Manor, Ealing, is now a library, while 13 Lincoln's Inn Fields is the Sir John Soane Museum, containing his collection of antiques and paintings.

**soccer** *See* FOOTBALL.

**Social Democratic and Labour Party (SDLP).** The SDLP was for many years the leading institution representing the catholic minority in Northern Ireland since the province's establishment. It was formed in 1971 as a coalition between the old Nationalist Party members, republican socialists, and civil rights campaigners. It was initially led by Gerry Fitt, representative of Belfast's Labour tradition. It joined the power-sharing executive of 1973–4 and suffered from its rapid collapse. In 1979 John Hume was elected leader and developed effective contact with politicians in Dublin, Brussels, and the USA. The SDLP's electoral dominance among the catholic community was challenged by *Sinn Fein and in the Assembly election in March 2007 it gained only 16 seats against 28 for Sinn Fein.

**Social Democratic Federation** Founded in June 1881, but did not add the 'Social' to its name until 1884. By then it had also become social*ist*, in a Marxist sense, under the influence of H. M. *Hyndman. It was never a mass party, but it did exert considerable influence, and assisted in the birth of the *Labour Party in 1900.

**Social Democratic Party** The late 1970s saw a marked rise of the left within the *Labour Party. Dissatisfaction with the *Callaghan government (1976–9) intensified such pressures. Leading ex-ministers began to contemplate breaking away from Labour to form a new party. The signal came when the party conference in January 1981 voted to vest the election of party leader in an electoral college, in which MPs would have only 30 per cent of the votes. Twelve MPs, led by Shirley Williams, Bill Rodgers, David *Owen, plus Roy *Jenkins (chancellor of the Exchequer in the 1966 Wilson government), formed a Council for Social Democracy, soon transformed into the SDP.

The first task was to create a party structure, the second to negotiate an alliance with the *Liberals. The Alliance involved a division of the constituencies between the two parties, and the nomination of a prime minister-designate, the choice being Jenkins. In the first months, the Alliance was highly successful, winning by-elections at Croydon NE, Crosby, and Glasgow Hillhead, where Jenkins was returned. By April 1982, 29 sitting Labour MPs and one Conservative had joined the SDP.

Early in 1982 polls indicated a falling-off of support. One factor was the *Falklands War, which rallied opinion to Mrs *Thatcher's Conservative government, and another was signs of economic recovery. In the general election of 1983, the Alliance won 26 per cent of the national vote, only 2 per cent behind Labour. But the working of the British electoral system awarded the Alliance only 23 seats, against Labour's 209.

Jenkins resigned as leader of the SDP at once and was replaced by David Owen. Relations with the Liberals became more strained. The Alliance was hampered by the retreat of the left inside the Labour Party,

and in the 1987 general election its vote dropped to 23 per cent. David Steel, leader of the Liberals, delivered an ultimatum—either a merger or the Alliance should be dissolved. Owen resigned when a majority of his members supported it. The two parties then formed the new Social and *Liberal Democrat Party. Owen and two other MPs stayed aloof in an independent SDP. Owen retired from Parliament at the 1992 election and the two other SDP MPs were narrowly defeated.

**socialism** The word first appeared in 1827 as a description of the doctrines of Robert *Owen. Socialists emphasized a social, as opposed to an individualist, approach to life, especially economic organization. Owenite socialism aimed to change society by the establishment of experimental communities, in which property was held in common and social and economic activity was organized on a co-operative basis. Between 1825 and 1847, seven Owenite communities were founded in Britain. None of them flourished long; but from the co-operative trading stores came the modern *Co-operative movement. The idea of co-operative socialism was continued by the middle-class *Christian socialists of 1848–54.

In 1884 came a revival, beginning with the *Social Democratic Federation (SDF), founded in 1881. It was basically Marxist. The Socialist League, under the leadership of William *Morris, split off from the SDF in 1884; and in the same year the *Fabian Society was formed by a group of middle-class intellectuals who derived their socialism not from Marx but from *utilitarianism. In 1893 the *Independent Labour Party was founded in Bradford, and despite its title was committed to socialism.

Numerically the socialists were only a small body—probably no more than 2,000 in the 1880s and perhaps 20,000–30,000 by 1900. In that year a Labour Representation Committee based on an alliance of socialist societies and trade unions was formed, and in 1906 this became the *Labour Party. It did not adopt a specifically socialist programme until 1918. Thereafter the Labour Party was the main vehicle for an empirical, reformist, welfare-statist type of socialism in Britain, which reached its apogee in the Labour victory of 1945 with its ensuing programme of nationalization and welfare legislation.

**socialism, Christian** The belief that Christ's teachings led to socialism and that the church should actively promote social reform. After the collapse of *Owenism and *chartism, a group of middle-class Christian socialists promoted co-operative socialism among working men from 1848 to 1854, led by F. D. *Maurice, Charles *Kingsley, and J. M. Ludlow.

**Society for Constitutional Information** Founded in 1780 by Major John Cartwright to promote parliamentary reform, the SCI flourished until 1783, but thereafter made little headway. The SCI actively promoted Paine's *Rights of Man* and other radical publications, and under the leadership of *Horne Tooke collaborated with other reform societies, metropolitan and provincial. After the government repression and treason trials of 1794, the SCI ceased to meet.

**Society for Promoting Christian Knowledge (SPCK).** Founded (1698) by Thomas Bray (1656–1730) and others to provide religious literature for those without nearby libraries and to promote the establishment of *charity schools. Though it handed over to the *Society for the Propagation of the Gospel its American and West Indian missionary work, SPCK, albeit Anglican, supervised the German-Danish Lutheran Mission in south India, which SPG took over in 1825. Printing and distribution of literature remains its major task.

**Society for the Propagation of the Gospel in Foreign Parts (SPG).** Founded on the recommendation of Thomas Bray, founder of the *Society for Promoting Christian Knowledge (1701). Its aim was 'to settle the State of Religion as well as may be among our own people [in the plantations] . . . and then to proceed in the best Methods towards the Conversion of the Natives'. At first it aimed at the American colonies and the plantations in the West Indies. SPG was instrumental in making mission part of Anglican life.

**socinians** denied Christ's deity, holding, however, that his birth was miraculous. Used, particularly in the 17th and 18th cents. as a term of abuse against any suspected of unorthodox views of the trinity, it in fact describes a stage of *unitarianism and underlines its international development, deriving from the Italians Lelio Sozzini (Socinus) and his nephew Fausto.

**Sodor and Man, diocese of** According to tradition *Patrick converted Man *c.*447. There were certainly Celtic bishops, but it was probably not until the reign of *Edward the Confessor that the present see of Sudreys (the southern isles) was founded to include the Isle of Man and the Hebrides. In 1152 the see was transferred from the *York province to the Norwegian archiepiscopal province of Trondheim. Sudreys itself was returned to York in 1542. There are Manx-language editions of the Prayer Book (1765) and the Bible (1772).

**Solemn League and Covenant** An agreement between the Long Parliament and the Scots brought about by the failure of Parliament's war against the king. Adopted by the Scots Estates on 17 August 1643 and sworn by members of the House of Commons on 25 September, the covenant promised to reform religion in England and Ireland on *presbyterian lines. In return, the Scots undertook to invade England with an army of 20,000.

**solicitor-general** The 'junior' of the two law officers of the crown. The precursor of this office was the 'king's solicitor' first mentioned in 1461 and the title 'solicitor-general' was first used in 1515. From 1525 onwards the office of solicitor-general was a 'stepping stone' to the office of attorney-general, whose deputy and subordinate he was. There is a separate solicitor-general for Scotland, who acts as deputy to the *lord advocate.

**Solomon Islands** The Solomon Islands are in the South Pacific, east of New Guinea, and export copra and coconuts. During the Second World War there was extremely heavy fighting, particularly on Guadalcanal, where Japanese and Americans struggled for control of an important airfield. They are an independent state under the British crown with a Governor-general.

**Solway Moss, battle of,** 1542. When war broke out in August 1542 between Henry VIII and his nephew James V of Scotland, an English raid was defeated at Hadden Rig. James then assembled a large army for a counter-stroke towards Carlisle. His troops under Oliver Sinclair moved south along the Esk valley. On 24 November, at Solway Moss, they were surprised and routed by a much smaller English force, led by Thomas Wharton, Thomas Dacre, and John Musgrave. The defeat broke the spirit of James, already in poor health.

**Somerled, lord of the Isles** (d. 1164). Somerled claimed descent from Gofraid mac Fherghusa, son of the founder of the kingdom of *Dalriada. He established his position in Argyll and Kintyre at the expense of the Norse and fought for David I at the battle of the *Standard in 1138. After a naval victory, he forced Gofraid of Man in 1158 to take refuge in Norway. Somerled was at peace with Malcolm IV, David's successor, in 1160, but four years later they clashed and Somerled took an expedition to Renfrew, where he was killed.

**Somers, John, 1st Baron Somers** (1651–1716). Lawyer and Whig politician. Called to the bar in 1676, Somers made his name as an outstanding barrister. He was elected in 1689 to the Convention Parliament and was among the principal draftsmen of the *Bill of Rights. After that his advancement was rapid, becoming solicitor-general (1689), attorney-general (1692), lord keeper (1693), lord chancellor (1697), and a peer (1697). A leading *Junto Whig, he was one of the few English politicians in whom William III closely confided, but in 1700 Tory jealousy brought about his dismissal. By 1708 the queen's coolness gave way to appreciation of his statesmanlike qualities and he became lord president, but went out with his fellow-Whigs in 1710. At George I's accession he was given a seat in the cabinet.

**Somerset** forms the southern hinterland of the Bristol channel and has an unusual variety of topographical features—the bare Mendips north of Wells, the marshes around Glastonbury, the wooded Quantocks west of Bridgwater, and the high Cotswolds north of Bath. Since, despite a vigorous cloth industry and substantial deposits of coal, iron, and

lead, it escaped the worst ravages of industrialization, it remains one of the most beautiful of shires.

In Caesar's time, the area was in the territory of the *Belgae. It fell speedily to the Romans, who were exploiting the lead-mines of Mendip as early as AD 49. The hot springs at Bath were almost certainly known before Roman times and the city, Aquae Sulis, grew up quickly. After the Roman withdrawal, the area was shielded from Saxon advance for some time by Selwood forest to the east, and the legends of *Arthur arose from British resistance. The battle of *Mount Badon, around AD 500, may have been at Little Solsbury Hill, near Bath; a British defensive victory, it held up the Saxon advance. But in 577 a Saxon victory at Dyrham, east of Bristol, gave them control of the northern parts, the rest falling after their victory at Peonnan in 658 when *Cenwulf drove the Britons in flight to the Parrett. The region then became part of the kingdom of Wessex. *Ine is said to have refounded the monastery at Glastonbury. His nephew *Aldhelm built a church at *Wells (c.704), which became a see in 909. By this time the region was acquiring its own identity as a shire, taking its name from Somerton, then the county town, and adding the suffix sæte—'the people of'. At the Domesday survey, Bath was a city of national importance; Ilchester, Milborne Port, Taunton, Langport, Axbridge, and Bruton of local significance.

After the Norman Conquest, Glastonbury abbey became one of the wealthiest monasteries in the kingdom. Work on the new Wells cathedral started c.1184. Somerton and Ilchester were in sharp decline by Tudor times, but Taunton, Frome, and Yeovil prospered as cloth towns. Glastonbury lost its estates at the *dissolution of the monasteries and its last abbot was hanged on the Tor. The shire gained a reputation for independence, to which was added, in the cloth towns, a strong tradition of religious dissent. In the Civil War, the towns were largely parliamentary in sympathy. Taunton, led by Robert *Blake, withstood a protracted siege from *Goring's men in 1645 and the royalist army was later routed by *Fairfax at *Langport. At the Restoration, Taunton was punished by the forfeiture of its charter and the demolition of the town walls. It gave a warm welcome to *Monmouth in 1685 and paid for it after *Sedgemoor in corpses swinging from innumerable gallows.

The 18th and 19th cents. saw great changes in the county. Bath's greatest period of fashion came under Beau *Nash in the 1750s. In 1801 Bath was still the ninth largest town in England. Street, which had been no more than a village, became a sizeable town after Clarks shoe factory was built in 1825; Bridgwater, long a local port, added brick- and tile-making, and Shepton Mallett grew on the production of cider. The Brendon hills produced iron for south Wales until the last mine closed in 1911. The Somerset coalfield had a brief prosperity. By 1868 there were 64 pits at work around Radstock. It declined sharply after 1945 and the last pit was abandoned in 1973. The most remarkable growth in the county was at Yeovil and at Weston-super-Mare. Yeovil had fewer than 3,000 people in 1801 but developed into a manufacturing town, specializing in aircraft. Weston's growth was even more spectacular. In 1801 it had only 138 inhabitants, but the cult of seaside holidays and the arrival of Brunel's railway in 1841 sent it into orbit. By 1914 the population had passed that of Taunton. Clevedon and Portishead, without the beaches to rival Weston, retained more of their Victorian charm.

By a strange piece of legislation in 1972 the northern parishes of the shire were hived off to form the southern part of the new county of Avon. Though Avon was itself abolished in 1996, the parishes were not returned to Somerset. Proposals to abolish the shire for all but ceremonial purposes were successfully resisted, but the northern region was divided between two unitary authorities, Bath and North East Somerset, and North Somerset (based upon Weston-super-Mare).

**Somerset, Edmund Beaufort, 1st duke of** (c.1406–55). Beaufort was frequently employed in the defence of Lancastrian France, with the backing of his uncle, Cardinal *Beaufort. He succeeded to the titles of his elder brother John (d. 1444), but not to his lands. To the chagrin of Richard of *York, Somerset was appointed lieutenant-general of France in 1447; by 1450 all Normandy had been lost to the French. York accused him of treason, but he became the dominant favourite of Henry VI, created duke in 1448. Having alienated the Nevilles

by a dispute with *Warwick, Somerset gained the support of the earl of *Northumberland; both were killed in the first battle of *St Albans.

**Somerset, Edward Seymour, 1st duke of** (c.1500–52). The foundation of Somerset's career was that he was elder brother of *Jane Seymour, Henry VIII's third wife, and therefore uncle to Edward VI. His progress was by no means spectacular until his sister's marriage in May 1536. A week later he was made Viscount Beauchamp and the following year earl of Hertford. Great honours followed—the Garter in 1541, lord high admiral 1542–3, lieutenant-general in the north 1544–5, when he waged war against the Scots. On Henry VIII's death in 1547, with his nephew aged 9, he became protector of the realm and duke of Somerset. For 2½ years he was the effective power in the land. In August 1547 he consolidated his position with a victory against the Scots at *Pinkie Cleugh.

During 1549 Somerset's position collapsed completely. The *prayer book issued under his auspices provoked a serious rising in Cornwall and Devon in June, and was followed in July by *Kett's rebellion in Norfolk. The second was put down by *Northumberland, who now emerged as Somerset's chief rival. In October Somerset was deprived of his protectorate and sent to the Tower. Though he was pardoned the following year and restored to the council, he was again sent to the Tower in October 1551 and executed in January 1552.

**Somerset case** In 1771 the American master of James Somerset, a negro slave, attempted to send him out of England to be sold. Abolitionists pleaded *habeas corpus on his behalf. *Blackstone, in his Oxford lectures, had already denied that English law recognized slavery. In a famous judgment on 22 June 1772, *Mansfield declared that slavery was odious and unknown to common law. Somerset was given his freedom.

**Somerville, Mary** (1780–1872). Mathematician and scientist. Born into genteel poverty in Scotland, Mary Fairfax married secondly her cosmopolitan medical cousin William Somerville (1812), leaving Edinburgh for London in 1816. She developed an interest in mathematics, and an informal

S

apprenticeship under the foremost philosophers led to a long and distinguished career. Her books brought knowledge and clarity to a broad public. Mary Somerville was widely accepted as the leading scientific lady in Europe, and posthumously commemorated in the foundation of Somerville College, Oxford.

**Somme, battle of the,** 1916. When he became commander-in-chief, *Haig wanted to advance from Ypres to liberate the Belgian coast. However, the allies had already concerted their operations for 1916, so he agreed to take part in an Anglo-French offensive further south, astride the river Somme. Haig hoped that he would break through the German defences in a single day. But despite a lengthy bombardment, when his infantry advanced on 1 July, they suffered nearly 60,000 casualties and only dented the German line.

**Sophia, electress of Hanover** (1630–1714). Sophia was a granddaughter of James I by his daughter *Elizabeth, who had married the elector palatine. On the death in 1700 of Anne's last surviving child, William, duke of Gloucester, Sophia was the next non-catholic heir, and was recognized in the Act of *Settlement of 1701. She died at Herrenhausen seven weeks before Anne and her son George Lewis succeeded as George I.

**Sophia Dorothea** (1666–1726). Divorced wife of George I. Sophia Dorothea married her cousin George in 1682, but in 1694 was surprised in a rendezvous with her lover Count Königsmarck. He was never seen again, and she was divorced and honourably confined at the castle of Ahlden in Celle until her death.

**South Africa, Republic of** Former British dominion. During the French Revolutionary War, British troops seized the Dutch settlement at the *Cape of Good Hope. Handed back in 1802, the Cape was again captured in 1806 and became Cape Colony. Many Afrikaners (Boers) were irked by British rule and migrated eastward and northward to found the self-governing republics of *Transvaal and the *Orange Free State.

Diamonds were discovered at Kimberley in 1868 and Cape Colony quickly claimed ownership of the district. When gold was found in the Transvaal in the 1880s there was no doubt about the ownership of the land but the exploitation of the discovery depended heavily upon outside capital. This became the excuse for British intervention in the Transvaal which led to war between British and Afrikaners from 1899 to 1902. After the war the republics became British colonies and were joined with the older colonies in the Union of South Africa in 1910.

The majority of white South Africans supported Britain during the First World War, but with Afrikaners in the majority among the white population there was growing opposition to membership of the British empire. South Africa's participation in the Second World War was less enthusiastically received by many whites. A policy of white domination had always been accepted by both British and Afrikaners, but the victory of the National Party in the 1948 elections saw the policy carried to such extremes as to arouse international condemnation, resulting in South Africa's quitting the British Commonwealth in 1961 and becoming a republic. It rejoined the Commonwealth in 1994 after the dismantling of apartheid and is a leading member of the African Union.

**Southampton** A seaport which gave its name to Hampshire as early as 755. Saxon Hamwic was the chief port of the kingdom of Wessex. Its successor, on a slightly different site, has been a major port since the 11th cent. It lost ground to London in Tudor and Stuart times, but recovered from the 1840s with new docks and the railway, and is now the leading British deep sea port on the Channel.

**Southcott, Joanna** (1750–1814). A religious fanatic, of Devon farming stock, Joanna was in domestic service in Exeter. Originally called to *methodism (1791), she soon had religious experiences and started 'sealing' her writings. She visited Bristol (1798), published *The Strange Effects of Faith* (1801), and moved to London (1802). She claimed to be 'the Lamb's wife' (Rev. 12) who would give birth to 'the second Christ' in 1814; instead she died of brain disease.

**Southern Rhodesia** See RHODESIA.

**Southey, Robert** (1774–1843). Southey had a strange career, moving from extreme radicalism in the 1790s to a gloomy conservatism by the 1810s. Born in Bristol, he was educated at Westminster and Balliol College, Oxford, where he met *Coleridge and planned a liberated American settlement, Pantisocracy, on the banks of the Susquehanna. In 1794 he joined with Coleridge in a drama, *The Fall of Robespierre*. An annuity enabled him to settle at Greta Hall (Keswick), with Coleridge and *Wordsworth nearby. He was made poet laureate in 1813 and from 1835 received a pension of £300 p.a. from the government. Of greatest historical interest was his *Life of Nelson* (1813), the *History of the Peninsular War* (1823–32), his essays for the *Quarterly Review*, and the curious *Colloquies on the Progress and Prospects of Society* (1829).

**South Sea bubble** The 1720 financial crisis resulting from the collapse of the South Sea Company. Founded by *Harley in 1711 as a Tory alternative to the Whig financial establishment, the company in 1719 proposed to take over three-fifths of the national debt (about £30 million). A fever of speculation followed and its shares rose from 130 per cent to over 1,000 per cent in six months. Panic selling ensued and the market collapsed, ruining thousands of investors.

**Southwark, diocese of** The see, founded in 1905, is roughly conterminous with Greater London south of the Thames, with east and mid-Surrey; an area originally under *Winchester, but after 1877 under *Rochester. The cathedral is the former Augustinian priory church of St Mary Overie, founded in 1106.

**Southwell, diocese of** This see, roughly conterminous with Nottinghamshire, was created in 1884, following rapid population growth in the 19th cent. The cathedral is the former minster church, founded in 1108, restored in 1558. It has a fine Norman nave and transepts with a 13th-cent. choir and chapter house, where the stonework with its distinctive Southwell foliage is unique.

**Southwold or Sole Bay, battle of,** 1672. Naval engagement off the Suffolk coast in the third *Anglo-Dutch War on 7 June 1672 between de Ruyter with 91 ships and a slightly larger Anglo-French force, under the command of James, duke of York. De Ruyter lost more ships but the English fleet was badly damaged and Lord *Sandwich, admiral of the Blue, drowned.

**South Yorkshire** *See* YORKSHIRE, SOUTH.

**Spa Fields riot,** 1816. One of a number of popular incidents provoked by hunger and revolutionary feeling in the wake of the French wars. A great meeting in north London on 15 November addressed by Henry 'Orator' *Hunt turned into a drunken quasi-insurrection when a part of the crowd marched threateningly into the city after arming itself with weapons stolen from a gunsmith's shop.

**Spanish Succession, War of the,** 1702–13. Britain's involvement in a new war with France so soon after the conclusion of the *Nine Years War in 1697 arose from William III's anxiety to prevent Louis XIV incorporating the Spanish kingdom into a French 'universal monarchy'. When the imbecile Carlos II of Spain died childless in November 1700 Louis disregarded his own agreement with William III in the *Partition treaty of 1699, whereby the Spanish possessions were to be divided between Bourbon and Austrian Habsburg claimants. In 1701 Louis provocatively declared his grandson Philip king of Spain, invaded the Spanish Netherlands, and recognized James II's son as 'King James III'. William III brought Britain, the United Provinces, and Austria together in a Grand Alliance which was later joined by Prussia, Hanover, and other German states.

Under *Marlborough's command Anglo-Dutch forces concentrated on driving back the French from their advanced positions in the Spanish Netherlands. His close accord with Lord Treasurer *Godolphin ensured that the British war effort remained well resourced. From 1704 the allies won a series of spectacular victories over the French. In that year, as the Franco-Bavarian forces were coming close to winning the war in Germany, Marlborough swiftly marched his 40,000-strong Flanders army up the Rhine and into Bavaria where, joining the imperial regiments under Prince Eugene, he defeated the French and their allies at *Blenheim on 14 August. Marlborough pressed on in Flanders and following his victory at *Ramillies in

**S**

May 1706 reconquered most of the southern Netherlands. In August 1708 he repulsed a major French counter-attack at *Oudenarde.

In Spain, Britain's war to replace Louis XIV's grandson Philip V with the allied candidate, the Archduke Charles of Austria, was less successful. Portugal joined the coalition in 1703. But while important strategic benefits were obtained, such as the capture of *Gibraltar (1704) and *Minorca (1708), advances on the Spanish mainland were short-lived. In 1709 the carnage and near-defeat for Marlborough at *Malplaquet demonstrated that the war on France's northern frontier had reached stalemate, while in Spain in December 1710 the allied army under General *Stanhope was humiliatingly beaten at *Brihuega.

In Britain the Tories had come to power in 1710 determined to end the enormous cost and stabilize the soaring national debt. In December 1711 Marlborough was removed from his command. Meanwhile, Archduke Charles's succession in April 1711 as emperor rendered the war for him in Spain unfeasible, as no one was prepared to countenance a massive Austro-Spanish monarchy. In March 1713 the treaty of *Utrecht was signed between the allies and France.

**spas** were places with springs or wells containing salts which were claimed to improve the physical, mental, and spiritual health of people drinking or bathing in the waters. The term became current during the 17th cent. to describe towns which emulated Spa in Belgium which had just risen to fame. Several British towns owed their prosperity to health-giving waters long before the 17th cent., for example, *Bath, whose hot springs were used in the Roman town of Aquae Sulis, and *Walsingham in Norfolk, a centre of *pilgrimage in the later Middle Ages.

Fashionable visitors, including royalty, gave prestige to Bath and Tunbridge Wells in the 17th cent. but these and other towns grew in prominence later. They had lodging-houses to let to wealthy patrons in the season. In the early 19th cent. Cheltenham offered the first purpose-built luxury hotel. 'Taking the Waters' did not occupy all the time and energies of visitors. Elaborate provisions were made: theatres, ballrooms, libraries, specialized shops and services, excursions to places of interest, and religious devotions. A late entrant was Buxton in Derbyshire which remained popular throughout the 19th cent. Failed projects included Glastonbury in Somerset during the 18th cent. and Ashby de la Zouch in Leicestershire in the 19th cent.

**Speaker** The office of Speaker originated as a spokesman for the House of Commons in its dealings with the crown in the 14th cent. The first formal acknowledgement of the Speaker as 'prolocutor' was to Sir Peter de la Mare, knight of the shire for Herefordshire, in 1376 at the end of the reign of Edward III. The office was at first highly political. The post of Speaker was one of considerable risk, physical and political, and the protestations of reluctance to serve, now a pleasant ritual, were once genuine.

The fierce disputes between the king and Parliament in the early 17th cent. placed the Speakers in an extremely difficult position. Speaker Finch reminded the Commons in 1629 that 'I am not less the king's servant for being yours': nevertheless, he was held down in the chair when he tried to carry out the king's instructions to adjourn. But in 1642, Speaker Lenthall defied Charles I demanding the arrest of the *five members, and declared, 'I have neither eyes to see, nor tongue to speak in this place, but as the House is pleased to direct me.' By the end of the century, the Speaker was relatively free from royal pressure.

In the last 100 years or so changes in parliamentary procedure have laid new duties on the Speaker. The two most important devices involving the Speaker are the closure and the selection of amendments (the kangaroo). The Speaker must see that the right of the majority (normally the government) to pass legislation is balanced by respect for the rights of the opposition. The closure is a motion 'that the question be now put'. The Speaker must decide whether or not to accept the motion: if carried, as is likely, debate ceases forthwith.

A bill may attract a lot of amendments and, indeed, one way of delaying its passage is to propose many changes. The Speaker has the power of selecting amendments for debate: those not called fall by the wayside. The decision whether or not to call an amendment may have important political consequences.

The modern Speaker has to be an impartial chairman. The office needs tact, sensitivity, and skills of an unusual order. The responsibility for calling members to speak (and even more for not calling) may become contentious; the use of unparliamentary language may have to be checked; members may need protection against unfair interruptions. The Speaker has a ministerial scale salary, a pension, a suite in the palace of Westminster, and a peerage on retirement. In precedence, the Speaker comes after the royal family, archbishops, lord chancellor, prime minister, and lord president of the council. In the House of Lords, the lord chancellor acts as Speaker, but may speak and vote in debate.

***Spectator*** The most famous periodical of Anne's reign appeared daily between March 1711 and December 1712, and was briefly revived in 1714. Professing to be 'above party', the *Spectator*'s essays on social, moral, literary, or philosophical themes, mostly written by *Addison and *Steele, subtly promoted Whig values.

## Speenhamland poor relief system
Growth of population and acute distress during the Revolutionary and Napoleonic wars placed great strain upon the poor law system. In 1795 the price of bread reached record levels. On 6 May 1795 the Speenhamland justices resolved to give outdoor relief to families on a sliding scale in proportion to the cost of a loaf. The system was widely adopted but increasingly criticized as ruinously expensive, an invitation to farmers to pay low wages leaving the poor rate to make up the difference, and an encouragement to farm labourers to breed without restraint in order to get extra assistance. The *Poor Law Amendment Act of 1834 accordingly moved against the system in favour of indoor relief in workhouses.

**Speke, John Hanning** (1827–64). British soldier and explorer. Speke became famous as the result of two exploratory journeys in eastern Africa. In the course of the first, led by another Briton, Richard *Burton, which reached Lake Tanganyika in 1858, Speke conceived the idea that Lake Victoria was the source of the White Nile. Speke led another expedition (1860–3) which confirmed his opinion.

**Spence, Sir Basil Urwin** (1907–76). Scottish architect who leapt to prominence with his prize-winning design for Coventry cathedral (1951; completed 1962). Spence trained at Edinburgh College of Art, worked for *Lutyens on the Viceroy's House, New Delhi, in 1929–30, and practised in Edinburgh during the 1930s. His other buildings include churches, housing, schools, and the chancery at the British embassy, Rome (1971).

**Spence, Thomas** (1750–1814). Artisan radical reformer and bookseller from Newcastle whose 'Plan' argued that all land should be publicly owned. Local hostility and personal misfortune in 1787 caused him to move to London, and from 1792 he was an active member of the London *Corresponding Society. His numerous radical pamphlets and token coins attracted government attention, and he was arrested and imprisoned in 1792, 1794, 1798, and 1801. Spence originally hoped to effect his plan by education, and indeed advocated language reform.

**Spencer, Herbert** (1820–1903). Philosopher. Spencer was the son of a Derbyshire schoolteacher of radical and dissenting views. In the 1840s he joined Sturge's Complete Suffrage Union and in 1848 became subeditor of *The Economist*. His *Social Statics*, published in 1851, allowed the state only the minimum of defence and police functions. He published *Education* in 1861, advocating a child-centred approach and emphasizing the importance of science. But his main thesis—the need to limit the intervention of the state—was at variance with the spirit of the times. The miscellany of his thought gave him influence, but he was not a trained thinker and his fame faded fast.

**Spenser, Edmund** (1552–99). Elizabethan poet, mythographer, and colonial administrator. Educated at Merchant Taylors' School and Cambridge, Spenser briefly belonged to the household of the earl of *Leicester. His pastoral, *The Shepheardes Calender*, effectively marks the beginning of the Elizabethan 'golden age' of poetry; his masterpiece, *The Faerie Queene* (Books 1–3, 1590), is the finest example both of the 'cult of Elizabeth' and of the project for a 'reformation' in English poetics. His last published work, *A View of the Present State of Ireland*, advocated harsh colonial measures.

**Spion Kop, battle of,** 1900. A battle of the second *Boer War (1899-1902). The battle arose from British attempts to relieve the siege of *Ladysmith. The highest point of the Tugela Heights, Spion Kop ('Lookout Mountain') was defended by a Boer force of about 7,000 under Louis Botha. Lieutenant-General Sir Charles Warren ordered a night attack by 1,700 troops under Major-General E. R. P. Woodgate to capture the heights. As the fog lifted after dawn on 24 January the British found themselves in a position completely exposed to enemy fire. After dark the British retreated, having lost about 250 dead including Woodgate, and 1,000 wounded.

**Spithead naval mutiny,** 1797. While this mutiny lasted a calendar month, 16 April to 14 May, its roots had a century's growth. The Channel fleet was immobilized, with men withholding further service until grievances over pay, provisions, and leave had been redressed. Not until 10 May could the seamen be satisfied, but Earl *Howe's prestige and conciliatoriness, buttressed by a pardon, was decisive in bringing what had in effect been a strike to an end.

**'splendid isolation'** For most of the 19th cent. Britain was diplomatically isolated, having what *Palmerston called 'no eternal allies' to whom she owed favours. The obverse of this, of course, was that no other country owed favours to her. This was the context of Canadian premier Sir Wilfrid Laurier's description of Britain's situation in February 1896 as one of 'splendid' isolation, arising, he claimed, 'from her superiority'. Others at that time were beginning to doubt this. Joseph *Chamberlain in particular feared for the future of the *British empire if it could not find an ally in Europe, and negotiated with Germany. That came to nothing; but early in the new century Britain did abandon isolation, at least partially, through a treaty with Japan (1902), '*ententes' with France (1904) and Russia (1907), and then, of course, involvement in the First World War.

**Spurs, battle of the,** 1513. In 1513 Henry VIII began his second campaign against France, in alliance with the emperor, and laid siege to the town of Thérouanne. On 16 August a French cavalry force, attempting to relieve the town, fled in disarray. Thérouanne surrendered the following week.

Magnified as the battle of the Spurs, the skirmish testified to the military prowess of the young king.

**squash rackets** derived from rackets and originated at Harrow. An Association was formed in 1928 and by 1939 more than 200 clubs were affiliated. The sport was given a considerable boost by the Royal Air Force, which built courts at almost all stations, and it became fashionable in the 1980s as fierce exercise for young business executives.

**squire** is a term which has come down in the world. Originally it applied to a young man attendant on a knight, bearing his shield, and, by the late 14th cent., entitled to his own coat of arms. By Tudor times, the terminology was changing. William Harrison (1577) referred to 'esquire, which we commonly call squire'. In the 17th cent. it developed into a general term for the lord of the manor, well below the level of nobility, but far above yeomen. The term 'esquire', like that of 'gentleman', was gradually applied to any man as a suffix, and its final degradation was as a 20th-cent. term of pert familiarity. *See* GENTRY.

**Sri Lanka** or Ceylon was settled during the 6th cent. BC by peoples from the Indian subcontinent, who subsequently converted to Buddhism. Hindu Tamils conquered the island in the 11th cent. AD but were eventually driven back to a northern enclave. The Portuguese in 1505 established a hold over the south-west coast until moved on by the Dutch in the 17th cent. When Ceylon was finally ratified in British possession at the treaty of Amiens (1802), it was made a crown colony. Ceylon was granted independence within the Commonwealth in February 1948 and, in 1972, adopted a republican constitution under the ancient name of Sri Lanka.

**Stafford, William Howard, 1st Viscount** (1612-80). Howard was a younger son of the earl of *Arundel and was brought up as a catholic. But he did little to help the royalists during the Civil War, which he spent mainly in Holland in some poverty. In 1678 he was accused by Titus *Oates of complicity in the *Popish plot, kept in the Tower until 1680, tried in Westminster Hall, and executed. *Evelyn, who attended Stafford's trial, commented, 'I can hardly think a person of his age and experience should engage men, whom he never saw before,' and his guilt seems very doubtful.

**Staffordshire** is one of the counties most affected by the industrial revolution. The county town has never dominated the shire. In pre-Conquest days, it was overshadowed by Tamworth and Lichfield, in modern times by the Black Country towns and the Potteries. The core of the county is the river Trent. The northern parts of the shire are hilly, running up to the Peak District. Cannock Chase, south-east of Stafford, was for centuries almost impassable, and the Staffordshire rivers were not navigable until the 18th cent. Even as late as the 19th cent., Arnold *Bennett could describe his county as 'lost in the midst of England'.

In Roman times, the region was part of the territory of the *Cornovii. It subsequently became the heartland of the kingdom of *Mercia. Tamworth was the royal city of the Mercian kings and Lichfield the ecclesiastical capital, St *Chad establishing the bishopric there in 669. In the later 8th and 9th cents. the power of Mercia declined, first defeated by Wessex, then overrun in the 870s by the Danes. Under *Edward the Elder, the Mercians counter-attacked. *Æthelfleda, the lady of the Mercians, recovered Tamworth and Stafford in 913 and fortified them. The outlines of the shire were now appearing and it is mentioned in the *Anglo-Saxon Chronicle* for 1016 by name.

Throughout the Middle Ages, Staffordshire remained remote and inaccessible. Poor communications and the relative insignificance of the county town meant that many market towns achieved a genuinely independent existence—Leek, Stone, Walsall, Wolverhampton, Newcastle under Lyme, Rugely, and Uttoxeter. *Defoe in the 1720s was greatly impressed by the horse fairs at Penkridge, but a little disappointed in Stafford—'we thought to have found something more worth going so much out of the way'.

The transformation of Staffordshire's economy came in the 18th cent., greatly assisted by the new canals. The outlines of the canal network were apparent in the 1770s, when *Brindley opened the Staffordshire and Worcester to link up with the Severn; the

Trent and Mersey, through Burton, Rugely, Stone, and the Potteries, brought access to the north-west; the Birmingham canal to the midlands and south; the Caldon canal linked Etruria to Froghall, with a branch to Leek. The work of the canals in bringing the county into a national orbit was completed by the railways. The effect upon the county was dramatic. The deposits of iron and coal in south Staffordshire began to be exploited on a national scale: Matthew *Boulton started his Soho works at Handsworth in 1762. In the north of the county, Josiah *Wedgwood opened his Ivy House works at Burslem in 1759, setting up as a master potter, and ten years later built the great Etruria works. Burton upon Trent, favoured by good water, was exporting beer to the Baltic by the mid-18th cent.: William Worthington set up in business in 1744, William Bass in 1777. The first census of 1801 registered the changing situation. The population of Stafford with 3,900 was already surpassed by Stone, Lichfield, Leek, Wolverhampton, Newcastle, Rowley Regis, and West Bromwich above the 5,000 mark, Burslem 6,500, Walsall 10,000, and Stoke, a comparative newcomer, at 16,000. In the course of the 19th cent. the southern parts of the shire were swallowed up in Birmingham, and the six pottery towns came together in 1910 to form the unique federated borough of Stoke-on-Trent. By the local government reorganization of 1972, Staffordshire lost Walsall and Wolverhampton to the new West Midlands authority. Staffordshire retained its own county council in the later 1990s, with Stoke and Sandwell (Smethwick) becoming unitary authorities.

**stage-coaches** were road vehicles offering public scheduled stage carriage of passengers. London had its hackneys by the mid-1620s, the first stage-coach—to St Albans—was recorded in 1637, and services developed on the radial routes to the capital 1650–1715. By the late 1750s, the London-based network was largely complete. Regular services between leading provincial centres developed only from the 1770s, apart from *Bath, which had coaches from Exeter, Salisbury, and Oxford 'in the season' from the 1750s. Manchester was 80 hours from London in 1750, 27 in 1808, and around 20 in 1832. Passenger mileages grew at least tenfold 1770–1840, and in the peak year, 1836, there were around 10 million passenger journeys.

The industry originated with services run co-operatively by owner-drivers, using inns as their infrastructure. Debts led to innkeeper control, largely complete by 1750, and thereafter concentration grew, with large firms predominant in the London trade by the 1820s. Stage-coaches collapsed precipitously in the 1840s and 1850s, relegated to feeder and link services, and to serving peripheral areas beyond the advancing tide of the railway.

**Stainmore, battle of,** 954. The death at Stainmore of *Erik Bloodaxe, son of Harold Fairhair of Norway, brought to an end the Scandinavian kingdom of York, which reverted to Wessex. The place of the battle, on the old route from Scotch Corner to Penrith, suggests that Erik was intercepted while escaping to Viking allies in Scotland or Ireland.

**Stamford Bridge, battle of,** 1066. A victory for King *Harold Godwineson over *Harold Hardrada, king of Norway, and his own brother *Tostig, both of whom were killed. Harold Hardrada was asserting a purported promise of succession to the English kingdom by King *Harthacnut. The battle took place just east of York. Harold's success indirectly assisted William the Conqueror, who was given time to establish a secure base on the south coast before the battle of *Hastings.

**Stamp Act,** 1765. The Stamp Act, introduced by George *Grenville, imposed duties on goods and services (legal documents, appointments to public offices, ship's papers, etc.) in the British colonies in order to raise money for military expenses in America. Protests against Parliament's right to tax the colonies, widespread discussions of political liberty, crowd violence, and trade boycotts followed. In Britain, petitions from British merchants led to its repeal by the *Rockingham Whigs in 1766. But repeal was accompanied by the *Declaratory Act.

**Standard, battle of the,** 1138. The border between Scotland and England was far from settled in the 12th cent. and David I of Scotland was eager to acquire Northumbria and Cumbria. The civil war in England between Stephen and *Matilda gave him an opportunity and a period of border campaigning ended in August with a Scottish foray into north Yorkshire. It was met by a local force under *Thurstan, archbishop of York, on the 22nd at Cowton Moor, near Darlington. The English fought under the banners of St *Cuthbert, St Peter of York, St John of Beverley, and St *Wilfrid of Ripon, which accounted for the name 'battle of the Standard'. Though the saints were successful and the Scots defeated, David retained possession of the northern counties and was residing at Carlisle when he died in 1153.

**Stanhope, James Stanhope, 1st Earl** (1673–1721). Soldier, diplomat, and politician. Stanhope came to prominence in the War of the Spanish Succession where he was largely responsible for the campaign of 1710, including the disaster at *Brihuega, where he was captured. He was a Whig MP 1702–13 and 1714–17, was created a viscount in 1717 and an earl in 1718. From the accession of George I, Stanhope was continuously in office as secretary of state for the southern department (1714–16), for the northern department (1716–17, 1718–21), and 1st lord of the Treasury and chancellor of the Exchequer (1717–18). Foreign policy was Stanhope's main interest, his aim being to safeguard the Hanoverian succession. He teamed up with the 3rd earl of *Sunderland, and together they dominated the ministry until Stanhope's death (particularly during the Whig schism of 1717–20 when *Walpole and *Townshend left the government). Stanhope's diplomatic triumphs were the negotiation of the *Triple and *Quadruple Alliances in 1717 and 1718. At home he supported Whig supremacy with the *Septennial Act (1716), the *Peerage Bill (1719), and the repeal of the *Occasional Conformity and *Schism Acts (1719).

**Stanley, Sir Henry Morton** (1841–1904). The most effective, if ruthless, of the 19th-cent. explorers of Africa, Stanley was born in a Welsh workhouse but became a journalist in the USA. Sent to Africa by the *New York Herald,* in October 1871, he uttered the immortal words 'Dr Livingstone, I presume' on finding the explorer at Ujiji on Lake Tanganyika. In 1874–7 he led an expedition across the continent which solved nearly all the remaining puzzles of Africa's basic geography. Engaged by King Leopold, he established the beginnings of the Congo Free State in 1879–84.

## Stanley, Thomas, 1st earl of Derby

(c.1435–1504). Thomas Stanley succeeded his father in 1459 as Baron Stanley. He served as steward to Edward IV and then to Richard III, who gave him the Garter. But his second wife, whom he married about 1482, was the widow of the earl of Richmond and mother of the future Henry VII. Before *Bosworth, Richard, suspecting Stanley's fidelity, took his son Lord Strange as hostage. Stanley took no part in the battle and his younger brother Sir William Stanley intervened against Richard at a critical stage. His reward was speedy. He was made steward of the duchy of Lancaster and created earl.

**stannaries** (from the Latin *stannum*, tin). The region of tin-mining in Cornwall and Devon, which acquired special jurisdiction. Tin- and lead-miners, being isolated communities, had their own customs. King John's charter of 1201 empowered the lord warden of the stannaries to try all cases except land, life, or limb. The jurisdiction of the warden survived until 1873, that of the vice-warden until 1898. The stannaries also had parliaments for both Devon and Cornwall: each consisted of 24 representatives, nominated by the four stannary towns in each shire. The Cornish parliament met last in 1752.

**staple** A staple was a trading centre in England or occasionally abroad, where traders deposited commodities, bought and sold there. Edward II is regarded as the 'father of the English Staple' since it was during his reign that the Ordinance of the Staple (1313) made the system compulsory. The aim was to regulate commerce in important commodities, especially wool, wool cloth, leather, and tin, and, by confining trade to a few named staple towns to facilitate the collection of tolls and the maintenance of quality.

**Star Chamber** The origins of the Court of Star Chamber have been disputed, but it undoubtedly arose as an offshoot of the king's *council. The name probably derived from the fact that the king's council sat as a judicial tribunal in the 'camera stellata', a chamber with a starred ceiling, built in 1347 at Westminster. It became prominent under

the Tudors as a court which would control 'over-mighty subjects'. At first popular, under the Stuarts it became hated because of its increasingly draconian rulings on libel and sedition and its savage punishments. A byword for tyranny, it was abolished by the *Long Parliament in 1640.

**statutes** *See* PARLIAMENT, ACTS OF.

**steam-engines** are machines employing steam pressure and condensation to generate motion. Thomas *Savery's device (1698) pumped water by partial vacuum, without moving parts, and while engines on his principles were still in use in the 1790s, *Newcomen's atmospheric cylinder/piston engine in 1712 established the fundamental principles of steam-power. James *Watt's separate condenser of 1769 became a source of much-improved technical efficiency once *Wilkinson's improved cylinder boring became available (1774).

Mine drainage was its primary application, many engines running on unsaleable slack, with brewing and milling, water supply, and textiles following. Wider applications from the 1790s owed more to *Trevithick's high-pressure non-condensing and direct acting engines, which powered the first successful marine applications with Symington's *Charlotte Dundas* (1802), steam carriage (1801), and locomotive (1804).

*Stephenson long-boiler and Kitson outside-frame locomotives established the basic pattern of railway motive power. From the Grand Junction's establishment of Crewe (1837), British railways manufactured their own locomotives. The economical compound steam-engine was little used on British railways, where coal was cheap, whereas it became a standard unit for factory power, and in its ultimate triple-expansion form (after 1880) the key to British shipping and shipbuilding dominance. From the early 1900s, *Parsons's marine steam turbine provided still greater speed and economy.

**Steel, David** (b. 1938). Politician. Son of a minister of the Church of Scotland, Steel was born in Kirkcaldy and studied law at the University of Edinburgh. In 1965, at the age of 27, he was returned to Parliament as the Liberal member for Roxburgh, Selkirk and Peebles. In 1976 he became leader of the party in succession to Jeremy *Thorpe and formed a pact with *Callaghan's Labour government. After the party merged with the *SDP in 1988, Steel resigned the leadership and was replaced by Paddy *Ashdown. He was made a life peer in 1997, and from 1999 until 2003 was Presiding Officer of the new Scottish Parliament.

**Steele, Sir Richard** (1672–1729). Irish writer, soldier, and politician. Educated at Charterhouse and Merton College, Oxford, Steele entered the army before turning to writing plays. Appointed gazetteer in 1707, Steele embarked on a hugely successful journalistic career, assisted by *Addison in the *Tatler* and then the enormously popular *Spectator*. MP for Stockbridge in 1713 and recruited by the Whigs to head their propaganda campaign against the *Harley administration, Steele responded with papers like the *Guardian* and the *Englishman*. Rewarded for his services on the Hanoverian succession, Steele was knighted and appointed supervisor of Drury Lane theatre.

**Steenkirk, battle of,** 1692. William III, defending Brussels against the French, launched a surprise attack on 3 August on Marshal Luxembourg, who was separated from Boufflers. William gained a temporary advantage but Boufflers's troops joined in at the end of the day. The struggle was bloody but inconclusive.

**Stephen** (c.1096–1154), king of England (1135–54) and duke of Normandy (1135–44), was the third son of Stephen, count of Blois, and Adela, daughter of William the Conqueror. During his reign England plunged into a civil war in which neither side possessed the resources to achieve outright victory. Stephen was brought up at the court of his uncle Henry I, becoming one of the wealthiest of the Anglo-Norman magnates. Although he had taken the oath to accept Henry's daughter *Matilda as heir to the throne, Stephen seized the kingdom in December 1135. But he lacked the capacity to command the loyalty of the magnates. Symptomatic were the sporadic revolts early in his reign, and the rivalries at court which led to the defection of Earl *Robert of Gloucester in May 1138. His rival Matilda had secure bases in Anjou provided by her husband *Geoffrey and in western England by Robert of Gloucester, and her supporters

included the king of Scots, David I. Stephen's cause declined once Matilda was established in England from 1139 and after his capture at the battle of *Lincoln in 1141. Although he was sustained in 1141–2 by his queen *Matilda and was released from prison in 1142 after the capture by his supporters of Robert of Gloucester, his position was seriously compromised. His enemies controlled western and parts of northern England and Count Geoffrey completed the conquest of Normandy in 1144–5. Stephen also fell foul of the papacy because of a disagreement over the succession to the archbishopric of York, which had serious consequences when the pope (Eugenius III) refused to accept Stephen's son *Eustace as his heir in 1152, and instead transferred his support to Matilda's son, the future Henry II, as the direct descendant of Henry I. In 1153, with the magnates refusing to fight a pitched battle, Stephen accepted Henry as his heir by the treaty of *Winchester. Henry's succession followed peacefully after Stephen's death on 25 October 1154, a sign that all were weary of the civil war.

**Stephen Harding, St** (d. 1134). Third abbot of Cîteaux. A native and monk of Sherborne (Dorset), Stephen joined the abbey of Molesme near Dijon. Fervently ascetic, he helped Abbot Robert tighten Benedictine life there, but, facing opposition, they left for Cîteaux to follow the rule more rigorously. Stephen, the driving force, became third abbot (1109), but Cistercian austerity caused numbers to decline until Bernard's arrival (1111) with 30 followers retrieved the situation. Stephen himself founded thirteen other houses and appointed Bernard abbot of Clairvaux. He wrote *Carta caritatis* (1119), which was Cistercianism's foundation document. Cistercianism spread rapidly—over 100 Cistercian houses were founded in Stephen's lifetime, the first in England at Waverley, Surrey (1128).

**Stephens, James** (1825–1901). Fenian. Stephens, a protestant railway engineer from Kilkenny, was one of the few who joined Smith *O'Brien in the abortive 1848 rising. He escaped to France and returned to Ireland in 1856. In 1858 he founded what later became the *Irish Republican Brotherhood, drawing on his experience with revolutionary groups in France. On a fund-raising trip to America 1858-9 he joined in founding the *Fenian Brotherhood and in 1863 launched the *Irish People*, a weekly newspaper.

**Stephenson, George** (1781-1848). Son of a colliery workman, without schooling, George Stephenson became one of the most famous of all engineers. Beginning work at the age of 8, in early manhood he earned a reputation for managing the primitive *steam-engines employed in collieries. In 1815 he invented a safety lamp for use in coal-mines, after risking his life repeatedly in tests. He was responsible for the adoption of locomotives by the Stockton and Darlington railway and then the Liverpool and Manchester railway. His *Rocket* was triumphantly successful in the Rainhill trials of 1829.

**Stephenson, Robert** (1803-59). Only son of George *Stephenson, Robert was born when his father was still an obscure north-eastern colliery workman. By mid-century, he had acquired an independent reputation as one of the world's most famous engineers. His achievements at home and abroad included railways and bridges, including the High Level bridge at Newcastle (1849), the Royal Border bridge, Berwick (1850), the Menai Straits bridge (1850), and the Victoria bridge at Montreal (1859). He was Conservative MP for Whitby from 1847 until his death.

**Sterne, Laurence** (1713-68). Novelist and humorist. Son of a low-ranking infantry officer but educated at Jesus College, Cambridge, where he embraced *Locke's philosophy and contracted tuberculosis, Sterne was ordained and collated to a Yorkshire living (1738). *Tristram Shandy* (1759) prompted applause and abuse for its sentimentality and salaciousness, though, freeing the novel from straightforward narrative, it has since been seen as begetter of 'stream-of-consciousness' writing.

**Stevenson, Robert Louis** (1850-94). Writer. A spirited but sickly child, Stevenson abandoned engineering studies at Edinburgh for law but never practised. Much of his life was spent in search of health after tuberculosis developed. His output covered essays, short stories, poetry (*A Child's Garden of Verses*), travelogues, and collabora-

tions with his stepson Lloyd Osbourne, while delighting readers with Scottish romances (*Kidnapped, Catriona*) and storytelling (*Treasure Island, Dr Jekyll and Mr Hyde*).

**Stewart, Alexander** *See* BUCHAN, 1ST EARL OF.

**Stewart, Dugald** (1753-1828). Philosopher. Son of a distinguished mathematician, Stewart studied under Adam Ferguson, Thomas Reid, and Adam *Smith. He was professor of moral philosophy at Edinburgh 1785-1820. A noted lecturer and teacher, Stewart's classes drew huge audiences and shaped the intellectual world of a rising generation of young Whig politicians. His philosophy was a critical distillation of the philosophy of the *Scottish Enlightenment. The *Edinburgh Review*, founded by his pupils, was an indirect but important monument to his teaching.

**Stewart, James** *See* ROSS, 1ST DUKE OF.

**Stigand** (c.1000-72), archbishop of Canterbury (1052-70), was a worldly prelate. Promoted rapidly by *Edward the Confessor, he held the bishoprics of Winchester and Canterbury in plurality after 1052. His appointment to Canterbury after the Norman *Robert of Jumièges had been forced into exile was deemed uncanonical by the papacy. He was at first apparently accepted by William the Conqueror, even though he had crowned *Harold Godwineson. This was presumably a consequence of William's early policy of trying to work with the native English. But in 1070 a case for his removal was built up from his numerous irregularities and he was deposed by a papal legate.

**Stilicho** Late Roman general. In AD 395 Honorius became ruler of the western empire, but effective power lay with the outstanding military personality of his time, 'enigmatic Stilicho, half-Roman and half-German'. His career impinged on Roman Britain: in 396-8 he ordered an expedition against the barbarians troubling Britain, restoring peace in 399; but in 401-2 he withdrew troops from Britain to defend Italy.

**stipendiary magistrates** are paid magistrates who are professional lawyers. The normal mode of trial of minor criminal offences is by a bench of lay magistrates, but in the 18th cent. the problem of crime in London, exacerbated by the lack of a police force, led to the establishment in 1792 of paid magistrates for the metropolis. Later legislation provided that boroughs and urban areas could request the appointment of a stipendiary.

**Stirling Bridge, battle of,** 1297. Edward I's victory at *Dunbar in 1296 did not keep Scotland subdued for long. On 11 September 1297 a large English army, under John de *Warenne, earl of Surrey, and Hugh de Cressingham, was caught by William *Wallace crossing the Forth near Stirling. Cressingham was killed and Edward's conquest had to begin again.

**Stirling castle,** which stands on a dolorite hill over 400 feet above sea level, occupies an important strategic position controlling the main ford of the river Forth; it is thus a link between the Highlands and the Lowlands of Scotland. Called the 'Key to Scotland', the castle changed hands many times during the Wars of *Scottish Independence.

**Stock Exchange** The London Stock Exchange was founded in 1802, providing a mechanism for the increasing volume and complexity of financial transactions which had developed in the 18th cent. The scale of formal investment increased massively in the second half of the 19th cent., with a marked orientation towards international operations which the city of London retains.

**stocks** The growth of government spending from the late 17th cent. onwards, frequently for war, stimulated the search for ways to raise funds. The issue of government stock, effectively a form of IOU, dates from this time. In 1696 the Exchequer Bill was introduced, offering 3 pence per day interest on a subscription of £100. In 1749 a plan was introduced to consolidate all the different loans taken out by the government, reducing the rate of return to a standard 3 per cent p.a. These consolidated loans were established in 1752 as '3 per cent consols'. They proved to be a secure and flexible monetary instrument, since they could be bought conveniently through any attorney.

**Stoke, battle of,** 1487. Lambert *Simnel, posing as Edward, earl of *Warwick, and

nephew to Edward IV, raised support in Ireland and was crowned in Dublin as Edward VI. He landed near Lancaster and was supported by the earl of *Lincoln. His forces met with those of Henry VII at Stoke, near Newark, on 16 June. After heavy fighting, Lincoln was killed and Simnel captured. With a humour or clemency not much apparent in the Wars of the *Roses, Simnel was given menial employment at court.

**Stoke-on-Trent** was formed in 1910 as a federation of six Staffordshire pottery towns—Tunstall, Burslem, Hanley, Stoke, Fenton, and Longton. The development of the conurbation was largely 19th cent. and owed much to the canal network, begun with the Trent and Mersey in 1775, which greatly facilitated the transport of pottery. By 1851 the total population was some 137,000 and by 1901 in excess of 300,000. There was considerable boundary extension and Stoke became a city in 1925.

**Stonehenge** (Wilts.) is the best-known archaeological site in the British Isles. It is spectacular, but what survives is but the ruin of the final phase of a structure dating from c.4000 to c.1500 BC. The monument was orientated to mark sunrise at the midsummer solstice (and sunset at the midwinter solstice), but whether it has further astronomical significance is debatable.

**Stopes, Marie** (1880–1958). Birth control pioneer. Methodical and brilliant as a palaeobotanist, but disarrayed in her emotional life, her radical vision of an ideal marriage and clarification of sexual conduct prompted deep changes in social attitudes. With her second husband, she opened Britain's first birth control clinic at Holloway (1921), and published a stream of successful sociological works, but indifferent poetry and plays.

**Stormont** is the grandiose building outside Belfast which housed the Northern Irish Parliament 1932–72. Its absurdly lengthy drive possesses an imposing statue of a defiant Sir Edward *Carson. The word became a synonym for intransigent unionism. Since 2007 it has housed the power-sharing executive of Northern Ireland.

**Strafford, Thomas Wentworth, 1st earl of** (1593–1641). Wentworth made his name as a champion of constitutional rule by opposing the *forced loan of 1626. However, in the 1628 Parliament he suggested the compromise which culminated in Charles I's acceptance of the *petition of right. This opened the way to a career in government, and in 1633 the king sent him to rule Ireland. Strafford did so in such a despotic manner that he aroused hatred in England. When Charles, after the disastrous *Bishops' wars, called Strafford to his side and made him an earl, he promised that he would not 'suffer in his person, honour, or fortune'. However, *Pym struck first by impeaching Strafford for alienating the king from his subjects. At his trial, in March 1641, Strafford defended himself so ably that acquittal seemed likely. The Commons therefore changed tack, passing a bill of attainder, which simply declared Strafford's guilt and sentenced him to death. The king delayed his response until Strafford urged him to give his assent, 'for prevention of evils which may happen by your refusal'. A few days later, Strafford was executed on Tower Hill.

**Stratford de Redcliffe, Stratford Canning, 1st Viscount** (1786–1880). Diplomat. Son of a London merchant and cousin of George *Canning, Stratford Canning was sent to Eton and King's College, Cambridge, before entering the Foreign Office. He was in Constantinople at the time of the battle of *Navarino (1827) and again as ambassador 1841–58. He urged the Turks to resist Russian demands in the exchange which led to the *Crimean War.

**Stratford-upon-Avon** Birthplace of *Shakespeare. For many years after the death of Shakespeare in 1616, Stratford remained a small Warwickshire market town. The event which put it on the map was *Garrick's Shakespeare Jubilee of 1769 which, though nearly washed away by rain, attracted great attention. The first Memorial theatre, completed in 1879, was destroyed by fire in 1926 and replaced by the present building in 1932.

**Strathclyde.** The name was adopted in 1963 by one of Glasgow's universities, and from 1973 to 1996 was used for an administrative region: it contained 2.3 million people, nearly half Scotland's population. The region was unpopular with people living in its more rural parts, who felt it was dominated by Glasgow. This unpopularity led to the abolition of the 1973 structure and its replacement, from 1996, by nineteen all-purpose authorities.

**Strathclyde, kingdom of** The kingdom of Strathclyde, at its greatest extent, stretched from Loch Lomond in the north to Cumbria in the south. Its kings were Brittonic/Welsh, though they are often referred to as kings of Dumbarton, the fort which tops the massive rock which projects from the north bank of the Firth of Clyde. The first king who can be identified is Coroticus (Ceredig) to whose warband St *Patrick addressed a scathing letter sometime in the 5th cent. The last Brittonic king was probably Owain the Bald who died in 1018 fighting in the army of *Malcolm II of Scotland at the battle of *Carham (south-west of Berwick).

Strathclyde was remarkable for being the only Brittonic kingdom outside Wales to survive the Anglo-Saxon onslaught of the 6th and 7th cents. It survived the aggression of Picts and Gaels as well as Angles, and scored some notable victories. For extended periods, however, they were clients of more powerful kings. They submitted to kings of Northumbria in the 7th cent. and again after an invasion by a combined force of Picts and Angles in 756, which led to Anglian colonization of Kyle (mid-Ayrshire). The kingdom fell increasingly under the power of kings of Scots after being weakened by the destruction of Dumbarton in 870 by Vikings and ravaged by *Edmund, king of the English, in 945. Although the kingdom disappeared as a political entity, it had a brief afterlife (1973–96) as the administrative region of Strathclyde.

**Stratton, battle of,** 1643. Much of 1643 was devoted by king and Parliament to establishing local domination. Even in Cornwall and Devon, royalist strongholds, there was considerable support for Parliament. *Hopton suffered an embarrassing ambush at the hands of James Chudleigh on Sourton Down, near Okehampton, on 25 April, but on 16 May caught Lord Stamford and Chudleigh at Stratton in Cornwall and defeated them heavily, taking Chudleigh prisoner.

**strict settlement** *See* ENTAIL.

**Stuart, Arabella** (1575–1615). The niece of *Darnley, first cousin to James VI and I, and a possible successor to Elizabeth on the throne of England. She avoided implication in the *Bye and *Main plots in 1603 but her secret marriage in 1610 to William Seymour (Somerset), who had royal blood, alarmed the king and she spent most of her remaining years in the Tower.

**Stuart, Charles Edward** (1720–88), the 'Young Pretender'. Elder son of James Francis Edward *Stuart, the son and heir of the exiled James II and VII, Charles was the Jacobite prince of Wales. Early in 1744 he left Italy for France, having been summoned to accompany a proposed French invasion of England. It was cancelled. In July 1745 Charles sailed for Scotland to raise a rebellion in the Highlands, with the hope of stimulating French aid. Total self-confidence, plus a limited grasp of reality, and the outstanding generalship of Lord George *Murray, carried him through a conquest of Scotland and march to Derby which made him a hero. His period of hiding after his defeat at *Culloden endeared him to romantics as 'Bonnie Prince Charlie'. The rest of his life was a protracted anti-climax, full of failed relationships and alcoholism.

**Stuart, Cardinal Henry Benedict** (1725–1807). The younger son of James *Stuart, and latterly Jacobite cardinal-king, he was born in Rome and was his father's favourite son. He was kept ignorant about Franco-Jacobite intrigues in 1744, but did go to France to support his brother Charles in 1745. In 1747, in political despair, he accepted a cardinal's hat. After the death of Charles in 1788, Henry styled himself 'Henry IX'. It was an empty title.

**Stuart, house of** One of Europe's most resilient royal dynasties, the Stewart or Stuart family ruled Scotland in direct descent from 1371 to 1688, inheriting also the thrones of England and Ireland in 1603. The family was of Breton origin, before settling in Scotland at the invitation of David I, who gave Walter FitzAlan the honorific title of high or royal steward in 1158. The title was subsequently made heritable and the family was known by the surname Stewart until the mid-16th cent. when, under French influence, it was modified to Stuart. The royal succession came through the marriage of Walter, 6th high steward, to Marjory, daughter of Robert I Bruce. In 1371, the death without issue of

Robert I's only son, David II, led to the accession of Robert Stewart (1316–90), the sole heir of Walter and Marjory, as King Robert II. The dynasty's luck finally ran out in 1688 when the 12th Stuart monarch, James VII and II, was ousted in the *Glorious Revolution.

**Stuart, James Francis Edward** (1688–1766), the 'Old Pretender'. Son and heir of James VII of Scotland and II of England and Ireland by his second wife, *Mary of Modena. The birth of Prince James in June 1688 precipitated the Glorious Revolution. The propaganda querying his parentage was false, but the decision by Louis XIV to recognize him as heir to the British thrones when his father died in 1701 helped precipitate the War of the *Spanish Succession. He participated in an abortive invasion of Scotland in 1708. In late 1715 he joined the Scottish rising, fleeing from Montrose in the following spring. He was in Spain during the 1719 rising in the Highlands, returning to Italy to marry the Polish princess Clementina Sobieska, by whom he had two sons, Charles and Henry, and little happiness.

**Stubbs, George** (1724–1806). English anatomist and animal painter, especially of horses, Stubbs's work captures the English gentleman's enjoyment of rural life, at its peak in the prosperity of the mid-18th cent. Stubbs's paintings of racehorses, often with owner or groom, were particularly popular both in original form and as prints. His anatomical skills ensured that the power and beauty of animals was captured without sentimentality.

**submission of the clergy,** 1532. By the submission, which convocation passed on 15 May 1532, the English church surrendered its right to make provincial ecclesiastical laws independently of the king. It promised to issue no new canons without royal licence, and to submit existing canons to a royally appointed committee for revision. Sir Thomas *More, a supporter of church immunities, surrendered the lord chancellorship the following day.

**Succession, Acts of,** 1534, 1536, 1543. Henry VIII used statutes to make the adjustments to the succession that his complicated matrimonial history necessitated. The first Act

(25 Hen. VIII c. 22) declared Mary illegitimate as a consequence of his divorce from *Catherine of Aragon. The second (28 Hen. VIII c. 7) after *Anne Boleyn's execution declared both Mary and Elizabeth illegitimate and vested the succession in any future offspring of Henry's new wife, *Jane Seymour. The third Act (35 Hen. VIII c. 1), while recognizing Edward's claim, declared that should he die without heirs, Mary and Elizabeth would succeed in turn. By his will, made in December 1546, Henry repeated these arrangements but added that the succession would then go to the Suffolk line, offspring of his younger sister *Mary. The Stuart line, descendants of his elder sister *Margaret, was ignored. These repeated changes, from a man anxious to establish a clear succession, could only store trouble for the future.

**Sudan** Former Anglo-Egyptian condominium. Britain became involved in the Sudan as a result of her occupation of *Egypt in 1882. Fearing that French colonial expansion might threaten her control of the Red Sea route to India, Britain agreed to assist Egypt in reconquering the Sudan, which was achieved at the battle of *Omdurman in 1898.

**Sudbury, Simon** (d. 1381). Archbishop of Canterbury. Sudbury was promoted to the bishopric of London in 1362. Appointed archbishop in 1375 he incurred odium for supporting *John of Gaunt. In 1380 he was appointed chancellor and asked Parliament to grant the third poll tax. During the *Peasants' Revolt, his reported hostility to the rebels caused them to hunt him down; he was captured in the Tower of London and beheaded.

**Suetonius Paullinus** Governor of Britain 58–61. A native of Umbria, he spent most of his governorship campaigning in Wales. When news came of the *Boudiccan revolt in East Anglia, Suetonius reached London with his cavalry, but could not save it or Verulamium. He rejoined his advancing infantry in the midlands, where he destroyed the rebel force.

**Suez canal and crisis** The 106-mile canal links the Mediterranean to the Red Sea. It was built by the international Suez Canal Company, under the guidance of Ferdinand de Lesseps, and opened in 1869. The British

gained an interest in 1875 when *Disraeli purchased 40 per cent of the shares from the khedive for the government. The canal was protected by British troops from 1883 until 1956. In July 1956 the Egyptian government, under Nasser, nationalized the canal despite the fact that the Canal Company's concession ran until 1968. Anglo-French military intervention in November failed to regain control of the canal, which reopened in April 1957. The canal was again closed during the 'Six Day War' of June 1967 and did not reopen until 1975.

**Suffolk** is one of the largest and most beautiful of shires and its greater distance from London has saved it from some of the ravages inflicted on its southern neighbour *Essex. The 'south folk', from whom the county took its name, formed part of the kingdom of the *East Angles. The twin pivots of the county are Bury St Edmunds, described by *Leland as 'a city more neatly seated the sun never saw', and Ipswich, in *Camden's words 'the eye of the county'. The division between east and west is of long standing and in 1888 the two sections were given separate county councils. They were reunited in 1972.

In Roman times, Suffolk was part of the territory of the *Iceni. By the 7th cent. the kingdom of East Anglia was of importance. The *Sutton Hoo ship-burial, near Woodbridge, dating from c.630, is almost certainly the grave of one of their kings, probably *Rædwald, who died c.625.

By the 8th cent. East Anglia was experiencing difficulty in fending off Mercia and Wessex. The area suffered severely from Danish raids from 861 onwards. In 870 King *Edmund was martyred, allegedly transfixed with arrows, and his body taken eventually to Beodricsworthe, to be known in future as Bury St Edmunds. The region fell under Danish rule from 878, but was recovered by *Edward the Elder in the 920s. Dunwich (founded c.630) lost its episcopal status to *Thetford, and then *Norwich.

Throughout the Middle Ages, Suffolk was dominated by the many religious houses. Strife between the abbot of Bury and the townsfolk was fierce. In 1327 the town rioted and burned much of the abbey: in 1381, during the *Peasants' Revolt, the lord chief justice and the abbot were beheaded. At the *dissolution of the monasteries, the abbey was ransacked.

Suffolk's prosperity was built on sheep, corn, and fish. The cloth trade, in the later Middle Ages, produced the profits for the fine churches at Long Melford, Framlingham, Lavenham, Eye, and Bury. In the absence of mineral resources or heavy industry, population grew slowly. Dunwich's decline, due to erosion, was evident by the 14th cent., but Ipswich remained a busy port and Lowestoft became a major fishing harbour. Felixstowe developed as a seaside resort in the 19th cent. and after 1945 became a substantial container-port, dealing with Europe.

### Suffolk, Charles Brandon, 1st duke of (1484–1545). Brandon managed a spectacular career from modest beginnings. Son of Sir William Brandon, standard-bearer for Henry VII at *Bosworth, where he was killed, Brandon's rise began with the accession of Henry VIII in 1509. They were both fond of athletic pursuits and Brandon excelled in jousting. In 1515 he was created Viscount Lisle. The Garter followed. He fought in the campaign in France in 1513 and in February 1514 was made duke of Suffolk. His most extraordinary advance came in 1515 when, six weeks after the death of her husband Louis XII, he married *Mary, queen of France and sister of Henry VIII. Brandon bought himself out of the king's anger with gifts. After this, he continued in favour, serving as earl marshal 1524–33, lord president 1530–45, chief justice in Eyre south of Trent 1534–45, and lord steward 1540–5.

### suffrage Since suffrage (the right to vote) can be the key to political power, it has been contentious since representative institutions came into being. The original county franchise seems to have included all freemen. But an Act of Henry VI's reign in 1429 declared that 'great, outrageous and excessive numbers of people' were voting at elections, and went on to limit the franchise to freeholders with land worth 40 shillings a year. This remained the franchise until 1832. The issue became lively after the Civil War. At the *Putney army debates, *Cromwell and *Ireton opposed Rainborough and the radicals who pressed for a great extension of the franchise: where would it end, demanded Cromwell, if men 'who have no interest but the interest of breathing' were given the vote?

In parliamentary boroughs the franchise had always varied but there were four main groups—corporation, freeman, burgage, and inhabitant householder. They ranged from Westminster and Coventry with thousands of voters, to Gatton, a *rotten borough with two voters. The Scottish representation was extremely narrow, before and after the Union of 1707.

In the 18th cent. arguments for extending the franchise were heard with increasing frequency. *Wilkes argued in 1776 that 'the meanest mechanic, the poorest peasant and day labourer' was entitled to a vote, but nobody supported him. From 1832 onwards, however, a number of measures, enlarged the suffrage to full democracy. By the *Great Reform Act the urban franchise was made uniform at the £10 householder level, and in the counties the £50 copyholder was brought in to join the freeholders. The Scottish electorate rose from some 5,000 to 65,000. Radicals were far from satisfied and within a few years manhood suffrage was one of the six points of the *charter. It was strenuously opposed, *Macaulay insisting in 1842 that universal suffrage was 'utterly incompatible with the very existence of civilization'. The second Reform Act of 1867 moved one step closer, giving the vote to borough householders, and the 1884 Act, by extending the same franchise to the counties, brought the total electorate to well over 5 million.

By the later 19th cent. the campaign to give the vote to women was under way, though they had to wait until 1918, and then were given the vote only if they were over 30. The electorate was more than doubled and, at 22 million, was fast approaching that universal suffrage Macaulay had feared. Women under 30 gained the vote in 1929 and in 1969 the inclusion of persons between 18 and 21 brought in another 3 million new voters. The vote is not available to convicted felons or certified lunatics, but is granted to resident citizens of the Republic of Eire. Hereditary peers, deprived of their seats in the House of Lords in 1999, were granted the right to vote and to stand for election to the House of Commons.

### suffragettes were feminists who adopted militant methods to campaign for the parliamentary vote for women. Though by far the

most famous members of the women's movement before 1914, their contribution to winning the vote has been much diminished by modern scholarship.

The term 'suffragette' was coined by the *Daily Mail* to distinguish them from the suffragists who had been working for the vote since 1866. The movement originated with Mrs Emmeline *Pankhurst and her daughters Christabel and Sylvia, who founded the Women's Social and Political Union in 1903. They regarded militancy as justified in view of the failure to achieve the vote after 40 years of campaigning. Initially this involved interrupting the meetings of leading politicians, attempting to enter the lobby of the House of Commons, and intervening at by-elections at which electors were urged to vote against Liberal candidates. However, the growing violence used by the police and the hostility of the public towards the suffragettes led them to change tactics. This involved window-breaking, setting fire to pillar boxes and buildings, destroying the turf at golf courses, and dramatic incidents like the slashing of a painting, the *Rokeby Venus*, by Mary Richardson in 1914.

As a result the authorities began to impose prison sentences on the suffragettes, who went on hunger strikes. In order to avoid the death of a suffragette in custody attempts were made at forcible feeding. However, this proved dangerous to health, and thus in 1913 the government resorted to special legislation, dubbed the '*Cat and Mouse Act', to allow the authorities to release hunger-strikers but rearrest them when their health had improved. In 1913 Emily Wilding Davison foiled the government's strategy when she threw herself under the king's horse on Derby Day and died of her injuries.

Their campaign clearly set back the cause by antagonizing many non-militant women and by alienating pro-suffrage members of Parliament. But the crucial weakness lay in the Pankhursts' failure to mobilize working-class men and women. This lack of a genuine mass movement explains why the government freely employed the police against them.

The outbreak of war in August 1914 rescued them from the impasse. They quickly accepted an amnesty whereby prisoners were released and militancy suspended. Mrs Pankhurst and Christabel effectively abandoned not only militancy but the women's cause itself. During the war they attempted to build a new role by speaking on recruiting platforms and urging workers not to strike. In the process they moved further to the right. In spite of, or perhaps because of, the suspension of the Pankhursts' campaign, the vote was granted to 8.4 million women in June 1918. Thereafter Mrs Pankhurst spent much of her time lecturing in North America, Christabel gave up politics for religion, and Sylvia adopted several causes including the British *Communist Party.

**Sullivan, Sir Arthur** (1842–1900). Sullivan was born in Lambeth Walk (London), son of a professional musician at one time bandmaster at Sandhurst. Blessed with a fine voice, Sullivan was a chorister at the Chapel Royal. In 1856 he won the Mendelssohn scholarship and entered the Royal Academy of Music. In 1866 he produced his only symphony and was offered the professorship in composition at the academy. The great collaboration with *Gilbert got off to a faltering start in 1871 with *Thespis* but took fire in 1875 with *Trial by Jury*. *Pinafore* (1878), *The Pirates of Penzance* (1879), and *Mikado* (1885) followed in quick succession. Sullivan's serious work continued with *The Golden Legend* (1886) and *Ivanhoe* (1891). The last of the collaborations, *The Grand Duke*, was put on in 1896. His popular pieces included 'Onward Christian Soldiers' (1871) and 'The Lost Chord' (1877). Sullivan possessed a wealth of melody, brilliant orchestration, considerable poetry, and much humour. The serious work is good; the comic operas incomparable.

**sumptuary laws** were enacted in many countries between the 14th and 17th cents., and sought to prevent ostentatious display by the wealthy, and to keep the lower orders in their place. A statute of 1337 in England restricted the wearing of furs to those with an income of £100 p.a. By the Tudor period, English laws applied only to clothing and were repealed at the end of the 16th cent.

**Sunday observance** *See* SABBATARIANISM.

**Sunday schools** The English Sunday school movement is usually associated with Robert Raikes of Gloucester (1735–1811), the founder of the Sunday School Union. From 1782 Raikes established classes, often on Saturdays as well as Sundays, for children of the poor who were in employment for the rest of the week. A century after the movement began, over 5¾ million children in England were attending these schools.

**Sunderland, Charles Spencer, 3rd earl of** (1674–1722). Whig politician. Son of the 2nd earl, he entered Parliament in 1695 and shone as a gifted Whig spokesman. His marriage in 1700 to a daughter of the *Marlboroughs enhanced his political connections, and it was to the duchess and Lord Treasurer *Godolphin that he owed his appointment as secretary of state (southern department) in 1706. Much to his mortification he was given only token office at George I's accession, and intrigued against the effective leaders *Walpole and *Townshend until in 1717 he replaced the latter as secretary of state (northern). In 1718 he became 1st lord of the Treasury and shared the lead with *Stanhope. His scheme for reducing the national debt led to the *South Sea bubble in 1720, the fall-out from which forced him to surrender the premiership to Walpole in 1721. Nevertheless he retained personal influence with the king, dying suddenly in 1722.

**Sunderland, Robert Spencer, 2nd earl of** (1641–1702). Clever, urbane, self-confident, Sunderland was undoubtedly the most durable politician of the late Stuart age. After an ambassadorial career, he was appointed in 1679 secretary of state but dismissed in 1681 for supporting '*Exclusion'. He was reappointed in 1683 and for the next six years was effectively chief minister. Upon William's 'invasion', Sunderland, recently converted to catholicism, insisted that James reverse his policy, but was dismissed. Briefly exiled in Holland, he returned in 1690, reconverted, and by 1693 had emerged as William III's political 'manager' behind the scenes, without taking office until 1697 when he was made lord chamberlain.

**Supremacy, Act of,** 1534 (26 Hen. VIII c. 1). This Act, passed in the sixth session of the Reformation Parliament in November–December 1534, claimed to 'confirm and corroborate' the right of the king to be supreme head on earth of the Church of England. On 15 January 1535 Henry included the supreme headship in the royal style, and transferred its authority to a spiritual 'vicegerent', the layman Thomas *Cromwell. The title of supreme head was abolished by Mary I in 1554–5, to be replaced under Elizabeth by the more muted title of 'Supreme Governor'.

**Surrey,** The meaning of the name—Suthrige—as the land or region of the south people prompts the suggestion that the area may have formed part, in the early Saxon period, of a larger kingdom with *Middlesex or *Essex. So small a kingdom was bound to have difficulty in resisting powerful neighbours, particularly *Kent, *Mercia, and *Wessex.

By the early 11th cent. Surrey had become a recognized county unit. Kingston upon Thames, close to the Wessex–Mercian border, was a royal town, and a number of Wessex coronations and burials took place there. But as early as the *Domesday survey in 1086 the future pattern of the county could be perceived. Only two towns were separately identified—Guildford, the county town, and Southwark, itself a suburb of London. Surrey remained a predominantly agricultural county, producing mainly for the London market. But *Defoe, surveying west Surrey in the 1720s, was less impressed: 'here is a vast tract of land, which is not only poor, but even quite sterile—much of it is a sandy desert.' Guildford was busy, though the assizes were not held there; Woking 'is very little heard of in England', Leatherhead 'a little through-fare town'. But towards London it was different. There were large numbers of gentlemen's seats, Croydon was 'a great corn-market' for the capital, and Southwark had 'a prodigious number of inhabitants'.

In the first census of 1801, we can trace the effects of the capital on the county. The inner towns were still small—Kingston 4,400, Epsom 4,400, Farnham 4,300, Godalming 3,400, Dorking 3,000, and Guildford 2,600. But Lambeth had 28,000, Newington 10,000, and Southwark 66,000. By the 1840s the railways were pushing out into the shire. In 1851 Lambeth was 139,000, Southwark more than 100,000. By 1901 the suburbs had taken over—299,000 in Lambeth, 259,000 in Camberwell, 169,000 in Battersea, 134,000 in Croydon. The county of market gardeners had become commuter land.

**Surrey, Henry Howard, Lord** (*c*.1517–47). Grandson of Thomas, duke of *Norfolk, the victor of *Flodden. In high favour at the court of Henry VIII, he was given the Garter and, at one time, considered as a possible husband for the Princess Mary. But in December 1546 he was accused of treason for quartering the arms of *Edward the Confessor and beheaded on Tower Hill on 19 January 1547. Surrey, though clearly proud and indiscreet, was victim of Henry's senile suspiciousness and the machinations of his rival the earl of Hertford (*Somerset). He was a poet of some note.

**Surrey, kingdom of** The name 'Surrey' means the southern region, and at some time must have been linked with Middlesex north of the Thames. There is no royal dynasty associated with Surrey, and the most impressive evidence for its early history is a charter of *c*.672–4 granting land at Chertsey to Eorcenwold, bishop of London, issued by Frithuwold, a subking for the Mercian ruler *Wulfhere. The fortunes of Surrey were naturally closely bound up with the fortunes of London. The powerful Mercian kings of the 8th cent. maintained control, but in 825, when *Egbert of Wessex defeated the Mercians at *Ellendun, the people of Surrey submitted to him. From that time forward Surrey was an integral part of greater Wessex.

**Susa, treaty of,** 1629. In 1627 Charles I, already at war with Spain, began a conflict with Louis XIII of France. Attempts to relieve the Huguenot port of La Rochelle, besieged by Richelieu's troops, having failed, peace was made at Susa in Savoy in April 1629.

**suspending power** Though the monarch could not arbitrarily repeal a statute, he claimed, as executive, the right to suspend its operation. Controversy began when Charles II, who disapproved of the penal laws against religious dissidents, issued a *Declaration of Indulgence in 1672 to circumvent them. He was forced by the Commons to withdraw it. James II repeated the attempt in 1687 and indicted the *seven bishops for questioning the validity of his actions. By the *Bill of Rights in 1689 the

suspending power of the crown was abolished. *See* DISPENSING POWER.

**Sussex** was for centuries a byword for inaccessibility, cut off by the north downs and the heavily wooded weald, and proverbial for muddy lanes. In Roman times the local tribe was the *Regni. At the time of the Roman conquest, the king was *Cogidubnus, who submitted and whose title was recognized. The Roman capital was *Chichester (Regnum). The Saxon settlement in the area is curiously and perhaps deceptively precise. The *Anglo-Saxon Chronicle* relates that *Ælle and his three sons came to Britain in 477 (perhaps earlier?) and that one of the sons, Cissa, took Pevensey in 491. By *Bede's time, the kingdom of the South Saxons—Sussex—was well established. The line of Sussex kings continued until the later 8th cent., when the region fell under *Mercia and then *Wessex.

The size of the area made it a manageable unit for the shire system which developed in the 10th cent., but there were local characteristics. First, the county was, uniquely, divided into six *rapes—strips centred on Chichester, Arundel, Bramber, Lewes, Pevensey, and Hastings. Secondly, the difficulties of east-west communication meant that Sussex fell naturally into sections. The rape of Hastings was probably the territory of the Haestingas, who formed a subkingdom. Later, the county divided into a western section, based on Chichester, and an eastern section, based on Lewes. When parliamentary representation developed in the later medieval period, the convention was to choose one MP from each section.

The sea coast being difficult and the only large harbours at Chichester and Rye, the Sussex ports remained local. The spectacular medieval development was in iron manufacture, eked out by smuggling. *Camden, writing in the 1580s, noted that Sussex was 'full of iron mines everywhere...for the driving of mills by the flashes; which beating with hammers upon the iron, fill the neighbourhood round about, night and day, with their noise.' But in the late 17th cent. cheap Swedish iron, the exhaustion of the forests, and competition from Shropshire led to a decline, and by 1788 there were only two furnaces left.

The transformation of Sussex from a remote rural county of farms and small market towns was the result of two developments—the growing taste for seaside holidays and the coming of the railways. Brighthelmstone was described by *Defoe in the 1720s as 'a poor fishing town, old built', fast eaten away by an 'unkind' sea. The prince regent's visit in 1782 and his plans for the Pavilion put *Brighton on the fashionable map and thereafter its growth was prodigious. By 1801 it was already nearly twice the size of Chichester and by 1851 bigger, at 65,000, than all the other Sussex towns put together. It was now pursued by other local resorts. Hove, its neighbour, had a population of 100 in 1801 but 29,000 100 years later. By 1901, Eastbourne had 42,000, Hastings 52,000, and Worthing 20,000. Bognor left its run until the 20th cent., profiting from the convalescence of George V in 1929.

**Sussex, East** By a long-standing tradition, the large county of Sussex had its eastern and western parts, looking to Lewes and to Chichester. The county courts, quarter sessions, and usually the assizes were held alternately, and in 1832 the Reform Act recognized the situation by giving two representatives to each division. In 1888 separate county councils were established for East and West Sussex. This arrangement was continued by the Local Government Act of 1972, but Brighton was subsequently made a unitary authority.

**Sussex, kingdom of** Sussex was ruled by its own kings from the time of *Ælle (c.477), who is said by *Bede to have been the first overlord (*bretwalda) of the southern English, to the end of the 8th cent., but for most of that period the kings were subordinate to other rulers. Sussex was a complex political unit. Its earliest charters show that it was divided among a number of kings at times with a marked division between East Sussex, probably centred at Lewes, and West Sussex with a centre in the Chichester area. Hastings and its immediate surroundings always preserved individual characteristics, closer to Kent. It was the last substantial kingdom to receive Christianity, owing its conversion to St *Wilfrid during his exile from Northumbria in the early 680s. After 825 the West Saxon dynasty under *Egbert and his successors took control, treating Sussex as a suitable subkingdom for West Saxon princes.

**Sussex, Thomas Radcliffe, 3rd earl of** (c.1525–83). Radcliffe's mother was a daughter of the 2nd duke of *Norfolk. He fought with distinction in the French campaign of 1544 and at *Pinkie in 1547. Though he signed the proclamation of Lady Jane *Grey in 1553, his father declared for Mary and was in command of her forces at Framlingham. Radcliffe's wobble does not seem to have done him harm. He was entrusted by Mary with the suppression of *Wyatt's rising. He succeeded as earl in 1557 and was given the Garter. In 1556 he was sent by Mary to Ireland as lord keeper with instructions to promote the catholic cause. Elizabeth reappointed him, making him lord-lieutenant, but his renewed campaign against the O'Neills made little progress. He resigned in 1565 and from 1568 to 1572 was lord president of the Council of the North, helping to put down the rising of the *northern earls in 1569. From 1572 until his death he was lord chamberlain.

**Sussex, West** Given a separate county council in 1888, with its county headquarters at Chichester; the arrangement was continued in 1972. Brighton is a unitary authority. *See* SUSSEX, EAST.

**Sutherland, Graham** (1903–80). Painter. Sutherland studied art at Goldsmiths College, London. His early work, influenced by Samuel *Palmer, was in etching and engraving, before he moved into ceramics and painting. During the Second World War, as an official war artist, he produced powerful studies of air-raid devastation in London and Swansea. A portrait of Somerset Maugham (1949) was the first of several strong representations of famous people. That of Winston *Churchill was commissioned by Parliament, but destroyed by the sitter's wife.

**Sutton Hoo** A site containing up to 20 Anglo-Saxon burial barrows (c. AD 400–700) on the east bank of the Deben estuary in south-east Suffolk. In 1939 the largest barrow, some 120 feet in length and over 12 feet high, was opened. The depth of its extraordinarily rich deposit, almost certainly the inhumation of a king, possibly *Rædwald who died about AD 625, had protected it from robbery. The deposit lay in the centre of a 90-foot-long rowing boat. The objects, of supreme local craftsmanship in gold, of lesser craftsmanship in eastern Mediterranean silver, and including a whetstone sceptre and a mysterious 'iron standard', immeasurably widened knowledge of 'Dark Age' culture. This revelation of the Germanic world of the 'Age of Migrations' stands comparison with the tomb of Tutankhamun.

**Swan, Sir Joseph Wilson** (1828–1914). Born at Sunderland and educated in local schools, Swan was apprenticed to a local pharmacist. At Newcastle upon Tyne he became a partner in a pharmacy. A photographic business and a scientific instruments department were soon added. Swan invented an improved photographic printing technique, which is still in use. In December 1878 and February 1879 he demonstrated his first incandescent electric bulbs. Legal disputes between the Swan and Edison lighting interests were solved by creating a joint venture.

**Swansea** Town of south Wales located at the mouth of the river Tawe (Abertawe). The name, Scandinavian in origin, reflects post-Roman Viking activity, but there is no evidence of settlement until the site was developed as a castle borough by Henry de Beaumont, the first Norman lord of Gower. After 1717 it became the centre of the early Welsh metallurgical industry, mainly copper, lead, and silver. Swansea acquired city status in 1969 and is now an industrial and administrative centre.

**Swansea and Brecon, diocese of** In 1923, three years after the disestablishment of the Church in Wales, those parts of the ancient diocese of St Davids within the counties of Breconshire, Radnorshire, and western Glamorgan were formed into a new see of Swansea and Brecon, with the cathedral at the medieval priory church of St John in Brecon itself. The name of the see reflects the two focal points.

**Swaziland** Former British high commission territory. In the 19th cent. the Bantu kingdom of Swaziland was under intermittent threat from Zulus, from would-be Boer (Afrikaner) settlers, and from British administrators in *Natal. In 1906, along with *Botswana and *Lesotho it was placed under the jurisdiction of a British high commissioner. The country became independent in 1968.

**Swedenborgians** were followers of Emanuel Swedenborg (1688–1772), a Swedish scientist and diplomat who taught that there are correspondences between the visible forms of nature and the invisible world of the spirit. In 1787 some of his followers started the New Jerusalem church. They were particularly strong in Manchester where they were known as *Bible Christians.

**Sweyn Estrithsson** (d. 1074), king of Denmark (1047–74). Overshadowed by his rival *Harold Hardrada, king of Norway, Sweyn nevertheless posed a significant threat to the rulers of England. The son of *Cnut's sister Estrith and Jarl Ulf, Sweyn's existence as a possible heir to the childless Edward the Confessor made him a consistent element in the tangled northern politics of the age. After the death of Harold Hardrada at *Stamford Bridge in September 1066 and the subsequent Norman conquest of England, Sweyn came to the forefront of English politics. In 1069 he sent a huge fleet which sacked York, inflicting a rare defeat on the Normans. William, however, came to terms, more or less buying him off, and Sweyn's death on 28 April 1074 signalled a virtual end to any revival of Cnut's Anglo-Danish kingdom.

**Sweyn Forkbeard** (d. 1014), king of Denmark (c.985–1014), king of England (1013–14). For 20 years before 1013 Sweyn Forkbeard was involved in heavy raiding against England. Attacks intensified after 1004, some said in revenge for the murder of his sister Gunnhild during the massacre of *St Brice's Day, 1002. His principal effort came in 1013 when, accompanied by his son *Cnut, he invaded England through the Humber and the Trent, setting up his base at Gainsborough, where he was recognized as king by most of Anglo-Danish England. He then moved south where Oxford and Winchester surrendered immediately and when London finally submitted towards the end of the year, Æthelred was forced to flee to Normandy. For five or six weeks Sweyn was thus in control of all his newly conquered kingdom of England, but on 3 February 1014 he died at Gainsborough.

**Sweyn Godwineson** (d. 1052). The eldest son of Earl *Godwine, a wild streak in his nature led to personal disaster. In 1046 he seduced the abbess of Leominster, fled to Denmark, and on his forced return to England, became responsible for the murder of his own cousin, Earl Beorn. By special procedures more Scandinavian than English, Sweyn was adjudged 'nithing' in an assembly of the whole army, that is to say 'a man without honour'. He was outlawed and took refuge in Flanders. The influence of his father and the support of Bishop Ealdred enabled him to return but he went into exile again in the autumn of 1051, this time with the rest of the Godwine family. He died on his way back from a penitential pilgrimage to Jerusalem.

**Swift, Jonathan** (1667–1745). Irish writer and clergyman. Educated at Kilkenny School and Trinity College, Dublin, Swift became secretary to Sir William *Temple, taking holy orders in 1695. The witty and notorious *A Tale of a Tub* (1704) established Swift's reputation, and in 1710 he was recruited as a ministerial propagandist, writing the *Examiner* (1710–11) and *The Conduct of the Allies* (1711), an influential pamphlet defending the Tory government's peace overtures to France. Rewarded for his services by the deanship of St Patrick's, Dublin, Swift became embroiled in Irish politics after 1714. Despite the enduring relevance of *Gulliver's Travels* (1726), Swift's reputation has suffered from the savagery and scatology of his satire.

**swimming** was until recently confined to those living by lakes, rivers, or near the sea. The development of public baths and pools in the 19th cent. gave, for the first time, a chance for large numbers of people to learn to swim. After some early unsuccessful attempts, the Metropolitan Swimming Association was formed in 1869 and later became the Amateur Swimming Association. The feat of Captain Matthew Webb in swimming the English Channel from Dover to Calais in 1875 captured much attention for the sport.

**Swing riots,** 1830. Collective action by agricultural workers began in east Kent late in August 1830 with two attacks on the hated threshing-machines, which were believed to take winter work away from agricultural labourers. The disturbances continued until December and spread to much of southern and eastern England. Barns and hay ricks were fired, and threatening letters—often signed by the mythical 'Captain Swing'— were sent in all directions. In the wake of the disturbances 19 people were executed, 481 transported, and more than 700 imprisoned.

**syndicalists** Disliking capitalism and fearing that the triumph of communism would merely introduce a different form of state oppression, syndicalists argued for the transfer of power to the trade unions. In Britain their main contribution was to the concept of *guild socialism. British trade unionists showed little interest in the theory and their creation of the Labour Party was a direct repudiation of syndicalist tactics. Though the slogan 'All power to the trade unions' does not seem to have much contemporary appeal, concern at the power of the state, capitalist or communist, remains a live issue.

**Synge, J. M.** (1871–1909). Most gifted of the dramatists in the early days of the *Abbey theatre. Visits to the Aran Islands encouraged the development of a poetic prose based on the patterns of native speech. In *Riders to the Sea* (1904) Synge invested the life of the islands with something of the dignity of Greek tragedy and *The Playboy of the Western World* (1907) better embodied the spirit of the new literature than the efforts of *Yeats and Lady *Gregory.

**synods** A synod is a meeting of clergy, or clergy and laity, convened to discuss and decide upon matters of doctrine, church policy, and discipline. Today in the Church of England a general synod meets once or twice a year with the traditional agenda.

**Tacitus** Roman historian born *c.* AD 55. He is the principal surviving historian of Roman Britain, dealing with the first 40 years of the province. In 77 he married the daughter of *Agricola, soon to be governor of Britain, and his biography of his father-in-law survives.

**Taff Vale judgment,** 1902. Over 1,000 employees of the Taff Vale railway went on strike in 1901. Their union, the Amalgamated Society of Railway Servants, was sued for damages, and in December 1902 the Taff Vale Railway Company was paid £23,000. A crippling blow to trade unionism, this judgment was one reason why unions supported the infant Labour Representation Committee.

**Talavera, battle of,** 1809. On 28 July Wellesley's British army of 20,000 men, co-operating with Cuesta's Spanish army of 34,000 men, were attacked by 46,000 French commanded by King Joseph Bonaparte and Marshal Jourdan. The French mounted a series of assaults against the British centre, followed by a turning movement in the north. All were unsuccessful. As a reward, Wellesley was created Viscount *Wellington.

**Talbot, William Henry Fox** (1800–77). Pioneer of photography. A prosperous country gentleman from Lacock abbey (Wilts.), Talbot went to Harrow and Trinity College, Cambridge. An amateur scientist, in 1833 he began experiments to see if permanent images could be recorded on sensitized paper. In January 1839 his progress was reported to the Royal Institution and the Royal Society, explaining how 'natural objects may be made to delineate themselves without the aid of the artist's pencil'. Talbot's book *The Pencil of Nature* appeared 1844–6, including 24 photographs, one of them a famous view of the boulevards in Paris, and a magnificently evocative 'The Open Door'.

**Talents, Ministry of All the,** 1806–7. A coalition government formed in February 1806, following *Pitt's death. Supposedly embracing 'All the Talents', it was composed of the followers of Lord *Grenville and Charles *Fox, bolstered by those of Lord Sidmouth (*Addington). The resignation of the Talents in March 1807 was precipitated by George III, who rejected a limited measure of catholic relief and demanded that this question never again be raised. This change-over did not, however, destroy the Talents' greatest achievement: the abolition of the slave trade in May 1807.

**Taliesin** (6th cent.). Bard. Taliesin and *Aneurin were two of the five great bards referred to by *Nennius in his *Historia Brittonum* (*c.*796). Taliesin's surviving work records the deeds of Urien, king of the Britons, in *Rheged and his struggle against the Anglo-Saxons, just as Aneurin does for *Gododdin: 'And when I'm grown old, with death hard upon me, I'll not be happy save to praise Urien.'

**tallage** was the valuable right of the king (and of other lords) to impose taxation on his demesne, including his boroughs. It could not be refused, though it could be negotiated. Edward I's incessant warfare placed severe tax demands on his subjects. In the crisis of 1297, after he had left for France, he was urged to let tallage come under parliamentary control. Tallages continued to be demanded at intervals until 1340, when Edward III agreed that the consent of Parliament must be obtained.

**Tallis, Thomas** (*c.*1505–85). English composer and organist, whose early career included short periods at Dover priory, St Mary-at-Hill in London, Waltham abbey in Essex, and Canterbury cathedral. By 1545 he was a gentleman of the Chapel Royal, where he remained, also acting as organist, until his death. Thus, unusually, Tallis served four monarchs, something apparent in his music.

**Tamworth manifesto,** 1835. *Peel's manifesto to his constituents is often regarded as the foundation document of modern Conservatism. The Tory Party, badly beaten at the election of 1832, faced another general election and could hardly campaign on repealing the Great Reform Act, depriving Birmingham, Leeds, and Sheffield of their new representation, and restoring Gatton and Old Sarum. Peel, leading a minority government, explained that he now considered the Reform Act 'a final and irrevocable settlement' and that his general policy would be 'the firm maintenance of established rights, the correction of proved abuses and the redress of real grievances'. This left open who was to decide what was proof, what the word 'real' signified, and what would happen if the reform of abuses threatened established rights. Peel conceded that his statement was 'necessarily vague'. The manifesto has been seen as the foundation for a policy of prudent adjustment or as a recipe for continual surrender.

**Tanzania** Formerly Tanganyika and *Zanzibar. Previously a German dependency, Tanganyika became a British mandated territory after the First World War. Having few natural resources, it proved unattractive to white settlers. This, together with the absence of any dominant ethnic group with aspirations to hegemony, meant that the country developed peacefully. Its progress towards independence in 1961 was equally without serious incident. The following year Tanganyika became a republic, and in 1964 joined with Zanzibar to become Tanzania.

**Tara, hill of** (Co. Meath). A sacred site for at least two millennia, going back as far as the Neolithic period, the hilltop shows evidence of many structures. It later became a central site for the five provinces to hold assembly and conduct markets and fairs. In Irish mythology Tara is the royal seat of kings.

**Taranto, battle of,** 1940. On 11 November 1940, 21 Swordfish aircraft from HMS *Illustrious* launched a torpedo attack at night on the Italian fleet at anchor off Taranto. Two aircraft were lost but heavy damage was done and the remaining Italian vessels sought more remote harbours.

**tariff reform** *See* PROTECTIONISM.

**Tasmania,** (formerly Van Diemen's Land) a member state of the federal Commonwealth of Australia, has a population (2007) of 478,000. Hobart (population 206,000), established 1803, is the largest city and state capital. Discovered by Dutch navigator Abel Tasman in 1642 and named Van Diemen's Land it became infamous, following British occupation in 1803, for its ill-treatment of convicts (especially at Hell's Gate and Port Arthur) and the extermination of its Aboriginal population. Its name was changed to Tasmania in 1856 to help rid the island of its evil reputation.

The island's agricultural settlements and typically small farms are concentrated in its northern and south-eastern lowland areas leaving the mainly rugged, mountainous, and high-rainfall forested western two-thirds largely uninhabited. Tasmania's natural beauty has encouraged a strong environmental movement.

**Tate Gallery** In 1890 the sugar magnate Henry Tate gave 60 modern English paintings to the National Gallery provided that a gallery was made available. Eventually the government offered the prison site at Millbank, London, and the Tate Gallery opened in 1897. Wealthy benefactors have continued to aid expansion; in 1987 the Turner bequest was finally housed as the artist intended, in the extension funded by the Clore Foundation. The Bankside power station was converted into the Tate Modern, opened in 2000, and the original gallery was renamed Tate Britain.

*Tatler* A periodical edited by *Richard Steele under the pseudonym 'Isaac Bickerstaff', it appeared three times a week between April 1709 and January 1711. *Addison was an important collaborator.

**Tawney, R. H.** (1880–1962). Tawney made a significant impact in four interrelated roles, as Christian *socialist, social philosopher, educationalist, and economic historian. In 1908 he became the first tutorial class teacher in an agreement between the *Workers' Educational Association and Oxford University. The classes he took became renowned for their excellence. As a socialist, he wrote *Secondary Education for All* (1922), which informed Labour policy for a generation. His two most influential books, *The Acquisitive Society* (1921) and *Equality* (1931), exercised a profound influence on socialists in Britain and abroad and anticipated the welfare state. Tawney was also a professor of economic history from 1931, having made his reputation with *Religion and the Rise of Capitalism* (1926).

**Tay bridge** The wide estuary of the river Tay on the east coast of Scotland presented a formidable obstacle to transport. The first bridge over the estuary was designed by Thomas Bouch for the North British Railway Company. It was almost 2 miles long and was completed in 1877. Queen Victoria crossed it in the summer of 1879, and knighted its designer on the spot. But at the end of that year, on 28 December 1879, several spans collapsed in a severe storm while a train was crossing, sending 74 people to their deaths. The subsequent inquiry concluded that the bridge was 'badly designed, badly constructed and badly maintained'. A new road bridge was opened over the estuary in 1966.

**Tayside** From 1973 an administrative region in east Scotland created from the city of Dundee, all Angus and Kinross, and most of Perthshire. In 1996 it was divided into three all-purpose authorities (Angus, Dundee, Perth and Kinross) whose boundaries are almost the same as the previous districts. In addition to survival of older industries—some jute is still spun and woven—agriculture (especially soft fruit), food-processing, and manufacture of hole-in-the-wall cash machines are important to the economy.

**Tedder, Sir Arthur** (1890–1967). Tedder read history at Cambridge, then joined the RFC in the First World War. He commanded the Middle East Royal Air Force, May 1941 to February 1943. Next he was in charge of allied air forces in the Mediterranean before becoming deputy supreme commander of 'Overlord'. Tedder's contribution to allied success, especially in Normandy, 1944, involved 'interdiction': preventing enemy supplies and reinforcements from reaching the battlefield by attacking road and rail transport, direct and prompt tactical support for ground troops, using fighter-bombers as mobile artillery, and his occasional diversion of British and American heavy bombers to support big offensives. He became marshal of the RAF and was made viscount in 1946.

**Teheran conference,** 28 November–1 December 1943. The first of the 'Big Three' wartime meetings. It was here that *Churchill became uncomfortably aware of the extent to which British power was declining in relation to his allies. He had to agree to the earliest possible second front in northern France (June 1944). Churchill did what he could to protect the future of the Polish government in exile, while broadly accepting the drastic post-war movement westward of Poland's frontiers.

**Teilo, St** (6th cent.). Teilo is associated in Welsh triads with SS *David and *Cadoc as one of the Three Blessed Visitors to the Isle of Britain. Twelfth-cent. sources claim that he met St David, whom he accompanied on a pilgrimage to Jerusalem. His ministry was centred, however, on his monastery at Llandeilo Fawr, where he eventually died.

**Tel-el-Kebir, battle of,** 1882. In the third quarter of the 19th cent. Egypt's external debt became so great that Britain and France took control of the country's finances. The heavily taxed peasantry, led by an army officer, Ahmed Arabi, rebelled. British troops under Sir Garnet *Wolseley landed in Egypt to support the khedive and in a surprise attack destroyed Arabi's army at Tel-el-Kebir, 130 miles north-east of Cairo.

**Telford, Thomas** (1757–1834). Civil engineer from Eskdale (Dumfries). Apprenticeship as a stonemason laid the basis for Telford's move via Edinburgh to London, where he worked on Somerset House (1782), being introduced to Sir William Chambers and *Adam, before work at Portsmouth dockyard (1784). Distinguished canal work followed with his aqueduct at Pontcysyllte (1805), the Caledonian canal (1822), contributions to Sweden's Gotha canal (1832), and the Birmingham and Liverpool Junction (1835). Between 1803 and 1824 he was responsible for the construction or remodelling of 1,200 miles of road. His creation of the Shrewsbury–Holyhead road (from

1802) was a parallel developmental project, and at Menai (1825) and Conwy (1826) led to his pioneering development of suspension bridges. He succeeded *Rennie as Britain's leading civil engineer, and was a founding member of the Institute of Civil Engineers in 1828.

**temperance movement** A powerful social and political force in Victorian Britain. Though it did not succeed in eradicating drink, it helped to control it. Between 1831 and 1931, spirit consumption per head p.a. fell from 1.11 gallons to 0.22, and beer from 21.6 gallons to 13.3. Direct propaganda was not the only factor in this change: others included growing respectability, improved amenities, more comfortable homes, and a decline in occupations of heavy labour where drink was a necessity. The chief support of the temperance movement was the dissenting bodies, who carried it as an issue into the *Liberal Party, which adopted local option on the sale of drink as part of its *Newcastle Programme in 1891.

The leading organizations were the British and Temperance Society (1831), the British Association for the Promotion of Temperance (1835), the National Temperance Society (1842), and the United Kingdom Alliance (1853). One of the best publicized groups was the Band of Hope, founded in Leeds in 1847 to appeal to children. A trusted technique was to persuade men to 'take the pledge'—an action first agreed in 1832 by seven workmen in Preston. The movement often took the form of a religious revival and was referred to as a crusade. Drink was 'the demon', the pledge echoed baptism, and the solemn reading of the names of backsliders was a form of excommunication.

**Templars** Established in Jerusalem in 1118 as a small group of knights pledged to protect pilgrims journeying to the Holy Places. In 1128 they gained papal support and a rule was compiled for them by St Bernard of Clairvaux. Their first house in England was established just outside the city of London and moved to a site (the 'New Temple') off Fleet Street in 1161. Their wealth (and ultimate military failure) led to accusations of heresy, particularly in France where King Philip IV in association with Pope Clement V brought about the brutal demise of the order, finally suppressed in 1312.

**Temple, Sir William** (1628–99). Diplomat and author. Educated at Cambridge, Temple moved from Ireland to England in 1663 and became *Arlington's protégé. Accredited envoy at Brussels (1665), he negotiated the *Triple Alliance as ambassador at The Hague (1668), but retired to England as relations deteriorated; pro-Dutch, he was recalled to negotiate the 1674 treaty ending the Dutch War, and then, with *Danby, successfully arranged the alliance between Charles's niece Mary and William of Orange (1677). He retired from politics in 1681 to pursue gardening, fruit-growing, and writing at Moor Park.

**Temple, William** (1881–1944). Archbishop of Canterbury. Born in Exeter, Temple was educated at Balliol College, Oxford. He was ordained while fellow of Queen's (1904–10). He was successively headmaster of Repton (1910), rector of St James's, Piccadilly (1914), bishop of Manchester (1921), archbishop of York (1929) and of Canterbury (1942). Influenced by the *Workers' Educational Association and Student Christian Movement, he was, like his friend R. H. *Tawney, socialist in his thinking. Later dubbed 'intellectually the most brilliant archbishop since *Anselm', he also had great administrative ability and towered over the English ecclesiastical scene.

**Tempsford, battle of,** c.918. *Edward the Elder and his sister *Æthelfleda, lady of the Mercians, launched a sustained counter-attack upon Danish-held territory. In c.918 he stormed a large Danish camp at Tempsford, east of Bedford, killing the leader Guthrum II. Danish resistance in East Anglia crumbled.

**Tenant League** The Irish Tenant League was formed in 1850 to agitate for tenants' rights, in part to replace the repeal campaign. One objective was to extend the *Ulster custom, which gave some protection over rents and evictions. *Gladstone's *Land Act of 1870 conceded some of the rights claimed.

**tenant right** was a phrase much in use in Irish politics, especially after the famine of 1846. Landlords complained that tenants devised new rights as soon as old ones were conceded. The three Fs for which the *Tenant League later campaigned were free sale, fixity of tenure, and fair rent—all of which were slogans difficult to quantify. *Gladstone's *Land Act of 1870 legalized the *Ulster custom where it existed. Gladstone's second Land Act of 1881 conceded free sale, improved security of tenure, and introduced a machinery for deciding what was a fair rent. *Palmerston's comment—'tenant right is landlord's wrong'—was the other side of the coin.

**tenants-in-chief** were those who, after the *Norman Conquest, held their lands directly from the king. Their names are given in *Domesday Book (1086) and are mainly those who had fought alongside William at Hastings or their descendants. Domesday records some 1,400 of them. They were under obligation to produce a quota of knights on demand, though they could sublet (subinfeudate) provided the obligation was met. The larger tenants-in-chief may be regarded as the forerunners of the later nobility.

**Tenerife, battle of,** 1657. On 20 April 1657 *Blake won his last great victory, attacking a force of sixteen Spanish vessels at harbour in Santa Cruz, protected by shore batteries. Every enemy vessel was destroyed and all Blake's ships, some of them badly damaged, survived.

**Ten Hours Act** (1847). This Act, limiting the work of women and young persons (aged 13–18) in textile mills to ten hours a day for five days in the week and eight hours on Saturday, was the result of a sustained campaign from the 1830s managed in Parliament by Lord Ashley (*Shaftesbury) and John *Fielden. The Act was a triumph of welfare legislation over *laissez-faire doctrine.

**tennis** *See* LAWN TENNIS.

**Tennyson, Alfred, 1st Baron Tennyson** (1809–92). Tennyson was the first poet to be made a peer of the realm, since *Macaulay, author of *Lays of Ancient Rome*, had been an active politician. He was the son of a Lincolnshire rector and attended Louth Grammar School and Trinity College, Cambridge. His first volume of poetry in 1830 sold badly, though it contained 'Mariana':

the next volume in 1832 included 'The Lady of Shalott'. His collected volume in 1842 established him as a major poet. He succeeded *Wordsworth as poet laureate in 1850, and was given his barony during *Gladstone's ministry in 1884.

**Territorials** With a large navy to support, it was always necessary for Britain to augment her army with a reserve force. The *militia was not always popular, nor particularly effective, and in periods of crisis was supplemented by *volunteer and fencible corps. In 1907, *Haldane, Liberal secretary of state for war, determined to bring order into a confused situation by establishing a Territorial Force, which absorbed the militia. In 1921 it became the Territorial Army.

**terrorism** In the early 21st cent. there were indications that terrorism, which had previously taken the form of isolated assassinations or bombings, was becoming endemic and had acquired a formidable international dimension. On 11 September 2001 two hijacked aircraft destroyed the World Trade Centre in New York, with the loss of nearly 3,000 lives. The immediate result was an economic crisis, particularly in air travel, heightened security precautions, a search for Osama bin Laden who had encouraged the strike, and an American-led attack upon the Taliban regime in *Afghanistan, to root out members of al-Qa'eda. This was followed in 2003 by a three-week campaign in *Iraq which overthrew Saddam Hussein. In March 2004 an attack on the train system in Madrid killed 191 commuters, and in July 2005 a coordinated terrorist attack upon London killed more than fifty people.

**Terry, Ellen** (1847–1928). Actress. Born into an acting family, Alice Ellen Terry left the stage for some years until concern for her children's future prompted a return in 1874. She joined *Irving as his leading lady at the Lyceum theatre (1878), where her beauty and grace enhanced his productions; appearing in Britain and America, their famous partnership lasted until 1902. Enormously popular, her vitality and stagecraft were underpinned by intelligence, yet all her successes, except in *Shakespeare, were in sentimental melodrama.

**Test Act,** 1673. Usually linked to the *Corporation Act, but a later addition to the code of laws excluding non-members of the Church of England from public office (25 Car. II c. 2). It required all office-holders under the crown, including MPs, to receive communion according to the rites of the Church of England at least once a year, and to make a declaration against transubstantiation. This was aimed at catholics and the repeal of the Test Act was the principal objective of the successful *catholic emancipation campaign led by Daniel *O'Connell in the late 1820s.

**Tettenhall, battle of,** 910. With the death of *Alfred the Great in 899, his son *Edward succeeded to the Wessex crown. Together with his sister *Æthelfleda, 'the lady of the Mercians', Edward began to forge a strong English kingdom. The Danes raided in 910 and the king marched his army to Staffordshire to intercept them. On 5 August Edward won a convincing victory and extended his kingdom as far north as the Humber.

**Tewkesbury, battle of,** 1471. The last and one of the bloodiest battles of the Wars of the *Roses. Queen *Margaret, still defending the claims of her husband Henry VI, landed at Weymouth the same day that Edward IV defeated *Warwick at *Barnet. She moved towards Wales and the north-west to collect support, with Edward marching from Windsor to intercept her. Her troops were caught before they could cross the Severn and forced to give battle at Tewkesbury on 4 May 1471. *Edward, the young Lancastrian prince of Wales, was killed, Queen Margaret captured, and Henry VI murdered the same month.

**Texel, battle of the,** 1673. On 21 August was fought the last battle in the third Anglo-Dutch War. The Dutch were expecting a large convoy from the Indies and were also threatened with an invasion. De Ruyter took the initiative against a joint Anglo-French fleet under *Rupert. Dutch superiority in gunnery gave them the upper hand, though no major ships were lost on either side. But the convoy came home and the proposed landing was abandoned.

**Teyte, Dame Maggie** (1888–1976). English soprano. After studying in London and Paris, Teyte made her public début while still under 18 in a Mozart festival at Paris in 1906. She was chosen and coached by Debussy in 1908 to succeed Mary Garden as Mélisande in his opera *Pelléas et Mélisande*. Between the wars her British activity centred on operetta and musical comedy, but later concerts and recordings returned particularly to French song.

**Thackeray, William Makepeace** (1811–63). Novelist. Born in Calcutta, he was educated at Charterhouse and Cambridge. This Indian background and his public school were to figure prominently in *The Newcomes* (1853–5). He was a notable early contributor to *Punch* (founded 1841) and to *Fraser's Magazine* (founded 1830) and in 1860 became the editor of the dynamic new *Cornhill Magazine*. His real breakthrough came with the monthly part serialization of *Vanity Fair* (1847–8), a novel set at the time of Waterloo and its aftermath.

**thanes** *See* THEGNS.

**Thatcher, Margaret** (b. 1925). Prime minister. Britain's first woman prime minister and one of the most controversial, she won three resounding election victories in a row for the Conservatives (1979, 1983, and 1987), before they rejected her as party leader and premier in 1990, a ruthless act of political ingratitude.

Educated at Kesteven and Grantham Girls' School and Somerville College, Oxford, she entered Parliament in 1959. Beforehand she had been a research chemist (1947–54) and a lawyer (she was called to the bar in 1954). Between 1970 and 1974 she was secretary of state for education. As leader of the opposition, between 1975 and 1979, under the influence of Sir Keith Joseph, she moved towards that ideal of political patriotism, low taxes, private ownership, balanced budgets, and individual initiative which later became known as Thatcherism. However, if the goal was financial stability, permanently low inflation, reduced government spending, and lower taxes, it proved illusory. Her record as prime minister began and ended with severe recessions (the worst since the 1930s) leading to a reduced industrial base and low overall growth rates. The trade unions were tamed; most state-owned companies were privatized; and income tax was significantly lowered. However, rising indirect taxes, rising interest rates, rising inflation, plus the introduction of the hugely unpopular *poll tax meant that when a crisis erupted over Europe in 1990, Mrs Thatcher lacked the political support needed to survive.

Just as she had not been expected to win the Tory Party leadership against Heath in 1975, her rapid rise to international fame took many by surprise. From the start of her premiership, she made her mark in international affairs. In 1979 a peace settlement was negotiated at Lancaster House which ended the Rhodesian question and paved the way for an independent *Zimbabwe. Her next triumph, which made her an international celebrity, came with victory over Argentina in the *Falklands War of 1982. The bravery and efficiency displayed by the armed forces, the collapse of the reactionary Argentine dictatorship, and the leadership provided by the prime minister, all enabled Mrs Thatcher to win a remarkable triumph in the 1983 general election. Thereafter she developed a 'very, very special relationship' with the US president, Ronald Reagan, and despite some differences worked closely with him to end the *Cold War. She also managed to develop a close relationship with the Soviet leader Mikhail Gorbachev. When she finally visited Moscow, she received a triumphal welcome.

Her policy towards the European Community was, however, most controversial of all. Her first instincts had been conventional. She had campaigned enthusiastically for a Yes vote in the 1975 referendum and always believed that her approach was constructive. On the other hand, she was horrified by Jacques Delors's ideas regarding a European Social Charter, and even more so by European economic and monetary union. In her famous Bruges speech (1988), she declared her opposition to future integration, although she was persuaded by her cabinet colleagues Sir Geoffrey Howe and Nigel Lawson to promise to enter the exchange rate mechanism. By 1990, however, after having rejected economic and monetary union at a summit in Rome, she was deserted by Sir Geoffrey Howe, who resigned from her government and challenged Michael Heseltine to contest the party leadership. In the ensuing contest, Mrs Thatcher won the first

round, but withdrew from the leadership race, rather than submit to a second ballot. She was succeeded by John *Major as Tory leader. She retired from the Commons in 1992 and was made a life peer.

**thegns** was a title given to those members of society in late Anglo-Saxon England who held at least 5 hides of land and were under the obligation of serving the king in battle. Though there were many gradations within the ranks of thegns, their *wergeld in Mercia and Wessex was six times that of a ceorl. The spelling has been preferred by historians to distinguish them from Scottish thanes, who were barons or clan leaders.

**Theodore of Tarsus** (*c.*602–90). Sent by Pope Vitalian as archbishop of Canterbury, Theodore arrived in 669. Two deaths had left the see vacant for five years. The church lacked organization and had not achieved the uniformity promised at *Whitby (664). Theodore toured his province, eliminating irregularities, consecrating bishops, and in 672 summoned the first synod of the whole English church at *Hertford.

**Thirty-Nine Articles** The articles are those finally agreed by the convocations of the Church of England in 1571. They comprise a set of doctrinal statements which were intended to define the position of the reformed Church of England. Printed as an appendix to the 1662 *Book of Common Prayer, their declared purpose is 'for the avoiding of diversities of opinions and for the establishing of consent touching true religion'. They steer a careful—and sometimes ambiguous—path between catholic and reformed doctrines. Subscription to them is still required of the clergy, but since 1865 only a general affirmation is required.

**Thirty Years War** The war, from 1618 to 1648, was primarily a conflict between the Habsburgs and their Spanish allies against France, Sweden, and the Dutch. There were two reasons why England might be drawn into it. The *casus belli* was the decision by the Bohemians to defy the Habsburgs and offer their throne to Frederick of the Palatinate, who was married to *Elizabeth, daughter of James I. Secondly, there was a religious element to the war which, despite France's opposition to the Habsburgs, was seen by many protestants as a catholic crusade. Charles I's attempts to intervene were disastrous. Fortunately his relations with Parliament were so bad that he was obliged to make peace. The conflict was concluded by the treaty of Westphalia in 1648, by which time Charles was a prisoner awaiting trial.

**Thistle, Order of the** The origins of this Scottish order of knighthood are unclear but it seems to have been founded by James III about 1480. It lapsed after the Reformation but was revived by James VII and II in 1687 and again by Anne in 1703. It now numbers sixteen, including the sovereign.

**Thomas, Dylan** (1914–53). Poet. Born in Swansea, son of a schoolteacher, Thomas began as a journalist, publishing his first book *18 Poems* in 1934 and following it in 1936 with *25 Poems*. He married in 1937 and settled in the coastal village of Laugharne, south of Carmarthen, working for the BBC and lecturing. Though he knew no Welsh, Thomas's roistering life-style led some to accuse him of being a stage-Welshman. His radio play *Under Milk Wood* (1954) was greatly acclaimed as a portrait of Welsh life in the fictitious village of Llareggub.

**Thomas of Lancaster** (*c.*1278–1322) was one of the most powerful magnates during the reign of Edward II and a thorn in the side of the king. He was the son of Edmund Crouchback, a younger son of Henry III and was therefore first cousin to Edward II. As soon as his cousin succeeded, Thomas moved into opposition. He took an active part against the royal favourite *Gaveston, was one of the *Ordainers appointed to supervise the young king, and brought about Gaveston's execution in 1312. He refused to serve in the *Bannockburn campaign of 1314 and profited from the king's humiliation to increase his own influence. But by 1321 he was once more at odds with the king over the *Despensers, whom he forced into exile. In 1322 he was captured at *Boroughbridge and executed at Pontefract in the king's presence.

**Thomas of Woodstock** *See* GLOUCE-STER, THOMAS, DUKE OF.

**Thomson, J. J.** (1856–1940). Discoverer of the electron. After study in Manchester, Thomson gained a scholarship to Trinity College, Cambridge. In 1884 he became Cavendish professor, working on electricity and gases. Michael *Faraday had thought that the rays coming from the negative pole, or cathode, were charged particles, but with Wilhelm Röntgen's discovery of X-rays, most Germans supposed that cathode rays were similar, radiation akin to light. Thomson devised an experiment in which the rays were deflected by a magnetic field, and then deflected back again by an electric field. This proved they were negatively charged particles, or *corpuscles* as he called them following Robert *Boyle. Thomson was master of Trinity College, Cambridge, from 1918 to his death.

**Thorfinn, earl of Orkney** (*c.*1009–*c.*1065). It is clear that 'Thorfinn the Mighty' wielded great power. He succeeded his father Sigurd as earl of Orkney when a small boy in 1014. He was a grandson of *Malcolm II of Scotland. He fought against *Duncan I, his cousin, and may have divided the kingdom with *Macbeth. They certainly defeated and killed Duncan, and seem to have stayed in harmony until Macbeth's own death at *Lumphanan: it is said that they visited Rome together.

**Thorpe, Jeremy** (b.1929). Politician. One of the more colourful politicians of his day, Thorpe was educated at Eton and Trinity College, Oxford. Elected to Parliament in 1959 for North Devon as a Liberal, he became leader of the party in succession to Jo Grimond in 1967. He survived a disastrous election result in 1970 when the Liberals were reduced to six seats but was brought down in 1976 by bizarre accusations about his relationship with a male model. Thorpe was acquitted of attempted murder in 1978 but lost his seat in Parliament. His later years have been dogged by illness.

**Three Choirs Festival** An annual festival, originally termed 'Music Meeting', based in turn on the cathedrals of Gloucester, Hereford, and Worcester. The festival was inaugurated around 1716 in aid of charity and its early years were increasingly devoted to the music of *Handel.

**Throckmorton plot,** 1583. This was one of many conspiracies to free Mary, queen of Scots, and put her on the throne in place of

Elizabeth. Francis Throckmorton was son of Sir John Throckmorton, chief justice of Chester, disgraced in 1579. Francis Throckmorton, a catholic, spent the early 1580s on the continent and in 1583 was acting as go-between for Mary and Mendoza, the Spanish ambassador in London. When he was arrested a list of catholic conspirators and details of possible invasion ports were found. Throckmorton confessed under torture and was executed at Tyburn in July 1584.

**Thurloe, John** (1616–68). The son of an Essex clergyman, Thurloe was a lawyer under the patronage of Oliver St John. He did not take up arms in the Civil War, but in 1652 was appointed secretary to the *Council of State and was soon put in charge of Commonwealth intelligence gathering. He was an MP 1654 and 1656 and a member of *Cromwell's second council. Remarkably efficient, devoted to Cromwell, Thurloe presided over an international espionage network. After the fall of Richard Cromwell, he was reappointed secretary of state and tried to dissuade *Monck from bringing back Charles II.

**Thurlow, Edward, 1st Baron Thurlow** (1731–1806). A distinguished lawyer who appeared with success in several important constitutional cases. He was solicitor-general 1770, attorney-general 1771–8, and became lord chancellor as Baron Thurlow in 1778. He was a formidable presence on the woolsack and dominated the House of Lords. Except during Fox's ministry of 1783 he remained lord chancellor until 1792, but he alienated *Pitt by intriguing with the prince of Wales during the *Regency crisis of 1788–9.

**Thurstan** (d. 1140). Archbishop of York. Born in Bayeux, Thurstan was secretary to Henry I. As part of the unending dispute between Canterbury and York he refused consecration in 1114 by the archbishop of Canterbury and was eventually consecrated at Rheims (1119), receiving the pallium from Pope Calixtus II. He vigorously championed the independence of York from Canterbury; the pope decided in York's favour (1126), though Canterbury with legatine authority could still claim obedience. He organized and inspired Yorkshire forces against David I of Scotland's invasion and defeated him at

the battle of the *Standard (1138). He became a Cluniac before dying at Pontefract abbey.

**Tien-Tsin, treaty of,** 1858. The second Opium War began in October 1856 when the Chinese authorities at Canton seized the British-registered *Arrow*. In June 1856 at Tien-Tsin, the Chinese agreed to receive a British diplomat at Peking, open up more treaty ports, pay an indemnity, and legalize the opium trade. A punitive expedition to Peking in 1860 forced the confirmation of the terms, and Kowloon, opposite Hong Kong, was ceded in perpetuity.

**Tierney, George** (1761–1830). Whig politician, MP 1790 and 1796–1830. An early devotee of democratic principles, nicknamed 'Citizen Tierney', he joined the Association of the *Friends of the People and helped to draw up their report criticizing the state of the representative system 1792–3. After 1801 he advocated co-operation between the Whigs and *Addington, and joined Addington's government in 1803 as treasurer of the navy. An intimate of the prince of Wales, he served as president of the India Board in the '*Talents' ministry of 1806–7. Returning afterwards to opposition, Tierney acted as chief whip to the Whigs under Grey and in 1817 was elected their leader in the Commons. He accepted office in *Canning's cabinet as master of the mint but failed to persuade *Grey to join the government.

**Tillett, Ben** (1860–1943). Trade unionist. A Bristol man, Tillett spent his early years in the navy and merchant marine. Coming to the London docks he was shocked at the misery and poverty of casual labour and organized a docker's union. The great dockers' strike of 1889, for a basic wage of 6 pence an hour, was a sensation, and succeeded, partly through the mediation of Cardinal *Manning. He continued to build up dockers' and transport organizations, which came together in 1922 to form the Transport and General Workers' Union. Tillett served in Parliament for North Salford 1917–24 and 1929–31, and was chairman of the TUC 1928/9.

**Tillotson, John** (1630–94). Archbishop of Canterbury. As a graduate and fellow (1651) of Clare Hall, Cambridge, Calvinistic writings impressed Tillotson. Charles II, who admired his preaching, appointed him royal chaplain and dean of Canterbury (1672). With *Baxter he supported comprehension of nonconformists (1674–5). Favoured by William III (1689), he became dean of St Paul's (1689) and was nominated by the Canterbury chapter to exercise archiepiscopal authority during *Sancroft's suspension, reluctantly accepting the see of Canterbury (1691) on Sancroft's deprivation.

**Times, The** This newspaper has come to represent the 'establishment' of Britain and British journalism in popular perception. Founded in 1785 as the *Daily Universal Register*, it adopted its current title three years later, and its masthead symbol of the clock in 1804. After its late 19th-cent. decline, *The Times* was bought and revived by *Harmsworth in 1908, since when it has belonged to Lord Astor, Lord Thomson, and currently Rupert Murdoch.

**Tinchebrai, battle of,** 1106. Henry I and his elder brother *Robert of Normandy had been in contention over the succession to England and Normandy since 1100, when William II 'Rufus' died. In 1106 Henry sought to settle the issue. Whilst besieging Tinchebrai castle (south-west Normandy), Henry was challenged by Robert, who had decided to risk battle. The battle, fought on 28 September 1106, lasted barely an hour and settled the political issue once and for all. Robert's army was destroyed and he himself was taken to England, where he was imprisoned for the rest of his life.

**Tindal, Matthew** (1655–1733). One of the leading deists of the early 18th cent., Tindal came from Devon and attended Lincoln College, Oxford. In 1678 he obtained a fellowship at All Souls. His most celebrated work came out in 1730. In *Christianity as Old as Creation*, Tindal argued the case for natural religion. Though frequently accused of freethinking, he retained his fellowship at All Souls until his death.

**tin-mining** was undertaken in Cornwall and Devon in prehistoric times and continued into the 20th cent. Early mines exploited alluvial deposits near the surface but by the 16th cent. underground working following veins of ore had become the norm.

Flood waters limited access to some tin deposits and deeper mining only became practicable during the 18th cent. when *Newcomen beam-engines made it possible to pump water from the workings. Cornish production supplied most of the needs of Britain and Europe until the mid-19th cent. when many mines were worked out.

**Tintern** (Gwent) a *Cistercian abbey, was founded in 1131 by Richard de Clare, lord of Chepstow, and was the first Cistercian community in Wales. Like most Cistercian abbeys, Tintern's economy declined during the late Middle Ages, and the number of monks fell. The surviving remains acquired fame from *Wordsworth's poem, and are amongst the finest of any Cistercian abbey in Europe.

**Tippermuir, battle of,** 1644. Fought on 1 September 1644, this was the first in *Montrose's great run of victories. Outnumbered by more than two to one, he routed Lord Elcho's poorly trained troops just outside Perth, and went on to occupy the city.

**Tippett, Sir Michael** (1905–1998). Composer. Of Cornish stock, hence his Celtic temperament, Tippett studied at the Royal School of Music. Disillusioned by the realities of the First World War, he turned to socialism, then pacifism (a conscientious objector in the Second World War, briefly imprisoned 1943). Tippett's own music was initially conservative, but he soon developed a strongly personal idiom based on complex rhythms and long lyrical phrases; to symphonies and chamber music were added oratorio (*A Child of Our Time*, 1941) and operas with his own librettos (*The Midsummer Marriage, King Priam, The Knot Garden*).

**Tiptoft, John, 1st earl of Worcester** (*c.*1427–70). Unusually for a peer's heir, Tiptoft spent three years with a tutor in University College, Oxford. He was treasurer of England from 1452 to 1454, and probably became a sympathizer with Richard of *York. In 1458 he distanced himself by going to Jerusalem, afterwards touring Italy and studying at Padua until 1461. Edward IV appointed him a councillor and constable of England, when he became notorious for his trials of traitors. He was captured when *Warwick restored Henry VI, and executed.

**Tironensians** Founded by St Bernard of Tiron (*c*.1046–1117), a former Benedictine monk of Poitiers, who became a hermit at Tiron (near Chartres), this Benedictine congregation was one of several ascetic communities established in the early 12th cent., of which the *Cistercians were the most successful.

*Titanic* The largest passenger liner afloat, until the early morning of 15 April 1912, on its maiden transatlantic voyage, when it struck an iceberg and sank. Altogether 1,513 died, out of a total complement of 2,224. The ship's band famously continued playing on the sloping deck as she sank, ending its selection with 'Nearer, my God, to thee'. The *Titanic* became a national symbol for both hubris and courage.

**tithe** The payment, originally in kind, of a tenth of the produce of land was at first a voluntary religious duty for the benefit of the poor, pilgrims, and churches, but by the 10th cent. it was compulsory. When lords built private churches on their land, tithe soon went to the lord's family with only a portion to the priest. With the spread of protestant nonconformity in the 17th cent., the payment of tithe became extremely contentious. Resentment of tithe was still a factor in the *Swing riots of 1830 and the *Rebecca riots in south Wales in 1842–3. By the Tithe Commutation Act (1836) all tithe was commuted to rent-charges.

**Tobruk, battle of,** 1941. The Libyan port of Tobruk, 50 miles from the Egyptian frontier, was captured from the Italians by British forces on 22 January 1941. Axis forces under Rommel subsequently defeated the British, but it was decided to hold Tobruk. The siege of Tobruk began on 10 April 1941, and the port was relieved by the British on 10 December 1941. Tobruk was subsequently captured by Rommel on 21 June 1942 and finally retaken by the British following the battle of *El Alamein in November 1942.

**Toleration Act,** 1689. Though the Act did not grant whole-hearted toleration, it has been hailed as 'the grand landmark...in the history of dissent', since it legally sanctioned schism. Those unable to accept Anglican liturgy could worship in *unlocked* meeting-houses, licensed by the bishop, provided that the minister subscribed to the Thirty-Nine Articles except on baptism and church government. Catholics and unitarians were excluded.

**Tolpuddle martyrs** In 1834 six agricultural labourers from the village of Tolpuddle in Dorset, who formed a trade union lodge, were sentenced to seven years' transportation under an Act of 1797 forbidding 'unlawful oaths'. Although unions were no longer illegal after the repeal of the *Combination Acts, the government feared rural unrest, including rick-burning and machine-breaking. The harsh sentence provoked a campaign of petitions and mass demonstrations. Two years later the six were pardoned. In 1838 they returned home, but five of them later emigrated to Canada.

**Tone, Wolfe** (1763–98). Irish patriot. Tone was born into a middle-class protestant family in Dublin, educated at Trinity College, Dublin, and later trained as a lawyer. He was an eloquent advocate of catholic relief, and assistant secretary to the Catholic Committee (1792). He was involved with the foundation, in 1791, of the United Irish Society, a constitutional radical organization. However, his politics grew more militant, and in 1794–5 he was implicated in the trial, for treason, of a French agent, William Jackson. After a brief exile in the USA (August–December 1795), Tone served as United Irish emissary in France (1796–8), seeking French military assistance for the Irish republican cause. He was involved with two abortive French expeditions (in 1796 and 1798), being captured in October 1798. Convicted of treason, he committed suicide rather than suffer a public hanging.

**Tonga** is a group of volcanic islands, forming an independent kingdom within the Commonwealth. It lies east of Fiji. Cook, who visited several islands on his second and third voyage in the 1770s, called them the Friendly Islands.

**tonnage and poundage** were customs duties which Parliament granted to Tudor monarchs for life. However, the crown's resort to *impositions led the first Parliament of Charles I to refrain from making the customary lifetime grant. The king reacted by ordering the collection of the duties on an *ad hoc* basis until such time as Parliament granted them. Parliament refused to do so, however, and the 1629 session concluded in uproar with the passing of a resolution against the collection of tonnage and poundage, framed by Sir John *Eliot. Only in 1641 did the *Long Parliament at last grant the duties, but for a limited period declaring that the earlier prerogative levies were illegal.

**Torres Vedras** The lines of Torres Vedras were a system of defensive fortifications constructed by *Wellington's engineers in 1809, and were situated 40 miles north of Lisbon to protect the city from French attack during the Peninsular War. Wellington fell back on the lines in October 1810 and held Masséna's French army at bay.

**Torrington, battle of,** 1646. By 1646, after the heavy defeats at *Naseby, *Langport, and *Philiphaugh, the Civil War had become largely a mopping-up operation. *Hopton took over the remnants of *Goring's army in the south-west, numbering some 3,000 men. At Torrington in north Devon, he was attacked on 16 February by Sir Thomas *Fairfax's much larger force, was wounded, and forced back into Cornwall, where he surrendered the following month.

**torture** In his important work *De laudibus legum Angliae*, Chief Justice Fortescue (*c*.1385–1477/9) describes torture as being foreign to English law, which he praised in comparison with the civil law of the European continent. However, although not used by the common law courts, it was used by the *council when investigating offences, particularly in the reigns of Henry VIII and Elizabeth I. Torture was permitted under Scottish law, but was abolished after the Union by 7 Anne c. 21 s. 5 (1708).

**Tories** The Tories were one of the two main political parties between the later 17th and mid-19th cents. The term Tory (from *toraighe*, Irish for bandit or bog-trotter) was first applied by the Whigs to the court supporters of James, duke of York, during the *Exclusion crisis, 1679–81. Their notions of God-ordained kingly authority, 'divine right',

entailed a deep attachment to the Anglican church. James II's catholicism forced them into choosing between their king and their church, and though most chose the latter, many were still unwilling to regard William III as rightful king. The Tories were more at ease under Queen Anne (1702–14), whom they regarded as a legitimate successor of James II. But despite their electoral popularity, they were frequently split ministerially and in Parliament over war strategy, the persecution of dissenters, and the Hanoverian succession.

The adherence of some die-hard Tories to the *Jacobite cause after George I's accession in 1714 allowed the Whigs to discredit all Tories as disloyal and dangerous, and until the 1760s they were kept out of government office. As a result of George III's ending of proscription during the early 1760s, the Tories went their different ways. Tory values, however, continued to have an important place in political argument, featuring significantly in the debates on America and in the 'conservative reaction' towards the end of the century. Under the impact of the French Revolution, the younger *Pitt's ministry was frequently derided by the Foxite opposition as 'Tory'. Out of the factionalism of the early 19th cent. gradually emerged the Toryism of *Liverpool and *Peel, the latter credited with the ideology of Conservatism.

**Tostig, earl of Northumbria** (*c*.1025–66), younger brother of *Harold, who was briefly, in 1066, king of England. With Tostig's appointment to Northumbria, his family seemed set to dominate the English kingdom. But he was driven out by a local rebellion in 1065. He blamed Harold for not attempting to secure his reinstatement, and in exile raised a force which raided the English coast. Achieving little, he joined the army led by *Harold Hardrada, king of Norway, and was killed at the battle of *Stamford Bridge.

**touching for the king's evil** was an instant medieval royal tradition. On learning that their rivals the Capetian kings of France claimed divine healing powers, the kings of England, from Henry I onwards, followed suit. Curiously it was only scrofula that could be cured. The ceremony developed into a very formal one. The Hanoverians gave it up,

t

though in France Charles X was still stroking when removed by revolution in 1830.

**Toulouse, battle of,** 1814. On 10 April 1814 *Wellington launched an assault against the city, losing 5,000 men. However, after fierce fighting, Marshal Soult and the French were driven out with the loss of 3,000 men. The victory came hours before Napoleon's abdication in Paris.

**tournaments** By the later Middle Ages, the term tournament covered all kinds of armed combat, both team and individual, performed competitively in public. Tournaments were essentially sporting and social occasions rather than a means of developing skills for war. It was possible for young men of relatively low status to make a mark through their prowess, but in general the participants were already of noble or at least knightly birth. Moreover, it was an expensive activity, requiring increasingly sophisticated equipment, not only for show and identification, but also for protection because the combats were often exceedingly dangerous.

**Tours, truce of,** 1444. With the struggle in France moving against them in the 1440s, the English wished to use a marriage negotiation for Henry VI to obtain a settlement. At Tours in May 1444, Suffolk (William de la Pole) promised to surrender Maine in exchange for a two-year truce and Henry was betrothed to *Margaret of Anjou, niece of Charles VII of France. The break in hostilities lasted only until 1449 when Charles attacked Normandy.

**Tower of London (White Tower).** Built by William the Conqueror within the southeast corner of the old Roman walls of London as one of three fortresses intended to secure the city. As London became increasingly important as the centre both of government and of commerce, the castle was enlarged and updated by successive kings, especially by Edward I and Edward III, until it became a complex concentric fortification.

Even in the later Middle Ages the kings had preferred to reside when in London at their palace at *Westminster. Traditionally, however, the new sovereign spent the night in the Tower before his coronation, going in procession to Westminster for the ceremony.

The last king to make this procession was Charles II. The Tower has gradually been stripped of most of its other functions. It is still a royal castle, houses the crown jewels, and retains a small military presence but its other offices have been relocated. The historic collection of weapons in the armouries is all that remains of the arsenal, moved to Woolwich after 1841, and to Leeds in 1995.

**towns** Though there were large settlements in Iron Age Britain, true urbanism began with the Roman occupation of southern Britain. Leading Romano-British towns included a strikingly high proportion of those towns which topped urban league tables until the industrial revolution—*London, *Lincoln, *York, *Winchester, and *Canterbury.

Some Roman towns may have continued, under native leadership and invading Anglo-Saxons, as 'central places', but true town life seems to have revived in the 7th and 8th cents. Large trading towns (wics or *emporia*) developed both alongside old Roman fortified sites (London, York, and *Southampton) and in at least one case on a new, non-Roman site (*Ipswich). Meanwhile small towns developed inland around royal and ecclesiastical centres, especially after the foundation of cathedrals and major churches. Under the kings of united England (954–1066) existing towns flourished and new towns were founded.

The Normans after 1066 further developed towns in England and also in south Wales, many of them protected by a castle. A developing commercial economy in the 12th and 13th cents. led to the expansion of many towns and the creation of many new ones. Large towns acquired communal defences and chartered privileges, and London rapidly acquired a unique status as a capital city and the only British town comparable to the great continental towns. The *Black Death of 1348–50 killed a high proportion of townspeople, and some historians have seen it as ushering in a period of late medieval urban decay. However, there is much evidence that many towns, though reduced in size, flourished.

The 16th and 17th cents. saw some recovery in the size of towns, since although their mortality rates were high, they attracted large numbers of immigrants. The most outstanding case was that of London, becoming by 1700 the largest town in western Europe.

In the 18th cent., however, industrial and commercial development, including better communications, allowed many other towns to grow rapidly. This huge urban growth disrupted old institutions and attitudes and led to the municipal reforms from the 1830s onwards.

In the 19th and 20th cents. towns continued to grow in relative as well as absolute terms, and nearly all British people have come to share an essentially urban culture, whether or not they live in towns. The total urban population of England and Wales reached 54 per cent by 1851, and 81 per cent by 1951 (for Scotland similar calculations give 52 per cent by 1851 and 65 per cent by 1891).

**Townshend, Charles** (1725–67). Townshend dashed across the political sky in the 1760s like a comet, blazed, and was gone. A grandson of 'Turnip' *Townshend, he was returned to Parliament for Great Yarmouth when he was 21 and held a variety of junior posts in the 1750s and early 1760s. In 1766 he became chancellor of the Exchequer in Chatham's (*Pitt) ministry. In May 1767 he pledged himself to raise a revenue in America by the imposition of a range of duties. Having lit the fuse for an American time-bomb, he died in September 1767 at the age of 42.

**Townshend, Charles Townshend, 2nd Viscount** (1674–1738). Townshend succeeded to his peerage in 1687. He became a Whig, specializing in foreign affairs. In 1713 he married Robert *Walpole's sister and the following year became secretary of state for the northern department. Shifted to the less powerful post of lord-lieutenant of Ireland in 1717, he resigned from the government along with Walpole and remained in opposition during the Whig schism until 1720 when he became lord president of the council, returning to the northern department the following year. From 1722 he and Walpole ran the administration. Disagreement over foreign policy led to his resignation from the ministry in 1730. In retirement he devoted himself to agriculture on his estate at Rainham, and has come down to posterity as 'Turnip Townshend'.

**Townshend, George** (1724–1807). George Townshend, elder brother of *Charles, had a distinguished military and political career. He was second in command to *Wolfe in Canada and took over when Wolfe was killed. He succeeded as viscount in 1764 and from 1767 to 1772 was lord-lieutenant of Ireland. On his return, he was master of the ordnance throughout the rest of North's ministry and held the post again in 1783 under the coalition. He was out of office after 1784, though he was promoted field marshal in 1796.

**townswomen's guilds,** emerging out of the women's suffrage movement and modelled on the remarkably successful rural *women's institutes, were founded in 1928 with a programme of 'comradeship, arts and crafts and citizenship' for the urban ordinary housewife. Membership began to fall in the 1970s as structural rigidity came under challenge and younger women failed to come forward. Learning how to serve had begun to yield to women's changing aspirations and increasing economic emancipation. Nevertheless the Guild is capable of expressing its opinions with some vigour.

**Towton, battle of,** 1461. Towton is unique among British battles for being fought in a blinding snowstorm. Edward IV, the 19-year-old Yorkist claimant in the Wars of the *Roses, was proclaimed king in London early in March 1461 and pursued his adversaries north. Queen *Margaret and her hapless husband Henry VI were at York. The armies clashed at Ferrybridge on 28 March and did battle the following day at Towton, near Tadcaster. The slaughter was great and the Lancastrians routed.

**tractarianism** was the name applied to the first stage of the *Oxford movement, derived from a series of *Tracts for the Times* written between 1833 and 1841 by a group of Oxford high churchmen, including Hurrell Froude, *Keble, *Newman, *Pusey, and Isaac Williams. Their context, signalled by Keble's Oxford assize sermon on 'National Apostasy' (14 July 1833), was alarm at the onslaught of Roman catholicism, dissent, and 'liberalism'. The furore provoked by Newman's Tract 90, on the Thirty-Nine Articles, ended the series but their influence set the Anglican pace for the rest of the century.

**trade** One of the reasons for trade is specialization of production. Some examples are obvious. European countries are not very successful in growing bananas. Similarly, the distribution of natural resources like coal, iron ore, and oil has always been unequal. Each country specializes in producing those commodities in which it has a comparative advantage. Specialization allows economies of scale because it is more efficient to produce for a large world market than for a much smaller national market. Trade is thus a benefit to all parties, irrespective of whether trade is fair or a country is competitive.

But the fact that trade is universally advantageous does not mean that the benefits are equally distributed. The impact of imperial free trade policies on 19th-cent. India boosted the export of raw cotton to Britain but had a devastating impact on Indian cotton manufactures. Variations in natural resources, in which some countries are rich (Russia) and some relatively very poor (Japan), and in technology, barriers to trade, and historical experience of development have maintained and augmented these differences.

There is little doubt that international trade and specialized production played a major part in the growth of the industrial economies in the 18th and especially the 19th cent. But the less developed countries have argued that trade has not been beneficial for them since they have been peripheral to those with greater comparative advantage. Indeed it has become a criticism of the free market system that it prospered through the exploitation of the less developed countries by the industrial nations. Hence the support for import substitution policies and attempts to persuade the developed world to help by allowing trade on terms favourable to the less developed.

**Trade, Board of** The origins of the department may be traced back to 1621 when, in the face of a trade recession, a number of committees were appointed, under the guidance of *Cranfield, to consider the matter. At the Restoration, Charles II appointed separate councils for trade and for plantations. In 1696 when the problem of coinage was again giving trouble, a permanent Board of Trade and Plantations was set up, with eight core

members. The business of the board was primarily colonial administration and policy. In 1782 the board fell victim to the *economical reform of the Rockinghams. Pressure of business soon demanded a replacement. As early as March 1784 *Pitt's government appointed a new committee, upgraded in 1786 to a board, with Jenkinson as president and given a peerage as Lord *Liverpool. As economic growth became a major consideration, the prestige of the department rose and politicians of the calibre of *Gladstone, Joseph *Chamberlain, *Churchill, *Lloyd George, *Cripps, and *Wilson took it on.

**Trades Disputes Act,** 1906. The Liberal government introduced a bill based on the recommendations of the royal commission (1903). Labour MPs were not satisfied with the government's bill and introduced a private member's bill. The Labour bill was accepted by the Liberals and formed the basis of the Trades Disputes Act. This indemnified unions against civil proceedings; their funds were protected against claims for damages, thus discounting the *Taff Vale judgment (1902). This very privileged position survived until 1927.

**Trades Union Congress** At an early stage of trade union development the idea of a co-ordinating body emerged and in 1834 the *Grand National Consolidated Trade Union was founded. It attracted many members but few funds, and the secretary absconded with what there were. But during the next three decades there was a substantial growth of trade union membership, particularly in the skilled trades. In 1868 a meeting of 34 delegates in Manchester resolved that annual meetings were desirable. The new organization set up a parliamentary committee in 1871 to lobby on legislation. In 1900 a Labour Representation Committee was established—the forerunner of the *Labour Party in 1906. The Scottish TUC was founded in 1897.

**Trade Union Act,** 1871. Passed by *Gladstone's administration following the recommendations of the Royal Commission on Trade Societies (1867), the Act clarified the legality of trade unions and provided for their funds to be protected under the Friendly Society Act 1855. *Disraeli's government legalized peaceful picketing in 1875 (Conspiracy and Protection of Property Act).

**trade unions,** retaining some of the benefit functions of the old craft guilds, emerged in the 18th cent. as conflicts between capital and labour increased and state protection collapsed before the rise of the *factory system. Fear of revolution led to the *combination laws of 1799–1800; this legislation was ineffective, forcing unions underground. Eventually, unions were given legal recognition under the Act of 1825. Most unions were local, small, and based on public houses or 'houses of call'.

Owenite utopianism stimulated the rise of general unions. Older unionism existed alongside attempts to found a *Grand National Consolidated Trade Union; when this grandiose organization collapsed in 1834–5, continuity was maintained by 'the aristocracy of labour'. After the depression of the early 1840s national unions of skilled trades either revived or were founded. Trades councils were created by unions; from the London Trades Council emerged the *Trades Union Congress (1868).

Membership of unions rose from about 750,000 in 1888 to over 4 million by 1913. Individual unions increased in size. Industrial strife was widespread in the years before 1914, provoked by falling living standards and a growing radicalism associated with *syndicalist ideas. The Triple Alliance of transport workers, miners, and railwaymen was in existence by 1914, with a strategy of sympathy strikes in place. Thus the ground was drawn for the sharp class conflicts of the 1920s including the *General Strike of 1926. Trade union membership declined during the Great Slump, only reviving in the late 1930s.

During the Second World War (1939–45) trade union membership increased from about 6,250,000 in 1939 to nearly 8 million in 1945. By 1979 there were about 13,500,000 members or 58 per cent of those in work. After 1979 trade union membership fell to under 10,250,000 by 1988 or 37.6 per cent of the labour force. Hostile legislation designed to remove union power was a feature of the policies of *Thatcherite Conservatism. Plant bargaining began to replace national negotiations. A significant change was the Labour Party's distancing itself from the

union movement, with which it had been closely associated since its birth.

**Trafalgar, battle of,** 1805. Fought on 21 October 1805, south of Cadiz and south-west of the shoaling Cape Trafalgar, this most famous of engagements in the era of sail lasted from midday to about 5 p.m. In the course of it, 18 of the 33-strong combined fleet of France and Spain surrendered to the British under the command of Lord *Nelson, supported by Cuthbert *Collingwood heading the fleet's southerly (lee) division, and Lord Northesk, in the rear of Nelson's northerly (weather) division, which he himself headed in *Victory. Villeneuve's disposition of his ships was fatally confused, though their often inexperienced crews fought with great bravery. The British engaged 'pell mell' at the closest quarters without losing a ship, Nelson's exhortation to 'every man to do his duty' being echoed by rates of fire which no other fleet of the day could approach. Nelson's victory, for which he gave his life, removed all possibility of Napoleon launching an invasion of Britain.

**trained bands** were the county- and city-based militia regiments, which, except for London and a few counties, played little significant part in the civil wars. The London regiments played a critical role at *Turnham Green, the siege of Gloucester, and the first battle of *Newbury. Increasingly unwilling to leave London, they saw their role taken over by permanent standing armies in 1643 and 1644.

**transportation** was a form of punishment devised in England to exile convicted criminals to the American colonies from c.1650 and after the War of Independence to Australia between 1788 and 1868, when it was abolished. The system arose out of England's lack of state-organized prisons and the overcrowding of what few prisons there were, including converted warships (hulks) anchored in the river Thames. It is estimated that some 210,000 convicts were exiled between 1650 and 1868; 50,000 to the American colonies, the remainder to Australia.

**Transvaal** Founded as an independent republic by Boers (Afrikaners) fleeing British rule in the mid-19th cent., the Transvaal was annexed by Britain in 1877 but regained its internal autonomy in 1881. The discovery of immense reserves of gold in the years which followed led to an influx of foreign, predominantly British, miners whose treatment by the Boer government was used by the British government as the pretext for demands which the Boers rejected, and which culminated in war in 1899. The Transvaal was again annexed by Britain and became part of the Union of South Africa in 1910.

**treason** For centuries the evolution of the law of treason was to extend the number of offences and the ferocity of the punishment. High treason was a crime against the state which meant, in practice, against the monarch. *Alfred's law declared that a man's life and property were forfeit if he plotted against the king. Edward I set the precedent for hideous punishments when *Dafydd ap Gruffydd at Shrewsbury in 1283 was drawn to the gallows on a sledge, hanged, cut down while alive, disembowelled, and his head and limbs exhibited in different towns. Edward III's statute of 1352, which became the basic definition, made it treason to encompass the death of the king, or to violate the queen, the king's eldest daughter (if unmarried), or the king's eldest son's wife. After the *Peasants' Revolt in 1381 it was made treasonable to start a riot, Henry V made it treason to clip the coinage, and Henry VI to extort money by threatening to burn down a house. The scope of treason was widened still further by 'constructive treason', which allowed judges to 'interpret' the Act of 1352. The Tudors added more than 60 treason statutes. Henry VIII made it treason to deny his royal supremacy, or to refuse to admit it, and each of his marriages, separations, or divorces was buttressed by a fresh treason law. His daughter Elizabeth made it treason to declare her a heretic or usurper.

Mitigating legislation was slow in making its appearance. An Act of 1695 allowed the defendant counsel, a copy of the indictment five days before the trial, and declared that two direct witnesses were necessary. In 1814 *Romilly succeeded in carrying an Act not to cut traitors down still alive and disembowel them, though the Lords insisted that they should still be quartered.

**treasurer** The official who guarded the Norman treasure at Winchester in the reign of William I seems to have been more of a custodian than a minister or counsellor. The modern office has been traced back to the reign of Henry I, c.1126, and quickly established itself as of major importance. The title lord treasurer, or lord high treasurer, came into use in the Tudor period. But from 1612 the practice grew up of putting the Treasury into commission and the last lord high treasurer was Lord *Rochester 1679–84. That opened the way for the 1st lord of the Treasury to become the head of government or first minister. As the demands on the prime minister increased and financial questions became more complex, the office of *chancellor of the Exchequer rose in importance.

**Treasury** The Treasury has its antecedents far back in time as all governments have faced the need to secure revenues to finance expenditure. But the recognizably modern Treasury has its principal roots in the late 17th and early 18th cents. Its emergence as a major organ of state was precipitated by a fairly sudden and large increase in government spending. Prior to the 20th cent. such an increase was invariably the result of military involvement. (*See* NATIONAL DEBT.) The increase in expenditure produced a proliferation of stratagems to pay for it. One means was, of course, new taxation, which was imposed on salt, stamps, hackney coaches, and, especially, on land. New customs and excise duties were introduced and there were increases in those already in operation. Such an expansion in taxation required a bureaucracy to organize the operation of the revenue system and this, in turn, needed to be managed. This became the task of the Treasury. The Exchequer and Audit Department Act of 1866 established the practice of consolidating the annual tax proposals into a single Finance Bill. This created the first effective machinery for a retrospective annual audit of government spending, and effectively established the Treasury as custodian of financial propriety. This perception was reinforced by two major concerns of 19th-cent. policy, elimination of the national debt and the preservation of *free trade, both of which required tight fiscal control.

As government involvement in economic affairs increased in the 20th cent. so the role and influence of the Treasury became extremely important. Very often, incumbent administrations have adopted the Treasury view and followed policies consistent with its aims. Its close links with the city of London and its control over the *Bank of England have secured the primacy of financial considerations in economic policy. The other part of the strategy has been control of expenditure, an uphill struggle given massive spending increases in two world wars and the demand-driven government commitments to pay pension, unemployment, and welfare benefits.

**Trenchard, Hugh, 1st Viscount Trenchard** (1873–1956). Soldier and airman. 'Boom' Trenchard began his service career as an infantryman. By 1912, when he learned to fly, he was a major whose career appeared to be going nowhere. But by 1915 he was a major-general in command of the *Royal Flying Corps in France. When the *Royal Air Force was established as the world's first independent air force in 1918, Trenchard became its first professional head as chief of air staff, a post he held with only a brief interruption until 1929.

**Trent, battle on the,** 679. *Æthelred, king of Mercia, defeated *Ecgfrith, king of Northumbria, and regained authority over *Lindsey. Bede relates a miracle story about Imma, a Northumbrian noble captured by the Mercians. It shows that it was normal for captured nobles to be killed, and that lesser captives were sold to a Frisian slave merchant, who took them, chained, to London for export.

**Trent case,** 1861. In November 1861, soon after the start of the American Civil War, a Federal warship, the *San Jacinto*, stopped the British packet *Trent* and took off two Confederate envoys, Mason and Slidell. *Palmerston suspended export of arms to the North and sent reinforcements to Canada. War seemed likely but the prince consort, a dying man, softened the cabinet's protest. The Federal government apologized, disavowed the captain, and liberated the envoys.

**Trenton, battle of,** 1776. *Washington's attack upon Trenton in New Jersey gave a welcome victory after the loss of New York in September 1776. Early in the morning of Christmas Day, the Americans attacked the Hessian garrison under the command of

Colonel Rall. Nearly 1,000 Hessians were taken prisoner and their commander killed.

**Trevithick, Richard** (1771–1833). Cornish engineer and inventor. A mine engineer from 1790 before erecting his first engine at Ding Dong (1795), he developed high-pressure, non-condensing engines from 1797 to patent both in 1802. His attainments include demonstrating the first practical steam carriage at Camborne (1801) and locomotive at Penydarran (1804); a hydraulic engine and plunger pump for mines (1798); a steam barge (1805); iron storage tanks and iron ships (1808–9); a near-complete Thames tunnel (1809); a Cornish boiler and engine (1812); a portable agricultural engine (1812); a screw propeller (1815); and a tubular boiler (1816). Bankrupt in 1811, mining ventures led him to South America, 1816–27. He died the employee of a Kentish foundry.

**trial by battle** Before the Norman Conquest, guilt or innocence in legal disputes were decided by *compurgation, where a party would summon a number of 'oath helpers' to swear to the reliability of his oath, or especially in cases of 'criminal' accusation by one of the ordeals, fire, cold water, hot water, or accursed morsel (*see* TRIAL BY ORDEAL). To these methods the Normans, with their strong militaristic tradition, added trial by battle. The parties, or champions on their behalf, would fight in formal single combat and the winner would be deemed to be the successful party in the case. It was not abolished until 1819, after the accused was challenged to combat in the case of *Ashford* v. *Thornton*.

**trial by ordeal** was used to decide the guilt or innocence of a suspected criminal by invoking divine justice. There were several forms of ordeal in Anglo-Saxon and Norman England. In one the accused held a red hot iron or put his hand in a flame. If the wound healed, the accused was deemed innocent. In ordeal by cold water, used particularly for villeins, the accused was thrown, bound, into a pond or river. If he sank, he was deemed to be innocent, but if he floated he was regarded as guilty. In ordeal by accursed morsel, the accused was required to eat a piece of meat with a feather or other foreign body in it, and was adjudged guilty if he choked. When in 1215 the Lateran Council of the church forbade clergy to take part in ordeals, they fell into disuse and were eventually replaced by *jury trial.

**Triennial Acts,** 1641, 1664, 1694. These were attempts to curb the prerogatives of the crown in summoning and retaining parliaments. The first, 16 Car. 1 c. 1, passed in February 1641 and committed Charles I to summon a Parliament at least every three years and to keep it for at least 50 days. This was repealed in 1664 and replaced by an Act, 16 Car. II c. 1, declaring that the king should summon Parliament at least every three years but providing no mechanism for enforcing it. Charles II was in breach of the Act from March 1684 and James II from November 1688. The third Act, 6 & 7 Wm. & Mar. c. 2, passed in 1694 after William had vetoed a previous measure. It laid down that Parliament must be summoned within three years of the previous one and could not be retained more than three years. The first provision was rendered nugatory by financial demands that necessitated annual sessions; the second was abrogated by the *Septennial Act of 1716.

**Trimble, David** (b. 1944). Politician. Educated at Bangor (Northern Ireland), Trimble studied law at Queen's University, Belfast. He was elected to the Westminster Parliament in 1990 for Upper Bann as an *Ulster Unionist and became leader in 1996. He played an important role in securing his party's assent to the Good Friday agreement and, with John Hume of the *SDLP was awarded the Nobel Peace prize in 1998. Trimble served as First Minister in the power-sharing executive but his party was outflanked by the *DUP and Trimble lost his seat in 2005. In 2006 he was made a life peer and joined the Conservative party. He is one of many who have found moderation a slippery slope in Northern Ireland politics.

**trimmer** The term acquired popularity from the publication in 1688 of *Halifax's pamphlet *The Character of a Trimmer*, which appealed for moderation in politics, condemning 'madmen in two extremes [who] agree to make common sense treason'. Why, asked Halifax, do we play the fool by throwing the names Whig and Tory at each other, as boys do snowballs? Since moderation is rarely admired, the term soon acquired a pejorative meaning of waverer or time-server.

**Trinidad** and **Tobago** (neighbouring islands) lie off the coast of Venezuela and form an independent republic within the Commonwealth. Trinidad was discovered by Columbus and colonized by Spain. In 1797 it was captured by Sir Ralph Abercromby and ceded in 1802. Tobago, originally a Dutch colony, was taken from the French in 1793, restored by the treaty of Amiens in 1802, and recaptured in 1803. The islands became independent in 1962.

**Trinity College, Dublin** Founded by charter of Elizabeth I dated 21 December 1591, Trinity was largely modelled on *Cambridge. The period of growth was in the 18th cent. when the lord-lieutenant, the duke of Dorset, entered his son as a student in 1731. The college thenceforth attracted the nobility and gentry and its graduates included *Berkeley, *Burke, *Goldsmith, and *Grattan. Unlike *Oxford and Cambridge at this time, Trinity practised religious toleration.

**Trinovantes** A British tribe and *civitas*. The Trinovantes are the first British tribe to be mentioned by a Roman author, appearing in *Caesar's account of his invasion of 54 BC. Caesar took them under his protection, but eventually they were absorbed by *Cunobelinus, who moved the Catuvellaunian capital to Camulodunum (*Colchester). Thus, at the time of the Claudian conquest, the Trinovantes had no independent existence. But the imposition of a Roman colony on their old tribal centre created resentments which spilled over at the time of the *Boudiccan revolt in AD 60-1. Despite their role in the rebellion, within fifteen years the Trinovantes had been given local self-governing status as a *civitas*. The seat of their government may have been Camulodunum but Chelmsford (Caesaromagus) is also a possibility.

**Triple Alliance 1.** 1668. Alarmed at the growing power of Louis XIV's France, the Dutch and the English formed a defensive alliance in January 1668, which was joined by the Swedes. Louis was obliged to make peace and at Aix-la-Chapelle his gains were modest. He set to work to break the alliance and succeeded in 1670, when Charles II of

England signed the treaty of *Dover at the expense of the Dutch. Louis's great invasion of Holland followed in 1672. **2.** 1717. Soon after the death of Louis XIV in 1715, the Regent d'Orléans of France sought a *rapprochement* with Britain to check the ambitions of Philip V of Spain. An understanding was reached in 1716 to guarantee the succession in France and Britain. By the accession of the Dutch in January 1717 this was converted into a Triple Alliance and when the Emperor Charles VI adhered to it in 1718 it became a *Quadruple Alliance. **3.** 1788. After the War of American Independence, Pitt's government was concerned at Britain's diplomatic isolation. Political instability in Holland in 1786 gave rise to fears of French aggrandizement and in 1787 the Prussian army intervened to suppress the pro-French party. This was followed by a series of treaties in 1788 between Prussia, Britain, and Holland to guarantee each other's territories. **4.** 1882. The adherence of Italy to the Dual Alliance of Germany and Austro-Hungary in 1882 produced the Triple Alliance, which lasted until the outbreak of war in 1914. France, Russia, and Britain responded with the Triple Entente, thus dividing Europe into two armed camps.

**Trojan legend** *See* BRUTUS.

**Trollope, Anthony** (1815–82). Trollope's reputation suffered from the frank admission in his *Autobiography* (1883) that he set out to write 1,000 words an hour, checked by his watch. Many took this as evidence that he was a mere journeyman, a word-spinner. But his stock has risen dramatically and, like *Eliot and *Bennett, he is a historian's novelist, filling in the social background with care. His political novels are greatly admired, but there is something in the criticism that they show the political world with politics left out. He is better at drawing clerics in his Barchester novels—Revd Obadiah Slope in *Barchester Towers* (1857) or Revd Septimus Harding in *The Warden* (1855); Irish plotters in his early novel *The Macdermots of Ballycloran* (1847); civil service rivalry in *The Three Clerks* (1858); or perhaps, most memorably, shady plausible swindlers like Ferdinand Lopez in *The Prime Minister* (1876), or Melmotte in *The Way We Live Now* (1875), a novel that haunts after more than 100 years.

Trollope's life was uneventful—that of a hard-working Post Office official, whose claim to fame was the introduction of pillar boxes in the 1850s.

**Trotskyites** Trotsky's condemnation of Stalinist Russia as a vicious state bureaucracy found considerable support in Britain, but his call for permanent revolution less so. After his murder in 1940, Trotskyism in Britain was disputed between the Revolutionary Socialist League and the Workers' International League, which joined forces in 1944 to form the Revolutionary Communist Party. Later parties sympathetic to his analysis were the Socialist Workers' Party and the Workers' Revolutionary Party, but more influential were supporters of Militant Tendency, who achieved considerable support in the *Labour Party in the early 1980s.

**Troyes, treaty of,** 1420. By this Anglo-French treaty, ratified on 21 May, Henry V became heir and regent to the mad Charles VI of France. After the death of Charles, France and England were to be under one ruler. The dauphin (later Charles VII) was thus disinherited. In fact Henry died first: it was his baby son Henry VI who became king of the 'double monarchy'.

**Troyes, treaty of,** 1564. At her accession in 1558, Elizabeth inherited from Mary a war against France in which *Calais had been lost. By the treaty of *Cateau-Cambrésis (1559), the French promised to restore Calais after eight years or pay a large indemnity. In 1562 Elizabeth was tempted to intervene in the French wars of religion, supporting the Huguenots and taking possession of Le Havre as a pledge for Calais. But the garrison was decimated by disease and Le Havre was forced to surrender. At the treaty of Troyes in April 1564 peace was signed, both sides reserving their rights on Calais which, in effect, meant that it was lost for ever.

**Truro, diocese of** The see, roughly conterminous with Cornwall and the Isles of Scilly, was created in 1877. The cathedral, which dominates the small town, was completed in 1903: the architect was J. L. Pearson and the style Early English neo-Gothic Revival.

**Tuam, archiepiscopal diocese of** Though this Irish see had bishops in the early 12th cent., the Council of Kells-Mellifont (1152) established it as an archbishopric, carved out of Armagh province, with six dioceses in the far west of Ireland. Tuam is still a catholic archbishopric, but in 1839 the Anglican province of Tuam was reunited with Armagh.

**Tudor, house of** This is something of a misnomer. The important descent for Henry VII, who founded the dynasty when he defeated Richard III at *Bosworth, was the direct line from Edward III through *John of Gaunt and the Beaufort dukes of Somerset. The Welsh link, of which Henry and the Welsh made so much, was quite subordinate. Henry V's widow *Catherine de Valois made a private marriage with a minor courtier, Owen *Tudor. Their son Edmund married Margaret *Beaufort, great-granddaughter of Gaunt, thus bringing a second royal link into the equation. The Tudors were in essence a Lancastrian dynasty and the red rose seems to have been one of the badges of the Beauforts.

**Tudor, Jasper, 1st earl of Pembroke and 1st duke of Bedford** (c.1431–95). The second son of Owen *Tudor and *Catherine of Valois, Jasper was created earl of Pembroke in 1452. He was one of the die-hard Lancastrians. Ruling Wales on behalf of Henry VI from 1457, he refused to come to terms with Edward IV after 1461. But after the defeat of the Lancastrians at *Tewkesbury in May 1471, he fled once more, taking with him his 13-year-old nephew Henry Tudor, earl of Richmond (later Henry VII). He remained in exile for fourteen years, returning in triumph in 1485. Thereafter, back in Wales, and promoted duke of Bedford, he remained until his death Henry VII's principal lieutenant in the principality and the marches.

**Tudor, Owen** (c.1400–61). A humble Welsh servant of *Catherine of Valois, widow of Henry V, he secretly married her about 1428. Their first-born Edmund was the father of Henry VII. Tudor's sons were promoted by their half-brother Henry VI. Owen Tudor was a victim of the Wars of the Roses, executed by Edward, earl of March (later Edward IV), at Hereford following the battle of *Mortimer's Cross.

**Tull, Jethro** (1674–1741). Once considered a pioneer of the *agricultural revolution through his invention of the seed drill c.1700 when he was farming near Wallingford. The 'invention' was made famous by his book *The Horse-Hoing Husbandry* published in 1733, but today his role appears less influential.

**Turner, Joseph Mallord William** (1775–1851). British land- and seascape artist. Born in London the son of a barber, Turner was precociously talented. He entered the RA Schools in 1789, had a drawing exhibited at the academy in 1790, and was elected a full academician in 1802. He became professor of perspective in 1807. A prolific artist of amazing range of subject and style, he began work in water-colours, quickly founding both a reputation and a fortune, which made him independent of changing public taste. His work was not appreciated by everyone, but his supporters included Thomas *Lawrence, John *Ruskin, and the earl of Egremont, whose large collection at Petworth (Sussex) now belongs to the National Trust. He died in eccentric obscurity under a false name.

**Turnham Green, battle of,** 1642. Charles I's best hope of winning the Civil War was to bring it to an end before the superior resources of Parliament could be brought to bear. After the indecisive encounter at *Edgehill on 23 October, the king resumed his leisurely march on London. By the time he reached Brentford on 12 November, the remains of *Essex's army had been reinforced by the trained bands, bringing it up to 24,000 men. After some skirmishing, Charles's advance came to a halt the following day at Turnham Green. Outnumbered and unable to use his cavalry, Charles retired to Oxford. He was never again as close to London until he was brought there for his trial in January 1649.

**turnpikes** were a means of financing road maintenance by tolls charged on users, named from the gate used to restrict access. First applied to part of the Great North Road in 1663 on a temporary basis, the principle was employed from 1695 in a series of private Acts to supplant inadequate parish repair under the statute of 1555. Initially administered by justices of the peace, management by trustees was introduced in 1706, and generalized by 1714. 'Turnpike mania' 1750–72 saw the addition of 500 trusts, covering 15,000 miles, and the spread of the system into Wales and Scotland. The benefits were reflected in reduced travel times: Edinburgh, ten days from London by the fastest coach in 1754, was only four days away by 1776, and 40 hours by 1840.

**Turpin, Dick** (1706–39). Highwayman. Dick Turpin became a popular hero and the stuff of legend. He was, in fact, a leader of a gang of Essex ruffians, whose speciality was robbery with violence. He went into partnership with Tom King, whom he accidentally shot in a skirmish. Turpin escaped to York, where he traded in horses, and was hanged on 7 April 1739 for stealing a mare. The story of the celebrated ride to York to establish an alibi was told of John Nevison, or 'Swift Nick', hanged at York in 1685.

**Tuvalu** became independent within the Commonwealth in 1978. It was formerly the Ellice Islands and was part of the Gilbert and Ellice colony. The nine small islands lie some 2,500 miles north-east of Australia.

**Tweeddale, John Hay, 1st marquis of** [S] (1625–97). Hay had been sympathetic to the *covenant and fought against the king at *Marston Moor, but in 1648 supported the Engagement and joined the Scottish army which was defeated at *Preston. He attended Charles II's coronation at Scone in 1651 and succeeded to the earldom in 1653. He then came to terms with the Cromwellian regime. After the Restoration he was a member of the Privy Council [S] 1661–74, dismissed through the influence of *Lauderdale, but reinstated in 1680. He gave strong support to William and the Glorious Revolution and was raised to the marquisate in 1694. From 1692 until 1696 he was lord chancellor [S] and served as commissioner to the 1695 Parliament. In 1696 he was dismissed by William as a scapegoat for England's anger at the *Darien venture.

**Twickenham stadium** (Middx.). The headquarters of the Rugby Football Union. The site was purchased by William Williams in 1907, laid out with stands and provided with a car park. It has since been added to and has a capacity of more than 60,000.

**Two Treatises of Government** (1690). Composed by John *Locke between 1681 and 1689, the treatises were not published until 1690. Locke's purpose was twofold: in Part I to demolish the *divine right of kings theory held by Sir Robert Filmer; and in Part II to establish his own theory of government, resting on the consent of the governed and respect for natural rights.

**Tyburn,** the name borrowed for the Middlesex gallows from a nearby tributary of the river Thames, was the principal place of execution in London from 1388 until 1783 (near the modern Marble Arch). In the hope that witnessing an execution might prove deterrent, hanging days were public holidays, hence enormous, unruly crowds (the more affluent on grandstand seating) awaited the carts from Newgate gaol.

**Tyler, Wat** (d. 1381). The most famous leader of the *Peasants' Revolt in 1381. He may have worked as a tiler in Essex; he was said to have served with Richard Lyons, a wealthy London merchant in France. He first emerged as a major leader in Kent at the end of the first week in June 1381, seizing Canterbury on 10 June and heading the march to London. On 15 June he was the spokesman at Smithfield. His demands were radical. The young king Richard II ordered the mayor, John Walworth, to arrest Tyler, and in a struggle he was killed.

**Tyndale, William** (*c.*1494–1536). Translator of the Bible. Tyndale was probably from a Gloucestershire family and entered Magdalen College, Oxford, in 1510. He became tutor to the children of Sir John Walsh of Old Sodbury, but soon removed to London and the continent, visiting Luther at Wittenberg. Meanwhile he worked on his English translation of the New Testament. Printed in Germany, copies smuggled into England were burned by the authorities. In 1535 Tyndale was seized by servants of the Emperor Charles V and burned as a heretic at Vilvoorde near Brussels in October 1536. Tyndale's translation, based on Erasmus' Greek version, was much used by the Authorized Version issued in 1611, and his great phrases roll round the heads of Christians and non-Christians alike.

**Tyne and Wear** was one of the six English metropolitan county councils that existed from 1974 until their abolition in 1986. Tyne and Wear is still used as a geographical description for the former council's territory, based upon Newcastle and Sunderland.

**Tynwald,** meaning the assembly field, is an institution unique to the Isle of Man and is the successor of the Norse meeting of freemen. The Tynwald shares with the Icelandic Althing the claim to be the oldest surviving parliamentary institution.

**Tyrconnel, Richard Talbot, 1st Earl** (I)(1630–91). Talbot, a younger son from Co. Kildare, fought for the king in the 1640s and escaped from the destruction of Drogheda in 1649. In the 1650s he was appointed a groom of the bedchamber to the duke of York in exile and for the rest of his life his fortunes followed his patron's. As soon as the duke became James II, Talbot was created earl and in 1686 appointed lieutenant-general of the army in Ireland. In 1687 he succeeded *Clarendon as lord-lieutenant and began consolidating the catholic position. Tyrconnel was the 'new deputy' whom 'brother Teague' welcomed in *'Lillibullero'. After the Glorious Revolution he was made a Jacobite duke, fought at the *Boyne, and died in Limerick just before it was forced to capitulate.

**Tyrone** was the largest of the six counties of Northern Ireland before the local government reorganization of 1973. Omagh, the chief town, suffered severely in a bomb attack in 1998 which killed 26 people. Strabane, Dungannon, and Cookstown are local centres.

**U**

**Uganda** Former British protectorate in eastern Africa. The search for the source of the White Nile first brought the region to Britain's attention in the 1860s. British missionaries reached Uganda in 1877 and the difficulties in which they became involved led to the declaration of a British protectorate in 1894. The road to independence in 1962 was bedevilled only by the problem of accommodating the powerful, centrally located kingdom of Buganda in a unified state.

**Ulster** The northern province of Ireland, comprising the counties of Antrim, Down, Armagh, Cavan, Monaghan, Fermanagh, Donegal, Tyrone, and Londonderry. The Norman intrusion was both socially and geographically confined: Ulster remained the most Gaelic, and—from the perspective of English governors in Dublin—inaccessible part of Ireland until the plantation of 1609. The Ulster plantation embraced the six central and western counties of Ulster. The victory of the Williamite forces in Ireland by 1691 confirmed this territorial distribution, and opened the way to further British migration into Ulster. The mid- and late 18th cent. was characterized by economic growth throughout most of Ireland, and at this time Ulster emerged as the centre of the Irish linen industry, and *Belfast developed as a significant industrial centre. By the time of the first *Home Rule Bill (1886), there was broad support for the maintenance of a constitutional link with Britain. In 1920 the island was partitioned, with the six most unionist counties—the new *Northern Ireland—obtaining a separate devolved parliament and government. However, the dominant unionist social and political culture of Northern Ireland came under increasing challenge from the nationalist minority. Between 1969 and 1994, in the context of a low-grade civil war conducted between loyalist and republican paramilitaries and the Royal Ulster Constabulary and British army, an untenable position of unionist political predominance was gradually undermined. But the re-introduction of a power-sharing executive in 2007 has been accompanied by some encouraging signs of economic and social progress.

**Ulster (Ulaid) kingdom of,** The most powerful of the four provinces, along with Connachta (Connacht), Laigin (Leinster), and Mumu (Munster). The province of the Ulaid consisted of the whole of northern Ireland with its high seat at Emain Macha, near Armagh. As a result of political upheavals and the rise of the Uí Néill in the 5th cent., Ireland was subsequently divided into fifths (coiceds). *Armagh became the most important Irish town and was subsequently the seat of an archbishopric. The kingdom of the Ulaid was gradually destroyed and partitioned by the sons of Niall Noígiallach. This conquest established the Uí Néill in the north, whose territory included Armagh, Monaghan, Tyrone, and the greater part of Fermanagh and Derry. The result was the creation of two new kingdoms of Airgialla in the first conquest and Ailech after the conquest of Donegal *c.*428. The Uí Néill kingdom was greatly weakened by Viking expeditions from the 9th cent. onwards.

**Ulster covenant,** 1912. The Parliament Act of 1911 reduced the Lords' veto to a delay and in April 1912 the third Home Rule Bill was introduced. The protestant response was to bring forward a covenant on 'Ulster Day', 28 September 1912, pledging the signatories to use 'all means necessary to defeat the present conspiracy to set up a Home Rule Parliament in Ireland'. Both sides began preparing for armed conflict and the *Ulster Volunteer Force was founded in January 1913.

**Ulster custom** was the name given to the informal rights of Ulster tenants. These included security of tenure so long as the rent was fully paid, and the freedom to sell the right of occupancy to any new tenant who met with the landlord's approval. In 1847 the *tenant rights advocate William Sharman Crawford attempted to gain legalization for the custom, but failed. Only in 1870, through *Gladstone's Land Act, was this objective nominally attained.

**Ulster Special Constabulary,** 1920–70. Formed as an auxiliary armed police force by the new Northern Irish government, the Ulster Specials in 1922 consisted of 'A' full-time, 'B' part-time, 'C' reserve with 5,500, 19,000, and 7,500 members respectively. Dominated by old *Ulster Volunteer Force and *Orange order members and seen as a ruthless sectarian force by the catholic minority, it was reluctantly paid for by the British Treasury. After the early turbulent years of province, the 'A's and 'C's were disbanded. The 'B' Specials were criticized for their biased policing of civil rights marches in the late 1960s. The Hunt Report (October 1969) recommended their replacement by a new part-time security force, soon known as the Ulster Defence Regiment. The new, avowedly non-sectarian, force also failed to recruit many catholics and became almost as controversial as the 'B' Specials.

**Ulster Unionist Council** Created in 1904–5 as a representative body for Ulster unionism. Comprising originally 200 members (100 representing the local unionist associations, 50 representing the Orange order, and 50 co-opted members), the council was subsequently expanded and restructured: it was governed by a standing committee of 30. A new constitution was accepted in 1946. Although the representative significance of the UUC was overshadowed by the Unionist parliamentary party in the Northern Ireland House of Commons, since 1972 its strategic importance has been restored.

**Ulster Unionist Party** Formed in 1904–5 as the *Ulster Unionist Council to resist the threat of all-Ireland devolution, it consisted of representatives of local unionist institutions, the presbyterian church, the Orange order, and loyalist MPs. It brought protestant landowners, businessmen, and working class together successfully to oppose the third Home Rule Bill, 1912–14. It was led by southern unionist Sir Edward *Carson 1910–21, and then by Sir James *Craig, key organizer in the preceding period and the first Northern Ireland prime minister 1921–40. The Ulster Unionists became the single party controlling the Northern Ireland government and Parliament 1921–68. The civil rights crisis from 1967 and the reluctant involvement of the British government placed enormous strains on party unity and resulted in a challenge from traditional unionist sources. It divided over the power-sharing executive 1973–4, the majority deserting Brian *Faulkner's leadership and helping its demise. It has remained the majority representative of Northern unionist opinion, despite an increasing challenge from the *Democratic Unionist Party. The UUP opposed the *Anglo-Irish agreement 1985, but extremely cautiously supported the Downing Street declaration of 1993, and the Good Friday agreement of 1998. The latter placed a severe strain on the party as the *IRA reneged on its commitment to decommission its weapons, and the UUP was heavily defeated by Paisley's DUP at the 2005 general election: at Westminster it gained only one seat as against 9 for DUP, and in the 2007 election for the Northern Ireland Assembly obtained 18 seats to DUP's 36.

**Ulster Volunteer Force (UVF).** Formed in 1913, as the military back-up to Ulster loyalist resistance to the third Home Rule Bill, the UVF achieved success in the Larne gun-running. It ceased with the First World War, but its veterans were the basis of the *Ulster Special Constabulary, formed in 1920–1. The name was resuscitated in the mid-1960s for a secret protestant paramilitary force. Outlawed in the 1970s, it remained less popular and active than the Ulster Defence Army (UDA), with which it frequently clashed.

**Ulundi, battle of,** 1879. Last battle of the *Zulu–British War of 1879. A force of 10,000 men under General Chelmsford headed for Ulundi, the seat of Zulu chief Cetewayo. On 4 July 1879 they engaged a Zulu force of 20,000 men. The Zulus attacked but were cut down by rifle fire, and harried by the cavalry as they fled.

u

**unauthorized programme,** 1885. Between 1883 and 1885 Joseph *Chamberlain and John *Morley organized publication in the *Fortnightly Review* of a series of articles—on land, housing, religion, education, and taxation—republished as *The Radical Programme* (1885). The programme was 'unauthorized' as it lacked the Liberal Party leadership's approval.

**undertaker system** For many years the English administration in Dublin castle kept control of the Irish Parliament by reaching agreements with leading Irish borough patrons, who 'undertook' to construct a government majority and see through business. In exchange they received extensive patronage. Lord *Townshend, appointed lord-lieutenant in 1767, resolved to end the system, but was unable to do more than shuffle the personnel.

**Uniformity, Acts of,** 1549, 1552, 1559, 1662. By enforcing the use of successive Prayer Books, the Acts provided liturgical conformity in Books of *Common* Prayer instead of the diverse uses of Sarum, York, Bangor, and Lincoln. Constitutionally and ecclesiastically, though not liturgically, the 1549 Act was 'a momentous moment', because Parliament set a precedent by itself authorizing doctrine and liturgy, a royal preserve since 1534. The 1552 book marked a Zwinglian shift; the mass became the communion, tables replaced altars, the surplice replaced eucharistic vestments. The 1559 book was decidedly comprehensive. Catholic elements were added to the 1552 book and vestments were to be as in 1548. The 1661 Prayer Book (authorized 1662) roughly followed 1559, and was uniformly used until the 20th cent. Two thousand clerics left the Church of England in protest, giving a powerful boost to *dissent.

**Union, Act of (Ireland),** 1801. United the parliaments of Great Britain and Ireland, abolished the Irish Parliament in Dublin, and ended Irish legislative independence granted in 1782. The Act originated from Britain's difficulties in governing Ireland especially after the *Irish rising of 1798, and was designed to strengthen British security against France. The Act came into force on 1 January 1801. In place of her own House of Commons of 300 members, Ireland was given 100 MPs at Westminster, while 28 Irish peers were elected for life by the whole Irish peerage to represent them in the Lords. The Act was intended to pave the way for catholic emancipation in Ireland but George III refused to consent and *Pitt, the prime minister, resigned.

**Union, Act of (Scotland),** 1707. United England and Scotland and established the kingdom of Great Britain. In 1603 there was a union of crowns when James VI of Scotland became James I of England but the two countries remained independent states until 1707. After 1688 William III was anxious to promote union but the Commons did not agree. The process was restarted on the accession of Anne in 1702, but commissioners did not meet until April 1706. The English government was driven to seek a union when in 1705, to try to extract economic concessions, the Scottish Parliament passed an Act allowing Scotland to choose a successor to the Scottish crown on Anne's death, putting the prospect of the Hanoverian succession in jeopardy.

The unitary state of Great Britain was established on 12 May 1707 with Anne as queen, and the succession guaranteed in the house of Hanover. The Scottish Parliament was abolished, and Scottish representation in the British parliament consisted of 45 MPs and 16 representative peers (the numbers based on the respective sizes of the two economies). Free trade between North Britain (Scotland) and South Britain (England) was established, and England's colonies were open to the Scots on an equal footing. The Scots retained their own legal system, as well as their own Privy Council (this, however, was abolished in 1708). The established churches were to remain the same: Anglican in England and presbyterian in Scotland.

**Union, Act of (Wales)** A 20th-cent. term applied to two Acts of Parliament (1536, 1542/3) in which Wales was declared 'incorporated, united and annexed' to the English realm. The 1536 Act laid down principles 'for laws and justice to be administered in Wales in like form as it is in this realm'; the Act of 1542/3 contained further details. The 1536 Act created five shires (Monmouth, Brecon, Radnor, Denbigh, and Montgomery) in addition to the six of the old principality (Carmarthen, Cardigan, Anglesey, Caernarfon, Merioneth, and Flint) and existing counties palatine, Pembroke and Glamorgan. Equality at law was granted to the Welsh, and English law became official usage. Each Welsh county had one MP (prosperous Monmouth two), and each county town had one parliamentary burgess (except poor Harlech). The 1542/3 Act created the Court of Great Sessions, with twelve shires grouped in four circuits and Monmouth joining the Oxford circuit, an anomaly that created uncertainty as to whether Monmouthshire was or was not Welsh.

**Union Jack** National flag of the United Kingdom. After his accession in 1603, James VI and I issued a flag of Great Britain with the red cross of St George (England), superimposed upon the saltire of St Andrew (Scotland) on a blue field. On the union with Ireland (1801), the diagonal red cross of St Patrick was added.

**Union of Democratic Control** Founded in September 1914 by a group of liberal intellectuals, including J. A. *Hobson, Norman Angell, and Bertrand *Russell, who believed that wars came about through secret diplomacy. During the war they agitated vigorously for a negotiated settlement. Afterwards they campaigned against armaments and alliances, until 1967, when the UDC was dissolved.

**unitarians** deny the deity of Christ. They believe that only the Father should be worshipped, but their attitude to Jesus varies, reflecting their application of reasoned individual judgement to the Bible, and their reluctance to formulate creeds. Their views developed with the Reformation, notably through Michael Servetus (1511–53), the physician burned in Geneva. By the 17th cent. they had communities in Poland, Hungary, and England, where John Biddle's (1615–62) *XII Arguments* qualify him as the father of English unitarianism. With no co-ordinating body before the British and Foreign Unitarian Association of 1825, they none the less produced a distinctive social, political, and intellectual culture, represented by such families as the Martineaus, Chamberlains, Wicksteeds, and Holts.

**United Empire Loyalists** was the term coined by the governor of British North America, Lord Dorchester, in 1789 to designate those citizens of the thirteen colonies who remained loyal to Britain during the American Revolution and fled to what is now Canada or returned to England.

**United Irishmen** A society formed in Belfast and Dublin in 1791 by Theobald Wolfe *Tone and James Napper Tandy to agitate for parliamentary reform and equal religious rights. Revolutionary events in France made them more radical in 1793, while fears of growing catholic strength caused many protestants to secede and form the *Orange Society. In 1795 the United Irishmen were reconstituted as a secret society pledged to work for a republic. A rising with French help was thwarted when the invasion force was scattered by a storm off Bantry Bay in 1796. Another rising fixed for May 1798 was aborted by the arrest or flight of the leadership and the peasants were routed at *Vinegar Hill in June, shortly before Tone arrived with a small French invasion force.

**United Kingdom** *See* GREAT BRITAIN.

**United Nations** The UN replaced the failed *League of Nations after the Second World War. Wartime negotiations between Russia, America, China, and Britain produced a blueprint for a new global security institution. The United Nations came into being on 24 October 1945 with 51 member states. The accession of Montenegro in June 2006 brought the total membership up to 192.

The institutions of the UN bore some similarity to those of the league, though the General Assembly was empowered to act on majority votes, rather than the principle of unanimity. But the five main powers, UK, USA, USSR, France, and China, gave themselves a power of veto in the Security Council, which Britain retains.

The effectiveness of the UN in maintaining global security has rested to a large extent on the superpowers being in agreement. UN peacekeeping activities proliferated at times of relaxation during the *Cold War, and after 1989, but were rarer when the two main powers were trading vetoes with each other in the 1950s or the 1980s. The UN was able to intervene in the *Korean War because the

USSR at the time was boycotting the Security Council. British soldiers have played a part in UN peacekeeping activities, notably in *Cyprus and in Bosnia. But UN authority was weakened by strong disagreements in 2003 over policy towards *Iraq, and it has always found difficulty in persuading some members to accompany good intentions by action.

**'Unlearned' Parliament,** 1404. This nickname was given to the Parliament summoned by Henry IV in 1404 to meet at Coventry, after the king ordered that no lawyers should be returned, since they concentrated too much on their own professional business. The instructions were resented and the rebels of 1405 demanded a free Parliament.

**Urien** was the late 6th-cent. ruler of *Rheged, the British kingdom centred on Carlisle. The 9th-cent. British writer *Nennius described his power and *Taliesin, poet at Urien's court, praised him as warrior and protector. He is said to have led a coalition against the Angles in the northern kingdom of *Bernicia and to have been killed c.590 besieging *Bamburgh.

**Uses, statute of,** 1535. The use was a legal device whereby property could be held by one person for the benefit of another, e.g. when a landowner was absent on crusade. But, by extension, it might be employed to evade or avoid obligations, defraud creditors, or escape legislation against *mortmain. Henry VIII pressed strongly that uses should be restricted, arguing that his revenue was affected, but the Parliament of 1532 was unwilling to legislate and was told sharply 'not to contend with me'. In 1535 Parliament accepted 27 Hen. VIII c. 10, which complained of 'subtle inventions and practices' and restored obligations to the beneficiary.

**Ushant, battle of,** 1778. After France's entry into the American war, Augustus Keppel was dispatched with a fleet of 30 ships to watch Brest. On 23 July he sighted a French fleet of similar size off the Breton coast under d'Orvilliers. Though manœuvring went on for four days and a good deal of damage was inflicted, the result was indecisive, no ships being captured or sunk. Keppel's court-martial, which acquitted him, became a Whig demonstration.

**Ussher, James** (1581–1656). Archbishop of Armagh. Born in Dublin and educated at Trinity College, Dublin, Ussher was successively professor of divinity, vice-chancellor (1615), bishop of Meath (1621), and archbishop (1625). On returning from absence in England (1623–6), he signed the Irish bishops' protest against toleration of popery (1626). Despite his predestinarian theology, he was friendly with *Laud. During his tenure the disputed primacy of Ireland was settled in Armagh's favour and the Bible in Irish language was permitted. After leaving Ireland (1640), he held the see of Carlisle *in commendam*. Ussher was a distinguished scholar, contributing to early Irish history and biblical chronology: his argument that the world was created in 4004 BC held the field for decades.

**usury laws** The idea that it is wrong to profit from lending money is found in the Old Testament, and was linked to the belief that there exists a just or fair price for every commodity. But church doctrine did not forbid interest being paid as compensation for the use of capital tied in some venture. This double standard endured throughout the medieval period.

**utilitarianism** is the moral philosophy which asserts that the maximization of happiness is the ultimate aim of all human conduct. According to Jeremy *Bentham, the systematizer of utilitarianism, an action is right if, and only if, it promotes the greatest happiness of the greatest number.

Bentham presented utilitarianism as a practical guide to both individual and collective decision-making, developing a 'felicific calculus' to measure the net amount of happiness producible by alternative courses of action. The practical influence of utilitarianism in shaping social policy in Britain from the mid-19th cent. has been considerable. It became the ideological driving force behind the reform movement known as *philosophical radicalism, which tested all institutions by the principle of utility.

However, utilitarianism has been much criticized. It has been objected that it is impossible to reduce complex moral issues to a simple mathematical formula, however elegant, and that no rational criterion exists for balancing the great harm done to an individual by taking away his property, against the potential happiness which could be derived by 200 other persons to whom it might be distributed. Critics argue, also, that justice demands protection of basic human rights such as life and liberty irrespective of calculations of utility. John Stuart *Mill sought to answer this criticism by pointing out that the principle of justice promoted social utility in the long term, if not always in the immediate short term.

**Utopia** Politico-philosophic work by Thomas *More (1516), initiating a literary genre. Steeped in literary *humanism, More sought for the best form of government through discussions with the fictitious Raphael Hythloday. This is followed by Hythloday's account of the 'New Island of Utopia' ('Noplace'), but its egalitarian commonwealth appears flawed since, despite religious freedom and absence of hunger and homelessness, personal freedom is restricted.

**Utrecht, treaty of,** 1713. This was part of the general settlement ending the War of the *Spanish Succession. France and Spain recognized the Hanoverian succession. Philip V of Spain abandoned his claim to the French throne. France retained Alsace, Philip retained Spain and the Indies but lost his other possessions in the Netherlands and Italy to the Emperor Charles VI, Britain gained French territory in North America, and Gibraltar and Minorca from Spain.

**Uxbridge, treaty of,** 1645. The so-called treaty of Uxbridge was in fact an abortive negotiation. The fluctuating fortunes of war in 1644 persuaded Parliament to propose an armistice for discussion. Commissioners met at Uxbridge on 29 January to negotiate on three main issues—the church, the militia, and Ireland. On none of these points was any progress made. The negotiation was abandoned on 22 February. The last chance of ending the war by compromise had gone.

u

**vaccination,** a term first used by *Jenner (1798) for inoculating cowpox matter (*vacca* = cow) to produce immunity from the far more virulent smallpox, has since come to mean the creation of immunity from infectious diseases in general. The 1840 Vaccination Act prohibited inoculation and permitted vaccination of the poor at ratepayers' expense; the 1853 extension made the practice compulsory, though it was not universally enforced. With compulsory notification of infectious diseases and better trained public health officers, vaccination rapidly reduced the prevalence and mortality of smallpox. Subsequent vaccines against diphtheria, polio, measles, whooping cough, and rubella have largely controlled these diseases.

**Vagrancy Acts** Vagrancy was a phenomenon which particularly worried late medieval and Tudor society, not merely because it often led to crime, but because 'masterless men' seemed to threaten the whole social structure. The breakdown of the authority of lords of the manor freed men and women to move, and unemployment, demobilization, enclosures, and high prices could combine to produce destitution and vagrancy.

One of the earliest government interventions came in 1351, after the *Black Death had caused an acute shortage of labour. The statute attempted not only to control wages and enforce contracts but declared punishment for persons fleeing from one shire to another. Another flurry of legislation came after the *Peasants' Revolt of 1381. An Act of 1383 authorized JPs to apprehend vagabonds and another Act of 1388 insisted that anyone leaving his abode or service must carry letters patent explaining the purpose of his journey. Tudor legislation on the subject was both frequent and fierce. The Parliament of Henry VII in 1495 enacted that vagabonds should be put in the stocks for three days and three nights on bread and water. In 1535 it was announced that on a second offence any 'valiant beggar or sturdy vagabond' would lose part of his right ear, and on a third offence would be hanged. After the Restoration the problem of vagrancy diminished, partly because paupers were given help in their parishes of origin, partly because an expanding economy provided better opportunities for employment. The increasing expense of *poor relief led in the early 19th cent. to reorganization of the whole system, but vagabondage had ceased to terrify.

**Valence, Aymer de, earl of Pembroke** (*c.*1270–1324). Valence's father William was a half-brother of Henry III, being a son of John's widow Isabella by her second marriage, and came to England in 1247. Aymer de Valence inherited in 1296 and spent his early years campaigning in Scotland, fighting at *Falkirk (1298) and defeating Robert I Bruce at *Methven in 1306. The following year he was himself defeated by Bruce at *Loudoun Hill. In 1307 he was recognized as earl of Pembroke by virtue of his mother, a granddaughter of William *Marshal, earl of Pembroke (d. 1219). In Edward II's reign he was at first an *Ordainer but switched to the king's side after the murder of *Gaveston, who was seized from his custody. He fought for the king at *Bannockburn and was subsequently employed watching the Scots and on diplomatic missions.

**Vanbrugh, Sir John** (1664–1726). Dramatist and architect. A good imitation of Renaissance Man, Vanbrugh was of Dutch descent. Vanbrugh began as a soldier, was made a captain, and spent 1688–92 in captivity in France. In 1696 he had an enormous success with his delightful comedy *The Relapse, or Virtue in Danger*, with its bravura role of Lord Foppington. He followed it in 1697 with *The Provok'd Wife*, and in 1705 *The Confederacy* was put on at the Queen's,

Haymarket, which Vanbrugh had built. Meanwhile, Vanbrugh's career as an architect developed after he began building *Castle Howard in 1701 for the earl of *Carlisle. He was appointed comptroller of the board of works in 1702, Carlisle herald in 1703, and Clarenceux herald in 1704. His work on Blenheim palace began in 1705 and involved him in protracted and rancorous exchanges with Sarah, duchess of *Marlborough. His usual style is an extravagant and idiosyncratic baroque.

**Van Dyck, Anthony** (1599–1641). Portrait painter. Born in Antwerp, in 1632 he became 'Principal Painter in Ordinary' to Charles I and was knighted in 1633, undertaking large compositions to project the mystique of the king's royalist convictions. In the course of one decade, Van Dyck mirrored the frailest of the European monarchies with such mastery that, in British portraiture, only *Gainsborough and *Lawrence may be considered rivals.

**Vane, Sir Henry the elder** (1589–1655) and **Sir Henry the younger** (1613–62). Politicians of contrasted character. The father was a worldly minded courtier, bent on accumulating a great landed estate. The son was a radical puritan with mystical leanings, and in middle life a doctrinaire republican.

Through purchase or patronage, the elder acquired a succession of posts in the royal household, won Charles I's confidence, and became a privy counsellor in 1630. Favoured also by the queen, he rose in February 1640 to secretary of state. Gradually he aligned himself with the future parliamentarians, until Charles stripped him of all his offices.

The younger Vane sacrificed a promising career at court in 1635 for the religious liberty of Massachusetts, where within six months he was elected governor. He got deep into religious controversy, clashed seriously with the general court, resigned, and returned home in 1637. In the Long Parliament he rapidly became a leader of the war party, and a close ally of *Cromwell. But by 1648 he and Cromwell were parting company, and he held aloof from the king's trial. He was very active, however, in the government of the *Commonwealth, and he regarded Cromwell's *Protectorate as a betrayal of its republican principles. He was excepted from

pardon at the *Restoration, and was executed in 1662.

**Vanuatu,** an independent republic in the Commonwealth, was formerly the islands of the New Hebrides, so named by Cook. Their main support is agriculture (cocoa, coffee, and copra), fishing, and tourism. From 1906 they were under a condominium run by France and Britain, but became independent in 1980.

**vassal** was the term used to describe a person who had taken a formal oath of allegiance to a superior and was derived from a Celtic word meaning 'youth'. In its simplest form it was no more than commending oneself to a lord for protection, but it became more complex when estates and benefices were granted in exchange for specified duties. It was upheld by the ceremony of *homage. The Normans introduced the continental practice of endowing the vassal with a *fief: this did not imply outright ownership of the land and the vassal could not alienate, though he could subcontract. In exchange, the vassal performed carefully defined duties, such as knight service, and aids for particular occasions. By the 13th cent. the arrangements were unravelling as lords increasingly paid *scutage rather than perform knight service and vassals tried to commute their own obligations.

**Vaughan, Henry** (1622–95). Poet and mystic. After two years at Oxford, Vaughan commenced legal training in London but returned home to Breconshire at the outbreak of war in 1642. He began to publish poetry in 1646, but George *Herbert's influence led to rejection of 'idle books', and it is for his religious poems that he is now best known. *Silex Scintillans* ('The Glittering Flint', 1650, Part II 1655) and the prose *The Mount of Olives* (1652) reflect his spiritual rapture and fresh creativeness.

**Vaughan Williams, Ralph** (1872–1958). English composer, who believed passionately in the need for direct communication with his audience. Vaughan Williams studied composition with Charles Wood at Cambridge and with *Parry and Stanford at London's *Royal College of Music, where he established a lifelong friendship with fellow-composer Gustav *Holst. He scored a great success with his first published work, the delightful song 'Linden Lea' (1902). Vaughan Williams drew heavily on his native heritage: he edited *The English Hymnal* (1906), and works like the *Fantasia on a Theme of Thomas Tallis* (1909) reflect his great interest in Elizabethan music. He also collected folk-songs, which influenced his modal harmony and melodic style, contributing to an influential 'Englishness'.

**Vauxhall gardens** (London), just south of the Thames, opened soon after the Restoration as New Spring gardens, and were visited by *Pepys, who complained of high prices. In 1732 Jonathan Tyers arranged a grand re-opening, attended by Frederick, prince of Wales. The central features were the Rotunda and a famous statue of *Handel by *Roubiliac, erected in 1738. In the 19th cent. there were increasing complaints of rowdiness and vulgarity, and the gardens closed in the summer of 1859. They were soon built over.

**Vereeniging, treaty of** This brought the second *Boer War to a close. On 31 May 1902 at Vereeniging in southern Transvaal the Boers accepted Britain's final offer: that they declare themselves subjects of King Edward VII, in return for which they would get their lands back, with compensation for buildings and crops that had been destroyed; be allowed the use of their language in schools and law courts; and be given self-government as soon as possible, with a racist franchise if that was what they really desired.

**Verneuil, battle of,** 1424. The first task of John, duke of *Bedford, regent for the infant Henry VI, was to preserve Henry V's gains in France. In the summer of 1424 he began a campaign to conquer Anjou and Maine, but was confronted at Verneuil on 17 August by a superior French force, under the command of two Scots, the earl of Buchan, recently made constable of France, and Archibald, earl of Douglas, veteran campaigner of Henry IV's reign. English archers repeated their success at *Agincourt, nine years earlier. Buchan and Douglas were both killed.

**Vernon, Edward** (1684–1757). Admiral. Second son of James Vernon, secretary of state to William III, Vernon entered the navy at the age of 15. In 1722 he came into Parliament as MP for Penryn but moved into opposition and lost his seat in 1734. At the outbreak of the war with Spain in 1739, Vernon offered his services and was sent to the West Indies with the rank of vice-admiral. On 21 November 1739 his forces stormed the fortress of Portobello in Panama. Vernon became a national hero. London made him a freeman, taverns were named after him, and the tiny resort outside Edinburgh commemorated his great victory. But attempts to repeat the success at Cartagena, Santiago, or Panama failed. Returned to Parliament for Ipswich he became a noisy critic of government and was dismissed from the service in 1746.

**Versailles, treaty of,** 1783. The treaty of Versailles, at the end of the *American War of Independence, was less disadvantageous to Britain than had seemed likely, partly because of *Rodney's naval victory at the *Saints in April 1782 and partly because of the failure of de Bussy's expedition to India. The independence of the thirteen American colonies had to be recognized, but that had been inevitable after the surrender at *Yorktown in 1781. The Americans retained their fishing rights off Newfoundland and Congress promised 'earnestly to recommend' the restitution of estates to the loyalists. In the West Indies, France restored her conquests, save for Tobago, and in India Britain restored France's conquered possessions. Britain gave up Florida to Spain, retained *Gibraltar, for which Spain had pressed strongly, but ceded *Minorca.

**Versailles, treaty of,** 1919. The peace treaty between Germany and the victorious allies at the end of the *First World War. It was signed on 28 June 1919 in the hall of mirrors of the palace of Versailles, where the German empire had been proclaimed in 1871. Germany had to surrender Alsace and Lorraine to France and considerable territory to the reconstituted Poland. She was not to be allowed to rearm. The Germans particularly resented the fact that they had to accept liability for all war damage and pay 'reparations' to the allies. The treaty also established the new *League of Nations.

**Verulamium** Romano-British town, capital of the *Catuvellauni, predecessor of St Albans (Herts.). In the late Iron Age Verulamium was a major *oppidum*. The Catuvellauni seem to have been pro-Roman and after only brief military presence the new Verulamium started to develop. By the time of its destruction by *Boudicca in AD 60 it had a small street-grid and Roman-style buildings. By 79 it was able to dedicate its elaborate new forum and in due course acquired public baths, a theatre and temple complex, a *macellum* (covered market), and monumental arches. Verulamium was the site of the martyrdom of *Alban. Bishop *Germanus of Auxerre visited his shrine in 429, and the present cathedral may perpetuate its site.

**Vespasian** Roman emperor AD 69-79. Titus Flavius Vespasianus was born in AD 9 at Reate in Sabine country. In 43 as legate of *legio II Augusta* he took part in the invasion of Britain, distinguishing himself at the *Medway battle and going on to reduce the south-west, defeating two powerful tribes and reducing 20 hill-forts. He was proclaimed emperor in 69 following Nero's suicide. In Britain the advance north was resumed under his kinsman by marriage, Petillius Cerialis.

**Victoria** (1819-1901), queen of the United Kingdom of Great Britain and Ireland (1837-1901) and empress of India (1877-1901). Victoria would have agreed that her life fell into three parts—before *Albert, with Albert, after Albert. The death in childbirth in November 1817 of Princess *Charlotte, only daughter and heir to the prince regent, prompted a famous 'rush to the altar'. The duke of Cambridge married in May 1818. His elder brothers, the dukes of Clarence and Kent, were married in a joint ceremony a month later. Clarence's two daughters died as infants, leaving the probable succession to the duke of Kent's daughter the Princess Victoria, born 18 May 1819, christened Alexandrina, and known at first as 'Drina'. Eight months later her father was dead, taken off by pneumonia in winter at Sidmouth, leaving her to be brought up in a household almost totally female and totally German. Her mother, Princess Victoria of Leiningen, was of the house of Saxe-Coburg: recently arrived in England, she found the language difficult. The other person in constant attendance was Fräulein Lehzen, brought over as governess and companion from Hanover when the princess was 6 months old. They lived at Kensington palace, Victoria sleeping in her mother's room until she came to the throne. The centre of the princess's life was

her 132 dolls, given imposing names and elaborate costumes.

Victoria grew up intelligent and self-possessed. Her upbringing, though sheltered, endowed her with an artlessness and directness—a lack of introspection—which is rare, and never left her. Inevitably the duchess of Kent was on bad terms with George IV and even worse with his successor William IV, to whose demise she looked forward with ill-concealed relish. A clash over precedence meant that the duchess and the young princess boycotted William's coronation in 1831, the princess writing that not even her dolls could console her. 'I longed sadly for some gaiety', she wrote to her uncle Leopold at 16, 'but we have been for the last three months immured within our old palace.' As news of the gravity of King William's illness emerged in 1837 she wrote to Leopold: 'I look forward to the event which it seems is likely to occur soon with calm and quietness: I am not alarmed at it.' At her first council, Charles Greville wrote that 'she appeared to be awed, but not daunted'.

Victoria's education for life started with her first prime minister *Melbourne, whom she liked from their first audience, and who stood for father-figure and first love. His kind and pleasant manner, mellow and relaxed, eased her into her new duties: after five days she wrote to Leopold, 'I do regular, hard, but to me delightful work.' Greville wrote, not unkindly, in 1839 when the queen's affection for Melbourne had dragged her into the *Bedchamber crisis, 'Melbourne is everything to her...her feelings are sexual, though she does not know it.'

She told Melbourne that she might not marry at all: 'I don't know about that,' replied Melbourne, sensibly. In October 1839 Leopold played his trump card, sending Victoria's cousin Albert over from Saxe-Coburg on approval. In the event, one look was enough. 'It was with some emotion that I beheld Albert,' she wrote, 'who is *beautiful*... so excessively handsome.' Two days later, even disconcerting the urbane Melbourne, she declared that no time should be lost, and the following day she sent for Albert to propose marriage. The second phase of her life had begun.

Victoria took to matrimony *con brio*. 'We did not sleep much,' she confided to her journal after the wedding night. Then, to her dismay, within six weeks there were signs of pregnancy. Victoria was quite unsentimental about babies—'nasty objects'—but after the birth of the princess royal in November 1840, eight more arrived in rapid succession. Her life became a strange juxtaposition of public and private. April 1841 found her with Princess Victoria 6 months old and at war with China: 'Albert is so much amused at my having got the Island of Hong Kong, and we think Victoria ought to be called Princess of Hong Kong in addition to Princess Royal.' Albert's influence grew with the years, particularly after the success of the *Great Exhibition in 1851, and in 1857 Victoria gave him the unprecedented title of prince consort. But pressure of work and his own sense of duty took its toll. In December 1861, he caught typhoid and died at the age of 42.

Victoria faced a widowhood of 40 years. To some, even in her own day, her grief seemed excessive. There was a touch of morbidness and some gestures were repeated when the estimable John Brown, her Scottish manservant, died in 1883. For several years, her disappearance from public life was total. But slowly the family took over as it grew inexorably—such 'swarms of children', wrote Victoria without enthusiasm. Life became a welter of match-making, weddings, christenings, teething, mumps, visits, and birthdays (remembered or missed)—and, the penalty of advancing years, of deaths. *Disraeli, once detested for his unkindness to Sir Robert Peel, long a dear friend, died in 1881, 'the Queen bowed down with this misfortune'. In 1892 a terrible shock when 'Eddy', the prince of Wales's eldest son, succumbed to pneumonia at Sandringham. And gradually the courts and thrones of Europe filled up with Victoria's relatives and descendants. The tiny lady in the wheelchair was 'the matriarch of Europe'.

Her political influence as queen has been much debated and analysed, but the more extravagant claims should not be entertained. The two politicians she most distrusted were *Palmerston ('Pilgerstein') and Gladstone ('half-crazy'), but this did not stop the former being prime minister for nearly ten years and dying in office at the age of 81, nor the latter being prime minister on four occasions. Her importance lies in her role, with Albert, in restoring the

dignity and reputation of the monarchy. Victoria's standing rose with the years, and she enjoyed memorable triumphs at her *Golden and *Diamond Jubilees in 1887 and 1897. Much of it, of course, was illusion. The queen mother and empress was a tiny, fat old lady, painfully shortsighted, gobbling her food and eating too much. But nobody took liberties. The ribald jokes about John Brown had bounced off her. Though the queen herself did not fit the stereotype of 'Victorian England' (she never quite got over the dislike she had taken to bishops as a toddler), the phrase took hold so firmly that one wonders how other countries manage without the adjective. She remained to the end a mass of contradictions—self-centred yet considerate and dutiful; homely yet grand; excitable and passionate but with shrewd judgement. She died at Osborne on 23 January 1901 and was buried alongside Albert in the mausoleum at Frogmore.

**Victoria and Albert Museum** After the success of the *Great Exhibition (1851), a museum of manufactures was quickly established in Marlborough House, but its collecting policies became increasingly antiquarian. The first director was Henry Cole, a pioneer of public relations, who oversaw the construction of new but heterogeneous buildings at South Kensington (opened 1857), a site suggested by Prince *Albert. The new, renamed building (imposing but impractical) was completed by 1908. The 'V. & A.' has since become a leading museum for worldwide decorative art.

**Victoria Cross** The highest award for conspicuous gallantry, instituted in 1856 during the Crimean War. Unlike most previous honours, it was open to all ranks and unclassified. The ribbon is crimson and the inscription 'For Valour' was Queen Victoria's suggestion. The original crosses were made from metal of Russian guns captured at *Sebastopol.

***Victory,* HMS** The oldest warship in commission in the navy, *Victory* serves as flagship to the commander-in-chief, Naval Home Command. She was designed as a 100-gun ship in 1759, but not launched until 1765 and only first commissioned in 1778 during the American War of Independence. She was the fifth ship of the name in the navy, wearing the flags of Keppel, Kempenfelt, and Lord *Howe before *Nelson hoisted his on 30 July 1803. As his flagship at *Trafalgar, Victory was severely damaged, but had further service before being hulked at Portsmouth in 1824.

**Vienna, Congress of,** 1814–15. Napoleon's abdication in April 1814 was followed by a preliminary settlement, the first treaty of *Paris, which restored the Bourbon monarchy, returned most of France's colonies, allowed her the boundaries of 1792, and approved the union of Belgium and Holland. In March 1815 everything was thrown into the melting pot by Napoleon's escape from Elba, and not until he had been defeated in June at *Waterloo were the arrangements safe. The terms of the Vienna settlement with France were then made more severe, giving her the 1790s boundaries, and insisting on an indemnity and an army of occupation. Belgium and Holland were united in the hope that they would be a more effective barrier to French aggression than either the Spanish or Austrian Netherlands had been; Piedmont was strengthened as a barrier in Italy, where Austria, with Milan, Lombardy, and Venetia, became the dominant power; a kingdom of Poland was established under the rule of Tsar Alexander; Prussia was compensated in the west for territorial losses in the east; the neutrality of Switzerland was guaranteed; Denmark lost Norway to Sweden, which had changed sides at the last minute; Hanover's gains included East Frisia; Britain retained the Cape of Good Hope, Ceylon, Tobago, St Lucia, Malta, Mauritius, the Ionian Islands, and Heligoland. The first piece of the settlement to collapse was the union of Belgium and Holland, which disintegrated in 1830.

**Vienna, treaty of,** 1731. By the second treaty of Vienna of March 1731, Britain guaranteed Maria Theresa's succession to the Habsburg dominions under the pragmatic sanction, while the Emperor Charles VI agreed to wind up the Ostend Company, a competitor to the *East India Company. But when Maria Theresa was attacked in 1740, British assistance was far from whole-hearted.

**Vigo Bay, battle of,** 1702. In August 1702, at the outset of the War of the *Spanish Succession, Sir George *Rooke and the duke of *Ormond led an abortive expedition against Cadiz. On the way back they received news that a large Spanish treasure fleet and its escort was harboured in Vigo Bay. On 12 October they annihilated the enemy, sinking 11 men-of-war and taking 10 war vessels and 11 galleons. Though most of the treasure had been landed, the gains were enormous.

**Viking** is an Old Norse term which only came into common usage in the 19th cent. to describe peoples of Scandinavian origin who, as raiders, settlers, and traders, had major and long-lasting effects across large areas of northern Europe and the Atlantic seaboards between the late 8th and 11th cents.

Archaeological evidence suggests that trading activity between Britain and Scandinavia had existed from at least the 6th cent. In the later years of the 8th cent., however, contemporary documents record the beginnings of more aggressive contact, with Viking raids on weakly defended coastal sites in both Britain and Francia; the sacking of *Lindisfarne in 793 was but one of a series of such attacks. This pattern of attacks on England changed significantly in 850 when a Danish army overwintered on Thanet in Kent; a more permanent presence was now envisaged. In 866 the 'great raiding army' invaded East Anglia, after several years fighting in the Carolingian empire, and one branch of this group subsequently captured the commercial and political centre of *York in 867; from this base attacks were launched on *Mercia, *East Anglia, and *Wessex. The final years of the century saw a military and political struggle for power in southern England between the Danes and *Alfred (871–99), who ruled the only remaining Anglo-Saxon kingdom of Wessex; during this period recognition of a distinct legal and administrative system in the Scandinavian-settled areas north of the Thames–Chester line emerged with the establishment of *Danelaw c.886. Alfred's successors in the early years of the 10th cent. gradually re-established their power over the Anglo-Scandinavian midlands and north but it was only with the expulsion of the last Viking king of York, *Erik Bloodaxe, in 954 that England achieved a precarious political unity under a single crown. The Danelaw Scandinavians in eastern England were largely of Danish origin. During the first two decades of the 10th cent.,

V

however, groups from Norway, together with second-generation settlers familiar with western Scotland, arrived in Cumbria.

The middle years of the 10th cent. were largely free of Scandinavian activity in England, but a second wave of widespread raids began early in the reign of King *Æthelred (978–1016). The ultimate aim was now political domination of England and this was eventually achieved by *Cnut who became king of England and of Denmark in 1017. Anglo-Scandinavian relationships had a complex history after his death in 1035 but the defeat of *Harold Hardrada at *Stamford Bridge represented the last important Scandinavian attempt to conquer England.

Elsewhere in Britain (outside Ireland) Scandinavian raids and colonization are less well recorded. Apart from a few coastal place-names there is little trace of any impact on Wales. By contrast archaeological and onomastic evidence in *Orkney, *Shetland, the Hebrides, together with the *Isle of Man, points to heavy Norwegian settlement from the early 9th cent. Much of this western area remained as a recognizable political entity (the 'kingdom of the *Isles') until 1266, whilst the Scandinavian settlement of Orkney and Shetland accounts for their continued allegiance to Norway which only ended in 1469.

**villas, Roman** 'Villa' is a Latin word for farm, which has been appropriated by antiquaries and archaeologists to denote Romano-British rural establishments which exhibit Roman-style architecture, however debased. Villas develop from the late 1st cent., often overlying Iron Age buildings and are seen as the indigenous aristocracy taking on Roman ways. By the first half of the 4th cent. there were probably 1,000 villas, ranging from simple cottages to vast palatial complexes such as Bignor (Sussex) and *Woodchester. Villas were in decline in the later 4th cent. and passed out of use in the first half of the 5th.

**villein** was the term used to describe a peasant in a state of *serfdom—i.e. subject to a lord and under obligation to perform labour services. The term 'villanus' was used in *Domesday Book without any derogatory flavour to indicate persons who lived in 'vills'—and therefore formed the largest social class. Though not free men, they were above the bordars and cottars who held less land, and well above the slaves, who had been numerous in Saxon England. But the term is not precise and status and duties varied from manor to manor, region to region, and over time. There were several ways in which they could escape from villeinage—by purchasing freedom from the lord (*commutation); by escaping to a town for one year and one day; by taking holy orders (with the lord's permission). By the end of the 14th cent. villeinage was clearly disintegrating, villeins changing their status to that of copyholders.

**Vimeiro, battle of,** 1808. The first major battle of the Peninsular War. British troops under Arthur Wellesley (*Wellington) landed in Portugal at Mondego Bay on 1 August 1808 to assist the Portuguese by marching on Lisbon 30 miles to the south. The French, under Junot, numbered 14,000 and attacked on 21 August but were repulsed by Wellesley with 17,000 men.

**Vinegar Hill, battle of,** 1798. Part of the Wexford rebels in the Irish rising made camp on Vinegar Hill, just outside Enniscorthy, where they terrorized the protestants of the neighbourhood. On 21 June 1798, government forces under General Lake stormed the hill. Pikes and numbers were no match for artillery.

**Virgin Islands** A group east of Puerto Rico, shared between Britain and the USA. The British islands form a crown colony. They were visited and named by Columbus but colonized by the English from the later 17th cent.

**viscounts** are the fourth highest grade in the peerage, taking precedence over barons. This was the last of the five grades to be created: in 1440 Henry VI made John, Lord Beaumont, a viscount. The title was never particularly popular. In 1838, when Melbourne was educating the young Queen Victoria, she remarked that there had been very few viscounts at her coronation: 'there *are* very few viscounts,' he replied, 'they are a foreign title and not really English.'

**Vitoria, battle of,** 1813. Decisive battle of the Peninsular War between Wellington with

75,000 men and Joseph Bonaparte with 58,000 men. Wellington launched an attack 8 miles from Vitoria. Despite a determined stand the French centre crumbled and both flanks were turned. Joseph lost 7,000 men, 143 guns, and much booty. The battle ended Napoleon's rule in Spain and the French retreated across the Pyrenees.

**Volunteer movement** (Ireland). After France and Spain had entered the American War of Independence, many Irish volunteered to defend their country against invasion. By 1780, 40,000 were under arms. This also gave them political leverage which they used to wring concessions from the British government—first commercial advantages offered by *North in 1780, then the repeal of *Poynings's Law and the grant of legislative independence from the *Rockinghams in 1782. But when the Volunteers moved on to discuss parliamentary reform, they split on the rock of the catholic question.

**volunteers** Since from time immemorial it had been regarded as the duty of free men to defend their country, governments could scarcely object if, in moments of crisis, volunteers came forward to offer their services. Yet they were not necessarily very efficient, often tiresome in their personal demands, and, as the case of the Irish Volunteers suggests, a potential political threat. A number of corps were raised in 1690 to deal with a threat of French invasion, again in 1715 and 1745 to cope with the Jacobite risings, and again in 1779 during the American War of Independence. But the biggest response was during the Revolutionary and Napoleonic wars, and again in 1859 when there was yet another threat of war with France. By 1901 there were 230,000 volunteers, augmented by the Royal Navy and Royal Artillery Volunteers, the *militia and the *yeomanry. *Haldane's reforms of 1907 reorganized them into the Territorial Force, later the *Territorial Army.

**Vortigern** A leader of the Britons in the immediate post-Roman period. *Bede gives AD 449 as the year of the *adventus Saxonum* (the coming of the Saxons) and the story of Vortigern falls into the years following this date. Vortigern appears to have been a sub-Roman ruler in southern England, who, in order to protect his realm, is said to have invited two Saxon warriors, *Hengist and Horsa, and their troops into Britain to act as a kind of *foederatus* or mercenary force. They revolted against Vortigern and set up their own rule in Kent in the 450s.

**Votadini** Indigenous British tribe of the Iron Age and Roman periods whose territory covered the eastern part of Lowland Scotland. The ancient geographer Ptolemy, writing in the mid-2nd cent. AD, names four tribes inhabiting the area south of the Forth–Clyde isthmus: the Novantae, the *Damnonii, the *Selgovae, and the Votadini.

V

**Wade, George** (1673–1748). One of the best-known soldiers of early Hanoverian Britain. Grandson of a Cromwellian officer who had settled in Westmeath (Ireland), Wade joined the army in 1690 and by the end of the War of the *Spanish Succession in 1714 had risen to major-general. In 1715 he was returned to Parliament for Hindon and in 1722 transferred to Bath, where he built up a powerful political base and where his fine house in the abbey courtyard still stands. From 1724 to 1740 he commanded in Scotland, where his programme of military road-building was designed to facilitate troop movements. He was given charge of the army at Newcastle during the Jacobite invasion of 1745 though his conduct appears to have been sluggish.

**Waitangi, treaty of,** 1840. In 1839 the British government dispatched Captain William Hobson to New Zealand where uncontrolled development had already undermined traditional Maori culture. At Waitangi in February 1840 a majority of the Maori chiefs present agreed to cede sovereignty to Queen Victoria in exchange for confirmation of their land and protection. But Maori disappointment at the persistent encroachments upon their land led to the *Maori wars from 1844 until 1872. In 1994 a New Zealand government apologized for breaches of the treaty and promised compensation.

**Wakefield, battle of,** 1460. The Yorkist victory at *Northampton in the summer of 1460 had put Henry VI in the power of Richard, duke of *York. In October a reconciliation was effected, whereby Henry continued as monarch but recognized York as his heir. Queen *Margaret refused to accept this and raised troops in the north. York and *Warwick's father *Salisbury marched to meet her but were routed on 30 December at Wakefield. Salisbury and York were executed after the battle, the latter's head being exhibited on the walls of the city of York, wearing a paper crown.

**Wakefield, diocese of** The see, comprising parts of south Yorkshire, was created in 1888 to cope with the rapidly rising population. It did not, however, include Sheffield, which remained fiercely independent. The cathedral is the former All Saints' parish church, dating mostly from 14th cent. with a 15th-cent. west tower and a 20th-cent. east end by Gilbert *Scott.

**Wakefield, Edward Gibbon** (1796–1862). Wakefield was a wild youth who demanded to be removed from Westminster School, disliked Edinburgh High School, and made a runaway marriage with a ward of Chancery. Released from that scrape by the death of his wife, he attempted a second runaway match with a schoolgirl and was sent to gaol for three years. On his release he took up the cause of colonization, urging emigration to Australia and pointing out that the policy of granting free lands produced an acute shortage of labour. He then transferred his interest to *New Zealand, organizing a company to send out settlers and contributing to the formal annexation of that country in 1840.

**Walcheren landing,** 1809. Britain did not find it easy to wage war against Napoleonic Europe. Despite the catastrophic failure of the landing in Holland in 1799, the British government resolved in 1809 to try again. The object was to capture Walcheren, the island on which Flushing stands, menace Antwerp, and encourage the Dutch to rise against the French. Lord Chatham commanded 40,000 men, with Sir Richard Strachan in charge of a very large fleet. There was no element of surprise, French resistance was fierce, the commanders quarrelled, and the army was decimated by dysentery and fever. Some 106 men died in action, 4,000 from disease. The enterprise was abandoned.

**Wales, march (or marches) of** Comparable to 'mark' (German) and 'marche' (French), signifying, from the 11th cent., the borderland between the English shires and unsubdued Welsh kingdoms. It arose from the Anglo-Norman conquests from the 11th cent. onwards, and parts were a theatre of war until the late 13th. By 1300 the march enjoyed stability, politically and militarily, governmentally and socially. Its distinctive society embraced native and immigrant, Welsh, English, and French languages, and peculiar customs and laws. 'Marcher lords' enjoyed great authority to govern and exploit; the king's writ did not run and the common law did not normally operate there. There was no effective, supervisory authority, and the march acquired a reputation for independence and lawlessness. These matters were seriously addressed from Edward IV's reign by a *Council of the March, developing from the councils of English princes of Wales. By the Act of *Union (1536), the marcher lordships were absorbed in new or existing English or Welsh shires; but marcher lords survived and so did some of their rights over land and tenant.

**Wales, principality of** The term refers to the territorial dominion of the last Welsh princes of Wales; the estate granted to English princes of Wales after 1301; and the entire land of Wales following the Act of *Union (1536). The first Welsh ruler to call himself prince of Wales (1244) was *Dafydd ap Llywelyn. Dafydd's nephew *Llywelyn ap Gruffydd (d. 1282), prince of Wales, had a more extensive principality in north, northeast, and central Wales of which he was either direct ruler or overlord; his title and principality were acknowledged by Henry III to be hereditary (1267). Llywelyn's brother *Dafydd (d. 1283) claimed to be prince of Wales, but his principality was swiftly conquered by Edward I, who annexed and united it to the English crown (1284). This modified principality was bestowed in 1301 on Edward I's eldest surviving son, Edward, as the first English prince of Wales. From time to time thereafter, this principality was

the territorial endowment of the heir to the throne. It covered half of Wales and should 'never be separated from the crown, but should remain entirely to the kings of England for ever' (1301).

Edward I outlined an elaborate scheme of government for the principality of Wales in the statute of *Wales (1284). It was based on existing arrangements and hence had two sectors, of three counties in north Wales (Anglesey, Caernarfonshire, and Merioneth) based on Caernarfon, and of two counties in west Wales (Carmarthenshire and Cardiganshire) based on Carmarthen. The two sectors were frequently referred to, inaccurately, as the principality of north Wales and the principality of west (or south) Wales. It was a development of Llywelyn's principality, rather than a clear break with it, and it was larger than Llywelyn's in some respects.

The council of Edward IV's eldest son began to undertake responsibility for order not only in the principality but also (by 1476) in the marcher lordships and border English shires and so had a Wales-wide supervisory authority (as the *Council of the March) that was the germ of the arrangements made by the Act of Union (1536). These arrangements consolidated Wales administratively and constitutionally by extending the machinery of government of the principality of Wales to Wales as a whole, including Flintshire and the March. This principality retained peculiar features of law and justice, with separate courts albeit dispensing English common law, until, first, the Council of Wales and the March was abolished as a prerogative court in 1689 and, second, the great sessions were abolished in 1830 and the judicial system assimilated to that of England.

The concept of the principality of Wales within the United Kingdom survived, largely because of the distinctive culture, language, and sense of identity of the Welsh. Although in modern times prior to the 20th cent. princes of Wales visited their principality rarely, both prince and principality were a focus of Welsh sentiment.

**Wales, statute of** *See* RHUDDLAN.

**Walker, George** (1618-90). Walker, an elderly Church of Ireland clergyman, was the heart and soul of Londonderry's resistance to James II after the Glorious

w

Revolution. He held a living at Donaghmore, near Dungannon, and began raising troops early in 1689. In April he went to London-derry and acted as joint governor throughout the siege. He joined William at the start of his Irish campaign and was shot dead at the battle of the *Boyne.

**Wallace, William** (d. 1305). Scottish patri-ot. Wallace came of a middling family, retai-ners of the Stewarts in the neighbourhood of Paisley. In 1297 there were many prominent Scots anxious to resist Edward's 'take-over' of the previous year, including Wallace's lord, James, the hereditary steward of Scotland. In May Wallace killed the English sheriff of La-nark in an affray. He was joined by Sir William Douglas in an attack on the English justiciar at Scone. Others, including Robert Bruce, earl of Carrick, the future Robert I, were also prepared to join in. This rising might easily have achieved nothing, but in May another movement had started in Moray, with an at-tack on Inverness led by the young Andrew *Murray. By August, Murray and Wallace had joined forces and threatened Stirling. Their astute tactics at the battle of Stirling Bridge, and the ineptitude of the English commander Earl *Warenne, resulted in a dramatic victory.

By early 1298 Wallace had been knighted, and emerged as sole guardian. But at Falkirk the English knights and archers were devas-tating. The Scots were routed and Wallace escaped into hiding.

His next task was abroad. In 1299 he led a mission to the French court to get more ac-tive support from Philip IV, and seems to have stayed in Paris for most of the next year. By 1303 Wallace was back in Scotland, again fighting in the south. By 1304, Edward had triumphed and almost all the Scottish leaders submitted on negotiated terms.

Wallace was now a fugitive. In August 1305 he was captured, and there followed a show trial on 23 August, and immediate execution for 'treason', of which, as he had never sworn allegiance to Edward, he could not justly be accused. From that day, Wallace has been regarded as one of the greatest heroes in Scotland's national history.

**Waller, Sir William** (1598–1668). MP and parliamentary general during the Civil War. Educated at Magdalen Hall, Oxford, and Gray's Inn, Waller saw military service on the continent during the Thirty Years War. He was elected to the *Long Parliament, commissioned colonel under *Essex, and later major-general for the region around Gloucester. Emboldened by early military successes, he became a critic of Essex's lead-ership, but his own reputation suffered with his defeats at *Roundway Down (July 1643) and *Cropredy Bridge (June 1644). His nick-name 'William the Conqueror' was turned against him.

**Wallingford, treaty of** *See* WINCHES-TER, TREATY OF.

**Walpole, Horace, 4th earl of Orford** (1717–97). The youngest son of Sir Robert *Walpole, Horace Walpole became the most gifted letter-writer in English history. When he entered Parliament in 1741 his father's long administration was tottering to its fall. Though he remained in the Commons until 1768 he made no mark and his preferred role was that of observer. The places and pen-sions provided by his father afforded him a comfortable bachelor existence and he lav-ished great attention on the Gothic villa at Strawberry Hill (Twickenham) which he pur-chased in 1748. Much of his time was devoted to correspondence with his many friends and acquaintances. But he also wrote substantial works. *The Castle of Otranto* (1764) was an early example of the Gothic horror novel and *Historic Doubts on Richard III* (1768) fathered a minor academic industry.

**Walpole, Sir Robert, 1st earl of Or-ford** (1676–1745). Traditionally known as Britain's first prime minister. From a Norfolk gentry family, Walpole was the Whig MP for Castle Rising (1701–2) and King's Lynn (1702–12, 1713–42). His first posts were as secretary at war (1708) and treasurer of the navy (1710). His part in the administration of the War of the *Spanish Succession and his management of the trial of Dr *Sacheverell earned him the hatred of the Tory Party and he was dismissed in 1710, impeached for corruption, sent to the Tower (1711), and expelled from Parliament (1712). At the Han-overian succession he rejoined the govern-ment, along with his brother-in-law Viscount *Townshend, as paymaster-general, being promoted to 1st lord of the Treasury and chancellor of the Exchequer in 1715. In

1717 he, Townshend, and several followers left the *Sunderland/*Stanhope ministry. During the ensuing Whig schism Walpole opposed the repeal of the *Occasional Conformity and *Schism Acts (1718), and successfully defeated the *Peerage Bill in the Commons (1719). In April 1720, with most of the schismatic Whigs, he rejoined the government in the office of paymaster-general, resuming in 1721 as chancellor of the Exchequer and 1st lord of the Treasury.

Despite his financial acumen, which saved the administration and the dynasty in 1720-1 from the disaster of the *South Sea bubble, he did not yet dominate the ministry. Both Stanhope (who died prematurely in 1721), and more particularly Sunderland (who also died unexpectedly in April 1722), retained the confidence of George I until their deaths. Until 1724, when he was manœuvred into the lord-lieutenancy of Ireland, *Carteret was a potential rival. Further, from the very beginning of the reconciliation of the Whigs in 1720, Townshend was a major force to be reckoned with, particularly through his control of foreign policy after 1721. Townshend remained in office until his resignation in 1730, and for most of the 1720s the ministry should be seen as a duumvirate. Only in the late 1720s did Walpole become the unquestioned prime minister, partly through forcing the most talented of his Whig opponents, led by *Pulteney, into opposition.

Walpole's major contribution to politics was his development of the cabinet system, of the 'party of the crown' (which he based on the work of Harley) through extensive use of patronage, and of the Commons as the centre of parliamentary power. Following the South Sea crisis, Walpole's establishment of the Whig hegemony was largely accomplished as a result of his handling of the *Atterbury plot in 1722-3, which he used to drive home the fear of *Jacobitism, a label he had great success in attaching to his Tory opponents.

His sure grip on politics occasionally wavered. One such occasion was the *Excise scheme in 1733, which aroused so much opposition that Walpole was forced into dropping the proposal before the second reading. Another was his opposition to war with Spain in 1739, to which he was forced to agree by both the patriot opposition and

members of his own government. The poor handling of the war eventually led to his downfall in February 1742.

Walpole was created earl of Orford upon his resignation, and helped from the Upper House to baffle efforts to impeach him for corruption. He continued to give advice to George II when asked. He devoted much of his time to Houghton in Norfolk, the palatial house he had built and stocked with art treasures. He died in debt.

**Walsingham** Marian shrine, Norfolk. The earliest shrine, dedicated to the Holy House of Nazareth, was built by the lady of the manor, Richeldis de Faverches, traditionally to commemorate her vision of the Blessed Virgin (1061). Both shrine and adjacent Augustinian priory gained fame and wealth from pilgrims and their bequests, until destruction 1538-9.

**Walsingham, Sir Francis** (c.1532-90). Walsingham matriculated at King's College, Cambridge, in 1548 and was taught by the prominent humanist (and *Cecil's father-in-law) Sir John *Cheke. He became privy counsellor and principal secretary in 1571 and held the post until his death. Walsingham was a strong protestant, watchful against catholic plots and anxious for a European coalition of protestant powers.

**Walter, Hubert** (c.1140-1205). Viewed by many as one of the greatest royal ministers of all time. Introduced into Henry II's service by his uncle Ranulf *Glanvill, his career blossomed under Richard I. Created bishop of Salisbury in 1189, he accompanied Richard as his chief of staff on crusade. His performance in such challenging conditions led to his being promoted in 1193 to take charge of both secular and ecclesiastical government as *justiciar and archbishop of Canterbury.

**Waltham Black Act,** 1722. The statute of 9 Geo. I c. 22 has long been held up as a specimen of draconian 18th-cent. legislation. It originated in response to an outbreak of organized poaching in Windsor Forest and near Waltham (Hants), and declared that to go abroad in woodland areas in disguise or with blackened face was a felony without benefit of clergy and punishable by death. The gangs were so intimidating that more and more offences were specified until the

Act became a compendium of rural disorder —cutting down trees, maiming cattle, setting fire to ricks, breaking down fish-ponds, writing threatening letters, and shooting at people. It was abolished, largely at the instigation of *Mackintosh and *Peel, in 1823.

**Waltheof** (d. 1076). Waltheof was the son of *Siward, earl of Northumberland and victor over *Macbeth, who died in 1055. Waltheof did not then inherit the earldom, presumably because he was too young, and it passed to *Tostig, brother of Harold Godwineson. But on Tostig's exile in 1065, Waltheof became earl of Huntingdon. In 1069 he joined the Danish attack on York, but submitted to William the Conqueror in 1070, and was made earl of Northumberland two years later. He was also given a niece of the king in marriage. But in 1075 he was on the fringes of another conspiracy against William, who had him executed at Winchester the following year.

**Walton, Izaak** (1593–1683). Biographer. Of Staffordshire yeoman stock and member of the Ironmongers' Company, this kindly Fleet Street tradesman is immortalized through the quiet charm of his *Compleat Angler* (1653). He was better known to contemporaries for his lives of *Donne, Wootton, *Hooker, *Herbert, and Sanderson. Later commentators have emphasized subjectivity and irregularities, though admitting his good intentions.

**Walton, Sir William** (1902–83). English composer. Walton was a chorister and undergraduate at Oxford, although he remained a largely self-taught composer. He was adopted by the Sitwell family, causing a stir with his 'entertainment' *Façade* (1921-2), in which Edith Sitwell's poems were recited through a megaphone. The Viola Concerto (1929) helped establish a less controversial reputation. The dramatic paganism of *Belshazzar's Feast* (1931), although initially startling to audiences with its raw energy and powerful orchestration, lies firmly within the English choral tradition. His film music is justly renowned, especially the score for *Olivier's *Henry V* (1943-4).

**Wandewash, battle of,** 1760. On 22 January 1760 Sir Eyre *Coote defeated the forces of the Count de Lally at Wandewash, in south India, to signal the dominance of the English *East India Company over its French equivalent. After Wandewash, Coote went on to capture the French capital of Pondicherry.

**Wantage code** King *Æthelred's third law code. Issued at Wantage (Berks.) possibly in 997, it showed royal confirmation of local court customs in the five boroughs of the *Danelaw. Twelve leading *thegns in each *wapentake were to swear on relics neither to accuse an innocent man nor conceal a guilty one, the earliest reference in English law to what was effectively a sworn jury of presentment.

**wapentakes** in England were, from the 10th cent., subdivisions of shires in the *Danelaw, corresponding to *hundreds elsewhere. The terms applied in Derbyshire, part of Lancashire, Leicestershire, Lincolnshire, Nottinghamshire, Rutland, and Yorkshire. The word signified the brandishing of weapons in approval at a meeting.

**Warbeck, Perkin** (1474–99). Warbeck was a troublesome pretender to Henry VII's crown. He claimed to be Richard, duke of York, the younger of the two princes, sons of Edward IV. He was in fact born in Tournai. When he appeared in Cork in 1491 he was taken up by a number of people who wished to embarrass Henry. James IV of Scotland welcomed him and gave him his cousin in marriage. In 1497 he landed in Cornwall, but failed to take Exeter or Taunton. He surrendered at Beaulieu and was spared his life on confession. In 1499, having attempted to escape from the Tower, he was hanged at Tyburn.

**wardrobe** Financial institution. As its name suggests, the wardrobe was originally the place in which the king's robes were placed for safe keeping, and where cash was held from which the king's personal expenses might be paid. The keeper of the wardrobe was also the *treasurer of the household; he received moneys for its upkeep, checked the accounts of its departments, and rendered them to the Exchequer. The wars of Edward I and his successors boosted the wardrobe's significance further by making it the equivalent of a war treasury which travelled with the campaigning king. Subsequent rulers, however, continued to use the wardrobe for both regular household and military expenses although the Yorkist and early Tudor kings placed greater emphasis on the chamber for their private and 'secret' expenses.

**Wards, Court of** This court was set up in 1540 by Henry VIII to enforce the lord's rights of wardship and marriage which had existed, since the Norman Conquest, as feudal incidents. The purpose of the Court of Wards was to enforce payment of these ancient feudal dues to the crown and thus to increase the income of the king. It was abolished in 1656.

**Warenne, John de, 7th earl of Surrey** (*c.*1231–1304). Warenne inherited the earldom in 1240 when a boy and in 1247 was married to Henry III's half-sister Alice de Lusignan. During the civil war he supported Henry and was on the losing royal side at the battle of *Lewes in 1264. The following year he joined Prince Edward and took part in the campaign that ended with de *Montfort's death at *Evesham. He was a guardian during Edward I's absence during the early weeks of his reign, was much employed in the later 1270s and 1280s against the Welsh, and in the 1290s against the Scots. In 1296 he inflicted a sharp defeat on the Scots at *Dunbar but the following year was badly beaten by *Wallace at *Stirling Bridge. He was retained for the 1298 campaign when Edward defeated the Scots at *Falkirk.

**Warham, William** (*c.*1450–1532). Archbishop of Canterbury. Born in Hampshire and educated in law at New College, Oxford, Warham frequently served as a diplomat (1491–1502) and negotiated Prince *Arthur's marriage to *Catherine of Aragon (1496). He was successively master of the rolls (1494), bishop of London (1502), archbishop (1504), and lord chancellor (1504–15). From 1515 *Wolsey, as cardinal, lord chancellor, and papal legate, constantly overshadowed Warham. Under pressure he signed the petition requesting papal consent for a divorce. Described as 'morose and inflexible', he was nevertheless competent and conscientious.

**War of 1812** The last conflict between Britain and the USA began when the British blockade of Napoleonic Europe and naval impressment of American sailors inflamed relations. Western American politicians campaigned for conquest of Canada to open land for settlement and eliminate Indian resistance. Congress declared war on 16 June 1812. The Americans failed to overrun Canada, despite battles including *Queenston Heights (1812). The British retaliated for the destruction of York (later Toronto) in April 1813 by occupying Washington in August 1814 and burning the White House. The war was ended by the treaty of *Ghent, with its causes unresolved.

**War Office** The centre of British army administration from at least 1661 until the emergence of the Ministry of Defence in 1963, the War Office was designed to impose civilian control over military affairs. Before 1855, it was run by the curiously named secretary at war, but in the light of disasters in the Crimea, all administrative duties were consolidated under the secretary of state for war, a cabinet post. As the need for military advice to politicians grew, clashes between the secretary of state and military men became inevitable. In 1914 these clashes were dealt with by appointing Lord *Kitchener, an experienced soldier, as secretary of state. During the Second World War Winston *Churchill, as prime minister, assumed the role of 'minister of defence' and downgraded the influence of the War Office. Although the War Office was revived after 1945, any hopes of continued independence faded in light of a need for consolidated inter-service policies and economy. The Ministry of *Defence was the answer.

**Warwick, Richard Neville, 1st earl of** (1428–71), known as 'the Kingmaker'. Warwick was the mightiest of overmighty subjects, who was instrumental in putting Edward IV on the throne in 1461, deposing him in 1470, and restoring Henry VI. Warwick owed his power to his vast estates, combining in his own hands no fewer than four earldoms. Neville resources enabled the Yorkists successfully to overthrow Henry VI in 1461. In the next four years Warwick proved indispensable to Edward IV. Lavishly rewarded and allowed to take virtual control of northern England, he resented loss of influence after 1465. He first withdrew from court (1467) and eventually after two

**w**

abortive rebellions (1469 and 1470) he resorted to the restoration of Henry VI. However, the restoration was short-lived and on Easter Sunday 1471 Warwick was defeated and killed by Edward IV at *Barnet. He was an inept general, and this, in the last resort, was his undoing.

**Warwick, Edward Plantagenet, 2nd earl of** (1475–99). Warwick's father was George, duke of *Clarence (brother of Edward IV and Richard III), who was murdered when Warwick was 3. After Henry VII's victory at *Bosworth, he was placed in the Tower. In 1487 Lambert *Simnel claimed to be him and was crowned in Dublin, whereupon Warwick was taken publicly to St Paul's to quell the rumours. He remained in the Tower until November 1499 when he was accused of conspiring with Perkin *Warbeck and executed.

**Warwick castle,** sited on a cliff above the Avon, was founded by William the Conqueror in 1068 and has been the seat of the earls of Warwick from the 11th cent. It began as a motte and bailey castle, a stone castle from at least the 12th cent. The present castle owes much to the major rebuilding under the powerful Beauchamp earls, Thomas (d. 1369) and his son, also Thomas (d. 1401).

**Warwickshire** was an archetypal Mercian shire, regular in shape and taking its name from the chief town. *Camden placed it in the territory of the *Cornovii and divided it into the arable south, or Fielden, and the wooded north around the forest of Arden. The Fielden territory had been part of the land of the *Hwicce. Warwickshire formed the heartland of the kingdom of Mercia: in the 8th and 9th cents. Tamworth was the chief residence of the Mercian monarchs and Warwick was refounded in 914 by *Æthelfleda, lady of the Mercians.

It remained a rural county throughout the Middle Ages. Warwick itself was a significant provincial city, *Kenilworth and *Warwick castles important until the civil wars, and *Coventry had a reputation for cloth-making. The gradual improvement in transport through inland navigation, turnpikes, and finally railways brought Warwickshire into the national orbit. The Liverpool to Birmingham railway opened in 1837, the London to Birmingham in 1838.

The modern history of the county is the development of industry in the northern parts around *Birmingham and Coventry, exploiting the proximity of woodland, coal, and iron resources. Camden described Birmingham in Elizabeth's reign as 'swarming with inhabitants and echoing with the noise of anvils'. It passed Coventry in size during the 17th cent. and by 1700 had grown to around 15,000 people. It was given two MPs by the Great Reform Act of 1832. In the later 19th cent. Birmingham was granted city status and under Joseph *Chamberlain led the way in progressive local government. To nail-making, small arms, cutlery, and button-making was added industry of all kinds: Cadbury's moved to Bournville in 1879 and the Austin Motor Company opened at Longbridge in 1905. By 1911 the population was well over half a million.

*Stratford-upon-Avon owed its fame as a tourist attraction largely to the Shakespeare Jubilee of 1769, organized by David *Garrick. The salt springs at Leamington had been known since Tudor times, but the expansion of the town was 19th cent., the Pump Room opening in 1814. Nuneaton developed as a textile centre, Courtauld's setting up a factory in 1920, and Rugby grew steadily after the opening of the London to Birmingham railway, on which it was an important junction.

**Washington, George** (1732–99). First president of the USA. Washington's ancestors came from Northamptonshire and settled in Virginia in 1657. He inherited the Mount Vernon estate in 1752 when his half-brother died. Washington's first military experience was gained in the Virginia militia. He was appointed commander of the Virginia forces at the age of 23, and elected to the state legislature. After attending the first and second continental congresses in 1774 and 1775, he was elected commander of the congress forces. His first victory of any importance was at *Trenton in December 1776 and he held his army together through the terrible winter at Valley Forge in 1777–8. At the end of hostilities, on 19 April 1783, he led the triumphal march into New York. When the Federal constitution was adopted, Washington was the obvious choice for the presidency, and was unanimously elected and re-elected in 1789 and 1793. He retired in 1797 to spend his last two years back in Mount Vernon.

**Washington, treaty of,** 1871. The USA claimed compensation from Britain for the depredations of the *Alabama*, a Confederate warship built in England during the Civil War. Also in dispute was access to the Canadian fisheries and ownership of San Juan Island off British Columbia. Britain agreed to arbitration: San Juan was awarded to the USA, and $15.5 million was paid for the *Alabama* claims. Although a poor settlement for Britain and Canada, the treaty was a milestone in international arbitration.

**watch and ward** was an attempt at a more effective policing system, which started in 1233 with a specific incident. After disturbances, Henry III ordered all vills (townships) to arrange guards at night and apprehend suspicious persons. The instructions were repeated in 1242, and in Edward I's reign were promulgated in the statute of *Winchester of 1285. Its modern echoes are the neighbourhood watches set up in many suburbs and villages in the 1980s.

**Waterford (Port Láirge), diocese of** Originally a Norse city and thus an object of Anglo-Norman colonization of Ireland, it was a suffragan see of *Canterbury from 1096. Waterford was first listed as a bishopric at the Council of Kells-Mellifont (1152), though there was no regular succession of bishops until 1175. Waterford and Lismore is still a catholic bishopric in the province of Cashel, but the Anglican see was merged with the Cashel diocese in 1833.

**Waterloo, battle of,** 1815. In June 1815, Napoleon struck into Belgium, hoping to destroy *Wellington's Anglo-Dutch army and Blücher's Prussians before they could unite. After the battle of *Quatre Bras on 16 June, Wellington's inexperienced army of 67,000 men fell back to a ridge near Waterloo. The 89,000 strong Prussian army, badly mauled at Ligny on the same day, also retreated.

The battle began on 18 June with an unsuccessful attack on Hougoumont, a fortified farmhouse on Wellington's right flank. The arrival of Prussian forces compelled Napoleon to send part of his élite Imperial Guard to his right flank. By 6.30 p.m. the key farmhouse of La Haye Sainte had fallen to the

French, and an all-out assault might have broken Wellington's lines. However, Napoleon prevaricated, and only released his reserve—the Imperial Guard—at 7.00. The repulse of the Guard was the signal for the rout of Napoleon's army. With Blücher's men pouring on the field, Napoleon was finally defeated.

**Watling Street** is the later name for the major Roman road from Dover through Canterbury to London and thence via *Verulamium to Wroxeter (later the basis for *Telford's Holyhead road, the A5). The Anglo-Saxon name *Wæcelinga Stræt*, meant 'the street of the people of Wæcel'.

**Watson-Watt, Robert** (1892–1973). Scientist. Born in Brechin of a family related to James *Watt, Watson-Watt studied engineering at University College, Dundee. During the First World War he was posted to the Royal Aircraft Factory at Farnborough, which had begun studying the use of radio to predict atmospheric storms. In the 1930s his team became involved in air defence against bombers. By 1935 Watson-Watt was able to present a paper on 'The detection of aircraft by radio method'. By 1938 the basis of a radar defence system had been established and played a crucial part in the Battle of *Britain in 1940.

**Watt, James** (1736–1819). Instrument-maker to Glasgow University, where he applied principles of latent heat to the *Newcomen engine to patent the separate condenser in 1769, and found a career as leading steam engineer, conducted mainly (1775–1800) in partnership with *Boulton. Watt stopped his assistant's experiments with steam carriages, enthusiastically protected his patents, remained committed to low-pressure operation, and probably retarded steam innovations before 1800. Other research led to his patenting of a damp-paper letter copier (1780); experiments with the properties of air; the principle of the marine screw; and many measuring devices, in addition to his respecification of *Savery's 'horsepower' as a standard unit.

**Waugh, Evelyn** (1903–66). Novelist and satirist whose early books *Decline and Fall* (1928) and *Vile Bodies* (1930) chronicle the

W

doings of the Bright Young Things at Oxford and after with an ironic detachment approaching the grotesque. The central event in his life was conversion to Roman catholicism in 1930. Though middle-class himself, son of a successful publisher, like the narrator of *Brideshead Revisited* (1945) he cultivated the aristocracy and the old order. If his latter-day persona as irascible country gentleman sometimes verged on self-parody, in *The Sword of Honour* trilogy (1962) he convinces us that the concept is more than another name for snobbery.

**Wavell, Archibald Percival** (1883–1950). British general, commander-in-chief Middle East from July 1939, he directed campaigns against Italians after June 1940. In Cyrenaica he won a series of spectacular victories from December 1940 to February 1941, taking prisoner 130,000 Italians. He was then ordered to give priority to helping Greece. There, and in Africa, German contingents inflicted defeat and in spring 1941 both Cyrenaica and Greece were lost. In July *Auchinleck took over and Wavell became C.-in-C., India. He could not stop the loss of Malaya, Singapore, the Dutch East Indies, and Burma to the Japanese. Promoted field marshal and viscount, he became viceroy of India in June 1943.

**Wealth of Nations, The** Adam *Smith's treatise was published in 1776 when the old mercantilist system was fast breaking down. In simple and direct language, Smith argued the case for *laissez-faire* with a minimum of government intervention, though he conceded the need for regulation to protect national security, such as fostering shipping. He did not believe that politicians had any competence in directing economic activity, nor did he like their motives—'there is no art which one government sooner learns of another than that of draining money from the pockets of the people'.

**Webb, Sidney** (1859–1947) and **Beatrice** (1858–1943). Fabian socialists, social reformers, and historians. Married in 1882, the Webbs formed a partnership of unparalleled significance for the development of left-wing social policies in Britain. Sidney served on the London County Council from 1892 to 1910, became a Labour MP for Seaham in 1922, becoming president of the Board of Trade in 1924, and as Baron Passfield in 1929 serving briefly as secretary of state for the dominions and colonies.

The Webbs' approach to social reform was gradualist. In the 1930s, however, they became disillusioned with the progress of socialism in Britain and turned their attention to the USSR, which they found so impressive that in their last substantial book, *Soviet Communism: A New Civilisation?* (1935), they abandoned their piecemeal approach to political and social change.

**Wedderburn, Alexander, 1st earl of Rosslyn** (1733–1805). Wedderburn, a member of a Scottish legal family, was called to the English bar in 1757 and entered Parliament in 1761. He supported *Bute, *Grenville, and *North, becoming solicitor-general 1771–8 and attorney-general 1778–80. He was an effective speaker in the Commons, with a reputation for self-advancement. Appointed lord chief justice of Common Pleas in 1780 as Baron Loughborough, he remained a follower of North and helped to negotiate the coalition with *Fox in 1783. After the French Revolution he attempted to negotiate a junction between *Pitt and the opposition to support war against France but was tempted by Pitt's offer of the lord chancellorship and crossed the House alone. He left office with Pitt in 1801 and received the earldom of Rosslyn.

**Wedgwood, Josiah** (1730–95). Potter, industrialist, and social reformer. Wedgwood was born into a Staffordshire family of potters and was at work by the age of 9. Shrewd and innovative in manufacture, design, and marketing, he capitalized on 18th-cent. fashion and snobbery, setting up on his own in 1758, and opening the great Etruria factory in 1769. A notable commission came from Catherine the Great in 1774: a 952-piece service, now in the Hermitage Museum in St Petersburg, decorated with exquisite and accurate detail of 18th-cent. houses and countryside.

Wedgwood was keenly interested in the social and political problems of his day, much involved in road and canal development, and constantly reviewed the working and living conditions of his employees. His views were liberal/radical, he was sympathetic towards American independence in the 1770s, welcomed the French Revolution, and was a fervent supporter of the abolition of slavery.

**Wedmore, treaty of,** 878. The agreement made between King *Alfred and the Danish leader *Guthrum at Wedmore proved a turning-point in the Danish wars. From their fortified position at Chippenham the Danes had threatened to overrun all Wessex, but Alfred emerged from his refuge at Athelney, inflicted a severe defeat on the Danes at *Edington, and forced peace on Guthrum on condition that he would himself accept baptism and that his army would leave Wessex. The Danes kept the substance of the arrangement, moving the army back to Cirencester and ultimately to East Anglia.

**Welles, Richard and Robert** (d. 1470). Lionel, Lord Welles, and his son Richard, Lord Willoughby, fought against Edward IV at *Towton in 1461, when Lionel was killed. By fighting for Edward against Lancastrians in 1464, Richard recovered his father's title and estates. Then, in a private feud, he sacked the house of Thomas Burgh at Gainsborough. Determined to restore order, Edward summoned Richard and planned a formidable royal visitation of Lincolnshire. At this point, apparently, *Warwick and *Clarence fomented a rebellion to oppose Edward's arrival. His rapid march caught them unprepared. The locals assembled by Richard's son Robert were scattered at Empingham, in an action known as *Losecoat Field on 12 March 1470. Richard and Robert Welles were executed; Warwick and Clarence fled to France.

**Wellesley, Richard, 1st Marquis Wellesley** (1760–1842). Eldest brother of the duke of Wellington, Wellesley entered Parliament in 1784 as MP for Beeralston. In 1793 he became a member of the India Board and from 1797 to 1805 acted as governor-general of Bengal. British rule was threatened by the French in alliance with Tipu Sahib of Mysore and the nizam of Hyderabad. Wellesley retorted by taking control of Mysore, the Carnatic, Hyderabad, and Oudh, bringing native princes under British influence. He served as foreign secretary in *Perceval's cabinet. Wellesley championed the rights of catholics in Ireland and in

1821–8 and 1833–4 acted as lord-lieutenant of Ireland. In 1835 he became lord chamberlain.

**Wellington, Arthur Wellesley, 1st duke of** (1769–1852). Soldier and prime minister. Arthur Wellesley was the third surviving son of the earl of Mornington, an impoverished Irish peer. After a year at a French military academy at Angers, he entered the army by purchasing a commission. Early experience in the campaigns in the Low Countries during the first years of the Revolutionary War showed how things should not be done. His great chance came in India, where his elder brother was governor-general. Arthur established his military reputation by winning the spectacular victories of Assaye and Argaum over the Mahrattas in 1803. In 1808 he was sent as commander of the first detachment of British troops to Portugal. Winning the battle of *Vimeiro he was recalled to face a court of inquiry after the armistice of *Cintra, which was seen in England as craven. Wellesley had signed the agreement under orders, but was bitterly attacked by opposition politicians. Cleared by the inquiry he resumed command of the British army in Portugal after the death of *Moore. Shrewdly exploiting natural features and the engineering skills of the British army to construct the lines of *Torres Vedras he ensured that the British army would not be pushed into the sea. But he was more than a defensive general. He was bold when necessary, as the assaults on the fortresses of Badajoz and Ciudad Rodrigo showed, and in the battles of *Salamanca, *Vitoria, and the *Pyrenees he was as resourceful in attack as he had been in defence. The end of the Peninsular War saw him as the most famous British general since the duke of Marlborough. The battle of *Waterloo in 1815 confirmed his stature and his fame. He cared for his men and husbanded their lives, scorned extravagant gestures, and despised popularity.

After 1815 Wellington was prominent as a diplomat and politician. He had owed much to *Castlereagh; now he became one of his trusted lieutenants in the complex diplomacy of the post-war era. He also became a member of *Liverpool's government, believing that it was his duty to serve the state in whatever capacity might

**W**

be required of him. After the death of *Canning and the failure of the *Goderich ministry, Wellington became prime minister in January 1828. When in 1828 a crisis erupted in Ireland he chose to grant catholic emancipation rather than risk civil war. This earned him the hatred of the ultra-Tories and he fought a duel with Lord Winchilsea. In 1830 Wellington attempted to rally conservative opinion by affirming his resolute opposition to parliamentary reform. The tactic failed to restore confidence in his administration. In November 1830 he was defeated on the civil list in the Commons and resigned. Although Wellington opposed the Reform Bill he realized that opposition had to be attuned to the realities of politics. He therefore led 100 Tory peers from their seats in the Lords to allow the Reform Bill to pass in June 1832, preferring reform to the prospect of the Upper House being swamped by newly created peers. In 1834, during the crisis provoked by *Melbourne's resignation, Wellington became a caretaker prime minister for some three weeks and after 1835 he played an important role as an elder statesman.

**Wells, H. G.** (1866–1946). Shopkeeper's son who jumped the counter to become successful author and eventually teacher-at-large to the human race. A scholarship to what is now Imperial College, London, where he studied under T. H. *Huxley, suggested the power of science to make us free, though it was an imaginative energy which fuelled his early romances *The Time Machine* (1895) and *The War of the Worlds* (1898). Moving in literary and *Fabian circles, he saw the novel as a medium for discussing contemporary problems. *Kipps* (1905) and *The History of Mr Polly* (1910) offer portraits of the little man, and *Tono-Bungay* (1909) of the world of commerce. The best-selling *Outline of History* (1920) offered mankind 'salvation by history', lasting world peace only to be secured by learning its lessons.

**Wells cathedral** *See* BATH AND WELLS.

**Welsh language** The oldest language spoken in Britain, with an unbroken history from Brythonic origins as part of the Celtic family of Indo-European languages from which most European languages derive. Germanic and English advances westward led to

the separate development of Brythonic Celtic in Wales, Cumbria, and Cornwall: only Welsh survives; Cumbric died out in the 11th cent. and Cornish in the 18th. Those who used this language called themselves *Cymry* (fellow-countrymen).

Welsh appeared as a recognizable language before AD 600; up to the mid-12th cent., when French and English influences became strong, Old Welsh has left few traces apart from inscriptions, manuscript glosses, and Welsh poetry in saga or prophetic vein. Middle Welsh from the mid-12th cent. to the early 15th was rich in prose and popular verse, whose writers were patronized by Welsh princes and then (after 1283) by gentry of Welsh and immigrant lineage. The same influences that enriched the language set the scene for its decline, for trends in government and society, immigration and town foundation, popularized Latin, French, and especially English in the later Middle Ages. The Act of *Union (1536) sought to replace Welsh with English in official contexts; it discouraged its use and patronage, and the gentry gradually ceased to speak Welsh, adopting English surnames instead of Welsh patronymics.

Salvation came with printing and the Reformation, especially with the translation of the Scriptures and the Prayer Book into Welsh (1567, 1588). Educational, antiquarian, publishing, and religious movements in the 17th and 18th cents. ensured its survival as a spoken and written tongue; indeed, the 18th cent. saw a renaissance in Welsh culture. Even after half a century of industrialization, in 1801 80 per cent of Wales was Welsh-speaking. Industrialization was not at first an enemy to Welsh, for many migrants to the southern valleys were Welsh-speaking, but as a proportion of the expanding population they were a declining number. The popularity of English among the upper classes, the demands of British education, the cosmopolitan industrial and commercial centres, immigration, and mass media and communications undermined Wales's linguistic character and portrayed the language as old-fashioned. By 1901, 50 per cent of Wales's population spoke Welsh; thereafter the decline was relentless.

Yet since the 18th cent., Welsh literary culture has shown some creativity: an interest in Welsh history and tradition (including the *eisteddfod), a vigorous Welsh press, active nonconformity, the growth of national sentiment, and the foundation of national institutions (notably a library, museum, and university) in the late 19th and early 20th cents. More recently, opinion has focused intently on the question of the language's survival. It has been buttressed by academic study and a literary renaissance, acceptance at all levels of education, as well as by pressure groups, even perhaps violent protests. It remains to be seen whether this nurturing will enhance its vitality and stem its overall decline.

**Welsh Nationalist Party** *See* PLAID CYMRU.

**Wembley stadium** The Great Stadium at Wembley Park, London, was built to coincide with the British Empire Exhibition of 1923. Work was completed just four days before hosting its first Football Association Cup Final on 29 April 1923. The Rugby League Cup Final was played at Wembley every year between 1929 and 2000 (except 1932). The greatest moments in its history were the hosting of the 1948 Olympic Games and the 1966 World Cup. The stadium was completely rebuilt from 2000 and opened in 2007 to hold 90,000 spectators.

**Wensleydale's peerage case** In 1856 Sir James Parke, judge of the Court of Exchequer, was raised to the peerage with the title of Baron Wensleydale. However, the patent which conferred the title stated his barony was to be held 'for the term of his natural life'. Lords *Lyndhurst, *Brougham, and Campbell were united in opposing the change. After great argument, the government gave way and conferred on Parke an ordinary patent of peerage. Life peerages were postponed until 1958.

**wergeld** was the fixed amount, or blood-price, payable by a killer and his kin to his victim's kinsmen. A man's kin was obliged to seek vengeance for his untimely death, but payment of wergeld was an alternative to blood-feud, and a means of keeping order in a violent society. The amount of wergeld was also an important mark of social status.

**Wesley, Charles** (1707–88). Hymn-writer. Like his brother John, Charles was educated at Oxford, ordained in the Church of England, and became a leading methodist preacher. Methodism, it has been said, was born in song; and this was facilitated by the magnificent collection of hymns written by Charles Wesley, perhaps the greatest hymn-writer England has ever known. Favourites like 'Hark! The Herald Angels Sing' and 'Jesu, Lover of my Soul' became familiar far beyond the bounds of methodism.

**Wesley, John** (1703–91). Founder of methodism. Educated at Christ Church, Oxford, and elected a fellow of Lincoln College, Wesley was ordained in the Church of England. At Oxford in 1729 he gathered round him a group of devout Christians who were nicknamed methodists because they sought to follow strictly the method of study and practice laid down in the statutes of the church. After a short-lived missionary journey to Georgia, during which he was much influenced by some Moravian brethren, Wesley experienced a sudden conversion (1738). For over 50 years Wesley travelled all over Britain on horseback, averaging 5,000 miles annually, preaching thousands of sermons, often three times a day. Wesley wished methodism to remain within the Church of England, but this was not possible, given official Anglican hostility and the desire of conference (the supreme body of methodism) for independence.

**Wessex, kingdom of** The origins of the kingdom of Wessex are obscure. Archaeological evidence shows that the communities of Germanic settlers established in the middle Thames region in the late 5th and early 6th cents. constituted one of the principal elements, but literary evidence emphasizes a more southerly origin in the movement of *Cerdic and his successors in the early 6th cent. from a base in the Portsmouth area into Hampshire and Wiltshire. Historic shape was given to Wessex in the reign of *Ceawlin (560–91), who claimed descent from Cerdic and was described by *Bede as a *bretwalda (overlord of the Germanic settlers in Britain). At the battle of *Dyrham near Bath in 577, he won a victory over the Britons which left him in control of Bath, Cirencester, and Gloucester. Under two powerful kings, *Cædwalla (685–8) and *Ine (688–726), the West Saxons extended their political control over Devon

W

and Somerset. Ine died on pilgrimage to Rome and for the rest of the 8th cent. Wessex played a subordinate part to *Mercia in English affairs. Revival came in the 9th cent. during the reign of *Egbert (802–39). After his defeat of the Mercians at *Ellendun in 825 the *Anglo-Saxon Chronicle* referred to him as bretwalda. This did not prove permanent, but the south-east and East Anglia continued to acknowledge his lordship. His son *Æthelwulf (839–58) and his grandsons, especially his youngest grandson, *Alfred the Great (871–99), consolidated the West Saxon hold over Sussex, Surrey, and Kent. But the whole political structure of England was changed in the second half of the 9th cent. by the Danish invasions. Alfred's heroic defence resulted in the peace of *Wedmore (878) which left all England north and east of Watling Street and the river Lea in Danish hands. Alfred regained London after 886 and skilfully exploited his position as sole surviving effective representative of the ancient ruling English dynasties. From that point onwards the story of the kingdom of Wessex folds absolutely into the story of the kingdom of England. Alfred's work was consolidated by the campaigns of his son, *Edward the Elder, who doubled the territory under the control of Wessex.

**West, Benjamin** (1738–1820). History and portrait painter. West was born a British subject in Pennsylvania, remaining a loyalist all his life. He learned to paint in America, and studied for three years in Italy before settling in London in 1763. He was a founder member of the Royal Academy, becoming the second president on the death of *Reynolds. His *Death of Wolfe* (1771) broke with the tradition of painting heroes in classical costume and showed contemporary dress.

**Westbury, Richard Bethell, 1st Baron** (1800–73). Lawyer. Bethell was born in Bradford on Avon (Wilts.) and went to Wadham College, Oxford. After Middle Temple he began practising with great success. In 1851 he entered Parliament for Aylesbury as a Liberal, was made solicitor-general in 1852 and attorney-general in 1856. His ambition for the lord chancellorship was widely known and he obtained it, with a peerage, in 1861. He began a series of legal reforms but in 1865, peculation having been discovered in his office, a

select committee found in him a 'laxity of practice and want of caution'. He was censured by the House of Commons and obliged to resign.

**Western European Union (WEU).** This international security organization was initiated on 6 May 1955 when the Federal Republic of Germany and Italy joined the existing *Brussels Treaty Organization. This was a consequence of the refusal of the French National Assembly to ratify the European Defence Community plan (EDC). The pledge made by Britain to maintain troops in Europe in peacetime was a major innovation in foreign policy.

*NATO remained the primary West European security organization, but from 1958 to 1973 the WEU structure allowed the British government to consult with the six WEU states that had formed the *EEC without involving other NATO members. The organization was reactivated from 1984 to strengthen European influence within NATO and to promote EC foreign policy coordination (European Political Cooperation, EPC). The WEU played a prominent role in the Bosnian crisis in the 1990s.

**Western Isles (Na h-Eileanan Siar)** is the name given to the administrative region which since 1973 has been the local government area for the Outer Hebrides (Lewis, Harris, North and South Uist, Benbecula, Barra, Eriskay, and other small islands). Although the islands are diverse geologically, they are mostly rocky or peaty with sandy shores, supporting very limited agriculture, mainly in crofting townships, which provide some of the raw material for the woollen goods manufacture for which Harris is famed. The isolation of the Western Isles has helped Scottish Gaelic to survive as a living language, with distinctive accents in the different islands.

**Western Samoa** is a group of mountainous South Pacific islands with a population of about 165,000. Since 1962 they have been formed into an independent nation and joined the Commonwealth in 1970. In 1899 eastern Samoa was annexed by the USA, Western Samoa by Germany. In 1914 troops from New Zealand occupied Western Samoa and it became a New Zealand *mandate in 1920.

**West Indies** is the general geographical term for the many islands of the Caribbean, the largest of which are Cuba, Hispaniola (politically Haiti and the Dominican Republic), *Jamaica, Puerto Rico, *Trinidad, Guadeloupe, and Martinique. After Columbus' landing on San Salvador in 1492, Spain claimed the whole region. Sugar plantations were established and black African slaves introduced. The first inroads into the Spanish monopoly came when Spain, in the early 17th cent., was still struggling to put down the Dutch revolt in Europe. English settlement started at *St Kitts (1623) and *Barbados (1627), followed by *Antigua and *Montserrat (1632), Anguilla (1650), and the conquest of Jamaica in 1655 by a Cromwellian expedition. Meanwhile, France had acquired Guadeloupe and Martinique (1635), *Grenada in the 1640s, and had established a foothold on the western part of Hispaniola. Dutch settlements were on Curaçao and St Eustatius in the 1630s. Control by European governments was fitful and the West Indies gained its reputation for piracy and buccaneering.

The 18th cent. saw incessant warfare between the colonial powers, towns repeatedly sacked, and islands taken and retaken. Tobago changed hands so often that its inhabitants were said to live in a state of betweenity: at one stage, Charles II, who did not have it, granted it to the duke of Courland. At the end of the *Seven Years War in 1763, Britain retained Grenada, *Dominica, *St Vincent, and Tobago at the expense of France. When British sea power wobbled during the War of *American Independence, the French and Spanish took Grenada, Montserrat, St Kitts, St Vincent, and the Bahamas, but had to return them at the treaty of *Versailles in 1783, retaining only Tobago.

During the *Revolutionary and Napoleonic wars, Britain added Trinidad from Spain (1802) and *St Lucia from France (1814). By this time the West Indies were beginning to lose some of their economic importance to Britain, and the West Indian lobby some of its influence in Parliament. The slave trade was abolished in 1807 and slavery in the British empire in 1833. British rule in Jamaica was shaken by a rising in 1865, and the governor Edward Eyre recalled in disgrace, but control was reasserted.

Since the Second World War, the great majority of West Indian islands of any size have become sovereign states. In 1945 only Cuba, Haiti, and the Dominican Republic were independent. In 1958 the British introduced the West Indian Federation, long an aspiration, to improve political and economic co-operation, but it rapidly fell victim to inter-island rivalries. The Federation was wound up in 1962. Jamaica and Trinidad then became independent, followed by Barbados (1966), Bahamas (1973), Grenada (1974), Dominica (1978), St Lucia (1979), St Vincent (1979), Antigua (1981), and St Kitts and Nevis (1983). Two of the enduring legacies of British colonialism are the use of the English language and an awesome addiction to cricket.

**West Midlands** The metropolitan county of West Midlands was the creation of the Local Government Act of 1972. It brought together the county boroughs of Birmingham, Wolverhampton, Walsall, Dudley, Warley and West Bromwich, Solihull, and Coventry. The county headquarters was at Birmingham. The authority was abolished by the Local Government Act of 1985.

**Westminster, palace of** From the time of Edward the Confessor to the early years of the reign of Henry VIII, Westminster was the main royal residence. The palace grew up around the abbey built by the Confessor on Thorney Island and consecrated in December 1065, a week before the king's death. William Rufus built the great hall and first held court in it in 1099: it was reroofed by Richard II and for centuries was the home of the law courts, the place of impeachments and state trials, and the venue for the coronation banquet. By the 15th cent., the palace was a rabbit warren of rooms and corridors, swarming with servants and lawyers, and liable to flooding. After the fire of 1834, only Rufus' great hall was left.

**Westminster, provisions of,** 1259. The provisions of Westminster formed a stage in the conflict between Henry III and his baronial opponents led by Simon de *Montfort. By the provisions of *Oxford in June 1258 Henry had agreed to a mechanism of control, including the appointment of a supervising committee of fifteen. On 13 October 1259 in Westminster Hall, a detailed and miscellaneous programme of law reform was approved in response to a number of petitions and com-

**W**

plaints. The provisions were reissued in 1262 and 1264 and incorporated in the statute of Marlborough of 1267.

**Westminster, statute of,** 1275. The first statute of Westminster, promulgated in Edward I's first Parliament in 1275, was a great survey of the existing law, whose 51 clauses dealt with a vast variety of problems. The intention was to redress some of the grievances which had been felt during the new king's absence and which had been revealed by the hundred roll inquiries of 1274–5.

**Westminster, statute of,** 1285. The lengthy statute 13 Edw. I, usually known as Westminster II, was designed to remedy miscellaneous grievances at law. The most important provision was to tighten up the donor's rights over gifts of property. The statute was part of a determined attempt by Edward I to regulate a mass of law and custom and impose fairer solutions.

**Westminster, statute of,** 1290. The statute 18 Edw. I, known as Westminster III, was intended to prevent magnates being deprived of their feudal rights, such as escheat, marriage, or *wardship, by the sale of estates. It is generally accepted that the statute failed to hold the position.

**Westminster, statute of,** 1931. The immediate cause of the statute was the complaint of Mackenzie King, prime minister of Canada, that the governor-general had acted unconstitutionally in 1926 in refusing him a dissolution. This led the imperial conference of that year to discuss constitutional relationships. *Balfour, philosopher by inclination, defined Britain and the dominions as 'autonomous communities, equal in status, in no way subordinate one to another'. The statute of Westminster, 22 Geo. V c. 4, confirmed this position, leaving the crown and membership of the Commonwealth as the only link.

**Westminster, treaty of,** 1462. Edward IV, hoping to recover some of the influence in Scotland lost by the Wars of the *Roses, agreed in 1462 at Westminster with John *Macdonald, lord of the Isles and earl of Ross, and James, 9th earl of Douglas, that they should become his vassals and help him to gain the Scottish throne. Nothing came of the grandiose plan and it took Ed-

ward 20 years to recapture the border fortress of Berwick.

**Westminster, treaty of,** 1654. Though the Dutch had suffered more during the first *Anglo-Dutch War, the treaty which concluded it was mild, since *Cromwell was anxious to bring to an end this damaging quarrel between two protestant nations. The English *Navigation Act of 1651 remained on the statute book and the Estates of Holland agreed to exclude the house of Orange from public life, thus removing a potential source of assistance to the Stuarts in exile.

**Westminster, treaty of,** 1674. The treaty, signed on 19 February, brought to an end the third *Anglo-Dutch War. Since the Dutch were anxious to make a separate peace in order to concentrate on defeating the French, they offered concessions which did not reflect the fighting. They agreed to salute the English flag, pay a small indemnity, and return New Amsterdam, recaptured in August 1673.

**Westminster abbey** has been the setting for the coronation of English monarchs since 1066, when William the Conqueror was crowned in the new church of *Edward the Confessor, perhaps to underline continuity; from Henry III to George II sixteen monarchs were buried there. The present abbey was begun by Henry III in 1245 and was much influenced by contemporary French styles: it is the highest of great English medieval churches and therefore seems narrow. The body of Edward the Confessor was moved there in 1269.

The abbey's close connection with the monarchy saved it from the fate of most other abbeys at the Reformation. Though it suffered from the iconoclasts of the 1640s, its prestige helped it during the Commonwealth: *Cromwell was given an elaborate funeral in the abbey, only to be disinterred in January 1661. *Wren began the work of restoring the fabric of the abbey after years of neglect but not until 1745 were the western towers completed, to the design of Nicholas *Hawksmoor. Among the host of memorials, the most moving is that which commemorates the dead of the Great War, a brass to a 'British warrior, unknown by name or rank'.

**w**

**Westminster Assembly,** 1643. Set up by the Long Parliament to reform the English church, it consisted of 30 members of both houses and 121 ministers of varying opinions. Though most members favoured *presbyterianism, a forceful minority of independents, to Scottish astonishment, opposed it. The Scots agreed to the *Solemn League and Covenant (1643), which resulted in English presbyterianism being firmly under parliamentary control.

**Westminster cathedral** Commissioned by Cardinal Herbert Vaughan, the third archbishop after the restoration of the Roman catholic hierarchy in England and Wales, it was designed by J. F. Bentley in neo-Byzantine rather than Gothic style and built 1895–1903. The neo-Renaissance exterior, which includes a lofty campanile, contrasts bands of Portland stone with terracotta brick.

**Westminster hall,** built by William Rufus (1097) as an extension of Edward the Confessor's palace, is the only surviving part of the original palace of *Westminster. Used initially for feasts, then early parliaments, it developed into an administrative centre, housing the Courts of Common Pleas, King's Bench, Chancery, Exchequer, and Star Chamber.

**Westminster School** was founded shortly after the building of Westminster abbey. Henry VIII made the last abbot the first dean of the school in 1540. It was refounded by Elizabeth I 20 years later, connecting the school closely with her father's foundations of Christ Church, Oxford, and Trinity College, Cambridge.

**Westmorland** was one of the smaller counties, about 40 miles from Stainmore in the east to Bowfell in the west. The greater part was fell country and the market towns—Appleby, Kendal, Kirkby Lonsdale, and Kirkby Stephen—were small. The administrative arrangements reflected the topography of the shire. It was divided into two baronies, north and south, each in turn divided into two wards. The barony of Kendal was in the diocese of York, and then of Chester: the barony of Westmorland was in the diocese of Carlisle. Not until 1856 were they both placed under Carlisle.

The name Westmorland seems to mean the country west of the moors—i.e. the Pennines. It formed part of *Brigantes territory, was occupied by the Romans, colonized by Anglo-Saxons pushing out the Britons, and became a rather loosely attached part of the kingdom of *Northumbria. From the early 10th cent. there was considerable Norse settlement, from Ireland and the Isle of Man, leaving evidence in words like fell, ghyll, tarn, and how. *Athelstan established political control in 927, but Westmorland remained very much a border area, not integrated into the kingdom of England, and too remote to receive much attention.

At the time of the Domesday survey in 1086, the Kendal barony was treated as part of Lancashire, while the northern parts of the area were not included at all. Much of the district remained under Scottish control until William Rufus in 1092 seized Carlisle. Its establishment as a recognized county may have been as late as the 13th cent. but by 1290 it was represented in Edward I's parliaments by two knights of the shire.

The natives of Westmorland relied heavily upon sheep-farming in the south, cattle-rearing in the north, with a useful cloth industry in Kendal. Appleby, the county town, suffered greatly from Scottish raids, since it was athwart an easy line of advance across Stainmore towards Durham and York. It was sacked in 1173 and again in 1388.

*Defoe, writing in the 1720s before the Romantic movement, found Westmorland 'eminent only for being the wildest, most barren and frightful of any thing that I have passed over in England, or even in Wales'. But by the mid-18th cent. travellers were discovering the charms of the Lake District and, with Ullswater, Helvellyn, Grasmere, and Windermere, Westmorland became better known. Its status as a national treasure owed much to the Lakeland poets in the early 19th cent. In the 1990s, tourism is still the salvation and despair of the region. But, with the passing of years, gondolas on Windermere, Coniston, and Ullswater and steam trains to Lakeside have come to symbolize a bygone age of tranquillity. By the local government reorganization of 1972, the county was merged with Cumberland and northwest Lancashire to form Cumbria.

**West Sussex** *See* SUSSEX, WEST.

**West Yorkshire** *See* YORKSHIRE, WEST.

**Whigs** The Whigs were one of the two main political parties in Britain between the later 17th and mid-19th cents. The term, which derived from 'whiggamore', the name by which the Scots *covenanters had been derogatorily known, was first used by the Tories during the *Exclusion crisis to brand the opponents of James, duke of York. Whiggery thus began as a distinctly oppositional and populist ideology, which saw political authority stemming from the people, a 'contract' existing between them and their king, whom they might resist if he overrode their interests. Early Whig principles played a key part in shaping the 1689 revolution settlement. As firm supporters of the Hanoverian succession the Whigs presided over George I's accession in 1714 and afterwards engineered the long-term proscription of their Tory rivals. The resulting 'Whig oligarchy' achieved a hitherto unseen stability in political life over the next few decades, with power concentrated in the hands of the great Whig families.

By the 1760s all politicians regarded themselves loosely as Whigs, but the term was consciously appropriated and used by the remnants of the old corps who had regrouped as an aristocratic country party led by *Rockingham. Their consciousness as a 'party' was promoted by *Burke in the 1770s and 1780s, with economical reform and the reduction of the power of the crown essential to their evolving ideology. The political crisis at the end of the American war brought them briefly to office until Rockingham's sudden death in July 1782. The Rockingham Whigs, now led by the duke of *Portland and Charles James Fox, split in 1794 over their reaction to the French Revolution, with 'conservative' Whigs under Portland joining Pitt's administration, and the Foxites remaining in opposition. The latter kept alive the name of Whig, associating it with political, religious, and social reform. The mid-19th cent. saw Whiggery largely subsumed into liberalism, and the Whig label disappeared from political vocabulary.

**Whistler, James Abbott McNeill** (1834–1903). Painter and etcher, born in Massachusetts. Dismissed from West Point, Whistler joined the US navy, where as a car-tographer he learned etching and decided on a career in art. He went to Paris in 1855 before settling in London in 1859, where he enjoyed an early success, not only for his art but also for his flamboyant life-style. In 1877 he sued *Ruskin for libel and although he won his case and was awarded one farthing in damages, the expenses bankrupted him. His later life saw both artistic and financial success, with his salon in Chelsea a fashionable gathering place.

**Whitby, Synod of,** 664. The Northumbrian church, which began with *Paulinus and Roman Christianity, was revived by *Aidan, who introduced Celtic customs from Iona. The most controversial difference, the dating of Easter, was the main issue at Whitby.

Key Northumbrians representing the Celtic cause at Whitby were Abbess *Hilda, Cedd, bishop to the East Saxons, and Bishop Colman of Lindisfarne. *Wilfrid was spokesman for the visiting Frankish bishop Agilbert from Wessex, and his priest Agatho, main advocates for Rome. King *Oswiu's decision to conform with the greater body of Roman Christianity may have been politically expedient. The synod prepared the way for unification of the English church by *Theodore, next archbishop of Canterbury.

**White, Gilbert** (1720–93). Naturalist. Born in his grandfather's vicarage in the village of Selborne (Hants), White was educated at Oriel College, Oxford (fellow, 1744), and ordained in 1747, but preferred a Hampshire curacy to a 'fat goose living' elsewhere to stay close to the family home The Wakes (inherited eventually, with tortoise). A scientific naturalist by intention and committed diarist and record-keeper, he started a 'Garden Kalendar' in 1751 which developed into 'The Naturalist's Journal' (1768); this, with letters and papers, provided source material for *The Natural History of Selborne* (1788), subsequently an English classic.

**Whiteboys** was the name adopted by agrarian rebels in Ireland from 1761 onwards. The immediate cause of the outrages seems to have been the enclosure of common land for pasture, but grievances soon included tithes and extortionate leases. The centre of the movement was Munster, where the native Irish were poorest. Supported by widespread intimidation, it was difficult to deal with and continued for some decades.

**Whitefield, George** (1714-70). Evangelist. Born at the Bell Inn, Gloucester, which his father kept, Whitefield entered Pembroke College, Oxford, as a servitor in 1732. Attracted by the Oxford *methodists, he openly joined them in 1735. Ordained deacon and then priest (January 1739), he went to America for the first of seven visits in 1738. His breakthrough as an evangelist came in February 1739 when he preached in the open air to 200 Kingswood colliers. His championship of predestination interrupted his friendship with *Wesley in the late 1740s and the breach between Calvinist and Arminian methodists remained unhealed. In 1744 he met Lady *Huntingdon, proving no match for her 'tiptop gentility'. He visited Ireland, Scotland, and Wales as well as America, where he died, worn out, at Newbury Port, New Hampshire, in September 1770.

**Whitehall palace** as a royal residence lasted some 150 years. It began life as the London residence of the archbishops of York and was called York Place. *Wolsey spent lavishly on it and, on his fall in 1529, it was seized by Henry VIII, who had lost the greater part of Westminster palace by fire in 1512. James I resolved to build a fitting reception hall. His first attempt was burned down in 1619, but the second, the *Banqueting House, designed by Inigo *Jones, was finished by 1622. A disastrous fire in 1698, which left only the Banqueting House standing, provided the opportunity to abandon a palace that was too sprawling, public, and inconvenient. By the 18th cent. it was being taken over for government offices.

**White Ship** Its wreck on 25 November 1120 destroyed Henry I's plans for the succession, because his only legitimate son William died aged 17 in the disaster. An immediate second marriage to *Adela of Louvain produced no male heir, so, in 1126, Henry nominated his daughter, the Empress *Matilda, as his successor. The *White Ship* was sailing from *Normandy to England when it hit a rock in the Seine estuary. Two contemporary chroniclers say that the crew was drunk.

**Whitgift, John** (*c.*1530-1604). Archbishop of Canterbury (1583-1604). Born in Lincolnshire, Whitgift was educated at Pembroke Hall, Cambridge, a centre of reform, where he remained throughout Mary's reign. Ordained (1560), he was successively Lady Margaret professor of divinity (1563-7), master of Pembroke Hall (1567) and Trinity College (1567-77), regius professor of divinity (1567-9), dean of Lincoln (1576), bishop of Worcester (1577), and archbishop in succession to Edmund Grindal. Though strongly Calvinist, he vigorously defended *episcopacy and Anglican liturgy and ritual. Despite his fierce offensive against puritans, he upheld Calvinist doctrines of predestination and election in the Lambeth articles (1595).

**Whithorn, diocese of** Established in 731 as one of the four northern bishoprics under *York, its centre in extreme south-west Scotland was on the site of a Celtic monastery founded by *Ninian (*c.*440). It failed to survive the Danish invasions of the 9th cent. and was not revived.

**Whittington, Richard** (d. 1423). Mercer, benefactor, and pantomime hero. Youngest son of a Gloucestershire landowner, Whittington established himself in London, dealing in valuable imported silks and velvets, and thrice becoming master of the Mercers' Company. A city alderman in 1393, he was elected mayor three times (1397-8, 1406-7, 1419-20). Dying widowed and childless, his executors devoted his great wealth to further public works, including improvements to St Bartholomew's hospital, Guildhall, and Newgate gaol.

**Whittle, Sir Frank** (1907-1996). Frank Whittle, the distinguished aeronautical engineer and inventor of the jet engine, began his career as an apprentice with the Royal Air Force at the RAF College, Cranwell. While still a student he developed the idea of the gas turbine or 'jet' engine. In the lead-up to the Second World War he was assigned to a special project to develop the engine, and despite shortage of materials and much official incomprehension was brilliantly successful. His team produced a viable gas turbine and installed it in an aeroplane to create the first British jet fighter in the closing stages of the war.

W

**Wiglaf** (d. 840), king of Mercia (827–9 and 830–40). Wiglaf came to power in 827 at a time when several cadet lines were competing for the throne and, perhaps to help consolidate his position, he married Ælfflæd, the daughter of Ceolwulf I. In 829 Wiglaf was expelled by King *Egbert of Wessex who had already greatly reduced Mercian control south of the Thames. Egbert ruled Mercia for a year, but Wiglaf returned in 830 and reasserted Mercian control in Middlesex and Berkshire. Wiglaf was the only one of his line to rule; his grandson Wigstan was murdered by the son of Wiglaf's successor Beorhtwulf.

**Wihtred** (d. 725), king of Kent (690 (as joint king), sole ruler 692, 694–725). Wihtred is chiefly remembered for laws issued in 695, the third and last of the surviving Kentish 'codes'. Much of its emphasis is ecclesiastical. The first clause grants the church immunity from taxation. Others seek to enforce the church's rules on marriage, fasting, and the observance of the sabbath.

**Wilberforce, William** (1759–1833). Evangelical philanthropist and anti-slavery campaigner. Born in Hull, the son of a merchant, and educated at Cambridge, he was MP for Hull (1780), Yorkshire (1784–1812), and Bramber (1812–25). Following his conversion (1784–85) he became a leading evangelical, helping found the Proclamation Society to prosecute blasphemy and vice (1787), the Society for Bettering the Condition of the Poor (1796), the *Church Missionary Society (1799), and the *Bible Society (1804). In 1787 he joined the campaign against the slave trade, which he promoted in Parliament through his friendship with Prime Minister *Pitt, and which succeeded in 1807. In 1823 he joined the *Anti-Slavery Society, though ill-health forced his retirement from public life in 1825.

**Wild, Jonathan** (*c.*1682–1725). Thief-taker and anti-hero. Trained as a bucklemaker, imprisonment for debt brought Wild into contact with the underworld, then into handling stolen property. His activities prompted a statute whereby receiving a reward for returning deliberately stolen goods was an offence comparable to the felony (1718), but his delusion that his public services outweighed his crimes eventually ended at Tyburn.

**Wilde, Oscar** (1854–1900). Dublin-born aesthete, dramatist, and, by his own declaration, genius. At Oxford Pater and *Ruskin entranced him more than his classical studies. His early *Poems* (1881) were derivative but his personality, extravagantly displayed on an American tour the following year, was original. 'To become a work of art is the object of living,' he wrote, anticipating *The Picture of Dorian Gray* (1891). At the height of his powers, his ambivalent relationship to Victorian society most subtly deployed with *The Importance of Being Earnest* (1895), disaster struck. Publicly reviled, convicted of sodomy, he was sentenced to two years' hard labour in Reading gaol. Five years later, neglected in Paris, he was dead.

**'Wild Geese'** was the name given to catholic Irish professional soldiers who served in the armies of European sovereigns, especially after the conclusion of the Williamite war (1689–91) in Ireland. In fact connections of this kind long pre-dated 1691, but the treaty of *Limerick of 1691 sent 12,000 Irish troops to join the French army.

**Wilfrid, St** (*c.*634–*c.*709). Bishop of Northumbria. Noble, Northumbrian, sent by Queen Eanflæd to study at *Lindisfarne, Wilfrid then travelled to Kent, to Lyons, and to Rome. Back home, he introduced Roman ways in the monastery of Ripon, given to him by Alchfrith of Deira, was ordained by Agilbert, Frankish bishop of Wessex, for whom he spoke at the Synod of *Whitby (664) in favour of the Roman Easter, and was sent for consecration in Paris as bishop for the Northumbrians.

His subsequent career was stormy, involving deprivation (664–9, 678–86, 691–706) and divisions of his see, appropriation of assets of his monasteries, disagreements with the Northumbrian kings Ecgfrith and Aldfrith and with the archbishops of Canterbury *Theodore and Berhtwald. While not at home, he worked amongst the South Saxons, the West Saxons in the Isle of Wight, and in Mercia. He died as bishop of *Hexham at Oundle in 709 or 710 and was buried at Ripon. His relics were moved to Canterbury, probably in 948, by Archbishop Oda.

Wilfrid was in many respects—his ferocity, retinue, the loyalty of his followers, and his death-bed distribution of treasure—an ecclesiastical version of a traditional aristocratic warlord. The stone seat in Hexham Abbey is believed to have been Wilfrid's episcopal chair.

**Wilkes, John** (1725–97). Described on his coffin as 'A Friend of Liberty', Wilkes was the central figure in a number of constitutional disputes which extended the political rights of ordinary citizens. After a rakish youth, he became MP for Aylesbury in 1757. A leading opponent of the king's favourite, Lord *Bute, Wilkes was arrested after the publication on 23 April 1763 of No. 45 of his paper, the *North Briton*, and charged with seditious libel. He successfully challenged the use of *general warrants which had been issued, but was condemned by Parliament for publishing a scandalous and obscene libel. Wilkes fled to the continent in 1764. On his return in 1768 he was treated as a popular hero and elected MP for Middlesex. However, he was imprisoned for libel and expelled from the Commons, despite repeated re-election for Middlesex. 'Wilkes and Liberty' became the slogan of the London crowds who demonstrated in his support. He was a champion of mass politics and an early example of journalistic radicalism.

**Wilkie, Sir David** (1785–1841). Scottish painter renowned for his lively representations of the commonplace in Scottish life. His first important work was *Pitlessie Fair* (1804), while *The Village Politicians* confirmed his reputation when it was submitted to the Royal Academy in 1806. He was painter-in-ordinary to three monarchs and knighted in 1836.

**Wilkins, John** (1614–72). One of the most prominent of the remarkable group of amateur scientists in the mid-17th cent. He attended Oxford and took holy orders, becoming chaplain to a number of noblemen. In his first book, *Discovery of a World in the Moon* (1638), he argued that man could reach the moon and that it could be made habitable. The 'invisible college' of scientists which he organized was the forerunner of the *Royal Society, established in 1660 with Wilkins as secretary. Joining the parliamentary side in the Civil War, he was

appointed warden of Wadham College, Oxford, in 1648 and in 1656 married a sister of Oliver *Cromwell, retaining his college headship. In 1659 he transferred to the mastership of Trinity College, Cambridge, and though he lost it at the Restoration, he was made dean of Ripon in 1663 and bishop of Chester in 1668.

**Wilkinson, Ellen** (1891–1947). One of Britain's best known and most successful female politicians. After completing a history degree at Manchester University, she became an organizer for the National Union of Women's Suffrage Societies and then, in 1915, for the National Women's Organization of the Amalgamated Union of Co-operative Employees. She became Labour MP for Middlesbrough (1924–31) and for Jarrow from 1935. It was in the 1930s that 'Red Ellen' made her reputation as a crusader for the unemployed with extensive involvement in the Unity campaign, the famous Jarrow march, and in the campaign against fascism in Germany and Spain. As minister for education 1945–7 she achieved much: the implementation of the 1944 Education Act, the raising of the school-leaving age to 15, despite Treasury opposition, the building of new schools, and the introduction of 'school milk'.

**Wilkinson, John** (1728–1808). One of the most remarkable ironmasters and entrepreneurs of his day, Wilkinson was born in Cumberland. His father made money producing box-irons and then moved near to Wrexham, where he made high-quality cylinders, much used by *Boulton and *Watt. John Wilkinson established furnaces at *Coalbrookdale, using coal in place of charcoal, and diversified his output. Iron barges on the Severn carried his wares, he provided the ironwork for the great Iron Bridge in 1779, and manufactured lead pipes. But his most profitable line was boring cannon. Known popularly as 'Iron-mad Wilkinson', he was buried on his Cumberland estate near Ulverston in an iron coffin inside an iron tomb, roofed by an iron pyramid, and with an inscription, in iron letters, that he had himself composed.

**William I** (1027/8–87), king of England (1066–87) and duke of Normandy (1035–87), known as 'the Conqueror', was born at

W

Falaise in central *Normandy. William's succession to the duchy occurred when he was 8 and had the prior agreement of the Norman magnates and of his lord, the king of France. The first years of his rule in Normandy were turbulent and his survival at times precarious. But after defeating Norman rebels in 1047 and 1053-4, he established a formidable control within the duchy which was never thereafter seriously threatened. William began to make territorial gains to the south of Normandy in the 1050s and in 1063 acquired the large county of Maine. In 1051 he received a promise of succession to the English kingdom from *Edward the Confessor, apparently out of gratitude for the protection which Edward had been given while in exile in Normandy, and in 1066 he defeated *Harold Godwineson at the battle of *Hastings to make good his claim. Six years of often brutal campaigning, which included the notorious 'harrying of the North' in the winter of 1069-70, were needed to complete the subjugation of William's new kingdom. After 1072 he visited England only infrequently, usually to deal with crises such as the revolt of the earls in 1075 or the threatened invasion from Denmark in 1085. On his death-bed, he divided his lands between Robert Curthose, who received Normandy, and his second surviving son, William Rufus, who was given England.

William's achievement was based on a powerful personality, which appears to have overawed almost all who came into contact with him, and a strong physique which made him one of the most formidable warriors of his day. A capacity for often excessive cruelty and for leadership in war was combined with an unbending will and a shrewd political mind. His wife *Matilda, to whom he was faithful in a way which is remarkable among contemporary medieval kings and aristocrats, often acted as his deputy in Normandy when he was in England. He maintained English overlordship over Wales and Scotland. He was lucky in that Harold Godwineson's victory at the battle of *Stamford Bridge over *Harold Hardrada removed a contender whom William would otherwise have had to fight and in that *Edgar the Atheling was not a credible alternative around whom the English could unite after 1066. William's death was followed by a civil war between his sons over his inheritance, which was not finally resolved until Henry I's reunification of Normandy and England in 1106.

**William II** (c.1060–1100), king of England (1087–1100), known as 'Rufus', the second son of William the Conqueror, was a ruler whose reputation has suffered because of the opinions of contemporary ecclesiastics, appalled by his sometimes cynical attitude to religion. William became England's king as a result of his father's death-bed bequest. Whether his succession should be interpreted as involving the disinheritance of his elder brother *Robert Curthose is a controversial matter which cannot be conclusively resolved from the existing sources. Whatever the case, the consequence was that William rapidly faced widespread revolt in England in 1088 in support of Robert, who had acquired *Normandy. After defeating his opponents, William set out to weaken Robert's increasingly fragile hold on the duchy, organizing expeditions there in 1091 and 1094. In 1096 Robert mortgaged the duchy to William in order to take part in the First Crusade, and from then until his death, William ruled over his father's cross-channel realm. William also consolidated Norman rule in northern England, establishing effective royal power at Carlisle, and he supported the continuing Norman-French penetration of Wales. His provocative remarks offended more scrupulous clergy and he lacked the sincerity of belief which had ensured his father's good relations with the church. These factors contributed to his quarrel with St *Anselm, the gifted theologian and philosopher whose appointment to Canterbury had been dramatically sanctioned by the king as he lay seriously ill at Gloucester in 1093. A series of arguments culminated in the archbishop going into exile in 1097 and remaining out of England until after William's death. William was killed while hunting in the New Forest on 2 August 1100. His death was probably an accident; all arguments that he was murdered rest on highly circumstantial evidence. The nickname 'Rufus' first appeared in the early 12th cent., and refers either to red hair or to a ruddy complexion.

**William I** (c.1142–1214), king of Scots (1165–1214), later known as 'the Lion'.

Younger brother and successor to Malcolm IV, he was granted the earldom of Northumberland by his grandfather David I in 1152, and never accepted the loss of the border counties to Henry II in 1157. When Henry faced a major rebellion in 1173–4, William invaded Northumberland and Cumberland in a disastrous bid to reassert Scottish control. Captured at *Alnwick, he had to recognize Henry as the superior lord of Scotland by the treaty of *Falaise. Although William's conflicts with the English crown distracted his attention from the Highlands and Isles, his long reign nevertheless saw important advances. New burghs were founded outside the traditional royal heartlands; Anglo-Norman families gained new estates, especially north of the river Tay; and the bishopric of Argyll was established in about 1192. But a contrast must still be drawn between the effectiveness of royal power in the Lowlands and its much more restricted nature in the far north and west. In addition, the Isles remained, however loosely, under the overlordship of Norway. William died at Stirling and was buried in Arbroath abbey. Not until the 14th cent. was he referred to as 'the Lion', an epithet evoking his reputation as an enforcer of justice.

**William III** (1650–1702), king of England, Scotland (as William II), and Ireland (1689–1702), prince of Orange. Appointed stadtholder of Holland and Zeeland, and captain-and admiral-general of all the Dutch provinces for life in July 1672, these posts were rendered hereditary in 1674 and 1675, when William was additionally elected stadtholder of Utrecht and Gelderland. He was the only child of William II of Orange and Mary Stuart, eldest daughter of Charles I, and was born on 4 November, eight days after his father's death, at a time of extreme crisis in Orange's relations with Amsterdam, always the seat of anti-Orangist sentiment. Twenty years of republican rule then ensued, setting the Orangist interest at a discount: it was excluded from all future participation in Holland's government, the young prince's upbringing being left to his mother and then to his redoubtable paternal grandmother, Amalia van Solms. Charles's restoration in 1660 in fact saw Orange's readmission to Hol-

land's public life, the 10-year-old William being ceremonially received at Amsterdam.

During the 1660s William, puny in stature and incurably asthmatic, reached manhood. The Anglo-French attack on the Dutch republic in 1672 brought forth so strong an Orangist reaction that the Dutch savagely discarded republican government and bore the 22-year-old William upwards as the embodiment of resistance to aggression. In the formation of an anti-French front, William attained European stature and, returning to England in October 1677, was able to take momentous advantage of Charles II's embarrassed foreign policies by marrying his 15-year-old cousin Princess Mary, the elder and indubitably protestant daughter of James, duke of York, a professed catholic since 1670. From different motives the British and French monarchs resolved to acquiesce in the Orange marriage. Difficult though the marriage proved to be for two people of very different temperaments, and remaining childless, it enabled William to play the dynast and laid the foundation for his intervention in England's affairs in November 1688.

In November 1685 James II's assertion of the prerogative on behalf of his non-Anglican subjects alienated the most loyal Parliament a Stuart king had known. That William could prepare to intervene in England in the spring of 1688, some three months before he received the celebrated 'Invitation' of 30 June to rescue English liberties 'before it be too late', was owing to a series of reverses for France, and misjudgements by Louis XIV.

William had no illusions about English dislike of his countrymen, but his experience as a Dutch prince with more influence than real authority was providential for his exercise of Britain's 'Revolution' kingship. He never doubted, and gratefully recognized, Mary's own contribution to the device of the joint monarchy, and her death on 27 December 1694 prostrated him for months. But his rule in Scotland, where he delegated too much, is a blight on his record; and those terms in the Act of *Settlement of 1701 which placed limits upon the executive were unmistakably censorious. His conduct of the war against France, once Jacobite forces had been defeated in Ireland in 1691, placed him and his ministries under unrelenting parliamentary scrutiny. William's contribution to the disclosure of foreign policy to Parliament, however unwilling, opened a new era in crown–Parliament relations. When he died on 8 March 1702 he had won a measure of international recognition for Britain's protestant succession. No British king has stood higher than William in international renown.

**William IV** (1765–1837), king of the United Kingdom of Great Britain and Ireland (1830–7), king of Hanover. The third son of George III, born 21 August 1765, he seemed unlikely to become king. He entered the navy at 13 as a midshipman and soon demonstrated that despite enthusiasm for the service, his talents were limited and his manners rough. He saw active service in the War of *American Independence, and became a warm admirer and friend of *Nelson, but his naval service was accompanied by a private life which was far from respectable. In 1790 he met Mrs Jordan, an actress, with whom he was to live for many years and who bore him ten children. Although he received promotions to rear-admiral, vice-admiral, and in 1799 admiral, the navy refused his pleas for a return to active service. His long affair with Mrs Jordan ended acrimoniously in 1811, the year in which he became admiral of the fleet.

The death of George IV's daughter Princess *Charlotte in 1818 led to William's marriage to *Adelaide of Saxe-Meiningen, a widowed Bavarian princess. The marriage was a generally happy one, with Adelaide taking care of William's illegitimate children. In 1827 he was given the resurrected dignity of lord high admiral, intended as an honorific title, but his clumsy attempts to make its nominal authority effective led to his resignation after only fifteen months. George IV died on 26 June 1830, and 'Silly Billy' became king, with little in the way of helpful previous experience. He marked his accession by the conferment of titles on his illegitimate children, and exhibited an obvious and sometimes undignified zest for his new role. He inherited a political crisis, as the end of a long period of Tory ascendancy approached. *Wellington's government faltered. Unlike George IV, William had no objection to Whig ministers, telling his new premier Lord *Grey that he had 'complete confidence in your integrity, judgement, decision and experience'. During the reform crisis of 1831–2, he facilitated the enactment of that *Great Reform Act which was crucial in ensuring the peaceful evolution

of Britain. William's enthusiasm for change was limited, and in November 1834, having tired of his Whig ministers, he dismissed the government and recalled the Tories under *Peel. This proved a premature and unsuccessful ploy. The new government made gains at the ensuing general election, but not a majority, and William was forced to take the Whig ministers back again for the remainder of his reign. William's relations with his sister-in-law, the widowed duchess of Kent, Princess Victoria's mother, were difficult. He was determined to survive to see the young princess achieve her majority and so prevent her mother's regency. He lived for a month after Victoria's 18th birthday and died on 20 June 1837.

**William, Prince** (b. 1982). Elder son of *Charles, prince of Wales, and Princess *Diana, and second in line to the throne, William was educated initially at Wetherby preparatory school and at Ludgrove. Eton, then a gap year, preceded further studies at St Andrews university. A tall, personable young man, with a striking resemblance to his mother, he is already attracting the media attention that pursued her. After taking a degree in Geography, the prince joined the Blues and Royals Regiment of the Household Cavalry, where he is known as William Wales. In 2008 he gained his pilot's licence in the Royal Air Force.

**William the Atheling** (c.1102–20). Heir to the thrones of England and Normandy, as the son of a Norman father (Henry I) and an English mother (Queen *Matilda), he represented the hope of reconciliation between the two peoples. But his father's careful preparations for his unchallenged succession were brought to nothing on 25 November 1120. Like nearly everyone on board the *White Ship, he was drowned when it hit rocks as it left the Norman port of Barfleur.

**William of Occam** (c.1289–1349). Occam is a village near Guildford in Surrey, from which William presumably took his name. An Oxford Franciscan, he is said to have been a pupil of *Duns Scotus. His thought developed when his order became involved in a protracted dispute with the papacy on the subject of evangelical poverty, which the Franciscans embraced. Occam's writings in defence of his order led to a summons to

Avignon and a condemnation by Pope John XXII. The continuing controversy led Occam to examine the relations of church and state. He argued that the papacy had no standing in temporal matters and that within the church it was subordinate to a general council. In his methodology, he emphasized both the power and limitations of logic: it could not touch revealed truth and faith, and since it dealt largely with terms of argument, the principle of economy should apply and as few assumptions as possible should be made—hence, 'Occam's razor'.

**William of St Carilef** (d. 1096). Bishop of Durham. A secular priest at Bayeux, he took monastic vows at St Carilef (Maine), became prior there, and then abbot of St Vincent. In 1080 William I chose him as bishop of Durham. William II made him justiciar, but after implication in the 1088 rebellion, he was arrested and tried. Restored in 1091, he surprisingly supported the king against *Anselm at the Council of *Rockingham (1095). A great builder, on his return from exile (1091) he brought plans for the magnificent new cathedral, started in 1093.

**William of Wykeham** (1324–1404). Bishop of Winchester, keeper of the privy seal, chancellor of England. Possibly the son of a Hampshire serf, he entered royal service (c.1348) and superintended the rebuilding of Windsor castle. As bishop of Winchester (1366) he was the greatest ecclesiastical pluralist of the century with twelve appointments, headed by the archdeaconry of Lincoln. As chancellor (1367) he was efficient rather than statesmanlike. The tide of anticlericalism forced him to resign (1371) to make way for laymen. He is chiefly remembered for his benefactions to education by founding New College, Oxford (1379), and *Winchester College (1382).

**Williams, Roger** (c.1603–83). Colonist. Williams was born in London, attended Pembroke College, Cambridge, and took holy orders. In 1630 he left England for Massachusetts but his belief that magistrates should have no power over conscience gave him an uncomfortable time when he was appointed to the church at Salem. Expelled from Massachusetts in 1636, he founded a settlement at Providence and in 1639 established a baptist church, though he subse-

quently became a seeker, acknowledging no creed. In 1644 he visited England and obtained a charter of self-government for Providence—the foundation of Rhode Island. The colony soon became known for its tolerant attitude and *Jews and *quakers were allowed to settle. In 1654-7 Williams served as governor.

**Williams, Rowan** (b. 1950). Archbishop. Born in Swansea and educated at Christ's College, Cambridge, Williams took an Oxford D.Phil in 1975. After working in Cambridge as a priest, he became Lady Margaret Professor of Divinity at Oxford in 1986. From 1991 he was bishop of Monmouth, becoming archbishop of Wales in 1999 and archbishop of Canterbury in succession to George *Carey in 2002. He has experienced difficulty in holding together diverse views in the Church on gay relationships and in 2008 provoked strong protests by suggesting that elements of Sharia law might be introduced. A learned man and a poet, he has sometimes seemed more confused than those to whom he is tendering advice.

**Willibrord, St** (658–739). Northumbrian monk and missionary to Frisia. He was educated at *Wilfrid's Ripon, then for twelve years at Rath Melsigi (Clonmelsh, Co. Carlow) in Ireland, under Egbert, who in 690 directed him to work, as Wilfrid had, in Frisia. Consecrated archbishop (as Clement) of the Frisians by Pope Sergius I in 695, he was given Utrecht for his see. His monastery at Echternach (in modern Luxembourg), founded in 698, became famous for its school and scriptorium. Willibrord took the cult of *Oswald to Europe and prepared the way for the missionary *Boniface.

**Wills, W. D. and H. O.** A tobacco firm established in Bristol which, by the end of the 19th cent., was the largest in Britain. In contrast with many other tobacco importers, by the mid-19th cent. the directing members of the Wills family understood the nature of retailing and in particular the significance of brand names. Their successes with distinctive pipe tobaccos and a diverse array of cigarettes built a strong market (Passing Clouds 1871, Three Castles 1877, Woodbine 1888). In 1883 they bought the rights to the Bonsack cigarette-making machine enabling them to dominate cigarette-manufacturing in Britain until the 20th cent. when they led mergers to form British and American Tobacco in 1902.

## Wilmington, Spencer Compton, 1st earl of (c.1674–1743).

A younger son of the earl of Northampton. He entered the Commons in his twenties and became Speaker in 1715. At the accession of George II in 1727 he was expected to become first minister, but was outmanœuvred by *Walpole without difficulty. Compensation came in the form of a barony (1728), an earldom (1730), and the lord presidency of the council from 1730 until 1742. A ponderous and formal man, he succeeded Walpole as first minister in 1742, but old, unwell, and with little taste for leadership, he merely presided for a year until his death.

## Wilson, Harold, 1st Baron Wilson (1916–95).

Prime minister. The son of an industrial chemist, Wilson won an exhibition in history to Jesus College, Oxford, taking a first in PPE. In 1940 he joined the war cabinet secretariat as an economist. Elected MP for Ormskirk in 1945, Wilson became parliamentary secretary at the Ministry of Works and in 1947 entered the cabinet as president of the Board of Trade, aged only 31. He resigned from the government in 1951 along with Aneurin *Bevan, which established his credentials—not entirely deserved—as a left-winger when Labour began to factionalize in the 1950s.

In opposition Wilson progressed steadily up the hierarchy of the National Executive Committee and shadow cabinet and was made shadow chancellor in 1956 soon after *Gaitskell became party leader. He was out of sympathy with Gaitskell's efforts to 'modernize' the party following Labour's third successive electoral defeat in 1959 and unsuccessfully challenged him for the leadership in 1960. Wilson's opportunity came with Gaitskell's unexpected death in January 1963: in the contest for the succession he emerged victorious over George Brown and James *Callaghan.

With hindsight it is clear that Wilson was the right man for the time. His position on the centre-left enabled him to unite the Labour movement in a way Gaitskell would have found difficult. His comparative youth and his call for a technological revolution

struck a chord with the optimism of the 1960s. In the circumstances, Labour's victory in the election of 1964 was less surprising than the narrowness of the overall majority of four seats.

Yet hopes that Wilson's election might mark a new beginning for Britain were largely disappointed. Wilson remained wedded to many traditional attitudes, especially Britain's role as a world power and the importance of sterling as an international currency. The creation of a new Department of Economic Affairs, designed to shake off the overweening control of the Treasury, proved a failure. The electorate, however, was ready to give Labour the benefit of the doubt, and in 1966 Labour achieved a comfortable majority at the polls.

Increasingly, however, Wilson seemed to lose any sense of direction, particularly after the belated devaluation of the pound in 1967. Politics by gesture appeared to replace long-term planning. Wilson maintained party unity, but at the expense of blurring over internal differences. There was no transformation of the national economy, though Roy *Jenkins, as chancellor, established a reputation for prudent administration. Britain's application to join the Common Market in 1967 came up against General de Gaulle's veto. The qualities of the government seemed to be encapsulated in Labour's attempt to reform the trade union movement. Wilson and his employment secretary, Barbara Castle, invested much of their credibility in the proposed 'In Place of Strife' legislation but were obliged to accept humiliating defeat.

Nevertheless, Wilson's defeat in 1970 at the hands of Edward *Heath came as a considerable shock. He returned to power in 1974 still exuding self-confidence but lacking the apparent dynamism of a decade earlier. The most threatening issue, however, as far as the internal dynamics of the party were concerned, was membership of the *EEC. Wilson had opposed Heath's action in taking Britain into the community on the somewhat spurious grounds that the terms of entry were unacceptable. In 1975, Wilson allowed the issue of continuing membership to go to a referendum with members of the cabinet openly opposing one another.

There seems little reason to doubt Wilson's assertion that he had decided to stand down early from the premiership at the time he returned to office in 1974. Yet his resignation in 1976 was met with disbelief. He stayed on in the Commons until 1983 without playing much of a role, perhaps because of the onset of a debilitating illness.

**Wilson, Richard** (1714–82). Landscape painter. Born in Wales, the son of a clergyman, Wilson's formal training and early career were in portrait painting, but, while in Italy between 1750 and 1756, he decided to concentrate on painting landscape in the classical style. On his return to England, his pictures brought him fame but little employment. He was a founder member of the Royal Academy and appointed librarian in 1776, by which time he had almost ceased to paint. He is now regarded as the first great British landscapist and an important influence on 19th-cent. landscape painting.

**Wilton diptych** A small portable altarpiece of two hinged oak panels, painted and gilded on both sides, almost certainly intended for the private devotions of Richard II and resplendent with exquisite tooling and expensive pigments. The artist is unknown and the date, author, and motive of commission remain uncertain, despite scholarly debate. It was reputedly given by James II to Lord Castlemaine, before purchase by the earls of Pembroke at Wilton House, from which it takes its name, but has been in the National Gallery since 1929.

**Wiltshire** is one of the larger counties, more than 50 miles from north to south. It is not easy to perceive much geographical coherence and the balance of the county has constantly changed. The northern towns of Cricklade and Malmesbury had little contact with Mere or Downton in the south, save occasionally at shire meetings, held often for convenience at Devizes in the middle. Most of Wiltshire was prosperous farming country, the north famous for cheese, the south for butter, and the middle, around Salisbury plain, given over to sheep. On the western fringes, around Trowbridge, Bradford, Westbury, and Melksham, there was a domestic cloth industry, described by *Defoe in his tour of the 1720s as very flourishing.

The county took its name from Wilton, on the river Wylye, a tributary of the Salisbury Avon. As Wilton declined, prosperity shifted first to Old Sarum, then to New Sarum or Salisbury, which, by Tudor times, was one of the ten largest towns in the kingdom, with a population of 8,000. In modern times, with the development of Swindon as a railway town, the balance swung again: a hamlet of just over 1,000 people at Old Swindon in 1801 became by 1881 by far the largest town in Wiltshire, with 17,000 people, and by 2001 had risen to more than 180,000.

In pre-Roman times, the area was one of the most thickly populated in the country, the settlers preferring dry chalk lands to the damp and heavily wooded valleys. Wiltshire is the richest of all counties in prehistoric remains, festooned with barrows, and in Stonehenge and Avebury claiming two of the greatest sites in Europe. Though the tribes of the *Durotriges and the *Atrebates had a reputation for bravery, the region fell easily to the Roman advance. By the later 6th cent. it had succumbed to the Saxons, who won a decisive victory at Old Sarum in 552. In the early 9th cent. it was heavily disputed between *Mercia and *Wessex and was a centre of *Alfred's struggles against the Danes. The first evidence of its emerging identity is a reference in the *Anglo-Saxon Chronicle* for 800 to the defeat of the *Hwicce from Gloucestershire by the Wilsætes, under their ealdorman Woxtan. The most remarkable survival from the Saxon period is the tiny church at *Bradford on Avon, used as a cottage for many years and only rediscovered in 1856.

During the Civil War, the region lay between royalist and parliamentary areas and saw much fighting. Wardour castle was held for the king by Lady Arundell, surrendered in 1643, but was retaken by her son and destroyed rather than let it be used by the enemy. *Hopton's victory over *Waller at *Roundway Down in 1643 delivered most of the shire into royalist hands and they held Devizes until 1645. *Penruddock's rising on behalf of Charles II in 1655 was a damp squib, captured Salisbury for one day, and fizzled out.

The 19th cent. saw considerable distress in parts of the county. The cloth industry found competition from Yorkshire hard to meet and there was agricultural depression, especially after 1815. Of Cricklade, Cobbett remarked in 1821 that, 'the labourers seem miserably

W

poor. Their dwellings are little better than pig-beds...in my whole life, I never saw such human wretchedness equal to this; no, not even among the free negroes in America.' 'This *Wiltshire*', he concluded, 'is a horrible county.' In the *Swing riots of 1830, there were more prosecutions in Wiltshire than in any other county, mainly for machine-breaking.

The diffuse character of the shire made it difficult to agree on a suitable administrative headquarters. Quarter sessions met in turn at Marlborough, Devizes, Salisbury, and Warminster. The county council, instituted in 1888, began by meeting at Trowbridge (twice), Salisbury, and Swindon. By 1930 the position was intolerable. It was carried to meet at Devizes, only for the vote to be reversed when the Trowbridge United football ground became available. County hall opened there in 1940.

**Wimbledon** The most prestigious lawn tennis club in the world. Wimbledon is the home of 'the Lawn Tennis Championships on Grass', the oldest of all the lawn tennis tournaments. The first championship was held on 9 July 1877 at the club's original ground in Worple Road, Wimbledon, in south-west London. In 1922 the club moved to its present ground in Church Road.

**Winceby, battle of,** 1643. Sir John Henderson, royalist governor of Newark, set out in October 1643 to relieve Bolingbroke castle, near Horncastle. His force was intercepted by parliamentary cavalry under *Manchester, *Fairfax, and *Cromwell and badly cut up on the 11th. Though a small-scale action, the victory was a valuable boost to sagging roundhead morale.

**Winchelsey, Robert de** (d. 1313). Archbishop of Canterbury. Born in Kent, educated at Paris where he was rector and at Oxford where he was chancellor (1288), Winchelsey was a distinguished scholar. Though elected archbishop in 1293, he only returned from Rome in 1295. As an unyielding upholder of ecclesiastical independence, he obeyed Boniface VIII's bull *Clericis laicos* by refusing Edward I's request for clerical taxation (1296) until the pope compromised (1297). Winchelsey again confronted Edward at the Lincoln Parliament (1301), removing Walter Langton, the treasurer, which Edward

never forgave. Suspended by Pope Clement V (1306), Winchelsey went into exile. Restored (1307), he actively opposed *Gaveston and was one of the lords *Ordainers (1310).

**Winchester** was Venta Belgarum, capital of the probably artificial *civitas* of the *Belgae. Extensive 4th-cent. cemeteries suggest that Winchester was still a major centre of population, but they passed out of use at the beginning of the 5th cent. Winchester revived as a bishop's seat (662), but urban life did not return until a planned and fortified town (burh) was laid out within the Roman walls, probably by King *Alfred. The city expanded dramatically between the 10th and 12th cents., ranking by c.1110, with Norwich, second in size after London, and sharing with Westminster the developing functions of a national capital. Besides the cathedral, it possessed royal and episcopal palaces, 57 parish churches, and one of the four great trading fairs of England. However, it declined from the 12th cent. as the close links with the monarchy slackened, and since the 15th cent. it has been only a modest, though delightful, provincial town.

**Winchester, battle of,** 1141. In February 1141 *Matilda captured her rival Stephen at Lincoln and imprisoned him at Bristol. But she quarrelled with his brother Henry of Blois, bishop of Winchester, and began a siege of his castle. Stephen's queen then led a relief force which, on 14 September, scattered the besiegers and captured *Robert of Gloucester, Matilda's illegitimate brother and chief supporter. When Stephen and Robert were exchanged, Matilda lost the advantage she had gained at Lincoln.

**Winchester, diocese of** Roughly conterminous with west and central Hampshire and the Channel Islands, Winchester is the fifth senior see after *Canterbury, *York, *London, and *Durham, and with them its bishop always has a seat in the House of Lords. The first signs of a bishopric were in c.660, when *Cenwalh appointed Wine as bishop. In 705 the diocese was divided, Hampshire, Surrey, Sussex, the Isle of Wight staying under Winchester, the remainder west of Selwood going to the new see of *Sherborne. In c.909 *Edward the Elder further reduced it to Hampshire and Surrey by removing Berkshire and Wiltshire for the new diocese of *Ramsbury. It was further diminished by the creation of the *Guildford and *Portsmouth dioceses in 1927. The hegemony of Wessex from *Egbert's reign onwards increased the see's importance, and in the 11th cent. Winchester became the national capital. The present cathedral, the longest in Europe (556 feet), begun in 1079 under Walkelin (1070–98), is still basically Norman with Early English and Perpendicular additions. The cathedral contains the remains of the Saxon kings and a shrine of St Swithin.

**Winchester, statute of,** 1285. Edward I's reign saw a determination to enforce law and order. After complaining that local people were reluctant to do justice to strangers, the statute (13 Edw. I) declared that each district or hundred would be held responsible for unsolved crimes. Each man was to keep arms to take part in the *hue and cry when necessary.

**Winchester, treaty of,** 1153. For many years this agreement between Stephen and his rival Matilda's son Henry was known as the treaty of Wallingford. In fact, the negotiations were at Winchester and were ratified at Westminster. The death of Stephen's son *Eustace, in his twenties, had broken the back of Stephen's cause, and on 6 November 1153 he agreed to recognize Henry as his heir. Stephen died the following year and the prince succeeded as Henry II.

**Winchester, William Paulet, 1st marquis of** (c.1483–1572). 'More of a willow than an oak' was reported to have been Paulet's engaging assessment of himself and, indeed, anyone who could negotiate the vicissitudes of Tudor politics and hold high office in four reigns needed to be pliant. For many years he was associated with the profitable control of wardships. In the Parliament of 1529 he sat for Hampshire. From 1537 to 1539 he was treasurer of the household for Henry VIII, created Baron St John in 1539, and given the Garter in 1543. From 1543 to 1545 he was lord chamberlain, lord steward 1545–50, lord president of the council 1545–50, and lord high treasurer 1550–72. Clearly he was a more than useful work-horse. In Edward VI's reign, he backed *Northumberland against *Somerset, was created earl of Wiltshire in 1550, and marquis of Winchester

1551. The only time when his footwork faltered was in supporting Lady Jane *Grey in 1553, but he abandoned her quickly enough to retain Mary's confidence, and continued in office under Elizabeth.

**Winchester Bible** The Winchester Bible (1160–70), probably commissioned by Henry of Blois, is the finest of several large bibles produced through 12th-cent. contact with Byzantine art in Norman Sicily. Designed for ceremonial use rather than individual study, the volume was, like altar-missals, ornately decorated.

**Winchester College** In about 1330 *William of Wykeham attended a grammar school in Winchester. He later incorporated it in a new establishment, St Mary College of Winchester, founded by charter on 20 October 1382. The scholars, selected on a nation-wide basis, were prepared for entry to New College, Oxford, which Wykeham had founded in 1369.

**Winchester palace** was started by Charles II in 1682 with *Wren as architect. Substantial progress was made but it was far from finished when Charles died in 1685 and his successor James II, beset with problems, abandoned the project. In the Seven Years War and the War of American Independence, the shell of the palace was used for thousands of prisoners of war. In the early years of the Revolutionary War it gave shelter to French refugee clergy, but in 1796 was handed over to the military for use as a gaol. What was left of it was destroyed by fire in 1894.

**Windham, William** (1750–1810). Statesman. Educated at Eton and University College, Oxford, Windham was a close friend of Edmund *Burke and Dr *Johnson, being a pall-bearer at the latter's funeral. In 1784 he became MP for Norwich and was one of the members charged with the impeachment of Warren *Hastings. He was secretary for war in the Pitt administration of 1794 to 1801 with a seat in the cabinet. Windham opposed the peace of 1802, an unpopular view at the time which cost him his Norwich seat. He returned to government at the War and Colonial Office in *Grenville's 'Ministry of All the *Talents' (1806–7). Windham died of a tumour in 1810. His diary was published in 1866.

**window tax** William III's window tax (1696) was imposed on every dwelling except cottages. The rates were 2 shillings for houses with less than 10 windows, 6 shillings for 10–20 windows, and 10 shillings for more than 20 windows. It led to the stopping up of windows, often temporarily until the assessment had passed. During the Napoleonic wars the tax was increased on several occasions and by 1815 the yield was a substantial £2 million. In 1823 the tax was halved and in 1851 abolished.

**Windsor, house of** The Hanoverians, who were summoned in 1714 as the nearest protestant heirs, were related to the Stuarts and previous British dynasties through Sophia, electress of Hanover, mother of George I and granddaughter of James VI and I. The original family name was Guelph. They were often known as the Brunswick line since the correct name for Hanover was first Brunswick-Calenberg-Gottingen and then Brunswick-Luneburg. The first six rulers, up to Edward VII, married Germans.

When war broke out in 1914 the German antecedents of the royal family were an embarrassment. Prince Louis Battenburg, 1st sea lord, was obliged to resign his post. In 1917 as a gesture of identification with the nation, George V declared that the family would be known in future as Windsor. The new image was perfect and well received, save for some ribaldry from the kaiser. Various alternatives had been mooted. Tudor was rejected because of the image of Henry VIII, FitzRoy as smacking of bastardy, Plantagenet as unintelligible, and Stuart as dispiriting.

**Windsor, treaty of,** 1175. In 1171 Henry II took an expedition to Ireland to establish his authority. He received the submission of Normans and Irish alike, save for Rory O'Connor, king of Connacht, who claimed the high kingship of Ireland. But in 1175 O'Connor came to terms at Windsor, becoming the king's man. In return, Henry recognized his authority as high king outside the Pale. The arrangement did not work well and in 1185 Henry sent his youngest son John to rule Ireland.

**Windsor castle** (Berks.) is the premier castle of England as well as its largest. It was founded by William the Conqueror, who adopted the typical Norman design of motte and bailey, and was first used as a royal residence by Henry I. The original wooden structure was replaced by stone from 1165 to 1179 by Henry II, who also constructed the prominent Round Tower. St George's chapel, Windsor—which has long served as the last resting place of sovereigns —was begun by Edward IV in 1475 and is notable for its fan vaulting, monuments, stalls, and stained glass. Subsequently extensive remodelling was carried out for George III from 1796 by James Wyatt, and by his nephew Sir Jeffry Wyatville for George IV from 1820 to 1830. At Frogmore nearby is the royal mausoleum (1862–71) containing the two white marble effigies of Victoria and the prince consort.

**Windward Islands** A southern continuation of the chain of islands in the Caribbean known as the Lesser Antilles, with Puerto Rico to the west and *Trinidad to the south. They include *Dominica, Martinique, *St Lucia, and *St Vincent, with *Barbados lying to the east. Martinique is a *département* of France.

**Wingate, Orde** (1903–44). Soldier. Wingate's father was a colonel in the Indian army and Wingate was born in India. Commissioned in the Royal Artillery in 1923, he was sent to the Sudan in 1940 to lead an invasion of Italian-held Abyssinia, and with a small force, assisted by supporters of Haile Selassie, captured Addis Ababa in May 1941. He was then put in charge of the Chindit force to operate in Burma behind the Japanese lines. A successful sortie in 1943 led to a more ambitious campaign for 1944, but Wingate was killed in an air crash in the jungle early in the operation.

**Winstanley, Gerrard** (b. 1609). Digger leader. Born in Wigan and apprenticed in London, he failed in trade, and from 1643 worked as a cowhand in Surrey. His 20 tracts (twelve being of substantial length) were all written between 1648 and 1651, and included manifestos for the *Digger movement. Before that they were strongly *millenarian: the millennium will come when the land is restored to common ownership and all live as equals. His final work, *The Law of Freedom*, proposed a polity for those who voluntarily embrace a communistic commonwealth. It is highly authoritarian, and its penalties for breaches of its code make chilling reading.

**Winthrop, John** (1588–1649). Governor of Massachusetts. Of a prosperous Suffolk clothier's family, Winthrop went to Trinity College, Cambridge, and then studied law at Gray's Inn. In 1630 he left for America with a group of Puritan families, having been elected governor of the tiny colony of Massachusetts, which had then no more than 700 settlers. Winthrop was governor until 1634, and then 1637–40, 1642–4, and 1645–9. He was involved in all the religious disputes of the day, gradually adopting a more austere line towards dissent.

**Winwæd River, battle of,** 655. Here *Oswiu of Bernicia successfully challenged the overlordship of *Penda of Mercia and was able to take temporary control of Mercia and permanent control of Deira. Penda was killed in the battle and many of his supporters drowned when they tried to escape across the flooded river. The battle would have taken place near the Mercian/Northumbrian border in the Leeds area.

**Wiseman, Nicholas** (1802–65). First cardinal-archbishop of Westminster. Born of Irish parents in Seville, Wiseman was educated in Co. Durham and at the English College, Rome, where he later became rector (1828–44) and titular bishop (1840). Pius IX sent Wiseman as pro-vicar-apostolic to the London district in 1848 and then (1850) appointed him cardinal, intending to restore the English catholic hierarchy with Wiseman as archbishop. So great was English resentment that Parliament passed the Ecclesiastical Titles Act (1851), prohibiting catholics from assuming episcopal territorial titles. Wiseman's moderation assuaged suspicions; the Act was repealed (1871) without ever being invoked.

**Wishart, George** (*c.*1513–46). One of the first Scottish protestant martyrs. Wishart came from Pittarrow near Montrose. After visiting Germany and Switzerland, he became a fellow of Corpus Christi College, Cambridge, before returning to Scotland in 1543. There he commenced itinerant preaching with John *Knox as a disciple. He was arrested in 1546, taken to Cardinal *Beaton's castle at St Andrews, and tried for heresy. Two months after Wishart was burned, Beaton himself was murdered in the castle by Wishart's friends.

**witan** is the plural of Old English *wita*, a wise man, a counsellor. It was used by Anglo-Saxons sometimes in composition with *gemot* (an assembly) to indicate a royal or national conciliar meeting. Some have seen all such conciliar assemblies as essentially under royal control: to the contrary was the Victorian view that these could be 'nationally' representative. *Bede, writing *c.*731, certainly believed that decision on the conversion of a kingdom could be the subject of possibly formal, conciliar debate.

**Wodehouse, P. G.** (1881–1975). Wodehouse was the son of a judge in Hong Kong but was born in Guildford. From the age of 2 Wodehouse was brought up in England by relatives or hired governesses. Dulwich College he thought 'like heaven'. He began as a bank clerk, which he hated, but made his way into journalism and in 1919 published *My Man Jeeves*. The success of these stories prompted an avalanche of Bertie Wooster stories. During the Second World War Wodehouse was captured in France by the Germans, who allowed him to broadcast to America. This foolish action gave great offence in Britain and after the war Wodehouse lived in the USA, becoming an American citizen. He was given a knighthood a few days before his death. Wodehouse's stories acquired in time a period flavour of bright young things and made a very successful television series. Like most good writers, he created his own imaginary world, full of daft men and determined women.

**Wolfe, James** (1727–59). Born in Westerham (Kent) into a military family, Wolfe was an intelligent and articulate professional soldier. He fought at *Culloden and with distinction in the Rochefort expeditionary force. Marked out by William *Pitt for Canadian service, he served bravely at Louisbourg in 1758. Appointed a major-general, he led the assault on *Quebec in 1759. His tactical success and youthful death in victory on 13 September 1759 ensured his entry to the

**W**

pantheon of British heroes. His statement that he would rather have written *Gray's 'Elegy'* than capture Quebec is not forgotten.

**Wollstonecraft, Mary** (1759–97). Author and early feminist writer. Mary Wollstonecraft worked for a London publisher, James Johnson, until leaving for Paris in 1792 to study the French Revolution. Returning to London, she became part of a group of radical and progressive thinkers who included William *Godwin, Thomas *Paine, William *Blake, and William *Wordsworth. In 1796 she became Godwin's lover, and they married the next year—only six months before her death, which followed the birth of their daughter Mary (future wife of Shelley and author of *Frankenstein*).

Mary Wollstonecraft wrote four books, the most influential of which was *Vindication of the Rights of Woman* (1792). This was the first major statement of feminism by an English writer, and in it Wollstonecraft argued that the revolutionary principles of liberty and equality applied to women as much as to men.

**Wolseley, Garnet, 1st Viscount Wolseley** (1833–1913). Soldier. The son of an Irish major, Wolseley joined the army in 1852 and served with distinction in the Burmese War and the Crimean War. He was in India at the time of the mutiny and took part in the second Opium War against China in 1860. From 1861 he was in Canada, where he crushed the *Red River rebellion in 1870 and then won more fame in the *Ashanti War of 1873–4. His victory at *Tel-el-Kebir in Egypt over Arabi Pasha in 1882 made him a national hero. Though his expedition in 1885 failed to rescue *Gordon, Wolseley was not held responsible and was promoted viscount. He finished in 1894 as field marshal, one of the busiest and most successful of Victorian soldiers.

**Wolsey, Thomas** (*c*.1472–1530). Cardinal. Thomas Wolsey, cardinal-minister to Henry VIII, dominated the political and ecclesiastical life of England from 1515 to 1529. His relatively modest origins (reputedly the son of an Ipswich butcher) were not unusual for a senior cleric; it was the contrast between his origins and his life-style which drew notice. He studied at Oxford and became a fellow of Magdalen College around 1497.

He soon left scholarship to serve as chaplain to Henry Deane, archbishop of Canterbury, from 1501, became a royal chaplain from 1507, and the king's almoner in 1509. For helping to organize Henry VIII's first campaign in France (1513), he was rewarded with the bishoprics of Lincoln and newly captured Tournai in 1514, and the archbishopric of York shortly afterwards. In 1515 he became both cardinal and lord chancellor of England. In 1518 the pope honoured him with the special status of legate *a latere*, outranking the legatine status held by every archbishop of Canterbury; in 1524 this title was, uniquely, given for life.

With such an accumulation of posts, and vast energy, Wolsey took responsibility under the king for nearly all areas of government policy. A primary aim was to win military and diplomatic success for Henry. After the costly first campaign in France, Wolsey tried to magnify his master through grandiose peace negotiations (the treaty of *London, 1518, and the *Field of Cloth of Gold, 1520). However, England was drawn into invading France in 1522 and 1523, forcing heavy and much-resented taxation, for which Wolsey was blamed.

In domestic affairs Wolsey used his position as lord chancellor to pursue traditional policies with unusual verve and aggression. He revived Henry VII's campaign against those gentry and nobles who 'retained' excessive numbers of supporters to overawe royal justice. In 1517 he instituted commissions to search out those who had broken the law against converting arable farms into sheep-runs. He expanded the scope of the prerogative courts' equity jurisdiction, attracting a flood of civil suits to *Star Chamber and offering redress to poor plaintiffs in what later became the Court of Requests.

Wolsey's management of the church was less creative. However, he had a good eye for intellectual gifts in others; and his educational foundations, including the great unfinished project of Cardinal College, Oxford (later refounded as Christ Church), allow him to rank with Bishops Richard *Foxe in Oxford and John *Fisher in Cambridge.

Henry's desperate need for the annulment of his first marriage required Wolsey to ask of the papacy the one thing it could not grant. Wolsey attempted to have the issue devolved to a commission composed of himself and the roving Cardinal Campeggio, but the queen's appeal to Rome thwarted this plan. Wolsey, who planned a diplomatic second marriage to a French bride for Henry, had no control over *Anne Boleyn, who fed the king anticlerical and anti-Wolsey propaganda in the months leading up to the sudden loss of all his offices in October 1529. Wolsey pleaded guilty to an absurd charge of *praemunire arising out of his legatine status, but died on his way to London to answer, at Leicester, on 29 November 1530.

**women's institutes** Founded in Canada (1897) for improving women's education in domestic science, the first UK institute was formed on Anglesey (north Wales) in 1915 and the first county federation (Sussex) in 1917. Written off as a wartime experiment that would not last, their determination to better the lives of rural communities led to rapid expansion. Their love of festivals has created a popular image confined to making jam and singing Blake's 'Jerusalem', but they have demonstrated that they can be a powerful pressure group for change.

**'Wonderful' Parliament,** 1386. Parliament met on 1 October and demanded the dismissal of Richard II's chancellor and favourite, Suffolk (Michael de la *Pole). Richard refused and talked wildly of seeking aid from the king of France. But he was forced to agree to Suffolk's impeachment.

**Wood, Sir Henry J.** (1869–1944). English conductor. Initially an organist and composer, Wood studied at London's *Royal College of Music. He made his conducting début in 1888; he also helped *Sullivan prepare *The Yeomen of the Guard* and *Ivanhoe* and conducted the British première of Tchaikovsky's *Eugene Onegin* (1892). In 1895 Wood founded the enormously influential Queen's Hall *Promenade Concerts, which he conducted until his death. His *Fantasia on British Sea-Songs*, an arrangement written in 1905 for the centenary of Trafalgar, has become an immovable part of the Last Night of the Proms.

**Woodchester** is a major Romano-British villa in the Cotswolds near Stroud (Glos.). It originated on a small scale in the 2nd cent. By the first half of the 4th cent. it consisted of at least three courts in echelon. The principal range of the inner court contained a huge reception room, floored with the largest mosaic in Roman Britain, depicting Orpheus and the beasts.

**Woodforde, James** (1740–1803). Woodforde was a country parson whose diary from 1758 to 1802 has survived. His life was uneventful. He was born in Somerset, son of a cleric, and educated at New College, Oxford. After ten years as a Somerset curate, he returned briefly to college before becoming rector of Weston Longueville, a college living near Norwich. He had a lively interest in food, in his servants, and he played whist and went fishing. The diary is full of little vignettes—old Mr Reeve who broke Woodforde's gum—'he is too old, I think, to draw teeth, can't see very well'; Andrews the smuggler, who 'frightened us a little by whistling under the parlour window just as we were going to bed'; 'Mr Townshend's gamekeeper who goes by the name of Black Jack' and shot Woodforde's dog, Pompey.

**Wood's halfpence,** 1722. There was a shortage of coin in Ireland in 1722 and much of it was old and worn. Since there was no mint in Ireland, a patent was granted to a Wolverhampton ironmonger, William Wood, to supply just over £100,000 in halfpennies and farthings. There was vociferous protest from Ireland and an almost total refusal to handle the money. Swift's anonymous *Drapier's Letters* in 1724–5 raised a flame. *Walpole revoked the patent in 1725 and Wood was privately compensated. The episode suggests how tense Anglo-Irish relations were.

**Woodstock, Assize of,** 1184. The king's hunting in royal forests was protected in the Norman period by severe laws. Henry II enforced them fiercely, partly because of his own love of the chase, partly to raise revenue. This assize, also known as the Assize of the Forest, summarized previous laws. Stubbs suggested that it was milder than previous practice, but since punishments included blinding, mutilation, and castration, that is not easy to credit.

**Woodstock, treaty of,** 1247. For some years the treaty of Woodstock was the high-water mark of English advance against Wales. When *Dafydd ap Llywelyn died in

W

1246 without sons, his nephews Owain and *Llywelyn ap Gruffydd made peace with Henry III. They gave up their lands east of the Conwy and agreed to hold north Wales by military service. But Henry III's struggle with his barons enabled Llywelyn to recover much of his power and in 1258 to declare himself prince of Wales.

**Woolf, Virginia** (1882–1941). The daughter of Sir Leslie Stephen, editor of the *DNB*, Virginia Stephen was a sensitive child. Abused at the age of 6, the death of her mother when she was 13 caused a breakdown. She was engaged at one time to Lytton Strachey but in 1912 married Leonard Woolf. The physical side of the marriage was unappealing to her given her preference for lesbian relationships. With her husband she founded the Hogarth Press and their house became a centre for the Bloomsbury Group of artists and writers. Despite her delicate health she sustained a large output of essays, reviews, and novels—*Mrs Dalloway* (1925), *To the Lighthouse* (1927), and *Orlando* (1928), which experimented with 'stream of consciousness' technique and was a great success. In 1929 she published *A Room of One's Own*, surveying the difficulties confronting women, which became a classic of feminist literature. A protracted bout of depression in 1941 led her to drown herself in the river Ouse in Sussex.

**Worcester** Cathedral city on the river Severn, and county town of Worcestershire. A modest Roman town, it was reoccupied by a cathedral (680) and later by a fortified town (burh) *c.*890. From the 14th to the 17th cents. it flourished as a river port and cloth-making city. Its peak national ranking came in the 17th cent. (twelfth largest English town in 1662), but it suffered severely for supporting the royalists in the civil wars.

**Worcester, battle of,** 1651. In July 1650 Charles II landed in Scotland and was crowned at Scone on 1 January 1651. But finding his army outflanked by *Cromwell, he moved south in August, making for the old royalist strongholds of Wales and the west midlands. Cromwell pursued him with an army almost twice the size of his own, and caught up with him at Worcester. Cromwell attacked on 3 September. Superior numbers prevailed and the royal army was wiped out

as a fighting force. Charles was swept out of Worcester to the north and began his extraordinary escape. In his report of the battle, Cromwell wrote, 'it is, for aught I know, a crowning mercy'.

**Worcester, diocese of** Now roughly conterminous with Worcestershire, it was created by *Theodore in *c.*679 out of the large Mercian see for the *Hwicce people who inhabited Gloucestershire, Worcestershire, and half Warwickshire. The Worcester diocese was reduced in size by the creation of the see of *Gloucester in 1541 and *Birmingham in 1905. The cathedral, though Norman in plan with Norman crypt and chapter house, was mostly refashioned in the 19th cent. with a Perpendicular cloister.

**Worcester, pact of,** 1264. After Simon de *Montfort's victory at *Lewes in May 1264, he attempted to subdue Roger *Mortimer and the marcher lords. On 12 December at Worcester, a compromise was reached whereby the lords were to go to Ireland for a year and a day, Prince Edward's possessions were to pass to de Montfort, but the prince was to be released. Everything was overturned by de Montfort's defeat and death at *Evesham in August 1265.

**Worcester, Thomas Percy, 1st earl of** (*c.*1344–1403). The younger brother of the 1st earl of *Northumberland, Percy had a distinguished career in the French war from 1369 to 1388. From 1390 he held office in Richard II's household and was rewarded with the title of earl and a share of the spoils for his part in the destruction of the king's enemies. In 1399, however, he abandoned Richard in favour of Henry IV and served as admiral, ambassador, and lieutenant in south Wales. As the Beauforts and Nevilles gained royal favour, Percy influence was threatened, and this helped to explain why Worcester joined Henry *Percy's rebellion. He was beheaded after the battle of *Shrewsbury.

**Worcester, treaty of,** 1218. After John's death in 1216, he was succeeded by his son Henry III, aged 9. *Llywelyn ab Iorwerth had profited from the divisions of John's reign and controlled most of Wales. At Worcester in 1218 his power was acknowledged, he was recognized as Henry's lieutenant during the minority, and the royal castles of Carmarthen and Cardigan were placed in his hands. The accommodation soon broke down.

**Worcestershire** is bisected by the river Severn, which enters the county at Bewdley and leaves it near Tewkesbury. The Malverns formed the boundary with Herefordshire in the south-west. The early importance of Worcester was as a river crossing and it retained its strategic significance until the 17th cent. One form of the name was Wigornaceastre, which may derive from the people of the Wyre forest. The area formed part of the territory of the *Hwicce and then of the *Mercians.

Though sheltered from Welsh attacks by Hereford to the west, the county was for centuries a border area, and fell under the jurisdiction of the *Council of the Marches in Tudor times. Four great abbeys were early established, at Pershore, Evesham, Malvern, and Worcester itself. The cathedral at Worcester was rebuilt several times before the Norman Conquest. The present building was started in 1084 by St *Wulfstan but not finished until much later.

In the 16th cent. *Camden wrote of Worcester that it 'really deserved admiration both for its antiquity and beauty' and noted that the shire was celebrated for its perry and for the salt springs at Droitwich. Worcestershire retained its prosperity in the 18th cent. but the character of the county was beginning to change. There had always been local industries and the Severn was always a busy thoroughfare. Droitwich salt-pans went back to Domesday, Kidderminster was famous for textiles and then carpets, while there were glass manufactories at Stourbridge from Tudor times. In the 17th cent. the Foleys established nail-making at Stourbridge on a grand scale. The development of a canal and railway network brought Worcestershire more into the national context, as it did Warwickshire. Stourport was scarcely more than a solitary inn in the 1770s when it became the junction of the new Staffordshire and Worcester canal with the Severn, but subsequently developed into a busy town. Great Malvern jumped from a small local spa to a national one in the middle of the 19th cent. with the popularity of hydropathy. The southern and western towns of Evesham,

Pershore, and Tenbury remained small, but the northern parts were sucked into the Black Country complex. Dudley developed into a great mining and industrial centre, far exceeding Worcester in population. By the local government reorganization of 1972, the county was merged with its neighbour Herefordshire. 'The Malverns are no more,' it was declared. But the forced marriage, resented by Herefordshire, ended in divorce in 1998.

**Wordsworth, William** (1770–1850). Greatest of the Romantic poets for 'the union of deep feeling with profound thought' his friend *Coleridge admired in his work. From Cambridge a visit to France on the first anniversary of the Revolution fired his enthusiasm for the people's cause. His loyalties divided by the outbreak of war and separated from the woman who bore his child, he settled in Dorset with his sister Dorothy. *Lyrical Ballads* (1798) was written to show that 'men who do not wear fine clothes can feel deeply' and a copy presented to Charles James *Fox. After 1800, back in his native Cumberland, a more subjective vein emerged in *The Prelude* (not published until 1850), the long poem on the growth of his own mind.

**Workers' Educational Association (WEA).** Founded in 1903 by Albert Mansbridge (1876–1952), a cashier at the Cooperative Permanent Building Society, whose own formal education had ended at the age of 14. Mansbridge considered that the University Extension movement, established in 1878, had been largely taken over by the middle classes. To remedy this, Mansbridge launched an Association to Promote the Higher Education of Working Men, changing its name to the Workers' Educational Association two years later. By the outbreak of the First World War the movement had proved a success, with every university providing tutors. But infiltration by the middle class persisted.

**workhouses** The workhouse as such was an Elizabethan invention designed to provide a disciplined and productive environment for the able-bodied poor. The idea was slow to spread until the 18th cent., and an Act of 1723 enabled parishes to band together to support a shared workhouse out

**w**

of their income from rates (local property taxes). Many of the resulting ventures soon became places of refuge for the aged and impotent poor and for unmarried mothers rather than supervised workplaces. Some attempts were made to make relief to the able-bodied conditional on entry into the workhouse, but outdoor relief in various forms continued. The workhouse really rose to prominence with the *Poor Law Amendment Act of 1834, which required each of the new unions of parishes to provide a central workhouse which would classify the poor by age, sex, and circumstances and accommodate them under conditions which were 'less eligible' than the worst that prevailed outside. No relief was originally to be given outside these workhouses. In practice, the system was generally less fearsome than intended. Outdoor relief continued to be provided in many places: it was cheaper and more flexible than the workhouse. In industrial areas such as south Lancashire new workhouses were not built for over 30 years in some unions.

But the great achievement of the 1834 Act was to attach such a stigma to poor relief, and create such a fear of the workhouse, that many proud and independent people preferred starvation or prostitution to admission into the 'bastille'. Conditions in workhouse hospitals could still be appalling in the 1860s and 1870s, especially in the venereal and insane wards. Even when the workhouse premises passed into the National Health Service as hospitals after the Second World War, the stigma remained and many elderly people were terrified of entering them.

**working men's clubs** Clubs which brought working men together sociably took many forms, including *friendly societies for mutual insurance and gatherings in pubs or beerhouses for news and information and to enjoy shared interests and pursuits such as music and gardening. But the working men's club movement, as such, was a product of philanthropic and controlling concerns within the mid-Victorian middle classes, anxious to reclaim the working man from the pub and its temptations to alcoholic, political, and other excesses. The prime mover in the foundation of the Workingmen's Club and Institute Union, established in 1862, was the Revd

Henry Solly, a unitarian minister whose experiments in Lancaster had convinced him of the viability of this approach to social reform. But the CIU itself soon threw off most of the restrictions intended by its original patrons, and beer soon appeared as part of the clubs' attractions, followed by musical and comic entertainment. As with other cultural initiatives promoted from above, working men took what they wanted from the CIU and rejected the rest.

**Workmen's Compensation Act,** 1897. This Act, passed by Lord *Salisbury's government, was a significant step in establishing employers' liability. The foundation of the *Trades Union Congress in 1868 saw increased pressure for compensation for accidents at work, and in 1876 a select committee was set up, under the chairmanship of Robert *Lowe. It resulted in an Act of 1880 which offered up to three years' wages in damages if the employer or an authorized superintendent had been negligent. In the 1890s Joseph *Chamberlain campaigned for compensation 'irrespective of the cause of accident' and, though colonial secretary, was largely responsible for the Act of 1897, which established that an employee was entitled to compensation for any accident not his own fault, even if there was no negligence on the part of the employer.

**World War One** *See* FIRST WORLD WAR.

**World War Two** *See* SECOND WORLD WAR.

**Worms, treaty of,** 1743. In an attempt to gain the balance in the War of the Austrian Succession, Lord *Carteret persuaded Maria Theresa and George II to sign the treaty of Worms with Charles Emmanuel of Sardinia, offering him subsidies and territorial concessions in exchange for support. But the move was cancelled by France bringing Spain into the war on her side.

**Wren, Sir Christopher** (1632–1723). Wren was an instinctive mathematician and geometrician, whence came the constructional resource evident in the span of the Sheldonian theatre, Oxford (1664–9), and the dome of St Paul's (1705–11). A more reticent individualist than Inigo *Jones, as an astronomer Wren's individualism was of the age of *Newton, in which spatial values were pre-eminent. His work ranges from the Royal Observatory, Greenwich (1675), to *Hampton Court palace (1689–1702) and *Greenwich hospital (1696–1702). Apart from his masterpiece, St Paul's, Wren designed some 25 churches for London between 1670 and 1694. In 1669 he became surveyor-general of the king's works, holding the post until 1718.

**wrestling** is one of the oldest sports in the world and has always had a large number of local and national variants. It was included in the Olympic Games in 704 BC. In Britain, Cumberland and Westmorland, and Cornwall and Devon, developed their own versions, and it formed an important part of the Cotswold Games which flourished at Chipping Campden in the 17th cent. Professional wrestling on TV had a considerable following in the 1970s but the bouts became so ludicrous that its appeal wilted.

**Wright, Joseph** (1734–97). Painter, known as Wright of Derby, where he was born and spent most of his life. He earned a living as a portrait painter, while he experimented with the effects of light and industrial and scientific subjects, reflecting the interests of his day. Two of his best-known works come from this period, *A Philosopher Lecturing on the Orrery* (1766, Derby) and *An Experiment on a Bird in the Air Pump* (1768, Tate). Although in 1775 Wright failed to replace *Gainsborough in Bath, some of his best portraits come from the early 1780s.

**writs** The writ was originally an administrative command issued by the king to a subject, often an official such as the sheriff. After the Norman Conquest, and especially after the reign of Henry I, the king might issue a writ to permit a subject to have his case heard before the king's person or his *curia regis. After this, the issue of writs by the *Chancery or writ office became the regular way of obtaining a hearing in the king's court. Each writ had its own procedure and special features.

**Wrotham Heath, battle of,** 1554. Widespread risings against Mary's marriage to Philip of Spain did not take place as planned, but Sir Thomas *Wyatt managed to rouse considerable numbers in Kent. Part of his force under Sir Henry Isley was

caught at Wrotham Heath, between Sevenoaks and Rochester, on 28 January, and dispersed by Sir Robert Southwell, sheriff of the county. The remainder went on to threaten London, but the rebellion collapsed in early February.

**Wulfhere** (d. 675), king of Mercia (658–75). Wulfhere was in hiding after his father *Penda's defeat and death until a successful rising in 658 expelled the Northumbrians and made him king. He was a Christian, and events in his reign illuminate the relationship between a king's role and his faith. Wulfhere had authority over Essex; his ecclesiastical interventions there were both edifying, and less so. He sent a mission to reconvert part of Essex which had apostatized (*c*.664). He sold the see of London to Wine in the first known English act of simony (666). His relations with Sussex also interwove power and piety. Wulfhere's power flagged at the end of his life: he was defeated *c*.674 by the Northumbrians and lost control of Lindsey.

**Wulfstan, St** (*c*.1009–95). Bishop of Worcester. Born near Warwick and educated at the monasteries of Evesham and Peterborough, he took vows at Worcester, where he became prior. Renowned for his sanctity and care for the poor, he reluctantly accepted the bishopric in 1062. Politically useful, he was Harold's emissary to win loyalty in the north, but after the Norman Conquest he swore allegiance to William I. He supported William II against the Welsh (1088). He was canonized in 1203.

**Wyatt, Sir Thomas** (*c*.1521–54). Wyatt's father was a poet, courtier, and diplomat, with extensive estates in Kent. Wyatt inherited in 1542. Outraged in 1554 at Mary's decision to marry Philip of Spain, on national and religious grounds, he joined in what was intended as a national rising but finished up confined to Kent. The rebels suffered a setback at *Wrotham Heath but recovered the initiative when the duke of *Norfolk led an ill-judged advance. Wyatt moved towards London but Mary refused to flee. Repulsed at London bridge and the Tower, he crossed the Thames at Kingston, but found Ludgate closed and his forces deserting. He was executed on Tower Hill on 11 April.

w

**Wycherley, William** (1641–1716). English poet and playwright, aptly said to have 'fondled his age whilst abusing it'. He was educated in France, at Queen's College, Oxford, and then in the Inner Temple before establishing his reputation for witty if risqué satire on contemporary morality with his four plays *Love in a Wood* (1672), *The Gentleman Dancing-Master* (1673), *The Country Wife* (1675), and *The Plain-Dealer* (1677),

**Wyclif, John** (c.1329–84). Religious reformer. An Oxford-educated Yorkshireman, he was the leading philosopher of his day, briefly master of Balliol (1360) and warden of Canterbury Hall (1377). As *John of Gaunt's protégé, he was diplomat and government propagandist, persistently attacking clerical wealth and privilege, but, when condemned by the pope (1377), he was protected by Gaunt and Oxford University. The papal schism (1378) fuelled his attacks on catholic fundamentals—papal authority, confession, transubstantiation, and monasticism. After condemnation by Oxford (1381) and Archbishop *Courtenay, he withdrew to Lutterworth (Leics.), where he died. The *Peasants' Revolt (1381) discredited his ideas which became 'the touchstone of heresy', pursued by the *lollards and in Bohemia by John Hus. The Council of Constance (1415) condemned Wyclif's views, and his remains were exhumed and burned.

**Wyndham, Sir William** (c.1688–1740). Politician. Wyndham owed his position as a leader of the Tories in the Walpole period to three things—his standing as a well-connected Somerset baronet, his debating ability, and the fact that he was one of the few remaining Tories who had any experience of office. He entered Parliament at 21 at a by-election in Somerset in 1710, just before the great Tory victory at the general election. Pushed by *Bolingbroke, he was made master of the buckhounds 1711–12, secretary at war 1712–13, and chancellor of the Exchequer in 1713. He was dismissed at once by George I in 1714 and after Bolingbroke fled to France in 1715 planned a Jacobite rising. Arrested in bed, he spent some months in the Tower, but was released through the influence of his father-in-law, the duke of Somerset. Thereafter Wyndham gradually loosened his Jacobite ties and protested himself a Hanoverian Tory.

**Wyvill, Christopher** (1740–1822). A Yorkshire squire and clergyman, Wyvill was the main instigator of the county movement for parliamentary reform. Disillusioned by the loss of America and the policies of Lord North, the gentry of Yorkshire in 1779 formed the *Yorkshire Association to press for curbs on government expenditure and patronage ('*economical reform'), an increase in the number of independent (i.e. county) MPs, and annual parliaments. Wyvill was secretary and then chairman of the association. The Yorkshire Association disintegrated after the ending of the American war; and Wyvill's efforts at reform were eclipsed by more radical movements inspired by the French Revolution.

W

**Yalta conference,** 4–11 February 1945. *Churchill was increasingly fearful of the rising power of the USSR, but agreed that she was entitled to a buffer zone in eastern Europe. He agitated for some western influence in the reorganization of the Polish government and strove to promote free elections in the east. He also ensured that France was given an occupation zone in Germany, but was less successful in resisting Stalin's demands for huge reparations. After Yalta Churchill briefly seemed hopeful concerning the future.

**Yeats, Jack B.** (1871–1957). Painter. Brother of W. B. *Yeats the poet, Jack Yeats became the best-known Irish painter of his day. He was born in London, son of a good portrait painter, and attended (sometimes) the Westminster School of Art. He began as a water-colourist and illustrator before turning to oils. Most of his life was spent in Ireland, his family originating from Sligo, about which he published in 1930.

**Yeats, W. B.** (1865–1939). Dublin-born poet, dramatist, and essayist. His early years were spent in England, where his painter father introduced him to William *Morris and his circle. *The Wanderings of Oisin* (1889) reveals a late Romantic fired with enthusiasm for things Irish. He preferred to associate himself with the Anglo-Irish, 'bound neither to Cause nor to State . . . the people of *Burke and *Grattan'. Though in England at the time of the *Easter Rising, in poetry he recorded its 'terrible beauty'. Honoured with the Nobel prize and a seat in the Senate, he had little liking for *de Valera's Ireland.

**Yeavering** Residence of early Northumbrian kings. *Bede records the existence of the *villa regalis* of Ad Gefrin on the river Glen where *Paulinus baptized newly converted Northumbrians in 627 in the presence of King *Edwin. Following the identification of cropmarks suggesting large halls in the vicinity of the British hilltop site of Yeavering Bell, the site was dug by Brian Hope-Taylor and the results published in 1977.

**Yellow Ford, battle of the,** 1598. Sometimes known as the battle of the Blackwater, this was one of the last great victories of the Irish over their English antagonists. The great Hugh O'Neill (*Tyrone) was in rebellion and had brought together, not a scratch army capable only of guerrilla warfare, but a trained and equipped body of troops who could engage the enemy in pitched battle. Sir Henry Bagenal's advance was fiercely resisted on 14 August 1598 and when he was killed, his army of 5,000 fled.

**yeomanry** A force of volunteer cavalrymen, formed on a county basis, and first embodied in 1794 to meet the challenge of the French Revolution. Despite regular training, discipline was not always good. The Irish Yeomanry, raised in 1796, was almost exclusively protestant and put down the 1798 rising with great severity. The Lancashire and Cheshire Yeomanry got into difficulties in 1819 trying to disperse the crowd at *Peterloo. The yeomanry was merged with the *Volunteers in 1907 to form the *Territorial Army.

**yeomen** Legally a yeoman was a freeholder who could meet the qualification for voting in parliamentary elections, but the term came to be employed more widely than this, to encompass freeholders, copyholders, and sometimes even tenant farmers. In 18th-cent. Cumbria, freeholders, customary tenants, and tenant farmers were all encompassed by the term yeoman, while in other parts of the country it was virtually unknown. In 1566 Sir Thomas *Smith defined his fellow-Englishmen as gentlemen, yeomen, and rascals. By the early 19th cent. a slightly narrower definition seems to have been gaining ground. For the agricultural writer Arthur *Young, yeomen were only free-holders who were not gentry, and the same definition was used by witnesses before the 1833 Select Committee on Agriculture. Since the 1960s historians have increasingly es-chewed the word because of its romantic and sentimental overtones, as the sturdy inhabi-tants of a long-departed rural idyll.

**Yeomen of the Guard** are a royal body-guard founded in 1485 for the coronation of Henry VII. They have retained their Tudor uniforms and their duties include searching the cellars of Parliament before a state open-ing. The Yeomen Warders of the Tower, or Beefeaters, established in Edward VI's reign, have a similar uniform.

**York** A Roman legionary fortress, *colonia*, and provincial capital, Eboracum was founded in the early 70s AD as a fortress for *legio IX Hispana*. After the withdrawal of *IX Hispana*, its place was taken by *legio VI Victrix*, which remained in garrison, probably until the end of the Roman period. The for-tress lay between the rivers Ouse and Foss. Across the Ouse a civil settlement grew up which was promoted *colonia*, probably when York became capital of the new province of Britannia Inferior at the beginning of the 3rd cent. York remained a provincial capital in the 4th cent. and a bishop attended the Council of Arles in 314. Fortress and *colonia* seem to have been abandoned early in the 5th cent.

York re-emerged in historical record in 627 when the first Christian king of North-umbria was baptized there, and a bishopric established (an archbishopric from 735). By the 8th cent. it was a flourishing river port; between 866 and 954 it was in Viking hands, and was the capital of Danish and Norwe-gian kings, who fostered a commercial city of international importance, revealed at Cop-pergate. In 954 it was absorbed into England, and by the 12th cent. it was the fourth wealthiest English town. From about 1460 it declined, despite strong support from Ri-chard III. A modest recovery began with the residence in York of the king's *Council in the North (1561–1641), although the civil wars (especially the siege of 1644) were dam-aging. Late Stuart and Hanoverian York flourished greatly as a social capital, but the

city fell back in importance in the 19th cent. Its relative lack of industrialization and war damage has left York with a rich legacy of historic buildings, including an almost intact circuit of medieval walls and gates.

### York, Edward of York, 2nd duke of

(*c.*1373–1415). The elder son of *Edmund of Langley (whom he succeeded as duke in 1402), in 1390 Edward was created earl of Rutland by Richard II. He was a prominent supporter of Richard's coup in 1397, when his rewards included the title of duke of Au-male, which he lost after Henry IV's usurpa-tion. He continued, however, to serve Henry in Wales and Gascony. Edward commanded the van of Henry V's army at *Agincourt, where he was killed.

### York, Frederick Augustus, duke of

(1763–1827). The second son of George III, Frederick was made bishop of Osnabrück when he was 6 months old, but pursued a career in the army. In 1793 he commanded an expedition against the French in Flanders. After a bright cavalry victory at Beaumont in April 1794, he was badly beaten at Turcoing in May, and recalled. In 1795 he was made field marshal and in 1798 appointed com-mander-in-chief. A second expedition to Holland in 1799 proved even more disas-trous. In 1809 after allegations in Parliament that his mistress, Mary Anne Clarke, had used her influence to sell army commissions, he was forced to resign, but came back in 1811 and held the post until his death. Baron Stockmar wrote of him that he was 'very bald, and not a very intelligent face'. But he was unlucky to be remembered chiefly in a nursery rhyme.

### York, Richard Plantagenet, 3rd duke of

(1411–60). The son of the earl of Cam-bridge, who had rebelled against Henry V in 1415, and the heir to the estates, titles, and claims of the earls of March. Because of his blood and claim to the throne (1447–53 he was heir presumptive) he was always kept at arm's length by the king and his court. He served twice (1436–7, 1440–5) with some dis-tinction as the king's lieutenant in Nor-mandy. Failure to be reappointed in 1445 led to a bitter feud with his successor Ed-mund Beaufort, duke of *Somerset. He was rescued from political oblivion by the col-lapse of the king's health in 1453 and his

y

appointment as protector of the realm. The recovery of the king in 1454 led to his renewed exclusion, and thereafter he was set on a course of armed opposition which led in 1460 to his laying claim to the throne. He was killed in battle at *Wakefield and his head stuck on the walls of York with a paper crown on it.

**York, house of** 15th-cent. royal dynasty. Historians from the Tudor period onward viewed the Wars of the *Roses as a dynastic contest between the houses of Lancaster and York. This interpretation appears in the papal dispensation for the marriage of Henry VII and *Elizabeth of York, daughter of Edward IV, in 1486.

The title was first created in 1385 for Edmund of Langley duke of *York, 4th surviving son of Edward III, and descended to his son Edward, duke of *York in 1402. His heir was Richard of *York, son of his brother Richard of Conisborough. A hereditary right to the throne by York was inferior to that of the Lancastrians descended from *John of Gaunt, Edward III's third son to reach maturity. In 1460 Richard claimed the crown as heir to Lionel, Edward's second surviving son. By this date there had been intermittent hostilities since 1455, and this was the second time victory in battle by York and his allies had won control of Henry VI's government. After York's death in 1460, his friends recognized his son as King Edward IV. His claim was confirmed by battles in 1461 and again in 1471, when the main Lancastrian dynasty was extinguished.

The Yorkist monarchy was destroyed by Richard III's usurpation. Courtiers of Edward, believing Richard had murdered Edward's sons Edward V and Richard, agreed to accept Henry Tudor as king if he married their sister. Lancastrian recovery was achieved at *Bosworth in 1485.

**York, kingdom of** The Viking kingdom of York has attracted great attention since the Coppergate excavations revealed so much about Jorvik and its inhabitants. In 867 York was seized by Danish raiders from the Viking kingdom of *Dublin, led by Ivarr and his brother Halfdan. Holding the new conquest did not prove easy. Halfdan was killed in Ireland in 877 trying to assert his claim to Dublin. Halfdan II, who held the kingdom in 910, was killed at *Tettenhall in Staffordshire

fighting against *Edward the Elder. York's next ruler, Ragnall, a grandson of Ivarr, submitted to Edward in 920. The later decades of the kingdom were chaotic. England's suzerainty seems to have lasted since Ragnall's successor *Sihtric was married to a sister of *Athelstan, who took over the kingdom on Sihtric's death in 927, turning out Sihtric's brother Guthfrith and ruling it until 939. Guthfrith's son *Olaf then recaptured York but died soon after. Sihtric's son *Olaf could not hold it. From 944 the kings of England took over again until 947 when *Erik Bloodaxe, the last of the York Vikings, established a shaky rule. He was killed at *Stainmore in 954, possibly fleeing to Dublin. Henceforward the kingdom formed part of England, under *Edred and *Eadwig. The relative prosperity of Jorvik—its busy international trade, thriving workshops, and well-established mints—is perhaps a warning not to judge exclusively by chronicles, which tend to record death, destruction, and disaster, rather than peaceful progress.

**York, metropolitan diocese of** The present province of York, founded in 735, comprises the fourteen dioceses of northern England. The York diocese itself, founded by *Paulinus in 625, is now conterminous with eastern Yorkshire. Disputes between Canterbury and York over primacy were protracted. York's claim to be a metropolitan see independent of Canterbury was enhanced by Kent's political decline and *Offa of Mercia's temporarily successful bid for a *Lichfield archbishopric. Under Thomas of Bayeux (1070–1100) the contest developed in earnest. With William I's support in 1072, *Lanfranc (Canterbury 1070–89) was successful in resolving the matter in his favour. The dispute, renewed in 1118 with Pope Calixtus II's support for *Thurstan of York, continued for two centuries until Innocent VI (1352–1405) effected a compromise, though in Canterbury's favour. York was to have metropolitan authority over the north as 'Primate of England', while Canterbury was to have national precedence as 'Primate of all England'. The cathedral, York minster, is of mixed styles (13th to 15th cent.) with the broadest and tallest nave in England and a Norman crypt.

**York, statute of,** 1322. Immediately after the execution of *Thomas of Lancaster, Ed-

y

ward II summoned a parliament at York and by this statute (16 Edw. II stat. 1) repealed the Ordinances of 1311 (*see* ORDAINERS) which had limited his authority. It added that matters concerning the king, the realm, and the people should be debated in Parliament with the assent of magnates and the community of the realm.

**York, treaty of,** 1237. The kings of Scotland had long-standing ambitions to acquire Cumberland, Westmorland, and Northumberland. In the 12th cent. David I ruled at Newcastle and died at Carlisle. But in 1237 at York, Alexander II and his brother-in-law Henry III reached agreement. The Scottish king abandoned any claim to the northern counties in exchange for estates within them, notably in Tynedale and at Penrith.

**Yorkists** The three kings of England between 1461 and 1485 (Edward IV, Edward V, and Richard III) were so named because they were descended from Richard of *York. The term is also applied to their retainers, recognizable on effigies by their collars of suns and roses; to their supporters during the Wars of the *Roses; and to those who challenged Henry VII after 1485.

**Yorkshire,** the largest county in England, is bounded to the south by the Humber (which formed part of the ancient dividing line between northern and southern England), to the north by the Tees, and extends east–westwards from the North Sea into the Pennine hills, corresponding to lands settled by Halfdan's invading Danish army after 876. They divided it into three ridings ('thridings') for easier administration, the meeting-place for the north riding being at the Yarles tree (probably near Thirsk), that for the east riding at Craikhow (near Beverley), and possibly York for the west riding; the subdivisions called *wapentakes took their names from the meeting-places of their courts. The Danes were by no means the first European settlers: Eboracum (York) had been provincial capital of the Romans' Britannia Secunda, 6th-cent. Angles had formed the nucleus of the kingdom of *Deira, and some Norse immigration had occurred in the west from Lancashire and Westmorland. After the Norman Conquest, William's 'harrying of the north' left devastation, reflected in the Domesday survey. The might of the Norman

barons was symbolized by their castles (Knaresborough, Richmond, Scarborough).

York and Beverley's decline in the Tudor wool trade was the West Riding's gain, and it became one of the three major regions of the English cloth industry; Sheffield's cutlery industry was well established, Hull became one of England's busiest outports, and Whitby a coaling port. Yorkshire's integration into national life steadily increased. *Defoe found early Georgian Yorkshire endowed with thriving market towns (Doncaster, Ripon, Richmond), though he was more impressed by its horses and stone bridges than its spas. But the pace of industry was increasing, aided by improvements in the road network, canals to implement an already extensive river system and accelerated enclosure; the east and north ridings remained predominantly agricultural or moorland, but the west riding was transformed, since it sat at the northern edge of a huge coalfield that additionally contained iron. Leeds became the principal seat of woollen manufacture, Bradford the centre of the worsted trade, and Sheffield the focal point of the iron and steel industry, all experiencing massive increases in population and associated social problems. The advent of the railway in the 19th cent. (including the heroic Settle–Carlisle line) opened up some once isolated places while York developed into an important railway centre. In the remaining decades before local government reorganization (1972), when the ridings were swept away, traditional industries (textiles, coal, iron and steel) declined, but the strong sense of community barely wavered. A separate country to many because of its intense local patriotism—cricketers born outside Yorkshire were long ineligible to play for the county—the blunt-spoken, thrifty inhabitants retain an identity that many other shires have lost.

**Yorkshire, North** The county of North Yorkshire was created by the Local Government Act of 1972. It was substantially different from the old North Riding, losing a slice to Cleveland, including Guisborough and Yarm, gaining Filey and Norton from the east riding, and adding a large part of the former West Riding, including Harrogate, Ripon, Knaresborough, Skipton, Selby, and Tadcaster. The county town is Northallerton.

**Yorkshire, South** Since there was no south riding to build on, the metropolitan county of South Yorkshire, set up by the Local Government Act of 1972, was a new creation. It was based on the county boroughs of Sheffield, Rotherham, Barnsley, and Doncaster, augmented by parts of the West Riding, and parishes taken from Nottinghamshire. It was abolished under the Local Government Act of 1985.

**Yorkshire, West** The new metropolitan county of West Yorkshire, established by the Local Government Act of 1972, was built upon the county boroughs of Leeds, Bradford, Halifax, Dewsbury, Huddersfield, and Wakefield. There were substantial changes compared with the old West Riding, which lost large areas in the north-west to Cumbria and Lancashire; Harrogate, Ripon, and Selby to North Yorkshire; and a slice around Penistone and Cudworth to South Yorkshire. It was abolished with the other metropolitan counties in 1985.

**Yorkshire Association** Formed in December 1779 to lobby for *economical reform—a reduction of places and pensions—at a time of high taxation during the American War. Though conservatives denounced associations as potentially seditious, a number of other counties formed committees and joined with Yorkshire in petitioning Parliament. Their greatest success came in April 1780 when *Dunning's motion, deploring the influence of the crown, was carried against Lord *North, and in 1782 the short-lived *Rockingham administration undertook some useful reforms. The association was a remarkable attempt to mobilize public opinion and bring it to bear on Parliament, looking back to the *Wilkites and forward to the *chartists.

**Yorktown, surrender at,** 1781. After his costly victory at *Guilford courthouse in March 1781, *Cornwallis moved north into Virginia. Early in August he dug in on the coast at Yorktown, where supplies could be brought in. But the ships which arrived were French. Cornwallis, with 6,000 men, was blockaded by 9,000 Americans under Washington and 6,000 French under Rochambeau. A rescue operation from New York arrived too late. On 19 October, the British surrendered with full honours of war,

marching out to the tune 'The World Turned Upside Down', when 'cats should be chased into holes by the mouse'. Back in England, *North received the news like a man taking a ball in the chest: 'oh God, it is all over', he exclaimed.

**Young, Arthur** (1741–1820). Farmer, journalist, and agricultural writer. Often regarded as a pioneer of the *agricultural revolution, Young began his working life as a small farmer at Bradfield, his family home in Suffolk. After two years in Ireland (1776–8) he returned to Bradfield, where he farmed and settled to work as a writer and journalist, founding in 1784 the *Annals of Agriculture*, which he edited until 1809. In 1793 he became secretary to the Board of Agriculture with a salary of £400.

**Young England** was a small Tory parliamentary group of the 1840s, which included Lord John Manners, George Smythe, Baillie-Cochrane, and *Disraeli. They were greatly concerned with the 'condition of the people' question and their vague solution was a restoration of the trust and respect which they believed had once existed between nobility and people and a reaffirmation of the position of the church. It was not difficult to ridicule. Lord John Manners believed that a reintroduction of the practice of *touching for the king's evil might raise the tone of society and produced the memorable couplet: 'Let wealth and commerce, law and learning die, But leave us still our old nobility.' Yet their attitude to the poor, if condescending, was generous, and echoes of Young England survived as elements in Disraeli's later vision of Tory democracy.

**Young Ireland** was a group of patriotic middle-class intellectuals associated with the repeal movement of Daniel *O'Connell: its original leaders included Thomas Davis (1814–45), John Blake Dillon (1816–66), and Charles Gavan Duffy (1816–1903). Gavan Duffy's journalistic experience was essential to the success of the *Nation*, a newspaper founded in 1842 to promote the inclusivist nationalism of the Young Ireland movement. Growing tensions between Young Ireland and O'Connell's Repeal Association came to a head in July 1846, when a split occurred on the issue of physical force: the more militant Young Irelanders seceded from the Association, and, led by William Smith *O'Brien (1803–64), formed the Irish Confederation. The militants staggered into rebellion in 1848, which was easily suppressed, but the intellectual legacy of Young Ireland had a lasting influence.

## Young Men's Christian Association (YMCA).

Founded (1844) by a group of twelve young draper's assistants headed by George Williams (b. 1821) for 'the improving of the spiritual condition of young men engaged in drapery and other trades', who then lived in appalling urban conditions. Meeting for prayer and Bible study, they impressed Lord *Shaftesbury, who became the YMCA's first president (1851–85). It spread rapidly throughout Britain and, after the *Great Exhibition (1851), world-wide.

## Young Women's Christian Association (YWCA).

Founded independently of the *YMCA (1855, but united 1877) by Emma Roberts with her Prayer Union of 23 young women 'to offer service with their prayers', and Emily Kinnaird whose London hostel, originally for Florence *Nightingale's nurses *en route* for the Crimea, became a hostel for girls in need of safe, cheap accommodation. Lord *Shaftesbury became its first president (1878).

y

**Zambia,** previously known as Northern Rhodesia, is a republic within the Commonwealth and has a population of nearly 9 million. The region came under the control of *Rhodes's British South Africa Company, until in 1924 it was made a British protectorate. In 1953 it was joined with Nyasaland and Southern Rhodesia to form the Central African Federation, but this was dissolved in 1963. It became independent in 1964 with Kenneth Kaunda as first president.

**Zanzibar** Former British protectorate. Britain first became involved in Zanzibar in the 19th cent. because the island was one of the main depots for the export of east African slaves. A succession of able British consuls-general exerted an informal protectorate over the island, and the arrangement was regularized in 1890 when Britain became responsible for the administration of Zanzibar on the sultan's behalf. The slave trade was formally abolished in the sultan's dominions in 1897. Zanzibar became independent in 1963 and joined with Tanganyika to form *Tanzania in 1964.

**Zeppelin raids** The first air raid on Britain by German airships took place in January 1915. In theory the Zeppelin attacks were directed against naval and military targets. In reality, poor weather, limited night-time visibility, and frequent navigation errors meant that they dropped their bombs indiscriminately on civilian targets. In 51 raids the Zeppelins killed 556 people and injured 1,357. These attacks caused localized panic which interrupted industrial production but in the longer term failed to have an appreciable impact on Britain's war effort.

**Zimbabwe** *See* RHODESIA.

**Zinoviev letter** Supposed to have brought down the first Labour government of 1924. It bore the signature of Grigori Zinoviev, president of the Communist International (Comintern) in Moscow, and was addressed to the *Communist Party of Great Britain, calling on it to sow subversion among the armed forces of the crown. There is a faint possibility that it was a forgery; and a stronger likelihood that it was deliberately 'leaked' by the British secret services, shortly before the October 1924 general election, to scare voters over to the Conservatives.

**Zoffany, Johann** (*c.*1733–1810). Painter of portraits, conversation pieces, and theatrical scenes, Zoffany was born in Germany and came to England about 1758 after studying in Italy. He began by painting clock faces and doing hack work, before turning to painting theatrical scenes, especially depicting David *Garrick. He was favoured by the royal family. George III nominated him for the Royal Academy in 1769 and recommended him to the duke of Tuscany.

**Zulu War,** 1879. The war was the unforeseen result of the desire of Lord Carnarvon, the British colonial secretary, to unite the British colonies and Boer (Afrikaner) republics in South Africa to guarantee the security of white settlers. Sir Bartle Frere, sent out as high commissioner to implement Carnarvon's plan, concluded that Cape Colony would not cooperate as long as the Transvaal Boers were at loggerheads with their Zulu neighbours. Frere accepted the assertion that Zulu military strength constituted a threat to stability in South Africa. Against Carnarvon's strict instructions, Frere demanded impossible concessions from the Zulu ruler and then invaded Zululand in January 1879. The British government accepted the *fait accompli* and superior British arms overcame the courage and inappropriate tactics of the Zulus who surrendered in July. The renewed aggression of the Boers after the Transvaal had reasserted its internal autonomy in 1881 induced Britain to recognize their claims over a portion of Zululand and the remaining Zulu territory was incorporated into the British colony of *Natal.

**Zutphen, battle of,** 1586. During the Netherlands War of Independence, Elizabeth I sent troops under the earl of *Leicester to aid the rebels. In 1586 they laid siege to Zutphen, defended by a Spanish garrison under Prince Alexander of Parma. The Spanish sent a relief column and on 22 September Leicester attempted to intercept it. He was forced to retire after suffering considerable losses, including the death of his own nephew, Sir Philip *Sidney.

# Useful Websites

 **SEE WEB LINKS**

This is a web-linked dictionary. To access the websites listed below, go to the dictionary's web page at http://www.oup.com/uk/reference/resources/britishhistory, click on the Web links in the Resources section and click straight through to the relevant websites.

**BBC History**
- The BBC's history web page

**British Library**
- Homepage of the British Library

**Centre for Contemporary British History**
- Homepage of the CCBH

**Commonwealth**
- Homepage of the Commonwealth Secretariat

**English Heritage**
- Website of the organization

**European History**
- Useful overviews of European history

**H-Albion**
- Discussion network for British history

**Historic Royal Palaces**
- Official website of the five historic royal palaces

**Institute of Historical Research**
- Homepage of the IHR, the national centre for history

**The Monarchy**
- The official website of the British Monarchy

**Nationalism**
- Detailed discussion of the concept

**National Archives**
- Website of the UK government records and information management

**National Assembly for Wales**
- The Welsh Assembly's homepage

**Northern Ireland Assembly**
- Homepage of the Northern Ireland Assembly

**Number 10**
- The official website of the Prime Minister's Office

**Oxford Dictionary of National Biography**
- (subscription) Biographies of people who shaped the history of the British Isles

**The Scottish Parliament**
- Official website of Scotland's parliament

**Spartacus Encyclopedia of British History**
- Hyperlinked guide to British history from 1700 to 1920

**Tudor History**
- Detailed and well-organized information on the Tudor dynasty

**Time Ref.com**
- Hyperlinked timelines of British History from 800 to 1500

**United Kingdom Parliament**
- Official homepage of the UK Parliament

# Chronology

|      | GOVERNMENT AND POLITICS | OTHER EVENTS |
|------|------------------------|--------------|
| 871  | **Alfred the Great succeeds**; victory at Edington 878 | |
|      |                        | *Anglo-Saxon Chronicle* started *c*.892 |
| 899  | **Edward the Elder succeeds** | |
| 937  | Athelstan's victory at Brunanburh | |
|      |                        | Hywel Dda's legal code *c*.943 |
| 973  | Edgar crowned at Bath  | |
| 978  | **Æthelred II succeeds**; Viking raids; St Brice's Day massacre 1002; archbishop Ælfheah martyred by Danes 1012 | Ælfric, *Homilies c*.998 |
| 1016 | Edmund Ironside dies; **Cnut succeeds** | |
| 1035 | **Harold I Harefoot succeeds** | |
| 1040 | **Harthacnut succeeds** | |
| 1042 | **Edward the Confessor succeeds** | |
|      |                        | Westminster abbey rebuilt 1050–66 |
| 1066 | **Harold II succeeds**; killed at Hastings; **William the Conqueror succeeds** | |
|      |                        | Bayeux Tapestry *c*.1080; Domesday Book *c*.1088 |
| 1087 | **William Rufus succeeds** | |
| 1097 | **Edgar of Scotland succeeds** | |
| 1100 | **Henry I succeeds**   | |
| 1107 | **Alexander I of Scotland succeeds** | |
| 1124 | **David I of Scotland succeeds** | |
| 1135 | **Stephen succeeds**; war with Matilda | Geoffrey of Monmouth, *Historia Regum Britanniae c*.1136; Orderic Vitalis d. *c*.1142 |
| 1153 | **Malcolm IV of Scotland succeeds** | |
| 1154 | **Henry II succeeds**; 'Strongbow' invades Ireland 1170 | Becket murdered at Canterbury 1170 |
| 1165 | **William I of Scotland succeeds** | |
| 1189 | **Richard I succeeds**; Third Crusade | |
| 1199 | **John succeeds**; Magna Carta 1215 | |
| 1214 | **Alexander II of Scotland succeeds** | |
| 1216 | **Henry III succeeds** | |
| 1249 | **Alexander III of Scotland succeeds** | University College, Oxford, founded 1249; Matthew Paris d. 1259; *Bracton* 1260; Bacon, *Opus majus c*.1260 |
| 1264 | Baronial wars; de Montfort killed at Evesham 1265 | |
| 1272 | **Edward I succeeds**; Wales subdued 1280s | Peterhouse, Cambridge, founded 1284 |
| 1286 | **Margaret of Scotland succeeds** | |
| 1292 | **John Balliol of Scotland succeeds**; Scottish Wars of Independence | |

| | GOVERNMENT AND POLITICS | OTHER EVENTS |
|---|---|---|
| 1306 | **Robert I (the Bruce) of Scotland succeeds** | |
| 1307 | **Edward II succeeds**; Scottish victory at Bannockburn 1314 | |
| 1327 | **Edward III succeeds**; French wars; Crécy 1346; JPs established 1361 | Black Death 1349 |
| 1329 | **David II of Scotland succeeds** | |
| | | Langland, *Piers Plowman* c.1370 |
| 1371 | **Robert II of Scotland succeeds** | |
| 1377 | **Richard II succeeds**; Peasants' Revolt 1381 | Wyclif condemned 1381; Chaucer, *Canterbury Tales* c.1390 |
| 1399 | **Henry IV succeeds**; Glyndŵr's revolt; Hotspur killed 1403 | |
| 1406 | **James I of Scotland succeeds** | |
| 1413 | **Henry V succeeds**; Agincourt 1415 | |
| 1422 | **Henry VI succeeds** | |
| | | James I, 'Kingis Quair' c.1424 |
| 1437 | **James II of Scotland succeeds** | |
| | | Dunstable, musician, d. 1453 |
| 1460 | **James III of Scotland succeeds** | |
| 1461 | **Edward IV succeeds**; Wars of the Roses; Towton 1461; Barnet 1471 | Fortescue, *On the Governance of England* c.1470; Caxton's first book in English c.1474 |
| 1483 | **Edward V succeeds**; Richard's coup | |
| 1483 | **Richard III succeeds**; Bosworth 1485 | |
| 1485 | **Henry VII succeeds** | |
| 1488 | **James IV of Scotland succeeds** | |
| | | John Cabot reaches Newfoundland 1497; Erasmus visits England c.1500; Dunbar, *Thrissill and the Rois* 1503 |
| 1509 | **Henry VIII succeeds**; Flodden 1513 | |
| 1513 | **James V of Scotland succeeds** | |
| 1529 | Wolsey disgraced; Henry marries Anne Boleyn 1533; More executed 1534; Anne Boleyn executed 1536; Henry marries Jane Seymour 1536; marries Anne of Cleves 1540; Thomas Cromwell executed 1540; Henry marries Catherine Howard 1540; Catherine executed 1542; marries Catherine Parr 1543 | Dissolution of monasteries begins 1536; Pilgrimage of Grace 1536–7 |
| 1542 | **Mary Queen of Scots succeeds** | |
| | | Cardinal Beaton murdered 1546 |
| 1547 | **Edward VI succeeds**; Kett's rebellion 1549; Somerset overthrown 1549 | Prayer Book riots 1549 |
| 1553 | **Mary I succeeds**; Lady Jane Grey executed 1554; Calais lost 1558 | Reconciliation with papacy; Cranmer burned 1556 |

| | GOVERNMENT AND POLITICS | OTHER EVENTS |
|---|---|---|
| 1558 | **Elizabeth I succeeds**; Mary, queen of Scots, flees 1568; rising of northern earls 1569; Mary executed 1587; Spanish Armada 1588 | Reformation in Scotland 1560 |
| 1603 | **James I succeeds**; Gunpowder plot 1605; Ralegh executed 1618 | Marlowe, *Tamburlaine* c.1590; Spenser, *Faerie Queene* 1590; Shakespeare, *Henry VI* c.1591 Jonson, *Volpone* perf. 1605–6; Harvey lecturing on circulation of the blood 1615; Inigo Jones begins Queen's House Greenwich 1617, Banqueting House 1619 |
| 1625 | **Charles I succeeds**; Buckingham murdered 1628; Bishops' wars 1639–40; Short and Long Parliament 1640; Strafford executed 1641 | Milton, *Comus* perf. 1634 |
| 1642 | Civil War begins; Edgehill Oct. 1642; Marston Moor July 1644; Naseby June 1645 | Milton, *Areopagitica* 1644 |
| 1648 | Second Civil War; Charles executed 1649, republic declared | |
| 1651 | Charles II crowned at Scone; defeated at Worcester Sept.; first Dutch War 1652–4 | |
| 1657 | Cromwell rejects crown | |
| 1660 | Restoration; **Charles II's return**; second Dutch War 1665–7; third Dutch War 1672–4; Popish plot and Exclusion crisis 1678–81 | Pepys begins diary 1660; Royal Society founded 1660; plague year 1665; Great Fire of London 1666; Milton, *Paradise Lost* 1667; Bunyan, *Pilgrim's Progress* 1678 |
| 1685 | **James II succeeds**; Monmouth rising 1685 | |
| 1688 | Glorious Revolution; James flees | |
| 1689 | **William and Mary succeed**; Nine Years War 1689–97; Mary d. 1694 | Purcell, *Funeral Music*, 1694; Congreve, *Love for Love* 1695; Vanbrugh, *The Relapse* 1696 |
| 1702 | **Anne succeeds**; War of the Spanish Succession 1702–14; Blenheim 1704; Act of Union with Scotland 1707; treaty of Utrecht 1714 | |
| 1714 | **George I succeeds**; Jacobite rising 1715; Walpole in power 1721 | Three Choirs Festival 1716; South Sea bubble 1720; Swift, *Gulliver's Travels* 1726; Newton's funeral 1727 |
| 1727 | **George II succeeds**; Excise crisis 1733; Walpole resigns 1742; War of Austrian Succession 1740–8; Jacobite invasion 1745–6; Seven Years War 1756–63; Newcastle–Pitt administration 1757–61 | Fielding, *Tom Jones* 1730; Hogarth, *The Shrimp Girl* 1740; Handel, *Messiah* 1742; Royal Society of Arts founded 1754; Gainsborough, *The Painter's Daughters* 1756 |

| | GOVERNMENT AND POLITICS | OTHER EVENTS |
|---|---|---|
| 1760 | **George III succeeds**; War of American Independence 1775–83; Grattan's Parliament 1782–1801; Pitt in office 1784–1801 | Brindley's Worsley canal 1761; Royal Academy founded 1768; Arkwright's water frame 1769; Boulton–Watt partnership 1775; Smith, *Wealth of Nations* 1776; Burke, *Reflections on the Revolution in France* 1790 |
| 1793 | War against revolutionary France; naval mutinies 1797; Irish rebellion 1798 | Wordsworth and Coleridge's *Lyrical Ballads* 1798 |
| 1801 | Act of Union with Ireland, peace of Amiens 1802; war against Napoleonic France 1803–15; Trafalgar 1805; Waterloo 1815; abolition of slave trade 1807; Regency 1810–20 | Byron, *Childe Harold* 1812; Austen, *Pride and Prejudice* 1813; Scott, *Waverley* 1814 |
| 1820 | **George IV succeeds**; catholic emancipation 1829 | Constable, *The Hay Wain* 1821; Stephenson's *Rocket* 1829 |
| 1830 | **William IV succeeds**; Great Reform Act 1832; abolition of slavery 1833; Municipal Reform Act 1835 | Dickens, *Pickwick Papers* 1836 |
| 1837 | **Victoria succeeds**; Peel's ministry 1841–6; Chartist agitation 1837–48; Irish Famine 1845–51; repeal of the Corn Laws 1846 | Talbot demonstrates photography 1839; Turner, *The Fighting Téméraire* 1839; Brunel's *Great Britain* 1843; C. Brontë, *Jane Eyre* 1847; Thackeray, *Vanity Fair* 1847–8; Great Exhibition 1851 |
| | Crimean War 1853–6; Indian mutiny 1857 | Darwin, *Origin of Species* 1859; Tennyson, *Idylls of the King* 1859 |
| | Second Reform Act 1867; Gladstone's first ministry 1868–74 | Carroll, *Alice in Wonderland* 1865; Eliot, *Middlemarch* 1871; Trollope, *The Way We Live Now* 1874; Tay bridge disaster 1879 |
| | Disraeli's ministry 1874–80 Gladstone's second ministry 1880–5; third Reform Act 1884; Irish Home Rule defeated 1886; second Boer War 1899–1902 | Gilbert and Sullivan, *Mikado* 1885; Shaw, *Widowers' Houses* 1892; Wilde, *The Importance of Being Earnest* 1895; Hardy, *Jude the Obscure* 1895; Elgar, *Enigma Variations* 1899 |
| 1901 | **Edward VII succeeds**; naval arms race with Germany; Anglo-French entente 1904; Liberal landslide 1905; suffragette campaign; Lloyd George budget 1909 | Kipling, *Just So Stories* 1902; Chesterton, *Club of Queer Trades* 1905; Galsworthy, *A Man of Property* 1906; Bennett, *The Old Wives' Tale* 1906; Wells, *Tono-Bungay* 1909 |
| 1910 | **George V succeeds**; Parliament Act 1911; Home Rule crisis 1912–14; First World War 1914–18; Easter Rising 1916; Irish Free State 1922; first Labour government 1923; General Strike 1926; National Government 1931 | *Titanic* sinks 1912; Joyce, *Dubliners* 1914; Holst, *The Planets* 1919; Eliot, *The Waste Land* 1922; Waugh, *Decline and Fall* 1928; airship R101 crashes 1930; Huxley, *Brave New World* 1932 |

GOVERNMENT AND POLITICS

OTHER EVENTS

1936 **Edward VIII succeeds**; abdication crisis

1936 **George VI succeeds**; Second World War 1939–45; Attlee government 1945–51; Indian independence 1948

Orwell, *Animal Farm* 1945; Britten, *Peter Grimes* 1945; Greene, *The Third Man* 1950

1952 **Elizabeth II succeeds**; Korean War 1950–3; Suez crisis 1956; direct rule imposed on Northern Ireland 1972; Britain joins EEC 1973; Thatcher government 1979–90; Falklands War 1982; Gulf War 1991; Blair government 1997; devolution for Scotland and Wales 1999; power-sharing executive in Northern Ireland 1999; direct rule reimposed in Northern Ireland 2002; golden jubilee of Elizabeth II 2002; war in Iraq to overthrow Saddam Hussein 2003; renewed fighting in Afghanistan 2003; terrorist attack in Madrid 2004; third general election victory for Blair's Labour Party 2005; terrorist bombs in London kill more than fifty people 2005; power-sharing executive in Northern Ireland 2007; Gordon Brown succeeds Blair as prime minister 2007

Golding, *Lord of the Flies* 1954; Amis, *Lucky Jim* 1954; commercial television (ITV) introduced 1954; Betjeman, *Collected Poems* 1958; Lee, *Cider with Rosie* 1959; Pinter, *The Caretaker* 1960; Larkin, *Collected Poems* 1988; Rowling, *Harry Potter and the Philosopher's Stone* 1997; Tate Modern opened 2000; Wembley Stadium demolished 2003, re-opened 2007; Lowry Art Gallery, Salford opened 2000

# Answers

1. Lord Randolph Churchill in 1886. *See* GOSCHEN.
2. The shooting of 400 people in India in 1922 poisoned relations between Indians and British.
3. Corruption of Indian name (*nawab*=ruler or governor) applied to a *returned* wealthy merchant or administrator of the East India Company in the mid-18th cent.
4. In 1819 after an attempt to revive it.
5. The *Titanic* was sinking (1912).
6. Henry VIII's complaint of Anne of Cleves.
7. Sihtric, d. 927.
8. Crown jewels in Edinburgh castle.
9. Regular payments to the papacy in Rome stopped by Henry VIII in 1533.
10. Calgacus, the Caledonian leader, according to Tacitus.
11. During the Opium War 1839–42.
12. Edward Gibbon, the historian, of his fellow members 1774–84.